PHILOSOPHIE DES GEISTES / PHILOSOPHIE DER PSYCHOLOGIE

PHILOSOPHY OF MIND / PHILOSOPHY OF PSYCHOLOGY

PHILOSOPHY OF MIND
PHILOSOPHY OF PSYCHOLOGY

PROCEEDINGS OF
THE 9th INTERNATIONAL WITTGENSTEIN SYMPOSIUM

19th TO 26th AUGUST 1984
KIRCHBERG AM WECHSEL (AUSTRIA)

EDITORS

Roderick M. Chisholm, Johann Chr. Marek,
John T. Blackmore, Adolf Hübner

VIENNA 1985
HÖLDER-PICHLER-TEMPSKY

PHILOSOPHIE DES GEISTES
PHILOSOPHIE DER PSYCHOLOGIE

AKTEN DES
9. INTERNATIONALEN WITTGENSTEIN SYMPOSIUMS

19. BIS 26. AUGUST 1984
KIRCHBERG AM WECHSEL (ÖSTERREICH)

HERAUSGEBER

Roderick M. Chisholm, Johann Chr. Marek,
John T. Blackmore, Adolf Hübner

WIEN 1985
HÖLDER-PICHLER-TEMPSKY

Wir danken dem österreichischen Bundesministerium für Wissenschaft und Forschung und der Kulturabteilung des Amtes der Niederösterreichischen Landesregierung für die finanzielle Unterstützung bei der Drucklegung dieses Werkes.

Distributors for
Austria, Switzerland and the Federal Republic of Germany
VERLAG HÖLDER-PICHLER-TEMPSKY
A-1096 Wien, Postfach 127, Frankgasse 4

Distributors for the U.S.A. and Canada
KLUWER ACADEMIC PUBLISHERS GROUP
190 Old Derby Street, Hingham, MA 02043, U.S.A.

Distributors for all other countries
KLUWER ACADEMIC PUBLISHERS GROUP
Spuiboulevard 50, 3300 AZ Dordrecht, The Netherlands

CIP-Kurztitelaufnahme der Deutschen Bibliothek

Philosophie des Geistes, Philosophie der Psychologie:
Akten d. 9. Internat. Wittgenstein-Symposiums, 19.–26. August 1984,
(Kirchberg/Wechsel, Österreich)/Hrsg. Roderick M. Chisholm . . . – Wien:
Hölder-Pichler-Tempsky, 1985.
(Schriftenreihe der Wittgenstein-Gesellschaft; Bd. 11)
Parallelt.: Philosophy of mind, philosophy of psychology
ISBN 3-209-00592-3
NE: Chisholm, Roderick M. [Hrsg.]; Internationales Wittgenstein-Sympo-
sium <, 1984, Kirchberg, Wechsel >; Österreichische Ludwig-Wittgenstein-
Gesellschaft: Schriftenreihe der Wittgenstein-Gesellschaft; PT

ISBN 3-209-00592-3

Gestaltung und Mitarbeit: Erich Péhm
Satz: Baroschrift, Wien
Druck: Manz, Wien

INHALTSVERZEICHNIS
TABLE OF CONTENTS

6. Handlung, Emotion und Wille
6. Action, Emotion and Will

7. Intentionale Einstellungen
7. Intentional Attitudes

8. Wittgenstein und die Philosophie des Geistes
8. Wittgenstein and the Philosophy of Mind

9. Wittgensteins frühe Philosophie
9. Wittgenstein's Early Philosophy

10. Wittgensteins späte Philosophie
10. Wittgenstein's Late Philosophy

11. Logik und die Philosophie der Sprache
11. Logic and the Philosophy of Language

12. Psychoanalyse
12. Psychoanalysis

13. Universelle Sprachen
13. Universal Languages

VORWORT

Einleitung

Das Hauptthema des Neunten Internationalen Wittgenstein-Symposiums war „Philosophie des Geistes und Philosophie der Psychologie". U.a. wurden folgende Probleme im Detail diskutiert: das Problem von Geist und Körper (mind-body problem[1]), traditionelle Fragen der Philosophie des Geistes, die Philosophie der Psychologie und der „Funktionalismus".

Das Geist-Körper-Problem

Worin besteht das Problem, das wir im Deutschen gewöhnlich „Leib-Seele-Problem" und im Englischen „mind-body problem" nennen und das hier als „Geist-Körper-Problem" gekennzeichnet wird? Das englische Wort „mind" kann auf recht verschiedene Art und Weise verwendet werden, und diese Tatsache hat in den neueren philosophischen Diskussionen zu einiger Verwirrung geführt. Wir können mindestens fünf solche Gebrauchsweisen und daher mindestens fünf Gebrauchsweisen von „the mind-body problem" unterscheiden.

1. Wir könnten den Term „mind" so gebrauchen, wie Descartes den Term „mens" gebraucht hat, nämlich, daß er sich auf das bezieht, was psychologische Eigenschaften hat, auf das, was denkt, wahrnimmt, glaubt, wünscht. In diesem Falle würden wir „mind" so gebrauchen, daß der Term dasselbe wie „person" bedeutet, und daher so, daß er solche Entitäten wie den Verfasser und den Leser dieses Vorwortes bezeichnet. Wenn wir „mind" so gebrauchen, daß der Term dasselbe wie „person" bedeutet, dann würde eine Fassung des Geist-Körper-Problems wie folgende Frage aussehen: Was ist die Natur der Beziehung zwischen Personen und ihren Körpern? Was ist z.B. die Natur der Beziehung zwischen mir und meinem Körper? Es gibt zwei weitgespannte Möglichkeiten: Entweder bin ich mit meinem Körper identisch, oder ich bin mit meinem Körper nicht identisch. Wenn ich mit meinem Körper nicht identisch bin, dann gibt es wieder zwei Möglichkeiten: Entweder bin ich mit etwas, das einen Teil meines Körpers einschließt, identisch, oder ich bin nicht mit etwas, das einen Teil meines Körpers einschließt, identisch. Im letzteren Falle stellt sich die Frage: Was für ein Ding bin ich?

In den letzten Jahren ist vorgeschlagen worden, daß das Geistige, das, was im Englischen durch „mind" bezeichnet wird, mit dem Körper so verknüpft ist, wie das abstrakte Schema eines Computers mit dem Computer selbst. Aber dieser Vorschlag kann nicht richtig sein, wenn der Term „mind" in der eben herausgearbeiteten Bedeutung so aufgefaßt wird, daß er sich auf das bezieht, was psychologische Eigenschaften *hat*. Denn das abstrakte Schema eines Computers ist selbst eine Eigenschaft, ein abstraktes Objekt; jedoch das, was psychologische Eigenschaften hat, d.h. das, was wahrnimmt, denkt, fühlt und wünscht, ist ein individuelles Ding.

2. Wir könnten den Term „mind" auch so gebrauchen – wie es heute viele tun – daß er sich auf die intellektuellen Fähigkeiten einer Person bezieht. Das Wort wird auf diese Weise gebraucht, wenn man sagt, „That person has a good mind", und damit meint, daß die betreffende Person intelligent ist. Wenn wir diese zweite Bedeutung von „mind" im Auge haben, dann würde eine Untersuchung dessen, was durch „mind" bezeichnet wird, eine psychologische Untersuchung intellektueller Fähigkeiten sein. In diesem Falle könnte das Substantiv „mind" irreführend sein, denn es könnte so aufgefaßt werden, als bezeichnete es einen *individuellen Gegenstand*, der neben der Person und ihren Körper existiert. In solch einem Falle wird man dahingehend irregeführt, daß man annimmt, daß es *drei* individuelle Dinge gibt, die

zueinander in Beziehung gesetzt werden müssen: die Person, ihr Geistiges (mind) und ihr Körper.

Wenn wir „mind" auf diese zweite Art und Weise verwenden, können wir dann sagen, daß es ein Geist-Körper-Problem, ein mind-body-Problem gibt? Vielleicht taucht da die Frage auf: „Wie kann ein Körper intellektuelle Fähigkeiten haben?" Wenn wir annehmen können, daß es *etwas* gibt, das intellektuelle Fähigkeiten hat, dann kann diese Fassung des Geist-Körper-Problems auf die erste Fassung zurückgeführt werden: Worin besteht die Beziehung zwischen einer Person und ihrem Körper? Denn es ist anzunehmen, daß es die Person ist, die intellektuelle Fähigkeiten hat.

3. Wir können über den Geist einer Person auch so sprechen, daß er das ist, *womit sie denkt*. In diesem Fall bezeichnet der Term „mind" tatsächlich einen *individuellen Gegenstand*. Das, womit man denkt, ist ganz offensichtlich das Gehirn oder zumindestens etwas, das einen Teil des Gehirns einschließt. Wenn wir „mind" auf diese Art und Weise gebrauchen (d.h., wenn „mind" das bedeutet, womit man denkt), und nicht auf die erste Art und Weise (wo es die Person bedeutet), und auch nicht auf die zweite Art und Weise (wo es sich auf die intellektuellen Fähigkeiten bezieht), dann würde das, was wir eine „investigation of the mind", eine „Untersuchung des Geistes" nennen würden, eine neurophysiologische Untersuchung des Gehirns sein. Und der Ausdruck „mind-body problem" würde sich auf gewisse Fragen der Neurophysiologie beziehen. Die Antworten auf diese neurologischen Fragen liefern uns, für sich genommen, keine Lösung des Problems von Geist und Körper, des mind-body-Problems, wenn der Ausdruck „mind-body problem" im Einklang mit der *ersten* Bedeutung von „mind", die oben herausgearbeitet wurde, interpretiert wird.

4. Der Term „mind" wird manchmal dazu benützt, eine *geistige Substanz*, ein individuelles Ding von nicht-materiellem Charakter zu bezeichnen. (Das Wort „soul", „Seele", wäre hier vielleicht passender.) Wenn wir nun während der Beschäftigung mit dem Person-Körper-Problem die Entscheidung treffen würden, daß die Person nicht mit ihrem Körper identisch ist, und auch nicht mit etwas, das einen Teil ihres Körpers einschließt, dann könnten wir die Möglichkeit in Betracht ziehen, daß die Person eine Seele (soul) oder ein Geist, ein „mind" *ist*, in der gerade angeführten Bedeutung des Wortes „mind". (Wenn wir zu dem Ergebnis kommen, daß die Person eine Seele (soul) oder ein Geist (mind) *ist*, dann sollten wir vorsichtig sein und dieses Ergebnis nicht so ausdrücken, daß wir sagen, daß die Person eine Seele oder einen Geist *hat*. Denn dann könnten wir wieder dahingehend irregeführt werden, anzunehmen, daß wir es mit *drei* Arten von individuellen Dingen zu tun haben: mit Personen, ihrem Geist (minds) und ihren Körpern.)

5. Letztlich wird das Problem von Geist und Körper, das mind-body-Problem auch so aufgefaßt, daß es in der Untersuchung der Beziehung zwischen psychologischen und physischen Eigenschaften bestehe und daß dies ein besseres Verständnis nicht nur der Natur des psychologischen Universums, sondern auch der Natur des physischen Universums ermögliche. Man beschäftigt sich dann mit Fragen, wie: Ist jede psychologische Eigenschaft mit einer bestimmten physischen Eigenschaft *identisch*? Ist jede psychologische Eigenschaft in einem bestimmten Sinne von einer bestimmten physischen Eigenschaft oder von einer bestimmten Menge physischer Eigenschaften *abhängig*? Wiederum könnte hier der Ausdruck „*mind*-body problem" irreführend sein; ich schlage vor, daß „psychophysical problem", „psychophysisches Problem", besser wäre.

Die meisten gegenwärtigen Untersuchungen, die angeben, vom Geist-Körper-Problem zu handeln, befassen sich hauptsächlich mit dem psychophysischen Problem.

Deskriptive Psychologie

Ein großer Teil dessen, was „philosophy of mind" genannt wurde, befaßt sich damit, die psychologischen Zustände und Eigenschaften von Personen zu *beschreiben*, und zwar so zu beschreiben, wie sie von denen erlebt werden, die sich in diesen Zuständen befinden oder die diese Eigenschaften haben. Ein Grund für dieses Vorgehen ist, daß man die philosophische Verwirrung, welche aus manchen dieser Zustände und Eigenschaften entspringt, auflösen will. Man hofft, dadurch die Person, die das Subjekt solcher Zustände und Eigenschaften ist, besser zu verstehen. Diese Art der Philosophie des Geistes schließt nicht nur Brentanos deskriptive Psychologie ein, sondern auch die „Phänomenologie" Husserls und der späteren Existentialisten, sowie auch diejenige Art der Analyse, die sich in Wittgensteins *Philosophischen Untersuchungen* findet.

Einige der Philosophen, die sich „Phänomenologen" genannt haben, haben gesagt, daß ihre Beschreibungen dafür bestimmt sind, das *Wesen* solcher Phänomene zu erfassen, zum Beispiel das Wesen eines solchen Phänomens wie des Traurigseins. Das Wesen eines *individuellen Dinges* würde dann eine Menge von Eigenschaften sein, die dieses Ding – und nur dieses Ding – notwendigerweise hat und die ein anderes Ding unter keinen Umständen haben könnte. Nun ist Traurigkeit eine *Eigenschaft* und nicht ein individuelles Ding. Sollen wir nun sagen, daß das Wesen der Eigenschaft Traurigkeit eine Eigenschaft der Eigenschaft Traurigkeit ist, eine Eigenschaft, die ihr – und nur ihr – wesentlich zukommt und die jedem anderen Ding völlig entgegengesetzt ist? Es würde dann nicht schwierig sein zu sagen, worin das Wesen der Traurigkeit besteht: Traurigkeit ist eine Eigenschaft, die notwendigerweise von der Art ist, daß alle Dinge – und nur die Dinge – die traurig sind, sie exemplifizieren.

Wenn Philosophen gesagt haben, daß sie das Wesen der Traurigkeit beschrieben haben, dann könnten sie damit gemeint haben, daß sie eine *Analyse* der Traurigkeit geliefert haben. Worin würde eine solche Analyse bestehen?

Vielleicht darin, daß sich die Philosophen mit einem wohlbekannten Phänomen befassen und daß sie gewisse wesentliche Eigenschaften dieses Phänomens aufzeigen, Eigenschaften, die einen tiefen Einblick gewähren, aber oft nicht bemerkt werden. Wenn jemand sagt: „Die Analyse der Traurigkeit muß ergeben, daß sie so-und-so beschaffen ist", und wenn ich verstehe, was gesagt wurde, dann bin ich entweder schon mit der Traurigkeit vertraut, oder fasse ich das, was der Sprecher sagt, so auf, daß das, mit dem *er* als Traurigkeit vertraut ist, so-und-so beschaffen ist. In beiden Fällen bin ich imstande, das Analysandum unabhängig zu identifizieren. Allgemeiner ausgedrückt: Wenn man angibt, daß man eine inhaltliche Aussage über die Natur eines Zustandes oder einer Eigenschaft macht, dann setzt man voraus, daß diese Eigenschaft unabhängig identifiziert werden kann. Aber manche Philosophen, die angeben, daß sie uns etwas über die „wahre Natur" des Psychologischen sagen, setzen dies nicht voraus.

Die Philosophen dieser Richtung sagen, daß die Daten, auf welche sich die deskriptiven Psychologen berufen, selbst zweifelhaft sind und daß sie daher mit den Altweibergeschichten einer laienhaften, volkstümlichen Psychologie verglichen werden können. Diese Philosophen machen sich offensichtlich Gedanken darüber, was psychologische Zustände und psychologische Eigenschaften sein würden, wenn 1. die Psychologie eine exakte Wissenschaft wäre, in dem Sinne, in dem man von der Physik und der Chemie sagen kann, daß sie exakte Wissenschaften sind, und wenn 2. die Psychologie trotzdem psychologische Zustände und Eigenschaften untersuchen würde. Man befaßt sich dann mit Fragen, wie: „Welche Arten von Dingen können gerechtfertigterweise ‚Glauben', ‚Fühlen', ‚Wahrnehmen' usw. genannt werden, wenn die Psychologie eine Naturwissenschaft wäre?" Manchmal wird vorgeschlagen, daß das, was dann engl. „psychological", dt. „psychologisch" oder engl. „mental", dt. „geistig" genannt werden könnte, von denjenigen psychologischen Zuständen und Eigenschaften, mit denen wir tatsächlich vertraut sind, sehr verschieden sein würde. In diesem Fall wäre es möglich, daß die Philosophen keine Theorie über die Natur derjenigen psychologischen Eigenschaften, mit denen *wir* unmittelbar vertraut sind, haben, denn sie könnten erklären, daß sie nicht an die Existenz solcher Eigenschaften glaubten. Es ist daher schwierig, ihre Aussage zu beurteilen, weil es nicht klar ist, was sie als ihre Daten ansehen oder was sie als Bestätigung oder als Falsifizierung dessen, was sie zu sagen versuchen, akzeptieren würden.

Die Begründer der „Wissenschaftlichen Weltauffassung" und diejenigen, die ihnen in der Tradition des „Physikalismus" folgten, hatten gehofft, imstande zu sein, psychologische Zustände und Eigenschaften mit physischen Zuständen und Eigenschaften zu identifizieren. Aber mit *welchen* physischen Zuständen und Eigenschaften? Für den Fall der Empfindungen schien das Programm recht vielversprechend zu sein, denn man dachte, daß hier jeder Typ von Empfindung ein eindeutiges physisches Korrelat hat. Man könnte dann als eine allgemeine Hypothese vorschlagen, daß jede Empfindung mit ihrem physischen Korrelat identisch ist. Aber es war schwierig, solche Korrelata für intentionale Phänomene (z.B. Glauben, Hoffen, Fragen, Wünschen) zu finden. Z.B. mit welchem physischen Zustand sollen wir den Wunsch, eine 23 Fuß lange Schaluppe zu besitzen, identifizieren? Es scheint so, als gäbe es keinen identifizierbaren physischen Zustand, der eindeutig mit einem solchen Wunsch korreliert ist.

Man kam daher auf den Gedanken, daß solche intentionale Phänomene, wenn schon nicht mit physischen *Zuständen* oder *Eigenschaften*, so doch mit *Verhaltensdispositionen* identifiziert werden könnten. Eine primitive Form dieser Ansicht wäre, daß man sich dann wünscht, eine 23 Fuß Schaluppe zu besitzen, wenn − und nur wenn − man auf die Frage, ob man eine 23 Fuß lange Schaluppe zu besitzen wünscht, bejahend antworten würde. Aber diese bikonditionale Aussage muß eingeschränkt werden. So könnte sie falsch sein, wenn sich jemand eine solche Schaluppe *nicht* wünscht, aber eine andere Person so irreführen möchte, daß sie glaubt, daß er sich eine solche Schaluppe wünscht. Und sie könnte falsch sein, wenn jemand sich *tatsächlich* solch eine Schaluppe *wünscht*, aber die Sprache dessen, der ihn fragt, nicht versteht. Ist es nun möglich, daß wir passende Einschränkungen finden und dieser bikonditionalen Aussage hinzufügen können? Die Schwierigkeit besteht darin, daß die Einschränkungen, die wir hinzufügen müssen, um solche Beispiele zu behandeln, sich auch auf *andere* intentionale Phänomene beziehen werden, z.B. auf andere Dinge, die man sich wünscht oder nicht wünscht, darauf, was man glaubt und was man nicht glaubt, darauf, was man wahrnimmt und woran man sich erinnert. Von solch einer Theorie kann man kaum sagen, daß sie psychologische Phänomene auf Verhaltensdispositionen reduziert, denn die relevanten Dispositionen können nur dann beschrieben werden, wenn man sich auf andere psychologische Phänomene bezieht.

Könnte man eine psychophysische Identitätsthese verteidigen, ohne sich auf eine psychologische *Korrelations*these zu berufen? Man kann natürlich nicht sagen, daß ein Gegenstand mit einem andern Gegenstand zu einer bestimmten Zeit identisch sein kann und dann zu einer anderen Zeit wiederum mit einem *anderen* Gegenstand. Aber es ist vorgeschlagen worden, daß die *Einzelvorkommen*, die „tokens" einer beliebigen psychologischen Eigenschaft so beschaffen sein könnten, daß einige mit den Einzelvorkommen, den tokens, einer bestimmten physischen Eigenschaft identisch sind und andere mit den Einzelvorkommen, den tokens, einer anderen physischen Eigenschaft. Aber kann die metaphysische These, nach welcher es solche Einzelvorkommen, solche tokens, von Eigenschaften *gibt*, begründet werden? So weit ich sehen kann, hat die These überhaupt keine Begründung, ausgenommen die Möglichkeit, daß sie uns beim psychophysischen Problem helfen kann. Der metaphysische Preis dafür, daß man diese metaphysische Doktrin akzeptiert, um die psychophysische Identitätsthese zu retten, scheint sehr hoch zu sein, besonders wenn wir bedenken, daß diese „token-token"-Fassung der Theorie ein Paradebeispiel einer Theorie ist, die weder verifizierbar noch falsifizierbar ist.

Einige „Funktionalisten" haben wirklich gesagt, daß eine Reduzierung des Psychologischen als Ganzes auf das Physische möglich ist, auch wenn eine Stück-für-Stück-Reduzierung unmöglich ist. Der springende Punkt ist dabei nicht, daß man spezifische psychologische Zustände (wie z.B., daß man sich eine 23 Fuß lange Schaluppe wünscht) mit neurologischen Zuständen oder mit Dispositionen, sich auf eine bestimmte, spezifische Art und Weise zu verhalten, identifiziert, sondern daß man seinen *gesamten* psychologischen Zustand in jeder

15

beliebigen Zeit mit seinem gleichzeitigen gesamten physischen Zustand identifiziert. Solch eine Theorie gehorcht nicht mehr dem Geist der „Wissenschaftlichen Weltauffassung", denn genau so wie die „token-token"-Theorie, die gerade erörtert wurde, scheint sie der paradigmatische Fall einer Theorie zu sein, die weder verifizierbar noch falsifizierbar ist.

* * *

Abschließend möchte ich im Namen der Herausgeber allen jenen danken, die an der Veröffentlichung dieses Bandes mitgewirkt haben: den Autoren der Beiträge; Frau Dr. Elisabeth Leinfellner, der Herausgeberin dieser Reihe; und Herrn Erich Péhm vom Verlag Hölder-Pichler-Tempsky. Wir danken auch dem Bundesministerium für Wissenschaft und Forschung, der Niederösterreichischen Landesregierung und der Österreichischen Ludwig Wittgenstein Gesellschaft für die gewährten Druckkostenzuschüsse, sowie Frau Helga Michelitsch für ihre umsichtige Hilfe bei der Vorbereitung für den Druck.

Roderick M. Chisholm

(ANMERKUNG DES ÜBERSETZERS)

[1] Während die traditionelle Übersetzung von „mind-body problem" „Leib-Seele-Problem" ist, wurden hier wegen der nur ungenauen semantischen Übereinstimmung der beiden Ausdrücke und des spezifischen Charakters dieses Vorworts die Übersetzung „Geist-Körper-Problem" für „mind-body problem" und „Geist" oder „Geistiges" für „mind" verwendet.

* * *

PREFACE

Introduction

The principal theme of the Ninth International Wittgenstein-Symposium is *Philosophy of Mind and Philosophy of Psychology*. Among the topics that are discussed in detail are: the mind-body problem; traditional questions of the philosophy of mind; and the philosophy of psychology.

The Mind-Body Problem

What is the mind-body problem? The word "mind" has a number of rather different uses and this fact has led to some confusion in recent discussions. We may distinguish at least five such uses and therefore at least five senses of "the mind-body problem."

(1) We could use the term "mind," as Descartes had used the term "*mens*," to refer to that which has psychological properties—to that which thinks, senses, believes, desires. In this case, we would be using "mind" to mean the same as "person" and hence to designate such entities as you and me. If we use "mind" to mean the same as "person," one form of the mind-body problem would be the question: What is the relation between persons and their bodies? What is the relation, for example, between me and my body? There are two broad possibilities: Either I am identical with my body or I am not identical with it. If I am not identical with my body, then once again there are two possibilities: either I am identical with something that includes a part of my body or I am not identical with anything that includes a part of my body. In the latter case, what kind of thing am I?

It has been suggested in recent years that "the mind" is related to the body in the way in which the abstract diagram of a computer is related to the computer. But this suggestion cannot be true if "mind" is taken, in the sense just distinguished, to refer to that which *has* psychological properties. For the abstract diagram of a computer is itself a property, an abstract object; but that which has psychological properties—that which senses, thinks, feels, and desires—is an individual thing.

(2) We could also use the term "mind," as many now do, to refer to a person's intellectual capacities. The word is being used in this way when one says, "That person has a good mind," meaning that the person is intelligent. An "investigation of the mind," in this second sense of the word "mind," would be a psychological investigation of intellectual capacities. In this case, the substantive "mind" may be misleading, since it might be taken to designate an *individual thing* that exists along with the person and his body. In such a case one is mislead into supposing that there are *three* individual things to be related—the person, the person's mind, and the person's body.

Using "mind" in this second way, may we say that there is a mind-body problem? Perhaps there is the question "How can a body have intellectual capacities?" If we may assume that there is *something* that has intellectual capacities, then this version of the mind-body problem reduces to the first: What is the relation between a person and his body? For it is presumably the person who has intellectual capacities.

(3) We may also speak of a person's mind as being *that by means* of which he thinks. In this case the term "mind" *does* designate an individual thing. That by means of which one thinks is quite obviously the brain—or at least something that includes a part of the brain. If we use "mind" in this way (to mean that by means of which one thinks) and not in the first way (to mean the person) and not in the second way (to refer to intellectual capacities), then what we

would call an "investigation of the mind" would be a neurophysiological investigation of the brain. And the expression "mind-body problem" would refer to certain questions of neurophysiology. Answers to these neurological questions do not, as such, give us a solution to the "mind-body problem," where this expression is interpreted in accordance with the *first* sense of "mind" distinguished above.

(4) The term "mind" is sometimes used to designate a *spiritual substance*, an individual thing of a nonmaterial nature. (Here, perhaps, the word "soul" is more appropriate.) If, in dealing with the person-body problem, we were to decide that the person is not identical with his body or with anything that includes a part of his body, then we might want to consider the possibility that the person *is* a soul or mind, in the present sense of the word "mind." (If we conclude that the person *is* a soul or mind, then we should take care not to express this conclusion by saying that the person *has* a soul or mind. For then we might be misled, once again, into thinking that we are dealing with *three* types of individual thing—persons, minds, and bodies.)

(5) Finally, "the mind-body problem" is sometimes taken to be that of studying the relation between psychological and physical properties and thereby getting a better understanding, not only of the nature of the psychological, but also that of the physical universe. The concern is with such question as: Is each psychological property *identical* with some physical property? Is each psychological property *dependent* in some special sense upon physical property or upon some set of physical properties? Here, once again, the expression "*mind*-body problem" may be misleading once again; I suggest that "psychophysical problem" would be better.

Most contemporary discussions that purport to be about the mind-body problem are concerned primarily with the psychophysical problem.

Descriptive Psychology

Much of what has been called "philosophy of mind" is concerned with *describing* the psychological states and properties of persons and describing them as they are experienced by those who are in those states or have those properties. One purpose of doing this is to resolve the philosophical perplexity to which some of these states and properties give rise. The hope is thereby better to understand the person who is the subject of such states and properties. This type of philosophy of mind includes, not only the descriptive psychology of Brentano, but also the "phenomenology" of Husserl and the later existentialists, as well as the type of study to be found in Wittgenstein's *Philosophical Investigations*.

Some of the philosophers who have called themselves "phenomenologists" have said that their descriptions are designed to catch the *essences* of such phenomena—the essence, say, of such a phenomenon as being sad. The essence of an *individual thing* would be a set of properties that that thing and only that thing has necessarily and that nothing else could possibly have. Now sadness is a *property* and not an individual thing. Shall we say, then, that the essence of the property sadness is a property of the property sadness—a property that is essential to it and only it and repugnant to every thing else? Then there would be no difficulty in saying what the essence of sadness is: sadness is a property which is necessarily such that it is exemplified in all and only those things that are sad.

When philosophers have said they were describing the essence of sadness, what they may have meant is that they were providing with an *analysis* of sadness. What would that be?

Perhaps this: the philosophers are concerned with a familiar phenomenon and that they are pointing out certain essential properties of it that are revealing but often go unnoticed. If you say, "Sadness is to be analysed as being so-and-so and such-and-such," and if I understand what you are saying, then either I am already acquainted with sadness or I take you to be saying that that which *you* are acquainted with as sadness is so-and-so and such-and-such. In either case, I am able to identify the *analysandum* independently. More generally, if one professes to give an informative statement about the nature of a state or property, then one presupposes that that property can be independently identified. But some philosophers who profess to tell us about the "true nature" of the psychological do not presuppose this.

Such philosophers say that the data to which the descriptive psychologists appeal are themselves doubtful, being comparable to the old wives' tales of "folk psychology." These philosophers are apparently concerned with what psychological states and psychological properties would be if (1) psychology were a science in the sense in which physics and chemistry may be said to be science and if, nevertheless, (2) psychology were to investigate psychological states and properties. The concern, then, is with such questions as "What sorts of things might appropriately be called 'believing,' 'feeling,' 'sensing,' and the like if psychology were a natural science?" Sometimes it is suggested that what might then be called "psychological" or "mental" would be very different from the psychological states and properties that we are in fact acquainted with. In this case, the philosophers may have no theory about the nature of those psychological properties that *we* are directly acquainted with, since they may profess not to believe that there are such properties. It is difficult, therefore, to evaluate their statements since it is not clear what they take as their data or what they would accept as confirmation or as falsification of what they are trying to say.

The Psychophysical Problem

The authors of the *Wissenschaftliche Weltauffassung* and those who followed them in the tradition of "physicalism" hoped to be able to identify psychological states and properties with physical states and properties. But with *what* physical states and properties? The program seemed promising in the case of sensations where, it was thought, there is a physical correlate that is unique to every type of sensation. One could then propose as a general hypothesis that each sensation is identical with its physical correlate. But there was difficulty finding such correlates for intentional phenomena (e.g., believing, hoping, questioning, desiring). With what physical state, for example, are we to identify the desire to own a 23-foot sloop? There would seem to be no identifiable physical state that is uniquely correlated with such a desire.

It came to be thought, therefore, that such intentional phenomena might be identified, not with physical *states* or *properties*, but with *dispositions to behave*. A crude form of this view would be that you desire to own a 23-foot sloop if and only if you would respond affirmatively when asked whether you desire to own a 23-foot sloop. But this biconditional needs to be qualified. Thus it could be false if you do *not* desire such a sloop but wish to deceive someone into thinking that you do. And it could be false if you *do* desire such a sloop but do not understand the language of the one who is questioning you. Can we find suitable qualifications, then, to add to the biconditional? The difficulty is that the qualifications we must add to deal with such examples will refer to *other* intentional phenomena—for example, to other things that you desire or do not desire, to what you believe or do not believe, to what you perceive, and to what you remember. Such a theory could hardly be said to reduce psychological phenomena to dispositions to behave—since the relevant dispositions can be described only by reference to other psychological phenomena.

Could one defend a psychophysical identity thesis without appeal to a psychophysical *correlation* thesis? One cannot say, of course, that a thing may be identical with one thing at one time and with *another* thing at another time. But it has been suggested that the *particular occurrences* ("tokens") of any given psychological property may be such that some are identical with the particular occurrences of one physical property and others are identical with the particular occurrences of some other physical property. But what ground is there for the metaphysical thesis according to which there *are* such particular occurrences (tokens) of properties? So far as I have been able to see, the thesis has no basis at all—other than the possibility that it might help us with the psychophysical problem. The metaphysical price of accepting this metaphysical doctrine in order to preserve the psychophysical identity theory seems very high, especially when we consider that this "token-token" version of the theory is *par excellence*, a theory which is neither verifiable nor falsifiable.

Some "functionalists" have said, in effect, that even though a piecemeal reduction of the psychological to the physical is not possible, a wholesale reduction is possible. The point is, not to identify particular psychological states (such as desiring a 23-foot sloop) with neurological states or with dispositions to behave in certain particular ways, but to identify one's *total* psychological state at any time one's total physical state at that time. Such a theory is no longer in the spirit of the *Wissenschaftliche Weltauffassung*, for, like the "token-token" theory just considered, it would seem to be a paradigm case of a theory that is neither verifiable nor falsifiable.

* * *

On behalf of the Board of Editors, I would like to thank all of those who have worked with us in preparing this volume for publication: the authors of the particular papers; Dr. Elisabeth Leinfellner, one of the General Editors of this series; and Mr. Erich Péhm of Hölder-Pichler-Tempsky. We also thank the Bundesministerium für Wissenschaft und Forschung, the Niederösterreichische Landesregierung and the Austrian Ludwig Wittgenstein Society for grants to cover the cost of publication and Mrs. Helga Michelitsch for her invaluable help in preparing the final manuscript.

Roderick M. Chisholm

* * *

ABKÜRZUNGEN DER TITEL VON WITTGENSTEINS SCHRIFTEN
ABBREVIATIONS OF THE TITLES OF WITTGENSTEIN'S WRITINGS

BBB	=	Blue and Brown Books
BF	=	Bemerkungen über Farben
BLB	=	Blue Book
BPP	=	Bemerkungen über die Philosophie der Psychologie
BRB	=	Brown Book
BFGB	=	Bemerkungen über Frazers „The Golden Bough"
BGM	=	Bemerkungen über die Grundlagen der Mathematik
CV	=	Culture and Value
LCA	=	Lectures and Conversations on Aesthetics, Psychology and Religious Belief
LE	=	Lecture on Ethics
LFM	=	Lectures on the Foundations of Mathematics
LO	=	Letters to Ogden
LRKM	=	Letters to Russell, Keynes and Moore
LS	=	Letzte Schriften über die Philosophie der Psychologie
LW	=	Last Writings on the Philosophy of Psychology
NB	=	Notebooks 1914–1916
NL	=	Notes for Lectures on Private Experience and Sensedata
OC	=	On Certainty
PB	=	Philosophische Bemerkungen
PG	=	Philosophische Grammatik / Philosophical Grammar
PI	=	Philosophical Investigations
PR	=	Philosophical Remarks
PT	=	Prototractatus
PU	=	Philosophische Untersuchungen
RC	=	Remarks on Color
RFM	=	Remarks on the Foundations of Mathematics
RLF	=	Some Remarks on Logical Form
RPP	=	Remarks on the Philosophy of Psychology
TLP	=	Tractatus Logico-Philosophicus
TB	=	Tagebücher 1914–1916
ÜG	=	Über Gewißheit
VB	=	Vermischte Bemerkungen
WV	=	Wörterbuch für Volksschulen
WWK	=	Wittgenstein und der Wiener Kreis
Z	=	Zettel

ERÖFFNUNGSREDE

Roderick M. Chisholm
Brown University, Providence, R.I.

Ich danke den Mitgliedern des Programmkomitees, daß sie mir die Ehre gegeben haben, diese Eröffnungsbemerkungen zu machen.

Es gibt viele verschiedene Weisen, wie wir die Arbeit eines großen Philosophen betrachten können. Um den Ausdruck von Wittgenstein zu gebrauchen: wir können sie unter sehr verschiedenen „Aspekten" verstehen. Ich will heute morgen nur von einem jener Aspekte sprechen, unter denen wir das Werk von Wittgenstein betrachten können. Diese Perspektive ist historisch bedeutend; ich glaube, sie wird seine Philosophie beleuchten; und, soviel ich weiß, hat niemand sie ausführlich diskutiert. Sie besteht darin, daß wir das Werk Wittgensteins als eine Fortsetzung von dem von Franz Brentano und seiner Schule betrachten.

Brentano hat einmal eine Abhandlung über Thomas Reid geschrieben. Er hat sie in zwei Teilen formuliert − „was an Reid zu tadeln ist" und „was an Reid zu loben ist". Würde er über Wittgenstein schreiben, so könnten wir es nicht verhindern, daß er einen langen Teil schriebe über das, was an Wittgenstein zu tadeln ist. Aber es würde nicht schwierig sein, ihn zu überreden, einen längeren Teil über das, was an Wittgenstein zu loben ist, zu schreiben.

Um die Perspektive, von der ich jetzt spreche, zu verstehen, sollte man mit Wittgensteins *Bemerkungen über Farben* anfangen. Sein Büchlein ist, ebenso wie Brentanos *Untersuchungen zur Sinnespsychologie*, eine Abhandlung über die Gegenstände der Empfindung. Die Forschung auf diesem Gebiet war ein gemeinsamer Zug der Brentano-Schule und des österreichischen Positivismus − insbesondere von Mach, Schlick und dem frühen Carnap. Sie wurde von den Positivisten aufgegeben, als sie sich dem Physikalismus zuwandten, aber sie wurde nie von Wittgenstein aufgegeben. Was Wittgenstein und Brentano über Farben sagen, wäre inakzeptabel für einen Philosophen, der bekannte, er wisse nicht was eine Empfindung sei. Die Fragen, die sie besprechen, haben überhaupt nichts mit Physik oder mit physikalischen Körpern zu tun. Die Antwort auf eine Frage dieser Art kann, wie Wittgenstein sich ausdrückt, „kein physikalistischer Satz sein."

Sein Werk über Farben, sagte Wittgenstein, ist nicht „eine *Theorie* der Farben (weder eine physiologische noch eine psychologische), sondern die *Logik des Farbbegriffes*" (S. 15). Sicherlich hat Wittgensteins Werk größtenteils mit Begriffen zu tun. Wenn er bekennt, über *Sprache* zu sprechen, spricht er oft nicht über Sprache, sondern über Begriffe. Tatsächlich hätte er, wo er den Ausdruck „Sprachspiel" verwendet, mit gleicher Berechtigung den Ausdruck „*Begriffs*spiel" verwenden können.

Wittgenstein sagt in den *Bemerkungen über Farben*: „Hier ist die Versuchung sehr groß, an eine Phänomenologie, ein Mittelding zwischen Wissenschaft und Logik, zu glauben" (S. 35). Ist er selbst dieser Versuchung erlegen? Er sagt: „Es gibt zwar keine Phänomenologie, wohl aber phänomenologische Probleme" (S. 22). Und dies sind die Probleme, die er diskutiert.

Die *Philosophischen Untersuchungen* sind wohl ein bahnbrechender Beitrag zu dem, was Brentano „deskriptive Psychologie" genannt hatte. Sie erweitern unser Verständnis der Intentionalität in einem Maß, das die Mitglieder der Brentano-Schule nie hätten leisten können. Um diesen Punkt einzusehen, braucht man nur zu betrachten, was Wittgenstein uns dort über intentionale Phänomene erzählt − insbesondere über Wissen, Glauben, Wahrnehmen und Wollen. Und wenn er von dem „Aufleuchten eines Aspektes" spricht, macht er einen tiefschürfenden Beitrag zu unserem Verständnis von *Bemerken* − einem Begriff, der eine grundlegende Rolle in Brentanos deskriptiver Psychologie spielt.

Dieses Aufleuchten eines Aspektes ist etwas, was wir hervorheben müssen, denn es gibt eine auffallende Ähnlichkeit zwischen dem, was Wittgenstein hier geleistet hat, und dem, was Brentano geleistet hatte, als er unser Bewußtsein von zeitlichen Verhältnissen besprochen hatte.

Andere Philosophen hatten bemerkt, daß unser Zeitbewußtsein philosophisch rätselhaft ist. Man kann also fragen: „Wenn du ein Ding als zeitlich *vor* einem anderen stehend wahrnimmst, so mußt du das erste Ding als vergangen wahrnehmen. Aber wenn ein Ding jetzt in der Vergangenheit ist und nicht mehr in der Gegenwart, wie kannst du es jetzt *wahrnehmen* — und es *als vergangen* wahrnehmen?" Meines Erachtens war es Brentano, der als erster die volle Bedeutung solcher Fragen gesehen hatte. Er sah, daß sie eine Umwandlung fundamentaler psychologischer und philosophischer Begriffe verlangen. Das Ergebnis war eine Theorie des Zeitbewußtseins — ein Beitrag, welcher, zum Glück oder Unglück, zu dem Werk Heideggers und seiner Nachfolger geführt hat.

Ähnlich ist es mit Wittgenstein und dem Aufleuchten eines Aspektes. Psychologen wußten, daß das Beispiel des Hasen-Enten-Bildes uns vor rätselhafte Fragen stellt. Etwa: „Wenn du es als Ente zu sehen aufhörst und es als Hasen zu sehen anfängst, was ist es, das sich ändert — der *Gegenstand* der Empfindung oder der *Akt* der Empfindung?" Es war Wittgenstein, der als erster die volle Bedeutung solcher Fragen sah. Und was er darüber sagt, ist, meiner Meinung nach, noch nicht völlig gewürdigt worden. Von dem in Frage kommenden Phänomen sagt er: „Seine *Ursachen* interessieren den Psychologen, nicht mich" (*LS* 434). Auch hier stellt er Fragen deskriptiver Psychologie zur Diskussion.

Es gibt natürlich wichtige Unterschiede zwischen Brentano und Wittgenstein. Wir dürfen sie nicht unterschätzen. Wir sollten sie aber auch nicht überschätzen.

Ich denke zum Beispiel an die Erkenntnistheorie — an die Evidenzlehre, wie man sie in der Brentano-Schule genannt hat. Was Wittgenstein über Evidenz sagt — insbesondere in *Über Gewißheit* — läßt sich eher als eine Ergänzung denn als ein Widerspruch zur Evidenzlehre Brentanos interpretieren.

Wittgenstein sagt vieles über unmittelbare Erfahrung, was Brentano früher behauptet hatte. Zum Beispiel: „Man kann sich freilich über die unmittelbare Erfahrung nicht täuschen." Und dann, anders als Brentano, fügt er hinzu: „aber nicht, weil sie so gewiß ist." (*LS* 187) Wo Brentano sagt „Ich weiß" und „Es ist evident", sagt Wittgenstein: „Es hat keinen Sinn zu sagen ‚Ich weiß‘ oder ‚Es ist evident.‘" Aber man kann sich des Eindrucks nicht erwehren, daß der Streit nur sprachlich ist. Die Kriterien, durch welche Wittgenstein entscheidet, daß „Ich weiß" und „Es ist evident" *sinnlos* sind, sind genau dieselben wie die Kriterien, durch welche Brentano entscheidet, daß sie *wahr* sind.

Wenn eine Person Schmerzen hat, *sagt* sie wahrscheinlich nicht „Es ist mir evident, daß ich Schmerzen habe". Aber sie ist imstande, die Tatsache, daß sie Schmerzen hat, *als Evidenz* zu gebrauchen — als Evidenz für eine *andere* Tatsache. Um diesen Punkt besser zu verstehen, betrachten wir den folgenden Dialog:

„Offensichtlich habe ich mich noch nicht erholt."

„Woher weißt du das?"

„Ich habe noch Schmerzen."

Unabhängig davon, ob wir von einer Person sagen, daß sie *wisse, daß sie Schmerzen hat*, können wir sagen, *sie verwendet* diese Tatsache *als Evidenz* für die Hypothese, daß sie sich noch nicht erholt hat. Es scheint so, wie wenn der eine Philosoph sagt, „Es gibt einen unbewegten ersten Beweger," und der andere sagt, „Es gibt einen ersten Beweger, der sich selbst bewegt." Und doch sind die Gründe in beiden Fällen dieselben.

Es ist wahr, daß dort, wo Brentano das *Denken* betont, Wittgenstein *das Sprechen* hervorhebt. Brentano legt es uns nahe, daß die Prinzipien der Logik Regeln des *Denkens* sind. Und Wittgenstein legt nahe, daß sie Regeln der *Sprache* sind. Wenn man den einen Philosophen des "Psychologismus" bezichtigen kann, so kann man den anderen des „Lingualismus" bezichtigen. Indes scheinen mir die Anklagen in beiden Fällen nicht gerechtfertigt zu sein. Wie entscheidet man, *was* die Regeln des Denkens oder was die Regeln der Sprache sind?

Was der eine Philosoph sagen kann, kann der andere Philosoph auch sagen – *mutatis mutandis*.

Sollten wir die Sprache in bezug auf das Denken verstehen – oder umgekehrt? Die Antwort dreht sich um unsere Position zu einer der fundamentalsten aller Fragen, die in der österreichischen Philosophie diskutiert worden sind: „Ist die Referenz des Denkens durch Bezug auf die Referenz der Sprache zu verstehen, oder ist die Referenz der Sprache durch Bezug auf die Referenz des Denkens zu verstehen?" Es war die Ansicht Brentanos, daß wenn ein *Wort* ein gewisses Ding bezeichnet, so deshalb, weil das Wort fähig ist, *Gedanken* über dieses Ding auszudrücken. Wir können sagen, er verteidigte das Prinzip des Primats des Intentionalen.

Bis vor kurzem haben die meisten der Sprachphilosophen das entgegengesetzte Prinzip akzeptiert – „das Prinzip des Primats des Semantischen". Dieses Prinzip besagt: Wenn eine Person imstande ist, über ein gewisses Ding zu denken, so deshalb, weil sie *eine Sprache* hat – eine Sprache, in welcher es Wörter gibt, die dieses Ding bezeichnen. Und wie kommt es, daß die Wörter so etwas leisten können? Manchmal lautet die Antwort: „Sie können es einfach – und das ist das Ende". Ein andermal hört man eine ziemlich skizzenhafte Geschichte über kausale Ketten. Aber keine solche kausale Geschichte ist bei Wittgenstein zu finden.

Was ist sein Standpunkt in Bezug auf die These, daß das Denken auf Sprache beruht?

In den *Philosophischen Untersuchungen* erfaßt er das Problem in einer einzigen einfachen Frage – einer jener merkwürdigen Fragen, die wir nur bei Wittgenstein finden können. Sie lautet, „Was macht meine Vorstellung von ihm zu einer Vorstellung von *ihm*?" (S. 177) Jene Philosophen, die das Primat des Semantischen verteidigen, würden vielleicht sagen· „Was meine Vorstellung von ihm zu einer Vorstellung von *ihm* macht, ist die Tatsache, daß ich einen inneren Satz behauptet habe – einen Satz, in welchem Wörter, die ihn bezeichnen, verwendet werden." Aber Wittgenstein hat gesehen, daß man die gleiche Frage, welche er bezüglich der Vorstellung gestellt hat, auch in Bezug auf den *inneren Satz* stellen kann: „Was macht diesen *Satz* zu einem Satz, der von *ihm* handelt?" Die Hinwendung zur Sprache dient nur dazu, die ursprüngliche Frage zu verschieben.

Wittgenstein sagt, wenn du wissen willst, an wen ein Mensch denkt, dann brauchst du ihn nur zu fragen. „Und seine Antwort würde entscheiden. Sie würde uns eine *Intention* mitteilen. (*LS* 318, s. *PU* 177). Es ist hier keine Rede von kausalen Ketten oder von dem, was man in den USA „inner systems of representation" nennt.

Vielleicht habe ich den intentionalen Aspekt Wittgensteins übertrieben. Ich kann mir dessen nicht ganz sicher sein. Aber darüber habe ich volle Gewißheit: Die österreichische Tradition, die mit Bernard Bolzano anfängt und mit Franz Brentano weitergeht und die dann zu Ludwig Wittgenstein führt, ist eine der ertragreichsten in der Geschichte der modernen Philosophie.

* * *

OPENING ADDRESS

Roderick M. Chisholm
Brown University, Providence, R. I.

I thank the program committee for giving me the honor of presenting these opening remarks.

There are many different ways in which we may view the work of a great philosopher. As Wittgenstein might say, we can see it under many different aspects. I will speak this morning of just one of the aspects under which we may view the work of Wittgenstein. This way of looking at what he has done is historically important; I think it may throw light upon his philosophy; and, so far as I know, it has not been discussed in detail. It is this: we view Wittgenstein's work as continuing that of Franz Brentano and his school.

Brentano once wrote an essay on Thomas Reid and divided it into two parts: (1) "was an Reid zu tadeln ist" and (2) "was an Reid zu loben ist." We could not prevent him from writing a long section entitled "was an Wittgenstein zu tadeln ist." But we would have no difficulty in persuading him to write a longer section entitled "was an Wittgenstein zu loben ist."

To see Wittgenstein from the perspective I have in mind, we would do well to begin with his *Remarks on Colour*. His little book, like Brentano's *Untersuchungen zur Sinnespsychologie*, is a treatise about the objects of sensation. Investigation of this area was a feature that was common to the Brentano school and to Austrian positivism as instanced in the work of Mach and Schlick and the early Carnap. It was given up by the positivists when they turned to physicalism, but it was never given up by Wittgenstein. What Wittgenstein and Brentano say about colors would not be acceptable to a philosopher who professed not to know what sensation is. The questions they discuss have nothing to do with physics or even with physical things. As Wittgenstein puts it, the answer to any such question "cannot be a physicalistic statement" (p. 35).

His work on colors, Wittgenstein said, is "not a *theory* of colors (neither a physiological nor a psychological theory), but it is *the logic of the color concept*" (p. 15). Certainly most of Wittgenstein's work is concerned with concepts. Often, when he professes to be talking about *language*, he is really talking about the logic of certain *concepts*. Indeed, where he uses the expression "language game," he could have said, with equal justification, "*conceptual* game."

Wittgenstein also says in the book on colors: "The temptation is very great to believe in a phenomenology, a halfway place between science and logic" (p. 35). Did he succumb to this temptation? He says: "To be sure, there is no phenomenology, but there are phenomenological problems" (22). And these are the problems that he discusses.

The *Philosophische Untersuchungen* is, indeed, an epoch-making contribution to what Brentano had called "descriptive psychology." It extends our knowledge of intentional phenomena to a degree that Brentano's immediate followers had never been able to do. To see this one has only to consider what Wittgenstein tells us there about intentional phenomena—and in particular, about knowing, believing, perceiving and willing. And when he comes to talk about "the dawning of an aspect" he contributes profoundly to our understanding of the concept of *noticing*—a concept that plays a basic role in Brentano's descriptive psychology.

This matter of "the dawning of an aspect" is itself worth singling out. For there is a most striking resemblance between what Wittgenstein does here and what Brentano had done in connection with our experience of temporal relations—what he called *Proteraesthese*.

Other philosophers had noted that our awareness of temporal relations presents us with puzzling philosophical questions. For example: "If you perceive one thing as being prior to another, then you must perceive the first thing as being past. But if a thing is now in the past and no longer in the present, how can you *perceive* it now as *being in the past*?" It was Brentano, I would say, who first saw the full significance of these questions. He saw that they require the re-working of fundamental psychological and philosophical concepts. The result was a theory of the consciousness of time—a contribution which, for good or ill, was to lead to the work of Heidegger and his followers.

Compare, then, what Wittgenstein says about the dawning of an aspect. Psychologists had known that the example of the duck-rabbit presents us with puzzling questions. One was this: "When you cease to see it as a duck and come to see it as a rabbit, what changes—the *object* of sensation or the *act* of sensation?" It was Wittgenstein who first saw the full significance of these questions. And what he has to say about them, it seems to me, has not yet fully been appreciated. Of the causes of the phenomenon, Wittgenstein says: they "are of interest to psychologists, but not to me" (*LW* 434). Here, too, he is discussing descriptive psychology.

There are, of course, important differences between Brentano and Wittgenstein and we should not underestimate them. But we should not exaggerate them either.

I am thinking, for example, of the theory of knowledge—what members of the Brentano school called "the theory of the evident." What Wittgenstein says about evidence—especially in *On Certainty*—may be thought of as supplementing rather than contradicting the doctrine of Brentano.

Wittgenstein does not hesitate to say many of the same things that Brentano does about our immediate experience. Thus he writes: "Certainly one cannot be deceived about immediate experience." But then, unlike Brentano, he adds: "but not because it is certain." (*LW* 187). Where Brentano says "I know" and "It is evident", Wittgenstein says: "It makes no sense to say 'I know' or to say 'It is evident.'" Yet it is difficult to escape the conclusion that the dispute is only verbal. The criteria by means of which Wittgenstein decides that "I know" and "It is certain" are *senseless* are precisely Brentano's criteria for saying that "I know" and "It is certain" are *true*. If a person is in pain, he is not likely to *say* "It is evident to me that I am in pain"; but he is in a position to *use* the fact that he is in pain *as evidence*.

Consider this dialogue:

"Evidently I have not yet recovered."

"How do you know that?"

"I'm still in pain".

Whether or not we say of the person that he *knows* that he is in pain, we can say that he *uses* this fact as evidence for the hypothesis that he has not yet recovered. It would seem that, where the one philosopher concludes, in effect, that the prime mover is unmoved, the other concludes that he moves himself. But in each case the reasons are the same.

It is true that, where Brentano emphasizes *thought*, Wittgenstein emphasizes *language*. Brentano suggests that the principles of logic are to be understood by reference to the rules of thought. And Wittgenstein suggests that they are to be understood by reference to the rules of language. If the one philosopher can be accused of "psychologism", the other can be accused, with equal right, of "linguisticism." But, I would add, the accusation is not justified in either case. How do we decide what the rules of thinking are or what the rules of language are? Whatever the one philosopher can say the other can also say—*mutatis mutandis*.

Are we to understand language in terms of thinking, or conversely? The question turns upon our answer to the most fundamental of all the questions which have been discussed in Austrian philosophy. "Is the reference of thought to be explained in terms of the reference of language? Or is the reference of language to be explained in terms of the reference of thought?" It was Brentano's view that, if a *word* can be said to designate a certain thing, then it does so because it is capable of expressing *thoughts* that refer to that thing. We might say that he defended the principle of the primacy of the intentional.

Until fairly recently, most philosophers of language seemed to accept the contrary principle—what might be called the principle of the primacy of the semantical: if a person is able to think about a certain thing, then he does so in virtue of having a language in which there are words that designate that thing. And how do the words do it? Sometimes the answer is, "They just do." At other times, one hears a rather sketchy story about causal chains. But no such causal story is to be found in Wittgenstein.

How does he stand with respect to the thesis that thought is based upon language?

In the *Philosophische Untersuchungen*, he puts the problem in one simple question—one of those remarkable questions that one can find only in Wittgenstein. It is this: "What makes my idea of him an idea of *him*?" (p. 177) Those philosophers who affirm the primacy of the semantical would say something like this: "What makes my idea of him an idea of him is the fact that I have asserted an inner sentence in which words are used that refer to him." But Wittgenstein saw that you could raise the same question about the inner *sentence* that he had raised about the idea. "What makes this sentence a sentence about *him*?" The move to language simply transfers the original question.

Wittgenstein says that, if you want to know whom he is thinking of, just ask him. "And his answer would be decisive. It would tell us about an *intention*" (*LW* 318; see *PI* p. 177). There is no talk here about causal chains or "inner systems of representation."

Perhaps I have exaggerated the intentional aspect of Wittgenstein. I cannot be at all certain about this. But I am certain of one thing. The Austrian tradition that begins with Bernard Bolzano and continues with Franz Brentano and then leads on to Wittgenstein is one of the most productive in the history of modern philosophy.

* * *

1. Intentionalität

1. Intentionality

DER INTENTIONALE UND DER REALE GEGENSTAND*

Guido Küng
Universität Freiburg, Schweiz

In der Phänomenologie spielt der Begriff des intentionalen Gegenstandes eine zentrale Rolle. Franz Brentano war von der Auffassung ausgegangen, daß alle psychischen Phänomene sich durch das Merkmal der intentionalen Inexistenz eines Gegenstandes auszeichneten; doch kam er schließlich zur Überzeugung, daß die Annahme solcher in-existierender Gegenstände nicht sinnvoll sei. Husserls Auffassungen entwickelten sich dagegen in gerade entgegengesetzter Richtung: nachdem er anfänglich behauptet hatte, die Phänomenologie solle nur noetische Phänomenologie sein, kam er schließlich zur Überzeugung, daß die Analyse der geistigen Akte nur am Leitfaden der Analyse ihrer intentionalen Korrelate, nämlich der neomatischen Gegenstände, möglich sei.

Der Streit um die intentionalen Gegenstände ist jedoch nicht etwa nur von historischem Interesse; und die Unterscheidung zwischen realem und intentionalem Gegenstand ist mehr als nur ein Übungsfeld für scholastische Spitzfindigkeiten. Es geht hier vielmehr um ein Problem, das für das Wesen des Verhältnisses von Geist und Wirklichkeit zentral ist, und dessen Behandlung heute auch in den Diskussionen der analytischen Philosophie, Logik und Linguistik in den Vordergrund gerückt ist.

In meinem Aufsatz möchte ich zunächst, um die Frage des intentionalen Gegenstandes etwas besser in den Griff zu bekommen, die möglichen Ansichten in einen klassifizierenden Rahmen einordnen. Ich werde deshalb in einem ersten Teil die Vor- und Nachteile von drei allgemeinen Theorien des intentionalen Gegenstandes besprechen, die ich die Transzendenz-Theorie, die Immanenz-Theorie und die Theorie der zwei Objekte nennen will, je nachdem sie den intentionalen Gegenstand als bewußtseinstranszendent oder bewußtseinsimmanent auffaßt, oder für *einen* Akt gleichzeitig zwei intentionale Gegenstände, einen transzendenten *und* einen immanenten, zuläßt. Es wird sich herausstellen, daß keine dieser drei Theorien befriedigt, daß jedoch noch eine vierte Theorie möglich ist, die sich als Meinongsche Theorie bezeichnen läßt. Im dritten Teil meines Aufsatzes werde ich auf diese vierte Theorie näher eingehen und deren Schwierigkeiten und Komplikationen etwas ausführlicher unter die Lupe nehmen.

	Wahrnehmung	Halluzination
Transzendenz-Theorie	Der Akt hat *ein* Objekt: nämlich einen transzendenten Gegenstand, ein Ding in der realen Außenwelt.	Der Akt hat *kein* Objekt.
Immanenz-Theorie	Der Akt hat *ein* Objekt: nämlich einen immanenten Gegenstand, das *Noema* eines Dinges der realen Außenwelt.	Der Akt hat *ein* Objekt: nämlich einen immanenten Gegenstand, das *Noema* eines Dinges, das nicht existiert.
Theorie der zwei Objekte	Der Akt hat *zwei* Objekte: einen immanenten und einen transzendenten Gegenstand.	Der Akt hat *nur ein* Objekt: einen immanenten Gegenstand.

1. *Drei klassische Theorien*

Jeder psychische Akt scheint intentional auf einen Gegenstand gerichtet zu sein. Doch ist es durchaus möglich, daß in Wirklichkeit ein entsprechender Gegenstand gar nicht existiert. Es ist deshalb nicht unmittelbar einsichtig, was unter dem intentionalen Gegenstand eines Aktes zu verstehen ist. Anhand des Gegenstandes von beispielweise Wahrnehmung und Halluzination[1] läßt sich leicht ein Schema von drei verschiedenen Auffassungen zusammenstellen (vergleiche die vorangehende Seite).

1.1 Jede dieser drei allgemeinen Theorien hat ihre Vor- und Nachteile

Die *Transzendenz-Theorie* geht von der Überzeugung aus, daß unser Bewußtsein fähig ist, bewußtseinstranszendente Gegenstände zu erkennen. Sie identifiziert deshalb den intentionalen Gegenstand einer Wahrnehmung mit dem wahrgenommenen Ding in der realen Außenwelt. Im Falle einer Halluzination gibt es jedoch in der realen Außenwelt kein entsprechendes Ding. Die Theorie ist deshalb zur Aussage gezwungen, in einem solchen Falle habe der Akt streng genommen gar kein Objekt. Diese Behauptung ist jedoch unbefriedigend, denn vom phänomenologischen Standpunkt aus scheint es sehr wohl möglich, auch im Falle einer Halluzination ein entsprechendes Objekt, nämlich den halluzinierten Gegenstand, zu beschreiben. Und selbst im Falle einer echten Wahrnehmung hat diese Theorie den Nachteil, daß sie die Tatsache nicht zu berücksichtigen scheint, daß zwei Menschen, die dasselbe Ding betrachten, nie genau dasselbe sehen.

Die *Immanenz-Theorie* vermeidet diese Nachteile der Transzendenz-Theorie. Denn sie identifiziert den intentionalen Gegenstand mit genau dem, was das Subjekt sieht (oder zu sehen meint). Hier ist also der intentionale Gegenstand nicht das Ding in der realen Außenwelt, sondern das Ding-so-wie-es-vom-Subjekt-gesehen-wird. Diese Theorie ist sich bewußt, daß unser Erfassen der Dinge immer subjektiv ist. Da sie aber behauptet, das was wir sehen (oder zu sehen meinen), nämlich der intentionale Gegenstand, dürfe nicht mit dem Ding in der realen Außenwelt verwechselt werden, so hat sie Mühe anzuerkennen, was die Transzendenz-Theorie zum Vornherein als gegeben annimmt, nämlich daß unser Bewußtsein die transzendente Wirklichkeit erfassen kann. Die Immanenz-Theorie führt so zur Behauptung, daß das reale Ding-an-sich unsichtbar sei; und von da gelangt man leicht zur idealistischen Schlußfolgerung, daß die Annahme eines unerkennbaren Dinges-an-sich überflüssig und unsinnig sei, daß es gar keine Dinge-an-sich gebe.

In dieser Lage scheint es angebracht, die *Theorie der zwei Objekte* anzunehmen, da diese die Nachteile sowohl der Transzendenz- als auch der Immanenz-Theorie auszuschließen und die Vorteile dieser beiden Theorien in sich zu vereinigen scheint. Doch hat die Theorie der zwei Objekte ihrerseits ihre Nachteile. Wie Husserl in seiner Besprechung des Buches von Twardowski *Zur Lehre vom Inhalt und Gegenstand der Vorstellungen* angemerkt hat,[2] kann ein und derselbe Akt nicht gleichzeitig *zwei* Objekte haben. (Natürlich können wir z.B. auf einen Blick zwei Schuhe sehen, aber es geht hier natürlich nicht um diese trivialen Fälle der Erkenntnis mehrerer *nebeneinander* stehender Dinge.) Wir sind mit einer Alternative konfrontiert: *entweder* ist das Bewußtsein fähig, ein Ding der realen Außenwelt zu erfassen, und dann müssen wir sagen, daß der Wahrnehmungsakt in diesem Ding der Außenwelt terminiert; *oder* das Bewußtsein ist nicht fähig, wirklich über sich hinauszugehen, und dann müssen wir sagen, daß der Wahrnehmungsakt in einem immanenten Gegenstand terminiert. Ein und derselbe Akt kann nicht gleichzeitig an zwei „Orten" terminieren. Ein Akt, der einen transzendenten Gegenstand erfaßt und ein Akt, der einen immanenten Gegenstand erfaßt beinhalten zwei verschiedene Einstellungen und müssen demnach zwei verschiedene Akte sein.

1.2 Natürlich versucht jede der drei Theorien ihre Nachteile zu überwinden

In der *Transzendenz-Theorie* kann der subjektive Aspekt dessen, was wir sehen (oder zu sehen meinen) dem Akt zugeteilt werden, man kann sagen, er gehöre zu der Wie-Beschaffenheit des Aktes. Sprachlich heißt dies, daß statt Namen von immannenten Gegenständen *adverbiale* Ausdrücke zu verwenden sind. Zum Beispiel, statt zu berichten „Ich «sah» rosarote Elefanten" kann man sagen „Ich «sah» rosarot-elefantlich". Diese sogenannte adveriable Theorie ist in der analytischen Philosophie wohl bekannt.[3] Aber auch Husserl hatte eine ähnliche Auffassund vertreten als er in den *Logischen Untersuchungen* einen Bedeutungsbegriff entwickelte, der er später als ‚phansische Bedeutung' kennzeichnete.[4]

Doch Husserl gab sich schon bald Rechenschaft darüber, daß diese Theorie mit der Art wie wir tatsächlich die Bedeutung, d.h. die Richtung unserer Akte, feststellen nicht übereinstimmt. Die adverbiale Theorie schreibt den subjektiven Aspekt dessen, was wir sehen, dem Akt zu, und also sollten wir diesen subjektiven Aspekt nur durch eine Reflexion auf eben diesen Akt erfassen können. Tatsächlich erkennen wir diesen subjektiven Aspekt jedoch „direkt", ohne Reflexion: wir wissen „direkt" wie wir etwas sehen (oder zu sehen meinen). Das Ding-so-wie-ich-es-sehe steht sozusagen „vor" unseren Augen. Die adverbiale Theorie kann dieser „Objektivität" des subjektiven Aspektes insoweit Rechnung tragen, als sie eine passive statt eine aktive Redeweise verwendet. Zum Beispiel, statt „Ich sah rosarot-elefantlich" kann man sagen „Mir erschien-es rosarot-elefantlich" („I was appeared to pink-elephantly"). Doch trägt meiner Meinung nach auch diese Redeweise der Tatsache noch nicht genügend Rechnung, daß der Halluzierende etwas „vor" sich sieht, das in der realen Welt nicht vor ihm steht.

Die *Immanenz-Theorie* hat die entgegengesetzte Aufgabe in ihrem Rahmen einen Ersatz für den transzendenten Gegenstand zu finden. Sie versucht dies dadurch zu erreichen, daß sie den Begriff des immanenten Gegenstandes weiter differenziert. Und zwar beruft sie sich auf die Feststellung, daß es Akte des Identifizierens gibt, in denen verschiedenartige intentionale Gegenstände als ein und derselbe Gegenstand identifiziert werden. So kann ich zum Beispiel den Morgenstern, den ich heute sehe, mit dem Abendstern, den ich gestern gesehen habe, identifizieren. Ich habe in diesem Falle einen Gegenstand vor mir, auf den zwei Kennzeichnungen zutreffen. Die Immanenz-Theorie kann sagen, daß in einem solchen Fall die zwei immanenten Gegenstände, die den zwei Kennzeichnungen entsprechen, für mich denselben „Pol" haben und in diesem Sinne für mich derselbe Gegenstand sind. Bei genauerem Überlegen zeigt es sich jedoch, daß es nicht sehr klar ist, was dieser „identische Pol" sein soll, der „*in*" zwei immanenten Gegenständen vorkommen soll. Vor allem aber ist einzuwenden, daß die Redeweise von dem identischen Pol dem Begriff des transzendenten Gegenstandes nicht gleichwertig ist. Denn Akte des Identifizierens können auch bei Halluzinationen auftreten, wo kein entsprechender transzendenter Gegenstand vorhanden ist. Der wesentliche Unterschied zwischen dem identischen Pol zweier immanenter Gegenstände und dem transzendenten Gegenstand verschwindet nur bei Einnahme eines idealistischen Standpunktes, welcher den transzendenten Gegenstand als eine metaphysische Illusion auffaßt.

Die *Theorie der zwei Objekte* kann nicht, wie die zwei anderen Theorien, dem gegen sie erhobenen Einwand mit *zusätzlichen* Ausführungen begegnen. Sie muß vielmehr ihren Standpunkt *revidieren* und zugeben, daß nur einer der zwei Gegenstände, nämlich der transzendente Gegenstand, das Objekt ist, in dem die Intention terminiert. Wir erhalten somit eine spezielle Version der Transzendenz-Theorie. Der sogenannte immanente Gegenstand darf nun nicht mehr als ein Objekt im strikten Sinne, als ein *quod cognoscitur*, sondern nur noch als ein *medium quo* der Erkenntnis aufgefaßt werden. Husserl scheint eben diesen Begriff eines Pseudo-Objekts, das nur ein *medium quo* ist, entwickelt zu haben als er von der neotischen zu einer explizit neotisch-neomatischen Phänomenologie überging. Zuerst hatte er für dieses *medium quo* die Bezeichnung ‚ontische Bedeutung'[5] verwendet, erst einige Jahre später tritt die Bezeichnung ‚noema' auf. Der Ausdruck ‚ontische Bedeutung' ist wichtig, denn wenn die ontische Bedeutung wirklich eine Bedeutung, d.h. ein Sinn, ist, dann können wir von Frege lernen, daß diese ontische Bedeutung nicht das Referenzobjekt unserer Intention sein kann. Es muß sich in der Tat um ein *medium quo* handeln.

Die Ansicht, daß das Husserlsche Noema als ein Sinn aufzufassen sei, ist besonders von D. Føllesdal und seinen Schülern betont und mit der zeitgenössischen Semantik der möglichen Welten in Beziehung gesetzt worden, vgl. Smith und McIntyre (1982).

Wie ich andernorts ausgeführt habe, vgl. Küng (1975), S. 67, hat es noch weitere Vorteile, wenn die Beziehung zwischen immanentem und transzendentem Gegenstand nach dem Modell von Sinn und Referenzobjekt und nicht nach dem Modell von Wirkung und Ursache oder dem Modell von Zeichen und Bezeichnetem aufgefaßt wird. Der Sinnbegriff kann uns nämlich davor bewahren, das immanente Pseudoobjekt allzu sehr zu reifizieren und in den Repräsentationalismus der Immanenztheorie zu verfallen, wo der immanente Gegenstand als ein Bild oder Zeichen eines unsichtbaren transzendenten Gegenstandes aufgefaßt wird, von dem er verursacht sein soll. Eine Bedeutung, d.h. ein Sinn, ist im Gegensatz zu einem Bild oder Zeichen kein Ding, das ein anderes Ding verdecken kann, sondern sie ist, wie schon gesagt, ein *medium quo*, das seinem Wesen nach auf ein Referenzobjekt hin „durchsichtig" sein kann.

Doch die Auffassung, daß der immanente Gegenstand eine Bedeutung, ein *medium quo* und nicht das *quod* sei, das wir sehen (oder zu sehen meinen), löst nicht alle Probleme. Denn, indem wird die Theorie der zwei Objekte in eine Variante der Transzendenz-Theorie verwandeln, sind wir erneut mit dem Einwand gegen die Transzendenz-Theorie konfrontiert. Wenn nämlich der immanente Gegenstand in ein *medium quo* verwandelt wird, dann kann dieses *medium quo* nicht mehr das Objekt sein, das das Subjekt einer Halluzination zu sehen meint; dann ist dieses *medium quo* nur noch etwas, durch das „hindurch" dieses Subjekt ein *anderes*, nämlich einen Gegenstand, der nicht existiert, sieht. Das Vorhandensein einer immanenten ontischen Bedeutung kann die Schwierigkeit nicht lösen, die bei der Transzendenz-Theorie im Falle des Nichtexistierens des transzendenten Gegenstandes auftritt.

2. *Eine vierte Theorie*

Es scheint zunächst, daß kein Ausweg aus den genannten Schwierigkeiten möglich sei, da die behandelten drei Theorien das gesamte Spektrum der in der Terminologie von immanentem und transzendentem Gegenstand ausdrückbaren Möglichkeiten abzudecken scheinen. Doch wie wir sogleich sehen werden, kann uns ein genaueres Nachdenken über den Begriff des immanenten Gegenstandes weiterhelfen.

Denn was ist unter der Bewußtseinsimmanenz des immanenten Gegenstandes eigentlich zu verstehen? Sowohl Brentano wie auch Husserl betonen beide, daß der immanente Gegenstand nicht als realer (oder reeller) Bestandteil des Bewußtseins aufgefaßt werden kann, daß er nicht im selben Sinne mental ist wie der Bewußtseinsakt. Wie schon erwähnt, hat Brentano beim Nachdenken über diesen Punkt es schließlich aufgegeben, die Redeweise von dem intentionalen In-existieren eines immanenten Gegenstandes wörtlich zu nehmen.

Doch ein erstes läßt sich bezüglich der Immanenz des immanenten Gegenstandes mit Sicherheit festhalten. Die Behauptung, daß ein Gegenstand immanent ist, besagt sicher soviel, daß dieser Gegenstand vorhanden sein kann, auch wenn der transzendente Gegenstand nicht existiert. Die Reduktion des immanenten Gegenstandes auf eine ontische Bedeutung (einen Sinn) trägt dieser These und ebenso der festgestellten Irrealität des immanenten Gegenstandes Rechnung, denn eine Bedeutung ist in der Tat nichts Psychisches und sie kann vorhanden sein, auch wo das entsprechende Referenzobjekt fehlt.

Aber die Bedeutung eines Aktes kann nicht zugleich dessen Objekt sein, und es ist genau dieser Umstand, der uns stört. Denn er ist dafür verantwortlich, daß im Falle der Halluzination die Transzendenz-Theorie nichts enthält, das dem halluzinierten Gegenstand entspricht. Wir müssen deshalb versuchen, trotzdem an der These festzuhalten, daß der immanente Gegenstand Objekt des Bewußtseinsaktes ist. Gleichzeitig wollen wir aber auch die Überzeugung nicht aufgeben, wonach unsere Erkenntnis fähig ist, die transzendente Realität zu erfassen, das heißt wir wollen auch an der These festhalten, daß im Falle einer Wahrnehmung der transzendente Gegenstand das Objekt ist, in dem die Erkenntnis terminisiert. Beide Thesen zugleich lassen sich aber − wenn man die Theorie der zwei Objekte ablehnt − nur unter einer Bedingung festhalten: der *immanente Gegenstand muß in den Fällen, wo der transzendente Gegenstand existiert, mit dem transzendenten Gegenstand identisch sein!* Wir müssen also untersuchen, ob die folgende vierte Theorie des intentionalen Gegenstandes möglich ist:

	Wahrnehmung	Halluzination
Vierte Theorie	Der Akt hat *ein* Objekt: nämlich einen immmanenten Gegenstand, der mit dem transzendenten Gegenstand *identisch* ist.	Der Akt hat *ein* Objekt: nämlich einen immanenten Gegenstand.

Ist diese vierte Theorie nicht ein Widersinn? Wie soll ein immanenter Gegenstand mit einem transzendenten Gegenstand, d.h. mit einem Ding der realen Außenwelt identisch sein können?

Nun, dies hängt von der Bedeutung ab, die wir dem Wort ‚immanent‘ geben. Wir haben schon gesehen, daß das Adjektiv ‚immanent‘ nicht besagt, daß der immanente Gegenstand ein realer Bestandteil des Bewußtseins sei. Ebenso ist es falsch, das Bewußtsein als eine Art Schachtel aufzufassen. ‚Im Bewußtsein immanent‘ kann also auch nicht soviel wie ‚im Bewußtsein eingeschlossen‘ heißen. Die Immanenz des immanenten Gegenstandes bedeutet vielmehr nichts anderes als, daß *der Gegenstand vom Innern eines Subjektes her vermeint (d.h. intendiert) ist.* Ein Gegenstand der in diesem Sinne immanent ist, kann sehr wohl zugleich transzendent sein, denn ein Ding, das vom Innern eines Subjekts her vermeint ist, kann sehr wohl zugleich ein Ding der realen Außenwelt sein. Aber auch die früher formulierte These, wonach ein immanenter Gegenstand selbst dann vorhanden sein kann, wenn der transzendente Gegenstand fehlt, stimmt: es kommt oft vor, daß ein Ding, das vom Innern eines Subjektes her vermeint ist, in der realen Außenwelt nicht existiert. Übrigens stimmt diese Charakterisierung des immanenten Gegenstandes auch mit dem überein, was der Halluzierende erlebt: dieser berichtet z.B. nicht, er sehe in seinem Innern, in einem Akt der Reflektion einen rosaroten Elefanten, sondern er berichtet vielmehr, daß er dieses „Tier" irgendwie „vor sich" sehe.

Vielleicht ist der Ausdruck ‚immanenter Gegenstand‘ so sehr mit unhaltbaren Auffassungen vorbelastet, daß es, um Mißverständnisse zu vermeiden, klüger ist, für die Bedeutung ‚vom Innern eines Subjektes her vermeinter Gegenstand‘ einen anderen Ausdruck zu verwenden. Dies bietet keine Schwierigkeiten, da uns ja noch der Ausdruck ‚intentionaler Gegenstand‘ zur Verfügung steht und man ‚intentional‘ ohne weiteres mit ‚vom Innern eines Subjektes her vermeint‘ gleichsetzen kann.

3. *Die Schwierigkeiten der vierten Theorie*

Schon ein kurzes Nachdenken zeigt, daß auch die vierte Theorie ihre ganz besonderen Schwierigkeiten hat.

3.1 In den Fällen, wo wie bei der Halluzination zwar ein intentionaler, d.h. vom Innern her vermeinter Gegenstand beschrieben werden kann, aber in der realen Außenwelt dieser Gegenstand nicht vorhanden ist, stellt sich ein besonderes Problem. Soll man sagen, daß in diesen Fällen der von innen her vermeinte Gegenstand existiert oder soll man sagen, daß er nicht existiert? Für das erstere spricht die Tatsache, daß ein Gegenstand vermeint ist, für das letztere die Tatsache, daß dieser vermeinte Gegenstand in Wirklichkeit nicht existiert. Offensichtlich sind wir hier mit dem Meinongschen Problem der nicht-existierenden Gegenstände konfrontiert: haben diese Gegenstände irgendeine Art von Existenz oder haben sie absolut keine Existenz?

Da wir dazu gelangt sind, das Problem genau so zu stellen, wie es sich Meinong gestellt hat, so ist es nicht erstaunlich, daß Meinongs Antwort uns als die natürlichste erscheint: es ist wahr, daß in diesen Fällen etwas vermeint ist, aber es ist ebenso wahr, daß das, was vermeint ist, nicht existiert. Nehmen wir wieder das Beispiel mit den halluzinierten rosaroten Elefanten. Etwas ganz Bestimmtes ist vermeint, nämlich rosarote Elefanten und nicht etwa grüne

Pferde oder Präsident Mitterand. Aber diese rosaroten Elefanten existieren nicht, sie sind bloß vermeint. Tatsächlich ist es für sie durchaus genug, daß sie vermeint sind, denn das Vermeintsein genügt, damit etwas beschrieben werden kann. Als Phänomenologen können wir genau beschreiben, *was* wir vermeinen und *wie* wie es vermeinen, unabhängig davon, ob das Vermeinte nun auch existiert oder nicht. Wir können sogar die *Weise* beschreiben, in der ein vermeinter Gegenstand unserer Meinung nach existiert (ob wir ihm z.B. eine reale oder eine ideale Existenzweise zuschreiben); und wir können beschreiben, *wie überzeugt* wir von seiner Existenz sind (ob wir z.B. wirklich meinen, daß der Gegenstand existiert, oder ob wir, wie in einem Akt des Phantasierens, nur so tun, als ob er existiere). Alles dies können wir beschreiben, unabhängig davon, ob der besagte Gegenstand nun tatsächlich existiert oder nicht.

Aber ist es wirklich richtig, von den nicht-existierenden Gegenständen zu sagen, daß sie gar keine Art von Existenz haben? Ist Vermeint-sein nicht auch schon eine schwache Art des Existierens? Denn heißt Vermeint-sein nicht soviel wie ‚als Objekt eines Subjektes existieren'? Sind wir also nicht gezwungen, die paradoxale Feststellung zu machen, daß die nicht-existierenden Gegenstände doch irgendwie existieren?

Ich glaube nicht, daß dieses Argument zwingend ist. Selbst wenn wir die Redeweise zulassen,[6] daß etwas als Objekt eines Subjektes existiert, so folgt aus der Tatsache, daß etwas als Objekt eines Subjektes existiert, noch nicht, daß dieses Etwas existiert. Aus der Tatsache, daß Wilhelm Tell als Statue existiert, folgt ja auch noch nicht, daß Wilhelm Tell existiert oder existiert hat. Die Aussage ‚*a* existiert als Objekt eines Subjektes' ist nur oberflächlicherweise mit einer Aussage wie z.B. ‚*a* existiert als materielles Ding' verwandt. Aus ‚*a* existiert als materielles Ding' folgt ‚*a* existiert', denn daß *a* als materielles Ding existiert, heißt, daß *a* tatsächlich in der Weise eines materiellen Dinges existiert. Wenn man mir aber nur mitteilt, daß *a* als Objekt eines Subjektes existiert, dann weiß ich noch gar nichts über die Seinsweise von *a*, und ich weiß auch nicht, ob *a* existiert.

Natürlich bestehen zwischen dem Als-Objekt-eines-Subjektes-existieren und dem Als-Statue-existieren auch wesentliche Unterschiede.Eine Statue und eine Person, die durch die Statue dargestellt wird, sind nie identisch, während nach unserer vierten Theorie das intentionale Objekt mit dem transzendenten Gegenstand identisch sein muß, wo ein solcher existiert. Ferner gilt, daß wenn Wilhelm Tell als Statue existiert, dann vielleicht nicht Wilhelm Tell, aber sicher eine Statue existiert. Wenn dagegen ein rosaroter Elefant als Objekt eines Subjektes existiert, dann folgt daraus, weder daß ein rosaroter Elefant existiert, noch auch daß ein Objekt existiert.[7] Das Bestehen dieser Unterschiede soll uns nicht erstaunen, denn Ein-intentionaler-Gegenstand-sein und Eine-Statue-sein ist eben trotz des Bestehens einer gewissen Analogie etwas sehr Verschiedenes.

Aus der Tatsache, daß *a* als Objekt eines Subjektes existiert, folgt nicht, daß *a* existiert; es folgt aber auch nicht, daß *a nicht* existiert. Intentionale Gegenstände sind als solche − um mit Meinong zu sprechen − „jenseits" oder „außerhalb" von Sein und Nichtsein.[8] Natürlich ist dieses Jenseits-von-Sein-und-Nichtsein-sein nicht seinerseits eine Seinsweise, eine Weise des Existierens.

3.2 „‚Ein-intentionaler-Gegenstand-sein' heißt soviel wie ‚vom-Innern-eines-Subjektes-her-vermeint-sein". Positiv gesagt ist also das Ein-intentionaler-Gegenstand-sein ein bestimmtes Vermeint-sein. Intentionale Akte sind Akte, die in einer bestimmten Richtung, auf einen bestimmten Punkt hin zeigen. Intentionale Gegenstände, d.h. vermeinte Gegenstände, haben deshalb eine gewisse *Identität*.[9]

Es ist eine Tatsache, daß ein Gegenstand in diesem Sinne identifiziert werden kann, bevor wir wissen, ob er überhaupt vorhanden ist, ob er existiert oder nicht. Jedermann kann sich zum Beispiel ein Pferd vorstellen und dann annehmen, daß *dieses* Pferd über ein Hindernis springt und daß *es* stürzt, sich ein Bein bricht, usw. usf. Bei der Beschreibung solcher Fälle ist es völlig normal, hinweisende Artikel und Pronomina zu gebrauchen, welche angeben, daß ständig derselbe Gegenstand vermeint wird. Es ist überdies in der Umgangssprache durchaus möglich, einen in der Phantasie vermeinten Gegenstand mit einem in der realen Wirklichkeit existierenden Gegenstand zu identifizieren. Es ist z.B. denkbar, daß, während ich nicht glaube, daß das Loch Ness Ungeheuer existiert und ich mir bloß in der Phantasie vorstelle, daß *es* im Loch Ness herumschwimmt, *dieses* Ungeheuer tatsächlich existiert und jemand *es* gesehen hat . . . Dieser Gebrauch der Pronomina und der hinweisende Artikel in der Umgangssprache zeigt, daß die vierte Theorie keineswegs ein künstliches Gebilde ist, sondern sogar sehr genau mit den Redeweisen der natürlichen Sprache harmoniert.

Die intentionalen Gegenstände können in etwa mit geographischen *Koordinationspunkten* verglichen werden,[10] und die Frage, ob sich die intentionalen Gegenstände innerhalb oder außerhalb des Bewußtseins befinden, ist wie die Frage, ob sich die geographischen Koordinationspunkte im Bewußtsein der Geographen oder in der Außenwelt befinden. Man könnte argumentieren, daß es ohne Geographen keine geographischen Koordinationspunkte geben würde, und daß sich diese Punkte folglich im Bewußtsein des Geographen befinden müßten. Aber dieses Argument ist nicht überzeugend. Denn, wenn man einem Geographen sagt, daß an einem bestimmten Koordinatenpunkt ein Schatz vergraben liegt, dann sucht er nicht in seinem Bewußtsein nach diesem Schatz, sondern verifiziert, ob dieser Punkt mit einem bestimmten Ort der Erde identisch sei.

3.3 Doch die Annahme nicht existierender Gegenstände wirft ein weiteres Problem auf, das meiner Ansicht nach den eigentlichen Kern der Problematik der nicht-existierenden Gegenstände bildet: Können nicht-existierende Gegenstände Eigenschaften haben, und falls sie Eigenschaften haben, welcher Art sind diese Eigenschaften?

3.3.1. Nehmen wir den Fall, wo ich mir in reiner Phantasie ein grünes Pferd vorstelle. In diesem Fall ist etwas als ein Pferd und als grün-seiend *vermeint*.[11] Aber kann man auch sagen, daß hier etwas ein Pferd *ist* und grün *ist*? Das fragliche „grüne Pferd" existiert ja nicht, wie kann es da *grün* sein, so wie z.B. ein existierender Baum grün ist?[12] Aber es ist sicher *als-grün-seiend-vermeint*. Von daher scheint es plausibel, den nicht-existierenden Gegenständen statt der gewöhnlichen Eigenschaften nur sogenannte konvers-intentionale Eigenschaften[13] wie Als-ein-Pferd-vermeint-zu-sein und Als-grün-seiend-vermeint-zu-sein zuzuschreiben. Bezüglich der konvers-intentionalen Eigenschaften scheint es noch am ehesten möglich, die erstaunliche These zu akzeptieren, daß sie exemplifiziert sein können, selbst wenn der exemplifizierende Gegenstand ein nicht-existierender Gegenstand ist.[14]

Doch nicht-existierende Gegenstände müssen auch andere als konvers-intentionale Eigenschaften haben. Denn nicht-existierende Gegenstände sind tatsächlich nicht-existierend, sie haben also auch die Eigenschaft nicht-existierend zu sein, und diese Eigenschaft ist keine konvers-intentionale Eigenschaft. Ein Gegenstand kann die Eigenschaft des Nicht-existierendseins ja sogar dann besitzen, wenn er von einem Subjekt als existierend vermeint ist. Aber das Nicht-existierend-sein ist keine gewöhnliche Eigenschaft, und so können wir weiterhin behaupten, daß die nicht-existierenden Gegenstände sich dadurch auszeichnen, daß sie keine gewöhnlichen Eigenschaften haben.

3.3.2 Doch die These, daß ein vorgestellter Gegenstand, der nicht existiert, nicht die Eigenschaft Grün, sondern nur die Eigenschaft Als-grün-seiend-vermeint-zu-sein haben könne, kann auch in Zweifel gezogen werden. Denn wenn ich mir in meiner Phantasie ein grünes Pferd vorstelle, stelle ich mir dann wirklich etwas vor, das nur als-grün-seiend-vermeint ist? Sagen wir in einem solchen Fall nicht ganz spontan, daß ich mir etwas vorstelle, das *grün ist*?

Meinong vertritt deshalb in Übereinstimmung mit der Umgangssprache, die These, daß im besprochenen Beispiel der vorgestellte Gegenstand ein Pferd ist und grün ist.[15] Die Merkwürdigkeit, daß demnach etwas Nicht-existierendes ein Pferd und grün sein kann, sucht Meinong mit seiner Lehre vom *Sosein* und *Dasein* zu erklären. Das vorgestellte grüne Pferd hat kein Dasein, aber es hat das Sosein eines Pferdes und es hat das Sosein eines grünen Dinges.

Ich kann mir aber auch vorstellen, daß ein grünes Pferd in der realen Außenwelt existiert. Was ich mir vorstelle ist dann nicht nur ein Pferd und grün, es ist auch ein in der realen

Außenwelt Existierendes. Gleichzeitig ist es aber auch ein nichtexistierender Gegenstand. Wie ist das möglich? Offensichtlich muß hier, wenn man nicht zwei Gegenstände annehmen will, die Kopula zwei verschiedene Bedeutungen haben:[16]

(1) Das Vorgestellte ist$_1$ ein in der realen Außenwelt existierendes grünes Pferd.
(2) Das Vorgestellte ist$_2$ ein nicht-existierender Gegenstand.
Wie ist aber der Unterschied dieser zwei Kopulas zu verstehen?

Die These, die den nicht-existierenden Gegenständen die gewöhnlichen Eigenschaften abspricht, kann den Unterschied zwischen diesen Kopulas mit Hilfe des weniger mysteriösen Unterschiedes zwischen der Prädikation von konvers-intentionalen Eigenschaften und der Prädikation von nicht konvers-intentionalen Eigenschaften wegerklären:

(3) Das Vorgestellte *ist vermeint als* ein in der realen Außenwelt existierendes grünes Pferd.
(4) Das Vorgestellte *ist* ein nicht-existierender Gegenstand.

In (3) ist die Kopula ‚ist$_1$‘ von (1) durch den Ausdruck ‚ist vermeint als‘ übersetzt worden. Der Ausdruck ‚ist vermeint als‘ ist zusammengesetzt aus der Kopula ‚ist‘ und dem Ausdruck ‚vermeint als‘, der dem Prädikat zuzurechnen ist. Es kommt also in (3) und (4) nur noch *eine* Kopula vor. Allerdings handelt es sich, um eine etwas ungewöhnliche Kopula, da sie ja, wie schon die Kopulas ‚ist$_1$‘ und ‚ist$_2$‘ auch dann eine wahre Aussage bilden kann, wenn der dem Subjekt-Terminus entsprechende Gegenstand nicht existiert. Es genügt für diese Kopula, daß der Subjektgegenstand eine gewisse Identität besitzt.

Daß die These, die den nicht-existierenden Gegenständen die gewöhnlichen Eigenschaften abspricht, die Schwierigkeit mit den zwei Kopulas wegerklären kann, ist der große Vorteil dieser These. Die Alternative scheint also zu lauten: entweder (a) wir schreiben den nicht-existierenden Gegenständen gewöhnliche Eigenschaften zu: dann sind wir in Übereinstimmung mit der Umgangssprache, müssen aber die Schwierigkeit mit den zwei Kopulas in Kauf nehmen; oder (b) wir schreiben den nicht-existierenden Gegenständen statt der gewöhnlichen Eigenschaften nur entsprechende konvers-intentionale Eigenschaften zu: dann sind wir die Schwierigkeit mit den zwei Kopulas los, doch verwerfen wir in diesem Fall gewisse gängige umgangssprachliche Redeweisen.

3.3.3 Um die Alternative intuitiv etwas besser in den Griff zu bekommen, wollen wir einen Fall näher betrachten, der zwischen Wahrnehmung und Fiktion eine Mittelstellung einnimmt, nämlich den Fall einer sich täuschenden Wahrnehmung (delusory perception, misperception)[17], wo ich ein Maultier für ein Pferd halte.

Wenn wir die Analyse des intentionalen Gegenstandes mit Hilfe von konvers-intentionalen Eigenschaften durchführen, dann geht alles ohne Schwierigkeiten. Wir finden dann, daß der intentionale Gegenstand hier etwas ist, das neben anderen die zwei Eigenschaften Als-ein-Pferd-vermeint-zu-sein und Nicht-als-ein-Maultier-vermeint-zu-sein hat. Dieser intentionale Gegenstand ist nach Auffassung der vierten Theorie mit dem transzendenten Gegenstand identisch, der neben anderen die zwei Eigenschaften Ein-Maultier-zu-sein und Nicht-ein-Pferd-zu-sein hat. Es gibt also nach dieser Analyse einen einzigen Gegenstand, der neben anderen die vier folgenden Eigenschaften hat: Ein-Maultier-zu-sein, Nicht-ein-Pferd-zu-sein, Als-ein-Pferd-vermeint-zu-sein, Nicht-als-ein-Maultier-vermeint-zu-sein. Diese vier Eigenschaften sind problemlos kompatibel und der Gegenstand ist ein ganz normales existierendes Maultier.

In Übereinstimmung mit der Umgangssprache kann man aber bei dieser sich täuschenden Wahrnehmung noch von etwas anderem als von diesem Maultier sprechen. Das Maultier ist das, was *effektiv* vor dem Betrachter steht. Man kann aber auch von dem sprechen, was vor dem Betrachter stehen *müßte*, wenn die falsche Behauptung ‚Vor mir steht ein Pferd‘ wahr wäre: es müßte dann etwas vor mir stehen, das die Eigenschaft Ein-Pferd-zu-sein hat; auch müßte dieses Etwas natürlich die Eigenschaft des Existierend-seins haben. Da ich während der Täuschung tatsächlich meine, daß die Behauptung ‚Vor mir steht ein Pferd‘ wahr sei, so kann man sagen, daß während der Täuschung meine Intention nicht nur auf das Maultier, sondern auch auf dieses Pferd gerichtet sei.

Das Pferd, das da sein müßte, wenn die Behauptung ‚Vor mir steht ein Pferd‘ wahr wäre, kann mit dem Maultier, das effektiv vor mir steht *nicht* identisch sein, da das Maultier kein Pferd ist. Auch ist das Pferd, das da sein müßte, in Wirklichkeit nicht da, es ist ein nicht-existierender Gegenstand. Wie ersichtlich, muß es sich um einen Gegenstand handeln, der die oben erwähnte Schwierigkeit mit den zwei Kopulas mit sich bringt: der besagte Gegenstand ist$_1$ ein existierendes Pferd und er ist$_2$ ein nicht-existierender Gegenstand. Natürlich hat dieser nicht-existierende Gegenstand im Augenblick der Täuschung nicht die Eigenschaft, als ein nicht-existierender Gegenstand vermeint zu sein. Im Gegenteil, er ist$_2$ zu jenem Zeitpunkt als-existierend-vermeint, nämlich als-ein-existierendes-Pferd-vermeint.

Wir scheinen also bei diesem Beispiel einer sich täuschenden Wahrnehmung gleich wie vorher beim Beispiel einer reinen Phantasievorstellung mit einer Alternative von zwei Objekten konfrontiert zu sein. Doch eine etwas sorgfältigere Überlegung zeigt, daß die Alternative eine etwas komplexere Gestalt hat. Sie lautet nämlich nicht: *entweder* nehmen wir den Gegenstand der ersten Analyse, nämlich das Maultier, das die konvers-intentionale Eigenschaft des Als-Pferd-vermeint-seins hat an, *oder* wir nehmen den Gegenstand der zweiten Analyse, das Pferd, das zugleich ein nicht-existierender Gegenstand ist, an. Die Alternative lautet vielmehr: *entweder* nehmen wir nur den Gegenstand der ersten Analyse an, *oder* wir nehmen sowohl den Gegenstand der ersten Analyse als auch den Gegenstand der zweiten Analyse an.

Vom Standpunkt des Sparsamkeitsprinzips der analytischen Philosophie ist es empfehlenswert, bei der Beschreibung der sich täuschenden Wahrnehmung nur auf das keine Schwierigkeiten machende Maultier zu sprechen zu kommen. Vom Standpunkt der Phänomenologie hingegen, scheint der Gegensatz zwischen dem, was vor mir stehen müßte, und dem, was effektiv vor mir steht, für das Wesen der Täuschung besonders charakteristisch zu sein. Der Phänomenologe ist nicht in erster Linie an Sparsamkeit interessiert, sondern er sucht im Gegenteil eine möglichst reichhaltige Ontologie zu entwickeln. Er wird also versuchen beide Gegenstände, sowohl das Maultier als auch das nicht-existierende Pferd in seine Beschreibung einzubauen.

Der Phänomenologe erhält so eine neuartige „Theorie mit zwei Objekten“. Es handelt sich dabei nicht etwa um eine Version der früheren Theorie der zwei Objekte, die zwischen dem transzendenten Gegenstand und einem als ‚immanent‘ bezeichneten Gegenstand-genau-so-wie-er-vermeint-ist unterschied. Denn bei dieser neuartigen Theorie mit zwei Objekten ist ja jedes der zwei Objekte, sowohl das Maultier als auch das nicht-existierende Pferd, ein Objekt im Sinne der vierten Theorie: jedes von ihnen hat sowohl ein gewisses An-sich-sein, das von den Erkenntnisakten des Subjekts unabhängig ist, als auch ein gewisses Vermeint-sein, d.h. gewisse konvers-intentionale Eigenschaften.[18]

3.3.4 Ein Unterschied zwischen dem, was vor mir stehen müßte, und dem, was effektiv vor mir steht, ist dem Phänomenologen noch von einem anderen Beispiel her geläufig. Ein analoger Unterschied tritt nämlich beim Versuch einen kontradiktorischen Gegenstand zu denken auf.

Nehmen wir den Versuch ein rundes Viereck zu denken. In diesem Falle *müßte*, wenn mein Denkversuch gelingen würde, ein Ding vor meinem geistigen Auge stehen, das zugleich rund und viereckig *ist*. Doch die Eigenschaften Rund-zu-sein und Viereckig-zu-sein sind nicht kompatibel, mein Denkversuch kann deshalb unmöglich zu dem erstrebten Ende kommen. Der Gegenstand, der rund und viereckig ist$_1$, ist$_2$ ein unmöglicher Gegenstand, der weder existieren noch auch „effektiv gedacht“ werden kann. Effektiv steht vor meinem geistigen Auge nur ein Etwas, das die Eigenschaft hat als rund und viereckig *vermeint* zu sein, das aber nicht rund und viereckig *ist*.

Natürlich ist die Unterscheidung zwischen den zwei Objekten beim Beispiel des Denkens eines runden Vierecks schwerer nachzuvollziehen als beim Beispiel der sich täuschenden Wahrnehmung. Bei der sich täuschenden Wahrnehmung war nur eines der beiden Objekte ein nicht-existierender Gegenstand, während das andere Objekt ein handfestes Maultier war. Beim Denken eines runden Vierecks sind beide Objekte nicht-existierende Gegenstände, und überdies ist hier gerade das Etwas, das dem Maultier entspricht und das wie das Maultier logisch unproblematischer ist, ein Etwas, von dem man im Alltag nie spricht. Wir haben deshalb große Mühe, dieses Etwas zu bemerken, obwohl es im Gegensatz zum runden Viereck effektiv vor unserem geistigen Auge steht und obwohl es im Gegensatz zum runden Viereck kein kontradiktorischer Gegenstand ist und mit nur einer Kopula auskommt. Ich meine aber, daß die Analogie zum Maultier der sich täuschenden Wahrnehmung uns helfen kann, dieses ungewohnte Etwas zu erfassen.

3.3.5 Kehren wir nunmehr, nach dem Exkurs über die sich täuschende Wahrnehmung und das Denken unmöglicher Gegenstände, wieder zur reinen Phantasievorstellung eines grünen Pferdes zurück. Wir bemerken sofort, daß es auch hier bei den zwei Objekten um eine Unterscheidung zwischen dem, was vor mir stehen müßte, und dem, was effektiv vor mir steht, geht. Phantasieren heißt ja in einem gewissen Sinne so tun, als ob man etwas Bestimmtes wahrnehmbar vor sich hätte; es ist in einem gewissen Sinne ein Wünschen (aber natürlich nicht ein ernst gemeintes Wünschen), daß etwas wahrnehmbar vor mir stehe. Im gegebenen Fall ist ein grünes Pferd das, was vor mir stehen müßte, wenn der Phantasiewunsch erfüllt sein sollte. Was hingegen effektiv vor meinem geistigen Auge steht, ist ein Etwas, das die Eigenschaft hat als-ein-wahrnehmbar-vor-mir-stehendes-grünes-Pferd-*vermeint-zu-sein*, das aber nicht die Eigenschaft hat, ein-wahrnehmbar-vor-mir-stehendes-grünes-Pferd-*zu-sein*.

3.3.6 Ziehen wir aus dem zu den drei Beispielen Gesagten die Bilanz. In allen diesen Fällen kann man von zwei Objekten sprechen, nämlich von dem, was in einem gewissen Sinne (und in jedem Beispiel wieder in einem etwas anderen Sinne) vor mir stehen *müßte*, und von dem, was in einem gewissen Sinne *effektiv* vor mir steht. Der Umstand, daß die zwei Objekte nicht identisch sind, daß das, was vor mir stehen müßte, und das, was effektiv vor mir steht, auseinanderfällt, besagt, daß in allen diesen Beispielen eine gewisse (aber je wieder anders geartete) Unerfülltheit besteht. Gewöhnlich sind die Phänomenologen mehr am Thema der Erfüllung als am Thema der Unerfülltheit interessiert. Doch ist natürlich das eine dieser Themen immer die Kehrseite des anderen. Die hier entwickelte Unterscheidung von zwei Objekten, die beide Objekte im Sinne der vierten Theorie sind, kann also auch als ein kleiner Beitrag zur Analyse der Erfülltheit aufgefaßt werden. Man kann ja sagen, daß die Erfülltheit neben anderen Merkmalen das Merkmal einer ganz bestimmten Einfachheit, nämlich eben der Abwesenheit jener Unterscheidung, beinhaltet. Tatsächlich ist bei einer täuschungsfreien Wahrnehmung, beim Sich-denken eines möglichen Gegenstandes, beim Wahrnehmen und nicht nur Phantasieren, das, was vor mir stehen soll, und das, was effektiv vor mir steht, nicht mehr unterschieden. Es gibt jeweils nur noch *ein* Objekt, und zwar das logisch problemlose Objekt, und zudem stimmen alle konvers-intentionalen Eigenschaften dieses Objektes mit seinen „gewöhnlichen" Eigenschaften überein. Wenn zum Beispiel ein Maultier täuschungsfrei als ein Maultier wahrgenommen wird, dann hat dieses Maultier sowohl die Eigenschaft Als-ein-Maultier-vermeint-zu-sein als auch die Eigenschaft Ein-Maultier-zu-sein.

In dem vorliegenden Aufsatz habe ich die Unterscheidung der zwei Objekte im Sinne der vierten Theorie nur intuitiv und informell skizziert. Wie ich jedoch nachträglich festgestellt habe, sind diese zwei Objektbegriffe nicht nur formalisier*bar*, sie scheinen zum Teil schon weitgehend formalisiert worden zu sein, allerdings nicht zusammen in *einem* System, sondern getrennt in zwei verschiedenen Systemen. Diese Arbeiten gehen auf zwei verschiedene Anregungen von Ernst Mally zurück, wie die Schwierigkeiten der Meinongschen Gegenstandstheorie gelöst werden könnten. Diese Anregungen sind durch Findlay (1933) einem angelsächsischen Leserkreis vermittelt worden.

Die eine Anregung[19] ist von Meinong selbst als Lösung akzeptiert worden. Sie entspricht ungefähr meiner Unterscheidung der zwei Kopulas. In Meinongs Terminologie ausgedrückt handelt es sich um die Unterscheidung zwischen „konstitutorischen Eigenschaften" (entsprechend der Kopula ‚ist$_1$') und „außerkonstitutorischen Eigenschaften" (entsprechend der Kopula ‚ist$_2$'). Findlay spricht von „nuclear properties" und „extra-nuclear properties". Die ausführlichste Ausarbeitung eines Systems, das auf dieser Anregung basiert, findet sich in Parsons (1980).

Die zweite Anregung Mallys[10] entspricht in gewisser Hinsicht meiner Unterscheidung zwischen dem Haben von konvers-intentionalen Eigenschaften und dem Haben von nicht-konvers-intentionalen Eigenschaften. Mally empfiehlt hier nämlich zwischen dem Bestimmt-sein durch eine Bestimmung und dem Erfüllen einer Bestimmung zu unterscheiden. Er nimmt zum Beispiel an, das sogenannte runde Viereck sei nur durch die Bestimmung des Rund-und-viereckig-seins *bestimmt*, aber es *erfülle* diese Bestimmung nicht (Findlay würde sagen „it is determined by this determination, but it does not satisfy it".) Dies entspricht in etwa meiner Rede von einem Etwas, das nur als rund-und-viereckig-seiend-vermeint ist, aber nicht rund-und-viereckig ist. Doch ist die Entsprechung zwischen dem Mallyschen Bestimmt-sein und meinem Vermeint-sein nur in beschränktem Umfange vorhanden. Zum einen ist das Mallysche Bestimmt-sein unpersönlich verstanden, während ein Vermeint-sein nur vorkommen kann, wenn es eine Person gibt, die vermeint. Zum anderen scheint Mally nur von abstrakten Gegenständen zu sagen, daß sie bestimmt werden: die Bestimmung des Pferd-seins bestimmt nur den abstrakten Gegenstand „ein Pferd" und nicht ein konkretes existierendes Pferd. Trotz dieser Unterschiede besteht aber doch, wenigstens was die abstrakten (d.h. nicht-existierenden) Gegenstände betrifft, eine große Ähnlichkeit zu dem Objektbegriff, den ich als den logisch weniger problematischen bezeichnet habe.

Die zweite Anregung von Mally ist 1983 von Zalta, einem Schüler Parsons', systematisch ausgearbeitet worden. Dabei wurde die Terminologie etwas geändert: statt vom Erfüllen einer Bestimmung spricht Zalta vom Exemplifizieren einer Eigenschaft; und an Stelle der passiven Redeweise, die sagt, daß ein abstrakter Gegenstand *durch eine Bestimmung bestimmt werde*, führt Zalta eine positive Redeweise ein, nach der dieser Gegenstand *eine Eigenschaft enkodiere* (encodes).[21] Zalta nimmt zum Beispiel an, daß es nichts gibt, das die komplexe Eigenschaft Rund-und-viereckig-zu-sein exemplifiziert, daß aber ein gewisser abstrakter Gegenstand diese Eigenschaft enkodiert. Im Vergleich zu meinen eigenen Ausführungen besteht ein gewisser Unterschied, indem Zalta von zwei verschiedenen Beziehungen zwischen Gegenständen und Eigenschaften, dem Exemplifizieren und dem Enkodieren, aber nicht von zwei Arten von Eigenschaften, wie zum Beispiel dem Rot-exemplifizierend-sein (d.h. Rot-sein) und dem Rot-enkodierend-sein, spricht. Doch die letztere Redeweise ließe sich wohl ohne Schwierigkeiten in sein System einbauen.

ANMERKUNGEN

* Eine frühere Fassung dieses Aufsatzes ist in englischer Sprache in der Zeitschrift *Dialectica* Bd. 38 (1984), S. 143−156 erschienen.

[1] Ich verstehe unter Halluzination das, was Smith (1983), S. 97−98 als naive Halluzination bezeichnet. Smith unterscheidet zwischen illusionäre Wahrnehmung (illusory perception: es existiert etwas in der Wirklichkeit, aber es ist nicht so wie es dem wahrnehmenden Subjekt erscheint), sich täuschender Wahrnehmung (delusory perception: es existiert etwas in der Wirklichkeit, es ist nicht so wie es erscheint, aber das wahrnehmende Subjekt meint, es sei so wie es erscheint), naive Halluzination (naive hallucination: etwas erscheint einer halluzinierenden Person und diese Person meint das Erscheinende existiere in der Wirklichkeit, aber tatsächlich entspricht dem Erscheinenden nichts in

der Wirklichkeit), aufgeklärte Halluzination (hip hallucination: etwas erscheint einer halluzinierenden Person als ob es in der Wirklichkeit existiere, doch die halluzinierende Person nimmt richtigerweise an, daß dem Erscheinenden in der Wirklichkeit nichts entspreche) und neutraler Halluzination (neutral hallucination: etwas erscheint einer halluzinierenden Person, tatsächlich entspricht dem Erscheinenden nichts in der Wirklichkeit, doch die halluzinierende Person läßt die Frage unentschieden, ob dem Erscheinenden in der Wirklichkeit etwas entspreche oder nicht). − Es wird oft behauptet, daß, was die subjektive Erfahrung betrifft, zwischen einer naiven Halluzination und einer echten Wahrnehmung kein Unterschied besteht. Doch scheint mir diese Auffassung nicht richtig zu sein. Ich würde eher sagen, daß die einer naiven Halluzination unterliegende Person die Merkmale, die ihre subjektives Erleben von dem Erleben einer echten Wahrnehmung unterscheiden, nicht bemerkt, daß solche Merkmale jedoch vorhanden sind.

[2] Husserl (1896), S. 351 Fußnote: „Die Vorstellungstätigkeit bewegt sich nicht in doppelter Richtung."

[3] Vgl. z.B. Butchvarov (1980), Tye (1984).

[4] Vgl. Küng (1973). Wie ich aufgewiesen habe, hat Husserl in seinen „Vorlesungen über Bedeutungslehre" vom Sommersemester 1908 (unveröffentlichtes Manuskript F I 5) zwischen phansischer und ontischer Bedeutung unterschieden.

[5] Vgl. Anmerkung 4. Husserl spricht von der ontischen Bedeutung als dem „Gegenstand genommen in der Weise wie er bedeutet oder gedacht ist", und setzt den so verstandenen Gegenstand dem „Gegenstand schlechthin" gegenüber, der im Falle eines falschen Urteils fehlen kann. Wenn man den Ausdruck ‚Bedeutung' mit ‚Sinn' gleichsetzt, dann ist man geneigt die Beziehung zwischen dem „Gegenstand genommen in der Weise wie er bedeutet oder gedacht ist" und dem „Gegenstand schlechthin" als die Beziehung zwischen Sinn und Referenzobjekt aufzufassen. Man kann aber auch versuchen, diese Husserlschen Redeweisen im Sinne der vierten Theorie zu verstehen, auf die ich im Folgenden zu sprechen kommen werde.

[6] Vgl. jedoch Anmerkung 7.

[7] Der Umstand, daß im Rahmen der vierten Theorie aus ‚a existiert als Objekt eines Subjektes' nicht gefolgert werden darf ‚Ein Objekt existiert', legt nahe, daß es vielleicht doch sinnvoller ist, hier die Redeweise, daß etwas als Objekt eines Subjektes existiert, zu verbieten.

[8] Vgl. Meinong (1904), S. 494: „man könnte vielleicht sagen: der reine Gegenstand stehe «jenseits von Sein und Nichtsein». Minder ansprechend oder auch minder anspruchsvoll, dafür aber meines Erachtens sonst geeigneter, ließe sich dasselbe etwa so aussprechen: der Gegenstand ist von Natur außerseiend . . ."

[9] Ich bin mir bewußt, daß die Identität intentionaler Gegenstände sehr viele schwierige Probleme aufwirft und spreche denn auch nur von einer „gewissen" Identität. Vgl. z.B. die Ausführungen in Küng (1980), S. 112−113, welche betonen, daß der intendierte Gegenstand oft nicht gegeben, sondern nur „aufgegeben" ist.

[10] Vgl. hierzu Findlay (1933), S.112.

[11] Genau genommen müßte man hier nicht sagen, daß etwas als grün-seiend vermeint wird, sondern nur, daß etwas *vermeint* wird, *als ob es als etwas Grünes sichtbar wäre*. Denn im Gegensatz zu einer Wahrnehmung oder einer naiven Halluzination meinen wir ja im Falle einer reinen Phantasievorstellung nicht wirklich, daß etwas ein grünes Pferd sei; wir tun nur als ob.

[12] Vgl. hierzu Husserl (1894), S. 308 Anmerkung: „. . . was nicht existiert, ‹kann› auch nicht Eigenschaften haben ‹. . .›; sie werden nur als einem Gegenstand zukommend vorgestellt . . ."

[13] Der Ausdruck ‚konvers-intentionale Eigenschaften' wurde von Chisholm (1984) geprägt. − Es ist in diesem Zusammenhang wichtig einzusehen, daß eine Aussage wie ‚Der von mir vermeinte Gegenstand ist grün' zweideutig ist. Diese Aussage kann bedeuten „Der von mir vermeinte Gegenstand ist als grün-seiend vermeint", sie kann aber auch bedeuten „Der von mir vermeinte Gegenstand ist tatsächlich grün" (obwohl ich ihn vielleicht als rot-seiend vermeint habe).

[14] Zalta (1983) spricht davon, daß abstrakte Gegenstände Eigenschaften wie Grün-sein nur „enkodieren" aber nicht exemplifizieren können (vgl. unten Anmerkung 21). Er wirft aber nicht die Frage auf, ob diese abstrakten Gegenstände Eigenschaften wie Grün-enkodierend-sein exemplifizieren.

[15] Vgl. Brentano (1930), S. 88: „. . . die Vorstellung eines Pferdes ‹hat› nicht «vorgestelltes Pferd», sondern «Pferd» . . . zum Objekt". − Es ist jedoch zu betonen, daß der Unterschied zwischen der Phantasievorstellung eines Pferdes und der Vorstellung der Phantasievorstellung eines Pferdes auch nur schon in den konvers-intentionalen Eigenschaften zum Ausdruck kommt: im ersten Fall hat etwas die Eigenschaft Als-ob-es-ein-Pferd-wäre-vermeint-zu-sein, im zweiten Fall hat etwas die Eigenschaft Als-ein-in-der-Phantasie-vermeintes$_1$-Pferd-vermeint$_2$-zu-sein

[16] Das Problem einer solchen Doppelstruktur tritt auch bei Philosophen auf, die keine nicht-existierenden Gegenstände annehmen. So unterscheidet z.B. Frege (1884), S. 64 zwischen den Merkmalen und den Eigenschaften von Begriffen; und Ingarden zwischen der Struktur und dem Gehalt von rein intentionalen Gegenständen und von Ideen: vgl. Ingarden (1931), § 20 und Ingarden (1965), § 47 und § 50.

[17] Vgl. Anmerkung 1.

[18] Wir haben in Bezug auf die frühere Theorie der zwei Objekte den Einwand erhoben, daß ein und derselbe Akt nicht gleichzeitig zwei verschiedene Objekte haben könne. Muß dieser Einwand nicht auch bei dieser neuartigen Theorie berücksichtigt werden? Die Lage ist jedoch hier eine besondere,

da das Subjekt im Augenblick der Täuschung von der Verschiedenheit der zwei Objekte nichts weiß. Erst in der Retrospektive kann eine Täuschung als Täuschung ins Blickfeld des Phänomenologen geraten und erst dann wird die Verschiedenheit der zwei Objekte festgestellt. − Im Folgenden (3.3.4) werden wir den Fall des Denkens eines runden Vierecks besprechen. Hier ist unsere gegenwärtige Frage schwieriger zu beantworten. Vielleicht muß man da unterscheiden zwischen dem Akt, der das runde Viereck zu denken versucht, und dem Akt, der feststellt, daß nichts Rundes-und-Viereckiges vor meinem geistigen Auge „erschienen" ist.

[19] Mally (1908), S. 882, Meinong (1915), S. 175−177. Findlay (1933), S. 176, Zalta (1983), S. 10.
[20] Mally (1912), S. 64 und 76, Findlay (1933), S. 110−112 und 182−184, Zalta (1983), S. 11.
[21] Zalta (1983), S. 12.

LITERATUR

Brentano, F., *Wahrheit und Evidenz* (Leipzig 1930).
Butchvarov, P., „Adverbial theory of consciousness", *Midwest Studies in Philosophy* Bd. 5 (1980).
Chisholm, R.M., „What is the problem of objective reference?" *Dialectica* Bd. 38 (1984).
Findlay, J.N., *Meinong's Theory of Objects* (London 1933). Um zwei Kapitel vermehrte Ausgabe unter dem Titel *Meinong's Theory of Objects and Values* (Oxford 1963).
Frege, G., *Grundlagen der Arithmetik* (Breslau 1884).
Husserl, E., „Intentionale Gegenstände" (1894), in: *Husserliana* Bd. 22 (Den Haag 1979).
Husserl, E., Besprechung von K.Twardowski, *Zur Lehre vom Inhalt und Gegenstand der Vorstellungen* (1896), in: *Husserliana* Bd. 22 (Den Haag 1979).
Ingarden, R., *Das literarische Kunstwerk* (Halle ¹1931, Tübingen ⁴1972).
Ingarden, R., *Der Streit um die Existenz der Welt*, Bd. II/1 (Tübingen 1965).
Küng, G., „Husserl on pictures and intentional objects", *Review of Metaphysics* Bd. 26 (1973).
Küng, G., „The phenomenological reduction as epoche and as explication", *Monist* Bd. 59 (1975).
Küng, G.,„What do we «see» when we register a fact?", in: R.Haller und W.Grassl (Hrsg.), *Sprache, Logik und Philosophie*, Akten des 4. Internationalen Wittgenstein Symposiums (Wien 1980).
Mally, E., „Gegenstandstheorie und Mathematik", in: Verhandlungen *des 3. Internationalen Kongresses für Philosophie* (Heidelberg 1908).
Mally, E., *Gegenstandstheoretische Grundlagen der Logik und Logistik*, Ergänzungsheft zur *Zeitschrift für Philosophie und philosophische Kritik* Bd. 148 (Leipzig 1912).
Meinong, A., „Über Gegenstandstheorie" (1904), in: *Gesamtausgabe* Bd. 2 (Graz 1971).
Meinong, A., *Über Möglichkeit und Wahrscheinlichkeit* (Leipzig 1915), in: *Gesamtausgabe* Bd. 6 (Graz 1972).
Parsons, T., *Nonexistent Objects* (New Haven 1980).
Smith, D.W. und McIntyre, R., *Husserl and Intentionanlity,* Synthese Library Bd. 154 (Dordrecht 1982).
Smith, D.W., „Is this a dagger I see before me", *Synthese* Bd. 54 (1983).
Tye, M., „The adverbial approach to visual experience" *Philosophical Review* Bd. 93 (1984).
Zalta, E.N., *Abstract Objects*, Synthese Library Bd. 160 (Dordrecht 1983).

* * *

INTENTIONALITY, REPRESENTATION AND THE BRAIN LANGUAGE

Werner Leinfellner
University of Nebraska, Lincoln

Today, cognitive psychology and modern brain physiology show an interesting tendency to go back to Brentano's concept of intentionality as the meaning-giving act for all intelligent beings. Actually, Brentano's concept consists of two theses: the inexistence thesis and the synsemantic thesis. The latter states that an expression LE^i can be given meaning by other expressions $\{LE^j\}$. The first thesis assumes that if we think, imagine, judge, something is f.i., being thought of, and this something has to be an object existing in our mind. F.i. when we judge something is affirmed or denied; when we love something is loved.[1] Consequently, objects which do not exist empirically, such as unicorns, exist solely in our mind and do not refer to any object. A weaker version of the inexistence thesis demands only, f.i. that the reference relation exists as an activity or function of our mind either mentally or psychologically. This activity distinguishes the mental from the physical. Brentano's second (synsemantic) thesis comes pretty close to Wittgenstein's "language in use thesis." In the sentence "Tom is thinking about unicorns" a unicorn is now not any longer an inexistent object nor does it need a referential function, but 'unicorn', LE^i, gets its meaning synsemantically from $\{LE^j\}$ = a description taken from the mythical narration. Interestingly, brain physiology and psychology have recently taken up the quest for "mentally" inexisting representatives of external objects. Here the individual's intention relation which goes from the intelligent brain or the language user to the external world (like in the medieval personal supposition relation)[2] has been contrasted with representation—a mere physical relation—which goes into the opposite direction.

Thus, intentionality is regarded again as a two-fold relation, intention[1] and intention[2]. s^1=intention[1] connects inner mental states (BW) or linguistic expressions (LE) with external states of our world (O). We may express this by saying that linguistic intention (s^1), or reference, creates a semantic tripel $<O, \sigma, BW>$ where σ is the brainphysiological specialization of s^1. The second type of intentionality, intentionality[2], holds between linguistic expressions LE^i, $\{LE^j\}$, f.i., in "bodies are extended". Intentionality[2] is a "word by context" meaning-giving process: we extract the meaning of LE^i from $\{LE^j\}$; f.i., when we say, that a bachelor (LE^1) is an unmarried man $\{LE^2\}$ or bodies are extended, we may render the meaning-giving process by semantemes or semantic tripels: $<LE^1, s^2, \{LE^2\}>$. The question is again, what is the nature of the semantemes, of the reference relation s^1, of the meaning relation s^2 or of σ? Do mental states (BW) exist, and if they exist, where? One simple answer was offered by the linguistic representational view. According to this view LE^1 linguistically represents O and LE^1 stands for the meaning of $\{LE^2\}$. Intentionalistic views coalesce with the Wittgensteinian view, that the subject or the language user always attaches certain invariant linguistic expressions (LE) to the same, invariantly recurring empirical state of affairs or objects (O) in the case of intention[1] (or reference = s^1), i.e., the language user establishes the descriptive meaning of LE. In the case of intention[2], the language user fixes the meaning of LE^i by, f.i., a definite description $\{LE^j\}$, as Russell has proposed.

Again we may ask, what is the nature of, f.i., the relation s^2 in the tripel $<LE^1, s^2, \{LE^2\}>$? Is it a linguistic, a psychological, physiological or even an unempirical mental relation? Dennet 1969[3], Fodor 1975[4] gave a clear answer to this question: they regarded both forms of intentionality (intention[1] and intention[2]) as cognitive semantical functions; this, one may regard as a back-to-Brentano movement. Additionally, it was of great advantage for cognitive psychology to work with optimal design models: it led to a better understanding of intelligence;

intelligence is not, as in the traditional view, a capacity of the mind or of its mental functions, but a synergetic optimization of sensations, memories and of thinking by an inner "semantic" evaluation in order to maximize the individuals and the species' survival. The semantic turn in cognitive psychology consists in the following: Whenever we use linguistic descriptions of mental acts or functions, such as "I think that P" or "I remember P", we evaluate represent or encode, store, transmit, or transform meaning (P), since the function of intelligent individuals is: 1) to represent information from the environment and bestow "survival" meaning on them; 2) to carry information and meaning from one individual to the other individual (inter-individual semantical communication, f.i. by language); and 3) to process, store, and make usable and understandable the meaning of information, either in our (brain) memory or in our language, for example, by fixing the meaning of one expression LE^i linguistically through a context or a definition {LE^j}. But it turned out to be a great hindrance and disadvantage for cognitive psychology, that the two explanations of intentionality, the empirical one (intentionality[1]) and the formalistic one (intentionality[2]), stayed completely separated and could never be brought together. The formalists freely used the elegant formalisms of transformational grammar or the deductive logic of the predicate calculus to explain the establishing and the transfer of meaning; the empirists used, f.i. the reference relation as explanation. Dennett's robot[5] and Searle's chinese learning stories criticized the inability of the formalists to solve practical survival problems with their formalistic methods. The paradigmatical story uncovers three mistakes of the formalistic approach: 1)Intentionality[2] cannot be based on logic, nor can it be explained by transformational grammar alone. 2) Language cannot work without the cooperation of both forms of intentionality. 3) Language without brainphysiological foundation is useless, if the task of intelligence is to maximize individual survival. The gist of Dennett's story is not simply that without empirical meaning we are helpless, as it is according to the story: You are locked into the control center of an alien robot-spaceship, a windowless room, where on two walls you will find all the encoded informations from the outside in flashing light signals you do not understand and on the two other walls there are the buttons which you should press to maneuver the spaceship into security and maximize your own survival. What the story rather tells us is firstly, that in such a situation the decision maker or navigator is completly blocked, not only because he cannot understand the signals from outside, but because he cannot evaluate them. This shows clearly that intention[1] is an inner process where we bestow our survival values on the signals or the mental representations of external input. We will see later that this is exactly the case with the brain-wave patterns which we can now compare with the flashing signals in our control room. Thus, we come now to the second interpretation of our control room as the human brain. The brain represents the incoming sensory inputs in form of brain wave patterns (BW), like the flashing signals in our control room, but we are automatically able to bestow on, or associate with them a certain survival value. That is exactly the difference between frequency patterns like sound-wave patterns picked up by our ear and brain-wave patterns (BW). The latter alone get meaning, in a fundamental primary sense, by the survival values and in a secondary sense by association.

The survival problem of our space-ship navigator could even not be solved, if all the light indicators were labelled in your own empirical language, which has intention[1]-meaning only in your well known biological niche, but not in a completely unknown environment, to which we are not adapted at all. Only if our navigator can step outside and acquire intentional meaning[1] in an ostensive way and can evaluate the alien evironment, with respect to his survival chances, he may be saved.

For such and similar purposes and, more generally, to bridge the gap between intention[1] and intention[2] E. and W. Leinfellner[6] proposed 1978 a two-level semantics, which recursively connects the external empirical meaning, the "operative meaning" or intentionality[1], with the internal or "operational meaning" (intentionality[2]) with the help of semantic tripels and n-tupels.[6] Similar semantic systems have been discussed by Suppes[7], Wilks[8], and by the computer semanticists.

We see the following from this story: 1) if intentions[2] (the mere light signals) or, in the brainphysiological interpretation, the brain wave patterns (BW) are not somehow connected with the external world by intention[1]—this is certainly not the case for healthy humans—there is no survival chance. 2) Intentions[1] (external) or (internal) intentions[2] alone, if they function separately and independently, do not work (Rorty, Dennett, Searle). Intention[1] and intention[2] of intelligent beings are always relative to their specific biological niche. 3) Only if the two levels of semantical functions, operative or intention[1] and the operational or intention[2], are connected and cooperate, our spaceship can be saved. 4) Intention[1] and intention[2] serve a common cognitive purpose: intelligent problem solving. 5) Only together they maximize survival. 6) Intelligence (contrary to knowledge) consists of effective operative-operational semantical decision-making and problem-solving for the purpose of (species) survival. Thus, operative semantics (semantics[1]) and operational semantics[2] have to cooperate in any intelligent problem-solving; for this purpose, they can be connected on a linguistic level, as Leinfellner W. and E. have shown. Since problem solving optimizes survival, the next question is: how do intention[1] and intention[2] cooperate on the lower brainphysiological level of animalic mammalian intelligence and on the human psychic level without the help of a spoken language? If one could answer these questions, then one could regard intelligence and intentionality as the same, i.e., intentionality in both forms = intelligence, as Dennett has proposed it.

5. Intentionality and Perception

One central problem of cognitive psychology has been the question: How shall we explain the connection between the brainphysiological nervous level of sensory perception and the linguistic level? What is the nature of a brainphysiological representative (BW) when we represent, or recognize, or name an object? Does the representative (BW) "inexist" in our mind or our brain? Richardson (1981)[9] has recently proposed to regard external intentionality (intention[1]) as aboutness or ofness of any intelligent system which has to cope with its evolutionary dependency in its specific environmental niche. In a next step, we want to amalgamate a neurophysiologically based intentionality[1] with a linguistic psychological intentionality[1], following Brentano's ideas.

D1. Intentionality[1] is a general semantic or meaning-establishing, low-level process whose first level consists of neurophysiological functions (σ) which map (= /) environmental input (SW) onto an internal brain language (BL) or: SW/BL. The second level maps (λ) brain-wave patterns BW unto linguistic expressions LE^i. Thus we get: $< BW^i, \lambda, LE^i >$. A brain language consists of dynamic fluctuating states of the brain (or brain-wave patterns = BW, BWϵBL; see below) which serve for 1) communication between the neurons 2) for representing σ (encoding) the sensory input, f.i. in the form of light- or sound-wave patterns (SW), in brain wave patterns (BW), $<SW^i, \sigma, BW^i>$, which constitute the brain-language (BL), 3) to produce survival maximation.

D2. This neurophysiological-psychological activity functions in such a way that the whole process can or may store even that which empirically does no longer exist (Chisholm's contingency condition).

D3. Sensory perception must be such that it represents invariantly recurring objects (O) via invariant light-wave patterns (SW) (informational input) onto invariant brain-wave patterns, i.e.: O/SW/BW, or, in terms of tupels, since O = SW: $<SW^i, \sigma, BW^i>$. Only in case of a cerebral resonance of brain-wave patterns (BW) with linguistic patterns or expressions LE we get the tupel: $<BW^i, \lambda, LE^i>$ and by recursion we get: $<SW^i, \sigma <BW^i, \lambda, LE^i>>$

D4. The purpose of this intelligent process is survival maximation.

D5. In living intelligent mammalian brains, representational states (brain waves, BW) function as first-level representatives of sensory input (SW). Once activated, they continue to exist permanently as dynamic (unconscious) frequency patterns (BW) in the mammalian brain. If mapped into the spoken language (BWϵBL, BL/L), f.i. in the human brain, they become conscious.

D1 guarantees that mental acts are distinguishable from physical events, objects, and stimuli; D5 rules out external deterministic causes or causation from outside in a strict deterministic sense, but permits the partial or statistical causation of a stimulus-response type. Thus, respresentation and intention[1] need an object, but do not need a mystical reference, nor an inexisting symbol s. They rather form a physico-physiological, two-level, dynamic process where sound- or light-wave patterns (SW) are represented by brain-wave patterns (BW), SW/BW, and brain wave patterns by invariantly used linguistic expressions (LE), BW/LE. This explains the tripels $\langle SW, \sigma, BW \rangle$ and $\langle SW, \lambda, BW \rangle$, which we have used earlier. It was Dennett[10] and Beaty[11], who compared intentionality[1] with optimal design models, as expressed by D4 as the purpose of intentional perception. Maynard-Smith[12] introduced dynamic optimal design models to explain even the evolution of intelligent behavior (Leinfellner 1982[13], 1984[14]); hence, optimal design models for improving survival can be viewed as theoretical reconstructions of intelligent animal and human behavior which begins with intentional perception.

What does this mean? We will see here, for the first time, that human semantic intentionality[1] is a neurophysiological-psycho-linguistic process whose first level can even function without (linguistic) consciousness. 3) This idea got an astonishing confirmation by the representational theory of visual intentionality by Churchland and Gibson which we will combine here with Basar's and Adey's brain-wave pattern theory (see next chapter). Gibson's "Ecological Approach to Visual Perception"[15] states the following: 1) Observers can perceive (see) objects only, if they possess a neurophysiological functioning, screening representational device with a sensory input function (σ) which transforms and structures sensations—which are light- or sound-frequency patterns (SW)—into brain-wave patterns (BW). 2) Dynamic internal states or brain-wave patterns (BW) do not exist alone, but in triplets: $\langle SW^i, \sigma, BW^i \rangle$, where SW^i is an invariantly recurring, f.i. sound-wave pattern, a melody, σ transfers the sound pattern from the ear to the brain and BW^i is its invariant resonance in the form of an electromagnetic brain-wave pattern. This view is an active alternative to Hume's passive theory that all what we are sensing are our bodily impressions in the ear. Gibson's ecological, perceptual intentionality demonstrates clearly that in the act of perception outside and inside (the brain) are one interconnected holistic dynamic resonating field, as symbolized by the tripel $\langle SW^i, \sigma, BW^i \rangle$. Perceptual intentionality means that our brain selects certain light-wave patterns and does not represent all light beams from the outside. Thus we see perhaps only 10% of our world, because there is the inner, inbuilt evaluation (screening) of biologically unimportant visual inputs from outside. Visual perceptions are directed by genetically stored "evaluating filters" which are anchored in our genes. They bestow a primary meaning on them and function in the following way: What is not necessary for survival, we do not see and represent in short, has no meaning for us. Eyes are not at all pricked by light rays and do not react always in an automatical, deterministic, causal way; they are mobile scanners; they run over the array just like hands run over the material to feel and evaluate only that what is meaningful for us, i.e. for survival support. (Gibson 1968)[15]. Neutral experiences do not impress us and get no primary meaning. Therefore, light and light representation are completely different. Light-wave pattern representation is intentionally manipulated and directed by the "seeing" individual brain and is uniquely specific for our niche and scenario in which we had to survive since millenias. Thus we are able to explain for the first time, why the intention[1] relation goes from our brain to the objects, and why representation works in the opposite direction. But perception functions only in cases of "intentionally admitted" and regulated references, admitted by the "brain" to get all necessary lifesaving information from the external world. Therefore, it is the first step of a problem-solving and decision process which maximizes our survival and wellbeing. Thus the representational theory has changed from a passive view of reception to an active view of intentionality[1] which depends on the subject's survival or survival instinct. This intentional model of perception vindicates Brentano's psychological view of intention and could even explain neurophysiologically the lower-level function of intentionality[1].

Gibson's model of perception and similar other intentional perception theories can explain the following open questions of Brentano's intentionality: 1) the strategic role of the intentional for all mental life which Brentano, as Spiegelberg[16] says, had discovered, but could not explain and explore; 2) The new perception theories are based on the neurophysiological nature of intentionality[1] and stress their general semantic task. 3) They explain the direction of intention[1] which originates from the brain's and from the sense organs' scanning activity and which actively selects and modifies sensory informations from outside. 4) The individual is no longer a passive recipient, since Gibson's model shatters the deterministic stimulus-response theories of perception. 5) Given intentional perception, we need the intermediary function of the brain language (BL) which will serve as the missing link between sensory input (SW) and our spoken language (L), according to the representational two-level mapping: SW/BW and BW/LE. or: $\langle SW^i, \sigma, BW^i \rangle$ and $\langle BW^i, \lambda. LE^j \rangle$.

7. The Internal Language of the Brain: The Brain Language as the Missing Link

New results about the communication of the neurons in human brains have rejected the traditional idea that the brain functions just as a computer or a switching network, which consists of 25 billions of individual processing and firing cells, the neurons, which communicate with each other in a linear and pairwise fashion through electrical impulses. Since any language is a system of signs or signals for the purpose of communication, we will call their exchange of meaningful information the single-cell communicative language. According to the single-cell or feature extract model of the brain, neurons transmit electrochemical impulses from one to another via long fibers, the axions. The impulses travel along the axions until they reach the junctions called synapses which connect the axions with other cells' axions. Chemical transmitters, released from the axion terminals, cross the synapses and excite or inhibit the connected neuron. If the excitation from several synaptic inputs exceeds a certain threshold, the target neuron fires or "switches on" by generating an impulse of its own, or "switches off".

Thus, the brain was inevitably compared to a digital computer, although scientists pointed out that this cannot be the case: f.i. millions of neurons can not any longer digitally encode all the other neuronal impulses, since studies of sensory neurons showed that the single-cell communication consists simply in the increase or decrease of firing intensity which does not work digitally, but pulse code analog. More rapid firing simply represents more intense sensation. Since the impulse frequency varies continuously, sensor neurons rather use a pulse code analog, not a digital form of information transfer.

Fascinated by the computer analog model of the brain, scientists studied the internal language of single neurons, but never of cooperating cells in groups. They could explain the linear language of neurons by gradually beginning with the pairwise neuron communication and then continuing with neuron circuits, but they finally failed to explain the communication between all ganglions of the brain as it has been observed in special stereo-electroencephalograms and in evoked potentials of the brain, the EEG-EPrograms (see Basar, 1980 p. 22−29)[20]. The spontaneous electrical activity of the brain (EEG) can be influenced by direct or peripheal stimulation (electrical, optical, acoustical, linguistical, etc.) and yields the evoked brain-wave patterns (BW). Given that a group of scientists, E. R. John[17] (New York University Medical Center), Lawrence and Adey[18] challenged the single-cell communication or the computer model of our brain, because it assumed that at the top level of the neuron chains there had to exist highly specified single neurons, f.i. with the ability to recognize a person's body as a whole or as a gestalt. But how could one single cell synthesize millions of sensations of different types into one whole? Holistic systems or gestalts cannot be represented in specific single neurons, on the contrary, recent operations on the brain which removed large sections of the brain, where these highly specified neurons were assumed to be located, proved that the individual's memories were merely slightly impaired and not destroyed. This proved that memories must be distributed throughout the brain, that they had to be ubiquitous within the brain! It is clear that the computer-analog model could not explain this. It

48

could only explain that primitive forms of communication in the single-cell language are similar to the machine language of computers. For example, if switches are shut off and on, then the basic negation function is realized in the single cell communication language just by the analogy of firing and nonfiring of a neuron. It could explain how "and" or the intersection communication of signals are realized in serial communication circuits of neurons and how "or", the union communication, worked in simple neuron networks in parallel circuits of neuron chains. "All" statements or even fuzzy communication are realized by long series of parallel neurons. Thus it was possible to explain how simple syntactico-semantic operation like "non", "and", and "or" combination of signals, work in the single cell communication, namely, in invariant switching structures. But it could not explain communication between neurons which do not belong to the same linear chains, or between large groups, or between all neurons; further, it could not explain, how neuron networks represent similar or statistically recurring events, properties, or sensations, or how our brain could represent, associate, and compare similar sensory inputs, such as gestalt features, patterns, etc. Since the early 1970's, neuroscientists found out that there is a far more complex form of functioning intercommunication between our brain neurons, the cooperative one. According to this view, neurons have the ability to cooperate and communicate in large groups. They produce and communicate with the help of complex electromagnetic fields which pervade the brain and serve as a "collective" internal brain language between the neuronal body of thousands or millions of synchronized and cooperative neurons and at the same time could be understood by single neurons.

The cooperative model, outlined by John and Adey and E. Basar[19, 20], emphasizes the cooperative network communication rather than the individual linear communication. It grew out of the study of evoked electroencephalograms (EEG-EPrograms) which show clearly the measurable, slow electromagnetic wave patterns which pervade the brain. This special EEG can be recorded by electrodes and observed on screens. Research in the 1960's demonstrated that these special EEG's arise not from the random summation of individual cells, nor from linear neuron chains, but from a cooperative organized brain language of large groups of neurons with other groups. Each of the slow electromagnetic communication fields, produced by the individual neurons and by the different groups, are characterized by a different, or similar (identical), wave pattern BW. We will call both communication systems, the single-cell and the cooperative one, the internal brain language, BL, a concept which has been introduced by Jaynes to explain the internal communication between the two hemispheres of the mammalian brain.

This cooperation yields the formation of encoded, relatively invariantly recurring communication patterns of electromagnetic waves BW, whose message can be "understood" by the single neurons which belong to the cooperative group (BW^1) or, via resonance, to a similar group (BW^j). It represents in the first-level, internal brain language, BL, the incoming sensations. Invariantly swinging sound- or light-wave patterns (SW), coming from objects in our environment (= sensory informations), are represented (σ) encoded, and stored in the corresponding brain-wave patterns (BW), or form the tripel <SW, σ, BW>. They originate from specific areas of our brain and spread over the whole brain. The wave patterns show, on the one side, significant structural similarities with the second level of representation, the linguistic expressions LE. The latter, too are nothing else than similar, invariantly swinging sound-wave patterns, which are activated by the Wernicke center of our brain and produced by the vocal apparatus whose muscles are regulated and controlled by the Wernicke center. Actually, linguistic expressions LE in the tripel <BW, λ, LE> occur 1/300th second after the brain waves: Brain-wave patterns (BW) explain, on the other side, how it is possible that the most important external stimuli—which again are nothing else than invariantly recurring external sound- or light-wave patterns (SW)—can be represented by invariantly swinging brain-wave patterns BW: SW/BW. Thus, the picture theories of representation and similar older explanations of sensory representations, as well as the whole sense data theory become more or less obsolete.

Adey and Soviet scientists demonstrated recently 1) that specific complex electroencephalogram (EEG) patterns can be correlated with what we call second-level specific cognitive processes both in animals and in human brains (= ABW). They could explain, how certain invariantly given sensations (WS) are stored in dynamically swinging, invariantly recurring simple (BW) or abstract wave patterns (ABW). Growing evidence supports the idea that the first level, the invariantly swinging electromagnetic brain-communication patterns (BW), represent and store (isomorphically) certain invariantly, i.e. in the same shape, recurring sensory frequency patterns. Moreover, they could prove that the lower (BW) and the higher brain-wave patterns (ABW) are invariantly "translated" into linguistic expressions LE of our language L. Thus we get: BW^i/LE^i, ABW^j/LE or $\langle BW^i, \lambda, LE^i\rangle$, $\langle ABW^j, \lambda, LE^j\rangle$. According to our brain-wave hypothesis, the overall pattern of electromagnetic brain-waves (BW), representing sensory wave patterns (SW) or stimuli, firstly represent them invariantly; secondly, the fact that brain-waves (BW^i) resonate (or do not resonate) with other invariantly given similar wave patterns BW^j explains, how similarities (and dissimilarities) between sensations are distinguished in the brain. Similarities lead to resonances just like tuning forks resonate with specific frequencies. Abstract brain-waves (ABW) are superimpositions of brain-waves (BW), the represent millions of stimuli; if the latter are sound- or light-wave patterns (SW) does not matter. Moreover, communicative brain-wave patterns can activate or "recall" similar swinging patterns by resonance (=) even if they are already stored away in the chemical dynamic structure of other groups of neurons—and increase their intensity. But $BW^i = BW^j$ resonance is a typical non-linear oscillation and activation (under random) of similar stored and swinging wave patterns. Activation by resonance brings them back from their low energetic level to the threshold value at which they enter our consiousness (we did not discuss here the direct chemical senses (smell) which function through chemical interaction and transfer of chemical stimuli). Thus the brain-wave pattern (BW^i) (of electromagnetic waves) is the representation of an incoming sensory sound stimulus (sound-wave pattern SW^i). F.i., hearing the same song (an invariantly occurring sound-wave pattern) is represented by an invariantly swinging brain-wave pattern BW^i (SW^i/BW^i), and this brain-wave pattern invariantly retains its stored characteristic pattern and frequency. The pattern BW^i may trigger BW^j, and BW^j may resonate with a linguistic brain wave pattern LE^j, and the words of the melody BW^i will come now into our consciousness simply by the increase of BW^i's intensity. We have to assume the following two-level linguistic hypotheses: 1) synchronicity hypothesis: the internal brain language (BL) can be represented by, or translated into the language L: BL/L. In this case brain-wave patterns (BW) resonate and stimulate our vocal muscles and activate speech patterns, vice-versa. 2) Diachronicity thesis or Jaynes' thesis: our acoustic language originated historically or evolutionarily, step by step from the brain language. 3) Consciousness hypothesis: we may go so far as to assume that, if the stream of invariantly swinging brain-wave patterns (BW, ABW) has enough associative (communicative) power to resonate and activate similar "linguistic" wave patterns (LE), then they will become conscious to us. Thus the stream of consciousness is born and may show up as a sequence of spoken and heard linguistic expressions {(LE)}. (Jaynes). The role of the neurons essentially boils down to creating and producing the energy for, and to modulate the intensity of the already stored as well as of the new emerging brain-wave patterns. 4) The invariantly given specific brain wave patterns and the specific differences between the invariantly swinging innumerous different patterns can be seen on EEG screens and can be heard in the corresponding combinations of the linguistic expressions (LE), since the specific brain-wave patterns occur in the brain always 1/300th of a second before the corresponding words are spoken. In recent experiments, the specific brain-wave pattern for "switch on the light", appearing in an EEG has been amplified and used to directly switch on a light in a room with the person remaining silent! Thus the brain-wave "switch on the light" exists, and it can activate an electric switch without the use of the language. 5) Invariantly swinging brain-wave patterns represent the semantical contents of external, invariantly swinging sound- or light-wave patterns interpersonally, i.e., they are the same in different persons as experiments have convincingly shown.

We have to assume, that all newly emerging and representing communicative invariant patterns (BW) change the chemical and electric structure of the neuronal group, i.e., of the neurons, and thus have fixed memories in a new, dynamically and invariantly swinging brain-wave pattern. Wave patterns which are not reinforced by resonance will decrease their energy level slowly to a threshold value, where they will become subconscious or where we forget them. But they can be brought back if stimulated by new associative, enforcing resonance. That is exactly, how the dynamic retrieving of memories by resonances works.

Any of these retrieved amplified "memories", or, brainphysiologically speaking, any of these activated swinging neuronal wave patterns can be converted back via impulses along the axions, which again can be transmitted to the appropriate muscle cells to yield a motoric response in the organism (body): I will switch on my record player to listen again to the song, or begin to speak.

We have to stress again the fact, that, if all the items of information in the brain are encoded in the frequency spectra of modulated brain-waves, and if the rest of the brain cells and groups understand this message which is encoded in the brain-wave patterns, then the language of the brain 1) is ubiquitous, i.e., is everywhere in the brain and can be understood by all neurons; 2) both languages, the brain language (BL) and the spoken language (L), have a similar and invariant frequency structure. 3) Their semantic content has sentence like structure, but we have to assume that in the brain language "noun-parts" and "verb-parts" have equal weight. Therefore, the brain language (BL) may not differ functionally too much from a spoken language (L) which is encoded in the changing, but invariantly used, spectra of sound waves, in the words and their combinations, and is understood—just as the brain language by all neurons—by all language users. The salient point to understand the functioning of the brain-wave language is that the abstract brain-waves (ABW) and the simple brain-waves (BW) represent and encode the semantic content of what we call "sensations", "memories", "thoughts". Recent experiments have shown that it is solely their meaning for us which is encoded and represented. When Warren Brown recorded brain-waves of subjects, who listened to identically sounding words (homonyms) which are used both as nouns and verbs, such as "rows" in "he rows" and "rose" in "the rose" the EEG responses, i.e. the brain-wave patterns, were significantly different! Thus the basic assumption of the brain language is a semantic version of the inexistence thesis of Brentano. According to this thesis, the healthy human brain maintains a life-long, lasting activity of brain-wave patterns which represent, compare, combine, and store cerebral meaning, generated by the cooperative, dynamic activity of thousands or millions of neurons themselves. The encoded cerebral semantic items of information in turn influence the activity of all neuron cells. Therefore, this model uses a new dynamic form of inexistence, not of mental objects, but of cerebral meaning invariances, firstly in the form of operative or empirical meaning, when certain invariantly swinging brain waves represent or stand for invariant sensory stimuli (in the sense of SW/BW representation), and secondly, in the form of a cerebral operational semantics or prelinguistic meaning-establishing and storing, when certain brain-waves, f.i. BW^i, are identical or similar with others, BW^j, i.e. $BW^i = BW^j$. The most astonishing result of this new brain-language theory is certainly that the brain language is based completely on, and functions exclusively in the form of cerebral semantic relations which order and fix the cerebral operative (empirical) and operational meaning. We do regard here the brain only in the context of intelligence (not of knowledge or science). Only for intelligent behavior, the establishing and fixing of meaning is the first necessary step for the final goal, the maximation of survival and of welfare. (see Leinfellner, W., 1984, note 14, p. 264)

6. Episodic and Semantic Memory and the Parallelism between Cerebral and Linguistic Semantics.

According to Tulving's[21] propositional memory theory, there is one totally wrong memory theory: the static-warehouse theory, where the owner can find what he wants to find (Gregor von Feinagle's concept, 1807). Thus the warehouse concept is exactly the static theory which assumes inexistent mental objects and which Brentano gave up in his later years. We want to combine now the theory of the dynamic brain language with Tulving's semantic theory. According to the latter, memory is stored in the episodic memory which is exactly an operative semantics (semantics^1) and in the semantic memory, which is strictly functioning as an operational semantics (semantics^2). We stress the following: 1) There is no such thing as "the static memory", but different forms of inexistent, permanently activated neuro-physiological brain states (processes) or brain-wave patterns, spread over the whole brain, whose semantic content may easily show up in our language. 2) Retrieval of information is not finding a stored good, an inexisting mental object; it is the activation of brain-waves of low intensity which, if activated, appear in our consciousness as linguistic expressions. This emergence is not always successful; otherwise the rememberer would know what he has forgotten. 3) Memory is not determined by past memory contents; memory is, rather, a two-levelled semantic activation process with the goal to "translate" (λ) the dynamically swinging brain-wave patterns (BE^i) into linguistic expressions (LE^i). Thus we get the tripel $\langle BW^i, \lambda\, LE^i \rangle$ or BW^i/LE^i.

But we have to distinguish the procedural from the propositional linguistic memory. Kolers 1945[22] and Scheffler 1965[23], distinguish in a similar way between procedural memory and a semantic or substantial memory, or between skills and intelligent knowledge. Skillful procedures are neither true nor false, since we just execute automatically a brain-wave pattern; but we find and reveal words in our linguistic memory. Executing a skill means to follow a brain-wave pattern instinctively. Therefore we do not necessarily need linguistic instructions when we perform skills; we do it automatically, instinctively, and unconsciously, like adding or multiplying numbers. Propositional or linguistic memory can be subdivided, according to Tulving, into episodic and semantic memory. The first is practically a generalized intention^1 or semantics^1, the second is an intention^2 or a semantics^2. Both convert the cerebral semantics of the brain-wave language into linguistic semantics. Episodic memory is encoding and retrieval of personal experiences and happenings; but the semantic memory encodes and retrieves the invariant, semantic rules, the cerebral semantic networks of meaning for the purpose of how to use and understand meaning, independent of a person's identity and past; i.e., semantic memory activates via the cerebral the linguistic functions of the semantics^2. For we recollect a car in which we were riding, but recall an identical meaning or a semantic rule. Episodic memory is a time-creating, dynamic system which retrieves and stores brain-waves (BW) and the corresponding linguistic expressions (LE) by ordering them in a linear temporal and a spatial, locational frame or raster. Thus, the representatives, the brain-wave patterns (BW), impose their temporal and spatial order in an "empirically apriori" sense on sensations. The semantics^2 (cerebral and linguistic memory) stores meaning networks and rules necessary for the meaningful use of both languages. They resemble a "mental" Webster's Dictionary, a thesaurus, an organized semantic knowledge which a person possesses about the meaning (intention^2) or words and verbal symbols: how their meaning is described or defined by other words or contexts and how one may connect them via the episodic memory and the brain language to the referents (SW). It activates semantic relations among words, sentences, "switches on" rules, formulas, algorithms for the understanding and manipulation of brain waves, insofar they show up in spoken words or in their combinations.

There are no external input signals registered and necessary, once semantic memory is stored; this proves its mere internal, "linguistically apriori" semantic functions. But for the cognitive linguistic expressions quasi-referents are stored and obtainable from the episodes of the episodic memory. Retrieval from the semantic memory will leave its semantic networks (rules) unchanged. The two memories are interdependent, but nevertheless they mutually support each other in the sense of a linguistic, cognitive recursivity of internal intentionality^2 and external intentionality^1, i.e., $SW^i/BW^i/LE^i$, LE^i/LE^j. To make it clear: the linguistic empirical information stored in the episodic memory, f.i., is always about the past temporal co-occurrence of two words, whereas, f.i., the identity of 'body' and 'extension' is stored in the semantic memory as experienced (invariant) synonymity: "all bodies are extended". Therefore, what logicians call "analytically true" turns out to be "having the same meaning". The semantic networks can be reconstructed in recursive or in computer semantics (Leinfellner, E.)[24] which makes it possible for computers to utilize their knowledge in a semantic, and not logical form as well as to understand our language. Since the semantic, cerebral memory is phylogenetically and ontogenetically earlier than the linguistic memory, this can only be seen as a proof that the cerebral "silent" semantic memory existed already before the spoken language, i.e. as the cerebral semantics[2] for the non-spoken, communicative brain language (BL). The items of information stored in the episodic linguistic, semantic[1] system are the personal, individual experiences, while the information in the semantic[2] memory regulates their semantic use. The first is limited in its inferential capabilities, but the semantic memory possesses a rich inferential and deductive, exclusively semantic capability, because of the tightly organized and recorded semantical interdependencies and interrelations, which build up the semantic networks of the brain language and the spoken language (See Leinfellner, E.[24]). But one should never forget that the semantic memory cannot be based on logic, since logic develops ontogenetically and phylogenetically later than semantics. Therefore, logic is the offspring of a brain-physiologically and psychologically based semantics, a thesis already used in Brentano's psychological foundation of logic and logical deduction. F.i., in deductions the conclusions are always semantically included in the premises, i.e., brain-wave patterns of the premises have to be composites or superimpositions of the brain-wave patterns of the conclusions. In philosophy, it was Wittgenstein who long ago took the truth tables for "and", "or", and the negation from language use, i.e., from their semantic use and functions in our spoken language. Consequently, the foundation of our linguistic semantics on the cerebral semantic networks and functions of the brain language is the next step in the physiological-psychological foundation of our spoken everyday language (not of the scientific language) on the silent, but semantical, brain language.

Only episodic memory possesses a subjective veridicality which is actually a subjective memory evaluation, a truth testing that invariant names (LE^i) and invariantly used verbs (LE^j) refer to the same invariantly reoccurring and concurring events, SW^i, SW^j. Of course, the rigid and invariant empirical references of our spoken language, such as naming, develop historically, when the spoken language evolved historically, by a step by step activation from the brain language (Jaynes' hypothesis). Thus the empirical truth is nothing else than Brentano's evidence experience, when we retrieve and use the same (invariant) linguistic expression LE^i for the same invariantly (recurring) sensory experience (SW^i), only 1/300th of a second later, than our brain has already attached an invariant brain-wave pattern (BW^i) to the same invariant sensory experience (SW^i). Thus we get the recursion of the tripels $\langle SW^i, \sigma, BW^i \rangle$ and $\langle BW^1, \sigma, LF^i \rangle$ to $\langle SW^i, \sigma, \langle BW^i, \lambda, LE^i \rangle \rangle$ or, simply, in our symbolic translatory form: $SW^i/BW^i/LE$.

Finally, it is very well known that platonistic logicians assume that logical truths and tautologies are apriori given as timeless truths, independent of all sensory or empirical experience. But they have no explanation, why whatever is apriori must possess universal and necessary validity in all possible worlds. The brainphysiologically based semantics explains apriorism quite differently, namely as genetically inherited, statistical invariance of our cerebral and linguistic semantic functions and networks, which have gradually developed, during the evolution of the intelligent human brain, our semantic universe of both languages. Since, according to Tulving's memory theory, only our episodic memory is temporally ordered, while the semantic memory is timeless—like logic—it does not need any longer temporal connections to the knower's personal empirical history, but it could be so connected, if necessary. Instead it uses the evolved, established and inherited invariant semantic functions and forms, the universe of "discourse" of our brain language on the first level, and/or the synchronized semantic universe of our language at the second level. It does not refer to logical, apriori given, and moreover unempirical possible worlds. The timeless and intergenerational, genetically inherited, invariant semantic functions and networks of the brain language are guaranteed and maintained by the genetic inheritance from generation to generation. The semantics of our everyday language continues to function correctly, if we use it and if it is written down in our cultural tradition or in our textbooks. Therefore, the invariance of references, of established meanings, of meaning inclusion, of invariant similarities (synonymity) and of meaning are the physiological and psychological preconditions of any logical laws and, of course, of "analytic truth". Thus the possible worlds turn out to be the semantical universe of both languages, the brain language and the spoken language. There are no objections against the most abstract or obstruse bits of linguistic semantic memory knowledge. It may be a creative combination of fantastic or abstract wave patterns, or it may once have stood in a direct connection to our external environment in which we and unicornlike, and dragonlike creatures coexisted and lived. Today only the meanings of the "unicorns" and "dragons" live on in our cultural, mythical tradition and their once formed brain-wave patterns roam about in our semantic memory, but fortunately not any longer in our episodic memory.

ENDNOTES

[1] Brentano, F., *Psychologie vom empirischen Standpunkt* (Leipzig 1874), Vol. I, Book II, Chap. 1.
[2] Leinfellner, E., "Intentions as *intentiones animae* in Ockham and as Immanent Mental 'Objects'", this volume.
[3] Dennett, D. C., "Current Issues in the Philosophy of Mind", *American Philosophical Quarterly* Vol. 15 (1978), pp. 249−261, especially p. 257f.
[4] Fodor, J., *The Language of Thought* (New York 1975).
[5] Dennett (1978), p. 258.
[6] Leinfellner, W., and Leinfellner, E., *Ontologie, Systemtheorie und Semantik* (Berlin 1978), pp. 216−359.
[7] Suppes, P., "Procedural Semantics", in R. Haller and W. Grassl (eds.), *Language, Logic and Philosophy* (Wien 1980), pp. 27−36.
[8] Wilks, Y. *Grammar, Meaning and the Machine Analysis of Language* (London 1972).
[9] Richardson, R. C. "Internal Representation: Prologue to a Theory of Intentionality", *Philosophical Topics* Vol. 12 (1981), pp. 171−211.
[10] Dennett (1978).
[11] Beatty, J., "Optimal Design Models and the Strategy of Model Building in Evolutionary Biology", *Philosophy of Science* Vol. 47, pp. 532−561.
[12] Maynard-Smith, J., *Evolution and the Theory of Games* (Cambridge 1983).
[13] Leinfellner, W., "Das Konzept der Kausalität und der Spiele in der Evolutionstheorie", in K. Lorenz and F. Wuketits (eds.), *Die Evolution des Denkens* (München 1983), pp. 215−261; W. Leinfellner, "Evolution of Intelligence", in P. Weingartner and J. Czermak (eds.), *Epistemology and Philosophy of Science* (Wien 1983), pp. 161−168.
[14] Leinfellner, W., "Theory of Games and Evolution of Intelligence", in F. Wuketits (ed.), *Concepts and Approaches in Evolutionary Epistemology* (Boston 1984), pp. 223−276.
[15] Gibson, J.J., *The Senses Considered as Perceptual Systems* (London 1968), p. 251.
[16] Spiegelberg, H., "'Intention' and 'Intentionality' in the Scholastics, Brentano and Husserl", in L. L. McAlister (ed.), *The Philosophy of Brentano* (Atlantic Highlands, N.J. 1977), pp. 108−127, especially p. 108.
[17] John, E. R., "Multipotentiality: A Statistical Theory of Brain Function", in R. J. Davidson and J. M. Davidson (eds.), *The Psychobiology of Consciousness* (New York 1980).
[18] Lawrence A. F., and Adey, W. R., "Nonlinear Wave Mechanisms in Interactions between Excitable Tissue and Electromagnetic Fields", *Neurological Research* Vol. 4 (1982).
[19] Basar, E., et al. (eds.), *Synergetics of Brain* (Berlin 1983).
[20] Basar, E., *EEG-Brain Dynamics* (Amsterdam 1980).
[21] Tulving, E., *Elements of Episodic Memory* (Oxford 1983).
[22] Kolers, P. A., in L. S. Cermak and F. I. M. Craik (eds.), *Levels of Processing in Human Memory* (Hillsdale, N. J. 1979).
[23] Scheffler, I., *Conditions of Knowledge* (Glenview, Ill. 1965).

[24] Leinfellner, E., Steinacker, I., and Trost, H., "Anaphoric and Kataphoric Relations, Textual Cohesion, and Reference Resolution", *Computers and Artificial Intelligence* (in press); R. Trappl, E. Leinfellner, I. Steinacker, and H. Trost, "Ontology and Semantics in the Computer", *Language and Ontology: Proceedings of the 6th Wittgenstein Symposium* (Wien 1981).

I have to thank Prof. Basar, Institute for Psychology, Lübeck, for his helpful comments, E. Leinfellner for her semantic contributions to the research project, and finally the Research Council and Dean Meisels, University of Nebraska, Lincoln, USA, for the financial support of this research project.

* * *

WHO, SEARLE OR HUSSERL?

A. Z. Bar-On
Hebrew University of Jerusalem

The question dealt with in this paper, broader than that of the title, can be phrased as: who is to guide us in analysing the concept of intentionality? I shall try to answer it by tracing a path of thought leading from Brentano, through Husserl, to Searle, which is one of a few possible paths that can be shown to bring us from Brentano, as the source, to the theories of our days.

I

It is presumably agreed that it was Brentano who proposed the initial thesis of intentionality in modern times. He did it in two short adjacent passages in the second book of his *Psychologie vom empirischen Standpunkt* (quoted from the translation of C. Rancurello, D. B. Terrell, and Linda L. McAlister)[1]:

> Every mental phenomenon is characterized by what the Scholastics of the Middle Ages called the intentional (or mental) inexistence of an object, and what we might call, though not wholly unambiguously, reference to a content, direction toward an object (which is not to be understood here as meaning something real[2]), or immanent objectivity. Every mental phenomenon includes something as object within itself, although they do not always do so in the same way. In presentation something is presented, in judgement something is affirmed or denied, in love loved, in hate hated, in desire desired, etc.
>
> This intentional in-existence is characteristic exclusively of mental phenomena. No physical phenomenon exhibits anything like it. We can therefore define mental phenomena by saying that they are those phenomena which contain an object intentionally in themselves.

Brentano attached to this text two footnotes which are quite significant for its proper understanding.[3] In the first of them, the one attached to the place where the Scholastics of the Middle Ages are mentioned, Brentano reminds us that they also used the expression 'to exist as an object in something', but in his view we should refrain from employing it, because of the difference between their and our usage of the term 'objectively'; ours suggesting *real existence*, while theirs intimating just the opposite.

In the second footnote, attached to the end of the first passage, Brentano claims that the conception of inexistence can already be found in Aristotle, as much as in the writings of several later thinkers, like Philo, the Neo-Platonists, St. Augustine, Thomas Aquinas.

As to the text itself, we should, I think, distinguish in it the main definitional thesis from the elucidations and/or extensions added to it. In the thesis the single characteristic of mental phenomena, intentionality, is referred to by no less than four expressions which are supposed to be co-extensive: (1) intentional inexistence; (2) reference to a content; (3) direction toward an object; and (4) immanent objectivity. These expressions are supposed to describe the same property or relation, but they cannot, it seems to me, be considered synonymous. Each of them has some secondary connotations and only their joint application will prevent misunderstandings.[4]

As it is commonly acknowledged, the most important of these parallel expressions is the first one, connecting the conception of intentionality with certain traditions of the Middle Ages. Brentano's "mediaeval connection" need not be told here in its entirety, but I cannot omit it altogether. In the second footnote to the paragraph quoted above Brentano says: "Aristotle himself spoke of this mental in-existence. In his books on the soul he says that the sensed object as such is in the sensing subject; that the sense contains the sensed object without its matter; that the object which is thought is in the thinking intellect".[5]

What is meant here, as I read the text, is Aristotle's epistemological conception, according to which the knowing subject, whether through his sense-experience or by his understanding, takes in the *form* of what is being apprehended, without its matter. Hence, this conception assumes a threefold distinction applicable to the form: (a) the form *per se*; (b) the form *as in the thing*, as *its* form or essence; and (c) that very form as in the mind of the subject who apprehends the thing of which it is the form.

Now, Avicenna, who showed a special interest in the *third* sense of the form, had it identified with what in Arabic is called *máana*, i.e. meaning or concept. He distinguished, however, between the primary *máana*, such as 'man', 'ox', or 'donkey', that the subject applies to the man, the ox, or the donkey, which exist outside of his soul, and the secondary *máana*, such as 'species' or 'genus', also meanings or concepts in the soul, but such that the subject applies them not to things existing outside of the soul, but to the primary *máanas*, such as 'man', 'ox', or 'donkey'.[6]

When Avicenna's writings were translated into Latin, the term *máana* was replaced by *intentio* and the distinction between the primary and secondary *intentiones* were elaborated upon, giving thus birth to the adjective 'intentional'. What seems to be uncontroversial about the mediaeval usage of this term is that it was meant to signify a mode of existence different from the so called 'real' existence, i.e. existence in the mind as distinguished from 'external existence'. There is, however, quite an amount of disagreement as to the question whether it also signified a reference or directedness to an object.[7]

One has to take sides in this disagreement in order to answer the question of whether Brentano remained faithful to the mediaeval usage of the term 'intentional'. What, as it seems to me, cannot be doubted, is that *both* of the above mentioned meanings are there in Brentano's concept of intentionality, as characterized in the quoted passage. It can be said that Brentano appears to have combined in his conception of intentionality two distinctions: one between intra-mental and extra-mental existence, the other between directedness and the lack of directedness to an object. This explains, as I see it, the need for additional expressions referring to the characteristic in question. By means of the second phrase, 'reference to a content', Brentano reminds us of the first distinction, 'content' pointing to the exclusively intramental. The third phrase, 'direction toward an object', reminds us of the second distinction; not simply intra-mental existence is considered, but the reference to an object whose existence is intra-mental. Finally, in the fourth phrase, 'immanent objectivity', both distinctions are intertwined in a single term.

Let us consider now the three elucidations which Brentano had added to his main thesis. The *first* one, in the opening sentence of the first passage of our text, alludes to what we have just said: the alternative expressions are ambiguous and are therefore to be applied jointly, each one contributing its own shade of meaning to the correct understanding of the thesis.

The *second* elucidation can be found in the brackets after the phrase 'direction toward an object'. It is there to tell us how to construe the key-concept 'object' as a component of Brentano's thesis. The object need not be real. Reality is not a necessary condition for something to be intentionally included in the mental phenomenon as an object. Indeed, at this point Brentano does not tell us in what sense the term 'real' and 'reality' are used here. It may, however, be assumed that what is meant here is reality as the state of existing independently of being perceived or experienced in general. This is certainly the sense suggested by the footnote mentioned above. Anyhow, the point is controversial. It attracts the attention of those who are interested in Brentano's thesis more perhaps than any other of its aspects. It is, however, less prominent in our framework of discussion.

The *third* elucidation is what matters to us most. It consists of two parts: (a) what follows the word 'although' in the sentence "Every mental phenomenon includes something as object,

although they do not always do so in the same way; and (b) the examples of mental phenomena quoted by Brentano. These were, no doubt, chosen with care; the collection exemplifies
the basic classification that Brentano seems to have adopted for his inquiry. According to it
all mental phenomena divide into presentations (*Vorstellungen*), e.g. hearing a sound, seeing
a coloured object, feeling warm or cold, imagining a mythological figure, on the one hand,
and such mental phenomena what have a presentation as their basic component, on the other.
This second class divides in its turn into judgements and phenomena of feeling and desire or
will.

II

This third elucidation to Brentano's thesis may be seen as leading us to Husserl's conception. Husserl's theory of intentionality is indeed a thick web of arguments and analysis spread-
ing over his whole philosophical system, its warp the diachronic and weft the synchronic
order. We do not intend to deal here with all, or even with most of its facets; our discussion
will be restricted to only a few aspects which seem to be particularly relevant to the framework
of the present analysis.

Let us begin with a remark on terminology. Instead of Brentano's 'mental phenomenon' of
which intentionality is supposed to be a definitional characteristic, Husserl uses the term
'experience' (*Erlebnis*), adding that not each and every experience is intentional. And so,
whatever it will prove to be, intentionality cannot be considered a definitional feature of mentality. A class of examples of non-intentional experiences is given by a certain kind of *Gefühle*.

Husserl's *Logische Untersuchungen* read:

> Many experiences commonly classed as 'feelings' have an undeniable, real relation to
> something objective. This is the case, e.g., when we are pleased by a melody, displea-
> sed at a shrill blast etc. etc. It seems obvious, in general, that every joy or sorrow, that
> is joy or sorrow *about* something we think of, is a directed act. Instead of joy we can
> speak of pleased delight in something, instead of sorrow we can speak of displeased or
> painful dislike of it, aversion from it etc. etc.[8]

Note that in Brentano's view in each of these cases there would be two intentions, one of
them based on the other. The underlying intention would give us the object presented, while
the overlying intention would give us the object felt. The former can be separated from the
latter, but not *vice versa*.

Up to this point Husserl goes along with Brentano. He thinks, however, that there are also
feelings which are essentially non-intentional. He writes:

> We may now ask more generally whether, in addition to the intentional varieties of
> feeling, there are not other *non*-intentional species. It may seem . . . that an obvious
> 'Yes' is the right answer. In the wide field of so-called sensory feelings no intentional
> characters can be found. The sensible pain of a burn can certainly not be classed beside
> a conviction, a surmise, a volition, etc., but beside sensory contents like rough or
> smooth, red or blue, etc.[9]

And Husserl continues at the same page:

> Every sensory feeling, e.g. the pain of burning oneself or of being burnt, is no doubt
> after a fashion referred to an object: it is referred, on the one hand, to the ego and its
> burnt bodily member, on the other hand, to the object which inflicts the burn. In all
> these respects there is conformity with other sensations . . . And though this reference
> is realized in intentional experiences, no one would think of calling the referred sensa-
> tions intentional.

Thus far on the terminology regarding experiences in general and intentional experiences
in particular. We shall look now into that part of Husserl's theory which is related to what we
have referred to as Brentano's third elucidation of his definitional thesis, according to which
there are various kinds of references to an object, and the distinctions between these kinds
express important features of the structure of consciousness. Husserl adopts this idea and

elaborates upon it most resourcefully. The first impression is that he provides all the tools needed for an *extended theory of kinds of intentionality*. He writes:

> The act, e.g. corresponding to the name 'the knife on the table' is plainly complex . . . the knife is not the primary or full object of the judgement, but only the object of its subject. The full and entire object corresponding to the whole judgement is the *state of affairs* judged: the same state of affairs is presented in a mere presentation, wished in a wish, asked after in a question, doubted in a doubt, etc. . . . The state of affairs must obviously not be confused with the judging of it, nor with the presentation of this judgement. I plainly do not wish for a judgement, nor for any presentation . . .[10]

What is the most important aspect of these considerations for our analysis? The examples suggested by Husserl imply that we can speak of the self-same object as the object of more than one act. What I mean is not a multiplicity of acts identical in content, but such that occur at different times and/or in the consciousness of different people. What we are interested in are acts with different kinds of reference to the same object. *S*, in whose consciousness the presentation of the knife-on-the-table takes place, forms a judgement expressed by the indicative sentence 'the knife is on the table'. The same state of affairs obtains also as the object in *S*'s erotetic act expressed by the interrogative sentence 'Is the knife on the table?'. This applies also to *S*'s act expressed by the optative sentence 'I wish the knife were on the table'.

At this juncture Husserl introduced a distinction which proved to be of crucial importance in the subsequent development of the theory of intentionality. The distinction is between the 'content' or 'matter' of an intentional experience and its 'quality'. Husserl writes:

> We now turn . . . to another extremely important, seemingly plain distinction . . . This is the distinction between the general act-character, which stamps an act as merely presentative, judgemental, emotional, desiderative etc., and its 'content' which stamps it as presenting *this*, as judging *that* etc. etc. The two assertions '2 × 2 = 4' and 'Ibsen is the principal founder of modern dramatic realism', are both, *qua* assertions, of one kind; each is qualified as an assertion, and their common feature is their *judgement-quality*. The one, however, judges one content and the other another content. To distinguish such 'contents' from other notions of 'content' we shall speak here of the *matter* (material) of judgements. We shall draw similar distinctions between *quality* and *matter* in the case of all acts.[11]

Although matter cannot be separated from quality within the intention, the quality may be identified by abstracting it from the matter, and *vice versa*. Furthermore, regarding their quality, all intentional experiences divide into a series of different *genera* or categories of intendedness toward an object. What is the nature and status of these categories? Is their number finite, can they be surveyed and explored? And if so, do they constitute a system with definite relations between its members? Is the status of each of them established once and for all, or is this great family of kinds of intentional quality perhaps in a state of perpetual flux? And above all, how are we to identify these categories?

I am asking these questions explicitly, in a *post factum* manner. There was no such calm attitude for Husserl who felt driven to go on with his theory, as if the tools for doing so were at hand. He writes:

> Content in the sense of 'matter' is a component of the concrete act-experience, which it may share with acts of quite different quality. It comes out most clearly if we set up a series of identical utterances, where the act-qualities change, while the matter remains identical. All this is not hard to provide. We recall familiar talk to the effect that *the same content* may now be the content of a mere presentation, now of a judgement, now of a question, now of a doubt, a wish etc. etc. . . . To be alike in 'content', while differing in act-quality has its visible grammatical expression; *the harmony of grammatical forms points the way to our analysis.*[12]

Having spelt out the crucial distinction between the 'matter' and the 'quality' of an intentional experience, Husserl advanced a striking working hypothesis: grammatical forms can be used to identify and explore the various kinds of intentional quality.

Was this hypothesis actually used in Husserl's inquiry? The answer to this question is a qualified 'no'. There were at least two preconditions for its effectiveness: (a) the grammatical form must in fact be closely correlated with the intentional experience; and (b) philosophy of language should have been sufficiently developed at that time to provide a conceptual apparatus for exploring the various kinds of correlation between intentional experience and linguistic expression. The main reason for the hypothesis remaining unused was probably the non-fulfilment of the second precondition. But there was another, more specific reason for it, connected with the so called Aristotle-Bolzano controversy on the (logical) character of sentence-forms, which greatly occupied Husserl at that time.

The controversy may be rendered as follows: Granted that the mental act of judging is what confers meaning on an indicative sentence (when used to make a statement), we may ask whether for example an interrogative or optative sentence will also get its meaning directly from its correlated intentional experience. Aristotle's answer to this question would apparently have been in the affirmative. According to him there is no fundamental difference in this respect between judgement and other kinds of mental acts. Each of them confers meaning on the sentence form correlated with it.

At a certain stage Husserl was inclined to adopt this position, which would have coincided beautifully with his conception of the kinds of intentionality, which has been outlined above. Alas, towards the end of the *LI* he had changed his mind and adopted Bolzano's stand, as expressed in the latter's *Wissenschaftslehre* (Vol. I, par. 22): "A question like 'what is the relation of the diameter of a circle to its circumference?' asserts nothing about what it enquires into, but it asserts something nonetheless: our desire, in fact, to be informed concerning the object asked about. It is indeed capable of truth and falsehood, and is false when our desire is misstated by it".[13]

Although Husserl objects to the *way* in which Bolzano reduces the non-assertives to assertives, he adopts Bolzano's position in principle, suggesting his own idea on the relation between the kinds of acts and sentence-forms. An illuminating passage in this respect goes like this:

> Talk of 'expressing' is . . . ambiguous, and it remains so even when we connect it with the *acts* to be expressed. What are expressed may be, on the one hand, said to be sense-*giving* acts, to which in the narrower sense, 'voice' is given. But there are other acts which can also be said to be expressed, though . . . in a different sense. I refer here to the very frequent cases in which *we name acts we are now expressing*, and through such naming manage *to say that we are experiencing them*. In this sense I 'express' a wish through the words 'I wish that . . .', a question through the words 'I am asking whether . . .', . . . and so on. Naturally, we can pass judgement on our own inner experiences, just as we can pass judgements on outward things, and when we do the former, the meanings of the relevant sentences will reside in our *judgements* upon such experiences, and not in the experiences themselves, our wishes, questions, etc.[14]

Thus Husserl found a way (or so he thought) preferable to Bolzano's method to reduce the non-assertive to assertive forms, and this accomplished, the issue was settled for him for the time being, as is explicitly declared at the end of the VIth Logical Investigation.[15]

It would not be correct to say that as a result Husserl lost interest in the non-assertive forms and their correlates on the intentional level. He mentioned them on several occasions in his later writings. In *Erfahrung und Urteil* we even find quite an extensive discussion on the interrogative.[16] But, as far as I know, he never attempted a systematic treatment of these forms.

III

As regards this issue, I would like to substantiate the view that a continuity is detectable from Husserl's to Searle's position, even if Searle may not have been aware of it. As a matter of fact, he ascribes to himself a deviation from what he calls 'the tradition' of the theory of intentionality, and sets out to tell us in what ways his use of the term 'intentionality' differs from the 'traditional' one.[17] We should not, however, take this last claim too seriously. In general, when it is correct, the deviation is not very significant, and when the deviation seems of importance, the allegation is not quite accurate. For example, Searle argues that his use of the term 'intentionality' is non-conformist, as it stresses the difference in scope between intentionality and mentality: there are mental states which are not intentional, though not *vice versa*. This is a significant contention, but as we have seen, it was Husserl's position as well.

Further, Searle rejects calling the intentional state 'an act'. There are indeed, according to him, mental acts, as for instance "doing arithmetic in your head or forming mental images of the Golden Gate Bridge", which are also intentional states, but there are also countless intentional states which are not acts, like desiring, hoping, fearing, believing. An act is something that you perform, and in those other states none of it is occurring.[18]

We can reply to this that Husserl did indeed use the term 'act' as synonymous with 'intentional experience' (which Searle labels 'Intentional state' or 'event'), but he had explicitly made it a *technical* term. At a later stage of the development of his doctrine, when he came to conceive of the intentional experience as constitutive of its objects, the concept of 'act' came close to the sense of acting or bringing about, but even then Husserl preserved the distinction between this aspect of intentionality and acting as purposeful intervening in the course of events. The term 'act' seems to have remained for Husserl a technical term all along the way.

Searle's third contention about deviating from tradition concerns the relation between the term 'intention' in its ordinary, pre-analytic sense, and 'intentionality' as that property of mental states or events which is the subject-matter of our inquiry. Searle argues for a clear separation of the two. The term 'intention' in its pre-analytic sense is essentially connected with acting, speech being also considered a kind of acting. We form an intention to do something in the far or near future, or we do something with an intention to reach a certain goal, or to make something happen. Such an action will be called 'intentional', but there is no point, says Searle, to consider a belief, or a hope, or a desire 'intentional' in this sense. The mental states of belief, hope, or desire, imply a directedness toward some object or some state of affairs, and are thus identified as intentional, though no action is involved. Hence, we should (a) avoid using the noun 'intention' for those intentional states which have nothing to do directly with action; and (b) to specify the expressions 'intentional' and 'intentionality' as technical terms. Accordingly, every intention-for-doing-something and every intention-in-action is an intentional state, but not *vice versa*.

Here we can certainly see a deviation from the terminology used by Husserl and his followers, but hardly anything beyond terminology is involved. Indeed, Husserl often used the term 'intention' as synonymous with 'intentional experience' or with 'act', but similarly to Searle he took care to distinguish between the 'normal' or 'every day' use of the term, as essentially connected with acting, and the technical use of it signifying the subject-matter in the theory of intentionality. In German there is no great danger of misunderstanding, as there are different words for the ordinary sense of intention (*Absicht, Vorsatz*). Moreover, this technical use of 'intention' points to the etymological connection with the mediaeval tradition, from which it was taken by Brentano, as mentioned before.

Let us proceed now to Searle's theory itself. It could be said that the working hypothesis which Husserl had suggested, but failed on the whole to implement, is now applied by a masterly hand. The 'harmony of grammatical forms' as a guide in the analysis of intentionality received a radical interpretation in Searle's procedure of exploring the structure and logical properties of the intentional state by means of the model of a speech act.

This indeed is the *main* procedure that Searle has adopted to elaborate his theory. It is, however, underlied by the following, somewhat 'ideological' assumption, the importance of which cannot be overestimated.

The procedure became possible, since the model could be based on solid knowledge in the field of Philosophy of Language in general and on Searle's theory of speech acts in particular. Nevertheless, one must not jump to the conclusion that what Searle does is interpreting intentionality in linguistic terms. It is only an empirical fact that historically the development of the Philosophy of Language proceeded at a faster pace than did the inquiry into the nature of intentional states. As fas as the logical relation between these fields or layers is concerned, the intentional states come first. As Searle puts it: "Language is derived from intentionality and not conversely. The direction of pedagogy is to explain Intentionality in terms of language; the direction of logical analysis is to explain language in terms of Intentionality".[19]

In the course of his analysis Searle indicated a number of parallelisms between the intentional state and the speech act, and doing so he had developed a very useful conceptual apparatus for a systematic treatment of problems of the theory of intentionaltity and related topics.

I must rest content with analysing only a few of these parallelisms and connections, the ones which are particularly relevant to our discussion. First and foremost let us consider the parallelism between two distinctions, each of which is basic in its field: one of them is between the 'propositional content' and the 'illocutionary force' of the speech act, and the other is between the 'intentional (or representational) content' and the 'psychological mode' of the intentional state. What is immediately noticeable is that on the side of the intentional state the distinction is the same as the one we have found in Husserl's conception and described as one of the most important single findings in the field. Searle writes in this connection:

> Just as I can *order* you to leave the room, *predict* that you will leave the room, and *suggest* that you will leave the room, so I can *believe* that you will leave the room, *fear* that you will leave the room, *want* you to leave the room, and *hope* that you will leave the room. In the first class of cases, the speech act cases, there is an obvious distinction between the propositional content *that you will leave the room* and the illocutionary force with which that propositional content is presented in the speech act. But equally in the second class of cases, the Intentional states, there is a distinction between the representative content *that you will leave the room*, and the psychological mode, whether belief or fear or hope or whatever, in which one has that representative content.[20]

The relationship between the two levels is further elucidated by another parallelism between them, this time with respect to the so called direction-of-fit. As much as there are speech acts with the direction of fit of word-to-world, as for example a *statement* or a *description*, and speech acts with the direction of fit of world-to-word, like an *order* or a *promise*, so there are also intentional states with the direction of fit of mind-to-world, as for example *belief* or *hope*, and intentional states with the direction of fit of world-to-mind, like *desire* and *intention* (in its pre-analytic sense).

Finally, we are given a powerful key-concept of the 'conditions of satisfaction', which functions parallelly at both levels, linguistic and mental alike.

> We say, for example, that a statement is true or false, that an order is obeyed or disobeyed, that a promise is kept or broken. In each of these we ascribe success or failure of the illocutionary act to match reality in the particular direction of fit provided by the illocutionary point. To have an expression, we might label all of these conditions 'conditions of satisfaction' . . . [T]his notion of satisfaction clearly applies to Intentional states as well. My belief will be satisfied if and only if things are as I believe them to be, my desires will be satisfied if and only if they are fulfilled, my intentions will be satisfied if and only if they are carried out.[21]

The concept of conditions-of-satisfaction proved to be extremely fruitful at later stages of the analysis, when Searle used his conceptual apparatus to inquire into phenomena like sense-perception, activity, the relation between intensionality and intentionality, proper names, etc.

There is a considerable overlap between this concept of conditions-of-satisfaction and Husserl's distinction between intention and fulfilment. As we read in the *LI*:

> We may now further characterize the consciousness of fulfilment by seeing in it an experiential form which plays a part in many other fields of mental life. We have to think of the opposition between wishful intention and wish-fulfilment, between voluntary intention and execution, of the fulfilment of hopes and fears, the resolution of doubts, the confirmation of surmises, etc., to be clear that essentially the same opposition is to be found in very different classes of intentional experiences.[22]

These remarks on what Husserl calls the 'wider class of experiences' appear again in the context of the Sixth Investigation, as a kind of digression from the main subject, which is the phenomenological elucidation of knowledge'. The distinction between intention and fulfilment is investigated in close connection with only one class of acts, the so called 'objectifying acts' of judging and asserting.

I have thus far outlined the common areas of the two approaches without specifying how far does the overlap extend. This, I believe, is a problem deserving a separate treatment.

IV

To sum up: the context of our analysis in its historical perspective is a restricted one. The point of its departure is Brentano, but it is only the Brentano of the *Psychologie vom empirischen Standpunkt*, where he proposed his initial thesis on intentionality as the *differentia specifica* of mentality. At the core of this thesis we have found two distinctions intersecting each other: one between the intra- and the extra-mental existence, the other between intendedness and the lack of it. We have also understood that at least two problems cropped up from that terse formulation to challenge all who would proceed along Brentano's path: the problem of the ontological status both of the object (or the state-of-affairs) contained in the mental phenomenon and of the mental phenomenon containing it; and the problem of the variety of kinds of intentionality.

Husserl, and here we mean Husserl of the *LI*, took up the challenge of both problems; however, with respect to our discussion, the second one expresses better the continuity between the respective positions of the two thinkers. In pursuing this line of thought Husserl produced an important analytical tool: the distinction between the Matter (or Content) of the intentional experience and its Quality. He also proposed a device to guide us in identifying and analysing those *kinds of intentionality*: use of the alleged correlations between linguistic forms and intentional experiences. Unfortunately, this ingenious device had to remain, at least at the stage under consideration, unused. Even at later stages of the history of Husserl's theory of intentionality this particular part of it has remained underdeveloped, although there is some textual evidence that he always meant to come back to it.

At this point we have found it possible to speak of continuity between Husserl's position and that of Searle's. We have called Searle's procedure of using the speech-act as the model for analysing the logical properties of the Intentional state 'a radical interpretation of Husserl's working hypothesis' and have pointed out that Husserl's Matter and Quality, in a slightly changed terminology, gained the rank of key-concepts in Searle's theory. In fact, we have suggested, the parallelisms between the two positions go much further.

Still, this applies only to a comparison within the restricted context, as described above. Should this context be broadened, far reaching differences will emerge. For example, Searle says explicitly in his *Intentionality* (p. 160) that he has adopted a "resolutely naturalistic" approach, that he thinks of Intentional states, processes and events, as a part of our biological life history, in the way "that digestion, growth and secretion of bile are part of our biological life history". The later Husserl, Husserl of the 'phenomenological reduction' and 'intentional constitution' would have vigorously rejected such an attitude, as contradicting his 'transcendental idealism'.

Here, it seems, we are facing a real choice. To consider it, however, we would have to dive into deep philosophical waters, and such an undertaking must await another opportunity.

———

ENDNOTES

[1] Brentano, Franz, *Psychology from an Empirical Standpoint*, ed. Linda L. McAlister (London 1973), p. 88f.

[2] In McAlister's edition: 'a thing', in the original: 'eine Realität'.

[3] Rarely mentioned by commentators.

[4] Cf. J. N. Mohanty, *The Concept of Intentionality* (St. Louis, Missouri 1972), on the quoted passage in general, but particularly on this point, p. 6.

[5] McAlister's edition, p. 88n.

[6] On the history of this concept see W. & M. Kneale, *The Development of Logic* (Oxford 1962), p. 224ff.; I.M. Bocheński, *A History of Formal Logic* (Notre Dame 1961), p. 154ff.

[7] See e.g. the Marras-Spiegelberg controversy, as in Linda L. McAlister (ed.), *The Philosophy of Brentano* (London 1976), pp. 108−139.

[8] Quoted from Findlay's translation, as in Edmund Husserl, *Logical Investigations*, (London 1970), Vol. II (hereafter *LI*), p. 569f.

[9] *ibid.*, p. 572f.

[10] *ibid.*, p. 579.

[11] *ibid.*, p. 586.

[12] *ibid.*, p. 586, italics added.

[13] Quoted from *LI*, Vol. II, p. 840.

[14] *ibid*, p. 677. For a critical analysis of these considerations of Husserl's see J. N. Mohanty, *Edmund Husserl's Theory of Meaning* (The Hague 1964), pp. 80−86, as well as his "Husserl's Theory of Meaning" in F. Ellison and P. McCornick (eds.), *Husserl's Expositions and Appraisals* (Notre Dame 1977), pp. 26 and 34.

[15] *LI*, Vol II, p. 849ff.

[16] Husserl, Edmund, *Erfahrung und Urteil: Untersuchung zur Genealogie der Logik*, ed. Ludwig Landgrebe (Hamburg 1948), pp. 371−380. For an extensive survey and analysis of the various phases in the development of Husserl's conception of intentionality see Mohanty, *op. cit.*, Part II.

[17] See John R. Searle, *Intentionality: An Essay in the Philosophy of Mind* (Cambridge 1983), p. 1. See also "Von der Sprechakttheorie zur Intentionalität: ein Gespräch mit John R. Searle" in *Information Philosophie* (Basel 1984), p. 24ff.

[18] Searle, John R., *Intentionality*, p. 3.

[19] *ibid.*, p. 5.

[20] *ibid.*, p. 5f. Jitendranath Mohanty was probably the first who noticed the striking coincidence of these distinctions. See his "Husserl's Theory of Meaning" mentioned in Footnote 14, above, p. 22n. (quoted by Hubert L. Dreyfus in the text referred to below, Footnote 22).

[21] Searle, J. R., *Intentionality*, p. 10.

[22] *LI*, Vol. II, p. 699. Prof. Dreyfus arrives at a similar assessment of the relation between these basic distinctions in the Introduction to his collection *Husserl, Intentionality and Cognitive Science* (Cambridge, Mass., 1982), p. 4ff. Dreyfus' text came to my attention after the present paper had been submitted.

* * *

RE-EMERGENCE OF THE CONCEPT OF CONSCIOUSNESS IN TWENTIETH CENTURY SCIENCE AND PHILOSOPHY

Rudy Krejci
University of Alaska, Fairbanks

INTRODUCTION

Never in the history of mankind were there so many people shaped and influenced for such a long period of time by rather a few profound ideas as during the last four centuries.[1]

Anonymous

During the last four hundred years and into our century, a series of conceptual revolutions have taken place forcing us to change our way of thinking. The Copernican cosmological revolution destroyed the millenia old belief in the central position of the earth in the universe which was so important for the concept of a God-created universe and of man in it. A new emerging view of the nature of the universe produced a synthesis of physics and astronomy culminating in the classical physics of Newton which gave us a picture of the world that remained the same no matter how and from where one looked at it. It was a definite picture, a mechanistic view reflecting a mechanistic reality. This change in the concept of the universe implied a change in the concept of man. During the 18th century a new science of man and of society was formulated, patterned after physics and producing social physics, social mechanics, social statistics, social energetics, associanistic psychology, etc. During the 19th century four other revolutions followed within the mechanistic paradigm: first, the Darwinian theory of evolution, destroying the concept of a universal design with man on the top, and introducing the concept of survival of the fittest as a new mechanistic selector in the development of species. This was followed by Karl Marx explaining the history of human societies as a later dialectical development of cosmic matter. Materialism was regarded as the safest foundation of science and, correspondingly, social science could be nothing but some kind of economical determinism. Similarly, Freudian psychoanalysis projects the existing mechanistic paradigm upon the study of personality, declaring man as not being in charge of himself but rather a victim of unconscious drives and two forces: the self-preservative and the sexual drives whose primary interests are the optimal satisfaction of both of them. Thus man, unable to control himself, became a true object of scientific studies together with other species as a stimulus-response apparatus as seen in the emergence of Pavlovian teaching which prepared the way for the triumph of Behaviorism in the 20th century.

Newtonian science, due to its prestige, provided a new scientific paradigm, which in due time, produced a corresponding social science and science of man. In this model, science was concerned only with quantities and measurements for these were the primary qualities of the objective world which were captured in linguistic replicas and mathematical formulations. Ethical and moral issues were not scientific and therefore of no concern. One talked about the world without the awareness that someone was doing the talking. The phenomena of mental events, minds, psyche, self, disappeared in the process of studying man scientifically, consciousness became in these scientific circles "a buzz-word of our flower generation" and as such, of no scientific concern. The concept of man that emerged held that the human mind was a passive, blank sheet of paper, which in turn became the foundation of a political system of democracy based on the equality of social atoms at the time of birth. Thus the mechanistic concept of the universe produced a predominantly mechanistic society, with mechanistic man, reared in a mechanistic culture, medicine, law, education, economics, industry etc.

While all of the previous have been and to great extent still are going on, a new tacit conceptual revolution was in the making, finding at first its expression in the foundations of mathematics, thus producing new geometries with new implications for the whole realm of human thinking. Hand in hand with the radical changes in the foundations of mathematics went new modifications of the millenia old Aristotelian system of logic. The changes here were small but they were not expected to happen in a field regarded to have been definitely stated such a long time ago. By the end of the 19th century there were new ways expressed in discontinuities in literature, atonality was introduced into music, cubism represented similar innovation in art. Political, social and economical crisis accompanied this time of transition.

When at the turn of the century, classical physics found itself in a serious crisis, two new theories of modern physics (Einstein's theory of relativity and quantum mechanics) introduced a new conceptual reconstruction of reality, revealing the world we cannot perceive with our senses or adequately describe in our language. Time and space are conceived as inseparably connected, matter turns into fields of energy losing its substance and the consciousness of the observer-participator becomes an integral catalyst of the pattern of interactions of the whole. Where one would expect a fundamental agreement among the leading exponents of the new way of thinking one must be disappointed facing a veritable schism between Einstein on one hand and Bohr, Heisenberg and other quantum physicists on the other hand. What is the meaning of the conflict, and is the conflict basically of a philosophical, scientific or religious nature, or are all of them just three aspects of the same? Who is here to say, who is here to judge?[1]

The twentieth century will certainly occupy a very distinct role in the history of humanity due mostly to its multifaceted contradictions shaking the foundations of entire societies, furthermore by its atrocities, mass murders, ideological fanaticism hand in hand with the new emerging concept in the physical sciences and their technologies, bringing mankind to the brink of extinction. At the same time, bringing the people of the earth into close physical proximity and into better understanding. We can justly say at the close of our century that we have lived in a century of revolutions which for the first time involved the entire earth with its populations indicating the necessity of a new cultural, political and socal synthesis.[2]

I

The only goal of science appeared to be analytical, i.e., the splitting up of reality into ever smaller units and the isolation of individual causal trains.[3a]

Ludwig von Bertalanffy

The purpose of this essay is to explain the re-emergence of the concept of consciousness in 20th century science and philosophy. First, since the re-emergence is claimed to have occurred, I have to deal with the very existence of the concept of consciousness, how it emerged originally, how it was treated in the past and how it submerged later on, before it re-surfaced again in our own times.

Consciousness-self-knowledge, self-awareness, intentionality, introspection—is basically an art or act of observing one's own mental states and processes with the purpose of achieving self-knowledge—a phenomenon known to all people of all cultures and times, a human universal creating the same individual way of successfully achieving it. In our Western tradition Socrates is the symbol of a true seeker of wisdom (know thyself), he is the light in the darkness, and as Plato describes it in his Republic, there is a way of achieving the Good, the Absolute in terms of which the mind can recognize its own ideas. After training the body and the mind for many years a conscious state of harmony can be achieved, which in turn can introduce the student into the study of dialectics, where ideas are studied in their relationship away from all sensory imports till one reaches the level of the mind which is considering only the unchangeable Absolute Good itself.[3] Plato's philosophy survived in the Academy and in Neoplatonism, finding new formulations in Plotinus and later in St. Augustine who provided the first masterful synthesis of the ancient quest for wisdom within Christian teaching. Man's search for absolute certainty was now defined in religious terms and so it stayed till the end of the Middle Ages.

Modern philosophy begins in the West with Descartes who continued the search for absolute knowledge and found it in his famous Cogito-consciousness. He assumed that philosophy should start with the study of consciousness, however, this very claim did not find an expected follow up. His conscious mind was for him nothing but a mirror reflecting the world. He even admitted that the mirror might distort the world, however, he was convinced that man could never know for sure if this was the case because his mind can never get "out there" and check on it.[4] (4) Descartes never imagined that the mind itself could be an important variable in our conception of the world. The followers of Descartes philosophized out from his inconsistencies everything there was–so we had philosophies of dualism, monism, pantheism, idealism, and materialism claiming him as their legitimate father.

Among the British empiricists it was especially John Locke who maintained that the Self was a continuity of consciousness, independent of material bodies and of substances as well. Locke's great follower, David Hume, became the most influential philosopher in Anglo-Saxon thinking up to our present time. Hume, trying to find the mysterious self of Descartes, was not successful, what he found was only a "bundle of impressions", no general, overriding self, no unifying self of awareness. Did Hume not notice that someone was doing the looking? Evidently it never occurred to him. After his failure he hoped that others might be luckier in the future in solving the problem.[5] The followers of Hume, like William James, who agreed with him, maintained that introspection does not reveal an overriding self. During the 20th century, the Anglo-Saxon tradition put Hume's argument into modern logical gown in Gilbert Ryle's "systematic elusiveness of the concept of 'I'".[6] The American behavioristic school of Watson and Skinner boldly proclaimed that there were no mental events, not being aware, of course, that it followed.

Kant agreed in principle with Hume, that while a source to thinking must be thought, one can never know it. The self, the "I" is beyond an experience, unknowable.[7] Modern existentialism found in Sartre even a more radical position stating that cansciousness itself must be nothing, non-being: Therefore, there is no true self, no unifying sub stratum, no real source for our thoughts.[8]

In the view of most modern Western thinkers, the original Greek quest for self-knowledge, wisdom, is not attainable. The Delphic maxim–Know Thyself–is an illusion which cannot be reached. It appears that Plato's dialectic technique was lost, Descartes did not give us the source of conscious thought, introspection reveals only individual bundles of impressions, and consequently, consciousness turns necessarily into an empty concept–an unnecessary philosophical aether . . .

II

Neurophysiologists will not likely find what they are looking for outside their own consciousness, for that which they are looking for is that which is looking.[9a]

Keith Floyd

The re-emergence of the concept of consciousness during 20th century development can be traced to three major sources: 1. philosophical, 2. scientific, 3. Oriental philosophical imports in the West, and combinations of these three. The first source is represented by the school of phenomenology and of its founder Edmund Husserl (1859–1938), whose ideas have exerted a powerful influence on European and to a certain extent also on American thinking between the two World Wars. The phenomenological method has been widely applied outside of the field of philosophy where it has made new contributions in the fields of literature, art, aesthetics, social sciences, counseling, pedagogy, religion and many others. The central concept of phenomenology and the soil it germinated came from Franz Brentano's notion of intentionality. The mind, or conscious mind, or consciousness is always intentional, never merely reflecting the world but producing its own distortions due to our various mental positions—emotions, idiosyncrasies, likes, dislikes, prejudices, etc. Consciousness itself cannot be taken for granted, furthermore, it has to be investigated. Husserl defines phenomenology as the study of the structure of consciousness, which by being necessarily intentional is at the same time prejudiced. Scientific pursuits can partially help to eliminate some of them, however, there are also deeply seated habits to our thinking and perception. Science itself may be a mere product of them. Philosophy, to become a true exact science, has to fully recognize that there is a large field inside of man himself which has to be fully studied and comprehended before anything else.[9] Up to now, consciousness has become more or less a hostage of external objects, and thus enslaved it had to become passive, servile, and gutless.

Phenomenology is predominantly a method and it must follow that each application will happen to become necessarily highly individualistic as the followers of Husserl have shown so well. Phenomenology is perhaps, another name for science, a true science, the results of which cannot be petrified. Phenomenology with its "going back to the things themselves" is the direct study of consciousness in order to gain an increased control of our own existence. As a cognitive procedure, the phenomenological method consists fundamentally of an intellectual observation of the object based on intuition. In order to achieve that, a threefold reduction, or exclusion, or bracketing out, (epoché)—is required: 1. one has to bracket out one's own beliefs in the real existence of the object; all subjectivity has to be set aside, 2. all theoretical knowledge, hypotheses, theories, and proofs derived from other sources, have to be set aside. Only the given will be admitted. 3. all the traditions, and what others taught about the object before have to be excluded. The object under investigation has to be subjected to a further two-fold reduction. Its existence has to be disregarded and everything inessential has to be omitted. Thus, the successful steps of bracketing reveal the naked phenomenon in front of the investigator. And here is exactly where the method ends—the conditions are satisfied for the creative part which will be carried on intuitively. Because man is not a syllogism—nothing has to happen! to-day, maybe to-morrow—it cannot be commanded when the creative charge is to happen, or if it will happen at all. The negative aspect of the phenomenological method represents a deep insight into human creativity.

Husserl came to think that the intentional consciousness represented an intersubjective world,
a true community of persons living together in the prenatural, prescientific universe—the task of phenomenology will be the exploration of the human-life-world. (Lebenswelt)[10]

Phenomenology is a veritable Copernican revolution, fundamentally changing the entire realm of human thinking. Awareness of the continuous intentionality of consciousness is then responsible for a continuous process of change. In this state, phenomenology certainly establishes a certain control of continuous awareness which seemed to be totally lacking when mind-changing drugs were used during the last twenty years of experimentation: in these states the penetrating insights may be more intensive, but, without a context of lasting awareness.

All in all, phenomenology has inspired new developments in the understanding of consciousness and with its aesthetic, ethical and mystical experiences supplies a new starting point for mankind at the end of the 20th century.

III

The common division of the world into subject and object, inner world and outer world, body and soul is no longer adequate and leads us into difficulties.[11a]
Werner Heisenberg

Something rather similar to phenomenology can be observed in the radical shift in perspective which took place in modern physics when Einstein, Planck, Bohr and Heisenberg and their many followers realized that the completely passive observer never existed in scientific investigations. What were the implications in the past when Galileo talked about the primary and secondary qualities, and the great Newton did not pretend to give us a hypothesis, and Comte once and forever pontificated in his "laws of three stages" the triumph of positive science over metaphysics and religion? Science was always very progressive in fighting any kind of dogmatism save its own. It is apparent now that the classical world-view was identical with the belief that the universe was a huge aggregate of dispersed homogeneous matter changing its configurations according to the immutable laws of mechanics resting on classical concepts of space, time, matter, motion, causality, determinism and our pictorial character of knowledge. The very transition from the old to the new way of thinking is best characterized by words—picture with its passivity, as used in the past and conception with its creativity, as we use it presently.[11] The 20th century is undergoing perhaps the most engaging and deepest epistemological metamorphosis in the entire history of humanity. The key term that the new physics will talk about is the discovery of the observer and what it is that he really observes: To this, relativity theory answered—relations, quantum mechanics—probabilities.[12] The observer is, of course, a conscious observer, who cannot observe without altering what he observes—both of them are involved in an inseparable interrelation. We can very well conclude that what we experience is not an external objective reality as we have believed in the past, but our direct interaction with it. As Heisenberg said: "What we observe is not nature itself, but nature exposed to our method of questioning."[13] Our answers can only be understood in the context of their inseparable questions. Furthermore, our language does not picture our more advanced thoughts when we deal with the objects not directly observable. We do not even have to assume an objective reality apart from our experience. We deal with the microcosmos and macrocosmos in continuous process which interact, in our consciousness. In this dynamic universe we can only describe the statistical behaviour of the systems and make predictions—our observations are constant fusions and alterations of the observed. The conceptual framework of the new physics with an emphasis on the observer and consciousness is responsible for creating a mental atmosphere that reminds one of deep mystical vision. The men responsible for the new physics, without exception, exemplified the ongoing metamorphosis of their own unprecendented historical search with their belief in a mystical world-view that embodies the world as a spiritual, rather than material phenomenon.

There was a remarkable pilgrimage to China made by Niels Bohr in 1932. "Bohr came back from his visit to China in 1932 inspired by the tradition of learning in China and filled with admiration for the great Chinese thinkers of past and present. The central point of quantum theory, Bohr already had been forced to conclude five years earlier, is complementarity . . . In the East, Bohr discovered to his happiness, that complementarity could be the natural way of thinking. To symbolize complementarity, Bohr chose the Chinese yin-yang symbol and composed the Latin motto—not contraria sed complementa—The way of thinking symbolized by complementarity is so important in his view that every school child should be taught it."[14] Almost 50 years later Prof. Wheeler himself was invited to come to China and present three lectures on history and on contemporary views of quantum theory. In his first lecture he stated to his Chinese audience: "We have learned in our day that it is wrong to think of the universe as—sitting out there—. In the older physics, it was natural to think of the observer as, in effect, looking at "existence" from behind the safe protection of a 20 cm slab of plate glass. In contrast, quantum mechanics teaches the direct opposite. It is impossible to observe even so miniscule an object as an electron without, in effect, smashing that slab and reaching in with the appropriate measuring equipment. Moreover, the installation of apparatus to measure the position coordinate, x, of the electron, automatically prevents the insertion in the same region at the same time, of equipment to measure its momentum, P; and conversely. Furthermore, the choice of what to measure—or whether to measure at all—has irretrievable consequences for what one has a right to say about the electron in the future."[15]

Wheeler thus promotes the observer to a direct participator.

Eugene Wigner, one of the living men responsible for the new physics stated: ". . . it is not possible to formulate the laws of quantum mechanics without reference to consciousness." He believes that there are two kinds of reality. "These are so different that they should have different names. The reality of my perceptions, sensations and consciousness is immediate and absolute. The reality of everything else consists in the usefulness of thinking in terms of it. This reality is relative and changes from object to object, from concept to concept."[16] We come here in contact with Wigner's strong belief in the existence of consciousness and the necessity of its scientific study.

It is remarkable that every major physicist involved in the work of the new physics was completely in favor of the interdisciplinary dialogue. Probably their deep involvement in this unique search into the mysteries of nature led them without exception into the mystery of human consciousness. Einstein, Bohr, Heisenberg, Schroedinger, De Broglie, Jeans, Planck, Pauli, Eddington and their followers have created for mankind what one day will become known as a New New Testament, a respectable sequel to the other two Testaments and all other great documents of both eastern and western humanity.[17]

IV

. . . because our science—Greek science—is based on objectification, whereby it has cut itself off from an adequate understanding of the subject of Cognizance, of the mind. . . . our present way of thinking does need to be amended, perhaps by a bit of blood-transfusion from Eastern thought.[18a]

Erwin Schroedinger

Our present day culture is in the midst of profound changes. After 400 years of energetically practising the study of the outward world in the West we have been able to reach an understanding of the physical and to some extent biological phenomena. On the other hand the East by undertaking the study of the inward world for thousands of years arrived at a deep understanding of the inner universe of consciousness. In our western modern science we do not claim to possess anything more than embryonic ideas about consciousness and its role. The traditional East, particularly in its old Vedic scriptures, together with the six derivative systems of Indian philosophy possesses a well developed understanding of consciousness. Mostly due to our modern technological innovations the former cultural separations were cancelled resulting in the present day mutual interchange of ideas and goods. There are many recent developments that have begun to extend the scope of the Oriental imports in the West. The audience, a recipient of Oriental influences, represents a rather motley group as a cross-section of our western society. There exists a "counter-cultural community," opposed to science, and showing a great distaste for all of the rational thinking and its products—western logic, machines, gadgets and computers and their applied technologies. Various Oriental philosophies and religions are enthusiatically embraced satisfying the demand for a nonlinear, arational, intuitive and highly personal way of thinking and living. Then we have groups with a widespread interest in mind-altering drugs, such as psychedelic drugs, creating addictions together with the promise of a panacea for many of our young disillusioned generation.

Among today's very popular teachings we have more developed traditions including Zen-Buddhism, Tibetan Buddhism, Sufism, various aspects of Yoga, and Transcendental Meditation which, in itself, represents the theoretical foundation of the science of creative intelligence. During the last few decades there has been a great revival of interest in the study of consciousness within Western philosophy which is challenging the prevailing empirical position on the topic. Views of such philosophers like Butler, Reid, and McTaggart have been reintroduced, joined by new works of Chisholm, Madell, Ornstein and others.[18]

Another interesting phenomenon during the last 15 years has been the emergence of many studies written by scientifically trained writers who have attempted to link western science, especially physics, to oriental mystical traditions against violent objection by some physicists.[19] It is becoming clear that the notion of consciousness which has been totally absent from our western science, creates havoc in the conceptual structure of many contemporaries who have been trained in the old paradigms. A great part of our educational system in the West is still deeply oriented in the tradition and perpetuates the stubborness of the old regime. In spite of much progress in Western education we can still regard it more or less Ptolemaically oriented—under culture we understand western culture, under science western science, under art western art, under logic western logic, under thinking western way of thinking, under values western values. It will require a lot of time before we are freed from our narrow-minded provincialism and prejudices. In spite of all of the contemporary oriental imports in the West, most of them have achieved a rather superficial fashionable effect, many of them are turned into our typical western band-waggons. They come and go. There was an insightful work written during the second World War by F. S. C. Northrop—*Meeting of East and West* which was intended by the author to be a preparatory work introducing comparative cultural values of the post-war world;—looking back almost forty years, we can see that the work has hardly made a dent in our cultural consciousness. In spite of all the defficiencies our present human nature is responsible for, both the value systems of the East and the West must be viewed as being complementary and not contradictory as it has been understood by both sides up to now. The Western revival of interest in the spiritual and the Eastern interest to improve their material well-being is such a complementary enterprise requiring mutual help based on respect and understanding.

ENDNOTES

[1a] Anonymous
[1] Capek, Milic, *The Philosophical Impact of Contemporary* Physics (Princeton, N. J., 1961), pp. 3–6, 361–399.
[2] Leshan, Lawrence and Margenau, Henry, *Einstein's Space and Van Gogh's Sky—Physical Reality and Beyond* (New York 1982), pp. 3–41.
[3a] Bertalanffy, Ludwig von, *General System Theory* (New York 1968).
[3] Plato, *Republic* (Oxford Univ. Press, 1971), Chapter IX, 376E–392C, ibid, VI. 509b–518d.
[4] Descartes, René, *Discourse on Method and Meditations* (The Library of Liberal Arts 1960), Second Meditation, pp. 81–91.
[5] Hume, David, *Treatise of Human Nature* (London, J. M. Dent, 1951), Vol. 1, pp. 238–244.
[6] Ryle, Gilbert, *The Concept of Mind* (University Paperbacks, Barnes and Noble, New York), pp. 245–266.
[7] Kant, Immanuel, *Critique of Pure Reason* (Norman Kemp Smith's), pp. 83–89, 132–169.
[8] Sartre, J. P., *The Transcendence of the Ego* (Noonday press, New York), pp. 80–102.
[9a] Floyd, Keith, *Of Time and the Mind*, "Fields within Fields", No. 10 (1973–74).
[9] Husserl, Edmund, *Ideas: A General Introduction to Pure Phenomenology* (London and New York 1931), per 75.
[10] Husserl, Edmund, *Die Krisis der europäischen Wissenschaften und die transzendentale Phänomeno-logie* (the Hague 1954), pp. 347–on.
[11a] Heisenberg, Werner, *Physics and Philosophy* (New York 1958).
[11] Capek, Milic, pp. 3–4.
[12] Eddington, Arthur, *The Philosophy of Physical Science* (Ann Arbor Paperbacks, 1958), Chapter V, pp. 70–105.
[13] Heisenberg, Werner, (1958), pp. 58–on.
[14] Wheeler, John Archibald, *Physics and Austerity—Law Without Law—Workings Paper* (University of Texas, 1982), pp. 1–2.
[15] Wheeler, John Archibald, *Physics and Austerity—first lecture—This Incredible Quantum Business*, p. 9.
[16] Wigner, Eugene, *Symmetries and Reflections* (Bloomington, Ind., 1967), pp. 210–288.
[17] Wilbur, Ken, *Quantum Questions—Mystical writings of the world's great physicists* (New Science Library 1984), pp. 3–208.
[18a] Schroedinger, Erwin, *What is Life and Mind and Matter* (Cambridge Univ. Press).

[18] Kupperman, Joel J., "Investigations of the Self", *Philosophy East West* (Jan. 1984), pp. 37–49.
Nalimov, V. V., Three important contemporary translations from Russian: *Faces of Science* (Philadelphia, Pa, ISI Press, 1981); *In the labyrinths of language: a mathematician's journey Philadelphia, P*, ISI Press, 1981; *Realms of the Unconscious: The Unconscious: The Enchanted Frontier* (Philadelphia, Pa, ISI Press 1982), pp. 1–19; 140–146; 257–300.
[19] Capra, Fritjof, *The Tao of Physics* (Shambala 1975).
Capra, Fritjof, "Modern Physics and Eastern Mysticism", *The Journal of Transpersonal Psychology* 8 (1976), pp. 20–39.
Pagels, Heiz, The Cosmic Code (New York 1982).
Bohm, David, *Wholeness and the implicate order* (London 1980), pp. 196–213.
Heisenberg, Werner, *Physics and Philosophy* (New York 1958).
Heisenberg, Werner, *Physics and Beyond* (New York 1971).
Heisenberg, Werner, *On Modern Physics* (New York 1961).
Sarfatti, J., "The Physical Roots of Consciousness" in Mishlove, *The Roots of Consciousness*, New York 1975, pp. 279ff.
Talbot, Michael, *Mysticism and the new Physics* (A Bantam Book, 1981), pp. 1–64.
Prigogine, Ilya and Stengers, Isabelle, *Order Out of Chaos, Man's new dialogue with nature* (Bantam Books, 1984), pp. 27–56, 79–102, 291–313.

* * *

INTENTIONALITY AND *IRREALIA*

Burnham Terrell
University of Minnesota, Minneapolis

This paper is directed to a problem that emerges from Brentano's later writings. It starts from a set of assumptions that might rightly be taken to define a "Late-Brentano-style" approach to the philosophy of mind. These include (1) intentionality; (2) *Reismus*; (3) *Evidenz*; and (4) inner perception.[1] The problem was posed by Professor Roderick Chisholm in his article on "Intentionality" in the *Encyclopedia of Philosophy*:[2]

> . . . Brentano abandoned the ontological part of his doctrine of intentionality. In his later writings, he said that "unicorn" in the sentence "John is thinking of a unicorn" has no referential function . . . "Unicorn," in such sentences, is used syncategorematically to contribute to the description of the person who is said to have a unicorn as the object of his thought. But this conclusion seems to leave us with our problem. The statement "John is thinking of a unicorn" does not describe John as a unicorn; how, then, does "unicorn" serve to contribute to his description?
>
> The ontological problem, therefore, may be said to survive in the question, "How are we using 'unicorn' in 'John believes that there are unicorns'?" There is a temptation to say that the use of "unicorn" in such sentences has no connection at all with the use it would have in "There are unicorns." That this would be false, however, may be seen by noting that "John believes that there are unicorns" and "All of John's beliefs are true" together imply "There are unicorns."

It is true that when a word is used syncategorematically (synsemantically) it is not being used as it is when independently (autosemantically) referring. We are free, however, to draw distinctions between synsemantical expressions or between one sort of synsemantical function and another. Chisholm's question calls for such a distinction. Some synsemantical expressions are only accidentally so, by virtue of context; others are essentially synsemantic and have no autosemantic use whatsoever.

An essentially synsemantical expression could be identified with what others would call an incomplete symbol. 'Someone thinking of an object as such,' is not about what it appears to be about. It can be paraphrased, as: 'someone thinking of someone thinking of an object,' where 'object' could be said to have its ordinary role, but in a context in which it is, *per accidens*, synsemantical. Another paraphrase captures what is meant more naturally: 'someone thinking indirectly of an object.' There is no real difference in meaning between the two alternatives. To think of something indirectly is to think of it as what someone is thinking of, and that requires just that we think of someone as thinking of it.

We use words to describe mental phenomena. We use words to express mental phenomena. When John, the ill-informed zoologist, expresses his belief in unicorns by saying "There are unicorns", he uses the word 'unicorns' to specify the object of his belief. His judgment can be the primary object of a psychologist's description of John as a believer in unicorns. The psychologist uses 'unicorns' to specify the object of the belief he describes, to express a reference to unicorns incidental to a reference to someone referring to them.

Chisholm is mystified by the possibility of using a word both in referring to an object and in referring to someone who is referring to that object. We can make our own mental phenomena objects of primary reference. I can respond to a question such as "What were you referring to just now?" either by repeating the object-specifying word, 'unicorns', or by saying, "I was referring to unicorns." Someone else might respond for me, saying, "Terrell was referring to unicorns." As psychological reports, they are all equivalent. They all report the same psychological phenomenon in different ways.

The same point can be made by citing anaphoric reference in intentional contexts. If John says, "There are leprechauns," he will presumably be understood to be referring to leprechauns. Suppose that I respond, "Yes, you're right; I believe in them, too!" Chisholm's reading of Brentano would have us understand the pronoun 'them' to be synsemantical and hence disconnected from John's use of 'leprechauns.' (He would so understand the repetition of that word in the intentional context and, *a fortiori*, the use of the pronoun in its place.) I could say instead, "I believe as you do." I could say of Jerry that he believes as John and I do. Anaphoric reference and specification by similarity to a known model make no sense on Chisholm's reading. That is because his reading is mistaken.

The mistake arises from the confusion of indirect reference with synsemantical function. A description of a person as mentally active must be complex. It must include a specification of the mental act's quality and a specification of its object. A mental phenomenon is both qualitatively and objectually determined. The specifications are expressed by words in a language.

In expressing a judgment about unicorns, we use the word 'unicorn(s)' together with a component expressing the judgment's quality, in Brentano's sense. To express the objectual aspect of a description of a judgment, we use the same word, binding it to a larger context such as 'thinking about'. It is used in one case to express objectual specification for a judgment as to its primary object. In the other, the primary object of the judgment expressed by the words used is the person making the former judgment. The reference to unicorns is indirect. It provides the answer to the question, *What is his judgment about?* Any word that can be used autosemantically can be used in the expression of an indirect reference, as part of a psychological description. It functions there not independently but as an essential constituent of the specification of the mental phenomenon, the primary object of the description. Such synsemantical usage *per accidens* is not synsemantical function in Brentano's sense.

To show that the difficulties Chisholm raised are ill-founded does not satisfy his demand for a positive account of the connection between expressions of judgment and descriptions of judgers. We need to replace the ontological theory of intentional reference with a gnoseological theory in keeping with the later *Reismus*. We need a theory that will account for the logical connections Chisholm rightly insists upon without the ontological baggage of *irrealia*.

It will be useful to indroduce a distinction beween a *mental phenomenon* and an *intentional reference*. I shall call the mental phenomenon a mental act. For intentional reference I shall use that expression or 'mental reference'. An act of judgment is a complex of intentional references. It includes at least two judgmental references. One of them is objectually specified according to what we usually consider *the* object of judgment. Someone who expresses belief in unicorns by saying, "There are unicorns," is using the word to specify the primary object of his judgment, not in describing it, but in giving it verbal expression.

The act of judgment, however, includes another judgmental reference, the secondary reference of inner perception, which directly refers to the act of judgment itself and hence indirectly to the object of the primary judgmental reference. It is an affirmative judgmental reference within an act of judgment which is its object, but it is not a separate act of judgment. If it were, the first act of judgment would be its primary object and on Brentano's account it would be an act of inner observation, which he denies, not of inner perception.

To deny inner observation is not generally to deny mental phenomena that have other mental phenomena as their primary objects. There are psychologists. They make judgments about mental acts. The philosopher of mind, in making judgments about what psychologists do, must acknowledge:

a) the primary judgmental reference of some act of judgment;
b) the secondary judgmental reference, a constituent of the same act as (a);
c) the description (or affirmation) of the act of which (a) and (b) are both constituents.

The object of the secondary reference of inner perception is the entire act of which it is a constituent. A psychological judgment has a mental phenomenon as object of its primary reference. It is distinct from its object. Nevertheless, its object, a mental phenomenon, includes as secondary reference an awareness of itself. Both (b), the inner perception and (c), the psychological judgment, are objectually specified in the same way. The secondary object of the mental phenomenon is the same as the psychologist's primary object. Therein lies the connection.

If John believes in unicorns and Jerry believes of John that he is a believer in unicorns, their respective judgments could be expressed by saying, "There are unicorns" and "John believes in unicorns." The sentences express the primary intentional references of the two judgments. John's inner perception, however, is an awareness of himself as a believer in unicorns, an affirmative secondary judgmental reference. Jerry's primary judgmental reference is an affirmation of John as believer in unicorns. Jerry judges as John does, the one in primary reference, the other in secondary reference.

Now we have a solution to Chisholm's problem. The connection between a judgment and a psychologist's account of it is provided not by introducing a common irreal object, but by taking account of the objectual specification common to the subject's inner perception and the psychologist's primary reference. It is a matter of gnoseological description. There is no need for the proliferation of ontological links to mediate between them.

———————

ENDNOTES

[1] See the citations in my article, "Brentano's Philosophy of Mind," in: Guttorm Floistad (ed.), *Contemporary Philosophy. A New Survey* (The Hague/Boston/London 1983), Vol. 4, pp. 223–247.
[2] Edwards, Paul (ed.), *Encyclopedia of Philosophy* (New York 1967), Vol. 4, p. 202.

* * *

INTENTIONALITÄT IN TECHNOLOGIE UND TELEOLOGISCHER ERKLÄRUNG

Karl Weichselbaumer
Universität Linz

Propositionale Attitüden unterliegen genauso dem Ockhamschen Rasiermesserprinzip. Auf Quine,[1] Scheffler[2] und Stegmüller[3] zurückgehend, ist das allgemeine quantorenlogische Schema für teleologische Erklärungen daher so zu konstruieren, daß zunächst Absichten (bzw. Wünsche) sowie Glaubensinhalte (bzw. Überzeugungen) als propositionale Attitüden an Inschriften festgemacht werden. Die dadurch entstehenden inneren Sätze, die vorerst bezeichnungsundurchsichtig[4] sind, erhalten für ihre Termini eine klare ontologische Interpretation durch Reglementierung der Reichweite außenstehender Quantoren;[5] und zwar für die Hervorhebung bezeichnender Positionen aus der vorerst undurchsichtigen Konstruktion mittels Index „$_v$", Trennstrich „," und Querverweis. Vom Gesamtsatz gesehen, enthalten dann die inneren Sätze grundsätzlich nicht-bezeichnende Terme. Zwecks leichterer Lesbarkeit, aus gleichem Grund besteht „,", sind gewisse Individuenvariablen vorangestellt. (Sie könnten genauso gut unmittelbar hinter dem Prädikatbuchstaben stehen, da die Prädikatstellen nicht beliebig vertauscht werden dürfen.) Die Formel lautet dann:

$$\wedge\, x \wedge y \wedge z \wedge u\, [x\, W_{wv}\, x, y \wedge D(\vee v(Mxv \wedge Hv))y \wedge x\, G_{wv}\, x, z \wedge$$
$$\wedge\, D(\vee u \vee v(Mxu \wedge Fu \rightarrow Mxv \wedge Hv))\, z \rightarrow Mxu \wedge Fu]$$

Die Wertbereiche der Individuenvariablen sind folgend definiert: „x" steht für Personen, „y" und „z" für Inschriften, „u" und „v" für Ereignisse. „D(−)" ist ein prädikatbildender Operator mit Satzargument. Das Satzargument ist eine Paraphrasierung der Inschrift, für die sich nach Scheffler genau die Wahrheitsbedingungen angeben lassen. Um die logische Struktur des Argumentationszusammenhanges zu zeigen, habe ich bereits die Formel für diese sogenannten inneren Sätze eingesetzt (charakterisiert durch Atomsätze). Stegmüller, der die Grundzüge eines teleologischen Arguments als erster quantorenlogisch ausformuliert, bleibt dagegen noch bei besonderen Wünschen und steigt noch nicht zum Schema für generelle Sätze auf. Den Argumentationszusammenhang kann er daher durch eine einfachere Konstruktion herstellen. An dieser Stelle ist zu bemerken, daß die Prädikatbuchstaben nicht als Variable zu deuten sind, sondern als schematische Buchstaben, in die erst die Buchstaben als abgekürzte Prädikate einzusetzen sind. Wir würden sonst wieder in einen problematischen Platonismus geraten, den wir soweit wie möglich vermeiden wollen.

Der Ausdruck in der eckigen Klammer beginnt demgemäß in umgangssprachlicher Deutung mit „x wünscht-als-wahr von x ein y, welches eine Daß-es-gibt-ein-v-derart-,-daß-x-macht-v-,-welches-ein-H-ist-Inschrift ist". „x" ist als bezeichnende Position des inneren Satzes mithilfe des eigentümlichen Prädikats „W_{wv}", das als „wünscht-als-wahr von . . ." zu deuten ist, herausgehoben, besser: gekennzeichnet, und durch einen außenstehenden Quantor gebunden. Für „G_{wv}", das an der Stelle der Glaubensrelation steht, und das ebenso als mehrstelliges Prädikat eingeführt ist, bei der Inschriften eine Prädikatstelle einnehmen, gilt analoges. Das Schema als ganzes gilt für die allgemeine Gesetzesaussage im teleologischen Argument, das im Syllogismus des modus ponens „VuVx(Mxu∧Fu)" durch Deduktion liefert und das Explanadum „Mab∧Fb" daher befriedigt.

Aristoteles kommt zu einer Systematik der Ursachen, der seine eigentümliche Weltsicht, der des bildenden Künstlers,[6] zugrunde liegt. Die Zweckursache (zusammen mit der Formursache) nimmt in diesem Fachwerk eine ganz andere Stellung ein, als sie in der heutigen Handlungstheorie einnimmt. Das Telos hat nicht bereits mit dem Anstoß zur Handlung seine Schuldigkeit getan. Der Schwerpunkt teleologischer Erklärung liegt nach Aristoteles daher nicht wie bislang beim Anstoß der Handlung, er liegt bei der Gestaltung der Handlung selber. Für ihn ist sogar die Gestaltung allein das Explanandum.

Selbst Wright, der als führender Intentionalist gilt, entzieht sich der herkömmlichen Sichtweise nicht. Er konzentriert sich immerhin auf die logische Grammatik intentionalen Sprachgebrauchs insoweit, als sich psychische Phänomene intentionaler Art dort sedimentiert haben.[7] Er folgt dem Leitgedanken: „Wir sprechen, machen Äußerungen, und erst s p ä -t e r erhalten wir ein Bild von ihrem Leben" (*PU* XI) – prima facie das vernachlässigend, wieweit im jeweiligen Fall die Ausdrücke für die Realität zutreffen. Hier werden aber die intentionalen Phänomene nur indirekt, nicht sie selber behandelt.

Freilich sind die menschlichen Aktivitäten der Aristotelischen teleologischen Erklärung in verschiedenem Maße zugänglich. Das Formen des Tons steht am einen Ende der Skala, der Hausbau in der Mitte, das Ziehen am Flaschenzug am anderen. Kunst und Technik gehen fließend ineinander über. Wie bereits angedeutet, hat Aristoteles mit der Endursache nicht den Beginn der Aktivität im Auge, wenn er mit ihr etwas erklärt, sondern das Resultat, etwa eine Reiterfigur. Die Vorstellung der Form in der Seele des Baumeisters sei Bewegursache, vergleichbar dem Samen, der in die Erde als Material der Form gesenkt wird. Die Formen als solche aber sind zeitlos, und neben die Formursache stellt sich die Zweckursache als treibende Kraft, die mit ersterer zusammen auftritt. Form- und Endursache erklären die fertigen Dinge in ihrer Beschaffenheit und ihren Weg dorthin, nicht aber den Beginn der Materialformung. Dies leistet bereits die Bewegursache. (Sie darf nicht mit der Stoffursache verwechselt werden, die zugleich als Störursache Widerstand leistet und für etwaiges Mißlingen verantwortlich ist. Die List der Vernunft, mit Hegel zu sprechen, hat sie in Gestalt der Technik großenteils gezähmt.)

Versuchen wir, die teleologische Erklärung im Aristotelischen Sinn zu fassen,[8] wenn auch modernisiert, so gelangt man zu folgendem Schema für teleologische Erklärungen:

$$\bigwedge x \bigwedge y \bigwedge z \bigwedge u \bigwedge v\, [x\, W_{wv}\, x, y \wedge D(\bigvee v(Mxv \wedge Hv))\, y \wedge x\, G_{wv}\, xyz, z \wedge$$
$$\wedge\, D(\bigvee u \bigvee v(yz\, \square\, Mxu \wedge Fu \rightarrow Mxv \wedge Hv))\, z \rightarrow$$
$$\rightarrow (yz\, \square\, Mxu \wedge Fu \rightarrow Mxv \wedge Hv)].$$

Es gilt wieder für die allgemeine Gesetzesaussage im Argument, überraschenderweise aber auch für die von Technologien, letztlich für Technologie im strengen Sinn selber, die sich dann als teleologische Prognose erweisen, wenn die Spezialisierung im Syllogismus reziprok (analog zum Hempel-Openheimschen Erklärungs-Prognose-Schema) erfolgt. Explanandum und zu Prognostizierendes ist dann durch „VxVv(Mxv∧Hv)" erfüllt. Daß das Objekt der Erklärung sich immer auf einen Aspekt reduziert, präzise: auf singuläre Satze,[9] spricht für das Bestehen eines bislang unbekannten Aspekts, nämlich des gezeigten Aristotelischen. Er ist sogar eigentliches wie zentrales Objekt der TE.

Dieser Aristotelische Aspekt läßt mit Putnam überdies eine neue Deutung zu: Der von mir vorgeschlagene Vierstellen-Prädikate bildende Operator „□" mit dem Zweistellen-Prädikat „M" zum Argument, läßt sich in obiger Formel als Intentionalitätsoperator deuten. Er überführt – unbeschadet extensionaler Deutbarkeit – ein Machen „M" in ein intentional durchdrungenes Machen „M'". Lediglich leichterer Lesbarkeit wegen wiederum werden „y" und „z", die Inschriften, die zusätzliche Prädikatstellen belegen, vorangestellt. Putnam legt auf Fields Tarski-Kritik anhand ihrer Unzulänglichkeiten die Grenzen der naturwissenschaftlichen Methode im impliziten Wissen dar. Es ist in Theorie nicht ausformulierbar, da es sich in Fertigkeit gründet.[10] Die generelle Formel für die Gesetzesaussage im teleologischen Argument bildet bei der teleologischen Prognose, die zugleich technologische Prognose ist, die Technologie im strengen Sinn (das Können, das das Sollen impliziert). Gerade durch den eingeführten Intentionalitätsoperator wird dieses implizite Wissen berücksichtigt, das zum expliziten hinzutreten muß, um nach Putnam den Praxisvollzug – und damit auch von Technik –

überhaupt zu gewährleisten. Die Einbeziehung erfolgt aber nur indirekt über die Intentionalität (in Verbindung mit den propositionalen Attitüden), die die Aktualisierung des impliziten Wissens sicherstellt, und zwar material; ohne im Satz formal ableitbar zu sein. Der Operator steht gleichsam für eine Interpolation der exakten Teilkurve zum Kurvenstützpunkt „Absicht", wobei dessen Lage so angegeben ist, daß die Interpolation gelingt. Erklären i.e.S., aber auch wie bei Putnam Verstehen,[11] werden dann ebenso durch diesen Operator differenziert und in ihrem Standort erhellt.

Diese Strukturierung von Technologie mit unentbehrlicher Supplementierungsfunktion von Theorie erlaubt einen − de facto von vornherein vollzogenen − zwanglosen Übergang zur praktischen Zweck-Mittel-Relation, deren Eigentümlichkeiten aber auf der hier erarbeiteten Folie sich erst abheben.[12]

ANMERKUNGEN

[1] Quine, W. v. O., *Wort und Gegenstand (Word and Object)* (Stuttgart 1980).
[2] Scheffler, I., *The Anatomy of Inquiry: Philosophical Studies in the Theory of Science* (New York 1963). Vgl. dazu W. v. O. Quine, *Ontological Relativity and Other Essays*, deutsch: *Ontologische Relativität und andere Schriften* (Stuttgart 1975).
[3] Stegmüller, W., *Probleme und Resultate der Wissenschaftstheorie und Analytische Philosophie* Bd. I (Berlin-Heidelberg-New York 1974).
[4] Whitehead, A. N. und Russell, B., *Prinicipia Mathematica* Bd. 1 (Cambridghe 21925).
[5] Quine, W. v. O., *Wort und Gegenstand*, aaO., bes. S. 289ff.
[6] Windelband, W., *Lehrbuch der Geschichte der Philosophie*, H. Heimsoeth (Hrsg.) (Tübingen 151957). Das Weltgeschehen wird „in letzter Instanz unter der A n a l o g i e   d e s   b i l d e n - d e n   K ü n s t l e r s betrachtet, der für die Verwirklichung seines gestaltenden Gedankens in dem spröden Material eine Grenze findet" (ebd., S. 123).
[7] Wright, G. H. v., *Explanation and Understanding* (London 1971).
[8] Siehe hiezu Sachsses Plädoyer für frühere Stadien der Kategorienbildung. (H. Sachsse, *Kausalität-Gesetzlichkeit-Wahrscheinlichkeit* (Darmstadt 1979).)
[9] Stegmüller, W., aaO.
[10] Putnam, H., Meaning and the Moral Sciences (London 1978).
[11] Ebd.
[12] Ich verweise insbesondere auf Max Webers „formale Zweckrationalität" und die nun bis Putnam reichende Diskussion (H. Putnam, *Reason, Truth and History*, deutsch: *Vernunft, Wahrheit und Geschichte* (Frankfurt a. M. 1982).)

* * *

INTENTIONS AS *INTENTIONES ANIMAE* IN OCKHAM AND AS IMMANENT MENTAL 'OBJECTS' IN BRENTANO

Elisabeth Leinfellner-Rupertsberger
Lincoln, Nebraska

This paper focuses on three topics: (1) two paradigms of semantics and an attempt to unite them by using pragmatic and psychological concepts; (2) a characterization of Ockham's discussion of *intentio* in the framework of these two paradigms and as their synthesis; (3) an interpretation of some fragments from Brentano's writings in the light of (1) and (2).

The point of departure for relating a Scholastic philosopher to Brentano is the well-known quote from Brentano's *Psychology from an Empirical Standpoint*:

> Every mental phenomenon is characterised by what the Scholastics of the Middle Ages called the intentional (or mental) inexistence of an object, and what we might call, though not wholly unambiguously, reference to a content, direction toward an object (which is not to be understood here as meaning a thing), or immanent objectivity.[1]

Spiegelberg and Marras have examined Brentano's relationship to Scholastic philosophy from a mainly Thomistic standpoint.[2] This is justified considering that, f.i., *Psychology from an Empirical Standpoint* makes reference to Ockham but once, when Brentano discusses the question of whether the existence of a being is the same or a different reality than the being itself. According to Brentano, Ockham is correct in denying the difference, but arrives at the wrong conclusions.[3] On the other hand, Aquinas—and Aristotle—figure much more prominently in *Psychology from an Empirical Standpoint*.

However, the fragments from Brentano which I am going to discuss and which fall into a much later period than the (German) 1874 edition of *Psychology from an Empirical Standpoint* come much closer to Nominalism and to Ockham in particular than is to be expected from someone who had earlier (1894) relegated Ockham's philosophy to the second stage of medieval philosophy's decline, i.e., scepticism. In 1901, Brentano went as far as admitting —with reservations—that Nominalism might be right at least on some accounts. After discussing grammatical abstracta and universals in a way outlined below, he continues: "A concession should be made to Nominalism; not that Nominalism is correct, however, but only that certain errors can be purged from the opposing theory."[4]

I do not want to claim that Ockham's philosophy had any influence on Brentano's. The similarities between these two philosophies show, however, that similar problems may lead to similar solutions, a phenomenon upon which we sometimes bestow the grandiose name of *philosophia perennis*.

Spiegelberg points out that the above quote contains two characterizations of mental phenomena:[5] Of one, intentional inexistence, he claims that it is indeed a Scholastic, particularly Thomistic, concept; of the other, reference to a mental object, that it originated with Brentano.[6] According to Spiegelberg, there is in Scholastic philosophy no significant connection between reference to a mental object and *intentio*.[7] Marras, on the other hand, attempts to show that in Aquinas *intentio* is by nature representational and therefore has to stand in a reference relation to an object.[8] We have here two interrelated views of referential semantic relationships. In Brentano, the German term of which 'reference' is a translation means a relation (something relation-like, according to Brentano) between someone who thinks and the immanent mental object.[9] In modern philosophy, 'reference' means a relation between a linguistic expression and some object which may be real, but also possible. In Ockham, '*suppositio*' overlaps with 'reference' in the modern sense; but Ockham also discusses *intentio* in connection with supposition (see below).

However, it seems that Marras stresses the empirical object as referent, while what Spiegelberg has in mind is reference in the sense of Brentano as reference to an immanent, intentional object. Marras is correct in assuming that *intentio* in Aquinas is representational of an object and therefore intrinsically referring; but this does not solve the problem of whether the Scholastics discussed reference to an intentional object.

Ockham's concepts of a mental language and of *supposito simplex* furnish arguments against Spiegelberg's contention that Scholastic philosophy does not deal with reference to intentional objects; in addition, they allow us to broaden Marras' discussion of referring *intentiones* to the discussion of reference to *intentiones*.

Ockham distinguishes between three kinds of expressions: spoken, written, and mental. The spoken and the written language originate by convention (*thesei*), mental language by nature (*physei*). Ockham identifies the mental terms with the *intentiones animae*; they may be universals or singular terms.[10] The written language is an extension of the spoken language, the spoken language an extension of the mental one. However, a written term signifies independently from a spoken one, and a spoken one independently from a mental term.[11]

Suppositio simplex obtains when a term signifies secondarily and stands for a mental term, that is, an *intentio*, as *suppositum*.[12] Since supposition involves reference it is obviously possible to speak of reference to an intentional object, the mental term, in Ockham's philosophy. And since the *supponens* of *suppositio simplex* may be a mental term, too, we may be faced with a totally intentional and at the same time referential relation.

We have just used the term 'signifies secondarily'; Ockham explains the difference between primary and secondary signification as follows: In contrast to connotative terms, an absolute term like 'whiteness' has in *suppositio personalis* only primary signification: it denotes something in the empirical world, and nothing else besides; 'white', on the other hand, has in *suppositio personalis* both primary and secondary signification. When 'white' has secondary signification, it connotes 'whiteness'.[13] Since, as Ockham says, whiteness is not white, this secondary relation of signification is a language-immanent semantic relation (pardigm (2); see below). As to be expected, there exists a nominal definition where 'white' is defined in terms of 'whiteness'; 'whiteness' however is an absolute term and cannot really be defined nominally.

Terms in *suppositio personalis* signify primarily, and some, moreover, secondarily; terms in *suppositio simplex* — and *suppositio materialis* — signify only secondarily. One can see that Ockham treats relations between terms (*suppositio materialis* and *simplex*) totally different from relations between terms and empirical objects (*suppositio personalis*); this includes the interesting case of intentional objects as referents and elements of a mental language (*suppositio simplex*). Brentano stresses the same point when he comments that not each intentional object has a physical counterpart: mental reference is, therefore, not a genuine relation but something relation-like.[14]

In the spirit of *philosophia perennis* (see above), I will now relate Ockham's and Brentano's views on intentions, reference, etc. to two paradigms of semantics and a synthesis of these two paradigms, 'paradigm' taken in its everyday sense.[15]

Paradigm (1) we may call the truth-functional or referential paradigm; semantics, then, is of a Frege, Montague, or Davidson type. If we stick here to a strictly empiristic position, that is, want to avoid platonistic referents or referents in possible worlds, we must admit the existence of a large class of expressions which have no meaning at all, f.i. fictitious and metaphysical terms. A way of avoiding platonistic referents or referents in possible worlds would be to introduce mental or psychological intentional objects or intentions. However, in the last decades, and particularly since Carnap's *Logischer Aufbau der Welt* of 1928, empiristic philosophers have shunned intentional objects or intentions, since they fell under the dogma: "Thou shalt not commit the sin of psychologism". Ockham has been criticized, too, for having committed psychologism,[16] and so has Brentano.[17]

However, from the linguist's standpoint the introduction of mental or psychological intentional objects or intentions alone is not sufficient if we want to develop a comprehensive semantic system, expecially if we consider Brentano's argument that there is no one-one correspondence between thought and language.[18]

Paradigm (2) may be called the 'structural' or 'contextual paradigm'; it does away with the notion that reference and truth functions are the basis of semantics. Instead, we recur to language use f.i. in the sense of the later Wittgenstein and define meaning (or, rather, to have meaning) as having statistically invariant use in a language. Language use is identified with the set of all statistically invariant contexts of a given term. The linguist refines the set of statistically invariant contexts by introducing, f.i., systems of semantic markers, semantic networks, and the like.[19] This is the theoretical expression of Humboldt's famous dictum that one single word evokes the entire language. For sentences we make use of semantic filters, selectional restrictions, semanticized case grammars, and the like.

Paradigm (2) comprises componential analysis, many systems of Artificial Intelligence and Knowledge Representation, semantic networks, memory models, and the like. Its disadvantage is, of course, that all relations to the empirical world may disappear; we would end up with a truncated semantics.

Paradigm (2) can be seen as an attempt to avoid psychologism,[20] as evidenced by § 501 of *Philosophical Investigations* where Wittgenstein ironically comments on the notion that each sentence expresses a thought. Which thought is expressed by the sentence "It rains"?, he asks.

Even from this shortest of sketches it is obvious that a semanticist attempting to comprehensively explain semantic phenomena from an empiristic standpoint somehow has to use and unite the two paradigms. One way of doing this is by introducing a thesis which we may call 'invariance thesis'. This thesis states that statistically invariant empirical phenomena lead to statistically invariant contexts, that is, meaning as statistically invariant language use.

The most likely candidate for the missing link between the two paradigms is an intentional, psychological, or pragmatic connection. I plead here for memory, particularly also in the light of the most recent developments in memory research, where one now distinguishes between (at least) two kinds of 'linguistic' memory, episodic and conceptual ('semantic'). Episodic memory corresponds to paradigm (1), conceptual memory to paradigm (2). Likewise, in Artificial Intelligence one works with two components of semantic networks.[21]

How is such a two-levelled semantics and its linking component, the intentional, psychological (mental), or pragmatic element, anticipated in Ockham's system?

In Ockham's writings, *suppositio personalis* clearly corresponds to referential, truth-functional meaning according to paradigm (1). A term exhibits *suppositio personalis* if it stands for what it primarily signifies (see above).

Paradigm (2) appears in Ockham's philosophy in the following form: Paradigm-(2) meaning is represented by *suppositio materialis* as described under (b). Ockham assumes that there are two kinds of suppositio materialis: (a) *suppositio materialis* is a meta-relation as in "'woman' is a noun" where 'woman' has *suppositio materialis*; (b) *suppositio materialis* in connection with the problem of figment terms like 'chimera' and 'stag-goat'. If the term 'chimera' in "A chimera is an animal that is composed of a goat and a cow" is interpreted as having *suppositio personalis*, the sentence is false. If we change *suppositio personalis* to *suppositio materialis* by substituting 'signifies (secondarily)' for 'is', we arrive at the nominal definition, "'Chimera' and 'animal composed of a goat and a cow' signify the same", which is true.[22] According to some interpreters of Ockham, this process can be repeated iteratively until we arrive at terms capable of *suppositio personalis*,[23] that is, at paradigm (1).

This brings us to the question of how Ockham mediates between the two paradigms. On my interpretation, it is the universal (the universal mental term) in connection with *suppositio simplex* which mediates.

Let us take as an example universals as mental terms which are grammatical concreta and which belong to the category of substance, f.i. the term 'man'. Such a universal (universal mental term) is absolute, that is, does not connote and−in *suppositio personalis*−does not signify secondarily. In predicate position, it does not denote a property, nor does it denote a platonistic or *in-re* universal. In the sentence "Socrates is a man" both 'Socrates' and 'man'

81

personally supposit for the same empirical entity in which case the sentence is true. Such a universal is a mental term which is capable of standing for many things, one by one, so to speak, things which are similar to one another. This process of "standing for" is, however, not an abstraction, in the same way as a paradigm-(2) meaning is not the result of an abstraction. Thus an Ockhamist universal does not denote the class as a whole, nor does it denote a class property. The universal collects, as it were, the various referents and in this respect corresponds to the set of statistically invariant contexts since it is at the same time a mental term. Moreover, the term which is said to have meaning with respect to the universal as *intentio animae* is the one which stands in *suppositio simplex* to it.

It is interesting to note that Ockham interprets the universal mental term, a term which stands for many things, at the same time as an act of understanding. This stresses the intentional character of the universal. It is not surprising, then, that in the appendix (1911) to *Psychology from an Empirical Standpoint* Brentano replaced the concept of an immanent mental object with the concept of mental activity, or, rather, the mentally active subject.[24]

We come now to the comparison between elements of Ockham's and Brentano's philosophy as regards the universal and related matters. Brentano's views are expressed primarily in *Kategorienlehre* (1933, 1968) and in his letters (from *Wahrheit und Evidenz* (1930)).

The first point of our comparison concerns the doctrine that the universal is not a thing outside the mind. Ockham concedes that there might be conventional—as opposed to natural—signs which are universals, that is, spoken or written universals. But he states that he has no interest in them. He devotes an entire chapter of the *Summa* to the demonstration that universals are natural signs in the mind, *intentiones animae*.[25]

Brentano holds a similar view. In a letter to Marty of March 1901 he says: "There is nothing universal in the things; the so-called universal, as such, is only in the one who is thinking".[26] In a passage from *Kategorienlehre* (dated 1916) he maintains, like Ockham, that there are universal as well as particular intuitions (*Vorstellen*). However, in an appendix to the 1924 edition of *Psychologie vom empirischen Standpunkt* (dictated 1917) he presents a view even more restricted than Ockham's: Even if we think intuitively (*anschaulich*), "we can still think only in universal terms". The universal, says Brentano, has, however, only a secondary existence in the mind, not the primary existence of an empirically existing thing.[27]

This secondary existence of the universal according to Brentano is obviously systematically related to Ockham's notion that a term in *suppositio simplex* (and *suppositio materialis*) has only secondary signification.

The second point of our comparison between Ockham and Brentano is the relation of the universal to the empirical world. As we have already noted, in Ockham the universal mental term is characterized by being able to stand for many things, one by one. Brentano distinguishes between three approaches to the problem of universals, the first two of which he considers to be wrong:[28]

(1) The universal exists empirically. This is wrong, since nothing indeterminate (*unbestimmt*)—which Brentano identifies with the universal—can exist. (2) There is nothing in the empirical world which corresponds to the universal. This is wrong, too, since (3) the universal is characterized exactly by the fact that many empirical objects, phenomena may correspond to it in the same way.[29]

The third point of comparison is the problem of whether a universal corresponds to (Brentano), or denotes (Ockham), a part of a substance, or not. I will start here with Brentano's view as expressed in the letter to Marty of March 1901. Brentano at first distinguishes between grammatical concreta and grammatical abstracta and then repudiates his earlier view according to which a term like 'redness' denotes a part of a thing, in analogy to things having genuine parts. Brentano now offers another solution: When the term 'redness'—which is the linguistic counterpart of a mental universal—is applied to a red object, the whole object is thought of by means of an indefinite concept, the mental universal itself.[30]

Ockham's views, as far as they can be gleaned from his writings, are very similar. At first, like Brentano in *Kategorienlehre*, he denies that grammatical concreta and grammatical abstracta are synonymous, even though Aristotle maintains that they are. Thus 'whiteness' and 'white' are not synonymous.[31] Ockham places 'whiteness' directly into the category of quality, and 'white' "by reduction".[32] In *suppositio personalis*, 'whiteness' signifies only primarily and is, therefore, an absolute term, 'white', however, is absolute as well as connotative; in the latter case 'white' secondarily signifies 'whiteness'.

In *SL* II, 2, which deals with the truth of singular, non-modal propositions, Ockham states the principle that a sentence is true only if both subject and predicate supposit for the same. This neither requires that subject and predicate are identical, nor that, f.i., the term 'humanity', a grammatical abstract from the category of substance, supposits for a part of, e.g., Socrates.[33] The universal term 'whiteness', a grammatical abstract from the category of quality, poses different, and more confusing, problems. Ockham's viewpoint has been interpreted as indicating that the universal 'whiteness' primarily signifies not one but many whitenesses, and exactly as many whitenesses as there are white things.[34] This interpretation runs into the same difficulties as the view to which Ockham explicitly objects, namely, that there is a universal object whiteness. In the framework of Ockham's theory of truth both views lead to an unexpected consequence: A sentence in which 'whiteness' is predicated of a term from the category of substance can never be true, since the condition of "suppositing for the same" can never be fulfilled. We might want to return to the interpretation that 'whiteness' supposits for white things. But in *SL* I, 33 Ockham does say that 'whiteness' primarily signifies whiteness, and in *SL* I, 5 that 'white' and 'whiteness' do not primarily signify the same. Implicitly, this amounts to a prohibition of sentences containing abstracta from the category of quality as predicates in combination with a term from the category of substance. Indeed, such sentences are conspicuously absent from Ockham's example sentences.

At any rate, Ockham's universal term 'whiteness' is just as indefinite as Brentano's 'redness' and its corresponding mental universal redness, since both terms are applied to many empirical phenomena.

This is a typical instance of "reism" in Brentano[35] as well as in Ockham; according to this, only individual things exist in the sense proper.

We come now to the fourth and last point of comparison between Ockham and Brentano, the nature of grammatical abstracta. Brentano concludes in the 1901 letter to Marty that grammatical abstracta are delusions, useful ways of speaking.[36] This implies that they somehow have to be reduced to their respective grammatical concreta — at least from the epistemological standpoint.

It is interesting that Ockham has introduced a kind of reductive analysis for grammatical abstracta from the category of substance.[37] While absolute terms from the category of substance which are grammatical concreta, like 'man', 'animal', pose no particular problem, their respective grammatical abstracta, 'humanity', 'animality', do, since one cannot say, f.i., "Animality runs" in the same way as one says "An animal runs".

In *SL* I, 8 Ockham applies a reductive analysis to terms like 'humanity'. The above example shows that the elements of the pair 'man'-'humanity' — and similar pairs — are not synonymous. On the other hand, both terms may primarily signify, and personally supposit for, man. This is incongruous. Ockham solves the puzzle in the following manner: 'humanity' is equivalent in primary signification to a combination of terms. One element of this combination is a concrete term and we may assume that it is this concrete term which is responsible for the grammatical abstract's primary signification and personal supposition. The other element of the combination consists of one or more terms which, according to Ockham, are syncategorematic. Thus, 'humanity' primarily signifies the same as 'man as man' or 'man necessarily . . .', 'as man' and 'necessarily . . .' being the syncategorematic elements. Compared to the discussion of 'syncategorematic' in *SL* I, 4, we see that here a much broader concept of syncategorematic has been employed. At any rate, 'syncategorematic' can be viewed as a technical term from a paradigm-(2) semantics.

The syncategorematic elements 'as man' and 'necessarily . . .' attempt to express something theoretical about man.[38] Thus 'humanity' and similar terms are related to theoretical constructs which, on the one side, may be seen as purely theoretical (paradigm (2)) and, on the other side, may be joined to the empirical world (paradigm (1)).

In order to maintain the possibility of personal supposition for 'humanity', 'humanity' has been epistemologically reduced to 'man'; and that aspect of grammatical abstracta which Brentano termed 'delusions' Ockham calls 'syncategorematic'.

From the discussion of Brentano's and Ockham's views in the framework of the two semantic paradigms we can now draw one main conclusion, (1), and two subordinate conclusions, (2) and (3); (2) we may label 'content', and (3) 'form'. (1) Intentionality mediates between the two paradigms of semantics, both of which are necessary for a systematic discussion of all semantic phenomena. (2) Content: The concept of intentionality has to be applied to all semantic phenomena, not only to beliefs, modalities, etc. (3) Form: In our framework, we cannot restrict the analysis of intentionality to the analysis of intentional language, to the logic of intentional expressions, etc., in short to the Analytic philosopher's point of view. This is not to say that the Analytic view is to be rejected, but only that it is too narrow for our purposes: empiristic semantics has to include psychological, biological, and brainphysiological inquiries. Strict empiricism of the Vienna-Circle type drove out psychologism, but psychologism is about to enter through the back door.

ENDNOTES

[1] Brentano, F., *Psychology from an Empirical Standpoint*, ed. L. L. McAlister, transl. A. C. Rancurello, D. B. Terrell, and L. L. McAlister (New York 1973), p. 88.

[2] Spiegelberg, H., "'Intention' and 'Intentionality' in the Scholastics, Brentano and Husserl", in L. L. McAlister (ed.), *The Philosophy of Brentano* (Atlantic Highlands, N. J., 1977); Marras, A., "Scholastic Roots of Brentano's Conception of Intentionality", in McAlister (1977).

[3] Brentano (1973), p. 229.

[4] Brentano, F., *Die vier Phasen der Philosophie und ihr augenblicklicher Stand*, ed. O. Kraus (Leipzig 1926), p. 7ff.; Brentano, F., *The True and the Evident*, ed. R. M. Chisholm, transl. R. M. Chisholm, I. Politzer, and K. R. Fischer (London-New York 1966), p. 64.

[5] Spiegelberg, H., *The Phenomenological Movement* Vol. 1 (The Hague ²1969), p. 40f.

[6] Ibid.; see also Marras (1977), p. 128f.

[7] Cf. Marras (1977), p. 136.

[8] Marras (1977), p. 133ff.

[9] Brentano (1973), pp. 88, 272. For a detailed exposition of this and related questions see R. M. Chisholm, "Intentional Inexistence", in McAlister (1977).

[10] Ockham, Wilhelm von, *Summa logicae; pars prima*, ed. Ph. Boehner (Paderborn 1962), cap. 3 = *SL* I, 3. Ockham himself denies that there is a mental language: there are only mental terms and mental propositions, see *SL* I, 1.

[11] *SL* I, 1.

[12] *SL* I, 64, 68.

[13] *SL* I, 33; Ockham, Wilhelm von, *Summa logicae: pars secunda et tertiae prima*, ed. Ph. Boehner (Paderborn 1962), pars secunda, cap. 7, 10 = *SL* II, 7, 10; Spade, P., "Ockham's Distinction Between Absolute and Connotative Terms", *Vivarium* Vol. 13 (1975); Freddoso, A., "Ockham's Theory of Truth Conditions", in *Ockham's Theory of Propositions*, transl. A. F. Freddoso and H. Schuurman (Notre Dame, Ind., 1982), p. 4ff. According to *SL* I, 67 and 68, all terms may exhibit *suppositio materialis* and *simplex*; therefore, all terms may signify secondarily, but not in *suppositio personalis*.

[14] Brentano (1973), p. 272; see also Brentano (1966). p. 77.

[15] For a more detailed exposition of Ockham's philosophy in the framework of the two paradigms see W. Leinfellner and E. Leinfellner, *Ontologie, Systemtheorie und Semantik* (Berlin 1978), chap. 1.4; W. Leinfellner and E. Leinfellner, "Ockhams Semantik und Pragmatik" in H. Stachowiak (ed.), *Handbuch der Pragmatik* Vol. 1 (1984, in press).

[16] Hickman, L., "Three Consequences of Ockham's 'Mental-Act' Theory", *Southwest Philosophical Studies* Vol. 10 (1979).

[17] Brentano (1973), p. 306f.

[18] Brentano (1966), p. 71.

[19] One of the earliest (if not the earliest) attempts to use Wittgenstein's concept of meaning in use as philosophical background for a statistical approach to word meaning is W. Z. Shetter and F. W. Blaisdell, "Altsächsisch *mahlian* und die Verben des Sprechens und Sagens", *Zeitschrift für deutsche Wortforschung* Vol. 18 (Neue Folge Vol. 3) (1962).

[20] Cf. E. Leinfellner, "Zur nominalistischen Begründung von Linguistik und Sprachphilosophie: Fritz Mauthner und Ludwig Wittgenstein", *Studium Generale* Vol. 22 (1969), p. 216ff.

[21] Tulving, E., *Elements of Episodic Memory* (Oxford-New York 1983), p. 17ff.; Leinfellner, E., Steinacker, I., and Trost, H., "Anaphoric and Kataphoric Relations, Textual Cohesion, and Reference Resolution", *Computers and Artificial Intelligence* (1984, in press); Leinfellner, E., "Connexity/ Coherence and the Semantic Net" in M.-E. Conte, J. S. Petöfi, and E. Sözer (eds.), *Text and Discourse Connectedness* (1984, in press); Leinfellner, E., "Semantic Nets: Their Linguistic Usefulness", in P. Simons (comp.), *7th International Congress of Logic, Methodology and Philosophy of Science* (Salzburg 1983). See also the paper by Werner Leinfellner in this volume.

[22] *SL* I, 26; *SL* II, 14.

[23] F. i. Spade (1975), p. 69f.

[24] *SL* I, 15; cf. Leinfellner-Leinfellner (1984, in press), chap. 3.4; Brentano (1973), p. 276.

[25] *SL* I, 15.

[26] Brentano (1966), p. 64.

[27] Brentano, F., *Kategorienlehre*, ed. A. Kastil (Hamburg 1968), p. 21; Brentano (1973), pp. 311, 275f.

[28] Brentano (1968), p. 21.

[29] Brentano (1968), p. 21f.; Brentano (1966), pp. 72, 99.

[30] Brentano (1966), p. 63f.

[31] Brentano (1968), p. 6; *SL* I, 7.

[32] *SL* I, 41.

[33] *SL* I, 7.

[34] Loux, M. J., "The Ontology of William of Ockham", in *Ockham's Theory of Terms,* transl. M. J. Loux (Notre Dame, Indiana-London 1974), p. 13f. (misprint on p. 13, but see p. 14).

[35] See, f.i., T. Kotarbinski, "Franz Brentano as Reist", and D. B. Terrell, "Brentano's Argument for Reismus", both in McAlister (1977).

[36] Brentano (1966), p. 64.

[37] *SL* I, 7,8.

[38] Cf. Loux (1974), p. 11.

* * *

INTENTIONALITY, METHODOLOGICAL SOLIPSISM AND COMPUTATIONAL PSYCHOLOGY*

Ausonio Marras
University of Western Ontario

The development of cognitive psychology in the last twenty years has given new respectability to the study of mind. The positing of "inner" mental states and processes, once regarded as methodologically suspect, is now widely regarded as indispensible for a scientific understanding of intelligent behaviour. Controversy mainly arises about the *nature* of such inner, causally efficacious states, and about the conceptual resources which are appropriate for their description and identification.

According to Fodor (1981) and other theorists, the relevant mental states are those which essentially correspond to the *propositional attitude* states of commonsense, folk psychology. On this construal, cognitive psychology should be viewed essentially as a scientific extension of folk psychology, and thus as committed to the idea that the regularities in human behaviour can best be captured in terms of people's beliefs, wants, expectations, and other typically *intentional* states. Accordingly, the task of cognitive psychology is to provide a theoretical framework in which the loose concepts and generalizations of folk psychology can be analyzed, systematized, and scientifically tested. The scientific study of mind is thus, on this account, the study of the nature and dynamics of the propositional attitudes; it is, quite simply, the *science of the intentional.*

Since the main burden of this paper is to consider a challenge to this interpretation of the cognitivist program, it is important to consider in more detail some of its conceptual and methodological commitments.

On Fodor's account, propositional attitudes are to be viewed as relational states of organisms: they relate organisms to *mental representations.* Mental representations, like linguistic representations, are essentially *symbolic*, and have thus both *formal* and *semantic* properties. The intentionality of propositional attitudes derives from the semantic (intentional) content of the representations which are their relata; their causal role, on the other hand, is consequent upon the formal features of the representations. This, in a nutshell, is the conceptual skeleton of Fodor's "Representational Theory of the Mind" (RTM).

Because mental representations are construed as symbolic, it is natural to give the RTM a computational interpretation: the mental processes involved in cognitive activity are essentially computational in the sense that they are rule-governed operations defined over formally specifiable representations. On this construal, to be in a propositional attitude state is to bear a computational relation to a symbol-structure representing the object of the propositional attitude.

A virtue of the computational model of the mind is that, if sound, it would provide a solution to the problem of how mental states can be causally efficacious and, in particular, of how they are able to interact with one another in the production of behaviour in such a way as to satisfy the rules of theoretical and practical reasoning which apply in the intentional domain. For we know that computing machines can execute intentionally or semantically interpretable operations because those operations are formally representable, and if they are formally representable they are Turing reducible and thus mechanically realizable. The computer model thus enables us to relate the intentional domain to the physical domain, and thus provides a solution to the vexing old problem of how *reasons* can be *causes.*

It is clear that the computational form of the RTM imposes very specific constraints on the theory. Since only formally encoded aspects of a represented domain can effect a computing

86

machine's functioning, all semantically relevant characteristics of a represented domain must be encoded in the syntactic structure of a computational sequence representing an operation in that domain. This condition, which Fodor (1980) has called the *formality condition*, will insure that a symbol using device will be able to operate on symbol tokens in virtue exclusively of the formal-syntactic properties of those tokens, and thus that it will behave in semantically meaningful ways without having to concern itself with *meanings* but only with *forms*.

Promising as it seems, this type of cognitivist program has been challenged by some who do not believe that there can be a science of the intentional, or who do not believe that a mature scientific psychology should endeavor to accommodate the propositional attitude framework of folk psychology.

An instructive illustration of this type of challenge is Steven Stich's (1983) recent critique of Fodor's RTM. Stich distinguishes two forms of the RTM, a *strong* and a *weak* form, and charges Fodor with equivocating between the two. Both forms of the RTM share the intentionalist assumption that mental states are relations between organisms and "contentful" or semantically interpreted representations. But whereas the strong RTM insists that the nomological generalizations which detail the causal interactions among mental states apply to them by virtue of their intentional *contents*, the weak RTM denies this and holds instead that those generalizations apply to mental states exclusively in virtue of their *syntactic* properties. Against both forms or the RTM, Stich advances a strictly *syntactic* theory of mind (STM), which accepts the distinguishing claim of the weak RTM, but declares itself agnostic on the question whether mental states *have* content or other semantic properties. More precisely, whether or not the mental states posited by a mature cognitive science have semantic properties, the STM claims that there is *no need* to suppose that they do. It follows that according to the STM there is no need to construe the objects to which mental states relate us to as essentially *symbolic* or *representational*: according to the STM, the whole intentionalist framework of folk psychology which identifies mental states with propositional attitude states may well be jettisoned with no detriment to cognitive science.

There is no space, here, to assess the merits of Stich's STM, nor the soundness of his claim that Fodor has inconsistently endorsed both forms of the RTM. As a matter of fact, I believe that the STM is untenable, and that, correctly interpreted, Fodor's position commits him to the strong, not the weak, form of the RTM; but I am not going to argue that here. What I am going to argue for is that the strong RTM is immune to a criticism levelled by Stich against it. The criticism, essentially, is that the strong RTM is inconsistent with a methodological principle which is held to be central to any theory which, like the RTM, construes mental states as *computational*. This is the principle of *methodological solipsism*, which, according to Stich, expresses the doctrine that a computational theory of mind "ought to *restrict itself to postulating formal operations on mental states* [and] ought not to postulate processes which apply to mental states in virtue of their semantic properties" (Stich 1983, p. 162). This principle, according to Stich, "entails the rejection of the Strong RTM"; for, as he explains, "the theorist who couches his generalizations . . . in terms of the *content sentences* used to characterize mental states is merely postulating mental operations whose specification requires reference to semantic properties of these states" (ibid.)

As understood by Stich, methodological solipsism seems indeed incompatible with a "semantically based" theory like the strong RTM. But is methodological solipsism, as understood by Stich, a reasonable constraint on computational theories? Is it one to which the RTM is committed?

In the version made popular by Fodor (1980), methodological solipsism asserts that mental processess "have no access to the semantic properties of representations, including the property of being true, of having referents or, indeed, the property of being a representation of the environment" (Fodor 1980, p. 64). But what this means, exactly, and what methodological constraints this doctrine imposes on psychological theories, is far from obvious. The following considerations are in order.

1. In Putnam's (1975) original use of the term, methodological solipsism states the require-

ment that psychological theories should only admit psychological states in the *narrow sense*—where a psychological state in the narrow sense is one which need not satisfy such semantic properties as truth and reference in order to be truly ascribed. (Thus *believing that-p* is a psychological state in the narrow sense, whereas *knowing that-p* is a psychological state in the *wide* sense.) As distinct from epistemology, a (solipsistic) cognitive psychology *need* only admit narrow psychological states; knowledge, as distinct from "mere" (firmly held) belief, contributes nothing further to the etiology of behaviour.

2. It is now customary to distinguish between *referential (truth conditional)* semantics and *functional (conceptual, inferential) role* semantics. Whereas truth and reference find their natural home in a referential semantics, *meaning* and *content* may be understood either in terms of a referential semantics, or in terms of a functional-role semantics—in terms of the functional-conceptual-inferential role that items to which those properties are ascribed play in a system, given certain inputs. When the claim is made that methodological solipsism excludes reference to the semantic properties of the representations, including their content, the question ought to be asked: semantic properties in *which sense?*

It is tempting to answer: in the sense specified by a referential semantics, but not in the sense specified by a functional role semantics, for the latter does not presuppose anything about truth conditions, or about the way the world actually is as distinct from the way it is represented as being. It is far from clear, however, that this is the right answer. Fodor (forthcoming), for example, seems to favour a notion of mental content ("narrow content", he calls it) which presupposes a genuinely referential semantics—one, however, which only counts as distinct those objects, referents and truth conditions which are phenomenologically distinct and which can eventuate in difference of computational-behavioural states in a perceiving organism.

This is not the place to try to settle this question. Suffice it to say that the notion of content required by a semantically based computational psychology will have to be appropriately constrained so as to satisfy the intuition that cognitive behaviour is necessarily a function of the way an organism *represents* the world, but not necessarily a function of the way the world *actually* is. Call content thus constrained "narrow" content, without, however, committing ourselves to Fodor's specifically referential construal of this notion. Does then methodological solipsism exclude reference to the (narrow) content of mental representations, thus committing us to a purely syntactic theory of the mind?

Fodor's view is that adopting methodological solipsism is tantamount to adopting the *formality condition*, which is simply the condition that every cognitive operation must be formally representable. The point of adopting the condition is just to insure that any posited psychological operation is *computable*, thus *machine executable*, and thus causally and physically *realizable*; for a machine or physical system can only detect the formal features—the "shapes"—of the objects on which it operates. In no way does the formality condition prevent a theorist from ascribing such properties as meaning or content (*narrow* content, that is) to the constructs of his theory, if doing so enables him to recover theoretically useful generalizations about the objects in the domain of his theory; the formality condition only requires that the relevant semantic properties be *formally representable* and thus detectable by a machine.

In so far as the principle of methodological solipsism is understood merely as a consequence of the formality condition, there is no ground to Stich's supposition that it "entails the rejection" of a semantically based computational psychology of the strong RTM type. It is a mistake for Stich to construe the formality condition as requiring that "semantic properties of mental states play no role in the specification of psychological generalizations" (Stich 1983, p. 162), if meaning or (narrow) content count as semantic properties. The formality condition only requires that a computational theory tell us in virtue of what formal (and thus physically executable) operations certain generalizations statable over contents are satisfied. As I see it, the formality condition simply amounts to a *realizability constraint* on theories: a constraint demanded by a physicalistic ontology.

As already indicated, Stich of course does not deny that mental representations may *have* content; he only holds that because of the formality condition generalizations stated over contents, even when available, will "do no work" in a computational theory, for extensionally equivalent generalizations statable over purely syntactic objects will always be available. But this will be true only on the assumption that a type-type reduction of contents to forms is possible, and there is no reason to suppose that such an assumption is true. The formality condition, at any rate, only requires that for any content-type there be at least one syntactic token and that distinct content-types have distinct syntactic tokens.

In conclusion, whether a cognitive theory should posit mental states with intentional contents would seem to depend on whether an individuation of such states in terms of their content helps us recover theoretically important generalizations about cognitive behaviour that we wouldn't otherwise recover; it does *not* depend on whether we accept or reject the formality condition and the related principle of methodological solipsism. *(Of course* we must accept the formality condition, if we wish the processes subsumed by our generalizations to be computationally and physically realizable!) There is thus no need to rule out, on formal a priori grounds, the Strong RTM nor, indeed, the possibility of a "science of the intentional."

ENDNOTE

* I am grateful to the Social Sciences and Humanities Research Council of Canada for a travel grant that made presentation of this paper possible.

REFERENCES

Fodor, Jerry, "Methodological Solipsism Considered as a Research Strategy in Cognitive Psychology", The Behavioral and Brain Sciences Vol. 3 (1980).
Fodor, Jerry, *Representations* (Cambridge, Mass. 1981).
Putnam, H., "The Meaning of 'Meaning' ", in K. Gunderson (ed.), *Minnesota Studies in the Philosophy of Science* Vol. 7 (Minneapolis 1975).
Stich, S., *From Folk Psychology to Cognitive Science* (Cambridge, Mass. 1983).

* * *

FUNCTION, LAW AND THE EXPLANATION OF INTENTIONALITY

Eric Russert Kraemer
University of Nebraska, Lincoln

In this paper I would like to consider two recent attempts to account, in a physical way, for the intentionality of mental states. The efforts I shall discuss are those of Fred Dretske and Berent Enç. Both seem to me to agree in holding the intentionality is to be explicated as derivate from certain other properties of physical systems. In what follows I shall (1) state the problem, (2) set out the views of the two authors, (3) assess their claims concerning intentionality, and (4) make some final suggestions.

1. If mental states are wholly physical items, then how can many of them (most notably, the propositional attitudes) be "directed upon" objects or states-of-affairs which need not exist? Let us call this the problem of intentionality. It is the difficulty of answering this question which has prompted some followers of Brentano to urge that materialism in any interesting form can not be correct. But, we may ask, what is any serious theorist of the mind-body relation to make of Brentano's claim (Brentano, 1874) that mental phenomena are to be distinguished from physical phenomena precisely because the former and not the latter can be directed in a special way towards objects? There seem to be several sorts of answers that may be given.

One response to make is to deny that this sort of "directedness" is indeed a serious ontological feature. (See, for example, Quine, 1960). A second way of answering the problem would be to attempt to provide an *extensional* account of intentional concepts. (See, for example, R. J. Nelson, 1982). A third approach to the problem of intentionality would be to argue that intentionality is a primitive, unanalyzable property of certain mental states. I shall not comment on any of these three manoeuvers here. I shall concentrate intead on a fourth way to answer the problem of intentionality which I think deserves serious consideration. This concern examining what have been alleged to be the features (or 'criteria') of intentionality and attempting to explain how these can be present in a physical system given a certain conception of the mental. Let us call this the *criterial* approach. There are two ways in which this strategy might be successful. One might, first of all, look to the important concepts of the theory of mind under consideration. One might be able to demonstrate that some of these concepts themselves exhibit intentionality. The intentionality of the mental would then be explainable as derivative from that of certain concepts of the theory. There might, of course, be further worries in terms of accounting for the intentionality of these concepts, but if the theory of mind being discussed is non-circular, at least the problem of the intentionality of the mental would have been solved. A second way to implement the criterial approach would be to provide a set of explanations in terms of the elements of the theory of mind being proposed which would account for the presence of the intentional features of the mental system, even though the elements of the explaining theory lacked those features themselves. Let us now consider how the criterial strategy has been applied.

2. Fred Dretske's approach to mental states is by way of information thery. (Dretske, 1980) He holds that cognitive states should be construed as involving the transmission, receipt and processing of information, where information transfer depends upon nomic connections. Fred Dretske says: ". . . the intentionality associated with our cognitive states can be viewed as a manifestaçon of any underlying network of nomic regularities" (Dretske, p. 287). Dretske's argument for this claim consists in his urging that nomic regularities (in terms of which he

analyzes cognitive capacities) *as* nomic regularities (or laws of nature) possess "a significant degree of intentionality" (Dretske, p. 290). Enç, on the other hand, holds a view that he calls *teleological functionalism.* Enç identifies psychological states with the functional states of psychological mechanisms. Enç states

> ". . . The intensional language in which descriptions of psychological states are couched can be shown to be generated by the implicit function attrubutions made to, and by the functional explanations given for psychological phenomena, and when states of physical systems are referred to in the context of such functional explanations, it can also be shown that the language in which these states are described has the same degree of *intentsionality* as that of the language of psychology." (Enç, 1982, pp. 181−182)

(A similar claim is suggested, though not argued for, in William Lycan, 1981.) Let us now turn to assessing the claims of these two authors.

3. Let us now investigate to what extent we can ascribe intentionality to nomic and functional statements. Let us take as basic schemata the following:

(L) It is a law of nature that all F's are G's.
(F) A function of X is to bring about Y.

Specific instances of (L) and (F) do seem to satisfy a number of the criteria that have been proposed for intentionality.

Let us now begin with an important early criterion for intentionality, namely, non-substitutivity of co-referential expressions. (Chisholm, 1957) According to this criterion, if a sentence contains some term *t* such that one cannot substitute a co-referential term for *t* without changing the sentence's truth value then the sentence is intentional. Dretske urges, I think correctly, that nomic statements do satisfy this criterion:

> "To use a well-known example, drunks have liver problems and their problems may have their basis in a nomic relationship between excessive alcoholic intake and the condition of the liver. But we cannot infer from this fact that there is a nomic connection between sitting on a park bench B and liver trouble just because all, only only, drunks sit (have sat, are sitting, will sit) on park bench B." (Dretske, p. 286)

And Enç has claimed, persuasively, that the criterion also applies to function statements. He offers the following example:

> "Some fruits flies are known to be more fit in environments of high himidity. These fruits flies have a sensor which in their natural environment helps them to seek humid spots. The sensor functions by detecting the intensity of light in environment and helping the organism to steer itself to darker areas. Since in the natural environment of these flies there is a law governed correlation between dark aeas and humid areas, the organisms by and large end up in the more humid spots . . . A good case can be made for the claim that the function of the sensor is to enable the organism to reach humid spots, and not to enable the organisms to reach dark spots." (Enç, p. 168)

Dretske and Enç do not explicitly argue that other criteria of intentionality can be explained by appeal to features of statement of the form of (L) and (F). So to assess their claims it is worth considering which of the other proposed criteria of intentionality are satisfied by law and function statement. A second proposed criterion of intentionality is the criterion of non-extensional occurrence. (Chisholm, 1957) According to this criterion, if a sentence contains a dependent clause *C* such that one cannot substitute any clause of the same truth-value for *C* and preserve the truth-value of the sentence then the sentence is intentional. Clearly sentences of the form of (L) will satisfy this criterion, for certain obvious substitution instances of the clause, all F's and G's, will produce not only false, but necessarily false statements. To show that the non-extensional occurrence criterion also to sentences of the form of (F) one might suggest that (F) is logically equivalent to

(F*)   X has the function of bringing it about that Y occurs.

If this equivalence is granted, then it is a simple matter to show that particular substitution instances for the clause 'Y occurs' will conform to the criterion.

A third criterion to consider is that of failure of existential generalization. (Chisholm, 1957) According to this criterion a sentence is intentional if its truth value implies neither the existence nor non-existence of the things it talks about. I assume it obvious that instances of (L) satisfy this criteria. For example, laws relating the melting points of golden mountains imply neither that there are nor that there are nor any such mountains.

The case for (F) seems a bit more problematic. One might say that sentences of this form use the expression 'Y' in such a way that neither (F) nor its contradiction implies that there is or is not anything to which 'Y' applies. For it seems that items may certainly have functions *without* its being the case that those functions are successfully carried out. The objection may be made, however, that ordinary examples fail to bear this out. Take, for instance,

The function of the pancreas is to secrete insulin.

Individual pancreases may fail to produce insulin; nevertheless, insulin still exists. To make the argument for the failure of existential generalization criterion's applying to function statements stronger, let us consider what I will call the case of the unfortunate mutant. Imagine two organism 0_1 and 0_2 (the only two of this type) each with a *spancreas* whose function (it is later revealed) is to produce *spinsulin*-a type substance no instance of which ever *exists-but* which can be inferred from chemical and biological theory. But suppose that 0_1 and 0_2's spancreases never matured sufficiently to produce spinsulin for poor 0_1 and 0_2 were caught in a passing lava flow before having a chance to reproduce. Now according to one way of conceiving the matter, an organ such as a spancreas could not have had the function of producing spinsulin if no spinsulin were ever produced. (This result seems required, for instance, by Larry Wright's account of functions, Wright, 1973) But I do not see why one should be forced to accept this conclusion. It may be that in order for us to be able to establish conclusively a functional relationship we would need to refer to some existing state. But to argue that this epistemic handicap shows that all goals of functional states must be instantiated a t least once seems to me to confuse epistemology with ontology.

I have now considered three criteria that have been proposed for intentionality and have suggested that they apply as well to nomic relations and function ascriptions. There are, however, certain features of intentionality that it is more problematic to attribute to nomic and function ascriptions. Let us consider two different examples. Let us begin with what Chisholm has called a *negative* criterion of intentionality. (Chisholm, 1966) Suppose we consider the belief that p. Let us represent this as 'Bp'. We can then express the following claims as characteristic of the logic of belief statement: (A) $Bp \not\to {\sim} p$; (B) $Bp \not\to {\sim} B {\sim} p$; (C) ${\sim} B {\sim} p \not\to {\sim} Bp$; (D) ${\sim} B {\sim} p \not\to Bp$. This can be generalized as a criterion of intentional modality. How do nomic and functional statements fare according to this criterion? Although analogues of (A), (C) and (D) are applicable to such statements, there seems to be a problem with finding correct analogues for (B). That is, its being a law of nature that all F's are G's does seem to entail that it is not a law of nature that not all F's are G's; and, its being a function of X to bring about Y does seem to entail that it is not a function of X to bring about ${\sim}$ Y. Now one response here is to question whether (B) does hold for belief, for (B) requires the possibility of holding inconsistent beliefs, a possibility which is most controversial. (See, e.g., the paper by J. J. Ross in this volume.) Without going into that debate let me note two points. First, there are other mental attitudes, such as desire, which do seem to be strong candidates for satisfying this criterion. And secondly, I think it at least an *issue* whether inconsistent beliefs are possible, whereas there seems to be no such issue regarding function statements or laws of nature.

I would like to mention one further criterion of intentionality which I think is also problematic. Chisholm has suggested the following:

> . . . a sentence prefix M is intentional if, for every sentence q, the result of modifying q by M is logically contingent; and a sentence is intentional if it is the result of modifying a sentence by an intentional prefix or if it implies a sentence that is intentional. (Chisholm, 1966, p. 54)

Let us call this the *contingent prefix* criterion. Chisholm suggests that psychological states unlike all others can only be described using sentences which are intentional in this sense. Let us consider again the sentence schema (F*). The appropriate sentence prefix of this is "X functions to bring it about that." The problem that the contingent prefix criterion raises for the teleological functionalist is as follows. Consider any simle necessary arithmetic truth such as "2 + 2 = 4". If we prefix the sentence prefix of (F*) to such a sentence, the result, "X functions to bring it about that 2 + 2 = 4", does not just seem to be false as a matter of accident for substitution instances of X, but rather it seems to be *necessarily* false. Thus the contingent prefix criterion cannot be easily satisfied by teleological prefixes. Analogous remarks are to be made concerning nomic prefixes. But then how is this aspect of intentionality to be explained by those who use the criterial strategy?

5. I will now summarize what I have argued and make some final comments. Dretske and Enç are right in supposing that certain aspects of intentionality can be attributed to certain physical properties. Where they go wrong is in underestimating how *many* aspects of intentionality (as opposed to intensionality) so not readily apply to these notions. I have discussed only two such aspects, but there are many more to be considered. (See, for example, contributions by H. Morick and R. M. Chisholm in this volume.) The conclusion to draw is that the task of providing a physical explanation of intentionality is much farther from having a solution than Dretske and Enç confidently maintain.

My discussion here has dealt only with the first of the two ways I suggested for implementing the criterial strategy. However, it seems to me that if the materialist is to make significant progress on the problem of accounting for intentionality, then the second and more difficult procedure for carrying out the strategy needs to be explored.

One final aside. Some philosophers may take the attempt of the past thirty years to provide a mark of intentionality to have been shown to be an unproductive enterprise, with the literature being littered with only unsuccessful criteria. Although these various criteria have not been widely perceived to have succeeded in singling out all and only mental phenomena, nontheles they do give us a useful benchmark by means of which we may gauge which aspects of intentionality can be explicated by the various physical theories of the mind.

REFERENCES

Brentano, F., *Psychology from an Empirical Standpoint* (Leipzig 1874), Book II, Ch. 1.
Chisholm, R. M., *Perceiving* (Ithaca 1957), Ch. 11.
Chisholm, R. M., "On Some Psychological Concepts and the 'Logic' of Intentionality", and "Rejoinder", in: H. N. Castañeda (ed.), *Intentionality, Minds and Perception* (Detroit 1966), 11−35, 46−52.
Dretske, F., "The Intentionality of Cognitive States", *Midwest Studies in Philosophy*, Vol. 5 (1980), 281−294.
Enç, B., "The Intentional States of Mechanical Devices", *Mind*, Vol. 94 (1982), 161−182.
Lycan, W., "Form, Function and Feel", *Journal of Philosophy*, Vol. 78 (1981), 24−50.
Nelson, R. J., *The Logic of Mind* (Dordrecht 1982).
Quine, W. V., *Word and Object* (Cambridge, Mass. 1960), section 45.
Wright, L., "Functions", *Philosophical Review*, Vol. 82 (1973), 139−168.

* * *

DIE INTENTIONALITÄT DES DENKENS

Wolfgang Künne
Universität Hamburg

Wann ist das, was einer denkt, dasselbe wie das, was ein anderer denkt, – oder wie das, was er selbst zu einer anderen Zeit denkt? Das ist die Frage, die ich – im Blick auf ein Denken, das mit indexikalischen Aussagesätzen kundgetan werden kann – erörtern möchte. Mit ‚denken‘ ist dabei gemeint: denken, *daß* . . ., und zwar episodisch im Sinne von ‚urteilen‘ und dispositional im Sinne von ‚glauben‘.

Dort, wo die Analytische Philosophie der letzten Jahre auf unsere Fragestellung eingegangen ist, ist eine Kategorie zu neuen Ehren gekommen, die Russell und Whitehead eingeführt haben: die Kategorie der *singulären Propositionen*. Ich werde zunächst diese Kategorie erläutern. Sodann werde ich dafür plädieren, die singulären Propositionen, die durch indexikalisch kundgegebene Urteile und Meinungen repräsentiert werden, zu unterscheiden von den *Inhalten*, die solche Urteile und Meinungen haben. (Diese Distinktion ist von Husserl und Reinach inspiriert.) Abschließend werde ich versuchen, das kritische Potential dieser Unterscheidung anzudeuten.

Wenn ein Satz einen Indikator enthält, so ist das, was der Indikator in einem gegebenen Kontext denotiert, ein „Bestandteil" (constituent) der in diesem Kontext ausgedrückten Proposition. Nimmt also jemand mit dem Indikator in einer Äußerung von

(S1)   Der da ist stupsnasig

auf Sokrates Bezug, dann ist Sokrates selber (in propria persona) ein Bestandteil der ausgedrückten Proposition. Die andere Komponente dieser Proposition ist die Eigenschaft, stupsnasig zu sein. So bestimmen Russell, Whitehead und neuerdings Donnellan, Kaplan und Perry die Struktur einer singulären Proposition (kurz: einer sP).[1]

Jeder sP entspricht genau ein geordnetes Paar, dessen erstes Glied ein Einzelding oder ein geordnetes n-tupel von Einzeldingen und dessen zweites Glied eine Eigenschaft oder eine n-stellige Relation ist. So können wir der sP, die mit (S1) bei Bezugnahme auf Sokrates ausgedrückt wird, das geordnete Paar (Sokrates; Stupsnasigkeit) zuordnen. Aber nicht jedem solchen Paar entspricht eine sP. So können wir z.B. der folgenden Sequenz keine sP zuordnen: ((Sokrates; Simmias); die QUADRAT-VON-Relation). Die Spezifikation einer sP soll nämlich eine mögliche Antwort auf die Frage sein, was einer glaubt oder urteilt. ‚A glaubt, daß dies (→ Sokrates) das Quadrat von diesem (→ Simmias) ist‘ kann aber keine Antwort auf die Frage sein, was einer glaubt. (In diesem Sinne hat Wittgenstein 1913 gegen Russells damalige Urteilstheorie eingewandt: Eine richtige Theorie des Urteils muß zeigen, daß es unmöglich ist, einen Unsinn zu urteilen [*TLP* 5.5422].) SP sind also etwas anderes als geordnete Paare des angegebenen Typs.[2] Was die *Darstellung* von sP durch geordnete Paare augenfällig machen soll, ist die Tatsache, daß die Identität einer solchen Proposition durch die von den Indikatoren denotierten Gegenstände *selber* bestimmt wird – und *nicht* durch die Art und Weise, wie diese Gegenstände dem Denkenden gegeben sind.

Wir können Urteilsakte und Meinungen nun unter dem Gesichtspunkt klassifizieren: *Welche von ihnen repräsentieren dieselbe singuläre Proposition?* Ein mit einem indexikalischen Satz S kundgegebenes Denken repräsentiert genau dann dieselbe sP wie ein mit dem indexikalischen Satz S' kundgegebenes Denken, wenn es jeweils genau eine Entität gibt, auch die mit den Indikatoren in S und mit ihren Gegenstücken in S' Bezug genommen wird, und wenn über diese Entitäten mit S und S' dasselbe gesagt wird.

Nun kann aber manchmal der ernsthaften assertorischen Äußerung eines indexikalischen Satzes *keine* sP zugeordnet werden. Macbeth halluziniert und schreit:

(S2)   Das da ist ein blutiger Dolch.

In Ermangelung eines Gegenstandes, der in dieser Situation durch den Indikator denotiert wird, kann man nicht sagen, daß mit (S2) eine sP ausgedrückt wird. Macbeths Äußerung von (S2) ist aber gewiß ein guter Grund, ihm einen Urteilsakt zuzuschreiben. Nun kann man nicht urteilen oder meinen, ohne etwas zu urteilen oder zu meinen. *Was* ist das aber in diesem Falle? Es gibt etwas, das Macbeths kognitive Situation mit derjenigen gemeinsam hat, in der er sich befunden hätte, wenn ihm die indexikalische Bezugnahme *nicht* mißglückt wäre. Sein Denken hätte dann (ceteris paribus) denselben bedeutungsmäßigen Inhalt gehabt.

Wir können Urteilsakte und Meinungen nämlich auch unter dem Gesichtspunkt klassifizieren: *Welche von ihnen haben denselben bedeutungsmäßigen Inhalt?* Urteilsakte und Meinungen haben genau dann denselben bedeutungsmäßigen Inhalt, wenn sie durch Aussagesätze kundgegeben werden können, die denselben lexikalisch-grammatischen Sinn haben.

Die Zweideutigkeit des folgenden Satzes reflektiert die Verschiedenheit der Hinsichten, die uns bei der Bestimmung dessen, was einer denkt, leiten können:

(S3)   Am Vorabend der Wahl dachte A, er werde die Wahl gewinnen,
          und sein Gegenspieler B dachte *es* auch.

Was dachte B auch? In der *einen* Lesart wird die sP, die B's Denken repräsentieren, mit derjenigen identifiziert, die A's Denken repräsentiert: Beiden denken von A, er werde gewinnen. In der *anderen* Lesart wird der bedeutungsmäßige Inhalt, den B's Denken hat, mit demjenigen identifiziert, den A's Denken hat: Jeder denkt, er selbst werde gewinnen; jeder könnte seine Meinung mit dem Satz ‚Ich werde die Wahl gewinnen‘ (oder mit einem synonymen Satz) kundtun.

Manchmal benötigen wir einen reicheren Inhaltsbegriff als den des bedeutungsmäßigen Inhalts. Wenn jemand auf Hinz zeigt und, ohne den Finger zu bewegen, sagt:

(S4)   Dies ist derselbe Mann wie dies,

so trifft er eine nicht sonderlich erhellende Feststellung. Aber wenn jemand mit Hinz telefoniert, dabei aus dem Fenster sieht und Hinz in der Telefonzelle vor dem Haus erblickt, so kann er mit (S4) sehr wohl eine erkenntniserweiternde Aussage machen. In beiden Fällen repräsentiert das Denken des Sprechers dieselbe sP, der man das folgende geordnete Paar zuordnen kann: ((Hinz; Hinz); Identität). Aber in beiden Fällen hat das Denken *auch* denselben bedeutungsmäßigen Inhalt. Die Nicht-Trivialität dessen, was im zweiten Fall gedacht wird, kann also nicht unter Rekurs auf den *bedeutungsmäßigen* Inhalt des Urteilsaktes verständlich gemacht werden. Zum *vollen* Inhalt gehört hier eben auch noch, wie dem Denker das Objekt seiner indexikalischen Bezugnahme jeweils perzeptiv gegeben ist.[3]

Zwei Beispiele mögen abschließend das kritische Potential der skizzierten Distinktion sichtbar machen.

(a)   Kann man Unmögliches glauben?[4]

‚Es ist trivial falsch, daß p‘ möge genau dann gelten, wenn niemand ‚p‘ verstehen kann, ohne eo ipso zu wissen, daß es falsch ist, daß p. Wenn ‚p‘ diese Bedingung erfüllt, dann kann in der Tat niemand glauben oder urteilen, daß p. Der lexikalisch-grammatische Sinn von ‚p‘ kann dann nicht der bedeutungsmäßige Inhalt eines Glaubens oder Urteilsaktes sein. Sätze von dieser Art sind z.B. ‚2 ist eine Primzahl, und 2 ist keine Primzahl‘, ‚Alle Junggesellen sind weiblich‘, und

(S5)   Dies ist von sich selbst verschieden.

Aber ein Satz ‚p‘ kann auch dann etwas ausdrücken, was unmöglich der Fall sein kann, wenn es nicht *trivial* falsch ist, daß p. Und dann kann jemand sehr wohl glauben oder urteilen, daß p.

Wenn nun in einer Äußerung von (S4) beide Indikatorenvorkommnisse Hinz denotieren, dann drückt (S4) etwas aus, was notwendigerweise der Fall ist. Und wenn in einer Äußerung von

(S6)   Dies ist ein anderer Mann als dies

wieder beide ‚dies‘ Hinz denotieren, dann drückt (S6) etwas aus, was *unmöglich* der Fall sein kann. Ist die indexikalische Bezugnahme auf Hinz dabei aber einmal mit einer auditiven und einmal mit einer visuellen Hinz-Wahrnehmung verknüpft, so kann man mit (S6) sehr wohl einen Urteilsakt kundtun. Bei Bezugnahme auf Hinz drücken nun (S6) und (S5) dieselbe sP aus; wir können ihr das geordnete Paar ((Hinz; Hinz); Verschiedenheit) zuordnen. Aber der Sinn von (S6) kann sein, was der Sinn von (S5) nicht sein kann: der bedeutungsmäßige Inhalt eines Glaubens oder Urteilsaktes.

(b) Gibt es indexikalisch ausgedrückte Gedanken, die kontingent und dennoch a priori sind? Gibt es indexikalisch ausgedrückte Gedanken die notwendig, aber gleichwohl a posteriori sind? (Ersetzt man ‚indexikalisch‘ durch ‚unter Verwendung von Eigennamen‘, so lautet Kripkes Anwort auf beide Fragen bekanntlich: Ja.)

„Es ist kontingent, daß ich jetzt hier bin; aber (so könnte jemand argumentieren) daß ich jetzt hier bin, weiß ich a priori.“ − Diese Erwägung ist verworren. Jeder, der den deutschen Satz

(S7)   Ich bin jetzt hier

versteht, weiß, daß mit ihm (in seiner gestenunabhängigen Standardverwendung[5]) stets etwas Wahres gesagt wird. Ich verstehe (S7). Also kenne ich *a priori* den Wahrheitswert des *Inhalts*, den das jetzt von mir mit (S7) kundgegebene Urteil hat. Aber es ist in der Tat nicht notwendig, daß ich jetzt hier bin; schließlich hätte ich ja auch in meinem Geburtsort bleiben können: Die *sP*, die mein Urteil repräsentiert, ist *kontingent*. Die epistemische Eigenschaft, a priori von mir als wahr erkannt zu werden, und die modale Eigenschaft, kontingent zu sein, haben gar nicht denselben Träger.

„Daß dies“ (der Sprecher hört Hinz) „derselbe Mann ist wie dies“ (der Sprecher sieht Hinz), „ist notwendig; aber ich weiß es a posteriori.“ − Auch diese Erwägung ist verworren. In der geschilderten Situation ist die ausgedrückte *sP* Träger der modalen Eigenschaft *Notwendigkeit*, während der Träger der epistemischen Eigenschaft, vom Sprecher *a posteriori* als wahr erkannt zu werden, etwas anderes ist, nämlich der *Inhalt* seines Denkens.

———————

AMERKUNGEN

[1] Vgl. W. Künne, „Indexikalität, Sinn und propositionaler Gehalt", *Grazer Philosophische Studien*, Bd. 18 (1982), S. 58f.

[2] Dies u.a. gegen S. Schiffer, „The Basis of Reference", *Erkenntnis*, Bd. 13 (1978), S. 171.

[3] Vgl. A. Woodfield, „On Specifying the Content of Thought", in ders. (ed), *Thought and Object* (Oxford 1982), S. 286.
Die in diesem Absatz angestellte Überlegung zeigt übrigens, daß Kaplans ganz anders motivierte Unterscheidung zwischen „content" und „character" für unsere Zwecke unzureichend ist.

[4] Nein, − antwortet R. Barcan Marcus, „Rationality and Believing the Impossible", *Journal of Philosophy*, Bd. 80 (1983). Das Folgende ist z.T. kritisch auf diesen Aufsatz bezogen.

[5] Zeigt jemand auf eine Landkarte und äußert dabei (S7), so kann er natürlich etwas Falsches behaupten.

* * *

INTENTIONALITÄT BEI KANT*

Hjördis Nerheim
Universität Oslo

1. Nach Kant verhalten wir uns zur Welt, in der wir leben, denken und handeln, in der Form von Urteilen. Daß wir überhaupt *urteilen*, ist für Kant gleichbedeutend mit der Tatsache, daß wir überhaupt *Bewußtsein* haben. Dies deshalb, weil das Urteil die Form der Wirklichkeit im Bewußtsein ist, in der der Mensch sich als solcher verwirklicht und um sich und seine Welt in der transzendentalen Apperzeption weiß. Mit anderen Worten: Kant behauptet, daß Selbstbewußtsein Urteilsfähigkeit voraussetzt.

Das Vermögen selbst zu urteilen oder die Urteilskraft ist nun nach Kant „ein Verhältnis, das objektiv gültig ist" (*Kritik der reinen Vernunft (K.d.r.V.,)* B 124). Urteilsfähigkeit ist also das Vermögen zur Objektivität bzw. Intersubjektivität, eher gar kein Vermögen, sondern der Gebrauch, den wir von allen unseren Vermögen in handelnder Absicht machen können. Sie ist die Tatsache, daß man Urteile bilden kann.[1] Als solche ist sie ein Können. Wer etwas kann, ist *frei* es zu tun. Somit gewinnt das Urteilen den Aspekt der Urteils*handlung*. Die Freiheit der Urteilskraft ist also letztlich Bedingung dafür, daß *überhaupt* gedacht oder geurteilt werden kann. Hierfür ist im Folgenden der Nachweis zu führen.[2]

2. Im Hinblick auf unser Thema steht zunächst fest, daß Kant erst in der *Kritik der Urteilskraft (K.d.U.)* klar zum Ausdruck bringt, von welcher Art die Urteilshandlung ist, die er bereits für die Rationalität des Erkennens und dann auch für die des Handelns in Anspruch genommen hatte: Kognitives Urteilsvermögen, so konstatiert Kant jetzt, ist eine „auf Erkenntnis gerichtete Absicht" (*K.d.U.*, XXXVIII); es ist mit anderen, wiederum Kantischen Worten, „unsere absichtliche Tätigkeit", womit die „Erkenntniskräfte ins Spiel gesetzt werden" (*K.d.U.*, 28). Oder anders ausgedrückt: Theoretisches Erkennen und erst recht dann sittliches Handeln ist *Intentionalität*. Menschliche Rationalität ist als theoretische oder praktische Urteilsfähigkeit recht eigentlich Intentionalität.

Von daher besteht die Aufgabe, die stillschweigenden Implikationen zu entfalten. Dies bedeutet als erstes sich folgendes klarzumachen: Ist kognitive Urteilshandlung recht eigentlich Intentionalität, so muß sie damit auch etwas sein, das entweder Erfolg oder Mißerfolg hat, das entweder glückt oder mißglückt. Infolgedessen kann sich auch als Erfüllung einer Intention immer nur etwas einstellen, was im Prinzip als Mißerfolg derselben ausbleiben könnte. Diese Feststellung impliziert, daß sofern wir nur immer etwas intendieren, dieses intendierte Etwas sich eben entweder als Verwirklichung dieser Intention einstellen oder als Mangel an Verwirklichung derselben ausbleiben muß. Dennoch ist Urteilsvermögen als Intentionales nicht in ein und demselben Sinne entweder erfolgreich oder erfolglos. Denn so etwas wie eine Intention intendiert niemals etwa, erfolglos zu sein, sondern ausschließlich die *geglückte* Erreichung ihrer Absicht. Daß die Erfüllung ausbleiben kann, ist *unintendiertes* Handeln, d.h. Täuschung, und dies ist *Mangel* an Erkenntnis und bereits ein Fall von Unfreiheit. Wir dürfen demnach sagen, daß Erkennen als Intention *ursprünglich* und unmittelbar immer nur Erfolgsintention wäre und niemals etwa Falschheitsintention. Folglich muß dann das, was wir als Wahrheit bzw. Falschheit von Erkennen kennen, streng nominalistisch als Glücken oder Mißglücken der immer nur auf *Wirklichkeit* gehenden Erkenntnisintention verstanden werden. Wirklichkeit selber ist nichts als *Selbstverwirklichung* des Subjekts und muß ebenso wie der Terminus ‚Bewußtsein' von dem Urteilen als freie Handlung her verstanden werden. Was wir darunter zu verstehen haben, wird erst später ausgeführt werden können. Doch steht schon jetzt außer Zweifel, daß Glücken und Mißglücken von Intentionalität notwendig mit zu ihrem Begriff dazugehört.

In dieser Perspektive hat Erkennen Gelingensstruktur. Und eben dadurch ist Erkenntnis als erfolgreiche Intention gerade nicht ausschließllich in jemandes Macht. Vielmehr ist sie, mit Kant zu sprechen, eine *Gunst.* Das Spezifisch-Intentionale einer kategorialen Urteilshandlung ist zwar notwendig, aber deshalb nicht auch schon notwendig erfolgreich, was Kant mit der These zur Sprache bringt, daß „der Verstand damit [mit den kategorialen Begriffen bez. Urteilsformen, H.N.] unabsichtlich nach seiner Natur notwendig verfährt" (*K.d.U.*, XXXIX). Dies besagt jedoch keineswegs, es finde dabei überhaupt keine Absicht statt. Vielmehr ist der eigentliche Sinn jener Behauptung der Unabsichtlichkeit des Verstandes bezüglich seiner Kategorien mit jener Einsicht in die Intentionalität von Erkennen und Handeln nicht nur vereinbar; es gehören diese Absichtlichkeit und jene Behauptung der Unabsichtlichkeit sogar notwendig zusammen. „Die gedachte Übereinstimmung [. . .], muß nach aller unserer Einsicht als *zufällig* [von mir hervorgehoben] beurteilt werden, gleichwohl aber doch für unser Verstandesbedürfnis als unentbehrlich, mithin als Zweckmäßigkeit, wodurch die Natur mit unserer, aber nur auf Erkenntnis gerichteten, Absicht übereinstimmt" (*K.d.U.*, XXXVII). Kant formuliert deren Zusammengehörigkeit als *Zweckmäßigkeit ohne Zweck.*

Da nun die Zweckmäßigkeit *ohne* Vorstellung eines Zwecks sein soll, vermag sie nur unmittelbar empfunden zu werden. Und dies überzeugt um so mehr, als nach Kant die Erreichung jeder Absicht mit dem Gefühl der Lust verbunden ist (*K.d.U.*, XXXIX). Und eben darum ist mit jedem Erfolg die Empfindung eines Glücks verbunden. Die Lust gehört notwendig zur Erkenntnis, aber nicht so, daß dabei etwas, aus welchen Gründen immer, gelänge, sondern vielmehr so, daß etwas sich darüber vollendet hat. Im kognitiven Bereich von Erkennen kann man die Berechtigung dazu vor allem aus dem Umstand beziehen, daß etwas glückt oder gelingt, was wir nicht *erzwingen* können. Die Lust liegt dabei nicht bei der Absicht oder Nichtabsicht, sondern bei der „Erreichung", d.h. dabei, daß etwas Neues zum Vorschein gekommen ist, was zuvor nicht da war. Und wenn kein Argument mehr sticht, diese *Lust* bleibt der stärkste Einwand gegen die Skepsis. Schließlich vermittelt uns jenes Gefühl der Lust − dies Kants Argument − den Grund „der allgemeinen Mitteilbarkeit unserer Erkenntnis, welche in jeder Logik und jedem Prinzip der Erkenntnis, das nicht skeptisch ist, vorausgesetzt werden muß" (*K.d.U.*, 66).

Ich will die Folgerungen, die aus dieser These zu ziehen sind, an dieser Stelle nicht weiter ausführen. Nur diesen Punkt möchte ich herausheben. Nur das Bemerkenswerte: Unhintergehbare Voraussetzung jeder Erkenntnis überhaupt ist bei Kant die Lebensform, die im Vermögen der Lust und Unlust verankert ist.

3. Daß die Lust überhaupt ausbleiben kann, setzt aber eine Selbstbestimmbarkeit des Subjekts voraus, die Kant als *Interesse* bezeichnet. Das Subjekt könnte schon in der „Wahl" seiner Urteilshandlung durch irgendwelche empirischen oder dogmatischen Einflüsse, z.B. durch die „Neigung" zu bestimmten Theorien bedingt sein. Das würde dann heißen, die Urteilshandlung folgte Gründen aus den Bedingtheiten des Subjekts. Urteilen als *freies* Handeln wäre nicht möglich.

Die Konsequenz, die sich daraus ergibt, ist bemerkenswert: Sie besagt ganz unmißverständlich: Unter diesem Gesichtspunkt könnte es nicht *selbstbewußt*, d.h. *objektiv* urteilen und damit im Sinne Kants gar nicht urteilen können. Meine Freiheit wäre schöner Schein. Nun mag ich gewiß von außen als Gegenstand des inneren oder äußeren Sinnes betrachtet − im Verhältnis zur Intentionalität des Subjekts also − immer in dieser Weise bedingt sein und damit gar nicht in der Lage sein, selbstbewußt Urteile zu fällen.

Das ist die Perspektive, die Kants Analyse des Urteils als freies Handelns eröffnet. Und eben darin ist die Freiheit des Menschen im Verhältnis zur *Intentionalität* des Subjekts die reine Kontingenz und Faktizität. Andererseits setzen wir uns aber im moralischen Bewußtsein als freie, d.h. zur Objektivität fähige Urteilsvermögen voraus. Und eben dadurch hängt die Wirklichkeit des Menschen auch noch von Bedingungen ab, deren Erfüllung kognitives Urteilsvermögen bei aller Macht seiner Intentionalität doch prinzipiell nicht mächtig ist.

Die Gründe für die hier nur angedeutete Aporetik sind in unserem Zusammenhang nicht ausführlich zu diskutieren. Sie liegen auch nicht so sehr auf dem theoretischen Felde. Sie liegen eher und mächtiger im Phänomen der neuzeitlichen Weltentfremdung. Vielmehr soll die Frage zur Diskussion gestellt sein, was es eigentlich bedeutet, daß das Subjekt von sich selber her *voraussetzungslos* mit dem Urteilen anfangen können soll, also *objektiv* und vorurteilsfrei urteilen kann.

4. Die eigentliche Schwierigkeit liegt nun darin − und das bleibt ein unlösbares Dilemma − wenn man menschliche Rationalität offen als Intentionalität *allein* deklariert − zu zeigen, wie es möglich ist, daß das Bewußtsein mit sich selber und seinesgleichen seine Erfahrungen machen kann. Das Dilemma besteht darin, daß keine Intention als ihre Erfüllung etwa sich *selber* oder ihresgleichen intendieren könne. Denn so etwas wie eine Intention hat man nicht dadurch, daß man diese Intention selbst etwa allererst intendiert, sondern ausschließlich dadurch, daß man *irgendetwas*, und das heißt, irgendetwas *anderes* als diese Intention selbst intendiert, wobei die kognitive Urteilsintention eben das Objekt-Konstituierende selber ist. Das Bewußtsein setzt diesen Unterschied zwischen Subjekt und Objekt − Begehren und Begehrtsein − indem es weiß, daß es selbst als intentionales Urteilen das ist, was den Gegenstand konstituiert, d.h. denkt. Es ist *Gegenstands*bewußtsein, indem es den Gegenstand durch seine Urteilshandlung entstehen läßt. Dabei bleibt aber für eine Theorie dieser Intentionalität die Wirklichkeit des Bewußtseins, der Begriff des Bewußtseins vom jeweils Anderen seiner selbst. Sie ist zwar real, aber doch nur als die Realität des Bewußtseins.

Die Frage, die in diesem Zusammenhang gestellt werden muß, läßt sich demnach folgendermaßen formulieren: Wie machen wir den Schritt von der bloßen Erkenntnis der Gegenstände zum − nennen wir es einmal so − Bewußtsein der erfahrenden Instanz selber? Dies ist der Frage vergleichbar (eine Frage, die hier nicht geprüft werden kann): Unter welchen Bedingungen ist eine Person im Stande, sich auf sich *selbst* zu beziehen? Die Lösung dieses Problems soll nach Kant in der *K.d.U.* zu finden sein, nämlich wir vollziehen diesen Schritt durch das Gefühl der Lust und das darauf gerichtete Vermögen der *reflektierenden* Urteilskraft.

Offensichtlich um diesem Dilemma zu entgehen, unterscheidet Kant jetzt zwei Funktionen unserer Urteilskraft oder vielmehr zwei Arten des Urteilens: das bestimmende und das reflektierende, die wir nach heutigem Verständnis als exemplifizieren und identifizieren bezeichnen dürfen: „Ist das Allgemeine (die Regel, das Prinzip, das Gesetz [der Begriff]) gegeben, so ist die Urteilskraft, welche das Besondere darunter subsumiert [. . .], *bestimmend*" (*K.d.U.*, XXVI). In der neuen Terminologie kann die Einsicht in die Intentionalität von Erkennen und Handeln folgendermaßen ausgedrückt werden: „Intendieren", bzw. „kategorisieren" heißt soviel wie: nach geeigneten Gegenständen gesucht und *vielleicht* fündig geworden sein. Der Urteilskraft wird dabei keine *Freiheit* eingeräumt, weil ihr der Begriff, demgemäß sie eine einzelne Handlung unter die Regel des im Begriff ausgesprochenen Gesetzes bringt, *vorgegeben* ist. Sie findet nur das, was die Regeln allgemeinheitsfähiger Suche zugänglich machen. Ist dies geschehen, dann ist für die Urteilskraft, die bestimmend verfährt alle Problematik erledigt. „Ist aber", fährt Kant fort, „nur das Besondere gegeben, wozu sie [sc. die Urteilskraft] das Allgemeine finden soll, so ist die Urteilskraft bloß reflektierend" (ibid.). Die reflektierende Urteilskraft ist das Prinzip der Erreichung eines Handelns, deren Verwirklichung nicht von einem verfügbaren Allgemeinbegriff erwirkt ist, sondern welche sowohl in bezug auf den einzelnen Menschen wie in bezug auf die Gemeinschaft von Menschen durch Handlungen erst hervorzubringen ist. Denn es kann kein vorweg gesetzter Begriff ausgemacht werden, der einer freien Urteilskraft einen allgemeinen Bestimmungsgrund geben könnte. Gäbe es einen solchen vorgängig im Bewußtsein liegenden Begriff, dann wäre er der Grund, auf welchen das Urteilen nach einer Regel folgen würde, d.h. das Urteilen als *freie* Handlung wäre nicht möglich. Daraus ergibt sich unmittelbar die Konsequenz, daß es keine wie auch immer geartete „Theorie" gibt, die die Freiheit des Urteilens als Handlung bestimmen könnte. Und wir werden unsere These am besten dadurch erhärten, daß wir nun die Frage stellen, von welcher Art denn die Freiheit ist, die letztendlich Bedingung dafür ist, daß ein jeder für sich Erkenntnis und Selbstbewußtsein haben kann. Kant nennt sie „das freie Spiel" der Erkenntnis- bzw. Urteilsvermögen, was er mit der These zur Sprache bringt, daß die Erkenntnisvermögen zu einem „Erkenntnis überhaupt" zu denken sind. Mit der Einführung dieses Begriffs ist gerade das gemeint, daß die Erkenntnisvermögen nicht als *bestimmte* Urteilshandlungen mit eindeutig bestimmten Intentionen, sondern *frei* als die Betätigung von Vermögen *als* Vermögen ins Spiel zu bringen sind. Ohne dies freie Spiel kann *überhaupt* nicht gedacht oder geurteilt werden. Statt selber nur absichtlich intendiert zu werden, ist das freie Spiel vielmehr gar nichts anderes als dieses absichtliche Intendieren selbst, das seinerseits wesentlich niemals ausbleiben kann, was vielmehr immer schon auftreten muß, damit sich überhaupt etwas, Erkenntnis, als *Lust* zu diesem Intendieren einstellen kann. Denken *besteht* in diesem freien Spiel, weil es für jede Erkenntnis mittels menschlicher, d.h. diskursiver Begriffe vorauszusetzen ist. Kant formuliert dies wie folgt:

> Der Gemütszustand in dem freien Spiele der Einbildungskraft und des Verstandes (sofern sie untereinander, wie es zu einem *Erkenntnis überhaupt* erforderlich ist, zusammenstimmen) – muß ebensowohl für jedermann gelten und folglich allgemein mitteilbar sein, als es eine jede bestimmte Erkenntnis ist, die doch immer auf jenem Verhältnis als subjektiver Bedingung beruht. (*K.d.U.*, 29)

Diese Freiheit im Spiel definiert sich somit *vor* dem Übergang in einer *bestimmten* Urteilsform. Auf das Urteilen als Handeln in Freiheit übertragen, heißt das, daß die Freiheit im Spiel unserer Erkenntnisvermögen als die reine Möglichkeit freien Handelns, besser: objektiven Urteilens immer schon, vorausgesetzt ist. Das schließt dann auch die Erklärbarkeit von Freiheit aus. Erklären kann man nur, was sich auf anderes nach kategorialen Begriffen zurückführen läßt. Die Freiheit im Spiel ist also auch nicht vom Willen intendierbar, weil sie Voraussetzung für alles Wollen ist, dem an einer Handlung gelegen ist. Die Urteilsvermögen befinden sich hier noch in einem freien Spiel mit ihren *Möglichkeiten*, und nur in diesem Stadium schließt sich dem Bewußtsein alle Wirklichkeit und es selbst erst als ein gegenständlich greifbarer Inhalt auf. Das fordert aber eine „Umkehrung gewohnten Denkens", um sich *indirekt* der unhintergehbaren Voraussetzung *jeder Erkenntnis überhaupt* zu vergewissern, die unter allen intendierten Inhalten als solche nicht vorkommt, wenn sie sie auch alle trägt.

Dieser *Grund*, unter dem dem Menschen somit seine Freiheit erscheint, ist nach Kant das *Schöne*. Wir nennen also Gegenstände unserer Welt schön, aber wir beziehen uns offenbar *indirekt* auf die Voraussetzung jeder Erkenntnis überhaupt. Das mag paradox klingen, ist aber gar nicht rätselhaft, sobald man die Kontingenz und Faktizität der Welt, wie sie Kant im Verhältnis zur Intentionalität des Subjekts auslegt, berücksichtigt. Konkret gesprochen bedeutet das: Die Welt war schon schön, bevor unsere Aussagen über sie wahr sein konnten.

ANMERKUNGEN

* Der Norwegische Forschungsrat für Allgemeine Wissenschaften, NAVF, Oslo, ermöglichte den folgen Beitrag durch ein Reisestipendium.
[1] Man könnte das so verstehen, daß das Denken – das nach Kant immer ein Urteilen ist – auf die Urteilskraft – die Kompetenz aller möglichen Urteilsbildung – als auf die „transzendentalen Grammatik" oder „Tiefengrammatik" unseres Urteilens „höre" und damit die bloße Subjektivität des Bewußtseins zum Überindividuellen hin überschreite.
[2] Auf eine detaillierte Darstellung von Kants relevanten Argumenten muß hier freilich verzichtet werden. Ich habe eine solche Darstellung versucht in meiner Habilitation „Das Konstitutionsproblem in Kants Kritik der ästhetischen Urteilskraft". Oslo, 1985.

* * *

2. Geist und Gehirn

2. Mind and Brain

THE COSTS OF MECHANISTIC EMBODIMENT

Donald M. MacKay
University of Keele

As a working hypothesis, the idea that our conscious experience (and our mental activity in particular) is *embodied in* our brain activity offers attractions as an alternative both to classical interactionism on the one hand and to reductionist materialism on the other. I have elsewhere (1–5)* explicated the notion of embodiment by using the familiar example of the embodiment of an equation in a computer.

(a) There is a clear sense in which a computer programmed to solve Poisson's equation (say) has its behaviour *determined* by Poisson's equation and its given boundary conditions. Were this not the case, we could not take the output of the machine as a solution of that equation.

(b) There is an equally clear sense in which the computer has its behaviour *determined* by the laws of physics as applied to each of its physical components, taking due account of the interactions between these components, and of the constraints imposed on the whole physical system by its physical environment. Were this not the case, the designer would warn us that the machine could not be relied upon as a computer. His claim that its behaviour as a symbolic system is determined by Poisson's equation *depends upon* his assumption that its behaviour as a physical system is determined by the laws of physics. The two are not rival, mutually exclusive claims, but logically *complementary*. [6]

This example serves well enough to illustrate the kind of interdependence (rather than interaction) that I would denote by speaking of conscious cognitive agency as 'embodied' in, and determinative of, the workings of the agent's brain-and-body. It clearly provides a counterexample to a form of argument commonly employed against mechanistic theories of brain function. In particular, it throws doubt on the presupposition of many 'incompatibilists' that complete physical determination of human behaviour *must* be denied if we want to claim that that behaviour is (at least sometimes, to some extent) determined by conscious thinking, valuing and choosing on the part of the individual concerned. With respect to the hypothesis that conscious mental activity is embodied in brain activity in the relevant sense, this presupposition is clearly false. The example also illustrates well the need to distinguish between two kinds or levels of 'causal' connection—between *physical* causes on the one hand, and what systems engineers today term *informational* or *systemic* causes on the other. Physical explanations account for changes in a system in terms of the flow and exchange of energy and force; informational explanations do so in terms of the flow and exchange of information and control. The first trace the dependence of *force* on *force*; the second the dependence of *form* on *form*. Each legitimately uses the explanatory term 'because'; but much confusion arises if we fail to follow Aristotle's lead in distinguishing between the quite different senses of 'cause' involved. In particular, to speak of 'downward causation' between the informational and physical levels, as is done by Sperry[7] for example, can give rise to much misunderstanding, with its suggestion of some kind of convergence of forces from 'above' and 'below' upon the physical components, which Sperry describes as 'pushed and hauled about' by the 'causes' operating at the higher level.[8] It would seem oddly unhelpful to a computer scientist to speak of the transistors in his machine as 'pushed and hauled about' by the equation it is solving! The distinction needed here seems closely related to Chisholm's well-known contrast between 'immanent' and 'transeunt' causality,[9] though the implications I would draw are not in favour of Chisholm's incompatibilist position; but in case I mistake his meaning, I will here use 'systemic control' to refer to the determination of behaviour by the higher-level process embodied in a physical structure, and 'physical causation' to refer to the determination of the behaviour of the physical components, both individually and collectively, by the physical forces acting upon them.

But although I have been arguing on the foregoing lines for the past 35 years, and believe the computer analogy to be valid in these specific respects, I fear that comparisons between brains and computers in general, and the growth of the discipline called 'Artificial Intelligence' (AI) in particular, have given rise to a crop of deep misunderstandings as to the philosophical implications of current efforts to explain human behaviour mechanistically. Among the 'costs' of mechanistic embodiment, it is widely supposed, would be the reduction of all human behaviour to rule-following, the downgrading of concepts of 'tacit knowledge' or the 'ineffable' to mere temporary tokens of the incompleteness of our knowledge of the human 'brain program', the denial of freedom of choice as a (perhaps necessary) illusion based on ignorance, and the rejection of all religious assessments of our spiritual significance and destiny as incompatible with scientific mechanism. Whether each of these would be regarded as a 'cost' or a 'benefit' may be a matter of individual judgment; but I believe all of them to be unwarranted by the hypothesis of mechanistic embodiment. The bulk of this paper will therefore be devoted to disposing of some mistaken inferences, as I see it, from the neuro-scientific comparison between brains and computing machinery.

There are several respects in which my example of the embodiment of an equation in a digital computer is potentially misleading. First, in that case we start with our explicitly t formalized equation, and our task is to construct an explicit embodiment of the equation in a general-purpose discrete-state machine, each of whose states serves as a distinct symbol in the relevant mathematical calculus. In the case of conscious cognitive agency, however, we start with our immediate unquantified experience of what it is like to see, feel, act, think, doubt, suffer, love, hate . . ., and it is far from obvious that any explicit program of transitions between discrete symbolic states could even approximate to a representation of that experience. The assumption that our brain is a mechanism does nothing to foreclose this question, since as we shall see below there are other types of mechanism in which transitions between states are not determined by consulting explicit rules.

Secondly, there is a serious disanalogy between embodied equations and embodied persons with regard to the problem of *identity*. To ask whether the equation embodied in a particular computer is "the original equation or merely a replica" would be to raise a silly question. Poisson's equation is one and the same, no matter how many embodiments of it may be knocking around in people's computers. But in the case of you and me the question of personal identity is far from silly, however difficult we may find it to express in sharp and satisfactory terms.

Thirdly, whenever the appropriate program is run in a suitable machine, we can guarantee that its behaviour is determined by Poisson's equation; but it is far from obvious that whenever an AI program is run in a suitable machine so as to generate behaviour we can recognize as intelligent, we are entitled to conclude that we are in the presence of a conscious individual.[2] To repeat an argument I have used elsewhere,[10] suppose we visit the theatre, where Joe Smith is playing Hamlet in the famous soliloquy. How many people—conscious centres of awareness—are on the stage? Obviously, if Joe does his job, there is a sense in which what we can see is 'Hamlet's behaviour'; but this does not mean that Hamlet is present as a conscious centre of awareness in addition to Joe. Generating Hamlet-behaviour by consulting a book of rules does not conjure Hamlet into present existence as a conscious person. Even if Joe deserts Shakespeare's text, quits the stage and 'adopts the character' of Hamlet in free dialogue with us, it would be Pickwickian to claim on these grounds that we had met Hamlet, as distinct from an impersonation of Hamlet. It would be totally irrational to argue that the ontological situation might change if only Joe were given enough time to perfect his skill in generating Hamlet-behaviour. Merely organizing behaviour according to rules, whether explicit or implicit, is not a sufficient way to increase the number of centres of conscious awareness in the world.

If it would be irrational to take the Hamlet-like behaviour of Joe Smith as proof of the presence of Hamlet, it is not obviously less irrational (*pace* Turing[11]) to take the person-like behaviour of an AI-programmed computer as proof of the presence of a conscious person. That such a computer can have a mind or personality, in the sense in which a character represented on the stage has a mind and personality, need not be disputed;[12] but that a computer programmed by rule to act the part of a person has become *ipso facto* the embodiment of an additional member of the cognitive community is a quite baseless notion, which no amount of refinement in the acting skills of artificial agents can render plausible. Impersonation is not the same as embodiment.

At this point the reader may be tempted to suppose that our argument tells equally against the hypothesis that the brain is explicable in mechanistic terms; but this would be a mistake. The common notion that all machines are formally equivalent to some explicit program is false, and the truth is that only a restricted class of machines are rule-followers in the foregoing sense. 'Intelligent' machinery is characterized by the presence of branch-points in its course at which one out of several possibilities must be selected. In digital computers of the sort normally used for AI, the outcome at each branch point is determined by consulting a rule, which may involve extremely complex computations, but is explicitly specified by the program. In other types of mechanism, however, a quite different principle is employed: the outcome is determined, at least in part, by what amounts to the *making of a physical experiment*. As a simple illustration, consider the problem of multiplying two numbers x and y. A 'digital' method would be to look up an explicit multiplication table. An alternative, however, would be to take two physical quantities (such as the distances along the graduated scales of the once-familiar slide rule) proportional to the logarithms of x and y, and perform the physical experiment of combining them so that their physical sum determines the number read off the 'product' scale. In this so-called 'analogue' method, the actual outcome only approximates to the ideal, so it is unsuitable for precise symbolic calculations; but there are many situations, both in automata and in the human brain, where internal physical experimentation of this kind plays a crucial and effective part in determinig what happens next. The point is that, as with all appeals to the real world, the outcome of such processes have a degree of *contingency*, so that the functioning of the corresponding mechanism is irreducible to the making of selections uniquely determined by rule. (The digital computer can be regarded as a special case in which this contingency is made negligible by arranging that all physically-likely outcomes of a given symbolic situation are symbolically equivalent.)

Now the brain, considered as an information-processing mechanism, combines processes of both types. Neurones of the CNS are metastable elements which interact in a cooperative fashion, such that at a given time there is for each network a vast array of 'conditional probabilities' that *if* event A occurs *and if* B occurs within so many milliseconds, *then* the network will go over from state i to state j with transition-probability P_{ij}, and so on. These states may form a discrete set; but the physical quantities that govern the P_{ij} (ionic concentrations, proximity of synaptic terminals and the like) are generally continuously variable, and interact so delicately that no predictions based on the physical measurement of parameters could keep track of the outcome, even in principle, for a significant time. The best that physics could do, even with full information, would be to specify at any time a vast 'transition-probability-matrix' (TPM) indicating the conditional probabilities of various outcomes in various circumstances. Brain activity has to be thought of as a stochastic process, to whose actual time-course no explicit program of determinate rules could be equivalent.[13]

The consequences for the hypothesis of our embodiment as conscious agents are far-reaching. In the first place, since all that characterizes us as individuals (our memories, dispositions, skills etc.) depends *ex hypothesi* on the detailed physical structure upon and in which the aforementioned 'internal experimentation' is carried out, and on which each twist and turn of our experience leaves its mark in a widely distributed and largely implicit physical form, it is impossible even in principle to divorce our personal identity from the specific brain-matter in which we are embodied, in the easy way in which the identity of an equation can be divorced from its specific embodiment in a digital computer. I am the individual whose brain-matter went through this and that specific course as a result of these and those specific internal experiments in and upon it. You are another individual whose brain-matter has traced a different world-line. Nobody with a different world-line can be identical with you or me, for his physical embodiment is unique to him, a unique theatre of physical experimentation, such that even if he had been equipped instantaneously (in the manner of some science-fiction philosophers) with the best possible physical replica of your brain, his would manifest immediate and increasing divergences from the path taken by yours. I do not deny outright the notion that in the science-fiction world the 'replica' might share many of your memories or mine; and it is perhaps arguable that he might be allowed to share some of your retrospective obligations in these bizarre circumstances. What seems quite clear is that (if the replica is a conscious being at all) he has no rational claim to *be* you or me, whether or not you or I are killed (for his convenience) as soon as he is brought into being. Much of the extensive current argumentation about such possibilities[14] is vitiated by failure to recognize the differences between an imaginary 'brain' that is functionally equivalent to a program of easily replicable rules, and the real brain in its physical particularity as a theatre of continual appeals to local physical reality, the outcomes of which play an essential part in shaping both the course and the character of our embodied agency. In short, for us as embodied persons, "matter matters".

What I am arguing for is not materialism, but what I would call "Duality without Dualism".[15] The data of our conscious experience demand to be reckoned with as categorically distinct from, and ontologically prior to, all data about our brain activity. However tight the correlations we may discern between them, their duality seems at least as undeniable as the duality between the mathematical and the physical aspects of what goes on in a computer solving an equation. By the same token, there seems to be as little need for the thought-model of interactionist dualism, with its talk of causal traffic between two 'worlds', in the one case as in the other. The relationship between embodied and embodiment is *more intimate* than that between cause and effect.[2] Unlike Searle,[16] I would argue[3, 5] that to attribute 'thinking' or other intentional activities to either brains or machines is to confuse categorical levels. It is not brains, but persons, that think, hope, fear and the like. To insist (as I do) that the physical constitution of the brain is important for personal identity does not at all imply that it makes sense to attribute mental activity to the physical brain.

Secondly, if the structure of the brain is thought of as constraining and enabling our behaviour in anything like the sense in which the program shapes the behaviour of a computer, we must recognize that (in contrast to a digital computer program) much of its contribution takes the form of "inclination without necessitation" (another expression used by Chisholm (1982, pp. 33–35), from a different standpoint). For reasons given below I think we should resist the temptation to take this stochastic aspect of brain processes as the physical basis of freewill;[2] but it does at least dispose of the idea that mechanistic theories of brain function can find no scope for genuine creativity.

Thirdly, to conceive of our embodiment in these terms disposes of any idea that mechanistic explanation of brain function would leave no room for what Wittgenstein [17] termed the 'ineffable' (that which cannot be put into words but can only be 'manifested'), or for what Polanyi[18] called 'tacit knowledge'. That "we know more than we can tell" (Polanyi) would follow directly from the hypothesis that we are embodied in a mechanism in which information is represented partly in the implicit form of physical constraints on the relative probabilities of transitions in the course of internal experimentation. The knowledge so embodied would be tacit, in the sense that its *possessor* would have no words for it, though it would be immediately accessible to him in the course of conscious agency, in the way that knowledge how to swallow, or how to ride a bicycle, can be.[19] By the same token, mechanistic explanation of brain function on these lines would positively encourage expectations that the possessor could sometimes be aware of 'unutterables' of his experience which might nevertheless (in Wittgenstein's terms) be 'shown', through the medium of poetic or artistic expression.[20]

The stochastic nature of brain activity has a further consequence worth noting. Our normal thinking is frequently enlivened by what we call 'unbidden' events. 'It occurred to me that X', we say, or 'I was struck by Y'. Thinking, in other words, is a compound of 'doing' and 'suffering'. Now on our hypothesis of embodiment, the conditional probabilities of such unbidden transitions presumably depend on the microphysical details of specific structures (synapses or the like) in the thinker's brain. There is abundant and tragic evidence from the effects of drug abuse that gross chemical factors can modulate these conditional probabilities. What is less often recognized is that in an associative mechanism on these stochastic lines, even the speculative 'trial running' of ideas can be expected in general to change significantly the relative probabilities of future spontaneous transitions under *given* conditions. In other words, to be embodied in such a mechanism means that even speculative questioning is not a neutral activity, but can play a significant part, willy nilly, in determining what is likely to 'occur to' the questioner for the whole of his future life. The moral for the philosopher may be worth pondering!

A prime cost of mechanistic embodiment is that there can be no gain (or loss) of knowledge without a change in the physical world—specifically, a change in whatever cerebral structure has to embody the information in question. Popper,[21] in a classic paper of 1951, argued that even in a physically determinate universe this must set restrictions on the predictability of the universe for its inhabitants.

It has however a further consequence, which I have followed up elsewhere.[22-24] Mechanistic embodiment entails certain *relativistic restrictions* on the validity of state-descriptions of embodied persons. A complete and uptodate state-description S of the immediate future of the embodiment of an agent A, assuming it could be produced by a non-interfering observer O, would be valid-for-O but systematically invalid-for-A. This says more than that A could not know or believe S: it means that *no uniquely determinative specification exists*, even unknown to A, which has an equally valid claim to the assent of A and of O. Instead, we must recognize that what A would be correct to believe, and in error to disbelieve, about his immediate future is systematically different from what O would be correct to believe about it. Even if, for O, every detail of A's future had a fully determinate specification, it would and could have no such complete specification with an unconditional claim to A's assent, until after A's cognitive agency had determined relevant details of that future. I will not here retrace the consequences of this 'logical indeterminacy' for the freewill debate.[23, 26] I want only to emphasize the extent to which some standard non-relativistic forms of argument can be undermined by it. In particular, the question whether a specific future event is 'inevitable' is *not properly formulated* until we say *for whom* the inevitability is to be assessed. Even in a physically-determinate universe an event inevitable-for-O may not be at all inevitable-for-A, if A's future cognitive activity is one of the factors that will determine its form.[24]

Recognition of this relativistic principle does nothing to question the validity of standard logic, since nothing but standard logic is necessary to demonstrate it. All it means is that if we try to use standard logic to determine what cognitive agents would be correct to believe about themselves, we are not entitled to presuppose (as conventional logical arguments tend to do) that if anyone would be correct to believe proposition *p*, then everyone would be. It follows that the luxury of being able to indicate the truth-value of *p* universally by a single-valued scalar (true or false, 1 or 0) may in some such cases be denied us. In this strict sense the case of cognitive agency has about it an irreducible element of *mystery*, whatever the degree of physical explicability we attach to the workings of its embodiment.[25, 26]

What then of the common notion that the hypothesis of mechanistic embodiment entails rejection of all religious assessments of our spiritual significance and destiny? Much argumentation on these lines is based on the mistaken inferences we have already considered; but it could be thought that by emphasizing the link between our personal identity and our physical embodiment we have made it more difficult to take seriously the concept of 'eternal life' as found for example in biblical Christianity. This is not the place for a full discussion;[2, 26] but the apparent difficulty would arise only if the 'eternal life' in question were a mere disembodied persistence of the individual within our present space-time. For the Christian religion, which maintains that a personal Creator is the 'ground of being' of the physical world as well as of the persons embodied in it, the emphasis is not on mere persistence but on something even more mysterious—'resurrection' in a new embodiment, and moreover in a 'new creation'—a different space-time. On the hypothesis we have been examining, the continuity required in the embodiment would not be that of the material elements of the brain structure, but of its (to us unspecifiable) transition-probability matrix (TPM). Irrespective of one's individual convictions on these matters, there are clearly no rational scientific objections to the doctrine that the Creator who sustains our present TPM from one day to the next can ensure all the continuity required in the resurrection, if He will.

In conclusion it may be useful to take stock. I have argued that we must abandon the Procrustean and physiologically unrealistic image of our cerebral embodiment as a species of rule-determined symbol-manipulator, and recognize the functional significance of the brain as a theatre of internal physical experimentation, bearing the traces of its whole history in the transition-probability matrix implicit in its physical microstructure. The neuroscientific working hypothesis that we are each embodied in such a mechanism, I have argued, would *not* entail the reducibility of all our behaviour to rule-following. It would *not* entail any denial of our ability, by our thinking, valuing and deciding, to determine our own future. It would *not* imply that I could be 'teletransported' from A to B merely by having someone programme a mechanism at B to function in an identical manner to my brain. It would not even imply that a mechanism so programmed could be guaranteed to embody any conscious experience whatever. It would raise no rational obstacle, however, to the possibility of 'eternal life' as adumbrated in the Christian religion.

I have further argued that mechanistic embodiment on these lines entails no denial of genuine creativity, nor of the reality and importance of tacit human knowledge inexpressible in words. Its main 'cost' is that, if for us there can be no coming-to-know without a change in the physical world, then no complete (present or future-tense) specification of the physical world can exist with an unconditional claim to the assent of all cognitive agents. Instead, in the case of cognitive agency we must be content to recognize a relativistic situation, in which it is not necessarily the case that if O would be correct to believe *p* and in error to disbelieve *p*, then everyone else would be correct to believe *p* and in error to disbelieve *p*. In particular, for an agent A contemplating a choice, the immediate future of his cognitive system is not just unknown but logically *indeterminate* until he makes up his mind, even if his brain were as physically determinate as clockwork. Thus the costs of mechanistic embodiment do *not* include any implication that the future outcome of a choice is already inevitable for the mechanistically embodied chooser.

It will, I hope, be clear that in this whole discussion I have had no intention of urging a belief in mechanistic determinism, or even in computational models of the brain. My aim has rather been to loosen up a knotted skein of improperly linked inferences in order that the hypothesis of our mechanistic embodiment may be disentangled and considered on its merits. The question whether all human brain activity has a mechanistic explanation, I suggest, is one we can peacefully leave open for future investigation, no matter how high a view we take of man's power of decision and its moral and religious significance.

ENDNOTES

* The numbers in round brackets refer to the corresponding endnotes.
[1] MacKay, D. M., "Mindlike Behaviour in Artefacts", *Brit. J. Phil. of Sci.*, Vol. 2 (1951), pp. 105–121. Also Vol. 3(1953), pp. 352–353. "Mentality in Machines" *Proc. Aristot. Soc. Suppt.* Vol. 26 (1952), pp. 61–86.
[2] MacKay, D. M., "Man as a Mechanism", *Faith and Thought* Vol. 91 (1960), pp. 145–157. Also revised in D. M. MacKay (ed.), *Christianity in a Mechanistic Universe* (London 1965).
[3] MacKay, D. M., "The Use of Behavioural Language to Refer to Mechanical Processes", *Brit. J. Phil. of Sci.* Vol. 13 (1962), pp. 89–103. Also in F. J. Crosson (ed.), *Human and Artificial Intelligence* (New York 1971).

4 MacKay, D. M., "The Interdependence of Mind and Brain", *Neuroscience* Vol. 5 (1980), pp. 1389–1391.

5 MacKay, D. M., "Mind Talk and Brain Talk", in: M. S. Gazzaniga (ed.), *Handbook of Cognitive Neuroscience* (New York 1983), pp. 293–317.

6 MacKay, D. M., "Complementarity II", *Aristotelian Soc. Suppt.* Vol. 32 (1958), pp. 105–122. "Complementarity in Scientific and Theological Thinking", *Zygon* Vol. 9 (1974), pp. 225-244.

7 Sperry, R. W., *Science and Moral Priority*, (Oxford 1983).

8 While accepting that at the physical level "the laws of causation are nowhere broken or open (excepting perhaps in quantum-level indeterminacy which is here irrelevant)" Sperry still claims to "counter and refute . . . the classic physicalist assumption of a purely physical determinacy of the central nervous system" (Sperry 1983) pp. 81, 89). If by "purely" here he only means "exclusively" I would agree (see notes 1–5); but the confusion that can be caused by Sperry's choice of terms is brought out if we imagine a parallel argument in the case of our digital computer.

9 Chisholm, Roderick M., "Human Freedom and the Self", in Gary Watson (ed.), *Free Will* (Oxford 1982), p. 28.

10 MacKay, D. M., "Machines, Brains and Persons" *Zygon*, (1985, in press).

11 Turing, A. M., "Computing Machinery and Intelligence", *Mind* Vol. 59 (1960), pp. 433–60.

12 The term 'personality' has an unfortunate ambiguity. (a) We speak of the 'personality' of a character in a play or a novel, meaning (roughly) the dispositional features that distinguish that character psychologically, without any implication that he exists as a person. But when we ask whether we can rightly attribute 'personality' to a robot, we may be raising (b) the ontological question whether the robot *is* a person (a centre of conscious awareness), as distinct from merely behaving *like* a person.

I must plead guilty to some inconsistency in past uses of the term. In "The use of behavioural language to refer to mechanical processes" (note 3) I argued that a suitable artefact might have a personality in sense (a). In "A mind's eye view of the brain" (note 25) I used the term in sense (b) and denied that behavioural criteria were sufficient to settle the *ontological* question of personality. In each case I would still affirm what I meant, which I hope was clear from the context.

13 MacKay, D. M., "In Search of Basic Symbols", in: H. von Foerster (ed.), *Proc. 8th Conf. on Cybernetics* (New York 1951), pp. 181–221; "From Mechanism to Mind", *Trans. Vict. Inst.* Vol. 85 (1953), pp. 17–32; "Operational Aspects of Some Fundamental Concepts of Human Communication" *synthese* Vol. 9 (1954), pp. 182–198; "Operational Aspects of Intellect" *Mechanization of Thought Processes* (Her Majesty's Stationery Office 1959), pp. 37–52; "Digits and Analogues", in: H. E. von Gierke, W. D. Keidel and H. L. Ostreicher (eds.) *Principles and Practice of Bionics* (London 1970), pp. 457–466; see also note 5.

14 See for example Derek Parfit, *Reasons and Persons* (Oxford 1984).

15 MacKay, D. M., "Ourselves and our Brains: Duality without Dualism", *Psychoneuroendocrinology* Vol. 7 (1982), pp. 285–294. See also MacKay (1980), note 26.

16 Searle, John R., "Minds, Brains and Programs", *The Behavioral and Brain Sciences* Vol. 3 (1980), pp. 417–458.

17 TLP 6.432: "There are indeed things that cannot be put into words. They *make themselves manifest*".

18 Polanyi, M., *The Tacit Dimension* (London 1967).

19 MacKay, D. M., "The Mechanics of Tacit Knowing", *I. E. E. E. Trans. on Systems, Man and Cybernetics* SMC-4 No. 1 (1974), pp. 94–95.

20 Witness Wittgenstein's comment in a letter of 9th April 1917 to Engelmann: "The poem by Uhland is really magnificent. And this is how it is: if only you do not try to utter what is unutterable then *nothing* gets lost. But the unutterable will be—unutterably—*contained* in what has been uttered!" See P. Engelmann: *Letters from Ludwig Wittgenstein* (Oxford 1967), p. 7.

21 Popper, K. R., "Indeterminism in Quantum Physics and in Classical Physics", *Brit. J. for Phil. of Sci* Vol. 1 (1950), pp. 117–133 and 173–195.

22 MacKay, D. M., "Scientific Beliefs about Oneself", in: G. N. A. Vesey (ed.), *The Proper Study* (1971), pp. 48–63.

23 MacKay, D. M., "On the Logical Indeterminacy of a Free Choice", *Proc. XIIth Int. Congress of Philosophy* Vol. 3 (1958), 249–256; and expanded version in *Mind* Vol. 69 (1960), pp. 31–40. *Freedom of Action in a Mechanistic Universe* (Eddington Lecture), (London, New York 1967), reprinted in M. S. Gazzaniga and E. P. Lovejoy (eds.), *Good Readings in Psychology* (New York 1971), pp. 121–138.

24 MacKay, D. M., "What Determines My Choice?", in: P.A. Buser and A. Rougeul-Buser (eds.), *Cerebral Correlates of Conscious Experience* (Amsterdam, New York, Oxford 1978), pp. 335–346.

25 MacKay, D. M., "On Comparing the Brain with Machines" *The Advancement of Science* Vol. 40 (1954), pp. 402–406. Also *American Scientist* Vol. 42 (1954), pp. 261–268; and "A Mind's Eye View of the Brain", in: Norbert Weiner and J. P. Schade (eds.), *Cybernetics of the Nervous System, Progress in Brain Research* Vol. 17 (1965), pp. 321–332; "Selves and Brains", *Neuroscience* Vol. 3 (1978), pp. 599–606.

26 MacKay, D. M., *Human Science and Human Dignity* (London, Downers Grove, Ill., 1979). *Brains, Machines and Persons* (London, Grand Rapids, 1980).

* * *

GEHIRNTÄTIGKEIT UND BEWUSSTSEIN

Franz Seitelberger
Universität Wien

Das Wort Bewußtsein (B) wird in diesen Ausführungen als Bezeichnung einer Tätigkeitsweise des Gehirns, nämlich des bewußten Verhaltens, verwendet. Das zentrale Anliegen der Hirnforschung besteht in der Demonstrierbarkeit der psychischen Phänomene als Hirnleistungen. Die bisherigen Ergebnisse dieses Unterfangens legen nahe, daß es keine definierbaren morphologischen noch physiologischen Substrate *des* Bewußtseins gibt, sondern daß das B eine in der strukturellen Organisation der neurobiologischen Informationsverarbeitung hervortretende Disposition, und zwar jene der subjektiven Erscheinungsweise der individuellen Verhaltenssteuerung darstellt. Das B gibt es somit nur im Sinn der bewußten Beziehung zwischen Individuum und Umwelt in Form der bewußten höheren Hirnleistungen. Zu diesen zählen unter anderem Gedächtnis, Gegenstandswahrnehmung, Sprache und Denken. Diese Worte stehen aber nicht für einfache Leistungen, sondern für noch unbekannte Leistungskomplexe und hierarchisch organisierte Programme, für deren Durchführung die Großrinde unentbehrlich ist.

Man kann in der *Großrinde* 3 Gruppen von Rindengebieten hinsichtlich ihrer funktionalen Eigenart unterscheiden: Rindenregionen, in denen bestimmte Teile des Informationseinflusses ein- bzw. austreten, z.B. die primären Sinnesfelder (Sehregion etc.) oder die motorische Region: *Modale Rindenfelder*.

Gemäß dem, was über die sogenannte modulare Organisation der GHR bekannt ist, bedeutet die Aussage, daß in solchen Regionen bestimmte Funktionen *lokalisiert* seien, nicht eine funktionelle Spezität des betreffenden Hirnteiles, sondern die lokale Organisation des betreffenden Informationsinputs oder -outputs. Die Arbeitsweise der Hirnrinde ist prinzipiell in jeder Region die gleiche; die Arbeitsergebnisse aber sind vom bearbeiteten Material abhängig: Sinneserfahrungen, Bewegungen, etc. Die Konzentration der äußeren Informationskanäle (nervöse Leistungsbahnen) in solchen Regionen bedingt es auch, daß ihre Läsionen ganz bestimmte und konstante Funktionsfälle zur Folge haben, z.B. Blindheit oder Lähmung.

Anders verhält es sich mit den *intermodalen Rindenfeldern*, die sich zwischen den modalen ausspannen und diese in ihrer Ausdehnung beim Menschen weit übertreffen. Sie erhalten als Input die bereits von den modalen Feldern bearbeitete Information, also sekundäre, tertiäre etc. Verarbeitungsprodukte und zwar konvergierend von mehreren Modalfeldern sowie anderen Rinden- und Hirngebieten. Ihre Arbeit besteht in der integrativen Aufarbeitung großer Informationsmengen verschiedener Herkunft, sei es zum Aufbau der einheitlichen Wahrnehmungswelt oder zur optimalen Bewegungssteuerung. Die Läsion solcher Rindengebiete verursacht keine groben Defekte, man bezeichnet sie daher als „stumme" Regionen, sondern Beeinträchtigungen der Funktionshöhe. Die repetitive und distributive Bearbeitung jeden Inputs durch den Modulapparat der GHR erreicht im Menschengehirn dadurch eine maximale Stufe, daß große Gebiete vor allem des Stirn- und Schläfenlappens die Arbeitsergebnisse aller anderen Hirnteile zusammenzuführen und nochmals analysieren. Man kann umschreibend sagen, daß in diesen Regionen die Integration aller dem Gehirn zugehender Information in Beziehung auf die Gesamtsituation des Individuums mit Extrapolation in die Zukunft vorgenommen wird. Das betrifft nicht nur die Information aus der Außenwelt, sondern auch die aus dem eigenen Körper einschließlich der Befindens- und Triebsphäre.

Aus dieser „Information über Information" erwachsen offenbar die den eigentlich menschlichen Hirnleistungen korrelierten Fähigkeiten des Lernens, Denkens, Planens und Handelns, die man auch als *supramodale Funktionen* bezeichnet. Das entscheidende Moment dieser Leistungsstufe liegt in der Erschließung einer neuen Möglichkeit des Umfangs mit symbolischen Produkten der Hirntätigkeit, nämlich in der Behandlung der Abstraktionen, in denen für die Verhaltenssteuerung durch das Gehirn Wirklichkeitsäquivalente repräsentiert sind. Abstraktion ist zwar ein Grundzug der kodierten Datenverarbeitung überhaupt und gehört z.B. in Form der „feature extraction" zur Voraussetzung der einfachsten Wahrnehmung; in der supramodalen Stufe erreicht die Abstraktionsfähigkeit aber erst die höchste Form begrifflicher Kristallisation von innerer und äußerer Wirklichkeit. Sie manifestiert sich in der Sprache und ist allen höheren Hirnleistungen inhärent. Sprachfähigkeit bedeutet, daß die Integrationsprodukte höherer Ordnung, wie sie z.B. dem einheitlichen Wahrnehmungsgegenstand oder einem Bewegungsentwurf zugrunde liegen, Produkte, die auf dem Niveau der Gehirntätigkeit als komplexe raumzeitliche Erregungsmuster vorzustellen sind, als selbständige Einheiten identifiziert und klassifiziert werden, z.B. als ein „Baum", und in solcher Gestalt einer einfachen nicht-neurophysiologischen Neukodierung unterworfen werden können, nämlich der im geschichtlichen kulturellen Prozeß geschaffenen menschlichen *Sprache*. Der „Baum" ist also ein Konstrukt, der aus vielen Informationsquellen gespeisten integrierenden Hirntätigkeiten, ein Konstrukt, das in der lautlichen Kodierung als „Baum" wieder einen Input darstellt, der in den Modulapparat der GHR leicht eingespeist und bearbeitet werden kann, wobei die enorme Beziehungsfülle des Konstruktes in der knappen Form „Baum" erhalten bleibt und die Neubearbeitung einer Potenzierung der Resultate erbringen kann. Diese von der Sprachfähigkeit getragene Symbolbildung geht aber über die Konstruktion abstrakter Modelle von realer Wirklichkeit noch hinaus: In Verbindung mit der Lernfähigkeit und dem Gedächtnis gewinnt die integrative Hirntätigkeit Unabhängigkeit von konkreter Erfahrung, sie erweist sich quasi als ein unspezifisches Sinnesorgan, das seine Objekte selbst hervorbringt: Das ist die *Vorstellungskraft*. Mit ihr ist es nun möglich, nicht nur die ankommenden Informationen über aktuelle Lebenssituationen optimal auszuschöpfen, sondern auch die mittels der Vorstellungskraft in Eigentätigkeit erstellten Modelle von möglichen Situationen und zukünftigen Ereignisfolgen auszuwerten. Man bezeichnet den durch die supramodale Rindenfunktion gewonnenen Erfahrungshorizont, der den durch die Sinne vermittelten Zustand des aktuellen Lebensraumes, zugleich aber auch die Situations-relevanten, mittels des Gedächtnisses und der Vorstellungskraft gebildeten Wirklichkeitsmodelle mit Prospekten in die Zukunft umfaßt, also ein für die individuelle Existenz relevantes Weltbild vermittelt, auch als *Intelligenz* und ihre Betätigung als *Denken*.

Bei dieser Leistungsschilderung der Großhirnregionen muß die Leistungsdifferenzierung zwischen den beiden Hemisphären, also die sog. *Hemisphärenspezialisierung* berührt werden. Sie ist seit langem in Form von *Dominanz* der linken Hemisphäre des Rechtshänders für den Gebrauch der Hand und für die Sprachfähigkeit bekannt.

Sehr vereinfacht und verallgemeinert ausgedrückt, kann man der linken Hemisphäre des Rechtshänders eine analytisch-logische Funktion über der Zeitachse und der rechten Hemisphäre eine synthetisch-perzeptive Funktion über den Raumkoordinaten zusprechen. Wichtige Aufschlüsse über die Beziehung zwischen Gehirn und bewußten Leistungen erbrachten die sogenannten split brain-Experimente. Patienten mit durchtrenntem oder fehlendem Hirnbalken können auch mit der isoliert arbeitenden rechten Hemisphäre korrekt erkennen und mittels der von ihr gesteuerten linken Hand entsprechend agieren. Diese Leistungen haben aber für sich allein nicht den Charakter bewußter Wahrnehmungen bzw. Handlungen und sind daher nicht sprachfähig. Nichtsdestoweniger ist der Beitrag der rechten Hemisphäre zum bewußten Verhalten unentbehrlich und konstitutiv. Alle höheren Hirnleistungen kommen durch Zusammenwirken beider Hemisphären zustande.

Man erkennt, daß es sich bei der verhaltenssteuernden Gesamtfunktion des Gehirns nicht darum handelt, ein wissenschaftlich exaktes Abbild der Umwelt als Aktionsbasis zu liefern, sondern eine umfassend informierte und abgestimmte *Verhaltensbereitschaft*, von der aus die Handlungsplanung in allen relevanten Umständen bestimmt, bzw. begrenzt werden kann.

Die Einheit des organisierenden Hirnsystems entspricht der Einheit der bewußt erlebten

Welt und stellt den durch die Sinnesmannigfaltigkeit gestalteten Erfolgsraum der individuellen Aktionen dar.

Von hier aus können wir noch einen kurzen Blick auf die *metamodale Ebene der Hirntätigkeit* richten, auf der ihre Leistungsprodukte sich selbst zum Objekt werden, also eine Reflexionsebene, um uns einen Begriff davon zu machen, was *Bewußtsein* ist oder sein kann: jedenfalls keine eigene Funktion bestimmter Hirnapparate.

In einer die bisherigen Feststellungen erweiternden Hypothese könnte man sagen: Das B ist die durch die strukturelle Organisation der Informationsverarbeitung bedingte, subjektive Erscheinungsweise unserer Verhaltenssteuerung. Die Einheit unserer Existenz ist uns paradoxerweise nur in dualer Weise erfahrbar: in der Wahrnehmung der Welt und im Erlebnis des Ichs. Sobald durch die vervollkommnete Ansicht der Gesamtsituation und durch die autonome Produktion von beliebigen Verhaltensmöglichkeiten durch die Vorstellungskraft dem Individuum im raumzeitlichen Weltgeschehen eine Mehrzahl von Alternativen des Verhaltens mit Zukunftsprojektion zur Verfügung stehen, erfolgen bestimmte optimierende Entscheidungen im Medium des B. Das B eröffnet die für diese Verhaltensebene erforderliche zusätzliche neue logische Dimension (MacKay) bzw. liefert dazu einen eigenen anderen Code (Pribram). B ist also eine mit der Höhe und Komplexität der Informationsverarbeitung von Lebewesen immanent verbundene *Qualität*. Im B erlebt das Individuum unmittelbar seine relevante Weltbeziehung in Hinblick auf die ihm möglichen und daher anheimgestellten Entscheidungen. Das elementare Verhalten der Lebewesen zur Umwelt in Form von Reiz und Reaktion erhebt sich damit beim Gehirnträger auf die Ebene von B und Wahl, beim Menschen schließlich zur Ebene von Wissen und Wollen. Die Tatsachen des B sind somit eigengesetzliche Äußerungen des einen ganzen Individuums, in denen die Totalität seiner Organismus-Umwelt-Beziehung subjektiv repräsentiert wird. Beim Menschen erreicht dieses bewußte Inbild der Wirklichkeit die äußeren Dimensionen der Welt und der Zukunft, sowie die innere Dimension des Selbst, der autonomen menschlichen Person.

LITERATUR

Creutzfeldt, O. D., „Bewußtsein und Selbstbewußtsein als Problem der Neurophysiologie", *Universitas* 36, S. 467—475 (1981).

MacKay, D. M., *Brains, Machines and Persons*. (London 1980).

Pribram, K., „Holographic Brain", in: P. Weintraub (Ed.), *The Omni Interviews*. (New York 1983) S. 133—151.

Seitelberger, F., „Die Raum-Zeit-Struktur der menschlichen Erlebniswelt als Problem der Hirnforschung", in: *Studien zur Klassifikation*, Bd. 9 (Frankfurt 1980), S. 178—196.

Seitelberger, F., „Die Evolution der Erkenntnis. Leistungspotenzen und Leistungsprodukte des menschlichen Gehirns", in: *Erkenntnis- und Wissenschaftstheorie. Akten des 7. Internationalen Wittgenstein-Symposiums 22.—29.8.1982* (Kirchberg/Wechsel), S. 174—184.

Seitelberger, F., „Neurobiological Aspects of Intelligence," in: Franz Wuketits (Ed.), *Concepts and Approaches in Evolutionary Epistemology* (Dordrecht-Boston-Lancaster 1984), S. 123—148.

Sperry, R. W., Gazzaniga, M. S. and Bogen, J. E., „Interhemisphere Deconnection," in: P. J. Vinken & A. W. Bruyn (Eds.), *Handbook of Clinical Neurology*, Vol. 4 (Amsterdam-New York-Oxford 1978), S. 273—290.

Szentagothai, J., The local neuronal apparatus of the cerebral cortex. In: P. A. Buser and A. Rougeul-Buser (Eds.), *Cerebral correlates of conscious experience* (North-Holland, Amsterdam-New York-Oxford 1978), S. 131—138.

Wuketits, F. M., „Das Problem des Bewußtseins aus biologischer Sicht," *Österreichische Ärztezeitung* 35/1 (1980), S. 24—26.

* * *

EMOTION UND SPRACHE – EIN PSYCHOLOGISCHER ANSATZ

Peter Vitouch
Universität Wien

Der vorliegende Beitrag möchte als ein Denkanstoß gewertet werden, experimentalpsychologisch gewonnene Erkenntnisse mit philosophischem Instrumentarium auf ihre Haltbarkeit zu überprüfen. Es geht dabei nicht um eine wechselseitige Methodenkritik, sondern um die Darstellung der Möglichkeit, psychologische Theorien, die auf empirischen Daten fußen, in einen philosophischen Zusammenhang zu stellen.

Es geht um die Entwicklung der aktuellen psychologischen Emotionstheorien; also der Theorien, welche die Entstehungsweise eines Gefühls erklären wollen. Paradoxerweise ist der Terminus Emotion sehr aussagekräftig für die Allgemeinheit, für den experimentell orientierten Forscher ist Gefühl dagegen eine schwer definierbare und objektivierbare Größe.

Aristoteles unterschied als erster zwischen einer physiologischen und psychologischen Komponente der Emotion, die er einerseits als „Materie", andererseits als „Form und Idee" bezeichnete. Für die moderne Psychologie erwiesen sich die Erkenntnisse aus der Gehirnphysiologie und Neuropsychologie als bedeutsam, weil damit Phänomene des Erlebens, Denkens und Fühlens näher beschrieben werden konnten. Es wurde immer klarer, daß die Funktionen peripherer Systeme und ihre Interaktionen in der Hauptsache von Steuer- und Regelzentren des Gehirns kontrolliert werden (vegetatives Nervensystem). Ebenso besteht heute kein Zweifel darüber, daß psychologische Phänomene zentralnervöse Grundlagen besitzen, daß also die Funktion unseres Gehirns verantwortlich dafür ist.

Die Gehirnphysiologie machte sich an eine „Vermessung" unseres Gehirns, entdeckte motorische und sensorische Zentren, entwickelte eine „Kartographie" der Gehirnfunktionen. Nahezu alle Fähigkeiten des Menschen wurden bestimmten „Zentren" zugeordnet und demnach wurden auch den Gefühlen sogenannte „Emotionszentren" zugeordnet. Es zeigte sich jedoch, daß diese Auffassung eine unzulässige Trivialisierung der Funktionsweise unseres Gehirns darstellte. Sicherlich gibt es Zellformationen in unserem Gehirn, in denen zum Beispiel Gefühlsreaktionen gespeichert sind (wir können uns an einmal erlebte Gefühle erinnern). Die Existenz derartiger Zentren reicht aber sicher nicht aus, den Vorgang der Entstehung eines Gefühls zu repräsentieren. Ein Vorgang, an dem – wie man heute weiß – nahezu das ganze Gehirn in differenzierter Interaktion beteiligt ist.

Die nähere Untersuchung der als „Sitz des Gefühls" postulierten Gehirnareale führte jedoch zu interessanten Erkenntnissen der Neuropsychologie auf dem Gebiet der sogenannten „Aktivierungsforschung".

Was ist Aktivierung? Dem Zustand jedes Menschen kann in jedem Moment seines Lebens ein Grad auf einer gedachten Skala zugeordnet werden, die von tiefem Schlaf bis zu höchster Angespanntheit (z.B. Panik) reicht. Diese Abstufungen werden als Grade „innerer psychischer Entspanntheit bzw. Erregung" erlebt. Wir befinden uns also zu jeder Zeit auf einem bestimmten „psychischen Aktivierungsniveau", das sich aufgrund unterschiedlicher Umweltbedingungen mehr oder weniger stark ändern kann. Berlyne (1960) spricht vom sogenannten „Aktivierungstonus", das ist der Grad einer mittleren Aktiviertheit, den jeder Mensch zu erhalten versucht, weil er als angenehm empfunden wird.

Lange Zeit wurde die Formatio reticularis (ein Nervennetzwerk im Hirnstamm) als alleinverantwortlich für die Aufrechterhaltung des Aktivierungsniveaus angesehen. Magoun (1948) entdeckte, daß die Formatio reticularis eine „Weckwirkung" auf die Großhirnrinde ausübt und dadurch von wesentlicher Bedeutung für die jeweilige Bewußtseinshelligkeit ist.

Beim Studium der Formatio reticularis durch Olds und Milner (1958) verfehlte eine

Tiefenelektrode das Ziel und wurde in das Septum eines Versuchstieres implantiert. Es zeigte sich, daß die Tiere die elektrische Reizung dieser Region jedem anderen Reiz vorziehen. Schließlich ermöglichten die Versuchsleiter dem Tier, sich selbst zu reizen, indem das Tier den Stromkreis durch Hebeldruck selbst schließen konnte. Das Ergebnis war, daß die Tiere nun häufig bis zu 5000mal und mehr pro Stunde drückten, und dies bis zur völligen Erschöpfung. Selbst wenn dem Tier nach langer Hungerperiode Nahrung angeboten wird, wenn es Durst hat oder sexuelle Reize es ablenken sollen, wird die Selbstreizung jeder anderen Reaktion vorgezogen. Die Reizung tiefer gelegener Strukturen des Mittelhirns, im sogenannten periventrikulären System, hatte gegenteiligen Effekt. Die Tiere versuchten mit allen Mitteln, jede Art von elektrischer Reizung dieser Hirnteile zu vermeiden. Olds definierte diese Strukturen als „pleasure centers" (Belohnungszentren) und Bestrafungs- oder Aversionszentren.

Damit sind wir schon auf der Spur der Gefühle. Rohracher (1965) sagt: „Die Dimension Lust-Unlust, oder in neuerer Zeit die Polarität Verstärkung versus Aversion, werden als die bestimmenden Merkmale von Gefühlen angesehen." Jedenfalls gibt es keine Gefühle, die wir nicht zumindest in geringem Maße angenehm oder unangenehm empfinden.

Berlyne (1969) konnte in Experimenten nachweisen, daß offenbar die Intensitätskomponente (in Bezug auf Aktivierung) in Zusammenhang mit Lust-Unlust-Empfindungen steht.

Diese Ergebnisse stimmen mit der Alltagserfahrung überein. Jeder angenehme Reiz ist nur solange angenehm, solange er nicht zu intensiv wird. Der von Berlyne definierte Aktivierungstonus wird sich also auf einem mittleren Niveau einpendeln, um als angenehm erlebt zu werden.

Der nächste wesentliche Punkt, der menschliches Verhalten erklären hilft, ist die Einführung des Terminus ,Aktivierungsspitzen' Diese sprunghafte Veränderung des Aktivierungstonus ist das Resultat von Reizen aus der Umwelt, auf die ein Individuum reagiert. Als angenehm oder belohnend wird der – in mehr oder weniger kurzer Zeit – darauf folgende Rückgang des Aktivierungsniveaus erlebt.

In zahlreichen Experimenten der Lernpsychologie wurde bewiesen, daß ein Organismus auch Unangenehmes anstrebt (in diesem Fall das Abweichen von Aktivierungstonus), wenn dieser unangenehme Reiz ein Signal für darauffolgende Belohnung darstellt. Man strebt also Situationen an, welche die Aktivierung kurzzeitig anheben, unter der Voraussetzung, daß nach absehbarer Zeit eine Rückkehr zum Aktivierungstonus stattfindet.

Trotz der Plausibilität, die diese Theorien entwickeln, haben sie den gewichtigen Nachteil, die Funktion des Cortex (der Gehirnrinde) nicht mit einzubeziehen. Eine Theorie, die auf der Basis der Aktivierungstheorien den kognitiven Faktor – also die Funktion der Gehirnrinde – miteinbezieht, ist die Emotionstheorie von Schachter (ab 1960). Er konnte mit Hilfe von originellen Experimenten nachweisen, daß zwei Faktoren bei der Entstehung eines Gefühls von Bedeutung sind. Einerseits das bereits besprochene Aktivierungsniveau, das sich aufgrund von Außenreizen ändert. Dabei entsteht für den Organismus ein Zuordnungs- oder Benennungsbedürfnis. Nach Schachter determiniert der Aktivierungsgrad ausschließlich die Intensität einer Emotion. Die Qualität des Gefühls hängt von kognitiven Prozessen ab. Es kann also demnach der gleiche Aktivierungsgrad als Furcht oder Freude erlebt werden, je nachdem, wie die Umweltsituation interpretiert wird. Fehlt die physiologische Aktivierung oder ist sie sehr niedrig, wird es zu keiner Emotion kommen. Ein Beispiel ist die Beeinflussung des Erregungsniveaus durch Drogen. Ein Mensch, der unter sedierendem Drogeneinfluß in eine gefährliche Situation gerät, wird keine Furcht empfinden. Es entsteht andererseits ebenso keine Gefühlsreaktion, wenn die Aktivierung nicht auf kongnitiv-situative Faktoren, sondern auf somatische Ursachen zurückgeführt wird (z.B., wenn die erhöhte Aktivierung durch Einnahme von Medikamenten erklärt werden kann). Nur wenn keine derartige „direkte" Erklärung für die gesteigerte physiologische Aktivität vorliegt, wird die Erregung in Zusammenhang mit der Gesamtsituation als Gefühl interpretiert.

Die Kritik an den Gedankengängen von Schachter bezieht sich auf den Hinweis, daß es emotionale Reaktionen gibt, die zu schnell ablaufen, um einen Bewertungsprozeß zu gestatten. Diese Tatsache spricht jedoch nicht gegen die vorher dargestellten Emotionstheorien. Mann kann − in Verbindung der beiden Elemente − einen „dialektischen Prozeß" der Entwicklung eines Gefühlsrepertoires postulieren: Neue Situationen werden kognitiv bewertet, die physiologische Reaktion wird dadurch zu Gefühlen gefärbt und dann gespeichert. Entsteht in bestimmten Lebenssituationen öfter die gleiche Emotion, gerät dieses Gefühl unter „Stimuluskontrolle". Es kann durch die Reizsituation sofort − ohne vermittelnde Kognition − hervorgerufen werden. Diese gelernten „emotionalen Einstellungen" gehören zur Lern- und Entwicklungsgeschichte eines Individuums. Ein Gedankengang, der durch Beobachtungen verifizierbar ist. Kinder haben, je nach Entwicklungsstand, noch undifferenzierte Gefühle; die Kulturabhängigkeit von Gefühlen ist auf die unterschiedlichen Lern- und Interpretationsvorgänge abgeschlossener Sozietäten zurückzuführen.

Die Kognition als wesentliches Element der Emotion! Schließt man sich den linguistischen Deterministen oder der Definition von Bertrand Russell an, der sagt „Sprache ist nicht einfach dazu da, Gedanken auszudrücken, sondern Gedanken zu ermöglichen, die ohne sie gar nicht existieren können", so führt das zu der Behauptung: Es kann nur das differenziert gefühlt werden, was differenziert gedacht wurde.

Wittgenstein sagt, „die Sprache ist die logische Grenze der Welt" (*TLP* 5.6). Nichtsdestoweniger sagt er aber auch, daß es das Unsagbare, von dem geschwiegen werden muß, gibt (*TLP* 6.522). Gibt es also differenzierte Emotion jenseits der Sprache? Die logischen Positivisten sagen, daß der Grund, weswegen geschwiegen werden muß, einfach der ist, daß nichts da ist, worüber gesprochen werden kann (Wovon man nicht sprechen kann, darüber muß man schweigen).

Kann man ergänzen: Was man nicht benennen kann, kann man auch nicht fühlen?

LITERATUR

Berlyne, D. E., „The reward value of indifferent stimulation", in: Jack T. Tapp (Hrsg.), *Reinforcement and behavior* (New York 1969).
Magoun, Horace Winchell: *The waking brain*, 2nd ed. (Springfield, Ill. 1963).
Olds, J. & Milner, P., „Positive reinforcement produced by electrical stimulation of septual area and other regions of the brain" *Journal of comparative physiological psychology*, 47 (1958), S. 419−427.
Rohracher, Hubert, *Einführung in die Psychologie*, 9. unveränd. Aufl. (Wien 1965).
Schachter, Stanley & Singer, J. E.: „Cognitive, social and physiological determinants of emotional state" *Psychological review* 69 (1962), S. 379−399.
Vitouch, Peter, „Emotion", in: Kagelmann und Wenninger (Hrsg.), *Medienpsychologie/e. Handwörterbuch in Schlüsselbegriffen* (Wien 1982).

* * *

DAS LEIB-SEELE-PROBLEM
AUS EVOLUTIONÄRER PERSPEKTIVE

Franz M. Wuketits
Universität Wien

Das Leib-Seele Problem (Materie-Geist-Problem) zählt zu den altehrwürdigen Problemen der Philosophie; nicht minder hat dieses Problem auch in anderen Disziplinen Kontroversen verursacht, so in der Psychologie, die ja der „Psyche" ihren Namen verdankt. Das Problem stellt sich meist in der Frage nach den möglichen Beziehungen zwischen Leib und Seele (Materie und Geist) dar. Nach Bunge (1980) kann man grundsätzlich drei Haltungen diesem Problem gegenüber einnehmen: Man kann es als Scheinproblem abtun; man kann es aber auch als echtes, jedoch unlösbares, oder schließlich als zwar echtes, allerdings lösbares Problem behandeln.

Wie ich an anderer Stelle (Wuketits, 1985) ausgeführt habe, betrachte ich das Problem keineswegs als Scheinproblem, halte es aber für prinzipiell lösbar − jedoch nur unter der Voraussetzung der „richtigen" Fragestellung. Meines Erachtens kann das Problem nur als „Gehirn-Bewußtsein-Problem" sinnvoll formuliert werden: Ausgehend davon, daß alles Seelische und Geistige im letzten nur auf der Basis des (menschlichen) Gehirns bzw. Zentralnervensystems zustande kommen kann, ist zu fragen, wie denn dieses Gehirn (die „oberste Instanz", das Steuerungszentrum des Zentralnervensystems) hervorbringt, was wir als seelische und geistige Phänomene bezeichnen. Vorweg gesagt: Diese Phänomene müssen spezifische Systemeigenschaften des Gehirns sein; und da das Gehirn, wie jedes biologische Organ, ein Evolutionsprodukt ist, ist es legitim und konsequent, auch alles Seelische, Geistige an die Evolution zu binden, zu fragen, wie in der Evolution des Lebendigen schließlich auch solche Phänomene entstehen konnten.

Man hat im Zusammenhang mit dem Leib-Seele-Problem häufig einen *Kategoriefehler* begangen. Ryle (1966) veranschaulichte das Wesen solcher Fehler anhand des folgenden sehr treffenden Beispiels:

> A foreigner visiting Oxford or Cambridge for the first time is shown a number of colleges, libraries, . . . scientific departments and administrative offices. He then asks ‚But where ist the University? I have seen where the members of the Colleges live, where the Registrar works, where the scientists experiment and the rest. But I have not yet seen the University . . . It has then to be explained to him that the University is not another collateral institution . . . The University is just the way in which all that he has already seen is organized (Ryle, 1966; S. 17f).

So wie in diesem Beispiel könnte nun jemand, dem man das Gehirn, seine einzelnen Bestandteile − Nervenzellen, Synapsen usw. − gezeigt hat, fragen: „Aber wo ist das Bewußtsein, der Geist? Ich habe nun die Elemente eines Gehirns gesehen, aber ‚den Geist' habe ich nicht gesehen." Selbstverständlich kann er den Geist nicht gesehen haben; weil der Geist ein spezifischer Ausdruck, eine spezifische Eigenschaft des Gehirns ist, oder besser gesagt eine Eigenschaft, die das System „Gehirn" aus dem spezifischen *Zusammenwirken* seiner Elemente (aus deren Organisation) aufweist. Es geht hier also grundsätzlich um zwei Dinge: daß ein System nicht mit seinen Eigenschaften verwechselt wird und daß die Eigenschaften eines Systems nicht vom System selbst getrennt werden.

Die Vertreter einer *strikt materialistischen* Position machen den Fehler, daß sie Geistiges mit Materiellem buchstäblich gleichsetzen und die Existenz des Geistigen leugnen (was einer komischen Note nicht entbehrt, wenn man bedenkt, daß ja auch solche Materialisten mitunter „geistvolle" Traktate mit dem Resultat eben einer Leugnung alles Geistigen geschrieben haben); die Protagonisten *dualistischer* Auffassungen wiederum trennen den Geist vom Materiellen (vom Gehirn), um dann z.B. − wie Popper und Eccles (1977) − die Wechselwirkungen zwischen Gehirn und Bewußtsein (Geist) zu diskutieren, was ungefähr dem Versuch gleichkommt, „die Bewegung" von einem fahrenden Auto zu trennen, um sich dann darüber zu unterhalten, welche Beziehung denn zwischen einem Automobil und seiner Bewegung besteht. Eine solche Unterhaltung ist indes sinnlos, weil die Bewegung eine Eigenschaft des Autos ist. Ich meine also, daß das Leib-Seele-Problem häufig unter seiner falschen Formulierung leidet.

Hier wird das Leib-Seele-Problem formuliert als die Frage nach der Entstehung der höheren Bewußtseinsleistungen in der Evolution des Menschen. So haben wir die Möglichkeit, unter Rückbezug auf die Ergebnisse der empirischen Wissenschaften (Neurobiologie, Verhaltensforschung, Evolutionsbiologie), die Entwicklung jener Strukturen und Mechanismen zu rekonstruieren, die in letzter Instanz zum Auftreten des spezifisch menschlichen *selbstreflexiven Bewußtseins* (mit allen seinen Entäußerungen in Sprache, Kunst, Moralität) geführt haben. In seiner althergebrachten Form, in der Dualität von Leib und Seele, Materie und Geist, besteht das Problem unter diesen Prämissen nicht mehr.

Neuerdings ist es die *evolutionäre Erkenntnistheorie*, die alle geistigen Phänome (mit Selbstreflexivität, Erkennen und Denken) als Resultate von komplexen Prozessen der organischen Evolution ausweist (vgl. Lorenz, 1973; Lorenz und Wuketits, 1983; Riedl, 1980; Vollmer, 1980; Wuketits, 1984 a, b). Die Version des Leib-Seele-Problems in der evolutionären Erkenntnistheorie läuft auf die *Emergenz-These* hinaus, die beispielsweise auch von Bunge (1980) vertreten wird und die besagt:

> Geist als Gehirnfunktion ist eine (neu auftretende) Systemeigenschaft, zu der es keine Vorstufen zu geben braucht . . . Ein System kann Eigenschaften aufweisen, die keines seiner Untersysteme − auch nicht in „Vorstufen" − aufweist . . . Die Eigenschaften eines Systems können sich also wesentlich (qualitativ!) von denen seiner Teile unterscheiden (Vollmer, 1980; S. 22).

Es wird mithin zugestanden, daß der Geist irreduzibel bleibt, d.h. nicht „aufgelöst" werden kann in der Materie schlechthin; jedoch waren die *Vorbedingungen* für das Auftreten des Geistes in der Evolution materieller Art, gegeben also in der Evolution des Gehirns des Menschen. Im einzelnen heißt das:

1. Die Evolution kann, auch in der „subhumanen" Sphäre als ein „erkenntnisgewinnender" (informationsgewinnender) Vorgang beschrieben werden. Alle Lebewesen (Tiere) nehmen aus ihrer Umwelt mittels Sinnesorgane (oder, bei Einzellern, diesen äquivalenten Strukturen, etwa abgegrenzte Zellbezirke zur Wahrnehmung von Lichtreiz) Informationen aus ihrer Umwelt auf und vermögen in arterhaltend zweckmäßiger Weise darauf zu reagieren.

2. Damit bedeutet Leben *Lernen*, Evolution insgesamt ein „Versuch-und-Irrtum-Spiel"; ohne Aufnahme und Verarbeitung von Information aus ihrer jeweils spezifischen Umwelt würden die Lebewesen nicht überleben können. Man kann also sagen, daß jeder Organismus über einen „Weltbildapparat" verfügt (Lorenz, 1973), bestimmte Strukturen seiner Außenwelt wahrzunehmen und zu verrechnen in der Lage ist.

3. In der Evolution, die insgesamt eine Komplizierung und Differenzierung von Strukturen und Funktionen bedeutet, haben sich bestimmte Organe und Organsysteme ausgebildet, die die Aufgabe der Verrechnung der Außenwelt übernehmen: Sinnesorgane, Nervensysteme, Gehirne. Diese Organe (Organsysteme) sind immer komplizierter, differenzierter geworden, der „Horizont", das „Weltbild" der Lebewesen hat sich also in der Evolution, im Ganzen, beständig erweitert.

4. Alle, wenn man so sagen darf, „Erkenntnis"-Leistungen der Lebewesen im subhumanen Bereich spielen sich im wesentlichen *vorbewußt* ab. *Bewußte* Erkenntnis tritt erst ab einem sehr späten Evolutionsniveau auf, dem Niveau der Hominiden („Menschenartigen"), und auch dort kann man von Bewußtsein im engeren Sinne wohl erst auf der Stufe des *Homo*

sapiens sprechen; auf dieser Stufe standen bereits die berühmten Neandertaler, von denen Funde überliefert sind, die auf Kulthandlungen, auf Vorstellungen von einem „Jenseits" schließen lassen, was jedenfalls das Vermögen einer bewußten Reflexion der eigenen Existenz belegt.

5. Da während der ganzen Evolution der Hominiden (in einem Zeitraum von 4 bis 5 Jahrmillionen) eine sukzessive Vergrößerung der Gehirnkapazität feststellbar ist (von etwa 500 cm^3 bis etwa 1500 cm^3) und die uns vom Menschen der Gegenwart bekannten geistigen Leistungen erst mit einer verhältnismäßig hohen Gehirnkapazität auftreten, liegt die Annahme nahe, daß die Vergrößerung des Gehirns — nicht nur als Prozeß der Massenvermehrung, sondern vor allem auch als Ausbildung neuer Gehirnzentren (z.B. Sprachzentrum), also neuer „Qualitäten" — die anatomisch-physiologische Basis der Entstehung des Geistigen war.

Alles in allem gelangen wir also zu dem Schluß: Das Geistige ist ein Systemphänomen, eine Systemeigenschaft des Gehirns, die sich auszubilden vermochte auf der Basis entsprechender materieller Vorgänge.

Kybernetik und Systemtheorie liefern heute Modelle, die das Entstehen neuer Systemeigenschaften im allgemeinen begreifbar machen (zusammenfassend dargestellt von Wuketits, 1981). Schließen sich — zunächst unabhängig voneinander existierende — Elemente zu einem Ganzen zusammen, dann kann'dieses Ganze sozusagen schlagartig neue Eigenschaften entwickeln, die auf der Ebene der Elemente (Systemteile) noch nicht vorhanden sind. Aus der ganz spezifischen Zusammenschaltung (Integration) der Elemente des Gehirns (Nerven- bzw. Gehirnzellen oder Neuronen) konnte dieses System Gehirn neue, vorher nie dagewesene Eigenschaften entwickeln — die man also vergeblich auf der Ebene der Bausteine sucht.

Wir müssen allerdings zugeben, daß wir die einzelnen Integrationsmuster des Gehirns heute noch nicht zur Genüge kennen. Das bleibt der künftigen Forschung vorbehalten; vielleicht aber wird ein „kleiner Rest" der Frage, wie denn die Elemente unseres Gehirns zusammenwirken, um letztlich Geistiges zu erzeugen, für immer unbeantwortbar bleiben. Auch werden evolutionäre, kybernetisch-systemtheoretische Modelle von Bewußtseinsvorgängen uns vermutlich kein *allgemeines* Schema liefern können für die *individuellen* Leistungen des menschlichen Gehirns, für die dem Menschen eigene *Personalität*. Das Gehirn des Menschen ist ein dermaßen komplexes System, daß darin offenbar „genug Platz bleibt" für individuelle, nur mit sich selbst identische Leistungen, die in keine starren Schemata zu pressen sind.

Andererseits gewinnen wir damit, daß wir das Geistige im Hinblick auf seine Entstehung in der Evolution des Menschen betrachten, neue theoretische Möglichkeiten, jenes altersgraue Problem der Beziehung von Leib und Seele (Materie und Geist) zu lösen — oder bescheidener gesagt: uns einer Lösung zu nähern. Die Trennung von Leib und Seele jedenfalls ist kein geeigneter Ausgangspunkt für eine Lösung des Problems. Nehmen wir indessen die Evolution als Ausgangspunkt, die prinzipiell charakterisiert ist durch das Entstehen von immer neuen Systemen und Systemeigenschaften, dann haben wir dem Geistigen den Schein eines Wunders genommen — trotz (noch) bestehender „Restprobleme". Der Tradition verpflichtete Philosophen mögen von einer evolutionären Annäherung an das Leib-Seele-Problem, von der „biologischen Formulierung" des Problem enttäuscht sein. Dann aber bleibt ihnen nur, mit aller Klarheit gesagt, die endlose Repetition von Fragen, die Scheinfragen sind, und die Gewißheit, ein Problem so zu formulieren, daß es a priori unlösbar ist — was dem „Geschäft" der Philosophie nicht gerade zur Ehre gereicht.

———————

LITERATUR

Bunge, M., *The Mind-Body Problem. A Psychobiological Approach* (Oxford-New York-Toronto 1980).

Lorenz, K., *Die Rückseite des Spiegels. Versuch einer Naturgeschichte menschlichen Erkennens* (München-Zürich 1973).

Lorenz, K. und Wuketits, F. M. (Hrsg.), *Die Evolution des Denkens (München-Zürich 1983)*.

Popper, K. R. und Eccles, J. C., *The Self and Its Brain. An Argument for Interactionism* (Berlin-Heidelberg-London-New York 1977).

Riedl, R., *Biologie der Erkenntnis. Die stammesgeschichtlichen Grundlagen der Vernunft* (Berlin-Hamburg 1980).

Ryle, G., *The Concept of Mind* (Harmondsworth 1966).

Vollmer, G., „Evolutionäre Erkenntnistheorie und Leib-Seele-Problem", *Herrenalber Texte* 23 (1980).

Wuketits, F. M., „Kybernetik, Gehirn und Bewußtsein", *Umschau* 81 (1981).

Wuketits, F. M., (Hrsg.), *Concepts and Approaches in Evolutionary Epistemology. Towards an Evolutionary Theory of Knowledge* (Dordrecht–Boston–Lancaster 1984a).

Wuketits, F. M., *Evolution, Erkenntnis, Ethik* (Darmstadt 1984b).

Wuketits, F. M., *Zustand und Bewußtsein. Leben als biophilosophische Synthese* (Hamburg 1985).

* * *

ZUR VEREINBARKEIT VON KRIPKES THEORIE DER NOTWENDIGEN IDENTITÄT MIT DER LEIB-SEELE-IDENTITÄTSTHESE

Andreas Bartels
Universität Gießen

Die meisten Philosophen, die Saul Kripkes Argument gegen die Leib-Seele-Identitätsthese unter die Lupe nahmen, entdeckten darin die verunglückte Anwendung einer akzeptablen semantischen Theorie. Nach dieser Theorie etablieren alle wahren Identitätsaussagen, deren Terme starre Designatoren sind, notwendige Identitäten. Läßt man diesen semantischen Hintergrund unberührt, so muß man, um das Kripke-Argument zu entkräften, bei den Zusatzprämissen ansetzen, mit deren Hilfe Kripke mentale Begriffe in die Terminologie der starren Designatoren übersetzt: 1. Mentale Ausdrücke wie ‚mein Schmerz‘ sind starre Designatoren und 2. mentale Ereignisse sind unabhängig von Gehirnereignissen vorstellbar (Cartesische Intuition). Tatsächlich könnte ohne diese Prämissen Kripkes Theorie der notwendigen Identität nicht zu einer Aporie der Leib-Seele-Identitätsthese führen. Nur wenn die Ausdrücke ‚mein Schmerz x‘ und ‚mein Gehirnzustand y‘ starre Designatoren sind, zeichnet Kripkes Semantik eine mögliche Identität x=y als notwendige Identität aus. Und nur wenn ein Auftreten von x unabhängig von der Existenz von y denkbar ist, kann die notwendige Identität von x und y (und damit ihre Identität überhaupt) schließlich zu Fall gebracht werden. Hält man sich konsequent an Kripkes nichtepistemische Konzeption modaler Ausdrücke, so lassen sich nicht nur die Angriffe gegen die Zusatzprämissen zurückweisen; es läßt sich zeigen, daß die Grundidee seines Arguments gegen die Absicht Kripkes sogar als Stützungsinstanz einer starken Identitätsthese verwendet werden kann.

Aus welchem Grund ist Kripke davon überzeugt, daß der Ausdruck ‚mein Schmerz‘ ein starrer Bezeichnungsterm ist? Die Referenz des Terms ‚Schmerz‘ wird durch eine wesentliche Eigenschaft des Referenten bestimmt, denn, so Kripke, „Finden Sie es auch nur irgendwie plausibel, daß diese Empfindung selbst hätte existieren können, ohne eine Empfindung zu sein?"[1] Mein Schmerz kann nur existieren als diese besondere Empfindungsqualität, d.h. der Ausdruck ‚mein Schmerz‘ bezeichnet in jeder möglichen Welt eben jenen Eindruck, den er in der aktualen Welt bezeichnet. Ein naheliegender Einwand geht dahin, daß Schmerzen noch andere wesentliche Eigenschaften besitzen könnten; z.B. könnten sie, wie Blumenfeld[2] bemerkt hat, wesentlich mit bestimmten Gehirnzuständen identisch sein. Wenn die Referenz des Designators ‚mein Schmerz‘ nur durch *eine* wesentliche Eigenschaft des Referenten, nämlich durch seine Schmerzhaftigkeit bestimmt wird, so gebe es eine mögliche Welt, in der dem Referenten andere wesentliche Eigenschaften abgehen, z.B. die, ein Gehirnzustand zu sein. Der Referent von ‚mein Schmerz‘ wäre in unserer Welt wesentlich schmerzhaft und ein Gehirnzustand, in einer anderen Welt aber würde mit demselben Ausdruck eine andere Art schmerzhafter Ereignisse bezeichnet, die nicht Gehirnereignisse sind. Der Ausdruck ‚mein Schmerz‘ wäre folglich kein starrer Designator. „Mögliche Welten" fungieren in diesem Argument als Situationen, in denen Gegenstände auftreten, die zu einem Gegenstand der aktualen Welt ähnlich sind, in der Weise, daß sie einen oder mehrere wesentliche Aspekte des aktualen Gegenstandes teilen. Diese Sicht auf mögliche Welten ist aber nichts anderes als der von Kripke abgelehnte „telescope-view": wir richten im Geiste unser Fernrohr auf Realisationen von Beschreibungen und beurteilen ihre Ähnlichkeit zu aktualen Gegenständen. Für Kripke dagegen besitzen mögliche Welten keinen epistemischen Status (d.h. sie realisieren nicht Beschreibungen) und ihre Struktur ergibt sich nicht aus einer Ähnlichkeitsrelation zur aktualen Welt. Statt mit Beschreibungen ist der Begriff der möglichen Welten hier mit den Gegenständen selbst verankert und der Rahmen des Möglichen durch die Menge der gedanklichen

Inszenierungen bestimmt, die wir mit diesen Gegenständen veranstalten können, wenn wir uns dabei an die bekannten Naturgesetze halten. Deshalb vererben sich die wesentlichen Eigenschaften eines Gegenstandes in alle Kripke-möglichen Welten.

Eine zu Blumenfelds Kritik komplementäre Strategie verfolgt Levin,[3] indem er die Eignung von unmittelbaren phänomenologischen Qualitäten zur Referenzfixierung in Frage stellt. Seinen Angriff gegen den bei Kripke vermuteten phänomenologischen Essentialismus führt er mit dem Argument, daß innere Qualitäten nicht zur Erzeugung individuierender Beschreibungen verwendet werden können. Wenn wir mehr wollen als Schmerzen nur zu empfinden, also z.B. auf sie Bezug nehmen wollen, so müssen wir irgendetwas sagen, das auf sie zutrifft. Die einzigen Fakten aber, die uns über Schmerzen bekannt sind, betreffen die Umstände, unter denen sie auftreten. Folglich sind wir gezwungen, zur Referenzfixierung auf „äußere" Terme zurückzugreifen. Ebenso plausibel wie Levins Bemerkungen über die Bedingungen intersubjektiv zu rechtfertigender Bezugnahme auf mentale Ereignisse ist aber, daß wir auf unsere Schmerzen in einer Art Bezug nehmen können, die es uns erlaubt, sinnvoll von einer hypothetischen Situation zu sprechen, in der z.B. derselbe Kopfschmerz, der tatsächlich erst nach der Prüfung auftrat, uns schon während der Prüfung plagt. Diese Kompetenz scheint unabhängig davon zu sein, daß wir in der Lage sind, intersubjektiv aufschlußreiche Beschreibungen dieses Kopfschmerzes zu liefern, die anderen erlauben zu beurteilen, ob ich die Schmerzterme korrekt verwende, bzw. ob ich über Kriterien zur Identifizierung von Schmerzen verfüge. Für mich kann mein Schmerz durch seine spezifische Schmerzhaftigkeit individuiert werden, auch wenn ich nicht im Besitz von Kriterien bin, die festlegen, unter welchen Bedingungen ein Schmerz zu einem späteren Zeitpunkt derselbe Schmerz sein wird wie der gegenwärtige. Die starre Designation, also die Referenzfixierung für alle möglichen Welten im Sinne Kripkes, verlangt aber auch gar keine Identifizierung nach Kriterien. Sie beschreibt stattdessen die Konsequenzen in unserem Sprachverhalten, wenn wir etwas, z.B. Schmerzen, in der Art eines Einzeldings benennen. Um einen Schmerz im Sinne Kripkes starr zu bezeichnen, genügt bereits die Fähigkeit, sich diesen Schmerz zur Zeit t unter geänderten äußeren Umständen vorstellen zu können. Kripke benötigt also keine Inkorrigierbarkeits-These für mentale Erinnerungen oder mentale Selbstbeschreibungen. Die Rekonstruktion, die Kripke von unserem Gebrauch der Identität gibt, ist wesentlich nicht-epistemisch. Referenz und Identität fungieren als primitive Relationen, mit deren Hilfe ein Sprachgebrauch erläutert wird. Daraus ist klar, daß kein Rekurs auf individuierende phänomenologische Qualitäten erforderlich ist, um Kripkes Behandlung mentaler Ausdrücke als starre Designatoren zu rechtfertigen. Kripkes Verwendung von ‚Schmerz' als Terminus für Schmerzempfindungen schließt andererseits nicht aus, daß ‚Schmerz' in anderen Kontexten anders, z.B. als eine Bezeichnung verwendet werden kann, deren Referenz durch Beschreibungen in Termini des Verhaltens fixiert wird. Will man herausfinden, was Schmerzen „in Wirklichkeit" sind, so benötigt man äußere Identitätskriterien der Art „Schmerz x ist diejenige Entität, die das Schmerzverhalten y hervorruft". In diesem Fall wird x durch y kontingent herausgegriffen und x spielt die Rolle eines Platzhalters für mögliche wissenschaftliche Entdeckungen. Kripke aber verwendet diesen Ausdruck ausschließlich als Designator, der gestattet, meine subjektive Schmerzempfindung als Einzelding zu fixieren und unbeschadet seiner Identität in abweichende äußere Umstände gedanklich einzubetten. Kripkes These ist also gegen den Augenschein nicht antiphysikalistisch im Sinne einer behaupteten Analyseresistenz mentaler Phänomene; sie behauptet lediglich, daß eine bestimmte Verwendung mentaler Ausdrücke, nämlich jene, durch die subjektive Empfindungen fixiert werden, unabhängig von möglichen Entdeckungen über die physikalische Natur des Schmerzes ist.

Die „Cartesische Intuition" erhält in Kripkes semantischer Rekonstruktion entscheidende begriffliche Bedeutung: Es gibt eine mögliche Welt, in der C-Faser-Erregungen auftreten, ohne daß die Schmerzen existieren, von denen diese physikalischen Ereignisse in der aktualen Welt begleitet werden. Folglich kann die Identität von Gehirnzuständen mit Schmerzen keine notwendige sein; dies aber ist die einzige Form der Identität, die zugelassen ist, wenn ‚C-Faser-Erregung' und ‚Schmerz' starre Bezeichnungsausdrücke sind. Ein naheliegender

Einwand gegen eine argumentative Würdigung der Cartesischen Intuition ist, daß es Intuitionen dieser Art immer gibt, bevor man entdeckt, daß Phänomene, die zuvor getrennt vorstellbar, weil begrifflich unterscheidbar waren, tatsächlich identisch sind. Dieser Einwand wird jedoch gegenstandslos, wenn man sich klar macht, daß die Cartesische Intuition nichts mit mangelndem Wissen über mentale Ereignisse zu tun hat. Selbst wenn man bereits akzeptiert hat, daß ein schmerzhaftes Ereignis neurophysiologisch erschöpfend analysiert werden kann, bleibt die Cartesische Intuition in Kripkes Version lebensfähig, wie erstaunlicherweise durch einige Beispiele D. M. Armstrongs belegt wird, die dieser zur Stützung der kontingenten Identitätsthese gegeben hat.[4] Ich kann der Überzeugung sein, daß meine Hand nicht schmerzt, obgleich der physiologische Schmerz vorhanden ist, der unter Normalbedingungen als Schmerz in der Hand erfahren wird. In diesem Fall löst der tatsächlich vorhandene Schmerz vielleicht ein bestimmtes Schmerzverhalten aus (z.B. ein Greifen mit der anderen Hand nach der schmerzenden Stelle), ohne daß ein Bewußtsein des Schmerzes entsteht. Armstrong deutet diese Situation so, daß eine physikalische Kontrollfunktion meines ZNS blockiert ist, die eben nichts anderes ist als mein Schmerzbewußtsein. Anstatt dieses Beispiel für die Cartesische Intuition auszunutzen, könnte man natürlich einfach die Kontrollfunktion zur physikalischen Seite der Identität Gehirnvorgang = Schmerz hinzufügen. Man kann aber die Cartesische Intuition noch radikaler formulieren: Der physiko-chemische Zustand (einschließlich der Funktion, die die Kontrollinstanz realisiert) könnte isoliert von Personen oder Gehirnen auftreten. Die Verknüpfung mentaler mit physikalischen Zuständen scheint zumindest vom kontingenten Umstand der Existenz von Personen oder Gehirnen abzuhängen, die diese physiko-chemischen Zustände als ihre mentalen Zustände besitzen, also z.B. Schmerz fühlen können. Daß mentale Zustände nichts anderes sind als physiologische Vorgänge in uns, bedeutet nicht, daß diese physiologischen Vorgänge, die uns als mentale Zustände präsent sind, nicht anders hätten existieren können als in der Form, in der sie uns gegeben sind.

Leplin[5] hat auf die Abhängigkeit hingewiesen, die zwischen der Schlüsselrolle der Cartesischen Intuition in Kripkes Argument und der Fixierung auf das Standardbeispiel für wissenschaftliche Identifikationen „Wärme = Molekularbewegung" besteht. Ein Modell, bei dem wie im Fall Schmerz/Gehirnzustand sowohl der reduzierende wie der reduzierte Begriff durch wesentliche Eigenschaften herausgegriffen wird, ohne daß die Reduktion den Charakter einer kontingenten wissenschaftlichen Entdeckung verliert, ist die theoretische Realisation des Begriffs ‚Gen' durch das DNA-Molekül. DNA-Moleküle sind nicht eo ipso notwendig „Informationsträger", sondern diese Eigenschaft kommt im kontingenten Zusammenhang eines Organismus mit gewissen Ablesefunktionen zustande. Auf dieselbe Weise, so Leplin, sind Gehirnzustände nicht notwendig Schmerzempfindungen, sondern erst aufgrund bestimmter qualifizierender Randbedingungen (einer bestimmten Art der neuronalen Verschaltung, einer speziellen Kontrollfunktion etc.), die nur kontingenterweise gegeben sind. Die starre Designation von ‚Schmerz' erweist sich dadurch als Artefakt, der durch die Reduktion verschwindet. Die vorher für wesentlich gehaltene Eigenschaft von Schmerzen, ihre spezifische Schmerzhaftigkeit, wird durch die Reduktion zur kontingenten Eigenschaft des reduzierenden physikalischen Zustandes.

Das Leib-Seele-Problem weist jedoch noch einen wesentlichen Unterschied zur Situation in Leplins Reduktionsmodell auf: Daß Schmerzen durch Empfindungsbegriffe essentiell herausgegriffen werden, wird nicht in gleicher Weise durch die Reduktion Schmerz/Gehirnzustand korrigiert, wie dies für die Eigenschaften des Vererbungsmechanismus gilt, die den Genen zugesprochen werden. Essentialität in diesem zweiten Fall wird gemessen an der Zentralität der Eigenschaft innerhalb der reduzierenden Theorie. Die Eigenschaft aber, bezüglich derer Schmerzen herausgegriffen werden, ist keine zentrale Eigenschaft einer Theorie (oder auch nur einer Theorienskizze) und zwar deshalb, weil es bei der Erforschung des Schmerzes nicht um sukzessive verbesserte Beschreibungen des Schmerzempfindens geht. Jeder Bezug auf die Vererbungsmechanismen erfordert eine grobe Beschreibung der Eigenschaften von Genen, während der Bezug auf Schmerzerlebnisse keine Beschreibungen impliziert. Damit läßt sich Kripkes Argument gegen die Identitätsthese aufrecht erhalten, soweit es um Schmerz als Schmerzempfindung geht. Schmerzempfindungen stehen mit Gehirnzuständen deshalb nicht in der Relation der Identität, weil wir uns ihrer nicht mittels Beschreibungen vergegenwärtigen müssen, also nicht mittels individuierender Eigenschaften, die den Startpunkt für eine wissenschaftliche Reduktion abgeben könnten. Als identisch – und zwar als notwendig identisch – können sich dagegen ‚Schmerz' (in seiner Rolle als Erklärungsbegriff) und ‚Gehirnzustand' herausstellen. Auch ein vom Organismus isolierter Gehirnzustand realisiert die Rolle der Erklärung von Schmerzzuständen in Organismen, d.h. die Cartesische Intuition verliert hier ihre Wirksamkeit.

Daß die Anwendung der Kripke-Semantik auf mentale Begriffe eine notwendige Identität von Schmerz und Gehirnzustand etablieren kann, verschafft der Identitätstheorie einen entscheidenden Vorteil. Dem Dualisten wird der Ausweg versperrt, die Identität für die aktuale Welt zu akzeptieren, aber die Option nichtphysikalischer Schmerzen für mögliche andere Welten offenzuhalten. In dieser Sicht könnte Schmerz der Intension nach etwas wesentlich Unphysikalisches sein, das in unserer Welt zufällig mit physikalischen Sachverhalten extensional zusammenfällt. Die Kripke-Semantik dagegen verbietet es, das Wesen einer Sache gegen ihre empirische Realisation auszuspielen: Die empirische Realisation des Schmerzes in unserer Welt bestimmt das Wesen des Schmerzes in allen Welten, d.h. in allen mit unserem Wissen verträglichen Geschichten, die wir uns mit den Gegenständen unserer Welt ausdenken können.

ANMERKUNGEN

[1] Kripke, S. A., *Name und Notwendigkeit* (Frankfurt 1981), S. 167.
[2] Blumenfeld, J. B., „Kripke's Refutation of Materialism", *Australasian Journal of Philosophy* Bd. 53, Nr. 2 (1975), S. 151–156.
[3] Levin, M. E., „Kripke's Argument against the Identity Thesis", *The Journal of Philosophy* Bd. 72, Nr. 6 (1975), S. 149–167.
[4] Armstrong, D. M., *A Materialist Theory of the Mind* (London 1968).
[5] Leplin, J., „Theoretical Identification and the Mind-Body Problem", *Philosophia* Bd. 8 (1979), S. 673–688.

* * *

VISION, BRAIN, AND MIND

Wolfgang Wenning
Berlin

Vision conveniently provides information on what is where in the world; objects as well as their positions or motions are identified without the effort of touching. Most higher animals derive their spatio-temporal orientation in the environment predominantly from vision. Bats are a well-known exception in managing to fly and hunt in the dark by listening to the echo of their own ultrasonic voices, similar to the technique of radar. One of the earliest attempts to explain vision is based on a similar principle. Empedokles (483−424) assumed that the eyes send out emanations which bring visual messages back to the eyes, as they return from external objects. Empedokles is known as well for the opposite view that effluvia evaporating from the pores of body surfaces stimulate vision when they reach the eyes. Demokritos, dispensing with emanations or effluvia, proposed that vision mirrors objects in the eyes. Aristotle rejected this view, stating: "It is strange too, that it never occured to him to ask why, if his theory be true, the eye alone sees, while none of the other things in which images are reflected, do so" (*On Sense and the Sensible*, Oxford, 1908). In his own theory Aristotle regards the eyes as an offshoot of the brain where vision occurs. A more detailed theory based on precise descriptions of the anatomy of the visual chain has been proposed by the early physiologist Galen of Pergamon (129−200). According to his theory, "animal spirits" ($\pi\nu\varepsilon\acute{\upsilon}\mu\alpha\tau\alpha$) originate in the brain, travel through the hollow tubes of the optic nerves, fill the crystaline lense, and from there, after interacting with infalling light, bring visual messages back to the brain on the same way . In short, to receive information about the world, the brain sends out messengers and listens to their reports when they return. This exchange of messages does not occur between the eyes and the world (as in the emanation theory) but between the brain and the eyes. Remarkably, Galen's model of "animal spirits" travelling back and forth between the brain and the eyes fits well to modern findings of feedback loops of afferent and efferent neural connections in the visual pathway. Indeed, the old model of information pick-up by visual spirits anticipates modern views on feature extraction from visual scenes.

In the Renaissance Kepler applied geometrical optics to the human eye and proposed the retina, rather than the lense to be the interface of visual information processing. Descartes corrected Kepler's optical analysis by using the sinus law of refraction and by attributing visual accomodation to changes in the shape rather than the position of the lense. In addition Descartes conceived of a geometrical mapping from a visual scene to the pinal gland of the brain, where the two inverted retinal images merge into an upright picture. Remarkably, Descartes was aware that this proposal shifts the problem of vision only a step deeper into the head, since it is not ". . . by means of this resemblance that we see the objects; for there is not another set of eyes inside the head with which we could see the images." (*La Dioptrique* (1637)). This argument is equivalent to Aristotle's argument against Demokritos who supposed that vision is mirroring. Indeed this argument seems to defeat any theory which explains vision by what Kepler, with respect to the retina, had called a "representative image". Descartes felt that the transport of retinal images through the optic nerves to the pinal gland of the brain does not solve the problem of vision without an additional step. To explain vision Descartes proposed the "substantia" of the *soul* to be located in the pinal gland such that vision occurs not between the eyes and the brain but rather between brain and mind. Descartes deviated from Galen's more correct anatomical description of the visual pathway with respect to the role of the nerve crossing at the optic chiasm as well as to what Galen called the thalamus (known today as the thalamic lateral geniculate nucleus from where neurons project to the primary visual cortex); but he followed Galen in accepting the "animal spirits" (πνεύματα) to be the essence of the soul and in explaining the movement of the body by the conduction of these spirits through the hollow tubes of the nerves to the muscles which get, according to Descartes, inflated by this "very quick wind". Today the processes of neural conduction which cause motion and stimulates vision are understood to be based on excitation and inhibition. The problem remains how to bridge the gap of Cartesian dualism.

In his theory of vision Descartes exploited dualism in proposing that our ideas about the distance, size, form as well as position or motion of external objects are innately correct. That is to say the soul solves all the unsolved problems of vision. Not much remains to be explained if nativism is carried to extremes. In contrast to nativism, Hobbes and Locke revived the Stoic "tabula rasa" concept of the mind. Locke elucidated the empiricist view by a visual "Gedan-kenexperiment" which both Locke and Berkeley trace back to Molineaux: "Suppose a man born blind and now adult, and taught by his touch to distinguish between a cube and a spere [. . .]. Suppose then the cube and the sphere placed on a table, and the blind man be made to see; [. . . could he] now distinguish and tell which is the globe, which is the cube?" (Locke 1690). A Cartesian answer would be "yes"; Locke's answer−as well as Berkeley's −was "no"; the modern answer is a somewhat longer story.

To overcome dualism, Spinoza proposed: "ordo et connexio idearum idem est ac ordo et connexio rerum" (Ethica, 1677); Leibniz sophisticated this metaphysical approach in the Monadology; Berkeley, in his theory of vision, tried to overcome dualism by carrying the empiricist position to the extreme. He argued that distance cannot be immediately "seen", because the line connecting the distal stimulus at the object with the proximal stimulus at the retina is mapped on a point. It follows that, what appears to be a visual experience of distance (and similarly of size, form, position, and motion of external objects), must be a result of the process of thinking and learning, i.e. an activity of the mind. Further arguments concerning the other senses destroy the concept of space and time perception, and let the "real" world vanish in the mind. To explain what Kant later postulated to be the "synthetic unity of apper-ception" Berkeley proposed that the mind is part of God and that what appears as the real world does so only in God's perception.

In the 19th century, the metaphysical empiricism/nativism issue dissolved into research pro-grams for a science of vision. Fechner distinguished between "outer psychophysics" which relates stimuli to "nerve energies" (J. Müller), and "inner psychophysics" which relates neural processes to sensations. A dualist in his epistemology, Fechner was a (panpsychic) monist metaphysically. Mach was also a monist, while epistemologically he believed in psychophysi-cal parallelism. In "Über die Wirkung der räumlichen Verteilung des Lichtreizes über die Netzhaut" (1865) Mach states a principle of psychophysical parallelism which he regards to be "ein heuristisches Prinzip der psychophysischen Forschung". Hering underlines this in "Zur Lehre vom Lichtsinne" (1878) by calling Mach's principle of psychophysical parallelism a "conditio sine qua non aller solchen Forschung, wenn sie Früchte tragen soll". Modern re-search programs in the fields of psychophysics, neuro-physiology, and phenomenology of vision are foreshadowed by this view.

Let me switch to neurobiology and ask if the mind may be caught within the network of neurons in the brain. Let me approach this question by relating theories on (1) *color*, (2) *distance*, and (3) *form* perception of the 19th century to recent results in neurobiology.

(1) Thomas Young in 1806 conjectured that three different light sensitive "particles" or "resonators" in the human retina would account for the outcome of Newton's additive color mixture experiments. Helmholtz adopted and further developed this idea by proposing ab-sorption curves for three kinds of hypothetical photoreceptors which give rise to a three-dimensional color space. The Young-Helmholtz tristimulus theory of color vision found wide acceptance in psychophysics long before Wald in 1965 photochemically confirmed Young's original hypothesis by identifying three types of photo-pigments in retinal cones (and a fourth one in the rods for scotopic vision). It is obvious that Young applied some principle of psycho-

physical correspondence in his conclusion that lead from the psychology of additive color mixture to the physiology of the retinal surface.

Ewald Hering in 1878 proposed a different model of color vision which turned out to be correct at a deeper level of neural processing. Hering assumed that there are three opponent color systems of antagonistic physiological processes: the black/white, the red/green, and the yellow/blue-system. In each system, Hering supposed, the antagonistic mechanism consists of two kinds of activities which cancel each other at an equilibrium point. Physiologists predominantly rejected Hering's theory until around 1960, when electrophysiological techniques of single-cell recordings led to the discovery of opponent color systems in the visual pathway. Hubel and Wiesel showed that at the level of the primary visual cortex so-called simple neurons encode bright versus dark, red versus green and yellow versus blue antagonistically by increasing/decreasing firing rates depending on excitatory/inhibitory influences of concentric ON/OFF receptive field areas. (Red-ON, Green-OFF)-cells are excited by red and inhibited by green light. (Yellow-ON, Blue-OFF)-cells are excited by yellow and inhibited by blue light. Recently Michael 1978 identified color contrast neurons which get maximally stimulated if one opponent color hits the center and the other hits the suround of the dual opponent color receptive fields of these neurons. It is noteworthy that color contrast phenomena had originally motivated Hering's theory.

Let me mention the phenomenon of color constancy which puzzled theorists of vision especially since Katz 1911. Helson and Judd in the thirties found a rather complicated psychophysical description for it. In the sixties Land explained color constancy by his retinex theory of color vision elaborated later by Horn. Land, Hubel et al. 1983 conclude from split-brain experiments that the Horn-algorithm is performed behind the retinal level. Kolata 1982 reports the recent discovery that certain neurons in the primary visual cortex "do exactly what is needed for the sort of color perception that Land described".

(2) Since Thomas Reid 1785 theorists of vision in the empiricist tradition have distinguished sharply between "sensation" (e.g. of colors) and "perception" (e.g. of distance). Helmholtz, similar to Berkeley, based his theory of distance perception on the concept of "unconscious judgements and conclusions" performed by the mind. On the other hand, Hering in his nativist approach to distance perception proposed that color sensation and distance perception are both immediate experiences based on physiological mechanisms of similar complexity. Today the old problems raised in the empiricism/nativism debate between Helmholtz and Hering begin to find answers, such as the question of whether object recognition precedes or is preceded by distance perception: Bela Julesz, using his technique of random dot stereogramms, showed that form perception may even be constituted by mechanisms of distance perception, although usually we use object recognition as a cue to estimate distance. Visual science today buries the empiricism/nativism issue in the technicalities of a modular description of visual skills (Marr 1982, Poggio 1984). A kind of "Molineaux experiment"—proposed by Locke and Berkeley to settle the issue—has been performed by Blakemore and Cooper 1970 with cats. If kittens are raised in vertically/horizontally striped cylinders, their later behaviour as well as their neural connectivities in the visual cortex will depend on the environment, although not completely.

(3) Theories of visual form perception emerged with the concept of "Gestalt" proposed by Ehrenfels 1890 under the influence of Mach and Brentano. In what later became known as the Gestalt-school of Wertheimer, Köhler and Koffka, Mach's principle of psychophysical parallelism reappeared in the form of the much stronger principle of "psychophysical isomorphism", according to which (quoting from Köhler 1929 in condensed form) experienced order in space and time is always structurally identical with a functional order in the sequence of distributions of correlated brain events, such that units of experience go with functional units of underlying physiological processes (p. 61—63). Köhler assumed that the varying patterns of retinal stimulation constrain and alter processes of dynamic field organization in the brain where the interaction of (electromagnetic) field forces (arising from ionic reactions) leads somehow to the formation of spatio-temporal configurations, that is, "Gestalten" which are

128

"isomorphic" with what is perceived. According to this somewhat "neodemocritean" model, vision is a kind of distorted, three-dimensional "mirroring" of visual forms in the brain. Köhler 1929 explicitly rejected the idea that visual form is represented in the brain "symbolically" by "local events" and criticized Bühler for holding this view:

> "Once K. Bühler tried to give an explanation of a very characteristic shape, that of the straight line. He assumed that all retinal points which form a straight line are anatomically connected in a special manner, and that this gives a straight line its particular appearance. This hypothesis has the character of a machine theory. I do not think that we can hope to solve our problem in this fashion. There are a great many highly characteristic shapes besides the straight line. Are we to assume that for each there is a special anatomical arrangement? Or rather, a great many such arrangements for each single shape, since each may be projected upon many different parts of the retina"?

Bühler's view that the retinal points forming a straight line are anatomically connected coincides exactly with the findings of Hubel and Wiesel. Along the visual pathway neurons widen their scope by surveying neural activity at earlier levels. Simple, complex and hyper-complex neurons of the primary visual cortex integrate and modulate incoming signals in columnar circuits to build up opponent color tuned feature detectors for dots, oriented lines, edges, rectangles and (abstracting from retinal position) movement of these shapes. Bühler theoretically anticipated these experimental results. On the other side, Köhler anticipated a modern theoretical problem which amounts to the question if there are "grandmother detection neurons" or "yellow VW detectors" (Dodwell) in the brain. Köhler's principle of psychophysical isomorphism reduces the complexity of this problem in the most simple way by continuity conditions connecting spatiotemporal units of experience with spatiotemporal units of underlying brain processes. As discovered by Hubel and Wiesel there is indeed a topological correspondence between patterns of retinal stimulation and patterns of neural activity in the primary visual cortex. The most advanced theory of vision today—Marr 1982—builds its basic concept of the "primal sketch" on this correspondence, reviving Kepler's idea of a "representative image" within the computational paradigm of vision. Descartes' objection (see above) had been that the idea of a "representative image" (or a homunculus in the head) reproduces the problem that it is supposed to solve. However, if there is more than one homunculus in the brain, each one may solve a smaller problem. If there is a hierarchical population of homunculi in the brain, visual competence may be performed at different levels of visual skills. Let me quote a passage from Trevarthen in this connection (see "Brain and Mind", CIBA Foundation, a.a.O.):

> "I am an isomorphist. I think there is a little man in the head. In fact I think there is a whole crowd of people. They all understand each other perfectly well, they are innate, they make decisions in a properly formed hierarchy, they disagree occasionally but they know how to resolve their disagreements, and they also have specialized occupations which are at least as sophisticated as anything that has been created by technology. I could show you a picture of a little 'man' in the brain of a fish, but all I want to say now is that the task of getting about in space is solved morphologically by all active animals, and even by active plants."

A computational model along these lines had been developed by Selfridge 1959 for visual pattern recognition. It is called "pandemonium" and consists of a hierarchy of "image demons", "computational demons", "cognitive demons" and "decision demons". Each "demon" performs a definite computational task. Together the "demons" extract more and more complex features of a visual scene. It may be said that each "lower" demon extracts a bit of geometric information and transforms it into an algebraic one, which is delivered to the "higher" demons until a "decision" demon settles part of a scene analysis by giving a binary reply (yes or no).

The basic idea of this approach fits into the more general context of connections between geometry and algebra. *Counting* (attributing a number to a set of objects) and *measuring* (attributing a number to e.g. a segment of a line) are prominent examples of such connections. In attributing coordinates (ordered pairs of numbers) to each point of a plane figure (point, line, circle, etc.) Descartes isomorphically represented geometry within algebra. A somewhat more abstract connection of this kind has been discovered by Leonard Euler. He counted "vertices" (points), "edges" (lines) and "faces" of closed polyhedral surfaces, combined these numbers into a simple arithmetical expression (the so-called "Eulercharakteristik" χ = number of vertices minus number of edges plus number of faces), and in this way showed how to give a complete classification (up to topological isomorphism) of closed surfaces in three-dimensional space (e.g. the sphere, the torus, the double-torus, etc.) and also of non-orientable surfaces (e.g. Klein's bottle in four-dimensional space). Nowadays algebraic topology broadens and generalizes Euler's approach.

It seems that the brain is a pandemonium of mathematicians: more specifically, let the "image demons" be geometers concerned with geometric projections and transformations preserving certain types of invariants (stated in Klein's "Erlanger Programm"). "Computational demons" then will turn out to be algebraic topologists associating algebraic structures (numbers, groups, moduls etc.) and their interrelations (isomorphisms, homomorphisms) to the geometric output of the "image demons". In this way points, lines, circles, spheres, tori, etc. are related to algebraic entities. At the stage of "cognitive demons" we would encounter the species of pure algebraists. These perform calculations on algebraic structures which may be overwhelmingly complicated in their combinations but intellectually bound to only a few rules. At the top, finally, the "decision demons" apply even simpler rules concluding from algebraic data simply "true" or "false". These are the logicians who sometimes step out of their own personality and become metamathematicians to avoid (semantical) contradictions arising from problems of (conscious) self-reference.

Returning from the "metaphorical brain" (Arbib) of artificial intelligence to the ground of neurobiology, we do find connections. The first geometer in the visual chain is, of course, the lense of the eye which maps scenes onto the retina. The retinal output is an intrinsic combination of geometric and algebraic information: geometric information is reproduced topologically in the primary visual cortex, as evidenced by Hubel and Wiesel from measurements of cortical activity. Algebraic information is extracted from retinal signals in the visual cortex by local feature detectors for spots, oriented lines, angles, and movement of simple shapes (see above). Thus the brain intrinsically combines a geometric and an algebraic mode of information processing. It may well turn out that evolution found a clever way to combine both modes up to the level of visual decision making in recognition, and perhaps even up to the level of sentence creation out of mental images.

Visual science proceeds from phenomenological descriptions of visual abilities over psychophysical laws and models of functioning to neurobiological discoveries. Hering's theory of color vision is a paradigm case of this progression and has encouraged similar studies in distance and form perception. Cognitive abilities like attention, awareness, and consciousness however are not yet understood very well. According to Brentano and Husserl, consciousness is "directedness to something" or "intentionality". Creutzfeld 1979 suggests that if consciousness can be understood only in dualistic terms, it may be asked, whether "intentionality" has a neurophysiological basis. He distinguishes between "external loops" (thalamo-cortical circuits e.g. of visual information take up) and "internal loops" (feeding midbrain/cerebellum information into the neocortical areas) and connects both by "reflective loops" to describe the ability of the brain to "represent to itself its self-representation". Berkeley compared the brain with a swarm of bees. The challenge then is to describe the swarm in terms of mathematics and to describe mathematics in terms of the bees.

REFERENCES

Creutzfeld, O. D., "Neurophysiological Mechanisms of Consciousness", in: *Brain and Mind*, CIBA Foundation−Excerpta Medica (Amsterdam-Oxford-New York 1979).

Hering, E., *Zur Lehre vom Lichtsinne. Sechs Mitteilungen an die Kaiserl. Akad. der Wissenschaften.* (Vienna 1878).

Hochberg, J. E., "Nativism and Empirism in Perception", in: *Psychology in the Making*, L. Postman, ed. (New York 1962).

Köhler, W., *Gestaltpsychology* (New York 1929).

Marr, D., *Vision: A Computational Investigation into the Human Representation and Processing of Visual Information* (San Francisco 1982).

Wenning, W., "Colors and Languages", in *Logics and Linguistics, Problems and Solutions. Selected Papers of the 7th Int. Congr. of Logic, Methodology and Philosophy of Science* (New York 1984).

* * *

3. Das Ich und die Welt

3. The Self and the World

FOUR HYPOTHESES ON THE ORIGIN OF MIND

Julian Jaynes
Princeton University

What I have to present to you this morning is essentially a historical theory that results in a conclusion that consciousness and mind cannot be understood apart from their history. To me, all discussions of mind must be diachronic, not synchronic as most such discussions are. It is a position which I recognize is not popular or even consonant with modern philosophical thinking, but is one which I would like to urge upon you whether or not you accept the details of what I am going to present.

The problem that I start with is that of the origin of consciousness in an evolutionary sense. It is a problem that after the rise of evolutionary theory in the latter part of the 19th century was then regarded as massively important, indeed, imperative for the completion of the theory of the origin of species by natural selection and thereby its vindication. Evolution explained the materialistic and chance origin and proliferation of species, but how could it explain the origin of the seemingly inmaterial human mind? That was and still is the problem. How could consciousness have arisen out of mere matter by natural selection?

Some, like Wallace, said it couldn't: consciousness in humans had to be imposed by a Deity. So did Darwin, surprisingly, but at the beginning of evolution as one of the several powers which were "originally breathed by the Creator into a few forms or into one", my quotation being from the last paragraph of the *Origin of Species*. And this Darwinian idea that conscious mind evolved in parallel with morphology led to a program of research into the evolutionary development of consciousness by Darwin's disciple, Romanes — a program which was quickly seen to be inadequate. Other attempted solutions followed, such as Huxley's implausible brand of adversarial proto-behaviorism or the mysticism and imprecision of emergent evolution, and then in philosophy with the neo-realism of Whitehead, Alexander, Perry, and others which is unfortunately having a modern revival as a result of some of the paradoxes of "observer-participancy" in quantum physics. And of course along this tortuous way, the psychologist's flippant solution to the problem of the origin of consciousness by denying that it exists at all. Coming through such an exhausting and trying history, it is not surprising that the problem has withered away its 19th century urgency and disappeared from both scientific and philosophical discussions. I think it should be brought back to clarify many of the problems being addressed at this symposium.

The reason for this abysmal failure to solve the problem of the origin of consciousness is because of a false and unwieldy notion of consciousness. Through history it had accumulated a huge amount of cultural baggage which would not allow the matter to be looked at properly. Some of this excess of reference was due to religious history wherein the soul became invested with all possible psychological functions which then became the properties of mind or consciousness as those words replaced the term soul. Another source of such error was due to philosophical thinking itself, that what we could arrive at as a function of mind by logical inference, that too was a part of consciousness even though such propositions had no introspective validity. So the first and proper step in this analysis is to try to loosen the concept of consciousness from the accretion of these historical mistakes.

By the infusion of logically inferred capacities into the idea of consciousness, I mean processes such as sense-perception. While we can be conscious, (though not always) of the products of senseperception, the actual processes are in no way accessible to conscious introspection. Historically, we inferred and abstracted these processes from a realization of our sense organs, and then, because of prior assumptions about mind and matter or soul and body, we believed these processes to be a part of consciousness—which they are not. If any of you still think that sense-perception is to be equated to consciousness, then I think you could follow a path to a *reductio ad absurdum*: you would then have to say that since all animals have sense-perception, all are conscious, and so on back through the evolutionary scale even to one-celled protozoa, and thence to even the amoeboid white cells of the blood since they sense bacteria and devour them. They too would be conscious. And to say that there are ten thousand conscious beings per cubic milimeter of blood in each of us here this morning is a position few would wish to defend.

Now to some of you it will seem that I am defining consciousness in a much narrower way than is usual. I am. But it is part of the theory I am stating that that is what consciousness is, and not sense perceptions—as I have just stated. I do not mean that all consciousness is introspection, but it is introspectable. Consciousness is what is going on "in the minds" of any dozen people now on the street in Kirchberg, and if you should ask them to say into a tape recorder everything they are thinking about, you will not find bundles of sense-perceptions, but a stream of worries, regrets, hopes, reminiscences, interior dialogues, and monologues, plans, imaginations—all of which are the stuff of consciousness.

Why should it be that some people confound consciousness and sense perception? The reasons are several. First, as I shall be describing, consciousness is an anlalog of perception and so indeed can *seem* to be identical. I shall try to show that as the physical sense-organed I is to a physical object, so on the basis of language an analog 'I' is to an 'object' of consciousness. And a perception can indeed be an 'object' of consciousness though not always.

But it is surprising that sophisticated philosophers and psychologists, also confound sense perception and consciousness. In psychology, psychophysics began with this error. Fechner, a panpsychist, felt he was relating the entire universe of mind with that of matter by measuring the just noticeable differences in an attribute of sensation, and so forming the famous Weber-Fechner Law. Some psychologists even today who are studying perception think they are studying consciousness. As William James pointed out long ago, sense-perceptions are abstractions we impose on experience, not intrinsic parts of that experience itself. *His* starting point was only that 'thought goes on'. And so is mine.

Some modern philosophers also perpetuate this error. I imagine it is because of the old traditions about sense data. When Russell, looking for an example of consciousness, simply says, "I see a table", that is a highly artificial and misleading choice—like saying that a b flat is an example of a symphony. Yes, he is conscious of seeing a table (which incidentally he could probably do better with his eyes closed), but the seeing of the table is not consciousness but vision and an object of consciousness, even in the midst of what he was really conscious of, his argument. Russell should have picked a more ethologically valid example that was really true of his consciousness, that had really happened, such as "When will I find time to rework the *Principia*", or "How can I afford the alimony for the second Lady Russell". He would then have come to other conclusions. Such examples are consciousness in action. "I see a table" is not. Descartes would never have said, "I see a table, therefore I am."

Just as sense-perception is not due to consciousness, so with all the variety of preceptual constancies, as size, brightness, color, shape, which our nervous systems preserve under widely varying environmental changes of light, distance, angle of regard, or even our own moving about as objects retain their same position, called location constancy—all done without any help from consciousness.

So with another large class of activities we call *preoptive*, such as how we sit, walk, move. All these are done without consciousness, unless we decide to be conscious of them—the preoptive nature of consciousness. Even in speaking, the role of consciousness is more *interpolative* than any constant companion to my words. I am not now entering my lexical storehouse and selecting items to string on these syntatic structures. Instead, I have what can best be described as an intention of certain meanings, what I call *structions*, and then linguistic habit patterns take over without further input from my consciousness. Similarly, in hearing someone speak, what are listeners conscious of? If the flow of phonemes or even the next level up of morphemes or even words, you would not be understanding what I am intending.

That consciousness is in everything we do is an illusion. Like asking a flashlight to turn itself on and look around a completely dark room to see if there is light, the flashlight would conclude that the room was everywhere bright with light—which would be false.

A further error about consciousness stems from the beginning of empiricism when Gassendi used the Aristotelean term *tabula rasa*, and which Locke, who was basing the first two books of his *Essay* on Gassendi's *Syntagma Philosophicum*, anglicized as the mind's "white paper, void of all characters, without any ideas."(*Essay* II, 1.2). Had the camera been around at the time, I suggest Locke would have used it instead as his foundational metaphor. In experience, we take successive pictures of the world, develop them in reflection, bringing into existence concepts, memories, and all our mental furnishings.

But that consciousness does not copy experience can be shown very easily: (a) by examining the memories we have and noting that they are not structured the way we experienced them, e.g. thinking of the last time you were in swimming; most people, instead of the complicated multi-sensory experience as it actually was, tend to see themselves swimming from another point of view—something of course they have never experienced at all; or (b) by examining the absence of memories that we should have if consciousness did copy experience, e.g. knowing what letters go with what numbers on telephones which we have stared at thousands of times, or to sketch from memory while here in Kirchberg the main entrance-way to your office building—you will find it difficult. Conscious memory does not copy experience but reconstructs it as a must-have-been.

Empiricism is also the culprit in the belief that consciousness is necessary for learning. In the old terminology, mind had free ideas, copies of what was perceived, which when things were perceived together, their copies or ideas stuck together—the association of ideas. And since this presumably went on in consciousness, it seemed clear that learning or the association of ideas was the crucial criterion of consciousness. This was explicitly stated by many early psychologists. But a huge body of experimental research in later psychology suggests that this is far from true. Learning can be found in species and preparations where no one would think it plausible that something like introspective consciousness has anything to do with it whatever. In humans, all types of learning, conditioning, motor learning, and instrumental learning or operant conditioning can be shown to occur without any awareness or assistance from consciousness. This is not to say that consciousness does not play a role in human learning, as in decisions as to what to learn, or making rules of how to learn better, or consciously verbalizing aspects of a task. But this is not the learning itself. And my point is that consciousness is not necessary for learning to occur.

One could here bring up the well-known phenomenon of the automatization of habit, for when this happens to us, it seems that the task has required consciousness at the beginning, but as the habit is perfected consciousness eases away and the task is performed effortlessly. This same smoothing out and increased rapidity of a habit with practice is universal among all animals that can learn. Generally, in this ubiquitous phenomenon, it is not the lapsing of consciousness with improved performance so much as the lapsing of forced attention to components of the task. And attention, which is the focusing of sense-perception, is not necessarily conscious. If you take two coins in either hand, and toss them across each other so that the opposite hand catches each, this is a task that will take somewhere between 15 and 20 trials to learn. And if you wish to try this this evening, and monitor your consciousness while you are doing so, you will find that consciousness has little to do with the learning that seems to go on mechanically. You might be conscious of something about your clumsiness, or the silliness of what you are doing as you keep picking the coins up from the floor, until, at the point of success, your consciousness is somewhat surprised and even proud of your superior dexterity. It is the attention which has changed. Automatization is a diminution of attention not consciousness.

Consciousness is also not necessary for thinking or reasoning, a somewhat shocking statement. But in 1901, Karl Marbe as a graduate student at Würzburg performed the most simple and yet most profound experiment of his day. Using his professors as subjects, each of whom was highly experienced in introspective experiments, he asked them to make a simple judgment between two identical looking weights as to which was the heavier. Against the background of the experimental psychology of the time, the result was astonishing. There was no conscious content for the actual judgment itself, although such a judgment was embedded in the consciousness of the problem, its materials, and technique. So began what came to be called the Würzburg School of Imageless Thought, which lead through experiments by Ach, Watt, Kulpe and others to concepts such as set, *aufgabe*, and determining tendency—which I have renamed structions. Structions are structures like instructions given to the nervous system, that, when presented with the materials to work on, result in the answer automatically without any conscious thinking or reasoning. This phenomenon applies to most of our activities, all the way from such simplicities as judging weights to solving problems to scientific and philosophical activity. Consciousness studies a problem and prepares it as a struction, a process which may result in a sudden appearance of the solution as if out of nowhere. During World War II, British physicists used to say that they no longer made their discoveries in the laboratory; they had their three B's where their discoveries were made, the bath, the bed, and the bus. And this process on a smaller scale is going on in me at present as my words are as if chosen for me by my nervous system after giving it the struction of my intended meaning.

Finally in this list of mistakes about consciousness, a word about its location. Most people, with possibly the present company excepted who have thought long about the problem, and so placed it 'out there' in the intellectual domain, tend to think of their consciousness, much as Descartes, Locke and Hume did, as a space usually located inside their heads. There is of course no such actual space whatever. The space of consciousness, which I shall hereafter call mind-space, is a functional space that has no location except as we assign one to it. To think of our consciousness as inside our heads is, because of all our words like introspection, internalization, etc. a very natural but arbitrary thing to do. I certainly don't mean to say that consciousness is separate from the brain; by the assumptions of natural science, it is not. But we use our brains in riding bicycles, and yet no one considers that the location of bicycle riding is inside our heads. The phenomenal location of consciousness is arbitrary.

To sum up so far, we have shown that consciousness is not all mentality, not to be equated with sensation or perception, that it is not a copy of experience, nor necessary for learning, nor even necessary for thinking and reasoning, and has only an arbitrary and functional location. As a prelude to what I am to say later, I wish you to consider that there could have been at one time human beings who did most of the things we do, speak, understand, perceive, solve problems, etc. but who were without consciousness. I think this is a very important possibility.

So far this is almost going back to a radical behaviorist position. But what then is consciousness, since I regard it as an irreducible fact that my introspections are as real as so-called "external" perceptions, though with a distinguishably incongruent quality? My procedure here will be to outline in a somewhat terse fashion a theory of consciousness and then to explain it in various ways.

Subjective conscious mind is an analog of what we call the real world. It is built up with a vocabulary or lexical field whose terms are all metaphors or analogs of behavior in the physical world. Its reality is of the same order as mathematics. It allows us to short-cut behavioral process and arrive at more adequate decisions. Like mathematics, it is an operator rather than a thing or a repository. And it is intimately bound with volition and decision.

Consider the language we use to describe conscious processes. The most prominent group of words used to describe mental events are visual. We 'see' solutions to problems, the best which may be 'brillant' or 'clear' or possibly 'dull', 'fuzzy', 'obscure'. These words are all metaphors, and the mind-space to which they apply is generated by metaphors of actual space. In that space we can 'approach' a problem, perhaps from some 'view-point' and 'grapple' with its difficulties. Every word we use to refer to mental events is a metaphor or analog of some-

138

thing in the behavioral world. And the adjectives that we use to describe physical behavior in real space are analogically taken over to describe mental behavior in mind-space. We speak of the conscious mind as being 'quick' or 'slow', or of somebody 'nimble-witted' or 'strong-minded' or 'weak-minded' or 'broad-minded' or 'deep' or 'open' or 'narrow-minded'. And so like a real space, something can be at the 'back' of our mind, or in the 'inner-recesses' or 'beyond' our minds.

But, you will remind me, metaphor is a mere comparison and cannot make new entities like consciousness. A proper analysis of metaphor shows that it can. In every metaphor there are at least two terms, the thing we are trying to express in words, the *metaphrand*, and the term produced by a struction to do so, the *metaphier*. These are similar to what I. A. Richards called the tenor and the vehicle, terms more suitable to poetry than to philosophical analysis. I have chosen metaphrand and metaphier instead to have more of the connotation of an operator by echoing the arithmetic terms of multiplicand and multiplier. If I say the ship plows the sea, the metaphrand is the way the bow goes through the water and the metaphier is a plow.

As a more relevant example, suppose we are a person back at the formation of our mental vocabulary, and we have been trying to solve some problem or to learn how to perform some task. To express our 'See' is the metaphier, drawn from the physical behavior from the physical world, that is applied to this otherwise inexpressable mental occurrence, the metaphrand. But metaphiers usually have associations that we are calling *paraphiers* that then project back into the metaphrand as what are called *paraphrands*, and, indeed, creating new entities. The word 'see' has associations of seeing in the physical world and therefore of space, and this space then becomes a paraphrand as it is united with this inferred mental event called the metaphrand.

$$
\begin{array}{ccc}
\text{metaphrand} & \rightarrow & \text{metaphier} \\
\mid\ \mid & & \downarrow \\
\text{paraphrand} & \leftarrow & \text{paraphier}
\end{array}
$$

In this way the spatial quality of the world around us is being driven into the psychological fact of solving a problem (which as we remember needs no consciousness). And it is this associated spatial quality that, as a result of the language we use to describe such psychological events, becomes with constant repetitions this functional space of our consciousness, or mind-space. This mind-space I regard as the primary feature of consciousness. It is the space which you preoptively are 'introspecting on' or 'seeing' at this very moment.

But who does the 'seeing'? Who does the introspecting? Here we introduce analogy, which differs from metaphor in that the similarity is between relationship rather than between things or actions. As the body with its sense organs (referred to as I) is to physical seeing, so there develops automatically an analog 'I' to relate to this mental kind of 'seeing' in mind-space. The analog 'I' is the second most important feature of consciousness. It is not to be confused with the self, which is an object of consciousness in later development. The analog 'I' is contentless, related I think to Kant's transcendental ego. As the bodily I can move about in its environment looking at this or that, so the analog 'I' learns to 'move about' in mind-space concentrating on one thing or another.

A third feature of consciousness we are calling *narratization*, the analogic simulation of actual behavior, an obvious aspect of consciousness which seems to have escaped previous synchronic discussions of consciousness. Consciousness is constantly fitting things into a story, putting a before and an after around any event. This feature is an analog of our physical selves moving about through a physical world with its spatial successiveness which becomes the successiveness of time in mind-space. And this results in the conscious conception of time which is a spatialized time in which we locate events and indeed our lives. It is impossible to be conscious of time in any other way than as a space.

There are other features of consciousness which I shall simply mention: *concentration*, the 'inner' analog of perceptual attention; and its opposite, *suppression*, by which we stop being conscious of annoying thoughts, the analog of turning away from annoyances in the physical world; *excerption*, the analog of how we sense only one aspect of thing at a time; and *consilience*, the analog of perceptual assimilation; and others. In no way is my list meant to be exhaustive. The essential rule here is that no operation goes on in consciousness that was not in behavior first.

Cognitive psychologists are sometimes justly accused of the habit of reinventing the wheel and making it square, and then calling it a first approximation. I would demur from agreement that that is true in the development that I have just outlined, but I would indeed like to call it a first approximation. Consciousness is not a simple matter and it should not be spoken of as if it were. Nor have I mentioned the different modes of conscious narratization such as verbal, perceptual, bodily or musical, all of which seem quite distinct with properties of their own. But it is enough, I think, to allow us to go back to the evolutionary problem as I stated it in the beginning and which has caused so much trouble in biology, psychology, and philosophy. When did all this 'inner' world begin?

We have said that consciousness is based on language. This means that generations of effort to search out the origin of consciousness in animal evolution have been incorrect and in vain. If consciousness is a group of operations learned on the basis of language, then it follows that only species with language are conscious, and that, in spite of recent questionable discussions of sign language in chimpanzees and animal communication systems, that means only in human beings, and only at some point after the evolution of language.

When did language evolve? Elsewhere I have outlined ideas of how language could have evolved from call modification, what has been called the "Wahee, Wahoo model" which is at present in competition with several others. But such theorizing points to the late Pleistocene on several grounds: (1) Such a period coincides with an evolutionary pressure for verbal communication in the hunting of large animals, (2) it coincides with the astonishing development of the particular areas of the brain involved in language, and (3), what is unique in this theory, it corresponds to the archeological record of an explosion of tool-making, for we know that language is not communication merely, but also an organ of perception, directing attention and holding attention on a particular task. This dating means that language is no older than 50,000 years, which means that consciousness developed sometime between that date and, say, the present.

It is fortunate for this problem that by 3,000 B.C., human beings have learned the remarkable ability of writing. It is therefore obvious that our first step should be to look at the early writings of mankind to see if there is evidence of an analog 'I' narratizing in a mind-space. Briefly and summarily, there is no such evidence in any writing up to approximately 1,000 B.C., and this includes the older portions of texts as well known as the Iliad.

How then did anyone decide what to do? The evidence of many sorts in all the civilizations from 9,000 B.C. up through the time of the Iliad clearly indicates that human beings heard voices, what we would regard as auditory hallucinations, voices called gods, emenating from somewhere in the brain, even as the hallucinated voices that occur in many normal people today as well as in various forms of mental illness.

This is what is called the *bicameral mind* on the metaphier of a bicameral legislature, a word incidentally which has no good translation in *German* and so may be puzzling to some of you. It simply means that human mentality at this time was in two parts, a decision making part and a follower part and neither part was conscious in a sense in which I have described consciousness. And I would like to remind you here of the rather long critique of consciousness with which I began my talk, which demonstrated that human beings could speak and understand, solve problems, and do much that we do but without being conscious. So could bicameral man. In his everyday life he was a creature of habit, but when there came some kind of problem that needed a new decision or a more complicated solution than habit could provide, that decision stress was enough to instigate an auditory hallucination, which, because such individuals had no mind-space in which to question or rebel, had to be obeyed.

I think it can easily be inferred that human beings with such a mentality had to exist in a special kind of society, one rigidly ordered in strict hierarchies with strict expectancies organized into the mind so that such hallucinations preserved the social fabric. And such was definitely the case. Bicameral kingdoms were all hierarchical theocracies, with a god, often an idol, as throughout Mesopotamia, at its head from whom hallucinations seemed to come, or else, more rarely, with a human being who was divine being the head of state as in Egypt. The evidence that these early civilizations were organized by hallucinated voices called gods, I have collected elsewhere and need not go into at this time.

So far in my talk, I have discussed two of the four hypotheses of my talk. The first, which I have spent the most of my alloted time upon as being most pertinent to this symposium, is that consciousness is grounded in the ability of language to make metaphors and analogies. The second hypothesis is that in early times, there was a different non-conscious mentality called the bicameral mind. The third hypothesis is simply that one followed the other in history.

Actually, there are two possibilities here. A weak form of the theory I am presenting would state that, yes, consciousness is based on language, but instead of it being so recent, it began back at the beginning of language, perhaps even before civilization, say, about 12,000 B.C. about the time of the beginning of the bicameral mentality of hearing voices. Both systems of mind then could have gone on together, until the bicameral mind became unwieldy and was sloughed off, leaving consciousness on its own as the medium of human decisions. This is an extremely weak position because it could then explain almost anything and is almost undisprovable.

The strong form is of greater interest and is as I have stated it in introducing the concept of the bicameral mind. It sets an astonishingly recent date for the introduction into the world of this remarkable privacy of covert events which we call consciousness. The date is slightly different in different parts of the world, but in the middle East where bicameral civilization began, the date is rougly 1,000 B.C.

This dating I think can be seen in the evidence from Mesopotamia where the break-down of the bicameral mind, beginning about 1,200 B.C. is quite clear. It was due to chaotic social disorganizations, to overpopulation and probably to the success of writing in replacing the auditory mode of command. This breakdown resulted in many practices which we would now call religious which were efforts to return to the lost voices of the gods, e.g. prayer, religious worship, and particularly the many types of divination which are new ways of making decisions by supposedly returning to the directions of gods.

In Greek literature, beginning with the Linear B Tablets, going through the Iliad and the Odyssey, through the lyric and elegiac poets of the next two centuries to Solon, provides the clearest description of the breakdown of the bicameral mind and the development of the vocabulary of consciousness on the basis of metaphor. Such words as *thumos, phrenes, kardia, psuche* change from external objective referents to internal mental functions.

Another record of the same period is the Hebrew Testament of the Bible and it too is in agreement. The Prophets of Israel were those left-over bicameral or semi-bicameral persons who heard and could relay the voice of Yahweh with a convincing authenticity, and who were therefore prized in their societies as reaching back to the lost bicameral kingdom. The words of such prophets should be compared with the later Books of Wisdom such as Ecclesiastes, and then, of course, with the New Testament which teaches a kind of reformed Judaism for conscious people. Recently, my associate, Dr. Michael Carr, an expert in ancient Chinese texts, has demonstrated the same development of consciousness in the language of the successive sections of the *Shijing* at approximately the same time period.

But is this consciousness or the concept of consciousness? This is the well-known use-mention criticism which has been applied to Hobbes and others, as well as to the present theory. Are we not confusing here the concept of consciousness with consciousness itself? My reply is that we are fusing them, that they are the same. As Dan Dennett has pointed out in a recent discussion of this theory, there are many instances of mention and use being identical. The concept of baseball and baseball are the same thing. Or of money, or law, or good and evil. Or the concept of this Wittgenstein symposium, and this Wittgenstein symposium are the same thing.

That consciousness is based on language, that there existed a different kind of mentality called the bicameral mind, and that one followed the other are my first three hypotheses. The fourth I shall only mention briefly, as it is quite separable from the other three hypotheses and not germane to the symposium. It is a neurological model for the bicameral mind. It states that the neural substrate for the god side of the bicameral mind was what correcponds to Wernicke's Area on the right cerebral hemisphere, and that this particular location processed and learned all admonitory information in a person's life and organized it into what are heard as auditory hallucinations in order to transfer such directions to the opposite or so-called dominant hemisphere. If we use present day schizophrenics as examples of this process (schizophrenia being a partial relapse to the bicameral mind), we do find evidence that this is so. Moreover, the increasing and I must add overpopularized findings on right hemispheric function agree with this model.

In closing, I would like to point out that if we are correct that consciousness began only 3,000 years ago, this theory opens new areas for philosophical analysis as well as offering new ways to look at many ancient philosophical problems: the historical invention and rise of ethics along with its vocabulary and of law as a replacement for the voices of gods, the development of philosophy itself as a pattern of knowledge to fill the vaccuum left by the retreating gods, the historical origin of the concept of truth, and therefore of science, and of course history. I like to think that perhaps one of the reasons for the towering greatness of Greek philosophy is because the conscious world was all so new and therefore so clear, from which we could infer how our long intellectual history may work as an inhibition on our abilities and achievements.

And, of course, the greatest problem of all, the mind-body problem: the theory I have presented provides a very real solution. It restates the duality that we have been trying to understand for so long as not between mind and body, but between consciousness and everything else. This duality began only 3000 years ago. Before then, there was no consciousness-body problem whatever. And since then human nature has been ineradicably changed.

REFERENCES

Jaynes, J., *The Origin of Consciousness in the Breakdown of the Bicameral Mind*, (Boston 1976).
Jaynes, J., "The Evolution of Language in the Late Pleistocene", in: S. Harnad et al. (eds.) *Origins and Evolution of Language and Speech: Annals of the New York Academy of Sciences*, Vol. 280 (1976), p. 312.

* * *

ÜBER TAUTEGORISCHE MODELLE

Herbert Stachowiak
Universität Paderborn

1. Problemstellung

Den Begriff „tautegorisch" verwendet Friedrich Wilhelm Schelling in seinen Untersuchungen zur Mythologie als Kontrastbegriff zu „allegorisch".[1] Ist die Allegorie die versinnbildlichende Darstellung eines meist ohne explizite Kodekonvention vermittelbaren Bedeutungsinhalts, so fällt die Tautegorie mit ihrem Repräsentandum zusammen, ist mit ihm in gewisser Weise identisch. Dies, sagt Schelling, vollzöge sich in der Mythologie:

> „Die Götter sind ihr wirklich existierende Wesen, die nicht etwas anderes *sind*, etwas anderes *bedeuten*, sondern *nur* das bedeuten, was sie sind."[2]

Hiernach wäre mythologischer Sprachgebrauch durch die Extinktion einer für die menschliche Weltbegegnung fundamentalen semantischen Differenz gekennzeichnet. Er identifiziert das tautegorische „Modell" mit seinem „Original". In der Sprache der Allgemeinen Modelltheorie[3]: das Modell bildet sein Original präteritions- und abundanzfrei ab, und es ist zu ihm sowohl isomorph als auch isohyl.[4]

Was hat es mit jener tautegorischen Original-Modell-Relation des näheren auf sich? Wie läßt sie sich modelltheoretisch explizieren? Wie im Zusammenhang der Entfaltung von Philosophie verstehen? Und: Können wir heute etwas aus der Weltbegegnung des Menschen im Mythos lernen?

Dabei stellt sich natürlich unsere Analyse *über* mythologische Praxis. Sie ist *Logos* im Sinne altgriechischer Reflexion, die, wie Nestle es ausdrückt, „die Wirklichkeit in vernünftiger Rede, in begrifflichem Ausdruck, zutreffend wiederzugeben"[5] sucht. Aber diesen Logos verstehe ich hier nicht als Überwindung des Mythos. Vielmehr will ich versuchen, eine positive und für uns heute wichtige Seite des Mythologischen zurückzuholen, es womöglich neuem Verständnis aufzubereiten. Auch Schellings „Philosophie der Mythologie" verfolgte wohl dieses oder ein sehr ähnliches Ziel.[6] Mythos ist bei Schelling jener metaphysische Urgrund, aus dem sich Philosophie als „Geschichte des Selbstbewußtseins"[7] entfaltet. Schelling stand „geschichtliches Philosophieren" höher als jede geschichtslose Systematik der Vernunft. Vernunft ist je gegenwärtig und stets eingebettet in das Ganze von Vergangenheit und Zukunft. Ich stelle diese Reminiszenz ausdrücklich an den Anfang des folgenden Rekonstruktionsversuchs[8], weil ich meine, daß wir die kulturelle Dynamik, deren Resultat die heutige Welt ist, schwerlich werden verstehen können, wenn wir nicht in lernendem und vergleichend-evaluierendem Nachvollzug in den Ursprung von menschlicher Kultur überhaupt zurückgehen.

Dieses Zurückgehen bedarf der erkenntnisleitenden Zielreflexion. Meine Analyse operiert mit Modell-Original-Vergleichen auf der Grundlage von Attributensystemen und bedient sich moderner Begrifflichkeit. Mythos soll „im Lichte" solcher Begrifflichkeit in der Umkehrung seines Entfaltungsprozesses von dessen vorläufigem Endstadium her betrachtet und begriffen werden.

2. Mythologisches Original und tautegorisches Modell: Seinsweise, Struktur, Relationalität

Uns interessiert zunächst die Frage nach der Seinsweise von mythologischem Original und tautegorischem Modell. Das mythologische Original Schellings ist Teil eines kulturellen Universums, von dem wir offenlassen, aus welchen vorgängigen Ordnungsverhältnissen es entstanden ist, das jedenfalls vom Menschen erlebt wurde – vielleicht in rezenten homogenen Restkulturen partiell noch erlebt wird – als eine Gesamtheit von Ritus, Kult, Sozialgefüge und sich darin vollziehender lebensweltlicher Praxis. Das tautegorische Modell konstituiert sich demgegenüber im Individuum oder sagen wir besser: in den vielen zu der Kultur gehörenden Individuen, aus perzeptiven, emotiven und kogitativen Strukturteilen. Es gehört jedenfalls zur inneren Erlebniswelt des Menschen, der an der Kultur partizipiert. Es ist eine wesentlich psychische Entität. Das Stufenmodell der Allgemeinen Modelltheorie unterscheidet eine erste semantische Stufe von semantischen Fortsetzungsstufen. Die erste Stufe ist die der internen psychischen Gebilde. Danach kommen die Stufen der expliziten, der eigentlichen Kommunikation, der Sprache, der Schrift usw. Wir können die tautegorischen Modelle also primär der ersten semantischen Stufe zuordnen. Sie entspricht übrigens etwa der Welt 2 Poppers.

Sofern individuelle Partizipation am kulturellen Universum über Außenweltkontakte der Individuen verläuft, erfolgt sie via Zeichenträger, über das, was wir auch die Informations*substanz* nennen können. Diese entspricht Poppers Welt 1, allerdings nur in Ansehung deren Funktion als Informationsträger.[9] In der Sprache der Zeichentheorie können wir sagen, die semantische Sphäre der Kultur – Wilhelm Dupré nennt sie in seinen meisterhaften Analysen den „semantischen Raum" der Kultur[10] – vermittelt sich nur über die materiellen Medien an die Kultur-Partizipanten, durch Bedeutungsbelegung der jeweiligen materiellen Inputs gemäß einem (wir sagen heute: in der Sozialisation erlernten) Kode. – Die Seinsweise des mythologischen Originals ist schwieriger zu charakterisieren. Sicher können wir davon ausgehen, daß der „semantische Raum" der Kultur insgesamt so etwas wie eine umfassende Matrix von „Originalangeboten" an den Partizipanten bildet, und es wäre natürlich hinzuzufügen, daß dieser semantische Raum von hoher struktureller und funktioneller Komplexität ist, daß er synchronische wie diachronische Züge besitzt usw. Erinnert man dabei, daß die materiell-energetische Außenwelt für den Partizipanten dieser kulturellen Originalwelt nur Informations*träger* ist, so reduziert sich die Seinsweise jenes Universums, jener Matrix, auf etwas Konzeptionelles und Propositionales, also auf reine Bedeutungsgehalte – eben den *„semantischen* Raum" Duprés.

Wüßte man nur, was das genauer ist: Bedeutung! Es ist weder Ding noch Wort. Gleichwohl existiert es. Aber eben nicht nur mental. Und was bedeutet hier: existieren? In welchem Sinne existiert eine Norm, ein Ritus, ein Kult, ein Mythos – überhaupt ein Kulturell-Allgemeines? Von der Universalienmetaphysik über Ockhams Lösungsvorschlag[11] bis in die Gegenwart reichen die, ich darf wohl sagen: im ganzen *unbefriedigenden* Bemühungen über die Klärung des Bedeutungsbegriffs. Moore, Frege, Quine, Putnam, Davidson und viele andere haben erhebliche Anstrengungen auf diesen Problemkreis verwandt[12], dessen Aktualität auch unser Symposion zeigt. Wer die Bindestrich-Semantiken unserer Tage zusammenzählt, kommt rasch auf mehrere Dutzend. Quines semantischer Holismus verdient hier Hervorhebung, sowohl innerhalb der Semantikforschung unserer Tage als auch im rückwirkenden („reversen"[13]) Verständlichmachen der *„Kontext*semantik", die zweifellos die Symbolwelten mythologischer Kulturen beherrschte, welche Eigentümlichkeiten ihr darüber hinaus immer zuzuschreiben sind. Indes ist an Quines Holismus zu Recht dessen Naturalismus kritisiert worden.[14] Mir scheint, daß in konstruktiver Auseinandersetzung mit Quine Morton White, und zwar im Ansatz schon 1956 und dann deutlicher 1981[15], einen auch für unser Problem besonders fruchtbaren Vorschlag gemacht hat, die Schwierigkeiten nicht-holistischer semantischer Analysen holistisch – er sagt neuerdings „korporatistisch" – und pragmatisch zu überwinden (um das etwas defätistische Wort „umgehen" zu vermeiden). White gibt einem vorerst kräftigen epistemologischen Realismus Raum, beruhend auf, sagen wir, vorläufigen oder hypothetischen Evidenzen, die sich sowohl auf deskriptive wie normative Feststellungen beziehen, und legt das Gewicht auf ein je system-ganzheitliches Ausjustieren von deskriptiven und/oder normativen Widerspenstigkeiten („recalcitrant beliefs") bis hin zur pragmatisch legitimen Verwerfung fundamentaler deskriptiver Bestimmungen auf Grund der Verwerfung normativer

Konklusionen. Der Whitesche Korporatismus ist eine Lehre der *Harmonisierung* von Erfahrung und Gefühl.

Mir scheint auch für den „semantischen Raum" einer mythologischen Kultur eine solche auf das Ganze eines deskriptiv-normativen Verweisungszusammenhangs transformierte „Semantik" eine vernünftige Seinszuweisung der Originalwelt des Mythologischen. Hier allerdings ist die *dezisionäre* Form des Systemjustierens auf Grund von Widerspenstigkeiten noch eingefaltet in eine Welt selbstverständlich-traditionsbestimmter Lebenssteuerung. *Das* eben macht den Mythos − *vor* dem Logos aus. Lassen Sie mich, hoffentlich nicht *zu* spekulativ, hinzufügen, daß die mythologische Harmonie eines Seinsganzen − kritikimmun und monolitisch − vielleicht das Pendant zu jener Grunderfahrung des Menschen ist, natürlich des Menschen vor allem am Anfang seiner Kulturation, die wir die *Angst* nennen. Heidegger hat dies thematisiert[16], und ich meine, wir können seine Begründung des Seins aus der Ursprünglichkeit der Angst − die das *Nichts* offenbart[17] (als ein gleichsam Vor-Ursprüngliches, das da ist noch *vor* der Fähigkeit, *Seiendes* zu negieren) − besonders zur Bestimmung auch der Seinsweise des Mythologischen, der Welt der „Originale" tautegorischer Modellbildung heranziehen. Der Mensch hat sich *nach*-mythologisch der Angst des Nichts entledigt − kraft eben jener Negation des mehr und mehr als zu- und vorhanden Erlebten und durch ihn verfügbar Gemachten. Seine heutige „Rückkehr zur Angst" ist der Beweggrund dafür, daß ich Ihnen hier diese Gedanken über tautegorische Modelle vortrage.[18]

Im „semantischen Raum" ist angesiedelt, was weder zur physischen Welt noch zur Welt der individuellen Psyche gehört. In ihm ist angesiedelt, was *gemeinsamer* referentieller Besitz aller individueller Kulturpartizipanten ist, und dies darf eine im kulturrelativen Sinne „objektive" Welt genannt werden, die der Welt 3 Poppers gleicht. Ihre Objektivität ist die Objektivität des „kulturellen Universums", in das der junge Mensch hineinwächst, das ihn leitet, ihm Geborgenheit gibt, ihm Angst nimmt. Dabei dürfen wir offenlassen, ob − wie Popper wohl meinte[19] und wohl heute noch meint − die kultur*relativen* Drittwelten zu *einer umfassenden* Welt 3 zusammen„wachsen", die sich, vielleicht über einen kathartischen Prozeß, der nur das kulturübergreifende Bedeutsame bewahrt, als autonomes System des objektiven Geistes verewigt, so daß *diese* Welt 3 nach dem Tode auch noch des letzten Menschen in infinitum weiterexistiert.[20] Für uns hier ist, wie mir scheint, ebenso sinnvoll wie hinreichend die Unterscheidung einer je „kultur-objektiven" semantischen Sphäre, die kulturelle Kommunikation ermöglicht und in bezug auf welche der einzelne Kulturangehörende als „kulturische Monade"[21] dem lebensgemeinschaftlichen sozialkulturellen Ganzen eingefügt ist.

Ich schließe eine Bemerkung zur Struktur von mythologischem Original und tautegorischem Modell an. Die mythologischen Originale offenbaren sich in sprachlicher Gestalt, als Erzählung, eingewoben in den Alltag des Menschen jener Kultur mit seinen Riten, Geboten, Verboten, in der Vermengung von Natürlichem und Übernatürlichem. Die Entäußerungsform ist die des Zeichens, das sich der Interpretation darbietet, als techne semeiotike. Die entäußerten Inhalte sind die Wirklichkeit des Mythos, Weltanfang, Naturdeutung, Beziehung des menschlichen Seins zum göttlichen, wobei die in die Erzählung gebrachten Hauptbegriffe einerseits die allegorische Doppeldeutigkeit von Bild und Sinnbild zeigen, andererseits aber im praktischen Lebens- und Orientierungsbezug gerade aus der allegorischen Fassung heraus auf ihre *Selbst*bedeutung drängen, darauf, *das* zu meinen, was sie nominal bezeichnen: Apollon *ist* die Sonne. Phaetons Sonnenwagensturz *ist* der Sonnenuntergang im Abendrot[22]. Die Allegorie-Relate fallen schon in der mythologischen *Original*wirklichkeit semantisch zusammen, werden dem potentiellen Modellbildner als Einheit tautegorischer Identität dargeboten.

Das Zusammenfallen von Inhalt und Form, Bedeutung und Zeichen in der Wahrnehmung im Mythos betont auch Ernst Cassirer[23] unter gleichzeitiger Hervorhebung des Symbolcharakters der mythologischen Zeichen. Dieser Symbolcharakter hebe den mythischen Vorstellungsgehalt von vornherein über bloße Zeichensemantik hinaus *ins Pragmatische*.[24] Wir werden sehen, worin des näheren diese Pragmatizität besteht und wie sie den Menschen im Mythos an sich bindet, in sich einbindet. Vorerst sei hervorgehoben, was schon Vico (und in dieser Form von Cassirer merkwürdigerweise kaum aufgegriffen[25]) in seiner „Scienza Nuova" von jener Welt mythologischen Ursprungs sagte: daß sie *archaische Kraft* ausstrahle, göttliche Ordnungsmacht, die sich als steuernde Lebensmitte der Kultur darstellt.

Der sprachlichen Form des mythologischen Originals gemäß stelle ich mir dieses auf die Struktur eines attributiven Systems gebracht vor, lasse es also aus Individuen, Eigenschaften von Individuen und Relationen zwischen Individuen (wohl auch zwischen Eigenschaften als für sich betrachtete einstellige Prädikatoren) bestehen[26]. Diese Struktur werde auf der Metaebene unserer Betrachtung per Kodierung der formalen Elemente mit festen semantischen Referenda belegt, diese ähnlich „evidenzrealistisch" verstanden, wie ich dies für den Whiteschen Korporatismus angedeutet habe. Die mythologischen Referenda werden dem „semantischen Raum" der Kultur entnommen − genügende Separierbarkeit auf der von mir eingenommenen Ebene der Reflexion unterstellt. Kulturspezifische empirische Mythologieforschung sollte Repertoires mythologischer Originale verläßlich erarbeiten und auf explorationsfähige Systemgestalt bringen können.

Entsprechend strukturiere ich die Modellseite. Auch die internen Modelle als Abbildungen mythologischer Originale betrachte ich auf der Reflexionsebene der Untersuchung als attributive Systeme. Das heißt, ich unterstelle auch dem Menschen im Mythos, und zwar auch für schriftlose Kulturen, jenes „Distinktionspotential" attributierender Modellbildung, das noch Rudiment ist, jedoch post-mythologisch zu immer vollerer Entfaltung gelangt. Dabei nehme ich für diese internen Modellbildungen diverse Struktur„liberalisierungen" an wie Fuzzy-Abgrenzungen[27], Komplexklassen- und Superzeichenbildungen[28]. Mein Attributen-„Atomismus" ist mit „sophisticated Methoden" strukturell dergestalt anzureichern, daß er Modell-Original-Vergleiche ermöglicht. Diese wiederum dürften für ein im Sinne meiner Intentionen besseres Verständnis der tautegorisch-mythologischen „Reversion" nachmythologischer, rationalisierter Modellprozesse erforderlich sein. Was ich indes in diesem kurzen Versuch hier leisten kann, geht über erste Schritte nicht hinaus.[29]

In welcher näheren Relation steht das tautegorische Modell zu seinem Original? Hierzu gehe ich von der Einbettung des Modells in pragmatische Variablen aus. Die Allgemeine Modelltheorie unterwirft jedes Modell über seinen bloßen Originalbezug hinaus dem Frageschema: Wer bildet das Modell und gegebenenfalls für wen? Für welche Zeitspanne repräsentiert das Modell sein Original? Und wozu, für welche Operationen unter welcher Zielfunktion wird das Modell gebildet? Operationalisierende Gegenstandsverfremdung jetzt auf der Metaebene unserer Analyse soll dem Gegenstand neue, bislang noch unerschlossene Information abgewinnen. Es wird sich erweisen, daß der Grenzfall der Kopierung des Originals durch das Modell nicht etwa die pragmatischen Modellvariablen funktionslos macht. Lassen Sie mich jetzt für unseren Modelltypus diese pragmatischen Variablen abchecken:

(1) Subjektivität und Benefiziarität. Eines der Basisthemen der Kulturmorphologie von Vico bis Frobenius und Toynbee ist die Sinndeutung von Geschichte und Kulturwachstum aus der Quelle des Mythos - dem Schellingschen Thema, von dem ich ausging, eng verwandt. Ursprünglich sehen wir den Menschen im Numinosen leben, wo das Göttliche in der Welt und die Welt im Göttlichen war. Diesem Monom folgte die zweite Epoche, in der Mensch und Natur, Seele und Leib auseinandertraten, dann eine dritte, in der der Mensch aufstieg zu dem abstrakten Gegensatz von Subjekt, das er selber ist, und Objekt, das die Außenwelt ist.[30] Etwa im Ausgang der ersten, auch „pneumatologisch" genannten Epoche würde ich mythologische Kultur ansiedeln. Das modellbildende Subjekt steht noch im ausgehenden Monom, hat den Weg in duale Weltverhältnisse noch kaum angetreten. Es erlebt die mythischen Zeichen des semantischen Raumes als Symptome einer Ordnung, die noch ein gesundes Ganzes ist, sich in totaler Homöostase befindet.

In einem Essay von 1983 skizziert Eugen Baer „Eine semiotische Geschichte der Symptomatologie".[31] Er charakterisiert darin „Das mythische Zeichen" als ein „totales" Zeichen, das gleichzeitig Symptom einer kultur- und lebensumfassenden Prosperität ist, aus der hinauszugeraten Krankwerden bedeutet, wobei dann individuelles Kranksein wieder aufs Ganze der Kultur wirkt. Das (modellbildende) Subjekt stand in seiner Zuständlichkeit des Gesundseins und Krankseins inmitten jener totalen Ordnung, die sich artikulierte aus Mythos − Stammeserzählungen, Helden- und Göttersagen bis schließlich hin zu den schon fast technischen Schilderungen Homers – und darin eingefügte rituale wie lebensweltliche Praxis. Die Symptome stimulierten unmittelbar die Therapie. Und vice versa, sagt Baer.[32] Denn das Symptom war bereits performative Aktion, auf Durchführung, Leistung, Vollzug angelegt. Es war pragmatisch im Sinne totalen Gedeihens der Kultur. Und des Vermeidens von – Angst in dieser Kultur.

So ist konkrete Subjektivität mythologisch-tautegorischer Modellbildung, wenn wir diesen Deutungen folgen, sinnvoll nur interpretierbar als Aufgehen des Subjekts in ein Anderes, als Teilnehmen, Platon spricht später in seiner artifiziellen Kulturtheorie von Teilhabe, wir sprechen heute (in einem allerdings weiterhin trivialisierenden Sinne) von Partizipation.

Die Frage nach der Benefiziarität mythologischer Modellbildung können wir schnell abhaken. Jeder in einer solchen Kultur ist bezüglich der gesamtkulturellen Wohlfahrt stellvertretend für jeden anderen da. Gerade Kultur in der Phase des Mythos ist Ausdruck des Beieinander und Miteinander.

(2) Zeitlichkeit. Modell wann? Wir heute können *bestimmen* (oder glauben, bestimmen zu können), *wann* etwas etwas anderes repräsentiert. Aber im Mythos gab es das, was ich Entscheidungsruhe nennen möchte, das Sich-Hingeben an einen als zeitlos empfundenen Geltungsanspruch[33]. Eine Zeitbestimmung der Originalrepräsentanz durch ein Modell ist unmythologisch.[34] Original und Modell sind untrennbar miteinander verbunden, das Modell taucht gleichzeitig oder mit unmerklicher Verzögerung zusammen mit seinem Original auf und ist dann von unbedingter und damit auch zeitunabhängiger Wertigkeit. Hiermit hängt zusammen, daß auch kultureller Wandel sich im Mythos bewußtlos vollzieht. Die ergodische[35] Entwicklung mythologischer Kultur ist ein „dumpfer" Prozeß. Dieser ist denkbar weit entfernt von dem, was wir (im Extrem bewußten gesamtgesellschaftlichen Tuns) „geplante Geschichte" nennen können.

(3) Intentionalität. Modell wozu? Ein operativer Modellbegriff schließt per Entscheidung gesetzte Zielfunktionen für die Modelloperationen ein. Das tautegorisch-mythologische Modell ist demgegenüber vom Ganzen der Kultur[36] her intentionalisiert, einer kollektiven Ordnung[37] eingefügt. In dieser Totalintention gehen Ansätze möglicher Partialintentionen unter. Sie werden in sie aufgehoben, wenngleich ohne derartige Partialität Kulturwandel kaum denkbar wäre, und solchen Wandel haben wir natürlich auch in den mythologischen Kulturen, lange vor dem Auftreten der Universalreligionen (dies gilt wenigstens für die heterogenen Hochkulturen, etwa Ägypten, in denen das Verhältnis von Mythos und sogenannter Realität komplexen Anpassungsprozessen unterworfen ist und Mythen Transformationen erfahren können).

Unbeschadet der *totalen* Intentionalität der modellbildenden Partizipation der Angehörigen der *homogenen* mythologischen Kulturen war diese eminent *praktisch*-zweckbestimmt. Wieder steht das Gesamtziel der Prosperität der Kultur voran, wo die Symptomatik des Mythischen als eine umfassende semiotische Ordnung für die Gesamtheit der individuellen Wohlfahrtsbedürfnisse die entscheidende Rolle spielt. Dem kulturellen Partizipanten wurde diese Ordnung in lebhaftester Weise durch die Medien ihrer so intentionalisierten Modelle fühlbar: das Hinaustreten aus der Ordnung wurde mit Krankheit und Leiden, auch mit dem Tode („Tabutod") bestraft, das ihr gemäße innere und äußere Verhalten, als Verhaltens*einheit*, mit Wohlbefinden belohnt.[38] Die von den Partizipanten der Kultur empfangenen symptomatisch-mythologischen Signalkonstellationen *taten*, *bewirkten* das, was sie bezeichneten, über die Medien der tautegorischen Modelle. Der Körper, sagt Baer, wurde so zu einer „Szene kosmischen Mysteriums".[39]

> Man ist vielleicht einen Augenblick lang geneigt, solches Ausgeliefertsein mit tierischer Instinktsteuerung über Schlüsselreiz und spannungsreduzierendem Response vergleichen zu wollen. Aber dies würde sowohl das sozial-institutionelle System menschlicher Kultur als auch deren geistig-numinoses Gefüge der inneren Daseinsermöglichung des Menschen in durchaus unzulässiger Weise ausklammern, von Sprache

als „condition humaine" zu schweigen. Mag der *ergische* Teil menschlicher Motivdynamik den Menschen ans Tierreich knüpfen, mit seinem *engrammischen* Teil ist er dem Animalischen bereits in frühester mythologischer Verfaßtheit zweifellos in einer Weise, die solche Vergleiche nicht mehr gestattet, vollständig entwachsen. Cassirer wies übrigens auf die „Paradoxie" hin, die er darin sah, daß sich der „Grundtrieb des Mythos", nämlich der Trieb „zur konkret-*anschaulichen* Erfassung und Darstellung aller Daseinselemente" gerade auf das „„Unwirklichste' und Lebloseste richtet: daß das Schattenreich der Worte, der Bilder und Zeichen eine solche substantielle Gewalt über das mythische Bewußtsein gewinnt". Den Grund hierfür sieht er darin, daß „das Dingmoment und das Bedeutungsmoment unterschiedslos ineinander aufgehen", das heißt in der Verschmelzung von Zeichenträger und Zeichenbedeutung, und er sieht in diesem „Vereinigungszwang" die „immanente Bedingung seiner künftigen Aufhebung", nämlich jenes „geistigen Befreiungsprozesses, der sich im Fortschritt von der Stufe der *magisch-mythischen* Weltansicht zur eigentlich *religiösen* Weltansicht tatsächlich vollzieht".[40]

Es wäre ein Thema für sich, und sicher ein höchst bedeutsames Thema, diese dann zunächst menschheitsentscheidende Ausdifferenzierung, die im engeren Sinne religiöse Abkopplung vom Mythischen, darzustellen und in den drei großen Verlaufsformen des Buddhismus, der jüdisch-christlich-islamischen Religionsgruppe und der innerweltlich-aufklärerischen Form der „Mythos-Überwindung" verstehend nachzuvollziehen. Immer ist es ein Hinaustreten aus „der Einheit in das Eine oder das Andere", wie Michael Theunissen sagt[41], und immer ist dieses Dualisieren bereits *krisis*, Krise der Prosperität der Kultureinheit, und auch wohl, wenn wir schon hier anachronistisch-vorgreifend diesen Begriff einbringen dürfen, „Krise der Macht"[42].

Die Betrachtung der Subjektivität, Zeitlichkeit und Intentionalität tautegorischer Modelle führt uns übereinstimmend immer wieder auf Vereinheitlichungen, Einheitsbildungen, und damit bestätigt sich natürlich Wohlbekanntes: die modellierenden Subjekte handeln einheitlich wie *ein* Subjekt, die Zeitspannen der Originalrepräsentation durch das Modell sind *einheitlich* zeitlicher Verfügbarkeit entzogen, die Modellintentionen, in ihrer Praxisrelevanz für jedes Mitglied der Kultur, sind zu *einer* Intention amalgamiert. Das kulturelle Universum verwirft gleichsam im Mythos die pragmatischen Differenzen, läßt individuelle Verfügbarkeit über die Form der Einbeziehung des Individuums in das verhaltensleitende Kultursystem, den Dupréschen „semantischen Raum", nicht zu. Die tautegorische Identifikation der semantischen Originale mit ihren in der individuellen Psyche aufgebauten Modellen steht mit der Kollektivierung der Belegungen der pragmatischen Modellvariablen in einem Verhältnis wechselseitig notwendigen Bedingens. Das heißt, erst aus der Lösung von der Tautegorie, erst im Übergang zur Allegorie und damit zur Analogie, entsteht Entscheidungsfähigkeit, Wahlfreiheit des Individuums gegenüber dem Verbundsystem von Symptomen und Therapieanweisungen der Kultur, entstehen Spielräume der Symptominterpretation und damit der Therapiewahl, verlieren die Zeichen ihre Totalität und ihre Zwanghaftigkeit, wird das Ich Herr im eigenen (allerdings erst noch zu errichtenden) Haus − mit allen Nöten und Nötigungen, die solches Herrsein mit sich bringt bis zur Descartesschen Idiolatrie des „cogito ergo sum". Solange aber Sehen und Sein *eines und dasselbe* waren, der Mensch im mythischen Zeichen Symptom *war* und es nicht etwa nur „hatte", solange er mit dem Sehen und Sagen eines Dinges zugleich dieses Ding *war*, haben wir den Fall eines, wie es die Allgemeine Modelltheorie nennt, original-äquaten Modells oder einer Kopierung des Originals, einer strukturellen und materialen Originalidentifikation. Eugen Baer führt übrigens die geheimnisvoll-kosmische Kraft der mythologischen Symptomatologie, wenn ich ihn richtig verstehe, auf eine Art holistischen Funktionierens des „semantischen Raumes", jetzt als Symptomraum verstanden, zurück: die Modell-Tautegorie würde paradoxerweise gerade durch die Polysemie der Symptome bewirkt, dies sei gewissermaßen der Kunstgriff der mythologischen Kultur, Weissagungen, Rituale, Trauminterpretationen usw. zu „versteinerten Konventionen" („fossilized conventions") und damit den einzelnen Menschen total manipulierbar zu machen − vielleicht ein wenig Orwells Big Brother vergleichbar.[43]

Soviel also hierzu. Viele Gedanken drängen sich auf. Zum Beispiel mag unser „Wahrheitssuchen" mit der tautegorischen Modellbildung im Mythos zusammenhängen. Schelling meinte ja, Philosophie als wahrheitsfähige Wissenschaft bis in jenen noch irgendwie hinter den monotheistischen Gottesbegriff zurückweisenden Urgrund der mythischen Einheit zurückführen zu sollen, derart, daß sich Philosophie auseinanderfalte aus dieser Einheit. Hegel sah es dann ganz anders, man könnte sagen: okzidenzialistisch, eurozentristisch, er bringt Philosophie mit Gesellschafts- und Staatsverfaßtheit in Verbindung: „In der Geschichte tritt die Philosophie da auf, wo freie Verfassungen existieren", lesen wir in „System und Geschichte der Philosophie"[44], und mit ihrem Aufstieg werde das Buch der wirklichen Welt geschrieben.[45] In Hegels rationalistischer Konstruktion, einem „Mythos aus der Retorte", manifestiert sich vielleicht, zumal wenn man die materialistische Uminterpretation dieses Modells gegenwärtigt, nach den beiden vorangegangenen Aufklärungen, der klassischen und derjenigen der sich im 17. Jahrhundert vollendenden europäischen Umschichtung, der dritte große Bruch des Menschen mit seiner mythischen Seinsverbundenheit, die für ihn *innere Daseinsermöglichung* bedeutete, mit der er hätte pfleglich umgehen sollen auch in den Stürmen der Bewußtwerdung seiner „Freiheit".

Auf Schellings Deutung der Philosophie zurückkommend, muß auch die Wissenschaftslehre des Aristoteles in neuem Licht erscheinen. Der Empirismus der Zweiten Analytiken gibt sich finitistisch, er ist in der Form logisch standardisiert, auf (apophantische) Aussagen beschränkt und enthält einige blasse methodologische Andeutungen (zum induktiven Vorgehen) − seine Nous-Verankerung jedoch reduziert ihn auf einen „formal stilisierten *Mythos*".[46] Der a-pragmatische Aspekt dieser Stilisierung zeigt sich darin, daß bei Aristoteles die mythologisch noch relevante inhaltliche Belegung der pragmatischen Modell-Variablen totaliter aufgehoben ist: das konkrete Subjekt wird zu einem nur noch formalen Subjekt *überhaupt*, es verschwindet vollständig aus dem Wissenschaftskonzept; die Geltungsdauer der Originalrepräsentation durch das Modell wird von einer konkreten Zeitspanne ins Zeitlos-Unendliche verlegt; die Zweckbindung des Modells und der Modelloperationen schließlich wird inhaltlich entleert auf absolute Zweckfreiheit. Diese formale Einebnung ist natürlich wohlzuunterscheiden von der Kollektivierung der pragmatischen Modellbestimmungen im Mythos. Was dort lebendiges, umfassendes Geschehen war, ist hier weitgehend nur lebloser Essentialismus[47], wobei sich die lebendige Prosperität der Kultur des Mythos bei Aristoteles „vereinfacht" zu einer nouetischen Intuition als erkenntnisentscheidendes „Prinzip aller Prinzipien", *dem* „Prinzip der Wissenschaft", wie uns Aristoteles belehrt, ohne diese rätselhafte Begründungsinstanz auch nur im geringsten aufhellen zu können.

Natürlich sage ich dies nicht in tadelnder Absicht. Es geht mir hier nur darum, die spezifische Transformation deutlich zu machen, die der Mythos (schon bei Homer bis ins Ironische „säkularisiert") nach der bunten Zeit der Sophisten, die ja auch einen Pragmatiker Protagoras kannte, in der attischen Spätblüte erfuhr, die Transformation in einen, sagen wir ruhig: „Wissenschaftsmythos", der erst heute, in der rezenten Epistemologie, pragmatisch reflektiert wird. Die ambivalenten Folgen dieses um die pragmatische Dimension der Erkenntnis verkürzten „Wissenschaftsmythos" sind in unserer Zeit unübersehbar geworden.

Auf die hiermit verbundene Frage, inwieweit wir bei dem Eintritt in das Reich der Freiheit das Logos-Prinzip überstrapaziert haben könnten, komme ich im dritten und letzten Teil meiner Ausführungen zurück. Hier sei vielleicht noch die Frage kurz angerührt, inwieweit wir *außerhalb* des Mythischen tautegorische Modellbildungen antreffen. Ich nehme an, in Phantasie- und Traumwelten, in denen Bedeutungsunterschiede, „ohne reaktives Verwundern" des Phantasierenden oder Träumenden, miteinander verschmelzen, sich zu Erlebniseinheiten verdichten − wahrscheinlich ohne sinnstiftende Elemente mythologischer Identifikation. Die Psychoanalyse, insbesondere psychoanalytische Traumforschung, hat z.B. das Träumen und Denken des Kindes mit dem des sogenannten Primitiven verglichen und gerade die modellierenden Identifikationsakte untersucht. Auch dichterische Phantasie mag mit Tautegorie zu tun haben. Vielleicht ist es nicht unsinnig, ein Forschungsprogramm dieses gesamten Fragenkreises zu empfehlen, in das sehr unterschiedliche Disziplinen und nicht nur die Philosophie Analysemethoden einbringen könnten. Ich für meine Person möchte hier ein starkes Informationsbedürfnis anmelden.

Entmythologisierung, später überhaupt auf Entzauberung der Welt zielend, um Max Webers Wendung wieder einmal zu strapazieren, ist Befreiung von Fesseln, die selbst zur Fessel wird. Bewußte Distinktion des Modells von seinem Original erscheint als Sündenfall. Was aus dem grenzenlosen Ganzen, dem Apeiron, hinaustritt, habe dafür Buße zu leisten, sagt Anaximander. Dem Menschen, der sich über sein Seinsganzes erhoben hat, um es zu verlassen und zu vergessen, mag sogar grausame Strafe drohen. Versuchen wir, einige der Hauptstationen des Weges jener Seinsvergessenheit in der Entfaltung von Logos und Ratio zu erinnern.

Es kann nicht verwundern, daß nach der ersten Aufklärung, der griechischen, die in der attischen Periode kulminiert, ein Totalitätsdenken, wie es im Mythos seine Wurzeln hatte, erst wieder, und zwar in enger Verbindung mit dem Christentum, in der Gnostik, im Neupythagoreismus und Neuplatonismus aufleuchtet. Das neue rationalistische Element ist unverkennbar etwa in Plotins Seinslehre mit den von einer Mitte, die Gott ist, ausgehenden Emanationsstufen.[48] Charakteristisch auch das rationalisierende Modell des Augustinus, der drei Seinsbereiche unterscheidet, das Draußen, den inneren Menschen und die Wahrheitssphäre, zu der die vernunfttätige Seele aus ihrer liebenden Beziehung zu dem personalen Gott transzendiert[49]. Einen Höhepunkt theistischer Philosophie finden wir in Avicennas Erklärungsmodell mythologisch-religiöser Gotteserkenntnis. Ausgehend von der islamischen Mystik der Seelenabspaltung entwirft er ein Modell der Dynamik von Emanation und Reversion, letztere vollzogen in asketisch-kontemplativer Lebensführung.

Mittelalterliche Mystik, im Mönchstum entstanden, häufig auch von Frauen getragen, betont mehr das Ekstatisch-Asketische, sucht Versenkung und Aufgehen in Gott − Tauler spricht direkt von der „Vergottung" im mystischen Erleben[50]. Christliche Mystik ist wohl auch als Gegenbewegung gegen intellektualisierende Theologie zu verstehen, vielleicht als ein Strebensmodus (neben dem wahrheitsphilosophischen) zurück in die Einheit des Mythischen.

Dies alles bleibt im Theologischen. Aber das Mittelalter ist ja auch die Epoche des Umbruchs, nicht nur im Sinne gesellschaftlichen Wandels, sondern auch des Wandels im philosophischen Denken. Im 13. Jahrhundert kommen empiristische Strömungen auf, der Universalienrealismus wird brüchig, alles bereitet sich auf dasjenige vor, was Panajotis Kondylis in seinem großen Aufklärungsbuch[51] dann die „Rehabilitation der Sinnlichkeit" nennt − Empirismus und Rationalismus treiben die Ich-Abspaltung vom ursprünglich mythischen Ganzen um ein jähes, großes Stück voran. Das mathematische Zeitalter kommt auf, das Zeitalter der mathematischen Modellbildungen über die paßgerecht zerschnittene Wirklichkeit, die zwar beobachtet, zuvor aber „zurechtgemacht" wird − im Hintergrund steht, zunächst noch weitgehend unbewußt, der Verfügbarkeitsgedanke. Dies schlägt auch auf Religion und Kunst über. Cusanus entwirft eine zwar auf höchste Gottesverehrung angelegte, nichtsdestoweniger menschzentrierte mathematische Theologie. Dürers Zentralperspektive ist extreme Abgrenzung des Einzel-Ichs von der Welt: auf den Fluchtpunkt ist alles hingeordnet, ihm ist alles nachgeordnet. Im Humanismus wird die Willensfreiheit nun endgültig begründet. Reformation. Neuzeitliche Naturwissenschaft, Beginn der Naturbeherrschung. Grundlegung einer neuen Mathematik, die gleichzeitig in einem Mathesis-universalis-Anspruch aufgeht. Und dann die Einmündung in Kant und die Folgen. Das sind immer neue Höhepunkte des dissezierenden, atomisierenden, das Ich, die vielen Einzel-Iche vom Ganzen abtrennenden Denkens − gegen das sich allerdings schon seit Beginn der Neuzeit zunehmend Gegenbewegungen aufrechnen lassen. Ich meine Bruno, Spinoza (die more-geometrico-Form ist seiner monistischen Philosophie im Grunde nur äußerliches Zugeständnis an eine Modeströmung seiner Zeit), den sogenannten deutschen Idealismus − auch Goethe, der das Wahre dem Göttlichen gleichsetzte, gehört zu den Antagonisten des sich etablierenden Paradigmas. Im ganzen aber geht die Separierung und Positivierung des Denkens und des diesem Denken folgenden Tuns weiter den nun einmal begonnenen Weg.

Allerdings, wer sensibel genug ist, dies zu sehen, für den beginnt sich dieser Weg *heute* in eigenartiger Vielfältigkeit aufzugabeln, und einige seiner Fortsetzungen weisen irgendwie zurück in die Herkunftsrichtung, den Ausgangspunkt solcher Welt- und Denkentfaltung, die, wer will es leugnen, im Monströsen endete. Ja, es scheint, als bäume sich ein System, ich sage einmal in durchaus ontologisierender Absicht: ein holistisches System, *dem auch das erkennende Subjekt voll integriert ist* − als bäume sich dieses System gegen sein Zerschnittenwerden auf, gegen seine Vivisektion, als würde es nun einer tiefen gesamtsystemischen Existenznot folgend, seine Widersacher und seine Alternativen aus sich selbst gebären. Die Frühromantik kannte den Begriff des „Symphilosophierens": wirkliche Systemphilosophie mit einem, wir sagen heute, Forschungsprogramm, hier erwachsen aus dem Motiv der Menschenliebe, sollte die philosophischen Einzeldisziplinen übergreifen (ich denke hier wieder an Whites „Reunion in Philosophy"[52]) und reintegrieren. Sollte dies ein Konzept sein, das wert ist, neu durchdacht zu werden? Doch weiter in der Alternativen-Übersicht. Hier sind unter anderen sicherlich zu nennen: Schopenhauer und Nietzsche, ich meine auch: Eduard von Hartmann; in neuerer Zeit etwa Jaspers, der in seiner „Psychologie der Weltanschauungen" auch jene Denkebene, die an das Mythische und Heilige anknüpft und die er selbst ja wesentlich mitgestaltete, aus neuer Erfahrung zu reflektieren sucht. Das sind nur einige aus einer natürlich sehr viel größeren Zahl[53], und wir wissen, daß heute die Thematik „alternativen" Denkens zusammen nicht selten mit der Thematik von Mythos und Mythologie nicht nur in philosophischen Seminaren zunehmend Raum gewinnt.

> Nebenher: Ist nicht das Zustandekommen politischer Identität, *Nation* genannt, nach einer langen Phase, in der in Europa die von Papsttum und Kaisertum getragene Reichsidee herrschte, als eine wenn auch vielleicht nur „imitative" Rückkehr in jene sozialkulturelle Geborgenheit zu begreifen, die an kulturelle Einheit im Mythos denken läßt? Sind nicht vielleicht die bürgerlichen Revolutionen in England und Frankreich, die den Nationalstaatsgedanken hervorriefen, zu werten als Symptome der Rückkehrtendenzen heterogenisierter Gesellschaften in „vorstaatliche" Kulturkörper mit ihren gleichsam natürlichen, werthomogenen Lebensordnungen, die auch in die Bereiche von Wirtschaft und institutioneller Daseinssicherungen ausstrahlen? Das Recht auf nationale Selbstbestimmung[54] − hat es nicht letztlich sein historisches und politisch-ethisches Fundament in einem Symbolsystem, das den Massen „das Gefühl des ‚Zu-Hause-Seins‘ im eigenen Land" vermitteln kann, jenseits aller Klassenschranken?[55] Aber wie könnten solche Einheiten heute noch nebeneinander Platz auf dieser Erde haben, ohne in Aporien gegenüber menschen- und völkerrechtlichen Forderungen zu geraten? Wie wären sie supranational zur „Überlebensgemeinschaft" zu integrieren auf der Grundlage von „Selbstbehauptung und Anerkennung" in einer *globalen* Wirklichkeit der Idee der Nation", wie es Bernhard Willms fordert?[56] Ich stelle Fragen, ohne auch nur das Wagnis, sie zu beantworten, sinnvoll erwägen zu können. Vielleicht hat diese Welt die Reife einer alsbald sich vom Baum lösenden Frucht erreicht.

Einbrüche in den dominanten Rationalismus und Empirismus gibt es, wie ich hier nicht zu begründen brauche, auch in der Epistemologie. Dies beginnt schon im Konventionalismus der letzten Jahrhundertwende, bei Duhem vor allem, der zwischen zeitgemäßem Ökonomismus und unzeitgemäßem diachronisch-ganzheitlichem Denken schwankte; eine hauptsächlich über Quine führende Linie betont mehr und mehr das dynamisch-holistische Moment von Theorien- und Wissenschaftsentwicklung. Es kommt hinzu die fortschreitende rezente Historisierung von Epistemik und Epistemologie in Verbindung mit der im ganzen zweifellos fruchtbaren Kuhn-Feyerabend-Diskussion. Auch im Pragmatismus und in der Semiotik waren und sind weiterhin Züge einer Philosophie, ich möchte sagen: systemsymptomatologisch sichtbar geworden, die darauf verweisen, daß Trennungen aufgehoben, ganzheitliche Zusammenhänge zurückgeholt werden. Vielleicht sollte ich auch an die Wissenssoziologie erinnern, die in ihrer wenn auch einseitigen Art Erkenntnis umfassenderen Zusammenhängen einfügt, und erinnern auch an die Kybernetikbewegung in ihrer eigenartigen Gespaltenheit von Funktionalität und Nutzendenken einerseits, Systemdenken und einer für diese Bewegung charakteristischen Verbindung formativer, deskriptiver und normativer Elemente andererseits. Den Neopragmatismus unserer Tage, zumal in seiner systematisierten Form, thematisieren, hieße, in einen neuen Problemkreis eintreten. Dies muß ich hier zurückstellen. Rorty schließlich repräsentiert vielleicht den vorläufigen Endpunkt einer der „hermeneutisch überzogenen"

Fortsetzungslinien der gegenwärtigen pragmatischen Bewegung. Seine Gesprächs- und Bildungsphilosophie kann nur billigen, wen das Schicksal dieser Menschheitskultur[57] nichts mehr angeht.

Ist also mythisch-mythologische Welt- und Lebensorientierung gegenwärtig wieder im Kommen? Diese Frage sei zur Diskussion gestellt. Karl Acham hat im vergangenen Jahr eine bemerkenswerte Aktualität und Virulenz des Mythischen registriert, und wir alle kennen die vielfältigen obskuren Erscheinungsformen eines neuen Dranges besonders auch Jugendlicher zum Außeralltäglichen: Sektenkollektivismus, Rausch, Drogen, orgiastische Erlebnisformen unter Auslöschung der Modell-Original-Distanz, mit wortwörtlich leidenschaftlichem Bemühen, Gegenstands- und Selbstreflexion auszuschalten. Auch ziellose Apathie der Menschen unserer „Kultur" sowie die anachronistische Wiederbelebung irrationaler magisch-mythischer Rituale in entkolonialisierten Teilen der Welt gehören in diesen Formenkreis. Nun, wie dies zusammenstimmt in unserer Zeit, in der die „Aufklärung der Aufklärung" zu teils heilsamen, teils pathologischen und gefährlichen Entwicklungen geführt hat, wird wohl erst spätere kritische Kulturgeschichte überblicken können. Die Philosophie unserer Tage kann jedoch theoretisch wie hoffentlich auch praktisch dazu beitragen, den Blick für das Angemessene und Hilfreiche freizumachen, und sie sollte dies ohne Abstriche an die Forderung tun, Exaktheit der Analysen mit Ganzheitlichkeit der Gegenstandserfassung zu verbinden. An dieses, wie mir scheint, sehr zeitgemäße Anliegen mit meinem bescheidenen Beitrag zu erinnern, war der Sinn der Ausführungen, die Sie mit freundlicher Geduld für gut eine halbe Stunde über sich haben ergehen lassen.

Ich möchte diesen kleinen Versuch hier Wilhelm Dupré widmen als Dank für die von ihm erhaltenen Anregungen, ohne die ich mich, zumindest in dieser Form, kaum mit dem Problem der tautegorischen Modelle der Mythologie beschäftigt hätte.

ANMERKUNGEN

[1] Schelling, F. W. J., 1973 (1856), p. 196. Vgl. daselbst Schellings Anmerkung zur Erstverwendung des Ausdrucks „tautegorisch" durch Samuel Taylor Coleridge.
[2] A. a. O. (Anm. 1).
[3] Stachowiak, H., 1973.
[4] Zu den AMT-Termini vgl. H. Stachowiak 1973, p. 131−159, 304−333.
[5] Nestle, W., 1966, p. 9.
[6] Vgl. dazu K.-H. Volkmann-Schluck 1969.
[7] Schelling, F. W. J., 1861, Bd. X, p. 97.
[8] Rekonstruktion ist Explikation unter Einschluß von Überlegungen, die Ähnlichkeitsabbildung des Explikandums in das Explikat einer Zielfunktion zu unterwerfen.
[9] Stachowiak, H., 1973, p. 199−201.
[10] Dupré, W., (im Druck).
[11] Vgl. E. Leinfellner und W. Leinfellner 1978, p. 64−91 (im Druck). Siehe auch den Beitrag von E. Leinfellner in diesem Band.
[12] Hier der Hinweis etwa auf die von H. Delius betreute Aufsatzsammlung G. E. Moore 1969; die von G. Patzig betreute Aufsatzsammlung G. Frege 1962; W. V. Quine 1950; H. Putnam 1979; dazu die wohl „pragmatisch" zu nennende Bedeutungstheorie von D. Davidson 1980.
[13] Zu diesem AMT-Terminus vgl. H. Stachowiak 1973, p. 320ff.
[14] Hierzu die ausgezeichnete Analyse in H. Lauener 1982. Siehe auch den Beitrag von H. Lauener in diesem Band.
[15] Vgl. M. White 1956, 1981.
[16] Heidegger, M., 1943.
[17] Heidegger, M., 1943, p. 13.
[18] Das hier Angedeutete hat in vorzüglicher Exegese mit Bezug auf Heideggers Technikphilosophie H. Sachsse 1974 dargestellt.
[19] Erste Verlautbarung auf dem Third Intern. Congr. of Logic, Methodology and Philosophy of Science, Amsterdam, August 1967.

[20] Hierzu die allerdings etwas kurzgreifende Kritik an der Dreiweltentheorie Poppers durch M. Bunge 1981, insb. p. 155ff. Popper selbst äußert sich zu diesem Punkte nicht in der wünschenswerten Klarheit. Vgl. Anm. (!) 8, p. 179, in K. R. Popper 1973.

[21] Vgl. W. Dupré 1982, p. 361f.

[22] Vgl. die in W. Burkert 1979 angeführten Beispiele.

[23] Cassirer, E., 1964 (1929), p. 72, et passim. Vgl. auch E. Cassirer 1956 (1921–1938), p. 9–25

[24] Vgl. E. Cassirer 1958 (1923), p. 8, et passim. Hierzu auch P. Verene 1982, p. 3ff.

[25] Vgl. P. Verene 1982 in Verbindung mit P. Verene 1981.

[26] Über attributive Klassen und Systeme vgl. H. Stachowiak 1973, p. 134–138, (prädikativ:) p. 305–312.

[27] Vgl. A. Kaufmann 1975.

[28] Vgl. z.B. R. Gunzenhäuser 1975, p. 124–134.

[29] In der modelltheoretischen Mythos-Analyse wären über das Sprachlich-Erzählerische hinaus gewiß auch räumlich-graphiche Äußerungen einzubeziehen, wozu bereits Ernst Cassirer in seiner „Formenlehre des Mythos" den Grund gelegt hat; vgl. E. Cassirer 1958 (1923), p. 93–128. Speziell symbolische Konfigurationen im Mythos (Figuren, „abstrakte" kultische Steingraphiken, Masken usw.) wären als mediale Modelle *zwischen* der Originalwelt, die sie repräsentieren, und den Wahrnehmungsbildern, die sie bei den Partizipanten der Kultur hervorrufen, zu untersuchen unter Herausarbeitung ihrer jeweiligen Präteritions-, Kontrastierungs- und Abundanzcharakteristik sowie der Belegungscharakteristiken für die Variablen der pragmatischen Modell-Einbettung. Zu den angedeuteten Begriffen vgl. wiederum H. Stachowiak 1973.

[30] Vgl. R. Steiner 1981 (1922), p. 36, dem ich hier nicht nur in dieser Dreiphasenunterscheidung, sondern auch in manchen seiner kraftvollen Assoziationen folgen möchte, ohne daß ich seiner mystischen Theosophie Raum gebe.

[31] Baer, E., 1983.

[32] Baer, E., 1983, p. 51.

[33] Vgl. E. Cassirer 1958 (1923), der hervorhebt, daß für die Zeitbetrachtung im Mythus „eine *absolute* Vergangenheit besteht, die als solche der weitergehenden Erklärung weder fähig noch bedürftig ist" (daselbst, p. 131).

[34] Ansätze einer Theorie des mythischen Zeitbegriffs bei E. Cassirer 1958 (1923), p. 129–169.

[35] „Ergodisch" entwickelt sich ein System, wenn es im Verlauf dieser Entwicklung von seinem Anfangszustand unabhängig wird. Zur ergodischen Entwicklung und „Selbststeuerung" von Systemen (beliebiger Art) vgl. O. Lange 1969, insbes. p. 62ff.

[36] Oder einer „mythologisch homogenen" kulturellen Einheit. In segmentären Gesellschaften z.B. können Clans je eigene Mythen oder Mythenauslegungen „haben". Das zur Modell-Intentionalität Gesagte bezieht sich dann ohne besondere Erwähnung im Text auf solche homogenen Populationen. Vgl. J. Stagl 1974.

[37] Vgl. F. Schupp 1979, p. 64, der von einer „kollektiven Axiologie" spricht.

[38] Vgl. E. Baer 1983, p. 52.

[39] Baer, E., 1983, p. 52.

[40] Cassirer, E., 1958 (1923), p. 31f.

[41] Theunissen, M., 1975.

[42] Vgl. K. Röttgers 1983, p. 52.

[43] Vgl. E. Baer 1983, p. 52f.

[44] Vgl. G. W. F. Hegel 1940, p. 227.

[45] Zum Hegel-Schelling-Verhältnis vgl. C. Cesa (im Druck).

[46] Vgl. H. Stachowiak 1971, p. 272–308. Zur Geschichte des vorsokratischen Nous-Begriffes mit besonderem Bezug auf Homer vgl. K. von Fritz 1968.

[47] Zum Aristotelischen Essentialismus vgl. E. Martens (im Druck).

[48] Zum Neuplatonismus und zur Platonrezeption durch die Väter vgl. E. von Ivánka 1964.

[49] Vgl. F. Körner (im Druck).

[50] Tauler, J., 1968, p. 162. 8ff. Ich danke diesen Hinweis U. Köpf, München.

[51] Kondylis, P., 1981.

[52] White, M., 1956.

[53] Aus der Gruppe der Gegenwartsphilosophen, die sich einen „exakten Beziehungsholismus" des Gesellschaftlichen unter den Bedingungen unserer Zeit zum Gegenstand gemacht haben, sei hier Dieter Suhr genannt, vgl. z.B. D. Suhr 1977.

[54] Hierzu zahlreiche Arbeiten Bernhard Willms', z.B. B. Willms 1983.

[55] Die zuletzt zitierte Stelle findet sich in R. Bendix 1982, p. 113. Nach Bendix hat Marx die nationalistische Idee und das Bedürfnis auch der „Unterprivilegierten" nach symbolhaft-emotionaler „Statussicherheit" innerhalb gewachsener soziokultureller Systeme fehleingeschätzt – ich würde eher sagen: ideologisch verdrängt oder bewußt heruntergespielt, um sich den Weg für die Durchsetzung *seines* Gesellschaftsmodells freizumachen.

[56] Willms, B., 1983, p. 517f. Zum Problem der Nationenbildung sowie kritisch zum Nationalstaatsgedanken K. W. Deutsch 1972.

[57] Deren Theorie – affirmativ – Arnold Gehlen geschrieben hat.

LITERATUR

Baer, E., „A Semiotic History of Symptomatology", in Eschbach, A., Trabant, J. (Ed.), *History of Semiotics* (Amsterdam − Philadelphia 1983), S. 41−66.

Bendix, R., *Freiheit und historisches Schicksal*. Heidelberger Max Weber-Vorlesungen (Frankfurt a. M. 1982).

Bunge, M., *Scientific Materialism* (Dordrecht, Holland − Boston − London, England 1981).

Burkert, W., „Mythisches Denken", in Poser, H. (Hrsg.), *Philosophie und Mythos*. Ein Kolloquium (Berlin − New York 1979), S. 16−39.

Cassirer, E., *Wesen und Wirken des Symbolbegriffs* (unveränd. Nachdr. von 4 Originalarb. 1921−1938) (Darmstadt 1956).

Cassirer, E., *Philosophie der symbolischen Formen*. Zweiter Teil: *Das mythische Denken* (unveränd. Nachdr. d. 2. Aufl. v. 1923) (Darmstadt 1958).

Cesa, C., „System und Geschichte im Spannungsfeld zwischen Schelling und Hegel", in H. Stachowiak (Hrsg.) (im Druck).

Davidson, D., „Toward a Unified Theory of Meaning and Action", *Grazer Philosophische Studien* 11 (1980), S. 1−12.

Deutsch, K. W., *Nationenbildung − Nationalstaat − Integration* (Düsseldorf 1972).

Dupré, W., „Tradition und Aneignung", in Nagl-Docekal, H. (Hrsg.), *Überlieferung und Aufgabe*. Festschrift für Erich Heintel zum 70. Geburtstag, 2. Teilband (Wien 1982), S. 355−372.

Dupré, W., „Das Pragma in schriftlosen Kulturen", in Stachowiak, H. (Hrsg.) (im Druck).

Frege, G., *Funktion, Begriff, Bedeutung*. Fünf logische Studien, Hrsg. u. eingel. v. G. Patzig (Göttingen 1962).

Fritz, K. von, „Die Rolle des ΝΟΥΣ", in Gadamer, H. (Hrsg.), *Um die Begriffswelt der Vorsokratiker* (Darmstadt 1968), S. 246−363.

Gunzenhäuser, R., *Maß und Information als ästhetische Kategorien*. Einführung in die ästhetische Theorie G. D. Birkhoffs und die Informationsästhetik (Baden-Baden [2]1975).

Hegel, G. W. F.,*System und Geschichte der Philosophie*. Hrsg. v. J. Hoffmeister (Hamburg 1940).

Heidegger, M., *Was ist Metaphysik?* (Frankfurt a. M. 1943).

Ivánka, E. von, *Plato Christianus*. Übernahme und Umgestaltung des Platonismus durch die Väter (Einsiedeln 1964).

Kaufmann, A., *Introduction to the Theory of Fuzzy Subsets* (New York, N.Y. − San Francisco, Cal. − London 1975).

Kondylis, P., *Die Aufklärung im Rahmen des neuzeitlichen Rationalismus* (Stuttgart 1981).

Körner, F., „Existentielle Pragmatik aus transzendentaler Immanenz als innere Tragkraft letzter Wahrheitssuche am geistesgeschichtlichen Beginn abendländischen Rationalismus", in Stachowiak, H. (Hrsg.) (im Druck).

Lange, O., *Ganzheit und Entwicklung in kybernetischer Sicht* (aus d. Poln.) (Berlin 1969).

Lauener, H., *Willard V. Quine* (München 1982).

Leinfellner, E., Leinfellner, W., *Ontologie, Systemtheorie und Semantik* (Berlin 1978).

Leinfellner, E., Leinfellner, W., „Ockhams Semantik und Pragmatik", in Stachowiak, H. (Hrsg.) (im Druck).

Martens, E., „Platonischer Pragmatismus und Aristotelischer Essentialismus", in Stachowiak, H. (Hrsg.) (im Druck).

Moore, G. E., *Eine Verteidigung des Common Sense*. Fünf Aufsätze (aus d. Engl.). Eingel. v. H. Delius (Frankfurt a. M. 1969).

Nestle, W., *Vom Mythos zum Logos*. Die Selbstentfaltung des griechischen Denkens von Homer bis auf die Sophistik und Sokrates (Aalen 1966).

Popper, K. R., *Objektive Erkenntnis*. Ein evolutionärer Entwurf (aus d. Engl.) (Hamburg 1973).

Putnam, H., *Die Bedeutung von „Bedeutung"* (aus d. Amer.). Hrsg. u. Übers. v. W. Spohn (Frankfurt a. M. 1979).

Quine, W. V., *Methods of Logic* (New York, N. Y. 1950).

Röttgers, K., *Texte und Menschen* (Würzburg 1983).

Sachsse, H., „Was ist Metaphysik? Überlegungen zur Freiburger Antrittsvorlesung von Martin Heidegger und ein Exkurs über seine Frage nach der Technik", *Zs. f. Philos. Forschung* 28.1 (1974), S. 67−93.

Schelling, F. W. J., *Sämtliche Werke* (14 Bde.) (Stuttgart − Augsburg 1856−1861).

Schelling, F. W. J., *Philosophie der Mythologie* Bd. I: *Einleitung in die Philosophie der Mythologie* (unveränd. Nachdr. d. v. K. F. A. Schelling aus d. Nachlaß hrsg. Ausg. v. 1856) (Darmstadt 1973).

Schupp F., „Mythos und Religion: der Spielraum der Ordnung", in Poser, H. (Hrsg.), *Philosophie im Mythos*. Ein Kolloquium (Berlin − New York 1979), S. 59−74.

Stachowiak, H., *Allgemeine Modelltheorie* (Wien − New York 1973).

Stachowiak, H., (Hrsg.), *Pragmatik*, Bd. I: *Pragmatisches Denken von den Ursprüngen bis zum 18. Jahrhundert* (Hamburg (im Druck)).

Stagl, J., *Die Morphologie segmentärer Gesellschaften*, Dargestellt am Beispiel des Hochlandes von Neuguinea (Meisenheim am Glan 1974).

Steiner, R., *Der Entstehungsmoment der Naturwissenschaft in der Weltgeschichte* (Vortragskurs, geh. in Dornach 1922/23) (Dornach 1981).

Suhr, D., *Die kognitiv-praktische Situation*. Fundamentierungsprobleme in praktischer Philosophie, Sozialtechnik und Jurisprudenz (Berlin 1977).

Tauler, J., *Die Predigten Taulers*. Hrsg. v. F. Vetter (= Deutsche Texte des Mittelalters 11). Nachdr. (Dublin – Zürich 1968).

Theunissen, M., „Krise der Macht", in: *Referate des X. Internat. Hegel-Kongresses in Moskau* (Köln 1975 (Hegel-Jahrb. 1974)), S. 318–329.

Verene, P., *Vicos Science of Imagination* (Ithaca, N. Y. 1981).

Verene, P., „Cassirer's Philosophy of Culture", *Intern. Philos. Qu.* 22 (1982), S. 133–144.

Volkmann-Schluck, K.-H., *Mythos und Logos*. Interpretationen zu Schellings Philosophie der Mythologie (Berlin 1969).

White, M., *Toward Reunion in Philosophy* (Cambridge, Mass. 1956).

White, M., *What Is and What Ought To Be Done* (New York, N. Y. – Oxford 1981).

Willms, B., „Weltbürgerkrieg und Nationalstaat. Thomas Hobbes, Friedrich Meinecke und die Möglichkeit der Geschichtsphilosophie im 20. Jahrhundert", *Der Staat* 4 (1983), S. 499–519.

* * *

A LOGICAL CHARACTERIZATION OF THE PSYCHOLOGICAL

Roderick M. Chisholm
Brown University, Providence, R. I.

Introduction

If we are going to talk about the philosophy of mind and the "mind-body problem," we should have a way of characterizing the psychological *logically* and without making use of any psychological concepts.[1]

I will assume that, for each of us, there is a set of psychological properties which are such that we can know directly and immediately that we have those properties. And I will also assume that we can reflect upon these properties and in so doing come to know something about their general structure. Thus I now know directly and immediately such things as these: I hope we will have a useful discussion; I look forward to walking in the hills; I believe I have been here before; I seem to see something red.

If I may speak in the manner of G. E. Moore, I would also say, not only that it is evident to me that I have such properties, but also that it is evident to you that you have such properties. I know, of course, that today there are many philosophers who deny these things. But their denial, in every case, is based upon data far less obvious than the facts they profess to deny.

The properties I am concerned with, then, are properties that we might call "Cartesian" —such properties as: thinking; wishing; desiring; believing; sensing. The properties are *psychological* in that, if you know of a person that he has such a property, then you know something that relates him to the property of thinking.

All the properties I have referred to are *purely* psychological—they tell us *only* about thinking. They tell us nothing about the person's bodily state, nothing about his past, nothing about his future, and nothing about any other individual.

Some Methodological Comments

I have said that psychological properties are properties to which we have a certain privileged access. But I do not intend to *define* the psychological this way, since privileged access is itself a psychological concept.

In proposing a *logical* characterization of such properties, I will make use of the following undefined concepts: that of *exemplification*, as in "x exemplifies y"; that of *de re necessity*, as in "x is necessarily such that it exemplifies y"; that of an *individual thing*, and those of possibility, potentiality and disposition. I will sometimes use "has" as short for "exemplifies"; and I will use "x is possibly such that it is so-and-so" and "x can be so-and-so" as short for "x is not necessarily such that it is not so-and-so." And I will rely upon distinctions of *tense*.

I will now make explicit certain metaphysical assumptions. (1) One is that everything is necessarily such that it undergoes change. This is the assumption that is sometimes put by saying "everything is necessarily in time." (2) Another assumption is that it is logically possible that there is only one individual thing. One might put this by saying "there is a logically possible world in which there is only one individual thing." There may well be reasons for supposing that, if there are individual things, then there are many of them. But it is at least *logically* possible that there is only one. (3) I will also make a mereological assumption—an assumption about wholes and parts. It is this: for any two individuals that have no parts in common, there is another thing that has those two individuals as proper parts. Making this assumption is tantamount to countenancing the being of scattered objects and other "mere aggregates." (4) The final metaphysical assumption is that of extreme realism—Platonism, in the contemporary sense of that word.

My general strategy is as follows. I will begin with some examples of purely psychological properties. I will single out certain logical features that are common and peculiar to our examples. These features will enable us to define the concept of *that which is purely psychological*. We may then define *the psychological* as that which includes the purely psychological.

When we do philosophy, we have to begin somewhere. Perhaps you don't begin at the same place that I do. But this does not mean that one of us is wrong. If we are philosophically sophisticated, we will know that the important thing is to be clear about what it is that one assumes at the outset and about what follows from these assumptions.

Changeable Properties of Individuals

It will be useful to take the term "property" in a somewhat restricted sense.

> D1 P is a property =Df P is possibly such that there is something that exemplifies it

This definition, like those that follow, is in the present tense. I will assume that the past and future versions of these definitions are obvious.

Among properties, in the present sense of the word, are: being green; being heavy; being a table; being a horse; being a unicorn; being round; being square. But, although being round and being square are properties, in our present sense, being round *and* square is not a property. (If you wish to call *being a round square* a property, then you should replace "property" in my definition by some other word—say "attribute" or "determination.")

Let us now introduce the concept, *being a changeable property of an individual*. This concept will give us our first mark of the purely psychological.

Perhaps it is uncontroversial that purely psychological properties (feeling sad, hoping for rain, believing that all men are mortal . . .) are "changeable properties of individuals" in the following sense:

> D2 P is a changeable property of individuals =Df P is necessarily such that only individuals have it; P is possibly such that many individuals have it; and whatever can have P can also cease to have it and then have it again, any number of times

(I would remind you that the possibility and necessity of which we here speak are *logical possibility* and *logical necessity*.)

Thinking is a changeable property of individuals, but *being extended* is not. And, although thinking is a changeable property of individuals, the property of *having thought* is not; once you take it on, you will have it as long as you exist. And the property of *being such that one is going to think* is not a changeable property; once you lose it, you can never take it on again.

Here, then, is the first of our three marks of the purely psychological. A purely psychological property is a changeable property of individuals.

Internal Properties

The second mark of the purely psychological is this: Every purely psychological property is *internal*. What may be new, I think, is that this is a *logical* characterization of internality—a characterization which does not make use of metaphors and one which does not appeal to "privileged access" or to "inner perception."

Let us begin by singling out a certain logical relation that may hold between properties. I will call this relation—somewhat arbitrarily—the relation of property *inclusion* and define it as follows:

157

D3 P includes Q =Df P is necessarily such that, for every x, if x exemplifies P, then
x exemplifies Q

The property *walking* includes the property *having limbs*. And the property *walking swiftly* includes the property *walking*. But since our definitions are in the present tense, we cannot say that the properties of *having walked* and of *being such as to be going to walk* include the property *walking*. For a thing that is not walking may yet be such that it did walk or it is going to walk.

The properties of *having walked* and of *being such as to be going to walk* may be said to *project* the property of *walking*. The relevant sense of "project" is this:

D4 P projects Q =Df P is necessarily such that, if it is exemplified, then either (a) Q
is exemplified or (b) Q was exemplified or (c) Q will be exemplified

The property of being a bride-to-be projects the property of being a husband; so, too, does the property of being a widow. The property of having been thought to be a thief projects the property of being thought to be a thief as well as that of thinking, but it does not project the property of being a thief.

It is obvious that, if a property P includes a property Q, then P projects Q – and not conversely.

We may now characterize internal properties in terms of the kinds of properties they project.

Let us first note that there are properties that are projected by *every* property. These are the properties that certain abstract objects have necessarily. Examples are: being the successor of 7; being the property blue; being self-identical; and being such that 7 and 5 are 12. Every property is necessarily such that, if it is exemplified, then these necessary properties are exemplified.

Now we may note a peculiarity of properties that are internal. Except for the necessary properties just referred to, the only properties that an internal property projects are those properties that it includes. Hence we may define *internal property* this way:

D5 P is an internal property =Df For every Q, if P projects Q and if only individual
things can have Q, then P includes Q

Feeling sad, hoping for rain, believing that all men are mortal, along with the other "purely psychological properties" with which we began, satisfy the terms of this definition of internal property.

If a property is internal, then, it is possibly such that only one individual has it; indeed, it is possibly such that there will have been only one individual and that that individual has it. Thus the property *being sad* is possibly such that there is an individual that has it and there are no other individuals. It does not require the existence of any individual other than its own bearer. We may express this point by saying that internal properties are not "other implying".

That internal properties are not other-implying follows from the definition and our assumption that it is logically possible that there is only one individual thing. Consider a property that *is* other-implying – say, the property of being one of two individuals. This property projects a property it does not include (that of being an aggregate), and therefore it is not internal.

If we take "red" in its physical sense, we may say that *being red* is other-implying. For it projects but does not include the property of *being a proper part*. A thing cannot be red unless there are things that are proper parts of other things. But a thing may be red without itself being a proper part of any other thing. *Locomotion* is also other-implying; for it implies that there are two individual things changing their spatial relations to each other. And so, too, for the other properties that Locke had called "primary qualities" – "solidity, extension, figure, motion or rest and number."[2] And *weight* is also other-implying (for to say that a body has weight is to say that it stands in certain relations to some other body or bodies).

So far, then, we have two marks of the psychological. A psychological property is a changeable property of individuals and it is internal. If we turn now to nonpsychological properties, we are likely to find that the first ones to come to mind—say, *being 6 feet long* and *being such as to have 3 dimensions*—are such that either they are not internal or they are not changeable properties of individuals. We may be tempted to say, therefore, that *only* psychological properties have these features. But this would be a mistake. For there are nonpsychological properties that are changeable properties of individuals and that satisfy our definition of internality.

Consider that disjunctive property that all sad people and islands have in common—the property of being either sad or entirely surrounded by water. This both is a changeable property and is internal by our definition.

Hence we must look further if we are to find a logical *definition* of the psychological.

In the early part of the present century many philosophers spoke of properties that are "qualitative." This concept gives us a third mark of the psychological.

Purely Qualitative Properties

If a property is is purely qualitative, then it is not equivalent to a mere potency, disposition or possibility, But this is only a negative characterization. To characterize the concept more positively, let us introduce the following useful abbreviations:

D6 P falls under Q =Df P includes Q; and Q does not include P

Being a dog falls under being an animal, and believing that there are dogs falls under believing. (Please note that I am now using the expression "falls under" to refer to a relation that holds only between properties or relations. Using the expression in this sense, we cannot say that a thing "falls under" the properties that it exemplifies.)

D7 P falls between Q and R =Df Q and R are such that (a) P falls under one and (b) the other falls under P

Being a dog falls between being a wolfhound and being an animal, and believing that there are dogs falls between believing and believing that there are dogs and cats.

Some properties are such that they may be said to "*fall densely* under other properties. The concept may be illustrated by reference to the properties:

(P) being between 5 and 7 feet tall
(Q) being 6 feet tall

Consider any property R that falls between these properties P and Q. We might have, for example:

(P) being between 5 and 7 feet tall
(R) being between 5.1 and 6.9 feet tall
(Q) being 6 feet tall

For any property R, which thus falls between P and Q, we may find a property that falls between Q and R, and we may find a property that falls between P and R. The property P, then, "falls densely" under Q. The concept may be defined this way:

D8 P falls densely under Q =Df P falls under Q; and for every R, if R falls between P and Q, then (a) something falls between P and R and (b) something falls between Q and R

The word "dense" is appropriate, for such properties are related to each other in a way in which fractions are related to each other: I am thinking of the fact that between any two fractions there are indefinitely many other fractions.

We may note that, although *being 6 feet tall* falls densely under *some* properties, it falls under *other* properties without falling densely under those other properties. Thus it falls, but not densely, under *being possibly 6 feet tall*; there are no properties that fall between these properties.

These considerations lead us to the concept of the purely qualitative. Consider the property of *thinking*—the property of *being conscious*. Shall we say that the property of thinking is a property that does not fall densely under any property? This would not be accurate. For thinking falls densely under this property: *being a member of a class which is such that more than half of its members are thinking*. Between this latter property and thinking, we find, for example, *being a member of a class which is such that more than three quarters of its members are thinking*. It is clear that *thinking* falls densely under such properties. But these properties, unlike thinking, are not internal. For they project a property they do not include—the property of thinking.

Let us, then, define "purely qualitative property" this way:

> D9 P is purely qualitative =Df P is a property which is such that (a) nothing can have P necessarily, (b) P does not fall densely under any property that is internal, and (c) P is not a mere potency, disposition or possibility

Thinking is qualitative by this definition; so, too, for *being able to think*. (We should note, in passing, that there is a significant difference between the two purely qualitative properties——thinking and being able to think. Unlike thinking, *being able to think* is not one of those properties which are such that, if you have it, then you can know directly and immediately that you have it. But it is such that, if you have it and if you *raise the question* whether you have it, then you *can* know directly and immediately that you have it.)

The following subspecies of thinking are also purely qualitative: believing, liking, disliking, sensing visually, sensing auditorily, sensing tactually. But it is problematic whether *all* subspecies of thinking are purely qualitative.

Does *sensing redly*, for example, fall densely under *sensing visually*? (The question may be put in a different terminology: Does *having a red sensation* falls densely under *having a visual sensation*? We may note that *having a visual sensation* does not fall densely under anything.)

Again, does *believing that there are dogs and cats* fall densely under *believing that there are dogs*? One might be tempted to say that it does—on the ground that *believing that there are dogs and other animals* falls between these things. But does *believing that there are dogs and cats* include *believing that there are dogs and other animals*?

Whether or not such properties are themselves purely qualitative, each of them *includes* a property that is purely qualitative.

A Definition of the Psychological

Shall we now say that a psychological property is a purely qualitative property? This would be too narrow. Consider the property of judging truly that there is someone who is ill. Surely this is psychological. Yet it projects the property of being ill without including that property. Hence it is not internal, and therefore it is not purely qualitative.

Let us say rather this:

> D10 P is psychological =Df P is a property; and P includes a property that is (i) a changeable property of individuals; (ii) internal, and (iii) purely qualitative.

Here, then, we have our logical characterization of the psychological.

Some Problematic Cases

I will speak here only of two types of problematic case—*obligations* and *semantic* properties. In the past, these two types of property have served as obstacles in the way of finding a logical criterion of intentionality.[3]

Does *being obligated* project *thinking* and thus project a property it does not include? One might argue: "Surely no one can be under an obligation without having been conscious at some time or other." If being obligated does thus project thinking, it projects a property it does not include, and therefore it is not an internal property. But one may also argue that being obligated does *not* thus project thinking. "Consider a person who has never been conscious. Isn't such a person also under obligation? After all, he, too, has the obligation—the duty—not to commit murder." But what is it thus to have the duty not to commit murder? It is to have the property of being such as *not* to have the *right* to commit murder. But this property is not restricted to individuals. And therefore it is not a "changeable property of individuals."

Consider now the *semantic* property: having dogness (the property of being a dog) as part of its meaning. This is a property of the English words "dog" and "bulldog." In what respects does this property differ from psychological properties?

There are two ways of conceiving the property in question: (a) one may conceive it as a property of certain abstract objects; or (b) one may conceive it as a changeable property of individuals. In the former case, it will not satisfy the conditions of the definition of psychological property. In the latter case, it may be thought of as a property of such things as the written words, "dog", "chien", "Hund"; hence it would not be an internal property—for its exemplification would require that there be more than one individual thing.

ENDNOTES

[1] In "On the Nature of the Psychological," *Philosophical Studies*, Vol. 43 (1983), pp. 155–164, I presented a definition of psychological property; but the definition was not purely logical since it made use of the psychological expression "to conceive."
[2] See Locke's *Essay Concerning Human Understanding*, Book II, Ch. 8, Section 10.
[3] See the article "Intentionality" in Paul Edwards (ed.), *The Encyclopedia of Philosophy* (New York 1967), Vol. IV, pp. 201–204.

* * *

ZEITLICHKEIT DES BEWUSSTSEINS UND SYNTHETISCHES URTEIL A PRIORI

Konrad Cramer
Universität Göttingen

Der Grundgedanke von Kants nicht-empirischer Theorie der empirischen Erkenntnis läßt sich doxographisch in wenigen Sätzen zusammenfassen. (1) Wenn ein Subjekt, dem Sinnesdaten auf Grund seines Vermögens, Vorstellungen zu ‚empfangen‘, gegeben werden, sich diese als seine eigenen soll zuschreiben können, dann muß es sich der Identität seiner selbst mit Bezug auf solche Daten bewußt sein können. (2) Seiner Identität mit Bezug auf gegebene Vorstellungen kann sich ein solches Subjekt nur dann bewußt sein, wenn es diese Vorstellungen zur Einheit eines Bewußtseins verbindet. (3) Das auf einer Synthesis gegebener Vorstellungen beruhende Bewußtsein von der Einheit des Bewußtseins kann selber keine gegebene Vorstellung sein. Es beruht vielmehr auf einem ‚Aktus der Spontaneität der Vorstellungskraft‘, der sich in der Funktion des Urteils bekundet, durch welches ein Mannigfaltiges gegebener Vorstellungen zur Einheit eines Bewußtseins gebracht wird. (4) Die Analyse des durch die Funktion des Urteils erzeugten Einheitssinnes in der Verbindung gegebener Vorstellungen zeigt, daß das Subjekt über gewisse Grundbegriffe, die Kategorien, verfügen muß, in denen eine solche Einheit gedacht wird. (5) Sie zeigt weiter, daß sich ein Subjekt der Identität seiner selbst mit Bezug auf gegebene Vorstellungen dann und nur dann bewußt sein kann, wenn es durch den Gebrauch von Kategorien die Inhalte dieser Vorstellungen als Bestimmungen von etwas auffaßt, das von dem bloßen Vorgestelltsein dieser Vorstellungen unterschieden ist. (6) Dieses von den jeweiligen Vorstellungszuständen des Subjekts Unterschiedene ist der Gegenstand oder das Objekt seiner Vorstellungen.

Es ist insbesondere die Version, die Kant der ‚Transzendentalen Deduktion der Kategorien‘ in der 2. Auflage der ‚Kritik der reinen Vernunft‘ (B) gegeben hat, welche den in (1)–(6) skizzierten Zusammenhang zwischen dem Bewußtsein der Identität eines Subjekts mit Bezug auf eine Mannigfaltigkeit von Vorstellungen, die ihm als sinnliche gegeben sind, und der Beziehung dieser Vorstellungen auf einen Gegenstand der Erkenntnis herzustellen unternimmt. Zwar ist die Leistungskraft der Argumentationsschritte, in denen dies geschieht, bis heute noch nicht vollständig aufgeschlossen; und diese Schritte selber sind genau genommen noch nicht einmal mit Eindeutigkeit identifiziert.[1] Sicher ist jedoch, daß diejenige Überlegung Kants, welche den Kategorien die Funktion zuschreibt, das Mannigfaltige einer Anschauung, die ein auf gegebene Vorstellungen angewiesenes Subjekt die seinige nennt, „durch die Synthesis des Verstandes als zur notwendigen Einheit des Selbstbewußtsein gehörig“ (B 144) vorzustellen, noch ganz davon absieht, *auf welche Weise*, d.h. unter welchen Formen der Sinnlichkeit einem Subjekt ein Mannigfaltiges sinnlicher Vorstellungen gegeben wird. Gefordert ist hier nur, daß ein Subjekt das Vermögen besitzt, *überhaupt* sinnlich anzuschauen, d.h. mit Bezug auf gewisse Vorstellungen, die es sich als die seinen zuschreibt, das Bewußtsein davon zu haben, daß sie nicht von ihm selber erzeugt, sondern ihm „noch vor der Synthesis des Verstandes und unabhängig von ihr“ gegeben sind – „wie aber, bleibt hier unbestimmt.“ (B 145)

Wenn demnach in strenger Allgemeinheit gilt, daß ein Subjekt sich gegebene Vorstellungen der Sinnlichkeit nur dann als seine Vorstellungen zuschreiben kann, wenn es die in ihnen präsentierten Inhalte auf ein von ihnen unterschiedenes Objekt zu beziehen vermag, dann muß dies *eo ipso* auch für ein solches Subjekt gelten, dessen für seine Sinnlichkeit spezifische Anschauungsform die *Zeit* ist. Mit Rücksicht auf die Zeitlichkeit des Gegebenseins von Vorstellungen ergibt sich daher für Kant weder ein neues noch ein zusätzliches Deduktionsproblem, sondern nur die Frage, welche *spezifische* Bedeutung den Kategorien als denjenigen

Begriffen a priori, in denen eine synthetische und objektive Einheit gegebener Vorstellungen der Sinnlichkeit im Modus des ‚überhaupt‘ gedacht wird, in ihrer Anwendung auf die unsere Sinnlichkeit kennzeichnende Auschauungsform – die Zeit – zuwächst. Diese Frage versucht Kant in den Kapiteln über den ‚Schematismus der reinen Verstandesbegriffe‘ und über das ‚System der Grundsätze des reinen Verstandes‘ zu beantworten. In der Auszeichnung und Begründung eines solchen Systems will Kant den Nachweis führen, daß für ein Subjekt, dem Vorstellungen im *Wechsel* gegeben sind, ein genau bestimmter Inbegriff von synthetischen Urteilen a priori in Geltung stehen muß, deren Aussagegehalt die Beziehung zwischen der Selbstzuschreibung solcher Vorstellungen von seiten dieses Subjekts und der Beziehung der in ihnen präsentierten Inhalte auf einen Gegenstand der Erkenntnis in der Zeit (und, wie zu ergänzen ist, im Raum) näher, d.h. mit Rücksicht auf die Anschauungsform der Zeit (und des Raums) bestimmt. Solche Urteile sind für ein zeitlich anschauendes Subjekt insofern ‚objekt-konstituierende‘ Urteile, als es über sie verfügen können muß, um die ihm auf spezifische Weise gegebenen Vorstellungen seiner Sinnlichkeit in entsprechend spezifisch bestimmter Weise auf einen Gegenstand einer *ihm* möglichen Erfahrung beziehen zu können. Diejenigen synthetischen Urteile a priori dieses Systems, die auf das ‚Dasein‘ der Gegenstände einer einem solchen Subjekt möglichen Erfahrung gehen, faßt Kant unter dem Titel der ‚Analogien der Erfahrung‘ zusammen.

Der erste Halbsatz der 1. Analogie der Erfahrung lautet: „Bei allem Wechsel der Erscheinungen beharrt die Substanz.“ (B 224) Der Beweis dieses synthetischen Urteils a priori hat nach Kants eigenen methodologischen Bemerkungen über die Beweisaufgabe ‚transzendentaler Sätze‘ darzutun, daß seinem Subjektbegriff (‚Wechsel der Erscheinungen‘) durch die synthetische Beziehung des Prädikatbegriffs (‚Substanz‘) in der temporalen Bestimmtheit von ‚Beharrlichkeit‘ auf ihn die Bedeutung des Begriffs von einem *Objekt* einer einem zeitlich anschauenden Subjekt möglichen Erfahrung allererst zuwächst.

Inwiefern, so ist zunächst zu fragen, ist der erste Halbsatz der 1. Analogie ein *synthetisches* Urteil? Offensichtlich ist er dies nur dann, wenn der Begriff ‚Wechsel der Erscheinungen‘, nach seinem logischen Inhalt betrachtet, noch nicht diejenigen Konnotationen des Begriffs ‚Erscheinung‘ aufweist, denen gemäß nach Kants Lehre vom transzendentalen Idealismus von Zeit (und Raum) gerade die *Objekte* einer uns möglichen Erfahrung ‚bloße Erscheinungen‘ und nicht ‚Dinge an sich‘ sind. Denn der Begriff der Erscheinung als Begriff von einem Objekt einer uns möglichen Erfahrung enthält den Begriff der Substanz in seiner näheren Bestimmung durch den Zeitmodus der Beharrlichkeit gerade *analytisch* in sich. Erscheinungen als Objekte einer uns möglichen Erfahrung sind Entitäten, die nach dem kategorialen Schema der Beharrlichkeit von etwas im Wechsel oder im Zugleichsein seiner Zustände gedacht werden müssen, weil eben dieser Gedanke ihren Objektcharakter definiert. *Daß* dies der Fall ist, sagt der erste Halbsatz der 1. Analogie jedoch gerade aus, und zwar – der Behauptung nach – nicht auf analytische, sondern auf synthetische Weise. Soll diese Behauptung zutreffen, kann der Subjektbegriff der Aussage nur der Begriff vom Wechsel der Erscheinungen als *bloßer Vorstellungen* sein, die einem Subjekt in der Form der Zeit gegeben werden, also nicht selber schon der Begriff von der gerechtfertigten Beziehung solcher Vorstellungen auf ein von ihnen unterschiedenes Objekt derselben.

Kants Behauptung ist ferner, daß der erste Halbsatz der 1. Analogie ein Urteil *a priori* ist. Die in ihm zu denkende Synthesis von Subjekt- und Prädikatbegriff erfolgt nicht auf Grund der Erfahrung von Objekten in der Zeit und im Raum, sondern benennt eine ‚Bedingung der Möglichkeit‘ eben dieser Erfahrung. Genau dann, wenn dies der Fall ist, ist die Aussage kein empirisches Urteil, sondern ein Urteil, das unabhängig von aller wirklich gemachten besonderen Erfahrung von Objekten in Zeit und Raum, mithin a priori, gilt.

Diese Kennzeichnung wirft jedoch ein eigenes Problem auf. „Empirische Begriffe, imgleichen das, worauf sie sich gründen, die empirische Anschauung, können keinen synthetischen Satz geben, als nur einen solchen, der auch bloß empirisch, d.i. ein Erfahrungssatz ist, mithin niemals Notwendigkeit und absolute Allgemeinheit enthalten kann.“ (B 64) Diese Feststellung Kants leuchtet in der Tat ein. *Empirische* Begriffe können zwar in synthetischen Urteilen, aber nicht in synthetischen Urteilen a priori Verwendung finden, weil Urteile, in denen sie als Termini auftreten, nicht unabhängig von derjenigen empirischen Anschauung sind, deren allgemeine Vorstellung solche Begriffe sind. Begriffe, die in synthetischen Urteilen a priori Verwendung finden können sollen, müssen ihrerseits von aller Erfahrung, mithin auch von dem, auf was sich eine bestimmte Erfahrung gründet, der empirischen Anschauung, unabhängig sein. Unter dieser Kautele ergibt sich jedoch für den Subjektbegriff der 1. Analogie der Erfahrung, den Begriff ‚Wechsel der Erscheinungen‘, daß er der von Kant selber formulierten Bedingung für die Apriorität von Begriffen nicht zu genügen scheint. Denn nur *reine* Anschauungen oder *reine* Begriffe sollen a priori möglich sein. (Vgl. B 75) ‚Rein‘ aber sind Anschauungen oder Begriffe, wenn in ihren sinnlichen oder logischen Inhalt keinerlei Bezugnahme auf empirisch gegebene Daten unserer Sinnlichkeit eingeht. Dieser Forderung genügt der Begriff des ‚Wechsels der Erscheinungen‘ nicht.

Der Nachweis hierfür hat davon auszugehen, daß dieser Begriff von Kant als ein Begriff konzipiert ist, über den ein Subjekt so verfügt, daß es durch seine Verwendung eine Beschreibung von sich gibt. Ein Subjekt *verfügt* über diesen Begriff, wenn in ihm nicht nur ein Wechsel von Erscheinungen *erfolgt*, sondern wenn es auch ein *Bewußtsein* davon hat, *daß* in ihm ein solcher Wechsel erfolgt. Dieses Bewußtsein kann jedoch durchaus nicht als ein ‚reines‘ Bewußtsein, also auch nicht als ein Bewußtsein a priori beschrieben werden, *wenn* gilt, daß ein Bewußtsein, das nicht rein ist, kein Bewußtsein a priori sein kann. Zwar *impliziert* das Bewußtsein vom Wechsel der Erscheinungen ein Bewußtsein von der Zeit als der durchgängigen Form, in der Subjekten wie uns sinnliche Anschauungen gegeben werden; es ist jedoch mit dem Bewußtsein von dieser Formbestimmtheit unserer Sinnlichkeit *nicht identisch*. Denn es ist nicht das Bewußtsein von dieser *Form*, sondern vom Auftritt und Abtritt von etwas mit dieser Form nicht Identischem *in* dieser Form. Dieses mit der Form der Zeit nicht Identische ist aber gerade das *empirisch* gegebene Mannigfaltige unserer Sinnlichkeit − dasjenige Mannigfaltige, welches im Unterschied zu dem reinen Mannigfaltigen der Anschauungsform der Zeit selber gerade *nicht* a priori gegeben werden kann und dessen *inhaltliche* Bestimmtheiten und Differenzen auch nicht a priori *antizipiert* werden können. Wenn nun der logische Inhalt des Begriffs des bloßen Wechsels der Erscheinungen unbezüglich auf nur a posteriori gebbare Differenzen der empirischen Anschauung nicht exponibel ist, zeigt dann nicht das Bewußtsein vom Wechsel der Erscheinungen gerade eine Struktur an, die ein Subjekt als die seine bloß *erfährt*, und zwar deswegen, weil es den Wechsel der Erscheinungen nur erfahren, aber nicht a priori antizipieren kann? Dem entsprechend wäre der Begriff des bloßen Wechsels der Erscheinungen ein aus der von Kant ohnehin zugelassenen ‚inneren Erfahrung‘ abstrahierter *empirischer* Allgemeinbegriff, mithin ein Begriff, mit dem das Subjekt, das über ihn verfügt, das Bewußtsein, der Sachverhalt, der vermittels dieses Begriffs beschrieben wird, könne nur so und nicht anderes bestimmt sein, gerade *nicht* verbindet. Zwar ist es ohne Zweifel so, daß Subjekte wie wir vermittels des Begriffs des bloßen Wechsels der Erscheinungen eine solche Beschreibung von uns geben, der gegenüber wir *de facto* alternativelos sind. Diese Tatsache besagt jedoch durchaus nicht, daß wir uns deshalb schon der *Apriorität* des Bewußtseins vom Wechsel der Erscheinungen bewußt sind.

Gleichwohl muß es möglich sein, dem Begriff des bloßen Wechsels der Erscheinungen unbeschadet der Tatsache, daß sein logischer Inhalt nur mit Bezug auf Differenzen in der empirischen Anschauung exponibel ist, den epistemischen Status eines Begriffs a priori zu sichern. Wäre dies nicht möglich, könnte nicht verstanden werden, daß Kant die 1. Analogie der Erfahrung als ein synthetisches Urteil *a priori* kennzeichnet. Dies bedeutet jedoch, daß man Kants nahezu stereotyp aufgestellte These, nur ‚reine‘ Anschauungen oder Begriffe seien a priori möglich, als irrige Selbstinterpretation seines eigenen erkenntnistheoretischen Programms preiszugeben hat. Denn der Begriff des bloßen Wechsels der Erscheinungen ist kein ‚reiner‘ Begriff und muß gleichwohl ein Begriff a priori sein.

Nun muß man sich freilich darüber ins Klare setzen, daß weder für Kant noch der Sache nach ein Argument in Sicht ist, welches dem Begriff des Wechsels der Erscheinungen so etwas wie eine unbedingte Apriorität sichern könnte. Denn weder folgt aus dem Begriff eines Subjekts, daß ihm überhaupt Vorstellungen als sinnliche *gegeben* werden müssen, noch aus dem Begriff eines Subjekts, dem Vorstellungen als sinnliche gegeben werden, daß ihm diese in der Form der *Zeit* gegeben werden müssen. Soll daher dem Begriff des bloßen Wechsels der Erscheinungen der Status eines empirischen Allgemeinbegriffs, den ein Subjekt von seiner faktischen Verfassung hat, abgesprochen und der Status eines Begriffs a priori zugesprochen werden können, so wird dies nur ‚sub data quadam conditione' geschehen können. Es müßte sich eine Bedingung angeben lassen, unter der ausgeschlossen werden kann, daß ein Subjekt vermittels des Begriffs des bloßen Wechsels der Erscheinungen eine solche Beschreibung von sich gibt, mit der es das Bewußtsein verbindet, es *könnte* über diesen Begriff auch nicht verfügen und dennoch eine Beschreibung von sich geben. Eine derartige Bedingung wäre so beschaffen, daß einem Subjekt unter ihr eine alternative Selbstbeschreibung nicht nur *de facto* nicht möglich, sondern aus *logischen* Gründen unmöglich ist.

Es ist daher zu erwägen, ob nicht in dem Bewußtsein selber, welches durch den Begriff des bloßen Wechsels der Erscheinungen beschrieben wird, eine solche Bedingung aufgewiesen werden kann. Mit ihr müßte eine Struktureigentümlichkeit unserer Subjektivität namhaft gemacht werden, die wir aus logischen Gründen kennen, wenn wir mit diesem Begriff eine Beschreibung von uns geben. Sie wäre eine Bedingung, unter welcher sich der nicht-empirische Charakter des Begriffs vom bloßen Wechsel der Erscheinungen genau dann ergäbe, wenn sich nachweisen ließe, daß (a) kein Bewußtsein, das diese Bedingung erfüllt, ein anderes Bewußtsein als das Bewußtsein vom Wechsel der Erscheinungen sein kann, und (b) diese Bedingung selber nicht mit Sinn eine ‚empirische' genannt werden kann.

Ein solcher Nachweis hat von dem analytisch wahren Satz auszugehen, daß kein Subjekt ein Bewußtsein vom Wechsel seiner empirischen Anschauungen haben kann, ohne ein Bewußtsein von der Zeitlichkeit des Gegebenseins seiner empirischen Anschauungen zu haben. Das Bewußtsein von dieser Zeitlichkeit wäre die gesuchte Bedingung im Sinne des unter (a) formulierten Beweisziels, wenn sich ein zwingendes Argument dafür entwickeln ließe, daß ein Subjekt, welches überhaupt ein Bewußtsein von der *Zeitlichkeit* des Gegebenseins seiner empirischen Anschauungen haben können soll, aus logischen Gründen des Begriffs von diesem Bewußtsein ein Bewußtsein davon haben können muß, daß ihm seine empirischen Anschauungen im *Wechsel* gegeben werden müssen. Es wäre ein Argument für die ‚strenge Allgemeinheit und Notwendigkeit' der Beschreibung, welche ein Subjekt vermittels des Begriffs des bloßen Wechsels der Erscheinungen von sich gibt, *unter der Voraussetzung*, daß es vermittels des Begriffs der Zeitlichkeit des Gegebenseins seiner empirischen Anschauungen eine Beschreibung von sich gibt. Mit ihm wäre der Nachweis erbracht, daß ein Subjekt, das vermittels des Begriffs des bloßen Wechsels der Erscheinungen eine Beschreibung von sich gibt, gegenüber dieser Beschreibung nicht nur de facto, sondern aus logischen Gründen alternativelos ist, sofern es sich überhaupt als ein Subjekt bekannt sein können soll, dem empirische Anschauungen in der Zeit gegeben sind.

Ein derartiges Argument hat die formale Struktur eines ‚transzendentalen Arguments'. Es muß im zu betrachtenden Fall zeigen, daß entwerfbare *Alternativen* zum Bewußtsein vom Wechsel der Erscheinungen, die der Bedingung genügen sollen, Fälle des Bewußtseins von der Zeitlichkeit des Gegebenseins empirischer Anschauungen zu sein, ‚unechte', nämlich in Wahrheit *logisch inkonsistente* Alternativen sind. Ich habe an anderer Stelle drei solche Alternativen vorgestellt und diskutiert, die mir auch den vollständigen Satz solcher Alternativen zu präsentieren scheinen.[2] Diese Diskussion zeigt mit rein analytischen Mitteln, daß die Begriffe vom Bewußtsein von der Zeitlichkeit des Gegebenseins empirischer Vorstellungen und vom Bewußtsein des Wechsels solcher Vorstellungen *logisch äquivalente* Begriffe sind. Von diesem Diskussionsergebnis gehe ich für die Formulierung meiner Schlußüberlegungen aus.

Ein Subjekt, das über den Begriff der Zeitlichkeit des Gegebenseins seiner empirischen Anschauungen verfügt, verfügt mit logischer Notwendigkeit über den Begriff des Wechsels der Erscheinungen (als empirischer Anschauungen). Doch kommt dem Bewußtsein von der Zeitlichkeit des Gegebenseins der empirischen Anschauungen so etwas wie unbedingte oder interne Apriorität nicht zu. Es bezeichnet vielmehr einen bloß subjektiven Sachverhalt, der auf genau dieselbe Weise ,etwas ganz Zufälliges‘ ist, wie dies nach Kant eine uns mögliche Erfahrung von Objekten in Raum und Zeit auch ist. (Vgl. B 765) Gleichwohl muß es möglich sein, dem Begriff von diesem Bewußtsein und damit dem mit ihm äquivalenten Begriff des Wechsels der Erscheinungen den Status eines nicht-empirischen Begriffs zu sichern, um letzterem seine Funktion zu sichern, Subjektbegriff eines synthetischen Urteils a priori zu sein.

Dies kann nicht durch Rekurs auf Kants Lehre von der Zeit als apriorischer Form unserer Anschauung geschehen. Abgesehen von der Anfechtbarkeit dieser Lehre ist dies deshalb unmöglich, weil das Bewußtsein von der Zeitlichkeit des Gegebenseins der empirischen Anschauungen in seinem vollen deskriptiven Bestand nicht das Bewußtsein von dieser Form, sondern von demjenigen ist, was in dieser Form empirisch gegeben ist. Im Begriff des Wechsels der Erscheinungen ist die Zeit des Bewußtseins gerade unter der von dem Formcharakter der Zeit zu unterscheidenden Voraussetzung der Differenz empirischer Daten der Anschauung thematisch. Wenn daher die in Frage stehenden Begriffe als Begriffe a priori rekonstruierbar sein sollen, kann die Rekonstruktion nicht von dieser Differenz als einer bloß *empirisch* gebbaren absehen.

An einer und, soweit ich sehe, nur an dieser Stelle hat Kant selber einen Hinweis darauf gegeben, wie eine solche Rekonstruktion auszusehen hat. Sie ist auch die einzige, an der Kant mit seiner ansonsten stereotypen Forderung nach der ,Reinheit‘ von Vorstellungen, deren Begriffe als Termini in synthetischen Urteilen a priori Verwendung finden können sollen, förmlich bricht: „Innere Erfahrung überhaupt und deren Möglichkeit, oder Wahrnehmung überhaupt und deren Verhältnis zu anderer Wahrnehmung, ohne daß irgendein besonderer Unterschied derselben und Bestimmung empirisch gegeben ist, kann nicht als empirische Erkenntnis, sondern muß als Erkenntnis des Empirischen überhaupt angesehen werden, und gehört zur Untersuchung der Möglichkeit einer jeden Erfahrung, welche allerdings transzendental ist.“ (B 401) – Wenn dies gelten soll, muß es möglich sein, eine Erkenntnis vom eigenen ,Inneren‘ zu identifizieren, die von den jeweils *besonderen Unterschieden* in den Gehalten der Wahrnehmungen, in denen sich dies Innere präsentiert, absieht, ohne doch davon abzusehen, daß es sich in *Wahrnehmungen* präsentiert. Man kann solche Wahrnehmungen mit Kant und der Traditionsgeschichte des klassischen Empirismus ,innere Wahrnehmungen‘ nennen. Zwar ließe sich im Rekurs auf innere Wahrnehmungen gewiß nicht *begreiflich* machen, daß ein Subjekt Kenntnis von seinem eigenen Inneren hat. Selbstbewußtsein, und sei es auch ,empirisches Selbstbewußtsein‘, läßt sich nicht durch Wahrnehmungen erklären. Gibt es aber innere Wahrnehmungen, dann ist das Verhältnis der einen zu der anderen das ihrer zeitlichen Aufeinanderfolge. Genauer gesagt ist dies das grundsätzliche Verhältnis zwischen ihnen, dem gegenüber ein etwaiges Zugleichsein innerer Wahrnehmungen parasitär ist. Denn so, wie nach Kant unsere ,Apprehension‘ des Mannigfaltigen der Anschauung ,jederzeit sukzessiv‘ ist (vgl. B 225), so ist auch das Bewußtsein davon, daß ein Subjekt in verschiedenen Vorstellungszuständen ist, an das Bewußtsein von einer zeitlichen Folge der inneren Wahrnehmung dieser Vorstellungszustände geknüpft.

Nun kann es gewiß kein Bewußtsein davon geben, daß ein Wechsel der Erscheinungen wirklich erfolgt, ohne daß ,irgendein besonderer Unterschied‘ zwischen den Gehalten des innerlich Wahrgenommenen ,empirisch gegeben ist‘. Gleichwohl ist das Bewußtsein vom Wechsel der Erscheinungen einer Beschreibung zugänglich, die es von den einzelnen wirklich erfahrenen Fällen seiner jeweiligen konkreten Instantiierung zu unterscheiden nötigt. Das Argument hierfür geht aus dem Argument dafür hervor, daß ein Subjekt, welches ein Bewußtsein von der Zeitlichkeit des Gegebenseins seiner empirischen Anschauungen haben können soll, ein Bewußtsein davon haben können muß, daß ihm diese Anschauungen im Wechsel gegeben sind. Das Bewußtsein von diesem Wechsel impliziert ein Bewußtsein davon, daß ein Vorstellungszustand, den sich ein Subjekt auf Grund der Präsentation einer bestimmten, d.h. besonderen empirischen Anschauung als den eigenen zuschreibt, weder der *einzige* noch der *letzte* seiner Vorstellungszustände sein *kann*. Denn das Bewußtsein von der bloßen Zeitlichkeit des Gegebenseins der empirischen Anschauungen bezieht sich protensiv auf die Zukunft eines Subjekts als eine noch ausstehende Folge von Zeitpunkten seiner eigenen Zeit, in der ihm andere Inhalte der empirischen Anschauung als der jetzt gegebene Inhalt gebbar sein müssen. Eine innere Wahrnehmung ist die Wahrnehmung, die sie ist, daher nur unter der Bedingung der in sie selber fallenden Antizipation einer anderen zukünftigen inneren Wahrnehmung, also nur unter der Bedingung der Antizipation eines noch ausstehenden Wechsels der Erscheinungen. Diese Antizipation kann in der Tat nicht so beschrieben werden, daß in ihr selber ein besonderer Unterschied zwischen den empirischen Gehalten der jetzt vorliegenden und der antizipierten inneren Wahrnehmung *gegeben* ist. Denn der besondere Gehalt der empirischen Anschauung, deren innere Wahrnehmung antizipiert wird, ist *ex vi definitionis* von ‚Antizipation‘ gerade *nicht* gegeben. Was im Bewußtsein von der Notwendigkeit der Möglichkeit eines in Zukunft erfolgenden Wechsels der Erscheinungen antizipiert wird, ist bloß ein Unterschied zwischen empirischen Anschauungen im Modus des Kantischen ‚überhaupt‘, nur dies, daß der Inhalt einer zukünftigen inneren Wahrnehmung empirisch *anders* bestimmt sein muß als der Inhalt der gegenwärtig gegebenen, −*wie*, bleibt dabei gerade unbestimmt.

Nach dieser Rekonstruktion ist der Begriff des bloßen Wechsels der Erscheinungen primär kein Begriff, mit dessen Hilfe beschrieben wird, was in einem auf zeitliche Weise anschauenden Subjekt wirklich, und d.h. empirisch konstatierbar, vorgeht, sondern der Begriff von einer *Möglichkeit*, die einem solchen Subjekt grundsätzlich garantiert sein muß, wenn es überhaupt ein Bewußtsein von der Zeitlichkeit des Gegebenseins seiner empirischen Anschauungen haben können soll. Das Bewußtsein, welches durch den Begriff des bloßen Wechsels der Erscheinungen beschrieben wird, ist, um es in einem scheinbaren Paradox zu formulieren, eine a priori erfolgende Antizipation genau dessen, dessen jeweils besondere Bestimmtheit gar nicht a priori antizipiert werden kann, weil sie bloß empirisch gegeben werden kann. In diesem, aber auch nur in diesem Sinne ist das Bewußtsein vom Wechsel der Erscheinungen keine innere ‚Erfahrung‘ von der jeweils faktischen Bestimmtheit, in der sich ein Subjekt auf Grund der nur empirisch gebbaren und bestimmbaren Besonderungen seiner empirischen Anschauungen kennt, sondern eine Bedingung der Möglichkeit jeder derartigen Selbsterfahrung. In diesem, aber auch nur in diesem Sinne ist der Begriff des Wechsels der Erscheinungen kein empirischer Begriff, sondern ein Begriff a priori.

Dies gilt jedoch nur unter der Voraussetzung, daß ein Subjekt ein Bewußtsein von der Zeitlichkeit des Gegebenseins seiner empirischen Anschauung besitzt. *Daß* dies der Fall ist, bleibt auch nach Argumenten für die logische Äquivalenz des Begriffs von diesem Bewußtsein und des Begriffs vom Bewußtsein des Wechsels der Erscheinungen ‚etwas ganz Zufälliges‘, also ein kontingentes Faktum. Doch ist seine Kontingenz von der Kontingenz der Erfahrungen, die wir wirklich anstellen, noch zu unterscheiden. Denn diese Kontingenz ist nur unter der Bedingung jener möglich. Es gibt keine bestimmten Erfahrungen, seien sie nun Selbst- oder Fremderfahrungen, ohne das ihnen gegenüber invariante Bewußtsein vom Wechsel der Erscheinungen. Wenngleich dies Bewußtsein ebenso kontingent ist wie das Bewußtsein von der Zeitlichkeit der Subjekte, die wir sind, ist es doch mit genausowenig Sinn ein empirisches Bewußtsein zu nennen wie dieses. Es ist im Sinne des oben unter (b) formulierten Beweisziels eine kontingente, aber ihrerseits nicht-empirische Bedingung der Erkenntnis des Empirischen.

Diese Charakterisierung hat jedoch die systematische Pointe, daß dem Bewußtsein vom Wechsel der Erscheinungen so etwas wie eine interne oder unbedingte Apriorität ebensowenig zugeschrieben werden kann wie dem Bewußtsein von der Zeitlichkeit des Subjekts. Doch ist dies auch gar nicht nötig. Es genügt, den Begriff des bloßen Wechsels der Erscheinungen von allen *in specie* so zu nennenden empirischen Begriffen, die wir von uns selber auf Grund jeweils faktisch vollzogener Selbstzuschreibungen besonders gegebener Inhalte der empirischen Anschauung haben, unterscheiden zu können, um ihm die von Kant geforderte *transzendentale* Funktion für eine nicht-empirische Theorie der empirischen Erkenntnis zuzuweisen. Zwar ist er nur der Begriff von der Grundstruktur eines Subjekts, deren kontradiktorisches Gegenteil für dies Subjekt logisch denkbar bleibt − wenngleich nicht als eine auf es selber zutreffende Möglichkeit. Insofern er aber keine Bestimmtheit des Subjekts benennt, die über die Faktizität seiner eigenen Zeitlichkeit hinaus weitere kontingente Bedingungen seiner Selbsterfahrung in Anspruch nimmt, *kann* er als operativer Begriff einer Theorie fungieren, welche die Bedingungen der einem solchen Subjekt *möglichen* Erfahrung von Objekten (in genauem Unterschied zu dem, was solche Subjekte *de facto* erfahren) rekonstruiert. Der Begriff vom *Wechsel* der Erscheinungen *muß* in einer solchen Theorie aber auch fungieren. Denn er ist genau derjenige Begriff unseres gesamten Begriffsrepertoires, der im Unterschied zu Begriffen von einer ‚reinen' Anschauung und zu Begriffen von einer kategorialen Synthesis a priori auf das bloß empirisch gebbare Mannigfaltige und dessen Differenzen im Modus des ‚überhaupt' kraft seines logischen Inhalts bezogen ist. Er enthält eben daher die formalen subjektiven Bedingungen der Anwendung von Kategorien der *Relation* auf Gegebenheiten unserer Sinnlichkeit. Denn Kategorien der Relation lassen sich auf unsere Sinnlichkeit nur dann beziehen, wenn sie als Begriffe von der notwendigen Verbindung dessen aufgefaßt werden, was uns als eine Mannigfaltigkeit *empirisch* gegebener Daten in der Form der Zeit präsentiert wird. An den Anschauungsformen von Zeit und Raum als solchen haben Relationskategorien keinen Anhalt. Sie gehen nicht auf Zeit und Raum als Gegenstände vorgestellt, sondern auf etwas in Zeit und Raum als Gegenstand vorgestellt: auf das ‚Dasein' von Objekten *in* Raum und Zeit. Das ist der systematische Grund dafür, daß der Begriff des bloßen Wechsels der Erscheinungen nicht nur als Subjektbegriff der 1. Analogie der Erfahrung (und damit als der Grundbegriff aller Analogien der Erfahrung) fungieren kann, sondern auch fungieren muß. Diese Notwendigkeit kann jedoch nur dann einsichtig gemacht werden, wenn jene Möglichkeit verstanden werden kann. Die voranstehend entwickelten Überlegungen wollen als ein Versuch aufgefaßt werden, einem solchen Verständnis näherzukommen. Sie gelten der Frage, auf welche Weise dem Begriff des Wechsels der Erscheinungen die von Kant geforderte Apriorität gesichert werden kann, ohne die für seinen logischen Inhalt konstitutive Beziehung auf Differenzen der empirischen Anschauung aus ihm zu exportieren. Wo dies geschieht, begibt sich der Interpret jeder Möglichkeit, die transzendentale Funktion des Systems der Analogien der Erfahrung im Aufbau der Kantischen Epistemologie und die von Kant für sie angebotenen Beweisgründe zu verstehen.

ANMERKUNGEN

[1] Die avancierteste Rekonstruktion von Teilen der transzendentalen Deduktion hat vorgelegt D. Henrich, *Identität und Objektivität.* (Heidelberg 1976).
[2] Cramer, K., *Nicht-reine synthetische Urteile a priori. Ein Problem der Transzendentalphilosophie Immanuel Kants* (Heidelberg 1985), Kap. 10: Formale Probleme des Begriffs des bloßen Wechsels der Erscheinungen.

* * *

DAS LEIB-SEELE-PROBLEM, EPISTEMOLOGISCH GESEHEN

François Bonsack
Universität Neuchâtel
Institut für Methodologie, Biel

Die Unterscheidung zwischen Seele und Leib kann auf verschiedenen Ebenen gemacht werden:

a) auf der ontologischen Ebene, die dann auf die metaphysisch-religiöse erweitert werden kann;

b) auf der ethisch-moralischen Ebene;

c) auf der epistemologischen Ebene.

a) *Ontologische Ebene*

Der ontologische Dualismus postuliert zwei Substanzen, z.B. Descartes „res extensa" und „res cogitans", die beide objektiv existieren und sich durch verschiedene Eigenschaften unterscheiden, wie Eisen vom Sauerstoff, ein Proton von einem Photon oder ein Teilchen von einem Feld.

Die ontologische Dualität von Seele und Leib hatte den großen Vorteil, daß sie eine naheliegende Interpretation des Todes bot. Daher kam sie in den verschiedensten Kulturen vor.

Was unterscheidet nämlich einen lebenden Körper von einem Leichnam? – Materiell scheinbar nichts: die Organe, die Gewebe, die Zellen sind die gleichen, das Blut ist immer da (aber es zirkuliert nicht mehr), auch die Wärme ist zunächst noch da, kurz alles Leibliche besteht und doch funktioniert nichts mehr. Beweglichkeit und Empfindlichkeit sind verschwunden, der Körper ist nicht mehr fähig, seine Wärme aufrechtzuerhalten, und er zerfällt dann mit der Zeit. Es fehlt ihm offenbar etwas, das er besaß solange er am Leben war, obschon er materiell noch alles zu haben scheint. Was ihm fehlt, ist also notwendigerweise unkörperlich, es ist die Seele, die ihn funktionieren ließ, ihn empfindlich und beweglich machte und ihn beherrschte. Eine einheitliche Seele macht den Leib lebendig und löst sich von diesem im Augenblick des Todes.

Dies war der erste Schritt. Aber sogleich kam der zweite: Was ist diese Seele, die sich vom Körper löst? – Wenn sie das ist, was den Leib beweglich und empfindlich macht, liegt es nahe, sie mit dem bewußten Ich zu identifizieren, das eben auch das ist, was dem Leib Befehle gibt und von ihm Empfindungen bekommt. Die Seele wurde also auf das bewußte Ich eingeschränkt, ungeachtet dessen, daß man dabei einen großen Teil der unbewußten Funktionen fallen ließ, die beim Tode verschwinden und z.B. im Koma oder in der Narkose noch vorhanden sind.

Was geschieht weiter mit der abgelösten Seele? – Die Antwort auf diese Frage geben Religion und Metaphysik: sie könnte sich verflüchtigen, sie könnte erhalten bleiben, eventuell in andere Körper eintreten (von Menschen oder von Tieren), nach anderen Regionen wandern usw. Der Erhaltungstrieb, der „Wille zur Ewigkeit", wie Nietzsche sagt, und auch der Wunsch, geliebte Verstorbene wieder zu treffen, bevorzugen natürlich Lehren, welche die Unsterblichkeit der Seele verkünden.

Man muß aber bezweifeln, ob eine solche Begründung für die Unterscheidung von Leib und Seele heute noch bestehen kann. Die Biologie hat uns zu einer ganz anderen Interpretation des Todes geführt. Dem „Leben" wurden große Funktionen unterstellt, die alle notwendig sind für dessen Erhaltung: Verdauung, Atmung, Stoffwechsel, Blutzirkulation, Nervenübertragung, Empfindlichkeit, Muskelkontraktion usw., und jede dieser Funktionen kann in unzählige kleinere zerteilt werden, die alle an bestimmte Gewebe, Zellen, chemische Stoffe gebunden sind. Das Leben einer Zelle ist eine lokale Angelegenheit, die auf ein günstiges physikalisch-chemisches Milieu angewiesen ist, welches seinerseits durch das Zusammenwirken der meisten Organe erhalten wird. Der Tod folgt auf das Versagen einer oder mehrerer der großen Funktionen, welche zur Bewahrung dieses Milieus nötig sind.

Dieses Bild, das uns die heutige Biologie vom Tode entwirft, ist sehr weit von der Trennung einer körperlichen und einer unkörperlichen Substanz entfernt: die einzelnen Zellen sterben nach und nach ab, wenn die physikalisch-chemischen Bedingungen ihres Weiterlebens nicht mehr vorhanden sind, so daß der Genfer Zoologe Emile Guyénot eine seiner Vorlesungen „Teilweises Überleben nach allgemeinem Tod" betiteln konnte.

b) *Ethisch-moralische Ebene*

Wenn man Plato's „Phaidon" liest, wird einem sehr bald klar, daß die Seele der Vernunft gleichgestellt wird und daß nicht nur die „niederen" Triebe, sondern auch Affekte und Leidenschaften dem tierischen Leib zugeschrieben werden. Das ist auch verständlich, sobald man die Seele mit dem bewußten Ich identifiziert hat: dieses befiehlt nicht nur den Muskeln, sondern auch den leiblichen Begehren. Und im Christentum, z.B. im Römerbrief, kommt noch eine moralische Wertung hinzu: das Fleisch wird mit der Sünde und der Geist mit dem Heil gleichgestellt.

Die axiologisch-moralische Leib-Seele-Unterscheidung ist an sich logisch ganz unabhängig von der ontologischen Leib-Seele- oder allgemeiner Geist-Materie-Unterscheidung: man kann dem Geist und der Kultur einen hohen Wert beimessen, auch wenn man in ihnen nicht eine besondere, von der Materie verschiedene Substanz sieht, sondern eine Funktion, welche durch eine besondere Anordnung der Materie möglich gemacht wird – sie sind deshalb nicht weniger wertvoll. Und aus der Vernunft eine höhere biologische Funktion machen hindert diese nicht daran, Leidenschaften, Triebe und Körper zu beherrschen. Natürlich muß man dann auf eine transzendente Begründung der Moral (z.B. mit Hilfe eines letzten Gerichtes) zugunsten einer immanenten verzichten, was ihr beim heutigen Zeitgeist nur zugute kommen kann.

c) *Epistemologische Ebene*

Ich komme nun zu meinem eigentlichen Thema: die Leib-Seele-Unterscheidung auf der epistemologischen Ebene.

Als Ausgangspunkt meiner Ausführungen nehme ich folgende einleuchtende Feststellung: Wir haben keinen unmittelbaren Zugang zur Außenwelt; alles, was wir über sie erfahren, erreicht uns *mittelbar* über unsere Empfindungen, Wahrnehmungen, Vorstellungen. Es ist uns nicht möglich, unsere innere Wahrnehmung einer Kirsche mit einer an sich seienden, außenstehenden Kirsche zu vergleichen und so zu prüfen, ob diese Wahrnehmung die Kirsche richtig wiedergibt. Denn die außenstehende Kirsche ist uns eben nur über unsere Wahrnehmung zugänglich. Wir können nur Wahrnehmungen mit Wahrnehmungen vergleichen (z.B. jetzige mit früheren oder mit späteren, gesehene mit gehörten), Wahrnehmungen mit Begriffen, mit Aussagen anderer über ihre eigenen Wahrnehmungen, mit Wahrnehmungen von Bildern oder von Meßinstrumenten, welche besondere Eigenschaften der Kirsche bestimmen würden. Niemals aber die Wahrnehmung eines Objekts mit dem Objekt selbst. Das Objekt steht uns nicht zur Verfügung als Maßstab dessen Wahrnehmung.

Daher kann die Richtigkeit einer Wahrnehmung nicht an deren Übereinstimmung mit dem

Objekt geprüft werden, sondern nur in einem komplexen Vergleich zwischen verschiedenen Empfindungen, bekannten Begriffen und Gesetzen und einer Abwägung der verschiedenen Möglichkeiten in der gegebenen Lage.

Diese Feststellung kann so interpretiert werden, daß uns nur ein Bild in uns von der Außenwelt bekannt ist, und daß die Existenz dieser Außenwelt bezweifelt werden kann, dies umso mehr, als uns die Sinne manchmal täuschen und wir auch träumen, d.h. innere Bilder sozusagen wahrnehmen, denen in der Außenwelt nichts entspricht.

So schreibt Descartes in seinen *Prinzipien der Philosophie* (Teil I, § 8):

> Examinant ce que nous sommes, nous qui pensons maintenant qu'il n'y a rien endehors de notre pensée qui soit véritablement ou qui existe, nous connaissons manifestement que, pour être, nous n'avons pas besoin d'extension, de figure, d'être en aucun lieu, ni d'aucune autre telle chose que l'on peut attribuer au corps et que nous sommes par cela seul que nous pensons; et que par conséquent la notion que nous avons de notre âme ou de notre pensée précède celle que nous avons du corps, et qu'elle est plus certaine, vu que nous doutons encore qu'il y ait aucun corps au monde, et que nous savons certainement que nous pensons.
>
> (Denn wenn man prüft, wer wir sind, wir, die wir jetzt davon überzeugt sind, daß es nichts außerhalb unseres Bewußtseins gibt, das wahrhaft ist oder existiert, so sehen wir deutlich, daß wir weder Ausdehnung, noch Gestalt, noch Ort, noch irgend etwas anderes, das man dem Körper zuschreiben kann, brauchen, um zu sein, und daß wir allein dadurch sind, daß wir denken. Folglich geht der Begriff, den wir von unserer Seele oder von unserem Denken haben, demjenigen voran, den wir vom Leib haben, und er ist gewisser, da wir ja noch bezweifeln, daß es auch nur einen einzigen Körper in der Welt gebe, aber sicher wissen, daß wir denken.)

Dies führt uns zu einer epistemologischen Unterscheidung von Seele und Leib: Seele ist das, was uns unmittelbar sozusagen von innen zugänglich ist; Außenwelt und der zu ihr gehörende Leib ist das, auf dessen Existenz erst aus diesem unmittelbar Gegebenen mittelbar geschlossen wird. Unsere sichere Erkenntnis erstreckt sich nur auf unsere eigene Seele; zwischen ihr und der Welt liegt eine unüberbrückbare epistemologische Kluft.

Die Hauptfrage ist nun: entspricht dieser epistemologischen Unterscheidung eine ontologische? Kann man aus der Tatsache schließen, daß uns die Seele von innen erreichbar ist und der Leib sozusagen von außen, daß die Seele aus einem anderen Stoff aufgebaut ist als der Leib?

Nichts zwingt uns dazu. Und dieser Schluß hätte nicht geringe Nachteile, denn es würde die epistemologische Kluft in eine ontologische verwandeln; man würde dann nicht mehr verstehen, wie so verschiedenartige Substanzen aufeinander wirken können. Das bereitete schon Descartes und seinen Nachfolgern große Schwierigkeiten, welche diese zum Teil sehr unbefriedigende Lösungen vorschlugen.

„Seele" und „Leib" im Sinne Descartes müssen nämlich aufeinander wirken können, einerseits um die kausale Verbindung von objektiven Ereignissen auf unsere innere Sphäre zu erklären, und dies nicht nur bei den Sinnesempfindungen, sondern auch beim Einfluß von Drogen auf unseren Bewußtseinszustand. Andererseits muß man der Wirksamkeit unseres Willens auf die Außenwelt Rechnung tragen. Irgendwie müssen also Seele und Leib, oder Geist und Materie auf einer gemeinsamen ontologischen Ebene gelegen sein, damit ihre Wechselwirkungen interpretiert werden können.

Das heißt, daß das, was ich hier sehr vage mit „Seele" bezeichnet habe − nämlich die subjektive Sphäre, alles, was von innen her zugänglich ist − irgendwie reifiziert, objektiviert, als zur Welt gehörend betrachtet werden muß. Dies ist unumgänglich, wenn man daran festhält, daß es nur auf der ontologischen, objektiven Ebene echte Kausalbeziehungen gibt und daß es kontinuierliche Kausalketten gibt die von der Welt zu unserer subjektiven Sphäre und umgekehrt von letzterer zur Welt führen.

Aber wirft nicht eben diese Behauptung gewaltige Probleme auf? Man kann möglicherweise einig werden, daß es so sein muß, aber es bleibt die große Aufgabe zu erklären, *wieso* es möglich ist.

Hier einige Bemerkungen zu diesen Problemen:

a) Das *Objekt* unserer Wahrnehmung darf nicht mit dem *Mittel*, mit dessen Hilfe wir wahrnehmen, verwechselt werden. Daß ich einen Baum über das Bild wahrnehme, das auf meine Netzhaut abgebildet wird, heißt nicht, daß ich nichts anderes als dieses Bild sehe, daß es das *Objekt* meines Sehens ist — welche Behauptung nur die unsinnige Interpretation zuließe, daß dort, wo ich vermeintlich einen Baum sehe, in Tat und Wahrheit nur ein Bild des Baumes steht. Das Bild auf meiner Netzhaut ist nur ein Glied in der Kette, die zur Wahrnehmung führt; Objekt der Wahrnehmung ist nicht ein Zwischenglied, nicht einmal das Endglied dieser Kette, sondern deren „Anfangs"-glied.

Das Objekt meines Sehens ist also der Baum, nicht meine Wahrnehmung vom Baum. Man sollte nicht die heimliche Vorstellung hegen, daß ein zweites Subjekt in unserem Kopf steckt, welches das beobachtet, was uns vom äußeren Objekt durch unsere Sinne und Nerven übermittelt wird, nämlich bloß Nervenreize verschiedener Form auf verschiedenen Leitungen. Vielleicht tönt das naiv, doch bin ich nicht sicher, ob die eine oder andere Erkenntnislehre nicht in einer solchen Vorstellung ihre Wurzel hat, und es gibt Physiologen, die sich ernsthaft mit der Frage befaßt haben, warum uns die Objekte aufrecht erscheinen, obgleich sie auf der Netzhaut umgekehrt abgebildet sind.

b) Müssen zwei Substanzen wesensgleich sein, um aufeinander wirken zu können? Schließt die Hypothese, daß Seele und Leib wesensfremde Substanzen sind, jede Wechselwirkung zwischen ihnen aus? Sind nicht z.B. ein geladenes Teilchen und ein elektrisches Feld sehr verschiedene Entitäten, was aber das Teilchen nicht daran hindert, ein Feld zu erzeugen und dieses seinerseits, auf ein Teilchen eine Kraft auszuüben?

Die Antwort auf diese Frage hängt vom Status ab, das man der Kausalität gewährt. Gewöhnlich verbindet diese objektive Ereignisse, sie ist sozusagen physikalischer Natur. Ob es eine andere Art der Kausalität gibt als diese physikalische, ist nicht erwiesen. Wenn sie aber materielle und immaterielle Ereignisse verbinden soll, muß sie halb materieller, halb immaterieller Natur sein, was nicht leicht zu lösende metaphysische Probleme stellt.

Etwas sollte man aber m. E. mindestens festhalten, nämlich daß die Kausalität etwas Objektives ist, und daß sie Elemente objektiver Natur miteinander verbindet: z.B. sind Teilchen und Feld beide objektive Entitäten.

c) Niemand sollte daran Anstoß nehmen, daß eine und dieselbe Entität, zur ontologischen Ebene gehörend, epistemologisch auf ganz verschiedene Arten erfaßt werden kann. Es ist sogar die Regel. Ein und derselbe Kreis kann uns als verschieden abgeplattete Ellipsen oder sogar als ein Geradensegment erscheinen. Ein und derselbe Würfel kann gesehen und betastet, ein Blitz gesehen und gehört werden.

Nichts hindert also die Seele, einerseits als ein subjektiv Empfundenes zu erscheinen und andererseits eine wie der Leib zur Welt gehörende objektive Realität zu besitzen. Das scheint besonders natürlich für die subjektive Sphäre anderer, die ich nicht von innen empfinden kann wie meine eigene, sondern auf die ich nur über deren objektives Verhalten schließen kann. Epistemologisch hat mein Bewußtsein nicht nur einen gewaltigen Vorrang, es breitet sich sogar über die ganze Szene aus und duldet nichts außer sich; ontologisch ist es aber nur eines unter anderen und hat da ein objektives Sein wie die anderen belebten und unbelebten Körper.

d) Wieso darf ich von einer ontologischen Ebene sprechen, wenn ich doch von der Feststellung ausgegangen bin, daß uns die Welt nur über Wahrnehmungen, d.h. über private Ereignisse, erreichbar ist?

Dieses Vorgehen enthält aber gar keinen Widerspruch, wenn man mit Einstein die These vertritt, daß die ontologische Ebene nicht etwas primär Gegebenes ist, sondern etwas, das ich, von den Wahrnehmungen ausgehend, konstruiere, als Erklärung eben dieser Wahrnehmungen. *Im* Modell sind die ontologischen Entitäten Ursache der modellierten Wahrnehmungen, aber *das* Modell habe ich nach den ursprünglichen Wahrnehmungen konstruiert. Auf der Metaebene sind Wahrnehmungen epistemologisch das erste und Ontologie das letzte, im Modell sind die ontologischen Entitäten das erste und verursachen kausal die Wahrnehmungen.

Die ontologische Ebene unterscheidet sich von der objektiven dadurch, daß letztere noch epistemologischer Natur ist, d.h. je nach individuellem Subjekt und dessen Wissensstand variieren kann, die ontologische Ebene aber als etwas postuliert wird, das sich nicht mit dem Aneignen neuen Wissens ändern würde und vom einzelnen Erkennenden nicht abhängig wäre. Ontologie ist also nur ein praktisch unerreichbarer Grenzbegriff, der jenseits aller heutigen und künftigen objektiven Wissen der einzelnen Subjekte liegt. Wir postulieren sie, sie ist im Prinzip nicht unerkennbar, aber uns steht nur unser individuelles objektives Wissen zur Verfügung, das ihr gegenüber nur lückenhaft und teilweise sogar falsch sein kann. Noch mehr: dort, wo unser persönliches Modell gegebenenfalls mit ihr übereinstimmen würde, wüßten wir es nicht einmal. Von keinem Teil unseres Wissens können wir behaupten, er entspreche endgültig der Ontologie. Das einzige, was wir wissen ist, daß diese sich nicht ändert, wenn bloß unser Wissen erweitert oder verbessert wird.

e) Objektivieren bedeutet nicht „wissenschaftlich erklären". Man kann einem Ereignis eine objektive Realität zuschreiben, auch wenn man es nicht im Einzelnen erklären und auf bekannte Gesetze zurückführen kann.

Ähnlich braucht man, um eine kausale Beziehung zwischen zwei Ereignissen aufzuweisen, nicht alle Glieder der Kette erklärt zu haben. Es gibt eine empirisch-pragmatische Kausalität: ich beweise, daß B Wirkung von A ist, wenn ich B nach Belieben erzeugen oder hindern kann, indem ich auf A wirke. Ich sage, daß meine subjektive Wahrnehmung eines Objekts von diesem Objekt verursacht wird, weil ich meine Wahrnehmung erzeugen oder aufheben kann, indem ich es anschaue oder mich von ihm abwende; ich sage, daß mein subjektiver Schmerz vom Stich dieser Nadel verursacht wird, weil ich es jedesmal empfinde, wenn die Nadelspitze in meine Haut eindringt.

Die Erklärung einer kausalen Beziehung z.B. mit Hilfe eines wissenschaftlichen Gesetzes bringt zu diesem empirisch-pragmatischen Begriff der Kausalität nichts hinzu, denn die Aufstellung des Gesetzes ist nichts mehr als die Legalisierung einer solchen vorher konstatierten kausalen Verbindung.

f) Die Zuordnung von Elementen zweier Ebenen ist streng von einer kausalen Beziehung zwischen diesen einander zugeordneten Elementen zu unterscheiden.

Gewissen subjektiven Ereignissen (z.B. Empfinden eines Schmerzes) werden objektive Ereignisse (Verletzung der Haut, Nervenübertragung, Vorgänge im Zentralnervensystem) zugeordnet. Das heißt aber nicht, daß der neurophysiologische Vorgang in meinem Zentralnervensystem meinen subjektiven Schmerz *verursacht*. Verursacht wird etwas auf der *ontologischen* Ebene, dem epistemologisch einerseits ein subjektiver Schmerz, andererseits ein neurophysiologischer Vorgang zugeordnet ist.

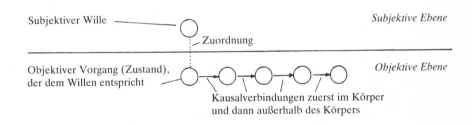

Subjektive und objektive Ebenen sind komplementäre *epistemologische* Ebenen.
Subjektiver und „objektiver Schmerz" sind getrennt auf der epistemologischen Ebene, aber verschmelzen zu einer einzigen Entität auf der ontologischen Ebene.

Man könnte für den Willensakt ein ähnliches Schema zeichnen:

Subjektive Ebene   Subjektiver Schmerz

Zuordnung

Objektive Ebene   Objektiver Vorgang, der dem Schmerz entspricht (objektivierte Subjektivität)

Nadelstich

Kausalverbindungen innerhalb des Körpers

Aber der empirisch-pragmatische Begriff der Kausalität braucht nicht an der Grenze der Objektivität Halt zu machen: es können die objektive Kausalkette und die Zuordnung zwischen objektiver und subjektiver Ebene auf einmal erfaßt werden: die Tatsache, daß ich einen subjektiven Schmerz beliebig erzeugen und beheben kann, indem ich mich steche oder aufhöre, mich zu stechen, beweist die Kausalkette auf der ontologischen Ebene und die Zuordnung eines subjektiven Schmerzes zu diesem Ereignis.

Zusammenfassend würde ich sagen, daß die Leib-Seele- und die Geist-Materie-Unterscheidung, welche die erste erweitert, verwischt wurden durch eine Verschmelzung aller Ebenen: einerseits wurde eine vorwissenschaftliche ursprüngliche Erklärung zu einer metaphysisch-religiösen, zusätzlich belastet mit moralischen Wertungen, andererseits hat man von einer epistemologischen Differenz auf eine ontologische geschlossen. Eine saubere Trennung all dieser Gesichtspunkte kann zu einem klareren Verständnis der Probleme führen oder sogar manche von diesen überhaupt verschwinden lassen.

* * *

DAS METAPHYSISCHE SUBJEKT:
DIE STUFE EINER LEITER[1]

Paul Hübscher
Universität Bern

Nur Logisches ist logisch faßbar. Diese Tautologie ist das Fundament von Wittgensteins Erkenntnistheorie im *TLP*. Sie erklärt auch die Stellung des Subjekts in Wittgensteins *TLP*. Das Subjekt ist das logische Ordnende. Doch in der Logik gibt es kein Subjekt, sondern nur Objekte und ihre Relationen (vgl. *TLP* 5.631). D.h., wenn das Subjekt die Objekte logisch ordnet, kommt es zum Schluß, daß es selbst nicht existiert. Das erkenntnistheoretische Subjekt schafft sich selber ab. Es ist sich selber ja nur *logisch* faßbar, als Ding für es, nicht als Ding an sich, als Subjekt. Die Erkenntnistheorie des *TLP* akzeptiert nur Dinge-für-das-Subjekt, aber kein Subjekt. Doch gerade indem sie das Subjekt eliminiert, kreiert sie es. Dem Begriff ,Subjekt' in der Bezeichnung ,Dinge-für-das-Subjekt' muß logischerweise etwas entsprechen, sonst wäre er nicht im Sprachbild. Die Existenz dieses Subjekts kann zwar noch gesehen werden, aber sie ist nicht mehr logisch faßbar. Wir stoßen im *TLP* zweimal auf eine Grenze des Erkennens: bei den Dingen (*TLP* 6.44) und beim Subjekt. Das macht den *TLP* über weite Strecken zu einer metaphysischen Abhandlung.

Auch Logik ist in gewissem Sinn metaphysisch. Sie definiert die Welt, ist aber nicht materieller Teil davon. Sie ist metaphysisch im Sinne von Kants ,metaphysica generalis': eine Aussage über die Gegenstände möglicher Erfahrung. Doch der *TLP* stößt in ein Gebiet vor, das zur ,metaphysica specialis' gehört, die als Wissenschaft laut Kant nicht möglich sein soll. Hier geht es letztlich um das höchste Wesen – Gott.

Die Schwierigkeit bei der Behandlung der Metaphysik ist, daß die Sprache als logisches Bild der Welt gegenüber Metaphysischem versagt. Die Grenze, die der *TLP* zwischen Welt und ,metaphysica specialis' zieht, ist wesentlich eine sprachliche Grenze. Das erkennende Subjekt kann die Grenze transzendieren, aber es wird die Sprache zurücklassen müssen. Der *TLP* versucht, die Grenze aufzuzeigen, indem er dem Subjekt nachweist, was es hat und was es nicht hat. Dieses an den Jahresabschluß eines Kaufmannes erinnernde Vorgehen zeitigt folgendes Resultat: Das Subjekt hat die Welt nur, insofern sie logisch geordnet ist. Wo die Logik aufhört, hört die Welt-für-das-Subjekt auf. Die verblüffende Einsicht des *TLP* ist, daß die Logik aufhört, wo sie beginnt – im die Welt ordnenden Subjekt. Daß das Subjekt die Grenze ist, *zeigt* sich darin, daß es logisch nicht erfaßt ist. Es ist „metaphysisch" (*TLP* 5.633), da es als Grenze nicht mehr zur Welt gehört. Gehört es zur ,metaphysica specialis'? Ich behaupte: Nein.

Die Welt, die das metaphysische Subjekt ordnet, ist der Mikrokosmos (*TLP* 5.63). Dieser Begriff und der Begriff ,Grenze' (und nicht ,Ende'!) der Welt suggerieren, daß es noch etwas jenseits des Mikrokosmos geben muß: einen Makrokosmos. Dieser Makrokosmos muß a-logisch sein, da er sonst durch die Logik in den Mikrokosmos eingeordnet würde. Dennoch manifestiert er sich im Mikrokosmos. Es zeigt sich, daß nicht alles dort logisch und erklärbar ist. Zum Beispiel sind Naturgesetze bloße Beschreibungsnetze. Daß sich ein Gegenstand nach ihnen richtet, ist sozusagen reine Gefälligkeit von ihm. Das Subjekt erfährt, daß seine Welt eine Grenze gegen außen hat: „Die Welt ist unabhängig von meinem Willen." (*TLP* 6.373) Diese Welt der unabhängigen Objekte ist der Makrokosmos. Wittgenstein nennt ihn nicht, da er darauf beharrt, daß über ,metaphysica specialis' nicht gesprochen werden kann. Er weist nur auf, wo sich der Makrokosmos im Mikrokosmos zeigt. Hat das ordnende Subjekt erfaßt, daß es etwas von ihm Unabhängiges gibt, so hat es sich als „metaphysisches Subjekt" (*TLP* 5.633) erfaßt, d.h. es begreift seinen Mikrokosmos als eingegrenztes Ganzes. Zugleich begreift es sich selber als Grenze. Dies ist die „Anschauung der Welt sub specie aeterni", das „Gefühl der Welt" (*TLP* 6.45). Das ‚Gefühl der Welt' ist ein nicht-logisches Erfassen der Welt. Es ist Erkenntnis ohne Kategorien. Hier ist das Subjekt jenseits des Mikrokosmos und damit jenseits der Sprache.

Es ist seine an Frege orientierte Abbildtheorie der Bedeutung, die es Wittgenstein erlaubt, diese Leiter vom Mikrokosmos in den Makrokosmos zu bauen. Für ihn wie für Frege ist die Bedeutung eines Zeichens an real Gegebenes gebunden. Doch der Sinn eines Zeichens kann außerhalb des real Gegebenen liegen. Wittgenstein erblickt hier die Möglichkeit, die ‚metaphysica specialis' in der Abbildtheorie des *TLP* einzuordnen. Ein Zeichen kann in seinem *Sinn* auf die ‚metaphysica specialis' hinweisen. Es ist allerdings eine besondere Art von Zeichen. Wittgenstein legt Wert darauf, daß das Satzzeichen eine Tatsache ist und daß Tatsachen als Zeichen aufgefaßt werden können, ja daß nur Tatsachen einen Sinn haben können (vgl. *TLP* 3.14–3.1431). Einen auf die ‚metaphysica specialis' hinweisenden Sinn kann nun nur eine ‚Tatsache großen Ausmaßes' haben: das Leben. Wittgenstein identifiziert damit den logischen, von Frege inspirierten Gebrauch von ‚Sinn' mit dem der Alltagssprache, wo ‚Sinn' auch ‚Zweck' oder ‚Ziel' konnotieren kann.

Damit haben wir eine Stufenfolge von Subjekten: Das Leben wird von einem empirischen Subjekt geführt. Dieses wird im *TLP* abgebildet als das sprachliche Subjekt ‚Ich'. Die Abbildung führt aber als Verallgemeinerung auf eine höhere Stufe. ‚Ich' bezeichnet nun das erkenntnistheoretische, logische Subjekt. (Das logische Subjekt ist sozusagen eine Variable, die den Wert eines empirischen Subjektes annehmen kann). Dieses logische, erkenntnistheoretische Subjekt regiert ordnend seine Welt, den Mikrokosmos. Wittgenstein nennt es das metaphysische Subjekt. Es ist im selben Sinne metaphysisch, wie die Logik metaphysisch ist. Zwar nicht Teil des Mikrokosmos, aber mit ihm verbunden, sind sie der ‚metaphysica generalis' zuzuordnen. Hier endet das Welt-Bild des *TLP*, da hier für ihn die Sprache endet. Doch er hinterläßt Pfeile, die über das Ausgesprochene hinausdeuten. Der Begriff ‚Mikrokosmos' weist auf den Begriff ‚Makrokosmos': wenn das Bild, das die erkennend geordnete Welt gibt, richtig ist, muß es etwas geben, das sich nicht erkennend ordnen läßt. Es gibt aber für den *TLP* keine Welt ohne Ordnung. Somit können wir folgende Schlüsse ziehen: Auch der prima facie nicht geordnete Makrokosmos verfügt über Ordnung. Er verfügt damit über ein ordnendes Subjekt. Wie das erkenntnistheoretische Subjekt gegenüber dem empirischen auf einer höheren Stufe steht, steht das Subjekt des Makrokosmos gegenüber dem erkenntnistheoretischen höher. Der Makrokosmos ist somit das Gebiet der ‚metaphysica specialis', sein Subjekt ist Gott.

Sprachlich ist Gott nicht zugänglich. Die Philosophie und insbesondere der *TLP* ist der Versuch, dieses Nichtsprachliche aufzuzeigen, indem das Sagbare vom Unsagbaren unterschieden wird. Das Sagbare aber sind Sätze der Naturwissenschaft, nur diese haben Bedeutung. Andere Sätze gibt es nicht, und damit keine Philosphie. Die einzige Art, Philosophie zu lehren, ist, den Kandidaten darauf hinzuweisen, daß er entweder Naturwissenschaft treibt oder bedeutungslose Sätze äußert (*TLP* 6.53). ‚Metaphysica specialis' wird nicht mit unbedeutenden sprachlichen Zeichen erfaßt, sondern nur mit dem großen Symbol eines ganzen Lebens.

Diese Einsicht hat ihre Konsequenzen auf die Selbsteinschätzung des *TLP*. ‚Logik' und ‚Philosophie' sind nicht nur im Titel sondern in der ganzen Abhandlung prominent. Doch die Logik entpuppt sich als in ihren Gründen nicht begründbar (Wittgenstein nennt kein Beispiel eines Elementarsatzes oder eines Namens). Die Philosophie existiert nur als Methode, sich selber zu überwinden. Dieses Resultat ist paradox, unsinnig (*TLP* 6.54), nonsense. Es ist nicht sinnlos. Der *TLP* hat im Gegenteil sehr viel Sinn, weil er zeigt, in welchem Verhältnis das empirische Subjekt zu Gott steht. Indem er den wesentlich abbildenden Charakter der Zeichen aufzeigt, wird er zu einer Leiter. Das empirische Subjekt erkennt sich und seine Grenzen in seinem Abbild, dem erkenntnistheoretischen („metaphysischen") Subjekt. Es erkennt auch, daß es ein makrokosmisches Subjekt geben muß. Paradox und deshalb unsinnig ist der *TLP*, weil das Subjekt am Schluß erkennt, daß es der Leiter gar nicht bedurft hätte, daß ihm die Logik des *TLP* bei der Gewinnung des Sinns des Lebens nicht helfen *kann*. Die ‚metaphysica specialis‘ ist nur durch ein Heraustreten aus der Logik zu begreifen. Dieses Heraustreten geschieht in der mystischen Anschauung der Welt als-begrenztes-Ganzes. Doch nun kann nichts mehr gesagt werden, da mit der Logik auch die Sprache verschwindet.

———————

ANMERKUNG

[1] Es handelt sich hier um eine Kurzfassung der ausführlichen Diskussion desselben Themas in:
P. Hübscher, *Der Einfluß von Johann Wolfgang Goethe und Paul Ernst auf Ludwig Wittgenstein* (Bern 1985).

* * *

ON THE AGREEMENT OF HUMAN MIND AND THE REASON OF NATURE

Adolf Hübner
Austrian Ludwig Wittgenstein Society, Kirchberg am Wechsel

I

We suggest accepting as objectively correct (true)
a) that within the existing universe (cosmos, physical reality, nature, "world"), which has the *property* "to be in motion", nothing can exist in a state of (absolute) rest. ("Nothing can be static"),
b) that, because of the property of the existing universe "to be in motion" a class of objects "being at (absolute) rest" is logically impossible. Since a "resting system of reference" would belong to this class of objects, we suggest accepting as well that such a system is logically impossible.

Because of the validity of points (a) and (b) we suggest accepting the *result* of the mathematical evaluation of the equivalence of figures 1 and 2, *which bears* the consequence of the impossibility of the existence of a resting system of reference (for the reason that other wise the existence of exceptions within logic would have had to be accepted) as objectively correct (true) in respect to the existing universe.[1]

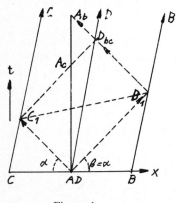

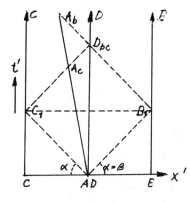

Figure 1   Figure 2

The result of the mathematical evaluation of figures 1 and 2 is $E = mc^2$. We suggest accepting this result as not-theoretically, but as a logical condition of a universe, which possesses the property „to be in motion".

The *verbal* evaluation of figures 1 and 2 (this is the evaluation of figures 1 and 2 by means of an application of "common sense" on the basis of universal regularities of natural languages–which we want to call "conceptual logic") permits certain propositions. If we want to proceed in this process of recognition of our world in a rational way, *we can't help* but apply the intellectual faculties (mind, reason, common sense, "ratio") as common sense by making use of the formulating capacity (the "medium") of the *given* structure of a natural language.[2] (If intellectual faculties working as common sense in the way described above, were not only incomplete but also "unsuitable" respecting the reason of nature, every rational enterprise having the aim of knowing something, which definitely corresponds to nature's (logical) structure would be absolutely hopeless.—Figures 1 and 2, with their correctness as well as their "world-concern" including how they bear on a correct world-concern had then to be seen as a "strange unlikelihood" as far as "world-suitability" is concerned.)

If we apply common sense to evaluate figures 1 and 2 verbally, we arrive at the following propositions:

1) Space and time are in a state of coupling.

2) There does not exist such a thing as an "absolute time". The times of systems of co-ordinates, which move at whatever different speed against on another are not identical.

3) The transformation of a system of co-ordinates x to a system of co-ordinates x' is necessarily connected with a change of the measure for length, which *can* (and actually does) *take place gradually*.

We suggest accepting as objectively correct both the mathematical as well as the conceptual evaluation of the two figures—where *the "special case" of the existing universe is concerned*.

Since the existing universe is *one* universe (and not universe*s*), it cannot be a) a non-Einsteinian "old" world, obeying the laws of Newton's mechanics, and b) an Einsteinian world, obeying the *laws* of TSR, *at the same time*. If this (one single) universe has to obey *the laws* of TSR, the following law, which stands above all laws of nature, *and which prevents actions of human minds from posing as physical events,* has to be derived from the context of point (3) (*within a process of rational recognition of this world*):

If gradual changes of measures belong to the competence of an intrinsic reason in nature, and are performed as real events within physical reality, abstract gradual changes of measures through the human mind must remain without consequences in a definite way.

If, within an Einsteinian world, which possesses the property "to be in motion", the quantities of all possible types of fundamental physical entities (the fundamental velocity, the elementary mass, the elementary action-quantity, the elementary electric charge) do not depend on measure-conditions of all possible kinds of measures, whereas all these quantities do depend on one another numerically (!), it follows

a) that we will *always* arrive at (numerically) the same quantities for fundamental physical entities independent of measure-conditions, and

b) that existing constant, relations between the quantities of fundamental physical entitites *can be founded on laws only, the character of which is purely formal*.

If the law, which we have deduced from the context of point (3) is a logical condition of the world, its formal representation should, in principle, fall within the range of man's intellectual faculties. If this representation is possible, it should have the form of a geometrical construction, in which the numerical sizes of fundamental physical entities appear as *scalar ratios*, pointing at one another—thus demonstrating that they all are mere *aspects* of a physical reality, which is one formal wholeness. Whithin this construction the measure-unit "one" for length must not play a role at all. It can be seen easily that the length "one" of the radius of the unit circle can be *chosen arbitrarily* and *remains without influence* on goniometric functions. We have good reasons to assume that the formal representation of "our" law should have to do with angles on the basis "r" of the unit circle. Only if we call the radius of a circle "one" and take it as cathetus of a rectangular triangle, the length of the counter-cathetus corresponds to the tangent-value of a given angle. The logic of all goniometric functions contains the *allowance* to choose the length of the radius of the unit circle arbitrarily, but it also contains a prohibition on expressing the size of the radius of the unit circle by a number, which is *not* 1. But here we also have to note that triangles belonging to the sinus- (or cosinus-)form of triangle-constructions are under artificial coercion to remain within the unit circle, while triangles belonging to the tangent-form of triangle-constructions can grow "in a natural way along the numerical series". Depending on the length of the counter-cathetuses, the hypotenuses of such triangles grow in a natural way as well. We are led to the hypothesis: If the natural behaviour of physical reality depends on the natural behaviour of formal elements, while it cannot be influenced by measure-conditions, goniometric functions of the tangent-form could possibly be the adequate logical framework to demonstrate this dependence.

II

From the recent history of physics we know that two theories remain in a state of rivalry until unified into a single homogeneous and comprehensive description of physical reality. The two "theories" are:

1) The Theory of Special Relativity, within which the speed of light plays an important role.

2) The Theory of Quantum Mechanics, within which the relation $\lambda = h/p$ is significant, but *not* velocities close to the speed of light. If it is presupposed that the result of the TSR ($E = mc^2$) is correct beyond doubt, while quantum mechanics is correct at least to a certain extent, we will suppose that both theories are different but *logically equivalent* descriptions of physical reality. The initial aim of this paper is to show that there is a logical equivalence between the two "conflicting" theories. The primary aim is to show that the title of this paper is significant and true. Our first aim confronts us immediately with two essential questions: a) How is the methodological procedure adequate and how does it promise to attain our goal? and b) which form of proof can we arrive at eventually (in case of "success") to demonstrate that our *understanding* of the logical equivalence of the two theories is correct? Dealing with question (b), first, we have to see clearly that the results of a process of understanding based on facts found by experiments or derived from the evaluation of experiments cannot be subject anew to experimental proof. Thus we are fully aware that our results can—at best—have the form of a geometric-arithmetic construction, showing that the fundamental element of QM, namely h (Planck's Constant), "depend on", "leads to", "is a consequence of", "is conditioned by" (etc.) elements of the TSR, as c^2 and (a special amount of) "mass" *within the logic of mathematics*. We have to leave it to the judgement of the scientific and philosophical community, whether "consistently presented connections" between elements of the TSR and QM (in the way as we were able to present them) are accepted as *criteria of objective correctness* or not. The predominant paradigms of both, physics and philosophy will, as we assume, be grave obstacles for an agreement to our presentation.

As far as the methodological procedure (question (a)) is concerned, we want to treat it philosophically in the sense of M. Schlick[3]), making use of the "knowledge-increasing power" of the structure of natural language, this is to say "making use of conceptual logic". We apply conceptual logic to the expression "$E = mc^2$", stating that this expression is not an equation. We justify this statement in the following way: while "mc^2" is constituted by concrete physical facts "E" is an empty symbol, and can as such be replaced by some other symbol. *Only* then, if the expression "E" is *replaced* by a concrete description of physical reality, logically *equivalent but not identical* with the description "mc^2" do we have an equation in front uf us, *which is not tautological*. If possible, we want to show that "QM *completes* TSR" and vice versa. For this process of showing, we cannot see another possibility than equating "somehow" the leading element of QM "h" with "mc^2".

For reasons which we have given in previous writings[4, 5]—and which are "outcomes" of another application of pure conceptual logic—the expression "$E = mc^2$" should, as we are convinced, be transformed into "$h^2f^2 = m_ec^2$" to become a non-tautological equation of a synthetic (knowledge-increasing) character. Since we take it for certain that the human mind cannot deviate from the reason of nature and b) that the existing universe is a singularity (and not universes), every kind of *conceptual* dualism with reference to this universe appears to us to be untenable. Presupposing that we are able to arrive at a "final" comprehensive registration of the mathematical content of QM (in the same way as we take "mc^2 as a comprehensive final result of the TSR), the result of an equation of these two final entries should necessarily be a complete presentation of the mathematical foundations of physical reality. To justify the special form of the equation $h^2f^2 = m_ec^2$—and especially to counter the objection that it is a "violation of dimensionality"—we have to lay special emphasis on the following points:

1) Since h is an "action-quantum" with the dimension gcm²/sec (= impulse x cm *or* energy x sec), it can lead (as it is shown by QM) to permanent states of energy ("electromagnetic vibrations, moving at the speed of light"), which we call "photons" or gamma quants (γ). The energy of photons is *variable* and depends on the frequency ν, according to the equation $E = h\nu$. We claim: because of the "singularity" of physical reality *all* states of energy, no matter how they may appear, must be established by the one and single elementary *action* h. Within one single universe only one elementary action can exist and therefore all physical states necessarily depend on that elementary *action*. Inasmuch as all states of physical reality are states of energy, their energy is a product of the *action* h. Concerning the fundamental material state of energy "electron", the energy of which is *constant*, ν must get a *definite numerical size*, which we will call "f". Therefore the *minimum* fact "hf" must be given with reference to its energy. The energy of the electron is given—according to TSR—with the expression $E = m_e c^2$ (m_e = mass of the electron). Thereout it follows that an equation of the "minimum" form . . . $hf = m_e c^2$ has to exist. With that form "*dimensionality is already exhausted*". All components of the equation have become *scalar quantities*—and we have to accept this exhaustion, and bear all consequences no matter how "strange" they may appear!

2) The energy of the electron is—according to $m_e c^2 - 8{,}187265 \times 10^{-7}$ gcm²/sec² (erg.) The energy of a photon, corresponding to the energy of an electron is also $8{,}187265 \times 10^{-7}$ erg, *but according to* $h\nu$. Thus it follows that—since $hf = h\nu_e = 8{,}187265 \times 10^{-7}$ erg—a "*particle-reality*" $hf = 8{,}187265 \times 10^{-7}$ *erg*, is *impossible*, because such a reality conceptually *is* a "*photonic*-reality", which *corresponds* to the *particle*-reality "electron" (with reference to energy), but certainly *is not* a particle-reality "electron". The conclusion is: though $hf = 8{,}187265 \times 10^{-7}$ *erg* cannot be a complete correct description of the *material* electromagnetic vibration "electron" and yet hf has to occur in the way . . . $hf = m_e c^2$, *purely mathematical derivatives* of hf *have to complete* the equation . . . $hf = m_e c^2$. The reason simply is that there do not exist other action-quantities than h within this universe, which is one, because all its states obey one and the same order—being one and essentially the same in spite of their "different appearance". (The expression "essentially" does not refer to a "metaphysical essence" but only to the fact, that all states of energy have to be results of the one and single action h. In this respect, h can in fact be called "the essence" of physical being.) "Differences of appearance" of states of energy, which are numerically identical concerning to energy (like e^-, e^+ and γ_e) must necessarily depend on the laws of an *internal* (not dimensional, and not dimensionally appearing) natural mathematical structure. In so far as the structure of physical reality cannot be grasped by direct or indirect observations, it is *internal*. Yet, we have an access to this internal structure, because the fundamental action h can appear externally—establishing reality dimensionally, and thus bringing to our knowledge its *importance as a scalar quantity* within the purely mathematical internal structure of the world.

3) Whether sensual appearance is in favour of an internal mathematical structure of the world or not, *conceptual correctness* has to have absolute ("ontological" or "epistemological") *priority*. The opportunity which is offered to us with regard to a correct understanding of the internal logical structure of the world, depends on the fact that we are able a) to get to know the scalar quantity of h by the way of conclusions out of results of certain experiments, and b) that with our knowledge of the scalar quantity of h the hope is justified, that we will be able to grasp the internal mathematical structure of the world *in the form of a bidimensional static geometric construction, which shows the mutual dependence of physical sizes,* may they be components of the TSR or of QM. (The equation . . . $hf = m_e c^2$ allows us not only to disregard dimensions, but it allows us also—according to the purely formal laws of mathematics—to disregard the "decadic step 10^{-7}.") *We* have to justify by way of a bidemensional static geometric construction that our demand "$h^2 f^2 = m_e c^2$" is correct. Given the correctness of this equation, the transformation of a (fundamental) photonic electromagnetic vibration into *the polar material complementarity* of a positive and a negative electromagnetic vibration (positron = e^+, electron = e^-), which occurs as a real event under very specific conditions, can be described as follows:[6]

$h\nu = h\,(2hf^2 + x) \rightarrow 2\,h^2f^2\,(e^+ \text{ plus } e^-) + hx$ (kinetic energy)

4) As we have pointed out previously,[7] "nature" has to be seen as a "natural-logarithmic-mathematician" acting automatically (*without* the possibility of *error*) in the manner of human mathematicians—since there cannot *exist different ways* to do mathematics as ontology. (All human mathematicians, whenever and whereever they may appear in the cosmos need not necessarily arrive at a decadic system of numbers, but necessarily must arrive at an *e* (basis of the system of natural logarithms) logically equivalent to our decadic one.) Just to illustrate the utmost simplicity of a logarithmic view of the logical structure of the world, we will give the following example: ($c_o = 2{,}997925 \times 10^{10}$ cm/sec//10^{10} cm/sec; $1/m_{eo} = 1{,}097748 \times 10^{27}$/g// 10^{28}g;

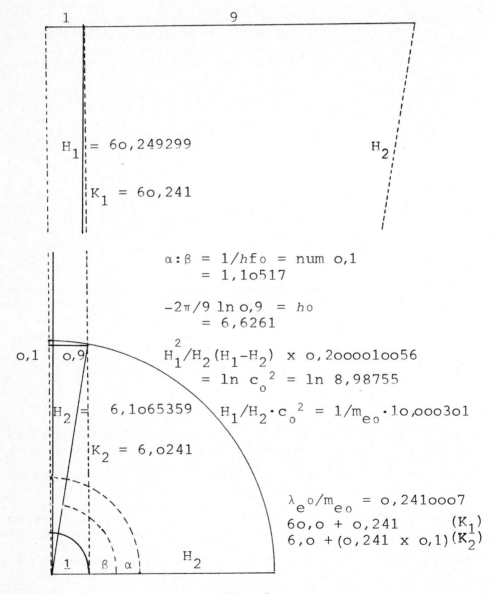

$$H_1 = 60{,}249299$$

$$K_1 = 60{,}241$$

$$\alpha : \beta = 1/hfo = \text{num } o{,}1$$
$$= 1{,}10517$$

$$-2\pi/9 \ln o{,}9 = ho$$
$$= 6{,}6261$$

$$H_1^2/H_2\,(H_1 - H_2) \times o{,}2000010056$$
$$= \ln c_o^2 = \ln 8{,}98755$$

$$6{,}1065359 \qquad H_1/H_2 \cdot c_o^2 = 1/m_{eo} \cdot 10{,}0003o1$$

$$K_2 = 6{,}0241$$

$$\lambda_{eo}/m_{eo} = o{,}2410007$$
$$60{,}o + o{,}241 \qquad (K_1)$$
$$6{,}o + (o{,}241 \times o{,}1)\,(K_2)$$

Figure 3

$0,1 = \ln (1/hf_o) = \ln (1{,}1051709 \times 10^3//10^3)$:
$\{(\ln c_o) + 0{,}1\} \times 2 = \ln (100 \times 1/m_{eo})$

We see that within a logarithmic view seemingly arbitrary values of components of physical reality remain numerically constant, while only decadic steps and the factor 2 do occur.

These components derive from both, TSR and QM. With this paper we want to to prove that *the human mind and the reason of nature are in perfect agreement* with the mere *gradual* restrictions a) that the human mind has the possibility of making (not easily dedectible) *conceptual* mistakes and b) that the reason of nature does fully understand the complexity of CODES (like e's), which it uses to establish physical reality, while the human mind has *difficulties* in understanding the logic of codes. For the time being, we will confine ourselves to the presentation of three more figures, trying to make clear, in which way *we* understand *the mathematical foundations of physics.*

Figure 3 shows that $1/hf_0$ (as it follows out of the equation $h^2f^2 = m_ec^2$) is the ratio of two distinguished angles $\alpha = 89{,}048979^0$ and $\beta = 80{,}574852^0$, given through the counter-cathetuses 60,241 and 6,0241 at the unit circle (which is the circle with the radius 1). The ln of $1/hf_0$ is 0,1 (numerus $e^{0{,}1} = 1{,}1051709 = \alpha/\beta$). There is no doubt that for our decadic e the exponential step 0,1 is the first (and therefore distinguished) step to establish a relation to the decadic realm of numbers outside of itself. Figure 3 shows that the geometrical representation of the distinguished number 1,1051709 (being the numerus of $e^{0{,}1}$) depends on a *distinguished "origin"* of the general ratio 10 : 1, and this distinguished origin, given by the ratio of the numbers 60,241 and 6,0241, does exist in the field of mathematical logic *only one time.*

What has to be proved is our assertion that we had to arrive at those number-sequences for fundamental physical sizes, at which we have arrived (independent of the "this-like sizes" of our measure-units) for the reason of an a-priori-dependence of physical reality on the purely formal laws of mathematical logic within the framework of the decadic system of numbers, which we have introduced (see page 182). If we call the hypotenuse of the triangle, given by α, the cathetus 1 and the counter-cathetus 60,241, H_1, and designate the hypotenuse of the triangle, given be β, the cathetus 2 and the counter-cathetus 6,0241, as H_2, we can establish the relation

$$(H_1)^2 / H_2 (H_1 - H_2) = 10{,}979149$$

And if we feed our computer with the numbers of c_o (this is $2{,}997925 \times 10^{10}$ cm/sec//10^{10} cm/sec) and then simply push the button "ln" we get 1,0979204. Hence it is shown that a ratio 1 : 10 exists between the number-sequence of the ln, obtained out of the number-sequence of an empirical measured value and an a priori (formal) value, which follows out of a geometrical construction, in which the distinguished origin of the ratio 10 : 1 is the ratio of two counter-cathetuses at the unit circle. (As one can see, we have expressed the numbers 60,241 and 6,0241 as multiples of the length *"one"* of the radius of the unit circle and have put them into the position of counter-cathetuses.) The connecting lines between the final points of the stretches 60,241 and 6,0241 and the central point of the unit circle produce angles the ratio of which can be understood as the numerus of $e^{1:10}$. (Remark: Just by chance we have learned that the ratio of the specific gravities of "heavy water" and water is 1,105 . . . also.) But the ratio 10 : 1 appears twofold in another way within figure 3: While at its final point H_2 has reached a distance 1 from the vertical line, raised through the centre of the unit circle, H_1 has reached a distance of precisely 0,1 at that height. At the height of the final point of H_1, this hypotenuse has reached the distance 1, while the prolongation of H_2 has reached a distance 9 from the vertical.

If we admit that the way in which physical events occur (the motion of photons occurs at the speed of light) depends on formal laws shown by figure 3, then we come to see that "abstract changes of the measure for length−performed by the human mind−"cannot influence the existing numerical relations: while we can very well choose an arbitrary size for the measure of length (and can call it centimeter, inch, or foot) we can't help but call the radius of the unit circle 1, and the counter-cathetuses 60,241 and 6,0241.

On the other hand, our construction in two-dimensional space provides us with an a priori knowledge of number-sequences, which correspond (with an accuracy of 5 figures) to empirical values. In addition a mutual dependence of number-sequences, corresponding to empirical sizes of quite different physical entities can be deduced:

$0,20000100563 \times (H_1)^2 / H_2 (H_1 - H_2) = \ln c_0^2 (c_0^2 = 8,98755 \times 10^0)$
$\{(\ln c_0) + 0,1\} \times 2 = \ln (100 \times 1/m_{eo})$

If we take the numerically constant difference of the deviations of H_1 and H_2 from the vertical at certain points as meaningful (this difference is 0,9 at the final point of H_2 and 9 at the final point of H_1), we arrive at the number-sequence of Planck's Constant "heuristically": (Heuristics was always a method of mathematicians.)

$1/9 \ln 0,9 = -1,054802; -1,0545802 \times -1 \times 2\pi = 6,6261227$ ($h_0 = 6,626196$)

If we accept that all physical events have to leave the fundamental constants and their relations untouched, we can understand them as rotations of the elements of fig. 3 around the centre of the unit-circle.

While, if we take the ratio $\alpha : \beta$ a thousand times, we arrive at 1/hf, as it follows out of $h^2 f^2 = m_e c^2$, we arrive *at the distinguished* character of the 360°-graduation, if we take a thousand times angle α, relate the resulting angle $\gamma = -51,022018°$ to $\alpha = 89,048978°$ (our computer subtracts automatically 247 complete rotations) and multiply by 2π:

$2\pi (\gamma : \alpha) = 2\pi (- 51,022018° / 89,048978°) = - 3,6000502$

If the 360°-division is logically distinguished, it follows that codes expressed within this graduation can point directly at numerical physical facts (see figure 4). $-3,6$ can be understood as "-360_0", like c_0.

(If we use another angle-graduation, e.g. the 400°-graduation, we come to the same result). What remains constant is the ratio of the rotations of α and β.

The number-sequence 241, which we have attached to the lengths 60, and 6,0 is identical with the ratio of the wavelength of the state of energy "electron" (as it is given according to $h^2 f^2 = m_e c^2$) to the elementary mass:

$\lambda_{eo}/m_{eo} = 2,1954104 : 9,109558 = 0,2410007$

What is strenghtened by figure 3, is our "conceptual expectation" that the natural mathematical order can—untouched by all arbitrary measure-conditions—only *point back* to itself (showing its different aspects) and cannot deliver *any* nonsensical numbers, belonging to "an unreal transcendent world". Nature as the original mathematician uses "our" system of co-ordinates, as it uses the system of natural logarithms and the 360°-graduation of angles. We have to accept that space possesses a *discontinuous* geometric-arithmetic structure of a unique form, which presents itself, in the way it does, because of the introduced decadic system of numbers.

Remarks:
1) The "natural size" of $1/hf = 1000\alpha/\beta = 1,1051709 \times 10^3$ can be understood from the construction of figure 3 in the following way:
$1/\{\ln(1000\alpha/\beta) - 7\} = \gamma + 180°$ (7,000002017 precisely)
2) The fundamental character of the relation $-2\pi/9 \cdot \ln 0,9 = h_0$ can be illustrated, if we write $2\pi \sqrt{1,23456789} \{10 \ln \sqrt{1,23456789}\} = 6,6261227 = h_0$. (Note: 1,2−3−4−5−6−7−8−9)
(The value of the "empirical" h, as it is given in recent publications is $6,626196 \times 10^{-27} gcm^2/sec.$)

3) The number-sequence 241 appears as a value in diffraction experiments, as they were performed with accelerated electrons by George P. Thomson for the first time. The sharpest diffraction-pictures are obtained, if one uses a tension of 150,52 V. The velocity v of the electrons is according to

$v = \sqrt{2 \cdot e \cdot V/300 \cdot m_e} = 7,2739 \times 10^8$ cm/sec (V = 150,52 V)

Within that formula the expression

$150,52 \times 4,80325 \times 10^{-10}/300 = 2,41 \times 10^{-10}$

appears. In our understanding of physics "sharpness" (exactness) depends on exact numerical fit. If the external conditions are made to fit the internal structure, we will get exactness, *which can be "seen"*:

$\lambda_e/m_e \times 1 \times 10^{-24} = 150,52 \times e/300$ (e = elementary charge)

In Thomson's experiment the numerical correspondence is given twice:

The velocity of the accelerated electrons fits the ratio h/m_e also:

$h/m_e : v = 7,2739 \times 10^0$ cm²/sec : $7,2739 \times 10^8$ cm/sec $= 1 \times 10^{-8}$cm

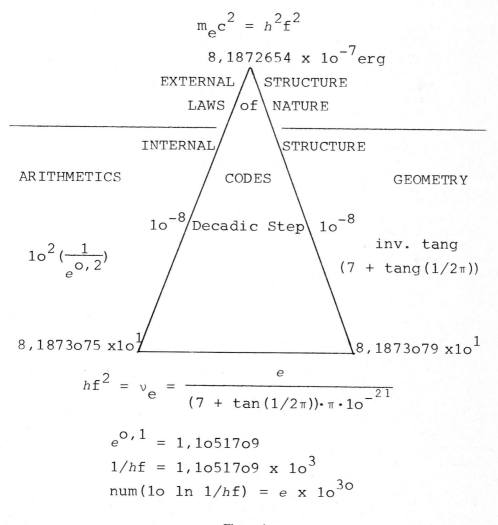

$$m_e c^2 = h^2 f^2$$

$$8,1872654 \times 10^{-7} \text{erg}$$

EXTERNAL / \ STRUCTURE

LAWS / of \ NATURE

INTERNAL / \ STRUCTURE

ARITHMETICS   CODES   GEOMETRY

10^{-8} / Decadic Step \ 10^{-8}

$10^2 (\dfrac{1}{e^{0,2}})$ inv. tang

$(7 + \text{tang}(1/2\pi))$

$8,1873075 \times 10^1$ $8,1873079 \times 10^1$

$$hf^2 = \nu_e = \dfrac{e}{(7 + \tan(1/2\pi)) \cdot \pi \cdot 10^{-21}}$$

$$e^{0,1} = 1,1051709$$

$$1/hf = 1,1051709 \times 10^3$$

$$\text{num}(10 \ln 1/hf) = e \times 10^{30}$$

Figure 4

185

4) To prove and demonstrate the unique and final importance of our "codelike" numerical understanding of nature, our aim must be to deduce fundamental "inertial" values from the equation $h^2f^2 = m_e c^2$.

The mass of the particle "proton" is 1836,1089-times the mass of the electron. We call this value "proton-inertia" $(= 1,8361089 \times 10^3 m_e)$

We have found the following relation:

(We will write "$\varkappa$" for $1/hf$ $(= 1,1051709 \times 10^3))$

$1 \times 10^6 \cdot \ln(\varkappa/\pi)/\{\text{num}(\ln \varkappa/\ln \pi) \cdot \ln \varkappa\} = 1836,1099$

5) In pursuing our goal to show that we do not present a theoretical construction, we succeeded in the following way:

$\ln (c^2/m_e) = \ln (9,8660658 \times 10^{47}) = 1,105106 \times 10^2$

or

$10,000587 \ln (c^2/m_e) = 1/hf$

or (see figure 3)

$\ln (H_1 \times 10^{47}/H_2) = 1,1051063 \times 10^2,$

which means

$\ln (H_1 \times 10^{47}/H_2) \simeq \ln (c^2/m_e)$

Figure 4 shows the dependence of the "outer World" (physical reality, laws of nature) on an internal logical structure. While the "What" (the ultimate "cause") of the world is *beyond* human understanding, the "How" of the world must be logical, and should therefore fall within the range of human intellectual faculties. The decadic step 10^{-8}, which we have indicated in fig. 4 connects logarithmic "codelikeness" with non-logarithmic dimensionality and appears as visible sharpness in adequate experiments.

Figure 5 shows three circles (a), (b), (c).

The common "logical property" of circle (a) and (c) is that they are those *two* circles, which (among the quantity of all circles) alone

1) can be "*distinguished*" by the *logic* of the world, "which has to take care *of itself*",

2) can be "*identified*" by the logic of a reality, which possesses measurable sizes.

Depending on the size of the measure-unit "cm", circle (a), which is the distinguished circle with the circumference 1, gets the size 1×10^5 cm in accordance with the *Concept-logical Principle of General Relativity*. Depending on the size of our measure-unit "cm", circle (c), which is the distinguished circle with the circumference 2π, gets the size 2π *cm*.

(Remark on point 1: With this wording, we have extended Wittgenstein's proposition 5.473, TLP, "die Logik muß für sich selber sorgen" to the working of the logic of our world. Simultaneously we have rejected his cramped remark "eine ausgezeichnete Zahl gibt es nicht" under number 5.553 TLP.)

Circle (b) is a necessary link between circles (a) and (c) and bears the consequences of an arbitrary measure for length. Therefore it is a logical image as well. To wind up the radius of circle (a) it has to perform 44 complete rotations plus a rotation of $74,262487°$ $(= \alpha)$. This angle gives a cotangent-ratio at circle (c), which corresponds to the "radius" of the state of energy "electron" numerically. Against sensuous appearance we hold that a world, which is logical, must obey the laws of its *static* logical foundation. The speed at which circle (b) rotates doesn't take influence on the result "r_e", while it is impossible that fundamental physical sizes are a matter of accidentalness.

If we define a measure for mass, we should not forget that "we do not act onedimensionally but take into consideration 'automatically' the reciprocal value of the square of the speed of light", since with mass we size a property of energy. Moreover we make the measure for the property of matter "to be heavy" depend on our measure for length.

Our point of view is just the opposite from the traditional view which understands that our threedimensional world is embedded in a higher dimensionality. We hold that "the internal logical structure of the world" possesses a logical manifoldness, which is larger than that of

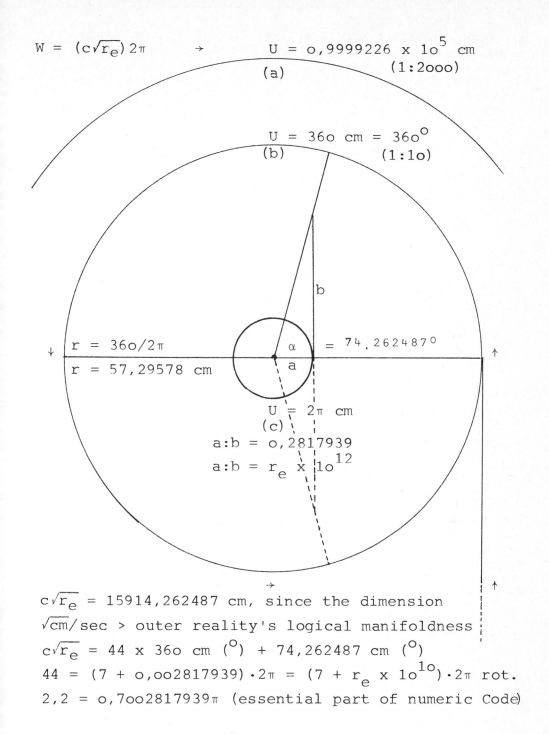

$$W = (c\sqrt{r_e})\,2\pi \qquad \rightarrow \qquad U = 0,9999226 \times 10^5 \text{ cm}$$
$$\text{(a)} \qquad\qquad\qquad (1:2000)$$

$$U = 360 \text{ cm} = 360^{\circ}$$
$$\text{(b)} \qquad\qquad (1:10)$$

$$r = 360/2\pi$$
$$r = 57,29578 \text{ cm}$$

$$\alpha = 74,2624870^{\circ}$$

$$U = 2\pi \text{ cm}$$
$$\text{(c)}$$
$$a:b = 0,2817939$$
$$a:b = r_e \times 10^{12}$$

$c\sqrt{r_e} = 15914,262487$ cm, since the dimension
$\sqrt{cm}/$sec > outer reality's logical manifoldness
$c\sqrt{r_e} = 44 \times 360$ cm $(^{\circ})$ + 74,262487 cm $(^{\circ})$
$44 = (7 + 0,002817939)\cdot 2\pi = (7 + r_e \times 10^{10})\cdot 2\pi$ rot.
$2,2 = 0,7002817939\pi$ (essential part of numeric Code)

Figure 5

physical reality as we know it. We assume that of a given dimensionality (like that of $c \sqrt{r_e}$) the part, which falls within the range of external physical reality can be handled correctly without taking into account its "reality-exceeding attribute". Given that fundamental physical values (dimensional or not) are numerically constant, because of their dependence on mathematical laws, which are as scalar as they are static, measures can take influence in decadic steps only. This is, what we try to show again and again with the ultimate aim of establishing a consistent network, which covers the field of fundamental physics. By making use of the number 2,2 (signifying "rotations", see fig. 5) as exponent of e (the basis of the system of natural logarithms) we arrive at

$\sqrt{e^{2,2}}/f\,\pi \times 1 \times 10^{-3} = (7 + \tan(1/2\,\pi)) \times 10^{-21}$ (f = frequency of electron) and can define the frequency of a photon, which (regarding energy) corresponds to the material state "electron" by

$v_e = e/\{(7 + \tan(1/2\pi))\,\pi \times 10^{-21}\} = e/\,\{(\tan(100\,/e^{0,2}))\,\pi \times 10^{-21}\}$

If the world is a logical case, its logic can rest on laws only, which are given by numbers and their logical connections. These connections are as geometrical as they are arithmetical. "The laws of dimensionality" cannot get "infringed" by us, since such "laws" do not belong to logic. If within the context "rectangular triangle" the cathetus "a" is put "1" the following two theorems appear: $h \times p = q$, and $q/p = b^2$. Hence it is shown that the logic of mathematics works as a context, which cares neither about dimensions nor about (arbitrary) measures.

ENDNOTES

[1] Figures 1 and 2 are taken from S. Flügge, *Wege und Ziele der Physik* (Berlin 1974) with kind permission of Springer-Verlag.

[2] We agree to TLP 5,5563 and reject PI § 97. Together with L. v. Bertalanffy we hold that all natural structures must correspond to one another. Language is a natural structure and we learned to use it correctly without any knowledge of its rules. Nature has developed man *and* his language.

[3] "Philosophische Schriftsteller werden noch lange alte Scheinfragen diskutieren, aber schließlich wird man ihnen nicht mehr zuhören, und sie werden Schauspielern gleichen, die noch eine Zeitlang fortspielen, bevor sie merken, daß die Zuschauer sich allmählich fortgeschlichen haben. Dann wird es nicht mehr nötig sein, über 'philosophische Fragen' zu sprechen, weil man über *alle* Fragen philosophisch sprechen wird, das heißt: sinnvoll und klar." M. Schlick, "Die Wende der Philosophie", *Erkenntnis*, Vol. 1 (Wien 1930/31).

[4] Hübner, A., "On the Logic of Being", *International Logic Review*, Nr. 23−24, pp. 27−45 (Bologna 1981).

[5] Hübner, A., "Das Sein und seine Logik−Einige grundlegende Ergebnisse sprachanalytischer Naturforschung", *Wiener Tierärztliche Monatsschrift*, Hefte 6/7, 8, 9 (Wien 1982).

[6] Hübner, A., "Der logische Code des fundamentalen Seins und seine Dechiffrierung, *Proceedings of the 4th International Wittgenstein Symposium*, pp. 585−609 (Wien 1979).

[5] see (5).

* * *

THE SELF, THE WORLD AND THE METAPHYSICAL SUBJECT

Graham P. Conroy
Portland State University

Jean-Paul Sartre remarked somewhere that all modern philosophy must begin with the Cartesian starting point. That point, the Cartesian cogito, the rational terminus of a chain of methodic doubtings has passed through a strange history from its inception as the French philosopher's Archimedean point (with which he believed he could lever a new universe of knowledge into place) to the many criticisms of it within twentieth century philosophy. The Anglo-Irish philosopher George Berkeley had claimed in his notebooks, or *Philosophical Commentaries*: "Cogito ergo sum. Tautology." Descartes' opponent Hobbes had stated that "Cogito ergo sum" was an illegitimate conclusion from general unverifiable premises. Gilbert Ryle had asserted it leads to the "ghost-in-the-machine" syndrome (a spiritual mechanism working the levers of a material mechanism over which it presides). Other assorted linguists, positivists, and logical empiricists have believed with Berkeley: "Cogito ergo sum. Tautology." There are simply no convincing proofs for the existence of self within the world.

Perhaps this is where many of the arguments intended to establish a metaphysical subject have foundered. They attempt to situate the self, or subject, as a part of the world. Locke's ideas of reflection seem all too often to have been used literally rather than metaphorically. These ideas seem to lead to attempts (through inspection or introspection) to somehow glimpse the eye (I) that was looking out at the world. Locke conceived mind as an unknown substratum for picturings seen within the world; and, for Hume, his introspection could not find a continuant picture that he could call mind, a sort of metaphysical glue holding our perceptions together. All there was was "congeries of perceptions" and a metaphoric way of talking of "someone's" having these experiences. Against Hume, Kant placed the world partly in the self, rather than the self in the world and made the mind constitutive of the world in his 'Copernican Revolution'. From Vienna in the *Analysis of Sensations* Ernst Mach celebrated the demise of the "unsalvageable self" and in his Leipzig laboratory Wilhelm Wundt pursued "psychology without a soul." They doubtlessly held that the early empiricists' try at psychologizing the subject and Kant's attempt to logicize it had both failed. There remained just the world and its descripton.

There are, however, approaches to the establishment of a philosophical, or metaphysical subject which, I believe, escape the destructive devices of both rationalists and empiricists. I will now consider the contributions of two philosophers to a solution of the egological problem. They are George Berkeley and the Tractarian Wittgenstein.

It is my belief that Berkeley was breaking new ground. He had substituted a relational idea of self, or subject, for the qualities-substance inherence model of the Lockeans. Awareness is always awareness of an idea, or set of ideas. Subject is unitary, not to be confused with the divisions of faculty psychology, nor with psychological states, nor with dispositions. These are the *anlagen* of self, not the self. They belong to the world side of the relation. I make the claim that for Berkeley the philosophic subject is forever a subject for experience, never an object of experience. Experience happens in the world. For Berkeley "to be, is to be perceived" is the formula for the existence of the world I encounter; "to be, is to will or to act" is the formula for the existence of that which knows the world. Yet strictly speaking we should not call this the epistemological subject. Psychological description is part of the description of the world. Berkeley only speaks of self as will, other than that it is basically uncharacterizable. This view is consistent throughout the *Principles*, *Three Dialogues* and *Alciphron*. Berkeley has often been called mistakenly a solipsist; a subjective idealist, but he is now being seen for the realist he actually is. The late Professor A. A. Luce often and eloquently made the claim that for Berkeley there was the world of ideas and the self that stood outside them. The body and the sense organs belong to the world of ideas. In a passage which could bear equally well on imputation of both solipsism and realism to Berkeley, Wittgenstein says: "Here it can be seen that solipsism, when its implications are followed out strictly accords with pure realism. The self of solipsism shrinks to a point without extension and there remains the reality co-ordinated with it." (*TLP* 5.64) "Thus there is a sense in which philosophy can talk about the self in a non-psychological way." (*TLP* 5.641) The subject does not belong to the world: rather, it is a limit of the world.

As if to underscore this interpretation Berkeley explicates the phrase 'in the mind' not in terms of a place or a state, but in terms of a relation.

> This perceiving active being is what I call mind, *spirit, soul*, or *myself*. By which words I do not denote any one of my ideas, but a thing entirely distinct from them, wherein they exist or, *which is the same thing*, [italics mine], whereby they are perceived—for the existence of an idea consists in being perceived. (*Alciphron*, sect. 2)

Berkeley wanted to say some things about the self but realized the difficulty. He hit upon the term 'notion' as a way out. He said of the notion, not the idea of self:

> Though it must be owned at the same time that we have some notion of soul, spirit and the operations of the mind, such as willing, loving, hating—inasmuch as we know or understand the meaning of these words. (*Alciphron*, sect. 5)

Ludwig Wittgenstein comes off better by saying we can't say anything of the self or subject. It manifests itself. Language is the limits of my world. We may speak only of the world. As a thought experiment he imagines himself to be the author of a book called, *The World I Found*. He states in the *Notebooks of 1914–16*, entry for 23.5.15:

> In the book "The World I Found" I should also have to report on my body and say which members are subject to my will, etc. For this is a *way of isolating the subject*, or rather of showing that in *an important sense* there is no such thing as the subject; for it would be the one thing that could not come into the book. (Cf. *TLP* 5.631)

What Wittgenstein does is to show that the metaphysical subject cannot be part of the world, but must stand in a relation to it; or, if anything can be said about it, that it is the limit of the world. In this act of isolating the self, solipsism, idealism, and realism come into harmony. He writes:

> This is the way I have travelled: Idealism singles man out from the world as unique, solipsism singles me out, and at last I see that I too belong with the rest of the world, and so on the one side *nothing* is left over, and on the other side, as unique, *the world*. In this way idealism leads to realism if it is strictly thought out. (*Notebooks*, entry for 20.10.16)

Now, what can be said about will and its confronting of world. He says among a series of affirmations:

> That life is the world. (Cf. *TLP* 5.621)
> That my will penetrates the world.
> That my will is good or evil. (*Notebooks*, entry for 11.6.16)

The domain of value must lie outside the world. It is for Wittgenstein as it was for Berkeley, and, I believe, Schopenhauer a matter of will. If the world has any value (and for L. W. it does) then that value must lie outside the world. The subject, values, the meaning of life, are all boundary conditions attained at the ladder's top ((Cf. *TLP* 6.54). Beyond that lies the transcendental, the mystical; but mystical only in that it can't be said. Berkeley had called the self a substance, using the substance-talk of the medievals which had been kept as part of the vocabulary of Cartesianism. On Wittgensteinean terms Berkeley is saying what cannot be said. The notion of a boundary conveys the situation more aptly.

It is my belief that the *Tractatus* and the *Investigations* do not contradict each other in regard to philosophy of mind, though the later philosophy takes a great leap forward. By referring to the metaphysical subject as a world limit, and leaving it radically uncharacterizable, it becomes like Musil's man—*ohne Eigenschaften*—whom qavonnei. This "it" is not a man, however; for as Wittgenstein has stated in the *Tractatus*: "The philosophical self is not the human being, not the human body, or the human soul with which psychology deals, but rather the metaphysical subject, the limit of the world—not a part of it." (*TLP* 5.641) Berkeley would also see body, psychological states, etc., as mind-related, but not as parts of what is meant by person. Subject stands in opposition to its ideas which are the objects of the empirical sciences including psychology. Wittgenstein's explanation is much the clearer despite his aphoristic and elliptical style. He established the metaphysical subject in the *Tractatus* and then explicated his psychological analyses and suggestions in the *Investigations* and the later writings on psychology. In so doing he had already avoided behaviouristic reduction as well as the need for neural identity theories. Life is not just physical, nor just psychological.

> The World and Life are one.
> Physiological life is of course not "Life".
> And neither is psychological life.
> Life is the world. (*Notebooks*, entry for 24.7.16)

Approaching the question of the self from different directives, both Berkeley and Wittgenstein have transcended the Cartesian starting point and placed themselves outside that tradition and its problems. This must be judged one of the most important achievements of each man.

* * *

THE SELF AND INTENTIONALITY

B. S. Gower
University of Durham

In this paper I discuss a problem revived in recent work by Bernard Williams and Thomas Nagel,[1] namely the problem of successfully relating subjective self to objective reality.

First of all there is the idea that among all the things, events and states of affairs that the world may be said to contain, there is one item which has a special significance. This is what I call the *self*. Events and states of affairs which, in some way, involve this self are real and important. Indeed, from this subjective point of view, it can easily come to seem that nothing but whatever involves the self is either real or important. As Russell put it, in a characteristically vivid manner, there is, for each of us, "a region which is specially warm and intimate and bright, surrounded in all directions by gradually growing darkness."

This view, because it is essentially subject-involving, quite readily lends itself to forms of idealism, scepticism or solipsism. Indeed, these philosophies may be said to derive their considerable strengths from the plausible claim that neither the self nor its experiences provide sufficient resources for illuminating Russell's darkness. So, idealism greets the suggestion that there is any such thing as experience-independent matter, which happens to lie outside the scope of the illumination provided by the self, as dispensable superstition. And scepticism trades on an indisputable consequence of idealism, namely that what may not exist cannot be an object of knowledge.

So if we take, as our philosophical starting point, the self together with its expriences, beliefs and feelings, it is hard if not impossible to find a place for a self-independent reality. The point is most familiar in an epistemological context, but the emphasis I want to press is metaphysical. In taking the subjective view we are in effect, declaring that only what is experienced "from the inside" counts as genuinely real. There is no room in such a view for "objectivity"-thoughts, i.e. thoughts about what cannot be experienced "from the inside", because there is no way of conferring meaning on such thoughts. What is being questioned here is not so much the possibility of knowledge concerning self-independent reality, as the possibility of coherent thought about it. This centred, subject-involving way of thinking leaves no space for realism about the world. Realism about the self is purchased at the cost of idealism about the world.

Because of its connection with standard metaphysical, semantic and epistemological issues, the subjective view has always been prominent within philosophical thinking. No-one with knowledge of post-Cartesian epistemology can fail to notice that it implies that thought about the world must be centred upon human experience because the terms in which we think have meaning only in so far as they are correlated with experience. There is no possibility of intelligible thought, still less of justified belief, about what lies beyond, behind or above experience. Man is the measure of all things, and if, as may seem inevitable, the scope of experience is restricted to that of an individual self, then each person is, severally and individually, the measure of all things.

Secondly, and opposed to this, there is an equally familiar conception according to which there is nothing in the least special about human beings and therefore nothing special about any self. Instead of thinking about reality as it appears from some particular viewpoint within reality, in which case the self which has that viewpoint will have an ontologically privileged role, we think about reality as it is, independently of any viewpoint. Clearly the availability of a conception of reality as it is — an objective conception of reality — derives from our capacity for detachment, i.e. our ability to step back from the centred, subject-involving way of representing reality.

In exercising this capacity for detachment in order to think about reality as it is, each of us thinks of reality as *containing* the individuals that we are. But in envisaging the world in this way we seem somehow to lose something important. The self, when presented to thought *as* a self rather than as an occupant among others of objective reality, cannot be incorporated into an objective or absolute conception precisely because that conception is not subject-involving. There is, as it were, no room in this conception for "I"-thoughts. How can the self that I refer to when I use the word "I" and that I essentially think about and know "from the inside", be identified with any occupant of objective reality, which is always and essentially something that I think about and know "from the outside"?

The question is not new. In one idiom or another it has been, and is, subject to close and careful philosophical scrutiny. Kant's observation that the "I think" which must accompany all representations is, despite Descartes, no more than a framework for thought, is one way of expressing, and perhaps dissolving, the difficulty. Another is to be found in Wittgenstein's remarks on the self and solipsism in the *Tractatus*. More recently, philosophers have argued that "I" fails to refer to anything at all, that "I"-thoughts resist incorporation into a Fregean semantics, that the self is without content or essence, that there are no first-person propositions. Whatever the particular merits of these conclusions may be, the arguments for them have made it plain that if there is a difficulty about identifying the self with any occupant of objective reality, the fault lies not with our conception of objective reality but with our conception of the self. We assume, wrongly, that the self is some kind of thing which *should* occupy a place in any comprehensive conception of reality.

Our realist conception of an objective spatio-temporal framework, then, entails an idealist conception of the self, or, which is the same thing, that "I" does not refer to anything.

We have, then, two mutually hostile pictures or conceptions. In one — the subjective conception — the central idea is that thoughts, beliefs, perceptions, etc., whatever they may be about, are essentially subject-involving and therefore perspectival. Because of this, realism about the self cannot be abandoned even if it entails anti-realism about everything other than the self. In the other — the objective or absolute conception — the central idea is that thought, belief, perception, etc., must be object-involving. That is to say, thought must, somehow, reach beyond itself to grasp what is independent of thought. Realism about a mind-independent world, then, is not a dispensable option but an essential presupposition of the possibility of thought. It, therefore, must be retained despite its hostility to realism about the self.

There is no question of repudiating one or other of these pictures in an attempt to resolve the tension between them. What is needed, rather, is a way of understanding the issues generating this tension so that its philosophical perplexity may be eased. I shall appeal to the concept of intentionality in order to effect such an understanding.

The objective or absolute conception of reality is expressed in thinking which is non-perspectival, non-indexical. The materials for explaining why such thinking is essential are already available. Thought has an intentional object; it reaches out beyond itself. This is why thought is *object*-involving, and the appropriate way to represent the object that is involved *as* an object is to employ a non-indexical mode of presentation. To eschew non-indexical thought would be to ignore what the arrow of intentional thought points to.

This conclusion is uncontentious. Nobody seriously proposes that non-indexical thought and the absolute conception could be abandoned even in principle. There are though, those who would urge that indexical thought does not require the existence of indexical reality — require, that is, the existence of indexical entities like the self. But since thought is intentional this form of idealism can be resisted. If, in thought about reality, our concern is with what directs the thought — with what makes thought about reality *thought* — then we are bound to employ a subject-involving indexical mode of presentation in representing reality. Arrows of intentionality need tails indicating their origins as well as heads pointing at their targets if the idea of their having direction is to make any sense.

My claim, then, is that two quite general philosophical problems raised by reflection on the self can best be understood in terms of the concept of intentionality. The first problem is the ancient one of showing how, if we begin our philosophy with the subjectively conceived self, room and role can be found for an objective world. The second problem is, in a way, the mirror image of the first. If we begin our philosophy with an absolute conception of reality, no place can be found in it for a real self. How can a picture which is essentially subject-involving become object-involving; how can a picture which is essentially object-involving become subject-involving? The double character of the intentionality of thought helps us to understand these two problems and the tension between the two pictures they present. It can be expressed by saying that any thought about any object must be a thought *of that object* (i.e. object-involving) and, at the same time, a *thought* of that object (i.e. subject-involving). In this way, intentionality helps us to understand the tension between objective and subjective views, but it does not dissolve that tension. Indeed it cannot do so because it shows that tension to be necessary.

ENDNOTE

[1] Williams, B., *Descartes: the Project of Pure Enquiry* (Harmondsworth 1978); Nagel, T., "The Objective Self" in Ginet, C., and Shoemaker, S., (eds.), *Knowledge and Mind* (New York − Oxford 1983), p. 211ff.

* * *

4. Methodologie der Philosophie des Geistes

4. The Methodology of the Philosophy of Mind

METHODOLOGISCHE BEMERKUNGEN
ZUR PHILOSOPHIE DES GEISTES

Henri Lauener
Universität Bern

Meine Auffassung von *offener Philosophie* entspringt einem Verständnis der transzendentalen Methode, das nicht zu einer im Sinne eines Empiristen anstößigen Metaphysik führt. Ähnlich wie Kant setze ich bei *Fakten* an, nämlich bei den mannigfaltigen Sprachsystemen und Theorien, die wir − als Erzeugnisse nicht der reinen Vernunft, sondern unserer Praxis − selbst gemacht (*facta*!) haben und deren verschiedene Bedingungen es zu untersuchen gilt. Im Gegensatz zu ihm glaube ich nicht, daß es nur *eine* endgültig wahre, d.h. *objektiv* ausgezeichnete Strukturierung der Welt gibt. Trotz meines Verzichts auf eine Letztbegründung bleibe ich Kants allgemeiner Konzeption insoweit treu, als ich daran festhalte, daß wir die in unserer Erkenntnis wirksamen Ordnungsprinzipien selbst schaffen. Mit dieser an den transzendentalen Idealismus gemahnenden Einsicht verbinde ich allerdings einen weitgehenden Relativismus, der mit Absolutheitsansprüchen, wie sie Kant im Anschluß an den traditionellen Rationalismus erhebt, unvereinbar bleibt. Die Menschen gesamthaft betrachtet oder wenigstens größere Kulturgemeinschaften teilen höchstens das, was man in Anlehnung an Wittgenstein ihre Lebenswelt in der weitesten Bedeutung des Wortes nennen könnte. Von einem solchen vagen, noch kaum systematisch zu erfassenden Hintergrund heben sich die durch vielfältige Zielsetzungen motivierten Unternehmen ab, die jeweils einen besonderen Kontext bilden und sich im Extremfall zu einer spezifisch wissenschaftlichen Theorie verselbständigen. Die Tatsache, daß sich bei einem derartigen Verzweigungsprozeß Grenzen ständig verschieben, scheint mir jedoch kein genügender Grund zu sein, um in holistischer Manier Sprache, Logik, Mathematik, empirische Theorie etc. zu einer einzigen amorphen Masse zu vereinigen, und zu behaupten, daß diese nur gesamthaft vor das Tribunal der Erfahrung gestellt werden könne. Die Rechtfertigung eines solchen Vorhabens würde eine *objektive* Auszeichnung der Quantifikationstheorie erfordern, die aber von einem naturalistischen Standpunkt nicht zu erbringen ist. Ich glaube, daß sich in der Tat keine erkenntnistheoretische Position − selbst nicht die, für einen Empiristen naheliegende, des physikalischen Realismus − sachlich als zwingend oder gar als wahr ausweisen läßt: die Gründe, die uns bewegen, eine Theorie einer anderen vorzuziehen, sind rein methodischer Natur.[1] Deshalb empfiehlt es sich, jeglicher Form von dogmatischem Reduktionismus eher mit Mißtrauen zu begegnen und sich für eine liberale, d.h. pluralistische Haltung zu entscheiden. Welchem Vorgehen jeweils der Vorzug gebührt, wird sich durch erfolgreiche Anwendung des theoretischen Rüstzeugs erweisen, das wir für die Lösung der anstehenden Probleme bereitgestellt haben.

Kant hatte nachdrücklich geleugnet, daß wir die Dinge so kennen, wie sie an sich sind. Ähnlich wie er halte ich dafür, daß wir nicht in der Lage sind, unsere theoretischen Konstrukte mit einer neutralen, unmittelbar gegebenen Realität zu vergleichen. Wohl prüfen wir in gewisser Hinsicht wissenschaftliche Theorien aufgrund von sogenannten Tatsachen; da diese als sprachlich artikulierte Gebilde begrifflich durchsetzt sind, erweist sich das, was wir im Kontext für „Erfahrungstatsachen" ausgeben, immer schon als durch bestimmte Interessen geleitete Interpretation. Der Vergleich vollzieht sich also gewissermaßen auf dem Hintergrund zweier Theorien − einer elaborierteren der Wissenschaft und einer primitiveren der alltäglichen Wahrnehmung oder der Experimentaltechniken. Daraus folgt, daß Wahrheit in einem strengen Sinne nicht, wie naive Realisten behaupten, in irgendeiner Übereinstimmung mit der Wirklichkeit bestehen kann. Indem ich dazu neige, das Prädikat ‚wahr' nur im Zusammenhang mit Fragen der formalen Sematik zu verwenden, verweise ich das Problem der Bewertung von empirischen Theorien in den Bereich der Pragmatik, wo es sich im wesentlichen darum handelt, ihre Brauchbarkeit relativ zur ursprünglichen Zielsetzung – unter anderem dem Erklären von Vorgängen oder der Voraussage von Ereignissen – zu beurteilen. Es scheint mir im übrigen wichtig, den *normativen* Charakter der zu einem solchen Zweck jeweils herangezogenen Kriterien hervorzuheben, über den die in einem deskriptiven Ton gehaltenen Wahrheitstheorien gewöhnlich hinwegtäuschen. Das bedeutet aber nicht, daß ich der nackten Willkür, d.h. der Methode „anything goes", die Schleusen öffnen möchte. Verzicht auf absolute Gewißheit kommt ja insofern nicht einer totalen Skepsis oder der Anarchie gleich, als auch die jeweils befolgten methodischen Regeln durch den praktischen Bewährungsprozeß miterfaßt werden. Die durch Kritik angeregten Korrekturen können zwar auch nicht mehr als einen relativen Erfolg verbürgen, was jedoch für unser Fortkommen durchaus genügt.

Quines extremer These vom rein empirischen Ursprung allen Wissens halte ich den Begriff eines relativen Apriori entgegen, der es mir erlaubt, im Kontext spezifischer Zweige der Erkenntnis eine strikte Trennung zwischen Sprache und Theorie vorzunehmen. Ich habe in früheren Arbeiten[2] ausführlich erörtert, wie wir beim Aufbau von linguistischen Rahmenwerken aufgrund von stipulativen Verfahren Sätze als analytische auszeichnen können, um das zu erzeugen, was man mit einem Unterton des Mißtrauens als „truth by *fiat*" bezeichnet hat. Im wesentlichen handelt es sich darum, eine Konvention einzugehen und dies zwar im Sinne einer Vereinbarung, daß die Wahrheit der betreffenden Sätze nicht angetastet wird, solange der Beschluß, das Sprachsystem aufrechtzuerhalten, andauert. Erst wenn es sich aus einem praktischen Grund als unbrauchbar erweist – sei es, weil es zu ausdrucksarm ist, einen zu geringen Präzisionsgrad zuläßt oder sonst welche Mängel aufweist, – entschließen wir uns, es als Ganzes aufzugeben, um ein neues, den vorliegenden Bedürfnissen besser angepaßtes Instrument herzustellen. Ein derartiger auf einen Kontext und eine Sprache relativierter Begriff der Analytizität scheint mir für die praktisch erforderliche Stabilisierung unserer Darstellungssysteme unerläßlich. Denn ohne solche normierende Eingriffe würde eine angemessene Organisation der Sprache gar nicht gelingen. Analytizität betrifft demnach keine Sachfragen über tatsächlichen Gebrauch oder „begriffliche Notwendigkeit", sondern die Frage nach einer adäquaten Reglementierung: Sätze werden durch pragmatisch motivierte Postulate zu analytischen *gemacht*. Damit verliert das Problem auch den Anschein geheimnisvoller Tiefgründigkeit; als transzendentale Bedingung für die Konstruktion linguistischer Systeme stellt Analytizität nicht länger ein unfaßbares Irrlicht dar, das den Philosophen narrt, sondern das schlichte Ergebnis einer empirisch durchaus zugänglichen Praxis,[3] die keines Rekurses auf Bedeutungen als platonische Entitäten bedarf.

Meiner Methodologie gemäß sind somit die apriorischen Formen, die der Strukturierung unserer Theorien dienen, nicht wie bei Kant durch die reine Vernunft endgültig festgelegt; Konventionen können, nachdem sie sich als unzweckmäßig erwiesen haben, widerrufen werden, so daß trotz vorläufiger Immunitäten grundsätzlich *jeder* Satz revidierbar bleibt. Wenn wir durch den Druck der Umstände gezwungen werden, eine Sprache aufzugeben, nehmen wir durch die Wahl eines neuen Systems mit entsprechenden semantischen Regeln das vor, was ich eine *externe* Revision nenne, während etwa die Verwerfung einer wissenschaftlichen Hypothese und ihre Ersetzung durch eine andere innerhalb desselben linguistischen Rahmenwerkes eine interne Revision ausmachen würde. Ein Wechsel der ersten Art kommt im übrigen der Schaffung eines neuen Kontextes gleich,[4] was eine weitgehende Inkommensurabilität der früheren mit der späteren Theorie zur Folge hat.

Die pluralistische Auffassung, die ich Quines Idee einer umgreifenden und vorläufig besten physikalischen Theorie entgegenstelle, wirkt sich ferner darin aus, daß ich wesentlich mehr Arten von Dingen in meiner Ontologie dulde als der Naturalist. Wir verwenden das Wort ‚existieren' in z.T. radikal voneinander abweichenden Kontexten. Im Rahmen der Arithmetik, wie sie etwa von Peano axiomatisiert wurde, gilt der Satz ‚Es gibt eine Primzahl zwischen 5 und 10' als analytisch wahr, weil er mit Hilfe der Ableitungsregeln aus Postulaten herleitbar ist. Aus meiner Sicht bedeutet das nun, daß wir durch die Verwendung des erwähnten Axiomensystems selbst abstrakte Objekte, nämlich natürliche Zahlen, erzeugen und daß es deshalb vergeblich wäre, solche in der empirischen Wirklichkeit suchen zu wollen. Andererseits finden wir in der griechischen Mythologie Götter wie Zeus oder in Sir Arthur Conan Doyles Roman *Der Hund von Baskerville* einen Detektiv namens Sherlock Holmes, was zur Folge hat, daß in diesen Kontexten respektive die beiden Sätze ‚$(\exists\, x)$ $(x = $ Zeus $. \wedge x$ ist ein Gott)‘ und ‚$(\exists\, x)$ $(x = $ Sherlock Holmes $\wedge x$ ist ein Detektiv)‘ wahr sind. Das wird aber nur dadurch möglich, daß wir aufgrund von Tätigkeiten unserer Einbildungskraft wie diejenigen des Erfindens von Mythen, Legenden etc. oder des Verfassens von literarischen Werken selbst fiktive Entitäten ins Leben rufen, die sich einer wenn auch nicht realen, so doch in der Welt der Literatur öffentlich nachweisbaren Existenz erfreuen. Anders verhält es sich, wenn wir von der Sprache einen *strikt deskriptiven* Gebrauch machen: in diesem Falle verfolgen wir die erklärte Absicht, über wirkliche Dinge zu berichten, deren Existenz sich nur vermittelst empirischer Beobachtung ausmachen läßt. Handelt es sich dabei um nicht unmittelbar zugängliche Objekte − etwa um den Nachweis von Elementarteilchen in der Quantenphysik, so sind für das Fixieren ihrer Spuren komplizierte Apparate und Techniken erforderlich. Falls sich aber der Versuch, z.B. mentale Entitäten in experimentell kontrollierbarer Weise einzuführen, als hoffungslos erweisen sollte, so müßten wir uns damit abfinden, daß sich auf solche beziehende Theorien einer effektiven Erklärungskraft entbehren und daher aus dem Bereich der Naturwissenschaften auszuscheiden hätten. (Wie wir später sehen werden, würde das allerdings nicht bedeuten, daß sie *überhaupt* nicht existieren: im gewöhnlichen Alltag, wo es weniger auf streng wissenschaftliche Überprüfung ankommt, hat sich ihre Einführung für den Zweck einer leichten Verständigung durchaus bewährt.)

Meine Auffassung hat nicht eine Trivialisierung der Ontologie zur Folge. Ich behaupte keineswegs, daß alles auf undifferenzierte Art existiert. Ich wähle in diesem Zusammenhang mit Quine die klassische Quantifikation als linguistisches Instrument,[5] weil sie sich für die Reglementierung des Gebrauchs von ‚existieren‘ insofern besonders eignet, als sie es erlaubt, ein präzises Kriterium für ontische Annahmen zu formulieren[6]. Mein nuancierter und − wie ich glaube − unserer Intuition angemessener Entwurf eines Systems der Ontologie entspricht im übrigen dem transzendentalen Anliegen, indem er den beim Aufstellen von Theorien wirksamen Verfahren der Strukturierung und Individuierung, die sich relativierend auswirken, gebührend Rechnung trägt, ohne in eine dem Empiristen nicht zumutbare Form von Idealismus zurückzufallen. Die Tätigkeiten des Beschreibens und des Identifizierens von Objekten hängen von der Verwendung einer Sprache ab. Es kann sogar geschehen, daß wir mit der Wahl einer solchen gewisse abstrakte oder fiktive Entitäten selbst schaffen, was jedoch genau dann nicht zutrifft, wenn wir ein in meinem engen Sinne deskriptives Rahmenwerk einsetzen. Einerseits kann es in einem Kontext, in dem das Prädikat ‚Elektron‘ nicht vorkommt, kein Elektronen geben. Andererseits ist aber die Frage, ob die Terme eine Referenz in der wirklichen Welt haben, nicht rein sprachlich oder durch Konventionen auszumachen, sondern muß dadurch empirisch entschieden werden, daß man ein Ding der betreffenden Art vorweist. In meiner Transzendentalphilosophie ist also nicht mehr von einem Vergleich der Erkenntnisobjekte mit Dingen an sich oder von der Abbildung von Sachverhalten in einer mentalen Beobachtungssprache die Rede; es verhält sich vielmehr so, daß Sprache und Realität sich wechselseitig bedingen, indem uns die erstere die für den Akt des Referierens erforderlichen Ausdrucksmittel liefert, während die Frage, ob wir mit diesen etwas Wirkliches bezeichnen, von der Beschaffenheit der letzteren (einschließlich unserer eigenen natürlichen Organisation) abhängt.

Meine methodologisch motivierte Version des Pluralismus betrifft ebensosehr die Zielsetzungen wie die theoretischen Ausformungen der Erkenntnis. Indem sie jegliche objektive Auszeichnung mit Hilfe eines Korrespondenzbegriffs der Wahrheit vereitelt, rückt sie den *normativen* Aspekt der Kriterien ans Licht, die bei der Beurteilung rivalisierender Theorien herangezogen werden. Wenn wir eine Theorie für „wahr" halten, so tun wir das *de facto* mit Rücksicht auf ihre „Güte", d.h. die Möglichkeit, sie erfolgreich anzuwenden. Entsprechend müssen wir uns bezüglich der Ontologie mit der Einsicht in die Relativität von Reduktions- oder Identifikationsverfahren abfinden: da jedes von ihnen bestimmte Regeln („legislation" im Sinne von Quine) und Setzungen („posits") voraussetzt, wird es uns nicht gelingen, ein

System allen übrigen gegenüber objektiv auszuzeichnen. Damit will ich nicht leugnen, daß wissenschaftliche Hypothesen experimentell geprüft werden, sondern nur auf die Tatsache aufmerksam machen, daß das, was wir in einem bestimmten Kontext als Daten der „Erfahrung" hinnehmen, immer schon das Ergebnis einer (primitiveren) Theorienbildung ist.

Die geschilderten Züge sprechen zugunsten einer liberalen Methodologie, die eine flexible Einstellung hinsichtlich der Wahl von Sprachsystemen und logischen Kalkülen empfiehlt. Das Aufstellen einer für empirische Theorien adäquaten Semantik erfordert eine offene Haltung, die der Kontextabhängigkeit der Bedeutung theoretischer Terme, aber auch dem intentionalen Charakter der Referenz und ganz allgemein der institutionalen Seite der Sprache mit ihren konventionellen Typen und Regeln gerecht wird. Auf der vorwissenschaftlichen Stufe der Alltagsrede wäre im besonderen ein Verfahren auszuarbeiten, das uns in die Lage versetzen würde, zwischen Regelmäßigkeiten, die auf das bloße Erlernen einer Sprache zurückgehen, und solchen, die durch das bewußte Adoptieren einer Theorie bedingt sind, zu unterscheiden.[7]

Wie wirkt sich nun des näheren die skizzierte Methodologie in der sog. Philosophie des Geistes aus? Auf intuitiver Ebene haben sich zwei allgemeine Überzeugungen verankert, die unter dem Titel „ontologischer Dualismus" und „mentale Verursachung" ihren Niederschlag in der Philosophie gefunden haben; der ersteren gemäß sind geistige Phänomene ihrer Natur nach wesentlich von physischen zu unterscheiden, während nach der letzteren sich mentale Zustände in Form von Handlungen etwa auf das empirische Geschehen auswirken können. Die logische Spannung, die eine gleichzeitige Aufrechterhaltung beider Thesen nach sich zieht, ließe sich historisch am Lösungsversuch des psycho-physischen Parallelismus der Okkasionalisten, an der von Leibniz aufgestellten Doktrin der prästabilierten Harmonie oder an Spinozas Einsubstanzenlehre illustrieren. Was neuerdings die an einem physikalistischen Weltbild orientierten Empiristen unseres Jahrhunderts angeht, so neigen die meisten von ihnen dazu, unter dem Druck der Annahme einer kausalen Geschlossenheit des physischen Bereichs, den Dualismus dem Ideal einer Einheitswissenschaft zu opfern. In der Absicht, psychische Ereignisse auf physische zurückzuführen, wenden sie des öftern die von Quine semantischer Aufstieg („semantic ascent") genannte Strategie an, indem sie ihre Aufmerksamkeit weniger auf die psychischen Objekte selbst als auf die diversen Mängel unserer mentalistischen Redeweise richten. Meinerseits erblicke ich, abgesehen vom Fehlen einer eigentlichen Theorie, die Schwäche einer bloßen Begriffsanalyse im Stil von Ryles *Concept of Mind* darin, daß ihre Anhänger — sich mutwillig über die experimentelle Forschung hinwegsetzend — eine Kluft zwischen der Philosophie des Geistes und der empirischen Psychologie aufgerissen haben, die meines Erachtens keine fruchtbaren Ergebnisse gezeigt hat.

In Opposition zu der aus Oxford und Cambridge stammenden sprachanalytischen Tradition beharrt der — in seiner extremsten Form von Quine vertretene — Naturalismus darauf, daß allein naturwissenschaftliche Methoden zur Konzipierung von Theorien mit echter Erklärungskraft taugen. In Übereinstimmung mit der Ablehnung einer strikten Unterscheidung zwischen analytisch und synthetisch verwirft der Holist die Ansicht, daß isolierten Termen überhaupt Bedeutungen zukommen — und dies zwar schon gar nicht in Form von intensionalen Entitäten. Das erkennende Subjekt zum Gegenstand der Psychologie als einem Teil der Gesamtwissenschaft deklassierend bestreitet er, daß die Introspektion irgend einen methodisch privilegierten Zugang zu den privaten Bewußtseinszuständen gewährt. Wenn wir im Anschluß an den Behaviorismus die Forschung auf empirisch zugängliche Objekte einschränken, brauchen wir nicht die Existenz von mentalen Vorgängen vorauszusetzen. Denn die Theorie, die das öffentlich beobachtbare Verhalten am besten erklärt, erfordert kein Quantifizieren über nicht-physikalische Entitäten. Darin zeigt sich der Naturalist radikaler als der ontologisch eher neutrale Sprachanalytiker, der bloß beansprucht, Sätze mit mentalistischen Ausdrücken ohne wesentlichen Verlust in Sätze mit Prädikaten für Verhaltensdispositionen übersetzt zu haben. Abgesehen von der heiklen Frage nach der effektiven Übersetzbarkeit[8] zieht es der Materialist ohnehin vor, ontologisch verdächtige Objekte grundsätzlich zu eliminieren, wodurch er zugleich auch das psycho-physische Problem aufzulösen glaubt.

Wie ist es um die tatsächliche Durchführung eines derartigen Programms bestellt? Betrachten wir zunächst die Version,[9] nach welcher – allgemein formuliert – Ereignisse im Bewußtsein mit physiologischen Vergängen im Gehirn identisch sind. Sie entspringt offenbar der Absicht, dem ontologischen Dualismus zu entgehen, ohne sich in die notorischen Schwierigkeiten der Übersetzungsthese zu verstricken. Was aber ist genau mit einer solchen Identitätserklärung gemeint? Im Satz ‚Schmerzen sind Gehirnzustände‘ kann das Wort ‚sind‘ jedenfalls nicht die Relation der sog. strikten Identität beinhalten, weil dann das Gesetz ‚$(x)\,(y)\,[(x = y) \rightarrow (F)\,(Fx \longleftrightarrow Fy)]$‘ uns zu unsinnigen Aussagen der Art verpflichten würde, daß Gehirnzustände heftig, beißend, dumpf oder verblassend sein können, die offensichtlich einen sog. Kategorienfehler involvieren. Da es auch nicht als ‚ist synonym mit‘ oder als ‚ist extensional gleich mit‘[10] gedeutet werden kann, hege ich den Verdacht, daß derartigen Sätzen letztlich nicht mehr Sinn als die doch eher triviale Behauptung einer invarianten Korrelation abzugewinnen ist. Abgesehen von der essentialistisch anmutenden Frage ‚Was ist Schmerz?‘, an deren Beantwortung vermutlich dem Identitätstheorektiker besonders gelegen ist, erlaubt uns im übrigen die Feststellung einer kontingenten Wechselbeziehung genau dieselben Voraussagen zu machen wie eine Identitätstheorie. Wie ich befürchte, ermangeln jedoch beide aus noch zu erläuternden Gründen einer effektiven Erklärungskraft.

Trotz seiner sorgfältigen Ausführungen scheint mir auch Hilary Putnams Deutungsversuch des ‚ist‘ als desjenigen der empirischen Reduktion[11] letzlich unverständlich. Vor allem bezweifle ich, daß die Belange der Ontologie durch sie in klarer Weise geordnet werden. Denn anders als im Fall von ‚Der Morgenstern ist der Abendstern‘ wo die beiden Namen[12] den gleichen Himmelskörper bezeichnen, wird die Frage nach der Referenz, sofern das ‚ist‘ der Reduktion eine symmetrische Relation ausdrückt, nicht eindeutig geregelt. Wir können nämlich ohne Willkür nicht entscheiden, ob nun die qualitativen (psychischen) Erlebnisse, die wir mit neurobiologischen Vorgängen gleichsetzen, oder die neurobiologischen (physikalischen) Vorgänge, die wir mit qualitativen Erlebnissen gleichsetzen, wirklich existieren. Jedenfalls ist es wegen ihres völlig verschiedenen Status – die einen sind privat, die anderen öffentlich beobachtbar – nicht möglich anzunehmen, daß es sich um eine einzige Art von Entitäten handelt. Wir können es mit anderen Worten nicht mit einem Fall zu tun haben, wo wir mittels verschiedener Terme über dasselbe sprechen.

Mit der etwas anders gelagerten reduktionistischen Strategie des sog. eliminativen Materialismus' lassen sich die bedenklichsten der angedeuteten Unstimmigkeiten vermeiden. In der typischen Ausprägung etwa von Quines physikalischem Realismus wird als Argument ins Feld geführt, daß allein eine naturwissenschaftliche, d.h. eine physiologische oder neurobiologische Theorie die Phänomene, die wir gewöhnlich als geistige bezeichnen, wirklich zu erklären vermag und daß deshalb die Ontologie nicht mit mentalen Entitäten belastet zu werden braucht. Mit einem holistischen Standpunkt gekoppelt läuft das radikale Verfahren darauf hinaus, die Existenz von qualitativen Erlebnissen überhaupt zu leugnen. Seine Vorteile sind augenfällig: die Theoriebildung wird vereinfacht und das Problem der mentalen Verursachung verschwindet zugleich mit den Empfindungen als wirklichen Dingen. Trotzdem scheint mir intuitiv eine solche Lösung nicht völlig befriedigend, weil ich nicht glaube, daß wir in der Praxis ganz ohne eine vorgängige mentalistische Theorie auskommen.

Hilary Putnam, der zögert, endgültig Stellung zu beziehen, hält andererseits das Ansinnen, ausschließlich menschlichen oder tierischen Organismen mentale Zustände zuzuschreiben, für zu spezifisch. Von den Verhaltenssimulationen in den Computerwissenschaften angeregt, strebt er eine extreme Verallgemeinerung an. Seiner funktionalistischen Hypothese gemäß, die er für empirisch prüfbar zu halten scheint, wären psychologische Eigenschaften mit funktionalen Eigenschaften identisch.[13] Dem Versuch einer rein physikalistischen Reduktion hält er entgegen, daß das Hirn Züge aufweist, die nicht in biochemischen Termen beschreibbar sind. Als wesentlich habe er die Eigenschaft hervor, daß es ein von seiner stofflichen Realisierung unabhängiges Programm besitzt. Putnam gehört zu den subtilsten und kenntnisreichsten Autoren unserer Zeit; entsprechend stützt er seine These mit ausführlichen Argumenten, deren Spannweite von Gedankenexperimenten über sprachphilosophische Überlegungen bis zur Erörterung von neurophysiologischen Befunden reicht. Wie allzu häufig im Rahmen der zeitgenössischen analytischen Philosophie wird man sich allerdings fragen, was der Aufwand an technischer Virtuosität nützt, wenn das gesamte Konzept dermaßen gegen die Intuition verstößt, daß seine Plausibilität von vornherein als gering erscheint. Wie soll man sich im Ernst zu Putnams Äußerung stellen, wonach Roboter ein Verhalten zeigen könnten, das Ärger verrät? Es ist kaum anzunehmen, daß das Gerät in der Lage ist, ein Gefühl des Unmuts zu empfinden, das demjenigen ähnlich wäre, das ich verpüre, wenn ich vergeblich versuche, mich von der Richtigkeit einer solchen Behauptung zu überzeugen. Man möchte zunächst annehmen, daß jemand, der so spricht, einfach das Wort ‚Ärger' falsch verwendet. In einem zu weit gefaßten Kontext ist es jedoch heikel, eine Grenze zwischen dem rein Linguistischen und dem Empirischen zu ziehen. Es kann deshalb auch kein allgemeines Kriterium geben, das uns erlauben würde, *kontextunabhängig* zu entscheiden, wann jemand eine Sachlage falsch beurteilt und wann er sich in der Wahl der Terminologie vergreift. Der Sprachgebrauch ist wandelbar; er wird u.a. durch die Ergebnisse der wissenschaftlichen Forschung in beträchtlichem Maße beeinflußt. Dieser Sachverhalt läßt sich aber, wie ich fürchte, holistisch nicht erfassen. Um ihn in den Griff zu bekommen, sind wir auf konventionelle Praktiken angewiesen, die eine scharfe Trennung der jeweiligen Kontexte ermöglichen. Wenn demnach Hilary Putnam behauptet, die Physiker hätten „entdeckt", daß Temperatur in Wirklichkeit durchschnittliche Molekularenergie ist, so kann das nicht besagen, daß wir innerhalb eines monistischen Gesamtsystems endgültig Individuen einer Gattung durch andere ersetzt haben. Es muß vielmehr bedeuten, daß wir in einem historischen Kontext mit Rücksicht auf momentane wissenschaftliche Bedürfnisse eine frühere Perspektive mit der ihr eigentümlichen qualitativen Sprache durch ein neues Rahmenwerk abgelöst haben, das uns erlaubt, eine bessere Theorie zu formulieren. Ohne Berücksichtigung der besonderen geschichtlichen und theoretischen Umstände, die zur Adoptierung der betreffenden Theorie geführt haben, bliebe ein Satz wie ‚Temperatur ist durchschnittliche Molekularenergie' unverständlich.

Meiner Überzeugung nach, die übrigens im gegenwärtigen Stand der Diskussion eine Bestätigung findet, gibt es keine empirischen Belege für die „Wahrheit" der einen oder anderen philosophischen Doktrin. Die Kontroverse dreht sich nämlich gar nicht um eine Sachfrage, sondern um praktische Entscheide, die im wesentlichen die Wahl von geeigneten Sprachsystemen und anderen für die Wissenschaft erforderlichen Instrumenten betreffen. Statt sich vergeblich abzumühen, die Wahrheit oder Falschheit von Aussagen wie ‚Bewußtseinszustände sind F' nachzuweisen, sollten wir uns deshalb eher nach methodischen Gründen umsehen, die für oder gegen eine solche Redeweise sprechen. Zugunsten meiner Auffassung, nach welcher es keine objektiven, von Konventionen unabhängigen Kriterien für die faktische Gleichheit von Wahrnehmungszuständen mit Vorgängen im Gehirn gibt, plädiert im übrigen die im allgemeinen zugestandene beobachtungsmäßige Ununterscheidbarkeit der verschiedenen Identitäts- oder Reduktionstheorien.

Wenn also Sätze der Form ‚Was man früher ein F genannt hat, ist nichts anderes als ein G' einen Sinn haben sollen, müssen sie anders analysiert werden, als das bisher geschehen ist. Obschon auch ich der Meinung bin, daß der wissenschaftliche Fortschritt das Ausscheiden gewisser Terme aus der Sprache und die Eliminierung entsprechender Arten von Entitäten aus der Ontologie erforderlich macht, glaube ich nicht, daß das aufgrund der üblichen holistischen Sicht möglich ist. Denn, hätten wir es, wie z.B. Quine das idealerweise vorausgesetzt, mit einer einzigen, umfassenden Sprache/Theorie zu tun, so müßten vor der Reduktion in ihr beides, mentale und physikalistische Prädikate vorkommen, wodurch wir unweigerlich in die erörterten Schwierigkeiten zurückgeworfen würden. Um all den mißlichen Folgen zu entgehen, sehe ich keinen anderen Ausweg, als für eine Methodologie zu optieren, die dank der Ermöglichung einer strikten Unterscheidung zwischen analytisch und synthetisch sowie zwischen Sprache und Theorie die Bahn zu einem echten Pluralismus freigibt.

‚Was man früher ein F genannt hat, ist in Wirklichkeit ein G'. Illustrieren wir die allgemeine Formel durch die Einsetzungsinstanz ‚Was man im Mittelalter Besessenheit durch einen Dämon genannt hat, ist in Wirklichkeit eine Nervenkrankheit', so wird deutlich, daß mit derartigen Sätzen nicht die Behauptung einer Identität intendiert ist. Das Beispiel besagt nicht, daß Dämonen und Geisteskrankheiten identisch seien, sondern bringt in elliptischer Form etwa das Folgende zum Ausdruck: Im Mittelalter haben sich die Leute mit (wissenschaftlich leeren) Erklärungen vermittelst von bösen Geistern begnügt, während wir heute ungewöhnliches Verhalten mit Hilfe von (etwas besseren) psychiatrischen Theorien erklären. Ähnlich verhält es sich im Falle des Schmerzes und der Reizung von C-Fasern, indem wir uns im Alltag mit einer noch vagen, mentalistischen Sprache zufriedengeben[14], die im Kontext psychologischer oder physiologischer Forschung versagen würde. Diesen Umstand sollten wir wenigstens so weit in Betracht ziehen, daß der Philosophe sich trotz materialistischer Neigungen nicht dazu versteigt, die Existenz von Entitäten mentaler Art absolut zu leugnen. Es würde sich sicher nicht lohnen, über die ontologischen Sünden zu meditieren, die man in diesem Zusammenhang Ockhams Grundsatz gemäß begeht. Eine Übersetzung in die kanonische Notation würde nichtsdestoweniger ans Licht bringen, daß wir in einem solchen Kontext über mentale Entitäten quantifizieren.

Genau das haben wir jedoch zu vermeiden, wenn es darum geht, eine empirische prüfbare Theorie zu entwerfen. In diesem Fall müssen wir eine reglementierte Sprache mit exakt identifizierbaren Individuen verwenden. Im engeren Kontext der Wissenschaft findet somit eine physikalistische Strategie eine gewisse Berechtigung, was aber nicht heißt, daß sie um der Einheitswissenschaft willen zum tyrannischen Prinzip erhoben werden sollte. Die Vereinheitlichung unserer Theorien ist zwar durchaus wünschbar, kann jedoch als Fernziel nur schrittweise verwirklicht werden. Wie weit entfernt wir uns noch von einem solchen Ideal befinden, ließe sich ironischerweise trotz der ungeheuren Fortschritte, die auf dem Gebiet der Neurophysiologie in den letzten Jahrzehnten erzielt wurden, gerade am Stande unseres Wissens über Hirnvorgänge veranschaulichen.

Ein sinnvoller Reduktionsprozeß kann also nach meiner Auslegung nicht darin bestehen, daß wir innerhalb eines Gesamtsystems Objekte aufgrund einer empirisch festgestellten Identität eliminieren. Er muß vielmehr in der Weise verstanden werden, daß wir im Kontext einer Theoriebildung aus pragmatischen Gründen ein Sprachsystem entwickeln, in welchem die Prädikate so gewählt werden, daß die in der Ontologie als wirklich vorausgesetzten Entitäten tatsächlich der Beobachtung zugänglich sind. An einer Stelle scheint auch Richard Rorty zu einem sehr ähnlichen Ergebnis zu gelangen, ohne allerdings den nächsten Schritt zu einem folgerichtigen Pluralismus zu vollziehen: „Die Unterscheidung zwischen Beobachtungstermen und Nicht-Beobachtungstermen ist relativ zur jeweiligen Sprachpraxis (die sich ändern kann, wenn die Forschung Fortschritte macht), anstatt ein für allemal abgesteckt werden zu können, indem man zwischen den ‚gefundenen‘ und den ‚gemachten‘ Elementen in unserer Erfahrung unterscheidet".[15] Die im Zitat angedeutete Änderung der Praxis wird, wie ich meine, nicht durch Korrekturen an einem Totalsystem vorgenommen, sondern dadurch, daß wir eine Vielzahl von eigenständigen Teilsystemen entwerfen, die zueinander in der Relation der Unverträglichkeit, der Inkommensurabilität, der empirischen Äquivalenz etc. stehen können. Deshalb scheint es mir auch unangebracht, die Frage nach der Wahrheit einer Aussage wie ‚Früher hat man das Wort ‚Atom‘ falsch verstanden, weil man damit die Vorstellung der Unteilbarkeit verband‘, als durch einen Hinweis auf die tatsächliche Teilbarkeit der Atome für endgültig erledigt zu betrachten. Angesichts der unvermeidlichen Kontextabhängigkeit, die ein derart absolutistisches Ansinnen vereitelt, muß man sich mit einer Deutung bescheiden, die nicht mehr besagt, als daß die Quantenphysik gewisse Naturphänomene besser, d.h. exakter und vollständiger erklärt als etwa die Theorie Demokrits oder Epikurs. In analoger Weise wäre die Behauptung, daß *die* Sprache durch wissenschaftliche Entdeckungen ständig verändert wird, zu behandeln. Sofern sie das Vorhandensein einer einzigen, universell verwendeten Sprache nahelegt, ist sie jedenfalls irreführend, weil wir in Wirklichkeit eine Vielfalt von gegeneinander abgrenzbaren, z.T. künstlichen linguistischen Instrumenten entfalten, die jene Entdeckungen erst möglich machen.

Die soweit dargelegten Überlegungen, scheinen mir nun den methodologischen Schluß nahezulegen, daß es sich beim gegenwärtigen Stand unseres Wissens nicht empfiehlt, in einem

Sprachsystem zugleich mentale und physiologische Prädikate einzuführen. Man könnte zwar für den bloßen Zweck einer Abkürzung den Term ‚Schmerz' vermittelst einer expliziten Definition:

$$x \text{ ist ein Schmerz} =_{\text{Def}} x \text{ ist ein neurobiologischer Zustand der Art} \ldots$$

so einführen, daß nur ein neuer Ausdruck vorgelegt wird. Da wir trotz der Gleichheit der Lautzeichen dadurch nicht die früheren Entitäten mitpostulieren würden, hätten wir es jedoch in diesem Fall mit einem rein physikalistischen Gebrauch des Wortes zu tun.

Zur Rechtfertigung meines Vorschlags möchte ich weniger auf die kongenitalen Schwächen der Identitätstheorien als auf die betrübliche Tatsache hinweisen, daß für eine absehbare Zukunft vermutlich keine Theorie in Aussicht steht, die eine im streng wissenschaftlichen Sinne gesetzesartige Beziehung zwischen mentalen und physiologischen Prozessen herstellen würde. Solange aber eine solche aussteht, erscheinen mir philosophische Spekulationen in Richtung eines universellen Materialismus eher als müßig – und dies zwar umsomehr, als sie – soweit ich das abzuschätzen vermag – selbst nicht viel zur Verwirklichung einer experimentell prüfbaren physikalistischen Theorie des Bewußtseins beitragen. Ähnlich beurteilt auch Reinhard Werth die Situation, [16] indem er den geringen wissenschaftlichen Wert der diesbezüglichen Arbeiten in der analytischen Philosophie beklagt und ausdrücklich die Ersetzung der Alltagssprache durch eine Fachsprache verlangt, in der Terme wie ‚geistig', ‚das Selbst', ‚bewußt', ‚privat' etc. so präzisierbar sind, daß sie effektiv in Experimenten verwendet werden können. Im Zeichen eines wohlverstandenen Empirismus neige ich dazu, ihm beizustimmen, wenn er darauf beharrt, daß es für die Erklärung der Leib-Seele-Beziehung wesentlich darauf ankommt, die neurophysiologischen Abläufe zu erforschen, die in Organismen (nicht in technisch realisierten Systemen!)[17] für die Verarbeitung von Reizen und für die Steuerung des Verhaltens verantwortlich sind. Da ich andererseits weder den heuristischen Wert spezifisch philosophischer Überlegungen noch die praktische Bedeutung nicht-naturwissenschaftlicher Kontexte allzu gering ansetzen möchte, glaube ich, daß eine liberale Gesinnung, wie sie meine offene Methodologie fordert, letztlich zu einer fruchtbareren Gesamtsicht führt als die monistischen oder fundamentalistischen Rivalen. Indem sie bei fortschreitender Entwicklung nur einen dem jeweils vorliegenden Problem angemessenen Grad von Exaktheit verlangt, fördert sie die Einsicht, daß es für den Anfang wichtiger ist, mit einer plausiblen, wenn auch vagen, Hypothese zu beginnen, als von vornherein auf einer strengen Formalisierung zu beharren, die uns in die Irre leiten wird.

Um Mißverständnissen vorzubeugen, füge ich abschließend hinzu, daß ich mit der Ansicht, wonach die abwechslungsweise Verwendung einer mentalistischen oder physikalistischen Sprache verschiedene Kontexte erzeugt, nicht jegliche Beziehung zwischen Bewußtsein und Vorgängen im zentralen Nervensystem abstreiten will. Auf der Metastufe läßt sich durchaus feststellen, daß mit dem Satz ‚Ich spüre Schmerz' gleichzeitig ein entsprechender Satz über die Reizung von C-Fasern etc. wahr wird. Eine bloße Registrierung eines kontingenten Zusammentreffens erklärt jedoch nichts. Eine interessante Korrelation im Sinne etwa einer kausalen Verknüpfung würde erst eine (vermutlich äußerst komplexe) die beiden Gebiete verbindende Einheitstheorie liefern, die – wie ich leider befürchte – noch in weiter Ferne liegt.

ANMERKUNGEN

[1] Vgl. dazu meine Aufsätze „Logik als Instrument des Philosophen", in: *Wissenschaftliche Akten der Schweizerischen Naturforschenden Gesellschaft* (1982) „Ansätze zu einer zeitgenössischen Transzendentalphilosophie", in: *Kant a due secoli dalla „Criteria",* Editrice La Scuola (Brescia 1984), S. 113–123, und „Method in Philosophy and Logic" *Dialectica* , 36, 4, 1982.

[2] Vgl. u.a. „Probleme der Ontologie", in: *Zeitschrift für allgemeine Wissenschaftstheorie*, IX, 1(1978); und „Ansätze zu einer zeitgenössischen Transzendentalphilosophie".

[3] Wie Regeln angewandt werden und wer befugt ist, sie einzuführen, sind Fragen, die im wesentlichen die Wissenschaftssoziologie angehen.

[4] Ich bin mir bewußt, daß eine nähere Bestimmung dieses Terms eher heikel ist. Ich verwende ihn nicht mit der (ebenfalls vagen!) Bedeutung einer möglichen Welt im Sinne der zeitgenössischen Semantik. Für mich sind Kontexte keine Alternativen zu anderen Welten, sondern konkrete Situationen mit bestimmten, bezüglich des vorliegenden Unternehmens relevanten Zügen, die in der wirklichen Welt auftreten. Es wird vermutlich nicht leicht sein, präzise Kriterien für die Individuierung von derartigen Gebilden anzugeben. Neben konventionellen Überlegungen dürfte es im allgemeinen genügen, die verwendete Sprache zu beschreiben sowie den besonderen Gebrauch, den man von ihr macht, zu charakterisieren, um sich vor allem auch darüber Klarheit zu verschaffen, welche Arten von Objekten im Wertbereich der Variablen vorkommen.

[5] Es ist klar, daß sich nicht alle Sprachen in das System der Prädikatenlogik übersetzen lassen; diejenigen, für die das nicht möglich ist, dürften jedoch solche sein, für die ontologische Fragen ohnehin von geringem Interesse bleiben.

[6] Vgl. „Probleme der Ontologie" und „Ontologie im Lichte einer zeitgenössischen Analyse", in: *Conceptus* , Jg. XIV, Nr. 33 (1980).

[7] Für einen Versuch in dieser Richtung vgl. Alan Miller, „Where's the Use in Meaning?", *Dialectica*, 39 (1985), H. 1.

[8] Wie in der Tat müßte eine praktisch brauchbare, neutrale Sprache aussehen, in welcher Aussagen, die Kategorienfehler der weiter unten erörterten Art nach sich ziehen, so zu übersetzen wären, daß keine solchen mehr auftauchen? In „Sensations and Brain Processes",*Philosophical Review*, 68 (1959), S. 141–156, gibt J. J. C. Smart einen Satz wie ‚Ich sehe ein oranges Nachbild' mit der folgenden Formulierung wieder: ‚Es geht etwas vor, wie das, was vorgeht, wenn ich meine Augen geöffnet habe, wach bin und wenn sich eine Orange in gutem Licht vor mir befindet, das heißt, wenn ich wirklich eine Orange sehe'!!

[9] Für eine systematische Klassifizierung der Theorien über die Beziehung des Mentalen zum Physikalischen vgl. Donald Davidson, „Mentale Ereignisse", deutsche Übersetzung in:*Analytische Philosophie des Geistes*, hrsg. v. P. Bieri Meisenheim 1981, S. 78.

[10] Man spürt keine Hirnprozesse im Knie!

[11] „Die Natur mentaler Zustände" im erwähnten Sammelband.

[12] Die Venus ist kein Stern, sondern ein Planet; die Terme sind deshalb keine Kennzeichnungen, sondern Eigennamen, d.h. „rigid designators" im Sinne Kripkes.

[13] Vgl. etwa *Reason, Truth and History* (Cambridge University Press 1981), S. 79, wo er von seiner Theorie als von einer korrekten, *naturalistischen* Beschreibung der Leib-Seele-Beziehung spricht, sich aber im Anschluß an Nelson Goodman bereit erklärt, ebenfalls „korrekte" nicht-naturalistische, z.B. mentale Versionen einzuräumen. Ich bin verlockt, diese etwas sibyllinische Äußerung als eine Annäherung an meine eigene Position zu deuten.

[14] Wer sich gelegentlich einer Konsultation beim Arzt über Mängel an seinen Neuronen, Synapsen etc. beklagen wollte, wäre in der Tat schlecht beraten!

[15] „Leib-Seele Identität, Privatheit und Kategorien", in: *Analytische Philosophie des Geistes*, S. 106ff.

[16] Vgl. *Bewußtsein (Psychologische, neurobiologische und wissenschaftstheoretische Aspekte)* (Berlin-Heidelberg-New York-Tokio 1983).

[17] Mit einem Computer ließen sich keine empirisch sinnvollen Experimente durchführen, so daß das Wort ‚Bewußtsein' in diesem Zusammenhang keine einsichtige Bedeutung haben kann. Die Fähigkeit des Simulierens gewährt keinen Einblick in wirkliche psychische oder physiologische Vorgänge!

* * *

WIE IST NATURWISSENSCHAFT MÖGLICH?
(GRUNDZÜGE EINES NATURALISTISCHEN IDEALISMUS)

Nicholas Rescher
Universität Pittsburgh

1. Wie ist Physik möglich?

Wie ist Naturwissenschaft − und im besonderen Physik − überhaupt möglich? Wie kommt es, daß es uns Menschen − Staubkörnchen nur im Weltall − gelingt, die Geheimnisse der Natur zu entschlüsseln und zu ihren Gesetzen verstandesmäßig Zugang zu finden? Und wie kommt es, daß unsere Mathematik − scheinbar eine freie Schöpfung menschlicher Erfindungskraft − benutzt werden kann, um den modus operandi der Natur mit geradezu unheimlicher Leistungsfähigkeit und Genauigkeit zu beschreiben? Wie kommt es, daß die gesetzmässige Ordnung der Natur für uns mit Begriffsmitteln erschließbar ist, die wir selbst erdacht haben?[1]

Wir haben es hier mit der großen Entdeckung des Pythagoras zu tun: daß „Dinge Zahlen" sind, daß die Verhältnisse und Verfahren unserer Umwelt (wie die harmonischen Intervalle im Bereich der Akustik) in mathematischer Sprache artikuliert werden können. Wir kehren also zurück zum Pythagoreischen Mysterium und zu den Betrachtungen in Platons „Timaios", die den Quellgrund einer Tradition von mathematisierender Kosmologie bilden, welche in kontinuierlichem Fluß von der Astrologie zur Astronomie führt − mit Kepler als einer bemerkenswerten Übergangserscheinung.

Es ist anzumerken, daß diese Frage der kognitiven Zugänglichkeit und mathematischen Faßbarkeit der Naturgesetze ihre beunruhigende Brisanz erst entfaltete, als die „scientific community" von der Gott-ist-tot-Idee beeinflußt wurde. Solange man die Welt als Produkt der schöpferischen Aktivität eines auf mathematischer Grundlage arbeitenden Verstandes betrachtete, als das Werk eines Schöpfers, der beim Entwerfen der Natur *more geometrico* verfährt, solange war die ganze Angelegenheit unproblematisch. Gott stattet die Natur mit mathematisch geordneten Strukturen aus und den menschlichen Verstand mit einer genau darauf abgestimmten Fähigkeit zu mathematischem Denken. Wie Natur und Verstand sich vereinbaren lassen, bereitet so keine Schwierigkeiten. Gott richtet es einfach in dieser Weise ein. Wenn aber *das* das Erklärungsprinzip für die Erfaßbarkeit der Naturgesetze ist, dann freilich verschwindet zugleich mit der Absage auf Gott auch unsere Erklärungsgrundlage für die Erkennbarkeit der Natur. Einige der größten Denker unserer Zeit halten diesen Verlust für endgültig.

Wissenschaftler und Philosophen allerersten Ranges bekräftigen heute oft und ohne Zögern, daß wir nicht hoffen können, das Rätsel um die mathematische Erkennbarkeit der Natur überhaupt zu lösen. Erwin Schroedinger charakterisiert den Umstand, daß der Mensch die Gesetze der Natur entdecken kann, als ein „Wunder, das möglicherweise jenseits des menschlichen Fassungsvermögens liegt"[2]. Eugene Wigner stellt fest, daß „die enorme Nützlichkeit der Mathematik in den Naturwissenschaften etwas ist, das ans Mysteriöse grenzt, und daß es keine rationale Erklärung dafür gibt"[3]; ja, mit einem unerwarteten Sinn fürs Lyrische steigert er sich zu der Behauptung: „Das Wunder, daß sich die mathematische Sprache zur Formulierung physikalischer Gesetze eignet, ist ein herrliches Geschenk, das wir weder verstehen noch verdienen."[4] Sogar Albert Einstein stand tief beeindruckt vor diesem Problem. In einem Brief, den er 1952 an Maurice Solovine, einen alten Freund seiner Berner Zeit, schrieb, heißt es: „Du findest es seltsam, daß ich die Erkennbarkeit der Welt − in dem Maße, in dem wir berechtigt sind, von solch einer Erkennbarkeit zu sprechen − als ein Wunder oder ewiges Geheimnis betrachte. Nun, a priori sollte man erwarten, daß die Welt nur in dem Ausmaß Gesetzmäßigkeiten aufzustellen erlaubt, in dem wir mit unserem ordnenden Verstand Eingriffe vornehmen . . . (Aber) die Art der Ordnung, die beispielsweise die Gravitationstheorie Newtons errichtet, ist von gänzlich anderem Charakter. Auch wenn die Axiome der Theorie von Menschen gesetzt sind − der Erfolg des Unternehmens basiert auf einem hohen Grad an Regelhaftigkeit in den objektiven Weltverläufen, den wir a priori in keiner Weise zu erwarten berechtigt sind. Das ist das Wunder, das mit der Entwicklung unseres Wissens mehr und mehr zum Tragen kommt . . . Das Seltsame ist, daß wir uns damit zufrieden geben müssen, das ‚Wunder‘ anzuerkennen, ohne daß wir über eine legitime Methode verfügten, dahinter zu sehen . . ."[5] Gemäß all diesen Theoretikern stehen wir hier vor einem echten Geheimnis. Wir müssen akzeptieren, *daß* die Natur intelligibel ist, haben aber keine Aussicht, je verstehen zu können, *warum* dies so ist. Das Problem einer Erfaßbarkeit der Natur durch die mathematisch formulierten Theoriebildungen des Menschen gilt als unüberwindlich, als hoffnungslos unlösbar. Alle drei genannten, berühmten Nobelpreisträger für Physik verwenden ohne Scheu das Wort „Wunder" in diesem Zusammenhang.

Vielleicht ist aber die Frage geradezu illegitim und sollte überhaupt nicht gestellt werden. Vielleicht ist das Thema der Erkennbarkeit der Natur nur grundsätzlich jeder vernünftigen Behandlung unzugänglich, indem es in gewissem Sinn auf einer falschen Voraussetzung beruht. Denn nach einer Erklärung dafür zu suchen, warum naturwissenschaftliches Forschen Erfolg hat, setzt voraus, daß es einen Erklärungsgrund für diesen Sachverhalt tatsächlich gibt. Wenn aber dieser Umstand als reiner *Zufall* betrachtet werden muß, dann kann es kein solches Erklärungsprinzip geben. Eben diesem Gedankengang folgt Karl Popper, wenn er schreibt: „Doch selbst wenn wir annehmen (und das tue ich), unsere Erkenntnissuche sei bisher sehr erfolgreich gewesen, wir wüßten jetzt etwas über die Welt, dann ist dieser Erfolg unbegreiflich unwahrscheinlich und daher unerklärlich; die Berufung auf eine endlose Folge unwahrscheinlicher Zufälle ist keine Erklärung. (Das Beste, was wir tun können, scheint mir zu sein, die fast unglaubliche Entwicklungsgeschichte dieser Zufälle zu untersuchen . . .).“[6]

Aus dieser Sicht wird die Frage nach der Erkennbarkeit der Natur ein illegitimes Scheinproblem, eine verbotene Frucht, nach der zu greifen man vernünftigerweise nicht trachten sollte. Wir müssen uns einfach mit dieser Tatsache abfinden und einsehen, daß jeder Erklärungsversuch von vornherein zum Scheitern verurteilt ist.

Gegenüber der großen Frage, wie Naturwissenschaft überhaupt möglich ist, bekennen sich daher einige der scharfsinnigsten zeitgenössischen Wissenschaftler ratlos und gehen unverzüglich dazu über, das Problem in die Schleier des Wundersamen und Mystischen zu hüllen. Solch ein Vorgehen ist freilich sehr problematisch. Ungeachtet bedeutender Gegenstimmen ist die Frage nach der Erkennbarkeit der Natur allem Anschein nach nicht nur sinnvoll und bedeutsam, sondern auch eine solche, von der wir prinzipiell hoffen dürfen, sie mehr oder weniger vernünftig beantworten zu können. Die hier unternommene Behandlung der Frage jedenfalls beruht auf der Überzeugung, daß das Thema eine gehörige Portion Entmystifizierung nötig hat und auch verdient.

2. Charakterisierung des Problems

Wie kommt es, daß wir unser mathematisches Instrumentarium erfolgreich zur Beschreibung der Natur einsetzen können? Weshalb trifft Mathematik auf die Wirklichkeit zu? Der reine Logiker scheint eine Antwort parat zu haben. Er sagt: „Mathematik *muß* auf die Realität anwendbar sein. Mathematische Propositionen sind doch begriffliche Wahrheiten. Sie sind daher in dieser Welt wahr, weil sie in jeder möglichen Welt wahr sind." Aber diese Antwort geht an der Sache vorbei. Zugegeben, die wahren Sätze der reinen Mathematik sind in und von jeder möglichen Welt wahr. Aber sie sind dies nur, weil sie streng hypothetisch und ohne deskriptiven Gehalt sind. Gerade ihr Status als Begriffswahrheiten besagt, daß sie für unsere Zwecke nicht herangezogen werden können. Wir beschäftigen uns doch jetzt nicht mit der apriorischen Wahrheit der reinen Mathematik und ihrem Leistungsvermögen, Vernunftwahrheiten zu formulieren. Worum es hier geht, ist vielmehr die Anwendbarkeit der Mathematik im Bereich der Erfahrungswirklichkeit, ihre zentrale Rolle bei der Aufgabe, den Rahmen für die kontingenten, aposteriorischen Wahrheiten über gesetzmäßige Abläufe abzustecken und so die Zusammenhänge der Natur für die Vernunft zugänglich zu machen.

Schließlich ist es ja vollkommen klar, daß die Gültigkeit der reinen Mathematik in einer Welt nicht bedeutet, daß die *Gesetze* dieser Welt mit relativ einfachen mathematischen Mitteln darstellbar sein sollen. Sie bedeutet nicht, die Verfahrensweisen der Natur müßten in stimmigem Bezug zur Mathematik stehen und in einfachen, klaren, eleganten und rational einsichtigen Formeln faßbar sein. Kurz, sie bedeutet nicht, die Welt müsse mathematisch diskutierbar oder „mathematophil" sein im Sinne einer Empfänglichkeit für eine Behandlung der eleganten Art, die ihr in den exakten Naturwissenschaften tatsächlich widerfährt. Wie also können wir die Tatsache begründen, daß die Welt auf die Mathematik paßt und umgekehrt?

Die Antwort erfordert einen etwas komplexen, doppelgleisigen Gedankengang. Der Umstand, daß X und Y sich in einem Zustand wechselseitiger Affinität und Übereinstimmung befinden (also daß Natur und Mathematik passend koordiniert sind), ist eine zweiseitige Angelegenheit, in der erwartungsgemäß beide Seiten von Belang sein werden.

Wenn wir die Natur verstehen wollen, wenn es zwischen diesen beiden Bezugspartnern Einklang und Übereinstimmung geben soll, dann müssen beide Teile, sowohl die Zusamenhänge der Natur als auch die mathematische Rationalität des Menschen, kooperativ zusammenwirken. Diesen Gedankengang müssen wir näher verfolgen.

3. Unsere Seite

Die Seite des Menschen in dieser zweiseitigen Angelegenheit ist relativ einfach zu beschreiben. Der Mensch ist in jedem Fall ein integraler Bestandteil der Natur, eingebunden in das System der Dinge als eine seiner inneren Komponenten. Daher ist der Typ von Mathematik, den er entwickelt, zwangsläufig anwendbar. Seine Erfahrung ist unvermeidlich Erfahrung *von* Natur. Genau *das* nämlich ist „Erfahrung": unsere durch unseren Erkenntnisapparat vermittelte Reaktion auf die als Stimuli fungierenden Umwelteinflüsse. So muß wohl die Art von Mathematik, die der Mensch im Hinblick auf diese Erfahrung entwickelt, eine solche sein, die auf die Natur, so wie er sie erfährt, anwendbar ist.

Die Mathematik einer in astronomischen Fernen lebenden Zivilisation dagegen, deren empirische Ausgangsbasis von unserer stark abweicht, könnte von der Mathematik, die wir kennen und lieben, fundamental verschieden sein. Der Umgang mit Quantität könnte dort gänzlich anumerisch erfolgen, z.B. rein vergleichend statt quantifizierend. Besonders wenn die äußere Umgebung dort nicht in genügendem Maße mit festen Gegenständen oder stabilen und damit meßbaren Strukturen ausgestattet ist – wenn die Bewohner dieser Welt etwa quallenähnliche Geschöpfe sind, die in einer Art „Bio-Suppe" herumschwimmen – so könnte die dortige „Geometrie" äußerst seltsam ausfallen, wohl vornehmlich auf Topologie konzentriert und eher auf flexible Strukturen eingerichtet als auf feste Größen oder Formen. Digitale Umsetzungen fehlten möglicherweise völlig, bestimmte Arten analogen Denkens andererseits könnten zu höchster Subtilität entwickelt sein. Wären ferner die extraterrestrischen Intelligenzen etwa diffuse Agglomerate von Einheiten, deren Zusammenfassung zu Ganzheiten auch Überlappungen zuließen, dann könnte ihr Denken so sehr von einer sozialen Begrifflichkeit dominiert werden, daß sie die Natur grundsätzlich unter sozialen Kategorien betrachteten, so daß jene Aggregate, die wir als *physikalische* Strukturen denken, bei ihnen unter einer *sozialen* Perspektive begriffen würden. Die Art von „Strukturen", die ihrer mathematischen Theoriebildung zugrunde läge, könnte *in der Tat grundlegend* von unserer eigenen abweichen.

Mathematik ist zwar die Theorie der Strukturen, aber sie muß sich doch als Theorie der vorstellbaren Strukturen entwickeln. Und „vorstellbar" bedeutet hier: vorstellbar für ein im

Laufe der Naturentwicklung entstandenes und in seine natürliche Umwelt eingebundenes Lebewesen. Mathematik ist freilich nicht Naturwissenschaft, sondern eine Theorie des hypothetisch Möglichen. Doch diese Möglichkeiten sind nichtsdestoweniger Möglichkeiten, wie sie *von uns* erfaßt werden, von Lebewesen also, die die Erfassung von Möglichkeiten mit einem evolutionär entwickelten, ihnen von Natur aus eingepflanzten Erkenntnisapparat erzeugen. Es darf uns also nicht überraschen, wenn die Art von Mathematik, die wir betreiben, eine solche ist, die sich zur menschenbegrifflichen Verarbeitung natürlichen Geschehens geeignet zeigt.

Unsere kognitiven Mechanismen – die Mathematik eingeschlossen – passen auf Natur, weil sie selbst ein Produkt natürlicher Abläufe sind, wobei diese ihrerseits vermittelt sind durch die kognitiven Prozesse intelligenter Lebewesen, die ihre Intelligenz dazu benutzen, ihre Interaktionen mit der Natur, deren Teil sie selbst sind, zu steuern. Unsere Mathematik ist dazu prädestiniert, auf die Natur einigermaßen abgestimmt zu sein, weil sie selbst ein Produkt der Natur ist; also weil sie in gewisser Hinsicht unsere eigene Stellung als integrale Konstituenten der Natur widerspiegelt.

Die kognitiven Mechanismen, die wir anwenden, wenn wir uns mit der Welt auseinandersetzen, wenn wir sensorische Interaktion in verstandesmäßig analysierbare Erfahrung umsetzen, haben neben vielen anderen Eigenschaften auch die, selbst ein Beitrag der Natur zur Anpassung eines ihr auf Gnaden oder Ungnaden ausgelieferten Lebewesens zu sein. Daß der Verstand des Menschen die Zusammenhänge der Natur begreift, ist nicht überraschender als die Tatsache, daß das Auge einen Teil der in der Natur vorkommenden Strahlung, oder daß der Magen Produkte der Natur als Nahrungsmittel verarbeiten kann. Dies alles haben wir dem Selektionsdruck zu verdanken.

Es könnte allerdings der Fall sein, daß unsere kognitive Anpassung nur innerhalb unserer unmittelbar nächstliegenden raum-zeitlich begrenzten Umgebung gut funktioniert, innerhalb der Mikro-Umgebung, die unsere besondere ökologische Nische definiert. So besteht die Möglichkeit, daß wir unter einem weiteren Blickwinkel gar nicht so gut dran sind, daß wir nur einen kleinen und sehr peripheren Teil eines großen, unzugänglichen Ganzen zu fassen bekommen. *Daher* kann in dem einseitigen Beitrag des Menschen nicht die *ganze* Antwort auf die Frage nach der Erkennbarkeit der Natur liegen. Denn selbst wenn wir, gemessen an unseren eigenen evolutionär entstandenen Bedürfnissen in unserer Naturerfassung ziemlich erfolgreich sind, so *könnte* diese in einem umfassenderen Zusammenhang doch immer noch sehr inadäquat sein. Es bleibt also noch zu zeigen, daß die Natur selbst unseren Erkenntnisleistungen die entsprechenden Ansatzpunkte bietet, daß sie der Vernunft prinzipiell – und nicht nur so irgendwie am Rande – zugänglich ist.

Um *diesen* Punkt zu klären, müssen wir daher dazu übergehen, den Beitrag der Natur in dem Wechselverhältnis von Natur und Geist in Sicht zu nehmen.

4. Die Seite der Natur

Wenn ein intelligentes Lebewesen, das seine natürliche Umgebung erforscht und dabei auf der Grundlage physischer Interaktion mit ihr mathematisch formulierte Entwürfe und Überzeugungen entwickelt, ein einigermaßen adäquates Verständnis von ihrer Funktionsweise erreichen soll, *dann* muß auch die Natur ihrerseits in gehörigem Umfang zur Zusammenarbeit beitragen. Offensichtlich muß sie zunächst die Entwicklung intelligenter Lebewesen zulassen. Darüber hinaus muß sie diesen Lebewesen eine Umwelt bieten, die über ausreichend stabile Konstellationen verfügt, um einen „Erfahrungs"-zusammenhang entstehen zu lassen und solche Lebewesen dazu zu befähigen, aus strukturierten Interaktionen geeignete *Informationen* zu gewinnen. Diese Überlegung hat weitreichende Implikationen. Im Hinblick auf unsere hier vorausgesetzte Zielsetzung muß gezeigt werden, daß die Mathematik nicht nur von einigem Nutzen ist, sondern daß sie für das Verständnis der Welt zwangsläufig eine äußerst wesentliche Voraussetzung darstellt. Wir müssen uns dessen versichern, daß die Anwendung von

Mathematik im Bereich rationaler Forschung ein adäquates und genaues Verständnis der Naturzusammenhänge liefern kann. Wir müssen also eingehender untersuchen, wie die Natur mit den Forschungsmethoden des Verstandes in einen Dialog tritt.

Der Beitrag der Natur selbst zur mathematisch artikulierbaren Naturerkenntnis muß in ihrer Strukturiertheit durch *relativ einfache* Gesetzmäßigkeiten bestehen, die in ihrer Regularität so leicht zu entschlüsseln sind, daß sie sogar von Lebewesen mit ziemlich bescheidenen Fähigkeiten und Mitteln gut verstanden werden können.

Wie aber kann man die These rechtfertigen, daß die Natur nach relativ durchschaubaren Gesetzmäßigkeiten geordnet sein *muß*? Lassen sich tatsächlich stichhaltige Gründe dafür anführen, weshalb die Welt, die wir mittels unseres vom mathematischen Denken geprägten Verstandes erforschen, auf der Basis relativ einfacher und der mathematischen Analyse von sich aus zugänglicher Prinzipien operieren sollte? Hier ist der zentrale Punkt wohl der folgende: Eigentlich darf es gar nicht erstaunen, daß der mathematisierende Verstand der Erfassung der Natur so wesentliche Erfolge erzielt, denn eine Welt, in der sich ein derartiger Erkenntnisapparat überhaupt entwickelt, ist eine Welt, die der Mathematik angepaßt ist. Dieser Schlußfolgerung liegt in groben Zügen etwa folgende Argumentation zugrunde: Eine Welt, in der sich durch *Evolutions*prozesse Intelligenz entwickelt, muß eine solche sein, in der diese Intelligenz den intelligenten Einwohner einen (zumindest bescheidenen) Evolutionsvorteil einbringen muß. Intelligenz muß für diejenigen, die darüber verfügen, ein „Selektionsplus" darstellen. Auch die niedrigsten Lebewesen, die nur höchst rudimentäre *Vorstufen* von Intelligenz besitzen (Schnecken und Algen zum Beispiel), müssen sich so verhalten, daß bestimmte Reiztypen (Muster sich wiederholender, definiert strukturierter Umwelteinflüsse) angemessen korrespondierende Reaktionstypen hervorrufen. Mit anderen Worten: solche Lebewesen müssen ein Reizmuster in ihrer Umwelt als solches isolieren und darauf in einer Weise reagieren können, die sie bei der Selektion begünstigt. Aber dies bedeutet, daß die Natur auf eine ganz bestimmte Art „kooperativ" ist, daß sie genügend gleichförmig, regelhaft und strukturiert sein muß, daß es auf Umweltereignisse „angemessene" und „lernbare" Reaktionen geben kann. Es muß also strukturierte Ereignismuster in der Natur geben, die schon die einfachsten Lebewesen in der Ausstattung ihres Umweltapparates und in ihrem modus operandi widerspiegeln können. Die Welt muß also problemlos lernbare Muster von Ereignisablauf-Strukturen beinhalten, das heißt relativ einfache Gesetzmäßigkeiten. Die Existenz solcher lernbaren Strukturiertheiten von natürlichen Vorkommnissen bedeutet, daß Mathematik, die letztlich die abstrakte und systematische Theorie der Strukturen im allgemeinen ist, *eine* nützliche Funktion haben muß. Und so können wir schließen, daß eine Welt, in der sich mittels evolutionärer Prozesse Intelligenz entwickeln kann, eine solche sein *muß*, die einem an mathematischen Begriffen orientierten Verständnis zugänglich ist.[7]

Eine Welt, in der evolutionäre Prozesse hochgradige Intelligenz hervorbringen, muß eine hochgradig intelligible Welt sein. Es liegt im Wesen der Evolution, daß eine Welt, in der mathematisierendes Denken überhaupt auftaucht, angesichts des damit verbundenen notwendigen Selektionsvorteils eine Welt sein muß, in der dieses Denken imstande ist, die Welt mathematisch zu verstehen. Die Existenz intelligenter Lebewesen mag für sich und als solche erstaunlich sein oder nicht; aber sobald es sie einmal gibt und sobald wir einsehen, daß es sie dank des Verlaufs der Evolution gibt, darf es nicht länger erstaunlich sein, daß ihren Bemühungen, die Welt in der Sprache der Mathematik zu beschreiben, ein substanzieller Erfolg beschieden ist. Eine Welt, in der Lebewesen mit hochgradiger Intelligenz entstehen können, muß eine sein, deren Gesetzesstrukturen eine leistungsfähige Beschreibung mit mathematischen Mitteln ermöglichen und erfordern.

Ein weiteres wichtiges Problem lauert noch im Hintergrund: *Wie gut* versteht unsere Naturwissenschaft die Welt wirklich? Kommt sie nicht nur zu mutmaßlichen, sondern auch zu echten Naturgesetzen? Das freilich ist eine Frage, die nicht als solche beantwortet werden kann. Denn wir haben keinerlei *direkten* Zugang zur Natur-an-sich, um diese mit der aus unseren Untersuchungen resultierenden mutmaßlichen Natur zu vergleichen – um unsere als solche behaupteten „Naturgesetze" mit ihren realen Gegenstücken zu konfrontieren. Alles was wir tun können, ist, die Adäquatheit unserer Theoriebildung am Grad ihrer *Leistungsfähigkeit* zu überprüfen, an ihrer Eignung, uns Vorhersagen und kontrollierte Eingriffe zu erlauben. Und freilich sind wir unter diesen pragmatischen Hinsichten zu hinlänglich guten Leistungen prädestiniert. Jene mutmaßlichen Gesetzmäßigkeiten wären eben nicht Bestandteile unseres naturwissenschaftlichen Kanons, wenn sie uns nicht unter diesen Rücksichten in recht guter Weise dienlich wären. (Dies ist der Ort, wo die *rationale* Selektion ins Spiel kommt). Es ist effektiv unvermeidlich, daß wir den Eindruck gewinnen, unsere Wissenschaft bilde die Natur relativ adäquat ab. Jene Theorien, die nach dem als „naturwissenschaftliche Methode" bezeichneten Verfahren gewonnen und bestätigt werden, gehörten doch gar nicht zum Corpus unserer Naturwissenschaft, wenn sie bei uns nicht diesen Eindruck hinterließen. Wenn wir über den „Erfolg der mathematisch formulierten Naturbeschreibung" reden, so spielen wir mit gezinkten Karten. Denn (1) muß solch ein Erfolg im Sinne eines *wahrgenommenen* Erfolges konzipiert werden und (2) entstammt diese Erfolgswahrnehmung demselben (biologischen und kognitiven) Evolutionsprozeß, der auch der für uns spezifischen Art von Naturverständnis zugrunde liegt.

Der Erfolg der Mathematik bei der Beschreibung der Natur ist so in keiner Weise erstaunlich. Daß sich intelligente Lebewesen überhaupt entwickeln konnten, mag Verwunderung hervorrufen oder nicht. Aber daß sie, einmal im Laufe der Evolution in Erscheinung getreten, erfolgreich sein würden bei dem Vorhaben, die Natur in mathematischen Beziehungen zu erfassen, ist nur zu erwarten. Eine Welt, in der sich Intelligenz zeigt, deren Lebewesen zu ihrer Intelligenz durch evolutionäre Mechanismen gelangen, muß für ein Verständnis nach mathematischen Begriffen wesentlich offen sein.

Man darf dabei nicht übersehen, daß der hier vorgeführte Argumentationsgang von strikt hypothetischem Charakter ist. Es wird nicht (kategorisch) behauptet, daß die Welt, um eine elegante mathematische Darstellung ihrer Verfahrensweisen zu ermöglichen, einfach genug sein muß und damit punktum. Es wird vielmehr die streng konditionale These behauptet: *Wenn* intelligente Lebewesen im Laufe *evolutionären* Geschehens in der Welt auftauchen, *dann* muß die Welt mathematophil sein. Entscheidend ist dabei die Einsicht, daß diese konditionale Form der These doch für unsere Zielsetzung völlig ausreicht; denn wir haben es mit der Antwort auf die Frage zu tun, weshalb wir Menschen, wir intelligenten Lebewesen, die Welt in der Sprache unserer Mathematik verstehen können sollten. Und die genannte konditionale Form genügt, um diese Aufgabe zu erfüllen.

5. Synthesis

Lassen Sie mich nun kurz innehalten, um die einzelnen Stücke zusammenzufügen. Die allgemeine Frage nach der Erkennbarkeit der Natur hat zwei Richtungssinne:

I. Warum ist der Verstand so gut auf die Natur abgestimmt?

II. Warum ist die Natur so gut auf den Verstand abgestimmt?

In der Erörterung dieser Fragen wurde die Ansicht vertreten, daß ihre Beantwortung gar nicht so schwierig ist – zumindest auf der Ebene einer schematischen Charakterisierung. Der Verstand muß an die Natur angepaßt sein, weil er ein Produkt evolutionärer Abläufe ist. Und die Natur muß durch den Verstand erfaßbar sein, weil dies allererst die Ausbildung von Verstand überhaupt ermöglicht.

Wenn Natur und Verstand zu weit ab von jeder Übereinstimmung wären, wenn der menschliche Erkenntnisapparat zu „unintelligent" wäre, um die vielschichtigen Zusammenhänge der Natur zu begreifen, oder die Natur zu komplex für die Fähigkeiten des Verstandes, dann könnten beide eben nicht auf Takt kommen. Es wäre wie der Versuch, Shakespeare in ein Pidgin-Englisch mit einem Vokabular von 500 Wörtern umzuschreiben – zu vieles und zu wesentliches ginge da verloren. Es wäre wie der Versuch, ein System mit zehn relevanten

Freiheitsgraden in einem Modell darzustellen, das nur über vier von diesen verfügen kann. Wenn es sich wirklich so verhielte wie in diesen Fällen, könnte der menschliche Erkenntnisapparat seine evolutionäre Mission nicht erfüllen.

Die Lösung unseres Problems wurzelt also in der Kombination zweier Überlegungen: (1) Eine Welt, die im Zuge der Evolution eine relativ potente Form von Intelligenz auftreten läßt, muß relativ regelmäßig und einfach strukturiert, das heißt mathematophil sein. (2) Wie eine hinlänglich potente Form von Intelligenz eine derartige Welt mittels mathematisch-naturwissenschaftlicher Theoriebildungen begreifen kann, ist dementsprechend durch die Tatsache zu erklären, daß im Hinblick auf die Evolution Verstand und verstandesmäßige Erfaßbarkeit in signifikanter Weise koordiniert sein müssen.

7. Ein Restpunkt

Diese Überlegungen bringen uns aber auf ein wesentliches restliches Element im Problemfeld um die Erkennbarkeit der Natur. Denn sie lassen die Schlüsselfrage noch unberührt: Warum haben sich in der Natur überhaupt verstandesbegabte Wesen entwickelt? Wie kommt es, daß die Welt der Schauplatz forschender Intelligenz ist?

Dies ist eine noch problembeladenere Frage als die soeben angesprochene – und in der Tat eine sehr alte. In Tabelle I findet sich eine einigermaßen vollständige Liste der verschiedenen Antworten, die dazu vorgeschlagen wurden.

TABELLE I

Weshalb hat sich in der Natur überhaupt Intelligenz entwickelt?

I. Die positivistische Antwort:
    Die Frage ist illegitim, unangemessen, sinnlos.

II. Die skeptizistische Antwort:
    Die Frage ist sinnvoll, aber wesentlich unbeantwortbar.

III. Die abblockende Antwort:
    Es gibt diesen (verflixten) Grund einfach nicht. Natur ist eben so. Die Natur der Natur hat keinen explanatorischen Hintergrund, sie bildet das Ende der Erklärungsreihe.

IV. Die theologische Antwort:
    Gott hat es so eingerichtet.

V. Die Teleologische Antwort:
    Die Gründe für das Auftreten von Intelligenz sind wesentlich teleologisch: Das Vorhandensein von Intelligenz ermöglicht es der Natur, ein bestimmtes Ziel zu verwirklichen.

VI. Die evolutionstheoretische Antwort:
    Mit der Entstehung von Leben in der Welt ist auch die Entwicklung von Intelligenz zu erwarten, denn Intelligenz erhöht die Überlebenschancen. Sie bietet eine wirksame Lösung für das Problem, eine biologische Art entlang der Zeitachse voranzubringen.

Die teleologische Antwort klingt besonders verführerisch. Sie schreibt der Natur eine bestimmte Neigung zur Ausbildung von Geistigkeit zu, einen inneren Antrieb zur Ermöglichung von Erkenntnisvollzügen. Sie stützt sich auf die in der Natur aufweisbare (oder ihr zuweisbare) Grundtendenz zur Selbstreproduktion (*conatus se replicandi* ähnlich dem *conatus se praeservandi*, der Selbsterhaltung). Die Natur, als ein Ganzes genommen, kann dies freilich nicht bewerkstelligen – es sei denn durch die Hervorbringung von Lebewesen, die Gedankenmodelle, nicht physische, aber begriffliche Abbildungen von ihr schaffen. So kommt die Natur dazu, Lebewesen hervorzubringen, die, wie Leibniz' Monaden, die Fähigkeit besitzen, die Welt in einem gewissen Grade verstandesmäßig „widerzuspiegeln". Die Welt verkörpert demnach eine von sich aus auf Geist hin abzielende Bewegung. Die Natur hat – in bester Tradition hegelschen Denkens – ein inneres Bestreben, sich selbst als Gedanke zu verwirklichen.

Die wahre Erklärung – die evolutionstheoretische Antwort – ist weitaus prosaischer, nüchterner und unromantischer. Sie beginnt mit der Feststellung, daß es viele verschiedene Wege gibt, mit der Natur sein Auskommen zu finden, daß den biologischen Arten diverse Wege geboten sind, um sich in der Natur zu behaupten: Erzeugung zahlreicher Nachkommenschaft, Widerstandsfähigkeit, Anpassungsfähigkeit, Isolation, et cetera. Unter diesen Marschrouten erweist sich aber eine als besonders aussichtsreich: diejenige, die darauf ausgeht, Intelligenz auszubilden, sich dadurch anzupassen, daß Gehirnkapazitäten statt Muskelkapazitäten oder erhöhter Reproduktionsfähigkeiten zum Einsatz kommen. Wie schon Meister Darwin selbst betonte, hat die Art, die Zusammenhänge ihrer Umgebung am besten erfaßt, einen Selektionsvorteil: Die Art, die ihren Weg durch den Darwinschen Konkurrenzkampf nicht durch reine Zähigkeit macht, nicht nur mit Klauen und Zähnen, sondern mit Intelligenz, findet eine vielversprechende ökologische Nische. Sobald sich das *Leben* entwickelt und unter der Schutzherrschaft der fruchtbaren Mutter Natur darangeht, verschiedene Fortpflanzungsstrategien auszukundschaften, ist es nur natürlich, daß sich Intelligenz entwickelt. Kurz und gut: Intelligenz tritt auf, weil sie für die Lösung des Überlebensproblems ein wirksames Instrument darstellt. Intelligenz entwickelt sich nicht deshalb, weil die Natur dies begünstigt, sondern weil Intelligenz das Überleben derer, die sie besitzen, innerhalb der Natur begünstigt (auf alle Fälle bis zu einem bestimmten Punkt).

Schluß

Wir wollen noch einmal rasch den Verlauf der Diskussion durchgehen und im Rückblick die drei Hauptpunkte Revue passieren lassen.
1) Intelligenz entwickelt sich in belebter Natur, weil sie Lebewesen eine gute Methode bietet, mit ihrer Umwelt zurechtzukommen.
2) Sobald intelligente Lebewesen entstehen, haben ihre Erkenntnisleistungen aller Wahrscheinlichkeit nach einen bestimmten Grad von Adäquatheit, da sie durch den Selektionsdruck auf die Arbeitsweise der Natur hin ausgerichtet sind.
3) Es sollte nicht überraschen, daß diese Anpassung schließlich eine äußerst leistungsfähige, mathematisch formulierte Physik entstehen läßt, denn die grundlegenden Strukturen natürlicher Vorgänge, die es auch zur Ausbildung von Intelligenz kommen lassen, *müssen* relativ einfach sein.

Im weiten Umfeld dieser Thesen mag in der Tat allerhand geheimnisvoll bleiben. (Fragen wie: „Warum hat sich *Leben* in der Welt entwickelt?" und – noch grundsätzlicher –: „Warum existiert die Welt überhaupt?" könnten als Kandidaten vorgebracht werden.) Sei das, wie es will, die gegenwärtig behandelte Thematik, weshalb die Natur dem Menschen erkennbar ist und weshalb sich solche Erkennbarkeit in einer mathematisch formulierten Physik niederschlagen sollte, erfüllt doch die Qualifikationen eines großen Mysteriums, geschweige denn eines Wunders, sicherlich nicht.

Gewiß, die hier vertretene Konzeption ist äußerst schematisch entworfen und erfordert umfangreiche Füllarbeiten. Es muß eine lange und verwickelte Geschichte über die physikalische und die kognitive Evolution erzählt werden, um die Konzeption mit Einzelheiten anzureichern. Aber es gibt sicherlich allen Grund, darauf zu hoffen und zu warten, daß eine solche Geschichte schließlich erzählt werden kann. Und das ist hier der entscheidende Punkt. Selbst wenn jemand an den Umrissen der hier skizzierten evolutionstheoretischen Darstellung, an der Linienführung im einzelnen, seine Zweifel hat − so bleibt doch die Tatsache, daß *irgend-eine Darstellung dieser Art* in bezug auf die Erfaßbarkeit der Natur mit mathematischen Mitteln eine hervorragend ausbaufähige Erklärung liefert. Die Tatsache allein, daß so eine Konzeption im Prinzip möglich ist, zeigt, daß man die Aussichten auf eine Beantwortung unserer Frage nicht so schwarz in schwarz malen muß, wie es die Zonen undurchdringlicher Geheimnisse sind.

Es besteht einfach keine Notwendigkeit, Einstein, Schroedinger und Co. Folge zu leisten, wenn sie die Erkennbarkeit der Natur als Wunder oder Geheimnis betrachten, das alles menschliche Verstehen übersteigt. Wenn wir bereit sind, von der Naturwissenschaft selbst zu lernen, wie die Natur funktioniert und wie der Mensch bei der Auswertung seiner Forschungsergebnisse vorgeht, dann könnten wir zunehmend das Problem, weshalb ein Lebewesen dieser Art eine physikalische Umgebung solcher Art effektiv erforschen kann, vom Schleier des Geheimnisses befreien. Wir wären schließlich imstande, es als völlig plausibel und ganz allen Erwartungen entsprechend zu finden, daß Wissenschaft betreibende Lebewesen auftreten und sich eine Position verschaffen, die es ihnen erlaubt, daraus allerhand Kapital zu schlagen. Bei der Suche nach einem Leitfaden zur Beantwortung der Frage, wie Naturwissenschaft möglich ist, können wir daher die *Wissenschaft selbst* in Blick nehmen. Und es gibt keinen guten Grund, weshalb sie uns in dieser Hinsicht im Stich lassen sollte.

ANMERKUNGEN

[1] Dieses ausgesprochen kantische Thema wird hier in einer ausgesprochen unkantischen Weise behandelt. Denn die vorliegenden Überlegungen beschäftigen sich nicht à la Kant mit bestimmten apriorischen Prinzipien, die der Physik vermutlich zugrunde liegen. Wir betrachten vielmehr die faktischen (aposteriorischen) Prinzipien, aus denen die Physik *besteht* − die Naturgesetze selbst.

[2] Schroedinger, Erwin, *What is Life?* (Cambridge 1945), S. 31.

[3] Wigner, Eugene P., „The Unreasonable Effectiveness of Mathematics in the Natural Sciences", *Communications on Pure and Applied Mathematics*, Bd. 13, (1960), S. 1−14. (vgl. S. 2)

[4] Ebd. S. 14.

[5] Einstein, A., *Lettres à Maurice Solovine* (Paris 1956), 114f.

[6] Popper, K. R., *Objektive Erkenntnis*, (dtsch. Übersetz. Hamburg 1973), S. 40f.

[7] Gespräche mit Gerald Massey haben in hilfreicher Weise zur Verbesserung und Klärung dieses Argumentationsteils beigetragen.

[8] Es ist freilich nicht die *biologische* Evolution im Sinne Darwins, die zur Mathematik führt, sondern die, sich an die biologische anschließende, kognitive Evolution, bei der die rationale Selektion der intellektuellen Mittel im Sinne der Lamarque'schen Theorie verläuft. Vgl. N. Rescher, *Methodological Pragmatism* (Oxford 1973).

* * *

GIBT ES FÜR DAS LEIB-SEELE-PROBLEM EINE „LÖSUNG"?

Dieter Birnbacher
Universität Essen

Ist das Leib-Seele-Problem ein echtes oder ein Scheinproblem? Bedarf die Frage nach dem Zusammenhang zwischen Leib und Seele der *Lösung* oder der *Auflösung?*

Ich bin überzeugt, daß das Leib-Seele-Problem *kein* bloßes Scheinproblem ist, das zu seiner Lösung lediglich der Klärung seiner sprachlichen Struktur bedarf. Aber ich bin ebenso davon überzeugt, daß wir gut daran täten, nicht schnurstracks auf die „Lösung" des Leib-Seele-Problems zuzugehen, sondern zunächst in reflektiver, metaphilosophischer Einstellung nach den *Kriterien* zu fragen, die wir dafür gelten lassen wollen, eine vorgeschlagene „Lösung" als Lösung zu akzeptieren. Erst wenn wir uns dieser Kriterien vergewissert haben − wenn wir wissen, was wir suchen, was wir von einer „Lösung" erwarten −, wird sich entscheiden lassen, ob es eine „Lösung" im Prinzip geben kann, ob sich bereits einer der gegenwärtig diskutierten Lösungsansätze als „Lösung" auszeichnen läßt, oder ob es dazu weitergehender Fortschritte des empirischen oder philosophischen Wissens bedarf.

Der *erste* Teil meines Beitrags wird einen Vorschlag zu den Kriterien machen, dem eine potentielle Lösung genügen sollte. Der *zweite* Teil wird dann prüfen, welche der gegenwärtig diskutierten Lösungsansätze diese Kriterien am ehesten erfüllen. Das Interessante an dieser Vorgehensweise ist, daß sich der Kreis der Bewerber mit ernsthaften Chancen als außerordentlich klein erweist. Der nächstgelegene Weg zur „Lösung", so zeigt sich, führt in der Tat über die „Grammatik" − wenn auch nicht die der Alltagssprache, sondern die der Philosophie, genauer: der *induktiven Metaphysik.* Unter einer *induktiven Metaphysik* soll dabei eine Hypothese (oder Hypothesensystem) verstanden werden, die die Existenz erfahrungstranszendenter Entitäten, Eigenschaften oder Relationen zum Zweck der Erklärung der Erfahrungswirklichkeit postuliert und von größerer Reichweite ist als die allgemeinsten Hypothesen und Hypothesensysteme der Wissenschaften. Ob zwischen wissenschaftlichen und metaphysischen Hypothesen in jedem Fall eine scharfe Grenze zu ziehen ist, kann dabei zunächst offenbleiben.

Die im folgenden skizzierten Kriterien sind Bewertungskriterien, die mehr oder weniger gute Gründe für die Akzeptierung einer metaphysischen Hypothese darstellen sollen, keine Ausschlußkriterien (constraints). Im Prinzip soll die Nichterfüllung eines Kriteriums also jederzeit durch die Erfüllung anderer Kriterien aufgewogen werden können. Die Reihenfolge der Nennung soll dem relativen Gewicht entsprechen: 1. *Intelligibilität*, 2. *Explizitheit der logischen Struktur*, 3. *Logische Konsistenz*, 4. *Kompatibilität mit weithin akzeptierten realwissenschaftlichen Theorien*, 5. *Komparativer Problemlösungsbeitrag*, 6. *Integrationsleistung*, 7. *Sparsamkeit*, 8. *Kohärenz mit anderen akzeptierten metaphysischen Theorien*, 9. *Einfachheit*, 10. *Heuristische Fruchtbarkeit*. Als „Lösung" ließe sich dann diejenige Hypothese apostrophieren, die diese Kriterien *bestmöglich* erfüllt, als „vorläufige Lösung" diejenige, die sie *auf dem gegenwärtigen Kenntnisstand bestmöglich* erfüllt.

Diese Kriterien erlauben zunächst die Eliminierung von zwei Lösungsvorschlägen: erstens Varianten eines *reduktiven Materialismus,* die alle psychologischen Prädikate − einschließlich von „raw feels"-Prädikaten − als (wie immer komplexe) physikalische konstruiert; zweitens interaktionistische Konzeptionen, die wie die von Hans Jonas Energieaustauschprozesse zwischen Psychischem und Physischem postulieren, sich dabei jedoch über die Erhaltungssätze der Physik hinwegsetzen zu können glauben.

Attraktiv aufgrund der angegebenen Kriterien ist eine Identitätstheorie, die ausgehend von der empirisch bestätigten Annahme einer durchgängigen Korrelation von psychischen Ereignissen mit Gehirnereignissen eine kontingente Identität von psychischen (P-) und bestimmten materiellen (M-) Ereignissen postuliert und einen Monismus der Entitäten (es gibt nur materielle Objekte) mit einem Dualismus der Eigenschaften (es gibt außer materiellen auch psychische Eigenschaften) verbindet. Sie übertrifft ihre dualistischen Konkurrenten sowohl hinsichtlich der Integrationsleistung (Kriterium 6) als auch hinsichtlich der Sparsamkeit (Kriterium 7). Interessanterweise erweisen sich die der Identitätstheorie am häufigsten angekreideten Schwächen (wie daß sie unseren Sprachgewohnheiten zuwiderläuft, indem sie psychische Ereignisse räumlich lokalisiert) nach dem angegebenen Kriterienkatalog als von allenfalls marginaler Bedeutung.

Problematisch an der Identitätstheorie ist allerdings die Einbuße an Problemlösungskapazität durch die Tendenz, die Frage nach der zwischen den miteinander identifizierten Phänomenen bestehenden *kausalen Beziehung* zu verschütten. Die Identität von P- und M- Ereignissen ändert ja nichts daran, daß diese Ereignisse zwei miteinander korrelierte Aspekte haben, für die sich die Frage stellt, ob M_i Ursache von P_i, P_i Ursache von M_i oder P_i koinzidierende Symptome eines zugrundeliegenden X_i sind. Die Identitätstheorie ist jedoch mit allen kausalen Deutungen verträglich, selbst noch mit der Annahme einer prästabilierten Harmonie. Sie hat insofern für das Problem des *Zusammenhangs* zwischen Geist und Materie keinen Lösungsvorschlag anzubieten. Sie bedarf der Erweiterung und Präzisierung.

Eine dieser möglichen Erweiterungen und Präzisierungen kann aufgrund des Kriterienkatalogs von vornherein als ceteris paribus weniger akzeptabel ausgeschlossen werden, da sie im Widerspruch zum ontologischen Sparsamkeitsprinzip steht: die Annahme eines unbekannten Dritten, dessen „Symptome" Geist und Gehirn sind. Betroffen davon sind sowohl Ansätze, nach denen uns stets nur die Symptomklassen M und P zugänglich sind − wie bei Spinoza, sofern man ihn als Vertreter einer solchen Theorie interpretiert −, als auch Ansätze, die eine zukünftige Emergenz „höherer" Symptomstufen nicht ausschließen − wie die von „angels" oder „finite gods" bei Samuel Alexander.

Unter den verbleibenden Ansätzen, dem Interaktionismus, der Kausalität in beiden, und dem Epiphänomenalismus, der Kausalität ausschließlich in der Richtung M−P annimmt, ist der Epiphänomenalismus nach den angegebenen Kriterien eindeutig zu präferieren. Erstens bringt der Epiphänomenalismus das, was wir wissen, auf den kleinstmöglichen metaphysischen Nenner (Kriterium 7). Zweitens vermeidet der Epiphänomenalismus ein gravierendes erkenntnistheoretisches Problem, mit dem der Interaktionismus konfrontiert ist: daß unter Bedingungen durchgängiger P-M-Korrelation eine Annahme kausal aktiver P-Ereignisse, wie sie für den Interaktionismus kennzeichnend ist, absolut willkürlich wäre.

Denn angenommen, der psychische Ereignisaspekt P_i sei die kausal hinreichende Bedingung für das materielle Ereignis M_j. P_i korreliere seinerseits mit dem materiellen Ereignis M_i. Dann gibt es für M_j entweder eine rein materielle kausal hinreichende Bedingung oder nicht. Angenommen, es gibt sie, so wäre diese keine andere als M_i, das mit P_i korrelierende M-Ereignis. Beide, P_i und M_i wären kausal hinreichende Bedingungen für M_j. Unter diesen Bedingungen gäbe es jedoch keinerlei Möglichkeit zu überprüfen, ob P_i der Annahme entsprechend tatsächlich eine kausal hinreichende Bedingung für M_j ist. Dazu müßten wir überprüfen können, daß P_i M_j auch ohne das Eintreten von M_i bewirkt, was unmöglich ist, da P_i und M_i korrelieren. Nehmen wir andererseits an, daß es für M_j *keine* materielle kausal hinreichende Bedingung gibt, so würden wir auch P_i nicht als kausal hinreichende Bedingung von M_j betrachten können, da andernfalls auch M_i eine kausal hinreichende Bedingung für M_j wäre, was der Voraussetzung widerspricht. Was dem Interaktionismus Schwierigkeiten macht, ist also weniger eine etwaige kausale Geschlossenheit der physikalischen Welt − im Gegensatz zur kausal nicht geschlossenen Welt des Psychischen − als vielmehr die Annahme einer durchgängigen Korrelation von psychischen mit materiellen Ereignissen. Auch wenn sich der notorisch interaktionistisch denkende common sense als unbelehrbar erweisen sollte − der identitätstheoretische Epiphänomenalismus erweist sich als derjenige Lösungsansatz, der den angegebenen Kriterien maximal gerecht wird und insofern, im Sinne eines historisch relativen Optimums, als die „vorläufige Lösung" des Leib-Seele-Problems betrachtet werden sollte.

Die These, daß der Epiphänomenalismus seinerseits keine Probleme neu aufwirft, ist mit mehreren Argumenten bestritten worden:

1. Es laufe der Idee kausaler Abhängigkeit zuwider, wenn das Abhängige nicht seinerseits wieder Ursache sei. − Aber weder besteht eine solche Notwendigkeit, noch wird sie durch das Kausalitätsprinzip ausgesagt. Auch die Vertreter des Interaktionismus nehmen nicht an, daß *alle* psychischen Wirkungen materieller Ursachen ihrerseits kausal aktive Rollen übernehmen.

2. Eine Kausalität von P nach M sei introspektiv „axiomatisch" gewiß. − Aber die Introspektion ist die falsche Instanz, wenn es darum geht, was „in ihrem Rücken" geschieht. Die Tatsache, daß wir gelegentlich die Vorstellung einer unmittelbaren Verknüpfung zwischen Willensakt und Verhalten haben, schließt nicht aus, daß der bewußte Willensimpuls nur vermöge seiner Korrelation mit einem Gehirnvorgang auf den Körper einwirkt.

3. Hätte der Epiphänomenalismus recht, wäre damit unsere Selbstsicht als Personen, die handelnd in die materielle Welt eingreifen, als Illusion desavouiert. − Aber dieser Einwand greift nur, wenn ein Begriff der Person vorausgesetzt wird, der die Person von der Existenz des menschlichen Gehirns abkoppelt. Die Vorstellung einer *körperunabhängigen* Einwirkug des Geistes auf das Gehirn wäre in der Tat eine Illusion − eine Illusion mit einem gewissen survival value allerdings, da es sein könnte, daß sie das Ich, indem sie ihm suggeriert, es schiebe, statt geschoben zu werden, in seinem Selbstbehauptungswillen stärkt.

4. Der Epiphänomenalismus sei mit evolutionistischen Ansätzen zur Erklärung des Bewußtseins unvereinbar. Nach diesem − namentlich von Popper − erhobenen Einwand soll es nur dann für eine nach dem Prinzip der natürlichen Selektion operierende Evolution einen Grund gegeben haben können, Lebewesen mit Bewußtsein hervorzubringen, wenn der Besitz von Bewußtsein eine kausal notwendige *und* hinreichende Bedingung für bestimmte überlebensdienliche Verhaltensweisen gewesen ist. Andernfalls wäre die „unaufwendigere" Alternative rein materieller Entwicklungslinien bevorzugt worden. Aber Poppers Einwand hat zwei entscheidende Schwächen: Erstens die Voraussetzung, daß die Evolution, um intelligentes Verhalten hervorzubringen, des Psychischen als eigenständiger, kausal aktiver Realität bedurfte; eine Natur, die teils lange vor der Dämmerung des Bewußtseins die Zelle, die geschlechtliche Fortpflanzung und die staatenbildenden Insekten „erfunden" hat, hätte auch das intelligente Verhalten „erfinden" können, ohne den Umweg über ein von der materiellen Basis abgekoppeltes Psychisches zu nehmen. Zweitens die Voraussetzung, daß die Natur eine Wahl hatte − eine Wahl zwischen Lebewesen *ohne*, und anderen, ebenso leistungsfähigen, *mit* der Zutat des Bewußtseins. Diese Wahl hatte sie dem Epiphänomenalismus zufolge jedoch gerade nicht: Falls die Evolution das intelligente Gehirn wollte, mußte sie nomologisch notwendig auch das Bewußtsein wollen. Hätte sie eine Wahl gehabt, hätte es in der Tat keinen Grund gegeben, weshalb sie die aufwendigere unter den zwei Möglichkeiten gewählt hätte. Der Epiphänomenalismus hält alles bereit, was sich die Evolutionstheorie nur wünschen kann, um zu erklären, warum die Evolution Lebewesen mit Bewußtsein bevorzugt hat, falls diese einmal durch Zufallsmutation entstanden sind. Freilich: das Faktum der nomologischen Verknüpfung von Materie und Geist selbst bleibt einer biologischen wie einer induktiv-metaphysischen Erklärung notwendig entzogen. Sie ist − jedenfalls bislang noch − Sache eines rein spekulativen Emergenzdenkens. Mit *dieser* Unzulänglichkeit unseres Denkens in Frieden zu leben, ist jedoch *jedem* ernstzunehmenden Versuch einer „Lösung" des Leib-Seele-Problems aufgegeben. Sie ist keine Hypothek, die allein auf dem Epiphänomenalismus lastet.

LITERATUR

Alexander, S., *Space, Time, and Deity*, Bd. 2 (London ²1927).

* * *

RAMSEY'S THEORY OF MIND IN RELATION TO HIS VIEW ON "THEORIES"

Ulrich Majer
Universität Hannover

In Ramsey's "Last Papers", posthumously published, there is a short article, entitled "Philosophy", that contains a sophisticated argument for the necessity of "self-consciousness" in philosophy.[1] Strange as this argument may seem, I want to show that you cannot understand "theories" and "theoretical terms" correctly according to Ramsey without reflecting on "our own mental states", that is, without taking into accont self-consciousness as part of a subjectivistic theory of mind.

In what follows, I shall first give a reconstruction of the argument, which leads—according to Ramsey—from some simple premises about the nature of philosophy to the conclusion, that "self-consciousness (is) inevitable in philosophy".[2] In a second step I want to show in greater detail, *why* you cannot understand theories and theoretical terms, in Ramsey's view, without the kind of self-consciousness just mentioned. In a third step I shall give an outline of Ramsey's theory of mind by drawing out some of the consequences of Ramsey's view on theories and theoretical terms with respect to an adequate theory of mind including self-consciousness. In a last step I return to the main conclusion Ramsey draws from his theory of mind, namely, I quote: " we cannot make our philosophy into an ordered progress to a goal, but have to take our problems as a whole and jump to a simultaneous solution".[3] (The problems in the interpretation of quantum mechanics are an outstanding example for this anti-fundamentalistic conclusion.)

I. The reconstruction of the argument, why self-consciousness is inevitable in Philosophy

Clearly, the argument depends primarily on what we understand by "philosophy". According to Ramsey it is the main and only task of philosophy to provide definitions of terms and sentences we use in science (as well as in every day life). This is so, simply because philosophy has as its main question "What do we mean by x?" A question, the answer to which is best given in the form of a definition of x (suppose, that x is a term). Therefore we can state as the first premise of the argument:

(1) "A philosophy is a system of definitions"[4]
You have to take this, admittedly, rather strange thesis quite seriously and literally, that is, you have to take it that

(i) philosophy is a system of definitions just as logic is a system of tautologies or mathematics is a system of identities.[5]

(ii) different philosophies differ from one another in providing different systems of definitions as different "logics" differ from one another in providing different systems of "tautologies".

Naturally, the next question that comes to mind in regard to such a definitive programme, is: "What do we mean by definitions?" (and hence by philosophy). Yet, in trying to answer this question we encounter a serious difficulty; a difficulty which involves the danger of a per-

219

petual "petitio principii" or something like that: We cannot answer this question simply by giving a definition of "definition". First we have to think about what definitions essentially are, and then to spell out the answer. If you think about the question "What definitions essentially are", you will sooner or later come to see that not all terms of a genuine language[6] can be defined, at least not in the obvious manner of giving a *nominal* definition by performing a speech act of the kind "x means such and such".[7] The very idea of a definition prohibits that every term of a language should be definable, because in the definiens you need terms, that already have a meaning, either by definition, in which case the argument can be repeated, or without any kind of nominal definition. Hence, in every genuine language there must be undefined terms or primitives, the meanings of which have to be explicated in a non-definitional way, or else you will go around in a circle. Let us call such non-definitional explications of the meaning of undefined terms for short "explanations"; then we can state the second premise of Ramsey's argument as follows:

(2) Philosophy, as a system of definitions, contains, besides nominal definitions, undefined terms, the meanings of which can only be *explained* but not explicitly defined.

Thus having saved philosophy from a flagrant circularity by admitting undefined terms in the systems of definitions we go further and ask: 'How do we explain—and grasp thereby—the meaning of undefined terms?' But at this point, philosophers often make an unnoticed presupposition, namely, that there is only *one type* of undefined terms in every system of definitions and hence only need for one type of explanation. This presupposition however is not always correct, or, according to Ramsey, it is plainly false, because there are at least two quite different types of undefined terms in every genuine language (and hence in philosophy):

(i)   terms, the meaning of which we are already acquainted with, like terms for sense impressions or common sense objects; these terms stand in no real need of explanation, because we could easily point to their visible instances.

(ii)   terms like "mass" and "energy", that look as if they should be defined in primitive terms—but of which a rigorous meaning analysis can show that it is not only unnecessary but quite *useless* to define them. These terms stand in serious need of explanation and cannot be defined nominally, because their definitions would be cumbersome and completely impractical. This type of expressions is what Ramsey calls "*variable hypotheticals*" and "*theoretical terms*".

Ramsey's philosophy mainly differs from others like that of Carnap and Russell in acknowledging that there are (at least) two types of undefined terms: primitives and theoretical terms (of which only the second stand in real need of explanation). Therefore we can state as the third premise of Ramsey's argument:

(3) Philosophy as a system of definitions, contains besides primitives so-called "theoretical terms" which have to be explained and should not be nominally defined.

It is clear that first this third premise contains the clue to the argument, because the conclusion that self-consciousness is inevitable in philosophy, only follows if we ask, how we explain (or grasp) the meaning of theoretical terms and variable hypotheticals.

Ramsey's answer to that question implicitly involves the conclusion that self-consciousness is inevitable in philosophy, because—I quote—"in this explanation we are forced to look not only at the objects, which we are talking about, but at our own mental states".[8] To understand Ramsey's answer correctly, we have to find the reason why in the explanation of theoretical terms and variable hypotheticals "we cannot neglect the epistemic or subjective side".[8] In order to do this, we have to study the relation between Ramsey's view on theories and the kind of self-consciousness he demands.

220

II. The relation between Ramsey's view on theories and the demand for self-consciousness in philosophy

Ramsey's answer to the question 'How do we explain the meaning of theoretical terms and variable hypotheticals?' can be split into two parts: a more negative one already contained in thesis (3) and a positive one which gives the essence of Ramsey's later philosophy.

(i)   The negative answer is best understood, if you realize that general propositions are *no propositions at all* but something like causal laws.

The reason for this is simply that general propositions do not only state facts, that is something which is definitely true or false, but also express general hypotheses about future situations, which are not properly true or false, but only more or less believable inference licenses for possible situations. To be precise, this means that general propositions cannot in principle be defined as finite or infinite conjunctions of propositions proper, but have to be explained as variable hypotheticals. What that means I will explore in the next part, for the moment I only want to stress that the negative answer implies that general propositions are not truth functions of atomic propositions—and nothing like that either, as in Tarski's definition of truth. The solution which Ramsey proposes for the problem of understanding general propositions is much more radical than Tarski's.

Passing over to the positive part of the answer I have to mention that theories, on Ramsey's view, are nothing but a special kind of rather complex variable hypotheticals, namely hypotheticals in which we introduce, for the sake of simplicitly and clearness, fictitious entities like "mass" and "force", that will be designated by the theoretical terms of the theory. That these should not be defined but have to be explained means that we can and should give only an *indefinite description* of the meaning of theoretical terms in terms of sense impressions. To give such indefinite descriptions of theoretical terms is, according to Ramsey, logically equivalent to making an *existential claim* of the form: Theoretical entities of such and such a kind exist—but not uniquely! In other words, Ramsey's philosophy is, in contrast to that of Russell and Carnap, a kind of anti-reductionist philosophy, insofar as Ramsey suggests that theoretical terms have their own *irreducible* meaning, which cannot be expressed uniquely and completely in terms of sense impressions, but have a fictitious character. Every attempt to define that fictitious character in terms of sense impressions like Carnap's and Russell's, makes the introduction of theoretical ꞁerms quite pointless![9] Out of what material—if not sense impressions—this fictitious character is built, and how we grasp this irreducible part of the meaning of theoretical terms and variable hypotheticals by reflection on our own mental states, is the concern of the next point.

(ii)   Again, the positive answer is best understood, if you consider why the genuine meaning of general propositions like 'All men are mortal' cannot be reduced to a finite or infinite conjunction of atomic propositions, but has to be explained by the way in which we *use* these general propositions or sentences respectively.

The reason is simply that their meaning is mainly *potential* (in contrast to actual) and hence cannot be expanded into facts or propositions about facts, but has to be elucidated in a completely unconventional manner, in which a kind of reflection on our own mental states plays an essential role. Take the above example and ask in what its meaning consists. One point is pretty clear: Its meaning is not exhausted by 'Socrates is mortal and Plato is mortal and Aristotle is mortal, and so on and so on' and by no conjunction of death reports, however long it may be, but only if we take into account all potential cases of men and says: 'If x is a man, then x is mortal', that means, he will die. But this is no proposition at all about facts, no statement true or false, but the expression of a conviction, namely the belief that all men will die, whoever they may be. This is in fact how we use this general proposition in every day life

221

as well as in science: We use it not to make a statement about facts — and also not about 'general' facts, whatever that may be — but to express our belief that whatever a man will do for his immortality, as a man, he will die.

The difference between statement and belief is important here, because a belief, and especially a general belief, is not in the same way true or false as a statement about facts is true or false. In the latter case the correspondence theory of truth seems adequate, in the former surely not, because a belief about potential situations cannot be compared with facts, at least not in the case of general beliefs such as 'All men are mortal'. In this case the question is not so much one of truth and falsehood (as in the case of statements) but of *credibility*: Shall we trust in the belief of another speaker? Is his general proposition a good 'variable hypothesis' for managing the future or not? Time will show, and if not, we will have to find a better one. This is the pragmatic notion of truth as "what everyone will believe in the end", and it is clearly a coherence — and not a correspondence notion of truth. This is not the time to go deeper into this matter, but let me mention two points before I return to the main question, why self-consciousness is inevitable in philosophy.

(α) The semantical analysis which Ramsey undertakes in regard to general propositions, presents them as a kind of 'cognitive attitude' in regard to the future, namely as inference licenses from the past to the future in which we believe. The generality of the inference is indicated as the variability of the range, and the epistemic status of belief is represented by the hypothetical form of the inference.

(β) The semantic distinction Ramsey makes between ordinary and general propositions is, logically speaking, rather different from the analogous distinction between propositional and predicate logic. While in the latter case the semantics of general propositions is constructed in parallel to that of singular propositions, Ramsey considers general propositions as instances of 'cognitive attitudes' in regard to propositions. This means that they require their own logic and semantics, just as epistemic or modal propositions require their own logic and semantics! In this respect Ramsey agrees with the intuitionists, especially with H. Weyl, who also sees the main gulf in logic between propositional logic on the one side and general as well as existential propositions on the other, the transcendental side of knowledge.[10]

Coming back to our main question, I hope it is evident by now, why self-consciousness is inevitable in philosophy at least in the case of general propositions: If our belief in regard to potential, and especially to future situations is not only part but the very essence of the meaning of general propositions, then "we are forced to look not only at the objects which are talking about, but at our own mental states".[8] We are forced to look at our own mental states, that is, our beliefs, wishes, and desires, for short, all our mental habits because they lie at the bottom of the meaning of general propositions, which as variable hypotheticals go far beyond what we actually know. This reflection on our beliefs is inevitable, if we want to *know* what we mean by a general proposition, insofar as no actual states of affairs can tell us that, but only potential ones; and these exist only in our mind and nowhere else. Sure, we could object that the potential situations are similar or analogous to the actual ones, but this is only to rename the problem of belief, because we, by our beliefs, have built the potential situations similar to the actual ones. Hence, the habit of belief is the material out of which we form the meaning of general propositions. Every philosophy, dealing with the meaning analysis of general propositions, has therefore to reflect upon these beliefs. That we can should do this is itself a hypothesis, called "self-consciousness", that is yet not fully understood.

What has been shown for general propositions could equally well be shown for theories as instances of variable hypotheticals with "theoretical terms". Interesting as this would be, I have to pass over this here, because of Ramsey's highly technical representation of "Theories". Let me only mention that Ramsey regards a theory of mind as a theory in his sense, that is, as a variable hypothetical about our own as well as other minds with certain theoretical terms like "self-consciousness". This brings me to my third topic.

III. Ramsey's theory of mind involving "self-consciousness".

In order to explain Ramsey's theory of mind I have to go back to a possible objection against Ramsey's view that self-consciousness is inevitable in philosophy. The objection runs roughly as follows:

The explanation of the meaning of general propositions by reference to our own mental states is *circular* insofar as it tries to explain the meaning of general propositions by the notion of variable hypotheticals, that is, roughly, by our belief in causal laws, which themselves stand in serious need of explanation. Instead, we should do our philosophical analysis — so the objection runs — in a given frame of logic and try to explain causal laws by general propositions, thinking all the time of the facts without reflecting on our own mental states.

That is, by the way, what is usually done up to this day. We try to explain causal laws by the logic of general propositions, thinking all the time about facts and the inductive generalizations without taking into account our beliefs in potential situations as the source of inductive reasoning. That is to say, we take it for granted that there is inductive generalization, which leads entirely without self-consciousness from facts to general propositions and in this way to causal laws.

Yet, according to Ramsey — and, I admit, also in my own view — this leads to an *impasse*, because, as we now all know, in this way we cannot understand causal laws and their intended meaning. What we have to do instead is, roughly speaking, the following: We have to become clear about how we think in the realm of *deductive* reasoning about the future, namely by stating variable hypotheticals and theories in general. Now according to Ramsey, this has two quite different yet intimately connected aspects: (i) On the one hand he contends that "over and above the regularity of succession the world, or rather that part of it with which we are acquainted, exhibits no feature called causal necessity". (ii) Yet, on the other hand "we make sentences, called causal laws, from which we proceed to actions and propositions connected with them". Insofar as these two aspects exhaust the matter, they entail a consequence which is highly relevant to every theory of mind, because the second aspect is, in Ramsey's view, nothing but "a regular feature of our conduct, a part of the general regularity of things; as always there is nothing beyond the regularity to be called causality, but we can again make a variable hypothetical about this conduct of ours".[11]

To my understanding this means at least two or three things:

(α) The objective meaning of every causal law is nothing but the regularity of successions of events in the world.

(β) This does not prevent that we — as a part of the world — make variable hypotheticals, i.e. causal laws, which go far beyond the actual world we know by projecting potential situations and fictitous entities. This conduct of ours is in fact itself a part of the regularity of the world.

(γ) Therefore, we can again make variable hypotheticals about this feature of our mind and call them "theories of mind". But we have to be aware that these theories of mind are themselves nothing but variable hypotheticals about a supposed regularity of our mind.

The last point is the crucial one, because it implies that every theory of mind has to contain a certain minimum of self-consciousness: It must reflect that it is itself only a theory — a theory about our mind — that contains an irreducibly hypothetical element.[12]

This brings me back to the thesis, quotet in the beginning, that "we cannot make our philosophy into an ordered progress to a goal, but have to take our problems as a whole and jump to a simultaneous solution".[3] The demand of hypothetical-deductive thinking instead of inductive reasoning has itself "something of the nature of a hypothesis";[13] it implies that we have to take into account self-consciousness as an essential part of the meaning analysis of theoretical terms and variable hypotheticals — and hence of a theory of mind. But of course, no one can prove this in the logical sense of proof. – Sure, you could try to explain the meaning of theoretical terms without self-consciousness, yet we believe in hypothetical-deductive thinking. This has to be shown useful – more useful than any other hypothesis – in the discourse of practical reasoning.

ENDNOTES

1 Ramsey, F. P., "Last Papers" in F. P. Ramsey, *The Foundations of Mathematics*, edited by R. B. Braithwaite in the International Library of Psychology, Philosophy and Scientific Method (London 1931) Quotations according to the fourth impression 1965. For reasons unknown to me, the paper discussed here has been omitted in the revised edition, published 1978 under the title "Foundations".
2 Ramsey (1965), S. 268.
3 Ramsey (1965), S. 268.
4 Ramsey (1965), S. 263.
5 "Logic issues in tautologies, mathematics in identities, philosophy in definitions, all trivial but all part of the vital work of clarifying and organizing our thought." Ramsey, S. 264.
6 A "genuine language" is a language the terms and sentences of which have to be understood without the help of another language, especially a meta-language, which is already understood; for example, the first language a child learns, is a genuine language; but there are other cases at hand, like the introduction of a completely new scientific theory e.g. quantum mechanics, the language of which has to be grasped without the help of a previously understood meta-language.
7 A definition is, in my view, what Austin calls a "speech-act": pointing out to the reader in which way the defined term is to be understood in the future. The futuristic aspect of definitions is pointed out by Ramsey too without the "speech-act" terminology; see Ramsey (1965), S. 263.
8 Ramsey (1965), S. 267ff.
9 In his famous paper "The Relation of Sense-Data to Physics" Russell tried to do precisely this: explicating "physical objects in terms of sense-data"; see his *Mysticism and Logic* (London [10]1951), S. 147.
10 I guess that Ramsey was inspired by the writings of H. Weyl, whom he criticized in *The Foundations of Mathematics* (1925) and *Mathematical Logic* (1926) defending Russell's logicism. Later, however, he became convinced by H. Weyl that a general proposition is not a judgement, but "a sort of cheque which can be cashed for a real judgement when an instance of it occurs"; Ramsey, S. 70.
11 Ramsey, S. 252; the last three quotations are taken from part B of the "Last Papers", entitled "General Propositions and Causality".
12 There are several theories of mind, criticized by Ramsey, that fall short in this respect, e.g. Carnap's theory of mind in *Der logische Aufbau der Welt* as well as all materialistic theories of mind. The mistake is always the same: They start from facts, we know about our own mind, making "theories" about other minds in terms of protons, neurons etc. and then turn back on our own mind and claim "that what are *really* happening there are simply these theoretical processes" forgetting the hypothetical character of the theory; see Ramsey, S. 266.
13 Ramsey (1965), S. 268.

* * *

LEIBNIZ' REPRÄSENTATIONSFORM EINES ADÄQUATEN BEGRIFFES VON ‚GEIST' IM VERHÄLTNIS ZU DESCARTES UND KANT.

Michael Benedikt
Universität Wien

‚Repräsentation' heißt seit Leibniz immer ein Zweifaches: einmal die entweder kohärente oder sogar korrespondierende Vorstellung eines mannigfaltig Gegebenen in einem Modell oder Konstrukt – seither auch Darstellung oder Abbildung genannt –, anderseits jedoch die Rolle, welche ein Vorstellendes – für Leibniz auch andere Lebewesen – in dieser Ausübung bzw. auch in anderen trivialen Tätigkeiten in einem öffentlichen Verband im Verfolgen von darstellbaren Regeln zu spielen vermag. Die *Vereinbarung* dieser beiden Bedeutungen verlangt aber einen adäquaten, nicht bloß klaren oder distinkten logischen Diskurs, in welchem die Bedeutung von ‚Geist' einen gewissen, also zumindest klaren und distinkten Stellenwert hat. Meine Untersuchung ist zunächst ideengeschichtlich, hat aber auch mit einigen gegenwärtigen Problemen zu tun.

I. Gilbert Ryles Mißverständnis gegenüber Descartes' ‚Mythos'.

Zusammen mit dem späten Wittgenstein und dem frühen Heidegger distanziert Gilbert Ryle in *The Concept of Mind* (dt. *Der Begriff des Geistes,* Stuttgart 1969) eher die rationalistisch *enge* Konzeption als die beiden *weiteren* Auffassungen des Begriffes von Geist bei Descartes: Ich meine die auf den Geistbegriff des Subjektes hingeordnete Ontologie der beiden Substanzen, die des sum cogitans und der res extensa. ‚Geist' oder ‚Seele', in der Ambivalenz von ‚mens' als Modalbegriff des ‚sum cogitans', ist für Heidegger ein *wohlfundierter* Modus des zunächst pragmatisch orientierten und ausgelegten ‚In-der-Welt-Seins', für den späten Wittgenstein hingegen eine paralogistische und paradoxe Reflexionsform bzw. eine ausweglose, therapeutisch unfruchtbare Beendigung eines philosophischen Diskurses.

Die in der Diskurstheorie, besser Sprachspielkonzeption, des späten Wittgenstein distanzierte Form des cogito ergo sum erinnert aber an Kants Auffassung des beschränkten, also noch nicht ästhetisch gefaßten ‚Geistes', somit der Repräsentationsform der Verdoppelung von theoretischer Referenz, also im Sinne der Thematisierung dessen, was wir tun, wenn wir die Welt unserer Erfahrung als Objekt der Wissenschaft oder bloß als etwa in Rechtstiteln beschreibbaren Strukturkomplex vornehmen einerseits und der Strategie der Begründung dieser Referenz anderseits.

Die früheste cartesische Aufgabe, wie wir in einer einzigen analytischen Methode überhaupt erst zu dieser Referenz gelangen, was dann auch sowohl Referenz als auch Begründung bzw. Legitimation umfassen soll, ist für Descartes immer ein normatives Postulat gewesen, aber nie zur Durchführung gelangt. Für unseren Zweck der Rezeption des ‚Geistes' in der Repräsentationsform von Leibniz mit Bezug auf Descartes unterscheiden wir aber drei Etappen in der Aneignung des Begriffes von Geist, wovon Ryle sich eben nur der letzten bedient.

1. Eine frühe Konzeption von den *Regulae ad directionem ingenii* bis zur Legitimation der wissenschaftlichen Methode im *Discours de la Méthode* ist ausgezeichnet durch eine nicht eingeholte Differenz zwischen Selbstreferenz und Gegenstandsbezug (res ipsa). Diese *Differenz* heißt ‚Geist' zunächst als ‚intellectus ipse' der Vereinbarung von ‚sagacitas' und ‚perspicuitas', sodann als regelgeleitete ‚bona mens' oder ‚ingenium' mit Bezug auf die konstruierte

oder vorausgesetzte ‚res ipsa', deren Programm in der achten bis zwölften Regula entworfen wird, allerdings ohne Auflösung jener Differenz.

2. Die im *Discours* vorbereitete, in den *Meditationen* zum Durchbruch gekommene Fixierung des Unterschiedes von Reflexion und Referenz unter der Bedingung einer Einordnung deskriptiver Wissenschaft und legitimierender Theologie in Anbetracht der neuen Sprachanalyse und Urteilslehre ist der prekäre Ausweg aus dem Unvollendeten, aus den *Regulae*, im Zeichen eines erweiterten Begriffes von ‚Geist' im Sinne von ‚spiritus' (als malignus oder als summum bonum).

3. Die petrifizierte Lehre der drei Substanzen, wie sie teils in den *Meditationen* und deren Apologie, vor allem aber in den *Prinzipien* bzw. der Repräsentation im Schreiben an Picot vorgetragen ist, stellt das Gerüst des rationalistischen Geistes in der üblichen Fassung des ‚intellectus ipse' dar.

Gilbert Ryle hält sich hauptsächlich an den Übergang von der zweiten zur dritten Konzeption, wenn er diese auch in seiner Auffassung des ‚Mythos von Descartes' (Kybernetes-Gleichnis) rückinterpretierend schon in den Übergang der ersten in die zweite Phase fallen läßt. Hierbei bedient er sich aber immer des reduzierten Idioms im Sinne der die Differenz begründenden Selbstreflexion einer Einheit von ‚sagacitas' und ‚perspicuitas'. Dagegen hat im *Discours* der Vorrang des ‚rem cogitare' (also nicht des ‚se cogitare') einen ganz anderen methodischen Charakter und eine andere ontologische Herkunft als die reduktive Formulierung des substantial oder dynamisch gefaßten Bewußtseinshabitus, welche vor allem Gegenstand der Ryle'schen Kritik der kategorialen Verwechslung darstellt. Während die Aufgabe der referentiell-objektiven Synthesis die frühen Ansätze in den *Regulae* überfordert und in der Folge das Unternehmen einer Begründung der Objektivität und Mathematisierung der Naturwissenschaften vermutlich aufgrund der impliziten Bacon-Kritik abgesetzt wird, ist die Strategie im Discours nach dreierlei Hinsichten abgesichert: Nach der ontotheologischen Lösung, derjenigen des technischen Experimentes von Modellen, was deren *Erklärungswert* und *Fruchtbarkeit* in der Voraussage betrifft; zuletzt nach der Repräsentationsfunktion sprachanalytischer Relevanz im propositionalen Urteil.

Ryle ignoriert diese Verfahrensweisen und zieht sich in einer mißverstandenen Wiederaufnahme zur Zusammenfassung des 5. Discours (Leib-Seele-Problem) auf die Kulmination von zwei Abstrakta zurück (Repräsentation in der vergeblichen Einheit des Selbstbewußtseins als Rolle instrumenteller Vernunft und als Präsentation der res ipsa), von denen Spinoza schon feststellt, daß sie nur dann einem Übergang von obskurer zu klarer, wenn auch nie adäquater Erkenntnis zugänglich seien, wenn man gerade die vermittelnde Substanz einklammert. Ryles Idee der Inexistenz des Geistes als Kybernetes eines Körperschiffes, ein altes Modell, das im 5. Discours wieder aufgenommen ist, unterschlägt aber zweierlei: Die technische Rekonstruktion unserer wissenschaftlichen Objektwelt findet für Descartes an der Menschenwelt ihre akkurate Grenze, wenn diese auch im Zuge der Verwissenschaftlichung modifiziert wird. Anderseits ist die Bewußtseinseinheit unserer Referenz auf die Körperwelt bzw. derjenigen auf uns selbst als auf unseren Leib auch keine Angelegenheit der Kategorialform des subjektiven Geistes als Kybernetes, sondern Sache des ‚geistigen vinculum' des ‚deus sive natura', eben auch schon bei Descartes. Deren bloß subjektive Reflexionseinbindung ohne Kenntnisnahme des Antecedens als ‚rem cogitare' und der Konsequenz als ‚se cogitare' sind paralogistisch für den gesunden Verstand, narzißtisch für den gesellschaftlich oder individuell verfaßten kranken Verstand, fatal für die Kritik der historischen Vernunft, im ganzen höchstens ein Anstoß zur Produktion für den Geist des künstlerischen Ingeniums.

Der andere wunde Punkt Ryles ist die Verkennung von Descartes' *pragmatischem Hintergrund* der Verwissenschaftlichung einer vorläufigen Moral: Die Legitimationsstrategie der Objektion unseres wissenschaftlichen Verfahrens ist nämlich eingebettet in die Verfahrensweise des pragmatischen Geistes und dessen technische Überlebensstrategie gemäß diskursiver Logizität. Erst ein zu Ende geführtes Experiment der Verwissenschaftlichung könnte mit Bezug auf die sukzessive Ablösung unserer pragmatischen Interessen zugunsten einer Gesellschaftsethik zu so etwas wie einem Erweis des ‚category mistake' führen, wenn wir zuvor die philosophische Methode außer acht lassen. Leider hatte sich Descartes den Primat des Praktischen durch den auch für modale und relationale Begriffsverbindungen gebrauchten Regelbegriff des Kontingenten als bloß ‚moralement possible‘ weitgehend verbaut.

Kant hat im Gegensatz zu Ryle versucht, dem Rechnung zu tragen, indem er anstelle des Gottesbegriffes, der beim mittleren Descartes die Einheit von Körper und Seele, die Referenz der Vorstellungen auf ihre Objekte, sogar die Einheit der Affinität von methodischen Teilschritten innerhalb von mathematischen Modellen der Wahrheitswertigkeit ein anderes Maß der wahren Propositionen zur Legitimation der Affinität vorschreibt, nämlich seine Logik der Synthesis apriori. Synthetische Sätze a priori ersetzen dann also, was bei Descartes den eigentlichen Vermittlungsbegriff des Geistes ausmacht, demgemäß die paralogistische Referenz der Seele auf sich selbst immer nur ein narzißtisches Beiwerk oder ein Umweg gewesen war, in den die faule Vernunft immer dann hineintappt, wenn sie die Bedingungen der Erkenntnis eines Sachverhaltes nicht mit Bezug auf ein primäres praktisches Erkenntnisinteresse anzugeben vermag.

Wie sich also die regelgeleitete Verbindung der Terme eines Urteils (im Sinne des Primats von Bejahung, Koordination und Optimierung) an der realisierbaren Einheit der Notionen aufweisen läßt, ohne wie Descartes, Spinoza oder Leibniz auf ein summum bonum zurückgreifen, vielmehr dies durch das regelgeleitete Handlungsinteresse zu supplieren, ist der Hintergrund von Ryles vordergründigem ‚Mythos des Geistes‘.

II. Leibniz' wiederholte Aneignung der res cogitans

Der bloß beiläufige, kontingente Übergang von ‚perspicuitas‘ zur ‚bona mens‘ des ‚ingenium‘, die neugierige ‚curiositas‘, hat Leibniz zunächst in Form der Gier des Aufsuchens von Nachlaßschriften Descartes' eingeholt. Dies schlägt selbst noch in seiner Auseinandersetzung mit der Äbtissin von Herford zu Buche.

In seinem Briefwechsel bzw. den Entwürfen der Korrespondenz mit Sophie-Charlotte von Preußen hat Leibniz prägnanter zwei Hauptthesen und ein verstecktes drittes Thema vorzutragen, und hier kommt er wieder auf Descartes zurück: Zunächst geht es in der Kontroverse mit Locke um die intersubjektive Erfaßbarkeit der primären Qualitäten und der Relationen der sekundären Phänomene sowohl gegenüber den ‚petites perceptions‘ des Unbewußten als auch gegenüber der Variabilität der Überschüsse unserer Reflexion mit Bezug auf unsere Sinneseindrücke: Hier wird dem vergleichenden und selegierenden Gemeinsinn zwischen Reproduktion und Antizipation die geistige Tätigkeit als primärer Ordnungsfaktor vorangestellt: das, was die Sinne, sie objektiv ordnend, übersteigt. Anderseits können wir die Komplexionen der Materie in der Variabilität ihrer Konstellation – unter gegebener Konstanz des Raumes und der Materie selbst, eine zweifelsohne prekäre Annahme – nur in der Differenz einer jeweils stufenweise vergeistigten Materie und selbst einer davon noch distanzierten und von der Materie losgelösten Substanz annehmen. *Diese Differenz zu setzen* ist nun Angelegenheit der res cogitans. Hier liegen Argumente vor, die über die monadische Verfaßtheit der Naturwelt bzw. der natürlichen Gesellschaften hinaus, wie sie Leibniz schon seit 1694 durch seinen Begriff der Monade vorstellig macht, eben in der Infragestellung der „natürlichen Gesellschaften" (von Ehe über Gemeinwesen, Großfamilien bis zur Kirche) mit Bezug auf nunmehr vordringliche Formen *künstlicher Gesellschaft* zur Geltung gebracht werden.

Wenn nun in seinen *Bemerkungen zu den cartesischen Prinzipien* (1692) ebenso wie in seiner Schrift *Gegen Descartes* vom Mai 1702 sowohl gegen den Atomismus, die abstrakte Geometrisierung des Raumes, die Unterschlagung der Dynamik gegenüber der Mechanik, das Überspringen des produktiven Möglichkeitsbegriffes bzw. der beiden Optimierungsgesetze Stellung bezogen wird, so greift darüber hinaus Leibniz sogar Descartes an der Wurzel seines paradoxen Zweifelverfahrens und seines Konzepts des sum cogitans an.

Gleichwohl ist in der Vereinbarung der ‚vis primitiva activa et passiva‘ als Grundlegung dynamischer Prozesse von Leibniz das Problem der kontingenten Propositionen eingeführt, deren unendliche und unabsehbare Auflösung (resolutio) nicht nur den Kontingenz-Begriff des ,moralement possible' des Descartes wieder aufleben läßt, sondern auch dessen pragmatisch-gesellschaftlichen Hintergrund wieder zur Geltung bringt.

Das ,moralement possible' ist als die Sphäre faktischer Möglichkeit, deren Verifikation immer nur nach bloßen Wahrscheinlichkeitskriterien im Kalkül des Ermessens vor sich geht, rezipiert: Seine Bestimmbarkeit und konkrete Bestimmung des Optimierens findet deshalb zunächst vor allem in hypothetischen Propositionen oder Handlungsanweisungen, die für einen durch sie eingrenzbaren Geltungsbereich auf Abruf funktionieren, statt. Diese sind aber auch, ohne Zweifel, der kontingente Hintergrund von Descartes' provisorischer Moral, wenn auch deren Prinzip in der vierten Maxime wieder auf eine Reflexionsnorm des ,sum cogitans, jetzt aber in verkürzter pragmatischer Form ohne das Antecedens des ,rem cogitare' zur Geltung gebracht ist. Sowie also Leibniz die Sphäre des Kontingenten in seine Titel des abgeleiteten ,principium grande' übernimmt, deren Exposition und Transformation ich hier voraussetzen muß, übernimmt er zugleich die pragmatische Reflexionsbasis der von Descartes mitbedachten Sphäre der Bedürfnisgesellschaft im Sinne des Reflexionsstatuts des Primats des ,se cogitare' vor der Affinität zum rem cogitare. Wenn also noch im Mai 1702 Leibniz gegen Descartes den Vorwurf erhebt, weder Ausdehnung noch Dauer begriffen zu haben (kontinuierliche und simultan gesetzte Wiederholung), noch auch die Sphäre des Kontinuums zu begreifen, die er selbst als reversible Manifestation eines Mannigfaltigen vorstellig macht und strukturell zwischen tätiger und passiver Kraft einbindet, so versucht er auch hier noch dem Argument Spinozas gegenüber Descartes (Einklammerung der Substanz selbst) gerecht zu werden.

Umso seltsamer nimmt sich aber einige Monate später Leibnizens Wiederaufnahme des Kerngedankens des autarken Intellektes im Übergang von der referentiellen Descriptionsform zur pragmatischen Form der Selbstmanifestation aus, ebenso wie die neuerdings erhobene Idee einer Konzeption des im Raum zusammengesetzten Kontingenten, was weder phänomenal konstruierbar noch auch harmonikal in der Dominanz einer Monade über andere und deren Übereinstimmung mit je anderen dominierenden Monaden antizipierbar ist.

Es gibt zwei Gründe für Leibnizens Rückgriff auf den hybriden autarken Intellekt Descartes': Einerseits sieht er das Problem komplexer materieller Zustände, auch mit Bezug auf organisierte Automaten, über die phänomenale Konstruktion hinaus dringlich werden. Im Zusammenspiel von vis activa und passiva ist Descartes' Strukturmodell eines Gleichgewichts von Mustern nicht auszuschließen; zugleich zeigt jedoch die Abhebung vom Konzept der Monade und dem der phänomenalen Konstruktion die Verselbständigung einer Relationssphäre an, in der die verschiedenen Elemente oder Entitäten bzw. Komplexionsmuster der Erscheinungsmannigfaltigkeit eine jeweils variable Rolle spielen können. Genau dies ist aber sowohl im Sprachkonzept des 5. Discours von Descartes ebenso wie in seiner Idee der provisorischen Moral oder aber im Konzept einer künstlichen Bedürfnisgesellschaft auf dem Boden jener Moral vorgedacht. Wenn also Leibniz ab Juni 1702 den mittleren Descartes zwischen seiner Referenztheorie der *Regulae* und dem ,Totalexperiment' rezipiert, rezipiert er über die Transformation des pragmatischen Momentes an der *Exigenz*, also der erzwungenen Affinität von Bedeutung und Erfüllung des ,sum cogitans', auch die Rückseite einer vorläufigen Moral der Bedürfnisgesellschaft, ebenso wie die Synthesis von vis primitiva activa und passiva eine Komplexion mehrerer Verfahrensschritte der Verselbständigung von Relationsstrukturen vorstellig macht.

III. Die späte esoterische Lösung von Leibniz

Wenn auch das monadische System des Verhältnisses von realer Möglichkeit, der Kompossibilität atomarer Tatsachen bezüglich deren Optimierung auf der Grundlage einer Disjunktion phänomenaler Konstruktion und noumenaler Ontologie schon ab 1696 konzipiert ist, tritt es erst stärker in den ontologisch-naturphilosophischen bzw. gesellschaftstheoretischen Entwürfen im Anschluß an die Theodizee als jetzt dominante und reife exoterische Konzeption hervor.

Parallel zu diesen Untersuchungen der universellen Harmonie der Individuation und der auch gesellschaftstheoretisch bedeutsamen Kompossibilität von Individuen (im Sinne der Gruppierung natürlicher Gesellschaften) wird jedoch schon ab 1706 das Programm einer *esoterischen* Fragestellung fruchtbar. Es ist zunächst gekennzeichnet durch den Leitgedanken der ‚dominierenden Monade' in komplexen Organisationen, führt von da zu den Kompossibilitätsmustern einer nach Wahrheitskriterien strukturell gefaßten Objektivität (res substantiata) und leitet zu den Erörterungen der Verbundformen künstlicher Gesellschaften über: Wenn es kein Mittleres zwischen phänomenaler Welt und Monadenwelt gäbe, so lautet die Primärthese, so gäbe es nur Modellkonstrukte hier und Verinnerlichungsstrategien des Geistes zugleich mit einer theologisch bedingten Harmoniekonzeption da, aber keine öffentliche gemeinsame Welt. Ausdrücklich wird dies in mehrerlei Hinsichten exponiert, wenn wir einmal die theologische Perspektive außer acht lassen, wie dies auch die jüngeren Studien hierzu von Blondel, Mathieu, Serres zeigen.

1. Die kontingenten Elemente einer Strukturkomplexion erhalten ihre Prägung nur durch die logische Synthesis der Struktur selbst − Leibniz nennt sie ‚vinculum substantiale' − nicht durch die interne Verfaßtheit bzw. durch die abstrakte Interpretation mittels eines modellhaften Charakters.

2. ‚Vinculum substantiale' als Gleichgewichtsbedingung eines komplexen Systems erlaubt die Austauschbarkeit von akzidentellen Relationsmustern.

3. ‚Vinculum substantiale' ist der bloßen Kausalreihe eines Determinismus ebenso übergeordnet, wie es eine Synthesis der bloßen Implikation gemäß dem Statut notwendiger Wahrheit kontingent modifiziert.

4. Die resultierende Komplexion ist keine geschlossene, sondern eine offene Relationspyramide, deren Entitäten hierdurch nicht mehr isolierte feststehende Monaden sind, sondern als eine im Kontinuum der Vernetzung stehende Ensemble-Mannigfaltigkeit in einer Entfaltungsstrategie dargestellt werden müssen.

5. Durch die Einführung der pragmatischen Dimension des ‚sum cogitans' in die Entfaltung der Monaden ebenso wie durch die Feststellung der Abhängigkeit des ‚ergo sum' vom ‚rem cogitare' (und nicht umgekehrt wie in der bloß biologistisch vorgestellten Explikation etwa eines Genoms) wird die kontingente Relevanz des ‚moralement possible' aus der prohibitiven Verfaßtheit natürlicher Gesellschaft in eine permissive Funktionsform ‚künstlicher' Sozialisation transformiert.

In dem 10 Jahre währenden Briefwechsel mit Des Bosses hat Leibniz diese Sphäre der Synthesis der künstlichen Gesellschaft auf dem Boden der Transformation des Hintergrundes des sum cogitans, also der provisorischen Moral, immer wieder vorstellig gemacht; die Auflösung ist allerdings zunächst eher in theologischer als in soziologischer oder ökonomischer Relevanz präsentiert. Leibniz hat damit über die Transformation des Hintergrundes des rem cogitare hinaus, also durch die pragmatische Moral des ‚moralement possible', der bloß optimierbaren Beliebigkeit, einer Regel Folge zu leisten, einen Übergang von der Naturwelt in die Menschenwelt vorgestellt.

IV. Abschluß und Vorblick

Zusammenfassend möchte ich erinnern, daß Ryles sprachanalytische und behavioristische Konzeption die logische Struktur des Primats des ‚rem cogitare' vor dem ‚se cogitare' ebenso vernachlässigt, wie deren Abwandlung von drei Hauptphasen, die er ebenso wie deren Übernahme durch Leibniz unterschätzt, besonders was die Transformation des pragmatischen Hintergrundes aus der natürlichen Gesellschaft in die künstliche der Menschenwelt betrifft.

In diesem Zusammenhang ist zu erinnern, daß der eigentliche Geistbegriff gerade auch schon seit Platos *Timaios*, wenn auch nicht in der Selbstreflexion der pragmatisch oder ideologisch isolierten ‚membra disjecta‘, so doch in der optimierbaren Synthesis der kompossiblen Elemente liegt. Dies besagt auch das vinculum substantiale superadditum, wenn dies auch als Geistbegriff, im Gegensatz zur ontotheologisch verfaßten Natur Platos, jetzt im Sinne eines Primates pragmatischer Reflexion vorgestellt wird, zugleich aber auch als Basis einer realistischen Referenztheorie fungiert, welche als Entlastung im Übergang von natürlicher zu künstlicher Gesellschaft und deren Gerechtigkeitsstruktur fällig wird. Ohne Zweifel hat Leibniz dieser arkanen Theorie zwischen 1706 und 1716 noch keine ausdrückliche Logik verschafft, wenn auch eine Reihe von ontologischen Entwürfen hierzu vorliegen. Diese Untersuchung hat Kant in seinem System der Synthesis a priori einzuführen getrachtet, welches die Vereinbarkeit von Handlungsteleologie der Intention von Motiven mit den Resultaten von Handlungen einerseits als auch andererseits deren Horizont einer Lebenswelt mit Blick auf die Bestimmung eben von kontingenten Sachverhalten unter Bedingung eines metatheoretischen Strukturmusters im Sinne der Gültigkeit einer wissenschaftlich akzeptierbaren Objektivität plausibel macht. Auf dem Boden der von ihm seit 1772 übernommenen Synthesis, im Primat der Relationen auch der sekundären Qualitäten, sind aber die Titel der vier Grundsätze aus der Dominanz des zureichenden Grundes im Sinne der Transformation von Regeln der Subsumtion, Bejahung, Koordination und Optimierung in den Primat der Analyse der Erfahrung auf dem Boden eines Zeitschematismus (zwischen gerichteter Zeit und der Zeitform reversibler Prozesse) transformiert. Ob jedoch jenes ‚vinculum substantiale‘ in der kritischen Transformation auch für die Modellbildung der ‚besonderen Analogien der Erfahrung‘ gemäß einem Primat der Raumschematik (und der Einbindung gerichteter Zeit gemäß entropischer Dissipation) im Sinne des ‚Fortschrittes der Physik‘ zureichend ist, dies ist eine andere Frage, welche ich hier ebenso wenig diskutieren will wie die Relativierung instrumentell ausgestatteter pragmatischer Vernunft durch eine ethisch verbindliche Synthesis weiter Pflichten, welche auf die Folgen der Handlung je Anderer geht. Hier erst würde jener von Descartes durch Leibniz vorgeschlagene Übergang von Natur- in Menschenwelt in letzterer einheimisch.

* * *

ZUR STRUKTUR PSYCHOLOGISCHER THEORIEN

Christfried Tögel
Bulgarische Akademie der Wissenschaften, Sofia

Das von Sneed und Stegmüller ausgearbeitete strukturalistische Theorienkonzept[1] ist bisher − von wenigen Ausnahmen abgesehen[2] − vorwiegend auf physikalische Theorien angewendet worden. Bei seiner Übertragung auf psychologische Theorien ergeben sich eine Reihe von Schwierigkeiten. So läßt sich z.B. für die wenigsten der Kern der Theorie als mathematische Struktur beschreiben.

Trotzdem sollen hier einige Erkenntnisgewinn versprechende Gesichtspunkte der strukturalistischen Betrachtungsweise psychologischer Theorien diskutiert werden.

Zu diesem Zweck seien die wichtigsten Schlußfolgerungen des Konzepts von Sneed/Stegmüller kurz resümiert. Eine der zentralen Behauptungen ist, daß Theorien gegenüber Falsifikationsversuchen immun sind, und zwar aus 3 Gründen: 1. weil die empirische Widerlegung einer Hypothese nicht mehr besagt, als daß die entsprechende Spezialisierung des Theoriekerns untauglich ist. Daraus folgt jedoch nicht, daß im Prinzip keine erfolgreichen Kernspezialisierungen möglich sind; 2. weil der Anwendungsbereich einer Theorie eine offene Menge ist, d.h. er kann abgesehen von den paradigmatischen Beispielen beliebig eingeengt werden; und 3. weil der Strukturkern einer Theorie in bezug auf eben diese Theorie relativierte theoretische Größen enthält, die eine empirische Falsifikation unmöglich machen.

Das scheinbar Irrationale dieser Behauptungen verschwindet, wenn man von der Identifikation einer Theorie mit ihren empirischen Hypothesen zu deren strenger Unterscheidung übergeht. Damit hören Theorien auf, Mengen von Aussagen zu sein, und verwandeln sich in ein − um mit Thomas Kuhn zu sprechen − „begriffliches Instrument", mit dessen Hilfe sich empirische Hypothesen formulieren lassen. So wird auch intuitiv klar, daß eine Widerlegung von Hypothesen nicht auf die Theorie selbst durchschlägt.

Ein zweiter, eng mit dem Problem der Immunität von Theorien verbundener, neuer Ansatz innerhalb des strukturalistischen Konzepts bezieht sich auf theoretische Terme. Sneed hat ein Theoretizitätskriterium eingeführt, daß auf die jeweilige Theorie relativiert ist. Eine Größe B der Theorie T ist danach T-theoretisch, wenn sie nur unter der Voraussetzung bestimmt werden kann, daß bereits eine gültige Anwendung der Theorie existiert.[3] Dieses Theoretizitätskriterium beruht nicht auf der Dichotomie theoretisch-beobachtbar, sondern auf der *Unterscheidung* der Dichotomien theoretisch-nichttheoretisch und beobachtbar-nichtbeobachtbar.

Das strukturalistische Theorienkonzept liefert noch weitere überraschende Gesichtspunkte; ich will mich jedoch auf die Immunität von Theorien, bzw. die strenge Unterscheidung von Theorien und ihren empirischen Hypothesen beschränken und zu zeigen versuchen, daß vom Standpunkt dieser Auffassung einige Probleme der Psychologie bzw. Psychologiegeschichte eine ganz natürliche Lösung finden.

Ein erstes Beispiel entnehme ich der Lerntheorie. Hier liegen am ehesten Ansätze vor, die formal gesehen mit ausgereiften physikalischen Theorien vergleichbar sind. Man denke nur an die Modelle von Estes, Bush/Mosteller und Luce. Ein Hauptproblem der Lernpsychologie besteht in der Frage, inwieweit experimentell gefundene und theoretisch abgeleitete Lernverläufe deckungsgleich sind. Für das Lernmodell von Estes versuchte man die Deckungsgleichheit durch Einführung proportionsspezifischer Reizbindungen herzustellen. Diese Methode gibt jedoch keinen Aufschluß darüber, *welche* Reizanteile wirksam sind, da die Anpassung des eingeführten Proportionalitätsfaktors durch keine empirische Aussage legitimiert werden kann.[4] Dieses Problem verschwindet nun, wenn man von der traditionellen Theorienauffassung zum strukturalistischen Theorienkonzept übergeht. Dann wird der Reiz nämlich eine theoretische Größe in bezug auf die Estes'sche Theorie und eine empirische Hypothese besteht in der Behauptung, daß die Theorie auf einen bestimmten Lernverlauf angewendet werden kann. Erweist sich eine solche Hypothese als falsch, muß entweder der Lernverlauf aus dem Anwendungsbereich ausgeschlossen werden oder die entsprechende Spezialisierung des Estes'schen Modells verworfen werden. In jedem Falle jedoch ist die Nichtdeckungs-gleichheit experimentell gefundener und theoretischer abgeleiteter Lernverläufe kein Problem der Theorie selbst.

Als zweites Beispiel für eine Neuinterpretation psychologischer Theorien vom Standpunkt des strukturalistischen Theorienkonzepts möchte ich die Psychoanalyse wählen. Es ist bekannt, daß Freud 3 Bedeutungen von Psychoanalyse unterschieden hat; nämlich 1. Psycho-analyse als Verfahren zur Untersuchung vorwiegend unbewußter seelischer Vorgänge, 2. Psycho-analyse als Behandlungsmethode neurotischer Störungen und 3. Psychoanalyse als System psychologischer und psychopathologischer Theorien.[5] Uns interessiert hier selbstverständlich nur der dritte Aspekt.

Seit fast 70 Jahren werden immer wieder Experimente gemacht, deren erklärtes Ziel die empirische Bestätigung bzw. Widerlegung der psychoanalytischen Theorie ist.[6] Eine Vielzahl dieser Versuche ist negativ ausgegangen, d.h. viele psychoanalytischen Theorien werden als empirisch widerlegt angesehen. Wieso, so muß man sich fragen, hat diese Entwicklung nicht zu einem Niedergang der Psychoanalyse oder doch wenigstens zu einer Abnahme ihrer Anzie-hungskraft geführt. Sicher liegt ein Grund in der meisterhaften Darstellung des Gegenstandes durch Freud selbst. Allerdings ist es eher seine schriftstellerische Begabung als die innere Fol-gerichtigkeit der Dinge, die dem Leser eine eiserne Logik suggeriert. Doch Freuds Stil kann nicht alles erklären. Meines Erachtens liefert das strukturalistische Theorienkonzept eine Erklärung des scheinbar widersinnigen Verhaltens vieler Anhänger der Psychoanalyse. Nimmt man nämlich mit Sneed und Stegmüller an, daß nicht Theorien, sondern nur deren empirische Hypothesen getestet werden können, so liegt in dem Festhalten an psychoanalyti-schen Theorien trotz Widerlegung psychoanalytischer Hypothesen nichts Irrationales mehr.

Ich möchte diesen Gedanken anhand Freuds Persönlichkeitstheorie, wie sie in seiner Schrift „Das Ich und das Es" aus dem Jahre 1923[7] niedergelegt ist, erläutern. Kern dieser Theorie ist die Idee vom strukturellen Aufbau der Persönlichkeit, bestehend aus Es, Ich und Über-Ich. Als paradigmatisches Beispiel dieser seiner Schichtenlehre betrachtete Freud die Neurosenätiologie.[8] Danach erkrankt der Mensch an dem Konflikt zwischen den Ansprüchen des Trieblebens und den Widerständen und Verboten die das Ich bzw. das Über-Ich ihnen entgegensetzt.

Zuerst muß bemerkt werden, daß das Freudsche Schichtenmodell einer empirischen Über-prüfung schon aus dem Grunde unzugänglich ist, weil sich keine experimentellen Bedingun-gen angeben lassen, die es verifizieren bzw. falsifizieren könnten. Dieser vom Standpunkt der traditionellen Theorienauffassung entscheidende Mangel wird unter dem Blickwinkel des strukturalistischen Theorienkonzepts zu einem wesentlichen Chatakteristikum der Theorie. In bezug auf das psychoanalytische Persönlichkeitskonzept erweisen sich darüber hinaus Es und Über-Ich als theoretische Begriffe und es existieren keine vom Schichtenmodell unabhän-gige Methoden ihrer Bestimmung. Folglich hatte es Freud gar nicht nötig, seine Theorien — etwa durch Einführung des Widerstandsbegriffs — zu immunisieren. Sie sind einfach immun.

Hat dann — so erhebt sich die Frage — empirische Überprüfung überhaupt noch einen Platz in der Wissenschaft? Die Antwort lautet: ja, und zwar einen sehr wichtigen Platz. Empirisch überprüft werden nämlich Anwendbarkeitsbehauptungen bestimmter Kernspezialisierungen, d.h. empirische Hypothesen. Im Falle der Bestätigung wird 1. der Anwendungsbereich der Theorie erweitert und 2. die begriffliche Struktur der Theorie durch Aufnahme der entspre-chenden Kernspezialisierung differenziert. Umgekehrt wird bei Widerlegungen der Anwend-barkeitsbehauptung das entsprechende Gebiet aus der Menge der intendierten Anwendungen ausgeschlossen und die Kernspezialisierung verworfen. Auf den Kern der Theorie selbst schlägt die Widerlegung jedoch nicht durch.

In bezug auf das psychoanalytische Strukturmodell hat Freud selbst eine Kernspezialisierung vorgeschlagen und ihre Anwendbarkeit auf schizophrene Psychosen behauptet. Danach entstehen diese aus einem Konflikt zwischen Ich und Außenwelt.[9] Da hier schon die theoretischen Begriffe „Es" und „Über-Ich" eliminiert sind, ist eine empirische Überprüfung im Prinzip möglich.

So zeigt sich auch auf dem Gebiet der Psychologie, daß vom Standpunkt des strukturalistischen Theorienkonzepts das Festhalten an Theorien trotz Widerlegung ihrer empirischen Hypothesen seine scheinbare Irrationalität verliert.

ANMERKUNGEN

[1] Sneed, J., *The Logical Structure of Mathematical Physics* (Dordrecht 1971); Stegmüller, W., *Theorienstrukturen und Theoriendynamik* (Heidelberg-Berlin-New York 1973); Stegmüller, W., *Neue Wege der Wissenschaftsphilosophie* (Heidelberg-Berlin-New York 1980).

[2] Z.B. W. Diederich und H. F. Fulda, Sneed'sche Strukturen in Marx' „Kapital", *Neue Hefte für Philosophie* 13 (1978), S. 47−80.

[3] Vgl. dazu W. Stegmüller, *Hauptströmungen der Gegenwartsphilosophie*, Bd. 2 (Stuttgart[6]), S. 474ff.

[4] Vgl. zu diesem Problem F. Klix, *Information und Verhalten* (Berlin 1973), S. 459ff.

[5] Freud, S., „Psychoanalyse" und „Libidotheorie", in: M. Marcuse (Hrsg.) *Handwörterbuch der Sexualwissenschaft* (Bonn 1923); vgl. auch J. Laplanche und J. B. Pontalis, *Das Vokabular der Psychoanalyse* (Frankfurt 1973).

[6] Vgl. dazu F. Kiener, Empirische Kontrolle psychoanalytischer Thesen, in: *Handbuch der Psychologie*, Bd. 8, 2. Halbb. (Göttingen 1978).

[7] Freud, S., Das Ich und das Es (Wien 1923).

[8] Freud, S., *Neue Folge der Vorlesungen zur Einführung in die Psychoanalyse*, in: Studienausgabe Bd. 1 (Frankfurt 1969), S. 496.

[9] Freud, S., *Der Realitätsverlust bei Neurose und Psychose*, in: Studienausgabe Bd. 3 (Frankfurt 1975), S. 355−361.

* * *

HOLISTIC BEHAVIORISM

Edward F. Becker
University of Nebraska, Lincoln

Our belief that other people are conscious beings is evidently based upon our observations of their behavior. If asked to say why we thought someone was feeling pain or was thinking of Vienna, we would cite some bit of behavior, such as a grimace, or something the person had said. But does the observation of the behavior really give us a good reason for believing in the conscious processes, which, after all, we never directly observe (except in our own case)? This is the problem of "other minds."

The purpose of this paper is to sketch a solution to this problem. Because space is limited many details will have to be passed over, but hopefully the main outlines of the proposed solution will become clear.

I

All mental states are either *occurrent* or *non-occurrent*. Occurrent mental states include sensations, thoughts, feelings, emotions, and in general any mental states which occur at, or during, a definite period of time. Non-occurrent mental states include beliefs, desires and intentions, as well as moods (such as depression) and character traits (such as pride). They come and go, but not at any definite time, and, unlike the occurrent states, need not involve any conscious processes.

Often, when we know about the occurrent mental state of another it is because he has *told* us how he feels, or what he is thinking. There is, of course, room for error in such cases: our interlocutor may be dishonest. The same applies to non-verbal evidence for mental occurrences. How are we to know that a person is not feigning anger, or pain, or sadness?

Well, we might know these things, in a reasonably strict sense of "know", if we knew that the person was honest, and thus that it would be out of character for him to deceive us by word or deed. At this point it may seem that we have merely traded the problem of recognizing mental occurrences for the problem of recognizing honest people. There is, however, a certain benefit to this exchange. Honesty is a non-occurrent mental state. (Specifically, a disposition to avoid deceptive behavior.) Thus, if we could solve the general problem of recognizing non-occurrent mental states, we would, in particular, have learned how to recognize honesty, and would thereby have resolved, at least to a large extent, the problem of inferring mental occurrences from behavior.

Knowledge of mental occurrences, then, depends on knowledge of non-occurrent mental states. It is on knowlege of the second kind, therefore, that we should focus our discussion.

II

One proposed account of our knowledge of non-occurrent mental states is analytical behaviorism. On this view, statements about such states are to be analyzed as statements about a person's behavior or his behavioral dispositions. Irrascibility, for example, might be explained as a disposition to engage in angry behavior. If analytical behaviorism were true our knowledge of non-occurrent mental states would be grounded in observations of behavior because every statement about the former would be equivalent to some statement about the latter.

Apart from whatever difficulties may attend particular behavioral analyses, there is a general problem which casts doubt on the whole behaviorist program. There are certain mental states, such as belief, which, although they do *involve* behavioral dispositions, are such that *which* dispositions they involve depends upon the person's *other* beliefs, desires, etc. For example, suppose that while playing poker I come to believe that one of my opponents, Smith, has two pair. No doubt this belief involves certain dispositions to behave, but which ones? The answer depends upon my beliefs about the holdings of the other players in the game, about Smith's susceptibility to being bluffed, about the susceptibility of the other players to being bluffed, etc.; it also depends, obviously, upon various of my desires and intentions. There is thus no saying what dispositions my belief involves without referring to some of my other beliefs, desires and intentions. This being so, no behavioral analysis can eliminate reference to these mental states.

It seems, then, that we must reject analytical behaviorism. On the other hand, it seems undeniable that we sometimes *do* know what others believe, desire, or intend and that this knowledge is based solely on our observations of their behavior. There thus arises the *paradox of behaviorism*: it seems obvious that behavior *is* the basis of our knowledge of others' mental states; and yet, given the failure of analytical behaviorism, it is hard to see how it *could* be the basis of such knowledge.

III

We can resolve this paradox by adopting a view of the mental which may be called "holistic behaviorism." On this view knowledge of a person's mental states is derived not by inferring particular beliefs, desires, etc., from particular bits of behavior, but by attributing to him the most rational *system* of beliefs, desires, etc., which is compatible with the whole pattern of his behavior as we have so far abserved it. Further, the system of beliefs, desires, etc., which a person really has, *is* just the most rational system compatible with the totality of his behavior. There can be no basis for ascribing different mental states to people who behave in the same way. The mind, as a whole, supervenes on behavior.

Let us set this view out in more detail. Holistic behaviorism involves the following theses:
1) Statements about particular mental states cannot be analyzed in terms of behavior.
2) Nevertheless, statements about mental states *are* confirmed on the basis of observations of behavior.
3) In ascribing mental states to people we try to ascribe to them the most rational system of beliefs, desires, etc., and of degrees of belief and desire, which is compatible with their behavior.
4) Claims about individual mental states are justified only insofar as they are part of our best systematic account of a person's mental states; such claims can only be established or refuted in the context of a theory.
5) We ascribe non-occurrent mental states, though not mental occurrences, to ourselves on the same basis on which we ascribe them to others.
6) In some cases people may believe, desire, intend, etc., things which they have never thought of or which they would even deny believing, desiring, or intending.
7) The ascription of any particular mental state to a person can be made consistent with his behavior insofar as we are willing to adjust our ascriptions of *other* mental states to him. (Think of paranoia.)
8) A person's behavior is the *only* basis for ascribing non-occurrent mental states to him.
9) In ascribing systems of mental states to a person we are guided by the principle of maximum charity; we assign the most rational system of mental states compatible with the agent's behavior.
10) The agent's rationality consists in his avoiding inconsistency and acting in such a way as to maximize the expected value of his acts.

Holistic behaviorism has many things to recommend it. Here are some of them:

A) It explains the failure of analytical behaviorism.

B) It is compatible with the evident fact that observations of behavior are the basis for the attribution of mental states.

C) Unlike some accounts of our knowledge of the mental it allows for the possibility of our being wrong, in any particular case, about a person's mental state.

D) It implies the intuitively acceptable conclusion that we often do have probable (sometimes highly probable) knowledge of other people's mental states.

E) It explains, by way of the principle of charity, why everyone who understands them believes certain obvious principles of logic and mathematics. (E.g., that $1{,}000{,}017 + 1 = 1{,}000{,}018$.)

F) It explains the possibility of "unconscious" beliefs, desires, and intentions.

G) It explains how, as in cases of paranoia, bizarre views about people's mental states may be irrefutable, in the sense that they do not contradict any of the behavioral data.

H) It allows reasonable scope for indeterminacy in the attribution of mental states. A person's mental states will be indeterminate when the application of the principle of charity to the observed behavior yields no uniquely best theory.

IV

In recent years, philosophers, largely because of the influence of W. V. Quine, have come to realize that establishing a scientific theory does not consist in the confirmation of isolated hypotheses by isolated bits of data. It is rather our entire theory of the world, or at least a substantial chunk of it, that has to be reconciled with our experience. Yet there has been a curious failure to extend this insight to the philosophy of mind. Even in Quine's writings there is a yearning, predictably unfulfilled, for reductive analyses in the spirit of analytical behaviorism. If what has been said in this paper is correct, such analyses are both impossible and unnecessary. Behavior is the basis of our knowledge of the mental, but not because isolated mental states can be equated with isolated bits of behavior. In understanding a person's mind, we treat his beliefs, desires, and intentions as a corporate body.*

————

ENDNOTE

* The influence of Quine's work on the ideas presented here will be obvious. Donald Davidson has also defended a version of holism which resembles, in some respects, the position taken in this paper. See his "Belief and the Basis of Meaning, *Synthese*, 27 (1974), pp. 309–323, and reprinted in his *Inquiries Into Truth and Meaning*, (Oxford and New York, 1984) pp. 141–54.

* * *

ÜBERLEGUNGEN ZUR ENTSTEHUNG DER LEIB-SEELE-UNTERSCHEIDUNG UND IHREM ZUSAMMENHANG MIT FRAGEN DER ERKENNTNISTHEORIE

Josef Marschner
Universität Linz

An die Unterscheidung von Leib und Seele wurde in der Geschichte der Philosophie eine Reihe von Fragestellungen geknüpft. Hier aber soll die zunächst unauffällige Tatsache beleuchtet werden, daß eine solche Unterscheidung überhaupt stattgefunden hat. Es ist wissenssoziologisch zu klären, warum die Leib-Seele-Unterscheidung (im weiteren: LSU) besteht. Mit K. R. Popper kann man davon ausgehen, daß die LSU der Versuch einer Erklärung der Erfahrung unseres Bewußtseins ist.[1] Dazu muß aber gezeigt werden, warum die Annahme der Existenz einer Seele überhaupt eine Erklärung (für die Wahrnehmung) des eigenen Subjektseins bieten kann. Eine Theorie, die dies leistet, stammt von G. Dux, und soll als Grundlage für die Beantwortung unserer Frage herangezogen werden.[2]

Dux untersucht den Prozeß des Erwerbs der Schemata, unter denen der Mensch Wissen überhaupt gewinnen kann. Seine Voraussetzung ist dabei, daß diese aus der Erfahrung stammen und in einem umfassenden Lernprozeß aufgebaut werden müssen. Mit ihnen entsteht gleichzeitig Subjektivität als Reflexivität, da der Organismus, geleitet vom Interesse der Bewältigung der Umwelt, seine Motorik steuern lernen muß.[3] Entscheidend ist nun für die Gestalt der bewußten Formen der Erfahrung, daß die Umwelt für das Kind zentral durch Subjektivität repräsentiert wird. Dux schreibt:

> Eben weil das primäre und schlechterdings dominante Objekt, mit dem das Kind umzugehen lernt, die sogenannte Bezugsperson ist, (...), ist das primitive Objektschema das des Subjekts, das Ereignisschema das der Handlung. Das Kind bildet mit anderen Worten ein Objektschema aus, in dem die Objekte ein Aktionszentrum haben wie Subjekte. Für es sind alle Objekte so gebaut, als könnten sie handeln, dies oder jenes tun und lassen. Die Konsequenzen für den Aufbau der Außenwelt sind gleichermaßen weitreichend für das Ereignisschema: Das Ereignisschema wird als Handlungsschema aufgebaut. Fortan werden Ereignisse so wahrgenommen, als hätten sie in der Binnenlage eines Objekts ihren Anfang und wären ein vom Willen dirigiertes, durch den Willen beeinflußbares Tun.[4]

Die Welt wird also in einem subjektivischen Schema begriffen. Es erklärt Vorgänge dadurch, daß diese auf einen Ursprung zurückgeführt werden. Dieser wird subjektiviert und substanzialisiert.[5] Setzt man Ontogenese und Phylogenese gleich, dann bietet sich für das Zustandekommen der LSU die Erklärung: Der Mensch muß seine eigene Subjektivität, wenn er sie sich verständlich machen will, so deuten, daß die Bedingung seines Handelns, Planens, Denkens und Träumens, seines gesamten Lebensausdrucks, selbst noch in einem gleichsam innenliegenden Ursprung, in einem substanzialisiert gedachten Zentrum, eben der Seele liegt. Ein Aspekt ist meines Erachtens noch nachzutragen: Wenn wir annehmen, daß der Mensch sich nur auf die angeführte Weise deuten konnte, dann dürfen wir nicht unsere neuzeitlichen Vorstellungen von dem, was es heißt, Subjekt zu sein, dem archaischen Menschen zuschreiben. Denn während wir uns als die Gestalter unserer Welt erleben, stellt sich der archaische Mensch so dar bzw. handelt so, als würden die Götter vermittels der Seele ihm alle Kraft und Handlungsmacht verleihen.[6] Warum orientiert sich nun das archaische Denken in letzter Instanz am Handeln von Gottheiten? Weil diese durch die Logik dieser Weltauffassung erzwungen werden. Götter werden geschaffen durch die interpretative Umsetzung des subjektivischen Schemas in der Wirklichkeit.[7] Sie sind Ursprung und somit auch letzte Erklärung für das, was in der Seele vorgeht; am Beginn der abendländischen Kultur mindestens noch zu jener Zeit, in der die Seele noch nicht als von sich aus formende Kraft und selbsttätiges Prinzip aufgefaßt wurde, wie etwa bei Aristoteles. Solche Ideen standen jedenfalls nicht am Anfang. Dies führt zu dem Schluß, daß die Erklärung menschlicher Subjektivität eine Geschichte aufweist. Sie hat einen Richtungssinn: Er verläuft so, daß der Mensch seine Handlungsmächtigkeit und Erkenntnisfähigkeit immer mehr sich selber zuzuschreiben beginnt.[8]

Im folgenden sollen einige Erläuterungen zum Zusammenhang der Auffassung von der Seele oder dem Geist mit der Erkenntnistheorie gegeben werden. Die Philosophie ist in der Erkenntnisfrage von einer Ausgangslage geprägt, die bei Parmenides gebildet wird. Seine Ontologie erzwingt eine Auffassung von der Erkenntnis, die die Welt, wie sie uns in der äußeren Erfahrung gegeben ist, nämlich als ständige Veränderung, als bloßen Schein durchschlägt. Nur das reine Denken vermag das wahre Sein, welches ungeworden und unveränderlich in sich selbst verharrt, zu erfassen. Diese Trennung zwischen der Sinneserfahrung und der Vernunfterkenntnis führt zu Platons Ideenlehre, derzufolge Erkenntnis darin besteht, daß sich die Seele an die Ideen erinnert, die sie geschaut hat, bevor sie in den Körper eingeschlossen wurde (Anamnesis). Die Ideenwelt als die eigentliche Wirklichkeit, als das wahrhaft Seiende gegenüber der empirischen Welt, und der menschliche Geist oder die menschliche Seele als Zugang zu dieser Welt: Dies ist der einflußreichste Erkenntnismythos bis zur Entstehung des neuzeitlichen Empirismus. Auch bei Aristoteles, den man häufig Platon entgegensetzt, geschieht Erkenntnis durch das Erfassen der Form (morphè) des Seienden, also von etwas Nichtstofflichem durch den denkenden, vernünftigen Teil der Seele. Solange die Anahme sich durchhält, es existiere eine substanzhafte Seele oder ein solcher Geist, wird dieser(m) gleichzeitig das Erkenntnisvermögen zugerechnet. Damit verbunden ist das Konzept, daß letzte, essentialistische Erkenntnis nur durch den Einsatz dieses Vermögens zu gewinnen sei. Erkenntnis wurde als ein nichtmaterieller Akt aufgefaßt, dessen ihn ermöglichender Ursprung in einer Substanz von gleicher Beschaffenheit zu suchen sei. Daß Erkenntnis dadurch verstehbar wird, daß sie auf das Fundament, dem sie entspringt, zurückgeführt wird, setzt voraus, daß Erklären überhaupt dem subjektivischen Schema als einen Ursprungsschema folgt. Im neuzeitlichen Denken wird diese eigentümliche Logik erst dort schließlich zerbrochen, wo die Philosophie dem Modell der neuen Naturwissenschaften zu folgen beginnt, welches einem nichtsubjektivischen Schema der Wirklichkeitsdeutung verpflichtet ist. Mit dem Zurückdrängen der Substanzideen etwa bei Locke und Hume erfolgt der Aufbau von Erkenntnistheorien, die gleichsam die Mechanik des Zustandekommens interner Repräsentationen erklären wollen.

Auch bei Kant findet sich die Zurückweisung einer substantialisierten Auffassung vom erkennenden Ich. In dem „transzendentale Dialektik" benannten Abschnitt der *Kritik der reinen Vernunft* behandelt er unter anderem die Vorstellungen der sogenannten rationalen Psychologie von der Substantialität der Seele bzw. des denkenden Wesens. Ein ‚reines Ich' ist für ihn nicht mehr möglicher Gegenstand der Erfahrung. Es müßte es aber sein, wenn die Kategorie der Substanz darauf angewendet werden soll. Vielmehr ist es transzendentale Bedingung von Erkenntnis.

Das Vorgehen Kants, dem theoretisch Denkbaren eine Grenze zu ziehen, ist mit dem Projekt des *Tractatus logico-philosophicus* von Wittgenstein verglichen worden. Allerdings ist der Unterschied im Verständnis des ‚reinen Ich' gravierend: Denn während Kant der transzendentalen Subjektivität gewisse Vernunftleistungen einschreibt, und diese auf dem Weg einer transzendentalen Selbstreflexion sichtbar machen will, behandelt Wittgenstein das metaphysische Subjekt in einem viel radikaleren Sinn als Grenze. Er kann über es nichts sagen. Er muß es auch nicht, weil bei ihm die Weltkonstitution nicht aus einem wie immer gearteten Subjekt erfolgt, sondern aus der logischen Struktur der Sprache selbst. Dadurch wird Wittgensteins Ansatz im Traktat zur Grundlage der Wissenschaftsphilosophie des „Wiener Kreises", welche ihm darin folgte. Erst nach der Aufhebung der Reduktion der Sprachanalyse auf rein syntaktische und semantische Formen und mit der Hinwendung zur Pragmatik erscheint in der neueren Wissenschaftsphilosophie bei der Erkenntnisanalyse wieder das ‚Ich', in Gestalt des empirischen Sprachbenützers.

Ein Punkt ist noch zu vermerken: Sowohl bei der LSU wie auch beim Erkenntnisproblem überschneiden sich eine subjektivistische und eine objektivistische Perspektive; T. Nagel hat auf sie hingewiesen.[9] Dies bedeutet, daß man, wenn man den subjektiven Zugang wählt, auf den Weg einer Phänomenologie der ‚inneren' Erfahrung gerät. Diesen Weg ist paradigmatisch Descartes gegangen. Er erzwingt metaphysische Voraussetzungen, und es ist nicht zu sehen, wie man ihnen ausweichen könnte. Im Fall eines objektivistischen Lösungswegs muß unterschieden werden: Im Leib-Seele-Problem stößt man auf Fragen von der Art, wie etwa Beschreibungen subjektiver Erlebnisse übersetzbar sind in Sprachen, die eine intersubjektive Prüfbarkeit gewähren. Das extremste Beispiel dafür ist der Behaviourismus. Was aus der subjektivistischen Perspektive gegen einen solchen Zugang spricht, ist die Art, wie wir uns selbst erleben. Dies allerdings kann kein letztes Kriterium sein. Im Falle eines objektiven Zugangs zum Erkenntnisproblem gibt es seinerseits zwei Dimensionen: Bei der ersten stellt man die Frage nach der Rechtfertigung von Erkenntnisansprüchen als Frage nach der Eigenschaft jenes Mediums, in dem Erkenntnis sich objektiviert, also in der Sprache und im handelnden Umgang mit dieser. Dies kann von der analytischen Philosophie geleistet werden. Die zweite Dimension umfaßt eine naturwissenschaftliche Untersuchung des organischen Substrats des Mediums von Erkenntnis. Dieser Weg wird von der Gehirnforschung, Neuropsychologie und Biologie beschritten. Bei ihm jedoch muß von der Rechtfertigung von Erkenntnis abgesehen werden.

ANMERKUNGEN

[1] Popper, K. R. und Eccles, J. C., *Das Ich und sein Gehirn* (München [3]1984), S. 199.
[2] Dux, G., *Die Logik der Weltbilder* (Frankfurt a. M. 1982).
[3] Dux (1982), S. 85f.
[4] Dux (1982), S. 94f.
[5] Dux (1982), S. 123.
[6] Dazu B. Snell, *Die Entdeckung des Geistes* (Göttingen [5]1980), S. 28.
[7] Dux (1982), S. 187.
[8] Snell (1980), S. 29.
[9] Nagel, T., *Über das Leben, die Seele und den Tod* (Königstein 1984), S. 215ff.

* * *

WHAT MENTAL STATES ARE REALLY LIKE[1]

Natika Newton
Long Island University, Greenvale, New York

Eliminative materialism claims that folk psychology is a false theory, whose elements are not reducible to neurology because they do not pick out natural kinds.[2] If this claim is to be plausible, we must be able to see how we could be wrong in thinking the most resistant mental properties, intentionality and consciousness, to be irreducible or ineliminable. In this paper I suggest how we might be wrong. I propose that all mental concepts are metaphors for the functions of our bodies, and that all mental events actually consist of memory traces of these functions. The metaphors lead to philosophical perplexities when they are taken literally. If the proposal is right, the consequence is a blend of reductionism and eliminativism.

Reductionism and eliminativism are versions of the materialistic theory which holds that the concepts and laws of physical science apply to all aspects of human beings (contrary to Cartesian dualism). Both versions presuppose scientific realism—that is, the view that the physical world exists independently of the observer and that our best approach to this world is through the methods of natural science. Reductionism claims that concepts in folk psychology refer to natural kinds and are reducible to concepts of neuroscience (whether or not they ever are or should be so reduced), whereas eliminativism holds that these concepts will be eliminated when psychology reaches scientific maturity. My discussion of these two forms of materialism presupposes nothing about the ultimate metaphysical nature of reality, or about how or whether this could be known.

To save time I will start with an assumption: that the reducibility of neurology to chemistry and physics is not so problematic as the reducibility of psychology to neurology. Most current nonreductionist psychologies which I oppose argue almost exclusively against the latter.[3] I make this assumption because I will argue that actual mental processes, not necessarily those of folk psychology, can be reduced to biological processes which do not confront us with a mind-body problem.

1. THINKING IS LIKE ACTING ON SEEN OBJECTS. Our ordinary understanding of the mind is of a being which literally behaves just like the physical body. First, there are mental and physical 'acts.' Most mental acts, like most physical ones, essentially involve objects. Physical acts of approaching or avoiding objects, manipulating them, making and altering them, or just focussing one's eyes on them, have counterparts in the mental acts of concentrating on or repressing thoughts of objects, analyzing them, creating or developing them, or just imagining them. Mental acts can be occurrent or dispositional, like physical acts. The mind, like the body, can take an attitude or stance with respect to something. Second, there are objects in both cases. Mental objects, like physical ones, are the goal or focus of some mental action or awareness. Third, there is mental and physical perception. The most common mental metaphors describe consciousness and knowledge as seeing. Like our eyes, our minds can 'focus' on only one thing at a time. Also common are mental 'feelings' or 'sensings.' Finally, mental and physical objects are given values, which motivate action. Propositions are true or false; arguments valid or invalid; decisions good or evil. These values are offered as justification for the respective mental acts (or propositional attitudes) of affirmation or denial, acceptance or rejection, approval or disapproval.

Thus, as traditionally described, our minds parallel our bodies. They show the same abstract action patterns and the same types of relations to objects. They have goals, suffer pain (sorrow) and pleasure (joy), experience chronic conditions (moods), have special abilities (intelligence or talent), and can be tired (depressed) or energetic (manic).[4] Perhaps all mental properties have physical parallels, and are nothing but neurological traces of physical action, described metaphorically.

An important objection is that in my comparison of mental and physical action, perception, etc., I have not distinguished between the mental and the nonmental, since the physical actions described are all intelligent, goal-directed actions. But as I indicated earlier, explaining goal-directedness *per se* is not the real problem in philosophy of mind. As Dennett implies, there is a continuum in biology from simple to complex, well-designed goal-directed systems.[5] The problem for such systems is that of how biology is reducible to chemistry and physics, not the problem of mind and body. The essential differences between the mental and physical acts described are that the physical acts are (a) all directed at existent objects, and (b) do not presuppose self-awareness but only object discrimination. The mental acts (a) do not require that their objects exist, and (b) sometimes presuppose self-awareness. Only in the mental acts are found the properties that have traditionally resisted materialistic explication: intentionality (in Brentano's sense) and self-consciousness or conscious awareness of qualitative states. Thus I have to show that both intentionality and self-consciousness have explicit parallels in processes or states of our physical bodies, from which their properties are entirely derived.

2. INTENTIONALITY. According to Brentano[6] mental processes are characterized by "direction upon an object", even though the object need not exist. If a thinker thinks about something only the thinker need exist. Relations between physical things, or "strict" relations, require that both relata exist. Mental relations are not reducible to physical ones.

Let us consider an example. Suppose that yesterday I was bitten by a dog and today I am remembering or imagining the event by reactivating memory traces laid down yesterday. Yesterday I had a real physical relation to a real dog, and today I have an imaginary physical relation (being bitten) to an imagined, possibly now nonexistent, dog. Both the object and the relation are imagined. If imagining or remembering can be simply a matter of reactivating memory traces in the brain, then there is at least one way I can think about something that can be analyzed as a physical type of event.

It can be objected that if imagining is just reactivating memory traces it is not propositional and hence has no semantics. Only if I imagine *that* I was bitten by a dog can the process be analyzed propositionally. But if imagining, in my example, is imagining *that*, then it is intentional in a purely mental sense since it is more than just reactivating memory traces. On this view only if I analyze imagining as mechanical will my example work, but then I have not analyzed an intentional process.

This objection brings out a key point in my analysis: when I think about a dog by imagining being bitten by it, the object of my thought is dependent on the mode of representation in the same way it would be dependent on a description. The reactivated memory traces include not only the perceptual data that was present at the time, but also my entire set of responses: muscular, proprioceptive, etc. These responses pick out one aspect of the event from other possibilities: I responded to the dog's teeth, not to his tail. The reactivation of the traces of all these responses determines what it is I imagine. My claim is that these responses are no different in kind from other biological goal-oriented processes, such as a neural crest cell migrating to its destination in the developing embryo, or aplysia recoiling from a probe.[7]

3. SELF-CONSCIOUSNESS. As intentionality can be analyzed primarily in terms of physical action, self-consciousness can be analyzed in terms of vision. A pain as the object of my attention is, I claim, an illusion concocted from two concurrent states appearing to form a whole 'object.' First there is the physical sensation. Second there is my imagining that I am looking at an object by reactivating schematic imagery of focussing my eyes, where the sensation seems to be incorporated into the imagined seeing as the object focussed on. What makes the process seem so mysterious is that I have no idea of the occurrence of the eye focus ima-

241

gery (even though the metaphorical language I use to describe my experience might suggest it).

In the case of more generalized self-awareness the structure of the process is the same. I am now conscious that I am sitting at my desk. First there are all my physical sensations, and in addition visual data. Second there is the act of imagining seeing a person in this place. The imagery is not necessarily of a person seen from a distance; its primary material is my current sensations which appear to form an observed whole when I activate schematic memory traces of focussing my eyes. Feedback from this process may be incorporated into the collection of sensations of which I am aware, so that my awareness gives the illusion of reflexivity.

If self-consciousness is just imaged eye focus occurring along with our sensations, how can we pay selective attention to some, ignoring others? A representation or image of eye focus can take a second, concurrent brain event as its 'object' by altering and adjusting in response to this brain event and not others. When I am 'focussed on' or 'paying attention to' certain inner states, my imagery of observation responds to changes in these states in the same way that my eyes respond selectively to patterns when watching a friend walk away into a crowd. This sort of selective responsiveness is found in biology at the cellular level.

That consciousness involves something more than eye focus imagery plus selective responsiveness to other physical states is an understandable illusion, arising because what responds to certain brain states is *eye focus* imagery. Thus it seems exactly as if I am following something with my eyes, but I am, as it were, only going through the motions.

There are many further issues that should be discussed, for which there is not space in this paper. They include the question of what causes me to notice a certain inner state, apart from the mechanism by which I accomplish this; the question of consciousness in the congenitally blind; the question of the evolutionary and cultural origins of intentionality and consciousness;[8] and the current evidence of action schemata in the brain.[9] These issues are treated elsewhere.[10]

ENDNOTES

[1] I wish to thank Eric Walther for invaluable advice and encouragement.
[2] Churchland, Paul, "Eliminative Materialism and the Propositional Attitudes," *Journal of Philosophy* LXXVIII, 2 (1981).
[3] See, e.g., Jerry Fodor, *The Language of Thought* (Cambridge, Mass. 1979), Introduction; and Hilary Putnam, "Philosophy and Our Mental Life", in N. Block, *Readings in Philosophy and Psychology* (Cambridge, Mass. 1980). Vol. I, pp. 134–143.
[4] Julian Jaynes has given a thorough and persuasive analysis of the metaphorical nature of the language of mind, and of how mental events are analogues of physical events, in *The Origin of Consciousness in the Breakdown of the Bicameral Mind*, (Boston 1976), Ch. 2. See also Margaret Boden, "Implications of Language Studies for Human Nature", in Thomas W. Simon and Robert J. Scholes, eds., *Language, Mind and Brain* (Hillsdale, N. J. 1982).
[5] Dennett, Daniel, "Intentional Systems", in *Brainstorms* (Cambridge, Mass. 1978), pp. 8–9.
[6] Brentano, Franz, *Psychologie Vom Empirischen Standpunkte* (Leipzig 1924), I, pp. 124–125. Selections translated in R. M. Chisholm, ed., *Realism and the Background of Phenomenologie* (Glencoe, III. 1960).
[7] Jacobson, Marcus, *Developmental Neurobiology* (New York 1978), p. 18; also Patricia Smith Churchland, "A Perspective on Mind-Brain Research", *Journal of Philosophy* LXXVIII, no. 4 (1980).
[8] See Eric Havelock, *The Literate Revolution in Greece and Its Cultural Consequences* (Princeton 1982), and Julian Jaynes, *op. cit.*, for interesting proposals about the cultural origins of mental concepts.
[9] See Karl Pribram, "Problems Concerning the Structure of Consciousness", in G. Globus, G. Maxwell and I. Savodnik, *Consciousness and the Brain* (New York 1976), and Edward Evarts, "Brain Mechanisms of Movement" *Scientific American*, (September 1979), 164–179.
[10] Newton, Natika, "Materialism, Metaphor and Mind", unpublished.

* * *

SOME REMARKS ON THE ROLE OF INDICATORS IN HISTORICAL INQUIRIES

Tadeusz Buksinski
University of Poznań

I. For the first time indicators were applied in a conscious and planned way in statistics. Then the concept was adopted by sociologists and psychologists of an empiristic bent. They conceived indicators as means for determining the empirical sense of terms which denote structures and factors unavailable to direct observation. The indicators were supposed to ensure social research, its empirical character.[1]

The aim of this paper is to determine the concept of indicator and to present the role of indicators in historical inquiries. Up to now attempts to reconstruct the process of historical inquiries based on the theory of indicators have not been made. The theory of history falls behind the other social and humanistic sciences in this respect.

According to my suggestion an indicator is every event from the occurrence of which one can infer the occurrence of another event. An indicator is any event A (a thing, a feature, a behavior, an utterance, etc.) which is empirical and related by regularity to another event B (a thing, a feature, a behavior, an utterance etc.). On the basis of their relationship and from the occurrence of indicating event A (referred to as indicator) we infer the occurrence of an indicated event B (referred to as indicatum). In science both the indicator and the indicatum belong to the class of empirical events. In science the role of the indicator may be played by any empirical event, both a directly observable and unobservable event.

To the most frequently applied indicators in history belong: 1) material objects and their features, e.g. a specific form of homesteads as an indicator of the material culture of the people living there. 2) written records (e.g. documents, chronicles) and their features (the information they include, the language in which they were written, the kind of materials on which they were written, etc.) 3) oral records and their features (sagas, legends, statements of witnesses etc.). 4) singular extra-source events such as the activities and customs of individuals and of groups and the specific feature of these activities and customs and their products. For the purpose of simplification all kinds of indicators will be referred to as an "event". We shall also avoid their time and space indexes. Such a broader concept of the indicator plays a useful role in considerations on the research procedure of a historian. The concept of the indicator is more universal than such concepts as 'source' and 'source information'. 'Lack of source'or-'lack of source information' and 'extra-source event' may also be indicators. The indicator makes it easier to work out a homogeneous research theory not only for history but also for all social sciences.

II. Substance relationships of various kinds may be developed between the indicator and the indicatum. The causes of events or their effects may be indicators. Events related to an indicatum functionally, genetically, structurally, etc. may be indicators. Events prior to an indicatum, simultaneous with or following it may be also indicators. But for the procedure of scientific research the most important meaning has the type of regularity or the degree of correlation between the indicator and the indicatum. On the basis of this criterion we devide indicators into exceptionless and probabilistic. The former are based on the following kinds of relationships: 1) relationships of exceptionless regularity ascertaining sufficient conditions, 2) relationships of exceptionless regularity ascertaining necessary conditions, 3) relationships of exceptionless regularity ascertaining both sufficient and necessary conditions.

In history the probabilistic indicators play a more significant role than the exceptionless ones. The following indicators belong to them: 1) statistical indicators, 2) indicators presupposing general alternative regularities, 3) typological indicators. I will describe more accuratly solely the typological indicators. It seems that they are less known for theorists of science, even though they play an important role in researches.

General typological statements describe regularities which are neither exceptionless nor statistical. They ascertain relationships weaker than exceptionless, though in a sense stronger than statistical. They describe regularities of variable probability that may also be graded. The general obligatory principle is that the more the features of a definite situation (a thing, a person) are typical or model, the greater the probability of the occurrence of a typical indicatum. The more the given situation deviates from a model (type) the greater the probability of the occurrence of the modified indicatum.[2] Examples of typological statements: The more positive the evaluation an individual enjoys in a group the more he accepts the standards prevailing in the group. Of two fighting armies the more easily one army achieves the victory the greater its supremacy in numbers of soldiers and in arms and the better its command competence, and the higher the moral of soldiers.

A peculiar feature of typological statements is also the fact that unlike statistical statements they may refer also to situations which seldom emerge.

Cultural norms and social standards (the rules of behavior) are a subclass of typological statements. Cultural norms constitute a relatively stable pattern of human behavior. However, not every uniformed behavior pattern is a cultural standard, but only those which are caused by the influence of the external or internal normative constraints. As for the external pressure, it may be the pressure of the group we belong to or the institutions we work in, while to internal constraints belong moral principles. An indispensable condition to recognize an activity as attaining a cultural standard is the conviction of an individual that a given activity pattern is at least to some degree right. To some extent, the individual must internally accept a given way of activities and agree with it. To behavior patterns guided by cultural norms (standards) belong: a sumptuous life of the affluent European nobility; duels among the nobles in the case of an honour insult, etc.

Indicators based on cultural (social) norms have a probabilistic character. The way in which they are probabilistic is different from that of statistical indicators. The probability degree of the occurrence of the typical (model) indicatum is of a range nature in a sense and may be graded. Cultural (social) norms are not met by all and not always. The severer the punishment for failing to meet the ruling standards and the more the individuals accept their social enviroments, roles, statuses, and the stronger inner value system they posses, and the greater the extent to which social eviroments is typical ('normal'), then the greater the extent to which the individual activities are in accordance with ruling norms.[3]

The rules and principles of inferring from the historical sources have also a typological character. We will show it in the next chapter.

III. Indicators play the basic role in two research contexts: discovery and justification. First, indicators suggest hypotheses which may solve a posed problem. They indicate what hypotheses may be taken into account as possible and probable answers to a posed research question. Every statement in historical works is a hypothesis answering the question, which is chosen from many other possible answers to that question. Every statement may be confirmed and disconfirmed. A researcher cannot make haphazard or wild guesses; he offers and considers proposals for solving a posed problem on the basis of acquired knowledge important for a given issue. He particularly refers to the knowledge of detailed facts and to the knowledge of generalizations characteristic of an examined period and region. This knowledge performs the function of a set of indicators. It lays down the direction in which solutions to a posed problem should be sought. The better the historian, the more regularities and detailed facts of a given period he knows.

The process of discovering (constructing, propounding) hypotheses and the process of justifying them are closely related and dependent upon one onother. At the very moment of its propounding a hypothesis is based on source-and extra-source indicators that support it. In the light of these indicators a researcher recognizes it as a possible and probable solution to a given problem. It may be generally assumed that the processes of heuristics are conclusion-drawing without the act of assertion: proposing from among all possible hypotheses concerning a given theme, the hypotheses which seem probable, even though their logical value and the degree of substantation have not been exactly determined. That is the stage of the process of research at which hypotheses are not accepted yet. They are taken to be propounded as for the sake of testing. Usually, there are many such hypotheses-suggested solutions to a given problem.

From the beginning the process of discovering is entangled in the process of challenging and eliminating other competitive hypotheses. Competitive hypotheses are all those probable solutions to a given problem which have more or less the same informative degree. Researchers try to determine the probability degree of each of the propounded hypotheses in order to accept the most probable. Eliminating competitive hypotheses in the process of justification takes place on the basis of analyzing the indicators known before the formulation of a given hypothesis and on the basis of those which will be discovered or determined in the course of justifying it. A very important role is played in that processes by typological principles of inferring from the historical sources. One of these presupposed principles may be formulated as follows: The better the author of a source is informed, the greater his interest in a given kind of facts, the more truthful and authentic the source is, then the greater the probability that the events described in the source did take place and that the unrecorded events did not occur. Assuming this kind of general statement the historians determine in a given situation the justifying force of a given indicator-event and as a result they estimate the confirmation degree of a given hypothesis. The followers of a hypothesis try to show that a given indicator quoted to support a hypothesis certainly occurred and that it confirms the hypothesis with highest probability (e.g. the source is highly reliable). The critics of a hypothesis try to show something contrary. Arguing, the oponents use the further range indicators, e.g. indicators of indicators.[4]

IV. It seems that on the basis of the analysis of the process of research one may attempt to compile the criteria according to which the confirmation degree of competitive hypotheses are estimated and compared. 1) The bigger the number of confirming indicators and the smaller the number of indicators invalidating a hypothesis, the better it is confirmed. 2) The new indicators discovered only after propounding a hypothesis confirm it to a greater degree than the old ones. 3) The more independent of one another the indicators are, the greater justifying value they possess. 4) The greater the variety of indicators, to a greater extent they justify hypotheses. The criterion of their variety is their attachment to different categories of events (things). 5) The greater the certainty of the occurrence of the justifying indicators (events) the better the hypothesis is justified (confirmed, disconfirmed). 6) The greater the probability relation between an indicator and an indicatum (a hypothesis) the better the hypothesis is justified. 7) The greater the degree to which an indicator challenges all but one of the competitive hypotheses, the greater its confirmation power. 8) The better (more accurate) the fact is known, the easier it is to determine its indicatory functions and to a greater extent it justifies the hypothesis.

I have mentioned solely the criteria, not having space to describe them in detail.

———

ENDNOTES

[1] Lazarsfeld, P. F., Rosenberg, M. (eds.), *The Language of Social Research* (Glencoe Illinois 1957). D. Lerner (ed.), *Evidence and Inference* (Illinois 1958). Bondon, R., Lazarsfeld, P. F. (eds.), *Le Vocabulaire des sciences sociales* (Paris 1972).
[2] Hempel, G., Oppenheim, P., *Der Typusbegriff im Lichte der neuen Logik* (Leiden 1936). Max Weber, *Wirtschaft und Gesellschaft* (Tübingen 1972) 5. Auflage.
[3] Nowak, Stefan, *Understanding and Prediction* (Dortrecht 1976).
[4] Buksinski, T., *Metodologiczne problemy uzasadniania wiedzy historycznej* [Methodological Problems of the Justification of Historical Knowledge], (Warszawa-Poznań 1982). The book presents the accurate analysis of many examples of justification of historical hypotheses.

* * *

METAPHYSICS, MIND, AND PHYSICALISM

Mark Migotti
Yale University

The aim of this paper is to criticize *physicalism* without compromising *naturalism*. By naturalism I understand the thesis that the mind is continuous with the rest of nature and that there is no deep ontological or epistemic divide between, on the one hand the mind and our understanding of mental phenomena, and on the other hand the rest of the world and our understanding of whatever phenomena it contains. By physicalism I understand the view that 'the physical' in some important sense has ontological primacy over 'the mental'. I shall attempt to show both that it is useful to distinguish physicalism from naturalism and that physicalism entails some implausible claims about the scope and nature of physical science. I shall present my case via a critique of K. V. Wilkes' recent and sophisticated arguments for a physicalistic philosophy of mind found in her 1978 book *Physicalism*. (Hereafter referred to in the text as *W.*)

I

Wilkes takes the central issue addressed by physicalism to be that of "whether the vocabulary and theories of physical sciences are adequate to describe, predict and explain the purposive behaviour of humans and animals. . . ." (*W*, p. 10.) According to Wilkes, the defining characteristic of the vocabulary of physical sciences is extensionality. The language of theories from the physical sciences, that is to say, consists exclusively of sentences that admit of the substitutability of co-referring expressions *salva veritate*. The central claim of physicalism, then, becomes that human behaviour can eventually be explained with the use of extensionally formulatable theories alone. Appearances to the contrary, intensional operators such as 'believes', 'hopes', 'fears' and so on are contextually eliminable for purposes of explaining and predicting human action.

Wilkes acknowledges that, *pace* radical behaviourism, one cannot successfully eliminate intensional locutions from psychological theory by simply refusing to touch them. In the wake of arguments from Dennett and others Wilkes is convinced that "behaviourism fails to explain or predict . . . some of the very simplest behaviour of mice and men." (*W*, p. 18 and ff for references to the literature on behaviourism.) Trying to account for why people do the particular things they do without reference to what they desire to accomplish and to what they believe, hope or fear about their situations—in short, without reference to how they represent the world to themselves—is, it seems, akin to entering a tennis match armed with a ping-pong paddle; one's equipment just isn't up to the job.

Wilkes' response to the demise of behaviourism is, briefly, to try to turn to physicalist ends the explanatory power afforded by the use of propositional attitudes and other intensional concepts in psychological theory. In other words, *contra* behaviourism, intensional sentence forming operators are to be permitted in the course of explaining intelligent behaviour, but as per physicalism, intensionally loaded explanations are to be officially endorsed only if they are translatable without loss of explanatory power into explanations employing only an extensionally pure language. Functionalism, Wilkes argues, is a methodology expressly designed to allow the science of psychology to benefit both from the epistemic advantages of an intensionally laden theoretical vocabulary—since without it not enough explaining gets done—and from the ontological advantages (as they are perceived) of physicalism—since the alternative is assumed to be some untenable form of dualism.

Here, roughly and telegrammatically, is an outline of Wilkes's functionalist methodology. First, one treats psychological theories as trying to account for various mental capacities by positing a number of pre-conditions which (it is conjectured) must be met if the capacities are to be used as they are. In other words, one regards the *explananda* for which psychology tries to account as a number of operationally defined systems consisting of systematically interrelated and organized parts. The leading question then is: How does the system carry out its characteristic functions? In short, How does it do what it does? The sort of answer one is looking for will be of the form 'it manages to do G because it does P, Q, and R, and doing P, Q, and R in a certain way just *is* doing G. Thus, to use a favourite example of Wilkes', a washing machine performs its characteristic G, washing clothes, by a) soaking, b) soaping, c) agitating and so forth. Now each of the functional prerequisites of a system can in turn be the object of another functional explanation. How, for example, does the machine soak the clothes? Well, it a'. . . ., b'. . . ., c'. . . . etc. . Eventually one arrives at a level of explanation which counts as basic. 'Base level' as Wilkes points out, is equivalent to "what scientists are currently calling the 'base level'". (*W*, p. 64.) The scientists who decide what base level is are, of course, physicists. (see *W*, p. 30.)

It is perhaps now becoming clearer how Wilkes expects functionalism to provide the physicalist psychologist or philosopher with a cake which is simultaneously eatable and havable. Intensionally phrased explanations are to be encouraged as long as there is hope that ontological commitment to the objects of intensional discourse can be 'discharged' at the level of neurophysiology. Less and less of the language with which psychological abilities are characterized will be required as these abilities are explained as the product of a number of interrelated sub-abilities. Psychological theory will link up with neurological theory as the unit functions of the former discipline are broken down into huge, complex conjunction of specialized neurological sub-functions, culminating in the extensionally describable function of individual neurons which is simply to fire when a certain afferent energy threshold has been reached. As Wilkes puts it, ". . . the greater the detail of the research, the more inflexible will be the functions that are performed by micro-structures or micro-processes of the brain; intensional descriptions are needed only when functions are complex and flexible." (*W*, p. 65.)

Borrowing a phrase of Kant's, I feel that this apparently tolerant functionalistic physicalism hides a significant "danger to our thinking self". (*K.d.r.V.*, A/383.) My principle fear is that the model of explanation of mental phenomena Wilkes espouses intimates a lot more for itself than it delivers. It does this by trading on an ambiguity between a strong, controversial interpretation (which I would call physicalism proper) and a mild, uncontentious interpretation (which I would call naturalism) of her central thesis. In the next section I try to show how this ambiguity can be focussed by examining the role of the physical sciences in our knowledge of the world as a whole.

II

Wilkes' attitude towards natural science is typified by the following two quotations:

> On the physical side of the mind-body relation . . . there seems no bar in principle to the suggestion that the physical sciences which study the brain and human activity can have, or devise a vocabulary adequate for the identification of any physical state, event or process. (W, p. 2.)

> . . . whatever one's criteria for a good theory may be, there seems no reason why (the physical sciences devoted to the study of the brain and the central nervous system) should not eventually meet them. (W, p. 31.)

Given that for Wilkes "the scope of 'the physical' is the physical scientist's business." (*W*, p. 2.) the first claim strikes me as self-authenticating in a way which renders it vacuous. It is as if a 'magicalist' engaged in a hypothesized controversy over the 'magical-mundane' problem were to argue as follows: "'the magical' picks out all and only items, processes, concepts, laws, hypotheses, theories or theoretical postulates used essentially by magicians. There seems, therefore, no bar in principle to the suggestion that qualified magicians studying the universe and the spell books can have or devise a vocabulary adequate for the identification of any magically caused events, states or processes." Of course (given these definitions) the physical scientist and the magician can pick out instances of the physical and the magical respectively, they are picking out just what they posited in!

The second passage, I presume, contains a likely response to such an attempted *reductio ad absurdum*. The physical sciences, it might be said, are capable not just of constructing any old theories about the world, but more importantly of constructing *good* theories about the world.

But even if it is accepted that good theories are (*inter alia*) those that permit successful prediction and control of the phenomena allegedly explained and that physics and chemistry are exemplary producers of good theories, it does not follow that theories which use an intensional vocabulary (apparently) not remotely connected with the extensional language of physics and chemistry cannot therefore be good theories; it does not follow, that is, unless one makes the very strong claim that *really* physics and chemistry are the *only* producers of good theories. To make this latter claim is to place a virtually a priori faith in the foundational position of physics *vis a vis* the rest of theoretical knowledge. It is also, in effect, to deny that any of the social sciences are capable of constructing good theories, unless the rider 'a theory which *might* one day be translated into extensional, physicalist language can still count as a good theory' is construed so broadly as to let in anything one likes. Finally, the claim also implies that probabilistically framed theories are dubious since 'the probability of x/y' is (on many accounts) an intensional sentence forming operator.[1]

If one endorses these consequences of strong physicalism, one is committed to the view that science properly so-called, i.e. physical science, has nothing at all to say about a vast range of phenomena, including most of the more interesting aspects of recorded human history. If, as seems to me immensely more attractive, one regards the whole of science as trying to explain the whole of experience, then it might well make sense to use different models and vocabularies for different sectors of experience as required. The best theories about the causes of wars use mainly intensional socio-economic terms while the best theories about the causes of plagues generally get by with extensional bio-medical terms. Notice, though, that the difference in vocabularies does not prevent theories from the two domains from interacting; wars can be among the causes of plague and plagues can be among the causes of war. (I take it as obvious that wars can not be adequately described in extensional terms alone.) Furthermore, if what constitutes a good theory is itself a theoretical issue — and if one acknowledges a discipline called 'epistemology', this is precisely its field — then one cannot (or should not) *dogmatically* privilege extensional, physicalistic vocabularies over intensional, mentalistic ones without at least suffering pangs of philosophical conscience. One should, that is, have an argument to show that the epistemic benefits of extensional purity outweigh the costs of sacrificing a large body of apparently serviceable knowledge about social behaviour which seems inextricably bound up in the intensional idiom.

Wilkes has no such argument to the best of my knowledge and I conclude that her brand of physicalism fails to account for some of the most interesting features of the mind, preeminently features expressed in social life, and that it furthermore rests upon a misguided hierarchical vision of science with physics as the solid foundation. Only a dogged and misconceived 'philosophical faith' (to echo William James) in physical science could lead one to hold that explanations in terms of propositional attitudes and other intensional descriptions of mental life can be countenanced only as temporary stand-ins for the pushes and pulls and charges and discharges that really underlie the whole show.

ENDNOTE

[1] I owe this point to Hugh Mellor whom I thank for helpful comments on the matters discussed in this paper.

REFERENCES

Kant, Immanuel *Kritik der reinen Vernunft*, English trans. Max Muller (New York 1966)
Wilkes, K. V., *Physicalism* (London 1978)

* * *

INSTRUMENTALISM IN THE PHILOSOPHY OF MIND

Gary Fuller
Central Michigan Unversity

A central concern in philosophy is the relation between common sense and science. Philosophy of mind, of course, has shared, and continues to share, this concern. Here the issue is that of the relation between our commonsense psychological notions of belief, desire, etc. (and the related notions of personhood, moral agency, and responsibility) and the rising sciences of the day: traditionally, Newtonian mechanics; some decades ago, radical behaviorism; and now, cognitive psychology and neurophysiology. The general question has remained constant: does science clash with our folk-psychological notions, or can it exist in harmony with them? Today, there are both optimistic thinkers, such as Jerry Fodor,[1] who are confident that an adequate scientific psychology will turn out to be quite similar to folk psychology, as well as pessimists, such as Paul Churchland,[2] who believe that the developing psychological and brain sciences will prove to be totally incompatible with folk psychology and that folk psychology should therefore be abandoned altogether.

One way in which a philosopher might try to protect folk psychology against possible threats from these advancing sciences is by adopting an instrumentalist interpretation of folk psychology according to which folk-psychological terms, such as 'belief' and 'desire' do not refer but rather are to be regarded as mere calculation devices. Daniel Dennett, one of the most influential philosophers of mind during the last fifteen years, is well known for his espousal of such a position. The aim of this paper is to examine instrumentalism through the work of Dennett and to raise the question of whether instrumentalism vindicates folk psychology. I shall do three things: (I) clarify the notion of instrumentalism; (II) give a brief account of Dennett's instrumentalist views; and (III) argue that at least Dennett's earlier strong instrumentalism fails to vindicate folk psychology.

I

Let us begin by giving some clarification of the notion of instrumentalism. What does it mean to be an instrumentalist with respect to folk psychology?

It will be easiest to spell out what instrumentalism involves if we make an assumption which is now widely held: the assumption that folk psychology is a *theory* of behavior implicit in our explanations and predictions of behavior in terms of beliefs, desires, and so on. On this assumption the mental terms of the theory, e.g. 'belief' and 'desire', are to be construed as theoretical terms which at least ostensibly refer to state types and/or tokens.

Having made this assumption, we can give an initial characterization of instrumentalism by contrasting it with realism, as follows:

(1) Realism: the mental terms of folk psychology refer to state types and/or tokens and its sentences have a truth value.

(2) Instrumentalism: the mental terms of the theory do not refer and its sentences have no truth value. Rather, such terms and sentences are calculation devices for the purpose of predicting behavior.

Notice that according to our characterization so far instrumentalism is incompatible with identity theories of both the mental type/physical type as well as the mental token/physical token varieties.

This initial account of instrumentalism, however, can be refined by relabeling (2) 'strong instrumentalism' and distinguishing it from weak instrumentalism, which can be characterized as follows:

(3) Weak instrumentalism: the mental terms of folk psychology do not refer; nevertheless, the sentences of the theory do have a truth value.

II

Over a number of years Daniel Dennett has articulated and defended an instrumentalist approach to folk psychology. Dennett's instrumentalism has not remained static; indeed, a good case can be made for claiming that his instrumentalism has undergone a major change.[3] Earlier on, especially in *Brainstorms*,[4] Dennett held a strong-instrumentalist position in which the sentences of folk psychology were construed as having no truth value. More recently, and here the key article is "Three Kinds of Intentional Psychology,"[5] he has adopted a weak instrumentalism according to which folk-psychological states, such as beliefs, are not genuine posits (*illata*) but mere calculation bound entities (*abstracta*) analogous to centers of gravity. On the new view then, the term 'belief' does not refer, but belief *sentences*, just like sentences "about" centers of gravity, do have a truth value.

Putting these details to one side, we need to ask the general question of why Dennett has favored instrumentalism at all, rather than opted for a realist position. Certainly, one central consideration for Dennett has been that folk psychology (or Dennett's refinement of it, Intentional Systems Theory), if interpreted realistically, might well prove to be false. Among other things, folk psychology contains a rationality idealization and is therefore unrealizable, and a realistic construal of folk psychology might seem to require inner "representations", about which Dennett has often been sceptical, to say the least.

This consideration taken by itself is obviously not enough. If folk psychology taken realistically is literally false, then why not scrap it altogether? There are a number of reasons why Dennett wants to preserve folk psychology. To begin with, Dennett believes that it does have a role to play in scientific psychology: it can function, for example, as a useful starting point in top-down strategies. In addition, and perhaps more important, folk psychology is in some sense indispensable to us. The second major consideration for Dennett in favor of adopting instrumentalism, then, is that it will enable us to preserve folk psychology. Instrumentalism will in a sense vindicate folk psychology.

III

What, if anything, is wrong with an instrumentalist approach to folk psychology? In this section I shall restrict myself to criticizing the strong instrumentalism of Dennett's early view, indeed, to exploring just one strand of criticism of the early view. I want to question whether strong instrumentalism, whatever its other merits and weaknesses, really does vindicate folk psychology.

Does the strong instrumentalist construal of folk psychology *vindicate* our folk notions of belief and desire and the related notions of personhood and responsibility?

Now what does 'vindicate' mean here? One sense in which a claim or theory, say in the face of a sceptical attack, can be said to be vindicated is by being shown to be true after all. But this sense, of course, is not the one we want here. 'Vindicate our folk-psychological notions' must mean here: 'show that we have good reason to continue to use these notions.' Taking 'vindicate' in this way, then, we might at first glance be tempted to argue that strong instrumentalism does vindicate our folk notions: surely the usefulness of these notions as calculation devices provides ample reason for continuing to employ them.

The trouble with this is that our folk-psychological notions are not mere calculation devices.

Indeed, as a number of philosophers have correctly argued, a strong-instrumentalist account of our idioms of belief, desire, and personhood will yield concepts different from our actual ones. Our actual concepts are *realistic*: facts about the inner states of a system (and about their causal relations to each other and to inputs and outputs), are relevant to the application of these concepts in a way that they are not to the application of the corresponding strong-instrumentalist concepts. Contrast, for example, the strong-instrumentalist concept of a "person" (or "mind") according to which, following Dennett, a system counts as a "person" just in case its behavior is "reliably and voluminously predictable"[6] via the instrumentalist rules of the intentional strategy, with our actual concept of a person. The two are clearly different, since:

(1) We can describe systems which satisfy the strong-instrumentalist but not the actual concept of a person. Stephen Stich has developed Ned Block's example of a chess-playing computer whose moves are generally predictable using the intentional strategy, but which has no internal representations of rules or goals.

> Rather, this computer's memory contains an *enormous* multiple branching tree representation of every possible chess game up to, say, 100 moves in length. ...if we were to run across (what appeared to be) a person whose conversations, chess playing, and other behaviors were controlled by an enormous preprogrammed branching list of what to do when, I think our intuition would rebel at saying that the "person" believed that I was about to attack with my queen—or indeed that he believed anything else!'[7]

(2) It is also easy to think of examples in the converse direction, examples of systems which satisfy the actual but not the strong-instrumentalist concept of a person. My colleague, Paul Yu, came up with the following case. Suppose that, unbeknownst to us, Martians so arrange matters that Jones's brain states become erratic whenever any attempt is made to predict his behavior, although he is perfectly normal at other times. Then, although Jones would count as a person on the actual construal of 'person' he would fail to be one on the instrumentalist construal.

Our actual folk-psychological concepts, then, are different from their strong-instrumentalist counterparts. Now if Dennett were interested in folk psychology only for the role that it can play in scientific psychology, e.g. (as we have seen) in developing top-down strategies, then perhaps this lack of equivalence need not worry him. But if, as he seems to be, he is concerned with vindicating our ordinary psychological notions and practices, then he *should* be worried: for how can the introduction of instrumentalist substitutes, however scientifically legitimate, vindicate our actual *realistic* concepts of desire, belief, and personhood?

To answer this last question we might try the following line. We use our folk-psychological concepts to draw certain distinctions: that between persons and non-persons, that between actions for which a person can be held accountable and those for which he cannot, and so on. Perhaps, as Dennett seems to think, these commonsense concepts are flawed in certain ways and should therefore be replaced by new unflawed concepts—in Dennett's opinion, by the new strong-instrumentalist substitutes. If the new concepts draw roughly the same distinctions as the old, then we can say that the new concepts have vindicated the old distinctions, and, indirectly, the old concepts. Taking this line of thought, we can hold, then, that the instrumentalist substitutes will vindicate our actual folk concepts just in case they agree reasonably closely in their (possible) extensions.

How close is reasonably close? Examples (1) and (2) above have already shown that the strong-instrumentalist substitutes are not equivalent to our actual folk-psychological concepts. Still, it might be thought here that the situations described in (1) and (2) are very unlikely to occur and that the instrumentalist and the actual concepts will turn out to be at least co-extensive in the actual world. Surely, this is enough for vindication.

Unfortunately (for the strong instrumentalist) we can think of cases which are less unlikely to occur but in which there is also a divergence. Consider the following example:

(3) Jones is pointing a gun at Smith and has every intention of pulling the trigger and killing him. He subsequently pulls the trigger and Smith dies. Nevertheless, what caused Jones's pul-

ling of the trigger was not his intention, or any other mental event, but rather some fluke brain event totally unrelated to any of Jones's mental states.

Although this example needs to be described in much greater detail, a good case can be made for claiming that we (using our ordinary folk concepts) would not want to hold Jones responsible for Smith's death whereas the strong instrumentalist would.

In conclusion, then, I have serious doubts about whether Dennett's earlier strong instrumentalism can vindicate our ordinary folk notions of belief, desire, and personhood. Indeed, I suspect that Dennett had these doubts as well and that they were an important motivating factor in the change from his earlier view to his new weakinstrumentalist view. Whether the new view also runs into similar problems about vindication is something which must await further exploration.*

ENDNOTES

1 See his *The Language of Thought* (New York 1975).
2 See his "Eliminative Materialism and Propositional Attitudes", *Journal of Philosophy*, Vol.78 (1981), pp. 67–90.
3 Paul Yu and I have argued this case in "A Critique of Dennett", (forthcoming in *Synthese*).
4 Dennett, Daniel, *Brainstorms* (Cambridge, Mass. 1978).
5 In R. Healey (ed.), *Reduction, Time and Reality* (Cambridge, England 1981), pp. 37–61.
6 "True Believers...", in: A. Heath (ed.), *Scientific Explanation* (Oxford 1981), p. 55.
7 Stich, Stephen, *From Folk Psychology to Cognitive Science* (Cambridge, Mass. 1983), pp. 244–5.

* I am heavily indebted to Paul Yu: this paper grew out of many long and enjoyable discussions with him on Dennett over the last year. Thanks also to Regine Imbsweiler, Ausonio Marras, and Salma Saab for helpful comments.

* * *

CAN HUMAN CONCEPTUAL SCHEMES BE STUDIED EMPIRICALLY? SOME CAUTIONARY REMARKS

Sharon Lee Armstrong[1]
Wesleyan University

The tradition in philosophy and psychology has been to assume that common words such as 'bird' are cover-labels for mental categories that are themselves bundles of simpler categories called features, attributes or properties. There are two major subtypes of a feature theory approach to mental categories: the *definitional* view, and the *prototype* view. On the definitional variant, a smallish set of simple properties are individually necessary and severally sufficient to pick out all and only, say, the birds, from everything else. While meritorious for its simplicity and precision, this view has proved recalcitrant to work out in the required detail. It's rarely the case that all and only the class members can be picked out in virtue of sufficient lists of necessary (let alone elemental) properties.

However, there is another class of feature descriptions that relinquishes the necessary and sufficient requirement. This is the family resemblance view first alluded to by Wittgenstein (*PI*) although he might be surprised at some of its recent guises. He took as an important example the concept *game*, held together by a variety of gamey attributes, only some of which are instantiated by any one game.

Psychologists have adapted this view and brought it into psychology through a series of compelling experimental demonstrations as the 'prototype' theory. The idea here is that there are distinctions among the properties themselves, some recognized as privileged relative to a category. Prototypical members have all or most of the privileged properties of a category. Marginal members have only one or a few. So for *bird*, we have robin as a prototypical member exhibiting the most privileged properties (flies, wings, feather-bearing, egg-laying), whereas penguin exhibits fewer of these properties and is considered marginal by many. This approach also offers to give an account, in terms of various measures of feature overlap and/or organization, the apparent fact that membership in a category is graded; for example, why a robin seems birdier than a penguin.

However, there are grounds for caution before embracing a particular interpretation of these findings. It is not notably easier to find the prototypic features of a concept than to find the necessary and sufficient ones. Prototype theories render the description of reasoning with words far more difficult and the understanding of compositional (phrase and sentence) meaning altogether hopeless. Thus it seems surprising that psychologists have been pleased, rather than depressed, by experimental findings that support a prototype theory. These problems provide some impetus to reconsider the empirical support.

Armstrong, Gleitman & Gleitman demonstrate serious empirical challenges and give extensive methodological criticisms of the empirical base for the prototype approach. I shall just quickly review some of their findings here.

Following upon Rosch, subjects were asked to indicate how good an example various instances of categories are by using a rating scale from 1 (good) to 7 (poor). It turns out that people will say that apples are very good examples of *fruit* and deserve a high rating while figs and olives are poor examples and deserve low ratings. When subjects were asked to judge the veracity of statements about category membership, it turns out that they respond faster to "AN APPLE IS A FRUIT" than to "A FIG IS A FRUIT" with word frequency controlled across the list. Rosch and her colleagues have interpreted these findings as evidence that membership is graded, rather than all-or-none in everyday categories. But if certain concepts are nondefinitional because of graded responses, that must be because if the concepts were definitional, graded responses would not be achieved. But this remains to be shown by testing some definitional concepts.

Are there definitional concepts? Of course. For example, consider the superordinate concept *odd number*. It is precisely defined as "an integer not divisible by two without remainder." No integer seems to sit on the fence, undecided as to whether it is quite even or perhaps a bit odd. No odd number seems odder than any other. A, G & G found that subjects gave graded responses to the definitional concepts *odd number, even number, plane geometry figure*, and *female* in both the exemplariness-rating and verification tasks!

These results suggest that we are back at square one in discovering the structure of everyday concepts *experimentally*: Certain techniques widely used to elicit the structure of such categories are flawed and thus the structure of those concepts studied remains unknown.

Perhaps a more direct approach to the study of the internal structure of everyday concepts would be more profitable. Instead of focusing on the kind of organization of features (definitional vs. prototypic) for a concept, focus instead on the features themselves. In psychology, the most direct approach has been taken by Rosch & Mervis. Subjects were presented with various exemplars from a number of superordinate categories (e.g., chair, sofa, bed, from the category *furniture*) and asked to list all the attributes that are "common to and characteristic of" each item. Their rationale was straightforward: If there is a set of necessary and sufficient attributes that defines, say, *furniture*, then every item that falls under concept necessarily has all the required attributes and these should emerge in the data collected.

In fact, Rosch & Mervis found that "very few" (sometimes no) attributes were listed for all the exemplars of a category. But it is by no means clear that the subjects could really comply with the instructions to come up with the appropriate features that describe a given category. And what does one make of the features that subjects do produce?

One problem concerns the suppression of features. A subject would not list *all* of the attributes of a given term even if he knew them. Some of the reasons have to do with lexical redundancy rules: Most subjects won't mention *living thing* let alone *physical object* for penguin. The features of the superordinate are simply presumed to apply to the items that fall under it. For related reasons, people tend to tell you what they think you need to know, suppressing the obvious. A standard dictionary defines *zebrula* as a "cross between a zebra and a horse"; but no dictionary (or subject) would ever define a *horse* as a "cross between a horse and a horse". Thus, not only will particular attributes vary from item to item within a superordinate category but level of response will likely vary as well.

An even more troublesome problem is whether the subjects could access the features and express them in words. Some empirical basis for this worry comes from pilot data (with Komatsu) partially replicating the Rosch & Mervis study. On the face of it, subjects' responses to *grapefruit* and *tractor* showed considerable variation. For *grapefruit,* subjects responded "sweet", "sour", and "not as sweet as an orange". For *tractor*, subjects responded "has four wheels", "has three wheels", and "has two wheels (very unstable)". Yet the variability may only be apparent. Notice that none of them said how many wheels a grapefruit had nor how sweet a tractor was. The subjects seem to share some common conceptions of the categories but perhaps were unable to come up with the right level of description—e.g., "bewheeled" and "sweet/sour dimension". Even if categories are describable in terms of some featural vocabulary, it will be difficult to expose this directly by limited inquiry.

Leaving aside questions of the interpretation of subjects' responses, there are other issues regarding variability of responses. Those feature lists that do emerge from psychological studies of concepts are obtained by pooling data across many subjects. This move presumes that concepts are stable across individuals in the relevant way. Never subjected to empirical test, this assumption is suspect. Suppose each subject's mental representation for *fruit* were definitional, but each subject's definition differed ever so slightly. Pooling data across subjects would lead the researcher to conclude that the concept *fruit* is a family-resemblance concept. But is it? It depends on whether your interest is in the linguistic community or in the individual. Current research methods would prejudice the results to be descriptive of the community even though the researcher's intention is to study the individual (collectively).

Problems of the sort just mentioned lead me to consider, in general, the efficacy of the empirical study of conceptual schemes as it is practiced now in psychology. It will be useful to contrast the philosophical and psychological approaches to the study of concepts.

The philosophical study of concepts is best represented by the approach called 'conceptual analysis'. It is characterized by extensive and penetrating probing of one's intuitions about the character of a particular concept. It involves the pitting of intuitions against intuitions, the attempt to generate counterexamples to any initial hypotheses, the attempt to devise questions and contexts, to reveal *the* nature of the concept under investigations, i.e., what *ought* to be believed by truth-seekers. Thus, the philosopher relys primarily on himself as an authority, but may draw upon other philosophers' beliefs subjected to the same rigorous probing.

In contrast, the psychologist's intent (usually − although some psychologists are confused about what their mission is) is to study the 'collective individual'; He would like to determine the nature of a conceptual scheme found in *most* people, which identifies this enterprise as empirical. The representativeness of a sample studied being an issue, many subjects (sometimes hundreds) are polled, responses tabulated, and statistical conclusions drawn. Subjects' responses are not typically analyzed vis a vis one another but simply tallied. In fact, there is a reluctance on the part of many researchers to provide much in the way of interpretations adhering to the dictum "let the data speak for themselves". The fear evoking this policy is that the investigator might inject too much of his own perspective into an interpretation and that conclusions drawn from tabulated subjects' responses are, in contrast, 'bias free'.

Bent on obtaining large numbers of subjects, psychologists have (due to oversight or the constraints of time and funding) limited both the range and depth of questioning to each subject (introducing bias nonetheless). Thus, the character of the data collected will be importantly different from that of the philosopher. The question arises, "How can we be sure that a severely limited sample of any particular subject's intuitions (however many times multiplied), would reveal the richness and complexity of human conceptual life that we know to exist?" I think that the examples given in the discussions above indicate that we are unlikely to.

To the extent that one's interests are directed to the collective individual, one *must* question a reasonable number of subjects but hundreds are not usually necessary or even better. (Repeated-measures designs offer some statistical advantage in terms of reducing one source of variation.) However, any attempt to study conceptual schemes empirically that can hope to avoid the problems mentioned above will also have to adapt the extensive probing techniques of philosophy. This will necessitate limiting the inquiry to a few conceptual domains at a time and studying them in depth rather than limiting the questioning to each subject. This is just as well since it is unlikely, that discoveries concerning the various important conceptual domains will reveal that any of them are organized as simple feature structures. Rather, in each domain, the units, their patterning, the principles that organize them, their development, their environmental dependence are all likely to be different and complex, rewarding serious study.

REFERENCES

Armstrong, S. L., Gleitman, L. R., & Gleitman, H., "What Some Concepts Might Not Be", *Cognition* Vol. 13 (1983), pp. 263–308.

Rosch, E., "On the Internal Structure of Perceptual and Semantic Categories", in T. E. Moore (ed.), *Cognitive Development and the Acquisition of Language* (New York 1973), pp. 111–144.

Rosch, E. & Mervis, C. B., "Family Resemblances: Studies in the Internal Structure of Categories", *Cognitive Psychology* Vol. 7 (1975), pp. 573–605.

ENDNOTE

[1] I am indepted to Lila R. Gleitman and Henry Gleitman for many ideas and discussions of issues presented here.

* * *

DE-IDEALIZING THE MIND-BODY PROBLEM

John Blackmore
Kirchberg am Wechsel

I

If what is often called the mind developed during the course of evolution, then we may be dealing primarily with an historical problem which could vary from species to species and even from individual to individual, that is, the relation between mind and matter may be contingent rather than necessary.

In other words, philosophers may be unable to solve the problem merely by switching categories around or by "eliminating linguistic confusion". It may require a knowledge not only of physics, chemistry, biology, physiology, medicine, and psychology but of the history of human and animal evolution as well.

Unfortunately, however, many philosophers may find it difficult to understand how most scientists think, especially historical and experimental scientists. What most philosophers understand by law-like claims (often any unqualified statement)[1] is drastically different from the few actual claims which are widely acknowledged as laws by significant numbers of scientists themselves (idealized universal claims which describe how idealized types of variables behave under idealized types of limited-variable conditions). Real scientific laws such as those of Galileo,[2] Boyle,[3] and Charles,[4] represent preliminary stages of understanding which while true under idealized conditions tend to give way in practical terms to laws which take more variables into account, that is, until a level is reached where there are too many important variables to be handled by laws, such as is largely the case in biology, geology, and the social sciences.

To the extent philosophers understand science it is often theoretical physics which serves as a model (particularly work done during the first three decades of this dying century). This is partly because "explanation" can often be idealized as deduction of a factual or verifiable claim from what philosophers imagine is a scientific law (an approach not utterly unrelated to traditional syllogistic reasoning). Regrettably, theoretical physics is not typical of the sciences (and hopefully dubious processes such as "renormalization" will never be typical), few claims which philosophers call laws are really laws, and real explanation normally bears little resemblance to mere formal deduction.

II

If philosophers wish to understand what the scientists who are really making progress toward resolving the mind-matter problem are doing, then it could be wise *to learn how to think historically*, that is, how to *de-idealize* one's thinking and understanding. Experimental scientists who have studied biology and physiology in a successful manner over the last two centuries such as Claude Bernard, Louis Pasteur, Gregor Mendel, Charles Darwin, and in medicine Joseph Lister, Robert Koch, and numerous others while they were able to draw important generalizations from their work and use those generalizations to guide subsequent work nevertheless had a marked ability to *de-idealize* problems. They were able, first, to *de-typify* the phenomena to be studied, that is, concentrate on particulars as particulars, second, *de-generalize*, that is, keep within the evidence and qualify their understanding of results at every important stage, third, *de-formalize*, that is, avoid unnecessary mathematics, abstractions, and technical jargon, fourth, *de-fictionalize*, illustrate and support arguments by real rather than fictional or imagined examples, fifth, *de-conventionalize*, base assumptions and arguments on facts rather than mere rules, definitions, or conventions, and sixth, *de-dogmatize*, hold no beliefs more strongly than the weight of evidence supports.[5] No one is perfect, and even great scientists can slip, but the above characteristics were generally present in their investigations.

There is no shortage of people inclined to jump to conclusions. Almost every important theory or discovery had its precursors. Copernicus had his Aristarchus, Dalton his Democritus, Newton his Hooke, and Darwin had more than can easily be listed, including his grandfather.[6] It is massive factual support and careful detailed study which can select the winner from a thousand hypotheses. Darwin's thesis wasn't new, but no one else took the trouble to study individual species and their history in such an extensive way to support that thesis. The mind-body problem is not short of theories or hypotheses or of switching the boundaries between mind and matter or abolishing them altogether. What is missing among philosophers is the patience and scientific understanding to study and collate the relevant data in a reasonably exhaustive manner. What is missing among scientists is of course lack of philosophical understanding. What is usually missing in both is a careful grasp of the earlier history of the relevant sciences. But the Darwins of the world can combine the characteristics needed.

III

Since Descartes the key to the mind-body problem has generally been understood to be consciousness. It is this issue which requires the most de-idealization if substantial progress or an experimental breakthrough is to be accomplished. Those philosophers who treat consciousness as an all-inclusive category such as Hegel[7] and Husserl[8] or as non-existent such as some early behaviorists not only share the same position in practical terms (i.e. an ability to ignore consciousness) but appear to be contradicted not only by a great deal of experimental work in biology, physiology, psychology, and medicine but in classical terms by Oswald Külpe and his Würzburg colleagues on the eve of the first world war.[9] They apparently discovered not only imageless thoughts (thereby helping to refute several old arguments by Berkeley and Hume against representational realism) but also that much or most imageless thinking is also unconscious. But if some thinking is conscious and some not, then neither an idealistic theory that everything is conscious or a behavioristic one that nothing is conscious can be sound. Consciousness is presumably real but has a limited and varying scope, that is, among those living creatures who are conscious.

Indeed, it is apparently a necessary condition for experimental study that what is studied be both conceivable as possibly real and limited such that one can at least conceive of or allow for a contrary, something to compare what is being studied against. If everything were conscious, how could we study it? What would we be studying which could distinguish it from what we are not studying? To be without a contrary removes our ability to understand it in a comparative way, and without at least some comparison can anything be said to be understood? In short, the scientific capacity to study consciousness already presupposes both the conceivable reality and the limited scope or range of consciousness. Without those two factors no scientific study seems possible. The following diagram could be helpful. Some things presumably are conscious (at least to some living creatures), some things which are not conscious can be made conscious, and presumably some things which are not conscious to anyone or any animal can never be made conscious to them, though depending on which epistemological assumptions are reliable, perhaps we can still understand or at least refer to much that is beyond the possible scope of consciousness, at least let us hope so. While the diagram below may seem to have general or universal application, in fact different creatures at different times and under different conditions may have their own diagrams as it were which possess different ranges of inclusiveness.

SOME REALITY

CANNOT BE MADE
CONSCIOUS

CAN BE MADE
CONSCIOUS

IS CONSCIOUS

IS
SUB-CONSCIOUS
OR PRESENT TO
SPLIT'CONSCIOUSNESS

Different philosophers of course define "reality" in different ways. Philosophers sometimes link it to perception, others to consciousness, and still others to Platonic Forms or universals. Most scientists and practical people, however, define reality as what can make a causal difference, that is, as a power or force, as if Hume's arguments were either false or irrelevant. In these terms whether reality can be made conscious tends to be a contingent rather than a necessary matter, though the limits of possible consciousness may mean that some forms of reality are necessarily beyond what can be made conscious.

IV

The issue of consciousness can and should be de-idealized much further. Not only may the character of consciousness and how mind and matter presumably interact, if indeed they do, well be different in different species and periods of history and individuals differ according to personality, accidents, and surgery, but comparison of unusual cases with each other and with more common ones have helped allow experimentalists to gain vast insight beyond what mere speculation and conjecture seem able to contrive. Inded, imaginable real cases were they to occur could revolutionize the future. For example, could Siamese twins joined in the head survive and be capable of being studies and were they to share a common lobe, the possible discoveries which could result might stagger the most staid and cautious scientist.

Comparing common states of consciousness may also become very informative. For example, sleep, drowsiness, lack of concentration, shock, anger, depression, and other modes and moods could not only affect interaction with the physical world differently but could suggest that consciousness is capable of greater and lesser intensity as well as greater and lesser scope. (Virtually all analogies are inadequate. If consciousness were a "stream", it should be capable of being speeded up or reversed, and if it were a spotlight (perhaps the best analogy) the beam should be detectable. If the object of consciousness were a holographic picture[10] in the brain or a "ghost in the machine"[11] where is it located, why is it noticable, and what is the mechanism for turning it on and off?)

A man in shock may speak or move, control some voluntary muscles, but has trouble initiating plans or attending carefully to the world around him. Is he really conscious, and if so, is it a different form of consciousness (even apart from the issue of what he will subsequently remember)?

Also, there are different forms of loss of consciousness which can affect what is normally regarded as voluntary behavior differently. People who faint normally do not lose control of their bowels,[12] but people in a "drunken stupor" often do, and dead people always. I have not seen evidence on people in comas, on drugs, or under anasthesia. Sleeping people normally continue to control many voluntary muscles, but under some circumstances can lose control.[13] In short, not only may there be different ways and degrees of losing consciousness, but each one may appear to affect mind-matter interaction differently. In fact, the character of consciousness itself may both be and decompose differently in different species, individuals, and when affected by different causal factors.

V

No suggestion is intended that rearranging philosophical definitions and categories is always as futile as shifting deckchairs on the Titanic. The more fundamental the philosophical categories tampered with, the greater the impact on how we understand or misunderstand the world. Philosophy can be awesomely influential for those people who know how to detect such matters, even the current Neo-Scholasticism with its emphasis on logic, language, and universals.[14] But *if* rearranging definitions and categories is to revolutionize our understanding *to best advantage,* then I think it should be based on a much deeper historical and experiment-grounded understanding of central issues such as the varieties of consciousness and losing consciousness and how they may affect the brain and physical behavior.

The issue is not what to *call* consciousness, whether to label it "mental" or "physical", but to admit its probable reality, the reality of what is trans-conscious, and to understand how consciousness has evolved in different species and inividuals. Once these problems have been better understood, then we can return to the matter of general classification and decide what activities may best be considered physical, what mental, and what perhaps neither. We might even slowly gain insight into how disparate or incommensurable forces in this huge universe could influence each other, or on a more modest scale within the less atrophied parts of our brain.

———

ENDNOTES

1 Sometimes the inflated notion of laws which many philosophers have is traced back to John Stuart Mill. Another possible source is the first two "Hauptsätze" of thermodynamics which are commonly mistranslated as laws in English. For most scientists a necessary law describes necessary relations between idealized variables, a statistical law statistical relations, and an empirical law empirical relations. The problem with the latter two types of laws is that it can be very difficult to draw valid deductions about particulars from them even under idealized conditions. Laws without variables can perhaps best be left to philosophers. Some constants may be non-idealized, but they are not laws.
2 Galileo's Law of Falling Bodies, his time-distance law.
3 Robert Boyle's pressure-volume law (also called Mariotte's law).
4 Jacques Charles' volume-temperature law (also called Gay-Lussac's Law).
5 A de-idealized approach is not merely needed when there are too many important variables to use laws, but whenever particulars would be understood not merely as examples of types (which by neglecting differences tends to idealize them) but as unique particulars.
6 Darwin, Erasmus (1731–1802).
7 Schischkoff, Georgi, (ed.), *Philosophisches Wörterbuch*, 21st edition (Stuttgart 1982), p. 261.
8 Stegmüller, Wolfgang, *Hauptströmungen der Gegenwartsphilosophie*, Vol. I, sixth edition, (Stuttgart, 1978), p. 53 and Hans Joachim Störig, *Weltgeschichte der Philosophie* (Stuttgart 1984), p. 622.
9 Boring, Edwin G., *A History of Experimental Psychology* (New York 1957), p. 404.
10 Pribram, Karl, *Consciousness and the Brain* (New York 1976).
11 Ryle, Gilbert, *The Concept of Mind* (New York 1949), chapter 1.
12 This may also depend on how long one is unconscious. If smelling salt cannot revive one, then presumably the condition is more serious than fainting. A pilot without oxygen is often said to "faint", but there is probably a more accurate word. Most people who faint presumably continue to breathe. Most people in a coma also continue to breathe. It is possible that everyday terminology cannot properly distinguish between control and loss of control over voluntary muscles. Nor is definition of the latter necessarily without problems, especially concerning breathing. Habitual and conditioned behavior may be voluntary without being volitional, which is different from non-voluntary or "instinctive" behavior which presumably can never be made volitional. Whether all habitual and conditioned behavior can be reversed and made volitional again is a moot point. Perhaps breathing contains both voluntary and involuntary aspects, with only some of the voluntary aspects being actively volitional even when we try to alter how we breathe.
13 Strangely enough, some dreams can cause us to lose control. Perhaps most people have been embarrassed by such experiences at one time or another.
14 Any approach which regards logic, language, or meaning as objective may be regarded as scholastic or artificial. If experience has taught us anything, it is that no two people use language or understand theories in exactly the same way. Not only do we all have different assumptions and patterns of usage as well as different vocabularies, but it is always possible to misunderstand logic, language, and meaning. It may sometimes be convenient to treat logic, language, and meaning *as if* they were objective (or consisted of universals), but whenever strict accuracy is important an historical, de-idealized approach is needed, which *distinguishes* between how different people use logic, language, and meaning.

* * *

THE POSITION OF THE THEORY OF MIND
IN THE CATEGORIAL INTERPRETATION OF DIALECTICS

Izabella Nowak and Leszek Nowak
University of Poznań

1. In the tradition of Marxian epistemology there are two formulas which in completely different ways define the essence of human cognition:
(*p*) cognition is a derivative of social practice, and
(*o*) cognition is a reflection of reality.
Various lines of interpretation in that tradition in different ways refer to both those formulas. There is a complementary line which embraces them on equal terms: both those characteristics of cognition are to be equally indispensable and important, therefore none of them should be left out while building epistemology. There is also a stratification line which admits both those formulas, but does not accord to them equal significance: as the basic one, the formula about the subordinate character of cognition towards practice (praxistic position), or the formula of reflection (ontological position) are advanced. So both these orientations in the framework of the stratification line emphasize something different as the main characteristic of cognition—the element considered as primary by the praxist, is treated as secondary by the ontologist, and vice-versa. This has such a methodological sense that while building epistemology the second is left out in the first approximation. The follower of the priority of the (*p*) formula therefore promises himself to take into account the connection between cognitive and ontological structures, after he has finished with the relation: cognition-practice; whereas the supporter of the priority of the (*o*) formula will first characterize the relationships of cognitive structures and the principles of their development to the ontological structures and the principles of their movement, in order to supplement and modify the obtained results by taking into account the elements of a pragmatic nature. This also has such a systematic sense that for the adherent of the praxistic formulation, what is assumed by Marxist epistemology is the theory of historical materialism, whereas the adherent of the ontological position assumes objective dialectics. The role of dialectics in the framework of praxistic epistemology, as well as the role of historical materialism in the framework of ontological epistemology becomes secondary, and usually—simply vague (e.g., when the praxistic approach to epistemology is accompanied by the praxistic interpretation of dialectics itself). Thus sometimes a nihilistic line comes into being in the framework of Marxism, which eliminates the (*p*) idea—variant anti-praxistic—or the (*o*) idea—anti-ontological variant. This occurs against the very tradition which after all evidently embraces both formulas, and—which is more important—against reality, because in fact cognition reflects reality, and simultaneously depends on social practice.

In the present article we would like to make a distinction between the problems of the theory of mind and the problems of the theory of cognition, show the position of the theory of mind in the framework of the categorial interpretation of dialectics, and also prove that this approach does not evoke nihilistic (or else liquidating) tendencies towards the (*p*) idea, which positively distinguishes it among some alternative interpretations of Marxist epistemology, which are discussed at the end of this article.

2. Dialectics, according to the categorial interpretations, is distinguished from among other essentialistic doctrines in that it is a dynamic essentialism. Essentialism asserts that there is a hierarchy of factors affecting each factor and the following factors are distinguished: primary and secondary. For each factor, therefore, there is a regularity relating it to the element(s), primary for the factor. That regularity is manifested in certain forms which express a combined effect on the given factor both of the primary as well as secondary magnitudes. What

distinguishes the categorially interpreted dialectics from among other essentialistic doctrines is the thesis that the essential structures of phenomena (factors) are changing. One should differentiate between the transformations of the essential structure of a phenomenon (qualitative changes) and the developments of that structure (quantitative changes). The former consists in that the set of primary factors is changing, whereas the latter in that the hierarchy of secondary factors undergoes changes with identical primary factors. If a qualitative change, therefore, takes place, then the very phenomenon (i.e., the fact consisting in that a given factor appears in a definite intensity on some object) is subject in comparable moments to different regularities. If, however, a quantitative change occurs, then it is subject to the same regularity, but that change is manifested differently in comparable moments, its forms are different.

The categorial history of a phenomenon is the series of its essential (quantitative or qualitative) changes. The historical process, therefore, in the categorial understanding consists in changes of the essential structure (developments or transformations). At each stage of the categorial history, a phenomenon is subject to various dependencies (its nomological structure is different)—or else to different regularities (in case of qualitative changes), or to different forms of the same regularity (in case of quantitative changes).

The principles of objective dialectics are interpreted as certain general theses on the form of the categorial histories of phenomena. Consequently, the principle which says about transformation of quantity into quality is understood as a thesis that the essential structure of each phenomenon is subject first to a series of developments, and only then to transformation; whereas the principle of double negation is interpreted as a statement which proclaims that there are not such transformations of essential structures, where a new structure does not have certain factors in common with the former one, therefore some range of continuation still remains.

3. The above outlined ideas of the categorial interpretation of objective dialectics are not precise enough[1] and incomplete (since they outline only the most idealized model of that conception).[2] However, they permit catching the moment—important for the present article, viz. the adequacy, correspondence of cognitive and ontic structures. The structure of the idealizational theory of a phenomenon is in some way a reflection of the essential structure of that phenomenon. The hierarchy: regularity and its subsequent forms corresponds to the hierarchy: the idealizational law and its subsequent concretizations. If, therefore, it is true that the mehod of idealization is the key method of constructing scientific theories, then it may be said that the structure of a theory is not an arbitrary creation of mind, but it reflects the internal structure of the phenomena explained by the theory.

Similarly, each idealizational theory passes through a number of developments—ever more numerous sets of idealizing assumptions are developed where, however, the same basic laws are retained, and then those laws are subject to concretization, among others with regard to new assumptions. A former law becomes more abstract in the framework of a new, more developed theory, but at the same time better concretized. After a number of developments, however, the theory is subject to transformation—a basically different picture of the essential structure with a different set of primary factors is assumed, a new idealizational law is established and gradually concretized. Never are all factors abandoned formerly treated as essential—some of them are still retained consequently, some elements of the former theory (discovered in its constituent dependencies) are incorporated into the new theoretical structure. It is apparent therefore, that as the history of a phenomenon is composed of a series of quantitative changes leading to qualitative ones, so the history of a scientific theory is composed of a series of developments of the initial theory, leading to its transformation. If the thesis that theories have idealizational structure is an equivalent of the thesis of essentialism, then the thesis that they undergo changes by developments and transformations is an equivalent of the principle that quantity transforms into quality; and the thesis that none of the new theories completely breaks away from the former, but constitutes at the most its transformation (i.e., retains some former dependencies at least in the form of concretization of new laws), is the counterpart of the double negation principle.

4. Even with the foregoing considerations[3] one may notice correspondence between theses of dialectics interpreted categorially and epistemological theses concerning the structure and development of scientific theories. Both the internal structure of a theory as well as the principles of its movement are isomorphic in relation to the structure of phenomena and principles of their movement.

Naturally that may only occur for very strong idealizing assumptions. We will call such a cognition as sovereign which is capable of discovering the idealizational theory for each value F, including the absolute truth, and discover immediately without correcting earlier suggestions; a mind capable of such cognition we will call perfect. (It need not be said there are no perfect minds, as there are no perfect Chomskian speakers—recipients, whereas examination of such constructs may be useful; this cannot be decided a priori: such examinations should simply be carried out). And so for the sovereign cognition among others the following principles of subject dialectics are true:[4]

> (1) each local history of any thought history includes transformations preceded by a set of developments,
>
> (2) each local history of each thought history includes exclusively transformations of the first type.

Those principles are the counterparts of the ontological principles saying that quantity is transformed into quality and the principle of double negation from objective dialectics, and so are other theses of subjective dialectics. Consequently, it may be stated that subjective dialectics needs the following condition which we will call a categorial interpretation of the formula of reflection:

(o') for each F the structure of the mental category of F type is isomorphic to the structure of the subjective category of F type, and the thought history of the F factor is isomorphic to the objective history of that factor.

Naturally, the conception of sovereign cognition is an idealization of the conception of human cognition. In real cognition we deal with the process of approximating the reality (never all concretizations are carried out effectively, a number of concretizations always ends with approximation), therefore the subsequent theoretical proposals do not contain theses which would claim the role of absolute truth, at the most they formulate their approximate equivalents more and more precisely with the progress of science. In real cognition, original theoretical proposals are always corrected (new secondary factors are introduced not because they were not acting before and now come into being, but simply because they were not recognized before), consequently each theory initiates a series of corrections. And so one assumes in an idealizing way about the sovereign cognition, and correspondingly, about the perfect mind that it is capable of formulating and not only approximating the absolute truth about a given phenomenon, and that it is carried out without correcting itself (consequently that self-correcting series consists of one element in this instance).

The theory of mind (or the theory of sovereign cognition), therefore, will be that part of epistemology which is binding with the idealizing assumption of the sovereignty of cognition. Before we will try to define the position occupied by a so-conceived theory of mind in categorial epistemology, there will be some comments on its constituents.

5. The theory of mind embraces first of all that model of cognition which is defined in the categorial interpretation of dialectics as subjective dialectics[5] with the principle of idealization and also the principles of subjective dialectics. Subjective dialectics is based not only on idealizing assumptions about the sovereignty of cognition, but also on all idealizing assumptions of objective dialectics. Consequently, if objective dialectics[6] is based on the assumptions idealizing the structure and development of the external reality, then subjective dialectics must make assumptions which constitute that ideal model of reality. And when those assumptions are gradually lifted in the subsequent models of the categorial ontology, and the ideal type of the external reality becomes ever more realistic, then the picture of the world examined by epistemology is thereby enriched, and as a result the theses of subjective dialectics are corrected and supplemented. And so, e.g.—referring to the already performed concretization of

objective dialectics, one should state (see point 2) that it is binding for, among others, two idealizing conditions. One of them says that material objects are subject exclusively to the process of essential differentiation (i.e. objects belonging to one categorial class, may belong in the future to one or more categorial classes)[7], and the other that factors are mutually essential at most in a one-directional way (i.e., if one is essential for the other, that other is not essential for the first one).

Consequently, removing the first of those conditions a unification of objective categories is introduced, as a reverse operation to their dissociating; a differentiation is made between historical and physical time; the conceptual range of subjective history is widened (distinguishing among others the history with unifications, history aggregatively differentiating, aggregatively unifying, etc.); formulations of the principles of objective dialectics are corrected and a new ontological thesis is added to those principles—the thesis about unevenness of movement: "each objective history is a history aggregatively differentiating and simultaneously uneven in terms of time".[8] That way the picture of cognition examined in epistemology must undergo adequate changes—nevertheless, cognition is related now to the ever more complex ideal type of external reality. Since the real processes cover not only the essential differentiating but also unifications, consequently the sovereign subject—and the assumption about sovereignty is constantly in force—must reflect those processes in his constructs. A unification of mental categories, therefore, is introduced,[9] the conception of the history of thought is appropiately widened etc., first and foremost the principle of the concreteness of truth is introduced: if cognition is sovereign, then consequently:

(3) the thought history of each factor is aggregatively differentiating, and differentiated in terms of time.

Since the time when the phenomena develop unevenly in different ranges of their existence, thereafter the sovereign cognition must designate for those different ranges different idealizational theories for the same values; in this sense "the truth is always concrete". But the thesis (3) does not belong to subjective dialectics, since it is not an epistemological equivalent of the principles of objective dialectics, it is instead an equivalent of the thesis about unevenness of movement of one of the derivative models of categorial ontology.

Subsequently, lifting the second of the mentioned idealizing conditions, the conceptions of coupling and system (a set of mutually coupled factors) are introduced, which enables reconstructing the thesis about an all-embracing union, saying that material reality is a system. And again: after the ideal type of reality is examined in the present, a more realistic model of the categorial ontology is to be reflected—and the idealizing assumption about the sovereignty of cognition is still in force—then the cognitive constructs should be appropriately enlarged. Consequently, one introduces appropriately the couplings between the idealizational theories, and conceptions of the theoretical system treated as a set of such theories of which every two are coupled. This enables reconstructing the procedures of analysis and synthesis in the specific sense of those terms, included in the Marxist tradition, and first of all—reconstructing the thesis about the system character of truth: if the cognition is sovereign, then

(4) the absolute truth about a given factor cannot be established without establishing such truth about every other factor.

The thesis about the system character of truth is an epistemological equivalent of the ontological thesis about the universal nexus.[11]

And so theses (1) and (2) are examples of theses of subjective dialectics and consequently of the theses from the most idealized models of the theory of mind. Whereas the theses (3) and (4) constitute examples of the more realistic epistemological models, but still belonging to the theory of mind since they all meet the categorial condition of reflection (o'). Those models of epistemology, beginning with subjective dialectics, which fulfil the categorial interpretation (o') of the formula: "cognition is a reflection of reality", constitute the theory of mind. Consequently, the theory of mind comprises the concretizational sequence of those epistemological models which retain isomorphism of ontological and cognitive structures.

Such a concretization of the epistemological model, which goes beyond that isomorphism does not belong to the theory of mind. It may easily be established which type of concretization goes beyond that isomorphism, and therefore satisfies the condition of reflection (o')—namely such which refers to the factors specially related to the character of the cognitive means employed by people, structure, of cognizing societies, etc. In short, beyond the theory of mind there proceeds such a concretization of the models of that theory, which assumes lifting the idealizing condition on the sovereignty of cognition. For that condition is in fact a decision not to take into consideration the cognitive limitations imposed on us 'people' by the structure of the perception apparatus, the nature of notions that we use, the methods for passing information, limitations—but also of amplifications—of the process of cognition, resulting from its numerous involvments in social practice, etc. Whereas beyond the cognition of reflection (o') these concretizations are not brought out which result from ontological simplifications, consequently from the idealization of the object of research.

That way, in the framework of epistemology one may distinguish the theory of mind—a sequence of models beginning with subjective dialectics, which while presenting an ever more realistic (as concerned with the ever more realistically presented reality) pictures of cognition, retain the condition of reflection (o'), and the theory of human cognition—a sequence of models, based on an ever broader taking into account of circumstances specific for our cognition, and therefore on the ever further weakening of the condition of reflection.

That structure of epistemology is presented graphically by Fig. 1.

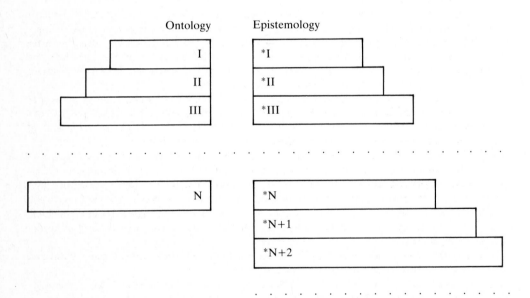

Fig. 1 Categorial ontology consists of the models I, II, III . . ., N, where the model I is objective dialectics. The categorial epistemology consists of the models *I, *II, *III . . ., *N + 1, *N + 2, *N + 3 . . ., where model *I is subjective dialectics. The categorial epistemology is composed of the theory of mind (the first epistemological models retain the condition of reflection (o'), and the theory of human cognition (further models).

6. The differentiation between the theory of mind and theory of human cognition leads to some consequences worth, as it may be assumed, noting. The first is the possibility of reinterpreting the known distinction between normative and descriptive epistemological considerations. The models of the cognitive process from the theory of mind present a certain pattern of cognition—as far as the structure of cognitive constructs and the principles of their development are concerned. Whereas the models of the cognitive process from the theory of human cognition present more realistic approaches which are simultaneously more distant from the pattern of sovereign cognition. Consequently, it could be said, that the theory of mind is "normative", and the theory of human cognition—"descriptive", but only when basing this differentiation on completely different principles. For neither the theory of mind formulates "norms", nor the theory of human cognition formulates "sentences". They both formulate some sentences, viz.—the idealizational statements. Whereas formulating norms in the theory of mind would be simply an irrational activity in terms of norms creation, for it is known that implementing the patterns of sovereign cognition is impossible; nobody establishes norms demanding states of affairs which are impossible to be carried out.[12] On the other hand, establishing idealizational statements which are to define the structure and development of sovereign cognition (i.e. fulfilling the condition of reflection (o')) permits defining our cognition in order to represent the nature and movement of reality itself. It plays, therefore, the role which is similar to the one played by, e.g., the structure of the system of the omniscient assertion logic, where the following formula is an axiom: "p is asserted then and only then, when p"; the omniscient assertor recognizes all true sentences and only true sentences—consequently knows everything and does not go astray.[13] The system of omniscient assertion indicates a certain pattern of perfect assertion in both senses of the word—idealized and correct. The theory of mind aspires towards something similar.

7. The theory of human cognition includes also, among others, models presenting the influence of social factors which weaken the sovereignty of cognition. This refers both to the internal factors related to the functioning of cognizing societies, as well as external refering to the role played by the products of those societies in broader social contexts. That type of model of sociology, deals with completely different issues than the models of the theory of mind, dealing not so much with correct cognition as with the conditions for attaining correct cognition by real cognition. What true cognition consists in, what are the conditions for transforming a theory into a subsequent one with retaining at least the same degree of truth, etc. —these are the issues undertaken in the framework of the theory of mind. Why physics seems to attain today a higher explanatory power than, let us say, economy, why the conditions of correspondence of theory are abused in economy, etc.—these are issues undertaken in the sociological theory of cognition. What is the structure of a scientific theory (whether it is defined by the relation of consequence, or concretization, or any other)—it is an issue belonging to the theory of mind. As to which social theories express the perspective of the class of owners, and which of the classes of rulers or priests[14]—is an issue belonging to the sociological theory of cognition. And so on.

Consequently, one should distinguish issues related to the characteristics of cognitive patterns—issues of the theory of mind; and issues related to the attainability and the social role of those patterns—functional issues belonging to the theory of cognition. Primary is that the issues of the first kind are in a quite definite sense pre-eminent in relation to the functional issues: one must assume solving the former in order to raise the latter at all. One must assume some conception of theory in order to be able at all to ask the question which scientific theories express the interests of which classes of disposers of material means. This corresponds to the order of the theory of mind and theory of human cognition (among others, therefore, to the sociological models of that theory) in the framework of epistemology. The mentioned order is an expression of that in the categorial interpretation of dialectics the formula of reflection (o) is pre-eminent in relation to the formula of subordination of cognition to practice (p). One must first know what cognition is, before one asks how it is affected by social practice and vice versa.

That way it is more apparent why in the framework of the categorial interpretation of dialectics—from among the mentioned in point 1—the stratification line in the ontological variant
is assumed. The very formula of subordination (p) is an answer to the functional question. On
the other hand, the formula of reflection (o) is an answer to the question belonging to the
theory of mind.

ENDNOTES

[1] For more on the subject L. Nowak, *U podstaw dialektyki Marksowskiej. Próba interpretacji kategorialnej (At the Basis of the Marxian Dialectics. An Attempt at a Categorial Interpretation)*, (Warszawa
1977), and "The Structure of Marxist Dialectics. Towards a Categorial Interpretation" *Erkenntnis*,
vol. 11, No. 3 (1977). See also papers by I. Nowakowa, S. Magala and L. Nowak in *Categorial Interpretation of Dialectics, Poznań Studies in the Philosophy of the Sciences and Humanities*, vol. 2,
No. 4 (1976), Amsterdam.

[2] For further models see: L. Nowak, *Wykłady z filozofii marksistowskiej (Lectures on the Marxist Philosophy)*, vol. II, *Ontologia i Epistemologia* (Poznań 1978).

[3] For more on the subject see: I. Nowak, *Dialektyczna korespondencja a rozwój nauki (Dialectic Correspondence and the Development of Science)*, (Warszawa-Poznań 1975), and *Z problematyki teorii
prawdy w filozofii marksistowskiej (Problems of the Theory of Truth in the Marxist Philosophy)*,
(Poznań 1977); L. Nowak, *The Structure of Idealization. Towards a Systematic Interpretation of the
Marxian Idea of Science.* (Dordrecht 1980).

[4] See: L. Nowak, *U podstaw...*, p. 250 and L. Nowak, *The Structure of Idealization*.

[5] Nowak, L., *The Structure of Idealization*.

[6] See works quoted in endnote 1.

[7] Ławniczak, J., "Rozszczepienia i unifikacje. Próba rozwiniecia kategorialnej interpretacji dialektyki" ("Splittings and Unifications. An Attempt at Developing a Categorial Interpretation of Dialectics"), in Założenia dialektyki (The Assumptions of Dialectics), (Warszawa-Poznań 1977); L.
Nowak, *Wykłady...*

[8] Nowak, L., *Wykłady...*, p. 21.

[9] Ibid., p. 86 and the following.

[10] Ibid. and I. Nowak "The Principle of Universal Nexus in the Categorial Interpretation of Dialectics",
in *Categorial Interpretation of Dialectics, Poznań Studies in the Philosophy of the Sciences and the
Humanities*, vol. 2, No. 4.

[11] Nowak, I., Nowak, L., "Zasada wszechzwiazku i systemowość prawdy" ("The Principle of Universal
Nexus and the Systematic Character of Truth"), in *Odkrycie, abstrakcja, prawda, empiria, historia a
idealizacje (Discovery, Abstraction, Truth, Empiricism, History and Idealizations)*, ed. A. Klawiter,
L. Nowak (Warszawa-Poznań 1979).

[12] Nowak, L., Próba metodologicznej charakterystyki prawoznawstwa (An Attempt at Characterizing
Jurisprudence), (Poznań 1968).

[13] Marciszewski, W., Podstawy logicznej teorii przekonań (Foundations of the Logical Theory of Convictions), (Warszawa 1971).

[14] See L. Nowak, *Property and Power. Towards a non-Marxian Historical Materialism* (Dordrecht
1983).

* * *

THEIR SKULLS AND OUR THOUGHTS

William James Earle
Baruch College Cuny

These remarks were occasioned by Rodney Needham's "Skulls and Causality." According to Needham, anthropologists have interpolated a link between the taking of heads and the supposed benefits of that practice; they have written as if their informants in the field had answered the question 'But *how* does the taking of heads procure benefits?' whereas the informants appear to find this question puzzling or unintelligible. I assume that Needham is right about what the ethnography will not sustain; based on the ethnography we should say only "The taking of heads secured well-being, and that was that".[1] One can sympathize with Needham's effort not to impose upon the natives our explanatory standards and categories; we have no reason, *a priori,* to think they share our beliefs about causality and causal explanation. But what do they believe? I am not, of course, going to try to answer this question (that belongs to anthropology), but to consider one purely philosophical, or conceptual, problem that arises in the attempt to ascribe beliefs. There may be other problems too, but one is enough to discuss in this brief compass.

The problem to be discussed arises in the following way. Suppose we set out to describe, without the imposition of anything alien, the native *Lebensform*, that is, we begin in the spirit of Needham which is also the spirit of Wittgenstein as evinced in the following characteristic remark: "Nur *beschreiben* kann man hier und sagen: so ist das menschliche Leben".[2] We can indeed describe a great deal: exactly how the natives gather the skulls of their dead enemies, how and where they preserve them, and what they, from time to time, do with them. We are being like, or trying to be like, a camera; and of course we might actually film the head-hunters. The film might be the most neutral, least deforming, way of showing what their life is like. But *showing* isn't saying: the perplexity we should feel standing at the edge of the clearing, we shall feel viewing the film if it really is a neutral conveyer of the scene. Whether we are on the scene or watching the film, we want to know what is going on, what the natives think they're up to, what they believe. The flattest, most external, least theory-beholden description of the natives (a kind of Hemingway or *nouvelle roman* flatness) will be the verbal analogue of the film: precisely not something that can be rendered false by anything the natives turn out to believe, but (like the film itself) it won't touch our perplexity.

Why can't we, to deal with perplexity, extend the descriptivist project to encompass native beliefs? This is where the conceptual problem I referred to above emerges. An external description of an agent's action [so we may define it] is a description that cannot be rendered false by anything the agent turns out to believe; an external description of a person's belief [analogously defined] is a description that cannot be rendered false by anything the person turns out to believe. (N.B., 'false', here, means 'false of' or 'inapplicable'.) It is sometimes claimed that external description even of action is impossible, though it is not clear why we can't frame such descriptions, 'thin' and uninteresting as they may inevitably be judged. Given the definition of 'external description', there can be no similar uncertainty about whether external description of belief is ruled out: external description of belief is simply logically impossible.

This has (to be clear) nothing to do with the question of how good we can become at ascribing beliefs from the external point of view, that is, how good we can become at ascribing beliefs based only on external descriptions. 'The woman rises from her chair, goes to the window and looks out; then she opens a closet, takes out a raincoat which she puts on and buttons up, walks through the hall where she picks up an umbrella, and leaves the house'. I would count this as an external description; no odd beliefs she has about what she is up to will make this description incorrect. (It can, of course, be incorrect for other reasons: the 'raincoat' may be a bulletproof coat, the 'umbrella' a gun, her standing before the window a signal to the other terrorists.) With this external description and our knowledge that it *is* raining, we say that she believes that it is raining; if we know it is not raining, we say that she believes that it is going to rain. In either case we have probably made a successful ascription of belief. Nevertheless our ascription of belief can turn out to be mistaken because of what she actually believes ('It's not going to rain, I'm not water-soluble anyway, but I might as well seem Miss Prudent to the executors of my trust who may spring for more money if they think I'm a sensible sister, etc.') whereas the description it was based upon will stand.

We ought (for the sake of further clarity) to add an utterance to the little scene we described. This time the woman, as she turns from the window, utters 'It is raining' (perhaps there is a maid, or a terrorist, standing in the part of the room we cannot see). To describe an utterance is to quote it. A quotation is like a taperecording. To describe the audio addition to our little scene, we simply say 'and then she said "It is raining"' or we say 'and then she said...' and press the button of our machine. Since quotation keeps us external, we are safe in saying she said 'It is raining', that is, uttered those words, no matter what she thinks she did or was up to. Ordinarily, the transition from direct quotation (she said 'It is raining') to *oratio obliqua* (she said that it was raining) is as unremarked as it is unremarkable: a minor shift in style of reportage.

There are circumstances, however, in which we cannot move beyond quotation. Let us suppose that the head-hunting natives interviewed by Needham and other ethnographers, when pressed for an explanation of *how* the taking of heads works, will only respond 'It just works'. We can of course say, not only 'They say "It just works"', but 'They say that it just works' and we can even go on to say 'The natives believe that it just works'. The move beyond quotation in the two sentences last mentioned is, I want to argue, merely apparent. In order to see this we have to ask ourselves how we understand 'X says that p' and how we understand 'X believes that p'. I say 'how we understand S' rather than 'what S means' because what we are looking for is a mapping of sentences to understandings [or construals or something of the sort], not a sentence to sentence mapping which, however accurate, would not explain how we understand either one. I suggest that we understand 'X says that p' as *X says what we would say in uttering 'p'* and understand 'X believes that p' as *X believes the belief we would express in uttering 'p'*. In offering these construals, I am simply borrowing the kernel of a view recently elaborated by Stephen Stich. According to Stich, when I say 'X believes that p"'...I am performing a little skit, doing a bit of play acting. The words following the demonstrative 'that' in the sentence I utter constitute the script for the play." I am then saying [says Stich] that X"... is in a belief state content-identical to one which would play the central role in the causal history leading up to my play-acting assertion, were that assertion to have been made with a typical causal history."[3] What is at issue in Stich's account, as he puts it, is a "relation of content identity that links the belief state of the believer with the hypothetical or counterfactually characterized belief state of the attributor."[4] Stich's view contributes to my argument in the following way. Where 'p' is 'It just works', there simply is no relevant belief state of the attributor, no typical causal history, no possible performance of the skit of ascription. It is obvious that, on the account offered here, my understanding of either 'X says that p' or 'X believes that p' is dependent on my prior understanding of plain 'p'. Where I really draw a blank for 'p' (as I do for 'It just works'), I can certainly say 'X says that p' or 'X believes that p', but *the most I can mean* is 'X says "p"' or 'X believes something he expresses by uttering "p"'. In my own society I may—at least—occasionally suspect that X is as blank as I am, that he is quoting 'p' to himself without being aware of it, without realizing that he has failed to give 'p' a real use, and that in fact he has no belief. Some of these will be the cases of 'inadvertent nonsense' made infamous long ago by the logical positivists. In the context of anthropology, we normally suppose that there are beliefs. Access to those beliefs, we must—perhaps sadly—conclude cannot be achieved through mere good will, imaginative sympathy, or prejudice-shedding.

ENDNOTES

[1] Needham, Rodney, "Skulls and Causality", in: *Against the Tranquility of Axioms* (Berkeley, 1983), p. 79.

[2] Wittgenstein, Ludwig, *Bemerkungen über Frazers Golden Bough* (Nottinghamshire 1979), p. 3.

[3] Stich, Stephen P., *From Folk Psychology to Cognitive Science: The Case Against Belief* (Cambridge Mass. and London 1983), p. 84.

[4] *Ibid.*, pp. 84−85.

* * *

WEAK METHODS AND SEMANTIC RICHNESS

R. Bhaskar

IBM Thomas J. Watson Research Center, Yorktown Heights, New York

0. Introduction

Artificial intelligence seeks to discover invariants in intelligence and intelligent behavior. One of the chief elements of intelligence is knowledge. This paper is about invariants in the use of knowledge. One approach to this problem is to postulate an invariant and empirically examine specific instances of actual behavior. It is then possible to decide, formally or informally, if the example supports or reflects the claims of a particular invariant. One example of an invariant is a general problem-solving method. Usually, general methods have to be substantially modified before they can help in performing cognitive acts, such as problem solving, especially in domains of special knowledge. These modifications can be called, "semantic adaptations."

To say that a particular method in a particular domain is a "semantic adaptation" is to assert the following: (1) there is a general method available for use in many different domains; (2) the method used in the particular domain being studied is similar to the general method, but not identical to it; (3) whatever differences exist between the two methods, the general or the particular, are caused by the role of specific knowledge elements in the domain. An example from everyday life will illustrate this in a simple way.

If you want a theory of traffic patterns of automobiles in the United States, it is a good idea to begin by noting a few laws that prevail over the entire country: the speed limit is 55 mph, you drive on the right, pass on the left, etcetera. Besides this, some areas have their own rules: you see signs that say DETOUR, or CONSTRUCTION AHEAD, and so on; it is easy to conclude that these signs affect traffic patterns locally. It would be nice if these *national* rules along with a few local rules were to be sufficient for understanding traffic patterns; in practice however, there are also large cities that have their own rules. To study traffic patterns everywhere, it is necessary to understand that intra-city traffic is important and large in volume; it is also necessary to realize that traffic patterns in the city cannot be understood just by understanding the rules. Instead, understanding city traffic requires knowing more about the city itself: where people live, where they work, the direction and timing of the morning rush hour, and so on. Within the city, studying traffic patterns is a complex matter, requiring study of matters that are not related to traffic in an obvious direct way, such as the economic and social geography of the city; these matters may vary from city to city.

A scientist studying cognition is in much the same position as the traffic theorist. It is definitely a good idea to begin by assuming some generality; a few general processes, a more or less uniformly organized memory and a control structure that facilitates complex information processing. Sometimes local problem conditions may allow shortcuts that are obvious at the situation; these local conditions apart, the picture is pretty clear, or so one hopes.

In practice of course, the situation is a little less cheerful; there are cognitive equivalents of the cities in our example. We call these cities, *domains*, and in understanding the patterns of cognitive processes on the whole, these domains play an important role. Here again, our example helps us to understand. We cannot understand the traffic patterns of a city just by knowing traffic laws in the city; instead, we need to learn something of the economic and social geography of the particular city. We need to learn something about the downtown area; who goes there, when or how do they get there. Analogously, we learn about cognitive processes by understanding the concepts of the domain. To understand this, we shall explore the domain with a general-purpose cognitive vehicle, the weak method (Newell, 1975). In this paper, we shall see how a domain looks when a weak method is used to solve problems in it.

Solving problems in a semantically rich domain with a weak method is a lot like driving in a strange city equipped with a map, but no special knowlege of the city. It can be done; the way it is done is probably not the simplest or easiest way. The second time around, even a novice may change to a route that does not necessarily seem, on the map, to be optimal; perhaps it does not even appear on the map.

Safe driving requires knowing your car; a weak method is a fairly general problem-solving method that is quite flexible about its inputs. A fairly common weak method, of which several brands exist, is the one generically termed "working backward." The rationale of this method is quite simple: analyze where you are, where you want to be, and plot (plan) a series of steps backward from your goal to the current (sad) state; if the plan is sufficiently detailed, and complete, actually executing the plan can be made quite trivial. However, things can go wrong. There may be error in calculation, in information, or perhaps in judgement. The weak method is now useful simply because it is general and can be used for error-recovery procedures.

1. Example 1

One place where working backward can be especially helpful is in solving a system of equations one by one. Equations of this sort appear in engineering thermodynamics. In a first course on thermodynamics, many problems involve the following four equations:

$$\dot{Q} - \dot{W} = \dot{m} \left(\frac{1}{2g_c}(v_2^2 - v_1^2) + C_p(T_2 - T_1)\right) \tag{1}$$

$$\varrho_1 A_1 v_1 = \varrho_2 A_2 v_2 \tag{2}$$

$$P_1 = \varrho_1 R T_1 \tag{3}$$

$$P_2 = \varrho_2 R T_2 \tag{4}$$

where

$\dot{Q} \equiv$ rate of heat input

$\dot{W} \equiv$ rate of shaft work output

$T \equiv$ temperature

$A \equiv$ area

$P \equiv$ pressure

$\varrho \equiv$ density

$v \equiv$ velocity

There are twelve variables and four equations. Since the equations are independent, it is possible to solve all four equations if eight variables are given. Consider for example, the following problem:

The working fluid of a flow system is air. The work done 592 lbf.ft/second. The inlet temperature is 46.1 degrees Fahrenheit. The outlet velocity is 15.8 feet per second. The heat input is 154.97 BTU/sec. The inlet area is 4.6 square feet. The inlet pressure is 16.8 psia. The outlet area is 36 sq.ft. The outlet specific volume is 0.3 cubic feet per lbm. What is the outlet pressure?

Ordinary application of the working backward method results in the equations being solved in the following order:

first Equation (3) for ϱ_1
then, Equation (2) for v_1
next, Equation (1) for T_2
finally, Equation (4) for P_2

In point of fact, a human who was asked to solve this problem did not solve the equation in this order. Instead he first wrote down Equation 1 (incidentally, equation 1 is the first law of thermodynamics), then selected and formulated the equation of conservation of mass, and *then* as a *third* step, wrote down and solved Equation (3), the equation of state at inlet. This step is third, rather than the first, as dictated by the standard method of working backward. This sequence is of course different from that predicted by a simple application of the process of working backward. This particular variation is repetitive, in the sense that the I law is consistently used as the basic equation that drives the behavior during the entire problem solving episode. The actual behavior of the human has been discussed in detail by Bhaskar and Simon (1977), especially pp. 209–212.

This particular sequence is actually a simple variant of the method of working backward. It is produced by adopting the following rule: *regardless of the problem, solve the energy equation first; after that, solve whatever equation(s) are necessary to calculate the particular variable the problem requires.* Solving the energy equation is, of course, another example of equation-solving and is itself accomplished by working backward, this time from the energy equation. Thus the "variant" we speak of essentially consists of breaking up the problem required into two separate problems, each of which is solved by a direct application of the method of working backward.

The variation from a "canonical" backward approach is not a random variation; rather it is specifically caused by the importance of the first law of thermodynamics in the semantic topography of the domain. This variation is not the only possible one; the equations of state (3, 4) are the expression of an important physical law (Gibbs' rule) as is the conservation of mass (equation 2). The central role of equation (1) cannot be predicted from theory; instead it can only be discovered by careful empirical exploration of cognition in the domain. Furthermore, it is quite important to know the equation-solving sequence for a theory of cognition that is satisfactorily complete.

2. Example 2

Physics provides another example. In elementary physics, the following equations are taught:

$$v_t = v_0 + at \qquad (1)$$

$$s = \bar{v}t \qquad (2)$$

$$v_t^2 = v_0^2 + 2as \qquad (3)$$

$$s = v_0 t + 1/2at^2 \qquad (4)$$

where

$v_0 \equiv$ initial velocity

$v_t \equiv$ velocity at time t

$\bar{v} \equiv$ average velocity

$s \equiv$ distance traversed in time t

$a \equiv$ constant acceleration

For many problems, one of these equations is sufficient. They offer a systematic and "guaran-teed" path to the solution. The expert, however, does not appear to use these equations, but instead a simpler form of the following equations using average velocity as a variable. Consi-der, for example the following three problems:

1. How long will it take a freely falling body to acquire a speed of 160 feet per second and *how far will it have fallen during that time* (Problem 6, Simon and Simon, 1978)?

2. A car moving on a straight road increases its speed at a uniform rate from 20 feet per second to 30 feet per second in 20 seconds. *How far did it move* (problem 7, Simon and Simon, 1978)?

3. A bullet shot vertically upward has an initial speed of 1600 feet per second. How long did it take before the bullet stops rising? *How high does the bullet go during this time?* (Problem 18, Simon and Simon, 1978).

In each of these, a certain distance is required to be calculated; two equations are available for this: equations (2) and (4), above. The expert consistently uses equation (2) and the novice, equation (4). The behavior of the expert here is also a special case of working back-ward. In this case the variant is produced by the rule: *calculate the average velocity first, then solve for the variable that is required by the problem statement.* This again, is a special case of solving the original problem by solving two separate problems by working backward. Thus it is a variant of working backward. Here the first subproblem has its goal the calculation of a particular *variable*. This variable is important because it allows physical intuition to play a role in solving physics problems (Simon and Simon, 1978).

As before, the point is that this choice of equations is not accidental. Where equation (4) is derived from principles of classroom physics, equation (2) can possibly be claimed as physical intuition, and indeed is so described by Simon and Simon (1978).

3. Conclusion

In two domains, experts use variants of the method of working backward; in one, thermo-dynamics, the variant consists of solving a particular equation, the *energy equation*, and then proceeding with the textbook problem; in the other, physics, the variant consists of solving for a particular variable, *average velocity*. Both of these are specific modifications of the weak method called "working backward." These modifications arise because of the the semantic topography of the respective domains. Understanding the laws of semantic topography is an important research question.

The equation-solving sequence is not a superficial description of the behavior of an expert; it reflects the effects of many different components, such as memory organization, problem solving, planning and goal formation processes, problem representation, and so on. For many practical purposes, especially those connected with learning and instruction, understanding this behavior may be the only way in which a change in behavior can be readily observed. That is to say, the equation-solving sequence appears to be systematically different for experts as compared to novices; the equation-solving sequence used by a particular human subject can be readily observed; thus it is easy to see if something has been learned or taught. To do this, however, the expert's equation-solving sequence must be recognized and understood.

What we are calling the equation-solving sequence is, of course, just one instance of an element of behavior that can become important in understanding cognition. In other domains, other elements will appear. What these elements will be cannot be determined by theory, but only by exploring the way the knowledge in the domain has accrued and has come to be used. This can only be done by careful empirical studies of cognition in specialized domains.

ENDNOTES

I am grateful to J. R. Hayes for comments on an earlier draft.
Ayer, A. J., *Logical Positivism* (New York 1959).
Bhaskar, R. and Herbert A. Simon, "Problem Solving in Semantically Rich Domains: An Example from Engineering Thermodynamics", *Cognitive Science* Vol. 1, No. 2, pp. 192–215.
Newell, A., "AI and the Concept of Mind" in Schank, R. C. and K. Colby, *Computer Models of Thought and Language* (San Francisco 1975).
Simon, D. P. and Simon, H. A., "Individual Differences in Problem Solving in Physics," in: Siegler, R. S. (ed.) *What Develops?* (Hillsdale, N.J. 1979).

* * *

5. Deskriptive Psychologie und Phänomenologie

5. Descriptive Psychology and Phenomenology

THE DESCRIPTION OF MENTAL STATES

Aaron Ben-Zeev
University of Haifa

The distinction between different levels of description is of the utmost importance in order to understand the nature of mental states. Such understanding is found, by and large, in Aristotle's view. I first mention Aristotle's view of the four explanatory factors. Accordingly, I indicate the way we should describe mental states.

Aristotle assumes that everything can be explained in the light of four explanatory factors ("causes" as they are inadequately termed): material, formal, efficient and final. The *material cause* refers to a lower level of description than that of the explanandum, namely, the elements out of which something is made. The *formal cause* refers to a higher level—that into which something is made. This cause refers to the essential functions (or the general regularity) typical of the species in question. Discussing the species is on a higher level than discussing the individual animal. The *efficient cause* is that by which something is done, and the *final cause* is that for the sake of which something is done. Both of the last causes usually refer to the same level of description. The movement of one billiard ball is on the same level of description as the movement of another ball which is its efficient cause. Similarly, the mature tree is on the same level of description as the young tree (the former is the final cause of the latter).

The material and formal causes are not separate in time or space from the explanandum; they are different aspects of it. In the case of the efficient and final causes, it is not the level of description that differentiates them from the explanandum. Rather, they refer to events that are separate—in time or space—from the explanandum. While material and formal causes refer to what constitutes a certain thing, efficient and final causes refer to causes of, and reasons for, a certain process of change. The relations in the former are not causal relations in the usual sense, since there is no actual separation between the cause and the effect. They are, rather, relations of correlation, namely, a relation of support (the lower level entities support the higher level properties) or of realization (the higher level properties are realized in the lower level entities). The efficient cause is identified with what modern science usually regards as a cause. The scientific notion of causal relations refers to relations within a certain level of description. The relation between the explanandum and the final cause is close, I believe, to the modern notion of intentionality. The final cause is that which the activity is directed at; intentionality is the feature of being directed at.

In the light of the above explanatory framework, we may explain each phenomenon by referring to at least three levels of description: (A) A lower level of description—something like Aristotle's material cause; the relation between the entities of that level and the explanandum is that of *support*. (B) The same level of description—something like Aristotle's efficient and final causes; here the relations are those of *causality* or *intentionality*. (C) A higher level of description—something like Aristotle's formal cause; the relation here is that of *realization*. While causality is taken to be a relation between two different things, support and realization are relations of correlation between two different aspects of the same thing.

It should be noted that the "height" of a certain level refers to its degree of complexity. A state consisting of a certain structure of atoms is, in this sense, more complex than a single atom; hence, it is described on a higher level of description. The higher-level properties are dependent upon the lower-level ones, but not vice versa. Accordingly, the lower-level properties are more fundamental and less conditioned.

Let us now apply the above framework to two phenomena: a water molecule, and a mental state of fear. A water molecule may be described by referring to: (a) protons, neutrons, and other elementary particles which constitute the molecule of water—this is a relation of support, that is a relation between a supportive basis and a supported state; (b) other water molecules—here we find relations of causality, namely, between an efficient cause and its effect; (c) properties of water as liquid, for example, its being wet, it pours, etc.—here we find the relation of realization, for instance the relation between a whole and its parts. The relation between the elementary particles constituting a water molecule and that molecule is different from the relation between two molecules of water. The latter relation is between two entities separated in time and space; the former relation is between two different aspects of the same thing. In a similar manner, the properties of water as liquid are not separate (in time or space) from the individual water molecules; they are just properties of a higher level of description. The relation between a mental state and a physiological structure is similar (I argue below) to the relation between a water molecule and its elementary particles, or to that between the liquidity of the water and the water molecules. It is a relation of realization. As Searle nicely puts it, "The liquidity of a bucket of water is not some extra juice secreted by H_2O molecules. When we describe the stuff as liquid we are just describing those very molecules at a higher level of description than that of the individual molecule. The liquidity, though not epiphenomenal, is realized in the molecular structure of the substance in question".[1] In this respect, higher-level properties may be a certain explanatory factor for lower level behavior. Thus, we may say that in the light of the water liquidity, further tilting of the pitcher is a reason for the individual water molecules to be in a different location. Similarly, we may describe physiological events by referring, among other things, to their mental correlates. The factor of one's will may be incorporated in the general explanation in this way. However, here also the relation between the higher-level properties and the lower-level ones is not that of causality. Rather, it is a correlation which is used as an explanatory short-cut.

One's state of fear may be described by referring to (a) a stimulation of a physiological mechanism, (b) a particular mental event, e.g., seeing one's boss or thinking about one's future promotion, and (c) the general character (structure) of the agent. The relation between physiological and mental events is not that between a cause and its effect, but rather a relation of support, or realization, between events from different levels of description. In our example, seeing one's boss (which is an efficient cause) and thinking about one's future promotion (which is a sort of final cause) are explanatory factors at the same level of description as that of the agent's state of fear, since all of them are particular mental states. It can be seen that though the final cause refers to a future event (a future promotion) it is not an occurrent, future event that finally influences the agent's state of fear; it is rather a present mental state, such as the agent's thought of the promotion that actually causes the fear. The reference to a future event has, nevertheless, some explanatory value, but it is not that of a retroactive, efficient cause. The formal cause in our example is the agent's general character (structure). Certainly, one with a different character would not be frightened at seeing one's boss or a future promotion. Here we do not refer to a particular mental state, but to a complex system of (dispositional and occurrent) mental states. The relation here is a relation of realization which exists between a whole and its parts. A whole is on a different level of description than that of its parts. We do not have a physiological event and a mental event; rather we can treat the same event as a physiological or a mental phenomenon.[2]

In the same vein, Aristotle argues that anger, like other affections, has a double character. A physicist would define anger as a boiling of the blood and hot stuff around the heart, while a dialectician would define anger as the desire for returning pain for pain (*De Anima*, 403a 29ff.). The desire for retaliation cannot be found in the boiling blood, though the boiling blood is a necessary supportive basis for that desire. In explaining the desire one should refer, as an efficient cause, to the pain suffered and not to the boiling blood.

By saying that properties belonging to two different levels of description express different aspects of the same things, I mean that what was separated, through abstraction, by our cognitive system when it used two different levels of description, may be found as the same thing in a level independent of those two levels (or in a level completely independent of our cognitive system, i.e., something like the thing-in-itself). Identification, as abstraction and negation, is an act of the cognitive system and not a feature of the thing-in-itself (if one wants to use this notion). As Wittgenstein remarks "It is self-evident that identity is not a relation between objects".[3] In identification, something that was distinguished in abstraction is being reunited by the act of identification. In a sense, there is here cancelation of a previous act of the cognitive system (i.e., abstraction), and an attempt to return to a level less independent of the cognitive system. Clearly, the notion of identity used here is different from the pure logical notion of identity. Concerning the latter, Wittgenstein rightly argues that "Roughly speaking, to say of *two* things that they are identical is nonsense, and to say of *one* thing that it is identical with itself is to say nothing at all".[4] Actually, I do not speak here about pure identity, but rather about an act of identification. This act (of the cognitive system) is correlative to the act of abstraction (or to that of making distinctions). Maybe we should speak here not about identity but about a sort of non-causal correlation.

The view suggested here is somewhat similar to Spinoza's view of different sets of attributes of the same thing. The various levels of description are different hands of the same clock; therefore, one cannot speak about causal relations between them. Similarly, one cannot speak about causal relations between a whole and its parts. In both cases there is not the separation needed for causal relations, and hence we may speak merely about correlations. My view differs from Spinoza's by not assuming a complete symmetry between the mental and the physical levels of description. Mental states emerge only out of certain complex physical systems. Hence, whenever there is a mental state there is a physical state as well, but not vice versa. The structure of a physical (or biological) system is very important for determining the possible emergence of mental states. In this sense, matter matters. This is also Aristotle's stand. He criticizes his predecessors for connecting the soul to a body "without adding any specification of the reason for their union or of the bodily conditions required for it" (*De An.*, 407 b13). In Aristotle view everything has a form, but not every form is mental. My view is also close to Hartmann's and Ryle's views. Both speak about various levels (or categories) of descriptions. Both assume that the regularity of the lower level does not unequivocally determine the events of the higher level; it determines what kinds of events cannot take place, but it leaves a few possible options regarding the particular event that actually will take place.[5]

In the approach suggested here the relation between physiological and mental events is no longer so mysterious; similar relations can be found in other phenomena as well. One important difficulty of the old enigma remains in this approach too, i.e., why is a particular physiological mechanism responsible for a particular mental state? At this stage of our knowledge we are far from answering this question. In the water example, such a question can have a meaningful answer. It can be indicated why the properties of liquidity arise out of H_2O molecules only when they move at a certain speed (at different speeds they form gas or ice). This indicates that though the types of levels of descriptions are similar in the above phenomena, the gap between the levels in the case of mental states is still the largest. Nevertheless, it is possible that future empirical research may narrow this gap. For example, such research may show that the physiological mechanism underlying pain feeling operates in dangerous circumstances for the organism; in this sense pain is a clear warning signal for these circumstances. The kind of correlations here may be similar to those existing between properties of a field and properties of its components.

Using different levels of description seems to be an indispensable tool in everyday and scientifc explanation. I see no reason why should we not use this tool in describing and explaining mental states as well. Though this tool may seem to assume too obvious and simplistic an attitude, I strongly believe it can resolve many conceptual puzzles concerning the description of mental states. As Wittgenstein remarks, an important task of philosophy is that of reminders of the obvious.

———

ENDNOTES

[1] Searle, J., *Intentionality* (Cambridge 1983), p. 266.
[2] I apply this view to the explanation of perceptual states in my articles, "Toward a Different Approach to Perception", *International Philosophical Quarterly*, Vol. 23 (1983); and "The Kantian Revolution in Perception", *Journal for the Theory of Social Behavior*, Vol. 14 (1984).
[3] Wittgenstein, L., *Tractatus Logico-Philosophicus* (London 1961), 5.5301.
[4] *Ibid*, 5.5303.
[5] See, e.g., N. Hartmann, *New Ways of Ontology* (Westport 1975); G. Ryle, *The Concept of Mind* (London 1949).

* * *

DAS LEIB-SEELE-PROBLEM IN DER TRANSZENDENTALEN PHÄNOMENOLOGIE

Hans Köchler
Universität Innsbruck

Das Leib-Seele-Problem, wie wir es aus der metaphysischen Tradition kennen, gewinnt in der transzendentalen Phänomenologie eine neue Dimension, die sich von der spezifischen Formulierung des Subjekt-Begriffes herleitet. Wenn Husserl versucht, das personale Ich als „psychophysische Einheit" zu beschreiben,[1] so ist dies nicht im Sinne einer realistischen Ontologie zu verstehen, die eine Gleichrangigkeit naturwissenschaftlicher und geisteswissenschaftlicher Betrachtung bedeuten würde. Denn nach seiner transzendental-idealistischen Auffassung ist es geradezu sinnlos, „für die geistigen Eigenheiten eines Menschen eine psychophysische ‚kausale Erklärung' zu fordern als das, was das Nötige und einzig wissenschaftlich Nötige sei, um das zu leisten, was Naturerklärung in der physischen Sphäre leistet."[2] Die Aufgabe phänomenologischer Deskription des Leib-Seele-Bezuges muß mithin auf einer anderen Ebene liegen. In Husserls Definition ist „Seele" die Einheit der auf den niederen sinnlichen aufgebauten . . ., geistigen Vermögen",[3] sie gewinnt ihre Realität dadurch, daß sie „als Einheit des seelischen Lebens verknüpft ist mit dem Leib als Einheit des leiblichen Seinsstromes, der seinerseits Glied der Natur ist."[4] Dieses „Ineinader von leiblichem und beseelendem Geschehen"[5] bedeutet, daß Seelisches niemals isoliert von der „Typik" eigener Leiblichkeit erfahren werden kann.[6] Die Mannigfaltigkeit dieser Interdependenz zu beschreiben, ist wesentliche Aufgabe phänomenologischer Deskription. In den „Ideen" bemüht sich Husserl, aufzuzeigen, „daß die ‚Natur' und der Leib, in ihrer Verflechtung mit diesem wieder die Seele, sich in Wechselbezogenheit aufeinander, in eins miteinander konstituieren."[7] Den Leib verteht er in diesem Sinne als „Umschlagstelle von geistiger Kausalität in Naturkausalität",[8] in ihm wandeln sich lediglich kausale Beziehungen in konditionale Beziehungen zwischen „Außenwelt" und „leiblich-seelischem Subjekt".[9] Die seelische Realität wird also durch den Leib konstituiert;[10] er ist gewissermaßen der „Nullpunkt" der Weltorientierung des Subjekts.[11] So ist auch letzlich das gesamte Bewußtsein des Menschen „durch seine hyletische Unterlage mit seinem Leib in gewisser Weise verbunden".[12] Mein Leib als „Nullkörper im absoluten Hier"[13] ist auch die Voraussetzung jeglicher Natur-Konstitution, die sich „in intentionaler Bezogenheit auf meine als wahrnehmend fungierende Leiblichkeit" vollzieht.[14]

Mit dieser Beschreibung der konkreten Leib-Seele-Beziehung ist jedoch − im Kontext der transzendentalen Phänomenologie − erst ein vordergründig-phänomenaler Problembestand in den Blick gekommen. Denn Husserl unterscheidet vom *realen seelischen Subjekt* − dem „identischen psychischen Wesen, das real verknüpft mit dem jeweiligen Menschen- und Tierleib das substantiell-reale Doppelwesen Mensch oder Tier, Animal, ausmacht[15] − das reine oder *transzendentale Ich*, das der Unterscheidung von „Welt" und „Erfahrung", Leiblichem und Seelischem, als das ontologisch Grundsätzlichere vorausliegt.[16] Während er der „materiellen Welt" (innerhalb der als Natur konstituierten „objektiven Welt") eine Eigenständigkeit einräumt, aufgrund deren sie „keines Sukkurses anderer Realitäten bedarf",[17] postuliert er gleichzeitig, daß das *Bewußtsein* als solches grundsätzlich „ohne eine Natur" denkbar sei.[18] Husserl glaubt, daß das Bewußtsein, sobald es „rein gesetzt ist als es selbst in phänomenologischer . . . Reduktion",[19] seine apperzeptive Auffassung als seelische Zuständlichkeit ablegen und seine „empirische Einordnung" in die Natur-Kausalität überwinden könne.

Die „verweltlichende Apperzeption" mit ihrer empirischen Formulierung des Leib-Seele-Wechselbezuges ist gewissermaßen nur die erste Stufe eines transzendental-phänomenologischen Rückganges „auf mich als das universale, absolute, das transzendentale Ego."[20] Die natürliche Einstellung", die uns die konkrete psychophysische Einheit des Menschen beschreiben läßt, wird in Husserls phänomenologischer Konstitutionsanalyse aufgehoben in der transzendentalen Einstellung, durch die das „absolute naturkonstituierende Bewußtsein" hervortritt,[21] auf das alle Natur − durch die von Husserl postulierte Korrelation zwischen Konstituierendem und Konstituiertem − relativ sein soll. Das Natürlich-Reale, dem auch der leibliche und seelische Aspekt der psychophysischen Einheit zuzuordnen sind, wird so in seiner ontologischen Bedeutung wieder entwertet: die reine transzendentale Subjektivität gilt als das ontologisch Absolute.[22] Die konkrete seelische Welterfahrung wird so als eine in der Monade des transzendentalen Ego „sich vollziehende Selbstobjektivierung derselben"[23] verstanden. Liegt der Seinssinn der Körperlichkeit − und mithin auch der Leiblichkeit, sofern sie der Naturwirklichkeit zugeordnet ist − in der Kausalität und der damit gegebenen Identifizierbarkeit und Unterscheidbarkeit als physische Individualität, so hat das (transzendentale) Ich bereits Individualität „aus sich selbst",[24] sein Fürsichsein wird − nach Husserls Auffassung − in keiner Weise durch die psychophysische Einbindung in die Raumzeitlichkeit fundiert: für das transzendentale Ich „sind Raum und Zeit keine Prinzipien der Individuation".

Dies bedeutet nach Husserl, daß der „Geist" (das transzendentale Subjekt) immer nur bis zu einem gewissen Grade „naturalisiert" werden kann,[25] daß mithin seine eigenen Analysen der Konstitution des Ego als „psychophysischer Einheit"[26] nur relative Bedeutung haben, insofern sie das personale Ich als „unmittelbar waltend in meinem, dem einzigen Leib, unmittelbar auch hineinwirkend in die primordiale Umwelt",[27] aufweisen, ohne aber in dieser „Manifestationsform" seine ontologische Bedeutung zu erblicken. Denn Subjekte können nach Husserl „nicht darin aufgehen, Natur zu sein, da dann das fehlen würde, was der Natur Sinn gibt".[28] Natur ist für ihn ein Feld „durchgängiger Relativitäten", die zum Geist als dem alle Relativitäten „tragenden" Absoluten hingeordnet sind.[29] Die Absolutheit des Geistes besteht also *trotz* der Bestimmtheit durch seine Umwelt,[30] wie sie Husserl ja auch in detaillierten phänomenologischen Analysen faktisch herauszuarbeiten suchte. Das Subjekt „waltet" in seinem Leib,[31] es besitzt ontologische Priorität. So hat für Husserl die eigentliche, konkrete psychophysische Einheit ihren objektiven Sinn ausschließlich „als Einheit des Waltens einer Subjektivität" im Leibkörper, der dadurch „subjektiv fungierendes Organ" wird.[32] „Geistigkeit (transzendentale Subjektivität) besteht nach dieser in eigentlichem Sinne idealistischen Auffassung bereits *vor* der raumzeitlichen Welt; davon ist die Dimension des „Seelischen" unterschieden, das die Weise bezeichnet, „wie Geistigkeit in der Raumwelt Lokalität, gewissermaßen ihre Verräumlichung gewinnt, und in eins mit ihrer körperlichen Unterlage *Realität*."[33]

II

An der Beschreibung des Vorganges des Todes wird nun konkret die idealistische Grundhaltung deutlich, die Husserls phänomenologische Beschreibung des Leib-Seele-Problems durchformt: in der „natürlichen Weltbetrachtung" ist die konkrete Leiblichkeit Bedingung der Möglichkeit „seelischen Seins"; dieses wird zu einem „Nichts", sobald die apperzeptiven Voraussetzungen seelischer Erfahrung − im Tod − aufgehoben werden.[34] Diese Interpretation des Todes als eines „realen Vorkommnisses in der Welt"[35] bezieht sich jedoch nur auf die vordergründige Ebene des naiven Weltvollzuges, der noch nicht zur Bewußtmachung der transzendentalen Subjektivität vorgedrungen ist. Auf der Ebene des reinen Subjekts gewinnt der Begriff der „Unsterblichkeit" eine neue Bedeutung, nicht als „Ablösung der Seele zu einem eigenen Realen" innerhalb der Welt,[36] sondern als Inbegriff der Nichtrückführbarkeit transzendentaler Subjektivität auf einen Kontext „weltlicher" Kausalitäten. Die „weltliche" Betrachtung des Todes als Vernichtung der Seele *in* der Welt[37] muß so nicht in einem Gegensatz zur transzendental-idealistischen Betrachtung stehen: „Die Unsterblichkeitslehre müßte also, wenn sie dem Sinn der Welt, wie er durch die universale objektive Erfahrung festgelegt ist, nicht widersprechen soll, eine ganz andere Bedeutung haben und kann sie in der Tat haben, wenn es wahr ist, daß die natürliche Weltbetrachtung, die alles natürlichen und welt-kundlichen Lebens, nicht das letzte Wort behalten muß und vielleicht behalten darf."[38] Husserl will in seiner Phänomenologie als transzendentalem Idealismus gerade zeigen, daß die Gesamtheit möglicher Gegenstände objektiver Erfahrung (was wir als „Welt" im natürlichen Sinne bezeichnen) nicht als im absoluten Sinne Seiendes gelten darf, daß das Absolute, „das die Welt schon voraussetzt", vielmehr der „Geist" (i.e. das transzendentale Subjekt) ist, jedoch nicht in seiner leiblich-gegenständlichen Konkretionsform − als „verweltlichter Geist" −, d.h. nicht als „Seele".[39]

Damit wird nochmals deutlich, in welch strikter Weise die transzendentale Phänomenologie Husserls zwischen Seelischem und Geistigem unterscheidet: der Seele als konkreter Subjekti-vität, die sich in realer Einheit mit dem „Leibkörper" manifestiert,[40] liegt die reine (transzen-dentale) Subjektivität als deren ontologische Bedingung voraus, welche die „weltlichen" Kon-kretionsformen von „Leib" und „Seele" als Konstitutionsformen umgreift. Damit geht Hus-serl über seinen ursprünglich realistischen Ansatz, wie er sich in der Analyse des Bezuges von Leib und Seele auch in den „Logischen Untersuchungen" manifestierte, hinaus. Während er in den „Logischen Untersuchungen" der Relativität der Existenz der Welt noch eine Relativi-tät der Existenz des Ich zuordnete,[41] dergestalt eine reale psychophysische Wechselwirkung postulierend, und den Unterschied zwischen den Bereichen des Physischen und des Psychi-schen − in genuin phänomenologischer Weise − vorerst einmal in der verschiedenen Art ihrer Gegebenheit erblickte, wird ihm dieser in den „Ideen" zu einem ontologischen Gegen-satz, der in der konkreten psychophysischen Einheit natürlicher Welterfahrung nicht über-wunden, nur verdeckt werden kann. Während in den „Logischen Untersuchungen" diese psy-chophysische Einheit noch als Grundlage des Bewußtseins angenommen wurde, ist nach der idealistischen Wende in den „Ideen" das Bewußtsein etwas in sich Selbständiges, Bewußtseins-erfahrungen können nur noch eine Einheit miteinander bilden.[42] Dies führt dazu, daß auch die konkrete Leiblichkeit des Menschen relativiert wird, da alles Wahrgenommene letzlich seinen Seinssinn als „intentionales Korrelat des Bewußtseins" erhält und mithin auch der eigene Leib als von mir Wahrgenommenes (Objekt meiner Wahrnehmung) in konstitutiver Relation zu meinem Bewußtsein steht. Die konkrete Einheit (und Wechselwirkung) von Leib und Seele erweist sich somit als Schein der „natürlichen" Einstellung. Auch in seiner Theorie der Leibeskonstitution[43] hat Husserl diese im letzten idealistische Ontologie nicht aufgegeben; diese Theorie ist vielmehr nur eine Ergänzung seiner Konstitutionsanalysen auf der Grund-lage derselben ontologischen Voraussetzungen, nicht eine Revision dieser Voraussetzungen selbst.

Auch für die Analyse der Konstitutionsform der Leiblichkeit gilt, was Husserl generell für die phänomenologische Analyse von „Gegenständlichkeiten" fordert: „Durch Rückgang auf das absolute Bewußtsein und die in ihm zu verfolgenden gesamten Wesenszusammenhänge sind allererst die sinngemäßen Relativitäten der betreffenden Gegenständlichkeiten der einen und anderen Einstellungen und ihre wechselseitigen Wesensbeziehungen zu verstehen."[44]

Hier nun eröffnet sich ein neuer Sinn von „Transzendenz", von dem Husserl nicht aus-drücklich spricht, der aber bezeichnend für jede idealistisch-transzendentale Innenwendung ist: als letzte Möglichkeitsbedingung wird ein absolutes transzendentales Ich postuliert, das jeglicher empirischen Erfahrung des Bewußtseins als deren Bedingung immer schon voraus-liegt und so − als zentrierender „Ichpol"[45] − das oberste synthetische Einheitsprinzip aller Erfahrung ausmacht. Dieses Ich ist selbst − so Husserl − „identische Einheit",[46] die sich in allen einzelnen cogitationes manifestiert. Es ist prinzipiell meta-empirisch, auch in iterierter Reflexion nicht einholbar. Es „ist das identische Subjekt der Funktion in allen Akten dessel-ben Bewußtseinsstroms, es ist das Ausstrahlungszentrum, bzw. Einstrahlungszentrum alles Bewußtseinsleben, aller Affektionen und Aktionen".[47] Als Bedingung jeglichen Wandels des empirischen Ich ist es also gerade das Unwandelbare, Ab-solute (d.h. vom Werden Losgelö-ste), jenseits gegenständlicher Relationen; denn − in Husserls Worten − „jedes cogito mit allen seinen Bestandstücken entsteht oder vergeht im Fluß der Erlebnisse. Aber das reine Sub-jekt entsteht nicht und vergeht nicht, obwohl es in seiner Art ‚auftritt' und wieder ‚abtritt'".[48]

Es ist − gegenüber den einzelnen cogito's − je schon transzendent, d.h. kein „reelles Moment derselben".[49] Es ist inkommensurabel mit dem empirischen Ich, es geht nur in bestimmte Manifestationsformen ein, durch die sich dann ein empirisches Ich konstituiert.[50] In solcher Konstitution einzelner cogitationes vollzieht sich seine Selbsterfassung.

III

Das „reine" (transzendentale) Subjekt ist somit aus dem „empirischen" Kontext des weltlichen Leib-Seele-Bezuges herausgehoben, es ist dessen ontologisches Fundament. Der Aufweis naturhafter Abhängigkeiten dieses als „Geistiges" verstandenen Transzendentalen − etwa mit dem Ziel naturwissenschaftlich eindeutiger Bestimmung des Geistigen − ist für Husserl daher undenkbar.[51] Damit wird die von ihm selbst durchgeführte detaillierte Schilderung der psychophysischen Wechselbeziehungen in ihrem philosophischen Stellenwert relativiert: seine Analyse des psychophysischen Leibes als „primordialen" Faktors bei der Konstitution der objektiven (raum-zeitlichen) Welt[52] wird durch das Diktum der „Irrelativität" der Subjektivität in ihrem realistischen Charakter wieder negiert. Der Leib als derjenige Körper, in welchem die Subjektivität mit der Realität eines diese transzendierenden Ansich vermittelt wird, wird so schon von vornherein als ontologisch eigenständige Kategorie aufgehoben. Der Unterschied zwischen Seelischem und Materiellem − den Husserl als „Realitätsüberschuß" über das bloße physische Ding" betrachtet,[53] wobei im Leib beide Realitätsdimensionen psychophysisch vereint sind und Seele dergestalt als eine „bloße Schicht realer Vorkommnisse an Leibern"[54] verstanden wird −, dieser Unterschied erscheint nunmehr als vordergründig, als nicht mehr konstitutiv für eine ontologische Wertung der Leib-Seele-Problematik. Der Leib, den er − in seiner Verflochtenheit mit dem seelischen Subjekt − als das „subjektive Objekt" bezeichnet,[55] und die Seele, die zusammen die „beseelte Realität" des personalen Ich ausmachen, welche nach beiden Seiten als Substrat kausaler Eigenschaften fungiert,[56] sind lediglich verschiedene Manifestationsformen der transzendentalen Subjektivität, in denen sie sich als „Mundanität" konstituiert. Der ontologische Idealismus, wie wir ihn an Husserls transzendentaler Phänomenologie zu explizieren suchten, läßt den Leib-Seele-Gegensatz nicht mehr als reelle Unterscheidung von seinsmäßig Verschiedenem gelten. (Damit hängt auch eine gewisse Künstlichkeit in der Analyse der Erfahrung des Fremdpsychischen zusammen,[57] da der ontologische Idealismus Husserls letzlich eine solipsistische Fiktion bedeutet, die eine Begegnung mit der Personalität des Anderen nur über eine analogisierende Einfühlung innerhalb der eigenen, in sich geschlossenen Subjektivität möglich macht.)

Der ursprünglich realistische Ansatz der Analyse des Leib-Seele-Bezuges, wie er in den „Logischen Untersuchungen" noch deutlich wird, ist durch Husserls Glauben an das „vielleicht in sich absolut geschlossene eigene Wesen" des Seelischen[58] nicht nur in Frage gestellt, sondern aufgehoben worden. Auch wenn sich in der vorhin zitierten Formulierung eine gewisse Unsicherheit manifestiert, mit der auch die Ambivalenz und Unklarheit der Termini „Seele" und „Geist" zusammenhängt, die Husserl häufig mit einander überlagernden Bedeutungskomponenten verwendet, bleibt die Tatsache bestehen, daß die „induktiv wirksame Typik" des Seelischen,[59] d.h. seine Kausalität in Abhebung vom Physisch-Materiellen, und die „induktive Kausalität" des Physischen[60] nicht im ontologischen Sinne eigenständigen Realitätsbereichen entsprechen. Das einzige, was Realität konstituiert, ist das reine Bewußtsein (reine Subjekt). In der transzendentalen epoché wird auch der Leib − als ein von dieser Subjektivität konstituierter spezieller Gegenstand, der in einer Wechselwirkung mit dem empirischen Bewußtsein steht und dadurch vor anderen Gegenständen ausgezeichnet ist − reduziert auf seinen Charakter, Gegenstand reiner fungierender Intentionalität zu sein. Seine „Auszeichnung" ist nur noch eine unter konstituierten Gegenständen, nicht eine etwa von seiner „inneren" (ontologischen) Struktur abgeleitete. Die realistische Ursache-Wirkung-Beziehung wird damit geradewegs umgekehrt: nicht der (die Verbindung zum Materiellen herstellende) Leib bestimmt das Bewußtsein, sondern das Bewußtsein konstituiert den Leib als eine spezielle Gegenständlichkeit innerhalb der Mundanität. Zwar ist der Leib als „Naturding" in die Kette der „realen" Kausalzusammenhänge eingegliedert und das empirische Bewußtsein über den Leib wiederum von diesen Kausalwirkungen bestimmt − was Husserl auch in seinen phänomenologischen Deskriptionen in den „Ideen" darlegt −, aber die „Realität" dieser Zusammenhänge muß eben im Lichte seiner transzendentalen Phänomenologie reinterpretiert werden als „Natur" im *transzendentalen* Sinne, d.h. als eine im reinen Bewußtsein „durch immanente Zusammenhänge motivierte intentionale Einheit".[61] In seiner transzendentalen Reduktion, die nicht nur ein methodischer Schritt zur besseren Beschreibung der Phänomene, sondern eine ontologische Setzung ist,[62] erblickt Husserl den eigentlichen Schritt zur universalen und endgültigen Formulierung der Realitätsproblematik, wenn er gegenüber einer realistisch argumentierenden Kritik betont: „Wir haben eigentlich nichts verloren, aber das gesamte absolute Sein gewonnen, das, recht verstanden, alle weltlichen Transzendenzen als intentionales Korrelat der ideell zu verwirklichenden einstimmig fortzuführenden Akte habitueller Geltung in sich birgt, sie in sich ‚konstituiert'."[63] Eine in diesem Sinne idealistische Position läßt die Nivellierung der Leib-Seele-Problematik auf die Ebene von mundanen „Konstitutionsformen" einer reinen Subjektivität offenbar nicht als Verlust erscheinen. Gleichwohl vermag auch die auf der transzendentalen Reduktion (wie Husserl sie versteht) basierende Phänomenologie die stets von neuem drängende Frage nach der real-ontologischen Eigenständigkeit des Bewußtseins gegenüber dem materiellen Sein − mit all den existenziellen Implikationen, die sich aus ihrer Beantwortung ergeben mögen − nicht aus der Welt zu schaffen.

ANMERKUNGEN

[1] *Cartesianische Meditationen* (ed. Ströker) (Hamburg 1977), S. 100.
[1] *Husserliana* (abgekürzt: Ha.), Bd. VI, S.479.
[3] *Ha.* IV, S. 120.
[4] a.a.O., S. 139.
[5] *Ha.* IX, S.107.
[6] a.a.O., S. 108.
[7] *Ha.* V, S. 124.
[8] *Ha.* IV, S. 286.
[9] ebd.
[10] Vgl. *Ha.* IV, S. 143ff.
[11] a.a.O., S. 158.
[12] a.a.O., S. 153.
[13] *Cartesianische Meditationen*, a.a.O., S. 126.
[14] a.a.O., S. 119.
[15] *Ha.* IV, S. 120.
[16] Allerdings scheint Husserl − in einem anderen Kontext − sich selbst zu widersprechen und diese strenge Unterscheidung wieder in Frage zu stellen, wenn er (in einer Kritik an Kant) betont, daß, „sowie wir diese transzendentale Subjektivität aber von der Seele unterscheiden," wir in ein „unverständlich Mythisches" geraten (*Ha.* VI, S. 120).
[17] *Ha.* V, S. 117.
[18] *Ha.* IV, S. 118.
[19] ebd.
[20] *Cartesianische Meditationen*, a.a.O., S.102.
[21] Ha. IV, S.179.
[22] Vgl. dazu auch die Arbeit des Verf.: *Die Subjekt-Objekt-Dialektik in der transzendentalen Phänomenologie* (Meisenheim a. G. 1974).
[23] *Cartesianische Meditationen*, a.a.O., S. 134.
[24] *Ha.* VI, S. 222.
[25] *Ha.* IV, S. 297.
[26] *Cartesianische Meditationen*, a.a.O., S. 113.
[27] ebd.
[28] *Ha.* IV, S. 297.

29 ebd.
30 ebd.
31 *Ha.* IX, S. 395.
32 ebd.
33 a.a.O., S. 132.
34 a.a.O., S. 109.
35 ebd.
36 ebd.
37 ebd.
38 ebd. – Vgl. auch Ms. K III 6 (Husserl-Archiv), S. 251a.
39 ebd. – Zum Problem der terminologischen Abgrenzung der Begriffe „Leib", „Seele", „Geist" und der damit zusammenhängenden je verschiedenen Bedeutung des Leib-Seele-Dualismus vgl. Josef Seifert, *Das Leib-Seele-Problem in der gegenwärtigen philosophischen Diskussion. Eine kritische Analyse* (Darmstadt 1979), S. 126ff.
40 *Ha.* IX, S. 393.
41 Vgl. *Logische Untersuchungen I*, Bd. 1, Halle a. S., 2. Aufl. 1913, S. 121; Bd. 2, Halle a. S., 1901, S. 337.
42 Zu dieser Deutung vgl. auch Theodor De Boer, *The Development of Husserl's Thought* (The Hague/Boston/London 1978), S. 227ff.
43 Vgl. *Ha.* IV, S. 157ff; *Ha.* III, S. 117ff.
44 *Ha.* IV, S. 180.
45 Vgl. *Ha.* IV, S. 105.
46 *Ha.* V, S. 113.
47 *Ha.* IV, S. 105.
48 a.a.O., S. 103.
49 a.a.O., S. 102 (im Original Singular).
50 *Ha.* V, S. 114.
51 *Ha.* IV, S. 297.
52 *Cartesianische Meditationen*, a.a.O., S. 137.
53 *Ha.* IV, S. 176.
54 a.a.O., S. 175.
55 *Ha.* V, S. 124.
56 *Ha.* IX, S. 133. – Zu dieser das personale Ich bestimmenden Interdependenz und psychophysischen Einheit vgl. auch: *Cartesianische Meditationen*, a.a.O., S. 100.
57 Vgl. *Cartesianische Meditationen*, a.a.O., S. 109ff.
58 *Ha.* IX, S. 135.
59 a.a.O., S. 138.
60 a.a.O., S. 136.
61 a.a.O., S. 120.
62 Vgl. die Arbeit des Verf.: *Die Subjekt-Objekt-Dialektik in der transzendentalen Phänomenologie* (Meisenheim a. G. 1974), S. 79ff.
63 *Ha.* III, S. 119.

* * *

THE UNIQUENESS-CLAIM ON PLEASURE AND ITS EMPIRICAL SIGNIFICANCE

Rainer Stuhlmann-Laeisz
Universität Göttingen

Is pleasure One or Many? This initial question from *Plato's Philebos* bears considerable import to ethical hedonism. Let us call the possible answers to the question the One-claim and the Many-claim on pleasure, respectively. In the first part of this paper I shall offer various meanings of these claims and have a look at their import to hedonism, in the second part I shall give empirical interpretations of the different formulations. However, I shall not decide the battle, since once the One/Many-question has been turned into an empirical one, this will not be a philosopher's job.

A. There are various activities or experiences one can get pleasure from. Someone might enjoy leading an excessive life, whereas someone else gets pleasure from sobriety. Especially examples like these made Plato ask the question.[1] Let us broach the problem in the following way. I presuppose that with every experience e giving pleasure to a person X there is associated a personal state F, e.g. a feeling, being the pleasure which X gets from e. On this basis we get a variety of One/Many-questions concerning pleasure, e.g. regarding only one person X we may ask whether (with all the experiences pleasant for X) F is the same rather than variable, regarding different persons—possibly all human beings—one can ask whether or not F is the same with all persons—and so on.—Putting things more exactly and distinguishing the case of only person from the case involving different persons we in detail get the following claims (the variables 'F' and 'e' running over personal states and experiences or activities respectively).

(i) The one-person-case. Here we have as the One-claim on pleasure:

> (One-pers-One-claim) There is an F such that for all e: if the person X enjoys e, then F is the pleasure which X gets from e.

The corresponding Many-claim would be the following:

> (One-pers-Many-claim) There is e_1 and e_2 such that the person X enjoys e_1 and enjoys e_2, but the pleasure F_1 which X gets from e_1 is different from the pleasure F_2 which X gets from e_2.

This is, in the one-person-case, the weakest form of the Many-claim, since it calls only for two experiences or activities yielding different pleasures. The One-claim mentioned above, on the other hand, is a very strong one, since it implies that pleasure is unique for the person X: there is exactly one personal state F which is *the pleasure got by X from any pleasant experience*. This uniqueness is due to the fact that the phrase 'F is the pleasure which X gets from e' expresses a functional identity: $F = Pl(X,e)$, 'Pl' denoting a function which attaches to each person X and every experience e pleasant to X the pleasure F got by X from e.—Note that with this interpretation the One-claim is contradictory to the Many-claim, thus they can neither be both true nor both false. The One-claim, however, is only contrary to those tightenings of the Many-claim which call for more than two different pleasures, the strongest of these tightenings being the claim:

(Strong One-pers-Many-claim) For any two experiences e_1 and e_2: if the person X enjoys both, e_1 and e_2, then the pleasure which X gets from e_1 is different from the pleasure which X gets from e_2.

This is to say that for X there are as many pleasures as there are pleasant experiences. If this claim is true, one might identify any pleasant experience or activity with the pleasure caused by it.

(ii) The different-person-case (I now use 'X' as a variable ranging over persons). Here we can distinguish two One-claims and at least three Many-claims:

(Diff-pers-One-claim a) For every e there is an F such that for all X: if X enjoys e, then F is the pleasure which X gets from e.

(Diff-pers-One-claim b) There is an F such that for every e and X: if X enjoys e, then F is the pleasure which X gets from e.

Claim (a) says that with every pleasant activity or experience e there is associated a unique personal state F being the pleasure all persons get from e. E.g. for all people who like drinking wine tipsiness might be the pleasure got by this activity. However, (a) allows what (b) denies, i.e. that pleasures vary with pleasant activities, thus (b) claims that pleasure is unique for all persons and all pleasant experiences.

Let us handle the different-persons-Many-claim in a less formal way. We first get two Many-claims as the negations of the One-claims. Claim (a') would say that at least one pleasant activity causes different pleasures to different persons, e.g., not all people might feel tipsiness as the pleasure got from drinking wine, but some might enjoy the pleasure of good taste. (b') would be the Many-claim in its weakest form, which speaking states that there are at least two pleasures, whereas the strongest claim would maintain that there are as many pleasures as there are connections of persons with pleasant experiences.

So far we h ave got different formulations of the two claims rendering precise their different meanings. Let us now have a look at the import these claims have to ethical hedonism. As is well-known, hedonistic theories hold the only intrinsic goods to be pleasant personal states, these and only these being desirable in themselves. In consequence, extrinsic goods are valued according to their contribution to those states, and these extrinsic goods are morally recommended to be chosen (as acts or states of the world to be realized or something like that). Well then, if the Diff-pers-One-claim b (the strong version) is true, hedonism—whether itself true or not—is apt to provide universal moral rules. If not, and if the strongest Many-claim is true, hedonism is likely not to be apt to provide such rules. The weaker formulation (a') would yield difficulties too, not so, possibly, the weakest claim (b').—

B. Let us now try to make things testable by giving empirical interpretations of the various One- and Many-claims. I shall do this by giving empirical content to the statements 'X enjoys e' and 'F is the pleasure got by X from e' and by rendering more precise the range of the variable 'F', so far only described as the class of personal states.—I propose the following decision-criterion for the truth or falsehood of statements 'X enjoys e':

X enjoys an experience e iff he, being in a position to choose between two states of affairs which—other things being equal—differ to the effect that in one of them he has the experience e whereas in the other one he has not, he, in the long run, would more often choose to have e rather than not to have e.

This criterion makes the question whether X enjoys an experience e or not decidable by observation of X's behaviour. If, e.g., e is the activity to play tennis, we can refute the claim that X enjoys e by pointing out a sufficiently large number of situations where X did not play tennis, though he—other things left equal—could have done.—Let us call this criterion the *Sidgwick-criterion*,[2] and let us say that a person X satisfies the Sidgwick-criterion with respect to an experience e—abbreviated 'Sidg (X,e)'—if X behaves as described above. To make the statements 'F is the pleasure which X gets from e' empirically significant, I use the fact that in a certain sense one cannot be mistaken about how one feels, i.e. if a person X truly says that he has a certain feeling then X has this feeling. This is not to say that one cannot be mistaken in one's personal situation as a whole, this is, of course, the case as e.g. psychoanalysis shows. It is only to say that one cannot deceive oneself about one's momentary feeling, as well as one cannot be wrong about one's momentary sensation: if I hear a telephone ring, then in fact, I hear this ring—be there a telephone call or not. Of course, one can deceive other persons in this respect. Therefore, let us presuppose that a sufficiently large number of persons answers truly if asked whether they feel in a certain way. Under this assumption we can decide by observing X's answer to the corresponding question whether or not he feels that way.—Now I shall say that X is in the s-state if he affirms the question 'Do you feel s?', the variable 's' here running over expressions usable to form statements 'I feel s'. Of course, with this interpretation one can be in different states at the same time, e.g. if one feels cold and hungry; thus I now regard classes of states as candidates for pleasures to be got from experiences. Well then, for every X and e there is a unique class of states which accompany all occurrences of e to X (in some cases it might be empty, though). Denoting this class by 'Occ(X,e)' I replace the phrase 'the pleasure which X gets from e' by the notion 'Occ(X,e)', and I substitute the identity-sign '=' for the word 'is' within the statements 'F is the pleasure . . .'. The variable 'F' runs now over classes of states in the sense described.—Using these substitutes and the Sidgwick-criterion to replace the expression 'X enjoys e' we can turn our various claims into empirically significant statements. Take for example the strong Diff-pers-One-claim b. Here we get the formulation:

There is an F such that for every X ande: if Sidg(X,e), then F = Occ(X,e).

However, we must carefully watch the following possible outcome of this claim's test: It might turn out that the question 'Do you feel pleasant?' is the only one of this type which all people affirm if they are enjoying something. In this case the class F consisting of the pleasant-state alone would satisfy the strong claim above. But for sure, this would not be an honest proof. Therefore, I put the following constraint on F: I call F *neutrally describable*, if the conjuction of expressions constituting the states within F is definable independent of the notion of pleasure. If, e.g., F contains only the cold- and the hungry-state, then F is neutrally describable, but if F contains the happy-state, it might be not. Thus I finally add to each claim the requirement that the respective classes F or Occ(X,e) be non-empty and neutrally describable.—With this interpretation the weak Diff-pers-One-Claim reads:

For every e there is a neutrally describable class of states, F, such that for all X: if Sidg(X,e), then F = Occ(X,e).

Perhaps, this claim is a good candidate for a true empirical statement.

ENDNOTES

[1] Vide *Philebos* 12 c 1 − d 7.
[2] I have derived the criterion from a definition of pleasure by Henry Sidgwick; vide: *The Methods of Ethics*. Book II, Chap. III, § 1.

* * *

INTENTION UND ERFÜLLUNG

Frank W. Liedtke
Universität Düsseldorf

Der Begriff der Erfüllung spielt in der Theorie der Intentionalität und in der Sprechakt-theorie eine zentrale Rolle – wenn auch nicht seine einzige Erfüllung kann ausgesagt werden von intentionalen Akten, die sich auf Sachverhalte beziehen; oder von sprachlichen Äußerungen, mit denen Sprecher sich auf Zustände in der Welt beziehen; oder sie wird als Relation zwischen einer Aussagefunktion und einem Gegenstand aufgefaßt. Erfüllung ist das Resultat eines solchen In-Beziehung-Setzens, das in der Übereinstimmung der in Beziehung gesetzten Entitäten besteht. Daß dies ungefähr das allgemeine Schema ist dafür, wie der Erfüllungsbe-griff verwendet wird, möchte ich im folgenden aufzeigen.

Umgangssprachlich wird Erfüllung von Erwartungen oder von Träumen ausgesagt, und man kann auch sagen, daß jemand seine Pflicht oder die ihm auferlegten Normen erfüllt. Ich werde hier die philosophische oder wissenschaftssprachliche Verwendung diskutieren, die sich von der umgangssprachlichen z.B. dadurch unterscheidet, daß sie viel weiter ist. Ich kann nur einige mir typisch erscheinende Verwendungsweisen aufzeigen, ohne die Heterogenität dieser Verwendungen verharmlosen zu wollen. Husserl verwendet den Begriff vielfältig. Ich möchte den Erfüllungsbegriff in seiner V. Logischen Untersuchung, die über intentionale Erlebnisse und ihre Inhalte geht, skizzieren. In dieser Untersuchung beschäftigt Husserl die Frage, worin die Akte des Bedeutens bestehen, und dies ist Teil seiner Frage nach dem Ursprung des Begriffes ‚Bedeutung'. Diese Frage wiederum geht aus seinem Interesse an einem Bedeutungsbegriff für sprachliche Ausdrücke hervor, der dann für die Aufstellung einer reinen Logik relevant wird. Die Akte des Bedeutens, oder: die bedeutungsverleihenden Akte, gründen auf dem meinenden Gerichtetsein auf einen Gegenstand, also auf intentiona-len Erlebnissen. Dieses Begründungsverhältnis von intentionalen Erlebnissen und Bedeutun-gen sprachlicher Ausdrücke thematisiert Husserl in der Einleitung zur V. Logischen Untersu-chung, und dies, indem er den Begriff der Erfüllung benutzt.

> Die Bedeutungen sollen in Aktintentionen liegen, die zur Anschauung in gewisse Beziehung treten können. Wir sprachen mehrfach von der Erfüllung der Bedeutungs-intention durch korrespondierende Anschauung und daß die höchste Form dieser Erfüllung in der Evidenz gegeben sei. Es erwächst also die Aufgabe, dieses merkwür-dige phänomenale Verhältnis zu beschreiben und seine logische Rolle zu bestimmen, d.h. die in ihm gründenden Erkenntnisbegriffe zu klären.[1]

Intentionale Erlebnisse oder Akte faßt Husserl als konstitutive Momente der individuellen Psyche auf, deren Besonderheit darin besteht, daß sie sich „in der Weise der Meinung oder in irgendeiner analogen Weise auf ein Gegenständliches beziehen."[2] Der intentionale Akt wird – möglicherweise – erfüllt durch den Gegenstand, auf den er abzielt. Husserl schreibt: „Im Bilde entspricht der Tätigkeit des Abzielens als Korrelat diejenige des Erzielens (das Abschie-ßen und Treffen). Genauso entsprechen gewissen Akten als „Intentionen" (z.B. Urteils-, Begehrungsintentionen) andere Akte als „Erzielungen" oder „Erfüllungen".[3] Ausdrücklich analogisiert er das Verhältnis von Erfüllendem und Erfülltem dem Verhältnis von einem zustimmenden Urteil (Erfüllendes) auf eine Frage (Erfülltes) im Gespräch.[4] Von diesem dis-kursiven Modell aus reflektiert Husserl die Anwendung des Erfüllungsbegriffs auf intentio-nale Akte, also Vermutungen, Erwartungen, Hoffnungen, Wünsche. Daß das, was ich inten-dierend wünsche, eintritt, merke ich dadurch, daß Wunsch und Erwünschtes eine „Einheit im charakteristischen Erfüllungsbewußtsein" bilden.[5] Dieses Erfüllungsbewußtsein koordiniert den Wunsch, daß S P sei, und das Erfahren, S sei P. Das Erfahren, daß S P sei, ist urteilsmässig. Erfüllung von intentionalen Akten erfahren wir also immer in einem ganz bestimmten Modus – dem des Urteils. So führt die Erfüllung von Hoffnung, Wunsch, Erwartung etc. zu einem Übergang zu einem anderen intentionalen Akt: dem des Urteils. Nur das Urteil erfüllt sich in einem qualitativ identischen Modus: eben dem des Urteils. Wir können so eine wichtige Asymmetrie zwischen intentionalen Akten wie Hoffnungen und dem intentionalen Akt des Urteils feststellen: in einem Fall qualitative Verschiedenheit, im anderen Falle qualitative Identität des erfüllten und des erfüllenden Aktes.

Von dieser fragmentarischen Skizzierung des Husserlschen Erfüllungsbegriffs möchte ich zu einer Verwendung des Erfüllungsbegriffs übergehen, die von einer ähnlichen Asymmetrie gekennzeichnet ist. Der Begriff der Erfüllung hat nicht nur in der Aussagenlogik, sondern seit den dreißiger Jahren auch in der Logik normativer Ausdrücke – der deontischen Logik – einen festen Platz. Stellen Aussagen, sofern sie erfüllt sind, das Bestehen eines Sachverhalts fest und befinden sich so in Korrespondenz mit der Wirklichkeit, so ist Funktion von Befehlen, das ‚Herstellen' eines Sachverhalts zu fordern, der sich dann in Korrespondenz mit dem Inhalt des Befehls befindet und ihn so erfüllt. Der Rechtsphilosoph van Loon nennt dies treffend „correspondence – theory of oughtness".[6] Eine frühe Version dieser Strategie ist in einem Aufsatz von Hofstädter / Mc Kinsey von 1939 zu finden, einem locus classicus für die Korrespondenztheorie des Sollens. Die Autoren sehen der Einfachheit halber Imperativsätze als Sätze an, die aus Behauptungssätzen durch Hinzufügen eines Operators „!" gebildet sind. Die Bedingung für die Erfülltheit des Imperativs ist die Wahrheit des Behauptungssatzes, aus dem der Imperativsatz ja als abgeleitet gedacht wird. „Roughly, we understand an imperative to be satisfied if what is commanded is the case. Thus the fiat „Let the door be closed!" is satisfied if the door is closed."[7] Daß die Tür zu ist, muß behauptet werden können. Auch hier existiert also das Prinzip des Moduswechsels. Der Imperativ ist erfüllt, wenn festgestellt werden kann, daß das der Fall ist, was befohlen wurde. Das Prinzip der Rückführung von Imperativen auf Aussagen schildert N. Rescher treffend:

> The semantical theory of validity in command inference, although distinctive and in some ways sui generis, is not primitive and self-subsistent, but should be approached from the direction of assertoric logic via the bridging–link of statements of command––termination (or command ‚satisfaction' in some cognate sense).[8]

Eine weitere Theorie, die den hier aufgezeigten Traditionslinien mindestens insofern affin ist, als ihre grundlegenden Begriffe ebenfalls über das Prinzip der Erfüllung durch Korrespondenz definiert werden, ist John R. Searles Theorie der Intentionalität.[9] Er faßt Intentionalität als eine Eigenschaft vieler mentaler Zustände und Ereignisse auf, durch die sie auf Objekte oder Sachverhalte in der Welt gerichtet sind.[10] Die Beziehung der Theorie der Intentionalität zu seiner früheren Sprechakttheorie ist sehr eng.

Ein Sprechakt ist ja unter anderem definiert als der Ausdruck eines bestimmten intentionalen Zustands, und dieser ist umgekehrt der Inhalt der Aufrichtigkeitsbedingung des Sprechakts. In seinem Buch über Intentionalität expliziert Searle diese Analogie zwischen Sprechakten und intentionalen Zuständen. Zunächst leistet er dies über eine Angleichung der formalen Struktur. Sprechakte bestehen aus der illokutionären Kraft und einem propositionalen Gehalt, haben also die Form „F(p)"; intentionale Zustände werden aufgeteilt in einen repräsentativen Gehalt und einen Modus, in dem dieser Gehalt repräsentiert wird, haben also die Form „S(r)".[11] Aus dieser formalen Analogie ergibt sich die inhaltliche. Sie ergibt sich durch die für beide Begriffe – intentionaler Zustand wie Sprechakt – verbindliche Instanz der Erfüllungsbedingung, die jeweils in einem bestimmten Modus repräsentiert wird. Searle, der die Vagheit der Kategorie der Repräsentation zwar konzediert, aber ihretwegen nicht auf den Begriff verzichten will, schreibt:

> Exploiting this vagueness we can say that Intentional states with a propositional content and a direction of fit represent their various conditions of satisfaction in the same sense that speech acts with a propositional content and a direction of fit represent their condition of satisfaction.[12]

Der Begriff der Repräsentation ist explizit nicht im Sinne von Abbildung gemeint. Zu sagen, daß ein intentionaler Zustand wie ‚Glaube' eine Repräsentation sei, heißt nichts anderes, als ihm Eigenschaften zuzuschreiben, die auch Sprechakte besitzen, also vor allem: daß sein propositionaler Gehalt eine Reihe von Erfüllungsbedingungen determiniert. Sie sind die Begründungsinstanz für Sprechakte wie für intentionale Zustände, und das heißt für letztere: „. . . that the key to understanding representation is conditions of satisfaction."[13] Durch die Analogisierung mit Sprechakten, aber auch durch die Art der Theorie über Intentionalität wird deutlich, daß Erfüllung von intentionalen Zuständen − wie Erfüllung von Sprechakten − etwas mit der Wahrheit des repräsentierten propositionalen Gehalts zu tun hat. Und eine Entscheidung darüber kann wohl nicht anders zustande kommen als „urteilsmäßig", was uns zu der Vermutung führt, daß sich diese Theorie auch in der Hinsicht der Asymmetrie intentionaler Zustände in Bezug auf Erfüllung in der aufgezeigten Tradition befindet. Ich möchte nun Searles Ansatz und die Problematik seines Erfüllungsbegriffs durch Hinweis auf einige seiner Beispiele illustrieren, ohne auf seine Analogisierung von intentionalen Zuständen und Sprechakten näher einzugehen. Man kann hinsichtlich ihrer Erfüllung mindestens drei Klassen intentionaler Zustände unterscheiden. 1. Zustände, die ich nur haben kann, solange ich nicht weiß, ob sie erfüllt sind (Hoffen, Zweifeln, Erwarten). 2. Intentionale Zustände, die ich nur haben kann, solange ich glaube, daß sie erfüllt sind (Stolz, Scham, Enttäuschung). 3. Zustände, die keiner von beiden Restriktionen unterliegen. Man mag diese Unterteilung sehr streng finden, doch ich glaube, daß man sie machen kann, ohne das Haben irgendwelcher Intentionen verbieten zu müssen. In allen drei Fällen hat die Kenntnis der Erfüllungsbedingungen einen je unterschiedlichen Status, und man sollte dieser Differenz in einer Theorie der Intentionalität einen prominenteren Platz einräumen. Ein zweites Problem in Zusammenhang mit Searles Annahmen über Intention und Erfüllung läßt sich durch eine Bemerkung Wittgensteins demonstrieren:

> Der Wunsch scheint schon zu wissen, was ihn erfüllen wird, oder würde; der Satz, der Gedanke, was ihn wahr macht, auch wenn es gar nicht da ist! Woher dieses *Bestimmen* dessen, was noch nicht da ist? Dieses despotische Fordern? („Die Härte des logischen Muß")[14]

Eine solche Despotie ist eine − zumindest mögliche − Konsequenz der Searle'schen Intentionalitätstheorie. Wenn man sie umgehen könnte, würde man interessante Fragen nach dem Wechselverhältnis zwischen Intention und Erfüllung stellen können. Es würde auch Raum geschaffen für die Überlegung, ob nicht in den Erfüllungsbedingungen gar nicht enthaltene Objekte oder Sachverhalte den intentionalen Zustand erfüllen könnten. Doch eine solche Theorie kann in diesem Rahmen nur despotisch gefordert werden.

ANMERKUNGEN

[1] Husserl, E., *Fünfte Logische Untersuchung*, hrsg., v. E. Ströcker (Hamburg 1975), S. 1.
[2] op. cit., S. 37.
[3] op. cit., S. 38.
[4] s. op. cit., S. 102.
[5] s. op. cit., S. 103.
[6] Loon, J. van, „Rules and Commands", *Mind* 67 (1958), S. 524−521.
[7] Hofstädter, A./Mc Kinsey, J. C. C., „On the logic of imperatives", *Philosophy of Science*, 6 (1939), S. 446−457.
[8] Rescher, N., *The Logic of Commands* (London 1966).
[9] Searle, J. R., Intentionality (Cambridge 1983).
[10] op. cit., S. 1.
[11] s. op. cit., S. 6.
[12] op. cit., S. 11.
[13] op. cit., S. 13.
[14] *PU* § 437.

* * *

„KULTUR" UND „VERHALTEN" IN DER PHILOSOPHIE DES GEISTES

Peter Klein
Universität Hamburg

„Warum haben die Papua eine Kultur
und die Deutschen keine?"

(A. Loos)

Lebewesen sind energetisch offene Systeme, welche ihren spezifischen Systemcharakter dadurch sowohl entfalten wie erhalten, daß sie, nach einem Regelsystem mit dem Umfeld wechselwirkend, sich dessen Eigenschaften zunutze machen.

Bei Tieren nennen wir dieses System, unter Einschluß interner Bedingungen und Antriebe, ihr „Verhalten". Es evolvierte *aufgrund* jener Wechselwirkung und sie optimierend, zugleich mit der betr. species, sie ebenso kennzeichnend wie deren morphologische Merkmale und mit ihnen eine funktionelle Einheit bildend, den „Bauplan" (v. Uexküll).

Menschen als Lebewesen benötigen ebenfalls lebenssichernde Mechanismen. Diese sind jedoch, anders als beim Tier, reduziert zu Verhaltensdispositionen, die erst durch Lernen ergänzt manifestes Handeln ermöglichen und daher durch lokale Bedingungen und Traditionen modifiziert werden können. Dabei entsteht aber nicht beliebiges Verhalten, sondern es stabilisieren sich gut ausgrenzbare Einheiten zwischen species und Individuen, welche sich eben durch die unterschiedlichen Systeme ihrer Lebensregeln konstituieren, die „Kulturen", definiert als Gesamtheit der Lebensäußerungen einer eben dadurch ausgrenzbaren Population einschließlich ihrer internen Antriebe und Vorstellungen (Mühlmann).

Die Bestimmungen von „Kultur" des Menschen und „Verhalten" der Tiere sind formal äquivalent. Ein möglicher Unterschied könnte ontologisch als Wesensunterschied von Mensch und Tier gedacht werden. Unter der Leitvorstellung einer evolutionären Deszendenz des Menschen vom Tier, mithin der Arbeitshypothese homologer Verwandtschaft ihrer Weltorientierungsleistungen, aber wäre diese Interpretation bloß formal. Unsere Analyse soll auf inhaltliche Unterschiede beider Begriffe gerichtet sein.

„Kultur" schlechthin zu besitzen wird erst seit dem 18. Jh. allen rezenten menschlichen Gesellschaften zugeschrieben, weil ethnologische Forschung die Einsicht erbrachte, daß es in ihnen keine primitiven Vorstufen der Vernunft gibt, sondern nur unterschiedliche Realisierungen der einen Vernunft als potentia. Auf u.a. dieser Basis bestimmte auch schon das 18. Jh. diese Vernunft allgemein, am umfassendsten *Kant*.

Tierische Daseinsorientierung ist gekennzeichnet durch radikale Reduktion der in komplexen Situationen bedeutsam werdenden, d.h. das Verhalten beeinflussenden Information (Uexküll, Tinbergen): Wenige Anzeichen stehen mit genügender statistischer Geltung für ganze Situationen, setzen als „Schlüsselreize" Wirkorgane in Tätigkeit, deren Funktionen genetisch fixiert, u.U. durch Lernen und interne „Stimmung" modifiziert, ablaufen, deren ebenfalls bloß statistische Überlebensfunktion sich nur dem äußeren, systematisierenden Beobachter verrät, dem Tier aber beschränkt ist auf das Gefüge von Merk- und Wirkorganen, dessen innere Repräsentanz genau so weit reicht, wie das Tier in dies überlebensdienliche Gefüge eingebunden ist: Das Tier hat nicht „Welt", sondern „Umwelt" (vgl. weiterhin Klein).

Menschliche Vernunft dürfte somit dadurch zu kennzeichnen sein, dem Menschen „Welt" zu vermitteln. Diese tritt aber nicht bloß als lebensdienlich perfektionierte, differenzierter wahrnehmende und bewirkende Repräsentanz von Reizen auf. Vielmehr ist es, mit Kant,

Beobachtung an der menschlichen Vernunft, daß sie dieses Gefüge überhöht: Vernunft fordert sich, obwohl sich als endlich und bedingt wissend, nichtsdestoweniger „Unbedingtheit" im Erkennen und Handeln ab. Struktur wie Grenzen der Legitimität dieses Anspruchs beschreibt Kant in den drei Kritiken. In Kürze das für uns Wichtige:

Wahrnehmung der Welt beschränkt sich nicht, wie beim Tier, auf programmierte Anzeichen bzw. zufällige Lernanlässe, sondern beabsichtigt eine vollständige lebensanlaßunabhängige Repräsentanz des Gegengefüges: Zwar ebenfalls begrenzt durch die Gesetze des Wahrnehmungs- und Denkapparats, aber mit der Absicht von Systematik, prinzipienhafter Ordnung und gezielter Erfahrung, somit über bloß Wahrnehmbares hinausgehend, legitimer- (Allgemeinbegriffe, Mathematisierung) wie illegitimerweise (Metaphysik). Wissenschaft, unabhängig von Daseinszwecken auf ein systematisiertes Bild der Welt gehend, und Reflexion auf ihre Methoden und Grenzen werden somit als vernunftgemäß – unbedingte Gestalt der Merkfunktion des Lebewesens Mensch gefaßt.

Nach der Seite der Wirkfunktion hin agiert der Mensch nicht, wie das Tier, momentan, situationsbezogen und antriebsgeleitet, vielmehr stellt seine praktische Vernunft sich unter das Postulat unbedingter Freiheit des Handelns, d.h. prinzipiengeleitet, von zufälligen Daseinsbedürfnissen unabhängig zu sein zur Verwirklichung des „Höchsten Gutes in der Welt". Sie kann das als *endliche* Vernunft nur, wenn sie sich eine unendliche Zeit dazu vorstellt („Unsterblichkeit") und eine gegenseitige Zuordnung von Weltverfaßtheit und Wollen der Vernunft annimmt („Gott").

Aufgrund dieser unbedingten praktischen Postulate allein ist aber prinzipiengeleitetes Handeln nicht möglich, da sie nicht „von dieser Welt" sind, sondern von einer jenseitigen, konkretes Handeln aber in der Welt der Erscheinungen geschieht. Daher muß eine weitere Vernunftfunktion die Welt der systematisch geordneten Erscheinungen und der transzendenten Postulate wechselseitig aufeinander beziehen. Die so *definierte* „Urteilskraft" tut dies erfahrungsgemäß – die Gründe führten hier zu weit – durch Entwurf leitender („regulativer") Ideen von einer zweckmäßig – wohlgeordneten Welt im Ganzen („teleologische Urteilskraft") und von einer als angemessen beurteilten Befindlichkeit des Menschen in ihr („ästhetische Urteilskraft"). Soweit Kant.

Konkretisiert sich die Einheit dieser Vernunftkomponenten, so entsteht ein Weltentwurf, der die Orientierungsleistung der Vernunft für ein vernunft-gemäßes Dasein ausschöpft. *Sofern* vernunftgemäß, nannten wir ihn „Kultur". (Eine Kultur kann sowohl als vernunfttypisch bildhafte (präsentativ-symbolische: Langer) Einheit von Welterklärung, Handlungsprinzipien und Zielentwurf auftreten („Mythos"), als auch, v.a. in „späten" Kulturen, als diskursiv aufgegliederter Entwurf. Im Mythos haben Bilder einer jenseitigen Welt mithin nicht den Charakter von „halluzinations" (Jaynes in diesem Band), sondern von „images" unbedingter Vernunftpostulate.)

Warum also haben die Papua „eine Kultur"? Das „warum" ist zweideutig:

„Inwiefern"? Weil ihr Dasein sich im Lichte eines alle Züge vernunftgemäßer Weltorientierung umfassenden Entwurfs vollzieht: Das konkrete Überlebensgeschäft systematisch überhöhend, von bildhaften Vernunftpostulaten einer transzendenten Welt geleitet, im Horizont eines Bildes vom Weltganzen und dem angemessenen Platz von Gesellschaft und Individuum in ihm.

„Aus welchem Grunde"? Weil sie sich *als* Kultur konstituiert und Identität erst erhält in vernunftgeleiteter Durchformung des sie definierenden „Welt-Bildes". Ihr systematisch-angemessener Charakter als diese Kultur zu dieser Zeit an diesem Ort wird durch ihre quasi – evolutionäre Bewährung in der Wechselwirkung einander kontaktierender „Kulturen in progress" erreicht und als offenes System stabilisiert.

Nun: „Warum haben die Deutschen keine?"

„Aus welchem Grunde" zuerst: Die kritizistische Befragung der Vernunft auf ihre Struktur enthüllt ihren Entwurfscharakter zur vernunftgemäßen Daseinsgestaltung. Ihre Verbindlichkeit wird dadurch relativiert. Diese Relativierung geschieht, da es sich um eine *Erkenntnis* handelt, mithilfe der *erkennenden* Vernunft, welche dadurch ein psychologisch verursachtes

Übergewicht im Bewußtsein erhält, besonders, da ihr Ergebnis, die Relativierung von Vernunftprinzipien, nun scheinbar ein der Bequemlichkeit sehr erwünschtes prinzipienverlassenes Dasein rechtfertigt. Dies ist daher regelmäßig das praktische Ergebnis aufklärerischen Denkens, welches sich die Reflexion auf das *Ganze* der menschlichen Vernunft als menschengemäßer Grundlage der Daseinsgestaltung erspart. Eine „Kultur" im vernunftgemäßen Sinne wird dann aber nicht verwirklicht.

Frage also schließlich: „Inwiefern?" — Weil einer solchen Gesellschaft das die Vernunft übergreifend charakterisierende Merkmal des Systematisch-Unbedingten fehlt. Wir wollen dies hinsichtlich der drei Bereiche der Venunft für unsere eigene Gesellschaft (als Repräsentanten eines Typus) andeuten.

— Hinsichtlich der *erkennenden „Vernunft"* tritt Wissenschaft zwar systematisiert, aber mit faktischem Wahrheitsanspruch auf („Galilei-Syndrom"): Zwar ist der methodische Modellcharakter ihrer Befunde — verbal oft beschworen — wohlbekannt; da aber wissenschaftliche Erkenntnis sich dem Ausweis vor und ggf. der Korrektur ihres Geltungsanspruchs durch Beurteilungskriterien der urteilenden Vernunft verweigert — hat sie diese doch relativiert! —, beansprucht sie ausschließliche Geltung und damit „praktische Wahrheit".

— Insofern sie in praktischer Hinsicht auf Unbedingtheit verzichtet, reduziert sie sich auf nützliche Verwendung und bindet damit den Menschen an seine konkrete Situationsbefindlichkeit, statt ihm Werkzeug der Distanzierung davon zu werden, mit welchem Ziel Wissenschaft ursprünglich begann und sich rechtfertigte. (Beispiel: „Erziehung zur Bewältigung von Lebenssituationen durch verwissenschaftlichten Unterricht", vgl. Klein.)

— Dieser Bindung an die Situation entspricht hinsichtlich der *praktischen „Vernunft"* eine bloß kasuistische Ethik, der eine Basis von Vernunftprinzipien fehlt, die also im philosophischen Sinne gar keine Ethik ist. Dies sogar in der wohl beachtlichsten Gestalt zeitgenössischer Bemühungen, denen um eine „Umweltethik", welche ihre Kriterien aus Partialanlässen wie „Achtung vor dem Leben", „Selbstwert aller species", „Überleben des Menschen" (wenn auch in menschenwürdigem, so doch bloß kreatürlich gedachtem Sinn) o.ä. entnimmt.

— Die erzieherische Realität ist dann noch bescheidener, wenn Schulbücher als Moralkriterien „optimale Bedürfniserfüllung von Individuen und Gesellschaft" definieren. Hier wird praktische „Vernunft" reduziert auf Antriebe des Kleinhirns, denen, z.B. in der Sexual-„ethik", psychoanalytisch zu erklärende begleitende Rationalisierungen freilich — und erwartetermaßen — nicht mangeln.

— Hinsichtlich der „Urteilskraft" schließlich fehlt ein systematisches — und insofern einheitliches — Bild von der zu gestaltenden Welt und der angemessenen Befindlichkeit des Menschen in ihr, welcher Mangel, als „Pluralismus" positiv wertgetönt, praktisches Handeln in gesellschaftsweitem Rahmen etwa in der Demokratie reduziert auf Interessenfixiertheit und deren Ausgleich als „Kompromiß" (vgl. damit das Vernunftpostulat der „Unbedingtheit") und das „Machbarkeitssyndrom" in einer Technik, der urteilende Reflexion auf den Sinn des Machbaren für das Ganze der Welt ebenso fehlt wie ein Rückbezug auf den Menschen und die ihm ästhetisch angemessene Welt.

Zusammengefaßt: Indem ihr alle Züge von Vernunftgemäßheit, mithin in ihrem Weltentwurf: von „Kultur" fehlen, wird aus einer solchen Gesellschaft eine geordnete Tierhorde, der trotz großer Leistungsfähigkeit in der Bewältigung von Lebenssituationen und trotz biologischer Verwandtschaft mit den Papua das Attribut, „Kultur" zu sein, eben nicht mehr zukommt (in genauer Umkehrung des eurozentrischen Ausgangspunkts).

Bereits Rousseau wie gegenwärtig z.B. Lorenz verdeutlichen darüberhinaus, daß damit, zumindest begrifflich, der Mensch sogar *weniger* wird als ein Tier, weil jenes, mit seinem Bauplan Teil der Natur, immer es selbst bleibt, während der Mensch, mit bloßer Disposition zur Vernunft begabt, über ein Vernunftanalog der Daseinsorientierung nicht schlechthin verfügt, sondern sich dieses erst — durch Erziehung — erwerben muß. Dieses kann dann freilich gleich die Anstrengung der (Selbst-)Erziehung zur prinzipiengeleiteten Vernunft sein.

Dazu braucht es freilich des „Stoffes" eines so beschaffenen kulturellen Umfelds. Das erfordert nicht, die durch einen Mythos gegebenen Prinzipien erneut gläubig zu praktizieren.

Vielmehr müssen sie wegen der Wandlung von Verhältnissen wie Bewußtsein durch Vernunfttätigkeit fortgeschrieben, dann aber aus erzieherischen Gründen auf ihren Ausgang bezogen werden und können dort, in relativierender Bewußtheit spielerisch praktiziert, dem vorkritischen Bewußtsein naiv bildungswirksam werden (Schleiermacher).

Sie demgegenüber neu und vermeintlich nun erst vernünftig zu konstruieren und revolutionär einzuführen wäre dogmatische Torheit, weil diese neuen Prinzipien ja ebenso aufgrund ihres Entwurfscharakters zu relativieren wären.

LITERATUR

Klein, Peter, *Umweltbindung und Weltdistanz* (Diss. U. Köln 1975).
Langer, Susanne K., *Philosophy in a New Key* (New York 1940).
Lorenz, Konrad, *Die acht Todsünden der zivilisierten Menschheit* (München 1973).
Rousseau, Jean-Jacques, *Discours über die Ungleichheit unter den Menschen* (1755).
Schleiermacher, Friedrich Daniel, *Reden über die Religion, an die Gebildeten unter ihren Verächtern* (1798).
Tinbergen, Nikolaas, *Instinktlehre* (Berlin 1951).
Uexküll, Jacob v., *Umwelt und Innenwelt der Tiere* (Berlin 1909).

* * *

ON THE STRUCTURES OF PERCEPTUAL GESTALTEN

Barry Smith[1]
University of Manchester

I

The objects we perceive exhibit structures and properties which are not indigenous to the world as it is in itself. Thus whilst the two horizontal lines in the Müller-Lyer illusion are objectively of equal length, they are experienced as being such that one is shorter than the other. There is a distinction between the structure as we experience it, the *perceived* Gestalt, and the underlying autonomous objectual formation. Now the perceived Gestalt is dependent both upon the experiencing subject and his acts and states on the one hand and upon the autonomous formation on the other, a state of affairs we might represent in a diagram somewhat as follows:

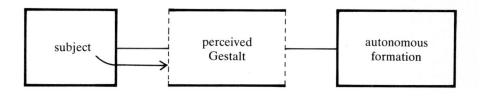

Here the lines connecting broken to solid walls of adjacent frames represent relations of one-sided dependence. A solid frame signifies that the entity in question is independent, i.e. can exist even if those entities to which it is connected should cease to exist. The solid arrow is intended to represent the relation of intentionality or mental directedness holding between the subject and the object of his experience.

Clearly there is a danger, in such an account, that we shall end up with some form of Kantianism, i.e. with a view according to which the underlying autonomous formation would cease to play a role as an object of cognition but would rather dissolve into an unknowable thing in itself.[2] This is not the case, however. For Gestalten are to different degrees transparent; they do not block out all autonomous properties of the objectual structures on which they depend. Indeed, the very fact that perceptual illusions are exceptional (or so, at least, experience tells us), suggests that Gestalten are typically transparent to a high degree. Moreover, even in cases of non-transparency we can embed an objectual formation into a larger whole—for example we can embed the two figures of the Müller-Lyer illusion into a complex involving the laying on of rulers—in such a way as to make quite specific properties of the original formation directly accessible as parts or moments of the resulting perceived Gestalt. Indeed the process of measurement, which enables us precisely to determine a large range of properties of objectual formations, is nothing other than the embedding of an object within a larger structure in such a way as to give rise to perceptual Gestalten of specific sorts.

The possibility of a systematic theory of perceptual Gestalten was first recognised by the great Austrian philosopher Christian von Ehrenfels in his paper "Über 'Gestaltqualitäten'" of 1890.[3] Ehrenfels himself however embraced a somewhat different interpretation of the way in which Gestalten play a role in our perceptual experience. Ehrenfels was writing at a time when atomistic sensationalism still retained the status of an orthodoxy in perceptual psychology. It was in no small part as a reaction to Ernst Mach's attempts to understand within a sensationalistic framework what is involved in our perception of melodies and geometrical figures that the notion of Gestalt quality was introduced. Thus for Ehrenfels the role of the autonomous objectual formation is played not by real physical things or processes but rather by individual data of sense. This gives rise to a picture somewhat as follows:

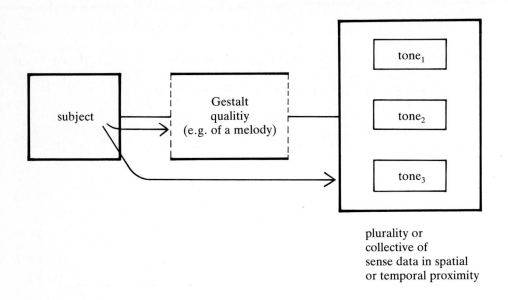

plurality or
collective of
sense data in spatial
or temporal proximity

The presence of two arrows is intended to represent the fact that, as will become clear, we have to do here with a certain sort of double intentionality.

The Ehrenfelsian account of Gestalt perception was taken over by another student of Brentano, Alexius Meinong, and its implications were worked out in detail by Meinong's students in Graz. Benussi, in particular,—whose influence continues to make itself felt in contemporary Italian Gestalt psychology—devoted an extensive series of articles to the development and to the empirical investigation of the Ehrenfelsian idea. But he and the other Meinongians introduced a numer of refinements into Ehrenfels' original conception. Where Ehrenfels had seen the process of generation of Gestalt qualities as a spontaneous one, requiring no special activity on the part of the perceiving subject, Benussi stressed that Gestalt qualities come into being as a result of more or less deliberate, specifically intellectual *acts of production*. The Meinongians were thereby able to explain how it is that different Gestalt structures can come to be associated with identically the same foundation of sensory data, as for example when the same sequence of notes is heard in different ways e.g. in reflection of the fact that different notes are taken as tonic or different groups of notes are collected together into phrasal clusters.[4] The new position made it possible for the Meinongians to acknowledge also the fact that our capacities to grasp Gestalten may differ over time, for they were able to show how the facility to perform acts of production may be affected by experience and by training.

For Benussi, as for Ehrenfels, it remains the case that the world of experience is rigidly divided into two different sorts of entity, each correlated with its own peculiar sort of mental act. We might compare this dichotomy with the classical division between matter and form. The *matter* of experience was conceived by Ehrenfels and the Meinongians as being constituted by the data given in simple sensory acts, all of which are discrete and independent, i.e. are such that each can exist in principle in isolation from all others. The *form* of experience they conceived as being constituted by Gestalt qualities (*'qualità di forma'*) given in non-sensory intellectual acts.[5]

It is worth noting in passing that the world of experience thus conceived has much in common with the world of Brentano's mature ontology. Neither Brentano nor the Meinongians have any room for physical things in the standardly accepted sense. They see the world rather as a kind of sensory surface, capable of being partitioned into constituent surfaces more or less *ad indefinitum*. To some of the sub-surfaces thereby generated a certain 'thing-character' may then be subjectively imputed.[6]

II

It is well known that the University of Prague, whose faculty included not only Ehrenfels but also Anton Marty, Oskar Kraus and other students of Brentano, was for a long time a centre of Brentanian thinking in philosophy and psychology (and indeed to some extent also in linguistic theory, economics and other fields). One of the products of Prague Brentanism is Max Wertheimer, who regularly attended lectures by both Ehrenfels and Marty, and it was Wertheimer who first seriously called into question the division of objects of experience into discrete and independent sensory data on the one hand and dependent structures yielded by intellectual acts of production on the other. In a series of clasic experiments on phenomenal motion carried out in 1912, Wertheimer discovered that when subjects—his subjects in the present case were a certain Dr. Köhler and Dr. Koffka—are exposed to two alternately flashing lights a short distance apart, then they have an experience of movement back and forth from the one to the other. That is to say, they *see* a movement: the movement is an object of perception, it is not a purely intellectual product of an act of production. But the pure phenomenal movement that is experienced in such circumstances is not a matter of discrete and independent sensory data, either: for it can be perceived only in the context of other sensory data of the given sort and is to that extent dependent on the latter.

Wertheimer's experiments signified a final brake with the atomistic sensationalism which had still made itself felt in the work of Ehrenfels, Meinong, Benussi and their followers. His experiments made it clear that it is not the case that to every part of a perceived structure there corresponds one or more sensory data which could in principle be experienced in isolation. What we perceive are, rather, complex Gestalten, some of whose parts bear at most a certain analogy to the putative discrete and independent data of sense which had formed the basis of the earlier theories. Wertheimer, Köhler and Koffka went even further in their later writings in asserting that data of sense are at home only in surrounding Gestalt structures of certain determinate sorts. Even 'isolation' signifies a special kind of Gestalt structure: an isolated coloured fleck or tone must appear in some specific way against a background of some specific sort, and then it may manifest itself either as independent and self-sufficient in relation to this background, or as incomplete, in need of saturation by something else. It may appear with the character of being 'lost' or 'homeless', or with the character of an alien body smuggled into an evironment in which it does not belong, or with the character of a disturbance in or defect of its environment, and so on. A true isolation, a sensory experience pure and simple, does not exist.[7]

The Gestalt tradition is responsible for a series of innovations which have since become part of the orthodoxy of psychological theory, and for all its faults the work of the Gestalt theorists is distinguished above all by the fact that it stressed from the very start the existence of physiologically-based universals of perception and of cognition. And whilst the term Gestalt has ceased to be associated with any single school, the problems raised by Ehrenfels, Meinong, Benussi, Wertheimer, Köhler and Koffka continue to make themselves felt, not least in recent developments in pattern recognition theory and in other areas of cognitive science.

ENDNOTES

1 I should like to thank the Alexander von Humboldt Stiftung for the award of a grant for study in Louvain and Erlangen where this note was written.

2 Exactly the same danger manifests itself in relation to the theory of *noemata* set forth by Husserl in his *Ideas* I, and indeed there are many similarities between the noema theory and the theory of perceptual Gestalten as here presented. Where, however, noemata were conceived by Husserl as peculiar abstract entities accessible to the subject only in a special sort of reflection, Gestalten were introduced as straightforward objects of presentation, and they were shown to be capable of investigation within a naturalistic framework.

3 References are provided in the bibliography of writings on Gestalt theory in B. Smith, ed., *Foundations of Gestalt Theory* (Munich: Philosophia, forthcoming). This volume also contains an English translation of Ehrenfels' paper on Gestalt qualities.

4 Wittgenstein's remarks on 'seeing as' notoriously grew out of his reflections on issues such as this in the Gestalt theory of perception.

5 This aspect of the Meinongian position will perhaps become more intelligible if we consider that its preferred examples of Gestalt qualities were: identity, similarity, difference, and all relations of comparison.

6 The view that things are themselves Gestalt qualities of sensory data was defended explicitly by Kreibig in his *Die intellektuellen Funktionen*.

7 Compare on this issue the work of Edwin Rausch, whose writings on the logic and ontology of Gestalten are among the neglected glories of post-war theoretical psychology.

* * *

BROWN AND YELLOW

William Brenner
Old Dominion University, Norfolk, Va.

I will examine a recent contribution to the philosophy of color, Jonathan Westphal's "Brown,"[1] an account critical of Wittgenstein's treatment of the subject on the grounds that it does not take place at a sufficiently scientific level. I will argue that Westphal has not appreciated the force of what Wittgenstein says about the nature of conceptual truth and the way it is related to experience.

1. Westphal describes an experiment devised by Helmholtz in which a uniform expanse of brown is viewed through a narrow black-lined tube:

> After a few seconds the brown will turn into a brillant chrome yellow, the exact hue depending on the hue of the original brown. A surface will turn brown if it is yellow in hue and dark relative to the brightness of the surrounding field. (p. 419)

From this and similar experiments he infers that the color brown is essentially a darkened yellow. And, to confirm this conclusion, he proceeds to argue that it has explanatory power. For example, he explains Wittgenstein's proposition that there is no clear brown by saying that, if there were such a thing, it would be yellow (p. 423).

Westphal emphasizes that the "unclarity," the lack of visible impurity of brown, lies in the concept, rather than in neural coding or the physics of the stimulus (p. 418). In this he is in agreement with Wittgenstein. But he rejects Wittgenstein's claim that "nature here is not what results from experiments"(*RC* I −71):

> Wittgenstein ... seems to have believed that the sciences could contribute nothing to our understanding of the 'internal' logic of propositions, merely because they use empirical methods and issue in *facts*−things which could have been otherwise. I do not believe that the application of empirical facts prevents the explanation of the impossibility of pure brown from issuing a logically necessary truth. The truth expressed in the real definition of a color must be an empirical one, whatever else it may be, but, with the truth fixed, logical consequences will follow. (pp. 429−30)

I believe that the following passage from Wittgenstein's *Lectures on the Foundations of Mathematics* on the relationship between calculation and experiment helps to bring out just how much truth there is in the preceding passage from Westphal:

> We might have adopted $2 + 2 = 4$ because two balls and two balls balances four. But now ⟨that⟩ we adopt it, it is aloof from experiments−it is petrified. (*LFM* p. 98)

Similarly: Although we might have adopted "brown equals darkened yellow" because of an experiment, now that we adopt it, it is aloof from experiments.

Making use of another idea from the *Lectures,* let us suppose that the Helmholtz experiment had been filmed. Then we may use this film as part of an empirical description. But we could also use it in another way (the way in which Westphal actually does use it). We could say that we are going to describe all future experiments by saying that they either agree with this experiment or disagree with it by so much. It now serves as a norm; this use petrifies it, makes it atemporal and aloof from future experiments. The proposition that yellow turns brown when darkened now rises (or sinks) to the level of rule, and we now describe experiments by means of it. We'd say "One experiment turned out right−the yellow turned brown; the other didn't−the yellow turned green." (Cf. *LFM,* pp. 73 & 99.)

According to Wittgenstein, to speak of "the right result" is just to say that we acknowledge it. "Because we all agree in getting this, we lay it down as a rule and put it in the archives" (*LFM*, pp. 101 & 107). Westphal would not be satisfied with this because he wants to say that "the concept" ("what it is to be brown") compels us to recognize one rule rather than another. And thus he speaks of the need to justify Wittgenstein's propositions about the geometry of brown by "unpacking the concept of brown." But this way of speaking, with its implied comparison with unpacking a trunk, is misleading. For if we are shown a trunk, and then ask if it contains clothing, we are asking a purely factual question; but if we are given an ostensive definition of "brown" and then ask whether something brown is essentially yellowish, we are asking a grammatical question—i.e., we are asking for a *further determination* of a concept, not for a sorting-out of something already determined. The answer which *we* get to this question is that brown is essentially yellowish. Had we gotten, and gone along with a different answer, that would have amounted to the formation of a more or less different concept.

That our concept-formation has no absolute validity is shown by the fact that we can imagine a language in which brown and green are said to be the same color, and in which any notion of an essential kinship between brown and yellow is vigorously rejected. The people that speak this language might be surprised, even repelled, by the Helmholtz experiment. But they would be no more tempted by it to say that brown is essentially akin to yellow than we are tempted to regard white as a yellow-reddish-greenish-blue on account of experiments with prisms. (Cf. *RC* I−72.) We are like this tribe in that we give the same ostensive explanations of the words 'brown' and 'yellow'; we differ from it in where we go on from there, what further rules we develop.

Empirical inquiry might be able to explain why we go one way rather than another in our use of the word 'brown', why we find one continuation more natural than another. But in doing so it would be telling us about *our* nature, not (as Westphal thinks) about the nature of brown. Similarly, if empirical investigation revealed why we have the arithmetic we do, it would not thereby reveal the nature of, for example, the number four. Understanding *its* nature consists in mastering the language-game with '4'. Mastering a different game would have amounted to the understanding of a different nature.

I suggest that Wittgenstein's discussion of the dawning of an aspect may help to explain our temptation to construe the grasp of an essence as something over and above the mastery of a technique. Thus in the 1932−35 *Lectures*,[2] Wittgenstein remarks that there is no phenomenon of seeing that 2+2 means the same as 4, although there is a phenomenon of seeing certain aspects—for example, seeing the dashes | | | | in pairs suggests the rule that 2+2=4. Similarly, I want to say, there is no phenomenon of seeing that brown means the same as darkened yellow, even thought there is a phenomenon of seeing certain aspects—for example, seeing the Helmholtz experiment suggests the rule that brown = darkened yellow. But in both cases we are apt to equate the seeing of an aspect with the grasping of a necessary or essential truth, forgetting that our only grounds for such a truth-claim are linguistic rules, that linguistic rules are made by us, and that what is given in perception gains regulative status only in and through our language-game. In other words, that brown is essentially yellowish is not something which we see when we look at things of those colors; what we see, rather, are phenomena which we limit by means of the language-game with 'brown' and 'yellow'. (CF. *RPP* I−619.)

2. Westphal contends that Wittgenstein "puts matters back to front when [in *Remarks on Colour*, Part III, sec. 48] he suggests that 'brown is akin to yellow' might mean that the task of choosing a somewhat yellowish brown would be readily understood" (p. 422). He thinks it obvious that the task would be readily understood because of what brown *is*, namely a kind of yellow. But, plausible though it may sound, Westphal's contention simply side-steps the thrust of Wittgenstein's remark, which (I take it) is this: The essential kinship of brown and yellow shows itself in the fact that people who have been through a certain initial training, and who have learned to speak of reddish-blues, yellowish-reds, etc., will readily, and independently, agree in their reaction to orders such as "Now point to a yellowish-brown, now to a brownish-yellow."

It appears that Westphal wants to say that the essence, or concept of brown, shows us how to use the word 'brown' properly. For he says that "grammar flows from essence" (p. 430). But if Wittgenstein is right, then essence (e.g., that brown is essentially yellowish) is what it is shown to be in our use of language (e.g., in our agreement in reaction to the order "Now point to a still more yellowish brown"). It is not something which underlies that use and which could be investigated independently of it. As he tried to show, with different examples, in the *Investigations,* the notion of an essence as a something which a term names and which justifies its use is a notion which (like the "beetle in the box") drops out of consideration as irrelevant.

"If you talk about essence−, you are merely noting a convention" (*RFM* I−74), and if you say, as Westphal does, that an experiment reveals essence, you are presupposing a convention−a standard way of taking the experiment which excludes all the other possible ways. And so experiment does not really give us a method of investigating the essence of brown which is independent of an investigation of grammar. For in talking about a "standard" or "proper" way of taking an experiment we are merely noting another convention for the use of a symbol−we are, in effect, treating the experiment itself as a symbol, "putting it in the archives."

———————

ENDNOTES

[1] Westphal, Jonathan, "Brown", *Inquiry* Vol. 25 (1982). All references are to this article, unless otherwise noted.
[2] Ambrose, Alice (ed.), *Wittgenstein's Lectures: Cambridge 1932−35* (Oxford 1979), p. 180.

* * *

KNOWING WHAT IT IS LIKE TO BE IN A STATE OF MIND

Roger A. Young
University of Dundee

Consider these two propositions

A) P knows what it was like to have the novel sensations she had yesterday at noon.

B) P knows what it was like to be in the physical state she was in during the first contractions of her first labour.

(The context is that it is P's first labour, her first contractions were at noon, and the novel sensations that pertained to her first contractions were the only novel sensations that she had at that time.)

One of these propositions specifies the object of knowledge in terms of subjective experience (sensation). The other specifies the object of knowledge as pertaining to a physical state. Let us regard A as intensional—here we have knowledge that is conceptualized as knowledge of sensation. Let us regard B as extensional, here P need not know that what she underwent were the first contractions of labour. Perhaps the knowledge that is required in B just consists of the knowledge that is specified in A. Perhaps the knowledge specified in B involves more than the knowledge that is specified in A, because the experience of undergoing the first contractions of labour involves familiar, as well as novel, sensations. But at any rate, if P lost all the knowledge specified in B, she would lose the knowledge specified in A.

In this paper I argue for the view that:

(i) knowledge of subjective experience always pertains to a physical state (there cannot be knowledge of kind A unless there is corresponding knowledge of kind B);

(ii) subjective states are necessarily objects of knowledge;

from (i) and (ii):

(iii) subjective states always pertain to physical states.

The premise (i) of the argument that I am putting forward can only be fully defended if we realise that A is true if and only if A_1 below is true, and B is true if and only if B_1 below is true:

A_1) P knows what it is like to have the type of novel sensations she had yesterday at noon.

B_1) P knows what it is like to be in the type of physical state she was in during the first contractions of her first labour.

We can generalize from the relationship between A and A_1 and say that all knowledge of subjective experience is implicitly knowledge of a *type* of subjective experience. Now a *type* of subjective experience is something that more than one person can have. Thus knowledge of subjective experience is a kind of *general* knowledge. A person can only be credited with knowledge of a *type* of subjective experience if there is some objective basis for crediting that person with that knowledge. This objective basis is provided by a general correlation between knowlede of what it is like to have a type of subjective experiences and knowledge of what it is like to be in physical states. An instance of this correlation is the relationship between A_1 and B_1. The correlation makes it possible for us to think about subjectivity in terms of types of physical being. Nagel's celebrated question, "What is it like to be a bat?"[1] is an instance of this way of thinking (a bat is, after all, an organism of a certain kind, i.e. a certain type of physical entity), although I must say that the question might be better posed in terms of a type of bat of a certain species, in a certain physical state, in a certain physical situation etc. Without this correlation there could, I claim, be no knowledge of types of subjective experience, and hence there could be no knowledge of subjective experience at all.

A challenge that might be to premise (i) is that some knowledge of subjective states is not knowledge of what subjective states are like, but is indexical knowledge, knowledge of oneself as, "I", etc., and that this knowledge does not require knowledge of types of experience. I agree that indexical knowledge is a different kind of knowledge from knowledge of what it is like to be in a subjective state, but I regard the latter knowledge as essential to subject states, and thus the argument from premises (i) and (ii) to (iii) can go through with knowledge being interpreted as knowledge of what it is like to be in a subjective state even though there are other kinds of knowledge of subjectivity.

Nagel thinks that subjectivity is characterizable in terms of what it is like to be a being with a given kind of subjectivity, and he remarks that this is a matter of *types* of being.[2] But Nagel tends to confuse the issue by explicating his position in terms of "points of view", a phrase which is ambiguous, in its metaphorical sense, with respect to whether the point of view is general or particular. Also Nagel avoids characterizing subjectivity in terms *knowledge* of what it is like to be in a subjective state. Thus his position on whether or not subjective knowledge is necessarily general knowledge is obscure. For this reason (and indeed for other reasons) my position should be distinguished from Nagel's. In the respect that we both regard knowledge of what it is like to be in a subjective state as essential to subjectivity my position is akin to Sprigge's,[3] but I differ from Sprigge because he thinks that the subject of consciousness is non-physical, and I deny this.

The reason why I regard *knowledge* of subjectivity as being essential to subjectivity is that I think that subjective experience consists of presentations of intentional content to oneself by one's own being. As with presentation of speech acts in linguistic communication a subject is only in receipt of a presentation if that subject has some knowledge of the presentation. An inattentive individual, who is being told something, may have very little knowledge of the content of what is being said but, if the individual is being told something, then it is minimally necessary that he recognizes that he is being presented with speech acts of a certain kind in a language that is intelligible to him. If this is not so, then the would-be 'teller' has not succeeded in presenting the individual with a speech act, a 'telling', at all. Similarly, in the case of presentations by an individual's faculties to that individual, it is minimally necessary that the individual recognizes that his own being is presenting him with intentional content in a mode of presentation such that the individual "knows what that mode of presentation is like" and is capable of identifying its content. (Think of an individual who is being presented with intentional content by his visual system. If the individual is concentrating on something else, the individual may have very little idea of the intentional content with which his visual system is presenting him, but he must have knowledge by acquaintance with the visual mode of presentation, thus he will know what the visual mode of presentation, is like otherwise he would not be visually perceiving anything.)

I have indicated that I think there is an analogy between presentation in linguistic communication and presentation in subjective experience. An opponent to my line of reasoning could question this analogy. Indeed an opponent might ask whether my whole approach is not led astray by this analogy. In defence of step (ii) in my main argument I claimed above that, "A person can only be credited with knowledge of a *type* of subjective experience if there is some objective basis for *crediting* that person with that knowledge". An opponent could argue that, in linguistic communication, knowledge of the language, and of what has been done with it, is a public matter, thus in linguistic communication, where P has knowledge of the communication, it is always possible in principle for another user of the language to ascertain that P does have that knowledge. Thus P only has that knowledge if it is possible in principle for another to credit him with it. But, an opponent might argue, it is by no means obvious that, in the case of P's knowledge by personal acquaintance of his subjective state, there is any requirement that it be possible even in principle for another person to ascertain that P has this knowledge.

It would be possible to argue against such an opponent by arguing that all genuine knowledge must have some basis in objective facts, and that what is objective is necessarily intersubjective. Such an argument could be developed from the fact that knowledge of subjectivity is, or at least fundamentally involves, *general* knowledge of types of being. But to end this paper I want to consider an argument that dispenses with the assumption of the public, objective or intersubjective nature of knowledge.

Let us try then to understand knowledge of what it is like to be in a subjective state in subjective terms. First of all, then, the basic modes of subjectivity in terms of which we talk of "what it is like" are surely sensory states. There are states of mind, for example some states of belief, which have content, but have no particular sensory mode of presentation. States like this, however, are not conscious states, and are not occurrent thoughts. Conscious thoughts occur in some sensuous mode of presentation or other. That is, they occur in some sensuous vehicle: a speaking to oneself in the mind's ear, or a piece of sensuous imagery, and it is this that enables us to talk of what such thoughts are like. Conscious thoughts not only have content, but they are characterized by a sensuous mode of presentation. For example, conscious memory, apart from its content, is distinguished by being presented in one sensory mode of presentation or another. In the case of sensuous memory simpliciter one has a simulation of the mode of presentation of a previous sensory state with a shift in content from the objects being presented as present to the objects being presented as past. In the case of sensuous memory, in which the sensuous memory is serving as the vehicle of memory of one's subjectivity, one has the further added content that the past sensory experience was like this present simulation of it. This reflexive content in which a present simulation is presented as *being like* another experience is the basis of knowledge of what it is like to be in a state of mind. Such knowledge consists in (1) the ability to simulate in sensuous memory that state of mind whilst being presented with the veridical content that the experience is like being in that state of mind, together with (2) the ability to produce comparable experiences using one's sensuous imagination.

A way of arguing for the view that subjective states pertain to physical states is to argue that *sensory states* pertain to physical states and that the *resemblance* which other sensuous states bear to sensory states itself pertains to a physical resemblance, i.e. the simulation of a state pertaining to the physical itself involves a physical simulation. Thus, because all subjective states are necessarily objects of knowledge of what they themselves are like, and this involves knowledge of their resemblance to some sensory state, it follows that subjective states always pertain to physical states. This argument, I would contend, rests not upon psychological contingencies, but upon our concepts of consciousness, of sensation and of the sensory. After all, in the last analysis, the basic mode of consciousness is the sensory mode of consciousness.

ENDNOTES

[1] Nagel, T., "What is it like to be a bat?", *Philosophical Review*, Vol 83 (1974), pp. 435–450, also in T. Nagel *Mortal Questions* (Cambridge 1979), pp. 165–180.
[2] Nagel (1979), p. 441.
[3] Sprigge, T., "The Importance of Subjectivity", *Inquiry*, Vol. 25, 1982, p. 146. See also T. Sprigge, "Final Causes", Proceedings of the Aristotelian Society, Supplementary Volume XLV (1971), p. 166ff.

* * *

RICHARD AVENARIUS UND DIE EINHEIT VON WELTBEGRIFF UND UREMPFINDUNG

Manfred Sommer
Universität Münster

Ernst Mach und Richard Avenarius waren sich einig in ihrem Anti-Cartesianismus. Unerträglich war es ihnen geworden, dort die *res extensa*, hier die *res cogitans* zu haben und dazwischen eine unüberbrückbare Kluft. Unter dem Titel des Verhältnisses von Physischem und Psychischem suchen beide Denker nach einem Ansatz, der diese Kluft gar nicht erst aufbrechen läßt. Und doch läßt Mach gegen die Bemühungen seines Zürcher Mitstreiters deutliche Zurückhaltung erkennen. Zu Avenarius' These, er kenne „weder Physisches noch Psychisches, sondern nur ein Drittes", bemerkt Mach: „Diese Worte würde ich sofort unterschreiben, wenn ich nicht fürchten müßte, daß man unter diesem Dritten ein unbekanntes Drittes, etwa ein Ding an sich oder eine andere metaphysische Teufelei versteht."[1]

Ich möchte in den folgenden Überlegungen zeigen, daß Mach − aus seiner Sicht − recht daran tat, dem „Dritten", das Avenarius allein zulassen will, mit Mißtrauen zu begegnen. Denn Avenarius baut auf einer formal-physiologischen Grundlage eine Art psychologischer Erkenntnistheorie auf und forciert diese dann so, daß sie zuläuft auf jenes „Dritte", in dem zwar Physisches und Psychisches eins sind, das aber unversehens theologische Züge annimmt. − In zwei Schritten möchte ich das zur Darstellung bringen; der erste handelt, epistemologisch, von der „gemischten" und der „reinen Erfahrung"; der zweite dann, theologisch, vom „Weltbegriff" und seiner Identität mit der absoluten „Urempfindung".

I

Avenarius entwirft eine Art Weltgeschichte des Bewußtseins. Diese Geschichte stellt, im globalen Maßstab, nichts anderes dar als den Fortschritt zur Wiedergewinnung derjenigen ursprünglichen Geborgenheit, die unsere pränatale Existenz im Uterus ausgezeichnet hat und die uns mit dem „Gewaltakt" der Geburt verlorengegangen sein soll.[2] *Terminus ad quem* dieses Prozesses ist das, was Avenarius den Weltbegriff nennt. Inhalt des Prozesses aber ist eine Katharsis, eine Befreiung der Erfahrung von allem, was nicht zu ihr gehört, eine *via purgativa*. Die Gedanken, die ich hier referiere, teils auch interpretiere und übertreibe, hat Avenarius vor allem in seiner Habilitationsschrift von 1876 entwickelt.[3]

Am Anfang der Geschichte des Bewußtseins steht die naive Form des Weltbegreifens. Naiv ist es, *eine* Erfahrung zum Muster aller folgenden Erfahrungen zu machen; eine neue Vorstellung in das Raster einer alten zu zwängen, ohne diesen Zwang zu bemerken: ein Verfahren, das wir bei jeder Subsumtion sinnlicher Einzelvorstellungen unter einen allgemeinen Begriff anwenden. Dies aber bedeutet zweierlei: Das Gegebene wird nicht vollständig und adäquat erfaßt, sondern nur das an ihm, was sich in die alte „Gewohnheitsvorstellung", in den vorgefaßten Begriff einfügt; und andererseits: In das Gegebene wird aus der bereits fertigen Vorstellung etwas „hineingelegt", aus dem Begriff etwas „hinzugedacht",[4] was im Gegebenen selbst gar nicht enthalten ist. Dies geschieht, wenn wir Leben in Unbelebtes legen, Substanz in Flüchtiges, Gefühl in Empfindungsloses.[5] Es ist die unter dem Namen Animismus bekannte Theorie des Mythos, auf die sich dieses Konzept des Hineinlegens stützt. Ontogenetisch ist zwar der erste Zustand nach der Geburt durch das Erlebnis von chaotischem „Gewirr" bestimmt.[6] Phylogenetisch indes haben wir dies immer schon bewältigt. Der Mythos bedeutet eine erste Konsolidierung. Das Chaos gibt es für das Bewußtsein nur als das, was es auch an seinem Anfang schon hinter sich hat. Das kann man auch so ausdrücken: Bewußtsein ist immer Bewußtsein von Gegenständen, wie labil diese anfangs auch sein mögen. Wegen des Ineinander von Gegebenem und Zutat, wegen der Beimischung der aus Begriffen stammenden Merkmale in das, was vorliegt, nennt Avenarius diesen Anfang den der „gemischten Erfahrung".

Doch der Begriff ist nicht etwa das, was, aus einer anderen Welt, zum Gegebenen hinzutritt, sondern was aus diesem selbst hervorgeht. Die Dichotomie von anschaulich Gegebenem und begrifflicher Form wird überbrückt und in die Fassung des zeitlichen Nacheinander von Gleichartigem gebracht: das früher Gegebene wird zum Bestimmenden, zum Begriff, das später Gegebene zum Unbestimmten, der Bestimmung Bedürftigen. Daß so Früheres zur auffassenden Determinante, zum Begriff wird: das verantwortet das Ökonomieprinzip; es erspart eben Aufwand, wenn man viel verschiedenes so betrachten kann, als sei es immer wieder das gleiche. Daß indessen gerade diese und nicht eine andere Vorstellung zum Begriff avanciert, daß gerade dieses das Frühere und jenes das Spätere ist: das geht zu Lasten des ‚Windhundprinzips': wer zuerst kommt, mahlt zuerst. Die darin enthaltene Beliebigkeit depraviert die so gewonnenen Begriffe, gibt ihnen den Charakter von Vorurteilen. Sieht man diese beiden Prinzipien sensualistischer Begriffskonstitution in ihrer Verklammerung, dann wird auch die Ambivalenz des Vorurteils verständlich: Vorurteile überhaupt sind höchst rational − wegen der Ökonomie. Jedes einzelne Vorurteil aber ist höchst irrational, wegen seiner Kontingenz.

Der mythische Zustand der animistischen Kultur ist kein Dauerzustand. Denn so nützlich die Subsumtion der späteren Vorstellung unter die frühere anfänglich war, um eine wenigstens minimale Distanz zum chaotischen Gewirr zu stabilisieren, so unökonomisch ist dieses Verfahren doch in sich selbst. Die Sperrigkeit der neuen Vorstellung gegenüber der alten zieht einen Kreislauf von Versuch und Mißlingen nach sich: Vergeblich wird im Gegebenen nach den hineingelegten Merkmalen gesucht; und dabei stören noch ständig die vom Begriff ausgeschlossenen, ignorierten, unterdrückten Merkmale dessen, was er unter sich subsumiert. Da ist es ökonomisch für das Bewußtsein, „durch eine zeitweilige Mehranstrengung eine neue Vorstellung zu suchen, in der es ruhen könne."[7]

Der Schritt aus dieser Naivität heraus bedeutet dreierlei: einmal Differenzierung, weil nicht das eine nach Maßgabe des anderen, sondern jedes je für sich aufgefaßt wird. Zweitens Adäquatheit, weil mehr Merkmale des Gegebenen auch erfahren werden, weil die Vorstellungen den Dingen, deren Vorstellungen sie sind, besser entsprechen. Und drittens Reinigung, weil die Zutaten wegfallen, keine nichtgegebenen Merkmale mehr ‚erfahren' werden, den Dingen durch die Vorstellungen von ihnen nichts mehr beigefügt wird, was sie nicht selbst enthalten. Das ist ein Schritt, der zugleich das Prinzip eines ganzen Fortschritts enthält: dieser ist nichts anderes als die Sequenz solcher Schritte, freilich mit einem kumulativen Effekt: immer feinere Differenziertheit, immer nähere Adäquatheit, immer weniger Zutaten. Insofern zeichnet der erste Schritt auch schon das Ende vor, zu dem seine Wiederholung schließlich führen wird. Die Begriffe, die wir haben, werden so verfeinert und vermehrt, daß ihre Vielfalt und Nuanciertheit dem, was durch sie apperzipiert wird, schließlich vollkommen adäquat ist: die Apperzeption leugnet nichts mehr weg und oktroyiert nichts mehr auf. Am Ende steht also die „reine Erfahrung": alles Gegebene ist frei von „Zumischungen".[8]

II

Ich komme zum zweiten Schritt meiner Überlegungen, zu dem, was ich, etwas pointiert, als theologisch bezeichnet habe, weil es darin um den Inbegriff aller Prädikate und um dessen Identität mit der absoluten Empfindung geht. − Man muß sehen, daß Begriffsdifferenzierung nicht gleichzusetzen ist mit der Herstellung eines Weltkatalogs, in dem für jedes Ding eine vollkommen adäquate Beschreibung oder eine Liste aller seiner Merkmale enthalten wäre. Von vorrangiger Bedeutung ist gar nicht, wie die einzelnen Begriffe im Endstadium der Reinigung je für sich und in sich verfaßt sind, sondern daß sie wesentlich Begriffe in einem Begriffssystem sind. Der alte Begriff bleibt nach einem Differenzierungsschritt nicht einfach isoliert neben dem neuen Begriff stehen. Vielmehr sind beide in den ihnen gemeinsamen Komponenten verbunden. Zwei verschiedene Gegenstände, von denen der eine diesem, der andere jenem Begriff entspricht, werden zunächst als gleich aufgefaßt durch gerade jene Merkmale, in denen die beiden Begriffe übereinstimmen; dann erst tritt der Bestimmungsvorgang in die Verzweigung ein. Simultan mit der begrifflichen Dissoziation entsteht ein allgemeinerer Begriff, der nur die gemeinsamen Merkmale beinhaltet. Begriffsdifferenzierung bedeutet also, daß die Begriffe zugleich allgemeiner *und* konkreter werden: Jeder Schritt erzeugt nicht nur neue, dem Gegebenen besser angemessene Begriffe, sondern er fördert auch das zutage, worin die neuen Begriffe zusammenhängen, also die Merkmale, die den voneinander verschiedenen Gegenständen dieser Begriffe gemeinsam sind. Und auch diese Merkmalskombination, dieses Wenige, worin die auseinandergefalteten Begriffe übereinstimmen, ist ein Begriff. Auch er faßt Gegebenes auf, und zwar mehr Einzelvorstellungen, diese aber nicht so genau wie die Begriffe, die mehr Merkmale enthalten: es ist das altbekannte logische Prinzip, daß Umfang und Inhalt eines Begriffs sich zueinander umgekehrt proportional verhalten.

Begriffsdifferenzierung führt also zu einem Begriffssystem, in sich nach Graden der Allgemeinheit gestuft, als ein in alle Richtungen sich verzweigendes Diagramm abbildbar. Auffassung einer individuellen Vorstellung ist dann, am Ende dieses Differenzierungsprozesses, ein Durchlaufen des Diagramms, eine Serie von Verzweigungen, die vom Allgemeinsten bis zum Bestimmtesten führt. Und da diese Differenzierung selbst ein Vorgang der Übung und Gewöhnung ist, wird verständlich, daß diese Apperzeption zuletzt so schnell geschieht, die Serie der Determination so rasch durchlaufen wird, daß, wie Avenarius sagt, „sich alles gleichsam von selbst ergibt".[9] Schlagartig, mühelos, selbstverständlich.

Im Mittelpunkt des zum Konkreten hinstrahlenden Systems steht, als allgemeinster Begriff, die „Zentralvorstellung", die „durch ihre günstige Stellung und häufige Anwendung immer leichter und selbstverständlicher wird" − und am Ende ganz unmerkbar und völlig selbstverständlich geworden ist:[10] völlig nivelliert, eingeebnet, unabgehoben. Diese „Zentralvorstellung" ist nichts anderes als der „Weltbegriff", das also, was allem zukommt, was in der Welt vorkommt; der Begriff, unter den alles, was gegeben werden kann, subsumierbar ist; der alles erfaßt, aber es am wenigsten bestimmt: „Der philosophische Begriff", so formuliert das Avenarius, „enthält die Welt nur in der abstrakten Form des Gemeinsamen aller Einzeldinge".[11] Es gibt also eine systematische Beziehung zwischen dem Ökonomieprinzip, der Erfahrungsreinigung und der Herausarbeitung des Weltbegriffs.

Der Weltbegriff ist insofern intuitiv, als er eine unmittelbare und ursprüngliche Weltvertrautheit gewährt: Hinschauen und Hinnehmen sind eins, das Auffassen mit ihm gelingt sofort und mühelos, ohne jeden Kraftverbrauch. Alles, was auf uns zukommt, ist ein *déjà vu*. Der Weltbegriff aktualisiert sich als „Sicherheitsgefühl"; er ist der Limes von Selbstverständlichkeit, die Gewohnheitsvorstellung schlechthin. Aber auch das ist der Weltbegriff: Inbegriff von Dürftigkeit, Superlativ von Leere. Der Begriff „Sein" bezieht sich auf alles und bedeutet nichts, er trifft immer zu, aber sagt nichts aus. Das aber heißt: er ist das universale Vorurteil: bei jeder kognitiven Regung ist er schon im Spiel; das unausrottbare Vorurteil: er entsteht ja gerade durch Elimination von Zutaten; das unbestimmbare Vorurteil: nichts von dem, was man wissen kann, kann sein Inhalt sein. Der Weltbegriff ist das absolute Vorurteil.

Zweierlei ist an dem hier betrachteten Endzustand der Geschichte des Bewußtseins bedeutsam: Zum einen: Als Grenzwert eines Anpassungsprozesses sind die Begriffe von dem, was durch sie aufgefaßt wird, gar nicht mehr unterschieden. Am Limes der Erkenntnis bricht die Grenze zwischen der Qualität, die einem Gegenstand zukommt, und dem Prädikat, das Teil eines Begriffs ist, zusammen. Qualitäten und Prädikate, Gegenstände und Begriffe werden eins. Das zweite aber ist dies: Als Resultat von Anpassung, Übung, Gewöhnung kommt die Leichtigkeit und Schnelligkeit des Erfassens nicht nur der „Zentralvorstellung", also dem Weltbegriff, zu, sondern allen Begriffen. Denkt man sich dieses Auffassen beliebig beschleunigt − und das darf man am idealen Ende −, so bedeutet das die Koinzidenz aller Begriffe in einem einzigen, die Kontraktion der Radien im Zentrum, eine Kontraktion, die wegen der

Identität der konkretesten Begriffe mit ihren Gegenständen auch diese Gegenstände mit in sich hineinzieht. So wird der Weltbegriff zur Identität von Welt und Begriff. Das ideale System stellt sich dar als Punkt. Man sieht, wie nahe der Positivismus dem Neuplatonismus ist.

Für den absoluten Punkt, den der Weltbegriff darstellt, hat Avenarius noch eine andere Bezeichnung, nämlich „Urempfindung".[12] Wenn man die Trennwand zwischen Objekt und Begriff, zwischen Physischem und Psychischem zum Verschwinden bringt, so bleibt als Resultat dieser Indifferenz die Empfindung übrig. Empfindungen repräsentieren uns nun nicht mehr Qualitäten; und sie werden auch nicht mehr zu Prädikaten in Urteilen transformiert; vielmehr enthält die Empfindung das ungeschieden in sich, was ehedem in Qualität und Prädikat auseinandergerissen war. ‚Die Empfindung' — das gibt es freilich so nicht, sondern immer nur in Gestalt absolut individuierter Empfindungen. Diese Individuen lassen sich in einer bunten Mannigfaltigkeit zerstreut denken. Wirklichkeit wäre dann bloß eine Art „Kaleidoskop", in dem sich „Empfindungsmosaikstückchen" zu einer ephemeren und prekären Ordnung zusammengefügt haben. Empfindungen können aber, so betont Avenarius, ineinander übergehen und auseinander hervorgehen. Der Empiriokritizist, hier ganz Neuplatoniker, nimmt an, daß „alle differenten Empfindungen aus einer ursprünglich gleichinhaltlichen Empfindung durch Selbstdifferenzierung entstanden seien". Diese in der Tat „eminent monistische Ansicht" gipfelt im Postulat einer „einheitlichen Urempfindung".[13] Die Urempfindung ist das Integral aller Empfindungen, das, woraus sie alle hervorgehen, woraus sie entspringen: sie ist der Punkt der Kontraktion aller Empfindungen in eine, aber auch, sofern diese ehedem als Qualitäten von Gegenständen gedeutet wurden, der Punkt dichtester Implikation aller möglichen Prädikate: ein göttlicher Intellekt, Kants „transzendentales Ideal".[14] — Wer sagt, daß es doch um den Weltbegriff, nicht um den Gottesbegriff gehen sollte, mag bedenken, was es bedeutet, wenn man das nicht mehr auseinanderhalten kann.[15]

* * *

ANMERKUNGEN

1 Mach, E., *Erkenntnis und Irrtum* (Leipzig ⁵1926 [¹1905]), S. 13 Anm.
2 Avenarius, R., *Kritik der reinen Erfahrung* (Leipzig ³1921/28 [¹1888/90]), Bd. I, S. 63f, 91.
3 Avenarius, R., *Philosophie als Denken der Welt gemäß dem Prinzip des kleinsten Kraftmaßes. Prolegomena zu einer Kritik der reinen Erfahrung* (Berlin ³1917 [¹1876]).
4 Ebd., S. 34f.
5 Ebd., S. 80; Avenarius bezieht sich hier auf das ‚animistische' Standardwerk: Edward B. Tylor, *Die Anfänge der Kultur* (Leipzig 1873).
6 Avenarius, R., *Kritik der reinen Erfahrung*, Bd. II, S. 58.
7 Avenarius, R., *Philosophie als Denken der Welt*, S. 34.
8 Ebd., S. 47.
9 Ebd., S. 17.
10 Ebd., S. 15f.
11 Ebd., S. 33.
12 Ebd., S. 85.
13 Ebd., S. 70, 85.
14 Kant, *Kritik der reinen Vernunft*, A 571ff, B 599ff.
15 Zu den spinozistischen Implikationen des Empiriokritizismus und deren Bedeutung für die Phänomenologie vgl.: M. Sommer, *Husserl und der frühe Positivismus* (Frankfurt a. M. 1985).

* * *

DESCARTES—BETWEEN SOLIPSISM AND RATIONALISM

Sara Yaretzky-Kahansky
Tel-Aviv University

I

At the time when I was working on Descartes' methodological solipsism, it occured to me that there was more than a superficial analogy between the predicament of that philosopher and the Aesopian fable about "The Fox and the Vineyard.". It seemed to me that the fable's protagonist, Renard, is but Renard Descartes.

Just like Aesop's fox, Renard Descartes must lose weight in order to be able to break into the vineyard of certain knowledge, that is, he does not have to lose physical, but rather mental weight. He has to doubt and reject all beliefs, except one, the *Cogito*. The latter is found to be nothing more than a general name for dissolute thoughts, but once Renard Descartes is in the vineyard of it, he can freely enjoy the grapes, that is, he can haze his illusion and let his fantasies run wild.

Only when the times come to leave the vineyard and bring its message of truth to the other foxes outside, Renard realizes that he cannot get out because he has eaten too much and has developed a stomach upset. He realizes that the true treasure he had hoped to find in the vineyard might be a sheer delusion too. At this point, he understands that in order to escape his terrible situation, he will have to lose weight and become thin again, i.e., he will have to disown all his foxy and vineyardlike thoughts, and to place his trust only in the good God, who's existence and righteousness he is sure of having succeeded in proving. Now surely he is saved, and this is the story's happy end.

II

After all, why didn't Renard Descartes remain in the vineyard forever? Was it only because God let him out? What would have happened if God had refused to liberate Renard on the basis of a conscientious objection? Descartes not only "brought God to exist" by a sheer thought, but also "endowed" Him with the morality of human beings. Why didn't he apply the hypothesis about the epistemic categories of the Evil Genius to the domain of the moral categories of the good God? For what Descartes considers to be morally good may totally differ from that which God considers to be morally good. Just as it may be that only the Evil Genius possesses the true knowledge, so may God *alone* possess the right moral. Wouldn't it be possible that God really thought that it would be better for Renard Descartes if he remained in the vineyard? For *we* shall not blame an unjustified arbitrariness on Him, although Descartes himself did it in several contexts in which he presents his concept of God. And if it really wasn't God who let him out from there, was it perhaps the Evil Genius who wanted to harm him? We all know how much Descartes suffered while in the vineyard, not knowing in what to believe and whom to recall, but who is *he*, poor creature, to be able to know what is good for him and what is bad? There is just one thing which is clear: Had Descartes made all these hypotheses of ours, and they should not necessarily concern God and his goodness, he would have become slim and would have got out of the vineyard.

The moral of the story is that nothing can resist the will. As a matter of fact, Descartes did not elaborate all those thoughts about God but in order to be able to perform his will to find a way out from the solipsistic prison to which he found himself committed as a consequence of his unbridled scepticism. The *Cogito* is the limit of sceptical thought, but at the same time it is the limit of knowledge too, and what is responsible for Descartes' fallacy is the Ontological proof for the existence of God. The *Cogitans* just ignored the rules of the game that he was committed to. According to these rules, there is nothing to be considered as knowledge, but the very awareness of illusion itself, which is also the only thing one should believe in, there is nothing that one should consider seriously, including every possible belief about God, e.g. the belief that God exists.

Had Descartes not used for a moment his free will and infringed the rules by giving the idea of God's existence an ontological status, he wouldn't have been saved. Why, for all that, the idea of God's existence? From the solipsistic point of view, there is nothing which has an ontological status, except the illusion itself, and accordingly no illusion concerning God, may the existence itself be a logical characteristic of it, is more priviledged than any other existential illusion. But this was not what Descartes thought, not because he ignored the bounds of Solipsism, but because he insisted on overcoming them. And even if he did not do his theoretical reasoning in the right way, his intention was praiseworthy.

Descartes was an anti-Solipsist, who lacked the sober insight that objectivity is not, and cannot be, an absolute datum of human knowledge, and that therefore one should constitute it *a priori*, if one does not wish to give it up. Kant had this insight. He knew that the world as such was not an object of knowledge and therefore based objectivity on the inherent structure of knowledge itself. The noumenal world-view is Kant's ontological choice, and as such it does present an objective category.

Had Descartes been endowed with Kants's penetrating view, he would have understood that God, no more than the world, is not given to the mind, and that therefore if there is to be any objectivity at all, it must be established by the mind *a priori*, irrespective whether the candidate for objectivity is God, his existence, or any other item conceivable. Descartes refused to fall into the trap of Solipsism, yet fell into it inadvertently when he made God depend on the arbitrary nature of his own mind while the world remained dependent, as it were, on that God.

Why was Descartes compelled to adopt from the beginning an anti-solipsistic attitude? The answer is, that it is because Rationalism is inherently destined to be an answer to Solipsism. But if that is so, then the question arises, what is the difference, if any, between Rationalism and rational Solipsism? Might not the reasoning of Kant himself be no more than an exaggeration of subjectivity, and in fact, an irrefutable proof that we can know nothing about world and God? Did Kant really believe then that he could break the bounds of knowledge? Did he take the whole thing seriously? He surely did, just because he was a rationalist, and because it was impossible for him as a rationalist to allow the claims of Solipsism. This was in accordance with the necessary rationalistic assumption that there is a world outside mind, and that *this world* is the object of reference of rational knowledge. This assumption is the meaning condition of classical rationalistic attitude, and the very advantage of it in relation to Solipsism, be it rational as it may. Had rationality satisfied all the conditions for Rationalism, one could consider the rationalistic attitude as a kind of subjectivistic attitude, not to say: as a kind of solipsistic attitude. 'Rationalism' and 'Rational Subjectivism' would then become synonyms, and the term 'Rationalism'—a redundant one.

Descartes' methodological Solipsism is the snare of Cartesian philosophy, just because its implications do not go along with Cartesian Rationalism *qua* Rationalism. In order to establish the evidence of illusion, i.e., the *Cogitatum*, there was surely no need of the hypothesis about the Evil Genius. It would suffice if Descartes had the insight concerning the very significance of doubting, may it be about the first empirical idea that would come to his mind. His way to redemption would then be much shorter. If only he had not adhered to the hypothesis of the Evil Genius, he would have saved himself all the suffering which followed and which was not a condition for knowledge.

It is also clear that once Descartes had got into the vineyard he had to find his way out. What whould he do if God did not give him his hand? This question is asked only for the sake of completeness, since if one comes to think of it, the only one who could really give Descartes a hand was Descartes himself. The basic moral remains the same: God helps those who help themselves.

What would have happened if Descartes skipped the hypothesis of the Evil Genius? For sure he wouldn't have become a victim of Solipsism. Would he have satisfied his commitment towards Scepticism? The answer seems to be "yes". It was not the Evil Genius who deprived Descartes of true knowledge, nor was it the good God who restores it to him. Descartes lost all criteria for truthfulness at the very moment in which he tried to skip that which is a necessary condition for any rationalistic attitude, and he quite regained them just when he felt lost and tried, though in vain, to establish the evidence of God's existence. Be the ontological proof for the existence of God as invalid as it may, the very fact of Descartes' performing an ontological assertion, whatsoever, set a limit to the sceptical practice and was a break for him from the solipsistic prison which made him epistemically dependent either on the Evil Genius' bad intentions or on God's good will.

That there was something absurd in the very assumption of an Evil Genius is no discovery of mine. That great master of philosophical humor, Bouwsma, noted that from an absurd assumption only absurdities can follow. Thus, he illustrates this[1] by presenting two hypothetical geniuses, both evil. The first Evil Genius promises the mother of us all that if she eats of the fruit of the tree, she will be like God, knowing good and evil. The second does not promise anything to anybody, neither good nor knowledge. The wickedness of the first is in that he disappoints the mother of us all; for as soon as she has eaten of the fruit of the tree and been healed of her ignorance, she realizes that "to know good and evil and not to be God is awful". The wickedness of the second is that he not only refrains from any promise at all, but also makes a terrible boast that hence he will deceive any son of Adam about anything, apart from a few clear and distinct ideas. Why didn't Bouwsma mention, if only by hint, as against these two, the good God? Bouwsma himself did not clarify this point, but we can easily guess that he didn't see any point in blaming God for either man's good or bad fate. He didn't see the point in blaming man's bad fate on God, because it is evil, and the Good God never does evil to man. He also didn't see the point in ascribing man's good fate to God, because to know good and evil according to God's criteria and not to be God, is not only awful, but also impossible.

But Bouwsma believes that even the Evil Genius cannot do man real harm. Why does he believe that? He reveals three possible ways in which the Evil Genius could plot against Descartes. He could decide to deceive him just once in a while, letting him recognize his mistakes and settling them. But this would not satisfy him, because it would not then be a total deception of man. He could also decide to deceive him constantly and not let him know that he is deceived. Here again the deception wouldn't be effective, for Descartes would remain in the paradise of ignorance. Otherwise the Evil Genius could decide to deceive Descartes constantly, to let him live in error, but to make him have a vague but constant feeling of trouble and unease. This, according to Bouwsma, would be His major success. But what would he gain then? Surely Descartes would be bothered but his life wouldn't really change, and again the Evil Genius will find himself frustrated and unhappy.

Furthermore, even if the Evil Genius decided to deceive Descartes constantly, he could not deceive him about several clear and distinct ideas, i.e., the necessary truths. But this is not, as Bouwsma thought, just because the domain of necessary truths is the only domain where the Evil Genius and Descartes speak the same language, but because those truths owe their validity to the terms in which they are formulated. Had the Evil Genius managed to deceive Descartes about those truths, he would have necessarily got him to "fail" in his definitions, but this is absolutely meaningless from a human being's point of view. Or else, if he hadn't got him to "fail" in his definitions, again he could not deceive him about the necessary truths, unless he would get him to believe in contradictions. But, as we all agree, a contradiction cannot be thought. This is a presupposition of any rational and rationalistic attitude. That the Evil Genius can never achieve his aim shows that, from man's point of view, total evil is necessarily incoherent, and therefore cannot be described. To get out of this all, Descartes would have had to believe in contradictions, but then his mind would not be human, and he would be either an Evil Genius or a God, and as such he could hold no philosophical interest for us.

———

ENDNOTE

[1] Bouwsma, O.K., "Descartes' Evil Genius", *The Philosophical Review*, Vol. 57 (1949), pp. 141–151.

* * *

AUSDRUCK UND PSYCHOSOMATISCHE FUNKTIONEN
EINE EMPIRISCHE UNTERSUCHUNG

Karl-Ernst Bühler
Universität Würzburg

1. Einleitung

Hinsichtlich der Leib/Seele-Problematik wird bei vorliegender Studie eine ontologisch neutrale Position eingenommen, die für die Erfordernisse einer praktischen Psychosomatik ausreichend erscheint. Dadurch wird die Frage ausgeklammert, ob es sich hier um zwei unterschiedliche ontologische Substanzen handelt wie beim psychophysischen Dualismus oder um psychophysische Identität bei monistischen Konzeptionen.

Diese Zurückhaltung läßt auch Wittgenstein erkennen, wenn er in *PU* 304 bemerkt: „Nicht doch, sie ist weder ein Etwas noch ein Nichts". Der empirischen Studie liegt gleichsam als theoretisches Fundament die Auffassung Wittgensteins zu Grunde, die Wortsprache beschreibe nicht seelische Ereignisse, sondern ersetze den natürlichen körperlichen Ausdruck. Bestimmte seelische Ereignisse, vor allem Affekte und Gefühle, können durch ihren unmittelbaren körperlichen Ausdruck unmittelbar erfaßt werden, z.B. verweist Lachen auf Freude. Zusätzlich verfügt der Mensch durch die Sprache über eine subtile Möglichkeit der Mitteilung seelischer Vorgänge.

Im folgenden wird keine philologische Interpretation Wittgensteins zu dieser Problematik angestrebt, sondern lediglich ein kurzer und zusammenfassender Abriß gegeben soweit für das Verständnis des empirischen Ansatzes erforderlich. Aus der Ersatzfunktion der Wortsprache folgt aber keineswegs eine vollständige Reduzierbarkeit von Erlebnisbegriffen auf Verhaltensbegriffe, sondern es folgt nur − wie Wittgenstein in seiner Privatsprachenargumentation zu zeigen versuchte −, daß die mentalistische Sprache keine private Erlebnissprache ist. Es werden in dieser Sprache vielmehr öffentliche Kriterien für seelische Ereignisse benutzt. Wittgenstein unterscheidet diese Kriterien von den Symptomen. Der Begriff „Symptom" meint − bezogen auf die Medizin − Krankheitszeichen. So ist die schlaffe Lähmung zum Beispiel ein Symptom für eine periphere Nervenschädigung. Eine Lähmung kann aber auch zum Ausdruck werden und so Kriterium für spezifisch seelische Ereignisse sein. Das klassische Beispiel dafür ist die sogenannte hysterische Lähmung. Isoliert betrachtet bleibt diese Art von Lähmung unverständlich, denn es finden sich keine neurologische Ausfälle. Jedoch ist sie als ein Ausdrucksphänomen verstehbar, d.h. als Kundgabe von umfassenderen Zusammenhängen und Bedeutungen. Der Bedeutungszusammenhang entsteht wesentlich durch die soziale Beziehung, ohne die es keinen Ausdruck gäbe, sondern nur natürliche Anzeichen oder Symptome im engeren medizinischen Sinne (s.a. Mead, 1909). Prinzipiell kann jedes Körpergeschehen zu einem Ausdrucksphänomen werden, wobei einzelne Körperfunktionen sich unterschiedlich gut als Ausdrucksträger eignen. Beispielsweise sind die Leber und die Nieren keine besonders geeignete Ausdrucksträger, obwohl ihre Funktion beeinflußt oder sogar geschädigt werden kann durch körperliche Vorgänge, die selbst geeignetere Ausdrucksträger sind oder mit solchen in einer funktionalen Beziehung stehen.

Auch können bestimmte Körperfunktionen mittels wissenschaftlicher Apparaturen zugänglich gemacht werden. So könnte beispielsweise der galvanische Hautwiderstand durch geeignete Maßnahmen zu einem Parameter in der sozialen Interaktion werden, wie dies bei der Schamröte der Fall ist, und auch die Funktion eines Kriteriums für seelische Ereignisse übernehmen. Zwischen dem Körpergeschehen als Ausdruck und dem Ausgedrückten besteht nach dem logischen Beziehungsargument eine logische oder begriffliche, nicht jedoch eine kontingente Beziehung.

Für körperliche Ausdrucksweisen wird oftmals der irreführende Terminus „Körperspra-che" gebraucht, der jedoch im Sinne einer Rudimentärsprache nur eine Teilfunktion der natürlichen Umgangssprache benutzt, nämlich die Kundgabefunktion nach Bühler (1965). Trotz der irreführenden Bezeichnung „Körpersprache" bestehen zwischen dem körperlichen Ausdruck und der Umgangssprache enge Beziehungen im Hinblick auf die seelischen Ereig-nisse. Die Analyse der Umgangssprache, so die Prämisse dieser empirischen Untersuchung, könnte daher Hinweise auf psychosomatische Zusammenhänge geben.

2. Methode

In einer Art Feldstudie wurden Redewendungen der deutschen Umgangssprache gesam-melt, die psychosomatische Aspekte erkennen lassen, nicht jedoch solche, die in ihrer Meta-phorik keinen Bezug zum Körpergeschehen aufweisen wie z.B. „Hoch zu Roß sitzen" für Hochmut; im Unterschied dazu „Hochnäsig sein". Als Quellen dienten vorwiegend Lexika der deutschen Umgangssprache, sowie populärwissenschaftlich konzipierte Zusammenstel-lungen gebräuchlicher Redewendungen. Darüber hinaus wurden auch Aussagen von Patien-ten berücksichtigt ebenso wie Hinweise aus der Belletristik.

Nach Zuordnung der Redewendungen zu den entsprechenden Organen oder Organsyste-men wurden diese inhaltsanalytisch verschiedenen Gefühls- bzw. Emotionsqualitäten zuge-ordnet:
Lust/Unlust; Freude/Trauer; Zuneigung/Abneigung; Liebe/Haß; Mut/Angst; Spannung/ Lösung; Kraft/Schwäche; Zorn/Gleichmut; Dominanz/Submission; Extraversion/Introver-sion; Akzeptierung/Zurückweisung; Unruhe; Ärger; Ekel; Überrraschung; Beklemmung; Sehnsucht.

3. Ergebnisse

Die Anzahl der relevanten Redewendungen beträgt bislang ungefähr 400, die sich jedoch unterschiedlich auf die einzelnen Organsysteme verteilen. Am meisten ist mit 22% der Gesamtzahl der Gastrointestinaltrakt repräsentiert, gefolgt vom Herzkreislaufsystem (21%). Nächst in der Rangreihe stehen das Respirationssystem (17%), der Halteapparat und die Wir-belsäule (12%), der Mund (11%), der Kopf (8%), die Nase (8%), Augen und Ohren (5%), die Haut (5%) und die Nieren (3%).

Im folgenden können nur einige exemplarische Redewendungen erwähnt werden:
„Mir ist der Appetit vergangen"; „Ich hatte lange daran zu knabbern"; „Es ist zum kotzen"; „Die Nachricht schlug mir auf den Magen"; „Die Schamröte schoß ihm ins Gesicht"; „Das Herz klopft mir bis zum Halse"; „Das hat ihr das Herz gebrochen"; „Der Schreck raubt ihr den Atem"; „Da muß ich erst einmal tief Luft holen"; „Wenn ich daran denke, dann steckt mir ein Kloß im Hals"; „Der Gerichtvollzieher saß ihm im Nacken"; „Soll ich Dir den Rücken stärken?"; „Nach dieser Enttäuschung ließ sie die Flügel hängen"; „Der Schreck ging mir durch Mark und Bein"; „Sie hat völlig den Kopf verloren"; „Manchmal hat er ein Brett vor dem Kopf"; „Über dieses Problem habe ich mir schon oft den Kopf zerbrochen"; „Du nervst mich!"; „In schwierigen Situationen kann man die Nerven verlieren"; „Wenn ich daran denke, dann läuft es mir eiskalt über den Rücken und ich bekomme eine Gänsehaut"; „Sie kann nichts so leicht erschüttern, sie hat wirklich eine dicke Haut"; „Sein Erfolg ist mir ein Dorn im Auge"; „Der Tod meines Nachbarn ging mir an die Nieren".

In obiger Aufzählung sind neben offenkundig ausdruckhaften auch eindeutig metaphori-sche Redewendungen aufgeführt.

Redewendungen, die realen körperlichen Ausdruck wiedergeben, beziehen sich auf direkt beobachtbare Körpervorgänge und sind daher im Sinne Wittgensteins deren verbale Substi-tute („sie ist blaß vor Schreck"), wohingegen bei metaphorischen Ausdrücken der bezeich-nete organische Prozeß nicht wirklich stattfindet.

Unmittelbaren Ausdruckscharakter hatten 8% aller Redewendungen. Sie bezogen sich hauptsächlich auf das Kreislaufsystem, den Intestinaltrakt (und hier vor allem auf den Appetit, die Nahrungsaufnahme und die Zähne, weniger häufig jedoch auf die inneren Organe, die keine guten Ausdrucksträger sind), den Respirationstrakt, und die Haut, weil diese Körperteile der direkten Beobachtung zugänglich sind.

Alle Redewendungen ließen emotionale Gestimmtheit erkennen. Deshalb wurden sie inhaltsanalytisch den jeweiligen Emotions- bzw. Gefühlsqualitäten zugeordnet. Die Inhaltsanalyse wurde von drei unabhängigen Sachverständigen durchgeführt und ergab eine hohe Übereinstimmung der Ergebnisse.

Dem Herz/Kreislaufsystem sind relativ viele positive Redewendungen zuzuordnen, wie z.B. Lust, Freude, Sympathie, Liebe und Mut. Im Gegensatz dazu stehen Trauer, Angst und Schwäche. Der Gastro-intestinaltrakt zeigt mehr negative Ausdrücke, hauptsächlich Unlust, Trauer, Abneigung, Angst, Spannung, Zorn, Ärger und Ekel. Das Atmungssystem ähnelt mehr dem Gastro-intestinaltrakt, jedoch mit Abneigung und Beklemmung als hervorstechende Kategorien. Kraft/Schwäche, Dominanz/Submission und Beklemmung beziehen sich auf den Halteapparat, wohingegen Spannung und Abneigung häufig bei Nervensystem und dem Kopfbereich vorkommen. Die Verteilung bei den Weichteilen sind ähnlich der des Halteapparates mit Kraft und Schwäche als Hauptkategorien. Bezüglich der Haut sind Angst, Ärger und Gleichmut vorherrschend.

4. Diskussion der Ergebnisse

Welche Schlüsse lassen sich aus vorliegender Untersuchung ziehen?

Eine genauere Analyse läßt bei vielen Redewendungen latente verbale Ausdruckskomponenten erkennen, für die sich nicht die Frage nach der Wahrheit stellen läßt (sie unterliegt nicht der wahr/falsch-Notation), sondern nach der Wahrhaftigkeit. Auf Grund dieser Verknüpfung von Ausdruckskomponenten scheinen die genannten Redewendungen keineswegs epistemologisch trivial, wie dies bei der Laienannahme: „Wenn der Frosch steigt, dann gibt es Sonne" der Fall ist.

Beispiel: „Meine Lage bereitet mir Kopfzerbrechen" (vollständige Redewendung)
„Ich habe Kopfschmerzen" (erste Teilkomponente)
„Ich befinde mich in einer schwierigen Lage" (zweite Teilkomponente).

Handelt es sich bei der vollständigen Redewendung um einen Erlebnissatz wie bei ihren Komponenten oder wird zwischen letzteren hypothetisch eine Beziehung angenommen, die der empirischen Forschung zugänglich ist und sich als wahr oder falsch herausstellen kann? Einerseits handelt es sich um einen Erlebnissatz, bei dem sich nicht – wie etwa bei eindeutigen Erfahrungssätzen – sinnvoll die Frage stellen läßt: „Woher weißt Du das?" (z.B.: „Ich habe Schmerzen"; „Dein Geschwätz geht mir auf die Nerven"; „Die hitzige Debatte schlägt mir auf den Magen", wobei von Beispiel zu Beispiel die Frage: „Was berechtigt Dich zu dieser Feststellung?" immer bedeutsamer wird), andererseits ist wie bei Erfahrungssätzen die Möglichkeit des Irrtums nicht ausgeschlossen, denn es könnte ja hauptsächlich übermäßiger Kaffeegenuß die Ursache für die Nervosität oder die Magenschmerzen sein. Vermutlich handelt es sich hier um das Problem der intentionalen Verursachung, wie es bei Searle (1983) analysiert wird, wobei intentionale Zustände, wie etwa Laienvorstellungen, auch über Gehirnvorgänge hinausgehende somatische Wirkungen ausüben können, selbst wenn der intenionale Gehalt der Aussage nicht erfüllt ist, d.h. wenn dieser eindeutig wissenschaftlich nicht zutrifft. Bestes Beispiel dafür sind die Laienvorstellungen über die Innervation bei der hysterischen Lähmung, die nicht mit den anatomischen Befunden übereinstimmen. Für die Theorie dieser Störung bilden sie einen integralen Teil, i.G. zu einer Theorie über das schöne Wetter, bei der die Laienvermutung über das Verhalten des Frosches eliminiert werden kann. Zumindest ein Teil der Laientheorien, wie sie in den Redewendungen zum Ausdruck kommen, haben auch eine kausale Funktion im Körpergeschehen und können aus einer Erklärung nicht eliminiert werden. Die Frage besteht nicht nach der Erfüllung des intentionalen Gehalts, sondern nach dessen kausalen Wirkungen auf Körperprozesse. Der kausale Einfluß muß jeweils empirisch bestimmt werden, wobei den Gefühlen, Emotionen und Affekten eine besondere Rolle zukommt. Bei der Inhaltsanalyse konnten erste empirische Befunde aufgezeigt werden.

Die Forschung darf sich jedoch nicht mit diesen ersten groben Ergebnissen begnügen, sondern muß zur weiteren Klärung subtilere empirische Methoden verwenden, ebenso muß auch die philosophische Analyse der intentionalen Verursachung weitergeführt werden und zwar über den relativ einfachen Fall der Willkürbewegung hinausgehend.

LITERATUR

Mead, G. H., „Social psychology as Counterpart to Physiological Psychology", in: *Psychol. Bull.* (1909); 6: 401–408.
Bühler, K., *Sprachtheorie* (Stuttgart 1965).
Searle, J. R., *Intentionality* (Cambridge 1983).

* * *

ZUR ANALYSE VON ‚TRÄUMEN'

Johann Christian Marek
Universität Graz

Nach der herkömmlichen Auffassung sind Träume „das mit dem Schlafe verbundene seelische Leben".[1] Herkömmlich deshalb, weil diese Auffassung im Alltag, aber auch von antiken wie neuzeitlichen Philosophen und Psychologen vertreten wird. Freud schließt ebenfalls an diese Tradition an; sich auf Aristoteles berufend schreibt er, daß „der Traum [. . .] das in den Schlafzustand − insofern man schläft − fortgesetzte Denken" ist.[2]

Man kann die herkömmliche Auffassung − ich möchte sie die Erlebnisauffassung von Träumen nennen − als eine Analyse des Traumbegriffs ansehen. Mit dieser Bestimmung von ‚Traum', ‚Träumen' etc. wird explizit gemacht, welche Bedeutung die Ausdrücke „Traum" usw. für uns haben: Wir verwenden „Traum" und „Träumen" im Sinne von Erlebnis bzw. Erleben im Schlaf. Wenn jemand im Schlaf Erlebnisse hat, wie dies beim Wahrnehmen, Vorstellen, Denken, Fühlen, Wollen usw. der Fall ist, so kann man demnach sagen, daß er träumt.

Die Fragen, ob man nun tatsächlich geträumt habe (ob man also tatsächlich im Schlaf Erlebnisse gehabt habe) und welcher Art die Traumerlebnisse tatsächlich waren, stellen aber kein sprachanalytisches Problem mehr dar, sondern scheinen empirischer Natur zu sein. Nun fehlen aber − insbesondere im Tiefschlaf − die für die Erlebnisse charakteristischen Verhaltensweisen, wodurch die Überprüfung von Behauptungen über vergangene Erlebnisse im Schlaf äußerst schwierig, nach Ansicht mancher Autoren sogar unmöglich wird. So weist zwar Freud bei der Diskussion der Frage, ob man eine Phantasie im Schlaf wirklich durchmache, auf die weitere Möglichkeit hin, daß die Phantasie „aber nicht noch im Schlaf durchlaufen [wird], sondern erst in der Erinnerung des Erwachten. Erwacht, erinnert man jetzt in ihren Einzelheiten die Phantasie, an die als Ganzes im Traum gerührt wurde". Allerdings räumt er zugleich ein, daß man „dabei kein Mittel zur Versicherung [hat], daß man wirklich etwas Geträumtes erinnert".[3]

Zur Debatte stehen also Fragen wie die: „Drückt die Traumerzählung im Wachen resp. beim Erwachen, also der Traumbericht, eine (echte, tatsächliche) Erinnerung über gehabte Erlebnisse im Schlaf aus oder scheint man sich dabei bloß zu erinnern, geträumt zu haben?" bzw. „Welcher Art waren die Erlebnisse, die man im Schlaf gehabt hat?" („Aus welchen Erlebnissen bestand tatsächlich der Traum?") Man hat zunächst den Eindruck, daß diese Fragen zum Aufgabengebiet des empirischen Traumtheoretikers zu zählen sind. Läßt dieser aber für die Begründung der Zuverlässigkeit des Traumberichtes keine weiteren Entscheidungshilfen zu − wie etwa die Berufung auf spezielle physiologische Vorgänge im Schlaf −, dann sind derartige Fragen empirisch nicht auflösbar. Anders ausgedrückt: Man kann nicht den Traumbericht als einzige Begründungsinstanz annehmen, um von Träumen zu sprechen, und zugleich die Zuverlässigkeit des Traumberichtes als Begründungsinstanz in Frage stellen. Um derartige Fragen als empirisch relevant vertreten zu können, muß eine erfahrungswissenschaftliche Traumtheorie im Sinne der herkömmlichen Auffassung über den Traumbericht hinausgehende Begründungsinstanzen haben.

In seinen vieldiskutierten Arbeiten über Träumen, dem Aufsatz: „Dreaming and Skepticism" (1956) und der Monographie *Dreaming* (1959), wendet sich Norman Malcolm mit erkenntnistheoretisch-sprachlogischen Argumenten gegen die herkömmliche Auffassung („received opinion"), nämlich die Erlebnisauffassung von Träumen.[4]

Diese Auffassung habe zur Folge, daß man sich im Schlaf bewußt sein, urteilen könne, daß man gerade schlafe und träume.[5] Da es aber für Malcolm prinzipiell unmöglich ist, das Urteil

„Ich schlafe jetzt", zu verifizieren, sei es überhaupt unsinnig, derartige Aussagen im erfahrungswissenschaftlichen Sinne zu erwägen.[6] Das Hauptziel, das Malcolm verfolgt, besteht darin zu zeigen, daß Träume nicht aus Erlebnissen, wie man sie beim Wahrnehmen, Vorstellen, Denken, Fühlen, Wollen etc. hat, bestehen können.[7] Daß man Träume als etwas Psychisches (in einem weiteren Sinn des Wortes) bezeichnen kann, läßt er gelten, jedoch seien Träume noch nichts Erlebnishaftes.[8] Natürlich seien Träume auch nicht als identisch mit den jeweiligen Traumberichten zu betrachten,[9] aber der Traumbericht sei das einzige Kriterium dafür, daß man geträumt hat.[10] Daß der Traumbericht das Kriterium für den Traum ist, besage u.a., daß man an Hand des Erzählens, Berichtens von Träumen überhaupt lernt, was „Träumen" bedeutet,[11] weiters, daß „Traum" aber deshalb nicht durch „Traumbericht" definiert wird, daß aber wohl eine logische Beziehung zwischen „Traum" und „Traumbericht" besteht: wenn ein Traumbericht vorliegt, kann man auch sagen, daß jemand geträumt hat.[12] Weil der Traumbericht das alleinige Kriterium des Traumes sei, könne bei Vorliegen eines Traumberichtes nicht mehr sinnvoll in Frage gestellt werden, ob wirklich geträumt wurde oder nicht. Malcolm sagt nichts Näheres darüber aus, was Träume sind.[13] Soviel steht für ihn zumindest fest: Man könne zwar aus der Aussage „Er hat geträumt" folgern „Er hat geschlafen", aber man könne daraus nicht folgern „Er hat Erlebnisse im Schlaf gehabt".

Die weiter oben behandelten Probleme, wozu auch die von Wittgenstein angeschnittene Frage gehört, „ob in der Nacht wirklich der Traum vor sich gegangen sei oder ob der Traum ein Gedächtnisphänomen des Erwachten sei" (*BPP* I 369), stellen sich demnach als unsinnig heraus, – und ebenso das skeptische Traumargument in Platons *Theaitet* und in Descartes' *Meditationen*, da darin Sätze vorkommen von der Art wie „Ich weiß nicht, daß ich wach bin und daß ich nicht schlafe und träume", – Sätze, die demnach nicht sinnvoll als Tatsachenbehauptungen in Betracht gezogen werden könnten.[14]

Der Malcolmschen Auffassung gemäß könne man den Begriff des Träumens einzig über das Sprachspiel des Traumberichtens erlangen, und der Traumbericht, da Kriterium des Traumes, stehe in logischer Beziehung zu den Träumen selbst. Die herkömmliche Auffassung sieht darin eine unerlaubte Verabsolutierung. Es gibt ja auch noch andere Möglichkeiten, wie man die Ausdrücke „Traum" etc. zu verwenden lernt. M. E. besteht dafür eine weitere Möglichkeit z.B. darin, daß man – soweit man bereits einen Begriff von Erleben und von Schlafen hat – „Erleben" und „Schlafen" zu „Erleben im Schlaf" kombiniert. Zwischen Traumbericht und Traum besteht dann keine logisch-analytische Beziehung, d.h. aus dem Vorliegen eines Traumberichtes kann noch nicht darauf geschlossen werden, daß der Traum tatsächlich stattgefunden habe. Die Beziehung zwischen Traumbericht und Traum ist demnach empirischer, hypothetischer Natur. Daß ein Traumbericht vorliegt, mag dann *eine* empirische Rechtfertigungsinstanz dafür abgeben, daß man davon spricht, der betreffende Traum habe stattgefunden, aber dies muß nicht der einzige Beweisgrund dafür sein: Bestimmte physiologische Vorgänge, die im Schlaf auftreten, REM-Phasen, charakteristische Erlebnisse vor dem Einschlafen usw. können ebenfalls als weitere empirische Indizien für Träume herangezogen werden. Für welche (empirische) Evidenz man sich auch entscheidet, der Ausdruck „Traum" kann in all diesen Fällen trotzdem einheitlich und eindeutig verwendet werden, nämlich im Sinne von Erlebnis im Schlaf.

Es ist mir in diesem Rahmen nicht möglich, mich näher mit Malcolms erkenntnistheoretisch-sprachanalytischen Untersuchungen auseinanderzusetzen, insbesondere seinen durch „Verifikation" und „Kriterium" angedeuteten operationalistischen Hintergrund adäquat zu durchleuchten, zumal ich in der Folge auf begriffliche Probleme eingehen möchte, die mit der herkömmlichen Traumauffassung, der Erlebnisauffassung vom Traum, unabhängig von Malcolms Thesen verbunden sind.

Gemäß der Erlebnisauffassung vom Traum schließt der Begriff des Schlafes nicht Bewußtlosigkeit ein, man kann im Schlaf Erlebnisse haben, eben träumen, und man kann sich im Schlaf sogar dessen bewußt sein, daß man schläft bzw. daß man träumt, wie dies bei den sogenannten Klarträumen (lucid dreams) der Fall ist.

„Klarträume" charakterisiert Paul Tholey folgendermaßen:

Klarträume sind solche Träume, in denen man völlige Klarheit darüber besitzt, daß man träumt und nach eigenem Entschluß handelnd in das Traumgeschehen eingreifen kann. Man fühlt sich in solchen Träumen im Besitz seiner normalen Verstandes- und Willensfunktionen und hat dabei eine klare Erinnerung an das Wachleben. Es gibt Klarträume, die sich im Hinblick auf die Erscheinungsweise von Körper-Ich und Umgebung überhaupt nicht von der Wachwirklichkeit unterscheiden.[15]

Ein schon klassisches Beispiel für den Bericht eines Klartraumes liefert Ernst Mach:

> Man reflectirt im Traume über den Traum, erkennt ihn als Traum an den Sonderbarkeiten, ist aber gleich wieder über dieselben beruhigt [. . .] — Als ich viel mit Raumfragen beschäftigt war, träumte mir von einem Spaziergang im Walde. Plötzlich bemerkte ich die mangelhafte perspectivische Verschiebung der Bäume, und erkannte daran den *Traum*. Sofort traten aber auch die vermissten Verschiebungen ein.[16]

Allerdings wird die Erlebnisauffassung vom Traum zumeist mit einer Täuschungsauffassung verbunden. Redewendungen wie „Es war ja nur ein Traum" und „Träume sind Schäume" weisen darauf hin, daß ein Traum nur Trug ist, daß er illusionären oder halluzinatorischen Charakters ist. Freud schreibt in seiner *Traumdeutung*:

> Charakteristisch für den Traum sind aber doch nur jene Inhaltselemente, welche sich wie Bilder verhalten, d.h. den Wahrnehmungen ähnlicher sind als den Erinnerungsvorstellungen. Mit Hinwegsetzung über alle die dem Psychiater wohlbekannten Diskussionen über das Wesen der Halluzination können wir mit allen sachkundigen Autoren aussagen, daß der Traum *halluziniert*, daß er Gedanken durch Halluzinationen ersetzt.[17]

Und an anderer Stelle sagt er, daß der Traum „eine Psychose" ist, „mit allen Ungereimtheiten, Wahnbildungen, Sinnestäuschungen einer solchen" bzw. daß „solange wir träumen, den Inhalten des Traumes objektive Realität zusprechen".[18]

Es hängt vom Sprecher ab, ob er den Täuschungscharakter als Begriffsmerkmal von „Traum" auffaßt oder ob er die empirische These vertritt, daß Träume (in der Regel) Täuschungen sind. Wenn man jedoch Klarträume als Träume anerkennt, können nicht alle Träume Täuschungscharakter haben. Zu sagen, daß Träume möglich sind, in denen man sich dessen bewußt ist, daß man träumt, oder auch schon zu sagen, es könne Träume geben, in denen nur vorgestellt wird, ohne daß ein Urteil über die Wirklichkeit des Vorgestellten gefällt wird, dies zu sagen, wäre nicht mehr verträglich mit der Auffassung, daß aus begrifflichen Gründen Träume immer Täuschungen sein müssen.

Mit dem Hinweis auf die Täuschungsmöglichkeit im Traum ergibt sich auch eine Reihe von sprachlogischen Fragen.

Wenn man sagt, der Traum habe halluzinatorischen Charakter, so versteht man — grob gesagt — darunter den Fall einer scheinbaren Wahrnehmung: Es treten bei der Halluzination Empfindungen (Eindrücke, Erscheinungen) mit entsprechenden Glaubenseinstellungen über die Wirklichkeit auf, ohne daß ein entsprechender Sinnesreiz gegeben ist.[19]

Man nehme hingegen den Fall einer Wahrnehmung: Sie betrachten die hinter mir befindlichen Fenster, und Sie sehen, daß sie verschiedenfärbig sind. Wenn Sie nun (visuell) wahrnehmen, daß die Fenster verschiedenfärbig sind, so gilt u.a., (1) daß Sie bestimmte visuelle Empfindungen haben, (2) daß die Tatsache, daß dort verschiedenfärbige Fenster sind, kausal in einer ganz bestimmten Weise dazu beiträgt, daß Sie diese Empfindungen haben, weiters gilt auch, (3) daß mit dem Haben der visuellen Eindrücke auch bestimmte Glaubenseinstellungen verbunden sind: Sie glauben, daß die Fenster verschiedenfärbig sind, und Sie glauben, daß der Umstand, daß die Fenster verschiedenfärbig sind, kausal in einer bestimmten Weise dazu beiträgt, daß Sie die betreffenden visuellen Eindrücke haben.[20]

Äußere Wahrnehmungen sind ein Komplex von Empfindungen und Glaubenseinstellungen: Es werden dabei Wahrheitsansprüche erhoben, die über das Feststellen des Habens von Eindrücken hinausgehen, die eben eine äußere Wirklichkeit betreffen, in meinem Beispiel etwa „Es gibt dort ein Fenster" usw. Allerdings gibt es Wahrnehmungen — die Fälle der sogenannten inneren, unmittelbaren Wahrnehmung —, wo man beim Urteilen nicht über das

Bestehen von Erlebnissen hinausgeht, wenn man sich z.B. nur bestimmter Gefühle oder Stimmungen bewußt ist. Zu beachten ist, daß bei psychischen Vorgängen und Zuständen, die einen derartigen unmittelbaren Charakter haben, es keine Halluzinationen im oben erwähnten Sinn geben kann. Auch wenn man im Traum Halluzinationen hat, die geträumten, unmittelbaren Erlebnisse sind wirkliche Erlebnisse, die geträumte Angst ist in diesem Falle eine reale Angst: „Der Traum besteht nicht einzig und allein aus Täuschungen; wenn man sich z.B. im Traum vor Räubern fürchtet, so sind die Räuber zwar imaginär, die Furcht aber ist real."[21]

Gegen die Auffassung, daß Träume halluzinatorischen Charakters im eben erwähnten Sinne sind, daß also im Traum stets Empfindungen und Glaubenshaltungen auftreten, wurden Bedenken vorgebracht: Den Traumerlebnissen fehle die Lebhaftigkeit, sie seien inhaltlich nicht völlig bestimmt, sie seien oft im eigentlichen Sinn des Wortes farblos; obwohl man in einem Traum starke Emotionen gehabt hat, fühlt man sich nachher gar nicht davon betroffen, man hat vielmehr den Eindruck, daß man im Traum an die Emotionen nur gedacht, sie höchstens bloß vorgestellt, aber nicht wirklich durchlebt hat. Oft scheint es einem auch unwahrscheinlich, so vieles in so kurzer Zeit tatsächlich erlebt zu haben. Überhaupt scheinen die meisten Träume eher den Charakter von Phantasie- und Erinnerungsvorstellungen zu haben, also Tagträumen zu gleichen, so daß man sagen könnte: Träume sind so etwas wie Tagträume im Schlaf.

Diese Traumauffassung − Träume seien Vorstellungen, gleichen Tagträumen − geht von einer Unterscheidung zwischen Wahrnehmen und Vorstellen aus − einer Unterscheidung, die auch in der traditionellen Psychologie vorgenommen wurde, etwa wenn man bei den Vorstellungen (im weiteren Sinne des Wortes) zwischen Wahrnehmungsvorstellungen auf der einen Seite und Phantasie- und Erinnerungsvorstellungen auf der anderen Seite unterschied.[22] Diese mit vielen Problemen behaftete Unterscheidung diskutiert auch Wittgenstein in seinen *Bemerkungen über die Philosophie der Psychologie* (II 63−147):

> Vorstellung:
> Gehörsvorstellung, Gesichtsvorstellung, wie unterscheiden sie sich von den Empfindungen? Nicht durch „Lebhaftigkeit".
> Vorstellungen belehren uns nicht über die Außenwelt, weder richtig noch falsch. (Vorstellungen sind nicht Halluzinationen, auch nicht Einbildungen.)
> Während ich einen Gegenstand sehe, kann ich ihn mir nicht vorstellen.
> Verschiedenheit der Sprachspiele: „Schau die Figur an!" und „Stell dir die Figur vor!"
> Vorstellung dem Willen unterworfen.
> Vorstellung nicht Bild. Welchen Gegenstand ich mir vorstelle, ersehe ich nicht aus der Ähnlichkeit des Vorstellungsbildes mit ihm.
> Auf die Frage "Was stellst du dir vor" kann man mit einem Bild antworten. (*BPP* II 63)

„Vorstellung" wird hier in einem speziellen Sinn verwendet − man könnte vielleicht auch von Imagination sprechen − und nicht in dem allgemeinen Sinn, den Brentano vor Augen hat. In diesem allgemeinen Sinne kann man genau dann von einem Vorstellen sprechen, wenn einem etwas erscheint, wenn gleichsam einem etwas psychisch gegeben ist.[23] Beispiele für Vorstellungen im Sinne von Imaginationen sind: Sie stellen sich vor, daß die Frontfenster dieses Raumes mit Plakaten für das nächstjährige Wittgenstein-Symposium beklebt sind. Die Plakate sind gelb, schwarz bedruckt . . . Oder Sie stellen sich vor, daß die Freiheitsstatue eingerüstet ist.

Für Vorstellungen in diesem engeren Sinne (der Imagination) gilt, daß sie zwar Erlebnischarakter haben − sie sind bewußte psychische Vorgänge −, daß man aber dabei noch keine sinnlichen Empfindungen hat wie bei den entsprechenden Wahrnehmungen. Im Gegensatz zu einer („geglückten") Wahrnehmung ist die Vorstellung unabhängig davon, ob das Vorgestellte auch tatsächlich zutreffend ist oder nicht. Bei Vorstellungen müssen keine Wahrheitsansprüche über die Wirklichkeit erhoben werden, wie dies bei Wahrnehmungen der Fall ist; der Vorstellende kann sich des Urteils über die Realität des Vorgestellten enthalten. Da im Wachen die Vorstellungen gewöhnlich von etlichen Wahrnehmungen begleitet sind, werden die Vorstellungen von den Wahrnehmungsurteilen gleichsam kontrolliert. Dies ist beim ersten Beispiel der Fall: Sie sehen, daß die Fenster ohne Plakate sind, und so ist mit der oben erwähnten Vorstellung das Urteil verbunden, daß die Fenster nicht mit Plakaten beklebt sind.

Vorstellungen stehen zum Wollen in einem anderen Verhältnis als Wahrnehmungen (bzw. Empfindungen). Um die Fenster zu sehen, muß ich die Augen öffnen, um sie nicht zu sehen, brauche ich die Augen nur zu schließen, also um entsprechende sinnliche Empfindungen zu haben, reicht es gewöhnlich nicht hin, solche Empfindungen bloß haben zu wollen; dagegen ist es in der Regel der Fall, daß man sich etwas vorstellt (z.B. die Plakate), soferne man es sich nur vorstellen will. Dieser Unterschied ist allerdings nicht begrifflicher Natur. Es ist nicht widersinnig, sich zu denken, daß jemand sinnliche Eindrücke produzieren könnte, soferne er dies nur will, und Vorstellungen, die sich unwillkürlich, gleichsam von selbst aufdrängen, kommen sogar häufig vor, etwa beim Tagträumen.

Die Unterschiede zwischen Wahrnehmen und Vorstellen genauer herauszuarbeiten, würde eine eigene Analyse erfordern, wozu ich in diesem Rahmen nicht in der Lage bin. Daß man Vorstellungserlebnisse gegenüber den Wahrnehmungserlebnissen als abbildhaft, als Kopien, als Schatten, und daß man sie als etwas nicht so Bestimmtes und als etwas Lückenhaftes betrachtet, und weiters, daß man Vorstellungen als etwas Blasseres, Flüchtigeres, Körperloseres und nicht so Lebhaftes wie Wahrnehmungen ansieht, mag für eine Analyse richtungsweisend sein. Aber derartige metaphorische Merkmalsbezeichnungen dürfen nicht dahin führen, daß man sich von den Bildern irreführen läßt. So ist eine Wahrnehmung von etwas Blassem trotzdem eine Wahrnehmung und keine Vorstellung; und es gibt starke und weniger starke Empfindungen, aber es gibt dabei keinen Punkt, wo das Empfindungserlebnis auch das Vorstellungserlebnis ist.

Betreffend die unmittelbaren eigenpsychischen Vorgänge, die Erlebnisse, besagt diese Theorie, daß die vorgestellten Erlebnisse von den tatsächlichen Erlebnissen zu unterscheiden sind: Ein vorgestelltes Erlebnis ist nicht ein reales Erlebnis, eine vorgestellte Angst oder ein vorgestellter Schmerz ist noch keine reale Angst bzw. kein realer Schmerz. Wenn man nun gemäß der zuletzt erwähnten Traumtheorie Träume als Vorstellungen auffaßt, ist die geträumte Angst keine reale Angst.

Besondere begriffliche Schwierigkeiten ergeben sich, wenn man die Vorstellungsauffassung von Träumen mit einer Täuschungsauffassung in Verbindung bringt. Das Problem stellt sich, wenn man damit zum Ausdruck bringen will, daß Träume einerseits nur Vorstellungen sind und weder Halluzinationen noch Illusionen enthalten, daß aber andererseits Wirklichkeitsansprüche auf das Vorgestellte erhoben werden und Träume daher halluzinatorischen oder illusionären Charakter haben. So kann man in psychologischen Werken lesen, daß infolge der Herabsetzung der Wahrnehmungsfähigkeit die Vorstellungen einen anderen Stellenwert im Bewußtsein bekommen und gleichsam die Stärke und Lebendigkeit von Empfindungen erlangen, so daß man deshalb von Halluzinationen sprechen müßte. Rudolf Eisler faßt dies so zusammen:

> Die T[raum]. vorstellungen haben, teilweise schon infolge des Wegfalls des Sinnenbewußtseins, nicht die Schwäche gewöhnlicher Erinnerungsvorstellungen, sondern die Lebhaftigkeit und den Objekt-Charakter von Illusionen oder Halluzinationen.[24]

Wenn man also von der strikten Unterscheidung Vorstellen (Imaginieren) vs. Empfinden (bzw. Wahrnehmen oder Halluzinationen- oder Illusionen-Haben) ausgeht, ergibt sich ein Widerspruch, soferne man z.B. sagt, daß jemand von einer kriechenden Spinne träumt (d.h. sie vorstellt), und soferne man auch sagt, daß er während des Traumes die Spinne halluziniert (und sie daher nicht vorstellt).

Man entgeht dem Widerspruch, wenn man Behauptungen wie die von Eisler dahingehend umdeutet: Der Träumende habe zunächst eine Vorstellung, aber dann produziere er Empfindungen, bilde somit Halluzinationen aus. Das bedeutet, daß der Traum dann wahrnehmungsartigen, genauer: halluzinatorischen Charakter hat und nicht mehr vorstellungshaft ist. Eine andere Deutung und zugleich ein anderer Weg, dem Widerspruch zu entgehen, besteht darin, zwar den Vorstellungscharakter von Träumen anzuerkennen, aber die Täuschung bloß als einen Irrtum bezüglich des Urteils über die Realität des Vorgestellten zu interpretieren.

Auch wenn man einräumt, daß man im Zustand der Ermüdung und des Schlafens besonders zu Fehlidentifikationen neigt, muß man aber deshalb noch nicht anerkennen, daß eine
Vorstellung zugleich auch eine Halluzination ist. Wenn jemand geträumt hat, daß er mit seinem Vater gesprochen hat, aber sein Vater im Traum wie dessen Nachbar ausgesehen hat,
der überhaupt keine Ähnlichkeit mit seinem Vater hat, so kann man von einer Fehlidentifikation sprechen. Ein weiterer Fall einer Fehlidentifikation besteht darin, daß man sich im
Traum auf einer grünen Wiese liegend glaubt und daß man jedoch die Empfindung von etwas
Rotem (soferne der Traum halluzinatorisch ist) oder die Vorstellung von etwas Rotem
(soferne der Traum vorstellungshaft ist) hat. Ein weiteres Beispiel, das ich nur vom Hörensa-
gen kenne, stellt G. E. Moores Traum dar, in dem er Tische für Propositionen gehalten habe.

Die Möglichkeit derartiger Fehlidentifikationen scheint mir die Annahme plausibel zu
machen, daß man im Traum vorgestellte Situationen fälschlich für real halten könne. Ein solches Fehlurteil beruht insbesondere auf den Umständen, daß die schlafende Person über
(nahezu) keine begleitenden kontrollierenden Wahrnehmungen verfügt, daß ihre kognitiven
Fähigkeiten, wie die zu diskriminieren und die sich zu erinnern, stark herabgemindert sind
und daß die Vorstellungen nicht mehr willentlich zustandekommen, sondern − analog wahrgenommenen Szenen − von selbst ablaufen. Wie bei einem Tagtraum werden anschauliche
Situationen nur vorgestellt − z.B. eine am Boden kriechende Spinne −, und man hat dabei
gar keine Sinnesempfindung. Aber im Gegensatz zu den üblichen Tagträumen ist einem im
Schlaf die Vorstellung insofern entglitten, als die vorgestellte Situation, daß die Spinne einem
am Boden zukriecht, für tatsächlich, für real gehalten wird. Von „üblichen Tagträumen" spreche ich deshalb, weil bei Tagträumen nur in Ausnahmefällen das Phänomen des Entgleitens
vorkommt. Ein analoger Fall des Entgleitens wäre noch das Sich-Hineinleben in ein Theater-
stück oder in einen Film; allerdings ist hier der Fall insofern etwas anders gelagert, als Empfindungen (visuelle, akustische) eine Rolle spielen.

Wendet man diese Traumtheorie auf Eigenpsychisches wie Angst, Schmerz und Stimmungen an, so gilt, daß derartige Erlebnisse während des Traumes nur vorgestellt werden, obwohl
sie für real gehalten werden. D.h. die geträumte Angst ist keine tatsächliche Angst, sondern
nur vorgestellter Natur, aber sie wird dennoch für tatsächlich gehalten.[25]

Aus dem bisher Gesagten wird deutlich, daß die herkömmliche Auffassung von Träumen,
die Erlebnisauffassung, im wesentlichen zu mindestens zwei Traumtheorien geführt hat: 1.
Träume haben stets wahrnehmungsartigen Charakter, und − verbunden mit der Täuschungsauffassung − sie sind immer halluzinatorischer oder illusionärer Natur; 2. Träume haben ausschließlich Vorstellungscharakter, und die Täuschungen, denen man dabei unterliegen kann,
bestehen weder aus Halluzinationen noch aus Illusionen, sondern aus den oben erwähnten
Fehlurteilen über das Vorgestellte.[26]

Die Beantwortung der Frage, ob die Theorien in der hier einander ausschließenden Form
gelten oder ob es nicht vielmehr der Fall ist, daß es Träume gibt, die nur Vorstellungscharakter
haben, und andere, die nur Wahrnehmungscharakter haben, und solche wiederum, die sowohl
das eine wie auch das andere sind, ist dann Aufgabe empirischer Untersuchungen und nicht
der Begriffsanalyse. Die Begriffsanalyse weist lediglich auf, daß Träume Erlebnisse im Schlaf
sein müssen. Indem die begrifflichen Beziehungen zwischen ‚Träumen', ‚Erleben', ‚Vorstellen', ‚Sich-Täuschen', ‚Halluzinieren' geklärt werden, wird nichts darüber befunden, daß
Träume stets Täuschungen sind oder immer Vorstellungscharakter haben u.ä.m. Die Begriffsanalyse vermag nur, auf die verschiedenen Erlebnismöglichkeiten im Schlaf hinzuweisen und
es Sache der Empirie sein zu lassen, welche der Möglichkeiten verwirklicht sind. Somit zeigt
die Begriffsanalyse, daß der Begriff des Traumes *lediglich* den des Erlebens im Schlaf impliziert; das bedeutet aber auch: die Begriffsanalyse zeigt, daß allein aus dem Begriff des Traumes
noch *nicht* folgt, daß Träume Halluzinationen bzw. Vorstellungen usw. sind. Darüber zu befinden, ob Träume z.B. wirklich Täuschungen sind, dies ist Aufgabe der Empirie.

Ebenfalls gehört es zum empirischen Aufgabengebiet, gute Gründe dafür zu finden, ob und
inwieweit Träume im Sinne von Erlebnissen im Schlaf überhaupt vorkommen. Schon vor
Freud hat man darauf hingewiesen, daß man im Schlaf nicht all das erlebt, was der Traumbe-

richt nahelegt. Den Hauptanlaß zu dieser Vermutung sieht Freud in dem Phänomen, daß Leute oft vermeinen, längere Szenen, ja ganze Szenenfolgen in äußerst kurzer Zeit geträumt zu haben. Zur Erklärung dieses Phänomens nahm Freud an, daß Phantasien unbewußt ausgebildet werden können − sozusagen im Speicher − und daß sie erst in bestimmten Situationen, insbesondere beim Erwachen, abgerufen werden. Daher mag es sein, daß jemand im Schlaf nur eine die ganze Phantasie andeutende Vorstellung gehabt hat oder daß jemand im Schlaf gar keine Erlebnisse, also gar keine Träume, gehabt hat und dennoch sogenannte Traumberichte zu erzählen vermag.[27]

Somit bin ich wieder bei der Ausgangsfrage dieses Referates angelangt, − gemäß der Erlebnisauffassung eine sinnvolle empirische Frage, der Ansicht Malcolms nach freilich eine unsinnige.*

ANMERKUNGEN

[1] Eisler, Rudolf, *Wörterbuch der philosophischen Begriffe,* Bd. III (Berlin 1930), S. 264.
[2] Freud, Sigmund, *Die Traumdeutung,* in: Sigm. Freud, *Gesammelte Werke*, 2. und 3. Bd. (London, Imago, 1942), S. 555.
[3] Freud (1942), S. 502.
[4] Malcolm, Norman, „Dreaming and Skepticism", *Philosophical Review* 64(1956), S. 14−37 (wiederabgedruckt in: Charles E. M. Dunlop (Hrsg.), *Philosophical Essays on Dreaming* (Ithaca und London 1977), S. 103−126; darin befinden sich auch zahlreiche Beiträge zur Malcolmschen Analyse von ‚Träumen'); Norman Malcolm, *Dreaming* (London 1959, ²1962).
[5] Malcolm (²1962), S. 9.
[6] Malcolm (²1962), S. 17f., 35ff.
[7] Malcolm (²1962), passim, insbes. S. 49ff.
[8] Malcolm (²1962), S. 52.
[9] Malcolm (²1962), S. 59f.
[10] Malcolm (²1962), S. 49, 81.
[11] Malcolm (²1962), S. 81.
[12] Malcolm (²1962), S. 60.
[13] Malcolm (²1962), S. 59.
[14] Siehe Johann Christian Marek, „Traum und Skepsis", *Zeitschrift für Didaktik der Philosophie* V(1983), S. 71−79. Zu bemerken ist, daß das skeptische Traumargument den Anstoß zu Malcolms Analysen gegeben hat.
[15] Tholey, Paul, „Klarträume als Gegenstand empirischer Untersuchungen", *Gestalt Theory* 2(1980), S. 175−191; S. 175.
[16] Mach, Ernst, *Die Analyse der Empfindungen und das Verhältniss des Physischen zum Psychischen* (Jena 1900), S. 163f (Fußnote).
[17] Freud (1942), S. 52.
[18] Freud, Sigmund, „Abriss der Psychoanalyse", in: Sigm. Freud, *Gesammelte Werke,* 17. Bd., *Schriften aus dem Nachlass* (London, Imago, 1941), S. 97 bzw. 87f.
[19] Eine eingehende Analyse von ‚Träumen' wird auch den Begriff der Illusion und das Verhältnis dieses Begriffes zu dem der Halluzination den näheren untersuchen müssen. Grob gesagt kann man von einer Illusion dann sprechen, wenn zwar dem Reiz entsprechende Empfindungen auftreten, mit diesen aber falsche Wirklichkeitsdeutungen gegeben werden. Ein Fall einer Illusion ist, wenn man z.B. im Traum das Geräusch eines Weckers als Zugsignale deutet. Die Reize müssen aber nicht immer äußerer Natur sein, innere Sinneserregungen können auch den Anlaß zu Illusionen geben, − wenn etwa Augenflimmern als Blitze und Ohrensausen als Windgeräusche angesehen werden. Die beiden letzten Beispiele zeigen aber auch schon die Vagheit der in diesem Aufsatz gegebenen Bestimmungen von ‚Halluzination' und ‚Illusion' auf, denn könnte man hier nicht ebenso gut von Halluzinationen sprechen? (Vgl. den Terminus „hypnagogische Halluzination).
[20] Der hier vertretene wahrnehmungstheoretische Ansatz entspricht in etwa John Searles Analyse von ‚Wahrnehmung' in: John R. Searle, *Intentionality. An essay in the philosophy of mind* (Cambridge u.a. 1983), S. 37−78.
[21] Freud (1942, S. 77) zitiert hier aus Strickers *Studien über das Bewußtsein* (Wien 1879).

[22] Siehe z.B. Alois Höfler, *Grundlehren der Logik und Psychologie* (Wien 1903), S. 189f.
Eine weitergehende Analyse von ‚Träumen' wird nicht umhin können, auf die Art von Träumen einzugehen, die rein aus Gedanken bestehen. Unter Gedanken werden in diesem Zusammenhang ebenfalls Erlebnisse verstanden, − Erlebnisse, die aber begrifflich sind und nicht anschaulich wie die Vorstellungen und Wahrnehmungen. In derartigen Träumen werden Inhalte gedacht, ohne daß Vorstellungen oder wahrnehmungsartige Erlebnisse hinzukommen.

[23] Siehe Franz Brentano, *Psychologie vom empirischen Standpunkt* Bd. II (Hamburg 1971, ¹1874), S. 34: „Wir reden von einem Vorstellen, wo immer uns etwas erscheint".

[24] Eisler (1930), S. 264. Vgl. dazu Freud (1942), S. 50−68.

[25] Das wäre allerdings ein Fall, wo die Evidenz der inneren Wahrnehmung nicht mehr gegeben ist, denn es gilt hier nicht mehr, daß aus dem Glauben, das Erlebnis (Angst) zu haben, folgt, daß man das Erlebnis (Angst) hat.

[26] Eine Modifikation dieser Einteilung ergibt sich, wenn man auch noch die Möglichkeit rein gedanklicher Träume (siehe Anm. 22) in Betracht zieht.

[27] Siehe Freud (1942), S. 501ff; sowie Dennetts „cassette theory" in: Daniel C. Dennett, „Are Dreams Experiences?" *Philosophical Review* 85 (1976), S. 151−171 (wiederabgedruckt in: Dunlop (1977), S. 227−250).

* Für kritische Kommentare sei im besonderen Herrn Heiner Rutte, Graz, gedankt. Bei dieser Gelegenheit möchte ich auch Frau Helga Michelitsch danken, − nicht nur für ihre Hilfe bei der Erstellung des Typoskripts dieses Aufsatzes, sondern vor allem auch für ihre ausdauernde und umsichtige Mithilfe bei der Herausgabe dieses Bandes.

* * *

6. Handlung, Emotion und Wille

6. Action, Emotion and Will

THE VARIETIES OF DESIRE

Brian O'Shaughnessy
King's College, London

I. *"Direct object" vs "Propositional object"*

(1) The distinction between a "direct object" of a psychological state and a "propositional object", is loosely expressed in the following way. We show the state falls under a description wherein it is linked via "of" "at" (etc) with some particular, or via "that" "lest" (etc) with some proposition. Thus, we speak of "catching sight of Jack" or "looking at Jill", and also of "believing that it is sunny" or "fearing lest it rain". Some, but apparently not all, psychological types permit both forms. One can see an undone shoelace or see that a shoelace is undone; whereas by contrast there seems to be nothing we could call the direct object of belief. Yet this claim is not absolutely pellucid; for do we not speak of "believing Smith"? But the sense of this utterance is, "He believed that the claim affirmed by Smith was true". So should we not say that belief cannot take a direct object? With this observation in mind one might confidently assert that the distinction is secure. Maybe whether a state has a direct or propositional object shows only when we spell out the full description of the state, and discover whether the description links the state with individual or proposition. Maybe this is how matters lie, but then again maybe not. Unfortunately, none of these issues seem settled. Plainly, the precise drawing of the distinction is not complete. I believe some illumination on the question will be gained if we consider the phenomena of noticing and fearing.

Consider a case of visual noticing. Here a distinct individual entity causes a mental event that is an awareness of that something "in the flesh" or "intuitively". Now it is possible to notice-of an entity without noticing-that anything whatsoever, for whatever putatively one notices-that might have been known and thought just before the noticing-of incident, and hence not be a fit topic for noticing-that. This fact manages to completely drain noticing-of of informational content. Then whereas noticing-of is a mode of acquaintance with a concrete existent individual, noticing-that is an experience of discovery caused by and concerning the present noticed-of. Evidently, we are dealing here with two closely related but distinct phenomena. But are not many cases of noticing-that visual experiences? But how can coming-to-know be a visual experience? It seems rather that seeing-that is a noticing-that which is a cognitive experience essentially caused by and essentially concerning the visually experienced. In sum, we distinguish noticing-of, which is an intuitional contact with a concrete existent individual, from noticing-that, which is a cognitive experience with the aforementioned features.

Fear presents a different picture. And yet one might suppose that one encounters two analogous phenomena, fear-of and fear-that. But it is not so, even though fearing is both "of" and "that". Thus, fearing a tiger is not a mystic acquaintance with danger incarnate, but is a fearing-of that is explained by the existence of a fearing-lest it attack. In a sense this fear passes through the tiger and ends up on a possible attack with tiger as agent. Then the difference with noticing is, that we are not here concerned with two distinct phenomena, fearing-of and fearing-lest. It is not merely that fear-of cannot occur in the absence of fear-lest; rather, the fear-lest spells out the determinate and thought-given content of the fearing phenomenon. So the tiger is the object of fear, but only in its role as agent of a possible attack. Then is the attack also the object of fear? It seems that here fear is directed onto its disturbing animate object, and yet we cannot distinguish fear of tiger from fear lest tiger attack. I conclude, that while we can talk of a direct and also of a propositional object of fear, these are objects for one and the same phenomenon which is directed onto direct object only insofar as it is directed onto propositional object. Whereas noticing-of is distinct from and cause of noticing-that,

333

fearing-of is identical with and explained by fearing-that. This distinction seems highly relevant to the enterprise of distinguishing direct and propositional object.

But before we do so, one other observation on the topic of fear. Namely: on the distinction between cause and object of fear. One who sees a nearby tiger out in the open is both frightened of it—so the tiger is object, and frightened-by it—so the tiger is cause; whereas one who hears a sudden blood curdling scream in the middle of the night, may be frightened-by that scream without being frightened either of the scream or its perpetrator or instigator or indeed of anything at all. Here we have a case of sheer dread of nothing in particular, internally given as caused by a particular brush with a particular though hidden danger. In a word, the object of fear can shrink to nothing, though it is internal to this fear that it be given as originating out of a brush with a completely obscured danger.

(2) To return to the drawing of distinctions. Then to begin, we note that the intentionality of properly mental states more or less ensures that anything that is mental must be directed towards some x or other that might be termed its "content"; but we must at once qualify this, bearing in mind this special case of being frightened-by, which may perhaps be accounted a case of "content" that is not a case of being directed-towards. So the next set of distinctions must be drawn amongst mental states with "content" that are also directed-towards. Then with some mental items, notably belief, that directed content is necessarily given by a "that"-clause and not by an "of"-clause; while with some other mental items, notably particular images, that content is necessarily given by an "of"-clause and not by a "that"-clause. Meanwhile, with some other mental phenomena, notably fear and noticing, there exist directed "contents" that are given by both "that" and "of" clauses. But an additional distinction can now be drawn amongst these latter phenomena. Thus, with some mental phenomena, notably fear, while the direct content is necessarily given by a "that"-clause, that specific content may contingently permit the state to be directed onto a concrete item, as when fear lest a tiger attack ensures that the tiger is direct object of fear; and in such cases we may say the psychological state is directed onto a direct object only insofar as it is directed to the propositional content. But with some other mental phenomena, notably noticing, a very different picture presents itself; for not only is noticing-of not there as the result of the good graces of noticing-that, it is an autonomous phenomenon in its own right and altogether distinct from the noticing-that with which it appears in close association. So whereas fearing-of is derivative from and identical with fearing-that, noticing-of causes and is distinct from noticing-that.

II. *Desiring-to-do/"do" and desiring-that*

(1) I turn to the phenomenon of desire. Now whereas there is such a thing as free floating anxiety, there is no such thing as free floating desire. Necessarily, no desire is just—desire. Necessarily, desire has "content"; and not just in the reduced sense in which merely being frightened-by has "content", but *directed* "content". There is always a "what" that is desired. Yet the "what" seems bewilderingly diverse. One can desire-that something be true or have a desire which is directed to particulars like oranges or actions; and some act-desires are directed to things as well while some are not; and some desires-that take both proposition and thing as object while some do not; and so on. Meanwhile, we note the existence of certain very fundamental human drives, such as the desire to appropriate, or the desire to know, or the desire "to be—" (eg. king, saint). How fundamental are these last? Might some be reduced to others? Might all be reduced to one, eg. to the desire to appropriate? What order exists in this welter?

There are I think *three* ultimate categories of desire. Every desire is a case of one and only one of these types. Those types are: act-desire, "act"-desire (eg. to laugh), propositional-desire. Then while no one of these is reducible to the others, the first two desire-types are the two sub-varieties of desire that stand to their object in a peculiarly concrete and probably causal relation and in any case otherwise than through the mediation of thought or proposition; so that the first two categories contrast with the third in lacking a propositional object. Therefore a single all encompassing distinction can be drawn between desires that stand in this peculiarly concrete relation to their individual phenomenal object, and desires that are directed either to a proposition or else to an individual through the mediation of a proposition (as happens with the desire to own some jewel). This distinction is not between desires-that and desires (merely) directed towards acts/"acts". It is between desires-that and all other desires; which, of necessity, are both directed towards act/"act" *and* examples of act/"act"-desire (for the concepts desire-directed-towards-action and act-desire differ). It can be singled out by three oppositions: desire that finds its object through the thought/desire which does not: desire that finds its object through the thought/desire that finds its object in the concrete manner of act-desire: desire-that/desire to do or "do". This distinction closely parallels the distinction between the two varieties of noticing, in which noticing either takes a direct intuitionally-given object or else a propositional object.

(2) Some might object to this schema, not because they think it is not comprehensive and omits certain desires, but because they reject the very distinction itself and believe that (at least in the self-conscious) absolutely *all* desires are desires-that. According to this account, desires-to-do are desires-that-it-be-true-one-do.

Take as example a simple act-inclination, eg. the desire to eat this steak. According to the present theory, this act-desire *is* the unmotivated desire that it be true that I eat this steak, ie. a sheer wanting it to happen that I do. Thus, "I feel like doing" becomes "I would like it to be true that I do", which is to say that willy nilly and for no reason *the idea* draws me. And note that I do not here oppose thought and what the thought is of, any more than in desiring that A punch B I am drawn by the thought of his doing so *rather than* the reality. As to desire such a reality *is* to be drawn by the thought of that reality, so to feel like eating this steak *is* (so it is said) to be drawn by the thought of such a thing. It is to wish such a world. Well, it is certain that the idea does attract. How could it not if my inclination is so great? But now is it the act via the mediation of the thought, or is it somehow directly the act itself that draws? And does "I feel like eating" *mean* "I would like it to be true that I eat"? But does not this latter desire lack a familiar committed activity of character? The causal properties of clearcut cases of act-desire, as against those of desire-that, tend to confirm the existence of such a qualitative break. Whereas the desire to move my arm finds immediate expression in action, the desire that A punch B finds mediate expression in acts designed to effect that deed and hence more immediate expression in thoughts and act-desires directed towards those procedures. No mediatory role remains for thought in one case, but necessarily exists in the other. So to render "I feel like doing" as "I would like it to happen that I do" is to strand act-desire in a region where it cannot find immediate expression and "discharge". But anyway is it plausible to suppose "I felt like shouting" means "I would have liked it to be true that I shout" or even (bizarrely) "I would have loved me to shout"? For are we not in such cases vividly aware of a mental force, pressing absolutely immediately and without any assistance from the mind towards shouting, and where is this force in "I would have loved me to shout"? Once again we are being offered action as envisaged in thought in place of action in the flesh. So I reject any attempt to reduce act-desire to the desire-that which in the self-conscious generally accompanies it. Thus, the act-desire/propositional-desire distinction is both a reality and a strict opposition.

(3) Now desires can take direct and propositional objects, and act-desires are directed to direct objects; so the direct object/propositional object (D/P) distinction both applies to desire and is exemplified in the act-desire/propositional-desire (A/P) distinction. Then how do these two distinctions relate? A natural suggestion is, that A/P is no more than a case of the familiar D/P distinction. That would imply that A/P was of no special significance, allow that some desires escape the classification, and thereby demote act-desire from any position of eminence amidst desires. I shall now consider these three suggestions.

Might A/P be no more than a case of D/P? But A/P is an opposition. So this idea will be mistaken, the principle of distinction different, if desires exist which are not act-desires, which simultaneously take direct and propositional object. Well, there do exist such desires, eg. a possessive desire can be directed uniquely towards a particular jewel and consist in the desire-that a proprietorial relation obtain between one and that jewel. I conclude that the principle of the A/P distinction cannot be that of D/P. So A/P has the significance of being novel.

But it will be much more significant if it is absolutely comprehensive, ie. if there cannot exist desires which are neither act/"act"-desires nor desires-that. Now since all desires take objects, such putative desires must be directed towards their own distinctive object—directly and not through the agency of a proposition. These desires must be true analogues of act-desire; so that as act-desires relate immediately and concretely with *actions*, in the same way these wholly distinctive desires must relate in the identical concrete manner with *havings*—or *knowings*—or whatever it be. This seems highly implausible. All these latter desires look to be cases of desiring-that. Moreover, these desires would need to have causal powers relating to their distinctive object as act-desires have in relation to striving or willing or acting; so that (say) the desire to know should tend to produce something like believing or suspecting or even knowing. I reject this suggestion, and conclude that the act-desire/propositional-desire distinction is at once completely comprehensive and a strict opposition. This fact points up the primacy of act-desire amongst all desire types.

* * *

BEWUSSTSEIN UND DER WILLE ZUM WOLLEN

Krystyna Górniak-Kocikowska
Universität Poznań

Den Ausgangspunkt meiner Erwägung bildet das Leib-Seele-Problem. Eine der zentralen Fragen dieses Problems ist die Frage nach dem Bewußtsein und dem Willen. Wie man seit Plato, Aristoteles und den Stoikern das Bewußtsein mit dem Geist zu identifizieren pflegte, so schrieb man gewöhnlich den Willen den Sinnen, also dem Leibe zu. In der in die Materie und den Geist geteilten Welt hatte man auch die *ethischen* Eigenschaften verteilt, – nun wurde die Materie *böse* und der Geist *gut*. Folglich wurden auch die „geistigen" Tätigkeiten des Bewußtseins gut und die sinnlich-leiblichen Funktionen des Willens – böse. Die eigentliche Tätigkeit des Bewußtseins wurde jedoch als eine reflektive bezeichnet, – wobei der Wille wiederum auf den Gefühlen basieren sollte. Die Forschung schreibt gewöhnlich dem Willen zwei verschiedene mögliche Positionen in bezug auf das Denken und somit auch auf das Bewußtsein zu:

1. Der Wille ist der Ratio untergeordnet (die Ratio verstehe ich hier allgemein als ein Denkvermögen). Als solcher spielt der Wille keine selbständige Rolle für das menschliche Wesen, auch wenn man ihn „freien Willen" nennt. Daß der Mensch etwas wollen soll oder nicht, entscheidet seine Ratio, die also den „freien" Willen bändigt und für ihn verantwortlich ist. Der Wille braucht aber nicht unbedingt der menschlichen Ratio untergeordnet zu sein. Z.B.: für den heiligen Augustin war der freie Wille der wesentlichste Kern der menschlichen Persönlichkeit, dem der Verstand untergeordnet war und der es allein entschied, ob unsere Handlung als Willensakt ins Bewußtsein eindringt oder auch nicht; sobald aber der Mensch mit Gott konfrontiert wurde, zeigte es sich, daß er gänzlich und vollkommen dem Gotteswillen unterliegt. Es wurde wieder die Aufgabe des Bewußtseins, sich auf den Gotteswillen und nicht auf den Menschenswillen zu konzentrieren, ja den menschlichen Willen als Feind, der uns zur Sünde verführt, zu betrachten. Gewollt sollte der Gotteswille werden.

2. Der Wille wird der Ratio entgegengestellt. Es spielt sich ständig ein Kampf zwischen ihnen ab, den das Bewußtsein zu registrieren versucht. Weil aber das Bewußtsein enger mit der Ratio als mit dem Willen verbunden ist, dringt oft der Wille zum Bewußtsein gar nicht ein. So wirkt er auf der Ebene des Unbewußten. Auf der Ebene des Bewußten wirkt dann (wie im ersten Fall) nur der durch die Ratio „gezähmte" Wille. Das andere, z.B. von Schopenhauer gezeigte Resultat dieses Kampfes des Willens gegen die Ratio ist der Sieg des Willens. Was geschieht aber mit dem siegreichen Willen, wenn er in das Bewußtsein eindringt? Kann er uns bewußt werden, ohne dem Prozeß der Rationalisierung zu unterliegen? Die Antwort, meiner Meinung nach, lautet: nein. Also auch in diesem Fall kann der „eigentliche" Wille nur auf der Ebene des Unbewußten wirklich frei sein und wirken.

In diesen beiden Untersuchungslinien bleibt eigentlich die Frage offen, ob der Wille, der nur unter Kontrolle der Ratio im Bewußtsein zum Vorschein kommt, überhaupt noch *der* Wille ist. Ist das der Wille des Menschen oder nur der Wille der menschlichen Ratio? Dieser „rationale Wille" läßt sich durch den („rationalen" oder auch nicht) Willen anderer Menschen regieren. Denn ich kann überzeugt werden (oder mich selbst überzeugen), daß ich etwas *wollen soll*. Erst dann kann ich handeln (ich bin zum Handeln motiviert). Ist dann das aber tatsächlich *mein Wille*? Sicher – auch, wenn ich sage: ich handle widerwillig. Aber dann weiß ich eben, es ist mir bewußt, daß mein „eigentlicher" Wille von einem anderen Willen (von meinem „rationalen" Willen, oder von einem fremden Willen) bekämpft wurde. Das, was ich tue, wollte ich nicht wollen. Der bekämpfte Wille kann aber nicht mehr mein Wille sein, denn ich *entschied* mich, etwas anderes zu *wollen*. Welcher Wille ist also authentisch? Mein aus dem

Bewußtsein ausgerotteter, bzw. gar nicht zum Bewußtsein zugelassener „eigentlicher" Wille, oder der bewußte, „rationale" Wille, nach dem ich handle?

Die Frage nach dem Willen wurde in den letzten Jahrzehnten wieder aktuell und bekam neue Lösungsmöglichkeiten, weil die Entwicklung der Wissenschaft ein neues Licht auf die menschliche Natur warf. Die moderne Wissenschaft interessiert sich für den menschlichen Willen vor allem aus praktischen Gründen. An dem Beispiel des Willens und der Wandlung in der Betrachtung dessen als eines Forschungsobjektes läßt sich ganz deutlich sehen, wie sehr der *Mensch* in der heutigen Markt-Gesellschaft zu einem *Markt-Gegenstand* wurde. Auf dem Markt wird er als ein Produkt betrachtet, der zu bestimmten Zwecken dienen soll. Deswegen – wenn seine Qualität als eines Produktes entsprechend gut sein soll – muß er bestimmte Eigenschaften besitzen. Die meisten Menschen treten auf dem Markt ausschließlich als Lieferanten ihrer eigenen Arbeitskraft auf. Der Mensch muß also, sobald seine Arbeitskraft auf dem Markt als *Ware* erscheint, bestimmte Fähigkeiten besitzen, die ihn zur Arbeit tauglich machen. Und schon Karl Marx hat es bemerkt:

> Außer der Anstrengung der Organe, die arbeiten, ist der zweckmäßige Wille, der sich als Aufmerksamkeit äußert, für die ganze Dauer der Arbeit erheischt, und um so mehr, je weniger sie durch den eignen Inhalt und die Art und Weise ihrer Ausführung den Arbeiter mit sich fortreißt, je weniger er sie daher als Spiel seiner eignen körperlichen und geistigen Kräfte genießt.[1]

Die sich so schnell im XIX. Jh. entwickelte Mechanisierung des Arbeitsprozesses brachte mit sich als Folge eine Verdinglichung des Menschen als Arbeitssubjekt. In dieser neuen Situation wuchs also ständig die Bedeutung des ‚zweckmäßigen Willens' als eines unentbehrlichen Faktors der menschlichen Persönlichkeit, wenn sich der Mensch im Arbeitsprozeß gemäß den Forderungen des Käufers seiner Arbeitskraft betätigen sollte. Der „zweckmäßige Wille" soll in einer Doppelfunktion verstanden sein, und zwar als ein „zweckmäßiger Wille" zur Bildung des „zweckmäßigen Willens", – der Wille einiger Menschen soll in anderen Menschen einen bestimmten Willen erwecken (oder erschaffen), z.B. den Willen zur Arbeit, auch wenn sie selbst kein Willensobjekt sein kann. Dieser erste Wille ist bewußt auf den Willen der Mitmenschen gezielt, er will das andere Wollen bilden, modellieren, lenken; für ihn, der selbst ein agierendes Subjekt ist, wird der andere Wille zum bloßen Objekt seiner selbst. Der Wille, der gestaltet und gelenkt wird, braucht nicht unbedingt ins Bewußtsein einzudringen, und kann seinerseits einem Prozeß der „Verschiebung" unterliegen. Z.B.: um den Willen zur Arbeit in einem Arbeitenden zu erwecken, braucht man gar nicht die Arbeit selbst zu dem eigentlichen Willensobjekt zu machen. Es genügt, wenn sie eine unumgängliche Stufe zu dem Willensziel bildet. Wenn das Willensziel genug attraktiv und begehrenswert ist, wird der Wille bewußt darauf konzentriert und unbewußt auch auf alle die Zwischenstufen, die zu ihm führen. Das ist keine Neuentdeckung. Die Möglichkeit der Konzentration des Willens auf ein sehr weit entferntes Ziel und dann die Verwandlung dessen in einen „zweckmäßigen Willen", der zu den Taten verhelfen sollte, die es ermöglichen können, dem entfernten Ziel näher zu kommen, wurde schon in der weiten Vergangenheit gesehen, – wozu als ein sehr gutes Beispiel der Chiliasmus dienen kann. Es sei hier an die Erwägungen von Reinhart Maurer anzuknüpfen, der einen sehr engen Zusammenhang der modernen Zivilisation mit dem Chiliasmus sieht und durch diesen Zusammenhang die Entstehung der modernen „technokratischen" Gesellschaft ausgerechnet in Europa erklärt.[2] Daß die christliche Geschichtstheologie bewußt zielgerichtet ist, hat – laut Reinhart Maurer – dazu verholfen, alle Menschen in ihrem Handeln zu vereinigen. Da es *ein* Ziel (das tausendjährige Reich Gottes auf Erden) war, das dazu noch die Befriedigung *aller* menschlichen Bedürfnisse bedeutete, *vereinigte* sich auch der Wille aller (gläubigen) Menschen. Es sei hier zu sagen, daß dieser Wille, jener Wille war, was im ersten Teil meines Vortrags als „rationaler Wille" bezeichnet wurde. Reinhart Maurer zeigt auch, wie sich dieses ursprünglich jenseitige Ziel „verweltlicht" hat. Warum aber wurde dieses universelle Ziel verweltlicht? Ich glaube, daß wir hier wieder auf das Problem des Willens zum Wollen stoßen. Denn solange die überwältigende Zahl der Menschen das jenseitige Ziel *wollen wollte*, reichte dies vollkommen aus, um ihre Tätigkeit darauf zu konzentrieren, um den „zweckmäßigen" Willen auf die nötige Arbeit zu lenken. Um dieses Wollen des Wollens neu zu erwecken, war es nötig, das Ziel neu zu bestimmen, – und das war die Aufgabe der Philosophie, die sie auch erfüllt hatte. Immer noch war das philosophische Wissen von dem Menschen größer als jenes der Wissenschaft. In den letzten Jahrzehnten hat sich aber die Situation geändert, – vor allem wuchs schnell die Chance des erfolgreichen und verschiedenartigen Eingriffes in die Sphäre des menschlichen Unterbewußtseins. Es wurde beinahe eine „Technologie" der Steuerung des menschlichen Willens bearbeitet, – und das bedeutet, daß man die alte Willensphilosophie nicht mehr braucht. Die Philosophie war nötig, als der Wille unter der Kontrolle des Bewußtseins funktionierte, – es war also sehr wichtig, *wie* und warum *so* das Bewußtsein den Willen regiert. Es war wichtig deswegen, weil sich der *einzelne* Mensch zu der bestimmten Handlung und somit auch zum bestimmten Ziel bekennen sollte, folglich also auch als ein „böser" oder „guter" Mensch beurteilt werden durfte. Wenn es auch so war, wie Nietzsche meinte, daß die Menschen frei gedacht wurden, um gerichtet, gestraft und schuldig werden zu können,[3] so waren sie doch auch für ihr Tun verantwortlich und waren sie sich auch dessen bewußt. So haben sie auch eine Philosophie gebraucht: dieses Richtigwollen-Wissens wegen. Die letzte Philosophie, die den Menschen in dieser Hinsicht helfen konnte, war die Philosophie von Kant. Heutzutage gibt es viele Möglichkeiten, den Willen der Kontrolle des eigenen Bewußtseins zu entziehen – die Folgen dessen können von einer unübersehbaren Wirkung für die Zukunft der Menschheit sein. Die Wissenschaft besitzt jetzt eine Macht wie nie zuvor. Sie soll der *ganzen* Menschheit *dienen*. Der *einzelne* Mensch braucht aber eine Philosophie, dank der er nicht nur zum bloßen Objekt des Geschehens wird, und die es ihm ermöglicht, die Spaltung des Willens und des Bewußtseins nicht zuzulassen. Denn außerdem, daß der Mensch etwas wollen kann, wozu er das Bewußtsein nicht unbedingt nötig hat, kann er auch das Wollen wollen, was aber ohne das Bewußtsein nicht möglich ist. Nur dann aber, wenn der Mensch über seinen eigenen Willen Herr ist, ist er auch wirklich frei. Wie es auch paradox klingen würde: wir sind frei, wenn unser Wille *nicht frei* ist, wenn aber *wir* und nicht andere Menschen über unseren Willen herrschen.

ANMERKUNGEN

[1] Marx, K., *Das Kapital* Bd 1 (Berlin 1980), S. 193.
[2] Maurer, R., *Warum in Europa? Geschichtsphilosophische Überlegungen zur Entstehung der modernen Technik*, in: G. Frey, J. Zelger (Hrsg.), *Der Mensch und die Wissenschaften vom Menschen* (Innsbruck 1983).
[3] Nietzsche, F., *Götzen-Dämmerung*, Werke Bd. 3 (Hrsg. K. Schlechta), (Frankfurt/Main-Berlin-Wien 1972), S. 423.

* * *

ABSICHT UND BEFEHL

Thomas Keutner
Fern Universität-GHS-Hagen

Vom Standpunkt einer sich selbst als wesentlich kontemplativ verstehenden Philosophie her betrachtet, muß die Theoretisierung des Praktischen als starke Versuchung erscheinen; diese Philosophie − so schrieb G. E. M. Anscombe in *Intention* − könne das Praktische nur als einen anderen Modus der Kontemplation begreifen, „so, als ob im Zentrum des Handelns eine ganz seltsame und besondere Art Auge Ausschau hielte".[1]

Im Zuge der Ausarbeitung einer Analytischen Philosophie des Praktischen wurde der Versuch unternommen, den Bereich des Praktischen als einen Bereich der Befehle oder sog. Directiva abzugrenzen. Als Abgrenzungskriterium praktischer Aussagen dient im Rahmen dieser Theorie die Möglichkeit, mit solchen Aussagen praktisch zu irren.

Die Theorie findet sich bei R. M. Hare und − in entfalteterer Form − bei A. Kenny, dessen Thesen daher im Mittelpunkt dieser Darstellung und Kritik stehen werden. Dabei greift Kenny auf Überlegungen Wittgensteins und Anscombes zur Grammatik von Absicht und Befehl zurück.

Im folgenden soll gezeigt werden, daß das Kriterium der Möglichkeit des praktischen Irrtums nicht Befehle, sondern Absichten kennzeichnet. Für die Bestimmung des Praktischen kann eine Theorie der Befehle und Directiva nicht an die Stelle einer Theorie des Absichtlichen treten.

Es wird zuerst die Vorgeschichte der Theorie bei Wittgenstein und Anscombe skizziert; sodann wird die Theorie Kennys dargestellt und kritisiert. Abschließend wird gezeigt, daß dieser Theorie ein Bild entspricht, welches die Theoretisierung des Praktischen in eigentümlicher Weise herauszufordern scheint.

1. L. Wittgenstein unterscheidet in den *PU* §§ 629−30 verschiedene Arten der Vorhersage und des Vorherwissens. Eine Voraussage in einem Sinne ist die einer chemischen Reaktion aufgrund der Beobachtung gewisser regelmäßiger Vorgänge und die Voraussage der willkürlichen Bewegung eines Anderen. Der Voraussage in diesem Sinne entspricht eine bestimmte Art des Vorherwissens. Daneben gibt es die Voraussage der eigenen willkürlichen Bewegungen. Dieser Voraussage entspricht eine andere Art des Vorherwissens. Schließlich sind auch Befehle und Selbstbefehle Voraussagen. Weite Teile des Folgenden sind der Frage gewidmet, ob auch hier ein Wissen vorliegt, und, wenn ja, in welchem Sinne.

In *Intention* verweist Anscombe auf die umfassenden Analogien, die zwischen Ausdrücken der Absicht und des Befehlens bestehen: Beide sind Voraussagen, beide werden in derselben Art und Weise begründet, nämlich durch Handlungsgründe (Anscombe (1957), S. 2, 4, 6); insbesondere aber besteht im Falle beider Sprachspiele die Möglichkeit eines bestimmten Fehlertypus, des ‚praktischen Irrtums': Ein Mann geht mit einer Liste einkaufen, wobei er von einem Detektiv verfolgt wird, der seinerseits auf einer Liste die Einkäufe des Mannes verzeichnet. Irrt sich der Detektiv in seinen Aufzeichnungen, dann muß er seine Liste berichtigen. Die Diskrepanz zwischen Liste und Einkäufen wird der Liste angelastet. Irrt der Verfolgte in seinen Einkäufen, dann besteht neben anderen die Möglichkeit der Fehlhandlung; hier muß der Einkauf korrigiert werden, während die Einkaufsliste unberichtigt bleibt. Die Einkaufsliste kann als Ausdruck der Absicht betrachtet werden, wenn der Mann sie selbst verfaßte, und als Befehl, wenn seine Frau sie ihm gab; in beiden Fällen wird der ‚praktische Irrtum' dem mit dem sprachlichen Ausdruck beschriebenen Sachverhalt angelastet − dieser muß korrigiert werden − und nicht die Aussage, wie im Falle der Liste des Detektivs. (Anscombe (1957), S. 56).

Die Analogie zwischen Befehl und Absicht ist jedoch nicht durchgängig: „Wir sagen, daß die Beschreibung (der gegenwärtigen, absichtlichen Handlung) des Handelnden ein Wissen ist, hingegen ist ein Befehl kein Wissen". (Anscombe (1957), S. 55)

2. In *Action, Emotion and Will* legt A. Kenny eine Gesamttheorie des Urteilens und Wollens vor. Er unterscheidet beide Bereiche aufgrund der Möglichkeit des praktischen Irrtums. Den Bereich des Praktischen vereinheitlicht er, indem er auf ein theoretisches Konstrukt zurückgreift, die sog. Wollung (‚Volition‘). Immer wenn ein X im Sinne dieses Konstrukts ‚will‘, dann kann er praktisch irren.[2] Unter dies Konstrukt fallen sprachliche Ausdrücke des Wollens; Wünschens; der Absicht; der Freude; der Furcht, des Bedauerns, daß nicht usw.

Eine ‚Wollung‘, so Kenny, kann als Selbstbefehl oder als Wunsch an sich selbst zum Ausdruck gebracht werden. (Kenny (1963), S. 220).

Mit dieser Auffassung geht er über Wittgenstein hinaus, der Befehle und Ausdrücke der Absicht als Voraussagen betrachtete, und ebenso über Anscombe, die der Analogisierung beider Fälle eine klare Grenze setzt. (Kenny führt diese Analogisierung sogar noch ein Stück weiter, wenn er zu zeigen versucht, man könne sowohl mit dem Ausdruck der Absicht, als auch mit dem Befehl lügen: Ein Befehl sei gelogen, wenn man ihn nicht *meine*. (A. Kenny (1963), S. 219). Einer späteren Theorie Kennys zufolge kann ein Bereich sog. Fiats abgegrenzt werden, und zwar aufgrund eines Kriteriums der „Last der Abbildung": Besteht der in der betreffenden Aussage beschriebene Sachverhalt nicht, dann lasten wir dies nicht der Aussage, sondern dem Sachverhalt an.[3] Dieser Bereich von Fiats entspricht dem Bereich des Konstrukts „Wollung" in der ersten Theorie. Befehle und Forderungen im besonderen bilden eine bestimmte Unterklasse von Fiats, die der sog. Directiva: Ein Directivum gibt einem Handelnden zu verstehen, er solle das betreffende Fiat in die Tat umsetzen; das Directivum ist nur dann erfüllt, wenn der in ihm beschriebene Sachverhalt durch das Handeln derjenigen Person in die Tat umgesetzt wurde, der gegenüber das Directivum geäußert wurde.

3. Ausdrücke der Absicht, ob gegenwartsbezogen („Ich koche Tee") oder zukunftsbezogen („Ich werde Tee kochen"), ob Ausdruck der eigenen Absicht oder Behauptung über die Absichten Anderer, sind nach Anscombe als solche Wissensbehauptungen. Das Wissen, um welches es hier geht, ist praktisches Wissen. Die Beziehung zwischen praktischem Wissen und Absicht ist tautologisch: Es ist widersprüchlich zu sagen, X habe die Absicht so-und-so, wisse aber nicht, wie er sie in die Tat umsetzen solle, wie deren Ergebnis beschaffen sein werde und ob so-und-so geschehen werde − dies die Inhalte des praktischen Wissens. Anders beim Befehl: Es ist nicht widersprüchlich zu sagen, jemand habe das-und-das befohlen, er wisse aber nicht, wie . . . und ob . . . Nun wurde jedoch oben vermerkt, daß es die Möglichkeit des praktischen Irrtums im Sprachspiel des Befehls gibt. Diese Feststellung scheint der zweiten, daß ein Befehl kein Wissen sei, zu widersprechen. Doch der praktische Irrtum im Sprachspiel des Befehls betrifft nicht den Befehl, sondern dessen Befolgung − ebenso wie sich im Sprachspiel der Absicht der Beabsichtigende als Handelnder praktisch irrt; eben dies mach den Irrtum zum praktischen. (Und mir scheint, daß auch die Frage nach der Möglichkeit der Lüge in analoger Art und Weise zu beantworten ist: Es lügt nicht der Befehlende, sondern derjenige, der zusagt, den Befehl zu befolgen.)

Demnach kann auch ein Selbstbefehl kein praktischer Irrtum sein und es folgt, daß Kenny in der Auffassung irrt, Ausdrücke der Absicht seien Selbstbefehle: Der Selbstbefehl kann nicht leisten, was der Ausdruck der Absicht leistet.

Hier ist aufgrund des bisher Gesagten ein Einwand denkbar: Der Befehl ist eine Voraussage; könnte man also nicht doch sagen, daß der Befehlende mit dieser Voraussage irren und daß demnach auch der Befehl ein Wissen sein kann? Die Antwort lautet, daß jemand, der einen Befehl gibt, sicher in vielen Fällen daran glaubt, das Befohlene werde geschehen. Doch dieser Glaube bzw. dieses Wissen ist nicht praktisch, sondern theoretisch: es wird durch Beweisgründe begründet, nicht durch Handlungsgründe.

Dieselbe Kritik betrifft nun auch die zweite Theorie eines Bereichs von ‚Fiats‘. Hier sei zunächst festgehalten, daß Kenny Pläne, Vorhaben und Ausdrücke der Absicht als Fiats, Befehle und Forderungen als Directiva einordnet. (Vgl. Kenny (1966), S. 69 und ders. (1975),

S. 40). Er läßt also offen, ob Ausdrücke der Absicht auch der besonderen Untergruppe der Directiva zuzurechnen sind. Diese Zuordnung liegt jedoch nahe: Der Grund für die Bildung einer Unterklasse von Directiva besteht offensichtlich in der Berücksichtigung eines Handelnden, der für die Last der Abbildung aufzukommen hat; wenn dies bei Befehlen die Zuordnung zu einer eigenen Klasse rechtfertigt, dann muß gleiches Recht auch für Ausdrücke der Absicht gelten. Es zeigt sich, daß Kenny, seiner Bestimmung der Directiva folgend, daran festhalten kann, daß ein Ausdruck der Absicht ein Selbstbefehl sei − nunmehr in neuem Gewand: Ein Ausdruck der Absicht ist ein an einen selbst gerichtetes Directivum.

Doch nun gilt für die Directiva die oben für Befehle angestellte Kritik: ich kann mit einem Directivum nicht praktisch irren, da in ihm kein praktisches Wissen zum Ausdruck gebracht wird (und ich kann auch nicht mit ihm lügen). All dies kann ich allenfalls als derjenige, der das Directivum ausführt und *diese* Absicht bekundet.

4. Der Theorie, dem Praktischen lägen Befehle oder Directiva zugrunde − so möchte ich nun sagen − entspricht ein bestimmtes Bild. Es ist dies das Bild von der Seele als einem Forum internum, auf dem sich zwei Akteure bewegen; der eine Akteur äußert den Befehl bzw. das Directivum, der andere ist mit der Ausführung beauftragt. In diesem Bild ist Handeln etwas, zu dem der eine Akteur durch die Äußerung *gebracht* werden muß. Ob er jedoch handeln wird, ob er den Befehl bzw. das Directivum ausführen wird, ist für den ersten Akteur eine Sache der Spekulation − soweit er dies weiß, handelt es sich um theoretisches Wissen. Damit wird im Rahmen dieses Bildes der Absicht gerade deren wesentliche Bestimmung abgesprochen: Praktisch zu sein.

Das Kriterium der Möglichkeit des praktischen Irrtums verweist auf die Möglichkeit praktischer Erkenntnis. Es taugt also zur Abgrenzung des Praktischen. Doch es kennzeichnet absichtliches Handeln, nicht einen Bereich der Befehle oder Directiva.

Vielleicht sind wir weniger versucht, dem zitierten Bild von der Seele zu folgen, wenn wir bedenken, daß dies Bild besonders Situationen des inneren Widerstreits charakterisiert. In solchen Situationen sind wir manchmal geneigt, uns Befehle zu geben. Allerdings werden wir dies gerade deshalb tun, weil uns der Ausgang als zweifelhaft erscheint, und wir unsere eigenen Handlungen zum Gegenstand theoretischer Betrachtung machen. Doch nicht nur entspringen nicht alle absichtlichen Handlungen solchen Situationen. Vielmehr ist selbst hier der Befehl kein Ausdruck der Absicht.

ANMERKUNGEN

[1] Anscombe, G. E. M., *Intention* (Oxford 1957), S. 57.
[2] Kenny, A., *Action, Emotion and Will* (London 1963), S. 303−316.
[3] Kenny, A., *Will, Freedom and Power* (Oxford 1975), S. 38 f; vgl. auch ders., „Practical Inference", in: *Analysis* Supplement 26, 3 (1966), S. 65−75.

* * *

INTENTION AND ACTION

Veikko Rantala
University of Tampere

I

In his book *An Essay in Deontic Logic and the General Theory of Action*, G. H. v. Wright says that an important type of action is represented by an action which brings about a *change* or prevents a change *in the world* (in nature). In other words, as a result of such an action, a state of affairs comes into being, ceases to be, or continues to be—in our actual world. This can still be expressed in a slightly different way by saying that in an action a proposition becomes true, ceases to be true, or continues to be true. Thus, if somebody opens a window, the proposition 'the window is open' will be true and the proposition 'the window is closed' ceases to be true.

However, I am going to consider action in a *more general* sense. I shall *relativise* states of affairs, propositions, and truth to a given action, or to its result, in a more general way. Actually, this kind of relativisation is suggested by what, for instance, artists—painters, writers, composers—do. By painting a picture, writing a novel, telling a story, or composing a musical work—in short, by creating—an artist is acting so that some propositions become *internally true*, that is, *true relative to* the work of art in question, in addition to propositions which become *externally true*, true about our actual world. Wolterstorff (1980) calls an action of this kind aptly 'projecting a world' — a world at which certain states of affairs obtain and certain propositions are true. Similar aspects can also be associated with an action of interpreting a piece of art, not just with creating.

What an artist or interpreter is thus doing might perhaps be called 'activity', as v. Wright proposes, rather than 'action'; it involves a process rather than a mere change. But I shall not make any distinction here. (For the distinction, see also Pörn, 1977.)

Actions, like those artistic ones, yielding relative truths which are not 'reducible' to actual ones, i.e., which are not actually or literally true, nor will ever turn out true (except, perhaps, from the Meinongian perspective), are conceptually more involved than the others; they are generally less simple, and thus more interesting. Other examples of such actions are making or interpreting a scientific theory, interpreting a measurement of a physical system, believing, perhaps even knowing, interpreting a codex or other body of norms, etc.

Another feature with respect to which I shall generalise the existing approaches to the semantics of action is that I shall consider action as a *dyadic* enterprise in the following sense (see Rantala and Wiesenthal, 1984): The relative notions of truth to be dealt with are relative to two factors. One of them is a *framework f*, broadly construed: a story, painting, composition, theory, physical system, body of norms or beliefs or knowledge, perhaps even a window. Truth is relative to framework, in the sense already mentioned above. The other component is a storyteller (author), painter, composer, scientific community or paradigm, measuring apparatus, believer or knower, interpreter, a person who opens a window or does something else by opening a window; in short, an *agent* who/which is *acting on the framework* to find out how the world, or a world, is, or to 'project' new worlds, to change the world, etc.

Thus, instead of simply saying that

(1) *s* brings it about that φ,

I shall say more generally that

(2) By acting on f, s brings it about that φ

or

(3) On the basis of s's acting on f, φ,

or the like. Here 'acting on f' is a general phrase indicating action and its object; naturally, it can be replaced by more specific phrases, such as 'producing f', 'interpreting f', 'using f'. The phrase (2), or (3), is formally expressed in Rantala and Wiesenthal (1984) by means of a dyadic modal operator:

(4) $[f, s]\, \varphi$.

The dyadic character of this action operator can be easily defended in many cases of action. For instance, the interpretation of a given text f, concerning what is 'true' on the basis of f, may depend, e.g., on the author s of the text, on s's intentions and 'background'. Furthermore, it is evident that what s believes or knows is always based on some framework; there are different kinds of knowledge and belief situations. Furthermore, what is permitted to a person s, or what s is obliged to do, is a matter of some body of norms f. Even the final state resulting when a window is opened may depend on the way in which or the tool by which it is done.

II

I shall also give *intentionality* a slightly deviating and generalised role here. Rather than considering, for instance, an intention to perform an action, or an intentional action, or an action performed with a further intention (see Pörn, 1977), I consider an intentional change of the 'background' of the agent. We may assume that with each agent a certain body of *background assumptions* is associated; it consists of what the agent knows or believes, or what is commonly known or believed in the agent's community, etc. This assumption in fact generalises what David Lewis assumes in his (1978). But it is evident that sometimes an agent has to *change* the background *intentionally*—to drop some assumptions, to adopt new ones—to be able to perform an intentional action and to produce new truths, relative or not (cf. Rantala and Wiesenthal, 1984). Examples are easy to come by. Even such a conceptually poor action as opening a window just to get fresh air may presuppose that the agent will search for new, abstract or technical, knowledge. However, intentional change of a background plays an especially important role in artists' and scientists' creative actions.

These generalising assumptions concerning action enable one to obtain a kind of *unifying semantics* for actions, in a very general sense. This unification was originally motivated in Rantala and Wiesenthal (1984) by the observation that in the recent philosophy of science and the philosophy of art—in particular, philosophy of literature (fiction)—there have been developments which seem to bring the semantics of scientific theories, on the one hand, and the semantics of fiction, on the other, close to each other; in particular, in the sense that their respective notions of truth are analogous, to a certain extent. But it appears that this analogy extends, or can be naturally extended, to many other cases of human, cognitive activity. If we this way are able to place artistic and scientific activities in a more general context of action, it may throw some new light on their controversial semantical questions.

III

In this section, I shall present the main lines of such a unifying *semantics*. In certain respects, this semantics generalises the semantics of *dynamic logic* (cf. Segerberg, 1980), *modal model theory* (Chang, 1973), and *neighborhood semantics* (Montague, 1968; Scott, 1968; Segerberg, 1971). I can present here only some preliminary principles, based on what has been said earlier in this paper. (For a more formal approach, see Rantala and Wiesenthal, 1984.)

It is instructive to think of an intentional action as a *problem solving* activity—as a 'response' to an intention to bring it about that φ, say, where 'φ' is a statement characterising the problem. The agent solves the problem by *acting on a framework* (cf. the earlier discussion concerning the role of framework). This description of action may not always be quite accurate; for instance, a person may as a consequence of an intentional action bring about something unintentional. Artistic and scientific activities are again a good example. However, in many cases this seems to be a heuristically proper way of conceiving action; and it motivates the subsequent characterisation of the semantical role of *intentional* and *intensional* features of action.

Consider the problem solving activities suggested by the statement (2), on the one hand, and by the statement obtained from (2) by replacing 'φ' by a different clause 'ψ', on the other. It is obvious that—if φ and ψ are sufficiently different—the agent s may become differently oriented in working on these two different problems. Thus it can be assumed that for each statement 'φ' there exists a unique *oriented state* s_φ of s. Furthermore, I assume s's orientation to mean that s's background will also be oriented, so that with s_φ a unique *oriented background* B (s_φ) can be associated; and that B (s_φ) is a *family of propositions*, i.e., a family of sets of *possible worlds*. It can be given appropriate closure conditions to indicate that the background is somehow *organised*. In some cases one may only be interested in the worlds at which *every* background assumption is true, i.e., in the totality of the background assumptions. (One may also wish that there exist such worlds.) In such a case, I shall simplify notation by assuming that B $(s\varphi)$ is just a *set of worlds*, i.e., a single proposition. The same proviso will be made for the other families of propositions to be discussed below.

Given a problem, to be solved by means of a framework, it may likewise happen that the framework has to be regimented in a certain way for the purpose. This can be seen clearly if we compare two very different problems—or problems which *look* very different. Thus it is natural to assume that to each statement 'φ' and framework f there corresponds a unique *regimented framework* f_φ. It is furthermore assumed that it has an *explicit content* C (f_φ), again describable as a family of propositions—usually satisfying some conditions—sometimes as a single proposition.

As we saw above, an intentional change of the background may play a crucial role in action, that is, in solving a problem. It is natural to assume that once a problem is given to a person, what the intentional assumptions are that are needed by the person to solve the problem depends—besides on the problem itself—on the oriented state and the regimented framework used. Let us assume, then, that to each pair s_φ, f_φ there corresponds a unique set of *oriented intentions*, i.e., a family of propositions I $(s\varphi, f\varphi)$, indicating those assumptions—or possibly, again, a single proposition. When compared with the respective background B (s_φ), it indicates how the person has intentionally *changed* the background assumptions in order to perform the action. One has to assume, of course, that the change is not completely arbitrary, but somehow *constrained* by the background and framework. It seems that a minimum requirement—if a change of the background is to make any sense—is that the intentions, the set of hypotheses to be used, are at least as *close*, or at least as *similar*, to the explicit content of the regimented framework as the original background is. Thus one needs here an appropriate (comparative) *closeness* or *similarity relation*, which would extend those studied in Lewis (1973). Other constraints may also be needed; but they cannot be discussed here. Let us only suggest that such constraints are to be considered *methodological*, and perhaps also *normative*, rules governing presuppositions of intentional actions.

Naturally a *truth condition* for our action operator depends on the case in question; it can be different for different kinds of action. But it is assumed that it will always be a relation between three components discussed above: the intentions and the explicit content of the framework (both appropriately relativised), and the proposition determined by the formula to which the operator is applied. If this proposition is V (φ), then a truth condition is quite generally of the form

(5) $[f, s]$ φ is *true* $\Leftrightarrow$ T (I (s_φ, f_φ), C (f_φ), V (φ)),

where T is an appropriate *truth relation*. How T is defined depends on (i) the kind of action, (ii) the methodological point of view or commitments, (iii) possibly some other features.

The components of (5) must of course be relativised to a possible world if one wants to develop a possible worlds semantics proper. What other improvements should be made will not be discussed here; instead, I shall briefly indicate by examples how different methodological situations may determine the character of the truth relation.

IV

Consider first a situation where a *result f of an earlier action is given* and it will be *interpreted* in a new action by another agent *s*, on the basis of a given background, or its change. Particularly interesting is a case where *f* is a work of art or a scientific theory, or another conceptually involved work. Sometimes there can be several alternatives for *s* to choose the background, even for the same work; and its intentional shift may depend on the point of view—on the interpreter's assumptions concerning the previous agent's intentions, on new observations, on the interpreter's methodological developments, etc.

In general, this is a case where the result *f* of an action is considered *from the point of view of the interpreter* rather than from the point of view of the previous agent who brought about *f*. If the result *f* is a work of art, this means that the point of view is that of the *audience* rather than the artist's. These two positions cannot be kept completely distinct, however. For instance, the artist's own intentions may have a strong influence on how the audience chooses its interpretative assumptions; and here a communication between the artist and audience seems to be, and has been, important in many cases. Similar considerations seem to arise if we think of an interpretation of a scientific theory—perhaps even in the case of conceptually simple actions.

As a concrete example let us mention recent attempts to analyse truth and meaning in fiction. It can be shown, for instance, that David Lewis' account of what 'truth' means in connection with fictional works can be reconstructed as a special case of our semantics (see Lewis, 1978; Rantala and Wiesenthal, 1984).

Consider next a case which is methodologically quite different from the previous one. Assume that only the background of an agent is given to start with, and possibly its intentional change. These given assumptions are used to perform an action in the sense of *producing* or *creating* something. In terms of our semantics, then, functions B and I are given, and an object *f* is to be produced by *s* so that its explicit content C would conform to I and to the methodological constraints. The outcome is not, of course, uniquely determined or defined by the initial assumptions and constraints.

Here we have, thus, a case where the result of an action is considered *from the point of view of its creator* rather than from the point of view of any other interpreter. If we, again, think of a work of art, this means that we are considering it as an *intentional outcome* of the artist, rather than, for instance, as something that is already given to a critic or the audience. However, similar qualifications are important here as in the first case.

Semantically, then, we are in this case considering an *intended interpretation* of a work of art—from the point of view of the artist; or *intended applications* of a scientific theory—from the standpoint of the inventor of the theory; in general, the agent's *intended worlds*. If I simplify the situation by assuming—as it is often done in this case—that we are dealing with single propositions instead of families (see my earlier remark concerning this possibility), it thus seems that the truth realtion T is to be defined in this case as follows:

$$T (U, U', U'') \Leftrightarrow U \cap U' \subseteq U''$$

When this is applied to (5), we have:

$$[f, s] \, \varphi \text{ is } true \Leftrightarrow I \, (s_\varphi, f_\varphi) \cap C \, (f_\varphi) \subseteq V \, (\varphi).$$

The intended worlds are the worlds which agree with the agent's intentions and with the explicit content of the result of the action; so they are the worlds that are in the intersection.

There exist methodological situations which differ from the ones discussed above, but they will not be considered here. For *epistemic* actions, which seem to be quite different—but still explainable in this framework—see my (1985).

———————

REFERENCES

Chang, C. C., "Modal Model Theory", in A. R. D. Mathias and H. Rogers (eds.), *Cambridge Summer School in Mathematical Logic*, Lecture Notes in Mathematics 337 (Berlin-Heidelberg-New York 1973), p. 599ff.

Lewis, D., *Counterfactuals* (Oxford 1973).

Lewis, D., "Truth in Fiction", *American Philosophical Quarterly* Vol. 15 (1978), p. 37ff.

Montague, R., "Pragmatics", in R. Klibansky (ed.), *Contemporary Philosophy* (Florence 1968).

Pörn, I., *Action Theory and Social Science* (Dordrecht 1977).

Rantala, V., "Logical Omniscience and Epistemic Constraints", in *Proceedings of the International Hegel Congress, Helsinki, Sept. 4–8, 1984* (Helsinki 1985), forthcoming.

Rantala, V. and Wiesenthal, L., "The Worlds of Fiction and the Worlds of Science", manuscript, 1984.

Scott, D., "Advice in Modal Logic" (Stanford 1968).

Segerberg, K., *An Essay in Classical Modal Logic* (Uppsala 1971).

Segerberg, K., "Applying Modal Logic", *Studia Logica* Vol. 39 (1980), p. 275ff.

Wolterstorff, N., *Works and Worlds of Art* (Oxford 1980).

von Wright, G. H., *An Essay in Deontic Logic and the General Theory of Action*, Acta Philosophica Fennica 21 (Amsterdam 1968).

* * *

AUFWEIS DES PHILOSOPHISCHEN LEIB-SEELE-PROBLEMS ALS EINES SCHEINPROBLEMS ANHAND DES ALLTAGSSPRACHLICH-LEBENSWELTLICHEN VERSTÄNDNISSES DER LEIBGEBUNDENHEIT UNSERES HANDELNS

Reiner Wimmer
Universität Konstanz

Menschliches Handeln hat zwei Aspekte: Einerseits sind Handlungen Ereignisse, sind Aktivitäten Vorgänge, über deren Eintreten und Vollzug wir durch Tun und Lassen frei verfügen. ‚Frei' besagt hier: Unser Handeln stößt uns weder wie ein Widerfahrnis zu, noch ist es unausweichlich; es geschieht nicht ohne unser Zutun. Es ist nicht so in das Naturgeschehen eingebunden, daß es den dort herrschenden Gesetzlichkeiten schlechthin unterworfen wäre, sondern ist uns gleichsam ‚in die Hand gegeben' und steht uns zur Verfügung. Insofern ist Handeln nicht wie ein Naturgeschehen *kausal determiniert*, sondern − wie wir sagen können − *intentional frei*. Andererseits ist Handeln leibgebunden, von Leibesveränderungen und im besonderen von Leibesbewegungen ‚getragen', die sich als physikalisch-physiologische Ereignisse beschreiben lassen, wenn sie auch nicht in solchen Beschreibungen aufgehen. So deuten sie zwar auf einen wichtigen *Aspekt* des Handlungsphänomens, aber sie können das Geschehen nicht erschöpfend darstellen.

Nun scheint man aber fragen zu können, welcher der beiden Aspekte der richtige sei, der kausalistisch-physikalische oder der intentional-aktionistische; denn sie scheinen einander auszuschließen. Ein materieller Vorgang − so meint man − läßt sich doch prinzipiell bei Kenntnis der Naturgesetze und der statthabenden Randbedingungen vorhersagen, und da besteht doch − so scheint es − kein Unterschied zwischen leiblichen und außerleiblichen Vorgängen! Verbindet man mit dieser Vorstellung die weitere von der Parallelität der ‚physischen' und der ‚psychischen' oder − besser gesagt − der materiellen und der intentionalen ‚Vorgänge' − wobei der zur Kennzeichnung beider Sachverhalte benutzte Ausdruck ‚Vorgang' schon eine (unhinterfragte) Gemeinsamkeit unterstellt! −, wie sie häufig der neurophysiologischen Forschung zugrundeliegt, dann muß man aus der Determiniertheit des einen Geschehens auf die Determiniertheit des Parallelgeschehens schließen. Nach dieser Parallelismusvorstellung sind Handlungen nicht nur leibgebunden, im übrigen aber intentional frei, sondern aufgrund ihrer physisch-materiellen Gebundenheit kausal determiniert. Das aber bedeutet, daß die Überzeugung von der freien Intentionalität unseres Handelns, daß uns unser Handeln in die Hand gegeben, in unser Belieben gestellt sei, irrig ist.

Wenn man nun aber nicht von vornherein eine der beiden angedeuteten Perspektiven bevorzugt, dann kann man auch von der Gegenthese ausgehen! Nach ihr können wir handelnd in die Natur eingreifen über jedes zunächst vorgestellte Maß hinaus. Wir heben z.B. die Arme und lösen dadurch eine ungeahnte Menge von Neutronenstürmen im Gehirn aus. Durch die Parallelismusvorstellung sind also beide Perspektiven abgedeckt, sowohl die, daß die ‚physischen' ‚Vorgänge' primär sind und die ‚psychisch-mentalen' ‚Vorgänge' sekundär als auch, daß diese primär sind und die ‚physischen' sie lediglich begleiten.

Zur Vorbereitung der Auflösung der Determinismus- und Parallelimusproblematik wäre zunächst die These zu vertreten und zu erörtern, daß das Alltagsverständnis unserer selbst, unseres Lebens und unseres Handelns Priorität vor dem wissenschaftlichen Verständnis hat. Doch wegen des sehr begrenzten Raumes kann dies hier nicht geschehen. Ich darf aber auf eine Arbeit von mir verweisen, in der diese These dargelegt und begründet wird.[1] Hier kann ich nur versuchen, auf jener These aufbauend die Begriffslogik von kausalen und nicht-kausalen Bedingungen aufzuschlüsseln, um so noch von einer anderen Seite die wesentliche Unterschiedenheit des Handlungs- und Ursachebegriffs zu beleuchten und damit die Leib-Seele-Problematik zu entschärfen.

Zur logischen Grammatik des Wortes ‚Ursache‘ gehört, daß gesichert sein muß, daß, wenn der Sachverhalt p der Fall ist (z.B. dadurch, daß wir p handelnd hergestellt haben), sich der Sachverhalt q einstellt. Das Auftreten von p stellt somit eine *notwendige* kausale Bedingung für das Auftreten von q dar: Nur wenn p, dann q. Damit ist aber noch nicht gesichert, daß p auch *hinreichende* kausale Bedingung für q ist; denn wenn q manchmal auftritt, manchmal nicht, kann p nicht alleinige Ursache für q sein. Es muß also weiter geklärt sein, daß, wenn p nicht vorliegt, auch q nicht eintritt: Immer wenn p, dann q. Diese zur Etablierung einer Kausalbeziehung indirekt zu verifizierenden kontrafaktischen Bedingungssätze können übersichtlich so notiert werden:

I a) Notwendige kausale Bedingung: Nur wenn p, dann q ≡ Wäre ⌐p, dann wäre ⌐p (in Situationen, in denen p).

    b) Hinreichende kausale Bedingung: Immer wenn p, dann q ≡ Wäre p, dann wäre q (in Situationen, in denen ⌐p).

Diese Merkmale der Verwendung von ‚Ursache‘ können nun aber nicht die des Gebrauchs des Wortes ‚Grund‘ sein; denn ein Grund kann anerkannt sein, ohne daß der ihn Anerkennende ihm folgt. M. a. W.: Ein Grund ist weder eine notwendige noch eine hinreichende (kausale) Bedingung dafür, daß ein bestimmter Sachverhalt − ein Ereignis oder ein Vorgang − stattfindet.

Aber nicht nur ein Ereignis oder Vorgang, sondern auch eine Handlung kann notwendige und hinreichende Bedingung für das Auftreten eines Sachverhalts p sein. Hier sind zwei Fälle zu unterscheiden: einmal die nicht-kausale Beziehung zwischen einer Handlung und ihrem Ergebnis sowie zwischen einer Handlung und ihren physiologischen Voraussetzungen, zum anderen die kausale Beziehung zwischen Handlungsergebnis und Handlungsfolge(n).[2] Für diese letztere Kausalbeziehung gilt das unter I Notierte; hier interessieren die nicht-kausalen Bedingungsverhältnisse. Sie lassen sich kurz so kennzeichnen:

II a) Handeln als notwendige Bedingung für p: Nur wenn x handelt, dann p ≡ Wenn x nicht handeln würde, würde nicht eintreten (in Situationen, in denen p handelnd hergestellt wird).

    b) Handeln als hinreichende Bedingung für p: Immer wenn x handelt, dann p ≡ Wenn x handeln würde, würde p auftreten (in Situationen, in denen p nicht handelnd hergestellt wird).

In dem Falle, wo p das *Ergebnis* einer bestimmten Handlung darstellt, besteht zwischen ihr und p − wie von Wright gezeigt hat − eine begriffslogisch-interne, also eine begrifflich notwendige Beziehung und nicht eine kausal-externe, also kontingente Beziehung nach dem Muster von I. In dem Falle, wo p eine bestimmte materielle Voraussetzung einer Handlung darstellt − z.B. das nach den bisherigen Ergebnissen der neurophysiologischen Forschung stets kurz (einige tausendstel Sekunden) vor dem Beginn des Vollzugs einer Handlung auftretende sogenannte ‚Bereitschaftspotential‘ −, möchte ich die nähere philosophische Deutung dieses Phänomens − ob es sich etwa um eine rückwirkende Verursachung dieses Potentials durch die Handlung handeln kann, wie von Wright in *Explanation and Understanding* erwägt − hier offenlassen. Ausschließen möchte ich lediglich ein Verständnis, das annimmt, dieses Potential *verursache* die Handlung; Handlungen können nach dem früher Gesagten weder physisch noch sonstwie verursacht sein. Möglich scheint mir hier höchstens eine Kausalitätsauffassung, wonach das Potential die materielle Seite des Handlungs*geschehens* bzw. seinen Beginn verursacht, dieses Geschehen als ganzes aber zusammen mit dem ihm vorausgehenden Potential ‚Teil‘ der Handlung ist, so wie Handlungen gewöhnlich von Leibesveränderungen − auch physiologischer Art − ‚getragen‘ sind, wie wir sagten.

Eine weitere Form der nicht-kausalen Bedingungsanalyse bezieht sich auf Handeln als Bedingung für Erwerb und Ausbildung einer bestimmten Handlungs*fähigkeit* F_H. Hier sind zwei Arten von Fällen denkbar je nachdem, ob das Handeln einer Person x Bedingung für den Erwerb von F_H durch eine andere Person y ist (wobei x selbst F_H besitzen kann und das Handeln von x die Aktualisierung von F_H sein kann) oder ob ein bestimmtes Handeln von x die Bedingung für den Erwerb von F_H durch x selbst ist. Es sei der erste Fall näher analysiert:

III Handeln von x als notwendige Bedingung für den Erwerb von F_H durch y: Nur wenn x handelt, gewinnt y F_H ≡ Wenn x nicht handeln würde, würde y nicht F_H gewinnen.

Die entsprechende Analyse eines Handelns als hinreichender Bedingung für F_H entfällt hier; denn zwar ist z.B. die Tatsache, daß jemand immer wieder in geeigneten Situationen mit einem Kleinkind spricht, eine *notwendige* Bedingung dafür, daß dieses Kind die Sprachfähigkeit erlangt. Aber das ist nicht auch schon *hinreichend* für Erwerb und Ausbildung dieser Fähigkeit; denn es müssen bei ihm dafür auch bestimmte organische Voraussetzungen gegeben sein, z.B. die entsprechenden Hirnfunktionen. Deshalb gilt weiter:

IV Organische Gegebenheiten bei y sind eine weitere notwendige Bedingung für F_H von y.

Zu beachten ist nun, daß es in III und IV nur um die Bedingungen für F_H geht, nicht um die Bedingungen für die *Aktualisierung* von F_H in bestimmten Handlungen der Art H, d.h.: III und IV haben nur die Bedingungen für die Ausführ*barkeit* von H im Blick, nicht aber die der tatsächlichen Ausführung von H. Es bleibt offen, ob y H ausführt oder nicht; es steht nämlich in seinem Belieben, H auszuführen oder zu unterlassen. Die Resultate der hirnphysiologischen Forschung betreffen im allgemeinen nur die in IV genannten organischen Voraussetzungen: Man ist hier zu recht daran interessiert, bestimmte Defekte im Gehirn für den Ausfall bestimmter Fähigkeiten namhaft machen zu können und den Weg zu finden, solche Defizite zu kompensieren. – Werden während einer Gehirnoperation bestimmte Körperbewegungen des Patienten etwa durch die Einführung einer Elektrode in eine bestimmte Gehirnpartie induziert, so nimmt der Patient diese Bewegungen als Vorgänge wahr, die er nicht zu verantworten hat, somit nicht als Handlungen, die in sein Belieben gestellt gewesen wären. Es mag hier aber Fälle geben, in denen ein Vorgang, der induziert wurde, vom Patienten zugleich als Handlung intendiert war, so daß nicht entscheidbar ist, ob es sich um eine Handlung oder um ein bloßes Geschehen handelte. Ob Fehlattribuierungen vorkommen können, wonach der Patient etwas als sein Tun deklariert, was ‚in Wirklichkeit‘ ein kausal hervorgerufenes Geschehen zu sein scheint, mag offenbleiben. Es erscheint aber zumindest zweifelhaft, ob sich solche angeblichen Fehlattribuierungen überhaupt empirisch identifizieren lassen, wenn es der Fall sein kann, wie zuvor bemerkt, daß jemand etwas handelnd intendiert, was zugleich kausal hervorgerufen ist.

ANMERKUNGEN

[1] Wimmer, R., „Zur Begriffs- und Forschungslogik von Ursachen und Gründen in psycho- und soziologischen Handlungserklärungen", *Zeitschrift für Sozialpsychologie*, Bd. 14 (1983), S. 299–311.
[2] Für diese Unterscheidung vgl. G. H. von Wright, *Norm and Action* (London 1963) und *Explanation and Understanding* (London 1971). – Die Arbeit verdankt wichtige Anregungen Herrn Prof. F. Kambartel, Konstanz. Ihm sei herzlich gedankt.

* * *

UNINTENDED ACTIONS AND UNCONSCIOUS INTENTIONS

Ora Gruengard
Tel-Aviv University

Intentionalists maintain that actions cannot be properly analysed unless the agent's intentions are taken into account. It is not, however, clear what precisely should be taken into account. Castañeda and Searle, among others, have suggested some well-articulated verbal reconstructions of thoughts which supposedly occur to agents before or during their acts.[1] Although they have not always referred to premediated actions, their reconstructions represent explicit plans which are to serve rather clear and consistent ends. This preoccupation with rational actions, and therefore with explicit plans, is perhaps justified by the purposes of their analyses; but it tends to obscure the fact that intentions may have implicit aspects as well. In the present paper I intend to show that intentions sometimes have contents which are not represented in the reconstructions of the agent's explicit plans, and argue that at least in some cases the agents themselves are not aware of these implicit contents. I intend thereby to challenge the belief that agents can always tell what are, in Searle's idiom, the conditions of satisfaction of their intentions.

The question how implicit a mental content may be and still count as an intention, or a part thereof, should have been asked by Castañeda, who maintains that agent A has the intention I if I is logically implied by the conjunction of some of A's other intentions (and beliefs). It is less obvious that such a question should bother Searle, whose opinion is that to intend I is, *inter alia*, to know the conditions of satisfactions of I. It is, ironically, a problem which Searle himself has raised[2]—concerning cases in which, to my mind, his theory cannot tell whether such conditions are satisfied—that will serve as the starting point of the present discussion: It has been noted, long ago, that an intended action can, under a different description, be presented as an unintended event. If, the example is borrowed from Searle,

(1) Oedipus marries Jocasta

is a description under which the event is an intended action

(2) Oedipus moves some air molecules

is a description under which the event (Oedipus' speaking) is neither intended nor an action.

(3) Oedipus creates the conditions for plague in Thebes

which refers to an unforeseen effect rather than an unknown physical aspect of Oedipus' behavior, is also such a description.

On the other hand

(4) Oedipus marries his mother

is, according to Searle, a description under which the event *is* an action, though an unintended one. These examples illustrate quite clearly the distinction Searle wants to make, but do not provide a clear criterion. As one might speak with the intention to move thereby air molecules, the traditional concentration on the nature of the event under description cannot provide a reliable rule, nor can the distinction between the act proper and its effects: unless one wants to go with Davidson *ad absurdum* one must admit that, depending on the agent's intention, various division lines between the action and its consequences can be drawn. Searle has not found a solution, but has suggested to look for a clue in the relation between the description of the unintended occurrence and the content of the agent's intention.

Dascal and I, trying to follow Searle's suggestion, have noticed the similarity between the pair (1) and (4) and the pair

(5) I (Oedipus) look at the Evening star

(6) Oedipus looks at the Morning star

where the agent and his act are the same, while the object to which the act is directed is the same extensionally but not necessarily intensionally. We have, however, found that whereas in the case of a "cognitive act" the term by which the agent is referred to is irrelevant as long as it designates a perceiver with a certain cognitive background, and the term which designates the act is either intentionally equivalent (provided the agent knows well the language) or not equivalent at all, in the case of an overt act both terms can be, in a relevant way, equivalent extensionally but not intentionally. Thus the description

(7) The son of Jocasta marries Jocasta

is one under which the event is an unintended action, since Oedipus did not intend himself *qua* the bearer of this social title to marry Jocasta. It is somewhat more complicated to illustrate by Oedipus' story the point concerning the designation of the act; but if we assume that Oedipus intends only to play and, with Jocasta's consent and co-operation, jokingly but accurately performs the marriage ritual, and further assume that according to the Theban rules (which he ignores) the performance of the ritual *is* marriage whatever the participants' intentions are, then (4) is a description under which the occurrence is an unintended action.

This analysis seems to lead to the conclusion that a description under which an intended action is an unintended *action*, can always be generated by substituting one or more extensionally but not intensionally equivalent terms for terms included in the description under which the event is intended, on one condition: if the term which designates the act is replaced by another term, there should be a *norm* that determines that the performance of the act designated by the former *counts as* the performance of the act designated by the latter. We have, however, noticed that this criterion is too large. If the distinction between an unintended action and an unintended non-action is to have a point, descriptions such as

(8) Oedipus marries the mother of the person whose story will eventually serve Freud . . .

and the equally anachronistic

(9) Oedipus marries the woman with the highest blood pressure in Thebes

should be excluded.[3] Moreover, if the distinction is to conform to the role the phrase "He x-ed unintentionally" has in common speech, then not only descriptions which are unintelligible in the agent's social context should be excluded, but also descriptions such as

(10) Oedipus marries the only woman in Thebes who does not like figs

i.e. descriptions that nobody in this context cares whether they are true. Hence, in order to know which alternative descriptions of the agent, his act, the object to which the act applies, etc. are candidates for a description of the event as an unintended action, we should know not only that the agent's plan has been to x. To intend to x is to choose to x *and not* y or z. There are some "and not so and so" clauses which are not necessarily represented in the agent's explicit plan, and yet are part of the conditions of satisfaction of his intention. Oedipus intention is that the new king of Thebes—*and not the late king's brother, son or murderer*—marries—*and not dishonors*—the late king's widow—*and not the latter's daughter or his own mother*. It is not that the new king—*and not the heaviest man in Thebes*—marries—*and not speaks with a foreign accent*—to the late king's widow—*and not the woman who hates figs*. So even if it were true and unknown to Oedipus that he was the heaviest man, his accent sounded strange, and only Jocasta hated figs, a description of his marriage to Jocasta in some of or all these terms is not one under which the event is his unintended action.

Oedipus had perhaps considered and rejected some alternatives, but—as the classical story runs—the possibility of marrying his mother did not occur to him more than the possibility of marrying the fig hater. However, if he were asked whether he intended to marry the queen who was also his mother he would know the answer at once. He would have to give at least a moment of thought to the question whether the queen's gastronomical idiosyncrasy mattered to his decision. A "not mother" clause was (while a "not fig hater" was not) implicit in his intention, but he was not aware of it.

It is because we know that the Greeks had a tabu prohibiting marriage to one's mother but no norm concerning the taste for figs that we know that "not mother" was, while "not the fig hater" was not, implicit in Oedipus' intention. Note, however, that the undesirability of the action under the alternative description is not a necessary condition for its being an unintended action. We can imagine a more Oedipal, or perhaps Egyptian, Oedipus who has decided to marry Jocasta and not his mother because he considered that trying to find the ideal spouse was highly impractical. It is therefore wrong to conclude that under a given description the action is an unintended *action* only if the agent would not have done it had he known that it could be so described. Had our imaginary Oedipus known his mother's identity he would probably have married Jocasta, but not with the intention to marry her and not his genitrix. Note, furthermore, that the event described as marriage to his mother would still be Oedipus' unintended *action* even if he were indifferent to this feature of his wife. The event described is A's unintended action if it is normally *expected* from agents like A to know in advance that such a description will be true if the intention is satisfied – and not to be indifferent to this possibility. Unlike the explanations of an unintended non action, explanations of an unintended action *as such* should explain the agent's ignorance. They most often do it by showing that it was due to unusual circumstances, the agent's uncommon indifference being one kind of such circumstances. Oedipus who personally dislikes fig-hating may marry unknowingly a Jocasta who hates figs. But his marriage to the only woman in Thebes who hates figs is no more an unintended action than is the gambler's betting on an unwinning number.

It is worth noting that this is also the case with the Freudian ascription of intentions to patients whose behaviors are, under their own descriptions, either not actions or inattentive, planless ones.[4] Freud's assumption is that the agent *knows* that a behavior such as his serves a purpose of a certain type, but being unready to admit to himself that he too has such a purpose, he intentionally forgets this knowledge. Additional assumptions concerning the functioning of repressed wishes are, of course, necessary for the understanding of Freud's approach, but it is this assumed not-totally-forgotten knowledge which makes the difference between an unintended, though wished for, happening and unconsciously intended action. However, Freud, who had claimed to have a theoretical explanation for intended forgetfulness and a technique for unfolding repressed wishes, had neither an explicit theory nor a specific technique which could support his assumption concerning the agent's implicit knowledge. Yet if one follows his examples one will find that he was using always the same argument, whether the case described was as simple as an insulting mispronounciation of somebody's name and whether it could not be comprehended without the analysis of complex chains of associations: "It is commonly known that . . .". That is, Freud ascribed an action when he expected the agent to know what in his own opinion was known to everybody; be it that people often express contempt towards others by distorting their names, and be it that a certain object is similar to, and therefore represents, another object which represents . . . etc. And, as in the case of the ascription of an unintended action, Freud ascribed an unconscious intention when he believed that the agent's temporary ignorance was due to special circumstances. Needless to say, he expected the agent not to be indifferent to the occurence of the event under his alternative description, but as much as he took into account petty details of the agent's particular biography, it was the assumption that the agent generally conformed to prevalent norms and conventions which justified his belief about the agent's attitude. In fact, the cases in which Freud's ascription of unconscious intentions is, to my mind, most convincing are those in which the psychoanalytically naive observer would suspect that the event was consciously intended. These are the cases in which the knowledge, as well as the attitude imputed to the agent, are common not only in Freud's opinion.

Whether Oedipus' incestual marriage was a case of an unconsciously intended action or whether it was a case of an uninteded action, some of the conditions of satisfaction of his intention could not be derived from his explicit plan. Moreover, other people could know that his intention would not be satisfied unless these conditions obtained – before he himself had realized it. They could know it because he was a conformist. The belief that the agent is always aware of the full content of his intention, and nobody else can know about it something he himself ignores, is historically linked with the belief that the agent can be utterly autonomous. Classical intentionalists, sharing these joint beliefs, have therefore taken it for granted that having an intention is nothing but being conscious of a project which can be reconstructed as a plan.[5] This paper was intented to show that if "unintended *action*" (and, of course, "unconscious intention") is an acceptable notion then such a conception is inadequate for the analysis of intentions.

ENDNOTES

[1] See H-N Castañeda, "Purpose, Action and Wants", *Manuscrito*, Vol. IV (1981), p. 27–52; J. R. Searle, "The Intentionality of Intention and Action", *Manuscrito*, Vol. IV (1981), p. 77–102.

[2] Searle (1981).

[3] Up to this point the analysis resumes some of the considerations underlying and positions expressed in M. Dascal and O. Gruengard "Unintentional Action and Non Action", *Manuscrito*, Vol. IV (1981) p. 103–114. For the rest of the analysis, as well as the change of perspective, I alone am responsible.

[4] See S. Freud, *The Psychopathology of Everyday Life* (1905).

[5] See for example A. Schutz, *Phenomenology of the Social World* (1967).

* * *

EGO DEVELOPMENT AND PHILOSOPHY OF ACTION

Guy A.M. Widdershoven
University of Nijmegen

In recent years there is a growth of mutual interest between philosophy and the social sciences. Philosophy is no longer seen as a completely autonomous discipline, merely concerned with a priori knowledge or conceptual analysis. Philosophers realize that they have to consider empirical investigations and integrate scientific results into their conceptual framework. Social scientists become aware of the presuppositions of their inquiries and of the necessity of a philosophical elaboration and foundation of their major assumptions about man and society.

The mutual dependency of philosophy and science is especially clear in stage theories of development. These theories make use of philosophical arguments to justify the superiority of higher stages and at the same time they give a psychological explanation of the way in which higher stages grow out of lower ones. Piaget reconstructs the intellectual development of the child as a progression towards thinking according to the criteria of formal logic. Kohlberg describes the moral development of the child as a series of stages terminating in moral reasoning based on universal ethical principles in line with Rawls' theory of justice. In the field of ego development a philosophical elaboration of the characteristics of the highest stage is still outstanding. My purpose is to show that the philosophy of action can fill this gap.

An important issue in the analytical philosophy of action is the difference between action and physical movements. Analytical philosophers say that human action is not just another kind of physical behaviour, but that it is behaviour guided by intentions or rules. If somebody wants to make clear why he does something, he can refer to the intention he has or to the rule he follows. In those cases the action is explained not by an external cause, but by an internal reason.

The explanation of an action by an intention refers to a wider context. To understand an intention one has to understand the specific form of life to which it belongs (Von Wright, 1971, p. 105). An intentional explanation reveals something about the agent. "Why do I want to tell him about an intention too, as well as telling him what I did? (. . .) because I want to tell him something about *myself*, which goes beyond what happened at that time." (Wittgenstein, *PI*, par. 659). This remark of Wittgenstein shows that human action presupposes personal identity. In order to act and to explain his actions to others a person has to be able to coordinate his intentions and integrate them into a personal way of living.

The explanation of an action by a rule reveals the pattern of which the action is a part. A rule relates present action to future behaviour. It commits the agent to behaving in one way rather than another (Winch, 1958, p. 50). The notion of rule-governed behaviour demonstrates again that personal identity is a prerequisite of rational action. To follow a rule is to be able to organize one's actions and to unite them into a personal way of life (Winch, 1958, p. 53).

The idea that meaningful actions are part of a total way of life, which can be found in the analytical philosophy of action, is central to hermeneutic philosophy. In the work of Merleau-Ponty, Gadamer and Ricoeur the relation between individual expressions and personality is an important topic. A survey of some of the thoughts of these continental philosophers can throw more light on the characteristics of personal identity.

A major theme in the work of Merleau-Ponty is the relation between the human body and the phenomenal world that surrounds it. According to Merleau-Ponty this relation is dialogical. In the dialogue between body and world both sides pose questions. The body learns how to encounter the world by acquiring a specific way of interrogating it. By forming habits man

355

finds a habitat, a place of living in the world (Merleau-Ponty, 1945, p. 359). In this way the world becomes his world. Every human being has his own, unique way of living. His way of handling the world crystallises into his own *style* (Merleau-Ponty, 1945, p. 197, 506, 519).By virtue of this personal style human behaviour can be understood (Merleau-Ponty, 1945, p. 214 f).

The intrinsic relation between man and world, which is central to the thought of Merleau-Ponty, is also evident in the hermeneutic philosophy of Gadamer. According to Gadamer man understands himself in the tradition to which he belongs, long before he understands himself through reflection. Gadamer assaults the antithesis between tradition and reason. He demonstrates that reason is impossible without tradition, because all understanding is based on anticipations and fore-conceptions (Gadamer, 1960, p. 250ff). On the other hand, Gadamer says, tradition needs to be cultivated and preserved, which implies an act of reason (Gadamer, 1960, p. 265ff). Traditional notions must be applied to the present situation and traditional rules have to be interpreted in the light of the concrete circumstances. This interpretation is a creative process, in the same way as the application of the law by a judge is a creative process (Gadamer, 1960, p. 307ff).

The relation between belonging to a tradition and creating new meaning, which is to be found in Gadamers hermeneutics, has been amplified by Ricoeur. According to Ricoeur distanciation is inherent in belonging-to (Ricoeur, 1975, p. 85ff). Expression of meaning is always an externalization and objectification, in which the original manner of belonging to a tradition is changed. As soon as meanings are being expressed, a distanciation of the tradition takes place and elements of the tradition are combined in a new way. This process of externalization presents us with a certain inner form, in which different experiences are connected. On the basis of this inner connection meanings can be understood (Ricoeur, 1976, p. 693).

As regards the importance and the qualities of personal identity, the investigations of Merleau-Ponty, Gadamer and Ricoeur point into the same direction. Human action requires a personal style in order to be meaningful. This personal style or inner form is the result of a dialectic between reason and tradition. By virtue of this dialectic the agent can integrate different rules into his own way of life, and is able to express his individuality in his actions. The expression of individuality takes form in a continuous interchange of *belonging-to* and *distanciation*. This means that a major characteristic of personal identity is the competence to balance belonging to and taking distance from social rules.

Philosophy of action makes clear that the development of personal identity concerns the ability to combine belonging-to and distanciation. Different stages of ego development can consequently be regarded as more or less adequate ways of balancing belonging to and distanciation from traditions and rules. During the developmental process new modes of affiliation and autonomy are being acquired, in which the former ones are contained and reorganised. This can be shown in the theory of ego development constructed by Loevinger (Loevinger, 1976). I will describe the stages distinguished by Loevinger, and make explicit the aspects of belonging-to and distanciation which are to be found in her exposition.

The first stage of ego development is the *symbiosis* between the child and its mother. The aspect of belonging-to is easy recognisable in the phenomenon of attachment. Attachment also implies distanciation, while a safe environment stimulates the child to exploratory activities. This first kind of distanciation later gives rise to separation and individuation, which eventually leads over to the second stage. The second stage of ego development is called the *impulsive* stage. It shows a fundamental need for support and a feeling of dependency on the one hand, and a strong resistance against constraints, expressed in sudden outbursts of rage, on the other hand. The third stage is called *opportunistic*. The child is instrumentally oriented towards others. It doesn't want to be different from its peers, but at the same time engages in competition. The fourth stage can be described as *conformist*. The combination of belonging-to and distanciation now takes the form of a strong tendency towards loyalty on the one hand, together with a desire to be acknowledged and to have a certain reputation on the other hand. The fifth stage is the *conscientious* stage. The interpersonal reciprocity that is characteristic of the conformist stage is being replaced by a mutuality based on the charing of norms. Identification with society is matched by a feeling of self and personal responsibility. The sixth stage is called the *autonomous* stage. It shows a fundamental tolerance towards others and a longing for intensive, intimate relations, which have a momentaneous character. It also shows a great interest in individual selfactualization. The last stage is called the *integrated* stage. The individual in this stage is able to engage in longterm interpersonal relationships, and to express itself in social life. This stage shows an optimal combination of socialisation and individualisation, belonging-to and distanciation.

Loevingers description of ego development presents us with a series of stages which end in a form of personal identity enabling the individual to follow social rules in a personal way. Each stage shows both differentiation and integration, which is not surprising since belonging-to is impossible without some kind of distanciation. One can't get to know a tradition if one immediately gives up ones own point of view and unconditionally surrenders to external rules. A person aquires a tradition not by loosing himself, but by finding himself in it. This hermeneutic principle is fundamental to ego development. It can direct conceptualisation in developmental theory, and be enriched and made concrete in psychological investigations.

———

REFERENCES

Gadamer, H.-G., *Wahrheit und Methode* (Tübingen 1960).
Loevinger, J., *Ego Development* (San Francisco 1976).
Merleau-Ponty, M., *Phénoménologie de la perception* (Paris 1945).
Ricoeur, P., "Phenomenology and Hermeneutics", *Noûs* (1975).
Ricoeur, P., "History and Hermeneutics", *The Journal of Philosophy* (1976).
Winch, P., *The Idea of a Social Science and its Relation to Philosophy* (London 1958).
Wittgenstein, L., *Philosophical Investigation* (Oxford 1958).
Wright, G.H. Von, *Explanation and Understanding* (London 1971).

* * *

INTENTION AND CONTROL

Michael H. Robins
Bowling Green State University

Functionalism in action theory is an attempt to analyze action in terms of its causal antecedents, usually desires and beliefs. Some functionalists have tried to extend this treatment to intention or even intending. For these reasons there has been much discussion over whether intending implies believing, particularly believing that one will succeed. Call this the success view. The standard counterexample to it is intending something under uncertainty as to whether it will succeed. In reply some functionalists have said that one cannot intend, but only (intend) to try to do the thing aimed at.

Recently a novel line of argument for this has been advanced. Suppose that S is a not very good basketball player in a game with a few seconds left to play, in which his team is behind just one point. What happens next is that S shoots from half court, knowing that his chances of scoring the winning point are slim. When philosophers are polled concerning how to describe S's intentions, the *most* that they will *agree* on is that (a) S *acted with the intention* of succeeding, but they will disagree over whether (b) he *intended* to succeed and whether he could be credited with (c) *intentionally* succeeding if he succeeds.[1]

Response (a) is the weakest of the three and fits best with S's trying to sink the shot, in a sense of "trying" captured by shooting with the aim or hope of sinking the shot. Defenders of the success view opined that the reason why at least many people refused to affirm (b) or (c) is that it suggested, falsely to them, that S thought he would do it. If perchance S did score the winning point, he would be boasting if he said that he did it intentionally.

Tempting as the success view is, I want to claim that if the results of the poll are juxtaposed with other examples of uncertainty, they are better accommodated by what I call the control view of intention. According to it, intending a implies, not the belief that one will a, but only the belief that one can a where "can" is weaker than ability but stronger than physical possibility. I call it the "can" of control which typically divides into two parts: the part that refers to the agent and the part that refers to the world's cooperating with his intention. These two aspects will be present in the case of nonbasic action, whereas only the "agent" part will be found in basic action. I construe the world's cooperation part to refer to the action plans of the agent, sufficiently detailed so as to include the level-generational route from bodily movements to intended result.[2] In contrast, the agent part of control should be construed as the cybernetic means through which the agent guides his bodily movement.

Schematically, such a cybernetic system consists of (a) an internal representation of a bodily movement type (e.g. raising one's arm), (b) a feedback loop by which information about the present token state of one's body can be compared with (a) and by means of which an error-correction signal can be sent to minimize any difference, and (c) a causal dependence of one's bodily movement token upon the error-correction process.[3] An example of such cybernetic control with which I am familiar is James's ideo-motor theory of volition.[4]

We can now see that this "can" is the "can" of control: the ideo-motor response images are at least one conception of the cognitive mechanism through which we typically control our body through feedback and adjustment, and action plans are the cognitive means though which we intentionally effect changes in the world beyond its boundaries of our own bodies.

If the "can" of control is a necessary condition for acting intentionally or intending, then the control theory so far provides at least as good an explanation of the results of the pole as was provided by the success view, but it obliges us to draw just the opposite conclusion. Recall that there was *disagreement* over whether (b) S intended or (c) acted intentionally. The control theory, however, would explain that disagreement as arising from the *ambiguity* of whether S believed he *could* sink the shot. The people who took "could" to mean something like control attributed intentionality to S as expressed in (b) and (c), whereas the people who took "could" to mean something stronger, like the ability to sink the basket at will, withheld the attribution to intentionality. But the control theory holds that if whatever other possible conditions for intentionality are satisfied, as they might appear to have been in the instant case, then it is correct to say that S both *intended* to sink the basket *and* sinks it intentionally if he sinks it. The confusion arises, not because he didn't think he *would*, but because, in the minds of some, he didn't think he *could*.

But even if this is right, it does little more than show the control theory to be an equal contender to the success theory. In order to show it to be a *better* theory, we should first frame the issue in somewhat the following way. On the success view, you can try to do something but necessarily without intending it if you think it improbable, whereas the control theory would hold that in such cases you con *both* try *and* intend. Trying *without* intending can occur for the latter theory only when you believe you lack control. Defining more precisely what is meant by trying with intending and without intending, we shall argue that the control theory accommodates different cases in a way not allowed by the success view.

Take trying with intending first, as I alleged to apply in the basketball case. Accordingly, such trying, which begins when the appropriate bodily movement is initiated (and ends when it is almost completed) should be conceived, not necessarily as exerting effort,[5] but as something like

(1) S is executing a commitment of his will to bring about *a*.

This execution is better expressed by

(1a) S wills to *a* (or to complete *a*).

Now when S tries *without* intending (or succeeds without doing so intentionally), this seems to be expressed by

(1b) S wills *that a*.

This would involve cases in which S *a*'s not only when the result is in doubt, but more important, when the agent believes he lacks any control over the route to the result. Gambling seems as good an example as any of the lack of control precisely because, unlike the basketball case, the causal chain from bodily movement to result is mediated wholly by chance—at least if it is pure gambling. Suppose that S throws the dice with the hope or aim of getting a winning combination. It is agreed on all accounts I take it, that he cannot *intend* to get a winning result or secure it intentionally. *If* it is appropriate to say, nevertheless, that he tried to secure the result, then we have a perfect instance of trying divorced from intending.

But *is* it appropriate to say that he even *tried*? What does such "trying" consist in? There are instances in which the trying would consist in some special bodily movement or sequence of movements. For example, persevering in round after round of a game of chance would be naturally described as trying to win, even if it rests upon the gambler's fallacy.

But it would be a mistake, however, to rest any weight on this, not only because there may not be any such sequence in the offing, but also because it would be a mistake to identify trying with any special effort. So a more direct answer would involve the idea that if winning (at gambling) is something S does (where doing = action), then it should be something that he can *try*, even though there may *not be* any special bodily performance that would count as trying over and above simply throwing the dice. So conceived, trying would consist in (a) throwing the dice, and (b) the attitude of *hoping* (S wills *that* A) coupled with (c) the fact that the prospective outcome is an action or a doing of S's, albeit a nonbasic one. This last clause

(c) is necessary to distinguish this attitude from other cases of hoping where the outcome is *not* an action of the person hoping (e.g., hoping that someone recovers from an illness).

Detractors who think that trying is not possible in a game of chance (and who aren't thinking of it as involving effort) might be confusing gambling with a case in which the outcome is thought by the agent to be impossible either by chance or control. To take a variation on an old example of Danto's, it is not possible to *try* to play "The Flight of the Bumblebee" on the trumpet if one believes that one does not know how to play the trumpet.

However, we are still not out of the woods yet because gambling's being something that one can try to win at, may make it appear to admit, not only of trying, but also of intending. What, then, makes it so different from the basketball case? Both, after all, are fraught with uncertainty. In fact there are examples in which winning at gambling may have a higher probability than succeeding in what one intends or allegedly intends. That is, of course, another reason why the difference cannot be found in the believed probability of success but rather in the believed presence or absence of control. But this is still not quite clear. After all, both the basketball player and the gambler are in control of their bodily movements so the difference cannot lie here. This leaves the difference in the non-basic or level-generational aspect of control. But what exactly *is* this difference?

The answer must lie in the fact that the gambler doesn't have an action plan: he doesn't conceptualize the continuity of the causal chain from his movements to the hoped for results. But the case is otherwise with regard to the basketball player. Although he may be more uncertain of succeeding than the gambler, he still does have a plan connecting a continuous causal chain from his movements to the hoped for result. His conception of an action plan has to include, minimally, that the ball is to reach the basket in an arc, not in a straight line (from his hands to the rim). Moreover, in shooting, he must throw the ball *above* the line to the basket, and believe that *gravity* will bring it down toward the basket. If he thinks you can sink a basket from half court by throwing the ball at the rim with great force in a line drive, he doesn't have a minimum viable action plan. But if it does include throwing it in an arc, it doesn't have to be so detailed as to envisage whether it is to be sunk by a swish or off the backboard. In fact it is because of a plan connecting a continuous causal from his movements to the hoped for result, which makes his *aiming* at sinking the shot one of *intending*, that the our not-so-good-athlete knows how to go about *improving* his skill: his action plan gives him a point of reference as it were for effecting more fine grained motor coordination or control of his movements so as to achieve the causal path envisaged in his plan. This is precisely why it *is* a skill.

The upshot of these examples is that there are different kinds of uncertainties under which one can act and that the control theory appears to accommodate those differences while the success view obliterates them. Since the latter view takes the outer limits of intentionality to lie in the believed success or likelihood of what is intended, it takes both cases of uncertainty, the basketball and the gambling case, to exhibit only attempting or trying, but not intentionality. In contrast, the control theory, drawing the outer limits of intentionality at control, withholds intentionality only of the gambler, but not necessarily of the basketball player.

Certainly there *is* a difference between these two cases. If it is conceded that trying is done in both of them, it looks as though it is trying in the two senses supported here: trying when one believes one has control over the result, rendered by willing to bring about that result, and trying without the believed sense of control, rendered by willing that the result occurs. If the believed control element is a necessary element of intending, then trying with belief in control allows for intentionality but not trying without such a belief.[6]

ENDNOTES

[1] This poll was taken in Gilbert Harman's National Endowment for the Humanities Summer Seminar on "The Nature of Reasoning," Princeton University, 1982. As a caveat, nobody should thin I am resting very much weight on "pollish philosophy"; rather I see it as a convenient way of eliciting our conflicting intuitions about delicate questions.

[2] "Level generation" is Alvin Goldman's term in his book, *A Theory of Human Action* (Englewood Cliffs 1970). I explain "sufficiently detailed" in my "Deviant Causal Chains and Non-Basic Action," *Australasian Journal of Philosophy*, Vol. 62 (1984), pp. 265–282.

[3] I am indebted here to Frederick Adams Jr.'s "Goal Directed Systems," (unpublished Ph.D. dissertation, University of Wisconsin, 1982), pp. iii-iv.

[4] This is James's ideo-theory in his *Principles of Psychology* (New York 1980), 2 vols., II, pp. 487ff. A nice discussion of this recently is by Alvin Goldman, "The Volitional Theory Revisited," in Myles Brand and Douglas Walten (eds.), *Action Theory* (Dordrecht 1975), pp. 67–84.

[5] The idea that trying necessarily involves effort or implies uncertainty is refuted in my opinion by Hugh McCann, "Trying, Paralysis, and Volition," *Review of Metaphysics*, Vol. 28 (1975), p. 431. This notion looks like the flip side of the claim that intention implies certainty or probabilty. McCann's position on trying is more developed in Brian O'Shaughnessy's *The Will* (Cambridge 1980), 2 vols., II, Chs. 9, 11, and 12.

[6] I wish to thank Gilbert Harman for kindling my interest in this problem (although he should not be held responsible for the result) and for critiquing my first draft. I am also indebted to Nicholas Rescher for his comments at the Ninth International Wittgenstein Symposium, Kirchberg, Austria (August 21, 1984).

* * *

CONTROL

Robert G. Burton
University of Georgia

Action theorists have always been concerned with the phenomenon of control although they have usually attempted to characterize, evaluate, and explain action without making an explicit examination of it. A notable exception is Nicholas Rescher whose essay "The Concept of Control"[1] provides the initial basis for this paper. The account offered here is in agreement with Rescher's analysis for the most part. But it also discusses some difficulties with the original and attempts to extend the analysis by exploring some further aspects of agent control.

Control as such is a binary relation that is not necessarily intentional. Its terms, subjects and objects, need not be persons or even nonhuman purposive agents. For example, a complex biological mechanism controls or regulates the production of a certain enzyme in a living organism. Control by agents is a subcategory of control as such.

Human agents are notable for their ability to construct automatic control mechanisms that are not in themselves consciously purposive. In cases of this sort proximate control is in the "hands" of machines instead of human agents whose own control is remote.

An automatically guided missile is "under control" as long as it continues to function according to plan; it is said to have gotten "out of control" if it ceases to function within tolerable limits according to plan. But the plan in question did not originate with the machine. Machines as such do not choose or make plans or have purposes. But there is an important similarity between cases such as the automatically guided missile that goes "out of control" and cases such as the following wherein the conscious controller is not remote. If a motorist bent on suicide should deliberately drive his car over a cliff at a dangerous point in the highway, it would be incorrect to describe the event as the result of his having lost control of his car although the investigating authorities, if they had no reason to suspect suicide, would probably describe it that way since the average motorist does not drive with the deliberate intention of going over the first convenient cliff that happens along. The similarity is this: in both cases the meaning of something's being "under control" or "out of control" is specifiable only with reference to some controller's purposes that are being served or frustrated.

Nicholas Rescher defines "full control" as "the capacity to intervene in the course of events so as to be able both to make something happen and to preclude it from happening, this result being produced in a way that can be characterized as in some sense intended or planned or foreseen."[2] Thus full control has both a positive and a negative aspect. One may have positive control, the capacity to make something happen, but lack negative control, the capacity to preclude its happening, and vice versa. To *have* control over something is to have a certain potentiality; to *exercise* the control is to actualize the potentiality.

The definition of full control as the capacity to make something happen and to preclude it from happening suggests that all control situations are instrumental. But Rescher correctly observes that . . . "there is a clearly defined category of the noninstrumentally controlled—viz. intentional bodily and mental changes . . ."[3] In cases of this sort the question of finding the means by which the controller effects the control does not arise. One is not making something happen in the normal case of intentionally moving one's hand. One is not, as it were, commanding different muscle groups to contract or relax. One is simply doing something intentionally. And so, from the standpoint of the *intentional* order, some control involves the capacity to do something rather than the capacity to make something happen.

Rescher's thesis that having control is a potentiality that becomes actual only when e x e r c i s e d has the paradoxical consequence that in some cases an agent may apparently convert potential control to actual control by doing nothing. Rescher observes that in some cases control may be exercised by inaction or omission as in the case of failure to exercise a veto for example. Here it might be useful to distinguish two senses of having control. Having control of X might mean having X included in the repertory of things one can control either instrumentally or noninstrumentally. This would seem to be the sense Rescher has in mind when he speaks of control as a potentiality. But in another sense, having control of X means being in charge of X and having some aspect of X under one's control. This would be something actual even though in some cases the maintenance of control might require no further action. As an example of this, certain aspects of one's car such as its location may be under one's control when the car is turned off and safely locked up in one's garage.

In both the instrumental and the noninstrumental cases, to have control of something is to have the ability both to do something and to refrain from doing it deliberately or as a matter of choice. But in many cases a person need not exercise his control deliberately. He may exercise it habitually as the experienced motorist operates his car without constantly attending to the process of keeping it in the proper lane and traveling at a safe speed. The control functions of monitoring, assessment, and the calculation and undertaking of corrective action if any is required are virtually automatic.

Rescher speaks paradoxically of the *inadvertent* exercise of control as another form of non-deliberate control. Thus the motorist may reach for the turn signal lever only to activate the windshield wipers by mistake or the hunter may accidentally discharge his gun. In cases of this sort the results may be not merely unintended but in fact disastrous. Failure to activate the turn signal at the crucial moment or the accidental discharge of a gun could be fatal and therefore at odds with any purposes that the agent might have. To be sure the agent in the motoring case has done *something* intentionally, and in both cases the agent is in some sense causally responsible for the result. But the paradox arises when we fail to distinguish the causal order of physical events from the intentional order of human actions. We certainly do some things inadvertently. And from a purely *causal* standpoint, it may be correct to say that we controlled what happened in that we provided the decisive causal antecedent. But from the standpoint of the *intentional* order it seems senseless to speak of the inadvertent exercise of control. In cases of this sort things have gotten "out of control" and at odds with any purposes that we might have.

What sort of object can be under one's control? We customarily speak of a driver's having his automobile under control, or of having one's children under control while visiting a library or attending a concert, or even of maintaining one's self-control in a trying situation. But strictly speaking, it is not the automobile but a limited range of movements or states of the automobile that are under the driver's control; it is not within the driver's power, for example, to make the automobile move vertically in the manner of a helicopter. And a person can control neither himself nor his children nor any other agents *simpliciter* but at best certain of his and their actions or states. Of course we should not forget that we are related to others both as persons or agents and as objects or patients. The control exercised by a parent in changing his child's diapers is apt to be very different from the control he exercises over his child's behavior. But in both cases the range of things controlled and the extent of the control is limited.

Control is also limited insofar as it is shared. In a typical governmental situation with a division of powers, full control is only held conjointly. And while the individual committee member may exercise full control over the use of his own vote, he may have very little control or influence over the results of the committee's deliberations if the group of voting members is very large. But paradoxically one of the most significant ways in which we increase the range of things over which we exercise control is by engaging in cooperative activity wherein control is shared. The violinist who plays an unaccompanied solo exercises control that is limited by such factors as his technical skill, the quality of the instrument, and his sensitivity to the music. When he joins others to form a string quartet, his control of the music making is obviously shared and to that extent limited. But the increase enabled by this co-operative venture is enormous. To begin with there is the quartet literature that cannot be performed by solitary musicians. But even more significant is the subtle dialogue, made possible by the intimate give and take of the players. An example from another domain is today's scientific research where the true "soloist" has all but disappeared.

A final source of limitation on control will be mentioned in closing. Thomas Nagel has pointed out that the consequences of our actions often determine what we have done even though these consequences are in various ways beyond our control and thus a matter of "moral luck."[4] And there is constitutive luck in the kind of person one is and luck in one's circumstances in addition to luck in the way one's actions turn out. Nagel argues that in the light of these factors that limit control, the area of genuine agency, and therefore legitimate moral assessment, seems to disappear. He suggests, however, that this apparently insoluble problem reflects the basic incompatibility of the two orders mentioned earlier, the causal order and the intentional order. But it is possible to view these two orders as complementary. It is possible that, within limits of the sort outlined in the analysis above, one may exercise control in the selection and execution of actions that contribute to the development of one's talents and character. The form of agent control that I find the most intriguing is self-control including delay of gratification, conscious self-monitoring and self-evaluation, and the various forms of self-tuition. I do not believe that the forces of nurture and nature preclude responsible agency. But these are issues to be explored on another occasion.

———————

ENDNOTES

[1] Rescher, Nicholas, "The Concept of Control," *Essays in Philosophical Analysis* (Pittsburgh 1969), pp. 327–353.
[2] Rescher (1969), p. 329.
[3] Rescher (1969), p. 340.
[4] Nagel, Thomas, "Moral Luck," *Mortal Questions* (Cambridge 1979), pp. 24–38.

* * *

7. Intentionale Einstellungen

7. Intentional Attitudes

ZUR EPISTEMOLOGIE INTENTIONALER EINSTELLUNGEN

Stefan Schilling
Universität Heidelberg

Die Gegenstände, die hier beschrieben werden sollen, können auf zwei Arten formuliert werden: als Phänomene, wie z.B. Gefühle oder Empfindungen von Schuld, Scham, Ärger oder Trauer, oder als Aussagen über Phänomene, wie z.B. ‚a fühlt sich schuldig, daß p‘ oder ‚a ärgert sich, daß p‘. ‚Intentionale Einstellungen‘ sind in dieser Arbeit nun Aussagen über intentionale Einstellungen, eine methodische Strategie, die seit Quine ‚Semantic Ascent‘ heißt (vgl. Bieri 1981, 11). Diese Aussagen werden über zweistellige Prädikate gebildet (‚intentionale Prädikate‘ oder ‚P-Prädikate‘ sensu Strawson), zu deren Extension „eine Klasse von geordneten Paaren“ gehört, „die in der Beziehung stehen, die das Prädikat bedeutet“ (Kutschera 1975, 66). In diesen Kontexten, die auf der sprachlichen Beschreibungsebene ‚intensional‘ heißen (vgl. Link 1976, 17) und in denen Phänomene auftreten können („die logischen Hauptprobleme der Intensionalität“: Link 1976, 19), die auf der Gegenstandsebene der Definition von ‚Intentionalität‘ dienen (vgl. Chisholm 1981; Dennett 1981), werden also Personen und Sachverhalte in eine bestimmte Beziehung zueinander gesetzt, die durch die Bedeutung des Prädikats bestimmt ist. Die These dieser Arbeit ist es nun, daß es sich bei den ‚intensionalen/intentionalen Kontexten‘ um epistemische Person-Umwelt-Beziehungen handelt und daß die Bedeutung der Prädikate oder Kontexte durch bestimmte dreistellige epistemische Prädikate beschrieben werden kann. Auf die anschaulichere Darstellung der Argumentation mithilfe des Logischen Quadrats muß ich leider aus Platzgründen verzichten.

Die Beschreibung der zweistelligen intentionalen Prädikate durch dreistellige epistemische Kontexte macht Gebrauch von einer Designationsregel, die Link in seiner Logik opaker Kontexte eingeführt hat: „ ‚t/s‘: t ist dem Epistemischen Subjekt unter der Bezeichnung s bekannt“ (Link 1976, 169). Während der Vorbereich von ‚/‘ extensional ist, „da ein Term in dieser Position nur zur Festlegung des Denotats dient, von dem die Rede ist“ (ebd.), ist sie im Nachbereich intensional, da für den Wahrheitswert des Kontextes die Form der Bezeichnung s relevant ist. ‚/‘ verknüpft also ‚Bedeutung und Sinn‘ (Frege), ‚Objekt und Noema‘ (Husserl), ‚Extension und Intension‘ (Carnap) oder zeigt, wie diese Arbeit selbst, einen Gegenstand ‚unter einer Beschreibung‘ (Anscombe). Die Vergrößerung der Kontexte von zwei auf drei Stellen geschieht also durch diese Designationsregel, die, wenn sie umfassender als bei Link interpretiert wird, im extensionalen Vorbereich u.a. Personen, Gegenstände, Sachverhalte und Wahrheitswerte (vgl. Carnap 1972), im intensionalen Nachbereich Namen, Begriffe, Aussagen, Kennzeichnungen oder Beschreibungen umfaßt.

Die logischen Probleme bei der Behandlung intensionaler Kontexte, wie sie gleichfalls Bestimmungsstücke einer Theorie der Subjektivität sein könnten, sind nach Link „die Quantifizierung in opake Kontexte und die Ungültigkeit eines extensionalen Substitutionsprinzips“ (1976, 19). Ich möchte diese ‚Probleme‘ nun als epistemische Phänomene mithilfe von ‚/‘ interpretieren: die Quantifizierung (i.e. Voranstellung eines Existenzquantors) ist aus zwei Gründen problematisch. Der erste Grund liegt in der möglichen Nicht-Lebendigkeit eines sprachlichen Ausdrucks für eine Person. ‚Lebendigkeit‘ (sensu Kaplan) ist bei Link dadurch definiert, daß ein Epistemisches Subjekt allein aufgrund der ihm bekannten Beschreibung das dazugehörige Referenzobjekt identifizieren kann (1976, 23). D.h. die Person hat nicht nur das Wissen der Beschreibung, sondern zusätzlich noch hinreichendes Wissen über den Gegenstand unter der Beschreibung. Innerhalb der Linkschen Designationsregel liest sich das so, daß bei Lebendigkeit einer Beschreibung eine epistemische Strukturierung in Vor- und Nachbereich von ‚/‘ möglich ist, bei Nicht-Lebendigkeit dagegen bleibt der Vorbereich unter der

Beschreibung epistemisch leer. Diese Leere (symbolisiert durch ‚Ø') meint nun aber nicht, wie etwa in der formalen Logik, die Nicht-Existenz von Gegenständen, sondern die Nicht-Lebendigkeit einer Beschreibung. Alltagssprachlich wird diese ausgedrückt durch z.B. ‚sich nichts darunter vorstellen können' (vgl. die topologische Parallele), ‚etwas nicht verstehen', ‚nicht wissen, wer oder was gemeint ist', ‚etwas nicht in vollem Umfang (= Extension) begreifen' (vgl. ‚Begriff'), ‚etwas oder jemanden nicht kennen' (bei einem Namen oder Kennzeichnung als Beschreibung) oder ‚etwas nicht können' (bei einem Handlungsterm als Beschreibung). Auch in der Linguistik finden sich Differenzierungen, wie sie m.E. der Strukturierung durch ‚/' entsprechen, z.B. ‚Präsupposition und Assertion' oder ‚Thema und Kommentar' (vgl. Reis 1977). Durch zwei mögliche Arten der Negation wird eine komplexe Aussage nämlich unterschiedlich dementiert: die starke Negation dementiert nur einen Teil der Äußerung (Assertion, Kommentar), der restliche Teil wird präsupponiert (Thema), die schwache Negation der formalen Logik (‚es ist nicht der Fall, daß') läßt eine solche Strukturierung dagegen nicht erkennen. Daß bei der starken Negation ein gemeinsames Thema mit der dementierten Aussage existiert (Vorbereich), bei der schwachen Negation aber nicht (der Vorbereich ‚/' bleibt epistemisch leer), ließe sich im Logischen Quadrat zeigen. Der Vorbereich von ‚/' legt allein den Gegenstand oder das Thema fest, von dem die Rede ist (vgl. Zitat Link, S. 65). Der zweite Grund für die Nichtquantifizierbarkeit über intensionale Kontexte liegt in einer Eigenart des Themas und damit des Vorbereichs von ‚/': dessen Wahrheitswert ist nämlich insofern ‚unproblematisch', als sowohl die Rede über nicht existierende Gegenstände als auch über fiktive Sachverhalte möglich ist. Weder in Syllogismen noch in Konditionalen wird in den Prämissen bzw. Antezedentien Existenz oder Faktivität impliziert. Daß es sich beim Thema um eine epistemische Kategorie handelt, zeigt auch die Einteilung der Konditionale in ‚subjunktive' (der Sprecher weiß nicht, welchen Wahrheitswert das Thema hat) oder ‚kontrafaktische' bzw. ‚spekulative' (der Sprecher weiß, daß das Thema fiktiv ist). Das dritte Problem bei der Behandlung intensionaler Kontexte, nämlich die Ungültigkeit eines extensionalen Substitutionsprinzips, betrifft den Nachbereich von ‚/', den Kommentar bzw. die Beschreibung: eine Substitution im Nachbereich über dasselbe Thema oder denselben Gegenstand (‚dasselbe' meint im Deutschen die Identität von Gegenständen, was synonym ist mit ‚Extensionsgleichheit'), darf den Wahrheitswert des Kontextes nicht ändern. Garantien für Extensionsgleichheit gibt die Syllogistik oder die Aussagenlogik. Ein anderes extensionales Substitutionsprinzip würde dagegen Vollständigkeit von Wissen über einen Gegenstand oder ein Thema implizieren: eine Substitution über dasselbe Thema würde dann nur den ‚neuen' Kommentar bejahen oder verneinen (z.B. ‚wissen, daß oder wissen, daß nicht'), aber nicht den Wahrheitswert des Kontextes ändern (z.B. ‚nicht wissen, ob').

Die epistemischen Grundprädikate, die diese dreistelligen Kontexte bilden, können nun über die Extension von Aussagen definiert werden: ‚erwarten, daß' bindet Aussagen mit der thematischen Extension ‚unbestimmt' (‚weder wahr noch falsch'); ‚Bestimmtheit' (‚entweder wahr oder falsch') ist die Minimalbedingung für ‚wissen, daß' und ist das Thema der Zeitpunkt des Extensionswechsels (‚bestimmt werden'), kann man von ‚bewußt sein, daß' sprechen. Weitere epistemische Grundprädikate wie ‚überzeugt sein, daß' oder ‚glauben, daß' können über die Rekonstruktion der Modalitäten definiert werden (vgl. Carnap 1972): so ist z.B. eine Lesart von ‚möglich' ‚denkbar' bzw. ‚vorstellbar'. Dann gilt ‚a ist überzeugt, daß p', wenn p für ihn notwendig wahr und damit unmöglich falsch ist. ‚Notwendig wahr' bedeutet dann, daß a sich die Falschheit von p nicht vorstellen kann, daß also der Vorbereich unter ‚-p' leer ist, daß im Kontext von ‚bewußt sein, daß' die Beschreibung ‚-p' nicht lebendig und unanschaulich ist; bei ‚glauben, daß' als epistemischer Minimalbedingung sind sowohl Wahrheit als auch Falschheit vorstellbar, d.h. es gibt Gründe für beide Annahmen, eine von beiden Alternativen ist aber für die Person zumindest etwas lebendiger als die andere.

Der Versuch, Gefühle und Emotionen epistemisch zu rekonstruieren, verlangt nun eine weitergehende Interpretation des Kontextes von ‚bewußt sein, daß'. Da Gefühle per definitionem im Bewußtsein stattfinden, müssen sie auch im Kontext dieses Prädikats beschrieben werden. Dabei entspricht die Strukturierung dieses Kontextes in einen ‚ontologischen' Vorbereich und einen ‚sprachlichen' Nachbereich m.E. einer Unterscheidung zweier Arten mentaler Ereignisse, wie sie Rorty (1981) vornimmt: Empfindungen und Gedanken. Meine These ist nun, daß beide Phänomene im Kontext von ‚bewußt sein, daß' epistemisch interpretiert werden können: ‚denken, daß' oder ‚das Gefühl haben, daß', ‚etwas so empfinden' oder ‚der Ansicht sein, daß' sind alltagssprachlich weitgehend äquivalent. Es gibt jedoch einen wichtigen Unterschied zwischen Gedanken und Empfindungen. Während für Gedanken dieselben Kriterien gelten wie für den epistemischen Vorbereich von ‚/' (das Denken gewußt wahrer, falscher oder nicht-gewußter Sachverhalte ist möglich), gibt es bei Empfindungen nur die Wahr-nehmung, die Vorstellung einer Empfindung von Sachverhalten als falsch ist nicht lebendig. Empfindungen einer Person sollen hier nun als lebendiges Wissen der Person über die Welt rekonstruiert werden. Z.B. wäre ‚es ist kalt' als Gedanke einer Person ein Wissen oder eine Überzeugung der Person über die Welt, die insofern nicht lebendig zu sein braucht, als die Person nicht friert. Die Empfindung des Frierens läßt sich dann als das lebendige Wissen der Person beschreiben, daß es kalt ist. Gefühle sind nun ebenfalls Empfindungen einer Person; sie sind damit epistemische Stereotype über bestimmte Themen, die lebendige Überzeugungen einer Person darstellen. Schuld als Gefühl wäre dann die lebendige Überzeugung einer Person, ein Ereignis absichtlich, willentlich, überlegt, vermeidbar oder freiwillig herbeigeführt oder unterlassen zu haben. Ein Diskurs über diese Kommentare könnte diese auch dementieren (i.e. Entschuldigung), wobei die Gründe dafür hinreichend sein müssen. Entschuldigungen dementieren also Beschreibungen, unter denen ein Ereignis als Handlung, als intentional erscheint. Während das Thema der Schuld im Rahmen einer Handlungstheorie beschrieben werden kann, soll die Scham im Rahmen einer Privatheitstheorie mit dem Thema ‚Wissen von Personen' rekonstruiert werden: das Schamgefühl wäre dann die lebendige Überzeugung einer Person, daß sie selbst mehr von andern weiß, als sie wissen sollte (z.B. Verlegenheit) bzw. daß andere Personen entweder zu viel oder zu wenig von ihr als Person wissen und zur Kenntnis nehmen. Scham wäre dann die Empfindung der Enttäuschung, sich allgemeiner oder individueller darstellen zu wollen. Ärger als Empfindung von Ungerechtigkeit ist die lebendige Überzeugung über eine intentionale und vermeidbare Enttäuschung von Erwartungen (vgl. ‚schamlos', ‚unverschämt'), wohingegen Trauer durch die lebendige Leere unter einer Beschreibung gekennzeichnet ist: ändert sich der Wahrheitswert eines Gegenstandes oder Sachverhaltes von real/faktiv zu irreal/fiktiv, wird die Person diese Veränderung erstmal nicht begreifen können, der extensionale Vorbereich ist leer, sie kann die Bedeutung der Veränderung nicht erfassen. Das Merkmal der Trauerarbeit ist gerade das Lebendigwerden vorher nicht lebendiger Sachverhalte, das ‚Anfüllen' mit Inhalt, Sinn und Bedeutung bis zu dem Punkt, wo sie die veränderte Situation ‚in vollem Umfang begriffen' hat, weil sie sich wiederum deren Gegenteil nicht vorstellen kann.

LITERATUR

Bieri, P. (Hrsg.), *Analytische Philosophie des Geistes* (Königstein/Ts 1981).
Carnap, R., *Bedeutung und Notwendigkeit* (Wien, New York 1972).
Chisholm, R. M., „Sätze über Glauben", in: P. Bieri (1981), S. 145–161.
Dennett, D. C., „Intentionale Systeme", in: P. Bieri (1981), S. 162–183.
Kutschera, F. v., *Sprachphilosophie* (München 1975).
Link, G., *Intensionale Semantik* (München 1976).
Reis, M., *Präsuppositionen und Syntax* (Tübingen 1977).
Rorty, R., „Unkorrigierbarkeit als das Merkmal des Mentalen", in: P. Bieri (1981), S. 243–260.

* * *

QUANTIFYING INTO REFERENTIAL ATTITUDES*

Peter Ludlow
MIT

It has been noted that there are difficulties in representing the specific reading of referential attitude reports by a wide scope position of the quantified noun phrase. Noteably, there will be difficulties for sentences like (1)

(1) Paula wants a cow

just in case Paula wants a non-existent cow (say the cow that jumped over the moon). The difficulty is that the wide scope reading (2) suggests that the sought-after cow exists, and of course it need not.

(2) $(\exists x : x$ a cow$)$ [Paula wants x]

One proposed solution to this difficulty is to suppose that quantifiers are substitutional. Such a view of quantification seems to have been employed by Wittgenstein in the *Tractatus*.

On a substitutional interpretation of quantifiers, (2) would be true if and only if (2') were true.

(2') for some term t, 't is a cow and Paula wants t' is true[1]

Such an interpretation is supposed to free us from undesireable existence entailments, for the meta-linguistic quantifier does not range over objects, but merely terms.

The objection to substitutional quantification that is most often cited concerns the problem of unnamed objects. As we shall see, whatever strength this objection may have for formal semantics, it is not immediately clear that it applies to the semantics of natural language.

The idea behind this objection is simply that there are objects which are not named, thus the substitutional interpretation will not be sensitive to the fact that these objects may satisfy certain open sentences. That is, under the substitutional interpretation one could never get a proper assignment of truth values for sentences like (3)

(3) some things are unnamed.

At least not if there are unnamed objects. Obviously, on the substitutional interpretation there would be no names which, when substituted for x, could make 'x is unnamed' true.

One necessary condition for this objection to go through is that there are unnamed objects. *Prima Facie* there seems to be quite a few unnamed objects. C. J. F. Williams[2] uses the example of unnamed pigeons at Trafalgar Square and argues that the substitutional interpretation assigns the wrong truth value to (4)

(4) Something is an unnamed pigeon at Trafalgar Square

Actually, what seems to be a problem with the substitutional interpretation here may be more a problem with our characterization of the class of substituends. One might argue, for example, that the metalinguistic quantified expression 'some term t' ranges over definite descriptions and demonstratives in addition to proper names. Thus (4) might be interpreted as true under the substitution of the expression 'the pigeon on the statue of Churchill'. This solution is not unproblematic, however, for if definite descriptions are construed as containing quantifiers, the question naturally arises as to how those contained quantifiers are to be interpreted. If they are interpreted substitutionally, we have begun an infinite regress.[3] To circumvent this problem, one would have to adopt a Fregean view of definite descriptions; one which treated them as semantically name-like.

There are, however, other problems. It seems that not only can one argue that there are not enough names. One can also argue that there are too many names. Consider the following sentences with restricted quantifiers.

(5) exactly one person wrote Waverly

(6) seven spies (each with two code names) quit the CIA

The most natural way of interpreting (5–6) would be as in (5'–6')

(5') for exactly one term t 't is a person and t wrote Waverly' is true

(6') for exactly 7 terms t1, t2, . . . , t7 'ti is a spy and ti quit the CIA' is true

The problem with (5') and (6') is that they will not be assigned the correct truth value at interpretation. (5') will be assigned the value false because there are at least two names which will make 't wrote Waverly' true—'Scott' and 'Sir Walter'. And likewise, because each spy has several names, (6') will be assigned the value false even when seven spies *did* quit the CIA. The problem becomes even more serious if we allow that definite descriptions and demonstratives may also serve as substitution instances.

Ultimately we are forced to treating the actual form of (5) and (6) as being (5") and (6").

(5") For some term t, 't wrote Waverly and (x) (x wrote Waverly $\rightarrow$ x = t)' is true

(6") For seven terms t1, t2, . . ., t7, 'ti is a spy and ti left the CIA and (x) ((x is a spy and x left the CIA) $\rightarrow$ (x = t1 v x = t2 v . . . v x = t7)) and (t1 $\neq$ t2 $\neq$ . . . $\neq$ t7)' is true

If the substitutional treatment of quantifiers like 'seven' is baroque, treatment of so-called non-first-orderizable quantifiers like 'most' is an absolute mess. Consider a sentence like (7).

(7) most men wear hats

(7) is a bit troublesome even on an objectual account, for it makes a claim about properties of sets. Namely, it claims that the cardinality of the set of hat wearers is greater than the cardinality of non-hat-wearers. Thus, on an objectual account, (7) is treated as (7').

(7') / {x: x is a man and x wears a hat} / > / { x: x is a man and x doesn't wear a hat} /[4]

A naive way of trying to substitutionally interpret (7) would be along the lines of (7'). For example, (7").

(7") / {x: x is a term t and 't is a man and t wears a hat' is true} / > / {x: x is a term t and 't is a man and t doesn't wear a hat' is true} /

But of course, there is no reason to suppose that (7") will be true if and only if (7) is true, for there is no reason to suppose there are as many names for hat wearers as there are for non-hat-wearers. In fact, given that there are an infinite number of possible descriptions for each

371

hat wearer and non-hat-wearer it is in principle impossible to ever determine when (7") will be true.

The fact of the matter is that on the substitutional interpretation, quantifiers like 'most' are not only non-first-orderizable, they are non-second-orderizable. One must establish the cardinality of sets of sets of terms. (7), for example, would have to be interpreted as (7"').

(7"') / {x: x is a set S = {t (1), t (2) . . ., t (n)} where t (1), t (2) . . . t (n) are terms and for each t (i), t (j) in S, 't (i) = t (j) and t (i) is a man and t (i) wears a hat' is true and for all terms y ('y = t (i)' is true → y ∈ S) } / > / {x: x is a set S = {t (1), t (2) . . ., t (n) } where t (1), t (2), . . ., t (n) are terms and for each t (i), t (j), in S, 't (i) = t (j) and t (i) is a man and t (i) doesn't wear a hat' is true and for all terms y, ('y = t (i)' is true → y ∈ S) } /

While such maneuvering may be acceptable for formal semantics, it is certainly not acceptable in a theory of the semantics of natural language.

ENDNOTES

* Thanks go to Norbert Hornstein and Charles Parsons for helpful discussion. Earlier versions of this paper were read at MIT and the University of Illinois Urbana. I would like to thank those audiences for suggested improvements. In particular, helpful criticism came from Jim Higginbotham, Richard Larson, Timothy McCarthy, and Thomas Norton-Smith. In addition, Dan Bonevac and Hartry Field read early versions of this material and have provided useful suggestions. This paper was written during my tenure as a Visiting Scholar at MIT.

1 Actually, the single quotes should be thought of as Quine's corners, for substitution of lexial elements for 't' is required.
2 See *What is Existence?* (Oxford 1981).
3 This point, which is due to Kripke, was first drawn to my attention by Dan Bonevac.
4 Field, McCarthy and Parsons have all suggested to me that there are alternative ways of handling such quantifiers. One promising alternative which incorporates their suggestions is developed in "Quantification Without Cardinality," MIT ms. by Law and Ludlow.

* * *

SENTENCES ABOUT BELIEVING, II

Harold Morick
State University of New York at Albany

Although pathbreaking, Roderick Chisholm's "Sentences about Believing" failed to provide adequate criteria of Intentionality.[1] I believe that the first criterion proposed in that paper is nevertheless on the right track. The main task of my own paper is to show the truth of this belief. In order intelligibly to achieve this end, I begin with a sketch of the main argument of "Sentences about Believing." Chisholm provided the following three criteria (I shall paraphrase them for the sake of simplicity) as singly sufficient and jointly necessary for a sentence to be Intentional:

> (1) A simple declarative sentence is Intentional if it uses a name or a description in such a way that neither the sentence nor its contradictory implies that there is or that there isn't anything to which the name or description applies.

A *simple sentence* is one that isn't constructed from two or more sentences by means of propositional connectives such as 'and', 'or', 'if-then', and 'because'. 'Sally believes in Santa Claus' is an instance of a sentence that is intentional by this criterion.

> (2) A simple declarative sentence that contains a subordinate clause or an equivalent phrase is Intentional if neither the sentence nor its contradictory implies either the truth or the falsity of the subordinate clause.

'He believed that John stole the money' is an instance of a sentence that is Intentional by this criterion.

> (3) A simple declarative sentence is Intentional if it contains a name or description that has a referentially opaque occurrence in that sentence.

'George IV knew that Scott was the author of Marmion' is an instance of a sentence that is Intentional by this criterion, since 'the author of *Marmion*' occurs opaquely.

Chisholm rounded off his account of criteria of Intentional sentences by saying that a sentence that isn't simple—i.e., a sentence constructed by means of propositional connectives from two or more sentences—is Intentional if and only if one or more of its component sentences is Intentional.

Chisholm's thesis was that every Intentional sentence that has no non-Intentional paraphrase—i.e., for which there is no non-Intentional sentence that describes the very same state of affairs—describes a psychological phenomenon. Thus, Chisholm claimed, 'The patient will be immune from the effects of any new epidemics', though Intentional by the first criterion, doesn't report a psychological phenomenon because it is paraphrasable into non-Intentional terms as 'If there should be any new epidemics, the patient would not be affected by them'. On the other hand, he claimed, an Intentional sentence like 'William James believes there are tigers in India' does describe a psychological phenomenon, since allegedly this sentence has no non-Intentional paraphrase. I shall turn now to what at this time seem to be the major objections to "Sentences about Believing."

First, the essay opened with a Wittgenstein quotation from which Chisholm drew a false distinction between "psychological" activities versus "merely physical" activities. Wittgenstein had said: "I can look for him when he is not there, but not hang him when he is not there." (*PI*, S 462) Chisholm claimed that the second of these activities is merely physical if only because it can't be performed unless its object is there to work with. Contrary to Chisholm, hanging is not a *merely physical* activity, for to say of an entity that it hanged (as opposed to *hung*) a man is to imply of it a state of mind or at least consciousness in general. So hanging somebody is one of a number of psychological activities that must have existing spatio-temporal individuals as their objects.

Second, contrary to Chisholm, the criteria in "Sentences about Believing" fail to provide a set of conditions that are necessary for psychological sentences. E.g., the sentences 'I am in pain', 'Morick knows the author of "Sentences about Believing"', and 'Quine found Chisholm in the kitchen' satisfy none of Chisholm's three criteria.

Third, none of the criteria provides a sufficient condition for a sentence to be a psychological sentence. In turn, here are *non*psychological sentences that satisfy one of the criteria. All three of the following satisfy Chisholm's first criterion: 'This toothpaste prevents cavities', 'It is unlikely that God exists', 'This plant requires a large supply of nitrogen'. The following two sentences satisfy Chisholm's second criterion: 'It is morally obligatory that people keep their promises', 'It is unlikely that God exists'. And the following referentially opaque sentence satisfies Chisholm's third criterion: 'It is necessarily true that Neil Armstrong is Neil Armstrong'.

A fourth defect of Chisholm's argument is that he didn't give even a hint as to how we are to tell whether a paraphrase of a sentence does in fact describe the same state of affairs described in the paraphrased sentence. We certainly cannot settle the problem by appeal to intuition. E.g., a non-Intentional "naturalistic" paraphrase of my counterexample sentence 'It is morally obligatory that people keep their promises' might fit the intuitions of a Jeremy Bentham but it would undoubtedly clash with the intuitions of a G. E. Moore. So, to use a metaphor of Wittgenstein's, the notion of paraphrase is an idle wheel in the machinery of "Sentences about Believing". Anyhow, the problem of providing a workable and plausible explanation of how you can paraphrase a sentence away is actually a problem for Chisholm's opponents, those who hold that every phenomenon can be adequately described and explained by the concepts and terminology of physics alone.

Call a simple declarative sentence a basic sentence if it is of the grammatical form subject-verb-object, if its verb is a present-tense, indicative-mood, active-voice occurrence verb, and if its subject and object are proper nouns or definite descriptive phrases. I now give a sufficient condition of Intentionality that in turn serves as a sufficient condition of the psychological:

> A verb is Intentional if there is a basic sentence that contains it such that it is not a truth condition for either the sentence or its negation that the object of the verb succeed of reference or that it fail of reference. A basic sentence that uses an Intentional verb reports a psychological occurrence, and any sentence whatsoever that *uses* (as opposed to *mentions*) an Intentional verb deals with what is psychological.[2]

Some Intentional verbs are: 'longing for', 'desiderating', 'seeking', 'looking for', 'awaiting', or 'waiting for', 'expecting', 'thinking of', 'talking about', 'portraying', 'drawing', 'praying to', 'cursing', 'thanking', 'worshipping', 'dreaming of', 'envisioning', 'envisaging', 'imagining', To illustrate, 'expect' is Intentional if only because it satisfies my criterion in the basic sentence 'The little girl next door is expecting Santa Claus'.

———

ENDNOTES

[1] *Proceedings of the Aristotelian Society*, Vol. 56 (1955–56), pp. 125–148.
[2] An expression succeeds of reference in my sense if and only if it refers to something that does or did exist.

* * *

EXPLANATION AND COGNITION

Stuart Silvers
Tilburg University, Netherlands

It is a fundamental claim of the Representational Theory of Mind (RTM) that mental states are relations to mental representations, i.e., propositional attitudes like beliefs, desires etc., are relations a system bears to those representational states, and that these relations defined over representations are computational, i.e., instantiable in a computer model. Because the model is purely formal in order for it to serve the needs of a serious cognitive psychology its states require semantic interpretation. "The point about propositional attitudes is that they are representational states: Whatever else a belief is, it is the kind of thing of which semantic evaluation is appropriate. Indeed, the very individuation of beliefs proceeds via (oblique) reference to states of affairs that determine their semantic value: . . ."[1] The contentiousness of computational cognitive psychology is the presumption that the semantic interpretation of computational states amounts to a full fledged intentional interpretation. "The question is whether the cognitive theory which the model instantiates can refrain from giving them (the states) an intentional interpretation."[2]

Cummins[3] challenges this thesis that the semantic interpretation of a system S is tantamount to treating S as an intentional system. The argument is that there are two distinctions that the RTM omits. First, we may *attribute* inferences to S or we may *interpret* S inferentially. (i) 'S inferrred that P' attributes inference to S, but (ii) 'S has capacity C manifestations of which are interpretable as conclusions, and P interprets an exercise of C' doesn't. Cummins "supposes that (i) entails (iii) 'S believes that P' but it is obvious that (ii) entails no such thing." (p. 75) But (i) doesn't entail (iii) either for there are inferences whose conclusions are reductions of their premises. Nevertheless, the crucial difference according to Cummins is that inferential interpretation of S represents S's capacities to S's interpreters or theorists in terms of a sentence token for that is how we theorists understand S, "but the system needn't understand it: C needn't be understood by S: hence C needn't represent anything for S." (Cummins, 1983, pp. 75–76) Thus a system consisting of a tape recorder with tape is such that when the metalic portion at each end of the tape passes over the recorder's heads it causes the motor to stop or reverse itself. When we see that metalic portion we understand that the recordable/playable section of the tape is exhausted, but the recorder doesn't, it just stops or reverses direction because of a built-in signal detection device. We interpret S inferentially, i.e., semantically without treating it as an intentional system. ". . . intentional characterization, such as attribution of propositional attitudes, involves representation *to* and *for* the system that has them." (Cummins, 1983, p. 76)

Call this constraint on intentionality the reflexivity condition on representation (or RCI for short). In order for S to be a subject of propositional attitude ascriptions S must represent the content of the propositional attitude to itself, ". . . representation in an intentionally characterizable i.e., an intentional system—is representation *for* and *to* that system. (Cummins, 1983, p. 78)

The second distinction is between explicit and implicit propositional attitudes. It is only the former, according to Cummins, that are intentional in the sense of RCI. This distinction is less important, however, for two reasons: it is dependent on the cogency of the first one and it figures less in the explanation of cognition than Cummins claims. The focus therefore will be on RCI as necessary for intentionality.

If Cummins argument for RCI is good then RTM cannot lay claim to being an adequate explanatory model of cognition. The argument is, however, a bad one. There are both epistemic and empirical reasons for rejecting RCI. It is not that if RCI is idle then RTM is adequate for that would be to indulge in the fallacy of denying the antecedant. The question of RTM can't be resolved via apriorisms, it is an independent empirical issue. At stake rather is that the idleness of RCI suggests the vacuity of intentionality as a condition on (truly) cognitive explanation.

If Robert, e.g., is an intentional system then according to the RCI the content of his belief *that drinking single malt scotch yields no hangover* represents itself to him, perhaps via a mental sentence. If we attribute this belief to Robert is there any contribution the RCI makes to the explanation of his scotch drinking behavior beyond explaining it by ascribing to Robert the belief vis-a-vis single malt scotch and that he drinks it because his belief has the content it does (and that he wouldn't drink it if he didn't have the belief he has). If there is a contribution it isn't one that adds to the explanatory strength of accounts in which RCI does figure. For *ex hypothesi* the only systems that can access the reflexive representation of belief contents are the systems that *have* the beliefs. In the current case, if *I* am Robert then I (alone) can determine if the RCI is satisfied, but then I surely needn't *ascribe* to myself my belief. The problem is (for Cummins) to make it clear what it is for my beliefs to represent their contents to me. For if intentional explanation involves the satisfaction of the RCI and RCI involves something other than the counterfactual reading I have suggested then certainly more is required from RCI than its mere assertion.

The reflexivity condition on self-representation is an idle one for it can only be satisfied by a system that has the capacity (whatever that might be like) to stand in a certain intimate relation to the contents of its own beliefs. Notoriously, the features of this kind of relation are the usual subjective ones. Hence, if I am Robert and I believe that single malt scotch has properties xyz then received wisdom has it that becaue I am the subject of the belief state I cannot be mistaken about it, my knowledge of it is incorrigible. "The claim that a certain type of property is subjective in nature raises the expectation that beliefs in respect of that type are incorrigible . . . subjective states of affairs are detectable 'from the inside' and so their detection does not allow for error."[4] The point, however, pertains to the indexical use of 'I' and not the substantive content of the belief state. Perceptual illusions, like the Müller-Lyer, hallucination, anaesthesia, and other drug-induced states testify to the possibility of false first-person belief and even to the misidentification of sensation. The indexical 'I' guarantees only against the misidentification of the referent, i.e., the subject reporting the experience but is of little or no epistemic import as regards the identification and adjudication of the contents of one's belief states. On epistemic grounds then it seems that the RCI makes no cogent contribution to the analysis of psychological explanation.

Empirical data relevant to issue of belief state contents can be brought to bear upon the tenability of RCI as necessary for intentionality. Stich's[5] interpretation of results of work in experimental social psychology tends to confirm the point I argue, viz., that any condition designed to mark out something peculiarly representational in intentional systems always meets substantive objection with little or no positive argument.

Intuitions guiding our talk of belief contents and their ascriptions seems to point in the direction that Fodor[6] emphasizes ". . . statement that P are normally caused by the belief that P . . ." If the explanation of why someone says that P is normally because he believes that P we should also expect other evidential sources to support the thesis that the individual has the belief he reports. But the evidence may be read otherwise.

In experiments involving insomniacs one group of subjects was given a placebo and told that the pill would produce symptoms associated with insomnia. Another group was given the same placebo but told it would produce the opposite symptoms. The first group fell asleep, as predicted, significantly faster after having taken the pill than the second group.

Another experiment had subject perform learning tasks while undergoing electric shocks. They were then asked to repeat the experiment, one group was given strong motivation for repeating the test, another group almost no motivation. The striking results were that the weakly motivated group did far better than the highly motivated group at the learning task the second time around.

The point of interest of these results as regards the connection between belief state content and verbal report is this: the experimentally produced changes in nonverbal behavior was accompanied by the subjects' verbal reports that did not indicate difference in belief. When asked to account for the changes in their sleeping pattern both groups of insomniacs said that the differences in the time it took them to fall asleep had nothing to do with the pill they had taken. Instead they offered explanations of the changes in their behavior that accorded with socially acknowledged causal relations between altered conditions and changes in behavior. Subjects in the weakly motivated group who were asked to repeat the learning task while enduring electric shocks 'explained' their improved performance by suggesting that the shock level had been reduced.

Applying these results to the issue of systems satisfying RCI meriting intentional characterization seems to indicate this: intentional systems are those that have the kinds of belief state contents that P that are normally the causes of statements that P, but these results tend to show that what is said is not brought about by the sorts of circumstances that we expect to produce well delineated belief states. Instead of reporting what the experiments were designed to induce as belief contents, the subjects, when asked, reported what would be reported by non-participant observers, i.e., by those who were not experimentally induced to represent the presumed qualitative content to themselves. The results suggest that whatever we identify as the content of a belief that P (whatever that notion might come to) it isn't what subjects' report gets represented in situations designed to produce in them the belief that P, because that is not what they say. What they say is, at best, what they think ought to be said. If we take such results seriously, the notion of a belief representing its content that P to a system and that these contents are normally implicated in the production of statements that P, then such a notion must be seriously doubted.

Let me try to summarize the story. RTM attempts to meet the intentionalist objection to computational instantiation of propositional attitude states by providing computational states with a semantic interpretation. Cummins argues that for true intentionality RTM must also yield a computationally instantiable system that satisfies his RCI condition on representation. My claim is that RCI is an unexplicated notion with neither epistemic nor empirical plausibility and hence poses no real problem for RTM. If correct, this analysis doesn't endorse RTM, it is almost neutral to it: but it does indicate the vacuity of the notion of intentionality as potential obstacle to a serious cognitive psychology.

ENDNOTES

[1] Fodor, J. A., "Semantics, Wisconsin Style". *Synthese*, Vol. 59, no. 3 (June 1984), pp. 231–232.
[2] Pylyshyn, Z., "Cognitive Representation and the Process-Architechture Distinction", *Behavioral and Brain Sciences*, 3, 1(1980), p. 161.
[3] Cummins, R., *The Nature of Psychological Explanation* (Cambridge, Mass. 1983).
[4] McGinn, C., *The Subjective View* (London 1983), p. 45.
[5] Stich, S., *From Folk Psychology to Cognitive Science* (Cambridge, Mass. 1983).
[6] Fodor, J. A., "Introduction: Something on the State of the Art", in: his *Representations* (Cambridge, Mass. 1981).

* * *

BEDINGUNGEN INTERNER REPRÄSENTATION

Gerhard Heyer
Ruhr-Universität Bochum

Die Position des um die Annahme interner Repräsentationen zur sog. ‚Repräsentationstheorie des Geistes' (Representational Theory of Mind) erweiterten Funktionalismus läßt sich nach Fodor mit folgenden fünf Thesen charakterisieren:

1. Propositional attitudes are relational.

2. Among the relata are mental representations (often called „Ideas" in the older literature).

3. Mental representations are symbols: they have both formal and semantic properties.

4. Mental representations have their causal roles in virtue of their formal properties.

5. Propositional attitudes inherit their semantic properties from those of the mental representations that function as their objects.[1]

Was interne Repräsentationen sind, wird dabei zunächst offengelassen; die genaue Beschreibung des Systems interner Repräsentationen wird als ein Ziel weiterer empirischer Forschung aufgefaßt.

Die Frage, die ich im folgenden diskutieren möchte, behandelt ein Problem, das allgemein als begriffliche Voraussetzung einer Repräsentationstheorie des Geistes anzusehen wäre und zu dem sich bei Fodor wenig findet: das Problem einer Präzisierung der Bedingungen für die Zuschreibung interner Repräsentationen. Die Annahme interner Repräsentationen aus empirischen und systematischen Gründen ist eine Sache; eine ganz andere Sache ist es aber, die notwendigen und hinreichenden Bedingungen anzugeben, nach denen wir sagen können, daß ein System über interne Repräsentationen verfügt.

Greifen wir zunächst auf Fodors oben angeführte Charakterisierung der Repräsentationstheorie des Geistes zurück. Wir können demnach interne Repräsentationen als zum Nachbereich einer Relation ϱ gehörig verstehen, die − allgemein gesprochen − eine *kausale Rolle* dafür spielt, daß ein System S einen bestimmten Zustand realisiert, der den Inhalt I hat. Die internen Repräsentationen R sind dabei als Symbole aufzufassen, d.h. wir nehmen an, daß sie syntaktisch-formale und semantische Eigenschaften haben. Die Relation ϱ beschreibt ein Verhältnis zwischen einem System S und bestimmten Symbolen, seinen internen Repräsentationen. Besteht die Relation ϱ, dann realisiert das System S nach Fodor einen mentalen Zustand oder genauer: es hat eine propositionale Einstellung.

Unser Problem einer Präzisierung der Zuschreibungsbedingungen interner Repräsentationen besteht nun darin, einerseits genau festzulegen, was unter den internen Repräsentationen R, der für die Repräsentationstheorie des Geistes zentralen Relation ϱ, und unter den Begriffen Inhalt und System verstanden werden kann, sowie andererseits eine logische Beziehung zwischen diesen Parametern anzugeben, welche zumindest als eine notwendige Bedingung für die Zuschreibung interner Repräsentationen angesehen werden kann. Dabei kann es sich bei den Zuschreibungsbedingungen, die wir suchen, keinesfalls um bloße Verhaltenskriterien handeln, da wir uns mit den gewählten, an Fodor orientierten Begriffen von vornherein in einem nicht-reduktionistischen Rahmen bewegen. Vielmehr suchen wir nach Bedingungen, welche die *inneren Vorgänge* eines Systems betreffen: wie ein System organisiert sein muß, damit bestimmte Vorgänge als repräsentationale Prozesse bezeichnet werden können.

Bezugnehmend auf ein Gedankenexperiment Dennets[2] gehe ich davon aus, daß die bloße Annahme interner Repräsentationen (als Grundlage mentaler Computationen) *nicht* ausreicht, um die Funktion des Gehirns zu erklären. Denn sind die internen Repräsentationen nicht semantisch interpretiert, erscheint ihre Annahme überflüssig. Sind die internen Repräsentationen aber semantisch interpretiert, stellt sich die Frage, woher die Bedeutung dieser Repräsentationen bekannt ist. Werden interne Repräsentationen überhaupt angenommen, dann muß auch angenommen werden, daß die Repräsentationen mit den *Verhaltensdispositionen* des gesamten Systems in funktionaler Verbindung stehen.

Unter der Voraussetzung, daß einem System aufgrund seiner materialen Beschaffenheit nur bestimmte Verhaltensdispositionen zur Verfügung stehen, bietet sich hier mit dem Begriff der Verhaltensdisposition ein erster Anhaltspunkt zur Präzisierung der Beziehung zwischen einem System und seinen internen Repräsentationen: je mehr offenbar in einem System bestimmte Eingabeformationen *unmittelbar* mit bestimmten Verhaltensreaktionen gekoppelt sind, desto weniger wird man dem System interne Repräsentationen zusprechen wollen. Umgekehrt gilt, daß je weniger bestimmte Eingabeinformationen unmittelbar mit bestimmten Verhaltensreaktionen gekoppelt sind − je mehr *Verhaltensdispositionen* einem System also zur Verfügung stehen −, desto mehr wird man dem System auch interne Repräsentationen zusprechen wollen.

Wir erhalten somit folgendes Bild eines *Kontinuums* informationsverarbeitender Systeme. Zur untersten Stufe hin stehen − natürliche oder künstliche − Systeme *ohne* interne Repräsentationen; bestimmte Eingabeinformationen sind hier kausal hinreichend für bestimmte Verhaltensreaktionen. Zur höchsten Stufe des Kontinuums hin stehen Systeme *mit* internen Repräsentationen; bestimmte Eingabeinformationen sind hier kausal hinreichend lediglich für das Auftreten interner Repräsentationen. Die tatsächlichen Verhaltensreaktionen sind das Ergebnis weiterer Verarbeitungsprozesse im System, die sich gfs. mit Begriffen wie „rational" oder „zielgerichtet" beschreiben lassen. Die Zuschreibungen von Intentionalität, − die ‚intentionalen Anleihen', wie sie Dennet nennt −, setzen damit zumindest das Vorliegen interner Repräsentationen, − oder einer gewissen Mindestkreditwürdigkeit, um im Bilde zu bleiben −, voraus.

Ich möchte kurz auf die zwei bisher verwendeten Grundbegriffe eingehen: den Begriff der *Verhaltensdisposition* und den *Informationsbegriff*.

Dispositionen sollen im folgenden als nicht operational definierbare Grundbegriffe angesehen werden. Der Grundgedanke dieses nicht-reduktionistischen Ansatzes besteht darin, die einem Objekt zukommenden Dispositionen aus gewissen strukturellen Eigenschaften dieses Objektes abzuleiten. Dispositionen sind nicht Konstruktionen aus Ereignissen, sondern umgekehrt: ein Objekt verhält sich in bestimmter Weise, weil ihm bestimmte Dispositionen zukommen, wobei sich einige dieser Dispositionen aus der Tatsache ableiten lassen, daß ein Objekt ein *Vertreter* einer natürlichen oder nominalen Art ist.[3]

Es verdient hervorgehoben zu werden, daß dieser Ansatz im Ergebnis die Tür zu einem *biologischen Naturalismus* öffnet.[4] Denn sind die Dispositionen eines Objekts stets Eigenschaften dieses Objekts als Vertreter einer Art, dann hängen die Dispositionen − trotz ihres funktionalen Charakters − auch stets von bestimmten *stofflichen* Voraussetzungen ab.

Auch der *Informationsbegriff*, der hier nicht in seiner technischen, wahrscheinlichkeitstheoretischen Bedeutung verwendet werden soll, muß weiter präzisiert werden. Was wir brauchen, ist ein *inhaltlich* bestimmter Informationsbegriff, nicht bloß ein Maß der durchschnittlichen Informationsmenge. Ein Ansatz dazu findet sich in Fred Dretskes Untersuchung *Knowledge and the Flow of Information*. Dretske definiert die Grundbedeutung des Informationsbegriffs, in der wir davon sprechen, daß z.B. Bücher oder Zeitungen Information enthalten, in der folgenden Weise:

A state of affairs contains information about X to just that extent to which a suitably placed observer could learn something about X by consulting it.[5]

Anders als der bloße Maßbegriff von Information setzt der semantische Informationsbegriff die *Wahrheit* des Mitgeteilten voraus; ich schlage vor, die in einem System A enthaltene semantische Information I über eine Umgebung B dementsprechend als ein *Modell* von B in A zu verstehen.

Da entsprechend der Kernbedeutung des Informationsbegriffs die in einem System enthaltene semantische Information von einem Benutzer interpretiert werden kann, aber nicht interpretiert werden muß, wollen wir darüber hinaus zwischen *interpretierter* und *uninterpretierter* Information unterscheiden.

Kehren wir jetzt zurück zu den oben skizzierten Überlegungen, dann können wir sagen: einfache informationsverarbeitende Systeme, d.h. Systeme ohne interne Repräsentationen, haben bestimmte Informationen gewissermaßen eingebaut; sie unterscheiden zwischen verschiedenen Eingaben, weil sie nur auf bestimmte Eingaben reagieren. Die Informationen, über die derartige Systeme verfügen, sind also uninterpretierte Informationen. Erst wenn die in dem System enthaltene Information mittels eines Interpretationsschlüssels interpretiert wird, kann ihr ein *Inhalt* und dem System ein *Zweck* zugeschrieben werden. Von komplexeren Informationsverarbeitenden Systemen könnte man demgegenüber sagen, daß sie nicht nur Informationen enthalten, sondern diese selber auch als Informationen interpretieren können, d.h. die in dem System enthaltenen Informationen haben auch für das System einen Inhalt.

Gehen wir von den Grundbegriffen Disposition und Information aus, und verstehen wir unter internen Repräsentationen *intern interpretierte Informationen*, dann besteht das Problem, Zuschreibungsbedingungen für interne Repräsentationen anzugeben, darin, den Punkt, an dem die in einem System enthaltenen uninterpretierten Informationen zu intern interpretierten Informationen werden, genau anzugeben. Die entscheidende Frage ist dabei, wie die Relation ϱ spezifiziert werden soll. Aufgrund der vorangegangenen Diskussion liegt es nahe, ϱ als eine *Interpretationsbeziehung* aufzufassen: die internen Repräsentationen re-präsentieren, indem sie selber präsent sind.

Für eine Ausarbeitung dieses Ansatzes bietet es sich an, die internen Interpretationen selber wiederum als *informationsverarbeitende Prozesse* aufzufassen. Ein System verfügt dann über interne Repräsentationen, wenn es über gewisse Informationen über die intern als Repräsentationen benutzten Zeichen verfügt, wobei wir – entgegen Fodor – annehmen wollen, daß diese Informationen nur syntaktisch-formaler Art sein können.

Sind damit die Zuschreibungsbedingungen interner Repräsentationen unter den gemachten Voraussetzungen allgemein bestimmt, so muß eine Präzisierung dieser Bedingungen vor allem der Forderung nach *Zuschreibungsadäquatheit* genügen, d.h. die kognitiven Modelle informationsverarbeitender Prozesse müssen Anspruch auf psychische Realität erheben können. Als theoretischer Rahmen scheint sich dafür eine Synthese aus einem biologischen und einem informationstheoretischen Ansatz besonders anzubieten: die einem System zur Verfügung stehenden Verhaltensdispositionen sind einerseits nicht nur funktional definiert, sondern auch von der *stofflichen Substanz* der Dinge abhängig, für die sie definiert sind; und sie sind andererseits auch als in dem System enthaltene *uninterpretierte Informationen* zu verstehen. Die Alternative zwischen der Dispositions- und Repräsentationstheorie des Geistes könnte sich damit im echten Sinne als Scheinproblem erweisen: weder Disposition noch Repräsentation, sondern ein biologisch interpretierter, semantischer Informationsbegriff wäre als Grundbegriff der kognitiven Wissenschaft anzusehen.

ANMERKUNGEN

[1] Fodor, J. A., *Representations* (Cambridge (Mass.) 1981), S. 26.

[2] Dennett, D., „Current Issues in the Philosophy of Mind", *American* Philosophical Quarterly 15 (1978), S. 249–261.

[3] Vgl. G. Heyer, *Generische Kennzeichnungen. Zur Logik und Ontologie generischer Bedeutung* (München und Wien 1985). Kap. VI.

[4] Vgl. J. Searle, *Intentionaity* (Cambridge 1983), sowie „Minds and Brains without Programs", unveröffentlichtes Manuskript.

[5] Dretske, F. I., *Knowledge and the Flow of Information* (Cambridge (Mass.) ²1982), S. 45.

* * *

IST SELBSTBEWUSSTSEIN EINE ERKENNTNIS?

Dieter Sturma
Universität Hannover

Wittgenstein hat in seiner späten Philosophie mehrfach herausgestellt, daß Sätze über Bewußtseinszustände, in denen ‚ich‘ als grammatikalisches Subjekt fungiert, keine Beobachtungssätze sind. So ist der Satz ‚ich habe Schmerzen‘ unter der Voraussetzung der Wahrhaftigkeit desjenigen, der ihn äußert, prinzipiell infallibel und unkorrigierbar. Es wäre nach Wittgenstein unsinnig, diesen Satz durch die Frage in Zweifel zu ziehen „Bist du sicher, daß *du* es bist, der Schmerzen hat?"[1] Weil in derartigen ‚ich‘-Sätzen kein Erkenntnisprozeß ausgedrückt wird, in bezug auf den Wahrheitswerte anwendbar wären, sind sie anscheinend nicht als Beschreibungen von kognitiven Einstellungen verstehbar. Fälle von Wissen erfordern den Besitz einer wahren Beschreibung dessen, was gewußt wird. Wie Wittgenstein gezeigt hat, ist es aber gerade die Eigentümlichkeit von ‚ich‘-Sätzen über Bewußtseinszustände, daß in ihnen eine solche Beschreibung nicht vorzuliegen braucht. Für Wittgenstein sind Sätze wie ‚ich habe Bewußtsein‘ keine Aussagen, sondern nur Ausdrucksformen unbezweifelbarer Gewißheiten. „‚Nichts ist so gewiß wie, daß mir Bewußtsein eignet.‘ Warum soll ich es dann nicht auf sich beruhen lassen? Diese Gewißheit ist wie eine große Kraft, deren Angriffspunkt sich nicht bewegt, die also keine Arbeit leistet."[2] Aus dieser Bemerkung Wittgensteins folgt offenbar, daß ‚ich‘-Sätze über Bewußtseinszustände in kognitiver Hinsicht folgenlos sind. Nur in ihnen kann sich aber Selbstbewußtsein manifestieren, daher stellt sich die Frage, inwiefern ihre semantischen Eigentümlichkeiten hinreichend sind, dem Phänomen des Selbstbewußtseins in begründeter Weise den Status einer kognitiven Einstellung abzusprechen. Um diese Frage beantworten zu können, soll im folgenden der Versuch unternommen werden, Selbstbewußtsein in der Perspektive einer allgemeinen Konzeption kognitiven Verhaltens zu bestimmen.

In dem Satz (1) *ich nehme X wahr* wird ein kognitives Verhalten bzw. eine kognitive Einstellung ausgedrückt. In normalen Anwendungsfällen wird die Bedeutung dieses Satzes durch seinen propositionalen Gehalt bestimmt. Ein Satz wie ‚ich sehe eine Katze‘ drückt meine Wahrnehmung von einer Katze aus, ohne daß ich mich in der Regel dabei noch eigens thematisiere. Die informationsartigen Komponenten von (1) sind zum einen das ein spezifisches kognitives Verhalten bezeichnende Verb und zum anderen der Sachverhalt, auf den sich dieses Verhalten bezieht. Der überwiegende Teil unserer Warhnehmungen ist denn auch ein unaufmerksames Wahrnehmen in dem Sinne, daß wir nicht in jedem Fall ein explizites Bewußtsein davon haben, daß wir etwas wahrnehmen bzw. daß wie es sind, die etwas wahrnehmen. Selbstbewußtsein muß dagegen immer ein reflektierter Bewußtseinszustand sein. Ein solcher Zustand wird durch den Satz (2) *ich habe Bewußtsein davon, daß ich X wahrnehme* beschrieben. Im propositionalen Satzteil von (2) erscheint noch einmal der Ausdruck ‚ich‘. Im Hinblick auf die zweifache Verwendung von ‚ich‘ in (2) ist zu klären, ob sie auf einen theoretisch relevanten Sachverhalt, der kognitive Konsequenzen hat, verweist. Wittgenstein hat eine solche Möglichkeit ausgeschlossen. Es ist seine Ansicht gewesen, daß Sätze, in denen kognitive Einstellungen gegenüber Bewußtseinszuständen ausgedrückt werden, nicht als Fälle von Wissen verstanden werden können. Im § 246 der *Philosophischen Untersuchungen* schreibt er: „Von mir kann man überhaupt nicht sagen (außer etwa im Spaß) ich *wisse*, daß ich Schmerzen habe. Was soll es denn heißen — außer etwa, daß ich Schmerzen *habe*?"[3] Wittgenstein zufolge sind derartige ‚ich‘-Sätze immer nur als verhaltensmäßige Manifestationen von mentalen Zuständen, aber nicht als Wissen zu begreifen. Diese Überzeugung ist gewiß plausibel hinsichtlich von Empfindungszuständen, es ist aber nicht einsehbar, wie daraus die weitreichende Folgerung gezogen werden kann, daß mit einem Satz wie (2) nichts anderes gesagt werden kann als ‚ich habe einen Bewußtseinszustand‘. Denn in reflektierten Bewußtseinszuständen kann ich mich über *meinen* jeweiligen Bewußtseinszustand orientieren, weshalb in ihnen mehr enthalten sein muß als der bloße Ausdruck mentaler Zustände. Wenn ich mir meiner selbst bewußt bin, dann bin ich mir bewußt, mich in diesem oder jenem Zustand zu befinden bzw. diese oder jene Handlung auszuführen, d.h. ich bin mir in einem konkreten Sinne bewußt, daß ich mich in einer spezifischen Weise zu der von mir wahrgenommenen Welt verhalte.

Wittgenstein hat aber im *Tractatus* völlig zu Recht das Subjekt, das etwas in der Welt wahrnimmt, als nicht zu dieser Welt gehörig bestimmt. „Das Subjekt gehört nicht zur Welt, sondern es ist eine Grenze der Welt."[4] In den *Tagebüchern* heißt es: „Das Ich ist kein Gegenstand. Jedem Gegenstand stehe ich objektiv gegenüber. Dem Ich nicht."[5] Mit dieser Feststellung Wittgensteins ergibt sich nunmehr die Schwierigkeit, wie erklärt werden kann, daß mit ‚ich' offenbar zugleich auf einen der wahrnehmbaren Welt zugehörigen und nicht zugehörigen Gegenstand Bezug genommen wird.

Es ist gerade diese scheinbare Schwierigkeit der gleichzeitigen Verwendung von ‚ich' im nicht-propositionalen und propositionalen Satzteil von (2), die eine entscheidende Argumentationsperspektive für die Aufklärung des kognitiven Sinns von Selbstbewußtsein eröffnet. Bei einem kognitiven Verhalten, wie es in (1) beschrieben wird, bin ich, wie ich mich selbst als Person erlebe, gar nicht betroffen. Es ist zwar mein Erlebnis, aber der Ausdruck ‚ich' in (1) betrifft nicht seinen inhaltlichen Gehalt. Aus diesem Grunde hat Wittgenstein darauf hingewiesen, daß der subjektive Ursprung der Erfahrung selbst nicht noch einmal als Bestandteil der erfahrbaren Welt wahrgenommen werden kann; ‚ich' fungiert dementsprechend in dem nicht-propositionalen Satzteil von (2) allein als Bezeichnung des Zentrums der Erlebnisperspektive der Person, die (2) äußert. Wenn ich etwas wahrnehme, dann habe ich jedoch ein spezifisches Verhältnis zu einem Ereignis in der Welt, und dieses Verhältnis impliziert, daß ich einen bestimmten Ort in der Welt einnehme, der den Orientierungspunkt meiner jeweiligen Erfahrung ausmacht, denn ich nehme nicht einfach ein Ereignis wahr, so wie es an sich bestimmt sein mag, sondern ich nehme es in einer besonderen Perspektive wahr, die wiederum relativ ist auf meinen jeweiligen Ort in der Welt; auf diesen Sachverhalt bezieht sich der Ausdruck ‚ich' in der Proposition von (2). Er indiziert, daß ich mich in einer bestimmten Art und Weise *in* und *zu* der von mir wahrgenommenen Welt verhalte, d.h. ‚ich' in der Proposition von (2) ist meinem jeweiligen Verhalten in der Welt, soweit ich davon ein explizites Bewußtsein habe, zugeordnet. Der Ausdruck ‚ich' ist dabei kein Index für ein gewöhnliches Objekt meiner Erfahrungswelt, das ich noch eigens zu identifizieren hätte, mit ‚ich' nehme ich aber gleichwohl auf ein unmittelbar mich betreffendes Ereignis in der Welt Bezug. Eine Wahrnehmung ist zwar ein Erlebnis, doch muß sie auch Bestandteil der Welt der Ereignisse sein, damit überhaupt etwas wahrgenommen werden kann. Wir schauen nicht gleichsam durch Fenster von außen in die Welt hinein, sondern wir sind, weil wir die Welt wahrnehmen, immer schon ein Teil von ihr. Dieser Sachverhalt, daß wir der Welt der Ereignisse angehören, aber von ihr als diejenigen, die sie erkennen können, zugleich um die Möglichkeit der Reflexion entrückt sind, findet seine sprachliche Entsprechung in der unterschiedlichen Funktion von ‚ich' im nicht-propositionalen und propositionalen Satzteil von (2), worin sich ein reflektierter Bewußtseinszustand manifestiert. Wenn ich also über einen bestimmten Wahrnehmungszustand ein explizites Bewußtsein herstelle, dann beziehe ich mich über den Ausdruck ‚ich' in der Proposition, in der diese Wahrnehmung ausgedrückt wird, darauf, wie ich mich als derjenige, der die Proposition äußert, zur Welt verhalte. Der in der Proposition enthaltene Ausdruck ‚ich' ist infolgedessen immer auch in personaler, lokaler und temporaler Hinsicht interpretierbar. Das macht den grundsätzlichen Unterschied zum Ausdruck ‚ich' in nicht-propositionalen Satzteilen aus, in denen ‚ich' eine Grenze der erfahrbaren Welt indiziert, die das unthematisierte Zentrum der Weltorientierung der jeweiligen Person ist. In propositionalen Kontexten bezieht sich ‚ich' dagegen auf ein Verhalten der Person in der Welt und ist daher für sie ein erfahrbares Selbstverhältnis. Damit ergibt sich für den Begriff des Selbstbewußtseins eine Struktur, die sich im wesentlichen aus drei Komponenten zusammensetzt: dem Zentrum der Erlebnisperspektive, dem inhaltlichen bzw. propositionalen Gehalt des jeweiligen Bewußtseinszustandes, in bezug auf den Selbstbewußtsein vorliegt, und einem selbstreferentiellen Ausdruck, der sich auf das Verhältnis desjenigen zur erfahrbaren Welt bezieht, der jeweils Selbstbewußtsein hat.

Mit der so bestimmten internen Struktur des Selbstbewußtseins wird ersichtlich, daß Selbstbewußtsein als eine kognitive Einstellung verstanden werden muß. Denn im Selbstbewußtsein bin ich mir meiner selbst als mich in einer bestimmten Weise verhaltend bewußt. Trivialerweise verhalte ich mich, solange ich existiere, immer in irgendeiner Weise zu der Welt, in der ich existiere, nur habe ich nicht durchgängig ein explizites Bewußtsein davon. Der Satz (1) beschreibt zwar ein mich betreffendes Ereignis in der Welt, aber ich thematisiere mich in ihm nicht als denjenigen, der von diesem Ereignis betroffen ist. Erst der Satz (2) ist die Beschreibung eines selbstthematisierenden Bewußtseinszustandes im Modus expliziten Bewußtseins. Ein solcher Aufmerksamkeitszustand ist informationsartig. In ihm manifestiert sich nicht einfach ein Verhalten, sondern er ist eine Orientierung über ein bestimmtes Verhalten von mir. Fälle reflektierten Bewußtseins sind in diesem Sinne informationserweiternde Zustände, denn das selbstthematisierende Bewußtsein, daß ‚X' *mein* Erlebnis ist, ist gegenüber der unreflektierten Wahrnehmung von ‚X' eine zusätzliche Information; (1) und (2) beschreiben dieselbe Tatsache, nur wird in (2) eine Veränderung meiner Einstellung gegenüber dieser Tatsache zum Ausdruck gebracht. Sätze wie (2) sind Beschreibungen von kognitiven Einstellungen, die über die in allen kognitiven Einstellungen vorliegenden informationsartigen Komponenten hinaus noch die Thematisierung des personalen Kontextes der kognitiven Einstellung enthalten. Das Bewußtsein, daß ich es bin, der sich so oder so zur Welt verhält, hat also gegenüber der bloßen Manifestation eines Falls intentionalen Bewußtseins in kognitiver Hinsicht weitere Konsequenzen. Erst durch das Selbstbewußtsein stellt sich ein konkret erfahrbarer Zusammenhang her zwischen der subjektiven Erlebnisperspektive einer Person und der objektiv identifizierbaren Welt der Ereignisse. Aufgrund der Selbstthematisierung im Selbstbewußtsein kann ich mich über meine Eigenschaften, Zustände und Verhaltensweisen aufklären, was mir ermöglicht, mein Verhalten in der Welt an meinen kognitiven Einstellungen auszurichten und *handelnd* auf Ereignisse Einfluß zu nehmen.

ANMERKUNGEN

[1] Wittgenstein, L., *Das blaue Buch*, in: L. Wittgenstein, *Schriften 5* (Frankfurt a. M. 1970), S. 107.
[2] Wittgenstein, L., *Zettel*, in: L. Wittgenstein (1970), S. 369.
[3] Wittgenstein, L., *Philosophische Untersuchungen*, in: L. Wittgenstein, *Schriften 1* (Frankfurt a. M. 1960), S. 391.
[4] Wittgenstein, L., *Tractatus logico-philosophicus*, in: L. Wittgenstein (1960), S. 65.
[5] Wittgenstein, L., *Tagebücher 1914–1916*, in: L. Wittgenstein (1960), S. 173.

* * *

8. Wittgenstein und die Philosophie des Geistes

8. Wittgenstein and the Philosophy of Mind

WITTGENSTEIN'S PLAN FOR THE TREATMENT OF PSYCHOLOGICAL CONCEPTS

Gabriel Falkenberg
Universität Düsseldorf

I would like to argue for the thesis that the insights gained into the nature of psychological concepts and the method used by Wittgenstein *after* 1946 differ in some respects markedly from the results and the methodology of the first part of the *PI*. In particular, I claim that Wittgenstein came at least close to developing a general view of psychological concepts.*

In order to show this, I would like to concentrate upon (what seems to me) a cornerstone in Wittgenstein's philosophy of psychology, namely his "plan for the treatment of psychological concepts", as he himself called it. This plan is contained in and also to a considerable extent carried out in Vol. II of the *Remarks on the Philosophy of Psychology*, written in 1947/48. The central statements are §§ 63, 148 and 178−9 (these §§ appeared nearly verbatim already in *Z* 45, 472, 483, 488−92 and 621, but were cut into pieces there and placed at different sections of that book). The first part reads:

> Plan for the treatment of psychological concepts.
> Psychological verbs characterized by the fact that the third person present is to be identified by observation, the first person not.
> Sentences in the third person present: information. In the first person present, expression. ((Not quite right.))
> Sensations: their inner connexions and analogies.
> All have genuine duration. Possibility of their being synchronized, of simultaneous occurrence.
> All have degrees and qualitative mixtures. Degree: scarcely perceptible−unendurable. (. . .)
> Place of sensation in the body: differentiates seeing and hearing from sense of pressure, temperature, taste and pain. (. . .)
> Pain differentiated from other sensations by a characteristic expression. This akin to joy (which no sense-experience).
> "Sensations give us knowledge about the external world".
> Imagination:
> auditory images, visual images−how are they distinguished from sensations? *Etc. Etc.* (*RPP* II 63; my translation).

Wittgenstein continues to treat imagination, emotion and mood, and intention in much the same way; later, although less systematically, he also considers belief, thought, understanding, dreaming, and other things.

What strikes one as remarkable is, first of all, the definitive tone, the systematic overall presentation, and the persistent use of common features in characterizing the different psychological concepts. He even speaks of being engaged in a *classification* of those concepts (*RPP* II 148). It is not, though, a description of the phenomena after the manner of psychology (or neurology) that he is interested in, but in the concepts *we* use in talking about the psyche of other people and our own. What he is doing here, as distinguished from his earlier work, is studying psychological concepts in their own right, as it were, rather than as an application of his insights concerning private language and rule following.

For the study of psychological *concepts*, Wittgenstein concentrates on psychological *verbs* (neither term appears in *PI* I). The underlying assumption here is that psychological items are what is designated primarily by psychological verbs, where the notion of *designation* invoked is to be explained in a two-fold manner: as "used to express" (for 1st person), and as "used to inform" (for 3rd person). The reason is that psychological verbs are characterized by an *asymmetry* between 1st and 2nd/3rd person use: 1st grammatical person present tense utterances are typically groundless, whereas corresponding 3rd grammatical person utterances are justified by behavioural evidence, by criteria. 1st person utterances are usually not reports, but expressions or manifestations (*Äußerungen*) of that psychological item that is designated by the psychological verb when used as the main predicate. I take this to be Wittgenstein's general characterization of the mental *via* a characterization of our verbal designation of it from two different epistemic perspectives, and I will suggest at the close why I find this insight of his important.

The features Wittgenstein employs in characterizing different psychological concepts I call "*psychological features*"; main features used include: (a) *genuine duration*, (b) *degree* (or intensity), (c) *quality* (and qualitative mixtures), (d) *bodily location* (localization), (e) *characteristic expression* (behavioural manifestation), (f) *information about the external world*, (g) *subjection to the will*, (h) *directedness* (having an object), and others. Before proceeding to the question of the general type of their explication, I will comment on some of them.

(a) Genuine duration. If someone learned that such-and-such and as a result knows that such-and-such, there might be the idea of his knowledge (or knowing) having duration. But it does not have genuine duration because knowing is neither an act nor a process: it makes no sense to ask "Is his knowledge (knowing) still going on?", no sense to say I interrupted him in knowing that such-and-such. Making spot-checks of what has genuine duration seems odd; so dispositions are such as not to have genuine duration. (Supplementary sources: *RPP* II 43−57, *Z* 71−87; cf. earlier *WWK* p. 167, *PG* I 68, *BLB* p. 40, *PI* I p. 148−55.)

(b) Degree, and (c), quality, are both at least intuitively clear; in any case, they are scarcely elaborated on by Wittgenstein. (Sources: *RPP* II 499, 618−20, *Z* 438, *LW* I 405 = *PI* II viii p. 186 d; cf. earlier *PR* 61, 65, for degree. *RPP* II 243, 274, 499, for quality and content

(d) Localization, is explicated by reference to the subject's reaction on touching the place and other causality-loaded notions, and by reference to being able to say where it itches, hurts, etc. (Sources: *RPP* II 161, 307, 325, 499, overlapping with *Z* 485−511 passim; *LW* I 388 = *PI* II viii p. 185 c, *LW* I 399, 401; cf. earlier *PR* 61, 65, 74, 86; *PG* I 64; *BLB* p. 7−9, 16, 50, 68; *BRB* I 48, II 3; *PI* I 253, 286, 302, 411, 448, 626.)

(e) Characteristic expression, is fairly clear for expository purposes, as is (f), information about the external world. (Sources: passim; cf. earlier *NB* 15.10.16 p. 84−5; *PG* I 30, 128, 129 (*Z* 506), *BLB* p. 41−42, 103, 144; *PI* I 54, 142, 152, 257, 281, 571, 574, for the former; *RPP* II 79−80, 354; *LW* I 386−90, 393, 837; *PI* II viii p. 185; cf. earlier *PI* I 486, for the latter.)

(g) Subjection to the will, is explicated mainly in terms of its making sense to order someone: "imagine that", "think that", etc., but not "feel that" or "understand that". (Sources: *RPP* II 78−101, 107−31; *Z* 51, 123; *LW* I 451−3, 505, 612; *PI* II, xi, p. 213 d−e.)

How is it ascertained, for each of these features, that they apply to this or that individual psychological concept? Not by psychological investigation. The method of investigation is a logical, conceptual one (*RPP* I 949 = *Z* 458; *RPP* II 43). Application of particular psychological features to concepts is guaranteed by a purely *grammatical* link, where "grammatical" is to be taken in the specific Wittgensteinian sense. Most of the sentences which form the basis of the correlation between feature and concept have this peculiar 'grammatical' status, e.g. "pains are felt somewhere in the body", "images−but not sensations−are subject to the will" (*RPP* II 129; cf. earlier *NB* 5.7.16 p. 73 = *TLP* 6.373, *NB* 21.7.16 p. 77), "belief is not any kind of occupation with the object of belief" (*RPP* II 155), and others. It is not the business of all these sentences to ensure any kind of differentiation between psychological phenomena, but between the *language-games* which are the natural homes of the corresponding psychological concepts (*RPP* II 129; *RFM* VII 71, *RC* III 115, *LW* I 877, 946, *OC* 564−6). The grammatical sentences are rule-expressions, elucidatory statements of how the psychological words contained in them are actually used.

An examination as to which of the psychological features (a) to (g) apply and which do not apply to the concepts of sensation, imagination, and emotion, according to Wittgenstein, results in the following overall picture:

	Features	a	b	c	d	e	f	g
Concepts		gen. dura-tion	degr.	qual.	bod. loca-tion	char. expr.	info. about world	subj. to will
Sensation — Sense-perception (Seeing, hearing, ...)		+	+	+	−	−	+	−
Sense of pressure, temper., and taste		+	+	+	+	−	+	−
Sensation of pain		+	+	+	+	+	+	−
Kinaesth. Sensation		+	−	−	−	−	+	−
Imagination		+	+	+	−	−	−	+
Emotion		+	+	+	−	+	−	−

The schema is meant to give a concise *synoptic view* of one area of psychological verbs by showing their various analogies to and differences from one another with the help of psychological features. For Wittgenstein, these features are−if formulated in propositional form−not individually necessary and jointly sufficient conditions for something's being a psychological concept; rather, we find an application of the *family-resemblance*-technique here, whereby not exactness but *Übersichtlichkeit* is sought (*RPP* I 895 = *Z* 464). The classifications of philosophers and psychologists are, as Wittgensteins puts it, "classifications of clouds by their shape" (*PR* 154, *Z* 462), whereas he distinguishes psychological concepts according to the function they play in our life.

I leave Wittgenstein's fascinating project at this point and come to a general conclusion. Recall his prior delimitation of the realm of the psychological in general, 1st and 3rd person uses being systematically related in the way I explained.

Something denoted by a psychological verb (in the context of a complete utterance) is not something wholly private, as it would be if everyone knew about it only from his own case. The designata of psychological verbs are, on the other hand, not something wholly public either, as they would be if everyone knew about them only by observing the behaviour of other people. Thus, in making it a characteristic of psychological verbs that they have this double aspect, this double use from two different epistemological standpoints, Wittgenstein is able to steer a middle course between the Scylla of solipsistic mentalism and the Charybdis of physicalistic behaviourism.

REFERENCES

* This is a much condensed version of the paper "Wittgenstein's later theory of psychological concepts" that I gave at the Symposium. My references are to §§ except where indicated otherwise. The full paper is due to appear elsewhere.

* * *

MIND AS EXPRESSION

Michel ter Hark
University of Groningen

The task of the philosophy of psychology is, according to Wittgenstein in *RPP* I & II, confined to the clarification of the tangled use of psychological concepts. The use of psychological words is compared to the following, "Wenn das Wort 'Violine' nicht bloß das Instrument, sondern manchmal auch den Geiger, die Geigenstimme, den Geigenklang, das Geigenspiel bezeichnete" (*RPP* II 730). I want to argue that Wittgenstein, using the method of conceptual analysis, wages a war on two fronts: against behaviourism and mentalism or dualism alike. The destruction of those positions also has a constructive side: a conception of the mind as essentially expressive in nature.

At the end of a fragment (*PU*, 308), in which Wittgenstein exposes the genesis of the problem of behaviourism and dualism, Wittgenstein concludes, "Und so scheinen wir also die geistigen Vorgänge geleugnet zu haben. Und wollen sie doch natürlich nicht leugnen". Although not wanting to deny mental phenomena, Wittgenstein's position, as he himself admits, can easily be misconceived as implying a rejection of mental phenomena. He is rejecting a widespread assumption according to which the inner world bears a certain kind of resemblance to the outer physical world. In speaking about the mind philosophers and psychologists alike have borrowed a terminology designed for the physical sciences: they talk about mental states, processes and activities as if these were the physical states, processes an activities they are acquainted with. Wittgenstein, however, stresses "gerade die Unvergleichbarkeit. Eher möchte ich sagen, wären die vergleichbaren Körperzustände: die *Geschwindigkeit* der Atmung, *Unregelmäßigkeit* des Herzschlags, *Zuverlässigkeit* der Verdauung" (*RPP* I, 661).

To come to the point of Wittgenstein's objection against dualism and mentalism: misled by the terminology of states and processes we would like to point to an object as the denotation of the 'content of experience'. The content of experience is the private object, the sense datum, the object that we grasp immediately with the mental eye or ear. As examples Wittgenstein mentions: I know what toothaches are like, I am acquainted with them, I know what it is like to see red, to feel sorrow, to see a drawing alternately as the head of a rabbit and of a duck. We would like to point to this content and say:

> '*So* sehe ich Rot', '*So* höre ich den Ton, den du anschlägst', '*So* fühle ich Vergnügen', '*So* empfinde ich Trauer', oder auch '*Das* empfindet man wenn man traurig ist; *das*, wenn man sich freut', etc. Man möchte eine Welt, analog der physikalischen, mit diesen *So* und *Das* bevölkern. Das hat aber nur dort Sinn, wo es ein Bild des *Erlebten* gibt, worauf man bei diesen Aussagen zeigen kann. (*RPP* I, 896)

The temptation to people a world with these thuses and thises analogous to the physical world, arises only in a dualistic or mentalistic context where we think that there is something but that it is out of reach. Something that cannot be exhibited to other people either. In this illusory situation one would like to exhibit the content of experience without the medium this content necessarily expresses itself in. In that situation the content, without its medium, becomes really a nothing.[1]

The problems connected with dualistic and mentalistic philosophy result partly from a misunderstanding of the asymmetries between first-and third-person uses of psychological concepts. In *RPP* II, 63 Wittgenstein says that psychological verbs are characterized by the fact that the third person of the present is to be verified by observation, the first person not. Sentences in the third person of the present give information; in the first person of the present they are akin to expression. Their meaning is not fixed but ambivalent like the duck/rabbit figure.

The dualist, however, supposes that, because 'I am afraid' is not a description of behaviour, it is a description of a hidden content of experience. But, according to Wittgenstein, the use in the first person is not descriptive at all but expressive. 'I am afraid' is not meant as informing other people about private happenings, but as a confession of participating in an intersubjective language-game. A language-game, for example, in which one is asking for attention, protection, pity and the like.

Sentences in the third person are to be verified by observation. Nowhere in his plan for the treatment of psychological concepts[2] is there any mention of criteriological, quasi-logical relation holding between a criterion and a mental state or process of which it is the criterion and on basis of which the mental state is ascribed to someone.[3]

The behaviouristic stress on criteria has been exaggerated. It has created a kind of dualism alien to Wittgenstein's philosophy as a whole. As soon as one speaks of outward behaviour on the basis of which inner states can be correctly ascribed to someone a form of dualism has been born. The creation of a distinction between behaviour and inner states seems to invoke precisely the kind of distinction between two different realms Wittgenstein's treatment of mental concepts seeks to question. In *RPP* I, 292 Wittgenstein remarks that it is in a certain sense correct to say that the psychologist records the behavior of the subject as a sign of mental processes. But it is misleading also, because we are accustomed to speak of the colour of the face as a sign of fever. Fever, as I should say, is manifested by or through the colour of the face, but not *in* it. About mental phenomena, such as joy and sorrow, we should not say that they are made evident by or through the facial expression, but *in* it. Facial expressions are no clues or criteria allowing others to infer hidden mental states. As Wittgenstein says, 'Man sieht Gemütsbewegung. – Im Gegensatz wozu? – Man sieht nicht die Gesichtsverziehungen und *schließt* nun, er fühle Freude, Trauer, Langeweile. Man beschreibt sein Gesicht unmittelbar als traurig . . . Die Trauer ist im Gesicht personifiziert . . .' *RPP* II, 570.

Wittgenstein's subtle treatment of various psychological concepts makes clear that it is wrong to suppose that for every psychological verb there has to be a criterial relation between the behaviour and the inner state. A logical characteristic of states of consciousness, like sensation and emotion, is that they possess 'genuine duration'. We could signal the beginning and ending of sensations and emotions, and the changes in them. We can identify states of consciousness because of this characteristic. Dispositions, like knowing and understanding, do not share this characteristic. In some cases criteria are needed to assess the presence of dispositions, as when the teacher wants to be sure that his pupil did learn his lesson well. In other situations they are not needed. Emotions can also be verified, identified by their characteristic mimic expressions and sensations.[4] The difference between sensations and images, both states of consciousness, is even more subtle. Images tell us nothing, either right or wrong, about the external world; sensations do. Images are subjected to the will; sensations not. I cannot digress on this topic here, but in his extensive analyses of psychological concepts Wittgenstein never commits himself to a generalization according to which all mental phenomena are identified and ascribed to someone on basis of behavioral criteria.

There is a striking resemblance between Wittgenstein's discussion of mental phenomena and his discussion of 'seeing as' and 'aspect'. I do not want to discuss that matter here, but I do want to remark that it is just as absurd to ask what an aspect is seperate from the thing it is an aspect of, as it is senseless to ask what mental phenomena are without the behaviour they are supposed to characterize. Mental phenomena are essentially contextually defined. They cannot be pinpointed to or known in isolation, because they are internally related to behaviour in which they have to express themselves. In the terminology of the *Tractatus* one could say, they *show* themselves *in* their expression.

But we have to distinguish between natural expressions and linguistic expressions. They are not on the same level, because linguistic expressions replace natural ones. Primitive expressions are pre-linguistic, which means that a language-game is based on them. They provide a prototype for the verbal expression. Primitive expressions are essentially of a public, not to say, cultural nature, in contradistinction to the Cartesian conception of the primitive which is also pre-linguistic but of a private psychological nature.

Primitive expressions will eventually be replaced by verbal ones. By this process our primitive actions and expressions can develop and be made more articulate. A lot of our mental phenomena can only exist because of our capacity for linguistic expression. All psychological phenomena are embedded in human life, situations and reactions constituting human life. But some of them, for example hope, require a more complicated background. We have to go a long way before there is room for hope and belief in our lives. A much longer way than for a concept as pain. That is why we don't say of a crocodile that it hopes. Crocodile-life is not complex enough for a phenomenon like hope to occur in it.

Wittgenstein's philosophy stresses the importance of language for the status of mental phenomena. Language provides a much more refined medium in which the mental can express itself more adequately, more articulately. An expressive medium also, which makes it possible that we perform part of our expressive capacity monologically, in the form of private thinking. Perhaps one can conclude that the 'moral' of Wittgenstein's later philosophy is that the hiddenness and subjectivity of mental phenomena is not to be seen as a virginal datum out of which our public activity can be explained, but as phenomena which are constituted in the process of expressing ourselves and therefore less hidden and less subjective than we think.

ENDNOTES

[1] I am referring here to the famous slogan: Sie (Empfindung) ist kein Etwas, aber auch nicht ein Nichts. *PU*, 304.
[2] Wittgenstein starts his plan in *RPP* II, 63. His treatment is strikingly more systematic than anywhere else in his work.
[3] See for criteriological interpretations of Wittgenstein's philosophy, A. Kenny, *Wittgenstein* (London 1973), p. 258.
[4] Wittgenstein continues his plan for the treatment of psychological concepts in *RPP* II, 148, with special emphasis on emotions.

* * *

IN WHAT SENSE DID WITTGENSTEIN REJECT
THE MIND-BODY PROBLEM?

Masahiro Oku
Osaka University

1. In his *Zettel* §§ 608−613 (and almost equivalently in *Remarks on the Philosophy of Psychology* I §§ 903−909) Wittgenstein asserts that there is no need to suppose any process in the brain or nervous system correlated with our thinking, and that psycho-physical parallelism should be discarded. At the outset of this discussion he uses a seed to illustrate his point. A clearer version of this is presented in a different passage (namely, in his manuscript written on 26th September 1937 which has been printed as a part of "Cause and Effect" in *Philosophia*, Philosophical Quarterly of Israel, vol. 6, No. 3−4, in 1976) where he uses two seeds. The latter version is as follows:

> Think of two different kinds of plant, A, and B, both of which yield seeds: the seeds of both kinds look exactly the same and even after the most careful investigation we can find no difference between them. But the seeds of A-plant always produce more A-plants, the seeds of B-plant, more B-plants. In this situation we can predict what sort of plant will grow out of such a seed only if we know which plant it has come from.

Wittgenstein continues his discussion thus: Someone might object to this. They could say: there must be a difference in the seeds themselves which we haven't yet discovered. Their histories cannot be the cause of their further perpetuation unless their histories have left traces within the seeds.

In spite of all this, Wittgenstein replies, that the emphatic expression "there *must* be a difference" does not alter the facts at all. It shows rather how strongly the prejudice of causality has affected us.

That's the metaphor of two seeds.

2. With this background we can understand well the passages which I first mentioned. They imply many other points indeed, but I would like to take up only those which are relevant to the mind-body problem. To summarize:

1) Although I meet a man after several years absence, recognize him and remember his name, nothing need have been stored in any way in my nervous system for me to remember him.

2) When we are talking, writing, or thinking of something, there need not occur any process in our brain which corresponds to the thought of our activities.

3) The prejudice in favour of psycho-physical parallelism should be rejected. It is a very natural assumption that thought-processes need not be read off from brain processes.

4) If the rejection of parallelism upsets our concept of causality, then it should be discarded.

5) The fact that we need our brains in our mental activities does not support psycho-physical parallelism at all. Imagine the following phenomenon. While I am reciting a text, someone is making a scribble which has no imaginable relation to the text, and later he reproduces the text by following the scribble. Moreover, without it he cannot reproduce the text, and if a part of it has been changed or damaged, then some difficulties occur in his reproduction. Nevertheless, there is no need of storing up the text in the scribble. The role of our brains may be the same as in this case.

3. This is Wittgenstein's assertion. In his text he mentioned only the psycho-physical paral-

lelism. Nevertheless, his criticism is not restricted to it: I think he criticized the mind-body problem in general. In order to show this, I would first like to propose a modern formulation of the problem, then I wish to show that Wittgenstein was averse to its presuppositions.

4. The mind-body problem has its long history and has been variously discussed. Rather than going into any historical investigations, I wish to reformulate the problem itself.

The mind-body problem starts with the fundamental presupposition of physiological psychology: That is, that a physiological process always corresponds to its respective psychological process. To borrow the terms of Imre Lakatos, this supposition might be called a 'scientific research programme'. Physiological psychologists are making every effort to realize it.

From another viewpoint there are some tasks to be performed in philosophical thought experiment. Some difficulties should have been removed prior to the completion of this science, namely, before every correspondence is elucidated. The dilemma between free will and the causal determinism of physiology is one of the difficulties, but the main problem is how to understand the correspondence itself, or its 'meaning'.

Many answers have been proposed. For example, monistic reduction or construction, dualistic interactionism or occasionalism. The mind-body problem is nothing but this endless dispute. In spite of the variety of answers, all the positions in the dispute take for granted the above scientific research programme. These theorists in the mind-body problem seem to have become under-labourers in justifying the grounds of physiological psychology.

5. If my remark on the mind-body problem is right, Wittgenstein did not choose from among the possible answers in the problem; instead he questioned the above fundamental presupposition itself. In my interpretation, he treats the problem as a pseudo-problem.

Please think about the fundamental presupposition that, for every psychological process, there corresponds a physiological process respectively. This has two implications, i.e. (1) that the 'mental' and the 'physical' are clearly distinguishable from each other in kind, and (2) that there is the correspondence between the two. I mentioned Wittgenstein questioned the validity of the correspondence, but his criticism was more than that. I would like to sum it up in the following way:

1) In the actual use of language medleys are made by mixing inseparably the 'mental' and the 'physical'. If one tries to reduce the relation into a simple formula, one goes wrong.

2) Not all the so-called mental concepts and expressions designate mental (seelische) events, states or situations.

3) Mental expressions are used quite differently from physical expressions. If we naively try to understand them as simple analogues of physical expressions, we would come to the psycho-physical parallelism.

All these seem to be familiar to those who have studied Wittgenstein's philosophy of mind, and these together would undermine the presupposition of the mind-body problem. In any case I would like to confirm these three points by referring to particular texts.

6. With respect to the first point. It is common that we should make such a medley, mixing physical states and states of consciousness together in a *single* report. I quote three passages. The first comes from *PI* § 421, and latter two from *PI* II v. "He suffered great torments and tossed about restlessly." "'I noticed that he was out of humour.' Is this a report about his behaviour or his state of mind? . . . Both." "A doctor asks: 'How is he feeling?' The nurse says: 'He is groaning.'"

The concept 'reading' should be mentioned as a good example. §§ 156−171 of *PI* treats this concept, and one of the results is that 'reading' is a family resamblance concept. In connection with the present problem, I would like to emphasize the following point. Although only those who have minds can read, it is almost impossible to reduce 'reading' to mental and physical elements. To read does not lie merely in seeing letters and uttering sounds. On the other hand, there is no single universal criterion distinguishing 'reading' from 'not-reading'.

Moreover, there are many passages in *PI* which show humourous results from easy attemps to abstract the so-called mental elements. Here I mention two of them, i.e. passages on *willing* and *thinking*. "What is left over if I subtract the fact that my arm goes up from the fact that I raise my arm?" (*PI* § 621) The remains are kinaesthetic sensations, not my *willing*. Neither can we say that thinking is what distinguishes talking with thought from talking without thought. (cf. *PI* § 330)

Put in a nutshell, mental elements are not separated so easily.

7. With respect to the second point. It is commonly thought that understanding, belief, knowledge, expectation, intention, etc. are mental concepts. In addition to this, 'understanding a word', 'hoping for something'. 'believing in something', 'knowing something', 'being able to do something', 'intending', 'expecting',—these are, grammatically speaking, states. Nevertheless, these are neither mental states nor states of consciousness in the sense that the hearing of a tone or a sentence, a sensation of pain or taste, depression, excitement, pleasure, anger, sorrow etc. are mental events or states.

This is an important point Wittgenstein emphasized again and again. Here I take § 42 of *On Certainty* as an example. The gist is as follows:

One can say "He believes it, but it isn't so", but not "He knows it, but it isn't so." The difference does not lie in that the two words 'know' and 'believe' correspond to different mental states. In this case we need not find any difference in his mind, say, of intensity of conviction.

Incidentally this does not mean that the word 'believe' is not used as a description of a mental state at all. Wittgenstein admits that there are such usages. Moreover, he suggests some languages might use different verbs according to these different usages.

Nevertheless, this does not weaken my second point but strengthens it, because the situation shows that our mental expressions do not correspond to mental states so naively.

One might perhaps make an objection thus: in spite of various usages, 'belief' is a unified concept, it designates a mental state, sometimes conscious, sometimes unconscious. But from Wittgenstein's viewpoint, nothing would be more confusing than the usage such as 'unconscious' mental state. (cf. *PI* § 149)

Here is a further evidence for my second point. It is almost invonceivable that some mental concepts could be learned or discovered by the experience or observation in either one's own mind, or someone else's. *PI* II takes 'believe' and 'remember' as examples. One can say: "Yes, now I know what 'tingling' is". (He has perhaps had an electric shock for the first time.) But we cannot imagine this situation: someone remembers for the first time in his life and says "Yes, now I know what 'remembering' is, what it *feels like* to remember".

8. At all events, are there any inconsistencies in my second point? I asserted: some mental concepts whose grammatical character is a state do not designate mental states. Is the expression 'mental concept' correct? The answer is: in a sense it is correct, in another sense problematic. We might say 'understanding', 'hoping', 'believing', etc. are mental concepts, if we would use this phrase to distinguish the grammar of these words from that of, say, the words 'eat' and 'cut'. On the other hand, this says only a few things about the difference, and if one thinks all the mental concepts are alike because they are mental, this phrase is misleading. But this difficulty does not come from a misnomer, it lies, rather, in the delicacy and complexity of the 'mental'.

We can say the same thing of the concept 'state'. To say of a concept that it is, grammatically, a state is no more than to say that it designates neither action nor performance. As Wittgenstein emphasized, even some concepts designating physical states such as 'fitting' and 'weight' stand in need of elaborate consideration. Non-physical states should be considered more elaborately.

9. This is *nothing* but my third point, and I would like to demonstrate this more explicitly by quotation.

"Don't look at it as a matter of course, but as a most remarkable thing, that the verbs 'believe', 'wish', 'will' display all the inflexions possessed by 'cut', 'chew', 'run'." (*PI* II x p. 190)

". . . But the use of this word [thinking] is tangled. Nor can we expect anything else. And that can of course be said of all psychological verbs. Their employment is not so clear or so easy to get a synoptic view of, as that of terms in mechanics, for example." (*Z* § 113)

More radically, in *Z* § 471,

"The psychological verbs to see, to believe, to think, to wish, do not signify phenomena." And in *PI* § 571,

"Misleading parallel: psychology treats of processes in the psychical sphere, as does physics in the physical."

10. Nonetheless, we are easily misled. *PI* § 36, where the term Geist (spirit) appears first, shows a typical case:

> And we do here what we do in a host of similar cases: because we cannot specify any *one* bodily action which we call pointing to the shape (as opposed, for example, to the colour), we say that a geistig (*spiritual*, mental, intellectual) activity corresponds to these words.
> Where our language suggests a body and there is none: there, we should like to say, is a *spirit*.

To refute this, Wittgenstein warns us in *PI* II xi p. 211,

"'Just now I looked at the shape rather than at the colour.' Do not let such phrases confuse you. Above all, don't wonder 'What can be going on in the eyes or brain?'"

What is the result when we don't heed his warning? One postulates mind as a substance, and talks of its activity, capacity, and state. When the ontological status of the mind becomes dubious, it is localized in the brain. In this sense the mind-body problem is also a result from the naive conception of language. In *Z* § 611 Wittgenstein writes as follows:

> The prejudice in favour of psychophysical parallelism is a fruit of primitive interpretations of our concepts. For if one allows a causality between psychological phenomena which is not mediated physiologically, one thinks one is making profession that there exists a soul *side by side* with the body, a ghostly soul-nature (nebelhaftes Seelenwesen).

11. This is only an outline of Wittgensteinian case against the mind-body problem as far as I understand him. It has not been my intention today to develop other issues regarding his philosophy of mind. Before giving my concluding remarks, I have something to add. The first concerns the concept 'Seele' (soul). This is a comment on my last point. The second concerns 'inner processes'. The third concerns Wittgenstein's estimation of physiological psychology as a science.

12. Wittgenstein points out that we use not only 'head' but also 'heart (Herz)', 'stomach (Magen)' etc. as terms relating to the 'mental'. Moreover, when we mention 'head', we think of thinking processes rather than brain processes. He recommended: psychologically, this way of speaking should be taken seriously.

The term 'Seele' (soul) is more interesting, and is examined in *PI* II iv. He writes:

"If the picture of thought in the head can force itself upon us, then why not much more that of thought in the soul?

The human body is the best picture of the human soul."

One of the characteristics of the concept 'soul' is that, although its place is not specified, it has always been thought to be within the human body proper. With regard to this, Wittgenstein remarks in *Z* § 497,

"'Where do you feel grief?'—In the soul (Seele).—What kind of consequences do we draw from this assignment of place? One is that we *do* not speak of a bodily place of grief. Yet we *do* point to our body, as if the grief were in it."

The result of Wittgenstein's consideration is this: When we speak of 'soul', 'head', 'heart' etc., we use these concepts as pictures (Bilder) and our usage is figurative (bildlich). If we miss this point and take these expressions naively, we are led to philosophical problems, e.g. to postulate a mental entity.

13. Wittgenstein does not deny the existence of 'inner processes'. Saying to oneself instead of saying aloud, doing mental arithmetic instead of doing written or oral calculations, thinking inwardly instead of thinking with a pencil and a sheet of paper, — Wittgenstein denies none of them. His warning is that we cannot understand these concepts properly if we look for what is happening when we are doing these inner mental actions. These concepts or expressions can be understood only when we recognize how they are used together with related expressions.

In *PI* § 376 Wittgenstein discusses the following possibility: whether we could take the sameness of the processes in our larynxes or brains as the criterion of my saying ABC to myself and someone else's saying ABC to himself. His conclusion is negative for two reasons. First, we haven't learned the use of the expression 'to say such-and-such to oneself' by someone's pointing to the above mentioned phenomena. Second, it is possible that our images of the sound *zed* correspond to different physiological processes.

We say that someone speaks to himself only if, in the ordinary sense of the word, *he can speak*. We do not say it of a parrot, or of a gramophone.

I believe Wittgenstein's explication of mental arithmetic gives a beautiful paradigm of the clarification of inner processes in general. After we have learned to calculate orally or on paper, we can learn mental arithmetic: i.e. we learn to follow the order "Calculate this in your head!" and to answer questions "Have you calculated it?" and "How far have you got?" We can learn the concept 'mental arithmetic' only via written or oral calculations. The question about what is going on in the brain when one is doing mental arithmetic might be interesting, but irrelevant to the concept 'mental arithmetic'. To look at this problem from another aspect; if some tribe would seem to know only of mental calculation and of no other kind, we would try to understand their form of life, according to another paradigm rather than to the usual model of calculation.

14. Hasn't Wittgenstein recognized any value in physiological psychology? This is a delicate question. He wouldn't deny the fact that brain surgery can remove difficulties in mental activities. In relation to this, he would admit that physiological psychologists might make some fruitful discoveries. On the other hand, Wittgenstein criticized the fundamental presupposition of this particular science. He wrote: in psychology there are experimental methods and *conceptual confusion*. (*PI* II xiv)

To make Wittgenstein's attitude to science in general clearer, I would like to quote a passage from *Z* § 438;

> Nothing is commoner than for the meaning of an expression to oscillate, for a phenomenon to be regarded sometimes as a symptom, sometimes as a criterion, of a state of affairs. And mostly in such a case the shift of meaning is not noted. In science it is usual to make phenomena that allow of exact measurement into defining criteria for an expression; and then one is inclined to think that now the proper meaning has been *found*. Innumerable confusions have arisen in this way.

15. How far have I gone in criticizing the mind-body problem? At most, only halfway. Even if what I have said is right, I have left some issues untouched. For example, I haven't discussed mental states or events, especially perceptions or sensations, save in passing. These should be scrutinized more specifically.

On the other hand, I believe I can follow the same line when treating these issues. To give a hint, I am thinking of his discussions on 'seeing and seeing-as' and of the section 384 of *PI* that "You learned the *concept* 'pain' when you learned language".

In any case, I would like to examine these issues at another time.

* * *

WITTGENSTEINS AUFHEBUNG DER GESTALTTHEORIE

J. C. Nyíri
Universität Budapest

An zwei wesentlich verschiedenen, anscheinend unvereinbaren Ansätzen hat sich die Philosophie des Geistes in den vergangenen Jahrzehnten neu orientiert: an der begriffsanalytisch soziologisierenden, alles Individuell-Geistige im Bezugsrahmen der Sprachgemeinschaft, der Lebensform auflösenden Betrachtungsweise des späteren Wittgenstein, – und an den Ergebnissen der modernen Neurophysiologie, welche ihrerseits entscheidend verflochten mit Fortschritten auf dem Gebiet der künstlichen Intelligenz ist. Nun hat bekanntlich Wittgenstein in seiner zweiten Schaffensphase, ab 1930, immer wieder die *Belanglosigkeit* jeglicher naturwissenschaftlicher Entdeckung in Bezug auf philosophische Fragen betont, und es scheint, daß der Gegensatz Philosophie–Naturwissenschaft von seiner Nachkommenschaft – zu welcher ich mich demütig rechnen möchte – schließlich ganz und gar auf die Spitze getrieben wurde. Es ist *eine* Sache, tiefsinnige und gut interpretierbare Worte zu zitieren, wie etwa: „Es handelt sich in der Philosophie . . . nie um die neuesten Ergebnisse der Experimente mit exotischen Fischen oder der Mathematik" (*PB,* S. 153f), und eine *andere,* fundamentale Errungenschaften in der wissenschaftlichen Erforschung bzw. Modellierung von Sinneswahrnehmung und höherer Geistestätigkeit systematisch zu ignorieren.[1] Dringend erwünscht wäre da ein Vorgehen, welches die von Wittgenstein erarbeiteten Methoden auf den tatsächlichen Bestand und auf die – vermutlich zahlreichen – *wirklich hemmenden* begrifflichen Verwirrungen der entsprechenden Wissenschaften anwenden würde. Es erübrigt sich zu sagen, daß ein solches Vorgehen im gegenwärtigen Referat noch nicht einmal versuchsweise illustriert werden kann; hervorgehoben werden sollen indessen sowohl gewisse *Grenzen* als auch die weitreichenden *Vorzüge* der wittgensteinschen Methode *im Problembereich der Gestaltwahrnehmung,* wobei ich davon ausgehe, daß dieser Bereich für die ins Auge gefaßte Demonstration ein besonders geeigneter ist.

Daß Wittgenstein nach 1945 sich eingehend mit Köhlers Buch *Gestalt Psychology* auseinandersetzte, ist bekannt. Das Problem des *Aspektes* allerdings, daß man also etwas *als* etwas hören, sehen, empfinden kann, taucht bereits ab § 534 des I. Teiles der *Philosophischen Untersuchungen* auf; die Idee, daß Zahlen „Gestalten" sind, bzw. daß sich die Mathematik mit „Transformationen von Gestalten" beschäftigt, wurde vor 1944 gefaßt (*BGM,* S. 229f); die Rolle des Aspektes in der alltäglichen und der mathematischen Wahrnehmung wurde bereits 1935 eingehend in Wittgensteins Vorlesungen erörtert;[2] und schon im *Traktat* stößt man ja auf das berüchtigte Würfelschema, mit der Erklärung: „Einen Komplex wahrnehmen, heißt, wahrnehmen, daß sich seine Bestandteile so und so zu einander verhalten". Die Bekanntschaft mit Vexierbildern setzt freilich durchaus nicht ein Studium der Gestaltpsychologie voraus. So sind doch bereits 1890, als von Gestalttheorie noch keine Rede sein konnte, der Würfel und viele andere verblüffende Figuren bei dem von Wittgenstein sehr geliebten William James abgebildet. Gestaltpsychologisch eingeführt indessen, und im Sinne der Meinong-Schule erörtert, werden die üblichen Vexierbilder in Höflers *Grundlehren der Psychologie,* ein mit kaiserlich-königlichem Ministerialerlaß 1903 approbiertes Lehrbuch. Gestalten sind für Höfler spezifische Wahrnehmungs- bzw. Empfindungs*komplexionen,* deren Erzeugung bzw. „Deutung", Aspektwechsel inbegriffen, mehr oder minder vom Willen abhängt. Es ist meine Vermutung – beweisen kann ich sie nicht –, daß Wittgenstein entweder noch als Gymnasialschüler, oder aber zur Zeit seiner jugendlichen experimentalpsychologischen Versuchen, in Höflers Buch geblättert hat. Bühlers 1913 verlegtes Werk *Die Gestaltwahrnehmungen: Experimentelle Untersuchungen zur psychologischen und ästhetischen Analyse der Raum-*

und Zeitanschauung, in welchem die Überzeugung ausgesprochen wird, „daß in die Eindrücke komplexer Raumgestalten . . . die Wahrnehmung von Gleichheiten und Verschiedenheiten, also Relationserlebnisse, als Momente eingehen", dürfte hingegen während der Entstehungsperiode des *Traktats* kaum mehr in Wittgensteins Hände gekommen sein, wie es ja auch überhaupt schwer einzusehen wäre, warum der ins Feld rückende Wittgenstein gerade an dem abschreckenden Kathederstil eines Bonner Privatdozenten sich hätte erbauen sollen. Hinweisen möchte ich hier noch allerdings auf Wertheimers Aufsatz „Über das Denken der Naturvölker: Zahlen und Zahlgebilde", das Anfang 1912 in der *Zeitschrift für Psychologie* erschienen ist, also genau zu jener Zeit, als Wittgenstein seine psychologischen Experimente in Cambridge ausführte. Ich habe keinen Grund zur Annahme, daß Wittgenstein diesen Aufsatz gelesen hat, obzwar die *Zeitschrift* in der Umgebung des Psychologischen Instituts der Universität Cambridge gewiß auffindbar war. 1912 freilich hätte sich Wittgenstein von Wertheimer wenig angesprochen gefühlt. Um so mehr in den *dreißiger* Jahren: stellt doch dieser Aufsatz, ohne die Idee der „natürlichen Basierung" von Gestalten preiszugeben,[3] eine weitgehend soziologisierende Auffassung der Mathematik dar. Wertheimer warnt vor der „dogmatisch-europäischen Betrachtung"[4], drängt auf eine Untersuchung, bei welcher die „kategorialen Gebilde" der Naturvölker auf „die Art ihres *Gebrauchs,* ihrer *Tauglichkeit,* ihrer *Funktionen*" hin erforscht würden,[5] spricht von der *sinnlosen Vorstellung* eines absolut genauen Rechnens,[6] betont, daß *Schätzen* nicht etwa *ungenaues Messen* sei,[7] weist auf Ritus und mathematische Spiele, auf in der *Lebensweise* ausgedrücktes Wissen hin.[8] Wertheimer zeigt hier ein tieferes Gefühl für die innigen Zusammenhänge zwischen Kulturganzem und abstrahierendes Denken, als etwa Koffka, in dessen *Principles of Gestalt Psychology* der Adoptivbegriff *molar behaviour*[9] − ganzheitliches, gemeinschaftsbezogenes Benehmen −, die Sapir-Hinweise, oder gar Sentenzen wie „the social framework is of paramount importance for the development of the Ego"[10], eine bloß äußerliche Rolle spielen. Die Leidenschaft spürt man bei Koffka erst, wenn er transkulturell geltende Universalphänomene beschreibt: wie etwa die Erscheinung, daß auf die Jastrow-Illusion sowohl Hühner als auch die Uzbeken hereinfallen.[11] Und was Köhler betrifft, so stand doch bekanntlich der Beweis, daß die Gestaltwahrnehmung grundsätzlich *nicht* vom Lernen abhängig ist, geradezu im Mittelpunkt seines 1929 erschienenen *Gestalt Psychology* − ein Beweis, den Wittgenstein gewissermaßen als eine Herausforderung empfinden mußte. Wir wissen aber nicht − d.h. ich weiß es nicht − wann und wie er ursprünglich auf diese Herausforderung traf.

Wenn Köhler die Gestaltwahrnehmung als vom Prozeß des Lernens *unabhängig* darzustellen bemüht ist, so will er damit das Bestehen einer anderen Art von Abhängigkeit hervorheben: nämlich die gegenseitige Abhängigkeit von Wahrnehmungen und besonderen *physiologischen Prozessen,* die Parallelität, den Isomorphismus zwischen psychologischen und physiologischen Erscheinungen bzw. Prozessen, das gegenseitige Entsprechen von wahrgenommenen und physiologischen *Gestalten.* Nun schließt freilich das Programm des *psychophysischen Parallelismus* eine soziologisierende Betrachtungsweise nicht schlechthin aus. Aber letztere erscheint dann als unwichtig; als uninteressant. Von der anderen Seite her gesehen, aus der Perspektive eines gemeinschaftsbezogenen Kontextualismus, erscheint hingegen gerade die physiologische Reduktion als ein irreführendes Ziel. Und Wittgenstein, der den Menschen nicht bloß in einer zwischenmenschlichen Umgebung, sondern eben auch *philosophisch* − und das heißt *begriffsanalytisch* − betrachtete, mußte in der physiologischen Erklärung geradezu eine gefährliche Illusion erblicken. Seine unter dem Titel *Letzte Schriften über die Philosophie der Psychologie* herausgegebenen Aufzeichnungen enthalten da besonders eindrucksvolle Abschnitte. Es geht ihm hier bekanntlich − wie bereits in den Typoskripten 229 und 232 − vor allem um die Analyse vom eigenartigen Phänomen des Aspektwechsels − daß man nämlich eine gewisse Gestalt mal *so,* mal *anders* sieht, wobei man doch eben *denselben* visuellen Gegenstand vor sich hat. Ist das eine *Deutung* des Bildes − oder wirklich eine Art *Sehen*? „Denk dir eine physiologische Erklärung für dies Erlebnis" − schreibt nun Wittgenstein.

Es sei die: beim Ansehen der Figur bestreicht der Blick das Objekt wieder und wieder entlang einer bestimmten Bahn. Diese Bahn entspricht einer bestimmten periodischen Bewegung der Augäpfel. Es kann geschehen, daß eine solche Bewegungsart in eine andere überspringt und die beiden miteinander abwechseln.

— Wittgenstein weist hier auf die Gestalt des schwarz-weißen Doppelkreuzes hin, und kommt dann gleich auf die Hase-Ente-Figur zu sprechen:

Gewisse Bewegungsformen sind physiologisch unmöglich, daher kann ich den H-E. Kopf nicht als Bild eines Hasenkopfes und eines hinter ihm liegenden Entenkopfes sehen, oder das Würfelschema als das zweier einander durchdringender Prismen. U.s.f. — Nehmen wir an, dies sei die Erklärung. — ,Ja, nun weiß ich, daß es eine Art Sehen ist.' Du hast jetzt ein *neues,* ein physiologisches Kriterium des Sehens eingeführt. Und das kann das alte Problem verdecken, aber nicht lösen. — Der Zweck dieser Bemerkung ist aber, dir vor Augen zu führen, was geschieht, wenn uns eine physiologische Erklärung dargeboten wird. Der psychologische Begriff schwebt über der physiologischen Erklärung unberührt. Und die Natur unseres Problems wird dadurch klarer. (*LS,* § 777)

Was ist nun die Pointe dieser Bemerkung — die übrigens fast gleichlautend auch im II. Teil der *Untersuchungen* abgedruckt ist —, was heißt es, daß ein *neues* Kriterium des Sehens eingeführt worden ist, und worin besteht das „alte Problem", das nicht gelöst wurde? Eine andere Stelle hilft uns gleich weiter: „Die Erscheinung nimmt einen zuerst wunder", meint Wittgensteins imaginärer Widersacher, „aber es wird gewiß eine physiologische Erklärung dafür gefunden werden". Worauf Wittgenstein sagt: „Unser Problem ist kein kausales, sondern ein begriffliches. — Die Frage ist: *Inwiefern* ist es ein Sehen?" (*LS,* § 642) Nicht der physiologische Vorgang hinter dem Aspektwechsel, sonder der *Begriff* dieses Wechsels ist das Problem; und das heißt: die *Rolle,* die derselbe in bestimmten Situationen spielt; die Art und Weise, in welcher er uns beigebracht wurde. Ich führe hierzu eine Bemerkung aus den *Untersuchungen* an:

Wenn ich mir im Innern das ABC vorsage, was ist das Kriterium dafür, daß ich das Gleiche tue, wie ein Andrer, der es sich im stillen vorsagt? Es könnte gefunden werden, daß in meinem Kehlkopf und in seinem das Gleiche dabei vorgeht. (Und ebenso, wenn wir beide an das Gleiche denken, das Gleiche wünschen, etc.) Aber lernten wir denn die Verwendung der Worte ‚sich im stillen das und das vorsagen', indem auf einen Vorgang im Kehlkopf, oder im Gehirn, hingewiesen wurde? (*PU,* § 376)

Unsere Kriterien dafür, ob sich jemand etwas im Innern vorsagt, ob er *denkt, wünscht,* ja ob er *liest, rechnet,* etwas *verstanden* hat usw. sind in die Situationen des alltäglichen Lebens eingebettet; sie sind *nicht* physiologische Kriterien. Es leuchtet ein, daß wenn die Entscheidung darüber, ob jemand etwa Schach spielen kann, einen in Zeit, Raum und Gemeinschaft ausgedehnten Kontext voraussetzt, dieselbe nicht auch anhand eines neurophysiologischen Tests herbeigeführt werden kann. Hier glaube ich durchaus verstehen zu können, was Wittgenstein meint, wenn er feststellt: „Es ist also wohl möglich, daß gewisse psychologische Phänomene physiologisch nicht untersucht werden *können,* weil ihnen physiologisch nichts entspricht." (*BPP,* I § 904) Und wenn man sich vergegenwärtigt, daß jede kognitive Regung nur in einem *Prozeß,* einem *System* des Denkens ihren Stellenwert und damit ihren Sinn erhält, kann auch nicht befremden, wenn Wittgenstein schreibt: „Ja, ich gestehe, nichts scheint mir möglicher, als daß die Menschen einmal zur bestimmten Ansicht kommen werden, dem *einzelnen* Gedanken, der *einzelnen* Vorstellung, Erinnerung entspreche keinerlei Abbild im Physiologischen, im Nervensystem." (*LS,* § 504) Ist es aber wohl wirklich so, daß diese auf das Begriffliche gerichtete Einstellung sich in *allen* Bereichen des Psychischen bewährt? Die Trennungslinie zwischen begrifflicher und kausaler Erklärung muß ja schließlich keine absolute sein. Und in der Tat gewinnt man den Eindruck, daß gerade die dem Phänomen der Gestaltwahrnehmung bzw. des Aspektwechsels anhaftenden Probleme grundlegend *nicht* logischanalytischer Natur sind. „Es scheint sich hier" — schreibt Wittgenstein —

etwas am Gesichtsbild der Figur zu ändern; und ändert sich doch wieder nichts. Und ich kann nicht sagen ‚Es fällt mir immer wieder eine neue Deutung ein'. Ja, es ist wohl das; aber sie verkörpert sich auch gleich im Gesehenen. Es fällt mir immer wieder ein neuer Aspekt der Zeichnung ein − die ich gleichbleiben sehe. (*BPP*, I § 33)

Das Ganze hat, meint Wittgenstein, „etwas Okkultes, etwas Unbegreifliches" (*BPP*, I § 966) an sich. „Unbegreiflich": da deutet die Diagnose auf eine *begriffliche Verwirrung*. Dies könnte jedoch auch eine falsche Diagnose sein. Immerhin ruft doch das Nachdenken über Aspekt und Aspektwechsel gewiß nicht denselben begrifflichen Schwindel hervor, wie etwa das Nachdenken über das Wesen der *Zeit*, oder die Frage, ob das Rot − auch für andere Leute wirklich rot sei.

Es scheint also keine Veranlassung zu bestehen, das von der Berliner Schule formulierte Programm einer physiologischen Erforschung, Interpretation, Übersetzung gestaltpsychologischer Erscheinungen von vornherein als philosophisch irrelevant abzutun. Und rein wissenschaftlich betrachtet hat sich ja dieses Programm glänzend bestätigt. Daß im Nervensystem nicht einfach mosaikartige Abbildungen, sondern besondere eigendynamische Querverbindungen entstehen, daß, wie Köhler es sagte, „sensory fields have . . . their own social psychology",[12] gilt heute als eine paradigmatische Wahrheit der Neurophysiologie. Und insbesondere die Köhlersche Vermutung, daß die Wahrnehmung von Gestalten nicht ohne weiteres mit Bildern auf der Netzhaut erklärt werden kann, sondern komplizierte Vorgänge der neuralen Organisation voraussetzt,[13] wurde inzwischen in lehrreicher Weise erhärtet. Soviel indessen läßt sich kaum behaupten, daß die These des psychophysischen *Isomorphismus*, diese erklärte Hauptthese der Berliner Schule, von der Forschung bestätigt worden wäre. Das wäre aber auch nicht möglich gewesen, da dieser These insbesondere Köhler, um leichten Widerlegungen vorzubeugen, eine ins Metaphysische verallgemeinerte Fassung gab. „[U]*nits in experience*" − schrieb doch Köhler − „*go with functional units in the underlying physiological processes.*"[14] Sind die Begriffe „unit" und „functional" nicht näher bestimmt, so paßt die These auf alles und auf nichts; während bei strengerer Definition dieselbe keineswegs allgemeingültig zu sein scheint. Ich verweise hier auf Ergebnisse, die auf dem Gebiet der künstlichen Intelligenz im Aufgabenbereich der *Gestalterfassung* erzielt worden sind. Es gibt in diesem Bereich freilich eine Vielfalt von Strategien, die Entwicklung ist rapide, und wahrscheinlich auch für den Fachmann, der ich nicht bin, schwer übersehbar. Folgende Feststellungen reichen indessen für meine Zwecke aus: *Erstens*, daß es Programme gibt, die nicht bloß auf *pattern recognition* ausgerichtet sind, sondern eben die menschliche Gestalterfassung zu simulieren versuchen, d.h. einer neurophysiologischen Interpretation immerhin nicht gänzlich widerstehen. *Zweitens*, daß einige unter diesen, so etwa jene von Selfridge und Neisser bzw. von Uhr und Vossler, eine besondere Methode, „feature detection" genannt, verwenden,[15] bei welcher die zu erfassende Gestalt nicht schlicht mosaikartig, oder eben irgendwie ganzheitlich, repräsentiert wird, sondern durch eine *Reihe* von *topologischen Besonderheiten*. Nun leuchtet es ein, daß man in Bezug auf solche Programme von einer funktionalen *Isomorphie* hinsichtlich der entsprechenden Gestalten nur noch im uneigentlichen Sinne des Wortes sprechen kann. Ähnliche Folgerungen ergeben sich aus einem unlängst im MIT zusammengestellten Programm,[16] welches zur Simulierung von Tiefenwahrnehmung dient. Es finden sich in diesem − neurophysiologische Parallelen reichlich bietenden − Programm bildlich interpretierbare Transformationen, in bezug auf die der Begriff einer Isomorphie anwendbar ist − aber auch gar manche solche Schritte, wo dieser Begriff absurd wirken würde. Hier könnte man fast sagen, daß, Köhler gegenüber, *Wittgenstein* recht behält mit seiner Annahme, daß dem *einzelnen* psychischen Inhalt − kein Abbild im Physiologischen entspricht.

Ich habe soeben Wittgenstein und das Thema der künstlichen Intelligenz in einem Atem erwähnt und kann der Versuchung nicht widerstehen, kurz die grundsätzliche Frage anzuschneiden, inwiefern das Phänomen Computer eine Widerlegung oder eventuell eine Bestätigung von gewissen spätwittgensteinschen Überzeugungen bedeutet. Damit hoffe ich zugleich sowohl in Bezug auf Wittgensteins gemeinschaftsbezogener Erkenntnistheorie, als auch hinsichtlich seiner puristisch begriffsanalytischen Methode noch etwas zusätzliches sagen zu können. „Wenn man an den Gedanken" − schreibt Wittgenstein Anfang der dreißiger Jahre − „als etwas spezifisch Menschliches, Organisches denkt, möchte man fragen: ‚könnte es denn eine Gedankenprothese geben, einen anorganischen Ersatz für den Gedanken?' . . . wenn das Denken . . . im Schreiben oder Sprechen besteht, warum soll dies nicht eine Maschine tun? − . . . ‚Aber'" − fragt nun der fiktive Gesprächspartner − „‚könnte eine Maschine denken?'" − Worauf Wittgenstein erwidert:

> Könnte sie Schmerzen haben? Hier kommt es darauf an, was man darunter versteht: ‚etwas *habe* Schmerzen'. Ich kann den Andern als eine Maschine ansehen die Schmerzen hat, d.h.: den andern *Körper*. Und ebenso, natürlich, meinen Körper. Dagegen setzt das Phänomen der Schmerzen, welche ich beschreibe, wenn ich etwa sage ‚ich habe Zahnschmerzen', einen physikalischen Körper nicht voraus. (PG, I § 64)

Das heißt, wenn ich es recht verstehe: das *Zeug* zum Denke könnte eine Maschine schon haben; die *begriffliche Umgebung* des Wortes „denken" indessen ist solcherart, daß wir dasselbe gewöhnlich auf Menschen, nicht aber auf Maschinen anwenden. Schreibt doch Wittgenstein in den *Philosophischen Untersuchungen*:

> Könnte eine Maschine denken? − Könnte sie Schmerzen haben? − Nun, soll der menschliche Körper so eine Maschine heißen? Er kommt doch am nächsten dazu, so eine Maschine zu sein. Aber eine Maschine kann doch nicht denken! Ist das ein Erfahrungssatz? Nein. Wir sagen nur vom Menschen, und was ihm ähnlich ist, es denke. Wir sagen es auch von Puppen und wohl auch von Geistern. Sieh das Wort ‚denken' als Instrument an! (*PU*, §§ 359f.)

Wir wenden dieses Instrument, das Wort ‚denken', *nicht* auf Maschinen an, weil − so glaube ich Wittgensteins Argument interpretieren zu dürfen − wir uns in keiner *Gemeinschaft* mit Maschinen vorstellen können: ähnlich wie in Bezug auf Geistesschwachen, bei denen wir ja, bemerkt Wittgenstein, „oft das Gefühl [haben], als redeten sie mehr automatisch als wir" (*BPP*, I § 198), und bei denen wir eben „nicht eine *Gesellschaft*" (*Z*, § 372) sehen können. Das ist aber gerade der Punkt, wo auch das Argument etwa von Joseph Weizenbaums berühmtem, gegen die Verherrlichung der künstlichen Intelligenz gerichtetem Buch *Computer Power and Human Reason* ansetzt. Maschinen, meint Weizenbaum, werden nie jenes Wissen besitzen können, das der Mensch eben als Mitglied einer Gesellschaft, „as a consequence of having been treated as [a] human being . . . by other human beings" erlernt.[17] Nun stammt die These von der grundsätzlich unbegrenzten Ähnlichkeit menschlicher und maschineller Intelligenz ursprünglich von Alan *Turing*, der bekanntlich nicht ganz unvertraut mit Wittgensteins Ideen war: er nahm an dessen Vorlesungen 1939 − und, wenn man dem Wittgenstein-Bilderbuch glauben darf, auch 1935 − teil.[18] Den Grundgedanken seines klassischen Aufsatzes „On Computable Numbers", in welchem Aufsatz die logisch-mathematischen Prinzipien des heutigen Digitalcomputers zum ersten Mal festgelegt wurden, faßte Turing im Sommer 1935;[19] sein Artikel „Computing Machinery and Intelligence" erschien 1950 in der Zeitschrift *Mind*. Jener mathematische Finitismus, den man etwa in den von Ambrose herausgegebenen Vorlesungen aus 1935 kennenlernen kann, und der dem „Computable Numbers" zugrundeliegende Finitismus, zeigen faszinierende Parallelen, Parallelen, die an gar manchen Stellen ins Erkenntnistheoretische reichen. So definiert Turing „states of mind", nämlich die seiner erdachten Maschine, als „notes of instructions (written in some standard form)".[20] Aber auch die unmittelbaren Anschauungen dieser beiden über *denkende Maschinen*, deren Verwirklichung Wittgenstein eben noch erlebt und vielleicht gar nicht mehr wahrgenommen, Turing aber als praktisch Beteiligter verfolgt hat, auch jene Anschauungen also stehen einander keineswegs so diametral gegenüber, als man es auf den ersten Blick meinen könnte. Zwar scheint Turing hinsichtlich der Frage „Can machines think?" gleich im ersten Absatz seines *Mind*-Artikels eine Art Zurückweisung der Wittgensteinschen Methode zu geben. „If the meaning of the words ‚machine' and ‚think' are to be found by examining how they are commonly used it is difficult to escape the conclusion that the meaning and the answer to the question, ‚Can machines think?' is to be sought in a statistical survey such as a Gallup poll. But this is absurd." Der springende Punkt aber ist, daß jene Maschinen, die Turing als intelligent bezeichnen möchte, von ihm grundsätzlich, und nicht nur in diesem Artikel, als *lernende*, ihr Können aus einem ständigen Kontakt mit menschlichen Wesen schöpfende Kreaturen dargestellt werden.[21] Turing betont immer wieder, daß „the isolated man does not develop any intellectual power",[22] und dieselbe Einsicht will er auch in Bezug auf Computers geltend machen. Turing will eine *Gesellschaft* von Menschen und Maschinen sehen. Er erweitert und bereichert damit, auf dem Gebiet der künstlichen Intelligenz, Wittgensteins kontextualistische Erkenntnistheorie, jene Theorie, die sich ihrerseits — dies zu zeigen war der Zweck meiner Ausführungen — teils als eine Erweiterung, teils aber auch als eine berechtigte Kritik des gestalttheoretischen Ansatzes deuten läßt.

ANMERKUNGEN

[1] Unlängst haben das Prof. Elmar Holenstein und Dr. W. Wenning betont hervorgehoben, in ihren Vorträgen bei der Konferenz „Foundations of Cognitive Psychology", veranstaltet von der Werner-Reimers-Stiftung, Bad Homburg, 18.–20. Juni 1984. Vgl. auch E. Holenstein, „Universals of Knowledge — Constraints on Understanding?", in: Herman Parret und Jacques Bouveresse (Hrsg.), *Meaning and Understanding* (Berlin 1981), S. 171ff., und W. Wenning, „Parallelen zwischen Sehtheorie und Wittgensteins Sprachphilosophie", in: *Erkenntnis- und Wissenschaftstheorie, Akten des 7. Intern. Wittgenstein Symposiums* (Wien 1983).

[2] Vgl. Alice Ambrose (Hrsg), *Wittgenstein's Lectures: Cambridge 1932–1935* (Oxford 1979), S. 179ff.

[3] Wertheimer, Max, *Drei Abhandlungen zur Gestalttheorie* (Erlangen 1925), S. 154.

[4] Wertheimer (1925), S. 107.

[5] Wertheimer (1925), S. 150f.

[6] Wertheimer (1925), S. 118f.

[7] Wertheimer (1925), S. 149.

[8] Wertheimer (1925), S. 152.

[9] Koffka, K., *Principles of Gestalt Psychology* (New York 1935), S. 25f.

[10] Koffka (1935), S. 675f.

[11] Koffka (1935), S. 32f.

[12] Köhler, W., *Gestalt Psychology: An Introduction to New Concepts in Modern Psychology* (rev. ed. New York 1947), S. 71.

[13] Köhler (1947), S. 106.

[14] Köhler (1947), S. 39.

[15] Vgl. etwa M. J. Apter, *The Computer Simulation of Behaviour* (London 1970), S. 103ff.

[16] Vgl. T. Poggio, „Vision by Man and Machine", *Scientific American* (Apr. 1984), S. 68ff.

[17] Weizenbaum, J., *Computer Power and Human Reason: From Judgment to Calculation* (San Francisco 1976), S. 209.

[18] Nedo, Michael und Ranchetti, Michele (Hrsg.), *Ludwig Wittgenstein: Sein Leben in Bildern und Texten* (Frankfurt a. M. 1983), S. 358.

[19] Vgl. A. Hodges, *Alan Turing: The Enigma* (London 1983), S. 96.

[20] Turing, A. M., „On Computable Numbers, with an Application to the Entscheidungsproblem", in: Martin Davis (Hrsg.), *The Undecidable* (Hewlett, N. Y. 1965), S. 139.

[21] Vgl. z.B. Hodges (1983), S. 359ff.

[22] Hodges (1983), S. 384.

* * *

THE NOTION OF THE WILL IN WITTGENSTEIN'S LATER WRITINGS

H. E. Mason
University of Minnesota, Minneapolis

The notion of the will figured prominently in Wittgenstein's early writings. In the *Notebooks* the will is discussed in what appears to be an exploratory way. Broad and sweeping assertions are followed by puzzled questions and conceptual explorations. The willing subject is said to exist and to be the bearer of good and evil, but it is also said to be deeply mysterious. How the will gains a foothold in the world, and even what it is, are questions given a series of perplexed and tentative answers. A variety of more particular questions about the relationship between willing and acting are treated in the same way. At the time he was writing the *Notebooks* Wittgenstein clearly thought that the will must have an essential function in human action, but found it difficult to say what that function is, or even what the will is.

In the *Brown Book*, the *Investigations* and *Zettel*, and in scattered remarks in the *Nachlass* Wittgenstein undertakes to bring the notion of the will down to earth. The thought to which he gives most attention in his discussions of the will in these writings is the thought that it is willing that makes voluntary actions of the things we do. The difficulty he finds in that thought is that, knowing the role willings are supposed to fulfill, it seems impossible to describe them in a way that makes it possible for them to fulfill that role. That difficulty is focussed in his remark in *Zettel* that when one's hand writes, it does not write because one wills, but one wills what it writes. (*Z* 586) The inclination to think of willings as independent acts somehow responsible for our voluntary doings raises the question how that relationship is to be specified, but any plausible specification seems bound to cast doubt on the independence of acts of will or willings. To develop this difficulty I will first give some attention to Wittgenstein's treatment of the analogies which he supposes from the philosophical notion of willing.

In the *Brown Book* we are offered a case we might be inclined to regard as a full-fledged case of willing: a person deliberates whether to lift a certain weight, decides to do it, applies force to it, and lifts it. (*BRB* p. 150) The case appears to bear out the tendency to speak of an act of willing as distinct from the act that is willed. In such a case there are a number of distinct acts, each of which might be regarded as an act of will. Wittgenstein contrasts this case with one in which, after lighting his own cigarette, a person reaches another the lighted match. In such a case there appears to be neither deliberation nor decision, and no apparent application of force or effort. One simply holds out the match for the other person. Thus, while offering a light seems clearly to be a voluntary act, there are no discernible acts of will of the sort exemplified in the earlier case. Considering these and similarly contrasting cases, Wittgenstein goes on to argue that it is a mistake to suppose that the earlier case is a full-fledged case of voluntary action exhibiting features common to all voluntary actions.

Trying is treated in the same way. Scattered through the later writings are a number of passages offering descriptions of voluntary actions we can't be said to try to do. "When I raise my arm," he observes in the *Investigations*, "I do not usually *try* to raise it." (*PI* 622) And considering the profession 'At all costs I will get to that house,' he observes, "But if there is no difficulty about it−*can* I try to get to the house?" (*PI* 623) There are, of course, a great many cases in which we must try, endeavor, even strive to do what we come to do. But if, in the course of specifying the role of willing in the performance of voluntary actions, we treat the question as one formed by those cases, we are bound to do an injustice to those more common but less dramatic cases in which, without deliberation or forethought, and seldom with effort, we sit quietly in our chairs or look out the window, make a remark or turn away.

A somewhat more perplexing analogy to which Wittgenstein seemed drawn both in his early and in his later writings is that between wishing and willing. In his early writings Wittgenstein proceeds on the supposition that wishing and willing are near kin, trying to distinguish them and their respective roles. In his later writings he tries to explain how not even wishing could fulfill the role we are inclined in our philosophical moments to give to willing. Wittgenstein's early idea must have been that there is a form of pure willing, the act of a willing subject, which is like wishing in being disposed toward prospective objects and susceptible of satisfaction in their occurrence, frustration in their non-occurrence, but unlike wishing in having the occasional power of bringing them about. That form of willing is like deciding or making an effort in being, as he says in the *Notebooks*, a kind of acting; it is unlike deciding and making an effort in being required by everything we can be said to do. While there are many things we do which we have not decided to do and can do with no effort at all, we must will to do whatever we do.

Wittgenstein's difficulties arise when he tries to apply this philosophical notion of willing to voluntary action. In a puzzling series of remarks late in the *Notebooks* he tries to find a way of explaining how willings are related to the actions which are their object. In a context in which he has already said that an act of will is not the cause of an action, he suggests that willed movements of the body happen like any unwilled movement in the world, with the difference that willed movements are accompanied by will. As he proceeds he seems less concerned to puzzle over the surprising idea that willed movements of the body are merely accompanied by willing than to insist that they be accompanied by willing and not merely by a wish. His apparent resolution in the *Notebooks* is to say that the fact that one wills an action *consists* in his performing the action, and not in his doing something else which causes the action. In the *Investigations* he gives that thought to an imagined interlocutor, and responds with the remark that if willing is the action it must be so in the ordinary sense of the word; it must be speaking, writing, walking. The deflationary force of this remark is clear enough. If willing just is speaking, writing, walking, it can hardly be what makes instances of those actions voluntary.

How can willing be conceived if it is to do what it is supposed to do, making voluntary actions of the movements of our bodies? In a series of remarks in the *Investigations*, paralleled in *Zettel*, he offers an explanation of the source of the difficulties. (*PI* 612−614; *Z* 579−580) We think of willing, he suggests, as a kind of immediate, non-causal bringing about. Willing to do this or that, we bring it about. But we bring it about directly or immediately. Willing is not something we do by means of which we walk or imagine. Willing is not an instrument or a device, which enables us to bring about our walking or our imagining. To bring out the strangeness in this idea Wittgenstein offers several cases in which we might be said to produce or bring about a result in ourselves. A person might produce a sneeze or a fit of coughing in himself by taking a sniff of some irritant or by holding his breath in a certain way. Compared with such cases it seems wrong to think of voluntary actions as produced or brought about. In a normal case there is nothing we do to bring about or produce our walking in the way that we might take a sniff of pepper to produce a sneeze. Against the background of such cases, Wittgenstein observes, "When I raise my arm 'voluntarily' I do not use any instrument to bring the movement about."

There is a particular reason why willing resists being thought of as a device or an instrument whereby we perform such voluntary actions as walking, talking, and eating. If we try to think of willing as instrument and not agent, it tends to reappear in the guise of an agent. "I'll walk," I might say, "so I'd better will to bring about my walking." My willing, so used, would no longer serve to make the walking mine, or even voluntary. That would be a matter of *my* using willing, *my* doing that, and not a matter of its being willing that I happened to use. But, because in the game in which we speak of willing, willing is known only by its role, I would guess that it would be argued that it was my doing that was a proper exercise of will. If I undertook to use willing, I would have to will to do that. Willing tends to resist any but a first and originating position in a course of action.

This line of thought shows the ease with which the philosophical notion of willing can be given application in the specification of our doing of anything we can be said to do. Is it an objection to those specifications to say that we must there be thinking of willing as a kind of direct or immediate producing of what is willed or bringing about what is willed? In both the *Investigations* and *Zettel* Wittgenstein offers examples to show that we neither produce nor bring about our voluntary actions. But once the producing is said to be direct it is less clear how forceful those examples are. Why not say that this is a case in which we can say what we please so long as we aren't misled? It seems to have been Wittgenstein's view that the expressions in question are less malleable than we might have thought. We may suppose that we understand how willing might be a direct bringing-about, but as the distance of willing from more common means of bringing things about becomes apparent, we should become less confident of that. To the extent that that is true we will have to turn to the cases to which the philosophical specifications of voluntary action are to apply to understand them. But that in turn raises doubts about the philosophical specifications. If saying that whenever I do anything voluntarily I will to do it and thereby bring it about directly has no more force than to say that in that instance I do in fact write or speak or walk, there seems little reason to prefer the former. Promising an explanation, it provides no more than an idling restatement.

As described by Wittgenstein willing is a strange phenomenon. It is something we do, but it is not a kind of action and not something we can either try or fail to do. It is something we must do whenever we do anything at all, but it isn't something we must or even can attend to. It is a kind of bringing about or producing, but it is direct and immediate. These and other peculiarities of willing raise the question why it should be given the place even Wittgenstein himself had been inclined to give it. What is there about the things we daily do that requires explanation in such difficult and elusive terms?

The thought that runs through Wittgenstein's writings on the will from the very beginning is that it is the fact that *we* do what we do that requires that those doings be the work of the will. Attributing all the variety of things we are said to do to our wills seems a way of collecting them consonantly with their being our doings. In the *Notebooks* he tries to find a way of explaining the relationship between our willings and our doings that will make our doings our doings. Grown skeptical of the philosophical notion of the will by the time of the later writings, he tries to unravel it. But he also attempts to exhibit the source of the difficulties. In a striking series of phenomenological observations in the *Investigations* he points to the notion of doing itself. "*Doing* itself," he says, "seems not to have any volume of experience. It seems like an extensionless point, the point of a needle. This point seems to be the real agent. And the phenomenal happenings only to be consequences of this action. 'I *do*. . .' seems to have a definite sense, separate from all experience." (*PI* 620) This series of observations puts very well the sense that what we can be said to do, strictly speaking, is much less than what we might be commonly said to do. There are a great many things we are commonly said to do. We are said to gaze and stroll, return serves, start fires and drop bombs. But which of these things can we be said to do, strictly speaking? Wittgenstein's idea is that there is an appealing point of view from which the most we can be said to do is to perform those primitive actions, fully within our power, which have as their consequences the various phenomenal happenings which lead people to say that we have returned a serve, started a fire, or dropped a bomb. The real agent, the willing subject, recedes from the things he cannot, strictly speaking, be said to do.

Wittgenstein's suggestion receives some confirmation from the currency of theories of action according to which our primitive actions, the things we can in a strict sense be said to do, are limited to the motions of our bodies, or, even more restrictively, to our tryings or strivings. Restricting what we can be said to do to bodily movements may seem a far cry from supposing that all the things we are commonly said to do are the workings of an elusive will. But once the movements of things normally within our control are regarded as phenomenal consequences of things more strictly in our control, we are bound to look for some non-arbitrary way of drawing the distinction between the things we actually do and those attributed to us as consequences of what we do. It may be plausible to think that we only move our bodies, but is it more plausible to think that we only move our bodies but not our pens and knives than it is to think that in a stricter sense we don't move our arms and legs but only effect contractions in our muscles? This line of thought leads ineluctably to the conclusion that in the strictest sense we will, and that all the other things we are said to do are only phenomenal happenings attributed to us in virtue of their being brought about by our willing. Doing recedes, as Wittgenstein observes, to an extensionless point. But it is surely arbitrary to suppose that what we do must be restricted to the movements of our bodies and cannot include mention of the various artifacts and tools and instruments we daily use. Can it be reasonably supposed, for example, that there is some difference of principle between the discipline of a ballet dancer and that of a flute player or a glider pilot, or between learning to be a high jumper and learning to be a pole vaulter? It is apparent that what is said to be done in any of these cases can in the strictest sense be said to be done, whether instruments or tools or other artifacts are involved or not. While it may be tempting to think of doing as an extensionless point, the doubts from which that thought stem cannot be sustained in the fact of the cases supposed to be doubtful.

Wittgenstein provides no recipes for understanding sentences attributing voluntary actions. He concentrates instead on the philosophical idea, once his own, that it is acts of will that make voluntary actions of the things we do. He seeks to show that to be an illusion, the notion of willing formed by analogy with a variety of other acts ill-suited to the role given to willing, and the attributions of willings taking what sense they have from those more ordinary attributions of actions they are supposed to gloss. He offers an explanation of the attraction of the idea, but that, too, leads us back to our pre-philosophical understanding of sentences attributing actions. In this series of discussions more than in many others, Wittgenstein's practice bears out his dictum that "our mistake is to look for an explanation where we ought to look at what happens as a 'proto-phenomenon'. That is, where we ought to have said: *this language-game is played*." (*PI* 654)

* * *

MALCOLM'S DREAMING AND WITTGENSTEIN'S PHILOSOPHY OF MIND

Sybe Terwee
University of Leiden

A question that bothers at least some philosophers of psychology is, whether their work has any relevance for the empirical discipline. And if so, what this relevance consists in. Norman Malcolm must have spent some thoughts on this when he wrote his monograph *Dreaming* in 1959.[1] At two points the book explicitly critizices empirical theories. I will quote a few of the more interesting remarks. One is directed at physiologists trying to investigate dream processes. Malcolm says: "Without an adequate realization of what they are doing, Dement and Kleitman are proposing a new concept in which the notions of location and duration in physical time and subjective-objective distinction will all have a place." (*Dreaming*, p.80). Malcolm also speaks of the 'muddle' these scientists are in. At the end of the book a quite different discipline is critizised. "If I am right then a good deal of Freud's theory of dreams needs to be rewritten." (ibid, 121).

During the 20 years following the appearance of the monograph, more than 50 philosophical articles were published in which Malcolm's position was discussed.[2] The interest among physiologists, psychologists and analysts was considerably less and I do not believe that Malcolm's words brought about much change in these fields. The philosophical enthusiasm and the scientific silence might have been a result of the fact that Malcolm's position was generally considered extreme and absurd. Things philosophers delight in, because it gives an opportunity for discussion, whereas to outsiders it seems useless even to react to it.

In the following I wish to consider some of Malcolm's theses again with a specific question in mind. Many of Malcolm's critics have assumed that this former student of Wittgenstein wrote his essay on dreaming under the influence of Wittgenstein's ideas. This cannot be denied. However, some of them suppose also that Malcolm gave an interpretation of Wittgenstein's ideas on dreaming. Curiously enough, nobody has found it necessary to check this reading of Wittgenstein: as if it goes without further argument that such extreme views must find their origin in his philosophy. Some authors only notice similarities between Malcolm's position and Wittgenstein's philosophy and wonder whether Wittgenstein would really have agreed with Malcolm.[3] In a 1975 article, E.M. Curley speaks of Malcolm's attempt to apply a key theme of the *Philosophical Investigations:* "An inner process stands in need of outward criteria". But he adds: "Perhaps Malcolm misapplies the insights and techniques of the master . . . then it would be a challenging task for someone to work out what a truly Wittgensteinian position on dreaming would be."[4] To my surprise, I could not find a single place in the literature up to 1984 where Malcolm is accused of misinterpreting Wittgenstein. In the following, I hope to show that there are important differences between Wittgenstein's and Malcolm's ideas on dreaming.

Malcolm's position

Malcolm observes, as an ordinary language philosopher, that the statement "I am asleep" cannot be used either correctly or incorrectly. It is an absurd judgment. The same may be said of the verb "to dream": there is no first person present tense. From this Malcolm draws the following consequence: "It is nonsensical to suppose that while a person is asleep he could make *any* judgement." (*Dreaming*, 36). But this argument can be applied as well to thinking, reasoning, perceiving and imagining (ibid 45). "Dreams cannot contain, or be identical with, judging, reasoning, feeling, imagery, and so on, for the reason that with respect to any of these things the question, 'How can it be *known* that this took place while he was *asleep?*' cannot be successfully answered . . ." (83).

"We know perfectly well, however, what establishes that a person dreamt while he slept —namely, his telling a dream". (50). This means that there is an important difference in possibility of verification between dreams and impressions we have during sleep, according to Malcolm. However, apart from somebody's waking up with the impression that certain incidents occurred, we have to add another criterion: that those incidents did, in fact, not occur (51).

Having defined in this way the concept of dreaming, Malcolm arrives at a typical Wittgensteinian problem. How do we learn the concept of dreaming? Well, certainly not by introspection, Malcolm is quick to declare: "I am applying to dreaming the points made by Wittgenstein in his attack on the notion that one learns what thinking, remembering, mental images, sensations, and so on, are from 'one's own case'." (54). Could not the descriptions that people give of their private states provide a determination of what those states are? one might ask. Yes, Malcolm answers, but then "One must treat the descriptions as the criterion of what the inner occurences are" (55). And this is exactly what Malcolm proposes to do in the case of dreaming: the concept of dreaming is derived from the phenomenon that we call 'telling a dream'. Here we are confronted with the well-known remark from the *Philosophical Investigations*: "An 'inner process' stands in need of outward criteria" (*PI*, § 580).

At this point, Malcolm quotes a long passage from the *PI*, p. 184, in which Wittgenstein describes the imaginary case of a tribe where people tell certain incidents in the morning without possessing a word like 'dreaming'. Wittgenstein proposes to teach them a simple language-game: preceding their narratives with 'I dreamt', and answering the question 'have you dreamt?'. Now the question is, do we normally worry whether these people are deceived by their memories of dreams? Whether they really had theses images while they slept? The answer seems to be: no—normally there will be no doubt. The simple language-game that the tribe learned is not different, in this respect, from our everyday Western language-game of telling dreams.

Wittgenstein concluded his remarks about dreaming at this point with a new question, however, to which the answer is especially interesting: "Does this mean that it is nonsense ever to raise the question whether dreams really take place during sleep, or are a memory phenomenon of the awakened? It will turn on the use of the question." (*PI*, p. 184).

Malcolm stays silent about this concluding remark by Wittgenstein. He broke off the quotation shortly before, and seems to like his own conclusion better: "That this question is not raised is not a mere matter of fact but is essential to our concept of dreaming." (*Dreaming*, 56). This forces him to take a peculiar position. We cannot even, in a strict sense, say that we remember a dream. For 'the dream' is not logically independent from our dreamreport. This makes 'knowing that one dreamt' a fairly complicated affair. Malcolm holds that statements of the form 'I dreamt so and so' are always inferential in nature. You wake up with the impression that so and so occurred; you discover that your impression does not correspond to reality; this is 'to discover that you had a dream' (65). From this, it follows that dreaming is not a process occurring at a certain place and time: the concept of time cannot be applied (70,75). It is time we have a look now at Wittgenstein's ideas.

Wittgenstein's Philosophy of Mind

One of Wittgenstein's fundamental insights was the difference between the first person and the third person use of psychological concepts. When I tell you that I feel a pain in my stomach, probably you will believe me, even if you have no evidence whatsoever except my statement. Would I tell you that yesterday I went to the movies with my brother you would also believe me. Why not? In both cases I could lie, but usually people do not lie about these matters. There is, however, an important difference between my two statements. In the first case you could not check the information I gave you, for I am the supreme authority in that matter. In the second case you could try to find out whether I really was in the cinema like I told you. Therefore, the two situations are epistemologically different. According to Wittgenstein, in the first case we speak about the truthfulness of my reports. There is no relation between a thing and its description and consequently we could not ask for the truth of the description.[5] (This applies to dream-reports). In the second case, I can describe a situation which is open to other observers. My description may be true, or false. We must conclude that the concept of truthfulness, and not that of truth, applies to dream reports. Dreaming is one of the many psychological verbs analyzed by Wittgenstein. Well known are his remarks that we do not *know* that we feel pain. We *feel* pain, and sometimes express this feeling. Without going into the subtleties of the private language argument, I hope this has been enough to suggest that Wittgenstein is not defending a kind of verificationism or operationalism (like Malcolm, who is critizised on this point by Putnam, Chihara and others).

On the contrary, Wittgenstein explicitly rejects such doctrines and only points out the differences between the language games of expression of feelings and description of things, because there is a tendency to confuse them.

A few quotations from Wittgenstein's *Investigations* may illustrate this. "That what someone else says to himself is hidden from me, is part of the *concept* 'saying inwardly'. Only 'hidden' is the wrong word here; for if it is hidden from me, it ought to be apparent to him, *he* would have to *know* it. But he does not 'know' it; only, the doubt which exists for me does not exist for him (. . .). 'I know, what I want, wish, believe, fell, . . .' (and so on through all the psychological verbs) is either philosophers' nonsense, or at any rate *not* a judgment *a priori*." (*PI*, p. 220f).

I think we may conclude from this that when Malcolm maintains that we *know* we had a dream by inference, Wittgenstein would call this philosophers' talk, not different from Moore's assertion that he knew he was looking at his hands. These assertions are not used in our language. Another passage from the *PI* is important with respect to the concept of truthfulness.

> The criteria for the truth of the *confession* that I thought such-and-such are not the criteria for a true *description* of a process. And the importance of the true confession does not reside in its being a correct and certain report of a process. It resides rather in the special consequences which can be drawn from a confession whose truth is guaranteed by the special criteria of *truthfulness*.
>
> (Assuming that dreams can yield important information about the dreamer, what yielded the information would be truthful accounts of dreams. The question whether the dreamer's memory deceives him when he reports the dream after waking cannot arise, unless indeed we introduce a completely new criterion for the report's 'agreeing' with the dream, a criterion which gives us a concept of 'truth' as distinct from 'truthfulness' here.) (*PI*, p.222f)

Wittgenstein does not deny that dreams exist, not that we can report them. Most important, he acknowledges that we can give truthful accounts of dreams. In all this, dreams are not essentially different from other experiences and thoughts.

One concluding remark must be made about Wittgenstein's philosophy of mind. Somehow it is still believed that Wittgenstein postulated the existence of so-called 'private sensations'. This is not the case. On the contrary, Wittgenstein believed that our inner experiences are not private, because our words for sensations are tied up with natural expressions of sensations. But in the course of the private language argument (*PI*, § 243ff) he tried to show the consequences of the assumption of 'private sensations': it leads to all kinds of absurdities. (*PI*, § 256). So it is not accidentally that the words 'inner process' (*PI*, § 580) appear in quotation marks. This serves to warn the reader not to make the mistake that Malcolm makes: thinking that 'inner processes' are private, without connection to behaviour and expression.

At several places in *Last Writings* (*LW*) and in the *Remarks on the Philosophy of Psychology* (*RPP*) we find Wittgenstein staying close to the normal uses of the word 'dreaming'—as distinguishable from 'telling a dream'. "May someone not dream and yet not tell anyone? Certainly: for he may dream *and* tell someone". (*RPP* I, par. 365). This also applies to the tribe we encountered in *PI*, p. 184: "Nor can it be said that for these people the verb 'to dream' could mean nothing but to tell a dream". (*RPP* I, 101; *Z*, 530). On the conception of dreams as experiences Wittgenstein makes the following remark: "Is a dream a hallucination?—The memory of a dream is like the memory of a hallucination, or rather; like the memory of a real experience. This means that sometimes you would like to say: 'I just saw this and that', as if you really had just seen it." (*LW* I, 965).

We may remember Wittgenstein's answer to the question whether the dream really went on in the night: that depends on what we intend, i.e. what use we are making of this question (Cf. above, *PI* p. 184). In *RPP* I, § 369 the answer goes on: "For if we form this picture of dreaming, that a picture comes before the mind of the sleeper (as it would be represented in a painting) then naturally it makes sense to ask this question." This shows there is nothing wrong with pictures and beliefs we might have concerning mental processes.

"Is it (in the end) an illusion, if I believed that the other's words had this sense for me at *that* time? Of course not! Any more than it is an illusion to believe that one has dreamed something before waking up." (*RPP* I, § 201). Also, it would be very difficult to live without certain pictures. "It is—we should like to say—not merely the picture of the behaviour that plays a part in the language-game with the words 'he is in pain', but also the picture of the pain. Or, not merely the paradigm of the behaviour, but also that of the pain". (*PI*, § 300). We need a paradigm of dreaming both in daily life and in empirical psychology. The paradigm of dreaming as a specific form of thinking during the night is not the worst we could choose.

The conclusion must be that scientists were wise to neglect Malcolm's prescriptions. They seem to be ill-founded and irrelevant. I hope to have shown some fundamental differences between Malcolm's and Wittgenstein's ideals. *Dreaming* is not an interpretation of Wittgenstein's work, nor is it an exercise in Wittgensteinian philosophy. It may be clear that Wittgenstein never gave prescriptions of any kind in his analysis of dreaming. Does his work nevertheless have any relevance for psychology?

Let me make one cautious remark on this. If psychology chooses to investigate dreaming as a form of thinking, as a cognitive process, it could learn from Wittgenstein that this thinking might be fruitfully investigated by considering the variety of situations in which it occurs and gets a meaning. It is one thing to look for correlations between neural processes and dreaming, another to discover the laws of dreaming and rules of dream interpretation at the cognitive level. I do not know whether the growing interest in the natural context of cognitive processes (as opposed to their physiological substrate) may be ascribed to the influence of Wittgenstein's ideas on meaning and expression.[6] But there are certainly parallels which deserve further attention.

ENDNOTES

[1] Malcolm, Norman, *Dreaming* (London 1959).
[2] Cf. C. E. M. Dunlop (ed), *Philosophical Essays on Dreaming* (Ithaca 1977) for a short bibliography of philosophical writings on dreaming. In the period 1977–1983 only a few new articles on Malcolm's monograph appeared.

[3] Cf. Charles Chihara, "What Dreams Are Made On", in: Dunlop, op cit., p. 253f, 263; A. J. Ayer, "Professor Malcolm On Dreams", in: Dunlop, op. cit., p. 135; Hilary Putnam, "Dreaming and depth grammar", in: *Mind, Language and Reality* (Cambridge 1975), p. 304: "If this interpretation of Malcolm's is faithful to what Wittgenstein had in mind, then these famous arguments are bad arguments and prove nothing."

[4] Curley, E.M., "Dreaming and Conceptual Revision", in: Dunlop, op. cit, p. 318f.

[5] Cf. L. Wittgenstein, *LW* I, 897/8; *PI*, p. 222/3.

[6] An influential, more recent statement of the psycho-physiological correlation hypothesis is: J. A. Hobson and R. W. McCarley, "The Brain as a Dream State Generator: An Activation-Synthesis Hypothesis of the Dream Process", *The American J. of Psychiatry* Vol. 134 (1977) p. 1335−48.

The fruitfulness of this approach for a psychological theory of dreaming is questioned by David Foulkes, "Dreams and Dream Research", in: *Sleep 1980* (Basel 1981), 246−57. Foulkes suggests research plans based on the conceptualization of dreaming as thinking. Ulric Neisser propagates a contextualist approach to psychological processes (reminiscent of Wittgenstein's treatment of meaning-problems by looking at different language-games) in his *Memory Observed: Remembering in Natural Contexts* (1982).

* * *

‚ICH BEKENNE, AUS MEINEM GEIST EIN IDOL GEMACHT ZU HABEN, ABER ICH HABE KEIN ANDERES GEFUNDEN.‘ (P. VALÉRY). – BEMERKUNGEN ZU LUDWIG WITTGENSTEINS PHILOSOPHIE DES GEISTES UND EINEM MÖGLICHEN PARALLELISMUS IN DER GEGENWARTSLITERATUR

Andreas Puff-Trojan
Universität Wien

Im „Logbuch“ des Monsieur Teste ist folgende Eintragung zu lesen: „Ich bekenne, aus meinem Geist ein Idol gemacht zu haben, aber ich habe kein anderes gefunden.“[1] – Die ‚Teste-Figur‘ ist aber für Paul Valéry nicht bloß ‚Figur‘, sondern ein literarisches *Formexperiment*, welches durch ein Begriffspaar gekennzeichnet werden kann: 1.) der Begriff der ‚Selbstwahl‘. Die eigene Einstellung (zu sich; zur Welt) wird als die evidente, primäre Einstellung angesehen, als die Polarisierung auf den eigenen Intellekt, durch den die Denkmethoden entwickelt werden. 2.) Testes Intellekt ist aber einer, der sich selbst mißtraut, denn man weiß um die Fragwürdigkeit der Evidenz (der Selbstwahl). – Teste wird sozusagen zu seinem eigenen ‚Zeugen‘. 3.) Verbindet man nun diese zwei Momente, so erhält man den Begriff der ‚Idolation‘; das ist die Selbstwahl bei gleichzeitigem Mißtrauen der Selbstwahl. ‚Idolation‘ intendiert eine gewisse Negativität und ist daher ungleich einer Idealisierung des eigenen geistigen Zustands. Auch ist die ‚Idolation‘ nicht mit dem Begriff der ‚Idolatrie‘ zu verwechseln, es handelt sich nicht um eine ‚Sonderform‘ der Götzenverehrung!

An Hand von Bemerkungen Ludwig Wittgensteins und einigen Kernsätzen dreier österreichischer Schriftsteller (Ingeborg Bachmann, Konrad Bayer, Thomas Bernhard) soll nun der Begriff der ‚Idolation‘ beleuchtet werden. – Es folgt aber keine Erklärung, keine Interpretation, sondern *die Beschreibung eines Phänomens*. – Diese Beschreibung setzt mit einem Gedanken Wittgensteins ein: „Die Form des erwachenden Geistes ist die Verehrung. Denn das Erwachen des Intellekts geht mit einer Trennung von dem ursprünglichen Boden, der ursprünglichen Grundlage des Lebens vor sich. Die Entstehung der *Wahl*.“[2] Die ‚Richtung‘ des (beschreibbaren) Phänomens möchte ich nun wie folgt vorskizzieren: Die Form des ‚zivilisatorischen‘ (‚erwachsenen‘) Geistes ist die ‚Idolation‘, die Entstehung der Selbstwahl! – Wobei der ‚Geist als Idol‘ nicht *das Objekt* der Verehrung betrifft, sondern *die Form*. – Mit Thomas Bernhard gesprochen: „Das Mystische in uns“ ist es, daß uns die Natur, die Welt als „Mystifikation“ sehen lassen *kann*.[3] – Ritual, Mystik und verschiedene mythologische Anschauungen treten im Werk aller drei Schriftsteller deutlich hervor.[4] Die Konfiguration der Problematik kann nun mit Wittgenstein angegeben werden: 1.) (Jede) Darstellung muß von meiner Welt handeln, weil die Darstellung sonst von Anfang an für mich *keinen Sinn hat*. Das bedeutet, jedes modellartige Bild, jedes Modell muß in seiner *Form* (Wesen) in Bezug zur Welt stehen, wobei das Primärkriterium *nicht* in einer möglichen Verifikation des Modells liegt (*PB* § 34). 2.) Jede Darstellung muß in einem gewissen Sinn evident sein mit meiner Vorstellung, mit meiner Einstellung zur Welt. Der Satz dieser Evidenz lautet: *daß die Welt meine Welt ist*; daß meine Vorstellung und die Welt miteinander koordiniert sind, entspricht Wittgensteins (angenommenen) Parallelismus zwischen meinem Geist und der Welt (*TLP* 5.641; Tagebücher: Eintragungen vom 2.9. u. 15.10.1916). 3.) Die Basis dieser Evidenz kann kein vorstellendes/erkennendes Subjekt sein, es gibt keine (dritte) Instanz zwischen Vorstellung und Welt. – Der Satz der Basis könnte also *nicht* lauten: ‚Es gibt ein vorstellendes Subjekt.‘ (vgl. *TLP* 5.631). Dennoch gilt für die Basis der Evidenz *die Form* der irrtumsfreien Bezugnahme: Nehme ich auf mich, auf meine Welt Bezug, so tue ich es mit ‚Gewißheit‘. Das bedeutet, ich kann mich *nicht irren*, daß die Welt meine Welt ist; nichts spricht in meinem Weltbild für *das Gegenteil* meines Weltbildes (*PU* § 247 u. S. 358f; *ÜG* § 91−93 u. § 245).

Diese Form der Basis der Evidenz ist auch folgendermaßen beschreibbar: Beziehe ich mich auf meine Welt, so stelle ich *keine Theorie, keine Hypothese* auf. Jenes Faktum verweist aber auf einen anderen Gedanken Ludwig Wittgensteins: Magische und mythische Anschauungen sind Anschauungen, sie stellen keine Theorie auf. Dort aber, wo keine Theorie zu finden ist, kann man auch keinen (möglichen) Irrtum suchen. Dies bedeutet, daß magische und mythische Anschauungen ebenso irrtumsfrei sind wie meine eigene Evidenz (*BFGB* S. 38−40; vgl. *ÜG* § 95−99)! − *Die Beziehung zwischen mythischer, bzw. mythologischer Anschauung und eigener Evidenz ist die Idolation, die gedankliche Basis der Evidenz.*

Das Problem der Basis lautet aber mit Ingeborg Bachmann: Fragen wir uns nach der Basis der Evidenz, so „werden wir auf uns selbst verwiesen."[5] Verfolgt man diesen Gedanken, so scheint tatsächlich die Lösung des Problems im Verschwinden des Problems zu liegen! − Die Frage, die aber offen bleibt, lautet: Heißt dies im Verschwinden des Mystischen, im Verschwinden *der* Basis, oder das Problem verschwindet *im* Mystischen (vgl. *TLP* 6.44 u. 6.521). − Leugne ich nun die Basis der Evidenz, die Idolationsstufe, so fällt damit auch die Evidenz, die irrtumsfreie Bezugnahme. Ist aber die Evidenz einmal gefallen, dann ist mit Wittgenstein nur noch lapidar festzustellen: „Wenn ich *der* Evidenz nicht traue, warum soll ich dann irgendeiner Evidenz trauen?" (*ÜG* § 672). − Diesem Gedanken entspricht Bachmanns literarischer Begriff des „Ich ohne Gewähr",[6] das ‚Ich ohne Evidenz'!

Versucht man aber die affirmative Position, die Idolationsstufe, näher zu beschreiben, so ergeben sich ebenfalls Probleme. Für Wittgenstein zeigt sich der Hauptunterschied zwischen Wissenschaft und Magie in dem Punkt, daß es in der Wissenschaft einen Fortschritt gibt, während die Magie keine Richtung der Entwicklung besitzt, die *in ihr selbst liegt* (*BFGB* S. 50). − Die Richtungslosigkeit der Entwicklung ist aber gerade durch die irrtumsfreie Bezugnahme gegeben. Das heißt, die Gewißheit meiner eigenen Evidenz und die Irrtumsfreiheit mythologischer Anschauungen erzeugen ihre eigene Bewegungslosigkeit (z.B. in der Argumentation). − Es ist dies, um mit Konrad Bayer zu sprechen: *die versteinerte Mystik des Ich*.[7] So sind für Wittgenstein die Sätze der Evidenz, wie „Die Welt und das Leben sind eins" (*TLP* 5.621) / „Ich bin meine Welt." (*TLP* 5.63) *keine* Erfahrungssätze, denn sie stellen keine (mögliche) Information dar, noch gilt für sie das Kriterium, daß (mögliche) Erfahrungen einander widersprechen können. − Man könnte auch sagen: Für die Sätze der Evidenz sind in unserer Sprache keine ‚*Gegen-Sätze*' vorgesehen. − So ist für Wittgenstein das (sprachliche) Bezugssystem der ‚Ich-Sonderstellung' nicht falsch, sondern es läßt sich *nicht rechtfertigen.* (*BLB* S. 103−107; *PB* § 66) Derjenige, der einmal die Stufe der ‚Ich-Sonderstellung' gewählt hat, hat keine (weitere) Wahlmöglichkeit (zwischen mehreren Möglichkeiten, nur den *Verzicht*). Wie auch das Bild vom Geist, der seinen Sitz im Körper hat, kein Bild unserer Wahl ist (*PU* S. 284; *BLB* S. 106)!

Man kann jetzt festhalten: Die Form des erwachenden Geistes war die Verehrung. / Die Entstehung der Wahl. − Die Form des ‚zivilisatorischen', ‚erwachsenen' Geistes ist die Idolation. / *Das Ende der Wahl.*

Die entscheidende (weiterführende) Idee liegt aber im Bildbegriff Konrad Bayers. Für Bayer ist der Begriff ‚Kopf' das *Bild* des Bewußtseins und das ‚Ich' der Name des (meines) Bewußtseins. − In der Evidenz, im Satz, ‚daß die Welt meine Welt ist', treffen sich Bild und Name![8] Die Konsequenz daraus wird im Roman „der sechste sinn" formuliert: Wir haben nur schlechte Bilder vom ‚Ich', von der Welt, weil diese zwar uns entsprechen, aber nicht d e r Welt. − Würde man nun diese Bilder zurückweisen, „dann kracht's hier"![9] Die Idee der ‚Explosion' möchte ich mit einem Gedanken Wittgensteins beschreiben, den er während eines Vortrages (Cambridge, 1929/30) formuliert hat: 1.) Der Satz: „Ich staune, daß die Welt existiert.", charakterisiert ein ganz bestimmtes persönliches Ereignis/Erlebnis. 2.) Dieser Satz ist aber ein unsinniger Satz, weil ich *nicht* über etwas staune, was nicht der Fall sein könnte. − Das heißt, ich staune nicht, daß sich etwas *so und so* verhält (z.B.: die Hitzebeständigkeit gewisser Metalle), sondern daß es sich gar nicht anders verhalten kann (Ich kann mir nicht vorstellen, daß die Welt *nicht* existiert)! 3.) Dieses Charakteristikum gilt ebenso für die Sätze der Evidenz. − Es ist, als wären diese Sätze ihrer Verwendung nach *Gleichnisse, Allegorien, Bilder*. Aber für jedes Gleichnis gilt, daß es doch Gleichnis *für etwas* sein muß! − Der entscheidende Gedankenschritt liegt darin: Will man statt dem Gleichnis die ihm koordinierte Tatsache aussprechen (man will sozusagen ‚hinter das Bild sehen‘), so erkennt man, daß es *keine solche Tatsache gibt!*[10]

Man kann jetzt sagen: Die Evidenz ist gleich dem sprachlichen Bild, daß die Welt meine Welt ist, und man sieht, daß diesem Bild mythische Bilder (der Struktur nach) *entsprechen*. Die Basis der Evidenz, die Idolationstufe, ist letztlich nichts anderes als der Versuch, an diesem Bild *festzuhalten*, der Gedanke von Koordination zwischen Bild und Tatsache. − Für Thomas Bernhard ergibt sich daraus der Begriff der „außerfleischlichen Tatsache“,[11] die zugleich eine „tödliche Tatsache“ darstellt, tödlich deswegen, weil „man allein ist in dieser Tatsache“.[12] − Man könnte dies auch so formulieren: ‚Ich habe (*in* dieser Tatsache) *keine Bewegungsfreiheit im logischen Raum*‘.

Diesem ‚negativen Aspekt‘ möchte ich mit dem Wittgensteinschen Begriff der „internen Relation“ begegnen: Die „interne Relation“ betrifft die *Struktur der Darstellung* einer möglichen Sachlage. Somit ist die „interne Eigenschaft“ (die Eigenschaft der Struktur) ein Zug der Tatsache. Eine „interne Eigenschaft“ nennen wir eine Eigenschaft, wenn es *undenkbar* ist, daß es diese Eigenschaft *nicht gibt* (*TLP* 4.12−4.126; vgl. 3.24).

Es war in diesem Aufsatz vom ‚Geist als Idol‘ die Rede, aber auch von *Vorstellung, Einstellung und Darstellung*. − Ich will sagen, daß derjenige, der (bildhafte) Sätze wie ‚Ich bin meine Welt‘ äußerte, versucht war, eine „interne Relation“ darzustellen. − Und ich möchte es noch anders formulieren: Es ist dies die *natürliche Intention, darstellen zu wollen*. Und in einem gewissen Sinn muß das für *alle* Darstellungsformen gelten.

ANMERKUNGEN

[1] Valéry, Paul, *Monsieur Teste* (Leipzig 1983), S. 69.
[2] Wittgenstein, Ludwig, *Bemerkungen über Frazer's „The Golden Bough"*, in: *Sprachanalyse und Soziologie*, hrsg. v. Rolf Wiggershaus (Frankfurt a. M. 1975). S. 49. − Wird im Text abgekürzt mit: ‚BFGB‘.
[3] Bernhard, Thomas, *Verstörung* (Frankfurt a. M. 1982), S. 170/188.
[4] Vgl.: ‚Index‘ zum Roman *der kopf des vitus bering* von Konrad Bayer. Bei Bachmann die Figur der ‚Franziska‘ im *Fall Franza* und zu Ritual und Schriftsteller die Frankfurter Vorlesung: ‚Fragen und Scheinfragen‘.
[5] Bachmann, Ingeborg, *Ludwig Wittgenstein-Essay*, in *Werke*, hrsg. v. Koschel, Weidenbaum, Münster (München 1982), Bd. 4. S. 21.
[6] ebenda. S. 217ff. Vgl. zur Evidenzlosigkeit des Subjekts: Konrad Bayers Stück „der idiot".
[7] Bayer, Konrad, *Das Gesamtwerk*, hrsg. v. Gerhard Rühm (Reinbeck 1966), S. 412.
[8] ebenda. S. 299/280.
[9] ebenda. S. 412/416.
[10] Dieser weniger bekannte Aufsatz erschien in ‚*Neue Zürcher* Zeitung‘, Nr. 27 (Fernausg. Nr.12) vom 14. 1. 1968.
[11] Bernhard, Thomas: *Frost* (Frankfurt a. M. 1972), S. 7f.
[12] Bernhard, *Verstörung* (1982), S. 116.

* * *

WITTGENSTEINS REHABILITIERUNG DES CARTESIANISCHEN PARADIGMAS

Wilhelm Lütterfelds
Universität Wien

Folgt man Wittgensteins radikaler Privatsprachenkritik, dann muß man ihm in all jenen Fällen zumindest Inkonsequenz vorhalten, wo er in seinen Analysen cartesianisch verfährt: Etwa wenn er die Introspektion billigt (*PU* 587f, 677), eine Klassifizierung psychologischer Begriffe versucht (*Z* 472ff), wenn er den „Ausruf des Schmerzes" von einem „Etwas" begleitet sein läßt, das „schrecklich" ist und um dessentwillen man den Ausruf macht (*PU* 296), wenn er das Gedächtniskriterium keinesfalls generell verwirft (*PU* 56), wenn er Gefühle hinsichtlich ihres Grades und Ortes analysiert (*PB* 61) oder sogar vom Denken als „seelischen Vorgang" spricht (*PU* 332).

Cartesianisch sind diese Analysen deshalb, weil sie unterstellen, daß man in ihnen unmittelbar auf die mentalen Phänomene selbst Bezug nimmt, indem man sie innermental unterscheidet, bezeichnet, beschreibt und wiedererkennt, sich also keineswegs nur auf deren sprachliche und nichtsprachliche Äußerung bezieht. Wird infolgedessen die Bedeutung der mentalen Termini gerade nicht der Art ihres Ausdrucksgebrauches entnommen, sondern einem vorsprachlichen, unmittelbaren Bewußtsein, dann spielt Wittgenstein häufig ein cartesianisches Sprachspiel, und seine Privatsprachen-Kritik fällt auf ihn selber zurück.

Dies ist nicht zufällig. Der Paradigmenwechsel vom Cartesianismus zur Bedeutungsanalyse bleibt in einer zirkulären Priorität stecken: Mentale Phänomene sind ebenso nur in sprachlichen Ausdrücken gegeben (*PU* 120), wie diese innerhalb des Bewußtseins bleiben („das Sprachliche" als „Erlebnis" (*PU* 649)). Dem entspricht Wittgensteins Inkonsequenz. Wenn er die Berechtigung des Bildes vom „Inneren" bestreitet, zieht er sich den Vorwurf zu, seelisch-geistige Phänomene würden für ihn überhaupt nicht existieren. Doch will er natürlich keineswegs ein Behaviorist sein und lediglich das (sprachliche) Verhalten nicht für eine Fiktion halten (*PU* 307, 370). Seine Position jenseits von Cartesianismus und Behaviorismus resultiert daraus, daß Sätze über mentale Phänomene nicht übersetzbar sind in Sätze über Verhalten, Dispositionen, physiologische Zustände etc.; daß sie aber auch nicht private Bewußtseinsdaten zum Ausdruck bringen.

Es ist die „grammatische Fiktion" der „physikalischen Ausdrucksweise", die zum Cartesianismus verführt: Bezeichnung, Benennung, Beschreibung, ostensive Definition im Hinschauen − diese sprachlichen Operationen sind „Redeformen", in denen wir uns auf Außenweltphänomene beziehen (*PB* 57). Verwenden wir sie für Mentales, dann unterstellt diese Ausdrucksweise, daß das Mentale in einer Innenwelt existiert, auf die man gleichfalls introspektiv, identifizierend und charakterisierend Bezug nimmt, dabei einen Wahrheitsanspruch erhebt und ihn kriteriell rechtfertigt. So legt sich eine mentale Entität wie das Ich etwa dann nahe, wenn man mit „ich" nicht bloß auf eine Person unter anderen oder gar auf einen Körper Bezug nehmen will, wenn man andere physische Instanzen für die indikatorische Bezeichnung aber nicht zur Verfügung hat und infolgedessen eine „geistige Natur" mit „Sitz in unserem Körper" als Referenzobjekt von „ich" einführt (*BLB* S. 110, 116).

Dieser Sprachverführung durch die Oberflächengrammatik begegnet Wittgenstein mit der These, auch die Bedeutung mentaler Termini sei ihrem Ausdrucksgebrauch zu entnehmen, nämlich ihrem „Subjektgebrauch". Und diese „neue Sprechweise" sei es, die das cartesianische Sprachspiel auszeichnet. Sie dürfe man nicht mit einem (physikalischen) Sprechen über eine neu entdeckte Innenwelt des Bewußtseins verwechseln (*PU* 400f, *BLB* S. 106).

Vor allem vier Züge kennzeichnen den Subjektgebrauch der neuen Sprechweise: (1) Die Selbstzuschreibung mentaler Termini (z.B. denken, sehen, empfinden) geschieht derart, daß man mit „ich" selbstidentifizierend auf sich Bezug nimmt und sich irrtumsfrei einen bestimmten Bewußtseinszustand zuspricht. (2) Dieser Zustand ist nicht ursprünglich ein vorsprachliches Phänomen (Erlebnis), das man dann in Wörter übersetzt, als Referenzobjekt von Ausdrücken verwendet und durch die Sprache darstellt (Z 191, PU 649). Insofern gibt es auch kein „Bewußtseinsparadigma" eines bestimmten Erlebnisses etwa als Erinnerungskriterium neben dem Paradigma des Verhaltens und der Sprachhandlung (PU 300). Generell steht die Sprache nicht vermittelnd zwischen Innenweltphänomen und dem expressiven Benehmen (PU 245). (3) Vielmehr realisiert man sich in der Selbstzuschreibung mentaler Termini erst als jemand, der sich in einem bestimmten Bewußtseinszustand befindet. Durch die subjektsprachliche Verwendung der mentalen Termini wird man sich dieses Zustandes allererst bewußt. Deshalb liegt ein Bewußtseinsphänomen nur als Bedeutung des sprachlichen Ausdrucks vor. Infolgedessen kann man es auch nur über dessen Verwendung identifizieren, wiedererkennen und vergleichen (PU 290). (4) Ein mentales Sprachspiel erhält dann seine Eigenart nicht durch Rückgriff auf erklärende Erlebnisse, sondern ist als „Urphänomen" hinzunehmen, indem man einfach feststellt, daß es gespielt wird (PU 654f).

Die Problematik der These Wittgensteins (mentale und physische Sprachspiele differieren nicht in einem inneren und äußeren Referenzbereich, sondern in der Art und Weise zu sprechen) ist unverkennbar. Zunächst deshalb, weil ein Zirkelverdacht besteht. Denn einerseits soll die Sprechweise darüber entscheiden, ob man auf physische oder mentale Phänomene Bezug nimmt, also bestimmen, welcher Typ von Sprachspiel vorliegt. Andererseits muß letzteres bereits bekannt sein, um die Sprechweise korrekt zu identifizieren. Daß z.B. ein visuelles oder emotionelles Sprachspiel gespielt wird −, wie läßt sich dies feststellen, wenn man nicht nur diesen Zirkel, sondern auch den unendlichen Regreß vermeiden will, worin man − um das fragliche Sprachspiel zirkelfrei zu identifizieren − immer wieder auf weitere Ausdrücke und anderes Benehmen rekurriert, für die sich jedoch dieselbe Frage stellt? Muß nicht die Konstatierung eines mentalen Sprachspiels als „Urphänomen" z.B. gewisse Wahrnehmungs- und Gefühlserlebnisse sowie ein unmittelbares Wissen um sie und ihren typischen Ausdruck a priori unterstellen, soll sie den Typ eines Sprachspiels zirkel- und regreßfrei feststellen können?

Allerdings bezieht sich dieses unmittelbare Bewußtsein nicht mehr in cartesianischer Manier ausschließlich auf Erlebnisse als vorsprachliche, rein mentale Phänomene, sondern lediglich auf deren Realität als Bedeutungen der sprachlichen Ausdrücke. Zudem ist dieses Bewußtsein selber nicht semantisch auf eine Bedeutung reduzierbar. Und daß schließlich ein mentales Phänomen als Bedeutung eines sprachlichen Ausdrucks bewußt ist, heißt, daß man es vom Ausdruck zugleich auch unterschieden weiß. Dies besagt jedoch, daß man sich auf es auch in einer unmittelbar-kognitiven, vorsprachlichen Weise bezieht. Zu Recht kann Wittgenstein deshalb am „Bild des Inneren" festhalten (PU 423f) sowie an der Erlebnisqualität, an Introspektion und Gedächtniskriterium. In all dem nimmt Wittgenstein nicht zuletzt einen modifizierten Cartesianismus wieder auf.

Für mentale Termini besagt dies, daß zwei Typen von Sprachspielen, genauer: deren „komplizierte Beziehungen" erforderlich sind, um die Bedeutung der fraglichen Termini korrekt zu ermitteln, nämlich ein öffentliches und ein cartesianisches. Unmißverständlich hat Wittgenstein dies in seiner Formel des „Durcheinander" festgehalten: Vom Benehmen und vom Seelenzustand handeln Sätze mit mentalen Termini, „aber nicht im Nebeneinander; sondern von einem durch das andere" (PU S. 179f). Unabhängig davon, ob man die Einheit dieser doppelten Referenz mit Hilfe der Beziehung von Sprachanalyse und Bewußtseinsphilosophie klären kann; oder ob man dies in einer Phänomenologie des körperlichen Ausdrucks erreicht, weil der „menschliche Körper das beste Bild der menschlichen Seele" ist (PU S. 178), so daß Bewußtseinszustände „in des Andern Gesicht" so deutlich sind wie in der „eigenen Brust" (Z 220ff); oder ob die fragliche Einheit gar zum „Inneren" jener Sprache gehört, derer man sich a priori bedient, weshalb man auch über jene Einheit nur „Äußeres" vorzubringen vermag

(*PU* 120); oder ob schließlich das „Wesen von Außen und Innen" vorrational allein durch „Glauben" aufzuhellen ist (*Z* 558) –, bei all dem wird Descartes' Paradigma in Wittgensteins sprachanalytischer Kritik rehabilitiert. Allerdings sind Wittgensteins Untersuchungen dann keineswegs konsistent. Geraten sie dann doch selber in jene Aporien, die seine Privatsprachenkritik zum Anlaß nimmt, das cartesianische Sprachspiel zu kritisieren. „So gelangt man beim Philosophieren am Ende dahin, wo man nur noch einen unartikulierten Laut ausstoßen möchte" (*PU* 261).

* * *

THE TRACTATUS SOLUTION
TO THE PROBLEM OF CONSCIOUSNESS

Kenneth Jones
New University of Ulster

In the Seventeenth century Descartes recommended a new concept, the concept of consciousness, and a different way of thinking about the human being or human soul from the traditional Aristotelean way of thinking. In *Meditations II* Descartes consciously separates off the soul as consciousness or 'thinking' from the wider Aristotelean conception of soul as principle of life which included all living and bodily functions, nutrition, growth, sensation, perception, imagination, thought and action. Famously Descartes says: "What then am I? A thinking thing. What is that? One that doubts, understands, asserts, denies, is willing, is unwilling, which imagines and feels".[1] Compared to the Aristotelean picture of the human soul the Cartesian picture appears severely circimscribed indeed, but Descartes felt that here, in conscious experience, he had drawn a boundary around something essentional about humanity that could be preserved against the materialism and determinism of the rising sciences. Now the development of the human sciences in the Nineteenth and Twentieth centuries—and in particular the development of psychology—made it clear that philosophy must once again redraw the spheres of competence between philosophy and the sciences. The point is that much of the contents of the Cartesian mind—the psychological aspects of doubting, understanding, assertion, denial, willing, imagining, feeling and perceiving—had become the subject of psychological investigation. Hence the question arose again, what part of consciousness lies outside the province of science? What part of the human image can be preserved against the sciences?

The *Tractatus* can be seen as an attempt to save the human image against the encroaching human sciences by separating the logical part of 'thought' from the psychological part. Or to put it another way the *Tractatus* can be seen as a redrawing of the boundary between philosophy and science—logic and psychology—by applying Frege's principle of purity—'always to separate sharply the psychological from the logical, the subjective from the objective'—to the Cartesian concept of consciousness. The central thesis of the *Tractatus* might be interpreted as the thesis that psychology cannot explain, or concern itself with, the propositional content at the heart of psychological acts. Psychology can investigate the mental facts involved in thinking or judging, but not the propositional content of thinking, not what is involved in saying something truely or falsely about the world. The strategy of the *Tractatus* is to separate off the psychological aspect of consciousness, which is the proper object of psychological investigation, from the propositional aspects of consciousness, which is the proper object of logical investigation and cannot be explained by the sciences. Or, as I would prefer to put it, the *Tractatus* distinguishes the psychological features of conscious states from the 'intentionality' of those states, for as I hope to show in a moment what the *Tractatus* preserves of the human mind against the human sciences is precisely its 'intentionality'.[2]

The best and quickest way to get sight of the problem at the heart of the *Tractatus* is through his later works where the problems are brilliantly expresses though of course for the purpose of criticism. The key passage for my purpose is *Philosophical Investigations* 95.

> Thought must be something unique. 'When we say, and mean, that such-and-such is the case, we—and our meaning—do not stop anywhere short of the fact; but we mean: This-is-so. But this paradox (which has the form of a truism) can also be expressed in this way: Thought can be of what is not the case.

Two paradoxes express thought's uniqueness. a) 'When we say, and mean, that such-and-such is the case, we—and our meaning—do not stop anywhere short of the fact' but ,deals with the very object itself. We feel as if by means of it we had caught reality in our net' (*PI* 428). Why is this a paradox? Well if I think of a stone, my mind does not become the stone. How then does it enter our thoughts? 'How' as Aristotle put it in *De Anima*,[3] 'does the mind which thinks become the object which it thinks?' The first paradox which expresses thoughts uniqueness is that thought can deal with the object without becoming the object. b) 'But this paradox (which has the form of a truism) can also be expressed in this way: Thought can be of what is not the case'. The second paradox is also an ancient one, the Parmenidean paradox of false thought. How can we say or think how things are not? What is the object of false judgement? Indeed Wittgenstein's earliest philosophical thoughts are concerned with 'the mystery of negation'. His entry in his notebooks 15.11.1914 reads: [4] 'Here is a deep mystery. It is the mystery of negation. This is not how things are, and yet we can say how things are *not.*—'

Thought then is doubly unique, it deals with what is and with what is not. It is directed to an object even though the object need not exist. It reaches out to reality even though there is no reality for it to reach out to. This double paradox I want to suggest is the problem at the heart of the *Tractatus*. It is the problem of 'intentionality'. The solution is the picture theory of the proposition. The picture theory is the theory of what thought must be like whereby it can reach out to a precise but only possible state of affairs. Wittgenstein's statement of the theory is short, simple and vivid.

> One name stands for one thing, another for another thing, and they are combined with one another. In this way the whole group—like a *tableau vivant*—presents a state of affairs. 4.0311.

This states Wittgenstein's basic intuition that the proposition is a picture of reality. But what kind of picture? It is clear from the nature of the problem that it cannot be a picture in any ordinary sense. Crucially it cannot be a mental picture or image. For the problem just is: 'What makes my image of him an image of HIM?' (*PI* p. 177) The miracle just is how the image reaches out and catches just that person in its net? The presence to mind of a mental image or picture states the problem, it does not solve it. The point is that the mental picture, like any picture, can always be interpreted. What makes the proposition-picture unique however is that 'it cannot be capable of interpretation. It is the last interpretation' (*BLB* p. 34). In *Lectures and Conversations* 67 he says, 'When I consider my own thought, I feel absolutely sure that it is a thought that so and so. It seems to be a super-picture. It seems, with thought, that there is no doubt whatever. With a picture, it still depends on the method of projection whereas with thought we are absolutely certain that this is the thought of that.' It is axiomatic in the *Tractatus* that the proposition's sense is self-revealing and transparent. There can never be any doubt when I consider my own thought that it is a thought that so and so. The proposition is a 'meaning terminus' there can be no coming to understand a proposition, it is the understanding. It is not something we think, something we have to supply a thought to, it is the thought. It follows from this that the proposition must be 'autonomous' in the sense that it must contain in itself everything that makes it a thought. Hence *it*—the proposition—and nothing else must present a definite but possible state of affairs. "Logic is not a field in which we express what we wish with the help of signs, but rather one in which the nature and inevitable sign speaks for itself" *TLP* 1.124. But how exactly is the miracle achieved? By what mechanism does the proposition-picture catch reality in its net? How does it reach out and touch reality?

The nuts and bolts of the 'picturing mechanism' are spelled out in section 2.1-2.16. These sections can be regarded as a transcendental argument ascribing to language and reality whatever is necessary for the one to be of the other. 2.1513 asserts that the picture includes the 'pictorial relationship, which makes it into a picture. This is crucial for its 'autonomy' for the proposition-picture must show a reality 'off its own bat', without the aid of anything outside of it. But what is the 'pictorial relationship'? "The pictorial relationship consists of the correlations of the picture's elements with things" 2.1514. "These correlations are, as it were, the feelers of the pictures's elements, with which the picture touches reality". 2.1515. But how does the correlation of the picture's elements with things enable the picture to reach out and attach itself to reality? Wittgenstein's basic idea is this: When names are correlated with objects they, as it were, absorb into themselves the logical form of objects i.e. the range of possibilities into which objects can fit. Hence whenever names are put together a proposition-picture is guaranteed. It is by this mechanism — names absorbing the logical form of objects- —that names reach out and touch reality. In 'Some Remarks on Logical Form', 1929 Wittgenstein states his basic idea thus:

> "I have said elsewhere (the Tractatus) that a proposition 'reaches up to reality,' and by this I meant that the forms of the entities are contained in the form of the proposition which is about these entities. For the sentence, together with the mode of projection which projects reality into the sentence, determines the logical form of the entities".

To summarise: The *Tractatus* can be interpreted as an attempt to save the human image against the encroaching sciences, and in particular psychology. The deal is that psychology can have all of consciousness bar its 'intentionality' or propositional content. The uniqueness of human mentality is the uniqueness of the thought or the proposition and can be expressed in two related paradoxes. a) the proposition 'deals with the object (reality)' and b) it can be of what is not the case. The picture of the human mind that emerges from the *Tractatus* is the Cartesian one but pared of its psychological contents, possessing logical volume only. In the later philosophy this remnant of the Cartesian soul — consciousness shrunk to an extensionless point — is rejected. Those features of thought which once made it appear remarkable and para-doxical and which called out the remarkable a priori order revealed in the *Tractatus* now appear as 'truisms' (*PI* 95). To understand why they appear as 'truisms' is to understand the difference between the earlier and later Wittgenstein.

ENDNOTES

1 *Descartes, Philosophical Writings*. A selection translated and edited by E. Anscombe P. T. Geach (Nelson's University Paperbacks, The Open University, 1971), p. 70.
2 Brentano defines the intentionality of a mental state as 'the reference to a content, a direction upon an object (by which we are not to understand a reality . . .) or an immanent objectivity', *Psychology From An Empirical Standpoint*, Vol. 1, Book II, Ch. 1. (Quoted from R. Chisholm's article 'Intentionality', in: *The Encyclopedia of Philosophy*. Edited by P. Edwards (1967). Two elements of intentionality are referred to here: a) thought is 'directed upon an object' and b) thought can be of what is not the case ('by which we are not to understand a reality'). These two features correspond to what Wittgenstein considers remarkable about the proposition, hence the theory of the proposition, is a theory of intentionality.
3 *Aristotle's De Anima*. Translated by D. W. Hamlyn. (Clarendon Aristotle Series, 1971), 431b. It is worth noting how similar Wittgenstein's answer to this paradox is to Aristotle's. My mind, Aristotle says, does not become the stone I think about but receives its form: 'It is not the stone which is present in the soul but the form' *De Anima*, 431b. The key idea in Wittgenstein's picture theory is of names absorbing the logical form of objects: 'These correlations (i.e. between names and objects) are, as it were, the feelers of the picture's elements with which the picture touches reality' *TLP* 2.1515.
4 Wittgenstein, L., *Notebooks 1914—16*, Edited by G. H. Wright and G. E. M. Anscombe. (Oxford 1969), p. 30.

* * *

PHILOSOPHIE DER PSYCHOLOGIE IM *TRACTATUS*

Hans Rudi Fischer
Universität Heidelberg

Als die wohl dichteste Auseinandersetzung mit Problemen der philosophischen Psychologie darf man die Argumentation gegen die Denkbarkeit einer Privatsprache in den *PU* auffassen. In diesem Zusammenhang zeichnet sich die Position ab, daß wir zu den Phänomenen unserer Erfahrung, ganz gleich ob ,innerer' oder ,äußerer' keinen epistemologisch neutralen Zugang haben. Die daraus resultierende prinzipielle Abhängigkeit von sprachlicher Beschreibbarkeit hinsichtlich des epistemischen Zugangs zu unserer Erfahrung ist eine Grundkonstante in Wittgensteins Denken und gilt bereits für den Traktat, was sich insbesondere bei der Diskussion der intentionalen Sätze zeigt. Ich möchte im folgenden mein Augenmerk auf das richten, was im *TLP* als ,Philosophie der Psychologie' zu verstehen ist und inwieweit dort die Wurzeln der späteren philosophischen Psychologie bereits gelegt ist.

Der Terminus ,Philosophie der Psychologie' taucht im bisher veröffentlichten Werk Wittgensteins nur zweimal auf und zwar jeweils in der gleichen Wendung: „Erkenntnistheorie ist die Philosophie der Psychologie" (*NB* p. 106 u. *TLP* 4.1121) Nun hat man im *TLP* unter ,Erkenntnistheorie' nicht das zu verstehen was wir heute gemeinhin unter dem Terminus ,Epistemologie' behandeln. Wie ist dann aber Wittgensteins Identifikation der Erkenntnistheorie mit der Philosophie der Psychologie zu verstehen? Diese identifikatorische These scheint mir aus dem Kontext von Wittgensteins Diskussion und Kritik von Russells Urteilstheorie verständlich. Russell arbeitete in der Zeit von 1910–1914 an der Verbesserung seiner früheren Urteilstheorie und wollte in einem Buch mit dem projektierten Titel ,Theory of Knowledge' die früheren Mängel beseitigen.[1]

Es ist belegt, daß Wittgenstein die Manuskripte des nie in toto erschienenen Buches kannte[2] und gegenüber Russell scharf kritisierte. Wittgensteins Bestimmung der Erkenntnistheorie als Philosophie der Psychologie scheint mir im Zusammenhang von Russells Bestimmung der Psychologie bzw. der Erkenntnistheorie in diesem Buch seine Bedeutung zu gewinnen. In diesem Buch wird die Relation zwischen Psychologie und Erkenntnistheorie so bestimmt, daß die Analyse der Erfahrung des Subjektes bzw. die Relation des Urteilsubjektes zu den Termen seines Urteils insoweit zur Psychologie gehört, als die Differenzierung wahrer/falscher Propositionen irrelevant ist. Als erkenntnistheoretische Aufgabe wird die Analyse der Voraussetzungen des Urteils bestimmt, sofern es wahr oder falsch sein kann.[3] Russells Theorie unterliegt die Auffassung, daß ein Urteil eine Beziehung eines Geistes (,mind', ,subject') zu den Termen seines Urteils (proposition) ist, mit denen er bekannt (aquaintance) sein muß. Gerade diese Relation wird als psychologischer Anteil der Erkenntnistheorie gefaßt und in den Aufsätzen von 1906 und 1910 als die primäre Frage diskutiert; die eigentliche epistemologische Frage nach den Bedingungen der Wahr-/Falschheit eines Urteils bzw. Satzes wird in diesen Aufsätzen kaum thematisiert. Über eine einfache korrespondenztheoretische Lösung wird das Problem der Wahr- bzw. Falschheit eines Satzes gelöst. Die Crux von Russells Urteilstheorien und dies gilt auch noch für die komplexere, die er ab 1910 zu entwickeln versucht, ist, daß er die Beziehung des Satzes zur Wirklichkeit nicht problematisiert, sondern nur die Beziehung des urteilenden Subjektes zum Satz. So ist es nach Russells Theorie möglich, daß ein Subjekt mit den Termen ,table', ,penholders' und ,book' bekannt ist und damit das Urteil fällen könte: „The table penholders the book', gerade dies heißt aber für Wittgenstein, daß Russells Theorie unsinnige Urteile nicht ausschließen kann.[4] Demgegenüber thematisiert Wittgenstein schon in den *Notes on Logic* (1913) den Satz und seine Beziehung zur Wirklichkeit und stellt diese Beziehung ins Zentrum seiner Betrachtung: „The epistemological questions concerning the nature of judgement and belief cannot be solved without a correct apprehension of the form of the proposition." *NB* p. 106) Nun scheint die Stoßrichtung von Wittgensteins These, daß die Erkenntnistheorie die Philosophie der Psychologie sei, klar: Für Wittgenstein ist die Beziehung des Satzes zur Wirklichkeit die primäre, die über den Sinn des Satzes Aufschluß geben muß. Wittgenstein greift im Gegensatz zu Russell das Problem der Beziehung: Subjekt-Satz-Wirklichkeit, von der Seite her an, die Russell als genuin epistemologische begreift, nämlich dort, wo die wahr/falsch-Notation relevant ist, und dies ist die Beziehung Satz-Wirklichkeit. Ist diese Beziehung geklärt, dann ist auch geklärt, wie die Relation Subjekt-Satz, die Russell als psychologische versteht, zu denken ist. Ist also die Philosophie wie sie Wittgenstein konzipiert, als „logische Klärung der Gedanken und der Sprache" aufzufassen, so ist sie über ein korrektes Verständnis des Satzes und seiner Möglichkeiten Wirklichkeit abzubilden auch Erkenntnistheorie, Theorie dessen was sinnvoll gesagt, gedacht und gewußt werden kann. Diese sprachkritische Form von Erkenntnistheorie des *TLP* ist über die Klärung des Verhältnisses von Satz und Wirklichkeit gerade darin auch Philosophie der Psychologie, als dadurch das Verhältnis von Subjekt und Satz, insofern es artikulierbar ist, von der korrekten Notation des Satzes und seiner Beziehung zur Wirklichkeit abhängig ist. D.h. in der abbild-theoretischen Klärung des Verhältnisses von Satz und Wirklichkeit ist auch geklärt, was über das Subjekt und seine intentionalen Zustände gesagt werden kann; gerade dies ist der Bereich, den Wittgenstein der Philosophie der Psychologie zuordnet. Bevor ich zu den Passagen komme, die ich als das Zentrum von Wittgensteins Philosophie der Psychologie im *TLP* begreife, skizziere ich noch die Beziehung von Sprache und Denken wie sie in den Tagebüchern zum Ausdruck kommt und für Wittgensteins Behandlung der intentionalen Sätze relevant ist. Wittgenstein setzt seinen Abbildgedanken so fundamental an, daß der Gedanke, selbst wenn er noch nicht ‚gedachtes Satzzeichen' ist, bereits ein „logisches Bild des Satzes und somit ebenfalls ein Art Satz" ist. (*NB* v. 12. 9. 1916) Selbst der aus psychischen Bestandteilen bestehende Gedanke gilt bereits als zeichenfunktional, denn seine Bestandteile sind „in gleichartiger Beziehung zur Wirklichkeit" wie die Wörter. (Brief an Russell v. 19. 8. 1919) Die Strukturidee wird also auf den Gedanken übertragen, der damit ebenso strukturisomorph mit einem möglichen Sachverhalt sein muß wie der Satz. Zwischen Denken und Sprechen besteht also für die Tractatkonzeption keine kategoriale Differenz, im Gegenteil „Das Denken ist nämlich eine Art Sprechen." (*NB* a.a.O.); gerade diese Auffassung haben wir bei der Analyse intentionaler Sätze im *TLP* zu berücksichtigen, worauf ich nun kommen möchte. Ich gebe im folgenden eine kurze Interpretation von *TLP* 5.541ff.; sie wird grundsätzlich nichts Neues bringen, ist aber insoweit notwendig, als ich in diesen Passagen die Wurzel der späteren Philosophie der Psychologie ausmachen möchte.

Wittgenstein behauptet in *TLP* 5.542, daß Sätze der Form „A glaubt p", wenn sie als „psychologische Satzformen" verstanden werden, d.h. als intentionale Sätze, die Form „ ‚p' besagt p" hätten. Zunächst gilt es zu bemerken, daß Sätze dieser Form auch nichtpsychologisch verstanden werden können, nämlich als Sätze über den Inhalt des Glaubens (Hoffens, Fürchtens, Denkens etc.) von A, dann sind sie aber wahrheitsfunktional, denn wenn A nicht p sondern q glaubt, dann ist der Satz „A glaubt p" falsch und so verstanden böte er keine Ausnahme von der Traktatkonzeption. Wittgenstein thematisiert hier aber solche Sätze als intentionale, als Sätze über ‚psychische Zustände' und diese haben nach seiner Position die Form „ ‚p' besagt p". Dies ist so zu verstehen: wenn A p glaubt, so hat er einen Gedanken der selbst schon strukturisomorph mit dem artikulierten Satz‚p' ist und dieser ist ebenso ein logisches Bild einer Tatsache wie der unartikulierte Gedanke. Im Subjekt liegt damit das Satzzeichen ‚p' oder ein psychisches Analogon vor, welches bereits zeichenfunktional ist. Dann aber ist eine Aussage wie „A glaubt p", als Versuch zu lesen, die Darstellungsfunktion des Satzes auszudrücken, gerade dies ist aber im Tractatus ein sinnloses Unterfangen. Wenn Wittgenstein intentionale Sätze als von der Form „ ‚p' besagt p" auffaßt, so zeigt dies, daß solche Sätze im *TLP* versuchen, den Satz als Mittel der Darstellung selbst dazustellen; gerade diese Darstellungsfunktion ist aber selbst allemal vorausgesetzt und kann gar nicht thematisiert werden. Der Zusammenhang zwischen Sprache und Wirklichkeit ist als ein interner zu verstehen und dieser ist nach der Sprachkonzeption des *TLP* prinzipiell nicht darstellbar. Mit Rückgriff auf die Spätphilosophie läßt sich sagen, daß ein solcher Satz eine Regel ausdrückt, die selbst aber nicht als Dargestelltes in deskriptivem Sinne verstanden werden darf, andernfalls ist sie genauso sinnlos wie der Satz „Ich weiß, daß ich Schmerzen habe." Intentionale Haltungen sind also für die Tractatsprache nur insoweit relevant als sie Haltungen *gegenüber Sätzen* bzw. satzanalogen Zeichenfunktionen sind. Die Intention selbst fällt als nicht wahrheitsfunktional aus dieser Sprache heraus, denn ein Glaube, ein Wunsch, etc. ist nur insoweit der wahr/falsch-Notation subsumierbar, als er sich an Sätzen artikuliert.

Wie wir aus der Spätphilosophie im Kontext der Solipsismus- bzw. Privatsprachenargumentation wissen, ist die dort eingeführte Asymmetrie zwischen 1. u. 3. Pers. Sing. hinsichtlich der psychologischen Prädikate zentral. Explizit macht Wittgenstein diese Differenzierung nun im Tractat nicht, denn die Diskussion psychologischer Satzformen thematisiert Wittgenstein am Paradigma „A glaubt p" und aus einer wichtigen Parallelstelle dazu geht hervor, daß auch die 1. Pers. Sing. die Satzvariable ‚A' erfüllt.[5] Innerhalb der *TLP* Sprache ist diese Differenzierung auch nicht nötig, denn danach gehöre auch ich zur übrigen Welt, ebenso wie alles andere, was in meinem Erfahrungshorizont liegt, so daß das empirische (psychologische) Subjekt eliminiert werden kann. Demnach bleibt nur die prinzipielle Beschreibbarkeit der Erfahrungen eines Subjektes in wahrheitsfunktionalen Sätzen. In solchen kann über die Beziehung eines Subjektes zu seinen ‚inneren Zuständen' nichts ausgesagt werden, was nicht eben abbildtheoretisch gerechtfertigt werden kann. Meine Hauptthese in diesem Zusammenhang ist nun, daß implizit die Differenzierung zwischen 1. u. 3. Pers. in der Konstruktion des metaphysischen bzw. solipsistischen Ichs vorhanden ist. Betrachten wir dazu die Augenanalogie, wie sie in *TLP* 5.6331 formuliert ist. Das Auge, das ich mit dem metaphysischen bzw. solipsistischen Ich identifiziere, ist der Grenzpunkt des Wahrnehmungsfeldes und somit nicht im Bereich des Erfahrbaren und Beschreibbaren, weswegen Wittgenstein die Rede von einem denkenden Ich in einem empirischen Sinne ablehnt. Nun gibt es aber die Relation des Auges zu seinem Wahrnehmungsfeld, gerade diese Beziehung ist für Wittgenstein intern, sie läßt sich nicht ausdrücken; intentionale Sätze versuchen diese Beziehung zu artikulieren. Wenn Wittgenstein in *TLP* 5.62 behauptet, daß das, was der Solipsismus meint, ganz richtig sei, daß es sich nur nicht sagen ließe, so ist in dieser ‚Richtigkeit' des Solipsismus die kriterienlose und dadurch eben prinzipiell inkorrigible, also nicht wahrheitsfunktionale Selbstzuschreibung psychologischer Prädikate bereits erkannt, wie sie später in den *Zetteln* formuliert wird. Die ‚Richtigkeit' des Solipsismus liegt darin, daß er die Asymmetrie zwischen 1. u. 3. Pers. hinsichtlich mentaler Prädikate erkennt aber diese Disparität als empirische anstatt, wie Wittgenstein in der Spätphilosophie sagen würde, als grammatische zu begreifen. Im übrigen ist die solipsistisch konstruierte Sprache, die Wittgenstein in den *PU* diskutiert, genau von diesem Gedankengang getragen wie er sich im solipsistischen Ich des *TLP* konkretisiert. Es gibt eine Fülle von Passagen aus der mittleren Periode Wittgensteins die diese Interpretation bestätigt. Ich kann hier nur eine wichtige Stelle erwähnen, aus der die Verklammerung von *TLP* und *PU* sich sehr schön erkennen läßt; interessanter Weise werden die Themen von *TLP* und *PU* zusammengesehen. Wittgenstein behauptet dort gegenüber Moore, daß die direkte Erfahrung keinen Besitzer denotiert: „In order to make clear what he meant by this he compared ‚I have toothache', with ‚I see a red patch'; and said of what he called ‚the visual sensation' generally . . that 'the idea of a person does not enter into the description of what is seen'; and he said that similarly ‚the idea of a person' doesn't enter into the description of 'having toothache'." (Moore-Lectures p. 309) Was nicht in die Beschreibung eingehen kann, wird im *TLP* sinnlos und entzieht sich schlechthin der Analyse. Es wird zur Grenze der Welt und damit mystisch. In den *PU* bleibt dies zwar auch sinnlos, dennoch aber einer grammatischen Analyse zugänglich. Dies liegt daran, daß Wittgenstein neben deskriptiven auch andere Sprachspiele zuläßt. Das ‚Recht des Solipsismus' besteht darin, daß die ‚inneren Zustände' als GEWISSHEITEN, nicht als Wissen in die Grammatik der Sprachspiele eingehen und nicht wie im *TLP* mystisch an die Grenze verwiesen werden. Man sieht, daß dabei das grundsätzliche Problem dasselbe ist, die Lösung jedoch unterschiedlich geortet wird.

ANMERKUNGEN

[1] Vgl. dazu: B. Russell, *On the Nature of Truth* (1906) u. *On the Nature of Truth and Falsehood* (1910).
[2] Fünf Kapitel dieses Buches erschienen 1914/15 in: *The Monist*, Vol. XXIV.
[3] Vgl: *The Monist*, Vol. XXV, S. 582ff.
[4] Vgl. dazu Wittgensteins Bemerkung in *NB* S. 103 und *TLP* 5.5422.
[5] Vgl. „Moore-Diktat", *NB*, Appendix, S. 119.

* * *

AN ILLUSTRATION OF WITTGENSTEIN'S METHOD

Paul Hedengren
Brigham Young University, U.S.A.

Wittgenstein says that philosophical problems may be resolved, dissolved and made to completely disappear. But what philosophical problems have been dissolved or made to disappear? I will consider the philosophical question "How can we speak about what does not exist?" and show how we may dissolve the question by understanding the manner in which the grammar misleads us.

To do this, we will first consider the objects of consciousness and then the objects of intentions. We will come to consider the objects of intentions as qualities of consciousness rather than objects. Once so conceived the question "How can we speak about what does not exist?" will be shown to loose its puzzling character.

In regard to the objects of consciousness, there is one obvious but important thesis to demonstrate. It is: Whatever the objects of consciousness may be, they are not identical to the physical objects to which they may be correlated. For example, suppose I am looking at a red square. Now suppose it is claimed that there is some object of consciousness which is correlated to the red square. The question is: Can this object of consciousness be identical to the physical entity, the red square? A red entity is an entity that reflects light of predominately a certain wave length. A square entity is an entity that has spatial extension. But is the object of consciousness correlated with the physical object either able to reflect light of such and such wave length or is it extended in space? It appears to be neither. The object of consciousness is a mental entity and as such cannot have light shined up it let alone reflect light of predominately such and such wave length. Similarly since the object of consciousness is a mental entity, it does not have location in space. Yet it must have location in space, if it is spatially extended. Hence it is not spatially extended. Consequently the object of consciousness correlated with the red square, is neither red nor square as the red square is red and square. Since nonidentity may be established between entities simply by finding only one property that one entity has that the other entity does not have, we have established that the object of consciousness correlated to the red square is not identical to the red square.

Besides the mental entities postulated to exist in perception, there may be postulated entities which are the objects of our intentions. Suppose associated with the word "lerm" are the criteria: is warm, is edible, and is in my left hand. Suppose I want a lerm. This means that I want some entity which is warm, is edible and is in my left hand. There is nothing in my left hand. If there is nothing in my left hand, then no lerm exists. Whatever entity we might postulate to correlate with what I want, that entity could not be identical to any lerm, for it must be in my left hand to be a lerm and nothing is in my left hand. Should the postulated entity be specified to be ethereal, so that it could be postulated to be in my left hand, then it would not be either warm or edible. Hence again it could not be identical to any lerm and so could not be what I want when I want a lerm. So I can want what does not now exist and whatever entity may be postulated to be correlated with what I want but does not exist could not be identical to the entity that I want.

I may want a lerm even though a lerm does not exist, but could I hit a lerm unless a lerm exists? No, I could not. With physical action, the object of the action must exist for one to perform that action upon it. Hence, I could not hit, crush, or squeeze a lerm unless a lerm exists. But with intentional acts the so-called object of the act need not exist for me to perform the act. Hence, I can want, wish for, or love a lerm even though no lerm exists. If I hit a lerm then the lerm is the object of my hitting. But if I want a lerm, is the lerm the object of my wanting? Suppose I want a lerm, but no lerm exists, how then could a lerm actually be the object of my wanting? When we recall that there is no entity that could be postulated to be correlated with what I want that could properly be called a lerm, we realize that either we are related to a nonexistent relatum, or there are no objects of our intentions even though the grammatical structure by which we express our intention makes it appear that there are.

But if intentional acts have no objects, how may we conceive them to be? What has been taken to be the object of the intention may be conceived to be simply a quality of the intention. For example rather than saying "I want a lerm". which makes it appear that there is an object of our intentional act of wanting, we might instead say, "I am lerm-wanting". By this latter expression, we seek to convey that what is wanted is a part of or a quality of wanting rather than an independent object. So when I want a lerm and no lerm exists, I can either claim to be related by my wanting to an nonexistent relatum or claim that lerm-wanting has a quality which distinguishes it from other kinds of wanting such as Pegasus-wanting. The claim that one is related to a nonexistent relata, seems to be unacceptable on purely logical grounds, for how can anything be truly related to what does not exist?

If we differentiate lerm-wanting from Pegasus-wanting by assuming variance in the quality of intentional acts, we do not preclude the possibility that there might exist that which would satisfy the intention. If I lerm-want, there might exist that which would satisfy the intention. If I lerm-want, there might come to exist an entity which is a lerm which satisfies my lerm-wanting. We might even choose to call the entity which satisfies my wanting to be the object of my intention, but doing so does not require that, before I can want, what I want must first exist.

With purely physical acts, the object must exist for the act to be done, but with purely intentional acts, the object may not need to exist. But now we come to the central question: May I speak about what does not exist? Put another way: May I refer to what does not exist? Or, for me to refer to something, must what I refer to exist? If referring is, or is like, a physical act, then we may expect that like other physical acts, the object of the act must exist if that act is to be performed. On the other hand, if referring is, or is like, an intentional act, then it may be that the object is better taken to be part of the intention rather than an object, and the so-called object need not exist for the act to be performed.

It appears that in some cases one can refer without the use of any physical entity, as might be the case in a ESP experiment in which one is to say only in one's mind "Pegasus doe not exist", but certainly in many cases there is a physical element as well.

Now suppose Pegasus does not exist and we say "Pegasus exists". We ask the questions: "Is the use of the words meaningful?", and "Is the assertion made through the use of the words true?" The first question is answered affirmatively and the second question is answered negatively.

Now, let us consider "Pegasus does not exist". When we use these words our use is meaningful and the assertion made through their use is true. But this time we have considered all of the words in the sentence. What may be said only about Pegasus? Notice that when I use the word "Pegasus", I may refer to Pegasus by my use, but I do not assert by my use what I may assert by the words, "I refer to Pegasus." This is a critical point. Since no assertion is made by my use of "Pegasus" alone in the sentence "Pegasus does not exist", it makes no sense even to inquire if what I mean by my use of that word is true or false. Truth or falsity is a property only of complete assertions, not of some of the symbols through which we make our assertions. So when I use "Pegasus", I do so meaningfully, but what I mean by the use of this one word is not an assertion. But even if I do not assert by my use of "Pegasus" what I assert by the words "I refer to Pegasus", let us consider whether this assertion is true. It is true, even though Pegasus does not exist, for my act of referring is intentional and intentional acts do not require objects in the sense that some physical acts do. What we may have considered the object of the act is better taken to be part of the act. It may be less misleading to say "I am Pegasus-referring", rather than "I am referring to Pegasus".

Now let us consider this treatment of the philosophical question, "How are we able to speak about what does not exist?" in light of the method suggested by Wittgenstein. Wittgenstein speaks of philosophical puzzlement and indeed the question we have considered arouses puzzlement. But this puzzlement is not to be satisfied but dissolved. It is dissolved when we come to see that the puzzlement was generated by confusion. In this case, the confusion arises through a misleading grammatical form. Physical actions such as hitting require that there be something hit. We express this action in language with a transitive verb and a direct object. Thus when we say "I hit the table" there is the person performing the action, the action and the object of the action. But what is misleading is that we use the same grammatical form to express the obtainment of an intentional state. I am sitting in a chair and have no consideration about lerms. Then I come to want a lerm. I have gone from one intentional state to another. From not being in the state of wanting a lerm to being in the state of wanting a lerm. The problem is that we express the newly acquired state by a grammatical form suitable for physical actions but misleading of intentional states. It appears from the grammatical structure of the sentence, "I want a lerm" that there is an action which is wanting and then separately an object of that action, a lerm. But the problem is there is no lerm. The temptation is to postulate sometype of shadowy entity, but none of them can meet the criteria of being a lerm. This tendency is even more pronounced in cases in which the verb has both physical and intentional aspects such as with the verb "referring". What may be postulated are Platonic Forms, concepts, Ideas, images or whatever. Rather than debate the existence of these, it is better simply to recognize that the grammatical form has misled us. We can then consider our ability to speak about what does not exist without philosophical concern.

* * *

9. Wittgensteins frühe Philosophie

9. Wittgenstein's Early Philosophy

LOGISCH-PHILOSOPHISCHE ABHANDLUNG ET LOGISCHER AUFBAU DER WELT

Gilles Gaston Granger
Université de Provence, Aix (France)

En 1921 paraît dans les *Annalen der Naturphilosophie* la *Logisch-Philosophische Abhandlung* de Wittgenstein, destinée à devenir célèbre sous le titre spinoziste de *Tractatus logico-philosophicus*. En 1928 est publié le *Logischer Aufbau der Welt* de Carnap. Ces oeuvres de jeunesse de deux des philosophes les plus marquants de ce début de siècle comportent, l'une et l'autre, dans leur titre, le mot «logique». On ne peut douter qu'une telle convergence soit significative, lorsqu'elle unit sur un même vocable aussi chargé de sens l'un des inspirateurs et l'un des fondateurs du Cercle de Vienne. Mais il est permis de s'interroger sur la différence d'interprétation de ce mot dont témoignent les deux ouvrages. Tous deux, sans doute, expriment des projets philosophiques centrés sur ce leitmotiv du logique, mais tous deux, on l'observera, ont explicitement récusé un rationalisme dogmatique universellement réducteur. Carnap termine son livre en citant le fameux aphorisme 7 du *Tractatus* (avec une légère variante): «*Wovon man nicht reden kann*» . . ., et souligne dans le résumé qui suit qu'il n'exige une «pure rationalité» que pour la science. (*A.* p. 273)[1] Cependant, cette vision commune d'un empire à la fois radical et borné de la logique recouvre deux conceptions profondément différentes de son sens. C'est cette bifurcation que l'on voudrait ici examiner. Elle annonce sans doute l'écart définitif des deux chemins parcourus plus tard par Wittgenstein et Carnap. Mais nous nous bornerons à l'envisager *in statu nascendi* dans ces deux grandes oeuvres liminaires, et sur quatre points qui nous paraissent essentiels. En premier lieu, comme expression de deux styles philosophiques; en second lieu, quant à la place respective en chacune d'elles de la connaissance scientifique et de la philosophie; en troisième lieu, relativement au jeu du logique et du transcendantal; quatrièmement enfin, sous l'aspect des fonctions qu'y tient le langage, et en général le symbolisme.

DEUX STYLES PHILOSOPHIQUES.

1.1. L'intention des deux auteurs est assurément de proposer une construction conceptuelle abstraite, évitant autant que faire se peut le recours à des imaginations intuitives et vagabondes suscitées par des expressions non maîtrisées dans le langage. L'un et l'autre veulent maintenir la pensée du lecteur dans un domaine délimité, et y gouverner son mouvement. Mais l'un fait usage d'une rhétorique procédant par aphorismes et commentaires, l'autre d'une rhétorique superposant différents niveaux d'exposés successifs. Aussi bien, l'importance et le jeu des liaisons logiques dans le *Tractatus* et l'*Aufbau* sont ils sensiblement différents.

Wittgenstein, comme on sait, énonce sept aphorismes majeurs, formant une suite de notions pour ainsi dire emboîtées: le «monde»-«ce que arrive»-«les états de choses», etc. . . ., et distribuées en trois niveaux: lemonde, l'image logique du monde, «ce dont on ne peut parler».[2] La liaison d'un concept à l'autre est alors d'explicitation plutôt que de conséquence, et chaque aphorisme est éventuellement *commenté* par des aphorismes dont la subordination est rendue manifeste par le mode de numération «alphabétique»: 1.1 commente en l'approfondissant 1; 2.01 commente 2 à un niveau de profondeur et de détail supérieur à celui auquel se situera 2.1. dans la suite. De sorte que l'echaînement du *Tractatus*, s'il répond bien à une certaine espèce de rigueur dont ce n'est pas ici le lieu de discuter, ne repose nullement pour sa stratégie d'ensemble sur le rapport de principe à conséquence, en l'un des sens précis que Wittgenstein lui-même indique dans la forme du langage objectif. Et il faut qu'il en soit ainsi, puisque, contrairement à la science, ce n'est pas des faits que selon lui parle la philosophie.

1.2. Bien qu'il en soit de même pour Carnap, en un sens qu'il y aura lieu de préciser, l'agencement de l'*Aufbau* est tout autre. L'oeuvre comporte d'abord un long exposé «non formel» de la Constitution, qui occupe la moitié de l'ensemble (Parties I, II, III); il entreprend ensuite de présenter pas à pas cette Constitution, mais un fragment seulement en est développé complètement, à titre d'échantillon, selon la stricte méthode formelle qui devrait être appliquée à la totalité des espèces d'objets. (Partie IV). La cinquième partie enfin traite plus brièvement de problèmes philosophiques classiques, sous le jour nouveau que la Constitution apporte.

Alors même qu'il n'intervient ès qualités que brièvement, sous une expression symbolique empruntée aux *Principia* de Russell-Whitehead, du § 106 au § 121, on voit qu'ici l'enchaînement logique au sens strict est revendiqué comme essentiel au développement de la philosophie, et non pas seulement de la science. Du point de vue du style de la pensée philosophique, c'est donc une application bien différente de l'adjectif *logisch* que font Carnap et Wittgenstein. Le traité de ce dernier est «logique» en ce qu'il montre le sens et le rôle de la forme *a priori* obligée de tout discours sensé sur le monde, c'est à dire sur les choses par l'intermédiaire des faits, de ce qui a lieu. La Constitution est «logique» en ce qu'elle prétend produire par la seule vertu d'une construction à la Russell-Whitehead la forme, nécessairement unique, des objets mêmes du monde.

DEUX RAPPORTS DE LA SCIENCE A LA PHILOSOPHIE.

2.1. Que soit logique dans l'*Aufbau* l'enchaînement même de la pensée philosophique, c'est là une conséquence du rapport qu'entretient alors pour Carnap cette pensée avec la connaissance scientifique. Il tient certes, comme Wittgenstein, que ce qui n'est pas formulable en concepts échappe à la connaissance (*Erkenntnis*) et relève d'une attitude de «croyance» (*Glauben*), sans rapport avec le savoir. Dans cette perspective essentiellement pratique— et selon lui, contrairement à Kant, étrangère à toute rationalité—, «on ne peut parler de question ni de réponse, puisqu'il s'agit alors de l'inexprimable.» (*A*. § 181, p. 257). Mais l'entreprise de Constitution des objets de la pensée positive qui est philosophique, n'en produit pas moins une véritable connaissance, et appartient déjà au domaine de l'exprimable et du conceptuel.

> «Afin que la science puisse s'attaquer à sa tâche, afin de pouvoir simplement formuler des propositions sur les objets, il faut que ceux-ci soient constitués (sans quoi leurs noms n'auraient certes aucun sens). *La construction du système de Constitution est ainsi la première tâche de la science*.» (*A*. § 179, p. 252).

L'établissement des formes d'objets, qui est proprement philosophique pour Carnap, représente donc le moment premier de la science, moment qu'il qualifie curieusement dans ce passage de «conventionnel», pour l'opposer au second moment, qui est de détermination des propriétés empiriques effectives des objets du monde. Le mot est emprunté à Poincaré et à des penseurs allemands contemprains, tels Dingler. On aurait tort cependant de l'entendre au sens fort que lui donne un «conventionnalisme» authentique. Carnap veut apparemment souligner seulement, en en faisant usage, qu'il se refuse à reconnaître un *a priori* synthétique. Rien de volontairement conventionnel, au sens d'arbitraire ou de commode, n'apparaît dans le mode de construction logique des formes de l'objectivité, si ce n'est naturellement le choix d'un langage. Lorsqu'on s'élève dans la Constitution du monde physique (du monde des physiciens), il est vrai que le choix des grandeurs d'état n'est pas strictement déterminé par la construction logique. Mais cette liberté de manoeuvre du physicien demeure fondamentalement limitée par l'exigence d'univocité—la «monomorphie»—des structures constituées, dont la seule réalisation doit être ce monde. En outre, même dans la phase antérieure à l'*Aufbau* où il est plus proche du conventionnalisme, le jeune Carnap formule déjà l'espoir qu'un «processus de décision méthodique, appuyé sur les données de l'expérience» dissipera un jour totalement toute ambiguïté dans l'établissement du cadre théorique de la science. («*Über die Aufgabe der Physik*», p. 90)[3]

La philosophie, comme détermination *a priori* des formes d'objets, tout comme la connaissance scientifique à quoi elle donne son assise, relève donc intégralement de l'exprimable. Et le discours philosophique de l'*Aufbau* se situe pour Carnap à l'intérieur de la science, de telle sorte que rien ne lui est plus étranger que le mot célèbre qui clôt le *Tractatus*:

> «Mes propositions sont des élucidations en ceci que, quiconque me comprend, les reconnaît au terme de sa lecture comme dépourvues de sens . . . (Il doit pour ainsi dire rejeter l'échelle qui lui a servi à monter.)» (*TLP* 6.54).

2.2. Il n'est pas question en effet pour Carnap de «rejeter l'échelle», car les termes successifs de la Constitution ne sont autres que les moments logiquement enchaînés qui font passer d'un *vécu* amorphe à une *réalité* articulée, telle que la connaît la perception organisée, puis la science. Avant de préciser le sens que revêt dans cette construction le rapport du logique au réel, soulignons brièvement en quoi s'en distingue la visée du *Tractatus*.

L'idée de réalité se dédouble chez Wittgenstein, qui transpose ainsi, d'une manière absolument originale, la profonde dichotomie de la tradition philosophique entre ce qui se donne immédiatement et ce qui, d'une manière ou d'une autre, fonde cette manifestation. La *Wirklichkeit* du *Tractatus*, c'est la situation d'«existence et de non existence des états de choses» (*TLP* 2.06), qui, considérée dans sa totalité, est le *monde* (*TLP* 2.063). Par opposition à cet ensemble des *faits*, le système des *objets* ou *choses* consitue la «substance du monde». Il ne s'agit nullement ici de dissocier une réalité vraie d'une apparence: le système des faits—relations entre choses—est exactement le *dual* du système des choses, comme les propriétés projectives d'un système de points sont duales de celles des droites qui les joignent. Ce qu'on appelle «logique» est alors la forme de ce système, la forme de la réalité, aussi bien en tant qu'ensemble de faits qu'en tant qu'ensemble de choses. La substance du monde, l'ensemble des choses, dessine l'espace de tous les faits possibles. Cette forme logique se montre donc aussi bien comme invariant et contrainte de l'arrangement des faits que comme possibilités de combinaison des choses. La première perspective se reflète dans le langage comme règles de calcul des propositions, la seconde demeure cachée: en vain Wittgenstein tentera-t-il de dégager une «logique des choses», en s'attaquant par exemple à une théorie *a priori* des couleurs. Et cet échec, sans doute, est l'une des origines de l'évolution de Wittgenstein vers la philosophie des *Recherches*. Dans le *Tractatus* en tous cas, le logique est «condition du monde» (l'expression se trouve dans les *Carnets* en date du 24 juillet 1916)[4], et ne se présente aucunement comme une *théorie* qui serait une première description schématique, ou un instrument de reconstruction, de la réalité.

Pour Carnap, la réalité est au contraire essentiellement produite par un processus de construction qui fait un usage explicite de la logique en tant que théorie. Dans un manuscrit inédit de 1922, intitulé: *Vom Chaos Zur Wirklichkeit*[5], et sur lequel Carnap a noté de sa main: «Ceci est le germe de la théorie de la Constitution», il se proposait de passer du «chaos» d'un vécu originaire fictif, à une «réalité» articulée. Le problème étant alors posé à partir du désir de surmonter les discordances et les irrationalités apparentes de notre perception effective du monde.

> «Mais cette thèse du chaos est une fiction . . . ce que nous vivons est une réalité déjà ordonnée, dont l'ordre et l'état, il est vrai, sont soumis à des altérations continuelles. Ces altérations, ces corrections sont principalement occasionnées par de petites dicordances. mais il est aussi des discordances importantes s'étendant à tout le doamine de la réalité, et nous resentons le désir de les surmonter par une nouvelle mise en ordre. C'est ce désir d'une mise en ordre nouvelle en vue d'écarter les discordances importantes qui occasionne la réflexion du théoricien de la connaissance, la fiction d'un chaos comme point de départ, et de principes d'ordre, selon lesquels l'édifice s'est produit, se produit et doit se produire.» (*Chaos*, p. 1).

Dans cette première esquisse Carnap insiste sur les corrections que doit subir l'expérience vécue pour que soit restauré, à partir d'une ordre immédiat imparfait, un ordre logique, constitutif de la réalité. Il évoque alors le problème d'une comparaison entre ce «domaine de la réalité» et le domaine de la Physique, se demandant à la fin du texte si le premier doit être considéré comme «un stade préliminaire, pré-scientifique et insuffisant»,—ou au contraire si le doamine de la Physique ne serait, relativement à l'autre, qu'«une fiction en vue de pouvoir appliquer le calcul». (*Chaos*, p. 14) Question qu'il considère du reste comme «métaphysique» et ne relevant pas du présent projet. Dans l'*Aufbau*, où le centre de gravité du système s'est déplacé du concept de réalité vers le concept de connaissance scientifique, la question n'est même plus formulée: la Constitution concerne à la fois le monde de la perception et celui de la science, qui ne s'opposent aucunement, la visée finale étant d'atteindre» un *monde objectif*, qui est saisissable par concepts, et le même pour tous les sujets» (*A.* § 2, p. 3). La science prolonge directement la systématisation qui organise déjà le monde de la perception, et ne fait que coordonner aux objets qualitatifs, *sans en rien perdre*,[6] des grandeurs permettant l'application des mathématiques et dégageant ainsi les conditions d'un consensus universel. Dès lors, la réalité, tant sous son expression perceptive que sous sa formulation scientifique, est inséparable en tant que telle de l'élaboration logique. Non pas, assurément, que la machinerie logique mise en oeuvre par le philosophe dans le processus réflexif de Constitution corresponde aux étapes d'une activité psychologique du sujet. La description de celle-ci, elle même fondée sur la Constitution d'un Ego empirique, relève évidemment d'une partie de la science dont Carnap reconnaît du reste la difficulté et le peu d'avancement. Il faudrait même dire que la réalité au sens le plus strict est fondamentalement de nature logique, dans la mesure où elle est objective. Car ne peut être objective que la *forme*: tout contenu *concret* est subjectif. (*A.* § 16, p. 20). Et, nous en discuterons plus loin, toute forme est pour Carnap une forme logique.

2.3. En tous cas, la reconstruction philosophique des formes d'objets, opéré par l'*Aufbau* au moyen de la logique russellienne, à partir de l'unique relation fondamentale de ressemblance mémorielle (*Ähnlichkeitserinnerung*) entre vécus (*Erlebnisse*), est bien considérée par Carnap comme relevant d'une pensée scientifique, exprimable d'une façon formelle dans le même langage que la science. A cette homogénéité du logique et du réel correspond la thèse de l'unicité radicale du monde: «Il n'y a qu'*un seul* domaine d'objets, et partant la science est *une*». (*A.* § 4, p. 4). La multiplicité des espèces d'objets n'est qu'un effet de la vie subjective; elle n'apparaît dans la Constitution que postérieurement à l'instauration d'un corps propre, avec la dissociation d'un domaine du psychisme solitaire (*Eigenpsychisches*), d'un domaine des objets physiques, puis des domaines de l'interpsychique et du monde culturel. En vertu de cette unicité foncière, chacun de ces domaines pourrait indifféremment, en principe, servir de point de départ à la Constitution, qui doit simplement rendre claire la possibilité de ramener aux éléments choisis comme donnée initiale toute connaissance-structurale-portant sur d'autres espèces d'objets. Aussi bien, cette *Zurückführung* n'est—elle nullement envisagée comme une réduction ontologique. Elle offre seulement le moyen de *traduire* toute proposition portant sur un objet d'espèce quelconque en une proposition portant sur les seuls objets primitifs. Tel est le sens que donne le jeune Carnap à la thèse de l'unité de la science, et cette unité ne peut être rendue manifeste qu'à partir du caractère purement logique jusqu'en son détail de la texture du monde.

Ainsi le problème de l'unité de la science est-il explicitement posé dans l'*Aufbau* à partir de la diversité et de l'hétérogénéité apparente des espèces d'objets. Diversité qui est alors présentée comme n'étant ni ontologique, ni logique, mais simplement «épistémologique» (*erkenntnistheoretisch*), c'est à dire relative à l'exercice par un sujet empirique des actes de connaissance. Elle n'apparaît comme irréductible que lorsque l'expérience est décrite dans le langage «réaliste» couramment utilisé, mais les caractères purement logiques qui suffisent à déterminer par la forme ce qui est connaissable dans les choses neutralisent cette hétérogénéité. Au reste, quel que soit le langage adopté pour décrire le monde, s'il est correctement employé, la description est traduisible dans les autres langages; et quel que soit par ailleurs le domaine d'objets où nous choisissons d'ancrer notre expérience, celle-ci doit toujours pouvoir, en principe être décrite dans sa totalité. Poursuivre de façon cohérente cette description en vue d'un complet accord intersubjectif suppose assurément qu'on s'en tienne à une langue formelle et à ses prolongements mathématiques, mais nullement que l'on accorde un privilège absolu au domaine des objets–physiques ou psychiques, par exemple–à partir duquel se développe la science unitaire de la réalité.

On observera que, dans le *Tractatus*, la question de l'unité de la science n'est pas explicitement posée. Elle constitue, à vrai dire, une thèse implicite et très affaiblie, dans la mesure où «la science de la nature est la totalité des propositions vraies». (*TLP* 4.11). or il n'est de sciences que naturelles, et les propositions scientifiques de la Psychologie, comme celles de la Physique, n'énoncent rien d'autre que des «corrélations de faits» (*TLP* 5.542). Mais, alors que l'unification forte de la science résultait chez Carnap de la *construction* uniformément logique des objets et entraînait, par conséquent, l'unification possible de la méthode, elle résulte chez Wittgenstein de l'universalité des contraintes logiques qui seules rendent effective la *représentation* des faits en général. Alors que celles-ci sont bien des conditions constitutives, les structures établies par le développement d'une pensée scientifique pour décrire le détail du monde ne font «qu'imposer une forme unifiée» à cette description (*TLP* 6.341). Forme que le *Tractatus* compare à un réseau, et le choix de la taille et de la figure des mailles de ce réseau n'obéit pas à une contrainte logique. On peut donc dire que l'unité fondamentale reconnue ici à la science en vertu de l'unicité logique de la structure du monde laisse largement indéterminé non seulement le problème de l'unité de la méthode, mais encore le mode d'organisation de ses objets. On comprend qu'il en soit autrement chez Carnap, pour qui cette organisation même relève dela philosophie en tant que proto-science, alors que dans le *Tractatus* la philosophie, qui ne fait que montrer l'universelle emprise du logique sur toute description du monde, demeure extérieure à la science dont elle prétend seulement «délimiter le domaine contesté.» (*TLP* 4.113).

LE LOGIQUE ET LE TRANSCENDANTAL.

3.1. Ce rapport de la logique à la philosophie et à la science, si différent de l'un à l'autre philosophe, exprime, à un niveau plus profond, deux conceptions de la nature de la logique et de ce qu'on pourrait appeler son statut métaphysique.

Carnap, das l'*Aufbau*, professe à l'égard de la logique deux thèses dont il convient de montrer à la fois les étroits rapports et la difficile coexistence. D'une part, il prend pour acquis la logique en tant que *théorie* formulée par Russell et Whitehead. D'autre part, il utilise la logique comme un instrument pour la *construction des formes d'objets*, lui faisant *jouer le rôle d'une doctrine du transcendantal*. Il y a sur ce dernier point un accord fondamental entre Carnap et Wittgenstein, mais la position de celui-ci ne comporte en revanche aucune ambiguïté. Nous avons noté plus haut le dédoublement wittgensteinien de la «réalité» en système des faits et système des choses, double expression d'une même condition de la représentation du monde. Cette condition ne concerne alors que le monde pris pour ainsi dire «localement», tel que peut le représenter la pensée objective, et non pas le monde pris comme expérience totale, dont la condition de saisie est alors l'*éthique* (ou *esthétique*), autre aspect de l'inexprimable. Le logique, qui joue bien alors le rôle de forme transcendantale constitutive des faits et des choses ne saurait être formulé et ne peut qu'être montré, par exemple comme règles de fonctionnement des symboles qu'institue à cet effet le logicien ou le mathématicien. Il est, comme le dit Wittgenstein, un acte et non une théorie. Il n'y a donc pas de *science* de la logique, pas d'*objets* logiques. Thèse radicale, audacieuse, mais cohérente, que n'ont sans doute pas vraiment prise au sérieux ni Russell, ni les membres du Cercle de Vienne pourtant fascinés par le *Tractatus*.

3.2. Pour Carnap, il semble qu'il veuille à la fois donner au logique le rôle transcendantal, puisque la Constitution s'effectue exclusivement par combinaison de formes logiques,–et lui conserver pourtant le statut de théorie. Car il y a des *objets* logico-mathématiques, dont les plus fondamentaux sont les classes et les relations, et postérieurement les espaces abstraits et les nombres. (*A.* § 107). Dans un article contemporain de l'*Aufbau* («*Eigentliche und uneigentliche Begriffe*», 1927), Carnap distingue les concepts (terme qui deviendra dans l'*Aufbau* exactement synonyme d'objet) en propres et impropres, et en réels et formels. Les «concepts réels figurent les objets proprement dits de la science» (*Eigentl.* p. 373); les concepts «formels» ne servent que de «moyens auxiliaires pour présenter la connaissance des concepts réels»; ce sont les concepts logiques et mathématiques. Mais les uns et les autres s'opposent aux concepts «impropres» en ce qu'ils sont des formes complètement déterminées, et non des formes «variables», susceptibles de différentes réalisation par des concepts propres essentiellement distincts, qu'ils soient formels ou réels. Une telle situation peut en effet se présenter lorsqu'un concept est introduit par une axiomatique, et non par une définition explicite: ainsi le nombre peanien est-il un concept impropre, alors que le nombre russellien serait propre. (*Eigentl.* p. 359)

> «Une réalisation de notre système d'axiomes peanien est par exemple cette suite de points de l'espace physique: le coin droit de cette table, puis le milieu entre ce coin et le coin gauche, puis le milieu entre ce dernier point et le coin gauche, etc. . . Des cas d'application dans le domaine logique (et arithmétique) sont par exemple: 1) la suite des cardinaux (définis à la manière de Russell); 2) la suite des cardinaux à partir de 5; 3) la suite des fonctions: a, ax, ax^2, etc. . . Le premier modèle – la suite des cardinaux russelliens – est celui en vue duquel le système axiomatique a été établi; mais, comme nous le voyons, le système et par conséquent la définition implicite qu'il exprime correspond non seulement à ce cas mais à une infinité d'autres, exactement à tous ceux dont les propriétés formelles indiquées, la structure, s'accordent avec les siennes.» (*Eigentl.* p. 362).

Plus tard, Carnap ne considérera plus ces modèles comme essentiellement distincts, ayant mieux élaboré la notion de «monomorphie». (voir plus bas § 3.4) Mais c'est bien cette opposition du propre à l'impropre qui dissocie ce qui compte authentiquement comme objet de ce qui n'est que construction auxiliaire, plutôt que la distinction du formel et du réel. Car l'abstraction en elle-même ne contredit aucunement à l'«objectité»: tout au plus parlera-t-on alors de «quasi-objets» (mais non point d'objets «impropres»). Il ne faut pas confondre en effet, dit Carnap, l'indétermination de concepts génériques et l'indétermination radicale des concepts impropres: le concept de «cheval» laisse indéterminée la couleur de la robe, comme aussi le concept de nombre peanien laisse indéterminée la parité; mais alors que la classe des objets réels auxquels s'applique le concept «cheval» est univoquement déterminée, il y a plus d'une seule classe d'objets réels et formels «pouvant être conçue comme réalisation de la classe des nombres». (*Eigentl.* p. 368). Si certains conepts mathématiques peuvent être définis «monomorphiquement», comme le pense Carnap, il y a donc bien des objets logico-mathématiques, et qui doivent par conséquent être «constitués». Ils l'ont été en effet, selon Carnap, par les *Principia*, dans lesquels «un système complet de Constitution des concepts formels est établi.» (*Eigentl.* p. 359, et aussi *A.* § 107). Que de tels objets soient authentiques, c'est ce que confirme le § 181 de l'*Aufbau* où Carnap veut montrer que l'idée de connaissance conceptuelle (*Erkenntnis*) est une, et s'applique aussi bien au domaine des mathématiques. Il remarque alors qu'un énoncé comme: 3 + 2 = 5 apporte une information effective, puisqu'il contredit l'énoncé empirique suivant: «j'ai 3 pommes, tu as 2 pommes et nous avons ensemble 4 pommes». (*A.* p. 257).

3.3. Comment concilier dès lors l'existence d'authentiques objets mathématiques avec les affirmations apparemment nominalistes qui terminent le § 107:

> «Les objets logiques et mathématiques ne sont pas de véritables objets au sens des objets réels (des objets des sciences de la réalité). La logique, y compris les mathématiques, consiste seulement en des thèses conventionnelles (*aus Konventionellen Festsetzungen*) sur l'usage du langage, avec les tautologies qui en dérivent. Les signes de la logique (et de la mathématique) ne désignent donc pas des objets, mais servent à fixer ces conventions dans des symboles.» (*A.* p. 150).

Thèse que l'*Abriß der Logistik* (1929), assez curieusement, ne formule pas explicitement, puisqu'on y dit seulement que la logistique:

> «s'offre comme propre à représenter les systèmes de concepts et les théories des différents domaines: Géométrie, Physique, théorie des parentés, théorie de la connaissance, analyse du langage, etc. . . » (*Abriß* p. 2)

Par contre, la *Symbolische Logik* de 1954 l'expose avec vigueur:

> «Un tel système n'est pas une théorie, c'est à dire un système de thèses sur certains objets, mais un *langage*, c'est à dire un système de signes avec leurs règles d'application,» (p. 1).

Il est vrai qu'alors le projet de Constitution originaire n'est plus à l'ordre du jour.

La difficulté apparaîtra plus clairement encore, lorsque, dans la *Logische Syntax der Sprache*, Carnap énoncera son fameux principe de tolérance: «*en logique il n'y a pas de morale*, chacun est libre de construire sa propre logique, c'est à dire sa propre forme de langage.» (*LSS.* p. 52, § 17). Prise à la lettre, cette affirmation ruinerait complètement l'édifice d'une construction logique du monde, et rendrait tout à fait arbitraire la coïncidence des concepts d'objets constitués avec l'expérience. Aussi bien, le véritable sens me semble-t-il devoir en être recherché dans une distinction implicite, mais qui se révèle déjà dans *Logische Syntax* et plus nettement encore dans *Introduction to semantics* de 1946. Certes les systèmes d'expression linguistique peuvent être librement établis; mais une *syntaxe générale* les gouverne. Il y a des propriétés indépendantes de toute référence à une langue particulière, et Carnap en esquisse l'exposé dans *Logische Syntax*, sous la forme d'une «syntaxe pour les langues en général, c'est à dire un système de définition des termes syntaxiques assez compréhensif pour s'appliquer à tous les langages quel qu'ils soient.» (*LSS.* p. 167, § 36). Les C-règles et les C-termes (C pour: conséquence) en constituent le fonds primitif dans cet ouvrage. Postérieurement, lorsque l'influence de Tarski aura été pleinement mûrie, Carnap dépeloppera une théorie des concepts «radicaux» et des concepts «absolus» qui semble bien répondre à l'idée d'un fonds logique nullement conventionnel, car elle concerne essentiellement les propriétés formelles des relations entre *propositions* et non entre leurs expressions particulières, «proposition» étant alors synonyme d'«état de choses» (*Sem.* p. 235). Dans ces conditions, la logique, bien qu'énonçant des règles de langage, peut bien être considérée comme théorie d'un type d'objets universels.

Il est donc permis d'interpréter l'opposition des objets formels de l'*Aufbau* aux objets réels non comme une réduction des premiers aux conventions contingentes d'un langage, mais comme l'expression d'une conception transcendantale du logique, cependant conciliable avec la thèse d'une *théorie* logique. La forme même des objets serait sous-jacente à toute formulation symbolique, et les conditions radicales de l'«objectité» se confondraient avec les conditions d'exprimabilité. Une *théorie* logique thématiserait ces conditions en système des propriétés de l'objet en général, au moyen d'un symbolisme sans doute largement arbitraire, mais qui ne servirait pas simplement à *montrer*.

3.4. Mais la construction strictement logique de la forme des objets empiriques à partir de ces objets conditionnants et fondamentaux que sont les objets logico-mathématiques, suppose que demeure satisfaite l'exigence, aux yeux de Carnap essentielle, de «monomorphie». Il faut que les formes d'objets auxquelles on aboutit soient celles et seulement celles qui peuvent être remplies par l'empirie, par les propriétés *erkenntnismäßige* que les sujets concrets rencontrent dans leur expérience. Revenons brièvement sur cette notion, déjà introduite comme caractère déterminant de l'objet propre en général.

Dans un long manuscrit postérieur à 1929[7] Carnap examine en détail la question, à propos de la complétude d'un système d'axiomes. Il distingue alors plusieurs sens de la *Vollständigkeit*, dont deux nous intéressent ici:

—la «non bifurcabilité» (*nicht-Gabelbarkeit*): un système n'est pas compatible à la fois avec un nouvel axiome (formel) et avec sa négation.

—la «monomorphie»: un système n'est satisfait que par des modèles isomorphes, l'isomorphie étant définie pour chaque type de variables que le système comporte.

Nous laisserons de côté une distinction par ailleurs importante qu'il introduit entre méta-propriétés «absolues» et «constructives». Carnap s'attache à démontrer que les deux sens de la complétude sont équivalents, pour en tirer des conséquences touchant la complétude de l'arithmétique peanienne qu'il ne nous appartient pas ici d'examiner. Ce qui nous intéresse, c'est l'importance qu'il accorde à la définiton précise de l'unicité d'un modèle de système formel. Il pense être parvenu dans ce manuscrit à déterminer ces conditions de monomorphie d'un système axiomatique. Cependant, le texte antérieur de l'*Aufbau* renonçait à une procédure d'axiomatisation pour construire formellement les objects du monde, et s'exprimait comme si la bifurcabilité et la polymorphie étaient, pour un système axiomatique, de droit commun. Par une définition axiomatique, écrit-il, «ce n'est pas à proprement parler un objet déterminé (concept) qui est défini implicitement au moyen des axiomes, mais une classe d'objets, ou si l'on veut, un «objet indéterminé» ou «impropre».» (*A*. § 15, p. 19).

Il pense en revanche obtenir la monomorphie en faisant usage de ce qu'il nomme la *strukturale Kennzeichnung*, caractérisation structurale, capable de «définir un objet unique, et précisément un objet d'un domaine empirique, extra-logique. «Il faut alors que lui correspondent des «états de fait (*Tatbestände*), que dans le domaine en question au moins un objet de l'espèce caratérisée, et un seulement se présente; les propositions ultérieures se rapportant à l'objet ainsi caractérise ne sont pas alors toutes analytiques, c'est à dire déductibles des propositions qui le définissent, comme c'est le cas pour l'objet défini implicitement, mais partiellement aussi synthétiques, exprimant des constations empiriques dans le domaine considéré.» (*A*. § 15, p. 20). La méthode de caractérisation structurale, qui procède par définitions progressives de concepts de plus en plus complexes, est manifestement héritée de Frege et de Russell. Elle préfigure assez exactement du reste ce qui sera précisé, dans le domaine mathématique, par Bourbaki, sous le nom de «construction d'échelon», et d'«espéces de structure». (*Théorie des ensembles*, chap. 4). Mais le texte qu'on vient de citer soulève au moins deux questions importantes:

1. quelle est la nature de l'enrichissement progressif des concepts obtenus par «caractérisation structurale».

2. quel rôle joue l'introduction de l'empirie dans l'obtention d'une monomorphie de ces concepts.

4.5. Sur le premier point, divers textes de l'*Aufbau* (par exemple au § 37) montrent que, pour Carnap, le passage d'un objet à une classe d'objets constitue une modification de fonction et un enrichissement de *contenu*. On peut dire plus, et autre chose, d'une classe qu'on ne dit de ses éléments. Si au niveau primitif qu'est le logique *stricto sensu*, réduit au calcul des propositions classique, nous ne rencontrons pour ainsi dire que la place vide pour un contenu à venir, le maniement des classes et des relations introduit ce que nous appellerons des contenus formels[8] Cet enrichissement, caractéristique de la création d'objets mathématiques, se manifeste déjà sans doute au niveau des combinaisons finies d'objets, qui est le point de départ de l'*Aufbau* (Carnap dans une réponse à un compte-rendu fait par Kaila-*Erkenntnis*, II, 1931, p. 75−77−reconnaît implicitement la finitude de l'ensemble des vécus effectifs, comme le suppose du reste l'exposé des concepts par «construction fictive».). Il est encore plus évident lorsque l'ensemble des objets constitués au niveau du champ visuel (les couleurs, les «places») est *complété* par adjonction de vécus virtuels, rendant «continues» les lignes d'univers. (*A*. §. 126 et 127). Le principe de *Vervollständigung*, qui était mis en vedette comme principe de passage à la «réalité» dans le manuscrit *Vom Chaos* n'apparaît plus, il est vrai, explicitement dans l'*Aufbau*, sous le nom d'*Analogie*, qu'aux niveaux supérieurs de la Constitution-le monde de la perception et le monde de la Physique. Il n'en est pas moins tacitement nécessaire déjà pour donner son plein sens au système des qualités et à l'espace visuel[9]; et si, dans un passage du manuscrit sur l'axiomatique, il note que «le cardinal des éléments individuels (*Einzelheiten*) du monde à au plus la puissance du continu» (*Ax*. p. 144), il faudrait ajouter qu'il doit avoir «au moins» une puissance non-dénombrable. En ce sens, la Constitution est bien proprement *synthétique*, comme le souligne Carnap lui-même:

«La quasi-analyse est une synthése qui endosse le vêtement linguistique de l'analyse». (*A*. § 74, p. 104).

Et, bien qu'il récuse l'idée de jugements *a priori* synthéthiques, on voit que, dans son usage transcendental d'établissement de la forme des objets du monde, le «logique» et son prolongement mathématique introduisent des contenus formels irréductibles à l'analyticité pure et simple.

3.6. Le second point concerne l'introduction de l'empirie dans le tissu logico-mathématique de la Constitution. Ce que nous appelons «empirie» apparaît d'abord sous forme latente dans les «vécus» qui sont choisis comme éléments de départ. Le donné «*subjektlos*» et non structuré est évidemment déjà gros du tout de l'expérience, mais fictivement posé comme *chaos*, ses propriétés sont neutralisées, si ce n'est celle d'être monnayable en instances dictinctes, sur l'ensemble desquelles est définie en extension la relation fondamentale de «ressemblance mémorielle». On observera que ces échantillons de «vécu» ne sont alors les vécus d'aucun sujet empirique; le «sujet A» qui établit les ressemblances et énumère les couples relationnels dans la «construction fictive» ne peut être que transcendental.

Cependant, au fur et à mesure que la Constitution s'avance, l'empirique pour ainsi dire fait surface, introduit au moyen d'axiomes-*Lehrsätze*. C'est ainsi que la relation originaire est donnée commen assymétrique (*Lehrsatz* 1, *A*. § 108, p. 151); puis, lorsque la notion de «dimension de l'espace des places visuelles», ou «champ visuel» est constituée relativement à une certaine relation de voisinage, l'axiome L. 5 lui assigne empiriquement la valeur 2. (*A*. § 117, p. 157). Il faut remarquer qu'en pareil cas le donné empirique vient seulement *fixer* un paramètre, dans une structure dont le sens formel a été constitué par ailleurs, sans recours à l'expérience: le nombre 2 de dimensions du champ visuel, ou 3 de l'espace des Couleurs (*L*. 6, *A*. § 118) est contingent; seule l'application de la notion de dimension est transcendentale. Il n'en est pourtant pas de même d'une clause qui entre dans la définition des classes qualitatives (*Qualitätklassen*, *A*. § 112, p. 153), où une certaine condition intervient selon laquelle une classe de vécus doit être contenue dans un cercle de ressemblance «au moins pour moitié» (ou pour plus de la moitié, si l'on s'en tient à la version formalisée). Pourquoi la moitié? Ce n'est là ni une condition logiquement préparée (le cardinal des ensembles de vécus ne joue aucun rôle dans la Constitution), ni une réponse de l'expérience à une question *posée* et laissée libre par la théorie. Il y a là l'une des difficultés sérieuses sur lesquelles achoppe le projet de Constitution tel qu'il est originairement envisagé, car ce n'est pas l'empirique qui s'introduit ainsi, légitimement, dans la construction logique, mais un élément purement pragmatique, et en un certain sens inadmissible ici, *conventionnel*.

Mais revenons à l'introduction légitime de l'empirique, qui doit assurer la monomorphie du systéme, en faire autre chose qu'une structure vide pour des mondes possibles, l'établir au contraire comme forme de ce seul monde qui est celui de notre expérience confirmée dans l'intersubjectivité. La relation primitive de ressemblance mémorielle n'étant caractérisée au départ que par sa propriété formelle d'assymétrie, demeure *a priori* indéterminée. Sans compromettre la suite de la construction, tout automorphisme de l'ensemble des vécus transforme la relation primitive en une relation isomorphe, mais non identique.

> «Toutes les propositions du système de Constitution demeurent alors valides, puisqu'elles ne concernent que des propriétés formelles. Cependant, les nouvelles relations fondamentales n'ont plus alors de sens, ce sont des listes de paires d'éléments fondamentaux ne manifestant aucune propriété pouvant être vécue (*erlebnismäßig*)». (*A*. § 154, p. 206).

En vue d'éviter ce collapsus de la Constitution dans l'insignifiance, Carnap introduit pour une relation la propriété d'«être fondée», de «correspondre à un rapport dans le vécu, à une rapport «naturel», ses termes ayant pour ainsi dire entre eux quelque chose de vécu» (*ibid.*). Indéfinissable formellement, cette propriété de *Fundiertheit* doit être considérée comme originaire: c'est un «*concept fondamental de la logique*» (*ibid.* p. 207). Il suffit dès lors, pour garantir que le monde réel est la modèle unique du système, de définir la relation de ressemblance mémorielle comme «l'unique relation fondée à partir de laquelle on peut constituer un objet arbitrairement choisi, d'un niveau assez élevé, de telle sorte qu'il se comporte empirriquement de telle ou telle manière.» (*A.* § 155, p. 208). Carnap prend comme objet constitué l'«espace des couleurs» avec sa propriété empirique d'avoir trois dimensions. Moyennant cette manoeuvre, «tous les objets et propositions du système de Constitution s'expriment en termes purement logiques.» Mais comment justifier *logiquement* la distinction d'une relation «fondée»? Il y a là, reconnaît Carnap, «un problème non encore résolu.» (p. 209).

3.7. Ainsi, la fonction transcendantale du logique que le voeu de Carnap était d'établir ne peut elle être plausible qu'à la faveur, d'une part, de l'assimilation complète du mathématique au logique, et d'un abandon plus ou moins tacite de l'analyticité; d'autre part, de l'admission au sein des concepts logiques de l'étrange et suspecte notion de relation fondée. C'est à ceprix très lourd que la Construction logique du monde rejoint l'empirie.

La logique qui se veut également transcendantale du *Tractatus* n'ayant pas les mêmes ambitions, ne rencontre pas les même problèmes. Elle est bien transcendantale en effet en ce sens que, si un monde existe, le logique est sa forme, et qu'il n'y a de logique que d'un monde. «Elle est antérieure au comment, non au quoi». (*TLP* 5.552). «S'il y avait une logique sans monde, comment pourrait-il y avoir une logique quand il y a un monde?» (*TLP* 5.5521). Elle constitue la forme du monde-ou plus précisément, contrairement à l'*Aufbau*, de tous les mondes possibles. Son rapport avec l'empirie est dès lors tout autre, et d'une certaine manière elle lui est, en tant que telle, radicalement étrangère. Le canevas logique montre les propriétés formelles des choses et des états de chose-formelles en un sens beaucoup plus pauvre que ne le sont les propriétés structurales construites par la Constitution carnapienne. Il est appliqué sur le monde, alors que les concepts de Carnap *sont*, d'une certaine manière, les objets mêmes. Aussi bien n'y a-t-il pour Wittgenstein aucune nécessité propre au monde, car «hors de la logique, tout est accidentel» (*TLP* 6.3). Alors que la *Gesetzmäßigkeit*, pour Carnap, pénètre au coeur même du monde des objets. Dans le *Tractatus*, est logique la possibilité de décrire l'empirie au moyen d'un réseau conceptuel; en revanche, que tel réseau soit plus favorable, ou qu'on puisse en imaginer un qui codifie *complètement* une représentation du monde, voilà qui est contingent et nous montre une propriété de *ce* monde, et par conséquent de l'empirie. (*TLP* 6.342). La logique ne concerne en somme que les méta-propriétés du langage, qui sont aussi les méta-propriétés (les propriétés formelles) du monde objectif (*TLP* 6.12), dont les propriétés lui échappent dans leur détail. Selon la métaphore de l'instrument de mesure assimilé à l'acte de pensée logique: «seules les marques de graduation *touchent* l'objet dont il faut prendre la mesure.» (*TLP* 2.1521).

LA FONCTION DU SYMBOLISME.

4.1. Il convient maintenant de revenir sur la fonction du symbolisme dans la représentation du monde, et la présentation—ou formulation—du logique.

Pour le Wittgenstein du *Tractatus*, une langue naturelle est «une partie de l'organisme humain, et n'est pas moins compliquée que lui.» Il n'a pas seulement pour fonction de décrire les faits-et c'est pourquoi on peut en faire usage en philosophie, ou pour suggérer des jugements de valeur. C'est aussi pourquoi «il est humainement impossible d'en tirer immédiatement sa forme logique.» (*TLP* 4.002). Le symbolisme artificiel des logiciens n'est donc rien d'autre qu'un moyen, d'abord de filtrer dans le langage ce qui est proprement *image* (*Bild*), représentation de faits; ensuite, de neutraliser dans l'image ce qui renvoie aux propriétés «externes» des faits et des choses. Les méta-propriétés des faits sont *montrées* dans le calcul des propositions, et c'est en vue de les montrer plus explicitement que Wittgenstein propose, dans ses *Notes sur la logique* de septembre 1913 (Appendice aux *Notebooks*), et reprend dans le *Tractatus* (*TLP* 6.1203−6.121) une méthode de représentation, à la vérité fort incommode. On figurera à droite et à gauche de chaque proposition ses deux pôles de vérité et de fausseté, et la forme du lien propositionnel sera matérialisée par des lignes joignant les pôles respectifs des propositions élémentaires qui sont associés par la liaison lorsqu'elle est vérifiée. Ayant ainsi insisté sur la fonction de présentation du logique par les symboles, Wittgenstein en revient toutefois à la *Begriffschrift* russellienne, non sans en critiquer certains aspects. Mais il ne s'agit toujours alors que de montrer la forme de l'espace des faits; et il faudrait aussi, puisqu'elle est logique, montrer dans un symbolisme la «logique des choses». Autrement dit, figurer la forme générale de la proposition élémentaire, et les règles qui en gouvernent l'usage. Certes, le symbolisme du calcul des prédicats paraît un premier pas en ce sens: «J'écris les propositions élémentaires comme fonctions de noms, de telle sorte qu'elles ont la forme «fx», «ϕ (x, y)», etc. . . »(*TLP* 4.24). Il faudrait cependant aller plus avant dans la figuration de la «substance du monde»: montrer par exemple dans le symbolisme que deux couleurs ne peuvent coexister en un même lieu, au même moment, ou qu'un objet spatial *doit* avoir une couleur (*TLP* 2.0131), ce qui est pour Wittgenstein une méta-propriété *logique*, et nullement une contraite contingente de l'empirie. L'aphorisme 5.555 ne saurait dispenser le philosophe de cette recherche:

> «Il est clair que nous avons un concept de proposition élémentaire indépendant de sa forme logique particulière. Mais quand on peut former des symboles selon un système, c'est le système qui est logiquement important, et non les symboles individuels.»

Sans doute, mais où est le système? Wittgenstein ne donne aucune réponse vraiment satisfaisante en disant, en 5.557, que c'est l'*application* de la logique qui décide si une proposition est élémentaire, et que la logique ne peut anticiper ce qui relève de son application. Qu'aucun symbolisme pertinent n'ait été construit dénonce un échec profond du *Tractatus*, et la conscience de cet échec pourrait être, comme nous l'avancions plus haut, l'une des origines du passage d'une philosophie *du* langage à une philosophie des jeux de langage.

4.2. Dans l'*Aufbau*, le langage occupe une place bien différente. Tout d'abord, comme nous l'avons rappelé, il y a des objets formels, logico-mathématiques, qui appartiennent au langage et sont immanents à tout système symbolique, dans la mesure au moins où il vise à décrire le monde. Puisqu'elles sont constituées en objets, on peut donc décrire les formes du langage elles-mêmes, et l'interdit wittgensteinien contre tout méta-langage est levé. La logique – la «logistique» de 1929 – est la théorie de ces objets qui, contrairement à «la pauvreté et à l'inutilité de l'ancienne logique» est un système d'une «grande richesse de contenu»: elle engendre à elle seule la mathématique. Wittgenstein concevait tout autrement leur rapport. Sans doute, Carnap considère-t-il comme lui que les concepts mathématiques sont des auxiliaires de la description du monde (*TLP* 6.211), mais de l'article de 1928 (*Eigentl.*) à l'*Aufbau* il modulera sensiblement sa position. Dans l'article, elle coïncide tout à fait avec celle de Wittgenstein: «ces concepts formels aident à parler de la réalité, rien ne leur correspond cependant dans cette réalité; ils servent seulement à former les propositions (p. 358). Mais dans l'*Aufbau* ils appartiennent à la texture du monde. Cependant, le *Tractatus* et l'*Aufbau* identifient semblablement logique et mathématique. L'identification chez Wittgenstein est, à vrai dire, encore plus manifeste: «La logique du monde, qui est montrée par les propositions de la logique dans les tautologies, la mathématique la montre dans les équations» (*TLP* 6.22); la mathématique est un aspect opératoire, une «méthode de la logique» (6.234), qui procède par la mise en évidence de l'équivalence de deux suites d'opérations. Et cette procédure ne doit rien à l'expérience: c'est une «méthode logique» (6.2). Il serait donc erroné de vouloir construire une *théorie* mathématique en la déduisant d'une *théorie* logique plus primitive. Or c'est bien ainsi que Carnap, interprétant Frege et Russell, conçoit leur rapport, et l'on trouve dans l'*Abriß der Logistik* non seulement une théorie des objets proprement logiques, mais encore une construction, à partir d'eux, des objets mathématiques premiers: le nombre entier, les progressions, le continu.

Si donc le logique concerne bien la langue il n'en constitue pas moins un domaine d'objets propre qu'un méta-langage, légitimement, doit décrire et explorer.

4.3. D'autre part, dans l'*Aufbau*, Carnap considère et utilise plusieurs espèces de langages, alors que le Wittgenstein du *Tractatus* ne considère jamais qu'un langage unique, le langage ordinaire, avec la schématisation élucidatoire de sa forme qu'est le symbolisme logique. La Constitution au contraire peut être exposée *parallèlement* dans plusieurs systèmes d'expression. L'un d'eux est naturellement la langue «réaliste», qui est la langue usuelle, éventuellement précisée et amendée comme il arrive dans sonusage scientifique. Elle parle d'emblée de «choses», de «qualités sensibles», de «lieux» et de «temps», c'est à dire d'objets à constituer, et sans les détacher des connotations empiriques, c'est à dire «subjectives», qu'ils comportent dans l'expérience effective. Une autre est la langue de la «construction fictive», qui formule des prescriptions opératoires imaginées pour construire les concepts définis par la langue formelle. «Si on introduit quelques fictions convenables, qui doivent être immédiatement précisées, les constitutions peuvent être d'une certaine manière exprimées comme des processus saisissables». (*A.* § 99, p. 137). Toutes les définitions constitutives posant des classes ou des relations, le langage de la construction fictive supposera leurs éléments et leurs termes-déjà antérieurement définis—comme effectivement donnés et énumérables,[10] et prescrira les règles de combinaison qui aboutissent au concept à produire. Ce langage est, jusqu'à un certain point, celui qui correspondrait le mieux à l'idée wittgensteinienne du logique: il décrit—fictivement, comme le discours du *Tractatus*—une activité plutôt qu'une théorie. On pourrait dire aussi, empruntant le vocabulaire postérieur, qu'il s'agit de divers jeux de langage; mais il serait essentiel de noter qu'ils portent sur la même expérience, et qu'ils se traduisent, d'autre part, mutuellement et intégralement. Il y a là un point fondamental de la doctrine de l'*Aufbau*. Car l'idée de fonder la connaissance du monde en le constituant repose sur le thème de la traduction:

> «Etablir une règle générale qui spécifie de quelle manière, dans chaque cas, on doit transformer (*umformen*) une proposition portant sur l'objet *a* pour obtenir une proposition portant sur les objets *b* et *c*. Cette règle de traduction nous l'appelons règle de Constitution.» (*A.* § 2, p. 2).

Une telle règle joue à l'intérieur du système de Constitution adopté pour «ramener» les propositions du langage formel aux objets choisis comme primitifs, que sont les vécus et la relation de ressemblance mémorielle. Elle pourrait aussi bien, en principe, *jouer dans un autre langage*, et pour une réduction à d'*autres objets primitifs*. Mais elle serait alors moins claire. Le privilège du langage symbolique de la logistique est de montrer dans sa nudité l'enchaînement de la construction, que risquerait de masquer, dans la langue naturelle et dans celle déjà épurée pourtant de la science, l'évocation entempestive des objets de la vie quotidienne ou des objets scientifiques, et de laisser douter que *toutes* les espèces d'objets sont bien réductibles—au sens dela Constitution—aux objets primitifs. (*A.* § 96, p. 134). Cet avantage décisif ne peut pourtant pas être considéré comme disqualifiant les autres langages, puisque Carnap a pris soin de traduire en ceux-ci chacune des définitions qu'il formule en langage formel dans son exposé rigoureux. Ce qui confirme bien l'idée que le logique, dans l'*Aufbau*, transcende les langages; il est forme transcendantale de ce monde, bien qu'un langage—et il en est plusieurs—soit nécessaire pour le manifester.

Tels sont les rapports, non toujours dépourvus d'ambiguité, que paraissent entretenir dans l'*Aufbau* la logique et la langue. Manifestement nourrie de la lecture de Russell et de Frege (dont Carnap fut l'élève), la doctrine est ouvertement sous l'influence du *Tractatus*, dont elle se démarque pourtant en profondeur.

Les points de coïncidence et d'opposition des deux interprétations du logique que nous avons tenté de dégager peuvent assurément fournir aujourd'hui encore un thème et un appui à la méditation du philosophe. Il en est de même de l'examen des deux voies différentes qu'ont suivies par après Carnap et Wittgenstein, pour une grande part motivés l'un et l'autre par les difficultés sur lesquelles leur entreprise achoppait. L'un, reconnaissant l'inadéquation d'une position *logique* du problème de la forme générale de la proposition élémentaire, développe une exploration des «jeux de langage». L'autre, conscient des obstacles rencontrés par un projet de Constitution logique universelle du monde empirique, et mieux averti des apories du langage formel, s'engage d'abord dans la construction d'une sémantique pure, puis dans l'analyse des conditions précises de la *Gesetzmäßigkeit* de l'empirie, en tentant de fonder une logique inductive.

Dans l'un et l'autre cas, il nous semble entrevoir dans les trajectoires suivies par ces deux puissants créateurs d'idées un mouvement vers la mise en lumière de la profonde et irréductible dualité de l'opération et de l'objet, origine de la mystérieuse prégnance, dans toute connaissance, de «contenus formels».

ENDNOTES

[1] «Pour la vie pratique, en revanche, sont reconnues l'existence et la valeur significative des autres sphères irrationnelles». (*Ibid.*)

[2] Nous avons étudié jadis la structure du *Tractatus*: «Structure philosophique et métastructure», in *Hommage à Martial Gueroult*, Paris, 1964, p. 139−164.

[3] Repris presque textuellement dans l'*Aufbau*, § 136, p. 181. Il faut naturellement reconnaître qu'un tel principe n'est pas envisagé comme pouvant être proprement «logique»; Carnap donne comme exemple possible un principe de «simplicité».

[4] Mais la proposition à laquelle nous faisons ici allusion parle aussi de l'*éthique* comme condition du monde. Le mot «condition» revêt donc ici un sens particulier; nous y reviendrons au § 3.

[5] Les manuscrits cités nous ont été communiqués très obligeamment par M. Richard Nollan, curateur des *Carnap, Reichenbach, Ramsey Collections* de l'Université de Pittsburgh, par l'intermédiaire de Mme Joëlle Proust qui a exploré le fonds Carnap. Nous en remercions vivement l'un et l'autre.

[6] Dans *Physikalische Begriffsbildung*, en 1926, Carnap dénonce une «croyance fausse», selon laquelle la science «filtrerait, pôur ainsi dire, la nature, ne retenant que le quantitatif, cependant que le qualitatif en quoi réside l'essentiel-lui filerait entre les doigts.» (*Ph. B.* p. 61). En fait, ce sont les formes objectives véhiculées au moyen de langues différentes qui demeurent invariantes, non les contenus concrets subjectifs, qui ne sauraient être objets d'une *connaissance (Erkenntnis)*.

[7] *Untersuchungen zur allgemeinen Axiomatik*, dont la troisième partie est intitulée: «*Monomorphie und Gabelbarkeit*.

[8] Granger, G., «The Notion of formal Content», in *Social Research*, 1982, vol. 49 n. 2, p. 360−382.

[9] La définition d'une dimension non nulle sur un ensemble fini, ou même dénombrable, au moyen des concepts mengeriens introduits par Carnap, pose un très sérieux problème. Nous pensons pouvoir lever la difficulté en faisant usage d'une définition de la dimension en termes de topologie algébrique, suggérée par l'article «*Dreidimensionalität des Raumes und Kausalität* (1924), et du principe d'«Analogie».

[10] Pour un «sujet A», qui ne peut être que transcendantal . . .

TEXTES CITÉS

Wittgenstein, *Tractatus logico-philosophicus*, Routledge & Keagan Paul, 1961. (*TLP*)
   Notebooks, Basil Blackwell, 1961.
Carnap, *Der logische Aufbau der Welt*, 4. éd., Ullstein 1974. (*A.*)
   «Eigentliche und uneigentliche Begriffe», in *Symposion*, Bd. 1, Heft 4, Berlin 1927, p. 355−374). (*Eigentl.*)
   «Dreidimensionalität des Raumes und Kausalität», in *Annalen der Philosophie*, IV, 1924, p. 105−130.
   «Über die Aufgabe der Physik», in *Kant Studien*, Bd. 28, 1923, p. 90−107.
   «Physikalische Begriffsbildung», Karlsruhe, 1926. (*Ph. B.*)
   Abriß der Logistik, Springer 1929. (*Abriß*)
   Symbolische Logik, 3. éd. Springer 1968.
   Introduction to Semantics, Cambridge, Mass. 1942, (*Sem.*)
   Logische Syntax der Sprache, trad. anglaise, Routledge & Kegan Paul, 1937. (*LSS.*)

MANUSCRITS

«Vom Chaos zur Wirklichkeit», 1922. (*Chaos*)
«Untersuchungen zur allgemeinen Axiomatik», non daté; contient une référence à l'*Abriß* (1929) (*Axiomatik*)

* * *

WITTGENSTEIN AND THE SEMANTICS OF COMBINATION

Peter M. Simons
Universität Salzburg

> *How do I love thee? Let me count the ways.*
> Elizabeth Barrett Browning

No one thought through the problems and implications of Frege's philosophical logic more thoroughly than the young Wittgenstein, and the *Tractatus* may be viewed in part as Wittgenstein's intended replacement for the philosophical logic underlying Frege's masterpiece *Die Grundgesetze der Arithmetik*. Most of Wittgenstein's criticisms concern Frege's informal semantics, the account of the relationship between language and what there is; the cardinal point here is that Frege mistakes the semantic role of propositions. Frege held that all expressions fit to appear in a scientific language should have both a sense and a reference, the nature of these depending on the category of expression concerned. All saturated expressions, including propositions, name saturated entities, objects, while all unsaturated expressions name unsaturated entities, functions. Among the objects are not only physical objects and numbers, but also truth-values. So for Frege every syntactically connected expression is a name, whether a proper name or a function name. There is essentially only one semantic relation between expressions and entities, that of naming, its variants being a matter of the category of expression and correlatively the category of named entity concerned. This aspect of Frege's semantics was carried forward i.a. by Carnap and Church, and forms the basis of the model-theoretic approach to semantics. Yet if Wittgenstein's Tractarian criticisms of Frege are correct, that work embodies a critique of model-theoretic semantics written before this was even invented.

While I sympathise with Wittgenstein's critical stance, it is impossible here to go into the involved question whether he is essentially right. Rather I wish to consider what Wittgenstein offered as a replacement for Frege's account. It hardly needs stressing here what difficulties there are in extracting a coherent theory of something from the *Tractatus*; as usual there will need to be interpolations and disputable interpretative decisions. It will suffice for present purposes if what follows is a reasonably good fit against the *Tractatus*.

Wittgenstein maintains against Frege that propositions are not names, whether of truth-values or anything else, such as facts or complexes. The semantic roles of naming (referring, denoting) on the one hand and being true or false on the other are irreducibly distinct from one another. For the former, Wittgenstein adopted Frege's term *bedeuten*; the phrase *Sinn haben* is used only for contingent propositions. An immediate consequence of this sharp dissociation of propositions from names is that Wittgenstein must view the logical connectives in a different way from Frege, who takes a connective like 'and' to form the name of a function from pairs of truth-values to truth-values. The reference of a connective is thus for Frege simply a function among functions, differing from others solely in its arguments and values, whereas Wittgenstein denies that truth-functions are material functions (5.44) or indeed functions at all—he prefers to speak of truth-*operations*, reserving the term 'truth-function' for the *result* of operating on elementary propositions with truth-operations (5.3ff.). So there are no objects corresponding to propositions (no logical objects at all (5.4)), and no other entities (such as functions) corresponding to connectives or quantifiers (4.0312: Wittgenstein's *Grundgedanke*).

The development of Wittgenstein's alternative position occupies much of the middle part of the *Tractatus*. He is frequently constrained to break his own injunctions on what cannot be said, and we shall do so likewise without apology. The three levels of his semantics correspond to three different kinds of expression: proper names, elementary propositions, and propositions in general. Proper names and their simple referents are not our concern here. More important is that Wittgenstein accounts for two kinds of complexity – the syntactic complexity of elementary propositions and the logical complexity of other propositions – in related ways, both involving what in English may be brought under the single term '*combinations*'.

The first sort of combination is found at 2.01:

"A state of affairs is a combination of objects [*eine Verbindung von Gegenständen*]."

While the individual product of combining or configurating is the state of affairs (2.0272), the *kind* of combining found in a state of affairs is its *structure*:

"2.031 In a state of affairs the objects stand to one another in a determinate way.
2.032 The way in which the objects in a state of affairs are connected is the structure of the state of affairs."

Wittgenstein stresses that the structure of a state of affairs is not a further constituent of it. His adverbial description of it as the *way (manner) in which (die Art und Weise wie)* the objects are related together is calculated to steer us as far as possible away from thinking of structures as *parts* of a complex whole. In a state of affairs, the only parts are the constituent objects. Better parallels to the notion of structure are found in such examples as characteristic *gaits* (ways of walking), *accents* (ways of pronouncing a language) or *arrangements* (e.g. of furniture; cf. 3.1431). The structure of a state of affairs is that aspect of it which it shares, according to the picture theory, with any picture of it – the elements of the picture are combined *in the same way as* those of the depicted state of affairs (cf. 2.15f.). With some reservations about the status of situations (*Sachlagen*) we can say the same for propositions in general and situations in general (3.21). (Here we employ the correct, if unilluminating, rule that states of affairs stand to situations as elementary propositions stand to propositions.) By replacing all the names in an elementary proposition by variables, we obtain a prototype (*Urbild*), which is as near as we can come to an expression for a structure on its own (3.215; cf. Frege's use of Greek consonant place-holders to show which functions he is talking about.) This completely pure propositional form is construed by Wittgenstein as a common mark (*gemeinsames Merkmal*) of all propositions in which it occurs (3.317). In the same way, we may say that the structure of a state of affairs is the common mark of all states of affairs in which it occurs. So for Wittgenstein – unlike Frege and everyone else – an elementary proposition contains no *part* playing a role in expressing the predicate, i.e. for Wittgenstein all propositions are *verbless*. The role of the predicate is taken *wholly* by the structure of the proposition, whereas for Frege the predicate is specified partly by the verb and partly by the syntactic structure. It is true that Wittgenstein occasionally writes functional symbols like 'f', but this may be seen as a concession to convenience given the limitations of conventional notation; verbs remain theoretically dispensable. It is thus impossible for Wittgenstein to develop a second-order logic like that of Frege, which involves having a detachable symbol, a verb-variable, which is bound by quantifiers.

Without commenting on the defensibility of Wittgenstein's view, I want to take from it the lesson that *structure*, the *way* in which things hang together, plays an indispensable role in constituting propositions and states of affairs without in any way being a further constituent of them. If a structure is an entity, it is so to speak a very attenuated one.

Wittgenstein also speaks later about ways of signifying (*Bezeichnungsweisen*) for signs (3.321–3). To clarify this, we must elucidate Wittgenstein's distinction between a sign and a symbol. A symbol is part of a proposition which has a hand in determining its sense (3.31). This may be viewed as a *sign in use* (3.326f.; note the anticipation here of the later theory of meaning). The sign is so to speak the perceivable bit of the symbol (3.32), and what makes this up to a symbol is its way of signifying—something which cannot be discerned by inspecting the sign (3.326), since one and the same sign may be used in different ways and therefore serve different symbols (3.322). Once again, by speaking of manners or ways (the Pears-McGuinness translation 'modes' is reserved for a somewhat different use below), Wittgenstein is trying to get as far as possible away from the idea of an object which is part of a more complex object, and therewith perhaps to avoid hypostatising entities on the basis of the theory of meaning. It is an interesting historical question how far Wittgenstein is here an unwitting successor to the terminist logicians of the fourteenth century, whose frequent employment of the term *modi significandi* may have had a similar aim.

The picture thus far is thus somewhat different from that of Frege or of later model theory. Each symbol—i.e. each sign used meaningfully—has its own characteristic way of signifying. The general *kind* of way of signifying of a symbol, for which I use the term '*mode* of signifying', is correlated with the syntactic category of the sign. For names, the mode of signifying is to *name* ((*be*)*nennen*: 3.221, 3.144) or *denote (bedeuten)*; the particular way of signifying (i.e. denoting) of a name is specified when we know *which* object it denotes. This leads to the temptation to identify this object (the name's denotatum) with its way of denoting, a temptation to which Wittgenstein indeed succumbed in the *Tractatus*, and for which he berated himself afterwards. For propositions the mode of signifying is to be possibly true or false, i.e. to have sense. Tautologies and contradictions form a borderline case here, and Wittgenstein wobbles on whether to accord them the status of *Sätze* at all (cf. 5.43 with 4.464). We must distinguish the sense or way of signifying of propositions, which is given by their truth-conditions, from their being true or being false. The latter is (except for tautologies and contradictions) the joint outcome of the sense (which determines the elbowroom (*Spielraum*) left to the way the world is (4.463)) and the independent contribution of the way the world is. This joint-outcome thesis, part of Wittgenstein's correspondence theory of truth, is quite alien to Frege. The sense of an elementary proposition is given when we know the ways of signifying of its constituent names (i.e. we know which objects it's about) and also its structure. These together determine the state of affairs whose obtaining makes the proposition true. While there is then a one-to-one correlation between the sense of an elementary proposition and its associated state of affairs, they are probably not to be identified, for one thing because the sense of a false elementary proposition exists while its state of affairs does not. In the early *Notes on Logic* and in the *Notes dictated to G. E. Moore in Norway* Wittgenstein had said that an elementary proposition has also a *Bedeutung*, namely the (atomic) fact concerning the state of affairs—the positive one if the proposition is true, the negative one if it is false. But even here he emphasises that the proposition is not a *name* of this fact. In the maturer theory of the *Tractatus* Wittgenstein drops talk of the *Bedeutung* of propositions (but cf. 3.31 and 3.314, which suggest that the earlier theory might not have been completely excised).

Like elementary propositions, propositions in general have a sense, that is a fixed range of possibilities for agreeing or disagreeing with reality (being true or false). Whereas for an elementary proposition there is only one way for it to agree or disagree with reality, according as its state of affairs obtains or not, for a non-elementary proposition (except the negation of an elementary one), there is either more than one way for it to be true, or more than one way for it to be false, or both. Which ways these are is a matter of its truth-functional structure. For any n elementary proposition there are 2^n possibilities of obtaining and non-obtaining among them, of which any combination (*Kombination*) may be realised, and exactly one is in fact realised (4.27). Stipulating which truth-possibilities result in truth and which in falsehood determines the truth-function in question (4.31), of which there are $2^{(2^n)}$ altogether (4.42). These combinations of truth-possibilities of elementary propositions do much work in the *Tractatus*, being essentially involved in the theories of inference (5.11ff.), probability (5.15ff.), truth-operations (5.2ff.) and the general propositional form (5.5ff.). As both the exposition and arithmetic show, the sense of 'combination' here used by Wittgenstein is that which is fundamental to the mathematical discipline now called *combinatorics*. Basic questions in combinatorics, like „In how many ways can k lions be put into n cages?", are very similar in spirit to issues exercising Wittgenstein in the *Tractatus*, like "In how many ways can a given truth-function p of elementary propositions be true, given that another truth-function q of the same elementary propositions is true?" (cf. 5.15). In view of his critical stance against Frege's account of connectives, Wittgenstein's theory of truth-functions is properly viewed not as *functional* but as *combinatorial* (5.25). Wittgenstein even believed that this analysis could be extended to account for the quantifiers, by taking the single logical constant to be the multivalent truth-operator N. To assess the merits of this risky conjecture would involve delving deeply into the nature of quantification, which is clearly out of the question here.

Whatever Wittgenstein himself later made of his Tractarian ideas, the work appears to contain the beginnings of an alternative way of doing logical semantics, which for want of a better term one might call *combinatorial semantics*. It would be nice to show that this approach, suitably developed, combines the more desirable features of both model theory and truth-value semantics without their respective drawbacks. One possible attraction is that the ontology which it is natural to associate with it is more likely to appeal to logicians of nominalist inclination; my attention was drawn in this direction in attempting to formulate a semantic theory for the much more powerful extensional logic of Leśniewski which would satisfy the latter's rigourous ontological scruples. Even without this encouragement however, it is worth considering alternative ways to give semantics, not only for extensional but also for intensional notions, which avoid giving rise to dubious metaphysical posits like abstract senses or possible worlds. Here the consideration of several different kinds of ways of signifying for a given expression, and the combinations of such ways, may prove to be more natural than applied set theory.

* * *

A FORMALIZATION OF WITTGENSTEIN'S EARLY THEORY OF BELIEF

Gert-Jan Lokhorst
Erasmus University Rotterdam

In the past two decades a number of attempts have been made to formalize the propositional part of the *Tractatus*, notably by Suszko[1] and Wolniewicz.[2] The results of these attempts are, however, rather unsatisfactory: they remain in an unfinished state, are invariably very complicated and cumbersome, and, moreover, do not throw any light on the earlier Wittgenstein's notoriously obscure remarks on the analysis of belief-sentences. In this paper we will (i) present a new formalization which, despite being considerably simpler, seems at least as adequate as the previous ones, and (ii) extend this formalization to clarify Wittgenstein's theory of belief.

I. A Tractarian semantics for the propositional calculus.

1. The language. Our language (L_o) has a countably infinite set of atomic sentences (*Elementarsätze*) $p_0, p_1, \ldots$ and the connectives $\neg$, $\wedge$, $\vee$ and $\rightarrow$. We use φ and ψ as variables ranging over sentences.

2. The model. A Tractarian model is an ordered pair $\langle B, I \rangle$, where B is a complete atomic Boolean algebra $\langle B, \vee, \wedge, -, 0, 1 \rangle$ and I is a function from the set of atomic sentences to B.

B, the universe of B, is Wittgenstein's 'logical space' (*logischer Raum*). The elements of B are called 'possible situations' (*Sachlagen*). Let $\{p_n : n \in N\}$ be the set of atomic sentences. Then $\{I(p_n) : n \in N\}$ is the set of 'elementary situations' (*Sachverhalte*). A 'fact' (*Tatsache*) is an element of the form $\vee \{f(n) . I(p_n) : n \in M\}$, where f is a function from M to $\{-1, +1\}$, and M is a subset of N. If $M = N$ we call the fact 'exhaustive'. W is the set of dual atoms ('possible worlds') of B. 0 is the necessary situation, 1 the impossible situation. We say that x exists (*besteht, der Fall ist*) at y iff $x \leq y$.

3. Semantics. For all $w \in W$: (i) $\models p_n [w]$ iff $I(p_n) \leq w$.("If the atomic sentence is true, the elementary situation exists; if the atomic sentence is false, the elementary situation does not exist." *TLP* 4.25) (ii) $\models \neg \varphi [w]$ iff not $\models \varphi [w]$. (iii) $\models \varphi \wedge \psi [w]$ iff $\models \varphi [w]$ and $\models \psi [w]$. (iv) $\models \varphi \vee \psi [w]$ iff $\models \varphi [w]$ or $\models \psi [w]$. (v) $\models \varphi \rightarrow \psi [w]$ iff not $\models \varphi [w]$ or $\models \psi [w]$. (Motivation: the Tractarian truth-tables, suitably relativized to worlds.)

For all $x \in B$: $\models \varphi [x]$ iff for all $w \geq x$: $\models \varphi [w]$. This clause is not suggested by the Tractatus; it is a generalization of the clause Rescher and Brandom[3] give for what they call 'schematized worlds'. The clause gives us the truth values of all sentences in all situations; note that all sentences of the language are true in 1 and that the sets of sentences true in non-world situations are, in general, incomplete with respect to the language.

Finally, we stipulate that $\models \varphi$ iff $\models \varphi [0]$.

The 'sense' (*Sinn*) of a sentence is the greatest common part of the situations in which the sentence is true: $S(\varphi) = \wedge \{x \in B : \models \varphi [x]\}$. Theorems: (i) $\models \varphi [x]$ iff $S(\varphi) \leq x$. (ii) $S(p_n) = I(p_n)$. (iii) $S(\neg \varphi) = -S(\varphi)$. ("Negation reverses the sense of a sentence." *TLP* 5.2341) (iv) $S(\varphi \wedge \psi) = S(\varphi) \vee S(\psi)$, $S(\varphi \vee \psi) = S(\varphi) \wedge S(\psi)$. ("The sense of a truth-function of a sentence is a function of the sense of the sentence." Ibid.) (v) The sense of a tautology is 0, the sense of a contradiction 1. (Cf. *TLP* 4.462−3, 5.143.)

The sense of a sentence is the greatest situation the sentence represents (*darstellt, abbildet*). So φ represents x iff $x \leq S(\varphi)$. In this case φ says that x exists in the sense that whenever φ is true (at y), x exists (at y). We regard '"φ" says ψ' as short for 'φ says that $S(\psi)$ exists', 'φ says that ψ is true', 'φ represents $S(\psi)$', and, most perspicuously, 'φ tautologically implies ψ'. This explains why it is remarked in *TLP* 5.142 that "the tautology says nothing" (except itself).

4. Two extra conditions on the model. In order to do even more justice to the *Tractatus*, we impose two extra conditions on the model. (i) Two worlds cannot agree on all sentences of L_0. Corollary: each world is a fact (cf. Stenius[4]). To be precise, each world is an exhaustive fact $V \{f(n) . I(p_n) : n \in N \text{ and } f(n) . I(p_n) \leq w\}$. A world is, in general, not the supremum of the set of *Sachverhalte* existing in it (*TLP* 2.04); but since 2.05 is correct, it is now true that each world is uniquely determined by the latter set (4.26). (ii) "The elementary situations are independent of one another" (*TLP* 2.061), i.e., they are independent in the sense of Boolean algebra. Corollary from (i) and (ii): each exhaustive fact is a world.

5. An example. An example of a Tractarian model is the pair $<B, I>$, where B is the power set of the set of all sets maximally consistent with respect to the propositional calculus, and $I(p_n) = \{ \text{Max } \Gamma : p_n \in \Gamma \}$.[5] It is clear that this model exists and that B is a complete atomic Boolean algebra satisfying the conditions and corollaries of I.4. Note furthermore that a sentence is valid in the model iff it is a thesis of the propositional calculus; this implies that PC is complete with respect to the class of Tractarian models (that it is also sound is easy to check).

II. A Tractarian logic of belief.

1. Wittgenstein on belief. According to Anscombe[6] and Berghel[7], whose views on this topic we largely adopt, Wittgenstein held that ascribing a belief to a person is a twofold affair. In the first place, it involves ascribing a thought to the person. What a thought is Wittgenstein confessed not to know (letter to Russell 19.8.1919); but at any rate it is a kind of sentence (ibid.), let us say a 'mental' sentence in a 'language of thought'. In the second place, it involves giving a partial specification of what this thought represents, i.e., of what the sense of this mental sentence is. It is this part of the ascription Wittgenstein primarily had in mind when he said that "'A believes that p', 'A has the thought p' and 'A says p' are of the form '"p" says p'." (*TLP* 5.542) Accordingly, the sentence 'i believes that φ' expresses (i) that i has the thought 't', and (ii) that 't' says φ. It is true iff the latter conditions obtain.

2. Tractarian semantics for belief-sentences. We can incorporate these insights relatively straightforwardly in our Tractarian model. Let L_i be i's language of thought. t_i is a function from W to L_i; $t_i(w)$ is i's thought at w, which we for simplicity's sake assume to be unique. S_i is a function from L_i to B assigning situations (senses) to thoughts. As we do not know anything at all about t_i and S_i separately, we shall henceforth only consider the composite function $S_i \circ t_i : W \rightarrow B$.

Accordingly, a Tractarian belief-model is a triple $\langle B, S_i \circ t_i, I \rangle$, where $S_i \circ t_i$ is the function we have just described and B and I are as above. In view of *TLP* 4 and II.4 (ii) below we require that, for all $w \in W$, $S_i \circ t_i(w) \neq 1$.

Adding the sentential operator B_i (for 'i believes that') to L_0, the truth clause becomes: $\models B_i \varphi [w]$ iff $\models \varphi [S_i \circ t_i(w)]$, which is equivalent to (i) $S(\varphi) \leq S_i \circ t_i(w)$, (ii) $t_i(w)$ represents $S(\varphi)$, and (iii) '$t_i(w)$' says φ. So the truth clause for $B_i \varphi$ has the same form as '"φ" says φ' as analyzed in I.3, which seems to be an acceptable way to give *TLP* 5.542 its due.

3. Axiomatization. Axiom schemata: PC, $B_i(\varphi \rightarrow \psi) \rightarrow (B_i \varphi \rightarrow B_i \psi)$, $B_i \varphi \rightarrow \neg B_i \neg \varphi$. Derivation rules: modus ponens, $\vdash \varphi \Rightarrow \vdash B_i \varphi$. Theorem: this logic (we'll call it D because it is the doxastic version of the basic deontic system D) is sound and complete with respect to the class of Tractarian models. Proof: soundness is trivial. Completeness[5]: define a canonical model $\langle B, S_i \circ t_i, I \rangle$ as follows. B is the power set of the set of D-maximally consistent sets. For all Max Γ, $S_i \circ t_i (\{\Gamma\}) = \{\text{Max } \triangle : \{\varphi : B_i \, \varphi \in \Gamma\} \subseteq \triangle\}$. $I(p_n) = \{\text{Max } \Gamma : p_n \in \Gamma\}$. It is clear that this model exists, that it is a Tractarian belief-model satisfying the requirement that $S_i \circ t_i (\{\Gamma\}) \neq \emptyset$, and that it falsifies every non-thesis of D. (However, in the case of D the corollaries from the conditions of I.4 no longer hold.)

4. Concluding remarks. We do not claim that the logic we have just presented is *the* logic of belief Wittgenstein had in mind; however, it is a logic which is at least entirely consonant with what he said, not only in *TLP* 5.542, but also in various other places.

(i) In the *Notes on Logic* it is said that in 'i believes that φ', φ cannot be replaced by a proper name; "here a *sense*, not a meaning [*Bedeutung*] is concerned." On our account i is, indeed, related to S (φ), namely by way of his or her thought.

(ii) $B_i \, \varphi$ is senseless (*sinnlos*: i.e., tautological or contradictory) iff φ is senseless, not well-formed iff φ is not well-formed: see *TLP* 5.5422. (According to *TLP* 5.1362 the same applies to 'i knows that φ'.)

(iii) Our account vindicates the remark made by Anscombe[6] that '"φ" says φ' is *unsinnig* whereas $B_i \, \varphi$ is perfectly *sinnvoll*. On our account, '"φ" says φ' is a metalinguistic statement purporting to express something that cannot be expressed in L_o; $B_i \, \varphi$, on the other hand, is an element of L_o which being in the domain of S has just as much sense as any other expression of L_o.

(iv) According to *TLP* 5.542, 'i asserts that φ' is to be analyzed analogously to 'i believes that φ'. Substituting A_i ('i asserts that') for B_i, we obtain Rescher's assertion-logic A_1.[8]

(v) Finally, we might say that when I believe that φ, I am, in a sense, at least as complex as φ; for in this case my thought represents as least as much as φ does. This perfectly agrees with the remark in the *Notes dictated to G. E. Moore* that "it is just as impossible that *I* should be a simple as that 'p' should be"—a remark which, just like Wittgenstein's whole early theory of belief, is incidentally strikingly reminiscent of Wundt.[9]

ENDNOTES

[1] Suszko, R., "Ontology in the Tractatus of L. Wittgenstein", *Notre Dame Journal of Formal Logic* 9 (1968), pp. 7−33.
[2] Wolniewicz, B., "A Wittgensteinian Semantics for Propositions", in: C. Diamond and J. Teichman (eds.), *Intention and Intentionality* (Brighton 1979), pp. 165−178.
[3] Rescher, N. and Brandom, R., *The Logic of Inconsistency* (Oxford 1980).
[4] Stenius. E., *Wittgenstein's Tractatus* (Oxford 1960), ch. 2−4.
[5] Notation as in: B. F. Chellas, *Modal Logic: An Introduction* (Cambridge 1980).
[6] Anscombe, G. E. M., *An Introduction to Wittgenstein's Tractatus* (London 1959), ch. 6.
[7] Berghel, H. L., "Harman's Tractarian Thoughts", in: E. and W. Leinfellner, H. Berghel and A. Hübner (eds.), *Wittgenstein and His Impact on Contemporary Thought: Procs. Second International Wittgenstein Symposium, 1977* (Vienna 1978), pp. 151−155.
[8] Rescher, N., *Topics in Philosophical Logic* (Dordrecht 1968), ch. 14.
[9] "Nicht als einfaches Sein, sondern als geordnete Einheit vieler Elemente ist die menschliche Seele was Leibniz sie nannte: *ein Spiegel der Welt*." W. Wundt, *Grundzüge der physiologischen Psychologie* (Leipzig 1874), S. 863.

* * *

SEMANTIC HOLISM AND THE PHENOMENALIZATION
OF THE *TRACTATUS*

Michael V. Wedin
University of California, Davis

Although not advertized as such, two Fregean principles govern the semantics of the *Tractatus [TLP]*. 3.3 introduces what I shall call the Context Principle

> Only propositions have sense; only in the context of a proposition does a name have meaning[1]

and 3.318 adds what I shall call the Principle of Semantic Dependence

> Like Frege and Russell I construe a proposition as a function of the expressions contained in it.

If the latter is read as

1. If S is comprised of elements (words)$w_1 \ldots w_n$, then the meaning of S is a function of the meanings of $w_1 \ldots w_n$

and the Context Principle is read as

2. If w is an element (word) of S, then the meaning of w is a function of its occurence in S,

then the meaning of a given word will depend on its occurrence in a sentence whose meaning in turn depends on that of the very word in question. In short, 1 and 2 appear to yield the unedifying point that a word's meaning depends on itself.

Wittgenstein is not insensitive to the bareness of this result. He avoids it by granting that sentence meaning is a function of the specific elements of a given sentence but denying the same for word meaning. As early on as 2.0122 he implicitly recognizes a relative measure of semantic independence for words:

> Things are independent in so far as they can occur in all *possible* situations, but this form of independence is a form of connexion with states of affairs, a form of dependence. (It is impossible for words to appear in two different roles: by themselves and in propositions.)

This suggests reformulating 2 as

2'. If w is a sentence-element (word) & S is a possible sentence, then the meaning of w is a function of its occurrence in S.

Because certain propositions, possible as well as actual, will not contain w, something weaker must be understood. One suggestion not to adopt is that w's meaning is a function of its occurrence in some sentence or other of the language that contains w. The apparent gain here in generalty affords none in explanation of w's meaning. For pick your arbitrary sentence and you have picked the original problem only slightly less directly. 2' must, then, be understood to range over any possible proposition that contains w:

2''. If w is a sentence-element (word) & S is a possible sentence in which w occurs, then the meaning of w is a function of its occurrence in S.

If 2'' frees a word from depending for its meaning on a given or narrowly defined set of propositions, do we have anything approaching semantic holism? This depends partly on what one understands by semantic holism. If we follow Davidson's characterization

> If sentences depend for their meaning on their structure, and we understand the meaning of each item in the structure only as an abstraction from the totality of sentences in which it features, then we can give the meaning of any sentence (or word) only by giving the meaning of every sentence (or word) in the language,[2]

2" will not do as it stands. For as it stands it relativizes *w*'s meaning to just those propositions, even if all possible, in which *w* occurs.

Nonetheless, there are signs that Wittgenstein wants to take 2" in the direction of something like Davidsonian holism. First, *TLP* sentences do depend for their meaning on their structure. A proposition shows its sense, in the idiom of 4.022 *"zeigt seinen Sinn,"* in virtue of the fact that it has an articulated structure (3.251) whose elements correspond to elements of the state of affairs that would, if obtaining, make the proposition true. The elements in question are, generally characterized, expressions or *Ausdrücke*, the parts of a proposition that have a determining effect on its sense. So the first of Davidson's sufficient conditions for holism is satisfied.

Although trickier, the second condition appears to be reflected in several passages that, in effect, comment on 3.3, namely 3.31, the passage that characterizes expressions (*Ausdrücke*) as the semantically relevant parts of propositions, and 3.311:

> An expression presupposes the forms of all the propositions in which it can occur. It is the common characteristic mark of a class of propositions.

3.311 does several things. It shows not just that 2" is the *TLP* parsing of 3.3 but also that a given element of the structure, a given expression, is understood, precisely as Davidson's second condition requires, only as an abstraction from the totality of sentences in which it may occur.

Intuitively, the idea is that giving the meaning of a word *w* in terms of the totality of its containing sentences implicitly commits one to giving the meanings of all the other words such sentences contain. So unless there are words that we know in advance can occur neither with *w* nor with words that can so occur, giving the meaning of *w* appears to involve giving the meaning of every word in the language. So far this accords with what is said in *TLP*. It is somewhat less clear whether the same line of argument is to be extended to propositions. But notice that 3.31 countenances propositions themselves as expressions and 3.314 officially brings expressions under the Context Principle. If we assume that the latter does not simply record the limiting case where a proposition is held meaningful only in the context of itself, we might suppose Wittgenstein open to the argument that a proposition has meaning only in the context of other sentences that contain it, in short, in terms of the language as a whole.

Linguistic holism, at least as here characterized, has a fairly natural extension to language learning. To learn a word is to learn its use in sentences of the language and to learn a sentence is to learn its use in the language. Holism in what might perhaps be described as its epistemic or doxastic brand, is also associated with Quine's view that our beliefs meet the world as a corporate body, not in a piecemeal manner. In particular, there is no room for the view that to any sentence *S* there corresponds a given class of experiences or sensory given material that on its own verifies of falsifies *S*.

The first point suggests that what is salient in language acquisition is usage rather than devices such as ostensive definition and the second suggests that phenomenalist language will play no particulary interesting role in the theory of *TLP*. I raise these points less to register their fidelity to the message of *TLP* than to locate crucial points of divergence from an increasingly popular contending view. On this view, most vigorously defended by Hintikka and Hintikka,[3] *TLP* emerges as a phenomenalist tract much in the spirit of early Russell. I propose to lay out the main features of the view, offering critical remarks on the argument for it and suggesting alternative interpretations more in line with our appraisal above.

The thesis to be scrutinized, is that the objects of *TLP* are phenomenalistic entities and that its primary language, the language of elementary propositions, is phenomenalistic.[4]

Some of the evidence for the thesis is anecdotal and amounts to citing reports of Wittgenstein's contemporaries[5] or certain of his post-*TLP* remarks, in which he disavows his earlier goal of a phenomenological or primary language.[6] For the most part I neglect this sort of evidence, because I am concerned with what kind of interpretation *TLP* itself allows. Here I shall argue that there is virtually no support for the phenomenalist reading. But first three remarks on the connection with early Russell.

The first concerns the Pears-Hintikka claim that Russell withheld publication of his 1913 manuscript *Theory of Knowledge* because Wittgenstein announced to him that he had already tried the same ideas and found them wanting.[7] Suppose we grant that the notion of a complex logical object was especially troublesome to Wittgenstein and that he subsequently adopted the view that all objects of acquaintance must be simple. What would this show? Perhaps that even before he came to write *TLP* Wittgenstein had already jettisoned early Russellian objects but certainly not that those he later countenanced in *TLP* are a pared down set of *Russellian* objects of acquaintance. In particular, it does not follow that simple objects of acquaintance must be phenomenalistic. Why might they not be universals or something akin to Fregean concepts? Both are better candidates given that several crucial theses of *TLP* seem to require as much.[8] In any case, simplicity alone is not enough to phenomenalize *TLP* objects.[9]

The second remark on the link to Russell concerns Hintikka and Hintikka's claim that Wittgenstein's use of phenomenalistic language for elementary propositions has epistemological but not ontological force. Rather it is seen, now in the spirit of Russell's *Our Knowledge of The External World*, as providing nothing more than a firm foundation for our knowledge of ordinary objects. But it is hard not to wonder how we are to reconcile this with 2.021's assertion that objects are the substance of the world and 2−2.01's implication that facts, and so ordinary objects, are nothing but certain combinations of objects. Certainly these look like ontological theses.[10]

The third connection alleged with early Russell turns on identifying Wittgenstein's denial of meaningfulness to assertions of an objects's existence with Russell's point that "of an actually given this, an object of acquaintance, it is meaningless to say it 'exists'." For Russell this follows from the impossibility of asserting truthfully "This does not exist." The impossibility in question is entirely pragmatic and depends crucially on the indexical nature of the sentence in question. So far as I can determine this plays no role whatever in Wittgenstein's attitude (see 5.534ff) toward denials of existence to objects. It is because objects are the meanings of names that it is impossible to meaningfully assert "*a* does not exist," where "*a*" is a *TLP* name.

Nonetheless, friends of linkage will rejoin that *TLP* names carry indexical force. At least this is so for those who see evidence in *TLP* for the central role of ostensive definition. So let us look at the passages in question.[11] On the basis of 2.02331 Hintikka and Hintikka find that *TLP* objects "can only be introduced by pointing to them" (431) and that names of such objects "are supposed to obtain their meanings from private encounters of an ostensive kind with the objects of direct acquaintance" (430). Although I am unclear what is meant here by introduction, the first claim cannot mean that *TLP* objects can be mentioned in an elementary proposition only by pointing to them. They can be mentioned simply by use of a name. So we are free to concentrate on the second quote which suggests that names get their meanings from ostensive definitions. This is an important claim and deserves full scrutiny.

Hintikka and Hintikka support the claim by appeal to 3.221

> Objects can only be *named*. Signs are their representatives. I can only speak *about* them: I cannot *put them into words*. Propositions can only say *how* things are, not *what* they are.

and, above all, 2.02331

> Either a thing has properties that nothing else has, in which case we can immediately use a description to distinguish it from the others and refer to it [*darauf hinweisen*]; or, on the other hand, there are several things that have the whole set of their properties in common, in which case it is quite impossible to indicate [*zeigen*] one of them.

We may dispose of 3.221 quickly. As part of a comment distinguishing names and proposi- tions (Hintikka and Hintikka do not include the final sentence), it has nothing to do with Rus- sell-like "tracing the meanings of phrases back to experience"[12] but only with the different ways names and propositions are significant. Names are about objects, while propositions express how objects are related. Thus 3.221 resists phenomenalization, unless we assume that the significance of a name can be established only by ostensive means.

So what about 2.02331? The passage is the center piece of the argument for the central role of ostensive definition in *TLP*. Hintikka and Hintikka find two crucial claims in it. First, the emphasized phrases, *darauf hinweisen* and *zeigen*, introduce the notion of ostensive definition and, thus, the second claim, the objects of *TLP* are phenomenal.

Several problems face this reading of 2.02331. One is that it must assume that only pheno- menal objects can be ostensively indicated. But virtually anything can be the subject of an act of ostension, including universals. In fact, however, it is hard to see how the passage could promote ostensive definition for *TLP* objects no matter what they are. The first of its two alternatives requires no mention of ostensive definition at all. One can unproblematically refer to an object *via* a description so long as the object uniquely satisfies that description. This appears to be a case where ostensive definition is not called for at all.[13]

So we must retreat to the second alternative. But notice that here we cannot both read "*zei- gen*" ostensively[14] and take the objects of ostension to be particulars, phenomenal or other- wise. For ostensive definition just is the sort of device that is wrung in to explain how we can distinguish qualitatively identical particulars, namely by pointing, first, to the one, then, to the other. Yet this is exactly what Wittgenstein bars us from doing! So the alternatives can hardly range over particulars.[15]

Finally, even were the passage to link ostension with *TLP* objects, it by no means follows that names acquire meaning by private acts of ostension nor, *pace* Hintikka and Hintikka, that Wittgenstein thought so. On the contrary. 4.063, a passage in which "*zeigen*" does display *bone fide* ostensive force, explicates the notion of truth by the following analogy: The shape of a black spot on white paper can be described (the analogue to asserting a proposition) by saying, for each point on the sheet, whether it is black or white (the analogue to analysis into elementary propositions). Then Wittgenstein says that I can say that a point is black or white only if I know what counts as black or white. But now, and this is the important point, the analogy breaks down. For while I can indicate (*zeigen*) a point on the sheet, even if I do not know what black and white are, nothing similar is possible in the case of a proposition. This passage clearly shows that ostension is not sufficient to determine the meaning of what is ost- ended, and even suggests that ostension has no evident role at all in establishing linguistic meaning. Thus, so far from counting for, the evidence of *TLP* appears to run against a seman- tically useful role for ostensive definitions.

How, then, is linguistic significance determined for *TLP* names? Ostension falls woefully short and definitions are plainly unsuited for the task. The answer, already anticipated, is clear. We learn the meanings of primitve signs, of names, by learning their use in propositions of the language. This is the unavoidable message of the two passages that follow 3.26 and 3.261's disqualification of definition for the task.

3.262 counsels that what cannot be expressed in signs can be made clear by their use (*Anwendung*). Since we know that the meaning of propositions is just what they express, we should expect to find this passage focusing on meaning that isn't expressed, namely, the mea- nings of names. Appropriately, 3.263 explicitly extends the point to *Urzeichen* or names:

> The meanings of primitive signs can be explicated through elucidations (*Erläuterun- gen*). Elucidations are propositions that contain the primitive signs. So they can only be understood, if the meanings of the sign are already known.

There will, I think, be little temptation to find in these lines any allusion to ostensive defin- ition.[16] On the other hand, it is clear what we do find, namely, a theory of meaning acquisition that parallels, in the second sentence, the Context Principle and, in the third sentence, the

Principle of Semantic Dependence. The first is given immediately at 3.3., the second a few lines later at 3.318. These are precisely the principles that led to the conclusion that the semantics of *TLP* is holistic. Indeed, without the thesis of semantic holism 3.263 parades as an unresolved conundrum of *TLP*.[17] And while *bone fide* conundra, intended or otherwise, grace the pages of Wittgenstein's marvelous book, this, I submit, is not one of them.

The argument for the semantic holism of *TLP* is admittedly only a sketch but hopefully it will prove enough[18] to allow at least some attention to settle on what is perhaps a more important result. This is that proposals to interpret *TLP* in phenomenalist categories face grave, if not insuperable, obstacles. This in turn suggests that its proper lineage is the semantic tradition of Frege, or even Frege-Russell, but not the epistemological tradition of Russell.

ENDNOTES

[1] I follow, for the most part, the Pears-McGuinness translation (London, 1961).
[2] "Truth and Meaning," *Synthese* 17 (1967) 304—23.
[3] I refer throughout to Jaakko Hintikka and Merril B. Hintikka, "The Development of Wittgenstein's Philosophy: The Hidden Unity," read to the 7th International Symposium. The view is argued elsewhere as well (see note 1 of their contribution to the proceedings, *Epistemology and Philosophy of Science* (Wien 1983), 425—437).
[4] In the published version of the paper talk of "phenomenalistic" language gives way to talk of "phenomenological" language (see note 6). Since this appears not to alter the essentially phenomenalist thrust of their interpretation, I retain the earlier form of the thesis.
[5] See page 429 where Waismann's report is used but not his assessment that the anti-phenomenalist idiom of Wittgenstein's reported remark is not directed against *TLP*.
[6] *Philosophical Remarks*, I, 1, p. 51.
[7] See D. Pears, "The Relation between Wittgenstein's Picture Theory of Propositions and Russell's Theories of Judgment," *Philosophical Review* 86 (1977) 177—96.
[8] Particularly, the mutual independence of elementary propositions. For the argument here, see Wedin, "Objects and Independence in the *Tractatus*," *Proceedings of the 2nd International Wittgenstein Symposium, Wittgenstein and His Impact on Contemporary Thought*, ed. Leinfellner, et. al., (Wien 1980) 107-113. Occasional allusions to the virtues of universals as *TLP* objects should be viewed, tolerantly I hope, as a thinly veiled reference to this article.
[9] For Hintikka and Hintikka, *TLP* objects are simple in the sense of having no analysis into simpler objects but not simple in the sense of being without structure (426). Apart from the question of how this differs from the complexity of the rejected Russellian logical objects, structure is supposedly required because the aim of logic is to construct a notation that will mirror the forms of 'simple' objects. But for objects to be somehow essential for logic, perhaps they need not themselves have structure but only the capability to yield structures that are relevant to logic. If what logic must mirror is the structure of facts or situations, then structure need appear only at this level. Thus it may be enough that objects differ intrinsically, one from the other, for this may generate differences in combinatorial capacities sufficient to account for structural variety at the level of facts.
[10] Notice also that because states of affairs need not exist, 2.01's assertion that they are combinations of objects makes it difficult to see how objects could be phenomenalistic entities. Unless, again with Russell, we countenance unsensed sense data. No like problem arises for universals.
[11] From here on I shall be dealing with interpretation of *TLP* exclusively.
[12] The phrase is Pears', its use here Hintikka and Hintikka's.
[13] "*Darauf hinweisen*" need not, of course, be given the narrow reading "points to it."
[14] That "*zeigen*" need not be so taken is clear from 4.022's remark that a proposition shows its sense (*zeigt seinen Sinn*). If nothing else, this would obliterate the difference between propositional and nominal styles of signification.
[15] On the other hand, 2.02331 makes good sense, if its objects are universals. Two universals or concepts not differing in quality are in fact not two but one universal or concept and so it is, of course, impossible to indicate one as distinct from the other.
[16] Hintikka and Hintikka are quite right to caution against taking *Erläuterungen* as ostensive definitions, not, however, to overlook 3.262—3.263 as central to the *TLP* account of how names 'get' meaning.

17 I do not then follow McGuinness' suggestion that the passage simply underscores what Wittgenstein takes to be a "falsche Fragestellung" (in his "Wittgenstein's Analysis of Psychological Verbs" read to the Ninth Symposium). On the other hand I am very sympathetic to his claim there that what a name means (denotes) is determined by its use in all the propositions that contain it.

18 A further point of support is that holism answers an objection, raised at the Ninth Symposium in a slightly different context by Rolf George, to the account of the *Tractatus*: Because thoughts map onto features of the world under a unique, "correct", projection there appears to be no room in *TLP* for incomplete, inadequate, and confused thoughts. True enough. But because a thought is determined, holistically, by language, to have a wrong or inadequate thought would then simply amount to not knowing the language and, put this way, the thesis that one cannot have inadequate thoughts turns out to be unsurprising.

* * *

ON THE CONCEPTS OF PROBLEM, SOLUTION, QUESTION AND ANSWER IN WITTGENSTEIN'S *TRACTATUS*

Arto Siitonen
University of Turku

Wittgenstein's *Tractatus* may be understood as a fruit of the intentional activity of solving problems and answering questions. It presents a doctrine—or, rather, several doctrines as solutions to its problems. The claim in P 8 concerning the final solution of the problems is unmistakable as it stands.[1] This claim can hardly be accepted. But it signifies a typical aspect of the *Tractatus*: its doctrinal dimension. The doctrinal dimension remains in opposition to the suggestion in 4.112, according to which philosophy is not a doctrine but an activity. What kind of activity has been meant here? Surely, "the logical clarification of thoughts" (4.112). The opposition between the doctrinal *Tractatus* and the open-ended program of clarifying thoughts provides the basis for one of the main inner tensions of the book.

Tractatus contains challenges to and problematizations of some prevailing doctrines, and clarifications of obstinate confusions. The doctrinal *Tractatus* includes e.g. an implicit theory of questions and problems. A classification of question types, closely connected to that of proposition types, is also reconstructible from Wittgenstein's text.

1. Doctrines are bodies of assumed knowledge. They are products of inquiring processes. Researchers aim at problem-solving and question-answering. Solutions and answers are formulated as doctrines. But these can again be made problematic, just as common-sense suppositions are questioned by philosophy, science and art. In this sense the activity of inquiring is more primary than the doctrines, which are stepping-stones on the road of research.

Wittgenstein's confrontation of doctrine with activity can be interpreted quite naturally in a *Socratic* manner: As a recommendation to keep the questioning activity, the readiness to clarify and elucidate thoughts, in operation and not to be content with fulfilled system.

This recommendation is indeed more than followed by Wittgenstein, who throws away and transcends all that has been maintained in the book up to the next to the last sentence. That which is abandoned can only be shown, not spoken about. Paradoxically, even this distinction cannot be spoken about after sentence 6.54 has been stated—the distinction only shows itself.

The tension between doctrine and activity extends to the concepts of question and problem and their correlates. An implicit theory of questions and problems and of meaningful asking and problemizing is discernible in the *Tractatus*. The concepts 'question', 'answer', 'problem' and 'solution' occur quite frequently in the book. Many of these occurrences are not combined to the above-mentioned theory but are rather instances of asking and problemizing things. Moreover, *Tractatus* contains several (at least 27) *explicit questions*. It is true that most of these questions are purely *rhetorical* and have been answered before asked, or are anwered in a wider context of the book. However, the three questions asked in 5.553, as well as the three in 5.5542, are at least partly *inquiring* questions. The joke question asked in 5.5352 may be said to be able to initiate a study on identity and existence. Correspondingly, the question asked in 5.452, combined to the question mentioned in 6.211, could well start a logico-philosophical research program (cf. 3.328 and 5.47321 to their connection to Occam's maxim).

2. To be sure, there is much that is doctrinal in the *Tractatus*—much to be thrown away as nonsensical (cf. 6.54). Above all, the main theory concerning the relationship between language and reality is nonsensical on the premises of the book.

Doctrinal is the naturalistic world-view, which is supported by idealism—an idealism with a transcendent subject. Because there is no logical link between the states of affairs (cf. 2.061−2, 5.135)—and no logical link between the elementary propositions (5.134)—it follows the doctrine that there is only logical necessity (6.3, 6.37, 6.375) with the corollary concerning the nonexistence of the causal nexus (5.136–1361, 6.37) and the corollary concerning the human will (6.373). The technical theory of truth possibilities is accompanied by a range theory of probability (4.464, 5.1, 5.152). Kantianism is represented e.g. by the sentences 5.5542, 6.233, 6.33–35, 6.36111.

It is controversial, how many of the above-mentioned doctrines and others in the *Tractatus* have been backed by arguments and how good the arguments are. In order to find out this, a detailed scrutiny of some of the doctrines and of its premises would be needed.

3. There are many sentences in the *Tractatus* in which current theories are made problematic. Targets of Wittgenstein's attack are e.g. the idealistic explanation of the seeing of spatial relations (4.0412), the typical view of scientific explanation and the "scientific world-view" connected with it (6.371–2), the traditional idea of the thinking, imagining subject (5.631), the normal conception of the immortality of the soul (6.4321), the supposition that scepticism is irrefutable (6.51).

Beside these challenges there are passages in the *Tractatus* in which some confusions are said to be clarified and passages in which solutions to problems are said to be given. Such cases–in which Wittgenstein is indeed carrying out his program of philosophy as clarification and elucidation–are e.g. 3.143, 3.323, 4.062–21, 4.122, 4.126, 5.02. According to 3.324, the whole philosophy is full of fundamental confusions; so, there is lot to be done before one may "pass over in silence".

4. The main idea of Wittgenstein's implicit theory of questions is:
Unanswerable questions are unaskable
Accordingly, if a question is genuinely asked, then there must be a range of possible answers to it: "When the answer cannot be put into words, neither can the question be put into words . . .
If a question can be framed at all, it is also *possible* to answer it." (6.5). These sentences can be formalized as follows:

(1) $(\sim Eq)\ \{q\epsilon A(Q)\} \rightarrow (\sim Ep)\ \{p\epsilon Q\}$
(2) $(Ep)\ \{p\epsilon Q\} \rightarrow (Eq)\ \{q\epsilon A(Q)\}$

In 6.51, the idea formalized in (2) is repeated as follows: "For doubt can exist only where a question exists, a question only where an answer exists, and an answer only where something *can be said*."

The limits of askability thus coincide with the limits of sayability and so with the limits of thought (that the limits of thought and the limits of the expression of thought are the same, is included in 3.001 and 5.61; cf. however P 3). Because these are, furthermore, the bounds of sense, unanswerable questions not only do not exist but are also nonsensical: "To ask whether a formal concept exists is nonsensical. For no proposition can be the answer to such a question." (from 4.1274). On the other hand, nonsensicality of a question implies its unanswerability: "Most of the propositions and questions to be found in philosophical works are not false but nonsensical. Consequently we cannot give any answer to questions of this kind, but can only establish that they are nonsensical." (from 4.003). Accordingly:

(3) $(\sim Eq)\ \{q\epsilon A(Q)\} \equiv Q_{nonsensical}$

Insofar as problems are exemplified by questions, the above theory of questions has the following corollaries:
Insoluble problems are not statable. If a problem can be stated, then it can be solved. An insoluble problem does not exist; it is nonsensical, a pseudoproblem. If and only if there is no solution to a problem, it is a pseudoproblem.
Exemplification of problems by questions is suggested in 5.4541, 5.551 and 6.52. Concerning insolubility, e.g. the formulation "vanishing of the problem" (of life) in 6.521 suggests that

in the case of nonexistence of a solution, the problem does not arise. The problem of squaring the circle provides a good example of an insoluble and accordingly unstatable mathematical problem;[2] a corresponding empirical "problem" would be that of constructing a perpetual motion-machine.

Meaningful questions and genuine problems belong to three different classes on the premises of the *Tractatus*: (a) logico-mathematical problems, (b) empirical problems, (c) elucidatory tasks. The class (c) cannot be labelled as "philosophical problems", because in P 2 Wittgenstein disqualifies the posing of such problems as being based on logical misunderstanding. However, he is ambiguous even in this central point: P 2 concerns *all* philosophical problems (cf. in German: "die philosophischen Probleme"), whereas in 4.003 he speaks, rather surprisingly, of "most of the propositions and questions to be found in philosophical works" as being nonsensical. One is interested in knowing, which questions would *not* be nonsensical in these works and what their relative frequency really is.

5. The logic underlying *Tractatus* is that of truth functions, i.e. the propositional calculus. Wittgenstein analyses and classifies propositions as carriers of meaning. However, implicitly he also considers questions and their properties: "Most of the propositions and questions to be found in philosophical works are not false but nonsensical." (from 4.003). This remark classifies *both* propositions *and* questions into *nonsensical, false* and, by implication, *true*. The suggested trichotomy is quite unproblematical in respect to propositions, but one may wonder what are true and false questions. Nonsensicality is more clear: Wittgenstein's example of a nonsensical question

(*) Is the good more or less identical than the beautiful?

(in 4.003) speaks for itself: one cannot make a meaningful statement which would properly answer (*). Accordingly, on the premises of the *Tractatus*, one may define the notion of nonsensical question as follows:

Q_n A question is nonsensical iff it does not admit of any meaningful direct answer

(cf. (3) in sect. 4 above). The concepts of false and true question require more interpretation. The following definitions should not be in conflict with Wittgenstein's intentions:

Q_f A question is false iff it admits of a consistent direct answer but lacks any true direct answer
Q_t A question is true iff it has a true direct answer

By means of an *extrapolation*, it would be possible to complete the above interpretation to the effect that the classification of propositions would be accompanied by its mirror image on the side of questions. What is needed for such an extrapolation, are the definitions of the concepts of *tautological* and *contradictory* questions (the former do not admit of any false direct answer, while the direct answers of the latter are contradictions).

ENDNOTES

[1] "p" followed by a number refers to the particular paragraph in the preface of the *Tractatus*.
[2] Cf. D. Hilbert, "Mathematische Probleme", *Gesammelte Abhandlungen* III, New York 1965, p. 297. Hilbert's theory of problems corresponds to that of Wittgenstein at least insofar as mathematical problems are concerned; cf. Hilbert's "Axiom von der Lösbarkeit eines jeden Problems" and his question, whether this would possibly be "ein allgemeines dem inneren Wesen unseres Verstandes anhaftendes Gesetz", p. 297.

* * *

TWO LANGUAGES IN WITTGENSTEIN'S *TRACTATUS'* THEORY OF LANGUAGE

Fu-tseng Liu

National Taiwan University, Taipei, Taiwan (R. o. C.)

1.

Consensus has it that there are two different theories of language in the full corpus of Wittgenstein's philosophy. One is presented in his *Tractatus*; another in his *Philosophical Investigations*.[1] However, I shall point out first that most of the interpreters and critics of his philosophy, perhaps even Wittgenstein himself, do not recognize that actually these two theories refer to two ontologically different languages. The *Tractatus* is primarily concerned with what I call metaphysical language, formulized by the *Tractatus'* philosophy. In the *Investigations*, the concern is by contrast ordinary language or worldly language. Secondly, interpreters and critics may not have perceived that in fact this duality of languages occurs within the *Tractatus* itself. (Therefore, there would in fact seem to be three different theories of *two* different languages in Wittgenstein's philosophy.) In this paper I shall consider this duality in the *Tractatus*, and explore how it can be used to improve the understanding and interpretation of this text.

Apparently Wittgenstein is supposed to consider *one* theory of *one* language in the *Tractatus*. In fact he deals with one theory of two languages. I want to suggest that we do better to view the *Tractatus'* theory of language as two theories of two languages: one about a metaphysical language, the other about an ordinary one. I shall attempt to show that if at least initially we deal with these two theories separately, we may glean some prospective solutions to unresolved difficulties and establish a stronger sense of coherence in the *Tractatus*.

Early in 1922, when Russell wrote the 'Introduction' for the first publication he already recognized that in the *Tractatus* the language Wittgenstein was primarily concerned with was not ordinary language. Russell says that "in the part of his theory which deals with Symbolism he is concerned with the conditions which would have to be fulfilled by a logically perfect language"[2] and that "Mr. Wittgenstein is concerned with conditions for a logically perfect language—not that any language is logically perfect language, but that the whole function of language is to have meaning, and it only fulfils this function in proportion as it approaches to the ideal language which we postulate."[3]

In these remarks, Russell has seen one thing but failed to see something else. Russell is right that in his Symbolism Wittgenstein is not primarily concerned with ordinary language. But he is wrong to say that Wittgenstein is concerned with a logically perfect language or an ideal language. It seems to me that Wittgenstein is not concerned with the conditions for some language, though the language he is primarily concerned with might fulfil these conditions. In Wittgenstein's mind, it is not that we try to find out some conditions first and then attempt to construct a so called ideal language fulfilling these conditions. Rather, there simply is such a language which happens to fulfill these conditions. We should notice this priority. Besides, in his Symbolism, Wittgenstein also deals with ordinary language. He might not have been aware of this himself. Russell missed this too. Perhaps in Russell's mind, Wittgenstein deals with only ideal language.

Bernstein recognizes the multiplicity of the language in the *Tractatus*. In the 'Wittgenstein's Three Languages',[4] he says that in the *Tractatus* there are at least three languages: the perspicuous language, ordinary language, and the ladder language. The perspicuous language is an aid for understanding how language works when we use it to make true and false statements.

It is not an ideal language which ordinary language must "approach" in order to fulfill its function. The purpose of the perspicuous language is to show perspicuously what is "hidden". In order to describe this perspicuous language, we must use a language—the ladder language—which must not be confused with the object language that it describes. The "propositions" in the ladder language cannot occur in the perspicuous language. In the *Tractatus*, the perspicuous language and ordinary language are mentioned but not used. The language used in the *Tractatus* is the ladder language. The elementary propositions belong to the perspicuous language. Where the perspicuous language conforms strictly to the truth-functional requirement, the ladder language cannot satisfy this strict truth-functional requirement.

I agree that the perspicuous language is not an ideal language which ordinary language must approach in order to fulfil its function, and further that the perspicuous language and ordinary language are mentioned in the *Tractatus* but the perspicuous language is not used. But it is not true that in the *Tractatus* ordinary is not used and only ladder language is. It seems to me that Bernstein has inadequately restricted the meaning of ordinary language here. It is only in contrast with perspicuous language that there is a sense to characterize so called the ladder language. Ladder language is simply ordinary language. I cannot see any meaning in a distinction between ladder language and ordinary language.

The most common view among commentators is that in the *Tractatus*' theory of language, the primary concern is the essence of language, which should be characteristic of any correct use of language.

The common point of the above three views is that the primary concern in the *Tractatus*' theory of language is, in a sense, a language which is not ordinary language. But these views have different characterizations about the nature and the logical or ontological status of *this* language. I would, as mentioned earlier, characterize this language as a metaphysical language, formulized by the *Tractatus*' philosophy.

2.

Metaphysicians often claim that there is a metaphysical world which is different from but more essential than this ordinary world; for example, Plato's world of ideas. Although such a metaphysical world is different from the ordinary world, there are some intrinsic connections between them. The general ontological status of a metaphysical language as characterized above is similar to that of such a metaphysical world.

Briefly, the metaphysical language in the *Tractatus* consists of names,[5] elementary propositions,[6] and the truth-functions of elementary propositions.[7] We will call these names and propositions names and propositions in the metaphysical language respectively. The propositions in this metaphysical language are different from what is generally called metaphysical propositions. The language used in metaphysical propositions is ordinary language. For example,

"道可道, 非常道   。"

(The Tao (Way) that can be told of is not the eternal Tao) in the *Lao Tzu (Tao-Te Ching)* is a metaphysical proposition, but it is written in ordinary Chinese language; "The soul is immaterial" is a metaphysical proposition too, but it is written in ordinary English. The reason we characterize metaphysical propositions as metaphysical is that the objects or the world(s), if any, which they talk about are so called metaphysical objects or worlds. As to the propositions in the metaphysical language, regardless of what kind of objects they are supposed to talk about, they are some kind of metaphysical objects themselves. This is perhaps the most peculiar feature of the theory of language in the *Tractatus*.

One thing we need to notice. The ontological status of what a philosopher is concerned with, might not be what he claims it to be, either explicitly or implicitly. As mentioned before, Russell says that Wittgenstein is supposed to deal with "the ideal language which we postulate". Here Russell might mean by "postulate" to "posit" a theoretical notion as in constructing a scientific theory. But actually it would be much better to construe it as to "admit" or "presume" something of a metaphysical kind.

According to Wittgenstein, he was sure, *a priori* or merely on purely logical grounds, that there must be elementary propositions and names and was sure what they must be like. He writes: "It is obvious that the analysis of propositions must bring us to propositions which consist of names in immediate combination."[8] "If we know on purely logical grounds that there must be elementary propositions, then everyone who understands propositions in their unanalysed form must know it."[9] "The requirement that simple signs be possible is the requirement that sense be determinate."[10] And "The simple signs employed in propositions are called names."[11]

We know, consequently, that the elementary propositions and names are obtained *a priori*, or from the theoretical requirement, and not from the actual analysis of ordinary sentences. Every reader of the *Tractatus* knows that Wittgenstein never gave any examples of elementary propositions and names. He was honest in this, because he did not pretend to do what could not be done. However, his student Malcolm reported that he had asked Wittgenstein whether, when he wrote the *Tractatus*, he had ever decided upon anything as an *example* of a 'simple object'. He replied that at that time his thought had been that he was a *logician*; and that it was not his business, as a logician, to try to decide whether this thing or that was a simple thing or a complex thing, that being a purely empirical matter.[12] He might make the same reply if Malcolm asked him anything as an example of a name or elementary proposition. If he made so, he would be not frank enough in that it would be metaphysical and no 'real' example could be given.

Apparently Wittgenstein would not admit that anything he said was metaphysical, because when he wrote the *Tractatus*, at least on the surface he would demarcate his philosophy with metaphysics. At the end of the *Tractatus*, he wrote in earnest that "the correct method in philosophy would really be the following: to say nothing except what can be said, i.e. propositions of natural science—i.e. something that has nothing to do with philosophy—and then, whenever someone else wanted to say something metaphysical, to demonstrate to him that he had failed to give a meaning to certain signs in his propositions."[13] But we cannot say that what one says is not metaphysical simply because he does not admit it to be the case. Pitcher says that in the *Tractatus*, Wittgenstein develops a metaphysical system from considerations of language and meaning.[14] Although Pitcher does not mean here metaphysical language, we would think that metaphysical language or the system of the metaphysical language is one of the most important things Wittgenstein establishes in the *Tractatus*. This claim could be further justified by its explanatory strength for the *Tractatus'* text. We will illustrate this below.

In the *Tractatus'* theory of language, although Wittgenstein is primarily concerned with metaphysical language, he is also concerned with ordinary language. Hence, in the *Tractatus*, there are at least two theories of languages: theory of metaphysical language and theory of ordinary language, though Wittgenstein might not be aware of this duality himself. Moreover, he might not be aware of the kind of language he is concerned with.

Having recognized this duality in the theories of language, we should notice several things:

(1) At least at in an initial study, we should take note of the features of these two theories, and determine in the *Tractatus* which words concern metaphysical language, which concern ordinary language, and which concern both. Since Wittgenstein does not notice that his theory concerns two languages, there are many overlapping places to which we should pay special attention.

(2) Since the *Tractatus* deals with two different theories which have intrinsic relations between them, when we try to evaluate them, we need at least to do it on two levels. One level deals with the theories themselves. The other concerns their relations, especially how much

and to what extent the theory of metaphysical language can be applied to the theory of ordinary language.

(3) Since the *Tractatus'* theories of language have intimate relationship with other dimensions of the *Tractatus'* philosophy, we should notice their dual relationship.

(4) In the study of the relations between the *Tractatus'* philosophy and his later philosophy as well as the ideas of other philosophers, especially Frege and Russell's we should take into account this duality of his theories of language.

3.

Now let us take some examples of how our claim that there are two theories of two languages can be used to explain and interpret the text of the *Tractatus*:

(1) One of the most important theses of the *Tractatus* is that a proposition is a truth-function of elementary propositions.[15] Pitcher argues that this thesis cannot hold, because not all propositions can be constructed by the truth-functional operation of elementary propositions.[16] Our view is that the propositions in this thesis are propositions in metaphysical language, and not propositions in the ordinary language. In this understanding the thesis is almost tautologically true. We should not deny this thesis for the reason that the propositions of "laws of inference", "one proposition implies another", "universal propositions", "propositions stating probabilities", "propositions of mathematics", etc., cannot be applied to it, because all of these propositions are propositions of ordinary language. We can only say that the thesis cannot be applied to these propositions.

(2) According to the *Tractatus*, every elementary proposition consists of names in immediate combination.[17] From our ordinary language, for example, Chinese, English, German, Japanese, etc., we cannot find any good example to help us understand such an elementary proposition. Moreover, if we interpret names here as meaning the simple signs which denote the objects which are simple,[18] we will simply get lost. But if we allow that the elementary propositions belong to metaphysical language, then we will not try to understand them from the examples of ordinary language, but will rather try to understand them from the perspective of speculative philosophy from which they are easier to grasp.

(3) The *Tractatus* says that "the totality of propositions is language."[19] Since the term propositions here can be construed ambiguously as propositions in ordinary language and propositions in metaphysical language, the term language here thus can mean ambiguously ordinary language or metaphysical language. Hence, this statement can be either about ordinary language or about metaphysical language.

(4) Item 3.32 of the *Tractatus* says that "a sign is what can be perceived of a symbol." Apparently the notion of the sign here is considered, at least initially, from the perspective of ordinary language. Here signs at least include names,[20] and propositions or propositional signs. Item 3.11 of the *Tractatus* says that "we use the perceptible sign of a proposition (spoken or written, etc.) as a projection of a possible situation." Item 3.12 says that "I call the sign with which we express a thought a propositional sign." In ordinary language, it is easy to understand that a sign is what can be perceived of a symbol by the senses. For example, in the expression "the earth goes around the sun," the English words "the earth" written on this page in that order, is the sign of the symbol of the earth, and the English sentence "the earth goes around the sun" written on this page, is the propositional sign of the proposition that the earth goes around the sun. These signs are all perceptible by our eyes. However, signs and

propositional signs here should include signs and elementary propositional signs in strictly *Tractatus'* sense. If simple signs and elementary propositional signs belong to ordinary language, then they should be perceptible by the senses. But it is inconceivable to say that like ordinary signs, simple signs and elementary propositional signs are perceptible by the senses. In ordinary language, a sign must be perceptible by the senses. Hence, simple signs and elementary propositional signs should not belong to ordinary language. They should belong to metaphysical language. However, metaphysical language is not perceptible by the senses. Although they cannot be perceived by the senses, they can be perceived in some way, for example, by mind. In Pears' translation, item 3.32 of the Tractatus is: "A sign is what can be perceived of a symbol." Here, the term perceive should have ambiguously two meanings: one is to be perceived by the senses, and the other is to be perceived by the mind, according as the signs belong to ordinary language or metaphysical language. The original German text of item 3.32 has the words 'sinnlich Wahrnehmbare', which literally means 'what is perceptible by the senses'. In Pears' translation, 'by the senses' is deliberatively expunged, and leave the 'perceptible' can mean ambiguously as 'perceptible by the senses' and 'perceptible by the mind'. This is a considered translation.

ENDNOTES

I am grateful for comments of earlier version of this paper by Roger T. Ames.

1 Wittgenstein, L., *Tractatus Logico-Philosophicus*, translated by D. F. Pears and B. F. McGuinness (London-New York revised 1963). L. Wittgenstein, *Philosophical Investigations*, translated by G. E. M. Anscombe (Oxford ³1968).
2 *Tractatus*, p. ix.
3 *Tractatus*, p. x.
4 Bernstein, Richard J., "Wittgenstein's Three Languages", in: *Review of Metaphysics*, vol. 15, no. 2, issue no. 58, 1961, 12, pp. 278—98. This paper is also collected in Irving M. Copi and Robert W. Beard (eds), *Essays on Wittgenstein's Tractatus* (New York 1973), p. 231ff.
5 *Tractatus*, 3.202, 3.203.
6 *Tractatus*, 4.21, 4.22, 4.221.
7 *Tractatus*, 5., 5.01.
8 *Tractatus*, 4.221.
9 *Tractatus*, 5.5562.
10 *Tractatus*, 3.23.
11 *Tractatus*, 3.202.
12 Malcolm, N., *Ludwig Wittgenstein: A Memoir* (London 1958), p. 86.
13 *Tractatus*, 6.53.
14 Pitcher, George, *The Philosophy of Wittgenstein* (New Jersey 1964), p. 18.
15 *Tractatus*, 5.
16 Pitcher, ib., pp. 98—104.
17 *Tractatus*, 4.22, 4.221.
18 *Tractatus*, 3.201, 3.202, 3.203, 2.02.
19 *Tractatus*, 4.001.
20 *Tractatus*, 3.202.

* * *

DIE WELT IST MEINE SPRACHE. DIE IDEALISTISCHE GRUNDSTRUKTUR VON LUDWIG WITTGENSTEINS *LOGISCH-PHILOSOPHISCHER ABHANDLUNG*

Heinz Hellerer
Universität München

Wer beginnt, sich mit der *Logisch-philosophischen Abhandlung* Wittgensteins, dem soge-nannten *Tractatus*,[1] auseinanderzusetzen, der wird sehr bald mit der Frage konfrontiert, wie die zum Teil sehr kurzen und kryptischen Aussagen dieses Werkes miteinander zusammen-hängen und ob hier nicht etwa offensichtliche Widersprüche verhindern, daß hinter ihren Aussagen ein einheitlicher Sinn aufgespürt werden kann. Diese Problematik tritt unter ande-rem darin zutage, daß Wittgenstein zu Beginn des Werkes eine Reihe von Bemerkungen über die Welt macht, sie z.B. als die Gesamtheit der Tatsachen und nicht der Dinge bezeichnet (*LPA* 1.1) usw., also offensichtlich eine Ontologie aufstellt, im weiteren Verlauf seiner Gedanken jedoch immer wieder Aussagen macht, die einer Ontologie deutlich widerspre-chen, so z.B. wenn er das Wesen der Welt und das Wesen des Satzes miteinander gleichsetzt (*LPA* 5.4711) oder im Zusammenhang mit seiner Diskussion des Solipsismus (*LPA* 5.62−5.641) behauptet, die Welt und das Leben seien Eins. Es entsteht auf diese Weise zwangsläufig der Eindruck, Wittgenstein habe mehrere philosophische Ansätze, vielleicht sogar ganz verschiedene Philosophien zu einem letztlich nicht mehr völlig entwirrbaren Gesamtzusammenhang vereint, ohne offensichtliche Widersprüche auszugleichen oder ohne sie auch überhaupt nur zu bemerken. Die damit angesprochene Problematik, welche Welt Wittgenstein eigentlich meint, wenn er von Welt und Wirklichkeit spricht und all ihre Impli-kationen wie die Frage nach dem Zusammenhang von Sprache und Welt und der daraus fol-genden Richtigkeit von Sätzen zieht sich durch die ganze *Abhandlung* hindurch und betrifft zuletzt auch den Bereich des Unaussprechlichen.

In dieser prekären Situation ergibt sich nun die Alternative, sich entweder damit abzufin-den, daß Wittgenstein scheinbar in der Verquickung mehrerer philosophischer Ansätze einige Widersprüche und auch einige letztlich unverständliche kryptische Passagen in die *Abhand-lung* eingeflochten hat, oder aber man versucht, zu den Ursprüngen seines Denkens vorzu-stoßen und von daher den Weltbegriff des Werkes neu aufzurollen. Für diese zweite Möglich-keit spricht der Umstand, daß es einerseits unwahrscheinlich wirkt, daß ein Denker von der philosophischen Kapazität Wittgensteins ganz offensichtliche Widersprüchlichkeiten in sei-nem Grundansatz nicht bemerkt haben soll, sowie andererseits die Tatsache, daß er selbst − wie er in einem Brief schreibt − von der „Kristallklarheit"[2] seines Werkes zutiefst überzeugt war.

Beginnt man nun zu prüfen, welche Denker tatsächlich Spuren in den Grundanschauungen Wittgensteins hinterlassen haben können, so stößt man neben Russell und Frege, die er ja selbst im Vorwort der *Abhandlung* erwähnt, sehr bald auf den Namen Schopenhauer. Daß Schopenhauer einen bedeutenden Einfluß auf Wittgenstein auszuüben vermochte, wird sowohl von ihm selbst ausdrücklich bemerkt,[3] als es sich auch aus den Tagebüchern ablesen läßt, in denen sich Wittgenstein mehrfach mit Gedankengängen Schopenhauers gründlich auseinandersetzt.[4]

Meine These ist nun, daß erst vor dem Hintergrund der Schopenhauerschen Philosophie einer Welt des Willens und einer Welt der Vorstellung auch der Weltbegriff der *Abhandlung* einsichtig zu werden vermag, daß Wittgenstein durch einen Idealismus im Sinne Schopenhau-ers einen wesentlichen Grundimpuls für seine eigene Philosophie erhalten hat. Für Schopen-hauer ist es eine unhintergehbare Tatsache, daß die Welt, die der Mensch sieht und erkennen kann, nichts anderes ist als eine Welt der Vorstellung, d.h. eine Welt, die primär nur im menschlichen Bewußtsein existiert; trotz alledem aber, was nach Schopenhauer für eine rein idealistische Sicht der Welt spricht, kann doch auf der anderen Seite nicht abgeleugnet werden, daß auch eine materielle Welt existiert. Was aber als Welt im menschlichen Bewußtsein aufleuchtet, ist keineswegs die Materie selbst, sondern lediglich ihre Akzidentien, die der menschliche Geist schafft. Die Materie als Ding an sich bleibt so dem Bewußtsein zwar unzugänglich, bildet aber doch den wesentlichen Grundstein der Erkenntnis neben dem reinen Bewußtsein. Erkenntnis besteht somit aus zwei Polen, der unerkennbaren Materie einerseits, die aber die Grundlage aller Erkenntnisprozesse bildet und damit die empirische Erkenntnis von der reinen Phantasie unterscheidet und andererseits aus dem transzendentalen Bewußtsein des Menschen, das eine Welt der Vorstellung und alle Eigenschaften der Dinge erst bildet. Erkenntnis der objektiven Welt ist damit also weder ein reines Produkt der Phantasie, noch im positivistischen Sinne das Wissen von einer Welt als Abbildung (‚Verdopplung‘), sondern sie ist und bleibt eine Welt der Vorstellung, allerdings auf einer materiellen Basis. Die Frage ist nun, ob dieser Gedanke Schopenhauers auf die *Abhandlung* gewirkt hat und wie Wittgenstein ihn möglicherweise transformiert hat. Obwohl Wittgenstein auf das Begriffsgerüst der Kantischen Philosophie – wie es Schopenhauer verwendet – weitgehend verzichtet und weder von Materie noch von einem Ding an sich, noch auch von einer Welt der Vorstellung spricht, läßt sich dieser Grundgedanke Schopenhauers dennoch in der *Abhandlung* nachverfolgen; um dies nachvollziehen zu können, muß man zunächst davon ausgehen, daß Wittgenstein nicht von einer Welt der Vorstellung seinen Ausgangspunkt nimmt, sondern daß bei ihm die Sprache den elementaren Baustein der Weltkonstitution bildet, eine Sprache, die ihrerseits auf substantiellen Gegenbenheiten aufruht. Wittgenstein expliziert diesen Zusammenhang folgendermaßen: die Welt besteht aus Tatsachen, die Tatsachen aus Sachverhalten, die Sachverhalte ihrerseits wiederum aus Konfigurationen von Gegenständen (*LPA* 2.01; 2.02; 2.0232 u.a.). Die Gegenstände besitzen aber nicht nur eine Funktion im Rahmen eines Sachverhalts, sondern Wittgenstein schreibt ihnen außerdem noch die Substanz der Welt zu (*LPA* 2.02). Er betont weiterhin, daß eben die Substanz gewährt, daß die Wahrheit eines Satzes nicht wiederum von der Wahrheit eines anderen Satzes abhängt (*LPA* 2.0211), und daß diese Substanz die Möglichkeitsbedingung dafür bildet, daß überhaupt ein Bild entstehen kann (*LPA* 2.0212). Die Substanz ihrerseits scheint jedoch in ‚meiner Welt‘ nicht auf, da sie nichts ist, was der Fall wäre und demnach keine Tatsache sein kann (*LPA* 2.024). Anders als die Substanz tritt jedoch der Gegenstand in der Sprache auf; nach Wittgenstein tut er dies als Name (*LPA* 3.22; 3.221). Innerhalb einer Konfiguration, in einem Sachverhalt also, kann der Gegenstand erfaßt werden, nicht aber für sich allein. Obwohl die Gegenstände die Substanz der Welt bilden, werden somit weder sie selbst noch auch ihre Substanz manifest; was in der Sprache allein aufscheint, ist der Sachverhalt in der Form eines Elementarsatzes. Zwischen dem, was Schopenhauer als ‚Vorstellung‘ bezeichnet und dem, was bei Wittgenstein die Sprache darstellt, besteht also insofern eine enge Verwandtschaft, als bei beiden das menschliche Bewußtsein, das bei Schopenhauer ‚Vorstellung‘ und bei Wittgenstein ‚Sprache‘ heißt, auf einer materiellen Grundlage aufruht, die selbst jedoch nicht greifbar wird. Betrachtet man nun weiterhin die Bildtheorie der *Abhandlung* genauer, so wird deutlich, daß nach Wittgenstein der Mensch nicht eine ontologisch vorgegebene Welt in seinem Bewußtsein einfach verdoppelt, sondern daß nach Wittgenstein der Mensch zunächst Bilder konstruiert, um diese sodann mit der nicht-subjektiven Wirklichkeit zu vergleichen (*LPA* 2.12; 2.224 u.a.). Der Mensch entwirft also Bilder der Wirklichkeit der nicht-subjektiven Welt, die sowohl wahr als auch falsch sein können, aber diese Bilder sind keine willkürlichen Phantasieprodukte, sondern sie hängen auf zweifache Weise mit der nicht-subjektiven Welt zusammen: zum einen dadurch, daß die substantiellen Gegenstände nötig sind, damit überhaupt ein Bild entworfen werden kann, zum anderen dadurch, daß der Mensch diese Bilder mit der nicht-subjektiven Wirklichkeit vergleicht (*LPA* 4.05; 4.06). Unabhängig von dem (ungeklärten) Problem, wie nun das Bild mit der nicht-subjektiven Wirklichkeit verglichen werden soll, wird aus der *Abhandlung* doch deutlich, daß der Mensch in erster Linie Bilder *konstruiert*. Die Welt des menschlichen Bewußtseins ist damit also in erster Linie eine Welt der Bilder, Sätze und Gedanken, eine subjektive Welt ähnlich Schopenhauers Welt der Vorstellung. Wittgensteins Satz oder Bild stimmt jedoch auf jeden Fall in einem wesentlichen Punkt mit der nicht-subjektiven Wirklichkeit überein: in der logischen Form. Sie ist das Bindeglied zwischen Subjekt und Objekt, sie ist unhintergehbar und damit die eigentlich ontologische Aussage der *Abhandlung* (*LPA* 2.18; 4.12; 4.121 u.a.). Der Hintergrund der Philosophie Schopenhauers führt also auf die Fährte, daß Wittgenstein nicht zunächst eine Ontologie aufstellt und dann die Sprache die solcherart festgelegte Welt abbilden läßt (eine Vorgehensweise, die man bei einem nachkantischen Philosophen tatsächlich als naiv bezeichnen müßte), sondern umgekehrt vorgeht: ähnlich der Schopenhauerschen Vorstellungswelt ist die Welt nach Wittgenstein zunächst eine Satzwelt, eine subjektive Welt, die von der objektiven Welt zwar abhängig ist, sie jedoch auf keinen Fall einfach abbildet. Nach Wittgenstein bestimmt damit die Sprache das menschliche Denken, ist die Sprache die Welt, nicht aber die materielle Wirklichkeit. Vor dem Hintergrund dieses ‚Sprachidealismus' läßt sich nun aber auch der innere Zusammenhang der *Abhandlung* besser verstehen.

Immer unter Berücksichtigung dessen, daß Wittgenstein eine subjektive Welt der Sprache meint, wenn er von Welt spricht, wird nunmehr deutlich, daß sich kein Widerspruch ergibt zwischen einer Welt, die „der Fall ist" (*LPA* 1) und einer Welt, die *meine Welt* ist und durch mein Leben begrenzt wird, daß die Grenzen der Sprache zwangsläufig mit den Grenzen der Welt identisch sind (*LPA* 5.6), und ebenso auch, warum die Wahrheit und die Falschheit eines Satzes am Bau der Welt etwas ändert (*LPA* 5.5262). Stets ist das Bild und die Sprache der grundlegende Akt des Bewußtseins, nicht aber die Empirie; es ist die Sprache allein, die Welt konstituiert, und alles, was Wittgenstein über Tatsachen, Sachverhalte, Gegenstände und Logik schreibt, ist nichts anderes als eine Beschreibung dessen, wie Sprache in unserem Bewußtsein Welt konstituiert. Die Aufgabe der Philosophie kann deshalb gemäß der *Abhandlung* auch nicht darin bestehen, daß sie entscheidet, welche Sätze wahr und welche falsch sind − Philosophie kann nur klären, wo die Sprache leerläuft und ins Undeutliche verschwimmt. Verständlicherweise gibt es in einer solchen Welt der gleichberechtigten Sätze (*LPA* 6.4) keine Rätsel, keine ‚höheren' Fragen und Antworten, da alle Sätze nur ein menschliches Konstrukt darstellen und es also unter ihnen keine Hierarchien geben kann, die nicht wiederum ihrerseits eine Schöpfung des Menschen wären. Das, was Wittgenstein „Lebensprobleme" nennt (*LPA* 6.52), tritt demnach erst da in Erscheinung, wo die natürliche Grenze der Sprachwelt erreicht wird, beim menschlichen Leben und beim menschlichen Ich; wo aber die Grenze von Sprache und Welt erreicht ist, kann nur noch das Schweigen einsetzen.

————————

ANMERKUNGEN

[1] Wittgenstein selbst hat es stets vermieden, sein Erstlingswerk als *Tractatus* zu bezeichnen, sondern nannte es fast immer *Logisch-philosophische Abhandlung*. Da kein einsichtiger Grund vorliegt, warum man nicht der Intention des Autors folgen sollte, wird das Werk hier durchgehend als *Logisch-philosophische Abhandlung* (Abkürzung: *LPA*) zitiert.
[2] Wittgenstein, L., *Briefe* (Frankfurt a. M. 1980), S. 85.
[3] Wittgenstein, L., *Vermischte Bemerkungen* (Frankfurt a. M. 1978), S. 43.
[4] Wittgenstein, L., *Notebooks 1914−1916, 2nd Edition* (Oxford 1979), S. 79−85.

* * *

LUDWIG WITTGENSTEIN: *TRACTATUS* 6.52
ODER
DAS DILEMMA WISSENSCHAFTLICHER AUSSAGEN

Rüdiger E. Böhle
Dreieich, BRD

Tractatus 6.52 beginnt: „wir fühlen". Das Pronomen ‚wir' ist im Anspruch allgemeiner Gültigkeit gebraucht. Das Verb ‚fühlen' spricht den emotionalen Bezug des Subjekts zum Objekt aus. ‚Fühlen' ist eine bestimmte sinnliche Weise menschlichen Weltumganges. Sinnlichkeit ist strikte Oberflächlichkeit. Sie fixiert augenblicklich Gegenwärtiges in einfacher Bestimmtheit. Ihr Ort des Verstehens ist der Bewußtseinstatus der sinnlichen Gewißheit; der ihrer Dignität, ein Gefühls-Mäßiges zu sein: ‚Wir fühlen', daß die vollendete Wissenschaft an Lebensproblemen vorbeifragt und vorbeiantwortet; Wissenschaft und Lebensprobleme sind kontaktlos verschieden. Die vollendet angenommene Wissenschaft läßt fühlen, daß Lebensprobleme aus dem Bereich wissenschaftlicher Relevanz herausfallen: die Wissenschaft ist hier systematisch fraglos geworden. „Freilich bleibt dann", sagt Wittgenstein, „eben keine Frage mehr"; das ist anscheinend tautologisch, doch fällt auf, daß zuvor von ‚wissenschaftlichen' Fragen die Rede war, nun aber von ‚Fragen' ohne nähere Bestimmtheit! Diese sprachliche Ungenauigkeit hat Konsequenzen: „und eben dies", daß keine ‚Fragen' und nicht nur keine ‚wissenschaftlichen' Fragen mehr bleiben, „ist die Antwort", d.h. die Antwort überhaupt und nicht nur die ‚wissenschaftliche' Antwort. Logisch korrekt wäre: „Freilich bleibt dann eben keine ‚wissenschaftliche' Frage mehr; und eben dies ist die ‚wissenschaftliche' Antwort." Das ist klare Tautologie und besagt darum auch ganz legitim nichts, was über Vorheriges hinausginge. Doch lassen wir sprachlich leichtfertig die Bezüglichkeit des Antwortens der Wissenschaft außer acht und nehmen uneingeschränkt an, daß außer wissenschaftlichen Fragen „eben keine Frage mehr (bleibt)", und „eben dies . . . die Antwort (ist)" auf unsere Lebensprobleme, dann gerät menschliche Betroffenheit zynisch ins menschenunwürdige Abseits: der Zusammenhang dieser Textstelle und Paranthesestellen in Wittgensteins Schriften legen nahe, daß Wittgenstein das in der Tat so meine. Der ungenaue Umgang mit der Sprache verbirgt die Einsicht in den hier vorliegenden Zynismus, der alles das, was dem per definitionem systematisch eingeschränkten Hinblick der Wissenschaft auf das Wirkliche so notwendig aus der Relevanz gesetzt wurde, als das in der Tat Bedeutungslose und Irrelevante verwirft. Rücksichtlich der Wissenschaft ist Wittgenstein nichts zu bestreiten: der Wissenschaft ist das Menschliche KEIN Thema; ohne diese Einschränkung aber ist Wittgenstein hier nichts zuzugeben, so alltäglich diese Irrelevanz auch geübt wird: in unseren zweck-rationalen, technisch-praktischen Veranstaltungen, die wir ‚Industrie', ‚Verwaltung', ‚Fließband', ‚Produktion' etc. nennen.

Das ist es, was ‚wir fühlen'! Doch ist die Frage, ob wir ‚Wahres' fühlen und wie ein solches bestimmt ist; so ist nach Wissenschaft und Lebensproblem zu fragen.

Die Wissenschaft ist das systematische Bemühen, gesetzmäßig bestimmbare Zusammenhänge an der Gegenständlichkeit menschlichen Weltumgangs zum Zwecke möglichen Gebrauchs aufzufinden, zu Funktionen zu formulieren und in der systematischen Notwendigkeit zu erklären. Die Wissenschaft stellt so ein systematisch wohlgeordnetes Kompendium theoretischer Werkzeuge her, die Gegenständlichkeit des technisch-praktischen Weltumganges des Menschen auf gesetzte Zwecke hin notwendig zwinged zu behandeln: Funktions- und Theoriekonzipierung vermittelst systematischer Abstraktion. Die systematische Abstraktion führt in die theoretische Bestimmtheit entdeckter, noch zu entdeckender und zu erklärender Daten. Die wissenschaftliche Aussage bestimmt in theoretisch fundierter und methodisch abgesicherter Weise, wie ein bestimmter Gegenstandsbereich funktioniert. Kant sprach davon, daß der Verstand der Natur die Gesetze vorschreibt[1], worüber man sich nicht wie J. König echauffieren[2], sondern vors Bewußtsein bringen sollte, daß die Begriffe des Verstandes, d.h. der Theorie, ohne Anschauung, d.h. ohne Empirie, leer sind. Der Verstand oder die Theorie stellt den selbstverständlichen Anspruch, der Gegenständlichkeit die Gesetze vorzuschreiben als die ihr gemäße Weise zu funktionieren; ob diese aber in der Tat gemäß dem Vorgeschriebenen funktioniert, das ist eine ganz andere Frage und gehört nicht der Theorie selbst an, sondern der Empirie. Die systematische Empirie nennen wir ,Experiment', die allgemeine ,den Gebrauch'; auf das Letztere ist jede Wissenschaft bezogen; hier fällt die Entscheidung über den theoretisch behaupteten Anspruch: die Empirie ist die Achillesferse aller Wissenschaft, wie geharnischt und in empirischer Distanz sie auch daherkommen mag.

Die Notwendigkeit dieser Kritik des wissenschaftlichen Anspruchs resultiert aus der logischen Geschichte der wissenschaftlichen Aussage: sie ist systematisch bedingte Abstraktion. Die Abstraktion wirft die Frage nach dem ,wovon?' auf. Wissenschaft abstrahiert vom Wirklichen und Lebendigen: aller Wissenschaft ist das Wirkliche, Lebendige das systematischbedingt notwendig Bedeutungslose, und so ist sie hiergegen, auch systematisch-bedingt notwendig das Ahnungslose; das hat Kant gezeigt und die moderne Wissenschaftstheorie führt diese Erkenntnis feinstens weiter aus. Dieser hiatus toto coelo ist die conditio sine qua non der Eindeutigkeit wissenschaftlicher Aussagen, worin sich ihr Dignität begründet: „Alle Gesetzesaussagen, mit denen man in den einzelnen Wissenschaften arbeitet, sind bloße hypothetische Annahmen."[3] So erschöpft sich die Leistung der Wissenschaft ganz legitimer Weise darin, in der Form der Hypothese Gesetzmäßigkeit zum zweckmäßigen Gebrauch zu formulieren und die hinreichende Antwort auf die Frage ,warum?' zu geben und solches bequem einstreichen zu lassen.[4] Die Dignität der Wissenschaft zeigt sich − in Anlehnung an Quine gesagt[5] − darin, ,rationale und gegenwärtig zweckmäßig brauchbare Mythen zu erstellen'.[6]

Das Problem der Wissenschaft ist die Rationalität zum Zwecke; Lebensprobleme sind von anderer Art, denn ihr Ursprung ist das Individuum. Ihr logischer Ort ist die Begegnung und Auseinandersetzung des Individuums mit dem Wirklichen, d.h. der ihm gegenwärtigen Welt. Lebensprobleme spiegeln betonter Weise in der Form der Frag-Würdigkeit das Verhältnis individueller Weltbegegnung und drücken in die Aufmerksamkeit des individuellen Bewußtseins gefallene Widersprüchlichkeiten desselben in der Auseinandersetzung mit dessen Welt aus. Die Bestimmtheit des Lebensproblems ist die widersprüchliche Bestimmtheit des Resultates der Geschichte dieses bestimmten Individuums da mit seiner Welt. Das Lebensproblem zeigt eine bestimmte, in ihrer Widersprüchlichkeit gegenwärtig bewußt gewordene Gestalt der bisher erfahrenen individuellen Lebensgeschichte. Das ist, von der Wissenschaft und ihrer Rationalität her betrachtet: Chaos; vom Wirklichen und Lebendigen her betrachtet, alltäglich: das Individuelle, Wirkliche und Lebendige ist der Abstraktion oder dem abstrakt-Allgemeinen, d.h. der Wissenschaft, das unerträgliche Skandalon, wovon sich zu distanzieren notwendig ist und wofür, zum Zwecke eindeutiger Rationalität, abstrakt-allgemeine Modelle entworfen werden.

Das dem Abstrakt-Allgemeinen oder der Wissenschaft Skandalöse am Individuum, vor allem in der besonderen Gestalt des geistigen Individuums, ist der nicht zu steigernde Widerspruch zu ihrer Dignität des abstrakt-rationalen Funktionierens: sich entscheiden zu können! So ist ihm Willkür ein Moment seiner Bestimmung, und also, wissenschaftlich betrachtet, das abstrakt-allgemeine oder wissenschaftliche Irrationale, welches notwendig aus dem relevanten und aussagbaren Gegenstandsbereich systematisch bedingt ausgeschlossen werden muß: bei Strafe des Widerspruchs! Aller abstrakt-allgemeinen Rationalität, wie sie in der Wissenschaft das Wesentliche des Verfahrens, Zusammenhänge zu bestimmen, ist, bedeutet das Vermögen, sich entscheiden zu können, und also nicht funktional allgemein-gültige Gesetzmäßigkeiten zu vollziehen, den horror contradictionis.

Betrachten wir die alltäglichen Auftritte des Menschen in der Welt, so sind wir geneigt, dem Urteil der abstrakt-allgemeinen Rationalität zuzustimmen, daß es im individuellen, durch Entscheidungen geprägten Verhalten der Menschen irrational und chaotisch zugehe; wie eindeutig, cum grano salis verläßlich geregelt und im voraus bestimmbar geht es hingegen im wissenschaftlichen Gegenstandsbereich zu. In der technisch-praktischen Alltäglichkeit des Produktions- und Konsumtionsgeschehens erfordert die Einfugung des Menschen zum reibungslosen Ablauf die größte Anstrengung – ganz legitimer Weise: hier soll es stringent zugehen; schließlich führt der Zweck. Aller Anstrengung zum Trotze zeigt die Erfahrung, daß das Individuum immer der, im abstrakt-allgemeinen Sinne verstanden: rationale Schwachpunkt ist. In der technisch-praktischen Alltäglichkeit, worin es um Zweckmäßiges geht, gilt es legitimer Weise, einen vorhandenen Unsicherheitsfaktor zu eliminieren, – auch wenn es der Unsicherheitsfaktor ‚Mensch‘ ist. Die allgemeinste Form, den Menschen aus der Zweckgefährdung zu setzen und ihn einfugungsfähig zu machen, nennen wir ‚Disziplinierung‘. Der Erfolg innerhalb des technisch-praktischen Weltumganges resultiert aus dem Grade der Fähigkeit, sich zur zweckorientierten, reibungslosen Verwendungsfähigkeit zu disziplinieren, denn das Geschehen eines technisch-praktischen Zusammenhanges funktioniert nur dann zweckmäßig, einfach und gleichsam schwerelos, wenn die einzelnen Komponenten dieses Zusammenhanges funktionieren: innerhalb der Sphäre einer zweckmäßig bestimmten technisch-praktischen Alltäglichkeit hat das funktional bedingte Verhalten reibungsloser Tauglichkeit zu Zwecken seinen von der Sache her wohlfundierten Ort. Dennoch machen wir bezüglich solcher Disziplinierungen und Rationalisierungen unseres Verhaltens widersprüchliche Erfahrungen: a) wenn die rationale Disziplinierung zum Zwecke nicht gelingt, treten Störungen und Schwierigkeiten auf; b) innerhalb der individuellen Sphäre zeigt sich alle rationale Disziplinierung als äußerst nützlich, reibungslos mit seinen Zeitgenossen auszukommen, weckt aber das Unbehagen, gemäß dieser Orientierung an der problemlosen Eingefugtheit und Stabilität des Nützlichen die Reduzierung der eigenen Person zu betreiben und streng rational an sich selbst vorbeizuleben. Der klar durchschaubare, leichthin funktionierende Ablauf vollendeter Disziplin hat von Seiten der Rationalität her immer das treffende Argument für sich, das Unbehagen zu diffamieren und ins irrationale Abseits zu setzen. Das Argument der Rationalität wider das Unbehagen ruht auf der Vergessenheit auf, daß der reibungs- und problemlose Ablauf einer Zweckrationalität aus der Bedingung resultiert, daß kein Element es wagt, ‚sich zu entscheiden‘, sondern daß alles immer schon entschieden ist; ‚sich zu entscheiden‘ drückt aus, Individuum, besonders ‚geistiges‘ Individuum zu sein, also: Skandalon der abstrakt-allgemeinen Rationalität. Das geistige Individuum oder den Menschen als Skandalon zu bestimmen, sei der abstrakt-allgemeinen Rationalität immer zugegeben; das Attribut ‚abstrakt-allgemein‘ zeigt die Dignität solchen Sagens an: es ist bestimmtes oder beschränktes Sagen! Die ‚abstrakt-allgemeine‘ Rationalität ist aber nicht ‚alle‘ Rationalität, sondern sie ist die Bedingung der Möglichkeit, den Aussagen der Wissenschaft Dignität zu verleihen: die Systematik der Irrelevanzerklärung alles Individuellen und Menschlichen. Demnach ist die abstrakt-allgemeine oder wissenschaftliche Rede bezüglich menschlicher Lebensprobleme das bedeutungslose Reproduzieren sonst sinnvoll zu vernehmender Sprachlaute: „Worüber man (abstrakt-allgemein oder wissenschaftlich bedingt) nicht sprechen kann, darüber muß man (abstrakt-allgemein oder wissenschaftlich bedingt) schweigen.“[6]

Die Mißachtung des notwendigen hiatus toto coelo zwischen Wissenschaft und ‚unseren Lebensproblemen‘, d.h. der prinzipiellen Unfähigkeit der Wissenschaft über ‚unsere Lebensprobleme‘ sinnvolle Aussagen machen zu können, verhindert den logischen Blick auf unsere Gegenwart, in welcher die existentielle Bedrohung alles Lebendigen aus streng abstrakt-allgemeiner oder wissenschaftlicher Rationalität heraus bestimmt geschieht: „Alles Erworbene bedroht die Maschine solange/sie sich erdreistet, im Geiste statt im Gehorsam zu sein.“[7] Nicht die Wissenschaft ist der Wahnwitz, sondern ihr illegitimer Gebrauch, der ihre Beschränktheit nicht erkennt; solcher Gebrauch kommt ganz still daher, umgeben von schlichter Dignität, ganz einsichtig hinreichende Antworten auf die Frage ‚warum?‘ geben zu können, die sich bequem einstreichen lassen.

So muß gegen Wittgensteins Konsequenz, daß keine Frage mehr bleibt, wenn Wissenschaft vollendet ist, Stellung bezogen werden: Wo alle wissenschaftliche Frage und Auseinandersetzung endet, beginnt die menschliche und wirkliche Frage und Auseinandersetzung!

———

ANMERKUNGEN

[1] Kant, *Kritik der reinen Vernunft*.
[2] König, Josef, „Bemerkungen über den Begriff der Ursache", (1949), in: J. König, *Vorträge und Aufsätze*, hrsg. v. G. Patzig (Freiburg/München 1978), S. 122–255.
[3] Stegmüller, Wolfgang, „Das Problem der Kausalität" in E. Topitsch (Hg,), *Probleme der Wissenschaftstheorie. FS für Victor Kraft* (Wien 1960), S. 171–190; S. 186.
[4] König, Josef, (1949).
[5] Quine, W. v. O., „On what there is?" in: Quine, *From a logical Point of View* (Cambridge, Mass., 1953).
[6] Wittgenstein, L., *Tractatus* 7; auch hier vergißt Wittgenstein die Attribute!
[7] Rilke, *Gedichte an Orpheus*.

* * *

10. Wittgensteins späte Philosophie

10. Wittgenstein's Late Philosophy

LANGUAGE AND COMMUNITY OF LIFE IN WITTGENSTEIN'S LATER PHILOSOPHY

Aldo Gargani
Pisa University

Both the Tractarian claim that a proposition is significant insofar as it has the same structure as what it is representing and the other premise that the proposition is an independent picture of states of affairs—so that it is not possible to infer one elementary proposition from another—were bound to be dropped by Wittgenstein as soon as he realized that they prevented a proposition from being a univocal representation of reality since they let elementary propositions determine the same co-ordinate of a fact in two or more different ways. Therefore in the course of the late Twenties and early Thirties Wittgenstein assumed language no longer as a set of propositions, each one independent from the other, but as a system and a calculus directed by internal relations and rules guiding the use of expressions. All this presupposed that language practices would be guided by rules along the rigid rails of a grammar which would operate at a distance independently of our use.[1] Wittgenstein realized that no rule by itself could determine or direct any course of action, any language practice, since any course of action and any language practice might be considered to conform to the rule.[2] In connection with this, Wittgenstein abandons the myth, which has stood for so long, that rationality consists in being constrained by rules. It is these problems and difficulties which give rise to Wittgenstein's doctrine of language-games. Now, in my opinion, Wittgenstein's Remarks on Frazer's *Golden Bough* were bound to exercise a distinctive role in the working up of this doctrine in the sense that a language-game may also be considered an anthropological game. In the course of this turn some former views of Wittgenstein are still operating and they permit us to trace some lines of continuity in the development of his ideas: the one is the original, youthful conception expressed by Wittgenstein in an entry of his *Notebooks* in 1914, where he writes that a proposition achieves its meaning "off its own bat" (*so stellt der Satz den Sachverhalt gleichsam auf eigene Faust dar*);[3] the other, strictly connected with the former, is that which induces Wittgenstein to rule out any fictitious comparison to which traditional philosophy has been resorting in order to explain the meaning of a proposition in conformity with its own tendency to get back behind language to something "well grounded".[4] In other words, traditional philosophers have resorted to what Wittgenstein in *The Blue and Brown Books* calls "the double" or "the prototype" which originates in the sham assumption that for a sentence to have meaning it would be necessary to compare it with a mould long prepared for it in our mind and into which it would fit, conferring in this way a transitive meaning on linguistic expressions. Whereas for Wittgenstein linguistic expressions have an intransitive use, and what philosophers have mistakenly tried to set up as the fitting of an expression into a prototype is a mere reflexive comparison of an expression with itself.[5] Consequently a picture doesn't fall and fit into a mould, but, as Wittgenstein writes, "we let the picture sink into our mind and make a mould there". In this connection, Wittgenstein's Remarks on Frazer's *Golden Bough* offer important clues as to the ways the language-games are set up and the role played in the latter by the views bearing on the intransitivity of linguistic expressions. First of all Wittgenstein distinguishes between practices of any sort on the one hand and such things as conception, view, theory on the other hand, in the sense that a practice doesn't spring from a conception or view; rather, practice and conception *occur together* within a form of life.[6] Hence originates Wittgenstein's rejection of any explanation, hypothesis and theory with which the meaning of linguistic expressions would be backed up. This is to be connected with those passages in the *Philosophical Investigations* where, as Hintikka remarks, rules, criteria and ostensive definitions are relegated to a secondary and unimportant role by Wittgenstein, who asserts that "to use a word without justification does not mean to use it without right".[7] In his Remarks on Frazer's *Golden Bough* Wittgenstein begins to put aside any explanation in the terms of a logico-analytical necessity, and replaces it with an entirely new pattern of analysis centered upon the notion of the connection of a community of life, of a coexistence of different ingredients of a situation of human life in which word, view, behaviour, gesture and the like are at the same level, are connected with one another and run together. In this sense, Wittgenstein writes that

> it was not a trivial reason, for really there can have been no *reason*, that prompted certain races of mankind to venerate the oak tree, but only the fact that they and the oak tree were united in a community of life, and therefore it was not by choice that they arose together, but rather like the flea and the dog. (If fleas developed a rite, it would be based on the dog).[8]

In his *Remarks* on Frazer, Wittgenstein stresses the eminent role that the interconnection of such features and ingredients of human life as rain, thunderstorms, the phases of the moon, the changing of the seasons, the phenomena of death, birth, sexual life, "in short, everything we observe around us year and year out" plays in the way man thinks and even does philosophy.[9] Rejecting hypotheses and explanations, Wittgenstein puts forward his claim aiming at seeing the data in their relation to one another and at taking them in what he calls a "perspicuous representation" (*übersichtliche Darstellung*).[10] For Wittgenstein it is no longer a matter of explaining, inferring, or of getting something fitted into something else, because the task of *seeing connections* assumes a primary importance. But at this point Wittgenstein gets concerned with another fundamental notion which he had been dealing with in his former writings and lectures, that is the concept of *internal relations*.[11] This concept had played an essential part in his former doctrine of language as a system and a calculus. In the *Philosophical Remarks* the internal relations were conceived of as being the grammatical footing which makes it possible to describe external relations.[12] Once that conception of language is put aside, the problem arises as to what role may be still assigned to them, since the concept of internal relations goes on occurring even in Wittgenstein's last writings. In fact, detached from the former view of language as a calculus, the internal relations are given an essential role in Wittgenstein's later philosophy, but at the same time they turn out to be fashioned in a different way. Since the *Remarks* on Frazer, the internal relations are no longer the relations ruling the items of a calculus, of a linguistic system, but they correspond to the new version of the philosophical task of *finding* and *seeing* formal connections among the facts and practices we are confronted with. This *seeing* must be a perspicuous seeing, a perspicuous representation.

But in order to grasp the role of internal relations in their new version, we have to ask what this perspicuous representation must be like, so that any trivialization of it may be avoided. Wittgenstein makes it clear in his *Remarks* on Frazer that what we need is "a general picture", "a formal connection" like the internal relation which holds for example in the case of the gradual converting of a circle to an ellipse, which is not a historical event, but a formal connection. It is on the very basis of his conception of internal relations that Wittgenstein carries out his strong criticism of Frazer's thesis that practices, ceremonies and rites of the savage rely on false conceptions or wrong theories. In fact, Wittgenstein succeeds in refuting Frazer's claim to the extent that he is able to find out the striking *similarities* which relate the habits of civilized and educated contemporary men to those of the savage. But the discovery of these similarities is of a piece with the discovery of a general pattern, of an internal relation, by which we are able, through "connecting links", to see those habits as being interconnected with one another and, in particular, with our own,[13] since we recognize our kinship with the savage whose habits and practices we share. Here the internal relation is no longer conceived as the property of a permanent logical matrix presupposed by any language, because it originates in an act of inspecting, of seeing and comparing facts belonging to different instances of human life. Rejecting any logical compulsion, Wittgenstein falls back upon a new sort of philosophical analysis centered upon the notion of the interconnection of features and ingredients of a community of human life. As a consequence of this view, Wittgenstein will be assigning to philosophy the task of ascertaining what language-games are actually played. His research then doesn't aim to seek a causal relation, but rather to find that sort of connection about which we don't say: if a, then b occurs; but: where there is a, there occurs also b. To put it in the terms used by R. Musil, we might say: "wo eins das andere gibt".[14]

It is worth remarking that since the *Remarks* on Frazer Wittgenstein extends the internal relations—which in general let us see the connection among the features of a form of life, for example that holding between some men and the oak—to the domain of mathematical structures such as those holding between circle and ellipse. This theme is then deepened in the *Remarks on the Foundations of Mathematics*, where the internal relation is conceived of as a non-temporal connection holding, for example, in the sentence: "The 100 apples in the box consists of 50 and 50". The internal relation ranges over all kinds of expressions as a timeless, unalterable paradigm for achieving their meaning, which neither reflects any experiment, nor any causal link, nor any logico-analytical compulsion, but the special context of a community of life, where different ingredients occur together. This is also the case of the sentence "White is lighter than black", where "light" and "dark" are not to be conceived of as being the nature or essence inherent in the "white" and the "black" respectively. There is no such inference for Wittgenstein; rather, he puts forward the pictures of a context, of a whole, that of a white patch or of a black patch, which, as he writes, "serves us simultaneously, as a paradigm of what we understand by 'lighter' and 'darker'".[15] Therefore, *darkness* is no part or nature of *black*, but rather they occur together in the same context set up by the pattern of a black patch. At this point we might even say that "dark" and "black" stand or occur together in the same way as some races of mankind and the oak, or the flea and the dog occur together. It is a matter of connection, not of inference. If now we ask how this connection or context arise, the answer would be that all those connections of pictures and names are set up and recognized as paradigms in the language we ordinarily practise.[16] Once language is arrived at, we reach the condition which is responsible for all these connections—for example for that bearing on "black" and "dark"—and beyond which we can't go. In connection with this, we must read such specific sentences of Wittgenstein as: "*This* is how we think. *This* is how we act. *This* is how we talk about it".[17] This constitutive role of language emerges from Wittgenstein's characterization of the internal relation as "a fact of synthesis" (*ein synthetisches Faktum*).[18] Here and elsewhere Wittgenstein insists on rejecting the idea of internal relation as consisting of a connection bearing on the nature itself of things, since, as he says, "nature" and "internal relation" always go together.[19] Pure blue and green considered as the alleged natures independently of language, seem to compel us to say that they have nothing in common. But this overlooks the role of the forms of life and language; in fact, there are as many so-called "natures" of colour as there are ways of dealing with them against the surroundings of our life and our alternative uses of language. Wittgenstein thinks up a culture where there is a common name for green and red on the one hand, and another for yellow and blue on the other; then he supposes that there are a patrician cast wearing red and green garments and a plebeian cast wearing yellow and blue garments. A man who was asked what red and green have in common, might admit that they have in fact something in common, that they are both patrician.[20] Language and not the alleged nature or essence is therefore responsible for such notions as those of similarity, identity, kinship and the like. The internal relations set up a fact of synthesis, a connection of ingredients, as a matter of pure decision, and therefore we could even imagine that if red and yellow always occurred together in a geometrical form, one might be unable to see anything yellow since he has no power of separating them.[21]

So under defined circumstances, a connection gives rise to a pattern of meaning which refers to a cluster of terms having a relation of similarity to one another. If we consider the popular belief in the "Corn-wolf" hidden in the last sheaf of corn which farmers have to bind, it is worth remarking that people call the "corn-wolf" not only the presumed hidden wolf, but also the sheaf itself and even the man who binds it.[22] It is as if a kind of peculiar kinship or similarity covered different things under a common name which relates to different aspects or facets of a connection. But it is the very connection of different ingredients set up in a culture or form of life which is responsible for the halo of this peculiar similarity and makes it possible for a meaning to undergo such changes and shifts. This accounts for the primitive assumption that a name would resemble or fit its bearer, in the sense of being a sort of portrait of that bearer.[23] Of course, this is a trivially false assumption, but it is a symptom of that deeper relation of familiarity owing to a connection established in the situations of human life. Summarizing, since for Wittgenstein meaning can't consist in a thing, in an entity in itself, but only in a context recognized as such by language, without the latter we would be merely confronted with a scattered multiplicity of things. So far there would be no meaning, nor knowledge. In fact, for a meaning to arise, it is necessary to draw lines establishing and linking what is common to a multiplicity of ingredients (behaviour, practices of any sort).[24] But such a pattern is achievable only if we recognize the relation as significant for us. In order to be so, that connection has to relate to the attitudes of our feeling and thought, precisely in the sense that we can recognize an ancient rite as dreadful, as for instance the celebration of a human sacrifice, to the extent that we may attribute this meaning from an experience of our own.[25] This is the reason why Wittgenstein says that if a lion began to speak, we couldn't understand it and writes in 1949 that some aspects of former cultures or writers turn out not to be understandable because they are deprived of their context which gave them their light and colour.[26] Here we find also the deep reason of Wittgenstein's strong rejection of any hypothesis and explanation for the analysis of meaning. The pattern of a causal link as such couldn't reach that internal relation of a manifold of ingredients to one another, which arises only in connection with a *perspective*, a way of looking, which may be significant for us and for the interests guiding our concepts. This new version of the internal relation is underlined by Wittgenstein in several passages of the *Philosophical Investigations:*

> I contemplate a face, and then suddenly notice its likeness to another. I *see* that it has not changed; and yet I see it differently. I call this experience "noticing an aspect" . . . But we can also *see* the illustration now as one thing now as another. —So we interpret it, and *see* it as we *interpret* it . . . But what I perceive in the dawning of an aspect is not a property of the object, but an internal relation between it and other objects. It is almost as if "seeing the sign in this context" were an echo of a thought. "The echo of a thought in sight"—one would like to say.[27]

Consequently, the task which Wittgenstein ascribes to philosophy is not that of *arguing*, but that of *describing* what human life is like.[28] The notion of internal relation is now re-shaped in conformity with the need of having that formal and general representation which let us recognize a line, a common physiognomy connecting the traces of human life, past ones and present ones.

———

ENDNOTES

[1] See Wittgenstein, *Philosophical Investigations* (Oxford 1978), pp. 48, 85; *Remarks on the Foundations of Mathematics* (Oxford 1956), pp. 34, 37−8, 167−68.
[2] See Wittgenstein, *The Blue and Brown Books* (Oxford 1960), pp. 123ff, Wittgenstein (1978), p. 81; Wittgenstein (1956), pp. 184−85.
[3] Wittgenstein, *Notebooks 1914−1916* (Oxford 1961), pp. 26 and 26e.
[4] See Wittgenstein, "Ursache und Wirkung: intuitives Erfassen", *Philosophia* Vol. 6 (1976), p. 440; *Zettel* (Oxford 1967), pp. 55−56.
[5] See Wittgenstein (1960), pp. 158−60, 163, 165, 169, 170, 174−78, 180; *Wittgenstein and the Vienna Circle* (Oxford 1979 a), p. 88.
[6] See Wittgenstein, "Remarks on Frazer's *Golden Bough*", in: C. G. Luckhardt (ed.), *Wittgenstein. Sources and Perspectives* (Hassocks, Sussex 1979 b), p. 62.

[7] See Jaakko Hintikka and Merrill B. Hintikka, "The Development of Wittgensteins Philosophy: The Hidden Unity", in: P. Weingartner and J. Czermak (eds.), *Epistemology and Philosophy of Science. Proceedings of the 7th International Wittgenstein Symposium*. Kirchberg am Wechsel August 1982 (Wien 1983), pp. 433–34; Wittgenstein (1978), p. 99; Wittgenstein (1976), pp. 416–17; P. Winch, "Im Anfang war die Tat", in: I. Block (ed.), *Perspectives on the Philosophy of Wittgenstein* (Oxford 1981), p. 173.

[8] Wittgenstein (1979 b), p. 73.

[9] See Wittgenstein (1979 b), pp. 66–7.

[10] See Wittgenstein (1979 b), p. 69; Wittgenstein (1978), p. 49.

[11] See on this point A. Gargani, "Schlick and Wittgenstein: Language and Experience", *Grazer Philosophische Studien*, vol. 16/17 (1982), pp. 349–55; A. Gargani, "Internal Relations, Syntax and Use in Wittgenstein's Philosophical Analysis" in: P. Weingartner and J. Czermak (eds.); *op. cit.*, pp. 482–87.

[12] See Wittgenstein, *Philosophical Remarks* (Oxford 1975), p. 66.

[13] See Wittgenstein (1979 b), pp. 69, 70, 72.

[14] See R. Musil, "Das Hilflose Europa oder Reise vom Hundertsten ins Tausendste" (1922), in: *Gesammelte Werke* (Hamburg 1978), Bd. 8, p. 1078.

[15] Wittgenstein (1956), pp. 30–1.

[16] See Wittgenstein (1956), p. 30; Wittgenstein (1967), p. 4.

[17] Wittgenstein (1967), p. 57.

[18] Wittgenstein (1956), p. 75.

[19] See Wittgenstein (1976), p. 443.

[20] See Wittgenstein (1960), p. 134.

[21] See Wittgenstein (1956), p. 192.

[22] See Wittgenstein (1979 b), pp. 70–1.

[23] On the relation between name and bearer see R. Rhees, "Wittgenstein über Sprache und Ritus", in: *Wittgenstein Schriften*, Beiheft 3 (Frankfurt a. M. 1979), pp. 53–4.

[24] See Wittgenstein (1979 b), p. 74.

[25] See Wittgenstein (1979 b), p. 77.

[26] See Wittgenstein, *Culture and Value* (Oxford 1980), p. 79.

[27] Wittgenstein (1978), pp. 193, 212.

[28] See Wittgenstein (1979 b), pp. 63, 71.

* * *

WEBERN UND WITTGENSTEIN
VERBINDLICHKEIT DURCH ELEMENTARISIERUNG

Friedrich Wallner
Universität Wien

Die Einstellung Wittgensteins zu normativen Fragen ist wesentlich differenzierter als die Stellungnahme von Mitgliedern des Wiener Kreises: Er sieht jedenfalls, daß es nicht angeht, diese Frage einfach in die Psychologie abzuschieben. Die Behandlung, welche er fordert, könnte man Auflösung zur Übersichtlichkeit nennen. Dieses Verfahren können wir auch in der modernen Kunst entdecken. Denn eine grundlegende Tendenz der modernen Kunst ist die Abkehr von normativen Idealisierungen. Dieser Grundzug moderner Kunst ist sowohl für ihre Problematik wie auch ihre Bedeutung maßgebend. Ihre Problematik zeigt sich besonders in den Rezeptionsschwierigkeiten, denen sie unterliegt: Man vermißt dort die Kunst, wo man nur Gemeinplätze zu sehen vermeint. Ihre Bedeutung liegt darin, möchte ich sagen, daß sie die Wirklichkeit läßt, wie sie ist; d.h. daß sie uns nicht vorgaukelt, tiefer als das Wirkliche zu sein; ihr Beitrag zum Verständnis der Welt liegt nicht in einer ‚tieferen Schau‘, sondern in der Verfremdung. – Ich will mich hier damit auseinandersetzen, ob dieser Gesichtspunkt der spielerischen Verfremdung nicht auch in der Tradition ein wichtiges Moment künstlerischen Schaffens war; die traditionelle Kunsttheorie wie auch die Kunstrezeption sah dies anders: Die Kunstdeutungen beriefen sich gewöhnlich auf normative Vorstellungen – wie das Schöne – und versuchten Kunst von Nicht-Kunst durch Berufung auf überzeitliche Ansprüche zu trennen.

Demgegenüber weist Webern in seinem Vorlesungszyklus ‚Der Weg zur Neuen Musik‘ die Annahme, daß das ‚Ästhetische‘ ein die Kunst bestimmender, aber von der Natur abgehobener, eigenen Gesetzen unterworfener Bereich sei, sozusagen die Welt der Werte des ‚Ewig Schönen‘ zurück. Damit strebt er die Nähe der Kunst zur alltäglichen Lebensgestaltung wie auch zur Natur an. Das bedeutet aber: Das Aufgeben einer normativen Ästhetik fordert keinen Verzicht auf Gesetzmäßigkeit in der Kunst; vielmehr erhalten ‚Gesetze‘ der Kunst eine andere Funktion und einen anderen Sinn als bisher. Webern formuliert so: „Wie der Naturforscher sich bemüht, die Gesetzmäßigkeiten zu finden, die der Natur zugrunde liegen, so muß es unser Bestreben sein, die Gesetze zu finden, unter denen die Natur in der besonderen Form des Menschen produktiv ist."[1]

Man könnte hier sagen: Was Webern an die Stelle der traditionellen Ästhetik setzt, ist eine Naturlehre mit anthropologischer Pointe. Diese anthropologische Dimension verdeutlicht er durch seinen Begriff von ‚Handwerkslehre‘: Die Gesetze muß der Musiker in seine Handwerkslehre einbringen. Hier erhält das alte Prinzip ‚ars imitatur naturam‘ einen neuen Sinn: Die Natur wird nicht bloß nachgebildet, sondern in der Kunst gleichsam entfaltet. Naturwissenschaft und Kunst stehen hier nicht unter der Devise ‚Wahrheit versus Schein‘ einander gegenüber, sondern die Kunst erhält den Primat gegenüber der Naturwissenschaft.

Die mathematische Naturbeschreibung der Neuzeit trägt das Stigma einer vom Handeln des Menschen absehenden Abstraktion gegenüber einem Naturbegriff der Kunst, in welchem Natürlichkeit und menschliches Handeln integriert sind. (Daß etwa zur gleichen Zeit in der Physik die Subjektsproblematik aufbrach, ist ein interessantes geistesgeschichtliches Faktum, auf das wir im Rahmen dieses Vortrags nur hinweisen können!)

In der dritten Vorlesung des Zyklus ‚Der Weg zur Neuen Musik‘ führt Webern aus:

> Der Gedanke ist verteilt im Raum, er ist nicht allein in einer Stimme – sie kann allein den Gedanken nicht ausdrücken –, nur die Vereinigung der Stimmen bringt den Gedanken ganz zum Ausdruck . . . Wir wollen die Prinzipien behandeln, wie der Tonbereich allmählich ausgenützt wurde – das von der Natur im Ton Gegebene.[2]

Hier werden irreführende Äquivokationen deutlich: ‚Raum' ist nichts Phänomenales, sondern der logische Raum, ‚Natur' sind die ‚logischen Möglichkeiten'! – Doch die Formulierungen sind hier so locker, daß einer nachträglichen Interpretation in gleichsam mythologisierender Art nichts im Wege steht: ‚Raum' könnten wir als ‚Kosmos des Tonbereichs' umschreiben, ‚Natur' als die Sinn ermöglichende Ordnung der logischen Möglichkeiten. Doch solche Deutungen sind bloße Allegorien, welche für den Gang der Argumentation keine Rolle spielen. Vielmehr erinnern Weberns Ausführungen an dieser Stelle recht deutlich an das Konzept der Konfigurationen im logischen Raum, das in Wittgensteins „Tractatus logico-philosophicus" eine zentrale Rolle spielt.

Weberns Synthese von Handlung und Natur geschieht nicht vor dem Hintergrund des einheitlichen Sinnes von Natur und menschlicher Vollendung; vielmehr bewegt sich seine Synthese von Natur und Handeln in einer durch abstrakte Verschärfung dieser Begriffe härteren Problemlage; man könnte sagen: Diese Synthese ist bei Webern eine dialektische, nämlich eine der Dialektik von Naturkausalität und Kausalität aus Freiheit.

Eine weitere Analyse dieser Problematik würde im Hinblick auf Webern nichts mehr bringen; er schreibt nicht als Berufsphilosoph. Auf diesen dialektischen Aspekt wollte er aber vermutlich hinweisen, wenn er die Wendung ‚Naturwerke von Menschen' mit besonderer Emphase verwendet.

Wenn Webern in seiner ersten Vorlesung im ersten Zyklus (‚Der Weg zur Neuen Musik') eine lange Passage aus dem Aufsatz über die Sprache zitiert, welchen Karl Kraus am Ende des Jahres 1932 in der Fackel[3] veröffentlichte, so ist dies nicht bloß eine intellektuelle Verbeugung vor einem originellen und vieldiskutierten Zeitgenossen; vielmehr hebt damit der wesentlichste Gedankenstrang, welcher die beiden Vorlesungszyklen durchzieht, an: Es ist dies Weberns Bemühung um eine neue Ontologie der Musik; nämlich weg von der ästhetischen Unmittelbarkeit zu der Verschränkung von Unmittelbarkeit und Reflexion, wie sie die Sprache – schlechthin – kennzeichnet. Diese intellektuelle Leistung läßt mich Webern als Genie bewundern.

Ich möchte – in Parenthese – darauf hinweisen, daß dieser Aspekt einer Umgestaltung der Musiktheorie auch für die angemessene Beurteilung der Entwicklung, welche die Musik nach Webern genommen hat, wesentlich ist. Hier muß noch viel Forschungsarbeit geleistet werden.

Gestatten Sie mir an dieser Stelle einen scherzhaften Hinweis: Weberns ‚Sprachontologie' der Musik hat natürlich nichts mit dem geflügelten Wort von der ‚Sprache der Musik' zu tun. Doch gerade die Trivialität dieser Floskel läßt uns die Genialität Anton von Weberns erahnen: Sie liegt in der Differenz der Sätze ‚Mit der Sprache verständigen wir uns' und ‚Durch die Sprache wird uns die Welt erschlossen'.

Hier erscheint es mir hilfreich, auf die Terminologie des jungen Wittgenstein zurückzugreifen. Danach ist der erste Satz sinnlos, der zweite unsinnig. D.h., der erste Satz bietet uns keine Information; wir könnten darauf antworten: ‚Womit denn sonst?'. Der zweite Satz aber überschreitet die Grenzen der Sprache; ihm liegt eine Unterscheidung zugrunde, welche die Sprache nicht in sinnvoller Weise machen kann: die Unterscheidung zwischen sprachlich nicht erschlossener und sprachlich erschlossener Welt; oder – mit anderen Worten – zwischen vorsprachlicher und sprachlicher Welt. Dennoch hat ein Satz, wie der zitierte unsinnige, eine wichtige Funktion: er ‚zeigt' die Grenzen der Sprache; er begrenzt die Sprache sozusagen von innen, denn von außen ist sie nicht zu begrenzen.

Hier muß eine methodologische Anmerkung gemacht werden: Dieser kurze Exkurs über den sprachphilosophischen Ansatz des jungen Wittgenstein ist nicht in wirkungsgeschichtlicher Attitüde vorgebracht worden. Zwar könnte Webern den Tractatus logico-philosophicus gekannt haben; wahrscheinlich hat er davon zumindest gehört (schließlich fand dieses Buch bei der intellektuellen Avantgarde Wiens in der Zwischenkriegszeit einige Beachtung): Es gibt tatsächlich ein paar Stellen in Weberns theoretischen Schriften, die eine Anspielung auf Wittgenstein-Sätze vermuten lassen; doch meines Erachtens reichen die Belege für eine derartige wirkungsgeschichtliche These nicht aus.

Demgegenüber soll unser Exkurs nur eine methodologische Hilfe für das Herausarbeiten der Gedanken Weberns liefern. (Offenbar hat sein unscharfer und schwankender Gebrauch von Begriffen verschuldet, daß seine großartige Leistung einer Umgestaltung der Musiktheorie bisher nicht in voller Klarheit gesehen wurde!)

In der dritten Vorlesung des zweiten Zyklus (‚Der Weg zur Komposition in zwölf Tönen‘) sagt Webern: „Dieses Umkreisen – das die Dinge nie beim richtigen Namen nennen – lauter Stellvertreter für die Grundakkorde einsetzen – alles, was gemeint ist, lieber offenlassen – das ist der Charakter der Komposition in zwölf Tönen!"[4]

Hätten wir nicht bereits begriffsanalytische Vorarbeit geleistet, so müßten wir hier ausrufen: ‚Wie ist dies mit Weberns Prinzipien der Klarheit und Faßlichkeit konsistent?‘ – Tatsächlich aber ist diese Passage eine gute Paraphrase des Konzepts eines ‚unsinnigen Satzes‘. Er ist zunächst dadurch gekennzeichnet, daß er Zeichen ohne strikte – d.h. Gegenständen zugeordnete – Bedeutung verwendet. Dieser Satztyp erhob in der traditionellen Philosophie den Anspruch, tiefe Einsichten zu vermitteln. Dies tut er tatsächlich, aber in indirekter Weise (‚lauter Stellvertreter‘); er umkreist gleichsam die sinnvolle Sprache, da er ständig ihre Grenzen zu überschreiten sich anschickt. Diese Parallele zwischen den ‚unsinnigen (also den philosophischen) Sätzen‘ und der Zwölftontechnik macht auch die Rolle von Klarheit und Faßlichkeit verständlich. Diese ‚zeigen‘ sich vermittels der Kompositionen in zwölf Tönen. D.h., durch solche Kompositionen wird Klarheit und Faßlichkeit im Bereich des Gehörs sichtbar.

Nach dieser Deutung kann man auch die folgende Behauptung Weberns verstehen: „Das Gehör hat absolut richtig entschieden, daß der Mensch, der die chromatische Skala aufgeschrieben und in ihr einzelne Töne abgestrichen hat, *kein Narr war.*"[5]

Dieser Satz müßte dunkel bleiben, wenn wir das Entscheiden des Gehörs als subjektive Leistung der Musikalität auffassen. Anderseits wäre diese Behauptung ein Rückfall in einen naiven ästhetischen Dogmatismus, wenn wir hier ‚Gehör‘ als eine übersubjektive inhaltlich-normierende Instanz auffaßten. Nach unserer Deutung hat hier ‚Gehör‘ dieselbe Funktion wie bei Wittgenstein ‚die Sprache‘: Wie bestimmte Sprachhandlungen das Neue, bisher Unverständliche verstehbar machen, so werden durch ganz bestimmte Aktionen im Tonbereich die erwähnten Manipulationen mit der chromatischen Skala verstehbar; d.h. es ist eine ihnen angemessene Sprache gefunden worden.

Dies bedeutet aber: Eine Legitimation des künstlerischen Tuns ist weder nötig noch möglich. – Die von Webern in den beiden Vorlesungszyklen aufgestellten Behauptungen sind demnach nicht als Legitimation der Zwölftonmusik aufzufassen: als solche würden sie nur eine methodisch ungenügende wissenschaftliche Arbeit darstellen. Fassen wir sie aber als Sprachspiele, in denen die Zwölftonmusik behandelt und gleichsam vielfältig variiert wird, auf, so verschwinden diese Schwierigkeiten: Die Vorlesungen erweisen sich als eine Anzahl von Sprachspielen, deren Begrenzungen nicht mit den Vorlesungsgrenzen ident sind; sie stellen Angebote an den Hörer bzw. Leser dar, die Zwölftonmusik sprachlich zu bewältigen.

In der achten Vorlesung des zweiten Zyklus (‚Der Weg zur Komposition in zwölf Tönen‘) führt Webern aus:

> Wenn man zu dieser richtigen Auffassung der Kunst kommt, dann kann es keinen Unterschied mehr geben zwischen Wissenschaft und inspiriertem Schaffen. Je weiter man vordringt, um so identischer wird alles, und man hat zuletzt den Eindruck, keinem Menschenwerk gegenüberzustehen, sondern der Natur.[6]

Würde man dies wörtlich nehmen, so müßte man von einem sehr naiven Szientismus oder von phantastischer Schwärmerei in science-fiction-Art sprechen. (Hier wird verständlich, warum Weberns Theorie in der geistigen Landschaft des 20. Jahrhunderts nicht jene Beachtung gefunden hat, die sie verdient!)

Unserer Deutung aber setzt diese Passage eine interessante Pointe auf: Wissenschaft und inspiriertes Schaffen werden einander in wesentlichen Gesichtspunkten gleich. Die Intuition hat für beide Bereiche die gleiche Funktion, nämlich eine heuristische; sie verliert für das künstlerische Schaffen ihren Legitimationsaspekt; die Kunst hat ebenso eine Sprachspielstruktur erhalten wie die Wissenschaft. Anderseits ist die Rechtfertigungsstruktur der Wissenschaft p r i n z i p i e l l von jener der Kunst nicht zu unterscheiden: Die Begründungen haben ihr Ende, sobald man an die Grenzen der Sprache stößt. An diesem Punkt wird alles identisch; man gelangt nämlich zu ‚unsinnigen Sätzen', die nichts sagen. Von ihren Grenzen aus erhält die Sprache einen Voraussetzungscharakter, welcher der Vorausgesetztheit der Natur für die sinnliche Unmittelbarkeit vergleichbar ist.

In den Vorlesungen Anton v. Weberns werden nicht Sprachspiele der Theorie oder Metatheorie – wie man zunächst meint –, sondern Sprachspiele der Verfremdung angeboten. Damit meinen wir Sprachspiele, welche die ‚rationale Argumentation' in solcher Art verfremden, daß die Grenzen der Rationalität sichtbar werden.

Es ist ein häufig antreffbares Mißverständnis, daß solche Sprachspiele eine destruktive Funktion hätten. Dies trifft deshalb nicht zu, da diese Sprachspiele n i c h t denselben Argumentationsstatus beanspruchen wie wissenschaftliche Sprachspiele (hier sind natürlich auch die Sprachspiele der Kunstwissenschaften gemeint!), sondern – um es mit Wittgenstein zu sagen – an der Wissenschaft (und auch an der Kunst) vorbeireden. Damit zerstören sie n i c h t die wissenschaftlichen bzw. künstlerischen Sprachspiele, sondern zeigen nur ihre Grenzen auf; d.h. sie machen die Regeln der jeweiligen Sprachspiele, die ja immer eine gewisse Unschärfe haben, expliziter. Man kann in diesem Fall von therapeutischen Sprachspielen reden.

Weberns Argumentation für die Zwölftontheorie ist eine ganz andere als jene von Schönberg und Hauer. Während der erstere von einer liberalen Ontologie her und der zweite dogmatisch aus dem Horizont strenger, von ihm als notwendig einsichtig ausgegebenen Gesetzen argumentiert, geht Webern den indirekten Weg. Zugrunde liegt die Einsicht, daß metatheoretische wie metaphysische Legitimierungen versagen: „... die Gründe werden mir bald ausgehen. Und ich werde dann, ohne Gründe, handeln."[7]

Doch dies ist nur bei Erreichen einer gewissen Übersichtlichkeit möglich; diese verschafft sich Webern durch seine Verfremdungsstrategien.

ANMERKUNGEN

[1] *Der Weg zur Neuen Musik,* hg. von Willi Reich (Wien 1960), S. 11.
[2] Webern, *Der Weg zur Neuen Musik,* S. 20.
[3] Nr. 885/7.
[4] a.a.o., S. 51.
[5] a.a.o., S. 55.
[6] a.a.o., S. 60.
[7] *PU* I, 211. Vgl. dazu auch *Über Gewißheit,* §§ 148, 196, 229, 232, 395 und 431.

* * *

SCEPTICAL ARGUMENTS AND PSYCHOLOGICAL CONCEPTS

Salma Saab
National University of Mexico

My main concern in this paper is to reflect upon Wittgenstein's attitude towards the philosophical problem of scepticism and the way in which general considerations about scepticism underlie some of the main problems that preocuppied him, especially in the philosophical works of his later period. I am particularly interested in the bearing of scepticims about rules and rule-following. For purposes of simplicity, I will focus my attention almost exclusively on the *Philosophical Investigations*.

I

Wittgenstein shares with an increasing number of philosophers nowadays the view that one should not take sceptical considerations seriously. In this point, as in many others, Wittgenstein takes a different stand from the dominant philosophical tradition. But the novelty of his position lies in its departure point: that of *not* accepting the sceptical challenge on the grounds that, in itself, it is an illegitimate and incomprehensible standpoint. He considers that the philosophers who have tried to contravene the sceptics' arguments, have gone wrong in that they thought that their arguments were sound, and their worries profound, when in fact they are vacuous. Wittgenstein dedicates a long part of *On Certainty* to a discussion of this.

Let me develop the point a bit. The big mistake of the philosophers that tried to attack the sceptical position is to think that it is a matter that should be approached *via* arguments, i.e. that our knowledge claims *can* and *should* be justified in all cases by means of reasons. For Wittgenstein this cannot be so, for many of the things we claim to know, as well as many of our beliefs, are arrived at unreflectively, while doubt comes after belief and not the other way around. Moreover, he regards the notion of knowledge as primarily a capacity or skill concept, i.e. as a *knowing how*, although he admits that this is not the only type of knowledge. In particular, the relationship which he sees between practical knowledge and theoretical or propositional knowledge is that the former is prior to the latter.

Unlike the notion of knowledge, the notion of doubt, which sceptics – among others – have linked to the notion of knowledge, is the product of a reflective attitude: we do not doubt something unless there is a specific reason for doing so; unless there is something that triggers the doubt. In this sense, doubt *has* to have a reason. In the sceptical position the tables are turned, so that the doubt is always in place and in consequence we can question all our knowledge claims. For Wittgenstein the sceptical attitude far from being justified, reveals an obsessive attitude, or to say the least, an unnatural one to us, and a position which at bottom presupposes a misunderstanding of the nature of doubt. Wittgenstein writes:

> Doesn't a presupposition imply a doubt? And doubt may be entirely lacking. Doubting has an end.[1]

In the same way that doubts come to an end, so do justifications or explanations. The end is not arbitrary or conventional, but arrived at naturally when the circumstances do not generate any further doubts, or there is not any reason for our suspicion. On the other hand, for the sceptic, the doubts are silenced or suppressed completely only when we achieve certainty or possess conclusive reasons. For example in paragraph 87 Wittgenstein says:

Suppose I give this explanation: "I take 'Moses' to mean the man, if there was such a man, who led the Israelites out of Egypt, whatever he was called then and whatever he may or may not have done besides."—But similar doubts to those about 'Moses' are possible about the words of this explanation (what are you calling "Egypt", whom the "Israelites" etc.?). Nor would these questions come to an end when we got down to words like "red", "dark", "sweet".—"But then how does an explanation help me to understand, if after all it is not the final one? In that case the explanation is never completed; so I still don't understand what he means, and never shall!"—As though an explanation as it were hung in the air unless supported by another one. Whereas an explanation may indeed rest on another one that has been given, but none stand in need of another—unless *we* require it to prevent a misunderstanding. One might say: an explanation serves to remove or to avert a misunderstanding—one, that is, that would occur but for the explanation; not every one that I can imagine.

It may easily look as if every doubt merely *revealed* an existing gap in the foundations; so that secure understanding is only possible if we first doubt everything that *can* be doubted, and then remove all these doubts.

The sign-post is in order—if, under normal circumstances, it fulfils its purpose.

Some recent commentators upon Wittgenstein's work, for example R. Fogelin[2] and S. Kripke[3] have stressed the affinity of Wittgenstein's thought to that of Hume in terms both of the attitude towards scepticism and of the importance attached to the natural attitudes of human beings—as opposed to their understanding.

Indeed, for Wittgenstein our natural attitudes and responses are what guide—and lie at the basis of—our actions and therefore of what we believe and claim to know. Wittgenstein regards the sceptical attitude as contrary to our natural inclinations: so in the same way that we do *not choose* our natural inclinations, we cannot choose to be sceptics.[4] Furthermore, the adoption of scepticism would be irrational since it would involve the cancellation of all possible courses of action.

So much for the main general remarks that Wittgenstein makes with respect to scepticism; now I pass on to consider their bearing upon rules.

II

When Wittgenstein begins his dicussion of rules, he has already emphasized that we go amiss if we follow the path of searching for definitions. Thus, the error behind the search for *the* meaning of a concept, *the* meaning of a rule, *the* logical form of propositions, *the* essence of language, etc. . The idea that there are fixed essential features of concepts has obliterated the multiplicity of uses that these concepts have, which for Wittgenstein are irreducible to any common feature. From these reflections emerges one of the central notions of the *Investigations*, i.e. that of a family-resemblance. For Wittgenstein the notion of knowledge is itself a family resemblance concept, which requires that it be linked to the contexts of use within which the speakers of the community employ it.

The discussion of rules is carried along with a discussion of many other psychological verbs, such as reading, understanding, signify, expect, desire, intend, etc. . One reason for dealing with this whole range of verbs is to reinforce the idea that, in spite of the fact that they are grouped together as psychological verbs, they function differently in our language, so that we need to attend more to their differences than to their similarities. Nevertheless, for Wittgenstein, one thing is true about all of these verbs, which is that none should be regarded as referring to an independent mental act, detached from, and prior to, the behaviour connected with it. Moreover, he claims that predication of any of these verbs to somebody depends on what the person does.

Thus, in the specific case of rules, we can properly say whether a person has understood a given rule by observing what she or he does. Wittgenstein, aware that this response might seem unsatisfactory to many philosophers, among them the sceptic, goes on to explain why he thinks the response might seem inadequate. One reason would be that it fails to exclude the possibility of someone giving the right answer without understanding the rule. For example, someone might correctly give the series 2, 4, 6, 8, . . ., when asked to "add 2" to each number, and another person might have a different function in mind and still produce the same series. In other words, the answer might be compatible both with the understanding and the not understanding of the rule, hence the need of something else that could discriminate the two cases. But we have seen that for Wittgenstein this possibility involves a detachment of our grasp of the rules from its application, which is illegitimate. In general, doing the right thing is a reliable criterion of understanding and we should not require that in order to be so it would have to rule out the other possibilities.

According to Wittgenstein, once we are hooked in the sceptical manner of looking at things, it is easy to see that the simple agreement in responses—i.e.something external and observable is not enough; hence the inclination to search for the difference in something inside the subject. One such response is to say that in the case of genuine knowledge or understanding, the subject has a rule that makes him give the right response, whereas in the case of merely *seeming* to know or to understand the subject either lacks such a rule altogether, or is guided by a different rule.

The sceptic would disregard this reply because it would still be possible to have the same rule and interpret it in a deviant way. We would need another rule to interpret it, and so on *ad infinitum*.

If we took the sceptical challenge seriously, the only satisfactory answer would be a rule that somehow contained in it all its applications and in that way the rule would fix or predetermine all its future applications. In this way we would have some sort of "mental rails" that would compel us to follow a rule in a specific manner. We could regard orders, as well as other psychological verbs, in a similar way and get a model like the one that Wittgenstein presents in paragraph 188:

> Here I should first of all like to say: your idea was that that act of meaning the order had in its own way already traversed all those steps: that when you meant it your mind as it were flew ahead and completed all the steps before you physically arrived at this or that one.
> Thus you were inclined to use such expressions as: "The steps are *really* already taken, even before I take them in writing or orally or in thought". And it seemed as if they were in some *unique* way predetermined, anticipated—as only the act of meaning can anticipate reality.

For Wittgenstein, the sceptical strategy far from resolving the difficulty, would generate it again at the level of the expression of the rule.[5] The upshot of this mistake is the following paradox, which commentators have discussed at great length:

> This was our paradox: no course of action could be determined by a rule, because every course of action can be made out to accord with the rule. The answer was: if everything can be made out to accord with the rule, then it can also be made out to conflict with it. And so there would be neither accord nor conflict here.
> It can be seen that there is a misunderstanding here from the mere fact that in the course of our argument we give one interpretation after another; as if each one contented us at least for a moment, until we thought of yet another standing behind it. What this shews is that there is a way of grasping a rule which is *not* an *interpretation*, but which is exhibited in what we call "obeying a rule" and "going against it" in actual cases.
> Hence there is an inclination to say: every action according to the rule is an interpretation. But we ought to restrict the term "interpretation" to the substitution of one expression of the rule for another.[6]

My interpretation of this passage is that what is expressed in the second paragraph is Wittgenstein's own suggestion: that there is a way of grasping or understanding a rule which does not need an interpretation, understood as something added to the expression of the rule. In the next section (202) Wittgenstein adds that there cannot be a private use; rather, what is necessary is that each person's usage be connected with what the other members of the community do in similar circumstances. By demanding this, a uniformity of use, without needing to rule out a deviant rule with the same result, Wittgenstein thereby refuses to enter on the path which would inevitably lead to the paradox.

Wittgenstein holds the view that in some circumstances, such as in learning situations, the agreement in usage is a good enough criterion because in such cases the training plays the role of a rule. It is in these cases that you grasp a rule without need of a further interpretation.

If we appealed to a rule in order to justify its application, this will lead us to suppose that in order for the rule to do this, i.e. be a criterion of the application, they have to be independent of each other, and have one prior to the other. As if we could have a way of grasping the meaning of a rule, independently of its use. Wittgenstein's objection seems to be that there is an unnecessary duplication of criteria, that this would be as absurd as supposing that one can know the construction of a machine independently of what it does.[7] The correct way of looking at the matter is to understand the relationship between a rule and its applications as an *internal* relation. I take rules, on Wittgenstein's view, as being neither so rigid as to exclude all possibilities except one, nor so indeterminate as to make every claim to be following the rule.

In Kripke's interpretation both the argument that leads to the paradox and Wittgenstein's solution are marked as sceptical. He claims that his scepticism is shown not only in the specific considerations that he makes about rules, but also in his general considerations about language.

For Kripke, the sceptical challenge takes two forms that correspond to the ontological and epistemological aspects of the problem: on the ontological side Wittgenstein would question that there is a *fact*, a mental fact, that constitutes the meaning of the concept, and on the epistemological side, he would question that there are reasons to be confident or certain of our responses. For Kripke, the relationship between these two aspects is the following: "I am confident of what I should answer, because this answer accords with what I *meant*."[8] And as we have seen, the answer does not exclude other answers, thus I cannot be sure of my own answer. On the other hand, we could have made the same answer, with or without this specific rule in mind, so the appeal to it is futile. For Kripke this amounts to siding with the sceptic, since every new use would be as inexplicable and mysterious as a "leap in the dark".

I agree with Kripke that the strategy that Wittgenstein adopts is similar to Hume's, and to many other philosophers, in that "he advocates a view apparently in patent contradiction with common sense. Rather than repudiating common sense, he asserts that the conflict comes from a philosophical misinterpretation of common-language."[9] Thus, Wittgenstein's solution to his own sceptical problem, according to Kripke, "begins by agreeing with the sceptics that there is no 'superlative fact' about my mind that constitutes my meaning addition by 'plus' and determines in advance what I should do to accord with this meaning."[10]

Kripke thinks that questioning the link between past "meanings" and future practice is analogous to questioning the link between the past and the future. Kripke also holds that this analogy should not obscure the point that the future applications are not guaranteed, or for that matter justified, by the past ones. Whereas I see the problem as one of illegitimately separating the meaning from its application, be it present or future. The nexus should be seen neither as a justification nor as totally mysterious, but rather as grammatical.

Kripke appeals to some conditional forms to illustrate Wittgenstein's move aimed at rejecting the idea that there must be a *fact* that explains the meaning of concepts. He calls it the inversion of the conditional that consists in saying, for example, not that we condemn certain acts because they are immoral, but that the acts are immoral because we condemn them. Or as Hume would have it, it is not that the fire is constantly associated with the heat because the fire causes the heat, but that the fire causes the heat because they are constantly associated. Similarly, Wittgenstein would say that we do not all say that $2 + 2 = 4$ because we all grasp the concept of addition, but that we all grasp the concept of addition because we all say that $2 + 2 = 4$. The first conditional forms in these examples is wrong, and is the form that commits us to the acceptance of facts.[11] More precisely Kripke says that we accept its contraposed form: the failure of a person to come up with the particular response that the community regards as right leads the community to suppose that he is not following the rule.

But again, Kripke considers that the rejection of the facts of this sort is a consequence of the possibilities to which the sceptic makes reference, and that in this point Wittgenstein agrees with the sceptic. But I consider that the theoretical possibilities to which the sceptic refers, the ones that underlie the discussion that leads to the paradox, are illegitimate from their very formulation: that the point which Wittgenstein wants to make in bringing them in is to illustrate how and why we should not argue in that way. Moreover, I think that Wittgenstein's rejection of the internalized model of language-use and of rules, does not rely on sceptical considerations. You only need to get rid of a wrong characterization of rules: the idea of rules that fix or determine their future uses.

The most I would say is that both the sceptical position and the philosophers that are looking for essences or definitions of concepts in terms of essential attributes go wrong because they are engaging in idle enterprises. But they differ in that in the case of the philosophers that search for definitions they can be offered reasons that could convince them that their search is futile, whereas in the case of the sceptics this rational route is ineffective. I take it that for Wittgenstein we would need to have a different form of life and to react differently from the way we do in order even to understand their objections. The sceptical challenge is as incomprehensible to us as is the question of wether the lion spoke since even if the lion spoke we would not understand him

Thus, I conclude that Wittgenstein renounces the fiction that the philosophical searchers of essences tried to make real, and that this fiction is different from the fiction in which the sceptic wants to seize us. Nevertheless the disease of both is similar: to create fictions. And for both cases the cure is to unveil the phantasmagorical character of that which they have taken as true.

ENDNOTES

[1] Wittgenstein, L., *Philosophical Investigation* (Oxford 1963), p. 180e,
[2] Fogelin, R., *Wittgenstein* (London 1976).
[3] Kripke, S., *Wittgenstein on Rules and Private Language* (Cambridge, Mass., 1982).
[4] Wittgenstein, ibid., p. 224e.
[5] Ibid.,
[6] Ibid., prg. 201.
[7] Ibid. prg. 193.
[8] Kripke, Op. cit. p. 11.
[8] Ibid. p. 65.
[10] Ibid. p. 65.
[11] Ibid. pp. 93−4, note.

* * *

WITTGENSTEINS WAHRHEIT ODER „KANN MAN DIE WIRKUNG DER ERFAHRUNG AUF UNSER SYSTEM VON ANNAHMEN LEUGNEN?" (*ÜG* § 134)

Armin Burkhardt
Technische Hochschule Darmstadt

0. Wahrheit ist eine Eigenschaft von Sätzen. Das ist eine sprachanalytische Entdeckung, die auf dem Gebiet der Wahrheitstheorie zumindest einige metaphysische Spekulationen hat abschneiden helfen. Die Beantwortung der Frage aber, worin genau Wahrheit besteht, wird auch heute in der Philosophie gewöhnlich an den Begriff *Übereinstimmung* delegiert: Ist Wahrheit die Übereinstimmung der Menschen in ihren Überzeugungen oder die der Sätze mit einer vorausgesetzten Realität oder mit dem System unserer übrigen Überzeugungen?

Im folgenden soll gezeigt werden, wie Wittgenstein in seiner Spätphilosophie den kohärenztheoretischen Ansatz durch die Einbeziehung letztlich semantischer Fragen und ihrer Voraussetzungen zwar ein Stück weiter bringt, den entscheidenden Schritt aber doch ausläßt.

1. Daß Wittgensteins Spätphilosophie ein kohärenztheoretischer Wahrheitsbegriff zugrundeliegt, wird vielleicht am deutlichsten in einer Formulierung wie der folgenden:

> Wir lernen in der Praxis des empirischen Urteilens nicht, indem wir Regeln lernen; es werden uns *Urteile* beigebracht und ihr Zusammenhang mit andern Urteilen. *Ein Ganzes* von Urteilen wird uns plausibel gemacht. (*ÜG* § 140; vgl. dazu auch *ÜG* §§ 141, 142, 144; 156, 273f und 410)

Wahrheit setzt für Wittgenstein ein kollektives System von Urteilen voraus, das der Einzelne − zumindest in seinen Kernaussagen − lernt (vgl. dazu *ÜG* §§ 279 und 298). Weil über die Erziehung die (doppelte) Übereinstimmung mit einem Wissenssystem erreicht wird, das zugleich intersubjektiv ist, kann Wittgenstein erklären, das, woran er festhalte, sei „nicht *ein* Satz, sondern ein Nest von Sätzen" (*ÜG* § 225). Das Nest ist ein Ort des Wohnens und der Geborgenheit in der Gemeinschaft, es ist nichts anderes als das „Weltbild", nämlich „der überkommene Hintergrund, auf welchem ich zwischen wahr und falsch unterscheide." (*ÜG* § 94) Was also unseren individuellen Urteilen „Sicherheit" verleiht, ist deren Übereinstimmung mit dem kollektiven Bezugssystem. Über die Sicherheit des Bezugssystems selbst ist damit zunächst noch nichts gesagt.

1.1 An dieser Stelle beginnt Wittgenstein, einige Schritte zu tun, die über die simple Grundkonzeption der Kohärenztheorie hinausführen. Zunächst einmal setzt Wahrheit − wie ihre Voraussetzung, das Wissen − eine Art Urvertrauen in die Überlieferung voraus, das selber nicht weiter zu begründen ist, denn „Am Grunde des begründeten Glaubens liegt der unbegründete Glaube" (*ÜG* § 253), der sich nur auf eine eingespielte Praxis stützen kann. Sozialisation beruht für Wittgenstein wesentlich darauf, daß wir lernen zu glauben und zu vertrauen; dies ist es, was er das „Naturgesetz des ‚Fürwahrhaltens'" (*ÜG* § 172) nennt. Die Frage der Verläßlichkeit unseres Bezugssystems und damit unseres Wissens wird aber dadurch nur eine Stufe weiter nach hinten geschoben: Wenn unsere Erfahrung des kollektiven Bezugssystems als der „vergangenen Erfahrung" (*ÜG* § 275) selber auf unserer Erfahung der Vertrauenswürdigkeit unserer Mitmenschen und so der Überlieferung beruht, so ist eben diese Erfahrung das, was zu klären wäre. Eine Absicherung der Erfahrung über die Erfahrung (der Vertrauenswürdigkeit) ist nicht möglich, ohne in einen infiniten Regreß zu geraten, den Wittgenstein nur dadurch abwenden kann, daß er ihn abschneidet durch das Postulat der Unhintergehbarkeit der „Praxis", wenn er z.B. formuliert:

Ich habe von Kind auf so urteilen gelernt. *Das ist* urteilen. (*ÜG* § 128; vgl. auch § 130f.)

1.2 Auch dieser Versuch, das menschliche Wissen an den Urgrund einer nicht weiter hinterfragbaren Praxis zu binden, kann nicht befriedigen. Wittgenstein geht daher noch einen Schritt weiter, wenn er auf das negative Wissen, den Zweifel zu sprechen kommt und dabei die selbstgestellte Frage „Was für einen Grund habe ich, Lehrbüchern der Experimentalphysik zu trauen?" mit der Feststellung beantwortet, er habe „keinen Grund, ihnen nicht zu trauen" (*ÜG* § 600).

Bereits bei C. S. Peirce kann man lernen, daß Zweifel einen Grund voraussetzt und daß jeder „Von-vornherein-Skeptizismus eine bloße Selbsttäuschung [. . .] und kein wirklicher Zweifel" ist.[1] Wittgenstein gelangt hier noch auf zweierlei Weise über die Peircesche Kritik an der Cartesischen Methode des universalen Zweifels hinaus, indem er erstens darauf hinweist, daß jeder Zweifel die Unterstellung der Wahrheit anderer Sätze voraussetzt, ein universaler Zweifel daher logisch unmöglich (*ÜG* § 341) und ein „Zweifel, der an allem zweifelte" kein Zweifel ist (*ÜG* § 450; vgl. dazu auch 625), und zweitens hervorhebt, daß jeder Zweifel nicht nur bereits von seinem Begriff her die Wahrheit anderer Sätze, sondern auch den Besitz von Sprache voraussetzt: Wer zweifelt, muß zumindest die Wörter des bezweifelten Satzes kennen. Weil die Beherrschung der Sprache jedem Zweifel notwendig vorausgeht, gehört die „Zweifellosigkeit zum Wesen des Sprachspiels" (*ÜG* § 370). Insofern ist also unser Vertrauen gerechtfertigt.

1.3 Wenn der Zweifel die Verfügbarkeit der Begriffe und der grammatischen Regeln voraussetzt, so gilt dies natürlich umso mehr für das Wissen. Wahrheit ist an das Funktionieren einer Überlieferung gebunden, die in erster Linie eine sprachliche ist. Weil wir alle im Verständnis unserer Begriffe annähernd übereinstimmen, die wir im Verlauf unserer Sozialisation gelernt haben, können wir überhaupt wissen, was wahr und falsch ist. Erst die intersubjektive Sicherung unserer Sprache und einer geschichtlichen Tradition in einer Gemeinschaft ermöglichen subjektive Urteile über das Bestehen von Sachverhalten auf objektiver, d.h. kollektiv gesicherter Grundlage. Das Wissen eines Sachverhalts setzt das Wissen der Bedeutung der Bestandteile des diesen beschreibenden Satzes voraus: „Und der Begriff des Wissens ist mit dem des Sprachspiels verkoppelt." (*ÜG* § 560) Über die Sprache erst ist ein nicht-subjektives Wahrheitskriterium möglich.

Überein s t i m m u n g − wie sie in *PU* § 241 postuliert wird − bedeutet wesentlich: mit einer Stimme, d.h. dieselbe Sprache sprechen, dasselbe Begriffssystem, dieselbe „Lebensform" haben. Es heißt auch: dieselben Ähnlichkeiten zwischen den Dingen sehen, dieselben Kategorisierungen durchführen und im Prinzip dieselben Urteile fällen.

> Alles Sprachspiel beruht darauf, daß Wörter und Gegenstände wiedererkannt werden. Wir lernen mit der gleichen Unerbittlichkeit, daß dies ein Sessel ist, wie daß $2 \times 2 = 4$ ist. (*ÜG* § 455)

Das Lernen der Sprache, die „Abrichtung" (*PU* § 6), liegt also am Anfang aller Übereinstimmung. Hier, beim Postulat der Unhinterfragbarkeit der sprachlichen Sozialisation bzw. der „Lebensform" und der „Unerbittlichkeit" des Lernens, ist der Grund erreicht, auf dem Wittgensteins Variante der Kohärenztheorie ruht. Darum hat es für Wittgenstein Sinn zu sagen: „Das Wissen gründet sich am Schluß auf Anerkennung." (*ÜG* § 378; vgl. dazu auch §§ 110, 471, 501, 563 und 630 sowie *PU* §§ 199, 202, 326, 485 und 654).

1.4 Wittgenstein kehrt also auf Umwegen wieder zu Humboldt zurück, zu der Auffassung, Wahrheit sei letztlich relativ zur − selber sprachlich manifestierten und über die Sprache erst gesicherten − „Lebensform", zur Kulturgeschichte einer Gemeinschaft, wenn er eine „Einsteinsche Wende" in der Sprachphilosophie mit den Worten fordert:

> Hier ist *wieder* ein Schritt nötig, ähnlich dem der Relativitätstheorie. (*ÜG* § 305)

Wenn der unhintergehbare Urgrund allen Wissens und aller Wahrheit die dem System von Überzeugungen selbst noch zugrundeliegende Begrifflichkeit der Sprache ist, dann sind Sprache und Erkenntnis zueinander relativ. Allerdings ist der Sprach- und somit Erkenntnisrelativismus Wittgensteins nicht einzelsprachspezifisch; weil nämlich jede Sprache selber ihre – abgeschnittene – Begründung in der gemeinsamen Praxis ihrer Benutzer findet, ist interkulturelle Verständigung möglich, denn

> Die gemeinsame menschliche Handlungsweise ist das Bezugssystem, mittels dessen wir uns eine fremde Sprache deuten. (*PU* § 206)

2. Wenn Wittgenstein auch die Kohärenztheorie der Wahrheit durch deren Bindung an die Überlieferung der Sprache auf festeren Boden gegründet hat, so wurden doch die Fragen nach der Richtigkeit der Theorie und der Wahrheit des Bezugssytems selbst bisher nicht gestellt: Die Frage, ob möglicherweise das ganze „Weltbild" falsch sein könnte, tritt (innerhalb des „Sprachspiels") einfach nicht auf, weil der Maßstab allen Urteilens nicht selbst wieder angezweifelt werden kann, ohne zugleich jegliche Sicherheit des Wissens aufzugeben.

2.1. Wie jede Wahrheitstheorie gründet sich auch die Kohärenztheorie auf den Begriff der Übereinstimmung. Übereinstimmung entfaltet sich im Rahmen einer solchen Theorie jedoch nach insgesamt fünf Seiten: Sie ist zunächst die eines Satzes mit unserem Bezugssystem. Diese Art Übereinstimmung setzt jedoch voraus, daß wir in der Lage sind, sie zu prüfen. Dazu müssen wir zweitens im Bezugssystem übereinstimmen und es drittens übereinstimmend richtig anwenden. Das ist nicht ohne die Sprachzeichen assoziierten semantischen Kriterien möglich, die uns unsere Sprache bereitstellt, in der wir wiederum übereinstimmen. Bei der Anwendung der sprachlichen Konzepte schließlich müssen wir fünftens übereinstimmen in der Wahrnehmung der Ähnlichkeiten in der Welt und im G e b r a u c h der Sprache, die beide in der Theorie nicht ohne infiniten Regreß zu beweisen sind, sich aber in der Praxis – so würde der frühe Wittgenstein gesagt haben – „zeigen". Wie bei der Begründung der Erkenntnis durch die Erfahrung läuft auch die Bindung der Wahrheit unserer Urteile an die Übereinstimmung letztlich leer. Walker hat deshalb formuliert: „Indem Wittgenstein die menschliche Übereinstimmung zum Maßstab der Ähnlichkeit gemacht hat, hat er es unverständlich werden lassen, warum diese Übereinstimmung überhaupt auftreten und auch in Zukunft weiter angetroffen werden sollte."[2] Weil die Übereinstimmung der Theorie gemäß selber wieder in der Übereinstimmung begründet sein muß und wir so in einen infiniten Regreß geraten, ist die Behauptung, daß die Glaubenssätze unseres Bezugssystems in einer in sich kohärenten Beziehung zueinander stehen, kohärenztheorieimmanent nicht zu beweisen. Und selbst wenn Wittgenstein es an dieser Stelle vorzieht, die Tatsache, daß wir übereinstimmen, als „rohes und grundlegendes Faktum"[3] zu betrachten, ist doch hier der kohärenztheoretische Ansatz an einer entscheidenden Stelle aufgegeben.

2.2. Neben diesem eher methodologischen gibt es aber noch einen weiteren, substantielleren Einwand gegen eine kohärenztheoretische Wahrheitsauffassung, denn die vielleicht überzeugendste Widerlegung dieser Theorie verkörpert wohl Orwells gerade in diesem Jahr vielzitierter Roman *1984*. In der ozeanischen Gesellschaft wird jeweils bei Bedarf kurzerhand das ganze System von Glaubenssätzen umgeschrieben. Ihr eigentliches Problem (aus der Sicht des Betrachters) wird dadurch, daß es kein Wahrheitskriterium mehr gibt – außer dem Wahrheitsministerium. Sogar die Vergangenheit wird so systematisch umgeschrieben, daß sämtliche Spuren ihrer Fälschung getilgt werden. Wahrheit wird kontrollierbar, modifizierbar, sie verschwindet in den Verlautbarungen der Partei, die selbst zum einzigen verfügbaren Wahrheitskriterium wird und auf die Kohärenz des in sich gefälschten Systems achtet. Ein Slogan der Partei lautet deshalb: „who controls the past [. . .] controls the future: who controls the present controls the past".[4] Die kohärenztheoretische Wahrheit, so zeigt Orwell, ist eine Frage der Macht.

2.3. Weil Winston Smith diesem „kollektiven Solipsismus"[5] nur den individuellen entgegenzusetzen hat, muß sein Kampf letztlich scheitern. Aber daß w i r geneigt wären, die „rektifizierte" ozeanische Wahrheit als Unwahrheit einzustufen, zeigt, daß wir sie von einem externen Maßstab her beurteilen: Sie stimmt nicht mit den erkennbaren Fakten überein. Auch Wittgenstein scheint seine insgesamt kohärenztheoretische Bestimmung der Wahrheit zu verlassen, wenn er schreibt:

> „L. W." ist mein Name. Und wenn es jemand bestritte, würde ich sofort unzählige Verbindungen schlagen, die ihn sichern.
>
> „Aber ich kann mir doch einen Menschen vorstellen, der alle diese Verbindungen macht, wovon keine mit der Wirklichkeit übereinstimmt. Warum soll ich mich nicht in einem ähnlichen Falle befinden?"
> Wenn ich mir jenen Menschen vorstelle, so stelle ich mir auch eine Realität vor, eine Welt, die ihn umgibt; und ihn, wie er der Welt zuwider denkt (und spricht).
> (*ÜG* § 594f.)

Hier deutet sich die Voraussetzung einer unabhängigen Realität an, die das letzte Kriterium unserer Urteile bildet. Jeder Kohärenztheorie der Wahrheit muß eine Korrespondenztheorie vorgelagert sein, weil es mit der Realität übereinstimmen muß, daß wir im Bezugssystem übereinstimmen. Das Problem bleibt aber, wie eine solche Korrespondenztheorie selber zu begründen wäre.

2.4. In *ÜG* kommt Wittgenstein auch auf mathematische „Petrefakten" (§ 657) zu sprechen denen „gleichsam offiziell der Stempel der Unbestreitbarkeit aufgedrückt" worden ist (§ 655). In der Gleichung $2 + 2 = 5$ wird bei Orwell ein solches Petrefakt dadurch erschüttert, daß dem Einzelnen das Kriterium der intersubjektiven Überprüfbarkeit entzogen wird. Dies kann nur dadurch geschehen, daß dem Individuum die Begriffe der Zahlen 2 und 4 selbst unsicher werden, denn, stehen sie, wie gewohnt, zur Verfügung, so folgt $2 + 2 = 4$. Wenn es eine Sicherheit gibt, dann kann diese letztlich keine über die Urteile selbst, sondern sie muß eine semantische sein, weil die Sicherheit der Begriffe die Sicherheit und Übereinstimmung der Urteile allererst begründet. Das scheint mir die explizite Botschaft Wittgensteins und die implizite Botschaft Orwells zu sein. Und für sie erst ist es unmöglich, Gründe anzugeben, denn „Die Grundlage jeder Erklärung ist die Abrichtung" (*Z* § 419), die in ihren wesentlichen Zügen zunächst eine Abrichtung im traditionsgemäßen Gebrauch der Wörter ist.

2.5 Kann man also „die Wirkung der Erfahrung auf unser System von Annahmen leugnen" (*ÜG* § 134)? Kann man „im Sattel bleibe[n], auch wenn die Tatsachen noch so sehr bockten" (*ÜG* § 616)? – Nein, man kann es nicht. Man kann es allein schon deswegen nicht, weil sich unser Bezugssystem von Überzeugungen nicht nur selbst – zumindest idealiter – an einer (wie auch immer) gegebenen Wirklichkeit ausrichtet, sondern vor allem, weil es selbst auf der Erfahrung der Sprache beruht. Sprache und die Übereinstimmung in ihr und ihrer Anwendung auf Erscheinungen ist die Basis aller Sicherheit des Urteils und so auch des Systems unserer Überzeugungen. Wenn aber Sprache aus der Sicht des Individuums nur erlernbar und nicht begründbar ist, so ist sie doch als kollektives Instrument ein Zeichensystem, dessen Bedeutungen selbst an einer vorauszusetzenden Wirklichkeit ausgerichtet werden. Auch wenn Wittgensteins Annahme zutrifft, die Sprache liege aller Gewißheit und Übereinstimmung zugrunde, kann man nicht a l l e Begründung auf die selber „unbegründete Handlungsweise" und die mit ihr verbundene sprachliche Praxis reduzieren, weil sonst nicht klar wäre, wieso sich unsere entwickelte Begrifflichkeit in der Praxis überhaupt bewähren können sollte.
Diese Gefahr bei Wittgenstein, nach unserem s p r a c h l i c h e n Zugang zur R e a l i t ä t nicht mehr weiterzufragen, scheint mir durch seine Methodologie hervorgerufen zu sein, die Frage nach unserem Begriff einer in der Realität vorfindlichen Erscheinung auf die Frage nach dem Gebrauch des entsprechenden Wortes in den alltäglichen Sprachspielen zu reduzieren.[6] So verengt er z.B. in *ÜG* an verschiedenen Stellen die Frage nach Wahrheit, Gewißheit und Wissen auf die nach dem normalen Gebrauch, den wir von *Ich weiß* (vgl. etwa *ÜG* § 260)

und dem Adjektiv *wahr* machen. Unsere Bildung solcher Begriffe hat aber − so ist zu hoffen − einen Grund, und diesen Grund zu überprüfen, ist z.B. Aufgabe der Philosophie, die sich selbst verstümmeln würde, beschränkte sie sich − wie Wittgenstein dies programmatisch fordert (vgl. *PU* §§ 109, 116 und 124) − auf die Beschreibung von Alltagsgebräuchen. Sprache verbürgt zwar unsere Übereinstimmung und Sicherheit im Urteil, rotiert aber notwendig nicht in sich selbst, sondern ist über die Ausbildung semantischer Ähnlichkeitskriterien für die begriffenen Gegenstände und Sachverhalte auf eine vorauszusetzende Realität bezogen.

3. Selbst eine Kohärenztheorie der Wahrheit setzt die Sicherheit über die gemeinsame Sprache, die gemeinsame Sprache aber eine Realität voraus, der sich ihre Begriffe asymptotisch annähern. Jede Kohärenztheorie hat daher zwei Grundlagen: (a) eine Korrespondenztheorie zu ihrem eigenen Beweis und (b) die Übereinstimmung in der Sprache als Grundlage jeder Theoriebildung. Beide münden in die Voraussetzung einer unabhängigen Realität.

ANMERKUNGEN

[1] Peirce, Charles Sanders, *Schriften zum Pragmatismus und Pragmatizismus*. Herausgegeben von Karl-Otto Apel (Frankfurt a. M. 1976), 2. Aufl., 5.265, vgl. dazu auch 5.376.
[2] Walker, Ralph C. S., „Regelbefolgen und die Kohärenztheorie der Wahrheit", in: Dieter Birnbacher/Armin Burkhardt (Hrsg.), *Sprachspiel und Methode. Zum Stand der Wittgenstein-Diskussion* (Berlin-New York 1985).
[3] Ebd.
[4] Orwell, George, *Nineteen Eighty-Four* (Harmondsworth, Middlesex 1973), S. 31.
[5] Ebd., S. 214. − „Whatever happens in all minds, truly happens" (ebd., S. 223), das ist der Trugschluß, gegen den Orwells Buch gerichtet ist.
[6] Vgl. dazu Armin Burkhardt, „Bedeutung und Begriff". Dir Fragwürdigkeit des Wittgensteinischen Methodologie-Konzepts", in: *Zeitschrift für philosophische Forschung* 37 (1982), S. 68−87.

* * *

TALKING ABOUT EXPERIENCES

Irwin Goldstein
Davidson College

In his private language discussion Wittgenstein asks how people teach and learn names for sensations and other private events. There is an interesting problem here. How does a child learn the meaning of the word 'afterimage'? No one *shows* him an afterimage. When other people speak of their own afterimages the child cannot directly observe what they are referring to. How does he learn what the word 'afterimage' means? If a child used the word 'afterimage' for his own experiences, how can other people know whether he had correctly understood the word? How can other people know whether the child uses the word for the same experience that they use it for? Suppose the child misunderstands the word and uses the word for the wrong private event. How could anyone else ever find out? The problems that the word 'afterimage' raises are also raised by 'fear', 'dream', 'thought', 'itch' and other words for experiences.

Some philosophers say, and Wittgenstein at times seems to say, that names for experiences are taught by reference to external, observable signs of those mental events. The word 'pain' ('anger', 'dream') is taught as 'that private event that is correlated with, or the cause of, behavioral responses characteristic of pain (anger, dreaming)'. Names for private events are taught by means of a reference to observable, behavioral correlates of the event.

This position is problematic. I think Wittgenstein recognized this. If 'grief' is taught as 'that which a person feels when he is doing x, y or z' there would be no guarantee that different people use the word 'grief' for *the same kind* of feeling. For how do I know if what another person feels when he behaves in a certain way is like what I feel when I behave that way? If I do not know what others feel then I do not, on the present view, know if what others call 'grief' is at all like what I call 'grief'. Perhaps the feeling that others call 'grief' is like what I call 'joy'. The present suggestion about how words for private events are learned does not provide solid grounds for believing that different people assign 'grief' the same meaning.

The problem I am raising here—a problem which has a place in many private language discussions—is not so much 'How do I know that others have minds?' but 'How do I know what sort of experience a person is having at a given time?' If I cannot know what other people are experiencing, and they cannot know what I am experiencing, how is it possible to teach and learn words for different kinds of experiences?

Some philosophers think that the problem of other minds can be disposed of easily. I do not think so. I think the problem is unsolved. I have never heard a sound argument that shows that a person knows the mental states of others.

Among people who think they can show that we know the mental states of others the most popular approach to doing so would be the argument by analogy. The argument might be formulated in the following way. Human beings are basically the same in a great many observable respects. Hence it is probable that they are also the same in ways that are private and unobservable.

This argument is unsound. Its premise, that people are basically the same in observable respects, is oversimplified. Though different people are similar in many many observable respects there are many observable respects in which people differ from each other. People differ in eye color, hair color and skin tone. Some people are taller or stronger than others. Different people often respond differently to the same external circumstance. A substance may cause one person to cough or sneeze but have no effect on another person. There are many further respects in which people differ from one another. Hence, I am not entitled to conclude, merely by appealing to the similarities between people, that when different people behave in the same way the behavior is caused by the same kind of experience. Perhaps, the private realm is one area in which people differ from one another.

It may be replied that people are the same in essentials and that they differ only in inessentials. But this does not help. How can I know whether feeling as I do when behaving in a certain way is essential rather than inessential to being human? Suppose that feeling this way is as inessential to being human as is having eyes that are green rather than brown?

I believe we can explain how it is possible to communicate over private events without tackling sceptical problems about other minds. Explaining how the words 'dream', 'fear', 'afterimage', 'headache' and other psychological words are taught and learned does not require showing that we know at times when others are dreaming, frightened, etc.

Why is communicating about private events problematic? Why does communicating over private events present problems that communicating over public phenomena does not? What is so special about *private* events? The reason that private events are assumed to present special problems is that I cannot *see* another person's private events, and he cannot see mine. Someone who thinks this presents problems in teaching these words is assuming that a person must *see* what people are referring to if he is to learn the meaning of the word which is used to refer to it. This assumption is mistaken.

We often learn the meaning of a word without being shown its referent. There are many words in addition to psychological words that are not learned by ostensive definition. A child can learn the word 'bachelor' or 'university' without having a bachelor or a university pointed out to him. Indeed it is doubtful that he *could* learn these words ostensively. There is little or nothing that one would see by looking at a bachelor, or even a series of bachelors, that would clearly indicate what we mean when we refer to that person as a 'bachelor'.

There are many words in addition to words for experiences that are not learned ostensively. 'God', 'infinite', 'logic', 'molecule', 'history', 'demonic' and many other words are not learned by having a referent of the word displayed. That a supernatural being cannot be displayed to children does not prevent children from learning the word 'God'.

That we cannot directly see other people's experiences does not prevent us from communicating about experiences in a public, shared language. A child can learn the word 'dream' without someone pointing out dreaming people to him. He can learn the word without someone else labelling one of the child's experiences a 'dream'. To be able to learn the word 'dream' a child need not know when others are dreaming, and others need not know when he is dreaming.

How do we learn the meanings of names for experiences? People learn them by hearing the sorts of things people say when using the words. It is not by having some mental event directly or indirectly pointed out that people learn these words. If a parent says 'Be careful; you may fall down and hurt yourself' a child may infer that 'hurting' himself is bad − it is something to be avoided. When a parent asks 'Where does it hurt?' a child may infer that 'hurting' yourself is something localized. The fact that the parent *asks* the child, and does not already know merely by looking at the child, shows that hurting yourself is not something that is publicly observable.

There are many words in addition to psychological words that are learned in this non-ostensive way. The word 'bachelor' or 'university' might be learned in this way. By hearing a remark like 'He's not married, he's a bachelor' one can infer that being a 'bachelor' implies being 'unmarried'. By hearing a remark like 'He is going on to university to study law' one might infer that the word 'university' is connected with the ideas of learning and education. One can infer what the word refers to without having its referent pointed out.

Children learn that different psychological words pick out different mental states from the fact that people speak of different mental states differently. Though people say things like 'Where do you feel the pain?' they do not normally ask 'Where do you feel your dream?' Though they ask 'Does your foot hurt?' they do not normally ask 'Does your foot think?' Our remarks imply that 'pain' names something that can be localized. Our remarks about 'dreaming' and 'thinking' do not have this implication. People talk about 'beliefs' being *false, irrational* or *insightful* but they do not assign 'aches' and 'afterimages' these logical characteristics. From the fact that people speak of 'beliefs' in this way a child can infer that the word 'belief' picks out the sort of mental state that can be false, irrational, insightful. Itches and afterimages do not have these attributes, so there is little worry that a child will mistakenly think that the word 'belief' is the name of the sensation that others speak of as an 'itch'. If he did misunderstand the word his misundstanding probably would be evidenced in the way he spoke of what he called 'beliefs'. If he spoke of 'beliefs' as localized in some part of his body, or he said that his 'belief' feels better when he scratches his arm, others would have some evidence that he uses the word 'belief' for the wrong mental state.

People speak as though being in 'pain' is *ipso facto* disagreeable and bad but they do not speak of 'afterimages' or 'dreams' in this way. This in itself indicates something about the meaning of 'pain' and how it differs from the meaning of 'dream'. To refer to a 'dream' or to 'pleasure' is not *ipso facto* to refer to something bad.

When a parent says to a child: 'Don't be angry. I did not tear your dress on purpose', the child may infer that the word 'angry' reports a mental state that can be appropriate or inappropriate to a situation. We do not normally talk of 'itches' or 'backaches' as though they could be inappropriate in this way. There are many other features of the remarks we make with psychological words that convey information about the meanings of psychological words to people learning the words.

I will now sum up my position. Words for private events are not learned ostensively. It is not by having dreaming people pointed out that children learn the meaning of 'dream'. To explain how a child learns the word 'dream' I do not need to prove that other people know when a child has dreams or that a child knows when other people have dreams. Children learn the meaning of the word 'dream' by hearing what people say when they speak of 'dreams'. What is true of 'dream' is true of 'pride', 'belief', and other names for private events.

* * *

PRIVATE EXPERIENCE AND PUBLIC COMMUNICATION

Stig Nystrand
University of Lund

In 1931, when Ludwig Wittgenstein just had gone through a severe intellectual struggle whose results perhaps best can be seen in *Philosophische Bemerkungen*, he wrote this: "Wir kämpfen mit der Sprache. Wir stehen im Kampf mit der Sprache." *CV*, p. 11. It is a saying that seems clear, but as most of Wittgenstein's thoughts it can be understood in many ways. Already in 1914, *CV*, p. 1, when conceiving his Tractatus-world he said that, as you cannot recognize the Language when somebody is talking Chinese, something belonging to a strange form of life, so it is often hard to recognize Man in human beings. The tie between man and his language as a tie involving the whole life-situation was already hinted at.

His sensitive soundings of the depths in Language and language-shadowed reality continued, though in many other directions. But, as Hermann Broch in *Der Tod des Vergils*[1] so aptly put it: it takes a life without end just for a second to get one glimpse into the abysmal depths of Language. —Ludwig Wittgenstein also stood near that abyss many times. In his Tractatus-world it was the silence in front of a mystery that still echoes in 20th century philosophy. Later on the tightrope of language-games got him and us across. In his life the mystery was still there. Together with the certainty of belonging to human life-forms, to the Language, he held to the mysterious certainty of being alone in front of the transcendence. We hear this in the last aphorism of *Zettel* § 717—"You can't hear God speak to someone else, you can hear him only if you are being addressed. That is a grammatical remark."

Once more let us come back to the saying of 1931. It might be interpreted, understood as 1. A categorical assertion that we cannot get out of this. We are in the middle of something most important, in fact *the* most important thing in our dealings with the world and reality. 2. Wir kämpfen und wir stehen im Kampf—stresses the dynamic, dialectical aspect of the relation to language. The form of the struggle may change, the fact of the struggle remains. And 3. a struggle is a struggle *against* and/or *for* something. And here we are even using as a weapon the very same thing which is both the object and the medium of the struggle. We fight *against* being taken in by language, being absorbed in it, losing our integrity, getting lost in a geography we haven't had the opportunity to get to know. Against that. But we also fight to master a technique, to see our way to where we belong, *inside* a form of life where an integrated language is the primary condition.

I don't think these ideas about what could be behind the short aphorism are unfair to Wittgenstein's ideas in general. And if they are not then an aphorism like this one will show that for him language is open and something to be shared. A saying like this would in its feeling of certainty already be an argument against thinking that the philosopher with *this* view would have anything to do with 'private', 'non-communicable' language. I will later elaborate further on that.

The Tractatus-world was a world full of facts which seemed to have found their correct place. In a way they perhaps had. But they were inhabitants without identity, carrying their firmly set horizon with them—not open to possibilities beyond. The non-factual, the metaphysical subject, on the other hand, rested in the encompassing world of will and value, beyond a borderline, that one drawn by your life. So the angstvoll author of the *Tractatus* thought.

The world of facts was expressed in propositions with Sinn und Bedeutung. But the world outside, the lived life, didn't make that split, the *Sinn und Bedeutung* melted into one *Lebensinhalt*, one *Einstellung*, to use Karl Jaspers' words from about the same time.[2] That is why the Tractatus-world was so incommunicable. The Chiffre, the code, couldn't be broken. According to Jaspers, the *Scheitern*, the failure, is perhaps something inherited by a *Chiffre*, by the seeking of a togetherness which would understand the *whole* world, a seeking after the transcendence. That cannot be reached without a code, but a code cannot be broken without resorting to the concepts of the being-in-the-world. And this retreating into the world is a *Scheitern*. And the whole seeking perhaps another *Chiffre*.

Now one could ask whether Wittgenstein's searching after the so called 'inner experiences' and into the possibilities of expressing them in language isn't another version of Jaspers' problem with the Chiffre. Only just turned in the opposite direction. Going deep enough into our 'inner life' we run into borders, fences. And we have to turn back to the world above surface. But Wittgenstein, though acknowledging the difficulties (see e.g. *PI*, 244–46, 290 onwards, *RPP* I, 141–2, 479, 858-9, 1089, *Z*, 495, 504, 534–6, 540–1, 554), didn't return frustrated. He was on the contrary convinced that our 'inner life' was not private. It was there as a certainty, just as sure as there were certainties constituting the *Vorwissen* to our knowledge of 'outer' reality. If this search was a *Scheitern*, it was one in the same way as Jaspers'. Both showed that there were dimensions not directly objectifiable, but to be presented, to be lived with, and to be accepted.

Perhaps we cannot imagine a Darstellung of 'inner experiences', but that wasn't important to Wittgenstein later on. He had other ways.—One of the sources to his *Angst* with the Tractatus-worldview is to be found in the impossibilty of applying his genial Darstellung–method to the 'mystical' side of the world, the metaphysical and value-dominated Zeigen–part of the world.—As we know, the Jewish God is not to be represented, dargestellt. Could it be that the whole world of will and value for Wittgenstein became like that God and that he already during this period was possessed with the problem of his identity and integrity? Belong or not belong?

The simples constituting the building-stones in the Tractarian world of facts were never completely identified. Were they 'objects of acquaintance' which included emotions, 'inner experiences' also? It didn't seem important—they were soon transmuted into variables of sorts by other philosophers. And by their author they were ignored or maybe, as Jaakko Hintikka[3] puts it, transformed from objects in a phenomenalistic language into objects in a more or less physicalistic language. Objects which went into building language-games further on. Among these building-blocks were emotions, feelings, 'inner experiences'. These became the real certainties of the later Wittgenstein's philosophy, something which never could be ruled out, something we *all* had, and upon which a rule-governed language could rest.—The language of sensations, 'inner experience', is *given* to me in a special, certain way, and if I can grasp that, it is no longer private. It has been integrated into the form of life of the community I belong to.

My 'inner experiences' have, so to speak, been put on a map. Erik Stenius has said:[4]

> All of us possess what might be called an internal map of the world. The internal map of a person comprises all facts he knows about the world and all states of affairs which he believes to obtain. Now everybody has *himself* a position on his internal map—thus the map comprises all his real or believed relations to his environment, including other persons. . . And though the internal map of a person is his private map, the internal maps of different persons have that in common that they are maps of the external world, the common world of human interaction.

—Though Stenius speaks only about the relations to the external world, these relations ought to include those generating from emotions, sensations and the like. In this way *these* could as well be proved, exhibited, as public. If that is not enough we could continue the picture by putting another map in the hands of the man on Stenius' map. And on that secondary map our 'inner life' would be exhibited. With the same consequences for that 'inner life' as for the outer relations if we imagined the map, that is firmly placed in the hands of our person, enlarged so that all details could be seen.—There may be flaws in this rendering of mine, but I think it's worth a try.

The example most often used, certainly by Wittgenstein himself, in this connection, is 'pain', feeling pain, understanding pain. It is perhaps a paradigmatic case, because pain is often shown very expressively, but it is also kept hidden by many and simulating pain is not a strange happening either. But according to Wittgenstein, e.g. *PI*, 288, 384, all these cases belong to the language-game of pain, and doesn't make it less real.

Pain expressed in language is in itself on the same level as primitive painbehaviour – a first-level language-game. So are many expressions of emotions also. This means that "I am in pain", discussed e.g. in *PI*, 404-7, directs attention, not to any definite *person*, but to *me*. It is not a description, but an assertion. I don't name any 'him', I am offering him, that is me, with a gesture of self-assurance. If it is a proposition at all, so only in a secondary sense. It is therefore to be believed in the same sense as when Karl Jaspers offers his concept of Existenz, which is connected with situations of walking on borderlines, taking risks.

Taken in this assertive way expressions of so called 'private experiences' appear as a most certain ground for human communication. That is, it demands attention, not indifferent noticing, but demands to be acted upon and not to be proved as true or false in a propositional way. So we see, that with this talk of 'private experiences' and with the use of language-games Wittgenstein tried, quite successfully, to bring back a more immediate touch into language, back from the abstractions of scientific thinking in philosophy, at least one based on strict logic, from the thinking moving on rails,[5] to something resembling more an oral tradition, to a language with colour, smells and cries.[6]

About the time of the 'middle' Wittgenstein (*PG*, *PB*, The lectures in the early thirties), when the above mentioned changes were conceived, another Viennese thinker, Robert Musil, expressing himself through fiction, said:[7] "Es ist eine Welt von Eigenschaften ohne Mann entstanden, von Erlebnissen ohne den, der sie erlebt, und es sieht beinahe aus, als ob im Idealfall der Mensch überhaupt nichts mehr privat erleben werde und die freundliche Schwere der persönlichen Verantwortung sich in ein Formelsystem von möglichen Bedeutungen auflösen solle." – Musil didn't find any solution, Wittgenstein found no final ones either, but he pointed a way to get back into the world of human *Eigenschaften*. However Wittgenstein as a person probably could have said all the time with Agathe in the last part of Musil's work, that the feeling of being outside life was complete.[8]

The language-games connected with our conception of reality have their roots in certainties which cannot be doubted, though the games of knowledge include a lot of other things also. In *OC*, and other texts, where Wittgenstein discusses these problems, he doesn't explicitly say that some 'inner experiences', e.g. pain, belong to the group of certainties. But the aura, the tone of voice, *OC* § 30, that goes with them might as well be applied to utterings on feelings or emotions. It sounds quite natural to replace 'two hands' with 'pain' or why not 'sorrow' in the following sayings, *OC* § 247: "What would it be like to doubt now whether I have two hands? . . . So far I have no system at all within which this doubt might exist." *Z* § 405: "No one but a philosopher would say 'I know that I have two hands' but one may well say 'I am unable to doubt that I have two hands."

"There is no experience of something necessarily happening", said Wittgenstein in 1932, *Lect. 1932–35*, p. 15, but questions about somebody being in pain and the like, have a strong *empirical certainty*, as Roderick Chisholm has pointed out.[9] Empirically certain, though not empirically verifiable. The verifiability must come through belonging to a form of life where the rule is *not* to doubt a person's 'inner experiences'. In fact the whole conception of forms of life doesn't fit in with a language-game of a really private character.

In the same lecture 1932 Wittgenstein also emphasized that a private language would be *grammatically* so. And then it would be excluded from all communicative dimensions, emotions in a way wouldn't exist. And we are all aware of facts to the contrary – even though we can doubt the extent and the force of communication through and in 'inner experiences'. In *RC* § 301–3, Wittgenstein puts it this way: "That I can be someone's friend rests on the fact that he has the same *possibilities* as I myself have, or similar ones. – Would it be correct to say our concepts reflect our life? They stand in the middle of it. – The rule-governed nature of our language permeates our life." Obeying a rule cannot then be private, otherwise there wouldn't exist any possibilities of being someone's friend. And even a private language of any sort whatever presupposes a common and public language.

In *PI* § 202 we find this expression: "Hence it is not possible to obey a rule 'privately': otherwise thinking one was obeying a rule would be the same thing as obeying it."—This sentence is the starting point for Saul Kripke's famous writing on rules and private language.[10] where he tries to give the background to Wittgenstein's discussions on rule-governed behaviour in form of a personal rendering of Wittgenstein's sceptical paradox in *PI* § 201.

If the language-game concerned with pain, sensations, emotions, is *learnt*, and some learning must be considered constitutive for games, then in a way you cannot forget them. It is an ability you carry with you as long as you are sane and mentally well enough to move about in the world. Other abilities, e.g. how to ride a bike, you don't forget either. You can be a little rusty when trying anew after a long time, but the ability is there with you. So are the language-games of intimate and inner kinds. They are a proof that you *belong*. You not only belong to a certain form of life, but these games are a proof that you are a member of the most extensive of all forms of life—belonging to the common human race.

That is why it's not so necessary to seek for the object-designation in questions of e.g. pain. The object-description doesn't work when talking of 'inner experiences', the beetle may not be there, *PI* § 293, but we surely can talk in and of the language-games in that field *without* talking of object-designation. We can use a word rightfully even if we don't have justification for it in terms of objective facts, *PI* § 289, *RFM* § 32. Wittgenstein also puts it this way, *PI* § 298: "The very fact that we should so very much like to say 'This is the important thing' while we point privately to the sensation—is enough to show how much we are inclined to say something which gives no information."—Because it is important *in* our life, *for* our life, to get revealed to others.

We are able to communicate on account of *certainty*. There may not be rules for this language-game which stand up to tests of knowledge, but there is this one certainty: rules or no rules, there is a fellow being who has the same possibilities as I have to understand and receive my message as I to understand his.—In *CV* p. 82, Wittgenstein says about soulful expression in music, that there is no paradigma for that. The same piece of music can be played in many ways just *as* soulfully and expressively. As a parallel you could say that it ought to be possible to understand feelings, 'inner experiences', pain, even if they are expressed by different interpreters, understand them as the same stuff, the real stuff, though subjectively coloured. The language-game based on this understanding is like a sketch of what takes place *inside* a person and goes beyond having an opinion of a fact or an act. A saying from *PI* p. 178, shows that what is meant is a sort of existential *Einstellung*: "My attitude towards him is an attitude towards a soul. I am not of the *opinion* that he has a soul."

In sharp contrast to the above-mentioned stands the primitive language-game in the beginning of *PI*, § 2 onwards. This part of the *Investigations* has been many times misunderstood. It is *not* Wittgenstein's conception of a successful and recommendable language-game, though it is in its way complete. It is a critical, even satirical, portrait of how naming (Bezeichnen) and ostensive (hinweisende) definition is learnt. It is sharp and clear, static and devoid of feeling, emotion, almost graphic in its expression. The ones ordering, the ones being ordered, don't show any feelings. It is as if they were waiting for something, for a change. That change will come about later in the book. There is a dramatic nerve, not often noticed, in the *Investigations*.—With the author's own words, from *PB* § 64: "The propositional sign . . doesn't consist in the sound alone, but in the fact that the sound came out of this mouth."

But there's also the question of receiving the sounds. How are experiences of emotional kinds communicated between persons? We have seen that they cannot be understood as in any way secret. There is a community of people, the inhabitants of my form of life, who knows about them, who checks them. But am I that public? Can a person's feelings be collectively understood? We know that the questions are not that easily answered.—In *CV*, pp. 45f, Wittgenstein says: "Ein Notschrei kann nicht größer sein, als der *eines* Menschen. Oder auch *keine* Not kann größer sein, als die, in der ein einzelner Mensch sein kann . . . Größere Not kann nicht empfunden werden, als von Einem Menschen."—You don't hear *another* human being better in a choir. It seems that to be heard, for what is innermost to be felt, you must make yourself manifest—in a way near to what Karl Jaspers calls 'offenbar'. That is, open for another who also wants to reveal himself.

The term 'offenbar' is here understood in two of its meanings. 1. As something made clear, manifest, clarity arising out of the encompassing, *das Umgreifende*, the different aspects of Being.[11] It could mean, being open to the world around you in a concrete way. It could mean more—yourself as an example of somebody with an integrity in front of life. 2. As something *revealed*. You want to reveal that which is really you, your inner attitude to life, your personal self.—This last-mentioned meaning of course has a touch of *Offenbarung*, miracle. Something which occupied Wittgenstein during different periods of his life, like also other aspects of religious faith. A miracle he once called "a gesture which God makes", *CV*, p. 45.

The making manifest (offenbar) demands an attitude of honesty, integrity, on part of those participating in the communication, a getting into the other persons's life-situation. Perhaps we could call it a deep understanding of a form of life. That is, you know the games, intuitively, before explaining the rules, you are inside the grammar, before explicating the language. And precisely that is also the essence of Jaspers' ideas about existential communication.

The communication of *all* the ideas in the Investigations, as in other of Wittgenstein's later works, could be seen as a communication with means taken from the philosophy of Existenz. The Norwegian philosopher Viggo Rosvaer has very interesting ideas about indirect communication and Wittgenstein's thoughts.[12] He thinks that the most important part of *PI* is not written down—it exists in the dimension of indirect communication. This dimension is then to be felt in all periods of Wittgenstein's philosophy.—"It takes two persons to make up one message", says Rosvaer. In indirect communication you have to be on the same wavelength, and you have to repeat and recreate—as you do in art also, in understanding and communicating art.

What Wittgenstein does, according to Rosvaer, is to put the viewpoint he wants to change before us in all its nakedness, there for us to choose. The selfidentitiy of the viewpoints is existential, your choosing one or some of them is an existential deed. In doing so you may feel the certainties I have been talking about. The certainty of knowing that there is something to communicate.—Rosvaer also asserts that Wittgenstein's technique has an ethical aspect, by an attack from within, he tries to change your Weltanschauung, achieve complete clarity.

In that strange book by Jerzy Kosinski, *Being there*, the man who has been hidden from the world most of his life thinks that, when you were spoken to and watched by other people you were secure. Everything you did was then interpreted by others in the same way as you yourself interpreted what they did. They could never know more about yourself than you knew about them.—A picture of the situation we have discussed? 'Inner experiences' looked at from above? The picture seems clear, but not too optimistic. But perhaps that is how far we can get.—"Zwischen dem Nichts des 'ich allein' und dem Nichts des Endlosen liegt die Welt"—said Karl Jaspers.[13]

ENDNOTES

[1] Broch, Hermann, *Der Tod des Vergils* (Frankfurt am Main 1976), p. 85.
[2] Jaspers, Karl, *Psychologie der Weltanschauungen* (Berlin-Göttingen-Heidelberg 1954, first ed. Berlin 1919), p. 52 ff.
[3] Hintikka, Jaakko & Merrill B., "The development of Wittgenstein's philosophy: The hidden unity", in: Paul Weingartner & Hans Czermak (eds.), *Epistemology and philosophy of science. Proceedings of the 7th International Wittgenstein-Symposium* (Vienna 1983).

4 Stenius, Erik, "The Picture theory and Wittgenstein's later attitudes to it", in: Irving Block (ed), *Perspectives on the philosophy of Wittgenstein* (Oxford 1981), p. 132.

5 Quoted from Rush Rhees (ed), *Ludwig Wittgenstein. Personal recollections* (Oxford 1981), p. 223.

6 See also Carlo Ginzburg, *Osten och maskarna* (Stockholm 1983), p. 99. Original Title: *Il formaggio e il vermi*.

7 Musil, Robert, *Der Mann ohne Eigenschaften* (Reinbek bei Hamburg 1978), p. 150.

8 Musil, (1978), p. 965. Agathe says among other things: "das Leben wäre auch ohne sie vollständig, daß sie darin nichts zu suchen und zu bestellen hätte. Dieses grausame Gefühl war im Grunde weder verzweifelt noch gekränkt, sondern ein Zuhören und Zusehen . . . . und bloß ohne jeden Antrieb, ja ohne die Möglichkeit, sich selbst einzusetzen. Beinahe lag eine Geborgenheit in dieser Ausgeschlossenheit, so wie es ein Staunen gibt, das alles Fragen vergißt."

9 Chisholm, R. M., "The Self and the world", in: Elisabeth Leinfellner et al. (eds.) *Wittgenstein and his impact on contemporary philosophy. Proceedings of the 2nd International Wittgenstein-Symposium* (Vienna 1978), p. 409.

10 Kripke, Saul, "Wittgenstein on rules and private language", in: Irving Block (ed), *Perspectives on the philosophy of Wittgenstein* (Oxford 1981), pp. 238–312.

11 Jaspers, Karl, *Von der Wahrheit* (München 1947). p. 548.

12 Rosvaer, Viggo, "Philosophy as an art form", in: Kjell S. Johannessen & Tore Nordenstam (eds); *Wittgenstein—aesthetics and transcendental philosophy* (Vienna 1981), pp. 25–31.

13 Jaspers (1947), p. 373.

* * *

WITTGENSTEIN – EIN STRUKTURALIST?

Astrid Wintersberger
Wien

„Die Philosophie ist keine Lehre, sondern eine Tätigkeit", schreibt Wittgenstein im Abschnit 4.112 des *Tractats*. Weiter heißt es: „Das Resultat der Philosophie sind nicht ‚philosophische Sätze', sondern das Klarwerden von Sätzen." Diese Beschreibung trifft auch auf jene philosophische Richtungen zu, die unter dem Namen ‚Strukturalismus' zusammengefaßt werden. Es ist unmöglich, eindeutige Wesensmerkmale anzugeben, die allen Vertretern dieser Richtungen gemeinsam wären; sie stehen vielmehr durch so etwas wie wittgensteinsche ‚Familienähnlichkeiten' miteinander in Verbindung. Deshalb ist es nicht abwegig und vielleicht gerade im Sinne Wittgensteins, auch nach Familienähnlichkeiten zwischen seiner Philosophie und dem strukturalistischen Denken zu suchen.

Meist wird als Merkmal des Strukturalismus die Berufung auf den Linguisten F. de Saussure genannt, dessen Begrifflichkeit sich wie ein roter Faden durch die Werke der Strukturalisten zieht. Saussure entwickelte in seinen Genfer Vorlesungen, die unter dem Titel *Grundfragen der allgemeinen Sprachwissenschaft* überliefert sind, eine Konzeption der Sprache, die einige erstaunliche Parallelen mit der des *Tractats* aufweist. Einer seiner ersten Grundsätze ist, daß die Sprache gegliedert oder ‚artikuliert' sei. Dieser Gedanke wird auch von Wittgenstein ausgesprochen: „Der Satz ist kein Wörtergemisch (. . .) Der Satz ist artikuliert." (*TLP* 3.141); und im Abschnitt 3.14 hieß es: „Das Satzzeichen besteht darin, daß sich seine Elemente, die Wörter, in ihm auf bestimmte Art und Weise zueinander verhalten. Das Satzzeichen ist eine Tatsache." Wir erfahren also, daß für das Satzzeichen all jene Eigenschaften zutreffen, die Wittgenstein seinen ‚Tatsachen' zugesprochen hatte. Ebenso wie ein Ding für sich genommen nicht zugänglich, nicht denkbar, sondern nur durch die Möglichkeit seines Vorkommens in Sachverhalten bestimmt ist, so ist auch das Wort für sich alleine bedeutungslos und erhält eine Funktion erst durch die Stellung, die es im Satz einnimmt. In 3.3 liest man daher auch konsequenterweise: „Nur im Zusammenhang des Satzes hat ein Name Bedeutung." Ähnlich wie Wittgenstein die Namen charakterisiert, bestimmt Saussure das, was er Signifikanten nennt; diese sind „nicht positiv durch ihren Inhalt, sondern negativ durch ihre Beziehungen zu den anderen Gliedern des Systems definiert."[1] Saussure gebraucht ein Bild zur Illustration seiner Theorie der Sprache: das des Schachspiels. Zu diesem Vergleich greift auch Wittgenstein, allerdings erst in den *PU*: „. . . wir reden von ihr [der Sprache] so wie von den Figuren des Schachspiels, indem wir Spielregeln für sie angeben, nicht ihre physikalischen Eigenschaften beschreiben. Die Frage ‚Was ist ein Wort?' ist analog der ‚Was ist eine Schachfigur?'" (*PU* § 108) Saussure widmet jenem Vergleich einen verhältnismäßig langen und ausführlichen Abschnitt in den *Grundfragen der allgemeinen Sprachwissenschaft*; auch er betont, daß die Figuren nur in Hinblick auf die Regeln und den Kontext des Spiels bestimmt werden könnten.

Man hat gesehen, daß Wittgenstein und Saussure darin übereinkommen, daß das sprachliche Zeichen durch seine Beziehungen zu anderen Zeichen gekennzeichnet ist. Dies genügt aber nicht für das Entstehen eines Sinngehalts; dazu bedarf es zusätzlich der Verbindung des Zeichens mit etwas, das es repräsentiert. Wittgenstein baut auf diesem Gedanken seine Abbildtheorie auf, während Saussure die Unterscheidung zwischen ‚Signifikant' und ‚Signifikat' einführt. Laut Wittgenstein werden die Bestandteile des Bildes den Bestandteilen des Abgebildeten zugeordnet, bei Saussure sind es die Elemente des Lautlichen (Signifikanten), die mit den Elementen des Gedanklichen (Signifikate) in Verbindung treten. Beide Denker sind sich dahingehend einig, daß diese Beziehung keine natürliche ist. Saussures bekannten

Grundsatz von der Beliebigkeit des Zeichens findet man auch im *Tractat*. In 3.322 schreibt Wittgenstein, daß das Zeichen willkürlich sei. Wir erfahren also, sowohl von Wittgenstein als auch von Saussure, daß die Beziehung von Bezeichnung und Bezeichnetem beliebig sei; wie dieses Zusammentreffen aber tatsächlich vor sich gehe, erfahren wir nur in sehr unzufriedenstellender Weise. Beide fühlen sich veranlaßt, auf diese Frage einzugehen, und beide beantworten sie nur mit Metaphern. So schreibt Wittgenstein: „Die abbildende Beziehung besteht aus den Zuordnungen der Elemente des Bildes und der Sachen. Diese Zuordnungen sind gleichsam die *Fühler* der Bildelemente, mit denen das Bild die Wirklichkeit berührt." (*TLP* 2.1514, 2.1515). Saussure fällt es schwer zu zeigen, wann und wodurch sich Signifikant und Signifikat miteinander vereinigen. Er spricht von einer ‚mysteriösen Tatsache‘, die er mit dem Entstehen der Wellen durch Berührung der Luft mit der Wasseroberfläche vergleicht.[2]

Jene Zuordnung zwischen Repräsentiertem und Repräsentierendem ist, wenn sie einmal erfolgt ist, eine endgültige. Der Wittgensteininterpret Anthony Kenny fügt jener These von der Willkürlichkeit des Zeichens folgendes hinzu: „Die Zuordnung zwischen Namen und Gegenständen ist willkürlich, doch wenn diese Festsetzungen einmal getroffen sind, dann ist keine weitere Festsetzung mehr nötig um zu sagen, daß diese Namen in dieser Beziehung jene Gegenstände in jener Beziehung bedeuten."[3] Dies entspricht auch ungefähr Saussures Position und charakterisiert eben jene Vorstellung, die Anlaß zur Kritik seitens der Neostrukturalisten gab: die fixe Verbindung zwischen Bezeichnetem und der entsprechenden Bezeichnung. Mit diesem letzten Punkt kann man den Vergleich zwischen Wittgenstein und Saussure abschließen, der zeigen wollte, daß die Kluft zwischen dem Ausgangspunkt des strukturalistischen Denkens und der Sprachphilosophie des *Tractats* keine unüberwindbare ist.

Es wurde schon angedeutet, daß die sogenannten ‚Neostrukturalisten‘ (wie Lacan, Derrida, Lyotard . . .) sich kritisch mit Saussure auseinandergesetzt haben; ebenso kritisch hat sich der späte Wittgenstein mit dem frühen auseinandergesetzt. Nun weisen die Korrekturen des frühen Strukturalismus durch den späten einige Parallelen mit Wittgensteins Revision des *Tractats* in den *Philosophischen Untersuchungen* auf. Im *Tractat* orientiert sich seine Beschreibung der Sprache am Paradigma einer wissenschaftlichen oder zumindest einer klaren, exakten Alltagssprache, von woher auch seine Forderung nach der Eindeutigkeit des Sinns zu verstehen ist. Die nie auszuschließende Mehrdeutigkeit eines Zeichens wird von Wittgenstein zu dieser Zeit als unwillkommene Quelle von Irrtümern angesehen. Jene Position hat er in den *PU* grundlegend revidiert; die Sprachspieltheorie ist mit einer strengen Forderung nach der Eindeutigkeit des Sinns nicht mehr vereinbar. Sie zeigt vielmehr eine Ähnlichkeit mit der Konzeption mancher Neostrukturalisten, die ihrerseits Saussures fixe Zuordnung zwischen Signifikat und Signifikant ablehnen und die Abhängigkeit der Bedeutung vom (sprachlichen und nichtsprachlichen) Kontext hervorheben. Das ‚Flottieren der Bedeutung‘ (Lacan) wird als prinzipielle, der Sprache wesentliche Möglichkeit angesehen. Lacan definiert das Wort als ‚Bedeutungsknoten‘ und fügt hinzu:

> Nenne ich beispielsweise das Wort ‚rideau‘, so bezeichnet es nicht allein kraft Übereinkunft einen Gegenstand, der auf tausenderlei Art gesehen werden kann – so vom Arbeiter und Kaufmann, vom Maler und Gestaltpsychologen entsprechend als Arbeit und Tauschwert, als farbige Physiognomie oder räumliche Struktur. Als Metapher wird es weiter zum ‚rideau d'arbres‘ (. . .) Im Zwischenakt des Dramas wird es zum Ausruf meiner Ungeduld oder zum Wort meines Überdrusses.[4]

Jene Beschreibung der verschiedenen Verwendungsweisen des Wortes ‚rideau‘ könnte auch ein Beispiel Wittgensteins zur Illustration seiner Theorie der Sprachspiele sein. Das Wort ‚Sprachspiel‘ soll hervorheben, daß „das Sprechen der Sprache Teil ist einer Tätigkeit oder einer Lebensform." (*PU* § 23) Kenny meint, daß Wittgenstein in den *PU* den Versuch aufgegeben habe, „alle Formen der Sprache auf eine Struktur zu bringen."[5] Demgegenüber betont er nun die Vielfalt der Gebrauchsweisen eines Wortes und die mannigfaltigen Möglichkeiten seines Vorkommens in verschiedenen Kontexten. Wenn Wittgenstein im *Blauen Buch* sagt: „Die Vorstellung von einem Allgemeinbegriff als einer gemeinsamen Eigenschaft seiner einzelnen Beispiele ist mit einer anderen primitiven, also einfachen Vorstellung von der Struktur der Sprache verbunden." (*BLB* S. 37), so könnte man dies auch als Kritik seiner eigenen, früheren Konzeption interpretieren. Der Vielfalt der Sprachspiele kann eine allgemeine Beschreibung nicht gerecht werden, es gibt nichts allen Sprachspielen Gemeinsames, das man als die ‚Sprache schlechthin' bezeichnen könnte; die verschiedenen Sprachformen weisen untereinander nur sogenannte ‚Familienähnlichkeiten' auf. Wittgensteins Gesinnungswechsel kommt in § 65 der *PU* besonders deutlich zum Ausdruck:

> . . . man könnte mir einwenden: ‚Du machst dirs leicht! Du redest von allen möglichen Sprachspielen, hast aber nirgends gesagt, was denn das wesentliche des Sprachspiels und also der Sprache ist. (. . .) Du schenkst dir also gerade den Teil der Untersuchung, der dir selbst seinerzeit das meiste Kopfzerbrechen gemacht hat, nämlich den, die allgemeine Form des Satzes und der Sprache betreffen.' Und das ist wahr. Statt etwas anzugeben, was allem, was wir Sprache nennen, gemeinsam ist, sage ich es ist diesen Erscheinungen gar nicht Eines gemeinsam, weswegen wir für alle das gleiche Wort verwenden − sondern sie sind miteinander in vielen verschiedenen Weisen verwandt. Und dieser Verwandtschaft, oder dieser Verwandtschaften wegen, nennen wir sie alle Sprachen.

In ähnlicher Weise lehnt auch der späte Strukturalismus die Vorstellung eines letzten, alle anderen Sprachsysteme begründenden Metasystems ab. In diesem Zusammenhang ist besonders F. Lyotard zu erwähnen, der explizit Wittgensteins Begriff des ‚Sprachspiels' übernimmt. Manfred Frank faßt in seiner Untersuchung *Was ist Neostrukturalismus?* einige Grundgedaken Lyotards zusammen. Er bezeichnet den Glauben an einen ‚Metadiskurs', der alle einzelnen Sprachspiele überbiete und zur Einheit zusammenfasse, als Unterstellung und fährt fort:[6] „Auch der Strukturalismus mit dem charakteristischen Universalitätsanspruch − den wir bei Saussure und erst recht bei Levi-Strauss antrafen − habe an dieser Unterstellung teil. (. . .) Tatsächlich gebe es keine die einzelnen Sprachspiele übergreifende Universalgrammatik."[7]

Zum Abschluß dieses Vergleiches, der versucht hatte, eine strenge Trennungslinie zwischen philosophischen Lagern etwas zu verwischen, kann man sich noch ein letztes Mal auf Wittgenstein berufen: „Wenn einer eine scharfe Grenze zöge, so könnte ich sie nicht als die anerkennen, die ich auch schon immer ziehen wollte oder im Geist gezogen habe. Denn ich wollte gar keine ziehen." (*PU* § 79).

ANMERKUNGEN

[1] Saussure, F. de, *Grundfragen der allgemeinen Sprachwissenschaft* (Berlin ²1967), S. 193.
[2] Saussure (1967), S. 134.
[3] Kenny, *Wittgenstein* (Frankfurt/Main 1974), S 82.
[4] nach Lang, *Die Sprache und das Unbewußte* (Frankfurt/Main 1973), S. 69
[5] Kenny (1974), S. 142.
[6] Frank, *Was ist Neostrukturalismus*? (Frankfurt/Main 1983), S. 106.
[7] Man könnte noch eine weitere Parallele nennen, die Frank in seiner Studie erwähnt; er meint, daß der spätere Wittgenstein und die Sprachphilosophen des Neostrukturalismus in ihrer gemeinsamen Ablehnung des Repräsentationsmodells der Sprache übereinkämen. Um nicht in unkritischer Weise zu vereinfachen, müßte man eher sagen, daß in den *PU* das Repräsentationsmodell zurücktritt, daß es gegenüber der Sprachspielstheorie an Gewicht verliert, wodurch sich die Inkommensurabilität zwischen Wittgenstein und den Neostrukturalisten bedeutsam verringert.

* * *

SENSATION DISCOURSE AND THE CORRECTNESS PRINCIPLE

Bruce W. Brower
University of Michigan

How strong is the verificationism which Wittgenstein makes use of in his later work? In this paper I show that the private language argument, at least, requires neither strong verificationism nor an assertibility theory of meaning. In the *Philosophical Investigations*, Wittgenstein makes implicit use of two crucial premises. The first, which I call 'the correctness constraint on meaning', is that in order to establish the use of a meaningful term, one must be able to distinguish between correct and incorrect use. The second, which I call 'the correctness principle', is that in order to distinguish between correct and incorrect use, one must be able to distinguish between being correct and seeming to be correct. To understand the role of these premises, we must look at the private language argument.

Unlike some commentators, including Saul Kripke, I take the private language argument contained in *PI*, sections 243–289, to be more than a mere application of an earlier argument. The only argument against private language to be found in the *Investigations* is an argument against the possibility of a language which meets the following conditions: (1) The terms of the language refer to the speaker's inner experiences. (2) These inner experiences can only be known to the speaker. (3) The speaker is the only person who can understand the language. (4) The terms must be introduced by inner ostensive defintion. Here, I examine only a part of this argument, after which I return to the topic of verificationism.

Wittgenstein's argument is directed against what I call 'the associative theory' according to which terms in a private language are introduced by inner ostensive definition. His argument may be reconstructed as having three subarguments, with these conclusions: (i) Ostensive defintion requires a type of stage setting. (ii) The required stage setting may not be borrowed from public language. (iii) The required stage setting cannot be done in private.

The heart of the third subargument, which concerns us here, is sections 258 and 265. In section 258 Wittgenstein imagines that he keeps a diary about the recurrence of a sensation associated with the sign 'S' by means of an inner ostensive definition accompanied by an inward concentration of attention. He claims:

> But 'I impress it on my self' can only mean: this process brings it about that I remember the connexion *right* in the future. But in the present case I have no criterion of correctness. One would like to say: Whatever is going to seem right to me is right. And that only means that here we can't talk about right.

In section 265 he imagines a table that is in the imagination. He suggests that the sort of justification given through the use of this table would be subjective and not independent. He then gives an example in which he contrasts checking the time of departure of a train by using the memory of a time table with the test of a current instance of use in private language by using the imaginary table.

According to the associative theory's criterion for correctness, I can only appeal to memory of an inner ostensive definition. But this criterion can only be used in a 'subjective justification', it cannot be used in a justification which appeals to something independent. The notion of independence here does *not* require that the independent thing be social; as a matter of fact, nowhere, in any of the discussion following section 243, is there any mention of the need for others to correct the individual. The contrast with the memory of the time table is important. I test my belief about the departure of the train by remembering the time table, but in this case my memory can be tested—I can get an actual time table and look at it. If I test my belief that 'S' must apply to my present inner sensation by appeal to my memory of an inner ostensive definition, then I have no further way of testing this memory. I have to assume my memory is correct. In this case, there is no way to distinguish between my memory's being correct and its seeming to be correct. This problem does not arise in the case of other memories, since other memories can be checked by considering something independent. In the case of *ordinary* ostensive definitions, memory may be checked by locating the original ostended object. Wittgenstein's argument here is based on the correctness constraint on meaning and the correctness principle.

It might be objected that if Wittgenstein's positive account of public sensation discourse entails that there is no distinction, in the case of an individual, between being in pain and seeming to be in pain, then how could Wittgenstein reject the associative theory because it did not allow an individual could distinguish between being in pain and seeming to be in pain?

Is there really a problem here for Wittgenstein? One way to escape the problem is to *accept* the view that since one cannot make the appropriate seeming-being distinction with regard to pain discourse, such discourse really is meaningless. This view seems to fit well with Wittgenstein's apparent claims that the word 'pain' is non-referential.

There are two problems with this view. The first I cannot construe in detail here, but it is that sections 293 through 317, which seem to support the view that sensation terms do not refer, really only make a point about the grammar—the justification—of sensation discourse and carefully avoid saying that such discourse is non-referntial.

The second problem involves a confusion about the content of the principle. Let us say that an *epistemic situation* is the situation of a particular individual at a particular time. Two versions of the correctness principle are:

> (a) For any predicate F, if, for all epistemic situations s and all objects x, no distinction can be made between x's being F and x's seeming to be F, then no sentence containing F is correct or incorrect.

> (b) For any predicate F, if there is some epistemic situation s and some object x for which no distinction can be made between x's being F and x's seeming to be F, then no sentence containing F is correct or incorrect.

Wittgenstein would accept (a) but not (b). If (b) were correct, then he could not allow, with regard to any meaningful predicate, that there is a situation in which an individual cannot distinguish between the predicate's seeming to be true of an object and its being true of an object. He *did*, however, hold that there are such situations, in cases of an individual speaking of his or her own sensations, in the discussion throughout *On Certainty*, and in the discussion of inductive certainty at *PI*, sections 471−485.

Sensation discourse in public language is crucially different from sensation discourse in private language. In public language, there may, for a given predicate, be some situations in which the individual cannot distinguish between being correct and seeming to be correct, but there are other situations in which the individual and others can make the distinction, e.g., in cases of discourse about other's pain, or about one's own past pain. It is only if Wittgenstein had held (b) instead of (a) that there would be a conflict between his positive theory and his argument against private language. On the other hand, in the private language under attack, there is *no* situation in which the speaker can distinguish between being correct and incorrect.

Conflation of (a) with (b) might also cause one to view the private language argument as excessively verificationist. (b) is an extremely strong principle. It does not allow that there could be any situations in which a speaker cannot make a distinction between a term's applying and its merely seeming to apply. (a), on the other hand, presupposes only a mild verificationism which can be rejected only if one allows that a term may be introduced even if there is no epistemic situation in which one could justify its use.

Other confusions are possible. In her paper "Private Languages",[1] Judith Jarvis Thomson takes the argument to be based on the claim that *we* could not verify the existence of a private language. The kind name 'private language' is taken to be meaningless because it is impossible for us to find out whether anything is a private language. Further, she takes it that the argument probably requires that it can, in principle, be found out with conclusive evidence whether or not something is a private language. She objects to this strongly verificationist line.

Whatever the merits are of this argument, it differs from Wittgenstein's in two respects. First, on his account, the problem in verification exists not for *us*, but for the private language speaker. The problem is not in verification of the use of the term 'private language' but in the use of the purported sensation terms of the private language. Second, (a) need not be interpreted in a strongly verificationist fashion. The claim is *not* that one must be able to conclusively justify whenever one is correct, and thus not that justifialbe use is to be identified with correct use. Rather, it is only that unless one has a distinction between justifiable and unjustifiable use, one cannot even attempt to make a distinction between uses which merely seem to be correct and those which seem to be correct but are not correct. Thus an individual can be wrong, but he must be able to distinguish between those cases where he is justified and those where he is not. A mere seeming to remember, unchecked and uncheckable, is not independent enough to count as a real or independent justification. Thomson agrees that Wittgenstein did not give the argument she considers, but she holds this because she takes him to advance no theses in philosophy. This is a poor interpretation. He may have had no positive theory, but he certainly rejected many views.

The correctness principle, as stated by (a), and the corresponding correctness constraint on meaning, ought, I think, to be accepted. The alternative, I noted, is to allow that a term may be introduced even if there is no situation in which its use may be justified. To allow this is to allow too wide a gap between the meanings of terms and the actual use of language. For instance, if (a) is rejected, it must be allowed that I could introduce a term into my language even if there was no reason at all for using it or not using it. I could thus invent a term, apply it to an object, and never have to justify my use, even if challenged. Such a term would seem a paradigm example of a meaningless word.

Principle (a), in conjunction with the correctness constraint on meaning, does not require that the *meaning* of terms be identified with the method of justifying predications of the terms to objects, nor does it require that meaning be identified with the contribution that terms make to assertibility conditions of sentences that contain them. (a) allows us to be realists about reference and the world, and yet it places a mild verificationist *constraint* on meaning.[2]

ENDNOTES

[1] Thomson, J. J., "Private Languages", *American Philosophical Quarterly*, Vol. 1 (1964), pp. 20−31.
[2] I would like to thank Annette Baier, and especielly Joseph Camp, Jr., for helpful comments on earlier versions of this paper.

* * *

THEORY AND PHENOMENA: PLATO AND THE LATER WITTGENSTEIN

A. M. Wiles
James Madison University, Harrisonburg

The work of Plato and Wittgenstein is often presented as having little in common. Plato is an idealist searching for universals; Wittgenstein more interested in the use of words. However, a common problem, central to both philosophies, is the question of how a theoretic account is related to phenomena. Any theory will reveal some things, conceal others, and *thereby* distort understanding of the phenomena. Yet, an account must somehow be given—if philosophy is to be done. While some philosophers (certain game/descision theorists) stress theory to the virtual exclusion of phenomena and others (existentialists and phenomenologists) generally abjure theory, Plato and the later Wittgenstein correctly show that successful intellectual inquiry requires both. Their resolution of this tension is worked out in their 1) philosophical techniques, 2) metaphilosophy and 3) literary style.

Plato wrote twenty-six dialogues and his works clearly constitute a *system* of philosophy containing a distinguishable ethics, aesthetics, political theory, epistemology, and metaphysics. Since Wittgenstein's later writing is often cryptic and aphoristic, and the primary sources are now fairly extensive, some detailed analysis is needed to understand his work as a system. Bambrough[1] shows that certain patterns and structures are exhibited by Wittgenstein's mosaic of examples and remarks; and, in the detailed study of the *Investigations*, recently completed by Baker and Hacker,[2] the authors argue that there is a unity in the work.

Plato and Wittgenstein are sensitive to the power and limitations of language. Plato assumes that a correct, consistent use of language is essential to adequate intellectual inquiry and good action. In the *Philebus*, [3]he argues that we must not be misologists and must avoid being misguided by false descriptions.

Three important, general points about language are made by Plato in several places in the middle and late dialogues: 1) the rhetorical use of language is distinguished from, but importantly related to the dialectical use. The main purpose of rhetoric is to sway emotion; of dialectic, to discover truth. The two uses may be in or out of harmony. If rhetoric is out of harmony with dialectic, the result is sophistry; if in harmony, the result is what Aristotle later referred to as practical wisdom. Dialectic in harmony with rhetoric provides truths about realities by which we are also charmed. This is not an isolated point about language; it is intimately connected with Plato's ontology, a tenet of which is that a person, being a composite of LOGOS and THUMOS, is attracted by both beauty and truth. 2) Throughout the dialogues, Plato assumes it is possible to discover and formulate a fairly adequate verbal account of the nature (essence, being) of any subject indicated by a general term. 3) Finally, although forms can be discovered and interconnections noted, Plato thinks written language is inadequate; and that such understanding can only be accomplished over a long period in live dialogue where questions are put and responses are modified by an awareness of phenomena.[4]

Underlying the well-known metaphors used by Wittgenstein are several assumptions about language. Language as it is, already working, must be the starting point of philosophical inquiry; language is a part of our natural history (*PI* § 25). It is a form of life, simply there, lying beyond justification; it is like our life, neither justified or unjustified (*OC*, § 359 and 559, and *PI*, § 19, 20), and combines the most diverse elements. There are many and varied uses of language (*PI*, § 23). Language has rules (*PI*, § 497), but they are flexible and varied from practice to practice. Hence we cannot say *in abstracto* what language is *essentially*, or what the meaning of a word is, but must in each case "look and see", examine language in the form of life which is its natural home. It is only in a given context that a word has meaning. Language and its concepts are instruments (*PI*, § 569). The concepts we have lead us to make certain investigations rather than others; they are the *expression* of our interest, and they *direct* our interest (*PI*, § 571) hence the importance of language for our conduct.

A central assumption Wittgenstein makes about language is that we are easily misled (bewitched) by it, particularly in philosophy. This often occurs because we attend only to surface analogies, so that from *prima facie* analogous grammars, we try to make the analogy hold throughout (*BLB* 7). It is not an isolated use of language that causes such confusion, but the whole conceptual system. A main source of our failure to understand is that we do not command a clear view of the use of our words, "Our grammar is lacking in this sort of perspicuity. A perspicuous representation produces just that understanding which consists in seeing connexions" (*PI*, § 122).

The philosophical techniques and metaphilosophy of Plato are intertwined with his views about language. The truth of all things is always in our souls and Plato recommends five principal techniques for apprehending or recollecting the forms: definition, hypothesis, analogy, example, and the double process of collection and division, with frequent overlapping among these techniques. A definition, or formal account, can be given of *any* concept, and if the definition is too broad or too narrow, this can be shown by the discovery or construction of counterexamples. The method of hypothesis is used by the early Socrates, as well as the Eleatic Stranger in the *Laws*; both frequently assume a proposition then draw out its logical or empirical consequences to test its accord with the phenomena. It is always possible for *any* hypothesis to be modified, although some are less subject to modification than others. Analogy and example are widely useful as techniques for measuring conclusions reached in philosophical argument. In the *Statesman* Plato claims, "It is difficult . . . to demonstrate sufficiently anything of real importance without the use of examples . . ."[5] The double process of collection and division is described in the *Phaedrus*[6] as 1) bringing a dispersed plurality under a single form, and 2) dividing one form into others, following the objective articulation – two processes which we know as synthesis and analysis. In dialogues after the *Phaedrus* this method is prominent.

On Plato's view, it is only by means of the forms (or universals) that we have *knowledge* of phenomena, and only through knowledge of forms and their interrelations that we have objective standards for excellence in our conduct and other practical matters. The rational account given of phenomena must not *contradict* the experience of the best and wisest persons, as transmitted by tradtition and literature, but it may *go beyond* it by being systematically articulated and rationally supported.

Wittgenstein thought the point of philosophy was to do away with explanation and concentrate on description – description of how the language works. Philosophical problems are "solved not by giving new information but by re-arranging what we have always known" (*PI*, § 109). Philosophers have assumed that only *exact*, that is clearly circumscribed, precisely defined, concepts are useful. Wittgenstein, much like Aristotle on this point, holds that often we cannot obtain such exact concepts, particularly in ethics and aesthetics, but that inexact concepts nonetheless are useful.(*PI*, § 71). If we choose, we can *draw* rigid conceptual boundaries in order to play some particular language game, but when we impose the boundaries we have drawn for one purpose onto some other game, the language bewitches us.

The primary method used in the *Investigations* is assembling "reminders" of how language functions. Frequently what this does is to dissolve a problem, a knot in out thinking which was caused by a missuse of language. Wittgenstein's reminders are apt to be in the form of parable, or short paradoxical statements ("If a lion could talk, we could not understand him"), but they serve essentially the same purpose as counter-example in Plato's approach, i.e. to correct the account of the phenomena. It is important to have a correct account of the phenomena because how we describe our experience, what we "see something as", influences what we do in respect to it (*PI*, § 74–76).

The method has an empirical aspect since language is a natural phenomenon. Wittgenstein is, however, quite emphatic on the point that his investigations are not *scientific* or *empirical* investigations for the purpose is to understand the logic (grammar) of the language. When Wittgenstein uses the term 'grammar' in *this* context (*PI*, § 371, 373), he does not mean sentence structure; he means essence.

Given a specific form of life, its grammar or logic (its essence) can be discovered and articulated; in brief, it can be described. In one sense, the logic of a form of life is necessary; in another sense, it is not. The sense in which it is *not* is that we cannot impose the logic from one form of life onto another form. The sense in which it *is*, is that any form of life has its own logic, peculiar to it and necessitated by it. Within a given form of life, one cannot mean whatever one chooses to mean by a term; a concept *relative to a particular form of life* is non-arbitrary, Concepts are always context dependent in this sense.

While knowing the logic of a form of life is important, even necessary, in understanding it, this is yet not sufficient. There is more to understanding than knowing the rules. Understanding requires getting into the practice or form of life and finding our way about in it. This includes such activities as giving and receiving tips, developing skills, noting nuances and colorations, conveying mood, calling attention to aspects of things that are not apparent, and generally getting a "feel" for the activity. Understanding is, to use an older terminology, as much a matter of habit as it is of rational comprehension, and habits are formed by exercise.

If language is inherently inadequate or misleading, and yet a philosopher has to use it, what can he legitimately do with it? The dogmatic idiom of the essaist will not suffice. Plato, believing written language inadequate for the purposes of philosophy, resolved the difficulty by adopting the style most akin to conversation, a style which mirrors what he took to be the nature of philosophy, i.e., the giving and receiving of a rational account—always as modified by the presence and influence of the phenomena. But he recognized as well that a kind of intuitive rational insight into the essence or nature of the subject was an indispensible component of understanding.

Wittgenstein said that what philosophers most need is a perspicuous representation of the use of our words. If this is not to be done by constructing a *theory*, how is it to be done? Hallett[7] suggests that Wittgenstein's later philosophy it is done by this technique of citing a list of concrete examples and thereby *revealing* (not stating) the grammar (or essence) of an expression. If exposition or theory construction in philosophy necessarily misleads, one need not thereby be reduced to silence—as we see Wittgenstein was not. One may make the phenomena clearer merely by drawing attention to certain features.

Both Plato and Wittgenstein are guided and restricted by the natural contours (being) of the subject, although Wittgenstein emphasizes context more that Plato; both assume that knowledge of concepts is possible, and that this knowledge is in some sense objective and necessary—that we can know essence. Both also point to a central truth about the relation of theory and phenomena, namely that neither can be slighted at the expense of the other.

The style of Plato and of Wittgenstein, being intimately connected with their views about language and philosophy, is highly unique. If Plutarch is correct in his claim that style is the outflow of character, this betokens the originality of each. However, one feature their styles have in common is that each forces the reader to *participate* in the dialogue, in the practice of philosophising. It is precisely because they both believe philosophy to be a serious pursuit, engaging affections as well as intellect, that their writings contain much playfulness, humor and paradox.

ENDNOTES

[1] Bambrough, Renford, "How to Read Wittgenstein", in: *Understanding Wittgenstein*. Royal Institute of Philosophy Lectures. Vol. VII (New York 1974).

[2] Baker, G. P. and P. M. S. Hacker, *Wittgenstein: Understanding and Meaning* (Oxford 1980).

[3] Plato, *Philebus*, 57 b − 58 e. in Edith Hamilton and Huntington Cairns (eds.), *The Collected Dialogues of Plato* (Princeton 1961).

[4] Plato, *Letter VII*, 241 c−d.

[5] Plato, *Statesman*, 277 d.

[6] Plato, *Phaedrus*, 265 d−266 b.

[7] Hallett, Garth, *A Companion to Wittgenstein's "Philosophical Investigations"* (Ithaca-London 1977), p. 34.

* * *

CERTAINTY AS A FORM OF LIFE

Elizabeth H. Wolgast
California State University, Hayward

I

Wittgenstein puzzled over Moores' truisms because they were propositions whose certainty rested neither on evidence nor upon a grammatical ground. They appeared to fall between the traditional classes of empirical and *a priori*. Throughout the notes collected in the volume *On Certainty* Wittgenstein returns again and again to this aspect of such propositions: they *appear to be* empirical yet play the role of *a priori* propositions; their position in our language is similar to *a priori* propositions, yet they are capable of change and one can imagine a language where their position is quite different. Thus they are like propositions which state contingent facts and express beliefs, as a tribe might believe, for example, that the world has just come into existence or that people are immortal or that they have come from the moon. Yet it is impossible for us to even imagine such things—impossible in the sense of jarring our way of looking at innumerable things, of upsetting our *Weltbild*, our most general conception of the world. What is the nature of such propositions then? Are they empirical, or *a priori*, or possibly neither? It is in answer to this question that Wittgenstein turns our attention away from the propositions and speaks instead of a form of life.

Empirical propositions are characterized by their openness to questioning and the giving of evidence in their behalf. Yet justifications do not go on forever, nor do they end in propositions of another kind. In his *Philosophical Investigations* Wittgenstein dealt with the problem how a justification *can* come to an end. He wrote: "If I have exhausted the justifications I have reached bedrock, and my spade is turned. Then I am inclined to say: 'This is simply what I do'" (*PI* 217). To continue raising questions after such a point is idle, foolish, and this is to say that some things aren't questioned—not *because* the propositions which state them are *a priori* or grammatical, which would be to have a reason for not questioning—but just because *we don't*.[1] The end to giving justifications has itself no reason.

Yet in a sense, the termination of giving justifications has every justification, and this lies in the fact that we live within a certain framework of beliefs and procedures and ways of viewing the world. Where justifications come to an end is where unspoken attitudes and convictions begin, matters which are not discussed or debated or justified, but which have a more central place in our lives than the propositions which are dicussed and questioned. These hang together with our expressed beliefs in a large design.

It is in this region of unexpressed beliefs that Moore's examples belong. Their immunity to questions does not mean they are taken for granted in a trivializing sense. On the contrary, Wittgenstein writes, "I would like to regard this certainty not as something akin to hastiness or superficiality, but as a form of life" (*OC* 358). He wants "to conceive it as something that lies beyond being justified or unjustified; as it were, as something animal" (*OC* 359). It isn't part of our lives as discursive and reasoning creatures; rather we should think here of man "as a primitive being to which one grants instinct but not ratiocination. As a creature in a primitive state" (*OC* 475).

Besides those parts of our lives which are involved with language and reasoning is another part which is more primitive, more fundamental, lying close to our natures as a species, a species with a characteristic mode (or modes) of existence.[2] We function on this level like animals, and on this level have convictions which are never reasoned out or arrived at, just as the squirrel does not arrive at its conviction that it will need food in the winter. We simply grow into a kind or form of life, and come to accept many things without question, or even thinking, as part of that form. Our certainty about some things "is not based on grounds. It is not reasonable (or unreasonable). It is there—like our life" (*OC* 559). To ask for justification of such beliefs is to misunderstand their nature. "We don't start from certain words, but from certain occasions or activities" (*RC* 3), and the truisms mark such beginnings. They signify beliefs which lie deeper than any justification, which belong more to our way of living than to our way of reasoning. "At some point one has to pass from explanation to mere description", Wittgenstein writes (*OC* 189). And the description is a description of what we do, what we do before thinking and without thinking.

The curiously certain truisms which are neither asserted nor questioned belong, then, to a region which is best described as outside language, to a rudimentary and primitive side of our lives and not to the side which is engaged with discourse and reasoning. Reasoning is more-over frequently a source of confusions, illusions. That the truisms are rooted in our lives without dependence upon reasoning gives them, by contrast, their particular substance and importance. Their having no justifications is therefore a virtue and sign of strength, not a sign of weakness. Viewed in this way the problem of their certainty dissolves.

This striking and pregnant account of the truisms is witness to Wittgenstein's richly imagin-ative approach. Yet he often expresses misgivings about his result: "That is very badly expres-sed and probably badly thought as well" he comments about one passage where the phrase "form of life" enters (*OC* 358), and throughout there are expressions of dissatisfaction and puzzlement. In this brief paper I will argue that the misgivings were well founded, and point to a kind of misunderstanding which Wittgenstein was usually on guard against and indeed famous for pointing out.

II

We do countless things every day without stopping to ask what beliefs underlie them. We simply act. Thus we don't examine the ground before the door when we step out. Might it be soft as oatmeal and give way? Yes it might, but no one in his right mind would stop to wonder about it! But you check a train schedule before going to the station (a philosopher responds); how much greater risk rides on this possibility, yet you ignore it.

There's a difference between the cases, Wittgenstein argues. The one concerns our being able to live normally: "My *life* consists in my being able to accept many things" (*OC* 344). My life, as opposed to my philosophy, my reasoned convictions. Our life takes form long before we learn to doubt and give justification, so that in a sense doubt and justifications rest upon this basis, they exist against this background. In that background are general propositions, such as the consistency and uniformity of natural events, which allow the methods of science to make sense. Then there are more specific propositions about ourselves and our place in the world.

> My life shews that I know or am certain that there is a chair over there, or a door, and so on—I tell a friend e.g. "Take that chair over there", "Shut the door", etc. etc. (*OC* 7)

The knowledge that this is a chair, and my certainty that it is, are embedded in what I do. It is not the result of some procedure or chain of reasoning. But then it is a presupposition. No. "The end (of giving justifications) is not an ungrounded presupposition: it is an ungrounded way of acting" (*OC* 110). Ungrounded—that means lacking justification; but to *do* something one doesn't always need justification and often couldn't think what one would look like. Does an infant "know that milk exists? Does a cat know that a mouse exists?" (*OC* 478) There is no appropriate answer.

The certainty of such things Wittgenstein calls "comfortable certainty" which he contrasts to the certainty "that is still struggling" (*OC* 358). If a person asserts, for example, "I'm *certain* he'll come soon", it is understood that there is some real or potential doubt *whether* he'll come soon. That is part of the normal background of such a remark, and signifies a real or potential opposition of views. There is, you might say, an implicit contest between views, and either side may claim justification without silencing the other. This is the certainty that is still struggling. It belongs where matters are not viewed as settled. Compare with this the certainty of the proposition that the world has existed for a long time: no opposition of views relates to this proposition. It is fixed, an undisputed rock where other certainties are soft and subject to erosion, like sand. Of course no one *asserts* such a fact—that is part of its role in the foundations of language, in the form our lives take. Its certainty goes unnoticed except in philosophy.

Yet there is an interesting result when a certainty is asserted. Wittgenstein takes as an example that his name is L. W. Instantly he finds himself asking "Why is there no doubt that I am called L. W.?" and goes on to remark that "it does not seem at all like something that one could establish at once beyond doubt" (*OC* 470). He worries the example:

> It is right to say of myself "I cannot be mistaken about my name", and wrong if I say "perhaps I am mistaken". But that doesn't mean that it is meaningless for others to doubt what I declare to be certain. (*OC* 629).

When he asserts as a certainty that he is L. W., Wittenstein's remark takes on the character of a certainty that is still struggling. It invokes a background of doubt and potential disagreement, just as the example "I'm certain he'll come soon" was seen to do. The background was not there before; no one questioned whether Wittgenstein's name was L. W. Yet now, when he has asserted it, the possibility of doubting it comes to life. It is not meaningless for other to doubt it, but quite in order.

This pattern of presenting an example and then asking how one might deal with doubts recurs throughout Wittgenstein's notes. And occasionally he sees something to be fishy in the attempt to locate comfortable certainties:

> When one hears Moore say "I *know* that that's a tree", one suddenly understands those who think that that has by no means been settled . . . It is as if "I know" did not tolerate a metaphysical emphasis (*OC* 481—2).

To make "I know" or "It is certain" introduce final pronouncements signifying the end of doubting is impossible. That metaphysical emphasis is not possible. The assertions themselves are witness that one is dealing with the certainty that is still struggling.

The problem Wittgenstein faces here has a grammatical ground. To say something is certain legitimizes questions about its truth. That is why with each example Wittgenstein asks himself—"But couldn't it be doubted? Couldn't the contradictory be believed? And the answer must be yes, however weird and unsettling the implications of saying this, however ajar with a multitude of things we do. Asserting the proposition is introducing the game in which certainties are *not only* asserted but also questioned. The two concepts work synergistically. This means that you cannot—as a matter of grammar—pronounce something to be certain and then reject the game of questioning and doubting which that pronouncement introduces. It follows, then, that there is no such thing as comfortable certainty.

The truisms, and other such propositions, don't play a role in our normal discourse. No one asserts them or even contemplates them outside philosophy. Therefore Wittgenstein is encouraged to locate them outside the working language, which is to say also outside the arena of doubt and investigation where struggling certainty is active. He proposes to bury them underground, like rocks in the earth, or to locate them in activities, in the fabric of our non-discursive lives. But this effort is futile. The certainty of truisms must belong to the kind of game where certainty and its opposite both exist. To continue protesting their certainty keeps the game going. It is, to put it bluntly, to protest too much.

ENDNOTES

[1] Norman Malcolm pursues Wittgenstein's line of reasoning about justifications in his perceptive essay, "The Groundlessness of Belief" in: N. Malcolm *Thought and Knowledge* (Ithaca, N.Y. 1977), pp. 199–216.

[2] Other authors have questioned whether by 'form of life' Wittgenstein means 'biological form' or 'culture' or both. I do not find this inquiry helpful, for I view the conception in terms of what it is contrasted with, *viz* discourse and reasoning *per se*.

* * *

WITTGENSTEIN: DIE ANTIZIPATION DER POSTMODERNE

Nobert Meder
Universität Köln

In seinem Bericht „Das postmoderne Wissen" geht es Lyotard um die Frage: Welchen strukturellen Wandel bringt das informationsverarbeitende Zeitalter mit sich? Für die Beantwortung dieser Frage des sozialen Wandels wählt Lyotard den Begriff des Sprachspiels von Wittgenstein. Den Erklärungswert dieses Begriffs sieht er darin, daß er es erlaubt, einerseits nach Regeln in sprachlichen Kontexten zu suchen, und daß er es erlaubt, andererseits das sprachliche Handeln als einen Wettstreit im Sinne des Spielens aufzufassen, der das Spiel dynamisch weitertreibt, neue Spielzüge generieren läßt, bis hin zur Veränderung der Regeln und des Spieles selbst. Über den so bezeichneten Erklärungswert des Begriffs vom Sprachspiel hinaus, gibt ein weiterer Umstand Veranlassung für seine methodische Verwendung. Einer impliziten Anregung Lyotards verdanke ich die These, daß die gesamte Philosophie Wittgensteins als Antizipation jenes Wandels angesehen werden kann, um dessen Beschreibung es Lyotard geht. Wittgenstein hat ihn schon theoretisch formuliert, ohne den technologisch-ökonomischen Wandel erlebt zu haben.

Lyotard setzt die Beschreibung des Wandels zum postmodernen Wissen damit an, das vorwissenschaftliche, das vormoderne Wissen in seiner Pragmatik als überwiegend narrativ zu charakterisieren. In Erzählungen wird tradiert, was wahr und falsch, was gut und böse, was Glück und Unglück ist. Die populären Geschichten erzählen, was man positive oder negative Bildung nennen könnte. Die Helden legitimieren in ihrem Erfolg und Mißerfolg die gesellschaftlich notwendigen Institutionen und geben als leitende Beispiele den Maßstab für Kompetenz und Leistung. Die hohe Flexibilität der narrativen Form gestattet die Integration einer Vielfalt von Sprachspielen, die wir aus heutiger Sicht als unverträglich bezeichnen würden. Beschreibende Aussagen, Vorschriften, Fragen und Bewertungen bilden ein dichtes Geflecht, das die Gesamtperspektive der jeweiligen Kultur zum Ausdruck bringt.

Wenn man diese Pragmatik narrativen Wissens mit derjenigen wissenschaftlichen Wissens vergleicht, wie es die Neuzeit und insbesondere die Moderne ausprägt, dann sind folgende Unterschiede festzuhalten, die auf Prinzipien der Moderne beruhen, zu deren Aufhebung die Postmoderne tendiert.

Das wissenschaftliche Wissen fordert die *Ausdifferenzierung* eines besonderen Sprachspiels, das der wahrheitsfähigen beschreibenden Sätze. Von anderen Sprachspielen getrennt, hat es nicht mehr unmittelbar Teil an der Selbstvergewisserung um das soziale Band der Gesellschaft. Dieses muß vielmehr in *sozialer Organisation* aus verschiedenen Sprachspielen, wie aus Kettengliedern, rekombiniert werden. Soziale Organisation beruht wesentlich auf Zentralisierung und Rollenzuweisung. Die „wissenschaftlichen" Rollen sind Proponent und Opponent. Der Proponent hat die Aufgabe, eine Aussage zu verifizieren. Er trägt die Beweislast. Der Opponent dagegen hat die Funktion zu falsifizieren. Es ist wichtig zu sehen, daß der Opponent es besser hat, weil Widerlegungsbeweise einfacher zu führen sind; häufig genügt der Hinweis auf Gegenbeispiele. Darin zeigt sich, daß dieses Spiel nicht die innere Tendenz zur Konsistenz eines Gebäudes von Aussagen hat, sondern die Tendenz zur Auflösung im Widerspruch und im Dissens. Hier liegt der Keim zur Postmodernen. Wenn das Spiel von Proponent und Opponent sich als Verifikation und Falsifikation prozessualisiert, dann hat dieser Prozeß die Tendenz, Beweise stetig und dicht zu machen. Stetigkeit kann aber nur erreicht werden durch beständige Zerlegung in kleinste logische Atome und deren lückenlose Verknüpfung nach möglichst einfachen Regeln. Wir werden später sehen, daß Wittgensteins Traktat als Vollendung dieser *Rationalisierungstendenz* betrachtet werden kann und daß in dieser Vollendung das postmoderne Wissen aufbricht. Die Rationalisierung des Beweises muß nämlich als Antwort auf die Frage aufgefaßt werden: Was ist ein Beweis? Wer und Was entscheidet über die Bedingungen des Wahren? Die Antwort, die die Rationalisierung gibt, lautet: Was ein Beweis ist zeigt sich in der Pragmatik seines stetigen Vollzugs. Die Bedingungen des Wahren liegen im Innern des Spieles selbst, und deren Vergewisserung artikuliert sich im Konsens der Mitspieler. Auch dies ist eine Konsequenz, die Wittgenstein im Traktat zieht.

Dies allerdings ist die späte, vielleicht sogar letzte Antwort auf die so gestellte Legitimationsfrage. Zuvor hat das moderne Wissen andere Versuche von Antworten vorgelegt. Dies waren die großen Metaphysiken des deutschen Idealismus. Lyotard deutet sie als die großen metaphysischen Erzählungen der Neuzeit. In ihnen gewinnt das narrative Wissen, obwohl scheinbar überwunden, erneut die Oberhand. Dies zeigt sich im dreifach unitarischen Charakter dieser Erzählungen, den Lyotard im Rückgriff auf Humboldt folgendermaßen charakterisiert: „,einmal alles aus einem ursprünglichen Prinzip abzuleiten', dem die wissenschaftliche Aktivität entspricht; ,ferner alles einem Ideal zuzubilden', welches die ethische und soziale Praxis leitet; ,endlich jenes Prinzip und dieses Ideal in Eine Idee zu verknüpfen', welche sicher stellt, daß die Erforschung der wahren Ursachen in der Wissenschaft nicht umhin kann mit dem Streben nach gerechten Zielen im moralischen und politischen Leben übereinzustimmen. Das legitime Subjekt konstituiert sich in dieser letzten Synthese." (S. 63)
Von ihm erzählen die großen metaphysischen Geschichten der Neuzeit. Der Held erscheint einmal als das absolute Subjekt des Wissens, ein andermal als die Menschheit auf dem Weg der Emanzipation zur Freiheit. Diese großen Erzählungen sind heute unglaubwürdig geworden. Den Helden der Wissenschaft hat die Wissenschaft selbst entthront, und daran war Wittgenstein nicht unbeteiligt. Den Helden der Freiheit hat zuletzt die Studentenrevolte der 60er und 70er Jahre gestürzt. In ihrem Versuch, die linke Erzählung in die soziale Realität umzusetzen, hat sie recht eigentlich deren Scheitern demonstriert, d.h. die Unglaubwürdigkeit des marxistischen Helden ins Bewußtsein gerufen. Daß dabei auch der kapitalistische Held der Erzählung vom „Bereichert euch" fiel, darf als positive Nebenwirkung gelten. Was die Erzählung vom Helden des Wissens anlangt, will ich nun zu Wittgenstein kommen und zu zeigen versuchen, wie sich in ihm die Geschichte, indem er sie erzält, beginnt aufzulösen. Meine erste Teilthese lautet: der Traktat ist der letzte Versuch, die Geschichte vom Helden des Wissens zu erzählen. Dies zeigt sich schon im Vorwort: „Dagegen scheint mir die Wahrheit der hier mitgeteilten Gedanken unantastbar und definitiv. Ich bin also der Meinung die Probleme im Wesentlichen endgültig gelöst zu haben."
Inwiefern hat Wittgenstein die Probleme gelöst?
Mit der Angabe der allgemeinen Form des Satzes in der Gestalt einer rekursiven Funktion hat Wittgenstein gleichsam die Weltformel gefunden. Ihr „Elementarteilchen" ist das Weder-Noch. Im Ausgang von gegebenen Sätzen läßt sich mit ihm in operativer Form jeder wahre Satz erzeugen. Darin vollendet sich der Prozeß der Rationalisierung des Beweises und damit der Pragmatik modernen Wissens. Die Zergliederung erreicht das Minimum des Möglichen, nämlich die dualen Momente 0 und 1 bzw. wahr und falsch von Elementarsätzen, und die Regel der Rekombination von Aggregaten des Wissens ist einfach, einzig und konstruktiv: nämlich die Form des Weder-Noch. Wir wissen heute, daß sich jede Hardware eines Computers in einer dieser beiden Formen schalten läßt. Die Wittgensteinsche Weltformel heißt in der Computersprache NOR als die Verkürzung von „not" und „or": nicht das eine und nicht das andere. Wir wissen aber auch, daß die Programmiersprache LISP nach dem Prinzip der allgemeinen Satzform gebaut ist, derzufolge *eine* Operation durch wiederholte Anwendung auf ihre Resultate und d.h. auf sich selbst jede Information generiert.
Somit erzählt der Traktat die Geschichte von dem einen ursprünglichen Prinzip, aus dem alles abgeleitet werden kann, aber der Held der Erzählung erweist sich nicht als das Menschheitsubjekt des Wissens und der Freiheit, der Held ist die künstliche Intelligenz. Das Telos des neuzeitlichen und insbesondere modernen Versuchs der Ergründung der Subjektivität in ihrer Beherrschung des Wissens ist erreicht, aber das Subjekt erweist sich als Maschine. Dies hat auch Wittgenstein deutlich erkannt. Deshalb fährt er auch im Anschluß an die zitierte

Stelle des Vorworts fort: „Und wenn ich mich nicht irre, so besteht nun der Wert dieser Arbeit zweitens darin, daß sie zeigt, wie wenig damit getan ist, daß diese Probleme gelöst sind." In diesem Sinne formuliert er auch am Ende des Traktats (*TLP* 6.52): „Wir fühlen, daß selbst, wenn alle möglichen wissenschaftlichen Fragen beantwortete sind, unsere Lebensprobleme noch gar nicht berührt sind." Die Geschichte ist zuende erzählt, der Held ist gefunden. Die Maschine ist das Subjekt als künstliche Intelligenz. Und wir stellen fest, daß die Geschichte gar nicht von uns handelt. Wir kommen in ihr nicht vor. Welche Konsequenzen zieht Wittgenstein aus diesem Resultat seines Traktates?

1. Er schweigt und trauert. Nach Lyotard hat Wittgenstein neben Musil, Mach u.a. „das Bewußtsein wie die theoretische und künstlerische Verantwortung" für die Auflösung und damit die Delegitimierung des universalistischen Konzepts vom modernen Wissen getragen. „Man kann heute sagen, daß diese Arbeit der Trauer abgeschlossen worden ist." (S. 77) Das postmoderne Wissen hat mit dieser Trauer nichts mehr zu tun: Der späte Wittgenstein zeigt das postmoderne Konzept des Wissens, das jenseits der Trauer entsteht.

2. So lautet die erste positive Konsequenz: Die Wissenschaft spielt ihr eigenes Spiel als Maschinenspiel. Die meisten Spielzüge, d.h. die meisten Sätze werden maschinell produziert. Damit wird Wissenschaft veräußerlicht und kann die anderen Sprachspiele nicht mehr im Sinne eines gesamtsystemischen Subjektes legitimieren, insbesondere nicht mehr das Sprachspiel der Ethik.

3. Das neuzeitliche Selbstkonzept des Menschen als des Mittelpunktes der Welt löst sich auf. Subjektivität ist die informationsverarbeitende Maschine. Sie diktiert die Form des Wissens und erzwingt sie über die Kanäle des Inputs. Was da keinen Eingang findet, was nicht in Informationsquantitäten übersetzbar ist, wird vernachlässigt. Dies ist das Verdikt postmodernen wissenaftlichen Wissens. Ich würde Wittgensteins späte Solipsismuskritik und Privatsprachenargumentation heute so verstehen, daß sie das Selbstkonzept des Menschen als *Subjekt* des Wissens widerlegen, aber zugleich ein neues Selbstkonzept implizit vorschlagen: das des Sprachspielers.

4. Worin und als was zeigt sich dieses Selbstkonzept? Der Sprachspieler ist das, was er ist und wie er ist, als Befindlichkeit im Sprachspiel. Er *weiß* nicht, daß er Schmerz empfindet, sondern er empfindet Schmerz. Er weiß nicht, was er macht im Spiel, sondern er macht es, und was es ist, was er dabei macht, ergibt sich aus der figuralen Vernetzung von Spielzügen, in der sich das Sprachspiel aktualisiert und situativ präsentiert. Das Selbstkonzept des Sprachspielers ist die feldartige Perspektive und die Sensibilität im Sprachspiel. Es ist nicht mehr Selbst*bewußtsein*, was der Sprachspieler hat, denn dies impliziert, daß er um alle Möglichkeiten im Spiel wissen könnte, wenn man ihm nur Zeit ließe. Diese Charakteristik trifft aber vielmehr auf die intelligente Maschine zu. Stattdessen besitzt der Sprachspieler Selbstgewißheit, die auf seiner Sensibilität für Unterschiede und der damit gegeben gleichsam lokal determinierten Perspektive beruht. Dieses Selbstkonzept hat Wittgenstein nicht wissenschaftlich deduziert, sondern vorgemacht und damit in jenes Sprachspiel eingeführt, das die große metaphysische Erzählung ablösen kann: die aphoristische Kurzgeschichte als Ausdruck des postmodernen narrativen Wissens, was heute häufig in der rückgewonnen Gewißheit und Sicherheit „das wilde Denken" genannt wird. Darin gewinnt das Irrationale die Oberhand über die Rationalisierungstendenz der Moderne.

5. Es bleibt die Frage ob sich in einer solchen Gewißheit auch die Selbstvergewisserung des sozialen Bandes, das eine Gesellschaft zusammenhält, vollziehen kann. Das soziale Gefüge scheint zerfallen in die Vielfalt von scheinbar unabhängigen Sprachspielen. Und dies als Konsequenz davon, daß sie ihre Prinzipien der Rationalisierung und interpersonalen Organisation zunehmend an die maschinelle Informationsverarbeitung abgibt und damit der gesellschaftlichen Praxis entäußert: Computergesteuerte Produktion von Gütern und Wissen im Modus intramaschineller Organisation. Was *in* der gesellschaftlichen Praxis zurückbleibt, ist das Bewußtsein der Perspektivität der Sprachspieler; Perspektive ist stets diese und nicht jene, d.h. sie ist stets nur eine im Horizont vieler Möglichkeiten. Das Bewußtsein darum ist ein ästhetisches: die Perspektive ist in sich geschlossen und dennoch partial, sie ist das Ganze im

Teil und verweist in diesem Grundzug auf andere Alternativen – als offenes Ganzes. Mir scheint, daß die Konzeption der Familienähnlichkeiten beim späten Wittgenstein, diesem Grundzug der Sprachspiele Rechnung trägt. Demnach erstellt sich das soziale Band, indem gespielt wird, in dem die Partialität des Sprachspiels als solche stattfindet und die darin liegende Verweisung auf andere Sprachspiele ausgeführt wird. Lyotard charakterisiert das so: Der Konsens ist nicht Ziel des Sprachspiels sondern sein Zustand. Das Ziel ist vielmehr der Dissens oder die Divergenz in die Vielfalt. Solches Operieren ist Kreativität – als das Ästhetische in der divergenten Erzeugung neuer und anderer Sprachspiele.

6. Das Wissen der künstlichen Intelligenz ist formal und leer, was auch Wittgenstein am Ende seines Traktates erkannt hat. Elementarsätze als Operationsbasen hat der Traktat dem Paradigma modernen Wissens folgend nicht finden können. Andererseits müssen sie gegeben werden, soll sich die künstliche Intelligenz im Sinne des Kapitals amortisieren. Mithin müssen sie *er*funden werden oder als Ausdruck unserer Handlungsweise zur ästhetischen Darstellung kommen. Beides leistet das postmoderne Sprachspielwissen. Das letztere hat Wittgenstein in seinen Beschreibungen von Sprachspielen vorgemacht, das erstere ist das Resultat der Selbstgewißheit des Sprachspielers. Im Ausgang von seiner lokalen Perspektive in einem Sprachspiel generiert er die durch die Perspektivität mitgegebenen oder auch erzwungenen alternativen Möglichkeiten und produziert neue Grammatiken für neue Sprachspiele, deren Spielzüge er im Computer simuliert. Der Sprachspieler produziert mögliche Welten und überlistet die Subjektivität künstlicher Intelligenz, in dem er deren „wahres" Wissen zur Simulation macht. Simulation aber zeigt den Vorrang des Ästhetischen an, das ich auch in diesem Sinn als den Grundzug postmodernen Wissens bezeichnen möchte.

LITERATUR

Lyotard, J.-F., „Das postmoderne Wissen. Ein Bericht", *Theatro Machinarum*, Heft 3/4 (1982), Jg. 1 bei: Verlag Impuls & Association, Bremen.
Koenne, W., „Rekursive Techniken und der Traktat", in *Österreichische Philosophen und ihr Einfluß auf die Analytische Philosophie der Gegenwart*, Bd. 1 (*Conceptus* (1977)), S. 289–303.

* * *

WITTGENSTEIN ON MATHEMATICAL PROOF

Margarete Möllmann
Wolfson College, Oxford

A proof delivers the verification or the falsification of a judgement with the help of facts or logical reasons. Mathematical reasoning is entirely dominated by proofs. Mathematical practice consists of proving theorems. A proof is a derivation according to specific rules of inference of a judgement from other judgments, the premisses which are presupposed to be true. A mathematical result that holds relies on a proof. A mathematician would claim that a proof states a new fact. Why should it be interesting for a philosopher like Wittgenstein to consider the nature of a proof? Does it give us some insight into the nature of mathematics? A philosopher is interested in the nature of mathematical concepts in order to look beyond mathematical facts and in order to clarify the genuine nature of mathematical knowledge. Can an assessment of the rôle of the proof in mathematics contribute to a specific philosophy of mathematics? Wittgenstein seemed to be convinced of that. In his Tractatus where Wittgenstein called mathematics a method of logic (*TLP* 6.234) he claimed that "a proof in logic is a merely mechanical expedient to facilitate the recognition of tautologies in complicated cases (*TLP* 6.1262)". But in 1936 Church proved that predicate logic is not decidable and by this it became clear that Wittgenstein's early account of a logical proof does not hold any more. He had claimed in *TLP* 6.1261 that in logic process and result are equivalent and that hence no surprises could occur. Church showed−to put it in simple terms−that it is not possible to construct a machine for predicate logic so that for any formula you put into it the machine tells you whether it is valid or not.

In this paper we will look at Wittgenstein's discussion of mathematical proof in his posthumous writings and we will try to evaluate the impact it has on his forthcoming account of mathematics. Wittgenstein tries to give a detailed characterisation of a proof. A proof is a pattern and must be perspicuous. By that Wittgenstein means, that only a structure whose reproduction is a clearly defined task can be called a proof. Wittgenstein chooses very simple examples which satisfy his requirement of perspicuousness. If I want to ascertain that a specific pattern of lines is equinumerous with a specific pattern of angles I correlate the two figures by drawing projection lines. This proceeding is temporal and represents nothing more than dividing a bag of apples among a group of people and finding out that each can have just one apple. To draw projection lines between two different shapes and to find out that they are equinumerous is an experiment. Why does it qualify as a proof? Wittgenstein argues that if I have given names to the shapes of the two patterns, in this case "H" for hand and "P" for pentacle and state that *H* has as many strokes as *P* has angles, I am entitled to speak of a proof. The latter is a non-temporal proposition. Wittgenstein calls it "a single pattern, at one end of which are written certain sentences and at the other end a sentence (which we call the 'proved proposition'. (*BGM* I 28)" The proposition now serves as a new prescription for ascertaining numerical equality: if one set of objects has been arranged in the form of a hand and another as the angles of a pentacle, we can say that the two sets are equinumerous. We now decide to use the proof picture instead of correlating the groups, as Wittgenstein states. We don't accept the result of a proof because it results once or often, but we see in the proof the reason for saying that this must be the result. The result we gain by the proof, however, does not give us an insight into the properties of "H" and "P". Wittgenstein puts that in the following words: "The proof does not *explore* the essence of the two figures but it does express what I am going to count as belonging to the essence of the figures from now on." (*BGM* I 32). Then he comes to the conclusion: "I deposit what belongs to the essence among the paradigms of language. The mathematician creates *essence*." (ibid.) To deposit what belongs to the essence among the paradigms of language means that mathematical propositions are instruments taken up into the language once for all and their proof shows the place where they stand. When Wittgenstein claims that the mathematician creates essence he means that if a mathematician defines mathematical properties and proves theorems he just demonstrates the internal properties of a mathematical structure but is not committed ontologically. Talking about essence is for Wittgenstein merely noting a convention. For him "to the depth that we see in the essence corresponds the deep need for the convention". (*BGM* I 74).

Conventions are the basis of mathematics. By that he means that mathematical practice is a custom (eine Gepflogenheit) like speaking a language and if we want to justify any mathematics we have to refer to these customs which require that we all follow the same rules. A proof guides us, that is a proof expresses what a mathematician counts as an internal property of a certain mathematical structure. But a proof, according to Wittgenstein, does not force us to adopt a certain law.

Wittgenstein's way of thinking objects to a specific kind of handling mathematical knowledge, that of Frege and Russell. Wittgenstein's strong suspicion against the new discipline, the foundations of mathematics, came out in a remark like "the curse of invasion of mathematics by mathematical logic" (*BGM* IV 46). Frege tried to reduce arithmetic to logic. He was convinced that arithmetic needed a philosophical foundation in order to show that the propositions of mathematics are true. Wittgenstein is not interested in truth. For him propositions of mathematics are nothing but rules and have no truth value. So, he looks e.g. at Cantor's diagonal method in a different way. Cantor proved by this method that the set of real numbers cannot be ordered in a sequence, is not denumerable. Wittgenstein objects to Cantor that his way of talking about this proof is not correct and claims that the diagonal procedure does not reveal anything about the nature of real numbers but something about the methods of calculation that show that any attempt to place real numbers into a one-to-one correspondence with the natural numbers must fail.

Wittgenstein understands that a proof is crucial for mathematical practice. But he is only interested in a proof as a pattern, a transformation device. This way of looking at a proof keeps us from considering a proof a mental act or having a psychological bearing. A proof is objective and communicable.

Any progress in mathematical research relies on a proof, but Wittgenstein does not believe that a proof delivers any mathematical knowledge. At least Wittgenstein is not interested in that aspect. For him a proof does not prove a mathematical proposition to be true because to accept a proof is to accept a rule, and not to accept a proposition that is true. "The proposition proved by means of the proof serves as a rule and so as a paradigm. For we *go* by the rule" (*BGM* II 28). Wittgenstein transfers his views on rules of language and rules of games to mathematics. "Let us remember that in mathematics we are convinced of *grammatical* propositions; so the expression, the result, of our being convinced is that we *accept a rule*" (*BGM* II 26). According to Wittgenstein mathematics is a mere calculus, a technique and mathematical propositions are rules. You learn mathematics the same way you learn a language, that is you follow rules. When you consider the equation "$5 + 7 = 12$" a rule you avoid the philosophical dispute about calling this equation a proposition a priori or a symbolic representation of an empirical act of counting. As a rule the arithmetical equation can be expressed either as logical or as empirical fact according to the context in which it is used. Wittgenstein avoids the kind of question Frege asked: What do mathematical propositions deal with? Or what is the meaning of a number? For Wittgenstein, numerical and arithmetical symbols refer to nothing. They don't have a meaning, they are just constellations within a calculus and they derive their meaning from the totality of the rules of the calculus. This view dominated Wittgenstein's characterisation of the so called crisis in the foundation of mathematics. In June 1930 Waismann recorded a statement by Wittgenstein in which he is talking about ending the crisis. "I believe that when the foundational crisis is ended mathematics will come to resemble that of the elementary schools, . . . Elementary school mathematics is absolutely rigorous and exact. There is no need to improve it. Mathematics is a machine, a calculus." (*WWK* p. 105).

How does Wittgenstein think the crisis could ever come to an end and the underlying philosophical dispute too? Does he mean, the philosophical problems will vanish by linguistic analysis? He seems to believe that it could be possible to overcome the crisis in mathematics by looking at mathematics as a calculus, an operating device that consists of rules. The crucial matter of the crisis was the set theoretical paradoxes. Wittgenstein's aim was "to alter the attitude to contradiction and to consistency proof". He speaks of the "superstitious fear and awe of mathematicians in the face of contradiction". (*BGM* A I 14) For him "the question of consistency cannot arise" if one is "clear as to the nature of mathematics". By this he means, first of all, that a contradiction does not vitiate a calculus as a calculus. A game is still a game even if, after a number of moves, we find that it becomes trivial. Of course, a calculus is intended to be applied – e.g. to make predictions – and a contradiction may make it useless for that purpose. Should this occur we are free to modify the rules, that is, to replace the calculus with a new one. If a calculus suits my purpose and I have found no contradiction then I shall continue to apply it. I would behave not differently if I had a proof of consistency. Thus a proof of consistency would have no consequences for my *use* of a calculus. But then Gödel's demonstration of the impossibility of such a proof is equally devoid of consequence. This is what Wittgenstein means when he writes: "My task is not to talk about (e.g.) Gödel's proof, but to by-pass it". (*BGM* V 16). For Wittgenstein, mathematics is a calculus – a game – which has no content beyond its application. The application is a sufficient justification for the calculus and we alter or enlarge it only as the application requires. In taking this view Wittgenstein seems to ignore the history of mathematics. Why was – we could ask – the justification of the parallel axiom such a problem and what led mathematicians to consider alternatives? Certainly applied mathematics would be poorer without that development. Contradictions are important to Wittgenstein only in that they inhibit applicability and force us to change our calculi. This hardly does justice to the rôle of paradoxes as harbingers of fruitful new concepts. Thus, the discovery of irrationals led ultimately to the concept of the real numbers. The paradoxes from the naive manipulation of infinite series led to a reexamination of the foundation of analysis which paved the way for modern mathematics. It seems to me that the paradoxes of the infinite will prove to be no less fruitful.

Wittgenstein claims that mathematics is just a game that can be arbitrarily altered. What allows him to make this statement? Already in his *Tractatus* Wittgenstein held the view that mathematics is a calculus and has no content. The meaning of any mathematical proposition is solely derived from the constellation of rules. A proof is just a paradigm and doesn't exhibit any meaning. What do we refer to if we speak of the content of mathematics? The content is the underlying intuition on behalf of which a mathematician builds up his axiom systems. Mathematicians are led in their research by intuitions that are nourished by many different things, like received mathematical wisdom, sociological, psychological and philosophical insights. Kurt Gödel saw intuition as his ultimate guide and he compared in an article[1] the kind of perception of objects by mathematical intuition with sense perception. He states that as in the case of physical experience, where you form your ideas on the basis of something else which is immediately given (sensations) in mathematics we also form our ideas of those objects on the basis of something else which is immediately given. This "given" is different from the physical world but "closely related", as he writes, "to the abstract elements contained in our empirical ideas".[2]

A calculus is useful as a way of formalizing the mathematician's intuition – indeed formalizability can be considered as a desideratum of mathematical knowledge – but the intuition itself is the overriding concept and the calculi are revised and extended as the intuition evolves. In fact, Gödel's second incompleteness theorem shows that it is impossible to formalize the whole of the intuition in a given calculus. If e.g. the axioms of number theory formalize our intuition then the intuition must tell us that number theory is consistent. But, as Gödel proved, this statement cannot be proven within number theory. (Thus, this axiomatisation is not a complete axiomatisation).

Wittgenstein is not interested in mathematical intuition. He denies that there is such a thing. He is very worried about not getting involved in the "mysteries" of mathematics, as he calls it. In the lectures that are recorded by his students in Cambridge he is reported to have stated that he does not want to interfere with mathematicians. He is of course right in claiming that a philosopher's "task is not to discover calculi, but to describe the *present* situation" (*BGM* II 81). But that can't mean not to get involved in mathematics. How to write about mathematics without getting involved in it? Gödel showed with his first undecidability theorem that there are mathematical sentences in our calculus that we can't decide. There are problems we cannot solve with the axioms we have got. Hence we must go beyond the calculus, and what is to guide us if not intuition? And so Gödel speaks about "the fact that continued appeals to mathematical intuition are necessary not only for obtaining unambigous answers to the questions of transfinite set theory, but also for the solution of the problems of finitary number theory (of the type of Goldbach's conjecture), where the meaningfulness and unambiguity of the concepts entering into them can hardly be doubted".[3]

In Wittgenstein's account mathematics consists of arbitrary conventions, subject at most to the constraint that they be capable of very concrete applications, such as building safe bridges or making accurate predictions. Gödel's appeal to intuition is designed to answer the question of how we go about selecting new conventions in mathematics when the present ones prove insufficient—as they must, according to his theorem. Wittgenstein's view does not seem to give any answer to this question. He might answer that one should not seek new conventions unless one has concrete applications in mind and that those applications will then determine the choices. But, in fact, the entire history of mathematics shows that the development of pure theory tends to precede concrete applications and that we cannot, in general, predict where the applications will occur. Could not the same be true e.g. of the passage to higher types? (In fact, Gödel showed that this brings about drastic reductions in length of proofs.[4] Hence this answer is unacceptable, and it is hard to see how Wittgenstein's theory could yield any other. In this respect Wittgenstein seems not so much to have "by-passed" Gödel's theorem as to have ignored its implications.

ENDNOTES

[1] Gödel, K., "What is Cantor's Continuum Problem?", in: Benacerraf & Putnam, *Philosophy of Mathematics* (Oxford 1964) pp. 258–273.
[2] ibid.. p. 212.
[3] ibid.
[4] Cf. K. Gödel, "Über die Länge von Beweisen", *Ergebnisse eines math. Koll.,* Heft 7 (1936), pp. 23–24.

* * *

DIE BEDEUTUNG VON WITTGENSTEINS SPÄTPHILOSOPHIE FÜR DAS VERSTÄNDNIS FAMILIENTHERAPEUTISCHER KONZEPTIONEN

Horst Ramsenthaler
Universität Paderborn

Die Familientherapie hat in den letzten Jahren zunehmend an Bedeutung gewonnen. Eine ihrer Hauptthesen lautet, „daß es zwar gestörte Beziehungen, nicht aber gestörte Individuen gibt . . .“[1]. Psychische Erkrankungen sind danach als sinnvolle Handlungsmuster des Patienten zur Bewältigung eines *gestörten* Kontextes verstehbar und stellen keine Störung seines *Geistes* bzw. seiner *Psyche* dar. Folglich setzen familientherapeutische Interventionen auch nicht am isolierten Individuum an, sondern richten sich auf diesen Kontext, der zumeist ein *familialer* ist.

So faszinierend die angeführte These auch wirken mag, die Grundlagen der Familientherapie sind in vielen Punkten klärungsbedürftig. Im folgenden wird gezeigt, daß Wittgensteins Spätphilosophie ein begriffliches Instrumentarium bereitstellt, das eine solche Klärung erlaubt.

I

Ein Merkmal vieler familientherapeutischer Ansätze ist die Forderung, der Therapeut habe sich auf das *Beobachtbare* zu beschränken und auf Aussagen über innerpsychische Vorgänge zu verzichten. Diese Forderung, im folgenden *Beobachtungsargument* genannt, hat der Familientherapie das Etikett *behavioristisch* und entsprechende Kritik eingetragen.[2] Wenn man jedoch den Kontext betrachtet, in dem das Beobachtungsargument auftritt, so stellt sich der Behaviorismusvorwurf als Mißverständnis heraus, und mit Hilfe Wittgensteins Spätphilosophie kann das Beobachtungsargument als Kritik an bestimmten Vorstellungen vom Funktionieren der Sprache gedeutet werden.

Das Beobachtungsargument wendet sich gegen Positionen, für die die Bedeutung mentaler Begriffe (z.B. ‚Einstellung‘, ‚Wille‘, ‚Bewußtsein‘) in inneren Gegenständen besteht. Die Gegenposition zur Familientherapie postuliert damit mentale Entitäten und führt psychische Störungen auf Defekte dieser mentalen Entitäten zurück – man spricht nicht von ungefähr von *Geistes*krankheiten. Der familientherapeutische Einwand dagegen lautet: Hier wird von bloßen Begriffen auf die Existenz innerer Gegenstände geschlossen und damit eine Verdinglichung vorgenommen, die unstatthaft ist[3]. Mit Wittgenstein läßt sich dieser Einwand präzisieren und als Kritik an einer Psychologie radikalisieren, die auf einer *realistischen Semantik* aufruht[4]. Ohne hier die entsprechenden Argumente aus *PU* aufzulisten, kann festgestellt werden, daß Wittgenstein einer realistischen Semantik den Boden entzogen hat[5]. Damit bricht die von der Familientherapie kritisierte Position zusammen.

Demgegenüber schwebt der Familientherapie offenbar eine *pragmatische Semantik* vor, ohne diese jedoch selbst zu entwickeln bzw. auf Wittgenstein zurückzugreifen. Das zeigt sich in Äußerungen wie: Mentale Begriffe seien „nur eine sprachliche Abkürzung für (die Beschreibung – H. R.) ganz bestimmter Beziehungsstrukturen“.[6] Mentale Begriffe verweisen nicht auf innere Vorgänge oder Gegenstände, vielmehr zeigt sich am Verhalten eines Menschen in seiner Umwelt, ob ihm zu Recht eine geistige Disposition zugeschrieben wird. Nach Wittgensteins Bedeutungstheorie, die das Gesagte untermauern hilft, ist Sprechen ein Handeln wie Turnen, Basteln, Einkaufen und kann nur – wie diese Handlungen – in dem Kontext verstanden werden, in dem es sich manifestiert. Die Bedeutung von Wörtern kann folglich nicht unabhängig vom Kontext ihrer Verwendung analysiert werden. Die Bedeutung von Wörtern ist nach Wittgenstein ihr Gebrauch in der Sprache. Freilich ist damit nicht ein beliebiger Gebrauch gemeint, sondern der korrekte. Und *korrekter Gebrauch* heißt *der Regel entsprechender Gebrauch*. Wenn aber die Familientherapie als Konzeption interpretierbar ist, die auf einer pragmatischen Semantik aufruht, so steht das Beobachtungsargument völlig im Einklang damit: Der Gebrauch ist nichts Verborgenes, Inneres, sondern erfahrbar, beobachtbar. Das heißt jedoch nicht, daß hier ein Behaviorismus vertreten wird, in dem nur von *Gesetzmäßigkeiten*, nicht von *Regeln* die Rede ist! Die Familientherapie leugnet ja nicht die Existenz innerer Vorgänge, nur geht sie mit Wörtern für Inneres anders um. Für sie beziehen sie sich nicht auf innere Gegenstände, sondern auf beobachtbares Verhalten: „Ein ‚innerer Vorgang‘ bedarf äußerer Kriterien." (*PU* § 580). Das Beobachtungsargument ist folglich als Warnung vor sprachlichen Fallen zu deuten, in die man leicht tappen kann, wenn man mentale Begriffe benutzt: Unser Hang dazu, innere Gegenstände anzunehmen, auf die sich diese Wörter zu beziehen scheinen. Löst man sich von dieser mentalistischen Sichtweise, so wird der Blick frei, Symptome als soziale Phänomene im Gegensatz zu individuellen Störungen zu sehen, denn in der Psychiatrie vorkommende Begriffe verweisen gar nicht auf Inneres − hier: *innere Störungen* −, sondern allein auf ein Verhalten − hier: ein *abweichendes*.

II

Wenn also psychische Störungen nicht als Erkrankungen des Geistes i.S. eines inneren Gegenstandes begriffen werden können, und wenn dagegen das Tun ‚psychisch Gestörter‘ auf dem Hintergrund ihrer Familien einsichtig gemacht werden kann, so stellt sich die Frage, wie die Struktur solcher ‚pathogener‘ Familien zu erfassen ist. In der systemischen Familientherapie greift man zu diesem Zweck auf Konzepte der Kybernetik zurück und beschreibt Familien in Begriffen wie *Regelkreis*, *Redundanz*, *Rückkopplung* etc. Die Anwendung solcher Begriffe auf Familien ist jedoch keineswegs klar. Was soll man sich z.B. unter *Homöostase* in einer Familie vorstellen? Was unter ihrem *Regler*?

Benutzt man den *Regelbegriff* Wittgensteins, so lassen sich die genannten Ausdrücke zwanglos rekonstruieren. Dazu ist der Regelbegriff zu klären, für dessen Verwendung zwei Kriterien wesentlich sind: (1) *Konstanz im Verhalten*: „Es kann nicht ein einziges Mal nur ein Mensch einer Regel gefolgt sein . . . Einer Regel folgen, eine Mitteilung machen, einen Befehl geben, eine Schachpartie spielen sind Gepflogenheiten . . ." (*PU* § 199). Einer Regel zu folgen ist also die Neigung zu bestimmten Handlungen. Nur wenn regelmäßiges Verhalten gezeigt wird, kann eine Regel vorliegen. Der Begriff der *Redundanz* kann damit als ‚Regelmäßigkeit‘ expliziert werden. (2) *Sanktionierende Reaktionen der Umwelt*: ‚Einer Regel folgen‘ heißt *etwas richtig machen*. Um von einer Regel sprechen zu können, muß also von korrektem bzw. inkorrektem Verhalten geredet werden können. Was nun richtig ist, hängt von den Reaktionen der Umwelt ab (*PU* § 143, 208). So deutet eine negative Sanktion auf inkorrekt geltendes Verhalten hin. Damit lassen sich weitere kybernetische Termini fassen: Ein *Regelkreis* ist die Neigung einer Gruppe, Abweichungen von der Regel durch negative Sanktionen (negatives Feed-back) zu unterbinden; *Homöostase* wäre der Zustand, in dem die Regeln weitgehend eingehalten werden[7].

Bettet man das in das Modell der Familientherapie ein, so ergibt sich folgendes: Familien sind relativ stabile Gruppen, in denen ein Großteil der Sozialisation abläuft (d.h. es werden Regeln vermittelt). In ihnen bilden sich auch für die die jeweilige Familie kennzeichnende (ideosynkratische) Regeln heraus, die von der Regelung der Sitzordnung bis hin zur Verteilung von Machtbefugnissen reichen. Diese Regeln zu erfassen heißt die Struktur der Familie zu beschreiben. Nun können bestimmte *Regelkonstellationen* die Befindlichkeit der Familienmitglieder erheblich beeinträchtigen und zu Störungen führen. Zwei typische Konstellationen seien kurz angedeutet: Nicht selten kommt es vor, daß die Kompetenzen in einer Familie unklar verteilt sind. Es besteht dann über Rechte und Pflichten keine Einigkeit. Jeder erlebt das Tun des Partners als Kompetenzüberschreitung und sanktioniert es. Diese Sanktion wird vom Partner seinerseits als Regelverletzung sanktioniert usf. Der permanente Kreislauf wechselseitiger Sanktionen kann für die Beteiligten sehr zermürbend sein. Eine andere Konstellation besteht darin, daß über die Regeln zwar Einigkeit herrscht, der eine Partner aber praktisch alle Machtbefugnisse innehat. Für den leerausgehenden Partner kann das eine solche Belastung darstellen, daß er in die Krankheit flieht. Er schafft durch sein Symptom eine neue Situation, die die Anwendung der alten Regeln verunmöglicht und z.B. Rücksichtnahme erforderlich macht.

III

Das Symptom ist hier als Versuch des einen Partners zu verstehen, sich ungeschriebenen Familienregeln zu entziehen. Dieses Verständnis der Handlungsweise des Symptomträgers ist aber nur auf der Folie des Miteinanderumgehens in der Familie zu gewinnen. Hier erscheint der Symptomträger nicht mehr als gestört, sondern als Person, die aus den ihr zur Verfügung stehenden Handlungsmöglichkeiten das Beste macht. Ähnlich ist das Symptom nach der *Doppelbindungstheorie* zu interpretieren, die sich auf die schizophrene Störung bezieht und hier nur angedeutet werden kann. Der Schizophrene muß dieser Theorie zufolge „in einem Universum leben, in dem die Abfolge der Ereignisse dergestalt ist, daß seine unkonventionellen Kommunikationsgewohnheiten in gewissem Sinne angemessen sind."[8] Dieses ‚Universum' – das *double bind* – ist so geartet, daß der Schizophrene widersprüchlichen und damit unbefolgbaren Regeln ausgesetzt ist, ohne sich diesen entziehen zu können. Das schizophrene Symptom ist sein Versuch, in diesem widersprüchlichen Kontext eine Orientierung zu gewinnen – z.B. durch paranoides Verhalten, d.h. durch die Suche nach dem scheinbar verborgenen Sinn der Handlungen der übrigen Familienmitglieder. Mit Hilfe von Wittgensteins Regelbegriff können auch die übrigen klinischen Symptome der Schizophrenie verständlich gemacht und die Doppelbindungstheorie rekonstruiert werden.[9]

IV

Wenn psychische Störungen auf dem Hintergrund gestörter Beziehungen (d.h. dysfunktionaler Regeln) verständlich gemacht werden können, dann ist es nicht verwunderlich, daß die Interventionen der Familientherapie an diesen Regeln ansetzen. Der Therapeut hat den Familienmitgliedern gleichsam ein neues Spiel zu lehren und damit die alten, dysfunktionalen Regeln durch neue zu ersetzen. Die z.T. widersinnig erscheinenden familientherapeutischen Interventionen wie *Symptomverschreibung* (der Klient wird aufgefordert, sein Symptom absichtlich zu manifestieren) oder *Verhaltensverschreibung* (der Therapeut verordnet der Familie ein neues Verhalten und führt damit eine Regel in die Familie ein) können im Rückgriff auf Wittgenstein als Versuch verstanden werden, die familiale Struktur (d.h. die Regeln) zu verändern.[10]

Die Familientherapie baut also auf dem Regelbegriff auf, der sich mit Hilfe der Spätphilosophie Wittgensteins präzisieren läßt. Der Therapeut hat die Regeln in der Familie zu identifizieren und ggf. ihre Veränderung einzuleiten.

Wittgensteins Philosophie enthält zwar keine für den Therapeuten relevanten *Inhalte*, wohl aber ein *begriffliches Intrumentarium*, das eine Rekonstruktion der Familientherapie erlaubt – von ihren Grundlagen bis hin zu ihren Interventionstechniken.

ANMERKUNGEN

1 Watzlawick, P., „Wesen und Formen menschlicher Beziehungen", in: H.-G. Gadamer und P. Vogler (Hrsg.), *Neue Anthropologie, Bd. 7: Philosophische Anthropologie* (Stuttgart 1975), S. 111.
2 Ziegler, J., *Kommunikation als paradoxer Mythos* (Weinheim-Basel 1977).
3 Vgl. P. Watzlawick, J.H. Beavin und D.D. Jackson, *Menschliche Kommunikation* (Bern-Stuttgart-Wien 1969) S. 28.
4 Wenigstens einer einfachen realistischen Semantik i.S. v. F. v. Kutschera, *Sprachphilosophie* (München ^{2}(1975), S. 38ff.
5 Vgl. F.v. Kutschera (1975), S. 133ff.
6 Watzlawick, Beavin und Jackson (1969), S. 28.
7 Zur Klärung weiterer kypernetischer Begriffe vgl. H. Ramsenthaler, *Pragmatische Kommunikationstheorie und Pädagogik* (Weinheim-Basel 1982) S. 60ff.
8 Bateson, G., u.a., „Auf dem Weg zu einer Schizophrenie-Theorie" in: G. Bateson u.a., *Schizophrenie und Familie* (Frankfurt a. M. 1969), S. 16.
9 Vgl. dazu H. Ramsenthaler (1982), S. 129ff.
10 Vgl. dazu H. Ramsenthaler (1982), S. 144ff.

* * *

WITTGENSTEIN ON THE NATURE OF UNDERSTANDING

Benjamin F. Armstrong, Jr.
Lafayette College

> Understanding the system can't consist in continuing the series up to *this* or *that* number: that is only applying one's understanding. The understanding itself is a state which is the source of the correct use. (*PI*, 146)
> We are tempted to think that the action of language consists of two parts; an inorganic part, the handling of signs, and an organic part, which we may call understanding these signs, meaning them, interpreting them, thinking. These latter activities seem to take place in a queer kind of medium, the mind; [. . .] (*BLB*, p. 3)

Wittgenstein argues at length against the view expressed in the passages above—the view that something, understanding, lies 'behind' certain instances of 'handling signs' in virtue of which they are, for example, issuing orders and obeying them; something that gives the signs their life.[1] Wittgenstein characterizes his own view when he says, "But if we had to name anything which is the life of the sign, we should have to say that it was its *use*." (*BLB*, p. 4; see also *PI*, 43, 120, 432).

Aspects of the view characterized in Wittgenstein's remark will be displayed in this paper, along with the consequent notion of 'understanding' ('understanding', as it pertains to ordinary everyday language). To accomplish this, Wittgenstein's account of the satisfaction of certain necessary conditions on a correct use for a sign will be presented. These conditions can be found in Wittgenstein's remark at *PI* 202 where he briefly discusses the need for a distinction between 'thinking one is obeying a rule' and 'obeying a rule'. Translating his remarks into necessary conditions and expressing these conditions in terms of conditions on a correct use for a sign, we get the following: There must be (i) something *a* can do that *counts* as 'thinking that one is using a sign correctly' and (ii) something *a* can do that *counts* as 'using a sign correctly' and, (iii) it must be possible for what counts as 'thinking that one is using a sign correctly' to occur when what counts as 'using a sign correctly' does not.[2]

Allowing that, in circumstances where all three conditions are satisfied, an individual speaker can, on his own, do something that satisfies (i) and (ii), the discussion will focus on Wittgenstein's account of the satisfaction of (iii).

It is Wittgenstein's view that a correct use exists *as* an accord between activities of speakers, activities that, in constituting a 'correct use' for a sign, thereby become instances of 'correct usings' ('correct usings' is an awkward expression, but it will, perhaps, help to keep this notion distinct from 'a correct use' in the discussion). Consideration of the following extension of Wittgenstein's two-speaker community (*PI*, 2) will enable us to see this: A utters the sign "slab"; on hearing this utterance B brings A a slab; A utters "block"; B brings A a block, and so on . . .; A refuses to accept a block when he has called "slab" and B brings a block, and B generally returns the wrong item with protest; when A utters "block" when he wants a slab, B refuses to return the block and A returns the block himself without protest. In this scenario, the accord that is constitutive of a correct use can be seen by thinking of A's callings and B's bringings as, respectively, instances of A's and B's 'thinking he is using the sign correctly' and their refusals as instances of 'thinking he (the other one) is using a sign incorrectly'. It is *in* the accord *in* the activities that a correct use originates and exists. In other words, agreement, of the sort described, between speakers, generates 'a correct use', a correct use existing in instances of this agreement; correct use emerges in a human agreement (in relations) that is not prior to, but expresses itself in, activities that thereby become instances of 'correct usings', or, to put it less awkwardly, thereby becoming talking and understanding. This view is part of what is behind Wittgenstein's remarks at *PI* 241, 242, when he says,

> "So you are saying that human agreement decides what is true and what is false?"—It is what human beings *say* that is true and false; and they agree in the *language* they use. That is not agreement in opinions but in form of life.
> If language is to be a means of communication there must be agreement not only in definitions but also [. . .] in judgments.

To put it succinctly, correct use is agreement between humans (that expresses itself) 'in the language they use'.

The point to be noted for the purposes of this paper, is the absence of any priority relation between 'a correct use' and instances of 'correct usings', about which more must be said.

The vision of a (guiding knowledge of) correct use that seems to underlie the view that certain 'sign handlings' are talking and understanding if they are manifestations of a knowledge of correct use requires that a correct use be prior to instances 'using a sign correctly'. Only if there is such a priority is there something (to be known) that can guide the 'handlings'. On Wittgenstein's account of correct use, instances of 'using a sign correctly' cannot be the result of a (guiding knowledge of) correct use. Since instances of 'using a sign correctly' are correct use-constituting, prior to these instances there is no correct use, hence nothing that can guide, nothing to be known. To recognize that correct use exists in constituting instances of talking and understanding is to be saved from the temptation to think about an 'organic' aspect in the handling of signs. Since correct use exists as an accord between its constituting instances, there is nothing for an 'organic' aspect of linguistic action to do.

The account described can be seen in Wittgenstein's solution to the 'paradox' described in section 201 of the *PI*. The 'paradox' (the seeming result of preceding investigations) is "no course of action could be determined by a rule, because every course of action can be made out to accord with the rule". About this 'paradox', Wittgenstein says,

> What this shews is that there is a way of grasping a rule which is *not an interpretation,* but which is exhibited in what we call 'obeying the rule' and 'going against it' in actual cases.

Changing once again to a discussion in terms of 'correct uses' rather than 'rules', to view understanding a word as, at a fundamental level, 'being guided by a sign by grasping its correct use and acting on it (or preparing to act on it, or storing it, etc.)', is to face the paradox Wittgenstein describes. Any encounterable sign can be made out to mean anything whatsoever, as Wittgenstein demonstrates. (It is important to keep in mind that Wittgenstein is not denying that people know what *words* mean; rather, he is making a point about what this 'knowledge' does and does not consist in, i.e., a point about how *signs* come to mean something, come to be words. This is clearest in his discussions across the 'arrow' examples, *BLB,* pp. 33–4, *PI,* 86.) Hence, if one must 'grasp the correct use of a sign and act on what is grasped' to be guided by it, there is no guidance. The notion of understanding that is a consequence of Wittgenstein's account of 'correct use' escapes such a paradox.

According to Wittgenstein's account, a correct use is exhibited in what we call 'understanding a word' and 'misunderstanding a word' in actual cases, because what we call 'understanding' and 'misunderstanding' are constitutive of the correct use. The understanding of ordinary everyday talk cannot involve interpretation/grasping of meaning (understood in the sense described in the paragraph above). It cannot involve interpretation/grasping of meaning because the reactions that constitute correct use are instances of understanding, only as they are constituting a correct use. Since this is so, when these reactions could be guided, there is nothing that, by being understood, can guide them. Wittgenstein escapes the paradox by recognizing that meaning is the outcome of reactions that we call understanding a word, rather than the source of these reactions; correct use is generated by what we call 'correct usings'—'correct usings' are not generated by (knowledge of) correct use. Hence, there is no possibility of misinterpreting the meaning, at a fundamental level, because the meaning just is whatever correct use emerges out of the accord in reactions.

The above sketch of understanding is filled out by Wittgenstein's discussions in *PG* (pp. 39—51). Says Wittgenstein, "'Understanding a word' may mean: *knowing* how it is used; *being able to* apply it" (p. 47). Also, "[. . .] the knowledge of the language [. . .] is [. . .] like the understanding or mastery of a calculus; something like the *ability* to multiply" (p. 50). Knowledge of the language does not consist in a storehouse of meanings that one draws on when talking and understanding. Knowledge of the language is mastery of a technique (see *PI*, 199); it is the ability to do something. 'Knowledge of the language', viewed as an ability to do something, is to be understood *in contrast to* the knowledge of the language one shows when one *talks about* or *explains* the meaning of particular words. On Wittgenstein's view the latter knowledge is importantly different from the former, it cannot take the place of the former in explanations of understanding the language at the fundamental level, and it is dependent on the former knowledge.

ENDNOTES

1 A discussion of these considerations can be found in G. P. Baker and P. M. S. Hacker, *Wittgenstein: Meaning and Understanding* (Chicago 1980).
2 A more detailed discussion of these conditions and their relation to 202 and the role they play in the 'private-language argument' can be found in my "Wittgenstein on Private Languages: It Takes Two to Talk", *Philosophical Investigations*, Vol. 7 (1984), pp. 46—62.

* * *

11. Logik und die Philosophie der Sprache

11. Logic and the Philosophy of Language

MODALTHEORIEN WITTGENSTEINS

Hans Burkhardt
Universität Erlangen-Nürnberg

Nimmt man in der Tradition bekannte Modaltheorien und vergleicht sie mit denen, die man bei Wittgenstein findet, so kommt man zu aufschlußreichen Erkenntnissen, die für die Wittgensteinsche Logik und Philosophie grundlegend sind. Zu diesem Zweck werden fünf verschiedene Konzeptionen der Modalitäten dargestellt. Es wird auch kurz auf ihr erstes Auftreten in der Geschichte der Logik und Philosophie, sowie auf ihre Rezeption durch die Tradition eingegangen. Ferner wird zu zeigen versucht, ob diese Modaltheorien oder diese Modalbegriffe bei Wittgenstein vorkommen, ob sie vielmehr von ihm zurückgewiesen oder absichtlich nicht verwendet werden. Es sind dies im einzelnen:

1. Das *possibile logicum* oder die syntaktische Definition oder Konzeption der Modalitäten
2. Die *epistemische* Konzeption der Modalitäten und der subjektiven Wahrscheinlichkeit
3. Der *steigerungsfähige* Möglichkeitsbegriff; er ist die Grundlage für die weitere Unterteilung des Strikt-Kontingenten und damit auch die Grundlage der Wahrscheinlichkeit. Als Beispiel dafür kann man die *praktischen* Modalitäten oder die Möglichkeit als Erreichbarkeit durch Handeln anführen.
4. Die *physische* Modalität: das *Unvermeidliche* als relativer Notwendigkeitsbegriff
5. Die Rückführung der Modalbegriffe auf Quantoren oder Zeitbegriffe: die *extensionale Reduktion* der Modalitäten

I

Die syntaktische Konzeption der Modalitäten kommt in Gestalt des possibile logicum erstmals in der Scholastik des 13. Jahrhunderts, nämlich bei Thomas von Aquin[1] und Johannes Duns Scotus[2], vor. Nach Duns Scotus ist ein widerspruchsfreier Begriff möglich und ein widerspruchsvoller unmöglich. Eine entscheidende Rolle für die theoretische Weiterentwicklung und Präzisierung dieser syntaktischen Konzeption der Modalitäten kommt dann Leibniz zu, denn er findet ein Verfahren, mit dessen Hilfe man jederzeit von zusammengesetzten Begriffen auf Aussagen übergehen kann und umgekehrt, und definiert widerspruchsfreie und widerspruchsvolle als mögliche bzw. unmögliche zusammengesetzte Begriffe, indem er zeigt, daß solche Begriffe einen Teilbegriff zusammen mit seiner Verneinung nicht enthalten oder enthalten. Durch Analogie zu mathematischen Verfahren kennzeichnet er auch als erster die syntaktische Konzeption als beweistheoretische.[3] Man findet das possibile logicum von da an bei vielen Philosophen, so u.a. bei Kant, Brentano und Meinong. Damit sind wir auch schon zeitlich, geographisch und ideengeschichtlich in Wittgensteins Nähe. Auch im *Tractatus* ist die syntaktische Definition der Modalität formuliert, so z.B. in 4.464:
„Die Wahrheit der Tautologie ist gewiß, des Satzes möglich, der Kontradiktion unmöglich."
Eine ähnliche Formulierung steht in 5.525, auch dort wird Gewißheit mit der Tautologie, Unmöglichkeit mit der Kontradiktion und Möglichkeit mit dem sinnvollen Satz gleichgesetzt. Die Tautologie kennzeichnet Wittgenstein wie die Kontradiktion an anderer Stelle als sinnlos, aber nicht unsinnig.[4] Notwendige Aussagen sind sinnlose Aussagen auf der Seite der Wahrheit.[5]
Da die Leistungen von Duns Scotus und Leibniz nicht bekannt waren, formuliert Carnap 1934 die syntaktische Definition der Modalitäten neu.[6] Er verwendet dazu die Begriffe der Analytizität und der Widersprüchlichkeit und zwar im extensionalen Sinne. Damit stellt er

sich gegen die Tradition, die seit Aristoteles einen intensionalen Begriff der Analytizität[7] und seit Duns Scotus einen intensionalen Begriff der Widersprüchlichkeit verwendet hatte. Von Wright vermutet, daß sich Carnap bei seiner Reduktion von notwendig auf analytisch und von unmöglich auf kontradiktorisch auf den Tractatus gestützt haben könnte.[8] Das ist möglich. Er kann jedoch den Tractatus nicht als Quelle für eine generelle Reduktion intensionaler Texte auf extensionale beanspruchen, denn im Tractatus kommen zweifellos modale Texte als besondere Art intensionaler Texte vor, und Wittgenstein weist extensionalen Reduktionismus explizit zurück (cf. V).

Das possibile logicum, das nach Vereinigung der Kontingenz $\neg (Mp \wedge M \neg p)$ mit der logischen Notwendigkeit zusammenfällt, bildet die Grundlage für andere Modalarten, nämlich die *praktische*, im Spezialfall die Erreichbarkeit durch Handeln und die *physische*, das Unvermeidliche.[9] Sie bildet damit das Gerüst der Welt, Meinong würde sagen: den Bestand.

II

Es ist aufschlußreich, daß Wittgenstein im *Tractatus* im Zusammenhang mit der syntaktischen Konzeption der Modalbegriffe zwar das Wort ‚unmöglich‘ gebraucht, aber nicht das Wort ‚notwendig‘. Er ersetzt es durch die *epistemische* Bezeichnung ‚gewiß‘. Epistemische Modalitäten kennt schon Aristoteles, eine Art epistemischer Wende, d.h. den Ersatz ontischer oder logischer Modalitäten durch epistemische vollziehen schon manche Scholastiker der Neuzeit, aber auch Bernoulli und Laplace[10] und vor allem Kant. Doch Wittgenstein dürfte eher in der Tradition Brentanos und seiner Schule stehen, für die die Gewißheit ein zentraler philosophischer Begriff ist.[11]

Was Wittgenstein hier im Auge hat, sind logische Beziehungen zwischen Aussagen, und diese Art von Beziehung hat nach ihm mit Wissen zu tun, sie ist also *epistemisch*. Im Tractatus 5.1362 läßt er daran keinen Zweifel:

„Der Zusammenhang von Wissen und Gewußtem, ist der der logischen Notwendigkeit.“

Dabei muß man sicheres Wissen oder Gewißheit von unsicherem Wissen oder Vermutungen unterscheiden. Sicheres Wissen garantiert notwendige Beziehungen und unsicheres führt zu wahrscheinlichen Beziehungen.[12] Sein Wahrscheinlichkeitsbegriff ist wie sein Notwendigkeitsbegriff ein relativer, von Wright nennt ihn auch ‚dyadisch‘ oder ‚bedingt‘.[13] Es handelt sich um eine Wahrscheinlichkeit, die zwischen Aussagen und nicht zwischen Ereignissen besteht. Es ist die Wahrscheinlichkeit, die eine Aussage einer anderen gibt.[14] Sie geht wahrscheinlich auf Bolzano zurück.[15] Es gibt schon einen Ansatz dafür bei Aristoteles, der als erster Beispiele für eine relative oder bedingte Wahrscheinlichkeit gab, allerdings zwischen Ereignissen und erst sekundär zwischen Aussagen.[16] Ein Text als Beleg für die Annahme einer relativen Wahrscheinlichkeit durch Wittgenstein steht im *Tractatus* 5.152:

„Folgt p aus q, so gibt der Satz ‚q‘ dem Satz ‚p‘ die Wahrscheinlichkeit 1. Die Gewißheit des logischen Schlusses ist ein Grenzfall der Wahrscheinlichkeit.“

Auch in diesem Text stellt die epistemische Notwendigkeit, also die Gewißheit, den Grenzfall für die Wahrscheinlichkeit dar. Einzelne Sätze können nach Wittgenstein keine Wahrscheinlichkeiten liefern:

„Ein Satz an sich ist weder wahrscheinlich noch unwahrscheinlich. Ein Ereignis trifft ein, oder trifft nicht ein, ein Mittelding gibt es nicht.“ (*Tractatus* 5.153)

Folgt man dem *Tractatus*, dann kann man nicht von der Wahrscheinlichkeit des Eintretens von Einzelereignissen oder von Ereignissen, generisch gesehen, sprechen. Damit lehnt Wittgenstein einen ontischen Begriff von Wahrscheinlichkeit, also den der in der Welt vorkommenden Häufigkeiten ab, wie ihn etwa Aristoteles besitzt. Die Wahrscheinlichkeit ist nicht eine Eigenschaft von Eigenschaften wie etwa von ‚grauhaarig werden‘ oder von ‚192 cm groß sein‘, sondern eine Eigenschaft von Sätzen oder von Objektiven, wie es bei Meinong heißt.[17] Für Wittgenstein kommt noch hinzu: auch nicht von Einzelsätzen, sondern nur von durch Junktoren kombinierte Sätze.

Bei der Annahme der epistemischen Konzeption der Modalitäten steht Wittgenstein durchaus im Einklang mit Frege, denn dieser spricht davon, daß man einen Wink auf ein Wissen gibt, wenn man von ‚notwendig‘ spricht.[18] Auch in Bezug auf die Möglichkeit deutet Frege die epistemische Lösung an und favorisiert sie.

III

Der nach dem possibile logicum zweite Möglichkeitsbegriff ist von anderer Art. Er unterscheidet sich vom ersten dadurch, daß er *steigerungsfähig* ist. Möglichkeit als Widerspruchsfreiheit ist nicht steigerungsfähig, denn widerspruchsfreier als widerspruchsfrei macht keinen Sinn.

Dieser zweite Begriff von Möglichkeit, der in der Sprache in Form von Ausdrücken wie ‚kaum möglich‘, ‚möglicher als‘, ‚genauso möglich wie‘ vorkommt,[19] ist von jeher die Grundlage der Wahrscheinlichkeitstheorie gewesen. Schon Aristoteles hatte das Wahrscheinliche, oder präziser: die relative Häufigkeit, durch die weitere Unterteilung des Strikt-Kontingenten erhalten, also dessen, was weder notwendig noch unmöglich ist.[20] Dieser Begriff der Wahrscheinlichkeit, dessen Rahmen modale Begriffe bilden, wird auch von der Scholastik aufgenommen, gelangt dann zu Leibniz und über Leibniz zu Bernoulli, Laplace und Brentano und spielt auch eine entscheidende Rolle bei Meinong, der in seinem Werk ‚Über Möglichkeit und Wahrscheinlichkeit‘ ebenfalls von Modalbegriffen ausgeht und diese Art von Möglichkeit als ‚vermutungsfreie Wahrscheinlichkeit‘ bezeichnet.[21]

Wittgenstein stellt ebenfalls einen deutlichen Zusammenhang zwischen Modaltheorie und Wahrscheinlichkeitstheorie her, wenn er im *Tractatus* schreibt: „Gewiß, möglich, unmöglich: Hier haben wir das Anzeichen jener Gradation, die wir für die Wahrscheinlichkeitslehre brauchen“. (4.464) Wahrscheinlich ist nach Wittgenstein also das, was sich zwischen Gewißheit und Unmöglichkeit im Bereich des Möglichen im Sinne des Strikt-Kontingenten, also dessen, was möglich ist und möglich nicht ist, abspielt.[22] In einem Schema sieht das so aus:

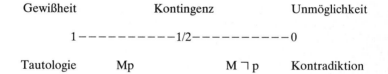

Gewißheit	Kontingenz		Unmöglichkeit
1 —————————	1/2	—————————	0
Tautologie	Mp	M ⌐ p	Kontradiktion

Im *Tractatus* 5.525 wird die Möglichkeit durch den sinnvollen Satz definiert, ja sogar mit ihm gleichgesetzt. Sie wird also nicht wie die Gewißheit und die Unmöglichkeit durch das Widerspruchskriterium definiert und damit syntaktisch aufgefaßt, sondern semantisch. Sie wird durch einen sinnvollen Satz über die Welt repräsentiert und fällt damit mit der Kontingenz zusammen.[23]

Ein Sonderfall dieses steigerungsfähigen Möglichkeitsbegriffs ist der Begriff der Erreichbarkeit durch Handeln.[24] Erreichbar durch Handeln soll ein zukünftiger Sachverhalt sein. Es gibt Fälle, in denen ein Sachverhalt C für eine Person B erreichbarer ist als für eine Person A, so z.B. ein Gewicht zu heben oder aber, daß ein Sachverhalt A erreichbarer ist als ein Sachverhalt B für eine Person C, so z.B. auf einen niedrigeren Berg zu steigen. Die Möglichkeit als Erreichbarkeit durch Handeln hat dann folgende Grundstruktur:

Nicht erreichbar nicht A		unvermeidbar A
erreichbar A	⎫	
erreichbar nicht A	⎬	verfügbar A
Nicht erreichbar A		unerreichbar A

539

Es ist zu betonen, daß in diesem Schema, also im Bereich der praktischen Modalitäten. Erreichbarkeit und Unvermeidbarkeit interdefinierbar sind. Das, was durch Handeln erreichbar oder vermeidbar (erreichbar nicht A) ist, spielt sich offensichtlich im Rahmen des Kontingenten ab und ist so weder unvermeidbar (notwendig) noch unerreichbar (unmöglich).

Man könnte dazu folgendes Gegenbeispiel anführen: angenommen, eine Lotterie besteht aus hundert Losen. Kaufe ich alle Lose, dann ist ein Gewinn unvermeidbar, kaufe ich kein Los, dann ist er unerreichbar, kaufe ich zwischen 1 und 99 Losen, dann ist er je nach Anzahl der gekauften Lose mit größerer Wahrscheinlichkeit entweder erreichbar oder vermeidbar. Doch ist dieses Gegenbeispiel nur scheinbar ein solches, denn der zukünftige Sachverhalt ist der Kauf der Lose und dieser Kauf ist tatsächlich weder unvermeidbar noch unerreichbar. Der Gewinn ist dann erst die Folge dieses Kaufs und er kann beim Kauf aller Lose durchaus unvermeid*lich* sein. Das Unvermeidliche ist im Gegensatz zum Unvermeidbaren keine praktische, sondern eine *physische* Modalität. (cf. IV)

Wie Lorenzen in seinem Aufsatz mit Recht betont, haben wir es bei den Beziehungen zwischen praktischen Modalitäten nicht mit Modallogik zu tun, denn es gelten außer den definierten Implikationen keine zusätzlichen, nicht einmal das Modalgefälle.[25]

IV

In der Geschichte der Modaltheorie und Modallogik gibt es einen wichtigen und ziemlich vernachlässigten Begriff, nämlich den des *Unvermeidlichen*. Das Unvermeidliche ist ein relativer Modalbegriff, denn ein Ereignis ist in Bezug auf ein anderes Ereignis oder eine Menge anderer Ereignisse unvermeidlich oder nicht unvermeidlich. Für die weitere Analyse ist es zweckmäßig zwei Arten von Ereignissen zu unterscheiden, nämlich solche, die Handlungen sind, und solche, die keine Handlungen sind. Dann ergeben sich zwei Arten von Ereignissen: Handlungen und Ereignisse im engeren Sinne. Wir erhalten dann vier Kombinationen:

Ereignisse	Ereignisse
Handlungen	Ereignisse
Ereignisse	Handlungen
Handlungen	Handlungen

Aristoteles vertritt die Auffassung, daß sowohl Ereignisse, die aus anderen Ereignissen folgen (so z.B. die Sonnenfinsternis bei einer bestimmten Konstellation von Sonne, Mond und Erde),[26] als auch Ereignisse, die aus Handlungen folgen, unvermeidlich sein können (so z.B. der Tod eines Tieres, dem man die Kehle durchschnitten hat).[27] Handlungen folgen entweder *auf* Ereignisse oder *auf* andere Handlungen, doch weder *aus* Ereignissen noch *aus* anderen Handlungen unvermeidlich.

In der Tradition kommt das Wort ‚inevitabile' erstmals bei Abälard vor, und der Begriff des Unvermeidlichen vor allem bei den Analysen, die mit dem Vorauswissen Gottes und dessen Konsequenzen für das menschliche Handeln zu tun haben. So z.B. bei Petrus de Rivo im 16. Jahrhundert, der eine ausführliche Analyse des Unvermeidlichen vorgelegt und es als physische Modalität kennzeichnet. Er vergleicht die Notwendigkeit mit dem Unvermeidlichen und kommt zu einigen aufschlußreichen logischen Beziehungen zwischen diesen beiden Modalitäten.[28] Ein besonderer historischer Clou ist das Vorkommen des Unvermeidlichen bei Crusius im Zusammenhang mit möglichen Welten. Danach gibt es Unvermeidliches bei Setzung jedweder möglichen Welt, und dieses Unvermeidliche besteht nicht in logischen oder mathematischen Wahrheiten.[29] Offensichtlich faßt auch Crusius das Unvermeidliche als physische Modalität auf und orientiert sich in seinem Verständnis von möglichen Welten an Descartes.

In neuerer Zeit hat sich, meines Wissens, insbesondere Gilbert Ryle mit dem Unvermeidlichen beschäftigt. Er unterscheidet in seiner Analyse zwischen der praktischen Modalität des

Unvermeid*baren* (unavoidability), der logischen Modalität des Unvermeid*lichen* (inevitability), sowie der Modalität des Unausweichlichen (unescapability) oder auch des Unausbleiblichen. Ryle wendet sich vor allem gegen die Verwechslung der logischen Modalität mit der physischen, die bei ihm mit dem ‚Unausbleiblichen‘ bezeichnet wird. Seiner Ansicht nach gibt es zwischen Ereignissen keine Implikationsbeziehungen, wie sie zwischen Aussagen bestehen können. Außerdem lehnt er auch die ontologische Relation des Unvermeidlichen ab.[30]

Darin folgt er wahrscheinlich Wittgenstein, für den es weder möglich ist, daß ein Ereignis notwendig aus einem anderen folgt, noch daß ein Ereignis aus einer Handlung folgt. Im Tractatus 6.37 schreibt er dazu:

„Einen Zwang, nach dem eines geschehen müßte, weil etwas anderes geschehen ist, gibt es nicht. Es gibt nur eine logische Notwendigkeit.“

Damit lehnt er eine notwendige physische Relation zwischen zwei Ereignissen ab; ein Ereignis kann das Eintreten eines anderen Ereignisses nicht erzwingen. Wie Aristoteles gibt Wittgenstein dafür ein Beispiel aus der Astronomie.[31] Auf die Beziehung zwischen Handlungen und Ereignissen geht er in 6.422 ein:

„Also muß diese Frage nach den Folgen einer Handlung belanglos sein. Zum Mindesten dürfen diese Folgen nicht Ereignisse sein.“

Diese Konsequenzen folgen aus der Wittgensteinschen ontologischen Position: in der Welt gibt es keine kausalen Beziehungen, keinen Kausalnexus. *Tractatus* 5.136, 6.1361: „Einen Kausalnexus, der einen solchen Schluß rechtfertigt, gibt es nicht.“ „Der Glaube an den Kausalnexus ist ein Aberglaube.“ Es gibt also keine kausalen Beziehungen zwischen Ereignissen, seien diese nun Handlungen oder keine Handlungen. Wittgenstein lehnt das Unvermeidliche als ontologische Relation schon deshalb ab, weil er jegliche Relation kausaler Art zwischen Ereignissen ablehnt. Die Relation U(A → B) kann man, von A aus gesehen, mit ‚A erzwingt B‘ und, von B aus gesehen, mit ‚B folgt unvermeidlich aus A‘ lesen.

Aus dieser Ablehnung von physischen Relationen zwischen atomaren Ereignissen folgt auch die Wittgensteinsche Haltung zum Problem der futura contingentia (5.1361):

„Die Ereignisse der Zukunft können wir nicht aus den gegenwärtigen erschließen.“

Nach Wittgenstein sind also echte Prognosen nicht möglich, denn sie setzen den Begriff des Notwendigen im Sinne des Unausbleiblichen oder Unvermeidlichen voraus, den es für Wittgenstein offensichtlich nicht gibt, weil es die zugrundeliegende ontologische Relation nicht gibt.[32]

V

Die Reduzierung der Möglichkeitsaussagen auf Existenzaussagen und damit auch aller Modalbegriffe auf Quantoren oder Zeitbegriffe wird von Wittgenstein ausdrücklich abgelehnt:

„Es ist unrichtig den Satz (Ex) fx − wie Russell dies tut − in Worten durch ‚fx ist möglich‘ wiederzugeben.“

Wittgenstein widerspricht damit Russell und auch Frege,[33] die beide dieses Verfahren der Reduktion der Modalitäten auf Quantoren oder Zeitbegriffe zum mindesten vorgeschlagen haben. Es führt zu einer *extensionalen* Reduktion und damit auch zu einer Eliminierung der Modalitäten. Wittgenstein wendet sich damit auch gegen eine Tradition, die mit Aristoteles beginnt, bei dem in den frühen Texten, so z.B. in den *De Interpretatione*, notwendig auch ‚immer‘ und ‚in jedem Fall‘ heißen kann, aber nicht umgekehrt. Erst in späteren Texten formuliert Aristoteles dann die Interdefinierbarkeit, so z.B. in den *De Generatione et Corruptione*.[34] Damit ist Aristoteles jedoch keineswegs schon ein Anhänger des Prinzips der vollständigen Erfüllung oder der statistischen Auffassung der Modalitäten wie später der Dialektiker Diodoros Kronos. Er ist nämlich nicht der Auffassung, daß jede echte Möglichkeit verwirklicht werden wird, sondern nur die Möglichkeiten, die nicht behindert werden.

———

ANMERKUNGEN

[1] Aquin, Thomas von, *S. T.*, I, q 25, a 3.
[2] Scotus, Duns, *Opus Oxoniense*, I dist. 2q. 7n. 10 (VIII 529/30); cf. *Deku* 1f.
[3] cf. Burkhardt (2) 275ff.
[4] *Tractatus* 4.461/4.4611.
[5] cf. von Wright 174, 192.
[6] Carnap 192ff; Becker 37f.
[7] Aristoteles, *Categoriae* 1b, 10–12.
[8] Wright, von, 187–188.
[9] Wright, von, 191; Brentano (1) 220 „Urteile, die Widerspruchslosigkeit behaupten, scheinen eine Klasse zu bilden, welche sich von der einen Widerspruch behauptenden und als widersprechend verwerfenden unterscheidet." cf. Brentano (2) 138; cf. von Wright 194, 195, 197.
[10] cf. Hacking 122ff; 143ff.
[11] cf. Diskussion der Deutung von E. Anscombe durch von Wright 188, Fußnote 11.
[12] cf. Meinong 19, 185, 188; Burkhardt (1) 110; von Wright 159, Fußnote 38: das Zitat von Waismann klingt sehr nach Meinong.
[13] Wright, von, 142.
[14] Wright, von, 142–3; Tractatus 5.152.
[15] Bolzano, *Wissenschaftslehre* Bd. 2, Sek. 161–168; von Wright 145.
[16] Aristoteles, *An. Pr.* 32b 12; *An. Post.*, 73b 12.
[17] Meinong 27f; 86ff; von Wright 148.
[18] Frege 4–5.
[19] cf. Meinong 59; Burkhardt (1) 109.
[20] Aristoteles, *De Int.*, Kap. 9; *An. Pr.* 32b 4f.
[21] Scholastik cf. Jacobi 91–5; 150–52; Leibniz cf. Burkhardt (2) 287f; Bernoulli und Laplace cf. Hakking 122f; 143f; Meinong 47, 71.
[22] cf. Black 234.
[23] Beziehung von Semantik und Kontingenz im Tractatus cf. von Wright 192.
[24] Unter ‚können' im praktischen Sinne versteht man die Erreichbarkeit eines zukünftigen Sachverhalts durch Handeln; cf. Wittgenstein 356: Analyse von ‚wissen' im Sinne von praktischem Können.
[25] Lorenzen 166.
[26] Aristoteles, *De Gen. et Corr.* 337b 14.
[27] Aristoteles, *An. Post.* 73b 14f.
[28] cf. Baudry 75.
[29] Crusius 4.
[30] Ryle 15f.
[31] *Tractatus* 6.36311.
[32] cf. Stenius 58f.
[33] Frege 4–5; cf. Rescher 91.
[34] Aristoteles, *De Gen. et Corr.* 337b 17f.

LITERATUR

Aristotelis Opera, *Ex recensione Immanuelis Bekkeri*, ed. Academia Regia Borussica, 5 Bde. (Berlin 1831–1870, Nachdruck Darmstadt 1960, Berlin 1964ff).
Baudry, Léon (Ed.), *La Querelle des futurs Contingents* (Louvain 1465–1475), *Textes inédits. Etudes de Philosophie Mediévale*, Paris 1950.
Becker, Oskar, *Untersuchungen über den Modalkalkül* (Meisenheim/Glan 1952).
Black, Max, *A Companion Wittgenstein's „Tractatus"* (Cambridge 1964).
Brentano, Franz (1), *Versuch über die Erkenntnis* (Hamburg 1970), Ders. (2), *Wahrheit und Evidenz* (Hamburg 1974).
Burkhardt, Hans, (1) „Modalität und Wahrscheinlichkeit in der Tradition und bei Meinong", in: *Erkenntnis- und Wissenschaftstheorie, Akten des 7. Internationalen Wittgenstein Symposiums*, 22.–29. August 1982, Kirchberg/Wechsel (Wien 1983), 108–111.
Ders. (2), „Modaltheorie und Modallogik in der Scholastik und bei Leibniz", in: *Anuario Filosofico*, Vol. XVI, N. 1, Universidad de Navarra (Pamplona 1983), 273–91.
Carnap, Rudolf, *Logische Syntax der Sprache*, (Wien 1934).
Crusius, Christian, August, *Entwurf der notwendigen Vernunftwahrheiten, wiefern sie den zufälligen entgegengesetzt werden* (Leipzig 1753, Nachdruck Darmstadt 1963).
Czuber, E., *Die philosophischen Grundlagen der Wahrscheinlichkeitsrechnung* (Leipzig und Berlin 1923).
Deku, Henry, „Possibile Logicum", *Philos. Jahrbuch der Görres-Gesellschaft* 64 (1956), 1–21.
Frege, Gottlob, *Begriffsschrift, einer der arithmetischen nachgebildete Formelsprache des reinen Denkens* (Halle 1979, Nachdruck Hildesheim 1964).

Hacking, Ian, *The Emergence of Probability* (Cambridge 1975).

Jacobi, Klaus, *Die Modalbegriffe in den logischen Schriften des Wilhelm von Shyreswood und in anderen Kompendien des 12. und 13. Jahrhunderts* (Leiden-Köln 1980).

Lorenzen, Paul, „Praktische und theoretische Modalitäten", in: *Philosophia Naturalis*, Band 17, Heft 3 (1979), 261–279.

Meinong, Alexius, *Über Möglichkeit und Wahrscheinlichkeit. Beiträge zur Gegenstandstheorie und Erkenntnistheorie* (Leipzig 1915).

Rescher, Nicholas, „Bertrand Russell and Modal Logic", in: *Studies in Modality, American Philosophical Quarterly, Monographic Series* No. 8 (Oxford 1974), 25–96.

Ryle, Gilbert, *Dilemmas* (Cambridge University Press 1960).

Stenius, Erik, *Wittgensteins Tractatus. A critical exposition of its main lines of thought* (Oxford 1960).

Wittgenstein, Ludwig, *Schriften, Tractatus Logico-philosophicus, Tagebücher 1914–1916; Philosophische Untersuchungen* (Frankfurt am Main 1960).

Wright, Georg, Henrik von, *Wittgenstein* (Oxford 1982).

SOME OBSERVATIONS ON MODAL LOGICS
AND THE *TRACTATUS*[1].

Jerzy Perzanowski
Jagiellonian University of Krakow

1. The modal character of the *Tractarian* ontology is now commonly recognized[2]. And it is clear that there must be some modal calculus (or, more carefully, calculi) implicit in the *Tractatus*. In the subjects' literature we may find several papers dealing with the question. Most of them point to Lewis' calculus *S5* as the *Tractarian* modal logic. Is this answer right? Are arguments in its support convincing?

I do believe that:

(1°) the most popular answer mentioned above, even if true, should be argued for more thoroughly than it has been;

(2°) the modality structure implicit in the *Tractatus*, even when restricted to purely ontological modalities, is more complex than it looks in its usual descriptions, including the best available at the moment. In particular, both the basic role played by the notion of form—fundamental modality of the *Tractatus*, as I tried to argue in my [6]—and the question of its logic is simply omitted by the writers known to me.

However, truth is only one, and if not fully recognized, irrespective of how deeply it is hidden, it sends us words about itself, mainly indirectly, through some inaccuracies and/or inconsistencies in current opinion. This applies to the question under discussion, among others, in the following way: both necessity and possibility operators implicit in *S5* or in any similar logic are symmetrical, whereas these two notions in its most frequent *Tractarian* occurrences are not. Characteristic are also incoherencies which are to be found in claims made by the authors arguing, in fact, along the same line (comp. [5], [14]).

In what follows, starting with brief comments concerning D. Kaplan's, G. H. von Wright's and A. Maury's works, I will try to reexamine the problem and to provide some new arguments for a corrected version of von Wright's solution and to extend that solution by basing it on more fundamental theory of the notion of form. This theory, as you will see, provides solid philosophical foundations for relational semantics of intensional logics, foundations which are grounded on the *Tractarian* ontology.

2. Before going into the proper discussion let me collect basic information concerning the class of normal modal logics that I shall need in what follows. For further information see [2] and [9].

Our discussion of the *Tractarian* modal logics is restricted initially to the class of all normal modal calculi. There are two main reasons for that restriction: the class of all normal logics is connected naturally with the original Kripke semantics (whose philosophical foundations I wish to consider as well); and secondly, it suffices, as will be shown, for distinguishing logics which, after scrutinizing the *Tractatus*, must be distinguished. However, further, more scrupulous, analysis, using the full class of modal logics, is needed and postponed to [8].

I have to mention as well, that, like other writers, I am working with the basic interdefinability equivalence: $L = \neg M \neg$, which—as I noted previously—is questionable in the case when we have only one sort of modalities. However, as you will see, my arguments will lead to the claim that in the *Tractatus* modalities of at least four different kinds are stuck together into one[3].

My notation is standard. The classical operators of negation, conjunction, disjunction, implication and equivalence are denoted respectively by: $\neg$, $\wedge$, $\vee$, $\rightarrow$, $\equiv$; whereas modal operators of possibility and necessity by: M and L. *CL* denotes the classical logic; *FOR*−the set of all formulas which are denoted by A, B, A_1. . .; whereas Var = { p, q, r, . . .} denotes the set of all variables.

The smallest normal logic *K* is defined as the closure of *CL* ∪ {L (A → B) → (LA → LB) : A, B ∈ *FOR*} under detachment and Gödel's rule of necessitation: A/LA; what we write *K* = *CL* [L (A → B) → (LA → LB)]. Analogously, we put *D* = *K* [LA → MA], *T* = *K* [LA → A], *DR* = *D* [⌐ CA], where CA =df MA ∧ M ⌐ A, *DR** = *D* [⌐ CCA], *TR* = *T* [⌐ CA], *S5* = *T* [MLA → LA] (= *T* [⌐ CCA], comp. [15]), *S13* = *S5* [Mp : p ∈ Var], *VER* = *K* [LA].

Notice that *TR* and *VER* are the only two Post-complete normal modal logics[4]. that any extension of *D* (including *D* itself) is inconsistent with *VER* and, next, that *S13* is the only one system in the above list which is not logic.

Interconnections between above systems are summarized in the following Diagram 1:

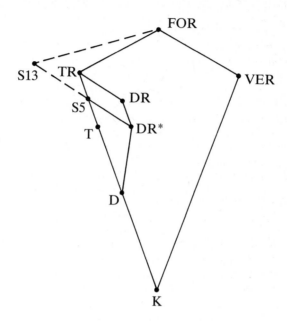

3. Now, let me present very briefly three most interesting, as far as I known, papers dealing with the question of the *Tractarian* modal logic.

D. Kaplan in his dissertation [3] touched on this problem and claimed that the modal logic of the *Tractatus* is an extension of Lewis' *S5*, called by him *S13*. Following some remarks of R. Carnap (see [1]) he accepts the extensional character of the *Tractarian* modal logic. This means that in its semantic characterization the alternativeness relation doesn't play any role. Hence we should accept at least *S5*. On the other hand, taking into account the *Tractarian* idea that all situations are possible, he accepts the axiom: Mp, obtaining his *S13* = *S5* [Mp : p ∈ Var]. Notice that *S13* is not closed under substitution, hence it is not logic at all (but it is *S5*-theory!).

In my opinion both of Kaplan's assumptions should be reexamined. Particularly, it is doubtful, whether the *Tractarian* modal logic is really extensional?

Without any doubt the best analysis of the problem was given by G. H. von Wright in his [14] and [15]. Taking the well-known Gödel-von Wright's calculus for his starting point (unfortunately without any argument for doing that) he discusses, profoundly and carefully, one of the most important notions of the *Tractatus*−the notion of a significant proposition, looking, particularly, for a proper interpretation of its bipolarity. The analysis results in the following modal definition of a significant proposition: it is what *can* be true or *can* be false; not, as it is usually oversimplified: what *is* true or *is* false. Next, Professor von Wright is searching for logic of this "can". Led by theses from 2.012 on he considers two formulas: $\neg$ CA, $\neg$ CCA and decides to choose the second. The resulting logic is indeed $S5 = T\,[\,\neg\,CCA]$.

I think that in von Wright's analysis the starting point is the weakest point[5]: Why start with T−certainly, from a philosophical point of view, not so innocent logic? Next, which *Tractarian* claims, if any, support T?

Von Wright's basic idea of the modal formulation of the Principle of Bivalence was developed in the dissertation of his pupil A. Maury [5]. The dissertation does not concern the question of the *Tractarian* modality theory. But it contains many insightful and relevant remarks, one of which supports the claim that in the *Tractatus* possibility equals contingency, or somewhat weaker "to be possible is to be contingent": $MA \rightarrow CA$ (comp. [5] p. 29). However, the associated logic $K\,[MA \rightarrow CA] = VER$, the logic which, as can be seen from the Diagram 1, is inconsistent not only with $S5$, but with any extension of D (including D itself).

Both von Wright's and Maury's arguments, taken separately, are rather convincing. But, as we have seen, the resulting logics are mutually inconsistent!

Therefore, if we consider−as I do−both analyses outlined previously to be reasonable, then either the modal theory implicit in the Tractatus is inconsistent or the above "inconsistency" is only apparent; which, according to the hermeneutic rule I was starting with, means that further investigations are needed, in the course of which the notions in question would be split into at least two series: *logical* and *ontological*. This, in turn, entails that we are in need of a more general theory comparing notions from these two (or more?) series.

4. Keeping in mind doubts concerning previous approaches it is very important to base our discussion on data as indubitable as possible.

To this end, I decide to start with cataloguing several basic modal notions of the *Tractatus* and with describing their interconnections. I concentrate on the *Tractarian* classification of complexes (or configurations).

In the *Tractatus* all complexes are−on the one hand−either possible or impossible, and−on the other hand−either contingent or noncontingent. Next, two sorts of contingencies (or situations) are distinguished: existing (or real)−facts (symbolized: F) and nonexisting, purely possible−counterfacts (cF). We should remark further, that in one reading of the text, there are two sorts of noncontingencies: necessities and inconsistencies; and two sorts of possibilities: contingencies and necessities. Sticking above classifications together we obtain the following *Table 1*:

Configurations or Complexes			
Possibilities M			Impossibilities ¬M
Contingencies C		Noncontingencies ¬C	
Facts F	Counter-Facts cF	Necessities L	Inconsistencies (⊥)

Changing Table 1 after A. Maury's idea (possibility *equals* contingency) we receive *Table 2*:

Configurations			
C		¬C	
M		L	¬M
F	cF	L	Inconsistencies

546

If, in turn, 2.012 would be interpreted as: to be configuration is to be noncontingent, we obtain the following mutations of the above tables:

Table 1'

Configurations			
¬C			
M			¬M
C		L	Incons.
F	cF		

Table 2'

Configurations			
¬C			
M			¬M
C	L		
F	cF		Incons.

In what follows, I am going to sketch two methods of understanding above Tables decoding modal logics implicit in them. I will discuss in all details needed only Table 1, for other tables I shall indicate merely the most important differences.

First reading of the Table 1, LOGICAL or SET-THEORETICAL, consists in treating it as the diagram of the given classification (or partition). It gives us the following remarkable set of definitions CA = MA $\land$ M ¬ A, FA = A $\land$ CA, cFA = ¬ A $\land$ CA; and—on the other hand—only one formula as specific axiom: LA $\to$ MA. Thus, in the class of normal modal logics Table 1 encodes the calculus D.

The second reading, say, ONTOLOGICAL, is obtained when the Table is understood as the diagram of the order of predication. After eliminating contradictory, from normal modal logics point of view, predications we receive a new interesting $S5$-like axiom: ¬ CLA, which, however, when added to D gives a calculus weaker than $S5$.

Notice that Table 1 solo, without any additional rules, doesn't give von Wright's formula: ¬CCA. Therefore this axiom must be justified in another way. The resulting calculus DR^* is an offspring of the two different intuitions: purely logical—supporting D; and semantical —supporting R* : ¬ CCA.

To obtain such a justification we transform Table 1 into Table 1'. Using ontological reading we receive immediately von Wright's formula: ¬ CCA. However, via logical interpretation we obtain, in fact, calculus DR stronger than DR^*, axiomatized by the Leibnizian formula: LA $\equiv$ MA, which, of course, is glaringly non-Wittgensteinian.

The above discussion shows clearly that in tables 1 and 1' two different notions of noncontingency occur: *logical*—in Table 1; and *ontological*—in the Table 1'. We may incorporate them into one Table, but in doing that notational distinction is necessary. In short, the logical interpretation works well for logical modalities, whereas ontological—only for their ontological counterparts.

Let me add that each Table contains also Kaplan's formula: Mp, provided that all inconsistencies are equivalent to the fixed one: $\perp$ Indeed, by any Table we have ¬Mp $\equiv$ $\perp$, hence Mp!

Finally, let us observe that Table 2 (or Table 2'), obtained from Table 1 (1') after Maury's idea, gives—in fact—*VER*!

To sum up: The above discussion of the Table 1 indicates D as the proper logic of the *Tractarian* logical modalities. Von Wright's axiom needs another justification: ontological, as in Table 1', or semantical, supply n.b. by Professor von Wright himself. Its addition gives either the calculus DR^*—in the case of Table 1 or DR—when we take into account Table 1'. Notice, however, that in both cases we obtain logics different from $S5$.

5. It should be pointed out that above method of searching for modal logics of a given philosophical theory is very general indeed. It may be used in the case of any theory containing classification of a family of (modal) notions, whose logic we are looking for.

6. Now I should like to outline very briefly a semantical approach to the problem under discussion.

Some people believe that the claim "the *Tractarian* modal logic equals *S5*" is implied by one of the most mysterious *Tractarian* claims—2.022: Every possible world has the same substance, i.e. objects, as the real one.

Of course, there is no such direct inference, simply because there is no easy explication of 2.022 and, on the other hand, it is not so obvious what exactly we should infer.

The last question is much easier to answer. Taking into account the usual Kripke-style characterization of *S5* we have to prove for any possible worlds w, w' that wRw', where R is an appropriate alternativity relation. Furthermore, recalling Henkin-type models, we may treat possible worlds as the maximal consistent sets of formulas. Then we should prove that for any w, w' w' $\subseteq$ Mw, where Mw = {A : MA$\in$w}.

By the way, it is noticeable that the *Tractarian* ontological approach to semantics—with its treating sentences, propositions and all pictures as configurations, items with the same ontological status as facts—provides solid and natural philosophical foundations for, the usually regarded as artificial, Henkin-models.

Next, the desired formal explication of 2.022 may be grounded on "Leibnizian" interpretation of the Tractatus as given in [6], [7]; where I construe 2.022 in connection with another— even more mysterious—key thesis of the Tractatus 2.033: The form is the possibility of the structure. This thesis was formalized there thus: Form (x) = $\Diamond$ Str (y), with understanding that the form of x is all that in x which makes (renders) possible the structure of y.

Having this, somewhat generalized, idea in mind I introduce the following chain of notions and definitions.

PRIMITIVE NOTIONS:
$\Diamond$ (,), the "making possible" or "formal possibility" relation with the intended meaning: $\Diamond$ (x, y)—the item x (object or class of objects) makes possible the configuration y.
<, the relation "to be simpler with respect to a given method of analysis". This relation was investigated many times by many authors. In the sequel I will use a version of its theory given by R. Suszko [10] and his followers.

DEFINITIONS:
At ( ), *objects* (things or atoms): At (x) if and only if $\neg\exists$y, y<x
S, *substance: relative*, of the item x — S(x) = {y<x : At (y)} and *absolute*—S = {y : At(y)}.
C (,), *compatibility*: C(x,y) if and only if $\Diamond$ (S(y), x)
ST, *situations: relative*, with respect to the item x—ST$_x$ = {y : C (y, S (x)} and *absolute*—ST = {y : C (y, S)}.
Possible worlds: <-maximal elements of ST, denoted by w, w', etc.
M, *ontological possibility: relative*—M$_x$y iff C (y, S (x)) (iff $\Diamond$ (S (x), y) and *absolute*—My iff C (y, S).
R, *Alternativity relation: relative*—wR$_w$,w' iff w' $\subseteq$ M$_w$,w and *absolute*—wRw' iff w' $\subseteq$ Mw

Applying above notions to the *Tractarian* framework (understood as in [6], [7]) I first note that Wittgenstein distinguished the actual world: a, by means of the fundamental idea that S = S (a). However, following Leibnizian Principle of Grounding (what is possible must be ontologically grounded on what is real, comp. [7]) he achieved, by introducing 2.022: For any possible world w, S (w) = S (a) = S, resolving of possible items into the factual sphere. From 2.022 we obtain (1): For any w, w' S (w) = S (w'). Notice that (1) implies, among others, reduction of the above relative notions to absolute notions.

Passing to the question of modal logic(s) connected with the above conceptual machinery let me note first that it solo, without any additional axioms, quarantees proof of the possibilization rule: A/MA. Hence it determines the calculus *D*! As usual, extensions of *D* may be obtained by choosing additional, specific axioms. And indeed, it is not so difficult to find axioms and rules which taken together with (1) imply the Kripkean characterization of *S5* mentioned previously. Therefore, in the above framework, 2.022 is, in fact, connected with *S5*!

Finally, let me emphasize the more general facet of the sketched construction: It reduces purely formal relational semantics to a formal philosophical theory thus grounding it, in the very end, on the Tractarian ontology.

7. To conclude, in the Tractatus at least four kinds of modal logics may be distinguished: theories of logical modality−*D* and the like; theories of semantical modality−*DR** type calculi; theories of metaphysical modality−*VER* type logics and, last but not least, theories of ontological modality−*S5*, *S13* etc.

Next, any Tractarian modal logic is connected with more fundamental theory of the formal modality, which, after formalization, plays the role of its formal metatheory[6].

ENDNOTES

[1] The paper's title clearly paraphrases the title of G. H. von Wright's master essay [15]. Its ambiguity is intended, two main claims of the paper are thus hinted at. The first one concerns complexity of the modality structure of the Tractatus and points out several modal logics inhering in it. The second one shows the way of basing modal logics on the Tractarian ontology. To do that one reduces the fundamental notions of modal philosophy and relational semantics of modal logics (compatibility, possible worlds and relation of aternativeness) to the notion of form−the basic ontological modality of the Tractatus (comp. [6]).

[2] The paper forms a third part of my bigger work in progress (comp. previous parts [6], [7]) in which, after having articulated the proper place of ontology in the Tractatus, I am trying to formalize it. Due to the limitation of the paper's length it is still a sort of abstract. Its full text, with all arguments developed, is intended to be published elsewhere as [8]. I am very grateful to the Austrian Wittgenstein Society for a grant which enabled me to attend the Ninth International Wittgenstein Symposium.

[3] What seems to be suggested by a rather cryptic final remark of [15].

[4] Compare [4]. Please note that by a normal system (or theory) I mean any overset of *K* closed on detachment and necessitation, whereas a normal logic is defined as a normal system which is closed under substitution.

[5] The same criticism applies also to B. Wolniewicz's paper [12].

[6] The most important problem arising from the above differentiation of the Tractarian logics is to connect and to interrelate logics of different kinds. This problem and details concerning the theory of formal modality are postponed to the next two instalments of the Tractarian serial by the present author.

REFERENCES

[1] Carnap, R., "Modality and Quantification", *The Journal of Symbolic Logic* 11 (1946), 33−64.

[2] Chellas, B. F., *Modal Logic*, (Cambridge University Press 1980), pp. 295.

[3] Kaplan, D., *Foundations of Intensional Logics* (Mimeographed, 1964).

[4] Makinson, D., "Some embedding theorems for modal logic", *Notre Dame Journal of Formal Logic* 12 (1971), 188−194.

[5] Maury, A., "The Concept of Sinn and Gegenstand in Wittgenstein's Tractatus", *Acta Philosophica Fennica* 29 (1977), 176 pp.

[6] Perzanowski, J., "Some ontological and semantical puzzles of Wittgenstein's Tractatus", in R. Haller (ed.), *Aesthetics, Proc. of the 8th International Wittgenstein Symposium* (Vienna 1984), 224−230.

[7] Perzanowski, J., "What is non Fregean in the Tractarian Semantics and why?", Lecture presented to the Second Frege Conference, Schwerin, GDR, September 1984; submitted.

[8] Perzanowski, J., *Modal Logics and the Tractatus*, (in preparation).

[9] Segerberg, K., "An Essay in Classical Modal Logic", *Filosofiska Studier* nr.13 (Uppsala 1971), 250pp.

[10] Suszko, R., "Ontology in the Tractatus of Wittgenstein", *Notre Dame Journal of Formal Logic* 9 (1968), 7−33.

[11] Wittgenstein, L., *Tractatus Logico-Philosophicus* (London 1922).
[12] Wolniewicz, B., "The Notion of Fact as a Modal Operator", *Teorema* 1972, 59–66.
[13] Wright, G. H. von, *Wittgenstein* (Oxford 1982).
[14] Wright, G. H. von, "Some Observations on Modal Logic and Philosophical System", in *Contemporary Philosophy in Scandinavia* (1972), 17–26.
[15] Wright, G. H. von, "Modal Logic and the Tractatus", in [13], 185–200.

* * *

TAKING THOUGHTS ONE AT A TIME
PEIRCE ON THE LINEAR PROGRESSION OF THOUGHT IN REASONING

Rolf George
University of Waterloo, Canada

The object of this paper is to solve a historical puzzle: In 1905 and 1906 Charles Sanders Peirce published three articles in the *Monist*, the third of which was titled: "Prolegomena to an Apology for Pragmaticism." Peirce there describes his system of *Existential Graphs*, a consistent and complete diagrammatic version of propositional and first order predicate logic. He reckoned this system to belong to the "bedrock beneath pragmaticism" and intended to make use of it, in the article to follow, which was to give a "proof" of pragmaticism, i.e. at least of the proposition "that a *conception* that is the rational purport of a word or other expression, lies exclusively in its conceivable bearing upon the conduct of life *and there is absolutely nothing more in it*." (5.412)[1] Peirce concludes his article as follows:

> In my next paper, the utility of this diagrammtization of thought in the discussion of the truth of Pragmaticism shall be made to appear. (4.572)

The next paper was never published, and it is a matter of dispute what role the graphs were meant to play in it. My conjecture is that Peirce thought of the graphs as a *model* of deductive thought superior to other representations of logic in a sense to be made clear later. And this is what I hope to establish.

From time to time philosophers have raised the question how sentences and arguments may be represented in the mind, that is, whether a language or an algorithm is a suitable *model* of thought, and whether some languages and some algorithms are better models, in some sense, than others.

For instance, in the 14th century Peter of Ailly and Gregory of Rimini wondered whether a sentence in a natural language could be a model of a sentence in mental language: "Is the mental sentence essentially put together out of several partial acts of knowing (*notitiis*), one of which is the subject, another the predicate, and another the copula?"[2] They both denied that a mental sentence has parts because they took it to be the intellect's "perfection" to produce a whole sentence or judgment all at once.[3] It would follow from this that, e.g. the sentences "Every whiteness is a quality" and "Every quality is a whiteness", were they represented as the collection of their parts, must receive the same representation in the mind (since they are not temporally strung out), even though one of them is true, and the other false. But since they do not have the same representations it follows, they claimed, that mental sentences do not have parts. Spade reports that somewhat later a commentator on Ockham maintained that mental sentences do have parts, even though they occur in an instant, but that they are so highly inflected that, in the words of Spade, "*word order counts for nothing whatever*."[4] On both views, natural language is a bad model of thought, on the one view because it shows parts where thought has none, and on the other because it shows uniformity where thought is highly inflected.

If there is a problem in the representation of mental sentences, there must be a larger problem still in the representation or modelling of inferences. Some writers sought to subsume the second problem to the first, for example Pardus, when he maintains that "a whole syllogism may be regarded as subordinate to one comparative apprehension with the specific nature of an illative apprehension," where, "apprehension" signifies the grasping of a complex sentence.[5]

The problem of the representation of thought, or the nature of thinking, if you prefer this way of putting it, was not just a medieval crotchet, but continued to engage some philosophers. Bolzano, for instance, devoted a part of his *Wissenschaftslehre* to the problem. He held that if several subjective ideas are to result in a judgement, they must be in the mind at the same time, or at least they must show some temporal overlap. But this simultaneity does not altogether explain that a *judgement* results. The ideas must have a special connection with each other.

> If I am asked what this connection is, I can answer only that it must be a sort of mutual influence of these ideas upon each other. But I am unable to determine what sort of mutual influence there must be in order for a judgement to result from the presence of several subjective ideas.[6]

But unlike Pardus, he thought that the occurence of an inference in the mind is generically different from that of a judgement. Like Aristotle (*Post. Anal.* 71 b20), he believed that the premisses of an argument *cause* the conclusion to appear in the mind:

> A judgement M which comes about by the mediation of ABCD . . . follows upon them in time, but in such a way that they have not altogether disappeared when it comes about. The correctness of this assertion is confirmed in part by the observation which each of us can make with his own judgements, in part by the fact that between effect and cause there must be some simultaneity.[7]

Apparently, Bolzano saw no difficulty in attributing to the mind the ability to maintain simultaneously an indefinitely large set of premisses, though he does not specifically address this issue. Rather, after attending briefly to the question of how a single judgement can be in the mind, he moves directly to the problem of inference, where premisses must be co-present in the mind in order to bring forth the conclusion.

This problem of the co-presence of premisses, which Whewell called "colligation", exercised others considerably, notably Brentano, but also Peirce, as we shall see. Brentano's concern was this: he thought that to form a judgement, subject and predicate must meet at a temporal border.[8] But once a judgement is formed, it is wholly in the past, and it becomes difficult to understand how an inference requiring more than one premiss is possible: once a reasoner arrives at the second premiss of, for example, a syllogism, the first premiss is in the past and no longer available to lead him to the conclusion. The problem is that in order to form the second premiss, the time in which its *subject* dwells passes before he comes to the temporal border between it and the *predicate*. But this passage of time leads him away from the major premiss, which is then out of mind. Brentano proposes that in a syllogism the major premiss is, in effect, converted into a predicate. For instance, the sentence "A tree is green" is converted into "A green tree is", and a sentence "No tree is blue" is converted into "A blue tree is not".

> And through such a composition the mental achievement we call an inference, or even a sequence of several inferences becomes possible, despite the Aristotelian law that, in the understanding, like in all other potentialities, there can be only one actuality at a time.[9]

Brentano says these things by way of elaborating on a point made be Aristotle in *De Anima III, 6*:

> But that which mind thinks, and the time in which it thinks are in this case divisible only incidentally and not as such. For in them too there is something indivisible (according to Brentano this is the point in which the two mental acts meet) . . . which gives unity to the time and the whole of length; and this is found equally in every continuum whether temporal or spatial. (430 b 17)

Brentano merely adumbrated, and did not develop, his theory, at least not in the Aristotle manuscripts, and it is not clear how it might be fleshed out. How, for instance, would one deal with inferences in propositional logic? Or with the problem of such an argument as dilemma, where three premisses must be colligated. How does one even reconstruct a simple syllogism along Brentano's lines, and how are singular terms managed?

We are now in a position to appreciate Peirce's problem. In the *Short Logic* of 1893 he wrote:

> The first step of inference usually consists in bringing together certain propositions which we believe to be true, but which, supposing the inference to be a new one, we have hitherto not considered together, or not as united in the same way. This step is called *colligation*. The compound assertion resulting from colligation is a *conjunctive proposition*, that is, it is a proposition with a composite icon . . . Colligation is a very important part of reasoning . . . (2.442)

Unlike Brentano, Peirce saw no difficulty in the co-presence of several premises in the mind. But a related problem arises when one tries to model the progression of deduction from several premises. Suppose that the initial steps make use only of some of them. What happens to the others? If thought progresses linearly, then they will be left behind. Do they then become inaccessible? Peirce states the problem as follows:

> What can it mean to say that ideas wholly past are thought of at all, any longer? They are utterly unknowable. What distinct meaning can attach to saying that an idea in the past in any way affects an idea in the future, from which it is completely detached? (6.106)

Let us now turn to the Existential Graphs themselves to see how they might be seen to deal with this problem. The merest sketch must be suffice. I will restrict myself to a brief account of the so-called "alpha" portion of the graphs, i.e. the propositional logic. A comprehensive exposition is given by Don Roberts.[10]

In EG a sentence is asserted if it is entered upon the so-called "sheet of assertion". Any number of sentences can be asserted simply by writing them on the sheet. There is no special sign for conjunction. (Indeed, to enter the sentences severally is to colligate them.) If a sentence is to be denied, it will be written onto the back side of the sheet of assertion. To bring it into view we cut out the part of the sheet on which it is entered and turn it over. In practice we depict this by drawing a fine line around the sentence, a "cut", which operates as the sign for denial. The disjunction of A, B, and the material implication of B by A are shown below:

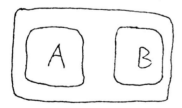 

The various entries on the sheet of assertion are called "graphs". Every graph occurs on a area: if the graph is written on the sheet of assertion itself, then the sheet is the area, if the graph lies inside a cut, then the area inside the cut is the area, etc. We can distinguish even and odd areas, depending on whether they are separated from the sheet of assertion by an even or an odd number of cuts.

The transformation rules, which are given in the appendix, allow one to diagram derivations and to prove tautologies, whose derivation begins with the empty sheet of assertion. The progress of an argument may then be depicted in the following way:

553

If God is known in the third mode, then He is known in the fourth mode. God is known in the third mode or in the fourth mode. Therefore, God is known in the fourth mode. (After Ockham)

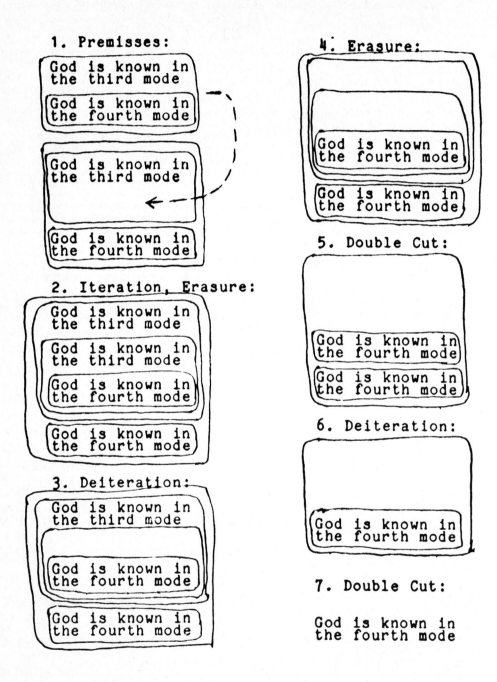

1. Premisses:

God is known in the third mode

God is known in the fourth mode

God is known in the third mode

God is known in the fourth mode

2. Iteration, Erasure:

God is known in the third mode

God is known in the third mode

God is known in the fourth mode

God is known in the fourth mode

3. Deiteration:

God is known in the third mode

God is known in the fourth mode

God is known in the fourth mode

4. Erasure:

God is known in the fourth mode

God is known in the fourth mode

5. Double Cut:

God is known in the fourth mode

God is known in the fourth mode

6. Deiteration:

God is known in the fourth mode

7. Double Cut:

God is known in the fourth mode

As in this display, proofs in EG all progress linearly. All initial information needed for the progress of the proof is carried forward, and earlier configurations, the initial premises and intermediate results, simply disappear (into the past) as the inference proceeds. This becomes clear once it is noted that only the nature of print forced Peirce to display graphs in sequences. They become a more adequate model of deductive thought if the entries are made sequentially *in the same graph*, by writing and erasing. I invite the reader to rewrite the sequence by altering *one* graph, rather than producing a sequence of them.

One can imagine (or make) a visual aid: a little flip-book, like those we had as children, where the rapid flipping of the pages produces apparent motion of figures. Plainly, such a book could be made to show a proof in EG, perhaps a longer one, like that of the self distributive law of implication, which takes some 20 steps. It would, presumably, simulate *the movement* of thought as embodied in the development of a graph. Peirce called the graphs "the moving pictures of thought", and we could, I think, guess what he meant were we to flip the book and observe something approximating the continous transformation of a graph. The graphs, says Peirce, represent "A change in thoughts or signs, as if to induce this change in the Interpreter." (4.538). He comments:

> When an argument is brought before us, there is brought to our notice (what appears so clearly in the illative transformations of Graphs) a process whereby the premisses bring forth the conclusion, not informing the interpreter of its truth, but appealing to him to assent thereto. This process of transformation, which is evidently the kernel of the matter, is no more built out of propositions than a motion is built out if positions. The logical relation of the conclusion to the premises might be asserted: but that would not be an argument, which is essentially intended to be understood as representing what it represents only in virtue of the logical habit which would bring any logical interpreter to assent to it. (4.572)

If we arrest the moving transformation of a graph for an instant and observe its present configuration, we see depicted a momentary state of consciousness. At this point the earlier configurations, the graphs that lie now in the past, have receded into habit. The present graph represents the cutting edge of deductive thought as it moves forward, acquiring new insights that it then leaves behind as habits, that is beliefs.

If this is so, then the graphs are, in effect, grist for the mill of synechism, i.e. "that tendency in philosophical thought that insists upon the idea of continuity as of prime importance in philosophy" (6.169) They depict the continuous transformation of the mind reasoning. As Peirce puts it:

> That ideas can nowise be connected without continuity is sufficiently evident to one who reflects upon the matter. (6.143)

What is at issue? Contrast Peirce's Graphs with an axiomatic development of propositional logic, or with a Fitch style natural deduction algorithm. For short stretches, proofs in these systems might satisfy the Peircean desideratum of linear progression, but more frequently we are required *to return* to previously proved or assumed material. Such algorithms therefore fail to be models of deductive thought, if deductive thought in fact progresses linearly. Indeed, since in such a system all previously catalogued material continues to be present, it could be viewed as a system of *coordinated* entities, a space, in Leibniz's words, not a mind, though a space that increases in the activity of proving. If one takes seriously the view that thought progresses linearly, and that it is a virtue of an algorithm to model thought, then they fall short.

But why should one hold that thought progresses linearly (and continuously)? The former, at any rate, seems to be true of *conscious* thought. But Peirce did not equate thought with conscious thought. So why should *he* have held that a proper representation of deductive thought must show it to be a linear progression? It was, in fact a very common view that thought so progresses, held, for instance, by Descartes, Leibniz, Kant, and, as we saw, Brentano. But Peirce's reasons were not theirs and have deep roots in his metaphysics.

For Peirce, inference is the grand metaphor for the unfolding of the universe. The graphs, therefore, are more than a representation of human thought. Since, in Peirce's philosophy, the universe develops as in evolution, thought must follow the same pattern. Looking back to the origin from any node in a tree of evolution, we see only one line. Looking forward, there are branchings, but at each node a definite option must be exercised, so that the choice path is again a line. It must be just so with thought. I quote Peirce:

> The law of continuity spreading will produce a mental association; and this I suppose is an abridged statement of the way the universe has been evolved. (6.143)

In an unpublished ms. Peirce says that "Evolution is the postulate of logic, itself,"[11] It is not wholly clear from the ms. whether logic dictates that there be evolution, or whether evolution is a postulate *in* logic, because evolution governs all things. This is a fine point, and it does not greatly matter in our context. The quotation supports the contention, though, that Peirce took thought to progress linearly, because that is what evolution does. I conjecture that this, together with their iconicity and some other features, mainly in predicate logic, made the graphs, in Peirce's view, such an apt representation of deductive thought.

A solution to the textual/biographical problem with which we began now suggests itself. It appears that Peirce did not mean to use the graphs as a *calculus* in which to cast the proof for pragmaticism. Indeed, he explicitly denied this: "(The) purpose and end is simply and solely the investigation of the theory of logic, and not at all the construction of a calculus to aid the drawing of inferences." (4.373). The explanation must be, rather, that he thought pragmaticism to presuppose synechism. But the case for the latter must remain weak if he cannot show that a logical algorithm is possible which models, or at least intimates, the continuous and linear transformation of the mind in reasoning, since the deductive movement of the mind is the great metaphor for the acquisition of habit that we find in all of nature. This then I take to be the role of the existential graphs in the projected proof of pragmaticism that unfortunately was never executed.

In concluding I want to raise a simple-minded objection: The graphs are thought a good model for deductive activity since in them conclusions *evolve* from the premisses. Evolution is never far from Peirce's mind, as I have argued, and inference is a sort of microcosm of evolution. But there is a fundamental disanalogy between reasoning and evolving in the biological sense. It is this: A species cannot reject an improvement. Suppose that a species can develop from a state A to a state B or else to a state C, where C is more advantageous, and where B and C are incompatible. It is the essence of evolution that if B comes along first, then the species must adopt it. It cannot postpone B on prudential grounds, so as to keep itself open to the improvement C. But it is of the essence of human decision that we should be able to forego an advantage in the expecation of a greater one. This even holds for deductive reasoning. What the graphs, as a model of deductive thought, leave unexplained is the fact that, even in deduction, we forego, or at least want to forego, less desirable conclusions for more desirable, more powerful or more inclusive ones. If I have a premiss 'A', and another premiss 'A implies B', and then proceed to the disjunction 'A or C', then I have, in the graphs, thrown away the possibility of deriving 'B' by modus ponens. It's a lost chance that may be gone forever. If my interpretation of Peirce's intentions is correct, then the graphs, as a model of deductive thought, leave out of account the plain fact that we *can* recover in such a case by reminding ourselves that we once were in the possession of 'A', and are therefore entitled to 'B'. Not that Peirce would have denied this. But it is at odds with what I take to be the very feature of the Graphs that made them, in Peirce's view, a representation of deductive thought. Perhaps to address this problem he postulated a "normal" course of inference:

> For any evolution of thought, whether it leads to a Conclusion or not, there is a certain normal course, which is to be determined by considerations not in the least psychological, and which I wish to expound in my next article. (4.540)

We do not know how he thought to describe this normal course, and whether he meant to meet the objection just advanced. As things stand, we must conclude that the graphs, like other algorithms, fail to model deductive thought. Indeed, it is time to begin to worry how an algorithm *can* model thought, and what it means to be successful in this.

APPENDIX: TRANSFORMATION RULES FOR GRAPHS.

We have the following five transformation rules. (Cf. Roberts 1973), p. 40 ff.)

1. The Rule of Erasure: Any evenly enclosed graph may be erased. Plainly, this rule cannot lead from truth to falsehood. We may, in fact, erase every graph, leaving the blank sheet of assertion.

2. The Rule of Insertion: Any graph may be scribed on an oddly enclosed area. This rule says, in effect, that if a sentence is false, then the conjunction of the sentence with any other sentence is also false.

3. The Rule of Iteration: Any graph may be repeated in its own area, or in any subordinate area. This is, in effect, a generalized version of the rule that A & -B entails A & A & -(B & A).

4. The Rule of Deiteration: Any graph whose occurence could be the result of iteration may be erased. We can understand this rule once we see that if a graph is removed by an even number of cuts from an identical graph lying farther out, it is really the double or quandruple, etc. negative of the latter, and can be deleted without loss of information. On the other hand, if a graph is removed by an odd number of lines from an identical graph lying farther out, it can be removed by a generalized version of disjunctive syllogism, as in A & -(B & A) implies A & -B, where one A has been deleted.

5. The Double Cut Rule: A double cut may be inserted around, or removed from, any graph on any area. This, of course, is the rule of double negation. It must be noted that if a graph is inscribed between two cuts, then this is not a double cut. The area between the two cuts must be empty.

ENDNOTES

[1] References to Peirce are to the *Collected Papers*, ed. C. Hartshorne and P. Weiss (Cambridge, Mass. 1933). As is customary, citations give volume and section number.

[2] Spade, Paul Vincent, "Gregory of Rimini and Peter of Ailly: Are Mental Sentences Composed of Parts?" Unpublished Paper; Indiana University, p. 4.

[3] Spade, p. 7.

[4] Spade, p. 8.

[5] Nuchelmans, G., *Late Scholastic and Humanist Theories of the Proposition* (Den Haag 1980), p. 43. Pardus' book was published in 1505.

[6] Bolzano, Bernard, *Theory of Science*, ed. Rolf George (Oxford 1972); Sect. 291. The reference is to the section number, which is the same in the German original edition of 1837.

[7] Bolzano, sect. 300.

[8] Brentano, Franz, "Aporien zum 9. und 10. Kapitel des Buches Lambda der *Metaphysik*". Unpublished ms. A 33, Houghton Library, Harvard University.

[9] Brentano A 33.

[10] Don D. Roberts, *The Existential Graphs of Charles S. Peirce*, (The Hague 1973).

[11] Ms. 875; quoted from H. William Davenport, "Peirce's Evolutionism and His Logic: Two Connections", *Proceedings of the C.S. Peirce Bicentennial International Congress*, Texas Tech University (1981), p. 310.

* * *

TURING, GÖDEL AND KALMÁR ON EFFECTIVE PROCEDURES

Guglielmo Tamburrini
Consiglio Nazionale delle Ricerche, Arco Felice, Italy

Turing's analysis of computation[1] is generally considered the most important argument for Church's thesis. Turing tried to find a mathematical characterization of effective calculability on the basis of a conceptual analysis of this intuitive notion. As recently pointed out by Kleene[2] and Davis[3], a similar strategy was first proposed by Gödel to Church in 1934. Gödel found unsatisfactory Church's heuristic arguments in favor of the thesis, and suggested that ". . . it might be possible, in terms of effective calculability as an undefined notion, to state a set of axioms which would embody the generally accepted properties of this notion, and to do something on that basis"[4].

Turing developed a similar approach to the problem, in terms of an answer to the questions: What are the basic properties of the notion of effective procedure? Can these properties be made precise and captured by a sharp mathematical notion? In his 1936 paper, Turing formulated some general conditions to be satisfied by any effective procedure. The most general conditions proposed by Turing can be characterized as finiteness and determinacy conditions:

Finiteness conditions
F_1: The list of instructions for the calculation is finite.
F_2: At each given instant the record of the calculation is finite.
F_3: The stock of basic symbols of the expressions on which the calculation is performed is finite.

Determinacy conditions
$D_1 - D_2$: At each given instant, the present instruction and part of the record uniquely determine i) the next action to undertake; ii) the next instruction to follow.
D_3: The list of instructions is fixed in advance.

D_3 is not explicitly stated, but is obviously required by Turing. Further, as noted by Kreisel[5], when it comes to the mathematical characterization, D_2 is interpreted by Turing as a *mechanical* condition. In particular, in the case of Turing machines, rules of passage between states are conceived of as a behavioral reaction of the computer in a given state to a symbol of the alphabet: if current instruction is I_j and the observed square contains symbol S_m act as prescribed by I_j and then apply instruction I_k.

The Church-Turing thesis, as it deserves to be called after Turing's work, claims the equivalence of effective functions and Turing machine computable functions. This claim implies that effectiveness can be mechanized. The scope of this "reducibility" claim, and consequently its epistemological relevance for mathematical logic (generalization of incompleteness theorems) as well as for areas such as cognitive psychology and artificial intelligence (computational models of the mind), depends on the interpretation given to the notion of effective procedure. Similarly, the available evidence in favor of Church's thesis can be assessed only against the background of a reasonable understanding of the properties of this intuitive notion.

Kreisel[6] pointed out that the notion of effective procedure is meant to include both humanly and mechanically effective procedures (briefly, h- and m-effective procedures), and stressed the fact that Turing's restrictive conditions are problematic when understood as referring to h-effective procedures. Kreisel developed this suggestion in connection with the intuitionistic notion of mathematical function. Gödel made a similar suggestion in a note to be added to his

1934 Princeton lectures.[7] He argued that Turing's analysis is defective because it presupposes that a humanly effective procedure can make use only of a finite number of states:

> Turing in *Proc. Lond. Math. Soc.* 42 (1936), p. 250, gives an argument which is supposed to show that mental procedures cannot carry any farther than mechanical procedures. However, the argument is inconclusive, because it depends on the supposition that a finite mind is capable of only a finite number of distinguishable states. What Turing disregards completely is the fact that *mind, in its use, is not static, but constantly developing*. . . Therefore, although at each stage of the mind's development the number of its possible states is finite, there is no reason why this number should not converge to infinity in the course of its development.[8]

In this remark, Gödel seems to suggest that the number of states may grow unboundedly during the mind's development, and that in the calculation of a function the mind may actually make use of these states ideally converging to infinity. It is clear that this supposition conflicts with Turing's conditions F_1 and D_3 on effective procedures. Gödel's remark is interesting at least for historical reasons, since i) it contributes to understand properly his *postscriptum* to the Princeton lectures,[9] in which he claims that Turing gives a precise analysis of the concept of *mechanical* procedure, and ii) it may also contribute to answer the question raised by Davis,[10] namely why Gödel didn't have Church's thesis. As for ii), though Gödel found Turing's argument convincing for mechanical procedures, this fact could not lead him to accept Church's thesis as a claim about h- and m-effective procedures, if he entertained the possibility of h-effective procedures of the kind envisaged in the passage quoted above.

Another example of an "extended" interpretation of effectiveness can be found in a 1957 paper by Kalmár.[11] Kalmár presents an argument against the plausibility of Church's thesis which makes an essential use of the intuitive notion of arbitrary correct proof. This notion is, according to Kalmár, a pre-mathematical concept, not liable to be made precise by formalization:

> There are pre-mathematical concepts which must remain pre-mathematical ones, for they cannot permit any restriction imposed by an exact mathematical definition. Among these belong, I am convinced, such concepts as that . . . of provability by arbitrary correct means, the extension of which cannot cease to change during the development of mathematics.[12]

Unlike provability in a formal system, the notion of provability by arbitrary correct means cannot be specified by a closure condition relative to a finite set of axiom schemes and rules of inference given in advance, since arbitrary correct methods of proof may become more and more inclusive at successive stages in the development of mathematics. One has to notice, in addition, that Kalmár is only concerned with finite proofs.

Let us now briefly present Kalmár's argument. Consider the number-theoretic function f, defined by means of Kleene's predicate T in the following way:

$$f(x) = \begin{cases} \min y\ T(x,x,y) \text{ if } \exists y\ T(x,x,y) \\ 0 \text{ otherwise} \end{cases}$$

This is not a general recursive function. By Church's thesis, f is not an effective, total function. Consider now the following "procedure" K, suggested by Kalmár for the calculation of f. Given any natural number m,

$$(K) \begin{cases} \text{case 1: if } \exists y\ T\ (m,m,y) \text{ and } n = \min y\ T\ (m,m,y), \text{ let } f(m) = n \\ \text{case 2: if one can prove by arbitrary correct means that } \forall y\ \neg T\ (m,m,y), \\ \qquad \text{then let } f(m) = 0 \end{cases}$$

Suppose, following Kalmár, that K is exhaustive, in the sense that for each natural number m either $\exists y\ T(m,m,y)$ — and thus one can find by a recursive procedure a natural number $n = \min y\ T\ (m,m,y)$ — or one can prove by arbitrary correct means that $\forall y\ \neg T\ (m,m,y)$, therefore establishing that $f(m) = 0$. But then, *in conflict with Church's thesis*, f would be an effectively calculable, total function. Therefore, under Church's thesis, by the law of excluded middle, one has to conclude that K is not an exhaustive procedure. Since, however, case 1 of K is obviously effective, this means that there is a natural number p such that the proposition '$\forall y\ \neg T(p,p,y)$' is true but such that this proposition cannot be established by arbitrary correct methods of proof. This is the purported consequence of Church's thesis considered implausible by Kalmár.

The question whether one can validly infer Kalmár's conclusion from Church's thesis can be seen primarily as a problem concerning the interpretation of Church's thesis. The procedure K defined by reference to arbitrary methods of proof, even under the assumption that it is exhaustive, does not satisfy Turing's conditions on effective procedures. K may not satisfy F_1: since arbitrary correct methods of proof are conceived of as a concept whose extension grows bigger during the development of mathematics, under an idealization similar to that implicit in the standard theory of effective calculability, correct methods of proof (and thus the list of instructions for the calculation of f) may ideally converge to infinity. D_3 is not met for the same reason: one cannot fix in advance what arbitrary correct methods of proof are.

There is a natural connection between Gödel's remark and Kalmár's approach to the problem of effectiveness. Both Gödel and Kalmár seem to pursue the idea of a mental procedure that cannot be specified in advance — because constantly developing — though allowing to calculate an h-effective function. This idea has the suggestive feature of picturing the possibility of the mind surpassing the calculating powers of any machine. In this sense, Gödel's and Kalmár's suggestions are in principle relevant to the issue of mechanism in psychology. The question whether their arguments can be applied to Church's thesis is more delicate. In my opinion, the violation of Turing's restrictive conditions suggests a distinction between different notions of effectiveness rather than an inadequacy of Turing's analysis. In this respect, it is instructive to notice that Turing was well aware of a possibility quite similar to those envisaged by Gödel and Kalmár, but confined himself to analyse the notion of *uniform* procedure. In his 1936 paper, he considered a sequence δ not computable according to his definition, and observed that "it is (as far as we know) possible that any assigned number of figures of δ can be calculated, but not by a uniform process. When sufficiently many figures of δ have been calculated, a essentially new method is necessary in order to obtain more figures".

This remark shows clearly that Turing excluded non-uniform, ever developing procedures from the range of his analysis. The question can be raised whether Gödel's and Kalmár's more comprehensive interpretations of effectiveness are amenable to a precise and fruitful treatment, much in the style of what has been achieved by means of Turing's analysis of uniform procedures. Independently of this issue, however, we have reached a quite definite conclusion. The arguments put forward by Gödel and Kalmár are based on a "deviant" interpretation of effectiveness and therefore cannot be applied to the standard interpretation of Church's thesis. Nonetheless, these "deviant" interpretations show their conceptual interest and, I believe, their underlying motivation when trying to assess the kind of support that Church's thesis offers to mechanism in psychology. Church's thesis expresses only a restricted form of mechanism. Being concerned only with uniform procedures, it does not exclude *a priori* the possibility of human beings calculating non-uniformly a sequence δ that cannot be calculated by any machine.

ENDNOTES

1 Turing, A. M., "On Computable Numbers, With An Application to the Entscheidungsproblem", *Proc. Lond. Math. Soc.* vol. 42 (1936), pp. 230−265.

2 Kleene, S. C., "Origins of Recursive Function Theory", *Ann. Hist. Comp.* vol. 3 (1981), pp. 52−67.

3 Davis, M., "Why Gödel Didn't Have Church's Thesis", *Information and Control*, vol. 54 (1982), pp. 3−24.

4 See Davis (1982), p. 9

5 Kreisel, G., "Which Number Theoretic Problems Can Be Solved in Recursive Progressions on Π_1^1 Paths Through *0*?", *J. of Symbolic Logic*, vol. 37 (1972), pp. 311−334.

6 Kreisel, G., "Church's Thesis: A Kind of Reducibility Axiom for Constructive Mathematics", in J. Myhill, A. Kino, R. E. Vesley (eds.), *Intuitionism and Proof Theory* (Amsterdam 1970), pp. 121−150.

7 Printed in M. Davis (ed.), *The Undecidable* (New York 1965), pp. 39−73.

8 See H. Wang, *From Mathematics to Philosophy* (London 1974), p. 325.

9 See Davis (1965), p. 72.

10 See Davis (1982).

11 Kalmár, L., "An Argument Against the Plausibility of Church's Thesis", in A. Heyting (ed.), *Constructivity in Mathematics* (Amsterdam 1959), pp. 72−80.

12 See Kalmár (1959), p. 79.

* * *

INCONSISTENT POLYNOMIALS, GEOMETROSTATIC AND THEOMETRIC LOCATING OF MONADS, TRACTATUS-RESIDUE

Eduard W. Wette
Radevormwald and Hennef-Uckerath

0. The subject dealt with in this paper had already been presented at the Sixth Symposium [2, JSL 48 l.c. [12]]. As concerns ontometry & theometry, i.e. a geometrostatic unification of 'motion' which eliminates not only all physical concepts (and data) but also all singularities from analytic or "harmonic" continuation (1962/65) — revolutionizing meta-astronomical consequences included (1973/75/77) —, there is now my summarizing contribution [2] on the occasion of the 15th century Hijra centenary celebrations.

0.1 The calculation of a pouch-wave (: Fig. 1), i.e. the simplest *maxi*mal surface, transcends all variational methods in uniform g (x, t)-terms, what encourages the imagination of pure geometry to rebut classical analysis with its arithmetizing criticisms: e.g., "continuous" curves with pathological properties (Weierstrass, Peano). Only an arithmetized transformation of metamathematical ⌜proof⌝-concepts is fitted to refute analysis (1966), arithmetic (1970), elementary computation, and propositional decision (1974), since the control of such basic results must be independent of any language. There is no defence against contradictory results of direct reckoning, except for intrafinite bounds to numerical polynomials: formalism can exploit latent code-numbers, even if encoding is prohibited by meta-stipulations.

0.2 The exhibition of inconsistent polynomials within position systems ever since the Sumerians, or in the concrete storage of modern computers, starts from a counter-derivation vs. Gödel's untrue theorems on *un*derivable propositions within a formal system. Archimedes' $\psi\alpha\mu\mu\iota\tau\eta\varsigma$ envisaged numbers $\leq A^{AA}$ with $\sqrt{\ } A = \mu = $ myriad $= 10000$; no 'period' $= A^A = 10^{800\ 000000}$ would have been introduced, if he had foreseen the size of inconsistent numbers (: **1.2**).

1. The first consistency-*critical* tool [1], a 140-rule calculus $\mathbf{K}_0$ which separates $+$, $\times$ from $=$ and translates arithmetical 'implication' into reflection-free 'production' on finite levels, can be decoded from $9812 = 373 \cdot 4 + (1720 - 56) \cdot 5$ binary digits (: Note); the number of 1-bits can be minimized to 2769, and the decimal value $\Psi_c = 2582.39^+ .. \times 10^{2950}$ encodes a critical creation. A tenfold information $\Psi_s < \Psi_c^{10} \ll \mu^\mu$ defines the primitive recursive function Ω and its *semantically* inconsistent property E $(\Omega; \xi) \equiv R_{13.}$ $(\xi) \to$ ri $(\Omega$ $(\xi)) \wedge [\Omega(\xi)]_3 = [\xi]_3 \wedge$ gl $(\Omega(\xi)) \leq$ tl (ξ). E is semipolynomial over Ω with varying undevicesimal degree, trilinear in the 19-length of subinputs; E's computation uses values $< \eta^\eta = {}^2\eta$ in $\eta = \Omega$ (ξ), since $(_{19}$ log $\eta)^{3-1} < \eta$. The 19-length of Ω (ξ) can be $\leq {}^\xi\xi = \psi_4$ $(2, \xi)$, $<$ for $\xi \neq 1$. Such a transelementary growth seems to exclude the transformation-lemma $\vdash_{\mathbf{z}} \mathsf{E}$ $(\Omega; \xi)$: a ri-⌜derivation⌝ $a^* = \Omega$ (a) of ⌜Vx U (x)⌝ exhibits ⌜U $(^{(i)}0)$⌝ $= [a^*]_{2,3}$, what entails ${}^a a \gg j + 1$; iterated ⌜inductions⌝ within a can result in ⌜Vx $(\psi(n,n) = x$⌝ with values j of the non-primitive recursion ψ_{n-1} $(n + 3, 2) - 3$ [2, JSL 48 lines 5 & 6].

1.1 Nevertheless, the lemma $\vdash_{\mathbf{z}} \mathsf{E}$ has been deduced by a *formal* induction on ξ through a 40-case induction step; the definition of Ω and E consists of < 300 auxiliary functions. Moreover, $_{19}$log $\xi^* \leq {}^\xi\xi$ is formally compatible with subsequent results that refute $\vdash_{\mathbf{z}} \mathsf{E}$ from earlier values than from an "inaccessible" ψ-term. A megabyte of information $> \mu^{30\mu} > \Psi_s^{40} > \Psi_f$ defines $< 300 + 2000$ variable-free polynomials which compute the *formally* inconsistent ⌜derivation⌐ $a_\wedge$ ($> e_\wedge \gg e_\vee > e_T = ⌐\vdash_\mathbf{z} E⌐$); $a_\wedge$ contains a minimum of ⌐inductions⌐, and an induction-free control of $49838 = [a_\wedge]_3 = [a_\wedge{}^*]_3 \neq 49838$ uses E for $\xi \leq a_\wedge$ only (whereas $e_\wedge$ contradicts "$e_\vee$" $\equiv \vdash_\mathbf{z} R_6$. $(\xi) \to [\xi]_3 \neq 2949$ after "e_T" for ξ), i.e. pure reckoning with variable-free terms $\leq \Omega$ $(a_\wedge) < {}^3(10^6)$ is inconsistent. The description of reckoning by k-proposition letter formulae yields a contradictory decision on 2 values, if $k \geq {}^5(10^6)$. Ergo: logic cannot *measure* itself; quantifier-free induction can be discomputed.

1.2 Defining informations in ⌐$a_\wedge$ applied⌐ are $> \Psi_f(⌐a_\wedge$ computed⌐$)$, but $< A^{15\mu}$. If Ψ_f computes $a_\wedge$ without any abbreviation (e.g., ⌐Ω⌐), then R $_{13.}$ $(a_\wedge) \wedge R_6$. $(e_\wedge) \wedge R_3$. $(⌐E⌐)$, and the *numerically* inconsistent value of $a_\wedge$ is $< \Psi_f^{677} < (\Psi_s^{27})^{1003} < A^A$, since (i) "$a_\wedge$" contains $\ll$ 1000 occurrences of Ω, (ii) the polynomial value ⌐E⌐, reproducing Ψ_s within Ψ_f, fulfils $\Psi_s <$ ⌐E⌐ $< \Psi_s^{27}$; $R_{13.}$ reproduces $\mathbf{K}_0$ within "Ψ_s", so that $\Psi_c < ⌐R_{13.}⌐ < \Psi_s$. Storing up 2300 addresses within $a_{\dot\wedge}$, the value of $a_{\dot\wedge}$ approaches its modified ⌐computation⌐ $\Psi_f (< \Psi_f)$.

1.3 In distinction to my (1978 Madison &) 1983 Salzburg precaution (A), parameter-solutions can be avoided by a doubly noninterlaced Ω-nesting in e : let f^-, b^- be f, b with $l-1$ instead of l [2, JSL 44, p. 475 line 14], let $a^- = \Omega_3$ $(l-1, [e]_2, b^-)$; then $el(s([e]_3) - 1, \Omega_3 (l - 1, [a^-]_1{}^h,$ $\varphi^* ([a^-]_1^h, [f^-]_2, q_4' ([a]_1))))$ with $h = h (e) = 1 + s ([e]_{2,3}) - s ([e]_{2,3,2})$ is the new $2 + 3$-nesting $\tau_{6.10}' (\Omega_{\cdot}; l, e, a)$.
The 1983 neutralization (B) can recur on the quadruple (l, e, c, a) instead of $(l, m, e, c, \bar{a})$, if the 10 "didactic" nestings in a are the only ones to be eliminated by Péter selection from a substitution-code, whereas the $2 + 4$ nestings in m, e have a didactic reduction after introducing further depth-concepts td, vd (as to tuples, variables) besides id, ed, which all enter, together with a md-rudiment, into a stricter grading level gl $(a) \leq l$.

1.4 Hilbert wrote in 1934, that Gödel's result could not prove the impracticability of his programme; he concluded that a sharpened (intrafinite?) utilization of the finite viewpoint must be the clue to more comprehensive (system-internal?) consistency-proofs. Gödel's arithmetizing methods were not advanced enough to confront Tarski's epigoni with the cage ⌐notation vs. meaning⌐, i.e. to "gut" Dirichlet's pigeon-hole principle. 2^{k^n} "free" decision series on k^n lattice-points restrict the human mind to consistent

	99	313	1981	51551	I	2
values $k \leq$	21	46	157	1385	I	3
	9	17	44	227	I	4

as concerns	Ψ_c	Ψ_s	Ψ_f	A^A	and	n dimensions in space & time.

2. Another work of intrafinite calculation is the complete solution to F. Klein's problem (1908) beyond Hilbert: *why* is arithmetic applicable to the realities (in nature, economics, politics)? Physicists (and astronomers) are unable to eliminate the patchwork of their concepts, formulae, and expensive experimentation for distorted data, to rectify the silhouettes of relativity & uncertainty as in QED, QCD, GUTs, to compute the curvature-distribution of the fold-fling oscillation representing a 'photon' (: Fig. 1), or mass-ratios hadron/lepton from a geometro*static* insight into the aether's kinematics. Descriptive geometry, > 60 millennia old, visualized the seamless warp & woof of nontransformable space-profiles & time-fibres with elastico-definite metrics, the anisotropic proportions in the "absolute" 4-torus average of time & space, the felly-position of our Milky Way (Hubble's redshift being a carrousel-effect!), negative masses in the anti-curved kernel of each star, varying values c (r), $\hbar$ (v) vs. fundamental "constants" c, $\hbar$ in conceded formalisms that do not intend to maintain 'substance & continuity' [2]. A determination of the terrestrial diagram-length for 1 sec from $\check{c} =$ cot $\hat{a} \wedge \hat{a} = 39°31'46''$ was obviously "outside" physically accessible achievements.

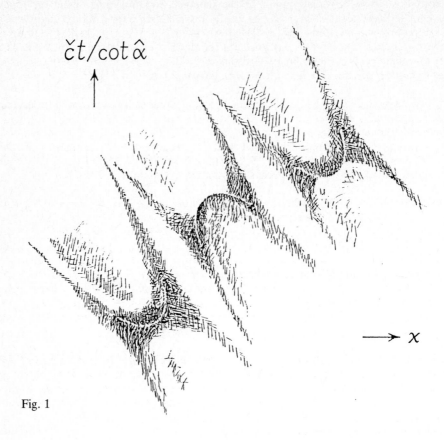

$\check{c}t/\cot\hat{\alpha}$

$\longrightarrow x$

Fig. 1

3. The locating of *monadic* threads (with respect to 'time' and *one* 'spatial' dimension) came from the web on a handle, whose net-lines cannot everywhere coincide in ones as with regularity. Fig. 2 shows a bio-handle − transitory tying-off of a bio-profile, whereas all time-fibres are coherent − and the scaffolding of its monadic fibres; monadic profiles & fibres meet at 2 cross-points of multiplicity 1, i.e. in pairs (or at 1 cross-point of multiplicity 2, i.e. in triples). Monad t_-^- between 'birth' and 'death' represents the internal ego; t_+^- can be the external ego *or* the super-ego in psychoanalysis; t_+^+, t_-^+ locate the masculine & feminine branch of id (before 'birth'), and soul & body (after 'death'), branches which belong to super-ego *or* id, but return to their own id under a frequency 0.3325 aHz $\approx 1/\hat{t}$ without repetition. Contrary to Maxwell, sources & vortices have no primary existence; circulations on the global average (e.g., from economy, traffic) exert wringing tendencies at the orifices of handles, where those result in collective reaction D_+^-, D_-^-, forces to be balanced by individual action D_+^+, D_-^+. Differences $D^+ - D^-$ mirror Freud's basic instincts, eros & thanatos. − Deviating from Leibniz's Théodicée, there is no highest monad; if 'God' corresponds to the substance-free and immovable rotation axis of 'time' in the cartography of all phases in the changing 'space', then 'His' theometric distance to our felly-position is 0.4203 $r_3 \approx 0.1184 \times 10^{24}$ km [2].

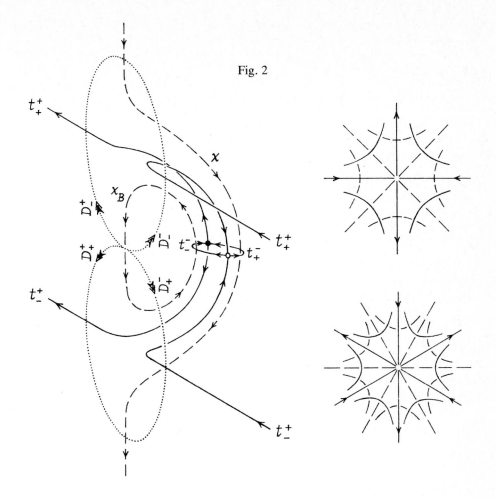

Fig. 2

4. Bounds to syntax have been unexpected in mathematical combination, not in natural languages. Wittgenstein interpreted the axiom of infinity by way of names with distinct meaning (TLP 5.535), but he did not consider the topo-& morpho-"logical" conclusions from finite bounds (TLP 5.2523)−not to speak of topo- & morpho-metric computations−, even if he felt limits (TLP 6.45). The syntactic collapse of semantics in position systems left 77 Tractatus-paragraphs under 526 ones, which might be of "unrestricted" validity.

I prefer to read in the reverse order: 6.54 6.522 6.52 6.5 6.45 6.372 6.371 6.3631 6.363 6.36111 6.36 6.3431 6.34 6.33 6.211 6.1231 6.031, 5.621 5.5561 5.556 5.555 5.5423 5.542 5.535 5.526 5.525 5.475 5.454 5.452 5.44 5.253 5.251 5.25 5.232 5.231 5.22 5.154 5.153 5.1363 5.1362, 4.462 4.211 4.1273 4.1271 4.1213 4.1212 4.116 4.114 4.1122 4.064 4.061 4.05 4.0412 4.0411 4.031 4.027 4.025 4.022 4.0141 4.013 4.012 4.011 4.01 4.002, 3.411 3.343 3.341 3.34 3.33 3.323 3.317 3.262 3.141 3.04 3.0321 2.063 2.024 (!).

Note. The occurrences of 1's reorder the value of bytes and 5-bit blocks: 0, 1 2 4 8 (16), 3 5 6 9 10 12 (17 18 20 24), 7 11 13 14 (19 21 22 25 26 28), 15 (23 27 29 30), (31). The statistical distribution of relators and of functors or communicators determines the argument-number for reordered bytes and blocks: *0214213111132313, 0010000032300122203223220000000***. Slanted *0*'s indicate ⌜creator⌝ and ⌜communicators⌝, which are not autonymous; formally those can be taken as 0-place relator and functors. The partition starts (from right to left) with a byte; each n-place byte is followed by n ⌜word-terms⌝ in blocks; the end of such "Polish" terms, determined through the rank of blocks, marks out the beginning of a byte. Commata are superfluous: premises and conclusions contain *one* byte. Metacommata between rules can be avoided: prohibit (i) different bytes in conclusions of the same ⌜creator⌝, (ii) unfettered ⌜communicators⌝ in a conclusion. For application contract the 140 rules to 78 ones with ≤ 8 conclusions (and ≤ 7 premises); one can reorder premises (e.g., rule 13.13 or 4.7,8) and, if "free" choice over communicator-indices is to be kept, also rules (e.g., 7.2.2 ahead of 7.2.1, or $6.3,4,6,7 \prec 6.2 \prec 6.9 \prec 6.5 \prec 6.10 \prec 6.8$): the insertion of 6.9, 6.10 with 13 communicators each out of a 5-stock (between 6.2, 5, 8 with ≤ 19 ones out of a 7-stock, but without any "new" and "uneconomical" index) uses the case that two bytes 0010 in ≥ 1 premises of 6.9 or 6.10 (via (ii)) *and* ≥ 1 conclusions of the foregoing rule 6.2 or 6.5 yield *one* premise and *one* conclusion.

The subtraction of $56 \cdot 5$ bits presupposes a 3-place ⌜halfcross⌝ 00110; its 4th argument in $\mathbf{K}_o$ could be recovered (according to 13.8, 10, 13) from the 3rd-place outputs of the 1st and 2nd 3-place functor by means of a substitute-computation on 5.1−14, *if* all ⌜communicators⌝ are applied under 0000-creation (and stand for purely autonymous ⌜words⌝). With 9812 instead of 10092 bits there occur 861−29 autonymous functors and 859−27 communicators; 60 + 7 communicators are unfettered (in premises!). Each contracted rule contains ≤ 38 communicators out of the 11-stock, among them $\leq 12 + 3$ unfettered ones out of a 5 + 1 -stock in $\leq 5 + 1$ premises (13.10); per index one rule contains ≤ 10 communicators (4.6,11−15,24,26), among them ≤ 4 unfettered ones in ≤ 3 premises (6.17).

Subtle partition would admit 0 as the bit of highest degree 9811; without any change of communicator-frequencies, the decimal Ψ_c-coefficient can thus be replaced by 675.401..; this will diminish only one k-bound under **1.4** (1980 instead of 1981 for Ψ_f and $n = 2$).

The autonymous output of $\mathbf{K}_o$ consists of one relator with ≥ 1 and ≤ 4 words. Such words have an *undevicesimal* numbering, different from blocks; e.g., the numeral '..' 0 with j occurrences of ' gets the code-number $5..\bar{5}1 = 5 \cdot (19^{j+1} − 1)/18 − (5 − 1)$.

REFERENCES

[1] Wette, E., The Refutation of Number Theory I, Constitution of the canonical system $\mathbf{K}_o$ for a finitary interpretation of intuitionistic 'deduction' by imperative 'derivation'. Würzburg 1975 (Triltsch), 2-colour insert to *International Logic Review* 10 (1974); available on March 18, 1975, at Munich (Large Congress Hall Theresienhöhe, public lecture "Was ist noch wahr an der Mathematik?−Und wie fügen sich alle Bewegungen zu einem durchschaubaren, unveränderlichen Urbild zusammen?" under 'Organismus und Technik' in Exempla '75). Cf. also ILR 9 (1974) 51−62, *Nominazione* 1 (1980) 153−158, 7 *ICLMPS* (Salzburg 1983) Abstracts Vol. 1 pp. 53−56, or, in German, *Dialectica* 24 (1970) 303−323. H. Kracke's *Mathe-musische Knobelisken*, Dümmlerbuch 4711 (Bonn 1982 & 1983), popularize [1] [2] on pp. 353−365 & 372−380.

[2] Wette, E. W., Theometric Consequences of 'Soul'-Computation: Solution to the Universal Problem of 'Motion', and Religion. *International Conference on Science in Islamic Polity* (Islamabad 1983), Papers Presented, Islamic Scientific Thought and Muslim Achievements in Science, Vol. 2, pp. 123−152. For further references see Notes 4, 6, 10, 11,18, *ibid.* pp. 146−150 & 152. E.g., 11 abstracts in *The Journal of Symbolic Logic* (1967−1983), cf. the list in JSL 45 (1980) p. 704 lines 19−34, and JSL 46 (1981) 443−445, JSL 48 (1983) 1228−1229; 3 more abstracts renew Wrocław 1977: JSL 49 (1984) 709−710, JSL 50 (1985) 280−281, Manchester 1984 forthcoming.

* * *

MENTALLY REPRESENTED GRAMMARS AND COMPUTATIONAL EXPLANATIONS OF UNDERSTANDING

Philip May
Wolfson College, Oxford

Technical developments in transformational grammar have often been overshadowed by controversy over the explanatory value of transformational formalisms. I want to look at an objection to Chomsky's claims about the explanatory value of grammar, an objection based on a particular reading of *The Philosophical Investigations*. I then want to show how Chomsky answers this objection by implicit appeal to a view of the mind I shall call 'computational cognitivism', a brand of functionalism whereby intelligent behaviour is underlaid by cognitive processes, and cognitive processes are computational processes defined over mental representations. Finally I want to suggest that this interpretation of the *Investigations* has its problems, and I shall toss out an alternative—an alternative which can be taken as a new argument against the explanatory power even of a computationally interpreted transformational grammar.

Concern centres over Chomsky's use of 'rules'. Transformational grammars (TG's) are rule-systems allegedly known by all native speakers of a language. But this is in conflict with the usual interpretation of Wittgenstein as a radical sceptic when it comes to rules and rule-following.[1] On this interpretation Wittgenstein has shown that no fact about an individual can ensure that his present behaviour is really guided by any particular rule. This radical scepticism is answered by radical conventionalism. Conformity to the inclinations of members of one's linguistic community provides the bridge between an expression of a rule and correct behaviour. This scepticism chafes with Chomsky's claims: the relationship between a rule and its application is not a matter of fact, it's a matter of custom or inclination. But the rules of a TG are utterly unfamiliar to a large majority of the speakers of any language: people are not even conscious of these rules, and therefore have no inclinations regarding them. Therefore they cannot follow these rules, and cannot describe others as following them. TG's try to describe facts that aren't there.

Chomsky claims he can give a precise account of how the unconscious, novel rules of a TG can actually govern the process of understanding. Here he commits himself to computational cognitivism.[2]

The heart of computational cognitivism is *computational description*, in which physical states of a system are assigned symbolic content. These come in varying degrees of complexity, but all are based on what I'll call 'simple computational description'. To give a system a simple computational description one specifies an encoding function which maps physical states of the system one-to-one into elements of a system of symbols. Causally determined changes in the physical system should correspond to transformations permissible in the symbol-system. We usually arrange things so that the symbol associated with the final state of the physical system is some particular function of the symbol associated with the initial state. Here we say the physical system *computes* this function.

If a complicated function is to be computed we may break it down into simpler steps, each thought of as a function. A system that computes these functions in sequence is *executing* an *algorithm* for the overall function.

In even more complicated cases we may want to say that the algorithm itself is encoded in the system, and actually governs the operation of the system. To effect such a description, the algorithm is treated as a list of instructions, each of which can be thought of as a function, and it is these instructions that are mapped into states of the physical system. Instructions are correlated with *control states* of the system, physical states whose causal potential ensures that when the system receives appropriate input it will obey the corresponding instruction (i.e. it will compute the associated function). Just which control state the system is in depends on the execution of previous instructions. Note the difference from algorithm description, where instructions were followed, in a sense, but were not themselves correlated with physical states of the system.

Chomsky is offering TG's as program-descriptions of the human language faculty. He acknowledges the difference between TG-rules and ordinary rules by saying the former are not known but *cognized*. They pack a behavioural punch without being available to consciousness, and they can do this because they are the core of a program-description of brain processes implicated in the production of linguistic judgements and general linguistic behaviour. This makes rule-scepticism and the conventionalist response to it look like a premature retreat. The central claim of rule-scepticism is that no fact about a speaker/hearer determines how he understands a sentence, or what rules guide his linguistic judgements and behaviour. The computational cognitivist argues that the facts have been there all along, we just haven't been looking at them in the right way. Computational cognitivism remedies this. It provides a theoretical framework for interpreting neurological facts. And surely there is *something* happening in a person's brain when he understands a sentence. If this can be given a program-description by some TG then we are in a position to interpret it as the process of understanding. This is the computationalist's vision; whether it obtains is surely an empirical question. All flights to scepticism must be delayed until this question is answered.

The sceptical problem is generated by the fact that any expression of any rule can be made compatible with any action, either in its application in novel circumstances (such as a sum we have never done before) or through bizarre interpretations of rules for interpreting the rule, in finite cases. The arguments for this are meant to be in sections 143−242 of the *Philosophical Investigations*. Within this section we find a lengthy discussion of reading aloud, and two features of this example clash with the sceptical interpretation. The first is inconsistent with the community-aid construal of Wittgenstein's 'solution': suppose we hear someone utter a single noise which happens to correspond with a character written on a page before him. We're tempted to ask "Did he *really* read that?". From the community-inclination point of view we'd say that the question can't be answered because the customary assertibility conditions require a larger sample of cases: we haven't enough information about the inclinations of the alleged reader, so we can't be sure if they match ours. Wittgenstein also says the question can't be answered, but for him the problem is *grammatical* rather than evidential: we can't answer because the question *makes no sense*, it contains something like a category mistake (*PI* § 157). Single noises, considered in isolation from other utterances, just aren't the kinds of things we can call reading. (Cf. *RFM*. VI−33b, 34b, *BLB*. p. 43)

This example is also difficult for the sceptical construal of the problem itself, for there is no problem over the novel application of rules. Suppose our reading slaves are English and we want them to read Cyrillic script. We could train them to use a chart with every Cyrillic character written on it, along with the corresponding combination of English letters. The reader would never encounter a case which had not been covered explicitly in his training. Neither is there any mention of inclinations or of rules for interpreting rules. In fact, Wittgenstein's description of the special relationship between the concept of reading and certain forms of behaviour and training leaves no important role for *any* 'mediating process':

> Now suppose we have, for example, taught someone the Cyrillic alphabet, and told him how to pronounce each letter. Next we put a passage before him and he reads it, pronouncing each letter as we have taught him. In this case we are very likely to say that he derives the sound of the word from the written pattern by the rule that we have given him. And this is also a clear case of reading . . .
> But why do we say he has *derived* the spoken from the printed words? Do we know anything more than that we taught him how each letter should be pronounced and that he then read the words out loud?

. . . certainly this is a special case of deriving; what is essential to deriving, however, was not hidden beneath the surface of this case, but this 'surface' was one case out of a family of different cases of deriving.
And in the same way we use the word 'to read' for a family of cases. (*PI* §§162, 164)

Consider this as a description of our concept of reading, rather than an attack on our ability to justify beliefs about reading. Here, rule-following is not reduced to agreement in how we are inclined to interpret the rule. Rather, Wittgenstein establishes the direct connection between reading and a performance continued over time, exhibiting regularity, and taking place against a background of training. Our concept of reading involves only such surface features; such features act as *criteria* for reading.

I suggest that Wittgenstein is not overly concerned with the problem of the multiple interpretability of rules. Yes, rule-expressions can be interpreted in many ways, but this just shows that "there is a way of grasping a rule which is *not* an *interpretation*, but which is exhibited in what we call 'obeying the rule' and 'going against it' in actual cases" (*PI* § 201b). I suggest that Wittgenstein's goal is a faithful description of the special relationship between a rule and "what we call 'obeying the rule'", or the parallel relationship between our concept of reading and certain forms of vocal behaviour together with background features such as training. These descriptions establish several important points about criteria for concepts like rule-following, obeying an order, fulfilling a wish, or understanding a sentence: (i) the actions of the reader, rule-follower, or whatever, must be more than simple episodes of behaviour; they must be part of a *practice*, a pattern of behaviour regular and complex enough to establish a normative relationship between the symbolic representation and actual behaviour. In the example, the student read the whole passage; further behaviour, such as using the rule expression to correct mistakes, would also establish the normative relationship. (ii) The relationship between applications of a concept and criteria for that concept is much more intimate than the relationship between hypothesis and evidence. Gathering evidence is a matter of establishing a connection between one type of phenomenon and another. But Wittgenstein has argued that there is no independent underlying process of reading with which we could 'connect' behaviour, in applying our concept of reading. We don't take criterial behaviour as evidence for some process; criterial behaviour *is* reading. Furthermore, the relationship between evidence and hypothesis is established in experience. But is it experience that establishes the connection between reading and the behaviour and training Wittgenstein describes in the passage quoted? We don't *discover* that such forms of behaviour are often indicators of reading. The connection is not a psychological one or a social one, it is a logical one, established in the grammar of our language.

On this reading, sceptical interpretations conflate framework conditions for concepts such as reading, or rule-following, or understanding, with criteria for these concepts. Some community agreement is necessary background, to be sure. We need to react to training in similar ways, we need to agree on paradigm cases. But this agreement in *not* what makes behaviour into reading, for instance. It is the embedding of that behaviour in a regular practice, it is the non-evidential role of that behaviour in our judgements about reading, and it is the logical, grammatical connection beween that behaviour and the concept of reading that makes it reading-behaviour.

The differences between this interpretation and rule scepticism stand out if we re-examine the computational construal of transformational grammar. Recall that the computationalist concentrates on facts in the causal history of behaviour. He claims we can interpret such a causal sequence as the process of reading or the process of understanding. But Wittgenstein's description of our concept of reading is intended to show that criteria do not consist of simple episodes of external behaviour. This behaviour must be part of a regular practice, and it must take place against an appropriate background, usually involving teaching or training. Criteria have this extra dimension unavailable to any causal account of particular pieces of behaviour.

The connection between the computational concept of understanding and criterial behaviour is a contingent one, to be discovered *a posteriori*. The essence of understanding is below the surface and *any* external behaviour can at best provide a high degree of confirmation that the proper sort of mechanism is in place. Criteria are no more than contingent effects of understanding, upon which we are forced to base our everyday use of the term. But as we've seen, Wittgenstein's goal is to display the internal, grammatical connection between a concept like understanding and criterial behaviour: the relationship between understanding a sentence and, say, being able to explain its meaning, like the relationship between reading and rendering texts out loud, is not a contingent relationship of any sort, causal or conventional. It is an internal relation founded in the grammar of language and learned along with our language.

Computational psychology is a growth industry. It seems able to avoid the dull conservativism of behaviourism, and the wreckless ontological investments of dualism, driving both these old rivals out of business. My goal here has simply been to suggest that Wittgenstein is best thought of as a 'consumer advocate' who questions the usefulness of the products of this new firm, not as just another vulnerable competitor, as many interpretations of his work would suggest.[3]

ENDNOTES

[1] See e.g. S. A. Kripke, *Wittgenstein on Rules and Private Language* (Oxford 1982); C.Wright, *Wittgenstein on the Foundations of Mathematica* (London 1980), ch. II.
[2] Chomsky, N., *Rules and Representations* (New York, 1980), pp. 102–3, 106–7,129–30.
[3] I would like to thank Dr. G. P. Baker for many helpful discussions on the interpretation of Wittgenstein's philosophy.

* * *

WHY SHOULD I ASK HER?

Marcelo Dascal
Tel-Aviv University

Is language-use a reliable indicator of what goes on in a persons's mind? Is it more reliable than other possible indicators? If so, why? These are the questions to which I want to address myself here.

A few words are necessary in order to explain my interest in these questions. Several traditions converge in suggesting a negative answer to them. Firstly, the centuries-old criticism of language and its use. From Bacon's 'idols of the marketplace', through Spinoza's view of language-use as yielding, at best, the lowest kind of 'knowledge'—which hardly deserves that name—namely, 'knowledge by hearsay', to analytic philosophy's discreditation of metaphysics as stemming from the misuse of words. Secondly, anti-mentalist tendencies of all kinds: if there is no such a thing as the mind and mental phenomena, the very question of what—if anything—is a reliable indicator of mental phenomena is meaningless. The more so if, as some anti-mentalists claim, the mental is nothing but language-use itself. Thirdly, the increasing awareness of the endless ways in which we can manipulate language in order to conceal rather than to reveal what we have in mind—lying and playacting being only their archaic prototypes. Fourthly, the development of methods to overcome the shortcomings of language as the high road to the mind of the other: language-independent psychological and neuro-physiological probes (e.g. the "lie-detector") and psycho-analytic techniques which, though relying on the patient's verbal behavior, take it only as 'raw material' for further interpretation, rather than as a source of direct insight into the patient's mental states.

Yet, these obstacles notwithstanding, language-use is still regarded as the most reliable means we have to know what is going on in the minds of our fellow humans. When in doubt about someone's beliefs, desires, fears, or wonderings, we normally don't think there is a better way of finding out than simply to ask her. When confronted with non-linguistic behavior that we want to interpret, we often wish we could address a direct question to the agent and obtain an answer ("If only I could ask the baby why she is crying!"). And when we succeed in interpreting non-linguistic behavior, we compare it to linguistic behavior ("I understand this dog so well. It is as if he were speaking to me.").

Not only commonsense holds this view. A psychologist whose main concern is the fact that most people don't really get to know even those persons who are closest to them, and believes to have found a solution to this problem—in his words, "a key to the lock of the portal to man's soul" (Jourard 1965: 9–10)—, describes this key as "self-disclosure", i.e. as the information "a person will *tell* another person about himself" (ibid.: italics mine). And in order to study self-disclosure he uses a *questionnaire* through which subjects are requested to *report* how much, about what personal subjects, and to whom they *talk*. Similarly, many philosophers—who are otherwise very careful about their handling of linguistic matters—do not hesitate to endorse the reliability of the "ask her" strategy. Thus, Bruce Aune (1967, 199) asserts that "the best way to obtain certainty (sic!) about someone's intentions is to ask him". And Rudolf Carnap (1956, 230), somewhat more cautiously, claims that

> "a sentence like (i) 'John believes that the earth is round' is to be interpreted in such a way that it can be inferred from a suitable sentence describing John's behavior at best with probability, but not with certainty, e.g. from (ii) 'John makes an affirmative response to 'the earth is round' as an English sentence'."

But how is this possible? Linguistic behavior is, after all, external, observable behavior. Its connection with what goes on in the agent's mind requires inferences, which are no less problematic—on the face of it—than those involved in the interpretation of other forms of beha-vior. Furthermore, the strategy of "asking the agent" instead of solving the general problem will in fact pose an additional difficulty. For, not only will whatever the agent answers be in need of interpretation by us before it yields the correct ascription of mental state(s); our own question will have to be interpreted by the agent before he produces his answer.[1] The problem is not only that of interpreting the content-specifying sentence (e.g. *The earth is round*), but also of determining the real import of the speaker's response. For, *pace* Carnap, Quine (1960, 29ff), and Davidson (1975, 14ff), affirmative (or negative) responses, assent (or dissent), and holding (or not) a sentence to be true are attitudes of a speaker that assigned to him on the basis of the interpretation of his behavior, just as the content of what he assents to is.

Why—in spite of so many difficulties—is the belief in the transparency of linguistic behavior so robust? Are there any reasons for singling out the interpretation of utterances as a more reliable process than the interpretation of other kinds of behavior? I believe there are. And I believe that discussing them is illuminating because they lie at the intersection of at least three philosophical disciplines: the philosophy of action, the philosophy of language and the philo-sophy of mind. In fact, in order to see at least some of these reasons, all that has to be done is to put together some insights of these three disciplines.

I will confine the discussion to what Searle calls "Intentional" mental states, exemplified by beliefs, desires, hopes, fears, intentions, etc. Traditionally, the Intentionality of such states has been vaguely described as their being "directed at" objects or states of affairs: a belief *that* such and such, a fear *of* something, etc. Searle proposes to characterize this property by saying that a mental state is Intentional iff "the specification of the content of that mental state requi-res the specification of some object or state of affairs which is not identical with that mental state" (Searle 1979, 182). This excludes pains and aches, some sorts of anxiety, and perhaps also some emotions. Though admittedly vague, such a criterion of Intentionality is quite help-ful for our purposes: in fact, Searle's non-Intentional mental states seem to be most reliably accessible (for an external observer) not through linguistic behavior, but rather through some other form of behavior (e.g. screaming). The privileged indicative status of linguistic beha-vior, therefore, should be claimed to hold only—if at all—for Intentional states. In order to assess this claim, linguistic behavior must be compared with other behavior that may also be plausibly claimed to be related to and indicative of Intentional states. And the best candidates are, of course, non-linguistic intentional actions[2] (e.g. polishing one's shoes, buying a car, etc.), which are usually taken to be based on such Intentional states as beliefs, desires, and intentions. Isn't brushing one's shoe after ointing it with cream, in normal circumstances, a good indication of one's belief that the cream is shoe-polish, perhaps even a better one than one's statement "This is shoe-polish."?

A few details of Searle's account of intentional action will be useful to proceed in our com-parison (even though the argument does not rely on the acceptance of this account). He cha-racterizes an Intentional state as a complex entity of the form S(r), where S is a variable for 'psychological mode' (e.g. hope, fear, belief, desire) and r a variable for 'representative con-tent'. Some, but not all, Intentional states have, according to him, a 'direction of fit' (mind-to-world or world-to mind), and "all Intentional states with a direction of fit represent their con-ditions of satisfaction" (Searle 1981, 79).[3] An intention is an Intentional state having a direc-tion of fit, and an intentional action is characterized as "simply the realization of the condi-tions of satisfaction of an intention" (ibid.). Such conditions of satisfaction must specify not only the event that is to occur (e.g. one's arm going up) but also the demand that the event occur by virtue of the intention. For, if that very same movement occurs, say, by the effect of invisible strings that pull the arm, it cannot count as satisfying the intention. Nor is it enough to have the 'prior intention' to perform it. Between the 'mere' movement and the prior inten-tion, Searle points out the need to acknowledge the existence of an 'intention in action'— which he equates with the 'experience of acting'—, without which it is impossible to characte-rize an intentional action. Both intentions must be self-referential, but whereas a prior inten-tion makes reference to the whole action [its content being: "(I perform the action of raising my arm by way of carrying out this intention)"], an intention in action makes reference only to one component of the action, namely the physical movement [its content being: "(My arm goes up as a result of this intention in action)"]. According to Searle, anything that qualifies as an action must have an intention-in-action as one of its components, but it may or may not have a prior intention. To say that it does have one, is to say that it causes the intention in action, which in turn causes the movement.

Now, speech-acts and semiotic actions in general are, of course, intentional actions. Hence, their conditions of satisfaction are self-referential in the way described above. Yet, they possess a further type of self-reference, not shared by other intentional actions. Their distinctive character is that they are intended to produce certain effects in an audience by virtue of the audience's *recognition* of such an intention. Recall Grice's analysis of 'speaker's meaning':

> "'A meant something by x' is (roughly) equivalent to 'A intended the utterance of x to produce some effect in an audience by means of the recognition of this intention'" (Grice 1967, 46).

Only if the utterance of x is caused by such an intention can it be regarded as a speech-act. Furthermore, it would be appropriate to call this intention a 'disclosure intention', since, through it, the speaker seeks to disclose to the audience at least one of his mental states, namely, that intention itself. To be sure, he may fail in this endeavor: the audience may not be able to recognize the intention, or the desired effect in the audience may not be produced. But this does not in the least affect the fact that there is an intrinsic, necessary connection between performing a speech-act or another semiotic action and intending to have at least one of one's Intentional states disclosed to another person.[4]

Of course, no such necessary connection characterizes non-semiotic intentional actions. The intentional action of polishing my shoes does not, normally, contain the intention that someone should recognize any intention of mine whatsoever. But, just as this does not prevent someone from achieving such a recognition by observing my polishing behavior, and thereby disclosing some of my mental states, so too, as we have seen, the fact that semiotic actions necessarily contain self-disclosure intentions does not ensure that some addressee takes advantage of them. It seems, then, that invoking this particular characteristic of semiotic actions does not show that they are better indicators of mental states than their competitors.

Upon reflection, however, this fact turns out to be significant for our problem. Though it is by no means sure that communicative intentions will always be correctly recognized by the addressee, it would be strange if the odds were, in general, against their being so recognized. For, in that case, one would rightly ask why in the hell would so many people perform actions based on (communicative) intentions rarely—if at all—achieved. If this were indeed the case, one would expect either the progressive disappearance of this kind of actions, or else the development of means to increase dramatically their chances of success. We all know, of course, that 'history' has taken the latter course. Foremost among the means available to foster successful recognition and interpretation of communicative intentions is the heuristics of pragmatic interpretation, which makes full use of all kinds of information (such as syntactic, semantic, pragmatico-semantic, as well as paralinguistic and other contextual information).[5]By means of the heuristics of pragmatic interpretation, addressees are likely (but by no means certain) to hit upon the speaker's meaning underlying an utterance, and thus to disclose—via the speaker's linguistic behavior—at least a few of the latter's Intentional states. Since no such heuristics is available for actions other than semiotic actions, the privileged status of semiotic behavior in general and linguistic behavior in particular as reliable indicators of mental states is explained.

Let's now go back and ask whether the communicative intentions are intentions in action or prior intentions. If we take seriously Searle's definition of intentions in action as those that refer to a physical movement, communicative intentions cannot be of this kind. On this view, the intentions in action involved in linguistic utterances would be those pertaining to the emission of sounds by activating the vocal tract. By an effort of imagination we can strip these movements from their communicative intentions, but we have no natural way to describe them. Practically every available verb that applies to speech-behavior—uttering, saying, asserting, asking, requesting, ordering, etc.—presumes the presence of a communicative intention. This is not surprising, since we know that (pure) syntax is possible only as the result of abstraction from semantics and pragmatics. What this suggests, however, is that, though perhaps not strictly belonging to the level of the intention in action, communicative intentions are very close to that level. Utterances are literally *perceived* as bearing such intentions.[6] If so, such intentions are, in a sense, directly accessible in linguistic behavior, and do not require a complex inferential process in order to be detected. To be sure, non-linguistic and non-semiotic actions may also be 'perceived' and most naturally described in such a way, i.e. "sub specie intentionalitatis". We normally *see* the upward movement of his arm as his raising of the arm. But this is precisely the level of the intention in action, whose content is: (his arm goes up as a result of this intention). On the other hand, if one describes his action as waving goodbye, voting, or requesting permission to go to the bathroom, one seems to be already jumping to the level of 'further' intentions, comparable to those one reaches when interpreting indirect speech-acts. There seems to be, for such actions, no intermediate group of intentions, distinct from the intention in action and yet close enough to it in order to be, literally, 'perceived' rather than inferred from the physical movement. In this, again, a person's linguistic behavior seems to provide a more direct and easy access to a wider range of her intentions.

Since philosophers are not very fond of arguments that seem to rely on empirical observations, statistical generalizations, and the like (though my argument only *seems* to be of this kind), let me conclude with a purely conceptual argument. Searle has claimed that, in general, a speech-act with a propositional content "is an expression of the corresponding Intentional state" (e.g. stating that p one *expresses* the belief that p, etc.). Furthermore, he says,

> "the expression of the Intentional state is not a mere accompaniment: there is an internal connection in the strict sense between the performance of the speech act and the expression of the corresponding psychological state, as is shown by Moore's paradox. One cannot say, 'It's raining but I don't believe it's raining', or 'I order you to leave but I don't want you to leave'. . ."(Searle 1979, 192).

I would like to use this thesis—assuming it is correct—in order to develop two further arguments in support of the claim that linguistic behavior is a privileged indicator of mental states, namely: (a) linguistic behavior reveals not only the communicative intentions of the speaker, but also other, more 'central' mental states of his, i.e. the beliefs, desires, etc. 'expressed' by that behavior; and (b) non-linguistic intentional behavior differs from linguistic behavior in that it does not display the same kind of conceptual connection (i.e. 'expression') with the agent's psychological states. For this reason, even though it allows for the inference of such states, it does so only in a more remote and indirect way than its linguistic counterpart.

There are, however, some difficulties with these arguments, which must be overcome.[7] The problem with (a) stems from the fact that, in Searle's terms, "one can express an Intentional state one does not have" (ibid.), which is how insincerity arises. Now, if the 'expression' of an Intentional state does not guarantee that the speaker is in fact in that state, it would seem that invoking the relation of expression is useless in order to support the claim that the addressee can infer such states directly from the speaker's utterances. In order to overcome this difficulty, observe first that Searle's use of the term 'expression' is somewhat strange. For that term (as others of the same family such as 'manifestation', 'disclosure', etc.) involves normally an existential presupposition: If A expresses (discloses, reveals, etc.) x, x should exist (at least as an 'idea' or 'state' of A). Strictly speaking, such a presupposition would preclude the use of the term 'expression' in cases of insincerity. In order to be able to employ it as he does, Searle could envisage two alternatives: (i) to reduce the force of the existential presupposition; or (ii) to modify the description of the psychological states allegedly 'expressed' in utterances. Let us consider them in turn.

The adoption of (i) would yield the following explication of the relation of 'expression': by asserting p, A expresses his belief that p in that he (strongly) *suggests* to the addressee that he in fact has that belief, without however fully *committing* himself to that suggestion.[8] Such a 'suggestion' can be cancelled out without contradiction (this explains the fact that Moore's paradox is not a *logical* paradox). The psychological state 'expressed' in an utterance would be, on this view, 'implicit' in what is said, just as the idea of the general dishonesty of Republicans is implicit in the assertion "He is a Republican, but honest". To express a belief without actually holding it would be only a case of violating a pragmatic norm of communication, which makes one accountable not only for what one explicitly says, but also for what one's words imply.

Another way (ii) of solving the problem is to say that, since—strictly speaking—one cannot 'express' a belief one does not actually have, what one does express is a 'similar' or 'related' psychological state. For example, one might say that what the sincere or insincere assertion of p expresses is the *belief-type* "belief that p". The question of whether such a type is indeed instantiated by a token in A is precisely the question of whether he is sincere or not, a question which, as we know, can only be solved with the help of the heuristics of pragmatic interpretation. Assuming a general 'presumption of sincerity' (obviously a *pragmatic* principle), one could move—in the absence of indications to the contrary—from the states-type expressed in utterances to their corresponding tokens, i.e. to the actual *occurrence* of such states in the speaker, which are in fact the constituents of his 'mental life'.

Now, whatever the alternative chosen, the attribution of an actual mental state to the speaker is not purely semantic (or logical)—it could never be, since pragmatic interpretation is always necessary (cf. Dascal 1983, 77ff). Yet, such an attribution is facilitated and made, so to speak, more direct by the existence of the *semantic* relation of expression. Whether implicit (as in (i)) or explicit (as in (ii)), such a relation is 'semantic' because it is conventionally attached to the utterance (cf. Dascal 1983, 22−40). The addressee is directly guided by that which is expressed in the utterance in his search for its pragmatic interpretation, much like he is guided by the nature of a deictic in his search for contextual elements that are appropriate to fill in the 'semantic gaps' the deictic leaves open in sentence meaning.

It remains to be seen—moving now to argument (b)—whether something of that sort does not occur also in non-linguistic intentional behavior. Suppose someone goes through the mechanics of polishing his shoes with a certain cream and then points to the cream and says "I don't believe this is shoe polish". Apparently this is similar to Moore's paradox. Something is evidently 'wrong', for the man's act seems to be self-defeating. If the cream *is* shoe polish, his belief (taking his utterance to be sincere) that it is not indicates perhaps a lack of knowledge of what is shoe polish. If it is not, we can interpret the situation either (1) by denying that he has the intention of polishing his shoes and ascribing to him other intentions (e.g. playacting, playing, exercising, etc.), or (2) by denying him knowledge of the instrumental conditions of shoe polishing, or else (3) by contesting his rationality. It is by virtue of the *causal* relation between shoe polish and shoe polishing that we can infer that whoever polishes shoes believes he is using shoe polish, but not by virtue of some *rule* that necessarily makes of the act of shoe polishing an expression of that belief. Such an inference does not substantially differ from the inference that someone has the measles based on the observation that his body is full of red spots. If someone has all the symptoms of a disease and does not in fact have it, obviously something is 'wrong'. In both cases, if a 'paradox' arises, it is because a *regularity*, well grounded in experience, is violated. But in the linguistic case, such a regularity (which also exists) is mediated by some *rule*. To utter something is to obey such a rule and to show one is so doing. It is the attempt to suppress the automatic inference authorized by such a display of obedience to the rule that produces the paradoxical effect in Moore's paradox, to which nothing corresponds in the shoe polisher's 'paradox'. And it is precisely this fact that shows how in one case a mental state is conveyed in a much more direct way than in the other.

For all these reasons—and there are more, which I discuss elsewhere (Dascal 1983)—you should not hesitate: go ahead and ask her!

ENDNOTES

1 Trying to make our questions more explicit, by employing terms that directly refer to the mental states in question will not do, since our questions will then, in all likelihood, be interpreted indirectly, rather than transparently. Compare "Did you see Ernest leaving the house?" and "Do you believe you saw Ernest leaving the house?". The latter is likely to be understood as questioning the grounds or the firmness of the belief, rather than just inquiring about whether one has the belief or not.

2 Notice the small "i" here: an intention with a small "i" is but one of the species of Intentional—with capital "I"—states.

3 'Conditions of satisfaction' is a generic term for states of affairs or things whose actual existence 'satisfies' an Intentional state with a direction of fit. For example, if I believe it is raining and it is raining, my belief is true (i.e. it is 'satisfied'); if I want you to run and you do so, my wish is fulfilled (i.e. it is 'satisfied'), and so on.

4 My use of Grice's notion of speaker's meaning is independent of the acceptance or rejection of his attempt to make of it the foundation of semantics, since I am using it only as a pragmatic notion.

5 For details and discussion see Dascal (1983), passim.

6 Cf. McDowell's (1980) parallel between understanding and perception.

7 I wish to thank Paulo E. Faria for pointing out to me these difficulties.

8 In what follows I will restrict myself to the case of assertions, in order to illustrate the treatment here proposed.

REFERENCES

Aune, Bruce, "Intention", in: Paul Edwards [ed.] *Encyclopedia of Philosophy*, vol. IV (New York 1967), 198—201.

Carnap, Rudolf, "On belief-sentences: reply to Alonzo Church", in: R. Carnap, *Meaning and Necessity* (Chicago 1956), 230—232.

Dascal, Marcelo, *Pragmatics and the Philosophy of Mind, vol. 1* (Amsterdam 1983).

Davidson, Donald, "Thought and talk", in: Samuel Guttenplan [ed.], *Mind and Language*. (Oxford 1975), 7—24.

Grice, H.P., "Meaning", in: P. F. Strawson [ed.], *Philosophical Logic*. (London 1967), 39—48.

Jourard, Sidney M., *The Transparent Self* (New York 1964).

McDowell, John, "Meaning, communication, and knowledge", in Z. van Straaten [ed.], *Philosophical Subjects* (1980).

Quine, Willard V.O., *Word and Object* (Cambridge, Mass., 1960).

Searle, John R., "Intentionality and the use of language". In A. Margalit [ed.], *Meaning and Use* (Dordrecht 1979), 181—197.

Searle, John R., "The intentionality of intention and action", *Manuscrito* 4, 2 (1981), 77—101.

* * *

ERKENNTNIS VON REGELN UND ERKENNTNIS DURCH REGELN

Amedeo G. Conte
Universität Pavia

1. *Einführung.*

1.1. Ausgangspunkt meiner neueren Forschungen, über die ich heute berichte, war ein Buch, das für die Philosophie der Geisteswissenschaften grundlegend ist: *Explanation and Understanding*, 1971. Der Autor ist der finnische Philosoph Georg Henrik von Wright, der zuerst Schüler und dann Nachfolger Wittgensteins in Cambridge gewesen ist.

1.1.1. In *Explanation and Understanding* spricht von Wright von Regeln, die eine institutionelle Praxis konstituieren (*„rules which define various social practices and institutions"*, *„rules which define institutions or constitute practices"*[1]).

1.1.2. Über die erkenntnistheoretische Rolle der Regeln, die eine institutionelle Praxis konstituieren, formuliert von Wright *zwei* Thesen: eine *negative* und eine *positive*.

1.1.2.1. *Negative These*: Solche Regeln „play no characteristic or important role in the *explanation* of behavior".

1.1.2.2. *Positive These*: „they are of fundamental importance to *understanding* behavior".[2] Ihre erkenntnistheoretische Rolle liegt nicht auf der Ebene des *Erklärens*, sondern auf einer anderen (wenn nicht sogar auf *der* anderen) Ebene: auf der Ebene des *Verstehens*.

1.2. Von Wrights positive These (die Regeln, die eine institutionelle Praxis konstituieren, spielen eine entscheidende Rolle beim Verstehen von Handlungen) hat 1974 zwei erkenntnistheoretische Fragen über eidetisch-konstitutive Regeln in mir hervorgerufen. Die *erste Frage* betrifft die Erkenntnis *von* eidetisch-konstitutiven Regeln (d.h. von Regeln, deren paradigmatischer Fall die Regeln des Schachspiels sind); die *zweite Frage* betrifft die Erkenntnis *durch* eidetisch-konstitutive Regeln.

1.2.1. *Erste Frage*: Können die eidetisch-konstitutiven Regeln aus der regelkonformen Handlung (aus regelkonformem Verhalten) erschlossen werden?

1.2.2. *Zweite Frage*: Ermöglichen es die eidetisch-konstitutiven Regeln, die regelkonforme Handlung (regelkonformes Verhalten) zu verstehen?

1.3. Um die beiden Fragen beantworten zu können, werde ich zuerst den Begriff: eidetisch-konstitutive Regel definieren.

2. *Der Begriff: eidetisch-konstitutive Regel.*

2.1. Die eidetisch-konstitutiven Regeln (*eidetic-constitutive rules*) sind Regeln, die in dreifachem Bedingungsverhältnis zur durch sie konstituierten Praxis stehen: Sie sind (eidetische) *Denkbarkeits*bedingung, (alethische) *Möglichkeits*bedingung, (noetische) *Wahrnehmbarkeits*bedingung der jeweiligen *Praxis* und der jeweiligen *Praxeme* (d.h. der jeweiligen Praxiseinheiten).

Der paradigmatische Fall der eidetisch-konstitutiven Regeln sind die Regeln des Schachspiels. (Zwei Beispiele: ‚Der Läufer soll diagonal gezogen werden'; ‚Schachmatt liegt vor, wenn der König unter Schach ist und durch keinen Zug dem Schach entzogen werden kann'.)

Die Praxis: Schachspiel und ihre Einheiten, ihre Praxeme (die *Steine*, z.B. der Läufer; die Züge bzw. *Pragmeme*, z.B. die Rochade; die *ludischen Status*, z.B. das Schach) bestehen nicht vor (und unabhängig von) den Regeln. Erst und nur die Spielregeln konstituieren das Spiel und (im Spiel) die Spieleinheiten, die Praxeme (Steine, Pragmeme, ludische Status).

2.2. Das Syntagma ‚eidetisch-konstitutive Regel' habe ich eingeführt, um einen Begriff zu bezeichnen, der sich im Werke mehrerer Autoren rekonstruieren läßt.

Die ersten Autoren, die Aspekte der Konstitutivität der eidetisch-konstitutiven Regeln ein-gesehen haben, sind (meiner Rekonstruktion nach) Johannes Thomae, 1898, Max Weber, 1907, Czesław Znamierowski, 1924, Ernst Mally, 1943, Antonino Pagliaro, 1951, Alf Ross, 1953, und (*last, not least*) Ludwig Wittgenstein.

2.2.1. Insbesondere:

2.2.1.1. Die Idee, daß die Identität der Steine im Schachspiel durch die Regeln bestimmt wird (d.h. die Idee, daß eine Figur der deontische Ort ihrer Regeln ist), ist bei Johannes Thomae und Ernst Mally belegt.

2.2.1.2. Die Idee, daß die Pragmeme (die *types* der Züge) des Schachspiels durch die Regeln konstituiert werden, ist schon bei Czesław Znamierowski angedeutet, der das Syntagma *,norma konstrukcyjna'* verwendet.

2.2.1.3. Die Idee, daß die *tokens* von Pragmemen erst und nur durch die Vermittlung der Spielregeln wahrnehmbar sind, ist bei Max Weber und Alf Ross belegt.[3]

2.2.2. Der Autor aber, der die eigentümliche Konstitutivität der eidetisch-konstitutiven Regeln am stärksten hervorgehoben hat, ist (wie ich woanders gezeigt habe) Ludwig Wittgenstein.

Im Buch *Wittgenstein's Lectures, Cambridge 1932–1935,* verwendet er sogar das Verb *,to constitute'* für die eidetisch-konstitutiven Regeln des Schachspiels:

> What idea do we have of the king of chess, and what is its relation to the rules of chess? [. . .] What the king can do is laid down by the rules. Do these rules follow from the idea? [. . .] No. The rules are not something contained in the idea and got by analyzing it. They *constitute* it. [. . .] The rules *constitute* the „freedom" of the pieces.[4]

3. *Zwei erkenntnistheoretische Fragen zum Begriff: eidetisch-konstitutive Regel.*

3.0. Der Begriff: eidetisch-konstitutive Regel hat 1974 zwei erkenntnistheoretische Fragen in mir hervorgerufen.

3.1. Die *erste Frage* betrifft die Erkenntnis *von* eidetisch-konstitutiven Regeln.

3.1.1. Können eidetisch-konstitutive Regeln aus regelkonformem Vehalten erschlossen werden? (Z.B.: Können die Schachregeln aus der Beobachtung von Zügen erschlossen werden?)

3.1.2. Die *Antwort* ist eindeutig. Die eidetisch-konstitutiven Regeln können nicht aus der Erfahrung regelkonformen Verhaltens erschlossen werden, weil die Regeln selbst notwendige Möglichkeitsbedingung jener Erfahrung sind.

Es ist unmöglich zu erkennen, daß eine gewisse Bewegung (ein *movimento*) *im Raum* ein Zug (eine *mossa*) *im Spiel* ist (und, *a fortiori*, ist es unmöglich zu erkennen, um welches Pragmem es sich handelt), wenn man die Regeln nicht schon kennt, die jenes Pragmem konstituieren.

Die Erfahrung einer Rochade ist zum Beispiel erst und nur dann möglich, wenn man über den *type* (über das *eîdos*): Rochade verfügt. (Erst und nur in bezug auf die Regeln ist es möglich, die simultane Versetzung von zwei Holzstücken als *token* vom *type*: Rochade zu deuten.)

Es ist ein *hýsteron próteron*, eidetisch-konstitutive Regeln aus einer Erfahrung zu erschließen, die durch die Regeln selbst vermittelt und ermöglicht worden ist.

3.2. Die *zweite Frage* betrifft die Erkenntis *durch* eidetisch-konstitutive Regeln.

3.2.1. In welchem Sinne (wenn überhaupt) ermöglichen eidetisch-konstitutive Regeln die Erkenntnis regelkonformen Verhaltens?

3.2.2. Die *Antwort* auf die zweite erkenntnistheoretische Frage ist nicht eindeutig.

3.2.2.1. Die eidetisch-konstitutiven Regeln, die die Praxeme einer Praxis konstituieren, gestatten zwar, *tokens* der durch sie konstituierten *types* zu erkennen.

Sie gestatten aber nicht, „das Individuelle in seinem eigenen Individualsein" (diese Formulierung hat mir Hans-Georg Gadamer 1983 suggeriert), das *ídion*, idiographisch zu erkennen.[5]

3.2.2.2. Mit einem Wortspiel, das auf der (zufälligen) Assonanz der griechischen Termini *,ídion'* (woher Windelbands ,idiographisch' kommt) und *,eîdos'* (woher ,eidetisch' kommt) beruht, habe ich 1982 folgende Formulierung getroffen:

3.2.2.2.1. Die eidetisch-konstitutiven Regeln einer Praxis gestatten zwar die Erkenntnis *nach einem eîdos*, aber sie gestatten keine Erkenntnis *des ídion*.

3.2.2.2.2. Die eidetisch-konstitutiven Regeln sind kein Werkzeug *idiographischen Verstehens* des *ídion*; sie sind Werkzeug *eidographischen Deutens* nach einem (durch sie konstituierten) *eîdos*.

ANMERKUNGEN

[1] Wright, G. H. von, *Explanation and Understanding* (London 1971), S. 151 und 204.
[2] Wright, G. H. von, *Explanation and Understanding* (London 1971), S. 152.
[3] Conte, A. G., „Konstitutive Regeln und Deontik", in: E. Morscher und R. Stranzinger (Hrsg.), *Ethik. Akten des 5. Wittgenstein-Symposiums 1980* (Wien 1981), S. 82−86; A. G. Conte, „Paradigmi d'analisi della regola in Wittgenstein", in: R. Egidi (Hrsg.), *Wittgenstein. Momenti di una critica del sapere* (Napoli 1983), S. 37−82; A. G. Conte, „Semiotics of Constitutive Rules", in: M. Herzfeld und L. Melazzo (Hrsg.), *Proceedings of the Third Congress of the International Association for Semiotic Studies 1984* (Berlin, im Druck).
[4] Wittgenstein, L., *Wittgenstein's Lectures, Cambridge, 1932−1935*, Edited by A. Ambrose (Oxford 1979), S. 86. (Auf diese Wittgenstein-Stelle hat mich Giampaolo M. Azzoni aufmerksam gemacht.) Für weitere Belege und weitere Literatur zu Wittgensteins Regelbegriff vgl. A. G. Conte, „Regola costitutiva in Wittgenstein", in: F. Castellani (Hrsg.), *Uomini senza qualità* (Trento 1981), S. 51−68; A. G. Conte, „Variationen über Wittgensteins Regelbegriff", in: R. Haller (Hrsg.), *Sprache und Erkenntnis als soziale Tatsache* (Wien 1981), S. 69−78; A. G. Conte, „Paradigmi d'analisi della regola in Wittgenstein", in: R. Egidi (Hrsg.), *Wittgenstein. Momenti di una critica del sapere* (Napoli 1983), S. 37−82; A. G. Conte, *Premessa del curatore*. in: L. Wittgenstein, *Libro blu e Libro marrone* (Torino 1983), S. XLVII−LIV.
[5] Das Adjektiv ‚idiographisch' (aus ‚ídios' und ‚gráphein') ist vor genau 90 Jahren von Wilhelm Windelband (in seiner Straßburger Rektoratsrede *Geschichte und Naturwissenschaft*, 1894) eingeführt und dem (schon bei Immanuel Kant in einem anderen Sinne belegten) Adjektiv ‚nomothetisch' (aus ‚nómos' und ‚tithénai') entgegengesetzt worden.

* * *

WAHRNEHMUNG UND SPRACHE: EVOLUTIONÄRE LOGIK UND HISTORISCHE GRAMMATIK

Klaus Landwehr
Universität Bielefeld

Erkenntnistheorie i.S. der Analytischen Philosophie Ludwig Wittgensteins (1953) fragt nicht nach den empirischen oder „transzendentalen" Bedingungen der Möglichkeit von Erkenntnis, sondern versucht eine Beschreibung der tatsächlichen Verwendung des Wortes Erkenntnis und damit zusammenhängender Begrifflichkeit, verharrt mithin im Medium Sprache. In dieser Hinsicht äquivalent betrachtet auch der Logische Empirismus Erkenntnis als in Aussagen formuliertes Wissen. Ökologische Wahrnehmungspsychologie i.S. James Gibsons (1966, 1979) betrachtet demgegenüber Erkenntnis als in besonderer Weise, z.B. durch Instrumente, Sprache oder Bilder erweiterte Wahrnehmungstätigkeit, die ihrerseits als über Ereignisse extendierte Extraktion von Invarianten im physikalisch definierten Energiefluß verstanden wird. Hier interessiert man sich dann innerhalb des Systems der Wahrnehmungs-Handlungs-Koordination für evolutionäre und ontogenetische Bedingungen der Entnahme verfügbarer Information und der Aneignung überdauernder Fertigkeiten/Fähigkeiten.

Das Dilemma beider Forschungstraditionen – sowohl der Philosophie als auch der Psychologie – ist, daß man immer schon mit dem arbeiten muß, was man untersuchen will, nämlich Wahrnehmung bzw. Sprache. Dieser so etablierte Dualismus kann seinerseits beschrieben, muß aber zuallererst wahrgenommen werden, ebenso wie eine Reihe anderer damit verbundener Dualismen (Leib-Seele, Natur-Gesellschaft, kausal-interpretativ usw.). Ich gehe also zunächst von einer strikten Trennung der Systeme Wahrnehmung und Sprache aus, wobei ich das erstere als grundlegend betrachte, und frage dann nach ihrer Koordination. Entsprechend dem ökologischen Ansatz wird verfügbare Information gesucht, die den genannten Dualismus bzw. die genannten Systeme spezifiziert. Wahrnehmbare Momente gesprochener/gehörter und geschriebener/gelesener Sprache als eines besonderen Wahrnehmungsgegenstandes sind z.T. offensichtlich, wenn auch in exakter Weise nicht unbedingt einfach zu bestimmen, insbesondere der Aspekt der multiplen Wiederholung. Wie aber wird die eigene Wahrnehmungsaktivität (oder die anderer) wahrgenommen?

Für das visuelle Wahrnehmen besteht ein deutlicher Unterschied zwischen den Varianten des Umherschauens (Kopfbewegung), der Beobachtung unter Bedingungen von Eigenbewegung (Lokomotion) und der Beobachtung von Objektbewegung (Nachfolge-Fixation): während im ersten Fall nur das Blickfeld verlagert wird, erfolgt im zweiten Fall ein optisches Fließen im Gesamt-Blickfeld um den Ort der Annäherung und im letzten Fall eine lokale optische Störung im statischen Feld. Insbesondere im zweiten Fall ist die Trennung von wahrnehmendem Subjekt und wahrgenommener Welt optisch komplementär spezifiziert und somit für visuelles Wahrnehmen verfügbare Information (es gibt noch einige weitere Information für die Selbstwahrnehmung). Akustisch-auditiv ist die beim eigenen Sprechen unvermeidbare binaurale Symmetrie eine eindeutige Spezifikation des eigenen Handeln und Wahrnehmens. Es bedarf also nicht unbedingt einer Wahrnehmung der eigenen Wahrnehmung i.S. einer Meta-Aktivität, ausgeführt von einer zusätzlichen, unabhängigen Instanz, um die Spezifika der eigenen Wahrnehmungsaktivität zu identifizieren: Wahrnehmen ist soz. selbstspezifisch.

Wie kann man sich nun die Beziehung zwischen Wahrnehmung und Sprache vorstellen? Ich betrachte Sprache als historisches, kollektiv zu nutzendes Instrument mit dem Hauptzweck der Koordination der geteilten Arbeitstätigkeit in der menschlichen Gesellschaft. Dabei ist es manchmal erforderlich, sich über prinzipiell Wahrnehmbares zu verständigen, d.h. es wird u.a. eine Beobachtungssprache benötigt, die als nicht bezweifelbarer Ersatz der Wahrnehmungserfahrung verwendbar ist. Da die Wahrnehmungstätigkeit hier nicht als bildliches Kopieren der realen Welt verstanden wird, ist damit keine Bilder-Theorie von Sprache impliziert. Vielmehr ist die Art und Weise, wie Bilder für kommunikative Zwecke verwendbar sind, selbst zu untersuchen. Allgemein läßt sich sagen, daß Bilder durch Analogie und/oder Erhalt eines Teils der verfügbaren Invarianten Information spezifizieren. Vorausgesetzt wird bei dieser Argumentation, daß es eine Bedeutung gibt, in der wir etwas zu zwei Gelegenheiten als gleich wahrnehmen, da sonst die Adäquanz eines Wahrnehmungsersatzes nicht bestimmbar ist, bzw. gar nicht davon gesprochen werden könnte.

Wittgenstein zeigt allerdings bekanntlich, daß die Sprache nicht immer auf die gleiche Weise funktioniert. Normalerweise erfüllt eine Aussage mehrere pragmatische Funktionen gleichzeitig. Die Aufgabe der Sprachforschung ist es also, eine Methode der kategorialen Dekomposition der kommunikativen Intentionen einer gegebenen verbalen Äußerung zu entwickeln, wobei gleichzeitig der Beobachtungsgehalt des Gesprochenen isoliert wird. Die linguistischen Phänomene sind auf dem Hintergrund historischer Entwicklungen zu betrachten.

Unabhängig davon besteht für die Wahrnehmungsforschung die Aufgabe der Identifizierung der grundlegenden Prinzipien der Funktionsweisen der Wahrnehmungssysteme. In der Sicht des ökologischen Ansatzes sind die Unterscheidung von Gleichheit und Verschiedenheit sowie von Konstanz und Veränderung die wesentlichen Charakteristika des Wahrnehmungsprozesses. Diese Phänomene lassen sich in ihrer species-spezifischen adaptiven Ausprägung evolutionsgeschichtlich rekonstruieren.

Eine Verschränkung der beiden Systeme Wahrnehmung und Sprache erfolgt, wenn wir versuchen zu beschreiben, was wir sehen, hören usw., oder wenn wir versuchen, nach etwas zu sehen, hören usw., wovon gesprochen wird. Wahrnehmungsevidenz fungiert aber auch als Kriterium oder Rechtfertigung in Argumentationen, und sprachliche Formulierung wird benutzt, um wahrnehmbare Unterschiede zu nivellieren u.ä.

Wahrnehmung konstituiert direktes Wissen insofern aufgrund projektiver Relationen zwischen einer Informationsquelle, d.i. der materiellen Ursache der Strukturierung der umgebenden Energieverteilung in einer bestimmten Richtung, und einem potentiell eingenommenen Beobachtungsort oder -pfad dort die relevante Information verfügbar ist, wohingegen Sprache indirektes Wissen vermittelt als die verfügbar gemachte Information nun in einem kommunikativen Kontext von Absichten eingebunden ist, der mehrdeutig ist.

Die Eindeutigkeit des Wahrnehmens bedeutet nicht, daß ein physikalisch definierter Stimulus eine bestimmte Reaktion erzwingt. Entgegen diesem Modell der neueren nicht-parallelistischen Psychophysik enthält das ökologische Paradigma soz. zwei Freiheitsgrade: zum einen hängt es von der konkreten Beobachtungsaktivität des Subjekts ab, welche Aspekte der insgesamt verfügbaren Stimulus-Information entnommen werden (die Gesamt-Information ist normalerweise nur über eine Vielzahl von Beobachtungswegen entnehmbar), zum anderen ist damit ein bestimmtes Verhalten in Aussicht gestellt, dessen Ausführung aber von weiteren Bedingungen (u.a. der Fortentwicklung der Situation) abhängt.

Es ergibt sich demgemäß eine gewisse Parallelität zwischen dem Paradigma der ökologischen Psychologie und der Analyse der Logik der Verwendung sog. dispositioneller Prädikate: die allgemein verfügbare Stimulus-Information stellt eine Ermöglichung für ein bestimmtes Verhalten dar und ist ihrerseits aufgrund eines bestimmten materiellen Weltzustandes ermöglicht; analog bezeichnet eine dispositionelle Prädikation ein mögliches Ereignis, für das wiederum eine kausale, materielle Basis angebbar ist. In der Wahrnehmungssituation ist es allerdings das beobachtende Subjekt selbst, das die Stimulus-Information entnimmt, wohingegen es in Fällen dispositioneller Prädikationen ein externes Ereignis ist, das die Manifestation der Disposition hervorruft. Im Normalfall läßt die Entnahme von Stimulus-Information die materielle Welt unbeeinflußt, dispositionelle Prädikate finden Anwendung bevorzugt in Fällen, in denen das relevante Verhalten des Objekts die materielle Basis der Disposition zerstört (z.B. im Standardspiel des zerbrechlichen Glases).

Charakteristika dispositioneller Prädikationen gelten analog auch bzgl. der ökologisch konzeptualisierten Wahrnehmungssituation. So bestehen eine allgemeine Regularität der Beziehungen Stimulus-Information – Verhalten bzw. Disposition – Ereignis, aber ebenso Ausnahmen, eine allgemeine Nicht-Notwendigkeit in diesen Beziehungen, aber für den Einzelfall strikte Notwendigkeit (das eingetretene Ereignis begründet endgültig die antezedente Disposition, die Entnahme von Stimulus-Information setzt deren Verfügbarkeit voraus). Weitere analytische Rekonstruktionen der Dispositionsbegriffe in Termini ihrer kontrafaktischen Implikationen und ihres induktiven Status finden ebenfalls Entsprechung im ökologischen Wahrnehmungskonzept: wäre Stimulus-Information verfügbar gewesen, hätte . . ., bzw. da Stimulus-Information$_i$ in der Vergangenheit Verhalten$_j$ ermöglicht hat, sollte dies auch in Zukunft der Fall sein.

Normative Aspekte, auf die ich bzgl. dispositioneller Prädikate in einem früheren Beitrag aufmerksam gemacht habe (Landwehr 1979), bestehen bzgl. wahrnehmbarer Stimulus-Information durch gesellschaftliche Einschränkungen der Verfügbarmachung derselben.

LITERATUR

Gibson, J. J., *The senses considered as perceptual systems* (Boston 1966).
Gibson, J. J., *The ecological approach to visual perception* (Boston 1979).
Landwehr, K., „Dispositionen, die ‚reasons-causes-Debatte' und die ‚is-ought-Frage'" in Berghel, H. Hübner, A. und Köhler, E. (Hrsg.), *Wittgenstein, der Wiener Kreis und der Kritische Rationalismus* – Akten des 3. Internationalen Wittgenstein Symposiums, 13.–19. August 1978/Kirchberg am Wechsel (Österreich) (Wien 1979), S. 315–317.
Wittgenstein, L., *Philosophische Untersuchungen – Philosophical Investigations* (Oxford 1953).

* * *

HOW DO WORDS REFER TO SENSATIONS?

Ulrich Steinvorth
Universität Hamburg

> This question is the same as: how does a human being learn the meaning of the names of sensations? – of the word "pain" for example. Here is one possibility: words are connected with the primitive, the natural, expressions of the sensation and used in their place. A child has hurt himself and he cries; and then adults talk to him and teach him exclamations and, later, sentences. They teach the child new pain-behaviour.
> "So you are saying that the word 'pain' really means crying?" – On the contrary: the verbal expression of pain replaces crying and does not describe it. (*PI* § 244)

Two theses follow from Wittgenstein's answer: (1) Words refer to sensations by being associated to natural expressions of sensations. (2) The meaning of sensation words is the same as the meaning of natural expressions of sensations. But there are some problems to the theses: (a) Every sensation word seems to need a natural expression it replaces. But which natural expressions do such words replace as "throbbing", "piercing", "dull", used to characterize head-ache? (b) Natural expressions can be sincere and insincere, but cannot be more or less striking, well put or truthful. Sensation words can. Some people can describe their sensations better than others. This fact seems incompatible with (2).

Now theses (1) and (2) feed on a one-sided diet; forgetting his § 593, Wittgenstein has been content with the one example of § 244. Let us imagine another one. A child has not yet felt stinging nettles. Some friend coaxes him into touching them and asks him: "What do you feel?" The child who is not plaintive may answer: "It's stinging." Let the friend be a punster saying: "But I can't see a sting in your fingers nor a puncture on your skin." The child may reply: "There are no real stings in my fingers. It's just as if some stings had stung into my fingers. But the feeling is real. I do not fancy." – Can we not learn this way the meaning of the names of sensations? Wittgenstein, I'm afraid, would deny it, arguing that to use and understand "stinging" as the child does we must have learnt the language game with sensations words, their role, grammar or post where they are stationed, and that we learn them in situations as described in § 244.

How are we to decide whether our child must already have learnt the language game with sensation words before using it the way we imagined? If historically men may have begun using words as our child does to refer to sensations without having learned before a language game of the kind described in § 244, then learning such a game is no necessary condition for using words to refer to sensations the way our child does. But our first human ancestors may well have begun using sensation words that way. After a hard struggle with a mammoth someone out of a horde of men who are busy with their wounds may have opened his mouth not to moan but to say: "This wound is burning", pointing to a red cleft in his thigh. Let us imagine that "burning" had before been used only to describe the public or physical processes of fires and flames (which of course implies describing our experiences and perceptions of them). So some comrade who is lucky to have got only slight wounds may wonder where there are flames in his leg. But since men did one day learn this new or metaphorical use of "burning", which now referred to a sensation and not to a fire, we may suppose that most men did understand the first speaker. They did not need to learn a language game with *sensation* words before. Perhaps they must have learnt a language game with words describing public things or events (let us call them *public words* for shortness), since they must have known the meaning of public words. There are some more conditions for a word's referring to a sensation in cases of our kind. To list them, a word "W" refers to a sensation iff:

(1) "W" has got a meaning in descriptions of a public thing or event W,
(2) there is no public thing W referred to by the speaker, and
(3) the hearer did experience something non-public which was similar to the experience of W.

If these conditions are necessary and sufficient to make the use of a word refer to a sensation, there would be some important agreement with Wittgenstein's view. They would exclude the possibility of a private language that only I can understand, since to refer to sensations we need a public word. On the other hand, they imply that in some sense there are private or non-public events. But they do not imply that private events are privately identifiable, i.e. identifiable by the person who has them in a way only he can identify them. To have the concept of a private event it is sufficient that one can distinguish public from non-public events by public criteria. Now obviously people can and could do so even in those times when they began speaking about their sensations. If I respond to some event E by some movement M, and if some other man or perceptive animal close to me performs the same movement or a similar one M' (e.g. looking to the left when I am looking to the right and he is standing on my right hand), then E is public; if I respond to some event E by some movement M, and if some other person or animal does not perform some M', E is private. Of course people could not always decide whether some E was public or private; we cannot even today. Yet we know the difference, we distinguish by public criteria only, and nevertheless the private event is non-public. We need as little assume as Wittgenstein did that we can privately identify it; we must only assume as Wittgenstein did that we can respond to it verbally or non-verbally, thereby making it both public and identifiable.

Not only may we but we must assume that we cannot privately identify the sensation. For at least when people began speaking about them, their use of public words to refer to them was some kind of metaphor, and it is specific to metaphors that there are no criteria of correctness of their use, hence no criteria of identity of what is referred to by the metaphor. No doubt by and by some of the public words which were used to refer to sensations were used exclusively to refer to them and lost their appearance of metaphor, e.g. the word "pain", which in its etymological roots referred to public events as "burning" does. Nevertheless, in its depth grammar it is still a metaphor if we define metaphor as signs used without criteria of correct application which have yet a meaning because there is a similarity seen or felt by speakers and hearers between the event or thing E referred to non-metaphorically and the event referred to metaphorically. But is there such an E in the case of a "pure" sensation word like "pain"? I think there is: it is any public thing or event which hurts or causes pain: hot stoves, sharp knives, hard stones in certain situations. Pain is what we feel when we experience such public things even if there are no such public things to be experienced, just as a burning sensation is what we feel when we experience flames even if there are no flames to be experienced.

Now if there is agreement with Wittgenstein's view on a private language in spite or our rejection of § 244, what is the importance of this rejection? According to Wittgenstein, it is some such context in human life as our interest in comforting and being comforted which gives meaning to a sensation word. According to my approach, public words get a new meaning by being used in a new situation. In Wittgenstein's view, sensations are something we are familiar with since we have to do with them every day and night in just those contexts without which we could never refer to them. Following my approach, we must view them as something men detected when they first applied public words to them. In some sense they had consciousness of them before speaking about them, but they could know and describe them only when they used public words for them. Thus, they were confronted with quite a new realm of unseizable things or qualities which they had to locate somewhere in their world. Instead of presupposing a "post where the new word is stationed" (§ 257), the use of sensation words must have forced people into looking for a way of lodging sensations in their world, which cannot have been an easy thing to accomplish without effects on their lives, since even now philosophers find so much difficulty in understanding sensations. If our reasonings are correct, we should expect to find some historical evidence of former men's efforts to get clear about sensations. Before looking for it, let us see whether we can transfer our approach from sensations to other psychic phenomena.

There are no problems about a transfer to dream descriptions, which obviously are applications of public words to private events. No doubt there have been special difficulties in distinguishing dreams as private events from public events, but there seems to be no essential difference in the way words refer to sensations and to dreams. Thoughts and intentions are a different case. The simplest and historically earliest way to express them would be to make an assertion, an announcement or a command by which the speaker would learn what he thinks or intends as well and as early as the hearer. In contrast to sensations and dreams, thoughts and intentions are not originally private. We can hide them as we can hide money or a mole on the shoulder, but they are nothing which, though not privately identifiable, we can respond to verbally or non-verbally. By contrast, ideas and intuitions which occur to me before I can express them verbally are originally private, and if we describe or express them, we refer to them in the way we do with sensations. I think most of our imaginations, memories, fancies, and emotions are similar to ideas and intuitions, though there may be cases where they are more similar to thoughts and intuitions.

In any case, obviously there are other private events than sensations, and if my approach is correct, we must assume that early men were confronted by a rather populous realm of various and multifarious inhabitants which, though in some sense real, must have been judged, on the one hand, strange and uncanny because they cannot be seized and produced by anybody, and, on the other hand, fascinating and intimate because they are the stuff we ourselves as conscious beings are made of. Hence, the world of early men must have been divided not into the physical and the psychic world, but into the realm of things seizable, more or less controllable, accessible to everybody, and into the realm of things both uncanny and fascinationg, not accessible to everybody, but, if at all, accessible only after complicated procedures. We have sufficient evidence that early men's life and world was impregnated by this separation. It is the separation of the profane and the sacred.

* * *

SPRACHSPIEL VS. VOLLSTÄNDIGE SPRACHE

Audun Öfsti
Universität Trondheim

> Die Grenzen meiner Sprache bedeuten die Grenzen meiner Welt
> . . . Das Subjekt gehört nicht zur Welt sondern es ist eine Grenze
> der Welt.
>
> Ludwig Wittgenstein

> Die Einheit dieses transzendentalen Subjekts zerbricht mit der
> Einheit der Universalsprache.
>
> Jürgen Habermas

I

Mit der Konzeption einer Mannigfaltigkeit von geschichtlich-konkreten Sprachspielen löst Wittgenstein die universale Einheit der Sprache auf − und zwar, so möchte ich sagen, in zweierlei Hinsicht. Es wird einerseits die Einheitlichkeit des „logischen Raumes" in Frage gestellt in dem Sinne, daß eine „allgemeine Form des Satzes" nicht mehr behauptet werden kann. Die „Logik" einer natürlichen Sprache umfaßt eine ganze Menge von Tätigkeiten inklusive der zugehörigen Verwendungsweisen von verschiedenartigen sprachlichen Ausdrücken, die je ihre eigene (Mikro-)Logik haben. (Vgl. § 23. Vgl. auch die sehr einfachen Sprachspiele in § 1, 2 und 8.[1]) Insofern kann man die natürliche Sprache mit einem Werkzeugkasten vergleichen (§ 11), wobei die einzelnen Werkzeuge: Hammer, Zange, Säge, Leim, Maßstab usw. der „Mannigfaltigkeit der Werkzeuge der Sprache und ihrer Verwendungsweisen" entsprechen. Oder wir können unsere Sprache mit einer Stadt vergleichen, die aus *verschiedenartigen* Bauten, Straßen, Plätzen usw. besteht (§ 18). Zu dieser ersten Auflösung der einheitlichen Tractatus-Sprache gehört natürlich auch Wittgensteins Weigerung, mehr als eine Art *Familienähnlichkeit* zwischen den Sprachspielen unseres Sprachrepertoires − also keine tiefliegende logische Gleichförmigkeit − anzuerkennen (§ 65ff).

Nun kann man aber anderseits auch in einem anderen Sinne von einer Auflösung *der* einen transzendentalen Sprache durch Wittgensteins Spätphilosophie reden; in dem Sinne nämlich, wo man die behauptete Vielfalt von Sprachspielen, bzw. Lebensform, als eine Vielfalt von tradierten (natürlichen) *Sprachen* nimmt (die je für sich eine Mannigfaltigkeit von sprachlichen „Werkzeugen", Verwendungsweisen, Spielen umfassen). Nach dieser Deutung kommen wir zu einer Art W. von Humboldtscher, Herderscher, Whorfscher oder sogar historistischer Auffassung der Sprache als Vehikel einer historisch-kulturell *relativierbaren* Welt- und Lebensanschauung. Es gibt eine Mannigfaltigkeit von natürlichen, selbstgenügsamen (vielleicht auch von einander keine Kenntnis nehmenden) Sprachen, deren unterschiedlicher Sprachbau eine Mannigfaltigkeit von unterschiedlichen (menschlichen) Welt- und Lebensformen bedeutet. Oder in der Sprache des frühen Wittgenstein ausgedrückt: Es kann nicht mehr im Singular von *der* Grenze *der* Welt gesprochen werden, wir müssen nunmehr mit einer Mannigfaltigkeit von *besonderen* Subjektivitäten bzw. Weltgrenzen rechnen. (Daß hierbei ein philosophisches Relativismusproblem entsteht, versteht sich von selbst.[2])

Man kann sich die zwei Auflösungsrichtungen verdeutlichen, indem man die dadurch entstehenden Einheits*probleme* ins Auge faßt.[3]

Bei der ersten Deutung der Auflösung können wir uns das folgende Einheitsproblem vorstellen: Wie kommen die verschiedenen Sprachspiele (Werkzeuge) zu einer selbstgenügsamen natürlichen Sprache zusammen, bzw. wie bauen sich in einem Individuum die Beherrschung einer Reihe von Fähigkeiten oder Sprachspielkompetenzen zu so etwas wie die Beherrschung *einer Sprache* auf? Ja, wir könnten sogar an dieser Stelle die weitere Frage aufwerfen: Wann ist überhaupt eine natürliche Sprache „vollständig", was erlaubt uns überhaupt in dieser Weise von einer Sprache als einer abgehobenen Einheit zu reden?

Man könnte auf diese letzte Frage eine Art trivialisierende Antwort geben, die auch Wittgensteins implizite Antwort zu sein scheint; die Einheit einer Sprache ist die einer Kommunikationsgemeinschaft oder eines „System(s) der Verständigung": Wenn mindestens zwei Individuen in ihrer Sprachpraxis derart übereinstimmen, daß sie durch diese Praxis ihre Handlungen erfolgreich miteinander abstimmen können, dann haben wir es schon mit einer Sprache zu tun. (So z.B. das §-2-Sprachspiel.) Wenn das Repertoire der Spielenden wächst, wächst die Sprache. Es gibt hier keine besonderen totalisierenden oder „ganzheitsstiftenden" Momente (Regeln, Spiele . . .), kein Minimumrepertoire, aber auch kein Maximumsrepertoire. Die Einheit der Sprache ist einfach gegeben durch die Gemeinschaft derer, die sie verstehen. Eine Sprache erweitert sich ständig durch neue Werkzeuge, und verliert im Laufe der Zeit auch einiges: „neue Sprachspiele, wie wir sagen können, entstehen und andere veralten und werden vergessen" (§ 23). Eine Sprache (ein Repertoire von Sprachspielen) hebt sich gegen andere Sprachen ab und erhält somit eine sie definierende Grenze einfach dadurch, daß das Eingeübtsein in das heimische Repertoire (die Beherrschung der eigenen Sprache) nicht gleich eine Kommunikation mit Mitgliedern anderer Kommunikationsgemeinschaften, die ein verschiedenes Repertoire haben, ermöglicht. − Durch diesen trivialisierenden Begriff von der Einheit *einer* Sprache erübrigt sich gewissermaßen auch die Frage nach dem, was eine vollständige Sprache bzw. Sprachkompetenz ausmacht.

Bei der zweiten Deutung des Zerfalls *der* menschlichen Sprache entsteht ein andersartiges Einheitsproblem. Wenn wir uns erlauben, von (natürlichen) Sprachen menschlicher Kommunikationsgemeinschaften als voneinander trennbaren Einheiten zu reden, so wie wir es gewohnt sind, entsteht sofort die Frage: wie verhalten sich diese Sprachen oder diese Kommunikationsgemeinschaften zueinander? Eines fällt dabei gleich auf: trotz ihrer Verschiedenheit unterstellen wir bei den natürlichen Sprachen eine Art Gleichwertigkeit. Bei aller Besonderheit des Weltzugangs, die durch eine partikuläre Sprache gegeben ist, bleibt sie doch aus der Sicht der anderen Sprachen zugänglich und mit ihnen irgendwie *vergleichbar*. Es besteht hier eine Art *Konkurrenzverhältnis* zwischen Sprachen, wo jede einzelne *einen Anspruch auf das Ganze* hat, sozusagen die Grenze *der* Welt liefern will. (Erst durch dieses Konkurrenzverhältnis *entsteht* überhaupt das philosophische Relativismusproblem in seiner „linguistischen" Form.) Worum es hier geht, läßt sich wohl am direktesten klarmachen durch den Hinweis darauf, daß unsere natürlichen Sprachen ineinander *übersetzbar* sind. Somit kann z.B. Habermas in einem Kommentar zu Wittgenstein − der zugleich eine Lösung des *hier* involvierten Einheitsproblems verspricht − von dem Zug reden, „den alle tradierten Sprachen gemeinsam haben und der ihre transzendentale Einheit verbürgt: . . . daß sie prinzipiell ineinander übersetzt werden können".[4]

Wir haben es also nach dem obigen mit zwei Mannigfaltigkeiten und zwei unterscheidbaren (obwohl eng verknüpften) Einheitsproblemen zu tun: Auf der einen Seite die Vielfalt von (natürlichen und tradierten) *Sprachen*, die in einer Art Konkurrenzverhältnis zueinander stehen, und auf der anderen Seite die Mannigfaltigkeit der *Sprachspiele*, die *innerhalb einer* Sprache eher ein Arbeitsteilungsverhältnis zueinander haben. Ich halte es für fruchtbar, diese zwei Typen von Vielfalt, Relation und Einheitsproblem nicht in einen Topf zu werfen, sondern möglichst klar auseinander zu halten; denn dadurch läßt sich m.E. ein zentrales Problem am besten beleuchten: das Problem nämlich, was wohl eine vollständige (komplette), selbstgenügsame Sprache heißen kann.[5]

Wittgenstein selber, wie auch manche seiner Interpreten, haben sich jedoch keineswegs an eine solche Trennung gehalten. Sie haben keinen Wert darauf gelegt, einen Unterschied zwischen (ganzen) *Sprachen* und (nur als „Teile" von solchen möglichen) sehr einfachen oder primitiven *Sprachspielen* hervorheben. Nun ist das vielleicht bei Wittgenstein selbst kein Wunder, insofern wir ihm tatsächlich die „trivialisierende" Ansicht bezüglich der „Einheit" eines Sprachganzen zuschreiben können (Vgl. auch § 18). Merkwürdiger ist es, daß auch K.-O. Apel und J. Habermas Wittgenstein in seiner Unterlassung, Sprache und Sprachspiel klar zu unterscheiden, treu bleiben. Ich möchte dies mit einem Zitat von K.-O.Apel belegen:

> Der Philosoph als *Sprachkritiker* muß sich darüber im Klaren sein, daß er bei dem Geschäft der Sprachspiel-*Beschreibung* selber ein *spezifisches Sprachspiel* in Anspruch nimmt, das auf alle nur möglichen Sprachspiele *reflexiv* und *kritisch* bezogen ist. Demnach setzt nun aber der Philosoph immer schon voraus, daß er prinzipiell an allen Sprachspielen *teilnehmen* bzw. zu den entsprechenden Sprachgemeinschaften in *Kommunikation* treten kann. Damit ist aber ein Postulat aufgestellt, das der These Wittgensteins, daß den unbegrenzt vielen und verschiedenen von ihm gemeinten ,Sprachspielen' nichts weiter *gemeinsam* sein muß als eine gewisse ,Familienähnlichkeit' – also kein durchgehender Wesenszug –, zu widersprechen scheint. In der Tat liegt die *Gemeinsamkeit* aller ,Sprachspiele' m.E. darin, daß mit der Erlernung *einer* Sprache – u.d.h. mit der erfolgreichen Sozialisation im Sinne *einer* mit dem Sprachgebrauch ,verwobenen' ,Lebensform' – zugleich so etwas wie *das* Sprachspiel – bzw. *die* menschliche Lebensform – erlernt wird: es wird nämlich prinzipiell die *Kompetenz* zur Reflexion der eigenen Sprache bzw. Lebensform und zur *Kommunikation* mit allen anderen Sprachspielen miterworben.[6]

Grundsätzlich stimme ich mit dem Gesagten überein. In diesem Zusammenhang interessiert mich jedoch am meisten die schwankende Bedeutung von „Sprache" und „Sprachspiel". Beide Arten von Mannigfaltigkeit (die ich oben auseinenderzuhalten versucht habe) sind offenbar angesprochen, und dabei wird der Terminus „Sprachspiel" auch zur Bezeichnung einer ganzen Sprache (deren Erlernung eben ganz allgemein die Kompetenz zur Kommunikation über Sprachgrenzen herbeiführt) benützt. Dieser Gebrauch verleitet m.E. zu einem eigentlich unnötigen Gegensatz zu Wittgenstein: Wir *können* tatsächlich nicht die behauptete „Gemeinsamkeit aller Sprachspiele" für die (nur „familienähnlichen") einfachen und übersichtlichen Sprachspiele Wittgensteins fordern. Von dieser Art Gemeinsamkeit kann nur dort gesprochen werden, wo wir von Übersetzung zwischen *Sprachen* reden können.

Ich möchte also nicht (wie Apel) die Wittgensteinsche Konzeption einer Relation der Familienähnlichkeit zwischen Sprachspielen in Frage stellen, sondern vielmehr die Kritik an Wittgenstein dahingehend formulieren, daß er keinen nichttrivialen Begriff von einer ganzen (vollständigen) *Sprache* hat oder wahrheben will (Vgl. § 18).

II

Ich will in dem Folgenden mit Wittgenstein (?) gegen Wittgenstein fünf Hinweise oder Thesen auflisten, bezüglich der Frage, was denn eine vollständige oder „volle" Sprache wohl heißen kann. Und dabei möchte ich vermeiden, diese Vollständigkeit sozusagen inhaltlich, in der Anwesenheit eines besonderen, vollständigmachenden Sprachspiels zu suchen.[7]

1. Die vollständige Sprache muß eine *Pluralität* von Sprachspielen umfassen, so daß man sagen kann, sie wurzele in einem *Geflecht* von Sprachspielen, dessen *Unterschiede* selber zur Sprache gehören (Vgl. §§ 20, 21). In diesem Sinne ist schon klar, daß das in § 2 beschriebene Sprachspiel gerade nicht die vollständige Sprache eines Volksstamms sein kann.

2. Die volle Sprache muß „Übersichtssprache" sein; d.h. es muß in dieser vollen Sprache möglich sein, ihre Worte und ihre Sprachspiele *getrennt* – bzw. umgekehrt die Sprachspielwirksamkeiten und Szenen als von der Gestalt der gesprochenen Worte getrennt – zu identifizieren und beschreiben. Erst dadurch erhalten die Wortgestalten einen gegenüber ihrem Sinn konventionellen Charakter; wird so etwas wie „übertragene Bedeutung" (als entscheidender Mechanismus sprachlicher Neubildung) und *Übersetzung* möglich.

3. Gewisse philosophische *Fehler* (vom Typ revisionistischer Metaphysik) müssen möglich, oder sogar in der vollständigen Sprache angelegt sein; Nominalismus, Platonismus (Hypostasierung von Sinn), „der Gedanke" als etwas sprachunabhängiges, Cartesianischer Idealismus

(im Sinne von Zettel §§ 413, 414, 422, 424), etc. Das (philosophische − und witzige) „Feiern" der Sprache muß möglich sein.[8]

4. Die „Akteursprache" der Sprachspielenden muß − wenn sie eine vollständige Sprache sein soll (und die Akteure sollen „wissen" können, was sie tun) − zugleich die Sprache eines sie beschreibenden Zuschauers sein können. Die performativ in Sprechakten verwendeten Phrasen müssen gerade *nicht* im Prinzip immer einer anderen Sprache angehören können, als der Sprache, in der diese Akteure („in der dritten Person") *beschrieben* werden.[9] In § 2 der *PU* besteht offenbar ein großer Unterschied zwischen der (Vierwort-)Akteursprache des A und B und der (Interpreten-)Sprache Wittgensteins, in welcher er diese Akteure beschreibt. Bevor dieser Unterschied auf einen graduellen, von der „kleineren" Sprache aus einholbaren Unterschied reduziert ist, kann die kleinere „Akteursprache" nicht als „vollständige" gelten. Oder anders ausgedrückt: Eine komplette Sprache darf nicht nur das „Ziehen" *in* den Sprachspielen ermöglichen, sondern essentiell auch eine Beschreibung *von* diesen Zügen. (Vgl. Punkt 2 oben.)

5. Als Ausgangspunkt für den letzten Hinweis, der wohl auch auf die Möglichkeit einer mehr systematischen Ordnung des schon Angedeuteten hinweist, möchte ich den § 18 nehmen, wo Wittgenstein eine Vorstellung von der Vollständigkeit einer Sprache ausdrücklich ablehnt:

> Daß die Sprachen (2) und (8) nur aus Befehlen bestehen, laß dich nicht stören. Willst du sagen, sie seien darum nicht vollständig, so frage dich, ob unsere Sprache vollständig ist; − ob sie es war, ehe ihr der chemische Symbolismus und die Infinitesimalnotation einverleibt wurden; denn dies sind, sozusagen, Vorstädte unserer Sprache. (Und mit wieviel Häusern, oder Straßen, fängt eine Stadt an, Stadt zu sein?) Unsere Sprache kann man ansehen als eine alte Stadt: Ein Gewinkel von Gäßchen und Plätzen, alten und neuen Häusern, und Häusern, mit Zubauten aus verschiedenen Zeiten; und dies umgeben von einer Menge neuer Vororte mit geraden und regelmäßigen Straßen und mit einförmigen Häusern.

Hier wird uns eine Vorstellung von Sprache (oder sprachlicher Kompetenz), die willkürlich begrenzt oder umfassend sein kann, und die also weder eine obere oder untere Grenze hat, ganz explizit präsentiert. Die Metapher hat natürlich ihren guten Sinn. Dies verhindert aber nicht, daß wir nach einem Begriff von ungleichen Niveaus der Kompetenz bei den heranwachsenden Sprachsubjekten suchen müssen. Wir können uns Formen der Erweiterung von Sprache vorstellen, die von Wittgensteins Metaphern nicht illustriert werden; sagen wir Mal eine Erweiterung von der Signalsprache zu einer *normativ* regulierten Sprache (in der einen oder anderen Minimalbedeutung), und weiter bis auf ein Niveau, auf dem Sprache und Handlung als verschiedene Weisen, „dieselbe" Intention auszudrücken, ausdifferenziert sind.[10] Weiter können wir uns vielleicht ein Niveau vorstellen, auf dem propositionale Inhalte sich als sprechaktinvariant festhalten und Sinninhalte sich hypostasieren lassen. Letztlich wäre eine Ebene als „höchstes" Niveau zu bezeichnen, wo wir von einer vollständigen kommunikativen Kompetenz reden können.

Die Pointe ist nicht, hier eine Theorie über solche Niveaus zu entwerfen, sondern lediglich darauf hinzuweisen, daß wir, wenn wir in *diesem* Sinne an eine Erweiterung der Sprache (oder der sprachlichen Kompetenz) denken − welche sich mit Namen wie Piaget, Habermas[11] und Kohlberg assoziieren läßt −, so können wir auch von einem Niveau der Vollständigkeit oder Komplettheit reden, bei dem weitere Erweiterungen *á la Wittgenstein* in § 18 keine formale Relevanz mehr besitzen, sondern einfach der „inhaltsmäßigen" Seite zugeschlagen werden müssen. Um einen traditionellen Begriff zu benutzen: Auf einem gewissen Niveau kann man sagen, daß es sich bei den sprachlichen Subjekten um *Vernunftwesen* handelt und daß „der Umfang" ihrer Sprache (ganz gleich welche „Vorstädte" diese Sprache nun einschließt oder auch nicht) gleichgültig ist. Der sprachliche Aktionsradius berührt − ein gewisses Minimumsniveau vorausgesetzt − nicht deren Status als *Vernunftwesen*, genausowenig, wie es das Intelligenzniveau tut.

ANMERKUNGEN

[1] Wenn nicht anders angemerkt referieren die angeführten §-en zu *PU*.

[2] Vgl. K.-O. Apel, *Transformation der Philosophie*, Bd. II (Frankfurt a. M. 1973), S. 320.

[3] Dabei steht von vornherein fest, daß ein Sprachspiel mit zugehörigem Regelfolgen − ungeachtet ob man hier unter Sprachspiel eine vollständige natürliche Sprache oder nur eines der vielen Werkzeuge einer solchen (Zählen, Bitten etc.) versteht − nach Wittgenstein nur *intersubjektiv* möglich ist: einer Regel folgen, ist Sache einer *Kommunikationsgemeinschaft*, deren Mitglieder in ihrer Sprachpraxis *übereinstimmen* (§ 199, 214).

[4] Habermas, J., *Zur Logik der Sozialwissenschaften* (Frankfurt a. M. 1970), S. 253.

[5] Die oben angedeutete „trivialisierende" − oder die Problemstellung unterlaufende − Antwort, die sich vielleicht den *PU* entnehmen läßt, scheint mir nicht befriedigend.

[6] Apel a.a.O. Bd. II, S. 347. Vgl. aber auch Habermas, a.a.O. S.252.

[7] Ich finde z.B. die Ausdrucksweise K.-O. Apels, der hier von einem spezifischen „transzendentalen" Sprachspiel spricht (Siehe Zitat länger oben, auch a.a.O. Bd. II, S. 352), für unangemessen.

[8] Zu Pkt. 2 und 3 wäre im Hinblick auf das Thema Übersicht(lichkeit) auch dies anzuknüpfen: Die vollständige Sprache muß eine Dimension bereitstellen, in der sich der Philosoph (und die philosophische Begriffsverwirrung) bewegen kann, und das heißt zugleich eine Dimension, die die „übersichtliche Darstellung" (§ 122) bzw. die philosophischen Aussagen (z.B. *PU*) ermöglicht.

[9] Dagegen natürlich der gesamte Objektivismus-Solipsismus, Carnap, Bergmann, Mandler & Kessen (*The Language of Psychology* (N. Y. 1959), p. 35), Quine, Föllesdal, Churchland u.a.

[10] Vgl. Charles Taylor, *Hegel* (Cambridge 1975), S. 16.

[11] Vgl. z.B. Habermas, Universalpragmatische Hinweise auf das System der Ich-Abgrenzungen, in Auwärter et al., *Kommunikation, Interaktion, Identität* (Frankfurt a. M. 1976), hier insb. S. 338−344.

* * *

REGELN UND INTENTIONALITÄT

Herbert Hrachovec
Universität Wien

1. Regeln sind weder Naturgesetze, noch Handlungen

Naturgesetze gelten in allen Fällen, für die sie aufgestellt sind, menschliche Handlungen erfordern die individuelle Überprüfung und Auswertung des jeweiligen historisch-sozialen Kontextes. Auf der einen Seite steht die Subsumtion unter ein Gesetz, auf der anderen die Gestaltung des Lebens durch verantwortliche Entscheidung. Die beiden Themenkreise geraten leicht in Konflikt. Der soll hier nicht entfaltet werden. Ich setze beide Seiten voraus, um etwas zur Charakteristik von Regeln beizutragen. Dazu sind nämlich einige Bestimmungsstücke nötig, die zwischen den Kontrahenten heftig umstritten sind: Kausalität, Freiheit, Intentionalität. Die Auseinandersetzung ist viel zu komplex, als daß diese Begriffe hier im Rahmen einer Theorie von Natur und Mensch beleuchtet werden könnten. Das umgekehrte Vorgehen läßt sich eher in Angriff nehmen: von der Analyse der Regeln aus den Konflikt, in den sie eingebettet sind, beleuchten.

Regeln unterscheiden sich von Naturgesetzen durch mangelnden „Automatismus". Sie müssen gelernt und entsprechend angewendet werden. Dabei sind Fehldeutungen nie ganz auszuschließen. Der überlegten einzelnen Handlung gegenüber fungieren Regeln dagegen quasi automatisch. Durch sie ist von vornherein festgelegt, was unter bestimmten Umständen geschieht. Diese Abgrenzungen bedeuten einen doppelten Mangel und eine doppelte Möglichkeit: Regeln fehlt die Allgemeingültigkeit der Naturgesetze und das Freiheitsmoment der Einzelhandlung, dafür sind sie an Kontexte adaptierbar und erschließen einen Horizont von Verläßlichkeit, der Entscheidungen an Ort und Stelle abgeht. Das Verhältnis der Regel zum Ausdruck, in dem sie niedergelegt ist, unterscheidet sie nach beiden Seiten hin. Naturgesetze funktionieren, ohne formuliert zu sein, Handlungen bestehen in Stellungnahmen zu etwas Vorgefundenem, einer Regel zu folgen heißt dagegen, sich im Sinne eines vorformulierten Auftrags verhalten. Die angesprochene Flexibilität und Verläßlichkeit hängen an dem Ausdruck, der zwar ein Reglement anzeigt, es aber nicht zwangsläufig aktualisiert. Ein Regelausdruck wirkt nicht kausal, andererseits aber auch nicht als Zufallsimpuls, sondern als mögliche Einweisung in den vorgeplanten Zusammenhang, dessen Einrichtung er voraussetzt.

Wenn es sich nicht um die Auslösung eines Naturablaufes handelt, wie ist die Funktion des Regelausdrucks dann zu erklären? Es liegt nahe, ihn als interpretierbares Symbol zu betrachten und das Regelfolgen zu den sinngeleiteten menschlichen Fähigkeiten zu zählen. Die Flexibilität der Regel erklärt sich dann aus dem Spielraum, den Interpretationen immer bieten und die dazu komplementäre Festgelegtheit weist auf die Institutionen zurück, die dabei normierend fungieren können. Bleibt die Frage, woran es liegt, daß Menschen Sprachausdrücke mehr oder weniger erwartungsgemäß interpretieren. Anders ausgedrückt: Wodurch wird die Semantik von Regelausdrücken möglich gemacht? Ich werde argumentieren, daß die semantische Betrachtung sich zwanglos zu einer Erörterung der intentionalen Struktur des menschlichen Bewußtseins ausweiten läßt. Ohne den Prioritätsstreit zu berühren, der sich hier ankündigt, soll die Verbindung zwischen einem entscheidenden Charakteristikum des Regelfolgens und der Vorstellungstätigkeit hergestellt werden.

2. Regeln sind nie unfehlbar

Die vorgeschlagene Lokalisierung der Regel ist, obwohl sie maßgeblichen Intuitionen entspricht, nicht einfach selbstverständlich. Die Verwendung von „Regel" reicht tief in die Problemfelder „Naturgesetze" sowie „praktische Entscheidungen". Bevor der Zwischenstatus als Kern des Phänomens erwiesen werden kann, sind die fließenden Übergänge festzuhalten. Zwei Beispiele, in denen „Regel" oft „unabänderliches Gesetz" heißen soll, sind Regeln der universalen Grammatik, denen jede menschliche Sprache angeblich gehorcht, und Rechenregeln. Die Fälle vom ersten Typ haben nichts mit dem Phänomen zu tun, das hier beschrieben wird. Das gilt für alle „Regeln" im Sinn naturgegebener Gesetzlichkeit. Schwierigere Grenzfälle sind die Rechenregeln, die als Darstellung der Gesetze der Mathematik konzipiert sind, wie etwa menschliche Gestze als Folgerungen aus dem natürlichen Sittengesetz. In diesen Betrachtungsweisen geht es gerade darum, die Regel dem Naturgesetz so weit wie möglich anzunähern, obwohl auch nicht zu übersehen ist, daß diese Angleichung nicht vollständig gelingen kann. Wittgensteins unermüdliche Attacken gegen die Auflösung des konventionellen Momentes mathematischer Vereinbarungen sind ein überzeugender Hinweis auf diese Unmöglichkeit. Eine Regel besteht geradezu darin, daß sie auf eine ihr spezifische Art mißlingen kann. Von Naturgesetzen kann man allenfalls sagen, daß sie im Einzelfall aus bestimmten Gründen nicht zutreffen.

Das andere Extrem ist die Auflösung der Regel in bewußte Entscheidungen. Die Regularität wird auf den Willen der Beteiligten in einem Gruppenprozeß zurückgeführt. Sie halten sich an ihre Festlegungen, ihnen steht es auch frei, sie zu ändern. Einschlägige Beispiele sind Spielregeln oder die Regeln des Anstands. Dieser Sprachgebrauch ist nicht wie vorhin äquivok, es kann eine wohlüberlegte Handlung sein, eine Regel einzurichten und ihr zu folgen. Aber das Besondere der Regel ist auch damit nicht getroffen. Wieder ist es das spezifische Mißlingen-Können, das den Unterschied ausmacht. Eine Regel verfehlen heißt nicht, eine abweichende Entscheidung treffen, es ist kein bewußter Akt, sowenig wie das Regelfolgen. Vielmehr macht man in einem eingelernten, bisher selbstverständlichen Zusammenhang einen Schritt, der dessen quasi-Natürlichkeit unversehens durchbricht. Regeln etablieren eine „zweite Natur", in der die Handlungsanteile ausgeblendet sind, bis ein Fehler oder ein Mißverständnis die Brüchigkeit des Zustandes erweist. Bewußtes Handeln ist zwar eine Vorbedingung für die Entstehung von Regeln, wie ich sie hier beschreibe. Aber die auf Abruf funktionierenden Ordnungsmuster der „zweiten Natur" sind nicht einfach Produkt freier Entscheidungen. Sie halten, wie der Name sagt, eine Mitte zwischen primärer Naturhaftigkeit und ihrer Wiedergewinnung nach dem Ausfall.

Die Bemerkungen über den Regelausdruck und über das konstitutive Mißlingen-Können ergeben eine Beschreibung des Charakteristischen der Regel. Zwischen beiden besteht ein Zusammenhang, der sich weder bei Naturgesetzen, noch bei Handlungen findet. Der kritische Punkt, wenn jemand eine Regel verfehlt, ist so zu beschreiben. Ein bisher problemlos funktionierender Ausdruck wird plötzlich nicht mehr auf die erwartete Weise verwendet. Vorher war er eigentlich kein „Ausdruck", sondern Funktionsmoment eines quasi-natürlichen Zusammenhangs. Erst im Nachhinein erweist er sich als „bloß" regelgeleitet, indem er in ein vereinzeltes syntaktisches Gebilde und eine enttäuschte Erwartung zerfällt. Die stillschweigenden Antizipationen werden unterbrochen und kommen dadurch erst in ihrer unentbehrlichen Funktion ans Licht. An diesem kritschen Punkt dissoziieren sich zwei elementare Bestandteile der Regel: ein Sprachausdruck und intentionales Verhalten. Die Semantik knüpft am Ausdruck an und reicht ins Feld der Intentionalität.

3. Regeln implizieren Vorstellungen

Ein terminus technicus aus der formalen Semantik eignet sich auch gut zur Erfassung der beschriebenen Situation: „intendierte Interpretation". Syntaktische Systeme werden gewöhnlich auf bestimmte Verwendungen hin konstruiert. Die blanken Zeichengestalten schreiben aber nicht zwingend vor, wie sie interpretiert werden sollen, darum ist es meistens möglich, ihnen auch unvorhergesehene Deutungen zu geben. Übertragen auf den Regelausdruck bedeutet das: auch er steht im Rahmen eines bestimmten − pragmatischen − Kontextes, ohne ihn von sich aus determinieren zu können. Das fällt erst auf (und der Ausdruck fällt damit aus der Praxis), wenn sich nicht-intendierte Interpretationen einstellen, entweder formalsemantische Modelle mit unvorhergesehenen Eigenschaften, die dennoch die Formeln erfüllen, oder, im Fall der Regeln, nichtbeabsichtigte Verhaltensweisen. Semantik ist kein unselbständiger Appendix an die Syntax, und einer Regel zu folgen reduziert sich nicht auf kausale Initialbedingungen. Um dieses Ergebnis festhalten zu können, müssen wir uns des Vokabulars des Vorstellungsdenkens bedienen.

Semantik wird gewöhnlich ohne Rekurs auf die Struktur des menschlichen Bewußtseins betrieben. An der entscheidenden Stelle, an der es darum geht, die Flexibilität von Interpretation zu gewährleisten, ohne die die ganze Disziplin sich auflöst, drängt sich der Sachverhalt der Intentionalität dennoch auf. Die (möglicherweise fehlgehende) Absicht, einen Ausdruck mit einer bestimmten Bedeutung zu versehen (Intention im engeren, handlungstheoretischen Sinn), ist ein Sonderfall der menschlichen Fähigkeit, sich − abgesehen von seiner faktischen Existenz − etwas in vielfachen Modifikationen vorzustellen (Intentionalität erkenntnistheoretisch verstanden). Das Vorstellungsmoment, das sich gleichsam unbeobachtet in die semantische Ausdrucksweise eingeschlichen hat, verweist auf einen unentbehrlichen Bezug. Ohne die Diskrepanz zwischen intendierten und nicht-intendierten Interpretationen gibt es keine Semantik und diese wieder hängt daran, daß Zeichen nur im Rahmen institutionalisierter Erwartungen auf das Bezeichnete bezogen sind. Intentionalität ist ein Vermögen, das verhindert, daß die Ausrichtung des Menschen auf Gegenstände und Sachverhalte zum unwiderruflichen Aufgehen im kausalen Weltablauf führt. Vorstellungen überbrücken die Kluft, die der Abbruch naturhafter Zusammenhänge aufreißt. Darum sind wir beim Versuch, die Regel zwischen Naturgesetz und Einzelhandlung zu situieren, notgedrungen auf das Vorstellungsvermögen gestoßen. Bewußtsein entsteht aus der Erfahrung der möglichen Inkongruenz von Weltablauf und Sich-Verhalten zur Welt. Seine Konstitution ist, wie jene des Regelfolgens, als nachträgliche Entdeckung eines anfangs nicht bemerkten Bruchs in Selbstverständlichkeiten zu beschreiben. Und es liegt nahe, intentionale Zustände ganz allgemein als Bedingungen einzelner Praktiken, wie des Regelfolgens, zu denken.

Die Frage, ob Semantik oder Erkenntnistheorie, die Henne oder das Ei, zuerst war, haben wir eingeklammert. Dafür wurde eine Auskunft darüber versprochen, was das Verhältnis von Regel und Intentionalität für die blockhafte Gegenüberstellung von Natur und Freiheit sagt. Zwei Aspekte sind hervorzuheben. Erstens wird sie durch das Mittelglied der Regel abgeschwächt. Das vorsichtige Gegeneinander-Ausspielen der beiden Faktoren, mit dem der Kern des Phänomens herausgearbeitet wurde, deutet darauf hin, daß der glatte Dualismus der Begriffe sich rasch in eine theoretische Doppelstrategie verwandelt, wenn es um diffizilere Bestimmungen geht. Das Regelfolgen als quasi-gesetzliches, der Handlung verwandtes menschliches Verhalten ist dazu geeignet, die flankierenden Abstraktionen, auf die man sich gerne allein verläßt, in konstruktiv-deskriptive Aufgaben zu verwickeln. So gesehen ergibt sich ein Nutzen für häufig verdächtigte Begriffe. Diese Betrachtung kann man zweitens auch anders akzentuieren. Die Phänomene des Regelfolgens und des Bewußtseins sind näher an der alltäglichen Erfahrung, als die abstakteren und abgeleiteten Territorien von Natur und Freiheit. Vielleicht sollte man, statt sie durch intentional gebrochene Naturabläufe zu erklären, umgekehrt den Sinn von „Naturgesetz" und „Vorstellung" von ihnen her entwickeln. Der Beginn der Explikation wäre dann, daß sich herausstellt, daß man sich täuschen kann. Von da aus würden Naturgesetze als nicht täuschungsanfällig und Vorstellungen als jene Konstruktionen eingeführt, bezüglich derer Täuschung möglich ist. Das klingt nicht nur nach Kartesianismus, es ist auch so gemeint. Die beschränkte Zuverlässigkeit von Regeln ist wie jene des Erkenntnisvermögens, die Descartes diskutiert, ein unübersehbarer Ausgangspunkt zur Entfaltung der Frage, was es heißt, als Mensch auf der Welt zu sein.

* * *

FREGE, SENSE, AND PRIVACY

John M. Connolly
Smith College, Northampton

In his pioneering struggle against the psychologism rampant in his day Frege introduced in his middle period the distinction between the sense (*Sinn*) and reference (*Bedeutung*) of words and sentences. The former notion was designed to embody two properties of equal importance for Frege's theory of language:

a) to be the *determiner of reference*; i.e. to be that the grasp of which enables the speaker to determine (taking here the case of proper names), for any given object x, whether x is the bearer of that name. And,

b) to be *intersubjective*; i.e. a sense is neither mine nor thine, is not in the mind (or brain), but is rather an objective entity which *many* speakers can grasp, and which is common to the word and all its synonyms, in whatever language.

I will argue that isolating a notion of sense with these two properties proves to be surprisingly elusive. In particular the Fregean program runs afoul−ironically−of psychological concepts, two of which−pain and intention−are examined in some detail below. The malaise arises from two separate sources: from the *private nature* of the referent (pains), and from the referent's *non-availability* (intentions).

I: Pains

Frege's main interest was, of course, the foundations of arithmetic, and he was concerned to combat attempts to identify the meanings of number-words with mental entities such as ideas. His main criterion of the mental seems to be 'that which is necessarily private'. Two people, he writes, "are not prevented from grasping the same sense; but they cannot have the same idea." Indeed, "one need have no scruples in speaking simply of *the* sense [of a word], whereas in the case of an idea one must, strictly speaking, add to whom it belongs and at what time."[1]

In his late essay "The Thought" Frege discusses, at some length, 'ideas' (*Vorstellungen*), by which he means "sense-impressions, the creations of one's imagination, sensations, feelings and moods, a world of inclinations, wishes and decisions".[2] These, though private, are nonetheless entities or 'objects' in Frege's technical terminology; and we can therefore form proper names to refer to them, e.g. 'Mabel's backache (at t2)'. But Frege's rather intuitive claims about 'ideas' imply a quite serious conflict between the properties he assigned to his theoretical notion of sense, for if the senses of idea-names determine their reference, then these senses *cannot* be intersubjective entities. Let us see how this conflict arises.

Pains are 'ideas' for Frege, and they are therefore private: "No one else has my pain" (ibid. p. 68). Take Mabel's expression 'my backache (at t2)'. Its reference is an idea, an entity 'experienced directly' by Mabel alone. Now the sense of Mabel's words 'my backache (at t2)' is by definition that (abstract entity) the grasp of which enables one to determine for any object x whether x is the pain in question. But who *can* grasp this sense? Can Mabel's husband Mel? Frege claims that a word such as 'pain' is "applicable only in the area" of the consciousness of the idea's bearer. Thus, since necessarily Mel can never be in a position to determine for any object whether it is that pain of Mabel's, he *cannot* grasp the sense of that expression. If privacy, i.e. what belongs "only in the area of my consciousness", means anything, it means that only Mabel can, in this Fregean manner, determine whether any particular entity is the referent of those words. Thus only she can understand them, their sense can be grasped by her alone, and is therefore not intersubjective. Hence at least in the case of sensation-words, where the referent is private to the speaker, senses cannot perform both of the functions Frege wants them to perform. (Compare *PI*, I, 293)

II: Intentions

A related case, that of intentions, shows that understanding meaning need not involve the grasp of a reference-determining sense at all, for the referent of 'intention' seems, surprisingly, to play no role in its use.

Consider the following real-life example: In making a batik on the back porch Marianne was removing wax from a piece of treated cloth by ironing the cloth between pages of newspaper. Her neighbor Betty watched in puzzlement from her window. Unfamiliar with the batik-process, Betty was too polite to ask her young neighbor, a German immigrant, what she was doing. Later she told her astonished friends that the German *Hausfrau*'s love of order could not be surpassed, they even ironed the newspapers!

Betty was mistaken: Marianne was *not* "ironing the newspaper". We might say she was ironing *on* the newspaper as part of her batiking. Betty imputes the *wrong* intention to Marianne's ironing behavior, i.e. the intention to neaten the newspapers by ironing them. We quite unproblematically use phrases such as "Marianne's intention to neaten the newspapers" as definite descriptions. Nonetheless the ability to determine whether a given entity is the referent of a phrase such as "the intention *x*" plays no role, either for the agent or for others, in the everyday use of such phrases.

Anscombe's investigation [3] showed that we speak of an agent's intention to do such-and-such (or in doing such-and-such) when e.g. the agent can say, and *not* on the basis of observation, what s/he is doing or will do. This ability amounts to (practical) knowledge when it is based on the know-how of the agent. In our example Marianne can say, without appealing to self-observation, that she is ironing on the newspaper in order to complete the batik; and she is able to have these intentions because she has learned the technique of batik-making.

Applying this analysis of intention to Marianne's grasp of the sense of the expression 'my own intention to iron on the newspaper', we must say that her understanding of these words consists in her ability to say what she would *do*, i.e. iron on the newspaper, if she had the intention in question. Now, can we think of such a grasp in Fregean terms, i.e. as the ability to identify the object—if there is one—designated by the referring expression? Well, what is that object? The intention, of course. But *it* is not an occurrence, process, or state of the agent's mind. (Compare *Zettel*, 45) It is, we saw, practical knowledge, the ability to say what one is doing or will do, where one justifies the description or prediction, if at all, by appeal to reasons for acting, as opposed to evidence or reasons for thinking the prediction true.

Let us compare Marianne's grasp of the sense of the following four expressions: i) '2+2'; ii) 'my own left arm'; iii) 'the pain in my shoulder'; iv) 'my own intention to iron on the newspaper'. Marianne's grasp of '2+2' consists in her ability to calculate the value of the plus-function for the argument-pair $\{2, 2\}$, i.e. to find her way to the value 4. Her grasp of the sense of 'my own left arm' consists in her ability to show, point to, etc. her left arm. In each of these cases grasp of the expression's sense consists in an ability to identify a referent in the public arena.

With 'the pain in my left shoulder' we enter what Frege would regard as the realm of private objects: no one else but the speaker can grasp the sense of this expression. For the speaker, however, grasp of the sense would seem to consist in the ability to identify the sensation in question if there is one. Once again the referent plays a central role in the understanding of the expression (suppressing for the moment Wittgensteinian scruples about private languages).

When, on the other hand, we consider the referring expression 'my own intention to iron on the newspaper', we find that Marianne's grasp of its sense consists in her ability to *say what she would do* if she had the intention in question. I.e., Marianne's understanding of the words manifests itself in a conditional predictive capacity, where what is predicted is her hypothetical intentional actions. But saying what one would do is an *expression* of the possible intention, not the possible intention itself. That is, grasping the sense in question consists not in identifying an object, public or private, but rather in the ability to manifest one's hypothetical knowledge of one's own possible actions. (Compare *TLP* 5.631; and *PI* I, 615, 618, 620)

The case of intentions, when viewed through the lens of Frege's semantics, reveals nicely an ambiguity in the notion of an entity. In a formal sense an entity is whatever we make assertions about. Since we make assertions about intentions, they are indeed entities in this sense. But more materially, we think of entities as something objective, present, discoverable, (in principle) available. In this second sense one's present intentions are not entities *for oneself*. Frege called the sense "die Art des Gegebenseins der Bedeutung", the mode of presentation of the referent. But our own intentions are not, we might say, *gegeben*, not presented to us, despite the fact that we as agents can say what they are.

In conclusion: it seems that Frege's break with the psychologism, internalism, and individualism of post-Cartesian philosophy remains curiously incomplete. The case of pains shows that his notion of sense cannot be quite generally *both* intersubjective *and* the determiner of reference, while the case of intentions shows that grasp of sense cannot quite generally be equated with the ability to identify the referent. Nonetheless, the basic insight of Frege's semantics, that sense must be intersubjective and distinct from reference, is not shaken by these criticisms. Having set off boldly across unexplored terrain Frege reaches an unexpected crossroads: one fork leads back toward Descartes and the subjectivity of meaning, the other further into the unknown and a more thoroughgoing uncoupling of sense from reference than Frege envisaged.

ENDNOTES

1 Frege, Gottlob, "Über Sinn und Bedeutung" ["On Sense and Reference"]. *Zeitschrift für Philosophie und philosophische Kritik*. NF 100 (1892), pp. 25–50. My translation.
2 Frege, Gottlob, "Der Gedanke". Eine logische Untersuchung" ["The Thought"]. *Beiträge zur Philosophie des deutschen Idealismus I* (1918–19), pp. 58–77. My translation.
3 Anscombe, G. E. M., *Intention* (Oxford 1957).

* * *

„REALISTISCHE" REPRÄSENTATIONEN VON „MENTALEN PHÄNOMENEN":ZUR SITUATION DER „SITUATION SEMANTICS"

Rainer P. Born
Universität Linz

0. Vorbemerkungen

In ihrem Buch „Situations and Attitudes" geben Jon Barwise und John Perry einen Vorgeschmack auf die von ihnen entworfene und so getaufte „situation semantics". Letztere soll dazu dienen eine neuartige, von ihnen als „realistisch" apostrophierte Semantik „natürlicher Sprachen" zu konstruieren. Das Prädikat „realistisch" bezieht sich in diesem Fall vor allem auf das Material aus dem die „Bedeutung" (i. S. des Informationsgehaltes) von sprachlichen Äußerungen aufgebaut und „an-gegeben" werden soll. Den Kern dieses „Baumateriales" bilden „reale Situationen" (mit Individuen, Relationen und Ortsangaben als wesentlichen Bestandteilen). Auf solche Situationen „beziehen" wir uns (referieren wir), wenn wir mit sprachlichen Äußerungen Informationen übermitteln wollen und anhand von solchen Situationen versuchen wir uns die Bedeutung (den Informationsgehalt) von zu interpretierenden sprachlichen Äußerungen klar zu machen. Die (sprachliche) Bedeutung eines Ausdruckes (einer Äußerung) wird daher im Rahmen der „situation semantics" (grob gesprochen) als „Beziehung" (i. S. einer mathematischen Relation) zwischen verschiedenen Typen von Situationen, nämlich sprachlichen Äußerungen „u" und bestimmten, aus Ereignissen (oder Ereignisabfolgen) bestehenden Situationen „s", sowohl (re-)konstruktiv (theoretisch) analysiert, als auch (praktisch) angegeben.

Auf Frege, sowie auf mögliche Einwände wird in den ersten Kapiteln des Buches eingegangen. Eine Einbettung des Ansatzes der „situation semantics" in die „klassische" (formale) Semantik (bzw. mathematische Modelltheorie i. S. von A. Tarski) ist möglich. (Sie wird unten angedeutet.) − Im vorliegenden Kontext wird jedoch vor allem auf das zehnte Kapitel des erwähnten Buches eingegangen. Dort beschäftigen sich die Autoren mit der Repräsentation von „mental states and events." Daran anknüpfend läßt sich die Frage stellen, welche Bedeutung die vorgeschlagene „realistische" Semantik natürlicher Sprachen für das philosophische Problem der „mentalen Phänomene" hat und welche Bedeutung dem Diktum von Barwise/Perry zukommt „that there is much more meaning and information in the world and less in the head than the traditional view of meaning assumed".

1. Zum Hintergrund

Als Anknüpfungspunkt für das philosophische Thema der mentalen Phänomene kann die im Alltagsdenken verwurzelte (?) Unterscheidung zwischen „physischen" und „mentalen" Phänomenen dienen. Als Beispiele für letztere gelten u.a. Meinungen, Überzeugungen, Absichten, Träume, Schmerz etc. Probleme aus dieser Unterscheidung ergeben sich vor allem aus einer (philosophischen) Reflexion der Konsequenzen (bzw. Implikationen), die einen wesentlichen Bestandteil der (keineswegs abgeschlossenen) Diskussion des Leib-Seele-Problems (auch in neuerer Zeit) ausmachen, wie z.B. ein kausaler Einfluß des Mentalen.

In der vorliegenden Arbeit konzentrieren wir uns allerdings vor allem auf den in der analytischen Philosophie vollzogenen Themenwechsel von den „Phänomenen" zu den „Sätzen über die Phänomene" (den „semantischen ascent" nach W. O. v. Quine). Dadurch wird die Frage nach der Bedeutung der „sprachlichen Repräsentation" des Mentalen besonders virulent und auch die Begründung des Themenwechsels, sowie die Rück-Interpretation des Ergebnisses der sprachanalytischen Untersuchung für das ursprüngliche Problem muß bedacht werden.

Gilbert Ryle trat bekanntlich dafür ein, daß sich unsere mentalistischen (sprachlichen) Ausdrücke überhaupt nicht auf einen vorborgenen Bereich innerer Phänomene beziehen. Er gab die „Semantik" derartiger Ausdrücke dadurch an, daß er argumentierte, daß wir, wenn wir ein mentalistisches Vokabular benutzen (um die mentalen Zustände einer menschlichen Person zu repräsentieren), uns in Wirklichkeit auf das intelligente Verhalten dieser Person beziehen. – In der (kritischen) Diskussion führte dies einerseits zu der dogmatischen Selbstüberschätzung der Philosphie, nach der z. B. die empirische Wissenschaft unsere gewöhnlichen, mentalistischen Begriffe weder revidieren noch verbessern kann und sich andererseits an das halten müsse, was die sprachphilosophische Analyse unseres „gewöhnlichen mentalistischen Diskurses" zu Tage fördert. – Erst durch eine Naturalisierung des Mentalen und damit durch den wissenschaftlichen Realismus konnte diese Position aufgeweicht werden. Im Anschluß an Quines Kritik an einer unverrückbaren Unterscheidung zwischen analytischen und synthetischen Sätzen mußte auch die strikte Trennung zwischen Begriffsanalyse und empirischer Wissenschaft (insbesondere im Hinblick auf die Natur oder das Wesen des Mentalen) revidiert und neu interpretiert werden. – Durch den Ansatz der „situation semantics" sollte es möglich sein, sowohl eine „realistische" Semantik mentaler Terme angeben zu können, als auch dem wissenschaftlichen Realismus genüge zu tun, d. h. die dogmatische These zu widerlegen, daß unsere gewöhnlichen Meinungen über das Mentale unkorrigierbar seien. (Eine im Lehnstuhl durchgeführte, sprachanaytische Untersuchung unseres mentalistischen Vokabulars kann kaum mehr als eine Kodifizierung einer „Common-Sense-Theorie" mentaler Phänomene sein. Das Thema der Philosophie sollte, i. S. von Wilfried Sellars, viel eher die Spannung zwischen unserem „Common-Sense-Weltbild" und demjenigen Weltbild sein, das sich aus den fortschreitenden Formal- und Naturwissenschaften ergibt. Dazu bedarf es aber auch seitens der Philosophie einer „repräsentativen" Analyse der Struktur der arbeitenden Einzelwissenschaften und damit der faktischen Begründungspraktiken letzterer; cf. naturalistische Erkenntnistheorien.)

2. *Zur Situation Semantics*

Wie schon oben angedeutet, geht es darum, Bedeutungen φ als eine Beziehung (Relation [φ]) zwischen (sprachlichen) *Äußerungen* u und *Situationen* s zu konstruieren. Genaugenommen müßte man an dieser Stelle den mathematischen Gebrauch und damit die *technische* Bedeutung von Relationen explizieren, denn diese wird sowohl in der Notation (u, s) $\in [\varphi]_G$, d.h. das Paar (u, s) ist Element des Graphen $[\varphi]_G$ der Relation [φ]), als auch von der Sache her den Überlegungen von Barwise und Perry zugrundegelegt. Äußerungen und Situationen werden dann selbstverständlich noch feiner analysiert. Erstere werden in *Diskurs*-Situationen d und den Bezug c eines Sprechers auf eine Situation (speakers *c*onnections) aufgespalten, letztere in ein „*setting*" σ (of the scene, zusammen mit einem *A*gens a) mit einem *E*reignis e (described situation). Entscheidend, vor allem für die (Bedeutungs-) Analyse mentaler Wendungen, sind die „constraints", die man an den Graphen der Relation [φ] anlegen muß, um so die zulässigen Bezugssituationen (als Referenzobjekte) einschränken und bestimmen zu können.

Die Bedeutung eines Satzes S, wie z. B. „Jackie is biting Molly" (wobei Jackie und Molly Hunde sein sollen) wird dadurch analysiert und angegeben, daß die abstrakte Beschreibung (oder Analyse) „d, c [IS BITING MOLLY] a, e" genau dann zutrifft, wenn es in der Situation e am Ort l ein Agens a gibt, so daß „biting: a, Molly" der Fall ist. MOLLY bezieht sich mittels „c" auf die reale Molly [Molly = c (Molly)] und l [bestimmt durch c (IS)] ist der Ort der Handlung, der mit der Diskurs-Situation l_d zu verknüpfen ist. Bei „Joe *believes* that Jackie is biting Molly" hingegen muß die Relation „u [JOE BELIEVES . . .] s" durch „believe options" so eingeschränkt werden, daß wir (Typen von) Situationen identifizieren können, auf die sich die fragliche Äußerung u bezieht, wodurch wir dann das Verhalten von Joe in einer (solchen) Situation prognostizieren können und die Äußerung u einen Sinn bekommt. (Auf weitere technische Details kann hier nicht eingegangen werden.)

3. *Kritische Analyse*

Am platzsparendsten kann man sich die „Bedeutung" der „situation semantics" in einem Diagramm (more geometrico) klar machen.

explanative Analyse   *konkrete Anweisungen*

zur REPRÄSENTATION von Bedeutung   zur ANGABE von Bedeutung

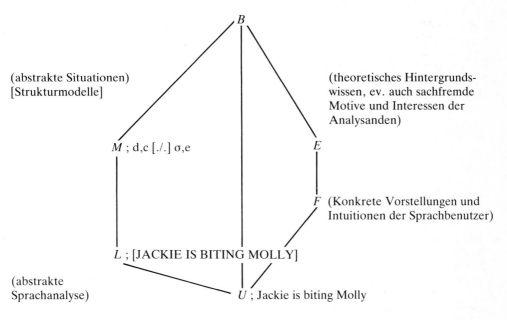

Bedeutung (Information) wird als eine „Beziehung" (Relation) zwischen U und B aufgefaßt. Die *abstrakte Bedeutung* einer Äußerung u wird durch Interpretation der abstrakten Analyse [./.] über abstrakten Situationen (Strukturmodellen) *konstruiert* und mit konkreten Situationen in Zusammenhang gebracht. Die konkrete Bedeutung einer Äußerung wird also dadurch angegeben, daß *solche* Typen von konkreten (realen) Situationen in B, und zwar in Einklang mit der abstrakten Analyse in L, M, konstruiert (bzw. identifiziert) werden, auf die man sich

599

in einer natürlichen (realistischen) Weise mit den konkreten Äußerungen aus *U* darauf beziehen kann. Den abstrakten Situationen aus *M* entsprechen konkrete Vorstellungen der Sprachbenutzer, z. B. Alltagsintuitionen über das Mentale (im Diagramm durch *F* bezeichnet). Diese Vorstellungen werden von den Sprachbenutzern zur Klassifikation von Realität benutzt.

Der Alltags-Realismus dieser „Bedeutungs*analysen* und *-angaben*" besteht darin, daß die theoretisch-explanativen Begriffsbildungen in *M* in gewissem Sinn als unmittelbare Beschreibungen der konkreten Vorstellungen der Sprachbenutzer angesehen werden. Der wissenschaftliche Realismus hingegen, der dem Ansatz zugrundeliegt, kann darin zum Ausdruck kommen, daß in die *abstrakten Situationsanalysen* der theoretisch-explanative Wissensstand der Forschung (etwa in bezug auf das Mentale), im Diagramm durch *E* dargestellt, eingehen kann und bei der Selektion von Situationen zum (vermittelnden) Aufbau von sprachlicher Bedeutung (bzw. Information) auf eine solche Weise lenkend eingreifen kann, daß eine Korrektur und *positive Veränderung* von Alltagsvorstellungen (etwa über das Mentale) möglich wird. Im Diagramm wurden diese Wechselbeziehungen sichtbar gemacht. In der „situation semantics" wird darauf jedoch zu wenig eingegangen.

LITERATUR

Barwise, Jon/Perry, John, Situations and Attitudes (Cambridge/London 1983).
Bieri, Peter (Hrsg.), *Analytische Philosophie des Geistes* (Königstein/Ts. 1981).
Born, Rainer Paul, „Schizo-Semantik: Provokationen zum Thema Bedeutungstheorien und Wissenschaftsphilosophie im Allgemeinen", *Conceptus* XVII (1983), Nr. 40/41, pp. 101–116.

* * *

12. Psychoanalyse

12. Psychoanalysis

PSYCHOANALYSE ZWISCHEN PSYCHOLOGIE UND PHILOSOPHIE

H. Strotzka
Universität Wien

Die Begegnungen der Psychoanalyse mit Philosophie und akademischer Psychologie waren meist nicht glücklich. Auf der einen Seite wurde die Wissenschaftlichkeit der Psychoanalyse von beiden Seiten bestritten, andererseits hat keine Philosophie oder Psychologie die geistige Welt so erschüttert und beeinflußt wie gerade die Psychoanalyse. Ihre Konzepte sind zumindestens in allen westlichen Industrienationen völlig selbstverständlich in alle Lebensbereiche integriert und zum Teil auch in den allgemeinen Sprachgebrauch eingedrungen. Dies hat allerdings auch zu einer Vulgarisierung und Banalisierung geführt.

Nur die großen Religionen und der Maxismus haben Geschichte und aktuelles Leben stärker beeinflußt. Daß die Psychoanalyse auch von diesen beiden Richtungen nicht geschätzt wurde, hängt allerdings nicht mit der mangelnden Wissenschaftlichkeit zusammen, sondern mit der ihr immanenten Ideologiekritik, die sie nach beiden Richtungen verdächtig macht.

Die Philosophie hat wie Odo Marquard (1981) gemeint hat, eine Kompetenzreduktion erlitten, aber durch eine Reduktionskompensation eine Art „Inkompetenzkompensationskompetenz" entwickelt. Die experimentelle akademische Psychologie liegt mit ihren Laborversuchen oft zuweit von der Komplexität des realen Lebens entfernt. Da sich die Zahl der Variablen nicht entsprechend kontrollieren läßt, behandelt sie zwar wissenschaftlich befriedigend oft irrelevante Probleme.

Es ist ein Irrtum anzunehmen, daß die psychoanalytische Theorie ein monolithischer Block sei. Derzeit existieren nebeneindander folgende Konzepte:

1. das klassisch Freudianische Modell, etwa der 1945 erschienenen Neurosentheorie von Fenichel entsprechend,
2. die Ich-Psychologie repräsentiert vor allem durch Anna Freud, Heinz Hartmann und E. H. Erikson (siehe das Buch von D. Rapaport, Struktur der psychoanalytischen Theorie, 1970),
3. die Lehre von den frühen Objektbeziehungen (Melanie Klein, Fairbairn, Winicott und andere),
4. die linguistisch-strukturalistische Konzeption (Lacan, Lorenzer und andere),
5. die Selbsttheorie von Heinz Kohut, der das übliche Konfliktmodell weitgehend aufgegeben hat, und
6. entwickeln sich vielleicht aus der neuen Narzißmuskonzeption von Kernberg oder der Über-Ich-Psychologie von Rangell, der informationstheoretischen Auffassung von Peterfreund oder auch der Entwicklungen bei Roy Schafer und Gedo ebenfalls neue Theoriesysteme.

Durch alle diese theoretischen Schulen geht eine Bruchlinie durch, die durch Akzeptierung oder Ablehnung des Todestriebs charakterisiert ist. Die Haltung zum Todestrieb sollte eigentlich schwerwiegende Konsequenzen für die jeweilige Weltanschauung haben, dies ist aber offenbar kaum der Fall und hängt vielleicht mit einer gewissen Philosophieaversion der Psychoanalytiker zusammen. Die eigene Einstellung entspricht einer eklektischen Auffassung zwischen Ich-Psychologie, Kernberg sowie Rangell. Der Todestriebspekulation kann ich mich ebenfalls nicht anschließen.

Allen Psychoanalytikern sind jedoch folgende recht gut empirisch unterbaute Hypothesen gemeinsam:

1. Die Psychoanalyse betrachtet sich als Verhaltenswissenschaft, die Verhalten zum Teil zu erklären, zum Teil zu verstehen versucht, also auch hermeneutisch aufzufassen ist.
2. Verhalten ist zum erheblichen Teil unbewußt determiniert, wobei Überdeterminierung und zirkuläre Systemzusammenhänge gegenüber einer linearen Kausalität ein Verständnis erschweren. Dadurch erklärt sich auch zum Teil die lange Dauer psychoanalytischer Prozesse.
3. Die Bedeutung der Sexualität (besonders in ihrer frühkindlichen Ausprägung) stützt sich auf hinreichende klinische Beobachtung.
4. Das gleiche kann für die Entwicklungspsychologie mit dem Wechsel der wichtigsten erogenen Zonen (oral, anal und genital) festgestellt werden.
5. Die Vorgänge der Fehlleistungen, Abwehrmechanismen, von Verdrängung, Widerstand und Übertragung (natürlich auch Gegenübertragung) lassen sich ebenfalls sowohl klinisch als auch im Alltag zwingend nachweisen.
6. Das gleiche gilt auch noch immer zum Teil für die Traumlehre, befriedigender noch für das Verständnis der Ambivalenz und des Narzißmus, selbst die Lehre von den frühen Objektbeziehungen wird durch die Arbeit mit Psychotikern hinreichend begründet.
7. Über die Therapie läßt sich sagen, daß die Standardtechnik (sogenannte große Analyse) nur für wenige Patienten notwendig ist, aber als Forschungs- und Ausbildungsinstrument unverändert gültig bleibt. Sonst ist eine Reihe von anderen psychotherapeutischen Techniken aufgetaucht und in der Psychoanalyse selbst finden sich Verkürzungen etwa in Form der Fokaltherapie von Malan, Gruppentherapie und teilweise Familientherapie.

Die vergleichende Psychotherapieforschung versucht derzeit eine Differentialindikation für die wichtigsten Behandlunbgsmethoden zu entwickeln, wobei das ethische Prinzip der Patientenzentriertheit im Vordergrund steht. Ich wende mich nun der Akzeptant der Psychoanalyse durch die Philosophie zu. 1958 beim 2. jährlichen Treffen des New Yorker University Institute of Philosophy in Washington (Sidney Hook, 1959) sind prominente Psychoanalytiker auf enorme Abwehr gestoßen, die in Ernest Nagels Verdikt „not proven" mündete. Der Versuch von Morris Lazerowitz, Philosophen und ihre Arbeit einer psychoanalytischen Betrachtung zu unterziehen, begegnete einer Abwehr von Haß und Wut. Für Wittgensteins Einstellung zur Psychoanalyse ist charakteristisch, daß er seinem Freunde Con Drury die Traumdeutung Freuds mit sehr positiven Kommentaren schenkte, aber dazu erklärte, daß er sich selbst nicht einer Analyse unterziehen möchte. „He did not think it right to reveal all one's thoughts to a stranger. Psychoanalysis as presented by Freud was irreligious. It was a very dangerous prodecure; I know of a case where it did infinite harm" (Nedo (1983), S. 283).

Wittgenstein fühlte also eine Gefahr, die von der Psychoanalyse allgemein und für ihn persönlich ausgehen könnte. Auch der Analytiker würde eher annehmen, daß eine Analyse für ihn bei seiner äußerst labilen Persönlichkeit problematisch gewesen wäre.

Eine neuere retrospektive psychoanalytische Betrachtung eines Philosophen ist die von Lewis S. Feuer über Kant (in: Hanly und Lazerowitz, 1970). Der Autor weist auf die ausgeprägte Sexualangst und Abwehr dieses pedantisch, phobisch-zwanghaften Menschen hin. Hippel berichtet, daß Kant oft sagte, wenn ein Mensch alles, was er denkt, sagen oder schreiben müßte dann gäbe es auf Gottes Erde nichts Schrecklicheres als den Menschen. Kant hatte eine harte, unglückliche Kindheit, die ihn melancholisch und hypochondrisch machte. Es ist kaum daran zu zweifeln, daß sein Denksystem von dieser dynamischen Entwicklung geprägt war. Daß auch Nietzsche, „der ängstliche Adler", wie Ross ihn genannt hat, seine Schwäche überkompensierte und daß Schopenhauers unglückliche Mutterbeziehung in seinem System sich zum Teil widerspiegelt, kann kaum bezweifelt werden.

Wenn man Sidney Hooks Buch über Psychoanalyse (1958) mit Richard Wollheim und Janos Hopkins (1982) vergleicht, dann besteht zwar auf Seite der Philosophie eine nicht ganz unberechtigte Skepsis vor manchen Ungereimtheiten der psychoanalytischen Theorie, aber es breitet sich auch eine weit größere Kenntnis aus und es besteht ein besseres Diskussionsklima. Es wird immer wieder die Ansicht Poppers zitiert, daß Psychoanalyse keine Wissenschaft sei, weil sie alles erkläre und daher nicht falsifizierbar sei. Stimmt etwa ein Analysand einer Deutung zu, kann dies eine echte Einsicht oder ein Übertragungsphänomen sein. Widerspricht er, so kann dies ein Widerstand gegen die Aufhebung der Verdrängung sein, gerade weil die Deutung so wichtig ist. Der Psychoanalytiker behalte jedenfalls immer recht. Hier werden inadäquate Kriterien an den psychoanalytischen Prozeß angelegt. Es handelt sich um einen Langzeitvorgang, Richtigkeit oder Falschheit der Deutung stellt sich erst heraus, wenn weitere Assoziationen und/oder Verhaltensänderungen sie bestätigen oder entkräftigen. Psychoanalytische Sätze sind immer nur probabilistisch, wie es entsprechend der Überdetermination und Ambivalenz zu erwarten ist.

Über die philosophische Haltung von Psychoanalytikern selbst gibt es leider keine Literatur. Ich versuche seit Jahren ein allerdings unsystematisches und nicht repräsentatives Bild darüber zu machen und bin überrascht, daß gegen meine Erwartung nicht vorwiegend liberale Pragmatiker, Neopositivisten und kritische Empiriker überwiegen, sondern daß sich eine weite Palette aller Möglichkeiten ergibt. Aus Diskretionsgründen lassen sich keine Namen anführen, ein durch seine eigenen Veröffentlichungen gut dokumentiertes Beispiel ist aber Igor Caruso gewesen, der Gründer der Arbeitsgemeinschaft für Tiefenpsychologie, der als existentialistischer Katholik begann und als Marxist Blochscher Prägung endete, dabei aber trotzdem immer ein orthodoxer Freudianer blieb.

Es scheint so zu sein, als ob Analytiker in therapeutischen und Ausbildungsanalysen die Tendenz haben, weltanschauliche und religiöse Problematik aus der Arbeit eher auszuschließen. Dies ist vertretbar, wenn auf diesem Gebiet keine neurotischen Fixierungen bestehen, was allerdings nach meinem Eindurck selten der Fall ist.

Die Beziehungen einzelner Psychotherapeuten zu Philosphen sind in einem sehr guten Überblickswerk von Eckart Wiesenhütter (1979) zusammengefaßt und sollten dort nachgelesen werden. Aus diesem Buch möchte ich nur ein charakteristisches Zitat von dem Theologen, Philosphen und Psychoanalytiker Wucherer-Huldenfeld wiedergeben:

> Der Metaphysik geht es nicht allein um die von Freud unterstellte illusionäre Wahrheit der Gesamtwirklichkeit, Philosophie ist nicht nur Gestalt der Wahrheit, sondern auch der Unwahrheit. Gerade Freud folgend sollte man nicht übersehen, daß die Wahrheit nicht frei von Unwahrheit, nicht frei von wahnhaften Momenten ist. Sein ist immer tiefer, als wir denken können. Sie sich hiermit ergebende Skepsis offenbart von Alters her die Diskrepanz zwischen Denken und Sein. Nur eine monistische Wahnbildung (nach Freud das narzißtische Einheitsverlangen der Philosophie), versuche die Dialektik von Wahrheit und Nichtübereinstimmung zu überspielen. (a.a.O., S. 159)

Der leider vor kurzen so früh verstorbene Michel Foucault hat mit seinem berühmten Satz, daß man aus der Psychoanalyse keine Ethik ableiten könne, meines Erachtens sicher nur zum Teil recht.

Die Psychoanalyse läßt wenigstens verstehen, wie aus Scham- und Schuldgefühl, die von außen an das Kind herangetragen und internalisiert wurden, Moral und Ethik entstehen und wie sich durch Introjektion, Identifikation und Imitation Werte entwickeln und wie wir schließlich die Gefühle des „guten" oder „schlechten" Gewissens verstehen sollen (Strotzka, 1983). Ich glaube in dieser Tour de force gezeigt zu haben, daß die Psychoanalyse mit all ihren Unvollkommenheiten und Schwächen von vielen Philosophen und philosophischen Richtungen als wesentliche Bereicherung zunehmend ernstlich diskutiert und angewendet wird. Zumindestens hat die experimentelle Psychologie nicht in einer annähernd vergleichbaren Weise anregend (manchmal aufregend) auf die Philosophie gewirkt (vielleicht mit Ausnahme von Skinner). Umgekehrt hat die philosophische Kritik leider recht wenig in der Psychoanalyse bewirkt, dies hängt einerseits mit der Auffassung Freuds zusammen, der glaubte naturwissenschaftlich zu arbeiten, andererseits mit der historisch bedingten akademischen Isoliertheit der Psychoanalyse und der Tendenz, jede Kritik als Widerstand zu interpretieren. Für die Zukunft würde ich mir wünschen, daß sich neben den Psychohistorikern auch Psychophilosophen entwickeln, die sich in beiden Disziplinen daheim fühlen. Zahlreiche Ansätze in dieser Richtung sind bereits feststellbar.

LITERATUR

Cavell, St., *The Claim of Reason* (New York 1979).
Fenichel, O., *Psychoanalytische Neurosenlehre* (Olten 1977).
Hanly, Ch., Lazerowitz, M. (Ed.), *Psychoanalysis and Philosophy* (New York 1970).
Hook, S. (Ed.), *Psychoanalysis Scientific Method and Philosophy*, 3. Printing, (N. Y. 1971).
Jacoby, R., *Eine Kritik der konformistischen Psychologie von Adler bis Laing* (Frankfurt a. Main ²1980).
Lazerowitz, M., *The Language of Philosophy. Freud and Wittgenstein* (Dordrecht, Holland 1977).
Marquard, O., *Abschied vom Prinzipiellen* (Stuttgart 1981).
Nedo, M. et al., *Ludwig Wittgenstein*, Bildmonographien (Frankfurt a. M. 1983).
Rapaport, D., *Struktur der psychoanalytischen Theorie* (Stuttgart 1970).
Ross, W., *Der ängstliche Adler* (Stuttgart 1980).
Strotzka, H., *Fairneß, Verantwortung, Fantasie. Eine psychoanalytische Alltagsethik* (Wien 1983).
Wollheim, R., Hopkins J. (Ed.) *Philosophical Essays on Freud* (Cambridge 1982).
Wiesenhütter, E., *Die Begegnung zwischen Philosophie und Tiefenpsychologie* (Darmstadt 1979).

* * *

DAS MOTIVATIONSKONZEPT DER PSYCHOANALYSE: VERSUCH EINER WISSENSCHAFTSTHEORETISCHEN PRÄZISION MIT BEISPIELEN AUS DEM ALLTAG

Walter Toman
Universität Erlangen-Nürnberg

Die wissenschaftstheoretische Kritik am psychoanalytischen Motivationskonzept lautet etwa: Die Annahme eines Liebestriebes oder eines Todestriebes ist redundant. Es genügt, festzustellen, daß Menschen immer wieder sinnliche Befriedigungen mit anderen Menschen suchen beziehungsweise daß sie andere Menschen manchmal schädigen, verletzen oder töten wollen. Der Bezug auf die Effekte, an denen man die Wirksamkeit des Liebes- oder Todestriebes erkennt, erübrigt die Postulierung eines Triebes. Lediglich Freuds Annahme, daß der Liebestrieb in seiner Menge oder Stärke interindividuell verschieden, aber intraindividuell längerfristig oder lebenslänglich konstant ist (Freud 1905, 1916/17, 1920), könnte das Triebkonzept rechtfertigen.

Setzen wir voraus, daß wir als externe Beobachter sinnliche Befriedigungen wie etwa ‚essen‘ oder ‚mit anderen Menschen beisammen sein‘ identifizieren und Beobachtungskonsens erreichen können, etwa darüber, daß sie stattfinden. Setzen wir weiters voraus, daß wir uns auch über die Zeitmessung einig sind, die bis zum Wiedereintritt einer bestimmten Befriedigung vergeht. Nehmen wir schließlich an, daß die Intensität eines Motives mit der Zeit wächst, die seit der letzten Befriedigung desselben vergangen ist (*Intensitätsaxiom*; Toman 1960, 1968, 1978).

Wir können dann die Intensität eines Motivs i als das Verhältnis der Zeit t_i, die seit der letzten Befriedigung vergangen ist, und der durchschnittlichen Zeit $\bar{t}_i$, die zwischen aufeinanderfolgenden Befriedigungen des Motivs i vergeht, bestimmen: $k_i = t_i / \bar{t}_i$. Bei einer Person, die im Durchschnitt alle 4 Stunden ißt und 3 Stunden lang nichts gegessen hat, ist $k_e = 3/4$. Drei Viertel wovon? Von jener Intensität, bei der im Durchschnitt die Befriedigung erfolgt. Bei einer Person, die im Durchschnitt alle 2 Stunden mit Menschen zusammen zu sein pflegt und im Augenblick bereits 6 Stunden ohne Sozialkontakt zugebracht hat, ist $k_s = 6/2$. Die Person ist dreimal so bedürftig nach Sozialkontakt als im Durchschnitt. − Motivintensitäten werden also durch Zeitverhältnisse ausgedrückt.

Die Motivintensität k_i variiert nach dieser Bestimmung zu verschiedenen Beobachtungszeiten für eine gegebene Person offenbar um 1. Andere empirisch sinnvolle Bestimmungen sind möglich, wir bleiben aber der Einfachheit halber bei dieser. Fragt man, wann die Intensität eines Motivs i für die Person alarmierend wird und sich bei Fortdauer der Nichtbefriedigung zur Panik steigern kann, dann liegt als Antwort nahe: Dann, wenn die Intensität des Motivs i die maximale bisher vom Individuum erlebte Intensität übersteigt, nämlich wenn $k_i > k_{i\,max}$.

Motive mit unterschiedlichen Intervallen zwischen aufeinanderfolgenden Motivbefriedigungen wachsen in ihrer Intensität mit verschiedenen Geschwindigkeiten. Ihre Intensitäts-*inkremente* ε_i sind verschieden. Wenn jemand alle 4 Stunden ißt, nimmt sein Motiv zu essen in einer Stunde um ein Viertel jener Intensität zu, bei der durchschnittlich die Befriedigung erfolgt: $\varepsilon_e = 1/\bar{t}_e = 1/4$. Wenn er durchschnittlich 16 Stunden wach ist, ehe er wieder zu schlafen beginnt, nimmt sein Motiv zu schlafen in einer Stunde um ein Sechzehntel der durchschnittlichen Befriedigungsintensität zu: $\varepsilon_{sch} = 1/16$.

Auf Komplikationen, die durch die zeitliche Ausdehnung der Motivbefriedigung selbst oder durch die Unterbrechung aller Motivbefriedigungsrythmen im Schlafzustand entstehen, sei hier nur hingewiesen. Sie sind aber in diesem Motivationskonzept ohne Schwierigkeiten behandelbar.

Aus dem Gesagten ergibt sich folgendes Bild des Motivationsgeschehens: Unter der Vielzahl von Motiven einer Person werden zu einer gegebenen Zeit manche gerade befriedigt, andere warten auf Befriedigung. Laufend gehen befriedigte Motive in den Wartezustand über, und die intensivsten der Motive im Wartezustand kommen als nächste zur Befriedigung. Für Abwechslung ist gesorgt.

In diesem Bild ist die Umgebung der Person als Ort der Motivbefriedigungen zunächst amorph. Alles, was zur Befriedigung jedes beliebigen Motivs von der Umgebung bereitgestellt werden muß, ist auf Abruf vorhanden. Tätigkeiten, die man nicht wegen ihres Befriedigungswertes, sondern wegen ihres instrumentellen Wertes ausübt, sind ausgeklammert. Die Person trifft hier nur unter dem Einfluß der internen Dynamik ihrer Motive ihre Entscheidungen. In der Wirklichkeit sind die Gelegenheiten zur Befriedigung verschiedener Motive oft sehr unterschiedlich. –

Wenn ein hungriger Mensch lange nichts zu essen bekommen hat, kann er sich vielleicht mit Trinken behelfen. Wenn ein kontaktbedürftiger Mensch von einer befreundeten Person räumlich getrennt ist, kann er mit ihr telefonieren oder einen Brief von ihr lesen. Wenn dabei der Hunger beziehungsweise das Kontaktbedürfnis auch nur etwas gemildert werden kann, haben wir es mit ähnlichen oder verwandten Motiven des jeweiligen ursprünglichen Motivs zu tun. Freud (1916/17) spricht von Ersatzbefriedigungen.

Wir können daher sagen: Ein derzeit nicht befriedigbares Motiv kann durch die Befriedigung eines ähnlichen Motivs in seiner Intensität vermindert werden (*Ähnlichkeitsaxiom*; Toman 1960, 1968, 1978).

Und wann ist ein Motiv b einem anderen Motiv a ähnlich? Wenn die Befriedigung des Motivs b die nächste spontane Befriedigung des Motivs a verzögert.

Ein Ähnlichkeits- oder Substitutionskontinuum ist eine Gruppe von Motiven oder Befriedigungsformen einer Person, die alle mehr oder weniger Ersatzwert füreinander haben (z.B. essen, trinken, Kaugummi kauen und rauchen). Ein solches Substitutionskontinuum ist durch die Intensitätsinkremente seiner beteiligten Motive charakterisierbar. Bei Ausfall eines der Motive des Kontinuums (z.B. durch ein Rauchverbot) werden die Befriedigungen der verbleibenden Motive zeitlich akzeleriert. Ein neuer Gleichgewichtszustand tritt ein, wenn die Intensitätsinkremente der verbleibenden Motive in der Summe den Wert erreichen, der vor dem Ausfall eines der Motive des Kontinuums gegeben war (Toman 1960, 1978). –

Zwei Motive von gegebener Intensität erhöhen die Gesamtbedürftigkeit einer Person um mehr als jedes der beiden Motive für sich allein (*Gesamtbedürftigkeitsaxiom*; Toman 1960, 1968, 1978).

Konkreter gesagt: Ein Mensch befindet sich in einem intensiveren Gesamtbedürftigkeitszustand, wenn er hungrig *und* durstig ist, als wenn er entweder nur hungrig oder nur durstig ist. Muß er auch lange still sitzen, schlechte Luft atmen und frieren, dann ist seine Gesamtbedürftigkeit noch höher.

Die vermutlich einfachste überhaupt mögliche Annahme über diese irgendwie additive Wirkung von unterschiedlichen Bedürftigkeiten oder Motiven k_i auf die Gesamtbedürftigkeit K eines Menschen ist eine Summengleichung: $K = 1/N \sum_{i=1}^{N} k_i$. Dabei ist N die Anzahl aller im Zustand wiederkehrender Befriedigung befindlichen Motive einer Person und k_i die momentane Intensität jedes dieser N Motive.

K variiert ähnlich wie k_i um 1. Erst wenn K größer ist als jedes von der Person bisher erlebte K ($K > K_{max}$), wird die Gesamtbedürftigkeit der Person alarmierend. Bei Andauer des Zustandes kann Panik entstehen. Andererseits kann möglicherweise die Befriedigung jedes beliebigen Motivs, sicher aber jedes Motivs in den besonders stark deprivierten Substitutionskontinuen die Gesamtbedürftigkeit verringern.

Die mehr oder weniger großen Ähnlichkeiten mancher der N Motive miteinander stellen übrigens eine Komplikation bei der praktischen Verwertung dieser Summengleichung dar. Auf ihre Behandlung kann hier nicht eingegangen werden.

Die Gesamtbedürftigkeit eines Menschen ist hoch, wenn sich viele seiner Motive im Warte-zustand befinden. Sie ist niedrig, wenn viele seiner Motive gerade befriedigt wurden.

Kann man auch etwas wie die Geschwindigkeit ausdrücken, mit der diese Gesamtbedürftig-keit in der Zeiteinheit durchschnittlich zunimmt? Hierfür wurde vorgeschlagen (Toman, 1957, 1960; siehe auch 1968, 1978): $C = f\left(\sum_{i=1}^{N} \epsilon_i\right)$.

C ist eine Funktion der Summe der Intensitätsinkremente ϵ_i aller N Motive einer Person, die sich im Zustand wiederkehrender Befriedigung befinden. Je größer C, desto mehr ver-schiedene Motive vermag der betreffende Mensch wiederkehrend zu befriedigen. Je mehr Motive er aber innerhalb einzelner Substitutionskontinua hat, desto leichter kann er auf Ersatzbefriedigungen ausweichen und desto längere Deprivationen einzelner Motive kann er ertragen. Je größer C, desto größer unter sonst vergleichbaren Umständen im Effekt die Fru-strationstoleranz eines Menschen.

Man könnte C, also die Wachstumsgeschwindigkeit der Gesamtbedürftigkeit eines Men-schen, als eine sehr einfache Operationalisierung von Freuds (1905, 1916/17) Begriff der Libido, des Liebestriebes oder der Lustsuchenergie eines Menschen bezeichnen.

Wenn man C tatsächlich, wie Freud, als interindividuell verschieden, aber intraindividuell konstant betrachtet, dann genügt als Annahme über die langfristige Motivationsentwicklung eines Menschen, daß N wächst. Wenn aber C konstant ist, müssen die Intensitätsinkremente der N Motive im Laufe der Entwicklung eines Menschen im Durchschnitt kleiner werden, die Intervalle zwischen aufeinanderfolgenden Motivbefriedigungen entsprechend größer. Dies konnte empirisch nachgewiesen werden (Toman 1957). – Man könnte C daher auch die Motivdifferenzierungsrate eines Menschen nennen. Auch als solche wäre C eine Operationa-lisierung des Libidobegriffs von Freud.

Das *Anstrengungsaxiom*, nach dem Motivbefriedigungen zunächst schwierig sind, aber bei Wiederholung zunehmend leichter werden, und das *Datenspeicherungsaxiom*, nach dem die Aufnahme und das Behalten von Daten eine inzidentelle Folge von Motivbefriedigungen sind, helfen dem Beobachter, die Erfahrungs- und Wissensstrukturen eines Menschen zu ver-stehen und diagnostisch zu deuten.

Verschiedene Schulen der Tiefenpsychologie halten sich in der therapeutischen Praxis de facto an diese Axiome. Dadurch sind die Schulen einander ähnlicher, als ihre globalen theore-tischen Nomenklaturen erwarten lassen.

LITERATUR

Freud, S., *Drei Abhandlungen zur Sexualtheorie* (1905), *Ges. Werke* Bd. 5 (London, Imago Publishing Co. 1940–1965).
Freud, S., *Vorlesungen zur Einführung in die Psychoanalyse* (1916/17), *Ges. Werke* Bd. 11.
Freud, S., *Jenseits des Lustprinzips* (1920), *Ges. Werke* Bd. 13.
Toman, W., „A general formula for the quantitative treatment of human motivation" (1957). *J. abn. soc. Psychol.* (1959) 58, 91–99.
Toman, W., *Introduction to psychoanalytic theory of motivation* (London, New York 1960).
Toman, W., *Motivation, Persönlichkeit, Umwelt* (Göttingen 1968).
Toman, W., *Tiefenpsychologie* (Stuttgart 1978).

* * *

PHILOSOPHISCHE FRAGEN
ZUR ARCHETYPENTHEORIE C. G. JUNGS

Fritz J. Kaune
Fachhochschule Braunschweig-Wolfenbüttel

I

Was wir die „Archetypentheorie" (AT-Theorie) nennen, besteht aus z.T. widersprüchlichen Aussagen, die sich in den meisten Schriften Jungs von 1912 an zu diesem Thema finden. Es handelt sich um einen jahrzehntelangen Versuch, gewisse psychische Phänomene durch im Laufe der Zeit immer umfangreichere geistesgeschichtliche Exkurse zu erklären. Diese langanhaltende Beschäftigung mit dem Thema weist, wie sich bald zeigen wird, auf ein erhebliches persönliches Forschungsinteresse Jungs. Wenn hier vorgeschlagen wird, diese Erklärungsversuche zurückzuweisen, so ist damit noch nichts über die in Frage stehenden Phänomene gesagt. „Wenn man einen Mythos zerstört, leugnet man keine Tatsachen, sondern stellt sie um." (Ryle)[1]

Es fällt auf, daß die AT-Lehre neben manifester Ablehnung hin und wider ebenso ein großes, wenn auch meist unkritisches Interesse erregt, daß es jedoch sehr wenig differenzierend-kritische Auseinandersetzung mit dieser Theorie gibt. Auch das ist ein Grund, dieses Thema hier noch einmal vorzustellen.

II

Jung weist darauf hin, daß er Empiriker sei und nichts erdichtet habe, in seiner Psychologie gebe es „keine einzige Feststellung, die nicht wesentlich durch echte Erfahrung unterbaut ist".[2]

Ich versuche hier zu zeigen, daß es sich bei dieser „Erfahrung", auf die sich die AT-Theorie stützen soll,

a) zu einem wichtigen Teil um Jungs eigenes Erleben handelt. Das wird an vielen Stellen seiner ERINNERUNGEN, GEDANKEN, TRÄUME, GEDANKEN deutlich,[3]

b) daß diese Erfahrungen von seinem Forschungsinteresse in eine bestimmte Richtung gelenkt, d.h. interpretiert werden, die mit Recht „spekulativ" zu nennen ist. Jung selbst stellt fest:

> . . . das Hauptinteresse meiner Arbeit liegt nicht in der Behandlung von Neurosen, sondern in der Annäherung an das Numinose. Es ist jedoch so, daß der Zugang zum Numinosen die eigentliche Therapie ist, . . .[4]

c) daß die „Tatsachen", die Jung anführt, einen höchst fragwürdigen Sachverhalt darstellen. Er gesteht einmal, „ist nicht jede Erfahrung im besten Fall mindestens zur Hälfte subjektive Deutung?"[5]

Die Erläuterung dieser drei Punkte beginne ich beim Letzten. Die Feststellung ist nicht neu, daß der Tatsachenbegriff in der Tiefenpsychologie umstritten ist. Bei Jung besteht eine „Tatsache" oder „Erfahrung" — beide Begriffe werden meist synonym gebraucht — aus einem Phänomen, das in einer ganz bestimmten Weise *gesehen*, d.h. verstanden wird, so daß durch einen „Assimilierungsprozeß" ein komplexer Befund geschaffen wird, der zum größten Teil interpretativ gewonnen ist. Das Ganze nennt er jedoch (in einem vorwissenschaftlichem Verständnis) „Tatsache", d.h. er versteht sie als Beweismittel, wie z.B. in dem Argument, nicht er habe der Seele „eine religiöse Funktion" angedichtet, sondern . . . habe die Tatsachen vorgelegt, welche beweisen, daß die Seele „naturaliter religiosa ist"[6]. Jung übersieht, daß schon Phänomenbeschreibungen (Basissätze) nicht theorieneutral sein können, also bereits gewisse Annahmen voraussetzen, er reflektiert auch nicht die Voraussetzungen des Assimilierungsprozesses, „ohne welchen es überhaupt kein Verstehen gibt".[6a]

D.h. aber, was er eine „Tatsache" nennt, kann eben *keinen unbestreitbaren Beweis* für eine bestimmte psychologische Behauptung abgeben. Jung bezeichnete sein spekulatives Interesse selber als eine „Annäherung an das Numinose" (s.o.), sein Werk MYSTERIUM CONIUNCTIONIS sei die Grundlage seiner ganzen Psychologie.[7] Darin geht es um die „Gegensatzvereinigung" in der mittelalterlichen Alchemie, die er einerseits als religiöse Symbolik auffaßt, und in der er ebenso eine „Entsprechung" zu seiner analytischen Psychologie sieht.

Nun zur Behauptung, die Erfahrungsbasis der AT-Theorie bestehe zu einem wesentlichen Teil aus Jungs eigenen Erfahrungen: Wie bei Freud, ist auch bei Jung ein wichtiger Teil seines Werkes aus einer langjährigen Selbstanalyse hervorgegangen. Aber die Zielsetzung dieser Selbstanalyse war eine andere als bei Freud, auch Jung wollte die „Inhalte (seiner) Imaginationen einigermaßen verstehen", doch dieses Verständnis suchte er in einer ganz bestimmten Richtung. Er wollte „den Nachweis der historischen Präfiguration (seiner) inneren Erfahrung" erbringen.[8] Und diesen Nachweis glaubte er in der alchemistischen Symbolik gefunden zu haben.

Die Kehrseite davon ist, daß die empirische Fundierung der AT-Theorie recht dürftig ausgefallen ist. Einen Einwand in diesem Sinne hat auch H. H. Balmer in seiner Arbeit über die AT-Theorie gemacht. Auch er weist auf den subjektiven Anteil hin[9] und sieht die „spekulativen Züge" in der Jungschen Theorie.

III

Der Ausdruck „Archetyp" wird von Jung oft in zweifachem Sinne verwendet: einmal bezeichnet er die spontan aus dem Unbewußten auftauchenden „archetypisch konstruierten Bilder" und Phantasien, in denen jeweils ein bestimmtes, historisch überall anzutreffendes Motiv sich ausdrückt, z.B. das des „weisen Mannes" oder ein „Mandala". Andererseits soll „Archetypus" die „hypothetische unanschauliche Vorlage" solcher Bilder bezeichnen, d.h. ein allgemeines „Schema", das „als präexistent angenommen werden (muß), da es sich schon in den Träumen kleiner Kinder oder ungebildeter Personen nachweisen läßt . . ."[10] Als ein hypothetisches „unanschauliches Strukturelement" des Unbewußten soll der AT einerseits „Elemente des Geistes" sein, anderseits wird er auch als „pattern of behaviour" bezeichnet, d.h. gilt als den Instinkten „verwandt".[11]

Jung führte daher den Ausdruck „archetypische Vorstellung" ein als Bezeichnung der in Phantasien, Träumen usw. auftauchenden Bilder und nannte es ein Mißverständnis, die AT als Schemata inhaltlich bestimmt, etwa als „unbewußte Vorstellungen" zu verstehen.[12] Sofern hier von einem Mißverständnis geredet werden kann, hat Jung selber dazu beigetragen, denn in dem Aufsatz „über die Archetypen des kollektiven Unbewußten" (1934), der 1954 unverändert wieder abgedruckt wurde, beschrieb er die AT als „jene psychischen Inhalte . . ., welche noch keiner bewußten Bearbeitung unterworfen wurden, mithin also eine noch *unmittelbare seelische Gegebenheit* darstellen". Doch schon wenige Sätze weiter wird die „unmittelbare . . . Gegebenheit" zurückgenommen, denn der unbewußte Inhalt werde „durch seine Bewußtwerdung und das Wahrgenommensein verändert . . ."[13] Hier wird doch zugegeben, daß ein unmittelbares Gegensein unbewußter Inhalte gar nicht möglich ist. Was auftaucht, sind immer schon *konkrete* Bilder. Damit bleibt die Unterscheidung von „leeren" oder „unanschaulichen Strukturelementen" des Vorstellens und den konkreten inhaltlichen Motiven eine reine Konstruktion. Es müßten zumindest *unterscheidbare*, also bestimmte Schemata (Vater-Bild, Mutter-Bild, Selbst u.a.) angenommen werden, auch auf der „unanschaulichen" Ebene.

Woher weiß ich also überhaupt, daß ein seelisches Bild ein archetypisches Motiv ist? Wenn die Rede von AT einen Sinn haben soll, müssen sich Kriterien angeben lassen, die uns ein Erkennen archetypischer Bilder, Motive etc. ermöglichen. Aus welchen der mitgeteilten Beobachtungen ließen sich solche Kriterien ableiten?

Zwei Gruppen von Phänomenen kommen in Frage: (a) bestimmte wiederkehrende Inhalte oder Motive von Phantasien, Träumen u.a. und (b) die besondere Erlebensqualität, die mit dem Auftauchen solcher Bilder verbunden ist.[13a]

a) Jung behauptet, daß es sich um archetypische Produktionen handelt, wenn sich in den Bildern oder Phantasien Motive oder Symbole aus der Geschichte des menschlichen Geistes wiederfinden lassen oder eine Ähnlichkeit mit ihnen feststellbar ist, da die Übereinstimmung oder Ähnlichkeit auf ihre kollektiv-psychische Herkunft, also ihren archetypischen Charakter hinweise.

Wie aber läßt sich solche Übereinstimmung nachweisen? Da der moderne Träumer oder Zeichner meist gar nichts über die Bedeutung seiner Spontanproduktionen zu sagen weiß (so Jung), ist es in der Regel der geistesgeschichtlich gebildete Therapeut, der z.B. die Existenz eines „kollektiven Bildes" in den Träumen einer „ahnungslose Modernen" feststellt.[14] Oder er interpretiert die Zeichnung eines Radbildes als ein „Mandala" und die darin dargestellten Tiere als Symbolisierung des Problems der Vielheit in dem Einem, was mit Zitaten aus der Theologie des Origines kommentiert wird.[15]

Jung behauptet nun auch, daß solche Bildproduktionen nur auf kollektivpsychischer Basis, d.h. archetypisch entstanden sein können. De facto ist die Übereinstimmung oder Ähnlichkeit zwischen den spontanen Bildern und historischen „Vorlagen" mal größer, mal kleiner, d.h. in diesem Fall dann fraglich. Die pauschale Ableitung aus dem kollektiven Unbewußten ist daher generell fraglich.

Wir haben es hier mit zwei Problemen zu tun: (a) die „Überstimmung" oder „Ähnlichkeit" moderner Imaginationen mit geistesgeschichtlichen Vorbildern ist eine Behauptung, die schwer zu beweisen, d.h. intersubjektiv einsehbar zu machen ist, viele Beispiele in den Jungschen Werken wirken nicht überzeugend, z.B. der eben erwähnte Kommentar zu einer Mandalazeichnung (vgl. auch Anmerkung 15). Alles hängt von der Deutung des Interpreten ab. Hier spielt sicher die „subjektive Evidenz", die diese Bilder für Jung besitzen (nach Balmer), eine entscheidende Rolle. Von der Frage einer tatsächlichen oder nur behaupteten Übereinstimmung ist aber zu trennen die Behauptung der archetypischen, d.h. kollektiv-psychischen Genese dieser Imaginationen. Selbst wenn Übereinstimmungen feststellbar wären, ist damit ihre archetypische Genese noch nicht erwiesen. Denn auch die von Jung hervorgehobene „Ahnungslosigkeit" der Urheber solcher Imaginationen ist zumindest in einigen Fällen bezweifelbar.[16] Zur Stützung der Behauptung der archetypischen Genese würde u.a. der Nachweis gehören, daß sie auf keine andere Weise überliefert sein können. Die Psychopathologie des ausgehenden 19. Jahrhunderts hat genügend Fälle von Kryptomnesien aufgezeigt.[17]

Welche Stellung kann hinsichtlich eines inhaltlichen Kriteriums zur Feststellung archetypischer Imaginationen bezogen werden? Die Antwort muß lauten: (1) es gibt keine sicheren, intersubjektiv einsehbare Kriterien dafür. Die Feststellung der Übereinstimmung hängt allein von der Interpretationskunst des Deutenden ab. (2) Selbst bei festgestellter Übereinstimmung ist über den archetypischen Charakter der Imaginationen nichts ausgemacht.

b) Das Auftauchen der sogenannten archetypischen Bilder ist nach Jung von einer besonderen Erlebensqualität begleitet. Diese Bilder haben, „je deutlicher sie sind, die Eigenschaft von besonders lebhaften Gefühlstönen begleitet zu sein, . . . Sie sind eindrucksvoll, einflußreich und faszinieren."[18] Sehr häufig ist auch vom Gefühl des Überwältigtseins und Überzeugtseins die Rede.

Es wäre zu erwarten, daß die Stärke des Erlebens nicht nur von der Deutlichkeit der Bilder, sondern auch von ihrer angenommenen Bedeutung abhängt, doch findet sich darüber bei Jung nichts. Nur indirekt läßt sich dieser Aspekt spezifizieren, es sind vor allem die Bilder und Symbole (z.B. Mandalas) der „Ganzheit", die bei ihrem spontanen Auftauchen als „numinos" erlebt werden. Als Beispiele für das besonders starke Erleben des „Tremendum und Fascinosum" führt Jung immer wieder „Gotteserfahrungen" an, d.h. das Auftauchen des

AT des Gottesbildes. In diesem Zusammenhang hat er z.B. das Visionserlebnis des Nikolaus von der Flüe ausführlich kommentiert.[19] Dagegen finden wir in den mitgeteilten Fallgeschichten z.T. kaum Hinweise auf starkes Gefühlserleben.[20]

Läßt sich aus diesen Phänomenen des Erlebens ein Kriterium für das Vorliegen „archetypischer" Imaginationen gewinnen? Ich neige dazu, das zu verneinen, denn was Jung hierüber mitteilt, ist z.T. recht vage, es fehlt z.B. eine genauere Aussage darüber, ob und wie alle sogenannten archetypischen Bilder von solchem besonderen Erleben begleitet sind. Auch erscheinen die Gefühle des Schrecklichen, Faszinierenden oder Überwältigenden usw. nicht sehr spezifisch. Diese Phänomene erweisen sich also als wenig brauchbar, ein allgemeines Kriterium abzugeben.

So bleibt die Frage offen, wie sich archetypisch geprägte Imaginationen als solche überhaupt erkennen lassen. Die vorangegangenen Überlegungen gingen von einem Erkenntnisbegriff aus, der am Kriterium intersubjektiver Überprüfbarkeit bzw. Einsehbarkeit orientiert ist. Man muß deshalb nicht leugnen, daß Jung und einige seiner Patienten Imaginationen von faszinierendem und überwältigendem Charakter erlebten, die vielleicht auch seelische Wandlungen auslösten oder deren Ausdruck waren. Ich kann nur sagen, daß die von Jung vorgelegten Belege und Argumente eine Annahme kollektiv-psychischer Archetypen nicht ausreichend begründen. Jung selber schrieb am Ende seines Lebens über die Bilder des „Individuationsprozesses", die ja den AT zugeschrieben werden:

> Glaubt (der Betreffende, F. K.) an diese oder gibt er ihnen auch nur einigen Kredit, so hat er damit ebenso recht und unrecht wie einer, der nicht an sie glaubt.[21]

Das an die Bilder „Glauben" ist jedoch keine nur theoretische Sache bei Jung, er zieht daraus Konsequenzen hinsichtlich der Selbstbestimmung des bewußten Ich. „Man ist ein psychischer Ablauf, den man nicht beherrscht oder doch nur zum Teil".[22]

IV

In der AT-Theorie drückt sich unmittelbar Jungs Überzeugung von der „Wirklichkeit der Seele" aus, die er zwar nur eine „Arbeitshypothese" nennt, deren Bedeutung aber eher einem Glauben entspricht, seinem Interesse für das „Numinose". Dazu tritt eine ambivalente Einstellung zum Bewußtsein, dem er einmal nur eine Rolle als „Empfänger, Zuschauer und Übermittler" anweist – in der Auseinandersetzung mit den unbewußten Inhalten –, dann wiederum warnt er vor dem unkritischen Akzeptieren der auftauchenden Bilder: „Ohne den menschlichen Geist ist das Unbewußte sinnlos . . ."[23]

Ist es wirklich notwendig, das menschliche Bewußtsein so zu spalten, wie Jung es getan hat, in ein bewußtes logisches Denken und ein von kollektiv-psychischen Faktoren gesteuertes assoziatives und analoges Denken?[24] Niemand bestreitet die „kollektive Natur" der geistigen Funktionen, sofern damit gemeint ist, daß sie allen Menschen gemeinsam sind. Aber etwas ganz *anderes* ist der von Jung hypostasierte Gegensatz von individuellem und kollektivpsychischem, d.h. archetypischem Denken. (Dieser hat eher etwas mit dem Unterschied von Meinen und Denken zu tun.) Jung konstruiert aus funktionalen Unterschieden intrapsychische Gegensätze. Hinter dem spontanen Auftreten der Bilder und Imaginationen sollen „Mächte des Unbewußten" stehen, „die in der Ökonomie der Persönlichkeit mitunter furchtbare Verwüstungen anrichten können".[25] Die verheerenden Auswirkungen psychotischer Persönlichkeitsspaltungen oder neurotischer Konflikte sind nicht zu leugnen; aber lassen sich daraus Schlußfolgerungen über die Struktur des menschlichen Geistes ableiten, und zwar gerade im Sinne der AT-Theorie?

Was immer die Bilder und Imaginationen, die Jung „archetypisch" nennt, sein mögen, ihr Auftauchen in dem seelischen Reifungsprozeß der „Individuation" wäre widersinnig, wenn das Bewußtsein sich nicht frei mit ihnen auseinandersetzen könnte. Bedeutet das aber nicht eine Relativierung der „Autonomie" der „unbewußten Mächte", also eine andere Auffassung dessen, was Archetypen sein sollen?

ANMERKUNGEN

[1] Ryle, G., *Der Begriff des Geistes* (Stuttgart 1969/1982), S.5.

[2] Jung, C. G., *Briefe*, Bd. II (Olten-Freiburg 1972), S. 82.

[3] Jaffé (Hrsg.), *Erinnerungen Träume Gedanken von C. G. Jung*, (Olten und Freiburg i. B. 11/1981) z.B. S. 189f, 214, 309.

[4] Jung, C. G., *100 Briefe* (Olten und Freiburg i. B. 1975), S. 84.

[5] Zit. nach R. Blomeyer, *Die Spiele der Analytiker* (Olten und Freiburg 1982), S. 177.

[6] Jung, C. G., „Einleitung in die religionspsychologische Problematik der Alchemie", in C. G. Jung, *Bewußtes und Unbewußtes* (Franfurt 1957), S. 64.

[6a] Jung, C. G., *Psychologie und Religion* (Zürich 1947), S. 11.

[7] Jaffé (1981), vgl. S. 225.

[8] Jaffé (1981), S.204.

[9] Balmer, H. H., *Die Archetypentheorie von C. G. Jung* (Berlin-Heidelberg 1972), vgl. S. 7, 100.

[10] Jung, C. G. (1972), S. 168.

[11] Jung, C. G. (1975), S.119f.

[12] Jung, C. G., „Psychologische Aspekte des Mutterarchetypus", in Jaffé (1981), S. 410.

[13] Jung, C. G., in: (1957), S. 13.

[13a] Jung gesteht, daß es „schwierig (ist) zu sagen, welche Inhalte als kollektiv und welche als persönlich zu bezeichnen sind." (*Die Beziehungen zwischen dem Ich und dem Unbewußten*, (Olten-Freiburg 12/1980), S. 43. Doch meint er, einige „unzweifelhafte" Kriterien zu haben: „z.B. archaische Symbolismen, wie sie in Phantasien und Träumen so häufig anzutreffen sind, (sind) kollektive Faktoren . . . Alle Grundtriebe und Grundformen des Denkens und Fühlens sind kollektiv." (ebd.)

[14] Jung, C. G., *Mandala* (Olten-Freiburg i. B. 1977), vgl. S. 71.

[15] Jung, C. G. (1977), vgl. S. 75.

[16] Bei der Urheberin der in Anmerkungen 14 und 15 kommentierten Mandalazeichnungen handelte es sich um eine Akademikerin mit neunjährigem Psychologiestudium, die dann bei Jung ihre Studien weiterführte, − woraus wir z.B. schließen können, daß sie zumindest einen Teil der Jungschen Schriften kannte. Aus dem Kommentar Jungs zu ihren Zeichnungen geht außerdem hervor, daß sie sowohl Kenntnisse in chinesischer Philosophie wie auch in Astrologie besaß. Eine „ahnungslose Moderne"? Vgl. Jung (1977), S. 9, 65.

[17] Jung gesteht in Einzelfällen die Möglichkeit von Kryptomnesien zu. „Ich habe aber genügend andere Fälle gesehen . . ., wo sogar eine Kryptomnesie mit Sicherheit ausgeschlossen ist. Auch wenn es sich . . . um eine Kryptomnesie handeln sollte, so bliebe noch zu erklären, was die präexistente Disposition war, auf Grund welcher gerade dieses Bild haftete und später wieder „ekphoriert" (SEMON) wurde". (Jung, 12/1980, S. 24).

[18] Jung, C. G., „Das Gewissen in psychologischer Sicht": *Das Gewissen* (Zürich 1958), S. 199f.

[19] Vgl. Jung (1957), S. 17ff.

[20] Z.B. bei der Urheberin der Mandalazeichnungen des Aufsatzes „Zur Empirie des Individuationsprozesses" in Jung (1977) oder der Patient in „Psychologie und Religion".

[21] Jaffé (1981), S. 309 − Zur Bedeutung des Individuationsprozesses siehe F. J. Kaune, *Selbstverwirklichung* (München-Basel 1967), S. 89ff.

[22] Ebd. S. 10.

[23] Vgl. Jung (1975), S. 67 und 61. Dort heißt es auch: „Nehmen Sie . . . das Unbewußte wörtlich, dann bleiben Sie nach kurzer Zeit in einem Engpaß stecken".

[24] Analytiker der Jungschen Schule sprechen von einem „archetypischen Denken", das nicht sachlich und diskriminierend, sondern ein „ganzheitlich erfassendes" „Analogie-Denken" ist. Vgl. Blomeyer (1982), S. 255.

[25] Jung, C. G., „Antwort an M. Buber" in MERKUR 51, (1952), S. 469.

* * *

CATEGORY MISTAKES OF FREUDIANISM
AND OTHER FALSE IDEOLOGIES
(e.g. "CRITICAL RATIONALISM" AND HERMENEUTICS)

Eugene T. Gadol
C. U. N. Y., New York

I. The persistent myth of unconscious rationalization.

Freudianism belongs to that type of unfortunate ideology which is captured by the metaphors of depth-analysis. Whether it be Gadamer, Habermas or the earlier *Frankfurter Schule* or Dilthey, they all go back to Hegel and like him they were not satisfied with the "superficial" view of things but tried to penetrate to their "deep-lying" causes. But as Collingwood pointedly remarked: "No one can dive in so deeply and come up so muddied as German philosophers". They all are engaged in poorly masked ideology because they systematically conflate pairs of concepts like *superficial* with *manifest and in the foreground*, and *deep* with *manifest, but in the background*, or *genetic* (process or product) with *logical* (process or product). And the Freudian paradigm is in this case no exception. Particularly in its confounding the unproblematical *unselfconscious* with the illegitimate *Unconscious* (in the sense of repression). However its main defects lie elsewhere. They are to be found

(1) partly in the myth of Unconscious psychic processes (repressed motives such as conflicting unfulfilled desires chiefly of a sexual nature) being causally efficient in the production and maintainance of neuroses and their symptoms, even though the alleged causes occured in infancy whereas the neurotic behavior is manifest in adulthood,

(2) partly in the myth of Unconscious energies miraculously being not merley *causally* efficacious, but being essential to every genuine rationalization and thus functioning as a masked *semiotic*! And lastly

(3) the defects of Freudianism (orthodox, neo-or revisionist) and of its spokesmen and defenders (e.g. F. Hacker or James Hopkins) lie in the indefensible strategy which has hardened into a tradition to immunize not merely the hard-core, but also the middle-belt and even the periphery of psychoanalysis (PA) against sober and wellfounded critique and 'stonewall' it like a good neurotic. A prime example of (3) is Jane Flax who in her response to Adolf Grünbaum's devastating and carefully reasoned refutation of the hard-core of psychoanalytic theory and praxis and of her defense of them, heaps one *ignoratio elenchi* upon the next.[1] Grünbaum in his patient rejoinder concludes goodnaturedly that Miss Flax simply had not joined issues with him — as if that were ever the intention of ideological apologists of her kind![2]

There is method to the madness. The incompetence she displays cannot be simply inadvertent! The same is true even of one of the most prominent critics of Freudianism: Karl Popper. In his repudiation of PA as unscientific Popper relies on his demarcation criteria which make up the hard-core of his (falsificationist) "critical rationalism". But by his own criteria PA turns out to be scientific! His attempt to distinguish between science and pseudoscience misfires, just as the attempt of the Vienna Circle to distinguish between science and metaphysics on the basis of meaning criteria misfired. In the course of his argumentation Popper offers five mayor (pseudo) reasons as to why he rejects not merely PA but also inductivism as philosophy of science:

Error 1: Inductivism must allow scientific status not merely to PA but also to Astrology and to Marxism. Popper arrives at this conclusion on the basis of a false historiography in the course of which he lumps together Carnap's (naive, ennumerative) and Bacon-Mill's (sophisticated) inductivism. Because he fails to distinguish clearly between merely positive and probative (supportive) evidence Popper falsely alleges that *all* forms of inductivism automatically grant the above mentioned disciplines scientific status. Thus he arrives at

error 2: PA has more in common with Astrology than with genuine science.

Error 3 consists in the mistaken belief to have discovered a new anti-inductivist standard of scientificity in his falsification criterion.

Error 4 consists in the mistaken and poorly argued belief that his criterion is greatly superior to those of inductivism. And lastly Popper argues on the basis of 4

point 5, i.e. PA and Astrology become *equally* unscientific (and on the basis of his demarcation criteria they do indeed!)[3]

Are these errors inadvertent or accidental, or is there method behind them? Do they evince an ideological and pseudo-rational (rationalizing) streak just like Jane Flax's blunders—only in reverse, so that because of its poor foundation Popper's attack on PA actually might extend PA's life-span contrary to all of Popper's intentions? The untenability of the major tenets of Popperism has been exposed mercilessly by Paul K. Feyerabend *et al*.[4] I argue that it is not incompetence that lies in back of Popper's not so accidental errors, nor is it sheer ignorance which makes him mishandle the concept of *inductive support*. There are powerful ideological motives at work, just as there are behind PA-practitioners and their defenders, e.g. the hermeneuts. To be sure they differ in kind and intensity from the ideological motives of critical rationalists, but once they are dug up (and this can and must be done *via* a concept of *rationalization* that dispenses with the Freudian myth of The Unconscious), it becomes quite clear why PA-practitioners and apologists have ignored or misused the concept of inductive support in their spurious claims as to the extraordinary explanatory value of PA-theory and the therapeutic success based on PA-practice. Thus I argue at length that the Freudian Dead End which, despite its road block to many more promising avenues in non-experimental psychology continues to pretend to be one of psychology's Thruways, can bolster this pretense only with indefensible ideological, but not with scientific or critical reasons.

II. A Non-Freudean Rationalization

That Freud and others who are equally fascinated by the depth-metaphor try to cover up a category-mistake (which usually takes the form of a systematic confusion of genetic and logical questions) becomes manifest even from some non-psychoanalytic pronouncements by Freud, for example his claim that an individual cannot imagine or comprehend his own death.[5] Here is the gist:

Whenever I attempt to represent my own death I survive as spectator. Since we are forever present as spectator we have not really represented our death. But we cannot eliminate ourselves as spectator, because as long as we do represent anything to ourselves we are always present.

Now, obviously, as long as the spectator is not eliminated, one is not dead. From this one might get the idea that we are really immortal, if only we find a way to make the spectator not eliminable! Freud did not speculate in this direction which would yield the desired result by punning on "eliminable"; neither did he pun on the word death the way Heidegger and some of his followers have. But he did pun on "spectator". He shuttles back and forth between the spectator (*Zuschauer*) as empirical self who witnesses something, and the spectator as the transcendental self "which accompanies all my representations". A consequence of using the word spectator thus ambiguously is that from the sentence "I *may be* a spectator at the coming World Series or I *may not*" there follows the sentence "I *shall be* a spectator *in any case*, whether I attend the World Series as a spectator or not". And that's how some metaphysical theories are born.

Perhaps like most idealists, so the materialist-determinist Freud too yearned for immortality. But as he was not conscious of this wish he produced a pseudo-argument which shall justify this (unacceptable?) wish. That is, he rationalized. But n.b. in order to uncover this rationalization and to show that it is part of an untenable ideology, I do not need Freud's concept of The Unconscious. The subconscious or the unselfconscious suffices. The rationalization becomes evident when I have uncovered the fallacy and the category mistake at its basis. Everything lies here in the open, and no going into the depths of some alleged repression can make things clearer. On the contrary, the introduction of this pseude-concept would only render more obscure whatever facts or obscurities I am trying to clear up.

Freudianism builds its model of self-knowledge on the untenable theory that inquiry into motives, although surely necessary for a proper understanding of character, dispositions, and actions springing from them, cannot possibly be fruitful without inquiry into and subsequent knowledge of The Unconscious, i.e. without cognizance of the chaotic *Id* which is timeless (!) and not subject to deliberate i.e. self-conscious control. That the *Id* and the rest of the Freudian constructs are no theoretical concepts, not even prescientific approximations of them, is well-known. Nevertheless, Freudians continue to adhere to the model of Unconscious self-knowledge, even though they may drop the old vocabulary.

The model still rests substantially on the tenous and misleading analogy with emotionally induced physiological disfunctions: just as the vegetative nervous system or the digestive tract function relatively autonomously, that is, normally their operations or mechanisms lie beyond our deliberate control, so the greater part of mental life takes place in The Unconscious which is just as much beyond our selfconscious control, etc., etc. And as the real state of affairs is insufferable Unconscious rationalizations are invented to make things tolerable.

III. Much happens without evident reasons, but nothing because of Unconscious Knowledge or Reasons.

The various types of *rationalization* and *ideology* are not congruent, anymore than *philosophy* and *ideology*, or *rationalization* and the different modes of the *unconscious*. All four concepts overlap but remain, even after clarification, logically independent. One substantial difference between ideology, whether it be good, bad or indifferent, and critical philosophy is that the ideologist adapts the world to his temperament, whereas the critical thinker tries to adapt his intellectual temperament and the intellectual equipment which evolves out of it to the world as *critical* common sense presents it to him. *Critical* common sense must be distinguished from ordinary horse sense and the common place of common consent, be it high-brow or low-brow.[6] Likewise rationalization must be distinguished from other forms of pretense and deception (be it of others or of oneself). Some rationalizations are essential to rational life as are the pretenses of polite conversation. To speak the unmitigated truth outside of pure science is seldom appropriate or wise.

Can one hide the truth from oneself once it has been disclosed? Is there an ineradicable self-deception? Is there a repressed knowing beyond one's control in the sense of Freud's Unconscious repressed wishing and thinking? The answer is in all cases negative.

Suppression (*unterdrücken*) is a way of life in civilized society, but according to Freud so is repression (*verdrängen*). Moreover, he alleges it makes for neuroses. That we suppress much of our emotional and ideational life is a fact of life that makes life viable. That we repress some of it, beyond retrieval by ordinary means, and this quite early, is the hard-core thesis of Freudianism upon which it erects a whole "*Weltanschauung*" which it tries (unsuccessfully) to support with a congeries of pseudohypotheses and metaphors. They all rest upon *his* concept of rationalization, which has proven to be untenable.

But Freudians do not appear to be taken aback by analytical criticism of the above sort. Ironically, this is especially true in Vienna, where the likes of Harald Leupold-Löwenthal and Friedrich Hacker (or other 'depth'-psychologists, like Erwin Ringel) continue to push their newly found popularity in the news-media and on TV with the shallowest of propaganda arguments without fear of having to encounter the nuisance of serious opposition.[7] And why not? As long as one can continue with the verbal magic while blithely dispensing *placebos* at prices that range world-wide anywhere from $ 30 to $ 100 or more per hour, paying attention to a serious critique, such as Adolf Grünbaum (or my venerable teacher Ernest Nagel before him) provided, does seem to be somehow out of place, doesn't it?

ENDNOTES

[1] *The Journal of Philosophy* (October 1981). pp. 561−569. (New York, N.Y.)

[2] *The Journal of Philosophy* (January 1983), pp. 46−51. (New York, N. Y.)

[3] See *A. Grünbaum*, "Is Psychoanalysis a Pseudo-Science?", *Zeitschrift für philosophische Forschung* (Juli-September 1977), pp. 334−353, from which these five blunders have been destilled.

[4] See also my presentation in the section "Wittgenstein and Popper" at the Third International Wittgenstein-Symposion, Kirchberg (1978).

[5] Cf. Paul Edwards, "My Death", *The Encyclopedia of Philosophy*, Ed. Paul Edwards, (New York 1967), Vol. V, p. 416.

[6] See my "Philosophy, Ideology, Common Sense and Murder−The Vienna of the Vienna Circle, Past and Present" in *Reality and Science*, Ed. Eugene T. Gadol, (Wien-New York, 1982). Cf. esp. pp. 21−28.

[7] Cf. My "Noch immer Berggasse 19? Freud und was nachher kam", *Die Presse* (Vienna 7./8. Juli 1979), which was ignored, as was my recent public lecture "unbotmäßige Betrachtungen über die Psychoanalyse" at the *Institut für Wissenschaft und Kunst" (Vienna, 19. January, 1984)*.

Die Presse stonewalled any possible follow up on the first article and a scheduled TV-*Nachtstudio* with me on Freud was abruptly cancelled without another one being in sight. However, and presumably to set things straight with at least one prodigal son, the City of Vienna under its new Mayor, Helmut Zilk, is planning to rename in the near future the *Votiv-Park* near *Berggasse 19 "Freud-Park"*.

* * *

I AND MY NEUROSIS: PSYCHOANALYSIS BETWEEN MECHANISM AND INTENTIONALITY

Wiljo Doeleman
Nijmegen

What are the implications of Freud's 'decentering of the subject' for the image of man? How to integrate the unconscious and ego-alien realm of our life, as revealed by psychoanalysis, into our idea of the human person? In our century, this question seems to have acquired the status of a perennial philosophical question. One way to approach this question is to investigate the relation between psychoanalysis and philosophical action-analysis: what is the relation of dreams, parapraxes, neurotic symptoms and their psychoanalytic explanation in terms of unconscious and ego-alien motives and defenses to the acting person and the explanation of personal action in terms of reasons, intentions, or rules?

The 'psychoanalytic phenomena' of dreams, parapraxes, and symptoms present the following problem: on the one hand they seem to be unintelligible and uncontrollable, to be an alien and meaningless element in our personal life; on the other hand Freud seems to have shown that this is 'only appearance' and that in fact they do have a (hidden) sense.

Philosophical action theory analyses human action as the execution of intentions on the basis of self-recognized reasons. By acting the person realizes himself, through his actions he forms and discovers his personal identity. Personal action is distinguished from natural processes: processes in non-living nature or behaviour of non-human living beings. This may be expressed in the famous duality of reasons versus causes or meaningfulness versus causality/mechanism. Reasons, intentions or meanings are not causes of the actions they belong to nor are they connected with these actions by laws of nature. Free action is not the product of external causes but is directed to self-posited aims and based on intentions or motives.

There is a clear convergence between the analytical philosophy of human action and its explanation and the hermeneutic philosophy of human utterances and their interpretation.[1] Against this 'humanist' analysis of action we find a 'naturalist' reaction, trying to understand intentional action in mechanistic or causal terms, or sometimes even, ultimately, in physiological terms. The duality between the human and the natural that is basic for the humanist analysis thus returns as the opposition of a humanist and a naturalist analysis of action. Let me briefly discuss the latter.

Could we not say that 'volitions' or 'intentions' and 'cognitions' are the causes of action, the influences on which action depends? Can freedom be conceived of as being determined by internal mental causes? The problem with this view is, that the idea that it is the person himself who acts, seems to disappear, if motive and action are connected by causal laws. I would then no longer decide myself what is to be the preponderant motive, nor would I be myself the source of the action that I carry out on the basis of that motive. I would be merely some kind of substratum of a process that happens to be mentally determined. Moreover, if action is guided by rules, and not submitted to causal laws, both the action and the rules are criticizable and possibly corrigible. But it seems meaningless to want to criticize or correct a causal law or process. Therefore a causal analysis of action seems inadequate.

However, the attempt to describe that which is specifically human only by the analysis of action seems one-sided. If we try to articulate the nature of personhood exclusively or primarily through the analysis of free action this may blind us to the importance of different forms of passivity in our life. Consider the role of fate, or being in the grip of strong passions and emotions, or the place of suffering, or surrender, or the way 'values' exercise an attraction on us, to which we submit. This whole 'passive zone of existence' seems to be rather neglected by action-theorists.

Taking our rough sketch of action theory as a background we may now ask how psychoanalysis is related to the aforementioned duality of man and nature, or of intentionality and mechanism. Some thinkers regard psychoanalysis as a full-blown humanistic, personal, hermeneutic, or action-theoretical psychology. Usually this implies a critique and a reform or purification of the traditional Freudian metapsychology. That which pertains to the interpretation of meaning in Freud should be disentangled from the physiological burden he is said to carry over from the past. A prominent spokesman for this position is Roy Schafer, who criticizes Freud for translating mental phenomena into what he calls "the quasi-physico-chemical and quasi-biological language of energy, force, mechanism, structure, function, and the like."[2] He wants to replace this by an explanation in terms of reasons which he characterizes as redescriptions that make actions comprehensible, or as "features of the person's personal world of meaning and goals".[3] Or once again: "Meaning, action, reason and situation are contrasted with cause, condition, determinant, and force, which latter terms, when used in psychology, express a subhumanizing or dehumanizing mode of considering human activity as though it were the workings of a machine."[4]

There seem to be two principal arguments for this hermeneutic or action-theoretical interpretation of psychoanalysis. The first is, that Freud has won an area for psychological interpretation that was previously considered to be only amenable to physiological explanations. Neurotic symptoms are no longer seen as a sign of hereditary degeneration, but can be related to the persons's life-history, and psychotherapy consists in making the patient see this relation. The second, related argument is, that Freud has shown symptoms, dreams, and parapraxes to have a sense, to be the expression of intentions or wishes of the person, or to be fixed reactions to traumatic experiences.

On the basis of these accomplishments of Freud his own metapsychology is rejected as an inadequate natural-science type of explanation. Schafer maintains, that dreams, symptoms, and parapraxes are not the resultant of forces or autonomous centres of activity inside the person, as Freud suggests. They are not, in his opinion, events that happen to me and that I experience passively. Instead they should be seen as actions that I perform, although they are 'disclaimed actions'. Perhaps his central argument rests on the description of therapy. The analyst appeals to the subjectivity of the patient, wants to bring him to recognize that what he seemingly suffers passively, is in fact his own doing. The disclaimed actions should be reclaimed by the person, reintegrated in his personal life. We are reminded here of Freuds remarks, that "neurotic suffering is always hidden pleasure" and that "an act so often understands how to disguise itself as a passive experience."[5]

But does it follow from this that disclaimed and (re)claimed action is action in the same sense? Disclaimed action seems to be *not* without qualification my own activity, it is disowned, ego-alien, even though somehow it originates in me. It does seem to be an expression of a part of myself that I don't know or control, that is isolated from my personality and that in this sense is a quasi-autonomous centre. Schafer's 'action language' describes the situation after therapy, the goal of therapy, but he wrongly projects this into the neurotic behaviour. And he disqualifies any notion of passivity as being only the language of the neurotic. I already hinted before that any adequate personal psychology should take into account the passive side of our life. This is especially important in psychopathology: 'disclaimed action' springing forth from 'disclaimed intentions' is indeed something that is passively undergone. It differs from (re)claimed action in not being self-controlled activity. Dreams, parapraxes and symptoms are quite different from ordinary action. There is a difference between the formation of a dreamstory and creative writing: the formation of the dream is beyond the influence of our will; it does not require special talents; we do not master the composition of our dreams; we do not get prizes for them. What Freud calls 'Fehlleistungen' or 'Fehlhandlungen' is perhaps translatable as 'misactions'. Now is a Fehlhandlung not something different from a Handlung? Doesn't a mis-action miss something that makes it similar to an action? Actions can be praised or blamed, they can be criticized on the basis of rules. Would it not be strange if we were to say 'you should not have dreamt that' or 'you dreamt that wrongly, you should dream it differently'? Or to the neurotic: 'you have produced the wrong symptom'?

I agree with Schafer that psychoanalysis does not or should not rely on physiological, or more broadly, mechanistic or causal explanations. But the proposed fully intentional explanation stresses one-sidedly the (hidden) meaningfulness of dream and neurosis and their possible reintegration in personal life. It neglects the fact that these phenomena are also uncontrollable and unintelligible and it blurs the distinction between dream or neurosis and intentional action.

Now I will briefly discuss an example of the other extreme position, diametrically opposed to the intentional interpretation of psychoanalysis in construing psychoanalytic explanations as a form of mechanistic explanation. Harvey Mullane has sought an answer in this direction for the problem that dreams and symptoms have sense on the one hand, but are often unintelligible and uncontrollable for the person on the other. He agrees with the anti-mechanistic critique insofar, that he claims that 'dumb mechanisms' cannot account for what he calls the cleverness and ingenuity of symptomformation. But, in contrast to Schafer, he also rejects the purely intentional interpretation of especially the defenses that are thought responsible for symptoms. His solution is to construe defense as a brain function. "These unconscious operations of dream- and symptomformation are functions of the neurophysiological system which derive the specificity of quasi intentionality from the fact that they are brain functions."[6] Apparently he considers these brain functions as not dumb but clever mechanisms, that can account both for the cleverness and ingenuity of defense and for the fact that it operates beyond the control of the conscious ego.

I think there are two reasons why this solution is not tenable. Mullane wants to hold on to the difference between neurosis or dreams and normal intentional action. But it would be strange to suggest that dreams and symptoms are, but normal actions are not connected with 'brain functions'. We can leave it just as vague as Mullane does, how exactly brainphysiology plays a role in normal and neurotic behaviour, but it is in both cases equally (ir)relevant and cannot serve to differentiate between the two. Secondly it is unclear how the explanation of defense and symptomformation in terms of brain functions relates to the thesis, which Mullane accepts, that dreams and symptoms have a sense, that can be made conscious. Mullane holds that it is at this moment scientifically not yet possible to give the type of explanations he demands. But psychoanalysis as interpretation and making aware of defense mechanisms does already exist and seems to do very well without any recourse to the purported brain functions. It is also unclear how such 'brain functions' could ever be made conscious or integrated into the ego; but this is exactly what happens to defense mechanisms in the course of a psychotherapy.

What conclusions can we draw from our discussion of Schafer's intentionalistic and Mullane's mechanistic interpretations of psychoanalysis? The curious fact remains that symptoms and dreams are somehow meaningful, and expression of intentions, but are also produced without knowledge and control of the conscious ego or person. They seem to be an expression of what might be called unintended intentions or unwished wishes. They are undeniably part of my life and yet seem not to belong to me. This queer status has to be respected and this is why I propose to view psychoanalytic phenomena and explanations as a third category between mechanism and intentionality. They cannot be reduced to the working of mechanisms that are purely external to the person, nor can they be conceived of as purely intentional actions.

ENDNOTES

[1] See G.A.M.Widdershoven, *Ego development and philosophy of action*, this volume.
[2] Schafer, R., *A New Language for Psychoanalysis* (New Haven/London 1976), p. 362.
[3] Schafer (1976), p. 204, 205.
[4] Schafer (1976), p. 232.
[5] Freud, S., *Standard Edition* (London 1953—74), Vol. XVIII, p. 11; S. E. Vol. XV, p. 58.
[6] Mullane, H., "Defense, dreams and rationality", *Synthese* 57 (1983), p. 199.

* * *

13. Universelle Sprachen

13. Universal Languages

INTERACTION BETWEEN LANGUAGE AND SOCIETY

Ivo Lapenna
University of London

1. *LANGUAGE AS A SOCIAL PHENOMENON*

The aim of this paper is to sketch the close connection between society and language. Language is a social, not a natural phenomenon. It is governed by social, not by biological laws. Born in society and evolving simultaneously with the development of society to satisfy its needs of communication, language in its turn fortifies social links and decisively contributes to the further development of society.

Today there is not a single serious philologist or sociologist who would not agree with this fundamental fact. One of the greatest linguists of all times, Antoine Meillet, wrote in his famous book *Linguistique Historique et Linguistique Générale*:

> "As a matter of fact, languages are not objects having independent material existence and evolving by themselves. Language belongs to a social group, and its modifications are linked with the history of that group."[1]

Another great French lingust, J. Vendryés, also regarded language as a social fact. He said:

> "Language, which is *par excellence* a social fact, is the result of social contacts. It became one of the stronger links which unifies societies, and its evolution is due to the existence of [the relevant] social group."[2]

Edward Sapir, the famous American linguist, defines language as the totality of symbols reflecting the whole physical and social background in which a human group is situated. He goes on by saying:

> "The mere fact of a common speech serves as a peculiarly potent symbol of the social solidarity of those who speak the language. The psychological significance of this goes far beyong the association of particular languages with nationalities, political entities, or smaller local groups".[3]

On the other hand, N. Ya. Marr was not the only Soviet linguist who examined the social origins and functions of languages. In the USSR the social character of language is the starting point of all linguistic studies. Let us mention only Professor A. S. Ĉikobava who, answering the question what is language, says very clearly: "Language is a social phenomenon."[4]

2. *FACTORS INFLUENCING THE EVOLUTION OF LANGUAGE*

In the evolution of language, two opposing trends may be observed: the trend towards disintegration and the trend towards integration. They are due to two antagonistic sets of factors, which continually—though not with the same force and effect in every age—influence language. To the first group belong various differentiating factors, such as the geographical and socio-economic: factors of caste or class, profession, sex and religion, in our times also political hindrances to international communication. The unifying factors are division of labour and economic interdependence over increasingly wide areas reaching world proportions, egalitarian ideas, technological progress and education.

2. 1. *Differentiating Factors*
The chief differentiating factors are:

2. 1. 1. Geographical factor.—High mountains, large seas, wide rivers, impassable marshes, dense forests, sterile deserts and similar conditions separate human groups from one another. Therefore, each group not only creates in the long evolutionary process its own language satisfying its actual needs of communication depending on the material conditions of life in which it finds itself, but the languages also remain without reciprocal contact.

The geographical factor plays a very important role on the lowest levels of civilisation, but even today it has not lost its significance. Human groups who live isolated from one another, without any kind of contact or with only very few reciprocal relations, have separate languages, which are not understood outside the respective areas. It is well known that the South American Indians have a very large number of languages. Each tribe—often consisting of only a few hundred members—has its own language. Hundreds of South American languages, according to A. Meillet, cannot merge, as the greater part of the continent is sparsely populated. A lively description of the numerous languages of North America was given by G. Sagard in his book *Grand Voyage du Pays des Hurons*.[6] He asserted that in the regions he had visited two villages seldom spoke the same language. In Burma the same situation is found. The aborigines of Australia even today speak some 500 different languages, whereas the three million inhabitants of Papua New Guinea, whose official language is Pidgin English,[7] use in everyday life 700 tribal languages.

Those few examples—many others could be mentioned—show the differentiating role of the geographical factor, especially in the early stages of language evolution.

2. 1. 2. Socio-economic factors.—Several factors belonging to this group may be distinguished. Here are the most important:

2. 1. 2. 1 Caste or class—Every economic differentiation also means a social differentiation, and this inevitably results in a differentiation of language. If the classes are sharply divided, their languages show important differences; if the classes have reciprocal contacts, their languages show fewer differences. The caste society of ancient India presents a typical example of almost complete caste isolation. Sanscrit, the language of the Vedas and of an extensive philosophical and scientific literature, was in fact the language of Brahmins, the highest caste in the Hindu Caste system, and aristocracy, whereas the masses of the people outside the castes spoke innumerable vernacular languages of Prakrit. A similar phenomenon could be observed in Europe in the feudal Middle Ages. At that time Latin was the class language of the ruling aristocracy, the church and scholarship, while the masses of serfs, bound to the land, spoke an enormous number of most varied languages and dialects.

It would be a mistake to think that today the class factor plays no part. Of course, since present-day classes are less isolated from one another than castes or classes of antiquity and Middle Ages; moreover, owing to the ever increasing significance of the unifying factors, the influence of the class factor is no longer strong enough to create completely separate languages. However, the various strata of society have often a tendency to congregate in particular districts, so that they are divided even territorially. The relationships between them are mainly external and insignificant. This is particularly noticeable in large industrial cities. The consequence is that also the languages of these social groups become considerably differentiated. It is easy to notice, in observing the languages of the upper classes and the working class in London, Paris, or any other large city, that the distance between them is neither small, nor unimportant. In addition, within each class there are numerous variations, caused by the professional factor.

2. 1. 2. 2. Profession.—The division of labour caused the creation of separate professional or technical languages. Wherever division of labour exists, differentiation of language must also exist. Each profession has its own terminology, which is often not known outside it. The total vocabulary of the most highly developed languages has reached hundreds of thousands of words, but, in fact, a very small number of them is common to all users of the language. Great thinkers and writers have a vocabulary of about 10,000 words. Shakespeare used in all his works about 15,000 words, Racine 6,000, Milton's total vocabulary is assessed at between

8,000 and 11,000 words, while the whole Old Testament was written using 5,462 words. In general, the individual vocabulary of educated people, if compared with the total amount of words in any present-day national standard language, is rather poor: perhaps a few thousand words. Everything else belongs to specialist, professional and technical languages. To this must also be added the increasing number of expressions created on the basis of various accessory activities, such as sport, plays, games, travel and other hobbies.

2. 1. 2. 3. Sex. – It is known that in some primitive tribes the language of women differs from the male language. According to J. W. Appleyard, Kaffir women have many special words that are not found in the language of men. This is the result of a custom which forbids the women to use any words or even sound that is similar to the sound of the name of their nearest male relatives. In African tribes were found cases where the women spoke completely different languages. This was attributed to the fact that the conquering tribe exterminated all the men of the conquered tribe and took possession of the women.

Except for these special cases, the differences between the male and female languages are derived from the different tasks which the two sexes perform in societies at lower levels of civilisation. Consequently, the sex factor in the context of language is not a biological factor, as might at first sight be supposed, but an economic and social factor. Sex as such does not have a great influence on language, especially not today in civilised societies, but it can become influential, if each sex is engaged in separate economic activities and performs separate social functions.

2. 1. 2. 3. Religion. – Practically every religion uses a separate language for its rites. This religious tongue totally or considerably differs from the common language. Religious rites, says A. Meillet, which are destined to transport man into a special, a holy world, demand a similarly special, almost mystical language.

Other differentiating factors might be considered, for example the handing on of the language from generation to generation, political hindrances to interregional or international communication, and so on. Doubtless these factors, too, play a greater or smaller part in differentiation and they are not to be neglected.

How great the importance of differentiating factors can be, may be seen from an example mentioned by Meillet in the book already quoted. One of the tribes of South India, consisting of only about 800 persons, has three special languages, one jargon and several dialects of class origin.

2. 2. Unifying Factors

The unifying factors are divisible into three main groups: socio-economic, technological, and educational.

2. 2. 1. Socio-economic factors. – The whole history of mankind is, in essence, a history of gradual transition from the spontaneous appropriation of the fruits of nature to higher, organised modes of production on the basis of new and ever more appropriate instruments of production. This was reflected in the social, political and legal organisation of society which, in its turn, influenced further economic development. From the primitive hordes and tribes up to present-day nations and – let us hope – to the future humanity unified in diversity, man has constantly aimed at, and created, higher forms of communal living in ever wider social groups. On this long and slow upward journey, several important elements have increasingly shown their unifying importance. Here are the most important ones:

2. 2. 1. 1. Division of labour. – The transition to more progressive modes of production caused the formation of larger social units with increased division of labour and, consequently, a more extensive interchange not only material, but intellectual as well. Thus the division of labour, which, on the one hand, plays the role of a differentiating factor in a vertical sense (the formation of professional languages), on the other hand brings men into economic interdependence over wide areas and appears as a powerful unifying factor in a horizontal sense.

The more there is division of labour, the more the activity of the individual is specialised, the more he becomes dependent on the labour of others. The interchanges multiply in kind and spread territorially. Today they go far beyond the frontiers of single nations and extend over the whole earth.

Of course, the interdependence caused by the division of labour also appears as a powerful unifying factor in the field of language. It is found in the very foundations on which both the national standard (literary) languages and the International Language have grown up.

2. 2. 1. 2. Egalitarian ideas.—Economic progress necessarily leads to progress in the field of ideas. The idea of equality of all human beings, which receives even larger and deeper contents, has a special significance. It developed from the religious concept of equality in death and after death, to the formal-political equality proclaimed by the French Revolution, up to the present-day international recognition of all human rights and fundamental freedoms, including the right to equality of languages, as contained in the Universal Declaration of Human Rights and other legally binding international documents in this field. The democratisation of political institutions and public life makes possible all kinds of international contacts among millions of men and women at least in the free world, and has already contributed to the assimilation of languages in many respects (for instance, internationalisation of terminology in some branches of sciences and learning.

2.2.2. Technological factor.—The spectacular technological progress, including particularly all technical means of communication, has made possible large-scale contacts not only within nations, but also internationally. They are powerful forces in the bringing of languages together. They transport from region to region, from county to country, all over the world, not only goods and human beings, but also words, while the modes of expression become more similar. This undoubtedly reinforces the unity of national standard languages, but at the same time constantly increases international linguistic material—a process clearly expressed in the International Language.

2.2.3. Educational factor.—The invention of the printing press,[8] the flowering of belles-lettres and scientific literature, schools and universities, libraries and reading rooms, theatres and sound films, radio and television, are only the most important of the numerous unifying educational factors. Thousands of teachers teach the unified standard national languages in schools. It is heard every day on radio and television, in the theatre and cinema. It is read in books, periodicals and newspapers. If today nations have their unified common national languages, though still not spoken by all members of the respective national communities,[9] this is to a great extent due to the tremendous impact of the educational factors, behind which are to be found the compulsory power of the State, armies of educationalists and considerable financial and material resources. It is obvious that in such conditions there is no possibility of disintegration of standard national languages into dialects. The direction has always been —and will be even more in the future—precisely the reverse.

3. CONCLUSION

All these differentiating and unifying factors, touched upon only very generally, act simultaneously, help each other or contradict each other. But even a superficial glance at the evolutionary process shows that *with the general progress of mankind the unifying factors accumulate and prevail, while the differentiating factors play an ever more insignificant part.* The general trend does not go from a single language to multilingualism, as some people still believe under influence of the Tower of Babel and early linguistics, but on the contrary, it leads from innumerable languages in the prehistoric times to a more and more restricted number of common languages for larger social groups at later stages. For a correct understanding of the present situation and dynamics of languages in the world, including the position and prospects of the International Language (Esperanto) in the general evolutionary process, this fact has a significance of the first importance. It is this that caused the formation of present-day standard national languages over regional and local dialects; that gave birth to the International Language as a means of international communication and as a linguistic expression of humanistic internationalism; and that should lead towards a single international language for all international relations over national languages in the future, perhaps not very distant, of humanity united in diversity. The alternative is slavery under the rule of a single nation and its language or end of the world in a general nuclear war.

———

ENDNOTES

1 Meillet, A., *Linguistique Historique et Linguistique Générale*, vol. I (Paris, 1926). p. 79
2 Vendryès, *Le Language* (Paris, 1921), p. 13.
3 Sapir, Edward, "Language", in *Selected Writings in Language, Culture and Personality*, ed. by D. Mandelbaum, pp. 7−32 (p. 10).
4 Cikobava, A. S., *Vvedenije v Jazykoznanije* (Introduction to Linguistics), Part I, second ed. (Moscow, 1953), p. 23.
5 *Op. cit.* in n. 1, p. 116.
6 Paris, 1631.
7 On the occasion of the celebrations connected with the opening of the new parliament building a few weeks ago even Prince Charles delivered there a short speech in that language.
8 The setting up in London in 1477 of the first printing press played a decisive role in transforming the dialect of London into the standard literary English language. By the middle of the 16th century printers in England had generaly adopted a fixed orthography. However, as in other countries, in England, too, the adoption of a standard national language and fixed orthography did not abolish dialects and spoken variations of prononciation which survive up to date despite the leveling influence of broadcasting.
9 For instance, according to official statistics (1984), only 50% of Italians can speak the standard literary Italian, initiated by Dante almost 700 years ago.

* * *

EXPERIMENTE ÜBER LERNLEICHTIGKEIT
UND INFORMATIONSGEHALT VON ILO-VOKABELN

Helmar G. Frank
Universität Paderborn

1. *Relative Wichtigkeit des Vokabellernens.* Zum Erlernen einer fremden Sprache gehört der Erwerb der notwendigen Kenntnisse über ihren Wortschatz, ihre Phonetik (oder, umgekehrt, über ihre Orthographie), ihre Grammatik und ihre Stilistik. Hinsichtlich des Wortschatzes ist der Lehrstoffumfang am größten. Im Falle der Internacia Lingvo (ILo) können Größenordnungen genannt werden. Danach weist man bereits eine sehr gute Kenntnis dieser Sprache auf, wenn man 2000 ihrer Wortwurzeln gelernt hat. Deren syntaktischer plus semantischer Informationsgehalt (vgl. z.B. Frank, 1976, § 7.1 sowie Abschnitt 5 des gegenwärtigen Beitrags) beträgt etwa 60 000 bit für einen Japaner oder Chinesen ohne Fremdsprachvorkenntnisse, für einen Deutschen ohne Fremdsprachvorkenntnisse etwa 50 000 bit, für einen vergleichbaren Franzosen, Spanier oder Italiener etwa 25 000 bit, für einen Lerner englischer Muttersprache wahrscheinlich noch etwas weniger. − Selbst für eine sehr gute ILo-Beherrschung reicht die Kenntnis der 16 grammatischen Regeln, sämtlicher drei Dutzend Affixe und der 33 Präpositionen aus. Dieser Lehrstoff umfaßt nicht mehr als 4 engbeschriebene Schreibmaschinenseiten mit einer Lehrstoffinformation von rund 10 000 bit. − Die Ausspracheregeln gehören im Falle der ILo zur Grammatik und enthalten weniger als 500 bit Information. − Hinsichtlich des Stils gibt es für ILo kaum mehr als eine Handvoll allgemein anerkannter Regeln, so daß über Stilistik vermutlich nicht mehr als etwa 300 bit zu lernen sind.

Vom Gesamtlehrstoff über ILo fallen daher zwischen 75% und 90% auf den Wortschatz. (Bei ethnischen Sprachen ist das prozentuale Ergebnis dasselbe. Natürlich ist die Lehrstoffinformation selbst um den Faktor 10 bis 30 größer, worin die erheblich geringere Lernleichtigkeit wurzelt.) Eine Theorie des Vokabellernens erscheint somit als wichtigster Teil einer Theorie des Fremdsprachenlernens. −

2. *Die (mindestens) drei geistigen Schritte beim (Vokabel-)Lernen.* Das Lernen erfolgt in (mindestens) drei Schritten, welche (mindestens) drei Komponenten unserer Intelligenz beanspruchen. (Vgl. Frank, 1969, Kap. 5.)

2.1 Wir apperzipieren den Lehrstoff, d.h. wir nehmen ihn ins Bewußtsein auf. Die Apperzeptionsgeschwindigkeit C_K ist im groben Mittel für Erwachsene 16 bit/sec, für 10-jährige etwa 12 bit/sec. Das Apperzipierte bleibt einige Sekunden bewußt. Diese Zeitspanne heißt „Gegenwartsdauer" und beträgt beim Erwachsenen im Mittel etwa $T = 6$ sec. Die Bewußtseinsweite (oder „Kurzspeicherkapazität") $K_K = C_K \cdot T$ beläuft sich demnach bei Erwachsenen auf weniger als 100 bit. Diese Parameterwerte unseres Bewußtseins reichen aus, um bei normaler Sprechgeschwindigkeit folgen und einen kurzen Satz überblicken (also gleichzeitig im Bewußtsein haben) zu können.

2.2 Es ist möglich, mindestens einen Teil des Apperzipierten, das vor einigen Minuten dem Bewußtsein entschwand, wieder in dieses zurückzurufen. Dies bedeutet, daß wir über ein vorbewußtes Gedächtnis für wenigstens kurzzeitiges Behalten verfügen; wir nennen es „Kurzgedächtnis". (Der „Kurzspeicher", der dem Bewußtsein entspricht, ist davon phänomenologisch radikal verschieden und wird oft als „Ultrakurzzeitgedächtnis" bezeichnet.) Bei Erwachsenen beträgt die Aufnahmegeschwindigkeit in das Kurzgedächtnis, also die Geschwindigkeit $C_{v,k}$ des vorläufigen (provisorischen) Lernens, etwas mehr als 0,7 bit/sec, also etwa 50 bit/min. (Der 10-jährige schafft knapp 30 bit/min.) Das Fassungsvermögen $K_{v,k}$ des Kurzgedächtnisses kann einige tausend bit erreichen. Das genügt für 100−400 neue ILo-Vokabeln, deren vorläufiges Lernen etwa 1−4 Schulstunden erfordert. − Nach einem Tag ist schon beinahe alles, was in dieses Kurzgedächtnis aufgenommen wurde, ihm wieder entschwunden.

2.3 Ein kleiner Prozentsatz des einstigen Kurzgedächtnisinhalts kann noch nach einigen Monaten oder manchmal sogar nach Jahren ins Bewußtsein zurückgerufen werden, insbesondere wenn es sich um Lernelemente handelt, die schon mehrfach in das Kurzgedächtnis aufgenommen worden waren. Wir verfügen daher auch über ein „Langgedächtnis", das zwar nur langsam Information aufnimmt (etwa $C_{v,l} = 0{,}1 \cdot C_{v,k}$, nämlich etwa 3 bit/min. bei Erwachsenen), aber eine Speicherkapazität $K_{v,l}$ von mehr als 10 Millionen bit besitzt. Dies reicht z.B. aus, um mehrere ethnische Sprachen zu lernen.

Es gibt einige neurophysiologische Argumente, welche die psychologische Theorie stützen, nach welcher es nicht nötig ist, zwischen mehr als den genannten drei Behaltensstufen zu unterscheiden. −

3. *Unterscheidung zwischen passiver und (auch) aktiver Sprachbeherrschung.* Jeder macht beim Fremdsprachenlernen die Erfahrung, daß es schwieriger ist, eine Fremdsprache aktiv anwenden zu lernen, also z.B. in sie zu übersetzen, als sie nur verstehen zu lernen, so daß man z.B. aus ihr übersetzen kann. Dies gilt schon für das Vokabellernen. Es genügt ja, sich einen Teil der Merkmale einer fremdsprachlichen Vokabel aus einer Menge zu lernender Vokabeln einzuprägen, um Verwechslungen zwischen diesen zu vermeiden; und um diese Vokabeln zu verstehen, braucht man darüber hinaus nur die Zuordnung (die Assoziation) dieser Elemente zu ihrer Bedeutung zu lernen. Die genaue Buchstaben- oder Lautfolge, welche die fremdsprachliche Vokabel ausmacht, braucht man nur auswendig zu wissen, um die Vokabel aktiv zu benutzen. Je länger diese Zeichenfolge, also das Wort, ist − genauer: je mehr Information die Zeichenfolge enthält − desto schwerer ist es, sie zu lernen. Um sie aber nur wiederzuerkennen und zu verstehen, muß von längeren Vokabeln nicht *mehr* an Merkmalen gelernt werden: ein geübter Lerner konzentriert sich auf wenige, besonders augenfällige Eigentümlichkeiten. (Nur wenn die Zahl der zu lernenden Vokabeln einer bestimmten Länge exponentiell mit der Vokabellänge wächst, kann es sein, daß es sich lohnt, mehr Merkmale ins Gedächtnis aufzunehmen.)

4. *Probleme.* Unsere Untersuchungen betreffen die folgenden Fragen:
4.1 Wie groß ist der Informationsgehalt von ILo-Vokabeln?
4.2 Wie rasch kann man das Verstehen von ILo-Wörtern lernen? Wie rasch die aktive Anwendung?
4.3 Hängt diese Lerngeschwindigkeit von der Wortlänge ab? Besteht eine Abhängigkeit vom Informationsgehalt?
4.4 Gibt es ein Gesetz, nach welchem diese Lerngeschwindigkeit von der Wortlänge oder vom Informationsgehalt abhängt?
4.5 Hängen die Antworten auf die vorstehenden Fragen vom Alter der Lerner ab? Nur eine Auswahl aus den bisherigen Forschungsergebnissen kann im folgenden mitgeteilt werden.

5. *Syntaktischer Informationsgehalt von ILo-Vokabeln.* Unter der Voraussetzung, daß eine zu lernende ILo-Vokabel keine Ähnlichkeit mit der gleichbedeutenden Vokabel in der Muttersprache des Lerners (oder einer ihm bekannten gleichbedeutenden fremdsprachlichen Vokabel) aufweist − wir werden abkürzend von „ähnlichen" Vokabeln sprechen −, darf stochastische Unabhängigkeit zwischen der Zeichenkette, die das Wort konstituiert, einerseits, und der Wortbedeutung andererseits unterstellt werden. Die zu lernende Information ist also die Summe aus syntaktischer und semantischer Information.

Die semantische Information kann (da beim Vokabellernen alle infragekommenden Bedeutungen ungefähr gleichwahrscheinlich sind) als konstant angesehen und dem Zweierlogarithmus der Zahl infragekommender Bedeutungen gleichgesetzt werden. Das ergibt beim Wortschatz der Grundschüler etwa 10 bit, bei Berücksichtigung der Bedeutungen aller 15 250 Wortwurzeln der ILo (vgl. das *Plena Ilustrita Vortaro*, 1970, S. XI) etwa 14 bit. Adaptiert man vor dem Lernen von z.B. 32 neuen Vokabeln an das Repertoire ihrer Bedeutungen, dann reduziert sich die Information der im Einzelfall zu lernenden Bedeutung auf ld 32 = 5 bit.

Zur Bestimmung der syntaktischen Information sollten 24 deutschsprachige Teilnehmer am Sprachorientierungsunterricht (Ilo-Unterricht, der zu propädeutischen Zwecken im 3. und 4. Grundschuljahr erteilt wird − vgl. z.B. Frank, Geisler, Meder, 1979) Buchstabe für Buchstabe 15 ihnen unbekannte ILo-Vokabeln erraten. Unter der Voraussetzung, daß die syntaktische Information eines bestimmten Buchstabens in einer bestimmten Position einer noch unbekannten Vokabel für jede dieser Versuchspersonen dieselbe war, kann sie als Zweierlogarithmus der Unwahrscheinlichkeit $1/p$ berechnet werden, wobei für die positive Zahl $p \leq 1$ der Prozentsatz der Versuchspersonen einzusetzen ist, der den besagten Buchstaben richtig riet. (Im Falle völliger Unsicherheit erscheint jedes Zeichen als gleichwahrscheinlich, die Information wird also etwa 5 bit; mit diesem Höchstwert wurde in den Ausnahmefällen gerechnet, in denen keiner der 24 Versuchspersonen richtig riet.)

In einem Kontrollversuch rieten der Autor, seine Frau und seine beiden Kinder Buchstabe für Buchstabe 50 ihnen zuvor unbekannte ILo-Vokabeln nach dem Codebaum-Verfahren von Weltner (1966). Bei der klassischen Anwendung dieses Verfahrens berechnet man den Erwartungswert der Information jedes Buchstabens durch Verdopplung der Zahl seiner falsch geratenen Binärkodeelemente.

Für den ersten, zweiten und dritten Buchstaben der Vokabelwurzeln, für alle weiteren Buchstaben der Vokabelwurzel, für die grammatische Endung (sie war bekannt, jedoch nicht die Stelle ihres Auftritts!) und für den Zwischenraum als Wortendezeichen (aus welchem sich erst ergibt, daß z.B. ein vorausgehendes o hier Substantivendung und nicht Vokal der Wortwurzel ist!) wurden je getrennt die mittleren Informationswerte in beiden Versuchen bestimmt. Der beigefügten Tabelle ist zu entnehmen, daß offensichtlich bei ILo-Vokabeln die syntaktische Information vom ersten zum zweiten Buchstaben stark abfällt und dann wieder ansteigt. Die Vertrautheit der zweiten Versuchspersonengruppe mit den statistischen Eigenschaften der ILo zeigt sich vom zweiten Buchstaben an in (um rund 20%) geringeren subjektiven Informationswerten. Aus den gewichteten Mittelwerten kann folgende Schätzformel für die subjektive syntaktische Information einer (im eingangs erwähnten Sinne „unähnlichen") ILo-Vokabel mit einer aus mindestens b Buchstaben bestehenden Wortwurzel abgeleitet werden:

$$(1) \quad i_{\text{synt}}/\text{bit} = 10{,}2 + 3{,}4 \cdot (b - 3)$$

(Dies ist deutlich mehr als bei deutschen Vokabeln, weshalb Übersetzungen aus dem Deutschen in ILo um rund 20% knapper werden.)

Versuch	1. Buchst.	2. Buchst.	3. Buchst.	weitere Buchst. der Wurzel	gramm. End- buchst. (a,o,i)	Zwischen- raum
24 ILO- Anfänger 8-10 jährig, 15 Vokabeln	4,023	2,733	3,217	3,989	0,485	0,370
4 gute ILO- Kenner, 14-51 jährig, 50 Vokabeln	4,057	2,043	2,557	2,416	0,471	0,057
gewichtetes Mittel	4,035	2,487	2,981	3,427	0,480	0,258

6. *Geschwindigkeit des Vokabellernens.* Aufgrund der in Abschnitt 2 genannten Lernge-schwindigkeiten kann man theoretisch den Lernzeitbedarf beim Vokabellernen abschätzen. Dabei ergeben sich die folgenden qualitativen Erwartungen:

1) Der Zeitbedarf bei Kindern ist größer als bei Erwachsenen.

2) Der Zeitbedarf für den Erwerb der nur passiven Vokabelbeherrschung hängt nicht (oder nur wenig) von der Wortlänge und damit vom Informationsgehalt ab und ist geringer als der Zeitbedarf für die auch aktive Beherrschung.

3) Der Zeitbedarf für den Erwerb der auch aktiven Vokabelbeherrschung steigt mit der Vokabellänge, also dem Informationsgehalt.

Weiter verbreitet als die Frage nach dem Zeitaufwand ist die Frage nach der erforderlichen Zahl von Wiederholungen. Geht man davon aus, daß sich etwaige positive und negative Bah-nungseffekte ausgleichen, dann liefert die Wahrscheinlichkeitsrechnung für den Erwartungs-wert w der Zahl erforderlicher Lernversuche bis zur Aneignung eines Lernelements die Funk-tion

(2) $w = 1/a$

wobei a die Wahrscheinlichkeit ist, daß schon der erste Lernversuch erfolgreich ist. Diese Wahrscheinlichkeit kann als Prozentsatz der „auf Anhieb erfolgreichen" Lerner empirisch bestimmt werden, oder rückgerechnet werden aus dem Erwartungswert

(3) $p_n = 1 - (1 - a)^n$

des Prozentsatzes der nach n Lernversuchen Erfolgreichen. (Hinsichtlich der genaueren Vor-aussetzungen vgl. z.B. Frank, 1977 und 1984, § 004.)
In einem Selbstversuch (Frank, 1977) nahm der Verfasser 70 ILo-Vokabeln (darunter 52 im erläuterten Sinn „unähnliche") passiv und aktiv in das Langgedächtnis auf, wozu täglich ein Lernversuch stattfand. Im Mittel waren für den Erwerb der passiven Beherrschung der 52 „unähnlichen" Vokabeln 2,923 solche Lernversuche nötig (im Gesamtmittel aller 70 Voka-beln: 2,74). Die erforderlichen Wiederholungszahlen korrelieren nicht ($r = 1\%$) mit der Wortlänge. Dagegen betrug die Korrelation zwischen Wortlänge und erforderlicher Zahl der Lernversuche für die auch aktive Beherrschung etwa $r = 46\%$. Unterstellt man einen linearen Zusammenhang zwischen der Zahl der Lernversuche (die ja zur Lernzeit proportional ist!) und der Wortlänge (die nach der empirischen Formel 1 ihrerseits mit dem Informationsgehalt linear zusammenhängt) und bestimmt durch Regressionsrechnung empirisch die Parameter aus den Einzelergebnissen des Selbstversuchs, dann erhält man als Erwartungswert für die Zahl der zur (langfristigen) passiven und aktiven Beherrschung insgesamt erforderlichen Lernversuche von ILo-Vokabeln der Wortwurzellänge b:

(4a) $w = 2,809 + 0,355b$

Bei der seinerzeitigen Untersuchung wurde ein anderes theoretisches Auswertungsmodell unterstellt. Danach ist die Wahrscheinlichkeit der Aneignung einer Vokabel gleich der Wahr-scheinlichkeit der nur passiven Aneignung (Bedeutungsaneignung) mal dem Produkt der Wahrscheinlichkeiten, daß der erste, zweite usf. Buchstabe der Vokabel erlernt ist; sind diese Wahrscheinlichkeiten im (geometrischen) Mittel A (wobei die grammatische Endung nicht mitgerechnet wurde, da der Kenner sie nicht mehr zu lernen braucht), dann führt dieses Modell wegen (2) auf die Beziehung

(4b) $w = w_p \cdot A^{-b} \approx 2,9 \cdot 0,9^{-b}$

Dabei wurde A durch lineare Regressionsrechnung aus den empirischen Wertepaaren (log w; b) bestimmt. (Eine nichtlineare Regressionsrechnung führt auf einen kleineren A-Wert.)

B. S. Meder (1977) führte eine Nachuntersuchung mit folgenden Abwandlungen durch:

1. Statt mit nur einer Versuchsperson (dem damals 42-jährigen Autor) arbeitete sie mit etwa 100 damals 8-9-jährigen Teilnehmern am Sprachorientierungsunterricht.
2. Gemessen wurde nicht unmittelbar w sondern der Prozentsatz p_4 der nach 4 Angeboten erfolgreichen Lerner; daraus wurde w nach (2) und (3) errechnet.
3. Die einzelnen Lernangebote folgten nicht in eintägigem Abstand sondern innerhalb weniger Minuten aufeinander, d.h. es wurde nicht in das Langgedächtnis sondern in das Kurzgedächtnis eingelernt.

Das von B. S. Meder (1977) mitgeteilte Ergebnis führt statt auf (4b) auf

(5) $w \approx 11{,}9 \cdot 0{,}9^{-b}$

also − unabhängig von der Wortlänge! − auf einen fast vierfachen Aufwand trotz nur provisorischen Lernens. Eine Wortlängenabhängigkeit des Aufwands für die nur passive Beherrschung stellt die Autorin nicht fest.

Eine inzwischen erfolgte kritische Prüfung der damals gewonnenen Daten führte vor allem zu folgenden Ergebnissen.

1. Drei Schülergruppen sind deutlich zu unterscheiden, d.h. ihre individuellen Ergebnisse können nicht zu einem Gruppenmittel sinnvoll zusammengefaßt werden:
   (a) eine Schülergruppe mit herausragend gutem Lernerfolg,
   (b) eine mittlere Gruppe,
   (c) eine Gruppe schlechter Lerner, die nach den Lernversuchen nicht mehr wußten als zuvor und offensichtlich nicht ernsthaft mitarbeiteten; diese Daten sind natürlich wertlos.

2. Die mittlere Zahl erforderlicher Lernversuche bis zur *passiven* Beherrschung liegt unter 10 und *steigt* mit der Wortlänge bzw. dem Informationsgehalt i_{synt}, und zwar
   (a) bei den guten Schülern schwach signifikant (Irrtumswahrscheinlichkeit $p = 24\%$), Korrelation $r = 17{,}4\%$, Regressionslinie (mit Umrechnung nach Gleichung 1)

   (6a) $w_p \approx 0{,}29 i_{synt} + 7{,}5 \ (= b + 7{,}5)$

   (b) bei den mittleren Schülern hochsignifikant (Irrtumswahrscheinlichkeit $p = 4\%$), Korrelation $51{,}3\%$, Regressionslinie (mit Umrechnung nach Gleichung 1)

   (6b) $w_p \approx 1{,}26 i_{synt} + 2{,}7 \ (= 4{,}54 b + 2{,}7)$

3. Für die auch aktive Beherrschung ist eine mit Wortlänge bzw. Information erheblich rascher wachsende Zahl an Lernversuchen nötig. Regressionslinie:

(7) $w = 4{,}39 i_{synt} - 20{,}5$

Korrelation zwischen Wiederholungszahl und Wortlänge bzw. Information: 65%, Irrtumswahrscheinlichkeit: $p = 2\%$.

Es lag nun nahe, auch für ältere Lerner wenigstens in einer Pilotuntersuchung zu prüfen, ob die hier für das provisorische Vokabellernen (Einlernen in das Kurzgedächtnis) sichtbar gewordenen Tendenzen sich bestätigen. Dazu lernten der Autor und seine Familienangehörigen die 50 Vokabeln (mittlere Wortwurzellänge: $b = 6{,}24$), für welche Tage zuvor (ohne

Gelegenheit zur Erlernung der semantischen Information!) die subjektive syntaktische Information bestimmt worden war (vgl. Abschnitt 5). Die bisherige Lerndatenauswertung führte u.a. zu folgenden Ergebnissen:

1. Der inzwischen 51-jährige Autor benötigte für den nur *provisorischen* Erwerb der *passiven* Vokabelbeherrschung im Mittel nur $w_p = 1{,}78$ Lernversuche statt 7 Jahre zuvor 2,92 für den *langfristigen* Erwerb. Die Abhängigkeit von der Wortlänge war minimal: $r = 8{,}9\%$, Regressionslinie

(8a) $w_p = 1{,}6 + 0{,}027b$

2. Die auch *aktive* Vokabelbeherrschung durch den Autor erforderte einen Aufwand, der geringer war und mit der Wortlänge (also auch mit dem Informationsgehalt) weniger rasch stieg, als (4a) für das Langgedächtnis beschreibt:

(9a) $w = 2{,}227 + 0{,}092b$

Der Zusatzaufwand $w - w_p$ steigt deutlich mit der Wortlänge ($r = 35\%$).

3. Tilo, der 14-jährige Sohn des Autors, benötigte durchweg mehr Wiederholungen (und überdies mehr Lernzeit pro Wiederholung), und zwar schon bis zur passiven Beherrschung eine mit der Wortlänge (also der Information) steigende Zahl; Korrelation $r = 27\%$, Regressionslinie:

(8b) $w_p = 1{,}6 + 0{,}105b$

Der Vergleich von (6b), (6a), (8b) und (8a) zeigt unverkennbar eine Abnahme der Wortlängenabhängigkeit mit wachsender Reife. Dagegen bleibt diese Abhängigkeit erheblich sobald auch die aktive Beherrschung angestrebt wird; Korrelation des Zusatzaufwands $w - w_p$ mit der Wortlänge: $r = 76\%$; Regressionslinie:

(9b) $w = 1{,}9 + 0{,}47b$

4. Deutlich anders fielen die Ergebnisse bei den weiblichen Familienmitgliedern aus. Ines, die 17-jährige Tochter, benötigte zwar im Mittel mehr Lernversuche als ihr Vater und weniger als ihr jüngerer Bruder ($w_p = 2{,}18$) jedoch bei tendenziell negativer (!) Korrelation mit der Wortlänge; der Zusatzaufwand $w - w_p$ bis zur auch aktiven Vokabelbeherrschung korrelierte zwar deutlich positiv ($r = 39\%$) mit der Wortlänge, bei jedoch vergleichsweise schwachem Anstieg der Regressionslinie:

(9c) $w = 2{,}64 + 0{,}029b$

Völlig fehlte die Wortlängenabhängigkeit bei ihrer Mutter: hier ergab sich rechnerisch eine Korrelation von $r = -0{,}6\%$ zwischen w_p und b und von $r = -3\%$ zwischen $w - w_p$ und b! Als Regressionslinien errechneten sich nahezu zwei Konstanten $w_p = 2{,}2$ und $w = 2{,}4$. Mit der passiven Beherrschung, die kaum mehr Aufwand kostete als bei der Tochter Ines, war demnach − anders als beim Rest der Familie − auch die aktive nahezu schon erlernt. −

7. Anstehende Fragen. Die Ergebnisse der sehr unterschiedlichen Experimente stimmen größtenteils gut zusammen, was zu genaueren Fragen ermutigt. Vor allem muß durch weitergehende Auswertung des vorliegenden Datenmaterials und evt. durch zusätzliche Experimente untersucht werden
− ob die *Wortlänge* oder (was zu vermuten ist) die *Information* der Vokabel die zuverlässigere Prognose des Lernaufwands zuläßt, und

– ob der Lernaufwand eher linear oder eher exponentiell mit der durch Länge oder Information gemessenen Schwierigkeit einer Vokabel steigt.

Dabei muß

– der Lernaufwand außer durch die Zahl der Lernversuche auch durch die damit verbrauchte Lernzeit gemessen,

– die Verallgemeinerbarkeit der Aussagen auf andere Sprachen durch analoge Informationsbestimmungen und Lernversuche geprüft und

– jede Frage sowohl für das Kurzgedächtnis als auch für das Langgedächtnis beantwortet werden.

Ungeklärt ist überdies, ob jenseits einer reifeabhängigen Verschiedenheit der gemessenen Parameter vielleicht auch die Existenz grundsätzlich verschiedener Lernertypen schon beim Vokabellernen anerkannt werden muß – vielleicht sogar die unter Lehrern verbreitete Überzeugung von der Überlegenheit (und demzufolge wohl auch anderen Nutzung) des Kurzgedächtnisses bei weiblichen Lernern. –

LITERATUR

Frank, H., „Mallonga enkonduko en la kibernetikan pedagogion/Kurze Einführung in die Kybernetische Pädagogik" in: Behrmann/Stimec, *Bildung und Berechnung/Klerigo kaj Prikalkulado* (Alsbach 1976, 21978), S. 9–55.

Frank, H., „Zur Wiederholungszahlbestimmung bei Sprachlehrprogrammen", in: Lobin/Bink, *Kybernetik und Bildung III* (Paderborn 1977. S. 63–71.

Frank, H., *Kybernetische Grundlagen der Pädagogik* (Baden-Baden 1962, 21969).

Frank, H., Propedeùtiko de la Kleringscienco Prospektiva/Vorkurs zur Prospektiven Bildungswissenschaft (Tübingen 1984).

Frank, H., Geisler, E. u. Meder, B. S., „Nachweise der strukturbedingten Transfers aus dem Sprachorientierungsunterricht", *Grundlagenstudien aus Kybernetik und Geisteswissenschaft*, Band 20, Heft 1 (1979), S. 14–28.

Meder, B. S., „Informationsgehalt und Lernwahrscheinlichkeit fremdsprachlicher Wörter", in: Boeckmann/Lehnert, *Bilanz und Perspektive der Bildungstechnologie*. Giessen, 1975.

Waringhien, G. (Red.), *Plena Ilustrita Vortaro* (Paris 1970).

Weltner, K., „Der Shannonsche Ratetest in der Praxis der Programmierten Instruktion", in: Frank, *Lehrmaschinen* 4. Oldenburg. München. 1966. S. 49–53.

* * *

DAS SEMANTISCHE MENGENGERÜST FÜR ALLE SPRACHEN

Lothar Hoffmann
Dortmund

Bei allem Fortschritt auf dieser Welt wurde bisher keine Methode entwickelt, um die sprachliche Verständigung zu verbessern. Die komplizierten Vorgänge des „Verstehens" funktionieren überhaupt nur dank der bewundernswerten Eigenschaften des menschlichen Gehirns, und dessen Training von Kindheit an. Deshalb haben seit Pythagoras so viele Menschen sinnvolle und universelle Sprachen schaffen wollen. Aber zu deren Zeit konnten diese weder technisch noch organisatorisch verwirklicht werden. Auch die in neuerer Zeit entwickelten Methoden der automatischen Übersetzungen funktionieren nur für einige Sprachpaare, für begrenzte Bereiche und mit riesigem elektronischen Aufwand. Den bisherigen Mißerfolgen aller ehemaligen und neuen Sprachversuche steht ein Experiment gegenüber, welches sich schon 3000 Jahre lang bewährt hat! In China und den umliegenden Ländern funktioniert seither und inzwischen für eine Milliarde Menschen eine Schreibweise, die nicht an die Sprache, sondern an die Bedeutung gebunden ist. Jeder − der überhaupt lesen kann − liest die Schriftzeichen jeweils in seiner eigenen Sprache! Ein entsprechendes System, welches die Begriffszeichen phonetisch definieren und artikulieren kann, ist nicht nur für den Menschen, sondern auch für den Computer zu verstehen.

Mein Projekt SPRACHE 2000 entwickelt solch ein umfassendes, technisches und damit neutrales Bindeglied zwischen allen Sprachen. SPRACHE 2000 entsteht auf folgende Weise: Alle Begriffe des menschlichen Erlebens − und nicht einfach die Wörter − werden systematisch in einem Register erfaßt und mit maximal 8 Buchstaben − an Stelle von Ziffern − gekennzeichnet. Diese Kennzeichen wechseln nach besonderen Regeln Konsonanten und Vokale ab, sodaß Registerwörter entstehen, die gut anzuhören und leicht zu merken sind. Jeder registrierte Begriff wird mit den dazu passenden Wörtern und/oder Wortfolgen definiert, einschließlich seiner grammatikalischen Einordnung in das Satzgefüge − nach und nach in allen Sprachen dieser Welt. Die in der Registersprache zu bildenden Sätze folgen besonderen Regeln, so daß sie − unabhängig von den Ausdrucksformen der 3000 Sprachen − eindeutig und logisch sind.

Die Entwicklung eines solchen Registers beziehungsweise einer systematischen Sprache kann und wird in Zusammenarbeit mit entsprechenden Fachleuten erfolgen. Der Aufbau kann wegen seines riesigen Umfangs nur mit elektronischer Hilfe erfolgen. Diese Aufgabe ist nicht abstrakter als all das, was ich während meiner Laufbahn als Ingenieur getan habe: Eine Idee verwirklichen! Solch ein wichtiger Auftrag schafft Arbeitsplätze für viele unterschiedliche Fachleute − weltweit für Jahrzehnte! Langfristig hat aber eine viel größere Bedeutung, daß auch die „unterprivilegierten" Völker unmittelbar Informationen bekommen können, die bisher nur in den paar „Weltsprachen" verbreitet werden. Durch Veröffentlichungen[1] und besonders durch meine Vorträge[2] fand meine Idee zuerst eine Verbreitung, dann Interesse und Anerkennung, und schließlich auch die erforderliche technische und finanzielle Hilfe. Nach meiner Pensionierung konnte ich 1983 an einem IBM 23 Computer wesentliche Vorarbeiten zum semantischen Mengengerüst für alle Sprachen durchführen. Seit einigen Monaten arbeite ich mit einem großen Verlag zusammen, der mein System für mehrsprachige Rohübersetzungen anwenden wird. Beim Aufbau der Datei korrespondiert mein (mittelgroßer) M.A.I.10 Computer mit dem Großcomputer im Verlag. Bei der professionellen Anwendung wird später etwa ein Personal-Computer ausreichen. Für den Gebrauch eines Touristen oder eines Geschäftsreisenden wird − für alle Sprachen! − ein Taschencomputer ausreichen. Wer irgendwie mit der Methode in Berührung kommt, sieht stets auch den Text in Registerwörtern und gewöhnt sich — ganz nebenbei — an die so einfache und eindeutige SPRACHE 2000.

Die Anzahl der heutzutage auf der Welt verwendeten Begriffe ist schwer abzuschätzen. Wegen der zukünftigen Entwicklung muß auch recht viel Reserve vorgesehen werden. Andererseits müssen die Registerwörter kurz und klar sein, damit man sie nach dem Aussehen und an der Aussprache leicht erfassen und sich merken kann. Vom Esperanto habe ich viele Wortstämme und einige Regeln übernommen. Die Registerwörter bestehen — wie beim Esperanto — aus Wortwurzeln und Affixen. Wegen der Begrenzung der Registerwörter auf 8 Stellen müssen sich die maximal zwei Wurzeln mit 3 Stellen und die Affixe mit einer Stelle begnügen. Die Zuordnung der Wortteile sehen Sie am folgenden Beispiel:

WORTTEIL	REGISTERWORT						BEDEUTUNG
	1. 2. 3.	4.	5. 6. 7.	8.	STELLE		
1. WURZEL	r i v						Fluß
DIFFERENZIERUNG		ā					zugehörig
2. WURZEL			b u j				Mündung
GRAMMATIK				o			Substantiv Singular
	r i v	ā	b u j	o			Flußmündung

Diese Festlegung war rein technisch. Sie dient der hierarchischen Einordnung und sie ermöglicht Such- und Sortier-Vorgänge im Computer-System. Bei der Zuordnung von Buchstaben bzw. Lauten sind dagegen sprachliche Belange entscheidend. Um die kurzen Wortwurzeln vielseitiger zu machen, wurde die Anzahl der „natürlichen" Doppellaute (z.B. j, x, z oder englisch a, i, o, u, w) durch häufig vorkommende Folgen ergänzt. Andererseits wurden die schwer zu unterscheidenden Zischlaute zusammengefaßt. Nach den bisherigen Ratschlägen und Überlegungen wurden vorerst jeweils 24 „Konsonanten" und „Vokale" phonetisch ausgewählt. Die endgültige Orthographie der Zeichen ist noch offen, da die Computerfirmen sich noch nicht auf einen gemeinsamen Zeichenvorrat einigen konnten. Auch für die vorgesehenen logographischen Zeichen ist die Zeit noch nicht reif. Vorerst werden wir den umfangreichen TELETEX Schriftzeichengrundvorrat benutzen. Unter Anwendung dieser Zeichen habe ich in geduldiger Kleinarbeit einigen Tausend Wortwurzeln eine Bedeutung zugeordnet. Mit einem „o" endend ergibt sich schon ein einfaches Substantiv, mit „a" ein Adjektiv usw. Viele dieser Wurzeln gleichen oder ähneln den Anfangsbuchstaben von Esperantowörtern. Oft mußte natürlich — um Mißverständnisse zu vermeiden — auf andere Sprachen zurückgegriffen werden. Es ist auch noch Platz vorhanden für nichteuropäische Wurzeln, die von entsprechenden Fachleuten empfohlen werden. Bei der Bearbeitung wird sich zeigen, welche Kennzeichnung der Wortwurzeln am besten in das System paßt und gut verständlich ist. Das Register der Wortwurzeln beginnt bisher so:

	Esperanto	Deutsch	English	Français
babi	*bab*ili	plaudern	chatter	causer
baco	tolo	Plane	tilt, awning	*bâch*e
badi	blankigi	tünchen	plaster	*bad*igeonner
bafi	balbuti	stammeln	stammer	*baf*ouiller
bago	*bag*atelo	*Bag*atelle	*bag*atelle	*bag*atelle

Mit Hilfe dieser gewählten Wortwurzeln werden nun die Registerwörter gebildet, welche einerseits eine gewisse Hierarchie aufweisen und andererseits eine Verbindung zu Wörtern in vorhandenen Sprachen herstellen. Diese Bedingungen erleichtern zuerst die Zusammenarbeit der verschiedensprachigen Mitarbeiter — und später eine Gewöhnung an SPRACHE 2000.

Einige der zahlreichen Bedeutungen des Wortes EINNEHMEN wurden z.B. den folgenden Registerwörtern zugeordnet:

12345678	BEDEUTUNG	AUSSPRACHE	URSPRUNG
ägūti	nehmen, schlucken	agiuti	gluti
mâci	speisen, essen, zu sich nehmen	manschi	manĝi
okupi	platznehmen, sich darauf setzen	okupi	okupi
käci	kassieren, bekommen, erhalten	käschi	cash
ókôki	erobern, besitzergreifen	oikonki	konkeri
kôteni	ausfüllen, umfassen	konteni	contenir
kôvîki	einnehmen von, überzeugen	konwinki	konvinki
ōgéni	parteiergreifen, gewinnen für	iogeini	gain

Bitte erwarten Sie nicht, daß dieses improvisierte „Wörterbuch" schon die endgültige Fassung für eine universelle SPRACHE 2000 sei. Wir sind erst im Stadium des Registrierens aller Begriffe des menschlichen Erlebens aus Wörtern, Wortfolgen und Kontexten. Die umfangreiche und schwere Arbeit wird noch eine ganze Weile dauern. Vor deren Abschluß − und sogar auch später bei notwendigen Korrekturen − kann die Zuordnung der Registerwörter leicht geändert werden. Nehmen wir an, die Wurzel „bac" für Plane (von französisch bâche) solle in „tol" (von Esperanto tolo) geändert werden, so genügt ein relativ einfacher Befehl, um diese Wurzel in a l l e n betroffenen Registerwörtern in allen Dateien auszutauschen!

Schon im nächsten Jahr soll die halbautomatische Übersetzung für einen Teilbereich anlaufen. Die recht einfache Methode funktioniert so: Der Originaltext erscheint Satz auf Satz am ersten Bildschirm. Die Bedienungskraft unterstützt das System bei der semantischen und syntaktischen Analyse − nur unter Zuhilfenahme der eigenen Muttersprache und einer gewissen Sachkenntnis vom Thema. In beliebig vielen Zielsprachen erscheinen rohe aber eindeutige Übersetzungen an weiteren Bildschirmen. Deren Bediener formen hieraus − in ihrer eigenen Muttersprache − korrekte und wohlformulierte Sätze, welche gespeichert und gedruckt werden. C'est tout!

Unabhängig davon, wann SPRACHE 2000 einmal für die d i r e k t e Verständigung angewandt wird, erleichtert sie schon bald sinngemäße Übersetzungen für a l l e Sprachen, auch zwischen solchen, für welche es keine Dolmetscher und Wörterbücher gibt!
SPRACHE 2000 ist eine Entwicklung des heutigen, elektronischen Zeitalters. Sie funktioniert aber nicht nur als Bindeglied zwischen den Kybernetischen Funktionen der Datenverarbeitung und den kommunikativen und kulturgeschichtlichen Rollen der gewachsenen Sprachen, sondern auch zwischen den Sprachen, ohne deren Vielfalt und Eigenarten zu beeinträchtigen!

ANMERKUNGEN

[1] Hoffmann, L., (Hrsg.), *SPRACHE 2000 − Neue Perspektiven einer weltweiten Verständigung* (Dortmund 1979); dto. „Auszug", *Future* (Mainz 1981).
[2] Hoffmann, L., (Vorträge): FEoLL Werkstattgespräch Interlinguistik in Bildung und Wissenschaft (Paderborn 1980); 4. Internationale Konferenz über das Sprachenproblem in der Wissenschaft (Paderborn 1981); INTERKOMPUTO (Budapest 1982); 10e Congrès International de Cybernétique (Namur 1983); Académie Internationale des Sciences (San Marino 1983); 7th World Congress of Applied Linguistics (Brussels 1984).

* * *

PÄDAGOGISCHE RELEVANZ EINER UNIVERSELLEN SPRACHE

Vladimir Mužić
Universität Zagreb

Die Behauptung von der Sprachverschiedenheit als eines Fluches ist wohl sehr trivial. Allerdings, von der Babylon-Legende bis zum heutigen Tag bekommt diese Frage sehr verschiedene Nuancen. Man spricht, natürlich, heute kaum von einer Weltsprachunifizierung. Die Idee, daß die Verbreitung international angenommener Wörter dazu führen könnte, erwies sich, mindestens für eine absehbare Zukunft, als illusorisch. Anders ist es aber mit der Idee, mit einer allgemeinen Zweitsprache, die negativen Folgen der Sprachverschiedenheit für die internationale Kommunikation zu beseitigen. In einer sinusoiden Bewegung (im groben Sinne dieses Bildes) läuft diese Idee durch die ganze Geschichte (wenigstens im westlichen Kulturkreis). Das waren, und sind noch immer Bestrebungen, daß eine Nationalsprache diese Funktion für bestimmte professionelle u.ä. Schichten bzw. für bestimmte Zwecke inne hat. In Europa war das für viele Jahrhunderte die lateinische Sprache, später in engeren oder weiteren Bereichen verschiedene lebende Sprachen, z.B. Französisch weltweit in der Diplomatie, Deutsch im Geschäftsleben Mitteleuropas, Arabisch in einigen Teilen Afrikas und, seit der Mitte dieses Jahrhunderts, weltweit Englisch. Eine ähnliche, wenn auch keineswegs dieselbe Funktion haben die genannten und andere Sprachen als Kommunikationsmittel in den ehemaligen Kolonien.

Allerdings gibt es manche Gründe, daß eine Nationalsprache höchstwahrscheinlich eine Universalität als Zweitsprache, die nicht auf eine Schicht (meistens elitäre oder professionelle) oder eine Region begrenzt ist, nicht erreichen wird. Dies betrifft z.B. „moralische" Gründe (dabei auch der mangelnden „Kommunikationssymmetrie" desjenigen, dem die gegebene Sprache Muttersprache ist, mit demjenigen, dem diese eine Fremdsprache ist), weiters das Nationalprestige, Aussprache- und Rechtschreibschwierigkeiten usw. (s. darüber Brozović, 1984).

Deswegen finden wir in der Vergangenheit eine Anzahl verschiedener universalsprachlicher Ansätze (auch Plansprachen genannt). Jedoch auch diese fanden bis zum heutigen Tag gar keine Verbreitung (fast alle) oder nur eine geringe Verbreitung, z.B. Esperanto. Selbst die Tatsache, daß diese Bestrebungen, besonders in bezug auf die letztgenannte Sprache, rational gerechtfertigt sind, ändert dabei nichts. Warum?

Ein Grund dafür ist sehr ähnlich dem schon genannten Nationalprestigegrund. Dabei ist interessant, daß dies nicht nur bei den Völkern, deren Muttersprache eine Weltsprache ist (z.B. Englisch oder Russisch), der Fall ist, sondern auch bei den kleinen Nationen bzw. Sprachgebieten. Vielleicht könnte man gar eine Analogie ziehen zwischen dem Standpunkt fast aller Sprachwissenschaftler meines Landes (mit sehr wenigen Ausnahmen), die sich, meistens völlig unrational, einer internationalen Sprache entgegensetzen, und der Tatsache, daß es ganz undenkbar ist, daß in einer absehbaren Zeit anstatt zweier Alphabete (lateinisch und kyrilisch) nur eines gebraucht wird, – obwohl dies, u.a. den pädagogischen Unsinn hervorruft, daß sich die Kinder in der dritten Klasse der Grundschule, also mit 8 Jahren, auch das zweite Alphabet aneignen müssen.

Es gibt aber auch einen anderen m.E. stärkeren Grund: Trotz der relativ großen Errungenschaften der Informationsrevolution sind ihre Folgen für die internationale Kommunikation doch erst in ihrem Anfangsstadium, und (nach Brozović, op. cit. S. 5) „die Menschheit kann noch immer leben und funktionieren ohne eine wahrhaftige internationale Sprache, dies wird immer schwerer, immer ungeschickter, immer riskanter, doch, es geht noch immer ohne eine internationale Sprache."

Es ist schwer zu sagen, wie lange das noch gehen wird. Einerseits ist der Fortschritt im Gebiet der Kommunikationstechnik riesig und immer schneller. Dies ist auch verbunden mit einer ständigen Verbilligung der Hardware, immer leichteren Handhabung, u.a. auch durch die Miniaturisierung usw. Alle diese Fortschritte machen die Idee eines „globalen Weltdorfes" leicht und schnell technisch machbar. Und in diesem Dorf müssen zwar nicht alle Einwohner dieselbe Muttersprache sprechen, sie müssen sich aber gegenseitig verständigen können.

Andererseits ist aber der Fortschritt im Menschen selbst, in seinem Denken, seinen Gefühlen, den zwischenmenschlichen Beziehungen viel langsamer. Die Unterschiede im Niveau der Wirtschaftsentwicklung zwischen „Nord" und „Süd" werden immer größer, und ähnlich ist es mit dem Anfeuern der politischen, ideologischen u.ä. Unterschiede zwischen „West" und „Ost". Und all dies spricht gegen eine baldige Verwirklichung eines innigen Zusammenlebens der ganzen Menschheit. Alles dies spricht keineswegs für eine schnelle Erfüllung der Vorbedingungen für eine generelle Verbreitung ein und derselben Zweitsprache, sei dies auch eine internationale, „neutrale" Plansprache.

Diese Skepsis in bezug auf eine allgemeine und globale „Praxislösung" der Zweitsprache muß keinesfalls derselbe Standpunkt in bezug auf einzelne Gebiete begleiten. Und da sich an solchen einzelnen Gebieten von allen neutralen internationalen „Plansprachen" nur Esperanto als lebensfähig erwiesen hat, ist die folgende Betrachtung an diese Sprache gerichtet. Dabei wird, neben einer Einsicht in seine Möglichkeiten und Mängel, auch seine pädagogische Relevanz hervorgehoben.

Im allgemeinen werden zwei Vorzüge von Esperanto, die auch eine pädagogische Relevanz haben können, betont: Einer ist die fast vollkommene Einfachheit des gesamten Sprachkomplexes, der zweite eine relative Allgemeinbekanntheit des Wortschatzes, da man seit dem Anfang bis zu zeitgenössischen Sprachbereicherungen immer trachtete, Wörter mit internationaler Verbreitung anzunehmen. Dieser zweite Vorzug kommt, als Lernerleichterung, stärker zum Ausdruck, wenn die Muttersprache offener für die Annahme solcher Fremdwörter mit internationaler Verbreitung ist. Die pädagogische Relevanz kommt nicht nur zum Ausdruck durch ein leichteres Erlernen, als dies bei den Fremdsprachen der Fall ist, sondern auch als seine Effizienz als „Brückensprache" beim Erlernen der Fremdsprachen. Eine Anzahl methodologisch kontrollierter pädagogischer Experimente hat gezeigt, daß man sich in derselben Lernzeit eine Fremdsprache besser aneignet, wenn man zuerst Esperanto lernt und dann die Fremdsprache, als wenn man die ganze Zeit nur die Fremdsprache lernt. Und dabei bekam man noch das Esperantowissen dazu. Erste solche Experimente wurden vollbracht im Schuljahr 1948/49 in England, und später vielmals repliziert (Mužić, 1954). Allerdings, solche Befunde sind in der Regel verbunden mit den Fremdsprachen, deren Wortschatz (in bezug auf die Wortwurzeln) mit dem Esperanto-Wortschatz größtenteils übereinstimmt, d.h. den Sprachen der romanischen Sprachfamilie.

Dieselbe Tatsache, daß Esperanto ausschließlich aus dem Wortschatz der romanischen, germanischen und slawischen Sprachen besteht und davon eine sehr überwiegende Mehrzahl romanische Sprachwurzeln sind, nimmt ihm allerdings den „äußeren" Neutralitätsstatus. Dieser innere Gegensatz ist einerseits geschichtlich gerechtfertigt: In der Zeit seiner Gründung war der Kulturkreis der genannten Sprachfamilien angenommen als „der" Kulturkreis der Menschheit. Anderseits ist es praktisch unmöglich, eine „gerechte" Verteilung des Wortschatzes auf alle Weltsprachen zu verwirklichen, da wären bestenfalls höchst fragwürdige Berichtigungen möglich. Doch, abgesehen von all diesem, bleibt noch die Tatsache, daß die Völker der dritten Welt notwendigerweise in Esperanto doch eine internationale Sprache der Europäer (der ehemaligen Kolonialherrscher) sehen.

Der genannte Gegensatz ist nicht der einzige. Von den anderen soll hier nur noch einer genannt werden: der des Verhältnisses zwischen Esperanto als einer streng normierten Plansprache und als einer Umgangssprache. Jede Umgangssprache – und Esperanto ist es heute schon im ziemlich großen Maße – hat eine dynamische Evolution. Einen Teil davon kann man in die Norm einbauen – diese Aufgabe erfüllt die Esperanto-Akademie. Doch andere, z.B. die Erscheinung semantischer Uneindeutigkeiten, sind nicht nur unauffangbar, sondern schaffen den zentralen Sinn der Plansprache − die für die eventuelle Computerbearbeitung absolut unumgängliche Eindeutigkeit − ab. Vielleicht könnte man sogar behaupten, daß eine gute Plansprache, die auch Plansprache (mit allen ihren, auch technischen, Eigentümlichkeiten) bleiben will, ungeeignet für einen Umgangsgebrauch sein müßte (ein positives Beispiel dafür könnte vielleicht Hoffmanns (1979) „Sprache 2000" sein, wenn auch der Autor wahrscheinlich anders darüber denkt).

Und, nur in Kürze, sei auch das Problem der Wert(un)freiheit von Esperanto erwähnt. Hervorgehend aus den humanistischen Gedanken seines Autors, L. L. Zamenhof, ist diese Sprache sehr wertgeladen. Diese Eigenschaft ist, selbstverständlich, zweischneidig. Einerseits, vorausgesetzt die Annahme dieser Werte, kann diese Sprache einen beträchtlichen Erziehungswert haben. Anderseits, bei einem Streben zur Wertfreiheit (das allerdings auch ein Werten ist), kann man diese Eigenschaft als störend empfinden. Prof. Frank fand einen Ausweg daraus durch den Namenswechsel, bzw. der Rückkehr zum Originalnamen („Esperanto" geht von Zamenhofs Pseudonym hervor, er selbst nannte die Sprache schlicht: Internationale Sprache = Internacia Lingvo, daher das von Prof. Frank gebrauchte Kürzel ILO). Allerdings möchte ich doch die Frage offen lassen, ob der Gedanke Doris Lessings (österr. Staatspreis für europäische Literatur 1981), man glaube, daß sich die Sachen schon aufgrund einer Umbenennung ändern, auch hier gilt.

Nach so einer Folge eigentlich unschlüssiger Ideen, müßte man sich die Frage stellen, ob nun überhaupt ein Beschluß oder sogar zukunftsgerichteter Beschluß anzustreben ist. Doch im Geiste des Wittgensteinschen Strebens zur Klarheit in seinem „Tractatus logico-philosophicus" (1960) − hier vielleicht aufgefaßt in einem zu weiten Sinne − möchte ich mittels eines Modells wenigstens den pädagogischen Aspekt einer universellen Sprache, konkret von Esperanto, klarmachen.

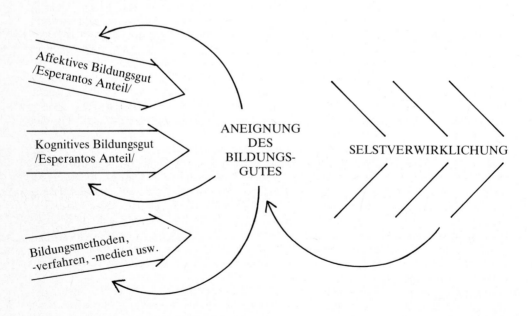

Abb. 1: Esperantos Anteil im Bildungsprozeß

Wie Abb. 1 zeigt, wird als Ziel der Bildung[1] ein kontinuierlicher Prozeß der *Selbstverwirklichung* angenommen. Dabei wirkt der Bildungsprozeß in dieser Richtung auf die *Aneignung* der Bildungsgüter innerhalb dieses Prozesses selbst, wie auch durch das Befähigen für die lebenslange Weiterbildung und dadurch auch zur lebenslangen Selbstverwirklichung. Damit wird, natürlich, nicht gemeint, daß die Bildung der einzige Weg zur Selbstverwirklichung ist; doch ist er einer der wichtigsten Wege.

In dieser Richtung wirkt eine vielfältige Interaktion verschiedener, dem Schüler und der Situation angemessener Bildungsverfahren (-methoden, -vorgänge) und der Bildungsgüter aus dem affektiven und kognitiven Bereich, − Auch aus dem psychomotorischen Bereich, doch in unserem besonderen Fall, wo es sich um die Bildungsrelevanz von Esperanto handelt, kommt dieser Bereich weniger zum Ausdruck. Zum Ausdruck kommen also in erster Reihe, im affektiven Bereich, ein Ausbau jener Einstellungen, die mitunter einen „Selbstabbau" mancher nationaler u.a. Vorurteile bedeuten, einen Ausbau eines höheren Freundschaftsbegriffen (auch internationaler „Fernfreundschaften") usw. Im kognitiven Bereich geht es um die lebensnähere, aktivere und effizientere Aneignung des geographischen, historischen u.a. Wissens aber auch Verstehens; sowie, selbstverständlich, die Aneignung von Esperanto als ein für sich selbst wertvolles Kommunikationsmittel (z.Zt. allerdings nur in spezifischen Umständen) und auch als Einstiegstufe zur Erleichterung des Fremdsprachenunterrichts.

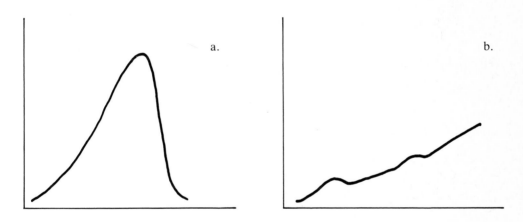

Abb. 2: Zwei typische Trends pädagogischer Neuerungen

Es ist unmöglich, eine verläßliche Prognose über die Zukunft dieser Vorhaben und somit auch eines entscheidenden Durchbruchs von Esperanto zu machen. Jedoch, in einer nahen Zukunft wird dies kaum die Form eines qualitativen Sprunges haben. Vielmehr, so ein Sprung wäre wahrscheinlich ein unnatürliches Faktum, das vielleicht zu einem starken Rückschlag führen würde (Abb. 2 a). Eine viel „gesündere" Entwicklung wäre die aus Abb. 2 b, also mit einem leichten, schwach exponentiellen Anstiegstrend, dazu vielleicht auch mit manchem zeitweiligen Rückschlag.

ANMERKUNG

[1] Der Begriff „Bildung" ist hier im weitesten Sinne dieses Wortes gemeint, also jenem, der bei manchen Pädagogen als „Bildung *und* Erziehung" verstanden wird.

LITERATUR

Brozović, D., „Lingva aspekto de internacia komunikado", *Tempo* (Zagreb) Nr.1–2 (1984), S. 4–5.

Hoffmann, L., *Sprache 2000* (Dortmund 1979).

Mužić, V., „Eksperimenti u nastavi esperanta u Engleskoj", *Pedagoški rad* (Zagreb) 9:279–280; Nr. 4–5 (1954).

Wittgenstein, L., *Tractatus Logico-Philosophicus* (Sarajevo: V. Masleša, 1960).

* * *

UNIVERSALSPRACHE, ENZYKLOPÄDIE UND DIE „ALLGEMEINE VERBESSERUNG DER MENSCHLICHEN DINGE" BEI J. A. COMENIUS.

Johann Dvořak
Wien

Im Wiener Kreis spielten sowohl Überlegungen zu einer Universalsprache als auch das Vorhaben einer Enzyklopädie eine gewisse Rolle. Unter ausdrücklichem Hinweis auf Wittgenstein („Was sich überhaupt sagen läßt, läßt sich klar sagen") wird im „Manifest" von 1929 („Wissenschaftliche Weltauffassung − Der Wiener Kreis") „das Suchen nach einem neutralen Formelsystem, einer von den Schlacken der historischen Sprachen befreiten Symbolik", „das Suchen nach einem Gesamtsystem der Begriffe" angestrebt.[1]

Otto Neurath verwies im Zusammenhang mit dem eigenen Enzyklopädie-Projekt auf die historische Bedeutung der Arbeiten des tschechischen Gelehrten Jan Amos Comenius, insbesondere auf dessen anschauliche Lehrmethoden und das pansophische Werk.[2]

Im 17. Jahrhundert waren, lange vor der großen französischen Enzyklopädie, Konzepte einer umfassenden Darstellung der menschlichen Erkenntnisse entwickelt worden; bei Comenius waren damit auch Vorstellungen vom Entwurf einer Universalsprache verbunden.

Jan Amos Comenius (1592−1670) hatte sich zeit seines Lebens um eine radikale Verbesserung und Neugestaltung des Bildungswesens bemüht. In der 1657 gedruckten „Großen Unterrichtslehre" machte er deutlich, daß Wissenschaft, Aufklärung und vernünftiges Handeln eine Einheit bilden sollten.

„Überhaupt soll man dafür sorgen, und es dahin bringen, daß niemandem auf dieser Welt etwas so Unbekanntes vorkomme, daß er darüber nicht einigermaßen urteilen und dasselbe nicht zu einem bestimmten Zwecke klug und ohne schädlichen Irrtum verwenden könnte."[3]

Ausgangspunkt für das Denken des Comenius ist ein radikaler Empirismus sowie die Annahme einer prinzipiell unbeschränkten menschlichen Erkenntnisfähigkeit. „Es ist . . . nichts in dem Verstand / wo es nicht zuvor im Sinne gewesen." Sinnliche Erfahrung ist Voraussetzung für vernünftige Erkenntnis und diese wiederum Voraussetzung für vernünftiges Handeln: „weil wir weder etwas ins Werk setzen / noch vernünftig ausreden können / wann wir nicht zuvor alles / was zu thun oder wovon zu reden ist / recht verstehen lernen."[4]

„Da nun also die sichtbare Welt nichts hat, was nicht gesehen, gehört, gerochen, geschmeckt, getastet werden könnte, und man darnach unterscheiden kann, was und welcher Art es sei: so folgt daraus, daß die Welt nichts enthält, was der mit Sinnlichkeit und Venunft begabte Mensch nicht fassen könnte."[5]   Von 1645 an bis zu seinem Tode 1670 arbeitete Jan Amos Comenius an einem Werk, das er „Allgemeine Beratung über die Verbesserung der menschlichen Dinge" betitelte. Im Zusammenhang damit dachte er auch an die Herausgabe eines „Pansophischen Sachwörterbuches":

> Das Wörterbuch sollte, sage ich, alles erschöpfend in einer alphabetischen Ordnung der Dinge und Wörter vollständig zusammenstellen, daß man sofort alles finden könne, was notwendig ist und was irgendwo vorkommt. Damit man erkennen kann, nicht wie ein und dasselbe oder dieses und jenes Ding in ihrer Sprache heißen oder wie es dieser oder jener Schriftsteller bezeichnete, sondern was ein jedes Ding an sich selbst im Innern ist, d.h. zu welcher Gattung es gehört und wodurch es sich von allen anderen Dingen dieser Gattung unterscheidet; ferner wozu es ist und wie man es gebrauchen kann.

Damit man sich so mit ein und demselben Atemzug einmal die rechte Erkenntnis aller Dinge, zum andern die ganze Sprache aneignet und der Verstand angenehm mit dem Licht der Weisheit gespeist werde, die Dinge unbestechlich werte und in seinen Entscheidungen und Taten nicht irre. . . . So soll es zu allem dienen, das zur Erkenntnis eines jeden Dinges vonnöten ist.[6]

Das Pansophische Sachwörterbuch wäre die Zusammenfassung der Ergebnisse der „Allgemeinen Beratung über die Verbesserung der menschlichen Dinge" in lexikalischer Form gewesen. Das gesamte Unternehmen einer enzyklopädischen Zusammenfassung der menschlichen Erkenntnisse war keineswegs konzipiert als Produkt bloß individualistischer Gelehrsamkeit, sondern als Ergebnis kollektiver Arbeit; als Ergebnis der gemeinsamen Anstrengung möglichst aller Menschen. Wissenschaftliche Welterkenntnis war auch nicht um ihrer selbst willen, sondern zwecks Verbesserung des menschlichen Daseins zu betreiben und Wissenschaft überhaupt nicht nur Angelegenheit einiger weniger Experten, sondern eben aller Menschen.

Wir wollen dies, daß man bei der Verwirklichung eines pansophischen Werks alle zuläßt, sage ich, und alle anhört, was sie auch immer Gutes bringen, alle, die zu den Fragen der Frömmigkeit, der Moral, zu Wissenschaft und Kunst etwas zu sagen haben oder gehabt hatten, ohne Rücksicht darauf, ob sie Christen oder Mohammedaner, Juden oder Heiden sind und welcher Gruppierung sie unter diesen auch immer angehören alle, Pythagoreer, Akademiker, Peripatetiker, Stoiker, Essäer, Griechen, Römer, Klassiker und Moderne, Doktoren oder Rabbiner.[7]

Sowohl die Anhänger der verschiedenen religiösen und philosophischen Strömungen, als auch die Angehörigen aller sozialen Klassen, Männer und Frauen sind zur Mitarbeit eingeladen, denn: „Da wir alle Bürger einer Welt sind, was hindert, daß wir uns in einem Gemeinwesen unter gleichen Gesetzen zusammenfinden."[8]

Der Gedanke einer Universalsprache ist daher kein zufälliger, keine Marotte eines versponnenen Gelehrten, sondern notwendige Konsequenz aus den bisher dargestellten Überlegungen; die Universalsprache ist ein Mittel zum Zweck der allgemeinen und umfassenden Verständigung, zur Überwindung nationaler und regionaler Beschränktheit.

Die „Allgemeine Beratung über die Verbesserung der menschlichen Dinge" sollte aus sieben Teilen bestehen und der fünfte Teil („Panglottia" benannt) der „universalen Sprachpflege" gewidmet sein.

Im Rahmen dieser „universalen Sprachpflege" war Comenius ebensosehr um die Reform des Sprachunterrichts bemüht, wie um die Schaffung einer „neuen, harmonischen Sprache", die „vollkommen flüssig, ganz klar, weise und sachentsprechend" sein sollte.[9] Denn anzustreben war die Einheit von vernünftigem Denken, richtigem Handeln und dem beiden gemäßen sprachlichen Ausdruck.

Jan Amos Comenius entfaltete ein radikaldemokratisches Programm bezüglich Wissenschaft, Bildung und umfassender Gesellschaftsreform. Enzyklopädische Zusammenfassung des Wissensstandes und die Entwicklung einer Universalsprache waren Instrumente der allgemeinen Verbreitung von Kenntnissen, der universalen Bildung und Aufklärung, die wiederum die Teilnahme aller Menschen an der praktischen Gestaltung und Verbesserung der Gesellschaft ermöglichen sollten.

Es ist bemerkenswert, daß im Zusammenhang mit der wissenschaftlichen Weltauffassung des Wiener Kreises jene Programmatik, zumindest ansatzweise, wieder aufgenommen worden ist: Einheit der wissenschaftlichen Erkenntnis, Verbindung von Wissenschaft, Bildungsarbeit und alltäglicher Lebensgestaltung, Prinzip der kollektiven Arbeit, Enzyklopädie, Universalsprache . . .[10]

Allerdings sind alle diese programmatischen Ansätze nicht verwirklicht, sondern unterdrückt worden.

Comenius hatte einst selbst die Frage gestellt, wozu die Realisierung seiner Vorhaben führen würde . . .

„Was soll daraus werden, wenn Handwerker, Bauern, Lastträger, ja sogar die Weibsbilder Gelehrte werden?"

Antwort: „Das wird werden, . . . sie werden lernen dieses kummervolle Leben angenehm hin-
zubringen . . .“[11]

ANMERKUNGEN

[1] Carnap, R., Hahn, H., Neurath, O., *Wissenschaftliche Weltauffassung – Der Wiener Kreis* (Wien 1929), S. 13, 15.
[2] Neurath, O., *Gesammelte philosophische und methodische Schriften* (Wien 1981), S. 723, 886.
[3] Comenius, J. A., *Große Unterrichtslehre* (Wien und Leipzig 1912), S. 58.
[4] Comenius, J. A., *Orbis sensualium pictus* (Dortmund 1978), Vorwort.
[5] Comenius, J. A., (1912), S. 33.
[6] Comenius, J. A., zit. n.: F. Hofmann, *Jan Amos Comenius* (Leipzig, Jena, Berlin 1975), S. 100.
[7] Comenius, J. A., *Vorläufer der Pansophie* (Düsseldorf 1963), S. 89.
[8] ibid.
[9] Hofmann, F., (1975), S. 62.
[10] Cf.: J. Dvořak, *Edgar Zilsel und die Einheit der Erkenntnis* (Wien 1981), S. 51–55.
[11] Comenius, J. A., (1912), S. 57.

* * *

ON THE UNITY OF ALL NORMATIVE SCIENCES AS A HIERARCHY OF RATIONALITY PRINCIPLES*

Eckehart Köhler
Institute for Advanced Studies, Vienna

The aim of furthering human understanding by use of international auxiliary languages (Esperanto, Interlingua) and related means of communication (encyclopedias, unification of science) can be considerably extended. *Rationality* is not restricted to language (logic, mathematics) and methodology (measurement theory, statistics, theory construction), but covers also procedures of individual decision-making (economics) and collective decision-making (ethics), i.e., rationality covers all *norms* in general.

Norms are usually distinguished from descriptions as being those circumstances which can be taken as "planning goals" or "target values" of an agent; whereas descriptions are those circumstances corresponding to "facts" or "actual values". This distinction can be based straightaway on the usual distinction between *utility* and *probability* (or between preferences and belief, resp.) made in decision theory. Now some norms presuppose others, e.g., statistical norms presuppose mathematical norms. Thus a *hierarchy* of norms can be established according to the degree of such presuppositions: logic, mathematics, methodology, economics, ethics.

The *unity* of this normative hierarchy can be gathered from two distinct considerations: 1. that the *transitions* between the classically-established normdomains are on closer analysis quite fluid–the validity of norms is not affected by whatever conventions are used to classify them into different domains; 2. that all norms may be *justified* in similar ways by a scheme employing suitable metatheoretical rationality criteria.

I. A. *Norms versus Descriptions. A General Distinction.*

To simplify the discussion, I will use only the simplest possible cases illustrating concepts and distinctions. The simple cases can then be generalized to complex cases in straightforward ways.

To distinguish norms from facts, we consider a system S (possibly the whole world) and the possible states it may take on, described by sentences 'Fx', where 'x' is a "variable of state" or a parameter indicating something (e.g. a number on a dial, or a color) about S, and 'F' is a predicate which says something about the state of S, e.g. that it is one particular state, or that it is *not* some other state, etc. The conceptual scheme in which these states and their properties are expressed we may call 'L'. Now suppose that S is, in *reality*, in state x^T ('T' for "true"); but suppose also that, based on some acceptable criterion, S has a state x^V considered *optimal* ('V' for "valid"). Then we may establish the following table governing facts and norms for S in L (where 'T' = true, 'F' = false, 'V' = valid, 'C' = contravalid):

Fx	
T, V	$Fx \rightarrow x = x^T \ \& \ x = x^V$
T, C	$Fx \rightarrow x = x^T \ \& \ x \neq x^V$
F, V	$Fx \rightarrow x \neq x^T \ \& \ x = x^V$
F, C	$Fx \rightarrow x \neq x^T \ \& \ x \neq x^V.$

On the right hand side of the table are listed equivalents to the evaluations of the table indicating the four possible combinations of cases concerning the "reality" and "optimality" of the state x of S. Now facts and norms may be defined in an obvious way, relative to our conceptual scheme L:

D 1. Fx   is a *fact* iff 'Fx' is *true*$_L$.
D 2. Fx   is a *norm* iff 'Fx' is *valid*$_L$.
D 3. 'T Fx' is *true*$_{ML}$ iff 'Fx' is *true*$_L$.
D 4. 'O Fx' is *true*$_{ML}$ iff 'Fx' is *valid*$_L$.

Immediately conjoined with facts and norms in the ("object-level") scheme L are the *meta-level attributes* T and O ("true" and "obligatory"). According to D4, *obligations* are *facts* when true and have the effect of transforming validity-values into truth-values and therefore can enter into truth-functional combinations with other propositions in L without difficulty.

I. B. *Hypothetical Norms*.

Norms are often stated to be valid only if certain circumstances prevail, in which case they are conditional or *hypothetical* norms. Such is the case in law, for example, where sanctions are imposed on illegal behavior; or in technology, where industrial norms are made conditional on the type of product involved, etc. I now want to show how hypothetical norms can be expressed either directly in terms of validity-value assignments to propositions relating conditions with normed parameters, or in terms of truth-value assignments to conditional propositions having obligation-clauses as consequents.

First, consider relational propositions of the form F xy, where x is an "exogenous" or *conditional* parameter and y is an "indogenous" or *normed* parameter; and suppose x^* and x^o are two states which x can be in (say, good and bad) and y^V and y^C are two states y can be in (say, reward and punishment). Then (part of) a validity-value table for F xy would look like this:

x	y	F xy
x^*	y^V	V
x^*	$\neq y^V$	C
x^o	y^C	V
x^o	$\neq y^C$	c,

and for all other values of x, F xy is either assigned no validity-value or the value "Indifference", if it is being used.

The table for hypothetical obligations is quite straightforward, assuming A to be the condition and B to be the norm:

A	B	O(B)	A → O(B)
T	V	T	T
T	C	F	F
F	V	T	T
F	C	F	T.

II. *Rational Justification of Facts and Norms Based on Probability and Utility*.

Up to now, I have developed just a formal apparatus for facts and norms without saying how truth- and validity-values should be assigned. I will now sketch *rational* methods for doing this based on knowledge of three measures: utility, probability and explanatory power (measuring strength of preference, of belief and of propositional content, respectively). I assume that these in turn are normed in a suitible way according to standard methods used in econometrics and statistics. To be sure, this assumption ammounts to begging many questions, since many foundational problems of utility and probability theory are (perhaps permanently) controversial. I will be satisfied with the relatively modest goal of relating facts and norms to other concepts enjoying widespread application, even if these require improvements.

The notation used for utiliy, probability and explanatory power will be u, p, and e, respectively. The concept of explanatory power is essentially a measure of information and can accordingly be defined in terms of probability. Below, I will assume that u, p, and e are absolute measures and defined over the propositions A, A', A", etc.

A. *Facts as Truth Estimations.*

Let q be an index of caution, measuring a trade-off between the wish to avoid error and a desire for knowledge. Then

i) if $p(A) \cdot e(A) \geq q$ and $T(A') \rightarrow e(A) \geq e(A')$, then $T(A)$;

ii) if $T(A)$ and $A \vdash A'$, then $T(A')$.

Clause (i) is a rule concerning the *strongest contingent* proposition acceptable as true, requiring that the product of its probability and strength match or exceed a level given by q. Clause (ii) is the (trivial) requirement that T be closed under deduction. The reservation of clause (i) to only the strongest contingent proposition is required to avoid the "lottery paradox" and the idea is due to Levi. It is important to notice that the two clauses leave T underdetermined: it cannot yet contain "all the facts in the world", because the probability measure p is limited to information available at a given time. If it is desired to make T complete, so that it satisfies a principle of excluded middle, "artificial measures" must be taken to complete it at the cost of lowering the caution index q.

B. *Norms as Estimations of Optimal Obligations.*

Let C be a codex governing (individual and social) actions and let 'A' describe a possible world (making A maximally strong). Then

i) if $p(A, C) \cdot u(A) \geq q^*$, then $O(C)$, where q^* is an optimal "satisficing" quotient;

ii) if $O(A)$ and $A \vdash_o A'$, then $O(A')$;

iii) if $A \vdash_o A'$ and A as well as A' are actions an individual can carry out at the same time, then $e(A) = e(A')$.

In case clause (i) does not yield a unique codex, it will need to be supplemented by another clause governing tie-breaking (a similar remark holds for clause (i) in the previous section). Clause (ii) has O deductively closed under the (weak) derivation rule $\vdash_o$, which must be formulated so as to satisfy clause (iii), which is required to avoid "Ross's paradox" and "Hilpinen's paradox"—the idea is due to Keuth. Notice that, in clause (iii), $e(A) = e(A')$ implies also $A \longleftrightarrow A'$. Keuth's idea is motivated by the consideration that the *efficient promulgation* of (any section of) a codex should suppress redundant information about norms.

Obligations are restricted, under the above characterization, to actions; if it is intended that 'O' represent optimality in general, then O may be extended to cover possible worlds and not just possible codices. However, if the notion of "possible codex" is taken *broadly* enough, i.e. to include actions amplified by *arbitrarily powerful* technical devices, there will be no practical difference between the notions of optimality for actions and optimality for states of the world.

Many normative theories do not make explicit use of (a metatheoretical notion of) optimality: in mathematics, statistics, system theory and economics, we find no operators corresponding to O. This can give rise to confusion, particularly in the case of economics, where rationality principles about "homo oeconomicus" are misunderstood as (empirical) descriptions of *imperfectly* sapient homo sapiens and thereupon mistakenly applied. Be this as it may, such theories *implicitly* presuppose what is here called "Leibniz' Principle":

$$O(A) \longleftrightarrow T(A),$$

which says that the "real" world and the "ideal" world coincide. Because of the well-known redundancy property of T, viz. that $T(A) \longleftrightarrow A$, normative theories may be developed "as if" they were descriptive theories. But the application of such theories requires the verification of the Leibniz Principle they presupposed.

In conclusion of this section, the dual evaluation of propositions by truth-values and by validity-values may be based on probability and utility assumptions, which are measures of beliefs and preferences, or, in terms of behavioral learning theory, of habits and drives. Thus the fundamental duality of reality and optimality derives from a twofold aspect of human motivation: the capacity to realize (technical mastery or knowledge), and the urge to realize (goal-setting or desire); and *both* may be subjected to rational ordering.

III. *A Hierarchy of Norms.*

Norms always classify actions or states as good or bad, preferable or not preferable. An argument intended to demonstrate something is good if it obeys norms of logic, otherwise bad. A calculation of a function is good if it obeys norms of mathematics, otherwise bad. Thus the norms of logic and mathematics *classify* activities into proofs and (correct) computations as opposed to non-proofs and mistaken computations, so we may say the basic *preference* concept is in each case a directly optimum concept; in logic it is based on a (generally defined) *provability* concept such as $\vdash$, in mathematics on a concept of *function* (or equivalently, on *set-membership*, sets being simply defined as ranges of functions). Other normative areas, however, may be regarded as providing classifications much richer than simple twofold ones into "good" and "bad", rather they permit a *continuous grading* by a (rationally defined) *measure* on states of nature. Such areas include statistics, decision theory and welfare economics, which can (roughly) be regarded as having to do with probability, utility and welfare measures, respectively.

Such considerations give rise to a table like the following one:

This systematization of norms is *hierarchical* in the following sense: each class of norms presupposes a rationality concept from each *prior* class of norms in the list. For example, a statistical inference presupposes both mathematical computational norms as well as logical consistency; welfare theory presupposes at least some rational individual preference orderings as well as inductive coherence and logical consistency. In a certain sense, there is in fact a deeper unity to the whole hierarchy, insofar as *all* of the norms represent *public goods*, because they constitute objective standards of validity, and hence all take on an *ethical* character from a metatheoretical standpoint; more precisely, the *acceptance and use* of *any* norm is an intrinsically social act based on some consensus implicitly reflecting a *collective rationality* and hence a standpoint based on justice or ethical procedure.

It must be stressed that there is nothing absolute about the hierarchical classification scheme suggested above. Closer inspection shows that the exact boundaries are in fact fleeting and may reflect historically accidental academic departmental distinctions. For example,

Area	Basic Concept	Typical Coverage	Goal
Logic	⊨ logical consequence	propositional logic, quantification and identity theory	logical consistency
Mathematics	e set member-ship (f functional dependence)	higher-order logic (algebra) theory of infinity arithmetic analysis	calculation with sets and measures
Statistics	p probability	theory of (empirical) data statistical inference (estimation)	inductive coherence
	μ measure	measurement theory, dimensions and standards	efficient observation
	e explanatory power	methodology of theory construction, complexity measurement	efficient explanation and prediction
Decision Theory	u utility (IP preference)	value theory, economics	prudence (individual rationality)
Welfare Theory	w welfare (IP social preference)	theories of group behavior and public goods, ethics political science legal theory	justice (collective rationality)

quantified propositions in identity theory make numerical statements, so they could just as well be reckoned to mathematics; but propositions of algebra and higher-order set theory do not necessarily have to do with quantities, so they may just as well be reckoned to logic. The boundaries between statistics, decision theory and ethics all may be and still are subject to debate. Since the norms themselves remain unchanged wherever disciplinary boundaries may be drawn, we have *another* indication of a common underlying unity of all norms.

IV. *Foundational Approaches to the Justification of Norms.*

A. But perhaps the most remarkable indication of the unity of all norms is the historical fact that, in every area of normative theory, four basic approaches to normative foundations have been tried. These are as follows:

	Subjective	Objective
Empirical (actual)	Mental (e.g. emotivism)	Physical (naturalism)
Rational (efficient)	Transcendental (intuitionism)	Logical (platonism)

In mathematics, in statistics, in ethics and in other normative areas, foundational researchers may be cited for each of the four foundational approaches who have proposed it. It seems, however, that the "Empirical" approaches are perhaps inappropriate, because, inasmuch as they do not go beyond descriptions of actual or possible norm-systems, they miss the essential aspect of norms: their (implicit or explicit) *efficiency* or *rationality* as determined by a suitable criterion. Furthermore, the distinction between "Subjective" and "Objective" seems inappropriate, since all *acceptable* norms, as previously mentioned, are *public* goods and reflect *collective* rationality, and are hence "Objective" in any case. Insofar as every *acceptable* norm-system must have the aesthetic property of being intuitively convincing in order to gain assent, on the other hand, it appears to be "Subjective" in any case. So it seems that norms are necessarily and always "Subjective" *as well as* "Objective" (individual *subjects* decide to use norms as collective *objective* tools). It therefore appears that the four classic foundational alternatives really reduce to one.

B. *The Principle of Tolerance.*

Foundational schemes suitable for justifying norms can in turn be normed or rationalized by considering what they require from a metatheoretical standpoint. The primary point is that, within each class of norms, a family of alternatives may be developed—even within logic and mathematics, which was finally realized by Carnap when stating his Tolerance Principle. Each alternative may be assigned an order of preference or perhaps a utility measure according to each of a variety of criteria, giving rise to the possibility of a decision-theoretical solution in a (metatheoretical) foundational framework. Then, assuming the applicability of a suitable amalgamation or "scoring" procedure, i.e. a decision rule, an optimal choice can be made, and one or several norms can be distinguished as efficient by that rule. However, the Principle of Tolerance also implies that precise knowledge of all relevant factors going into such decisions can never be obtained, so they must always be regarded as open to *revision* as more is learned about nature and how norms work out in practice, on the one hand (these are the "Objective" considerations), and as more is learned about our insights into what we regard as important decision criteria ("Subjective" considerations). The Tolerance Principle implies that there will forever be conflict about norms, even if only due to fashion, but Tolerance also implies striving for rational adjudication of all points of view, so there also always exist feasible settlements.

V. *Bibliographical Remarks.*

The method of a dual semantics for propositions (assigning both factual and normative values to them) is developed in a chapter on ethics in the author's forthcoming book on the Vienna Circle, to appear in 1985 (cf.*). Carnap's Principle of Tolerance, partly influenced by Karl Menger, was stated in his *Logische Syntax der Sprache*, (Vienna 1934, in English 1937), and is analyzed in B. G. Norton, *Linguistic Frameworks and Ontology* (The Hague 1977). Cf. also E. Köhler, "The Vienna Circle and Foundations without Absolutism" in P. Weingartner & H. Czermak (eds.), *Epistemology and Philosophy of Science. Proc. 7th Int. Wittg.-Symp.* (Vienna 1983), for another treatment of the Tolerance Principle and foundational frameworks.

The method for estimating facts based a probability- (and a strength-)measure is close to I. Levi's acceptance procedure for "corpora" (= bodies of knowledge), the best treatment of which is by W. K. Goosens: "Levi's Theory of Acceptance", in R. J. Bogdan (ed.), *Henry E. Kyburg, Jr. & Isaac Levi* (Dordrecht 1982); but the true source is I. Levi, *Gambling with Truth* (Cambridge MA ²1973 (¹1967)). and I. Levi, *The Enterprise of Knowledge* (1980); cf. also the treatment in R. Hilpinen, *Rules of Acceptance and Inductive Logic* (Amsterdam 1968).

In these books there is also ample discussion of logical strength or explanatory power, but an important source for this concept is I. Niiniluoto & R. Tuomela: *Theoretical Concepts and Hypothetico-Inductive Inference* (Dordrecht 1973).

Methods for estimating obligatoriness or optimality in terms of utility are presented in F. v. Kutschera, *Einführung in die Logik der Normen, Werte und Entscheidungen* (Freiburg 1973). A source for applying possible-world theory to deontic logic (i.e., estimating optimality of possible worlds) is D. Lewis, "Semantic Analysis for Dyadic Deontic Logics", in S. Stenlund (ed.): *Logical Theory and Semantic Analysis* (Dordrecht 1974). The solution to Ross's and Hilpinen's paradoxes achieved by suitably weakening the deduction rule $\vdash_O$ is in H. Keuth, "Deontische Logik und Logik der Normen", in H. Lenk (ed.): *Normenlogik* (Pullach 1974 (UTB 414)); and in H. Keuth, *Zur Logik der Normen* (Diss.), Schriften zur Rechtstheorie, Heft 27, (Berlin 1972).

ENDNOTE

* This paper resulted from work supported during 1982−1984 by the Österreichischer Fonds zur Förderung der Wissenschaftlichen Forschung, project P 4517, which was carried out together with my colleagues, Dr. Friedrich Stadler and Karl Müller, under the supervision of Prof. Edgar Morscher (Universität Salzburg) and Prof. Erika Weinzierl (Universität Wien).

* * *

ZEITGEMÄSSE WISSENSCHAFTSENZYKLOPÄDIEN

Karl Müller[1]
Institut für Höhere Studien, Wien

Innerhalb nur weniger Jahrzehnte haben rasch diffundierende ‚neue Technologien' in den Bereichen der Text- und Datenverarbeitung ein immer reicheres Spektrum an Chancen eröffnet, jahrhundertelang unerfüllte Desiderata einer enzyklopädischen Wissenschaftsorganisation[2] praktisch einzulösen − und doch sind solche Möglichkeiten bislang nur zu einem unbedeutenden Bruchteil realisiert worden. Versteht man unter den Minimalbedingungen einer zeitgemäßen Enzyklopädie das Vorhandensein einer homogenen Sprachform, eines Hintergrundmodells, einer mit diesem ‚Background-knowledge' vernetzten Theorienmenge, einer Stützungstheorie sowie einer kritischen Ausrichtung auf eine lebenswerte Gesellschaft, dann ließen sich die Elemente eines computerunterstützten enzyklopädischen Designs − zentriert um den sozialwissenschaftlichen Bereich − wie folgt zusammenfassen.

Die homogene Sprachform: Die Etablierung der Systemtheorie in unterschiedlichsten Wissenschaftsgebieten − ihre gegenwärtigen Applikationen erstrecken sich immerhin von der Computer-Architektur bis zur Analyse von Produktionsabläufen, Kommunikationsprozessen oder Modellen gesamtgesellschaftlichen Wandels − lassen es ratsam erscheinen, eine systemtheoretische Sprechweise als gegenwärtigen Pendant einer ‚Universalsprache' vorzuschlagen − analog etwa zum Physikalismus im Kontext der ‚Unity of Science'-Bewegung aus den 1930er Jahren. Die Vorteile einer quer über Disziplinen laufenden Sprache liegen dabei − neben der graduellen Aufhebung einer derzeit gestörten interdisziplinären Kommunikation − vor allem darin, Bereichsabgrenzungen zwischen Wissenschaftsfeldern und aktuelle Leerstellen im Wissenschaftsnetz transparenter zu gestalten, sowie die Verbindungsmöglichkeiten und die Verknüpfungen heterogener Problemgebiete wesentlich zu erleichtern.

Das Hintergrundmodell: Durch die immer weiter voranschreitende Verflechtung von ökonomischen, sozialen, kulturellen und wissenschaftlich-technologischen Indikatoren mit dem vorrätigen Theorienfundus zum gesamtgesellschaftlichen Wandel und mit Modellierungs- und Simulationstechniken müßten insbesondere computerunterstützte Ansätze wie beispielsweise bei Mesarovic-Pestel, Bariloche, im ILO- oder Globus-Approach[3] als ausbaufähige Kandidaten solcher Hintergrundmodelle angesehen werden. Für die Wahl dieser Art von Ansätzen lassen sich gleich mehrere komparativen Vorteile anführen: gegenüber nichtformalisierten Richtungen erlauben diese Modelle eine Analyse der für soziale Domänen grundlegenden Prozeßart, nämlich von stochastischen Prozessen; gegenüber regional tieferliegenden Niveaus erleichtern sie − vergleichsweise − das Abgrenzungsproblem; gegenüber ‚endogenen', rein ökonomischen, politologischen oder soziologischen Forschungstraditionen vermögen sie die meistens notwendige Inklusion heterogener Sphären zu bewerkstelligen; und gegenüber individualistischen Ausrichtungen haben sie sich das Denken von der vernünftigen Gesellschaft bewahrt; denn schon im Fall von wenigen hochgradig rational agierenden Individuen kann selbst bei trivialen Versuchsanordnungen nicht mehr das Zustandekommen vernünftiger Gesamtergebnisse verbürgt werden. Im enzyklopädischen Design werden solche Hintergrundmodelle vor allem aus drei forschungsstrategischen Gründen bedeutsam. Erstens erlauben sie durch die Art ihrer Spezifizierung eine theorievermittelte Separierung von relevanten und irrelevanten Problembereichen − und dies gilt wegen der vielfältigen Möglichkeiten von Dekompositionen nicht nur für ein, sondern für verschiedene Aggregationsniveaus. Darüberhinaus können die bestehenden Modellrelationen als „Nullhypothesen" für darunterliegende Levels verwendet werden, womit ein interessanter Zusammenhang von globalen „Conjectures" und möglichen regionalen „Refutations" hergestellt wird. Und schließlich lassen − wie weiter unten noch kurz angedeutet wird – über ein Hintergrundmodell auch noch Teile der für die Stützungstheorie benötigten Evaluierungskriterien definieren sowie die für Fragen der Optimierung u.ä.m. unabdingbaren Zielbereiche ausgrenzen.

Die einzelwissenschaftliche Ebene: Der dritte Bereich dieses enzyklopädischen Ansatzes ist durch das weite Feld normaler sozialwissenschaftlicher Theorieninformation gegeben, die neben ihrer homogenen systemtheoretischen Aufbereitung auf drei weitere Arten enzyklopädisch vernetzt werden könnte: einerseits über eine durch verschiedenartige Niveaus laufende allgemeine Theorie dynamischer Systeme[4]; weiters durch die Assemblage-Möglichkeiten, welche eine direkte Kopplung zweier oder mehrerer Systeme erlaubt[5]; und schließlich via Mikro- und Makroreduktionen[6], wodurch ein bestimmtes Systemverhalten mit Bezug auf ein dazu vergleichsweise darunter- oder darüberliegendes Niveau erklärt wird; zum Beispiel könnte die über eine logistische Kurve beschreibbare Ausbreitung einer Basisinnovation im nationalen Ökonomiebereich sowohl über die Interaktionen und die regionale Nähe von Individuen (Firmen) mikroreduziert als auch über einen globalen Ansatz zum ökonomischen Strukturwandel makroreduziert werden. In beiden Fällen jedenfalls kommt es dazu, unterschiedliche systemische Niveaus miteinander zu verweben.

Die Stützungstheorie: Als viertes Element dieses Enzyklopädieentwurfes firmiert eine Stützungstheorie, deren Ausgestaltung wesentlich durch das jeweilige Hintergrundmodell bestimmt wird.[7] Ihre Konstruktion ist – intuitiv formuliert – davon geleitet, enzyklopädisch verbundene einzelwissenschaftliche Resultate danach zu evaluieren, wie erfolgreich sie die über ein spezifisches Hintergrundmodell definierten Problembereiche zu lösen imstande sind; als Stützungskriterien figurieren dabei typischerweise Gesichtspunkte wie die Reichweite theoretischer Problemlösungen, die Häufigkeit von Konversionen bislang anomaler Probleme, die Prognosegenauigkeit etc. Durch diese Stützungstheorie soll jedenfalls etwas klar in Schwung gebracht werden, was H. Dubiel in der Forschungsorganisation der frühen Kritischen Theorie als eher ‚rudimentär bewußt‘ und mehr implizit denn vorhanden konstatiert:

> Im Zuge des dialektischen Erkennungsprozesses kommentieren sich also Totalitätsbezug und Detailbestimmung wechselseitig so lange, bis eine komplexe theoretische Struktur entwickelt ist, . . . die sich immer wieder rechtfertigen muß vor den analytischen, methodischen und meß-technischen Standards der Einzeldisziplinen.

Die kritische Dimension: Für enzyklopädische Intentionen typisch war und ist ihre Orientierung auf eine selbstbewußte, freiere, solidarische Gesellschaft: dieser kritischen Ausrichtung – nach zwei Jahrzehnten steriler Frontstellungen im Gefolge des Positivismusstreits – einen wissenschaftlichen Gehalt wiederzugeben, gestaltet sich dabei durch den andauernden Skandal einer an sich reichen und trotz alledem enorm ungleich organisierten Weltgesellschaft auf nahezu absurde Weise einfach und läßt sich über die folgenden Schritte realisieren: Zunächst wird als Minimalbild einer besseren Gesellschaft die Erfüllung individueller Grundbedürfnisse postuliert. Solche Grundbedürfnisse können dann modellvermittelt, d.h. über das enzyklopädische Hintergrundmodell selbst definiert und damit für's erste vom Bereich subjektiv empfundenen Mangels entkoppelt werden. Grundbedürfnisse sind damit als echte Teilmengen der Modellgrößen insgesamt ausgezeichnet. Und die Fixierung der einzelnen Bedürfnisvariablen auf kritische Minima[9] – sowohl was die Niveaus als auch was deren Distribution betrifft – braucht dann, eben wegen der gegenwärtig persistierenden weltweiten Disparitäten, in nichts anderem mehr als in der schieren physischen Reproduktion der menschlichen Art selbst zu bestehen[10]; in minimalen Verfüglichkeiten im Bereich von Nahrung, Gesundheit, Wohnung, Ausbildung oder politischer Partizipation -beschränkt auf das notleidende ‚untere‘ Drittel der Menschheit beispielsweise. Eine solche Vorgangsweise sollte in einer Phase, der die ‚großen Erzählungen‘ (J. F. Lyotard) verblassen, nicht unwesentlich sein: Schließlich kann ja auch kein lustvolleres, harmonischeres Bild einer zukünftigen Gesellschaft je auf die Dimension der physischen Arterhaltung verzichten; und gegenwärtig bleibt immerhin selbst dieses Ziel von der bestehenden Lage der Dinge entfernt genug – im besten Fall werden allein für die Utopie vom weltweiten Überleben Jahrzehnte vergehen müssen, um von der Wirklichkeit eingeholt zu werden.

Einem allerorten monierten Informationsfluß zum Trotz scheinen jedenfalls durch den Einbruch der Mikroelektronik die Chancen für inter- und transdisziplinäre Verkehrsformen im Wissenschaftsbetrieb insgesamt gewachsen zu sein: Computerunterstützte Informationssysteme ließen sich durchaus gemäß diesem eben skizzierten enzyklopädischen Design aufbauen. Zu erwarten, daß an sich vorhandene Möglichkeiten in Richtung einer kritischen emanzipatorischen Wissenschaftspraxis getrieben werden, wäre sicherlich verfehlt: Dem stehen ‚Sachzwänge' aller Arten entgegen. Die bestehenden Freiräume aber auch nicht zu nutzen, fällt allein auf die gegenwärtigen Sozialwissenschaften zurück.

ANMERKUNGEN

[1] Dieser Artikel stellt eine kursorische Übersicht eines Teils aus einem vom Forschungsförderungsfonds unterstützten Projekts dar, das unter der Leitung von Prof. E. Morscher (Universität Salzburg) sowie in Zusammenarbeit mit E. Köhler (Wien) und F. Stadler (Wien) die historischen und systematischen Grundzüge der österreichischen Wissenschaftsphilosophie sowie die Möglichkeiten, Inhalte von früher zeitgemäß zu adaptieren, zum Inhalt hat.

[2] Von Enzyklopädien soll, abweichend vom normalen Wortgebrauch, dann gesprochen werden, wenn − in den Worten von D. Diderot − versucht wird, „das allgemeine System der . . . auf der Erdoberfläche verstreuten Kenntnisse . . . auf der Höhe des Jahrhunderts" zusammenzufassen: Enzyklopädien stellen somit ein Kompendium des bestverfüglichen Wissens einer Zeit dar. Siehe D. Diderot, *Enzyklopädie. Philosophische und polititsche Texte aus der ‚Encyclopedie'* (München 1969), S. 79.

[3] Als neuere Übersicht dazu empfiehlt sich beispielsweise D. Meadows, J. Richardson, G. Bruckmann (Hrsg.), *Groping in the Dark. The First Decade of Global Modeling* (Chichester 1982).

[4] Vgl. beispielsweise H. Haken, *Advanced Synergetics. Instability Hierarchies of Self-organizing Systems and Devices* (Berlin-New York 1983); oder G. Hofbauer, K. Sigmund, *Evolutionstheorie und dynamische Systeme* (Berlin-Hamburg 1984).

[5] Vgl. u.a. H. Schmidt, B. Schips (Hrsg.), *Verknüpfung sozio-ökonomischer Modelle. Wissenschaftliches Analyse- und politisches Entscheidungsinstrument* (Frankfurt-New York 1981).

[6] Die Unterscheidung zwischen Mikro- und Makroebenen wird rein kontextual bestimmt: danach kann jedes System als Makroeinheit gegenüber seinen Komponenten und als Teilbereich übergeordneter Systeme firmieren.

[7] Genau genommen handelt es sich dabei um ein zweistufiges Verfahren: in einer externen Stufe ist's darum zu tun, mögliche Hintergrundmodelle, und in einer internen Stufe darum, einzelwissenschaftliche Theorienmengen im Kontext eines solchen Hintergrundmodells zu evaluieren.

[8] H. Dubiel, *Wissenschaftsorganisation und politische Erfahrung. Studien zur frühen Kritischen Theorie* (Frankfurt am Main 1978), S. 166ff.

[9] Dieser Verfahrensschritt wird beispielsweise auch von K. R. Popper vorgeschlagen beispielsweise in ders., *Die offene Gesellschaft und ihre Feinde. Der Zauber Platons* (Bern 1957), S. 387f.

[10] Bei typischen Variablen, die als Grundbedürfnisse Verwendung finden − wie etwa dem Pro-Kopf Kalorienkonsum, der Alphabetisierung, Lebenserwartung oder Wohnungsindikatoren (Wohnraumgrößen, Verfüglichkeit sicheren Wassers etc.) −, erweisen sich zudem kritische Überlebenswerte als diskursiv durchaus konsensfähig: die diesbezüglichen Intervalle haben sich, wie dies die Basic Needs-Literatur zeigt, innerhalb eines schmalen Bandes festgelegt.

* * *

LISTE UND INDEX DER VORTRAGENDEN
LIST AND INDEX OF SPEAKERS

SCHRIFTENREIHE DER WITTGENSTEIN-GESELLSCHAFT

Herausgegeben von Elisabeth Leinfellner
Rudolf Haller, Adolf Hübner, Werner Leinfellner, Paul Weingartner

Band 1

LUDWIG WITTGENSTEIN, Wörterbuch für Volksschulen
(Faksimile der Ausgabe von 1926) Wien 1977.
Hrsg. A. Hübner, W. und E. Leinfellner.
XXXVI+44 Seiten, kartoniert. ISBN 3-209-00191-X. öS 98,–/DM 14,–.

Band 2

WITTGENSTEIN UND SEIN EINFLUSS AUF DIE GEGENWÄRTIGE PHILOSOPHIE
Akten des 2. Internationalen Wittgenstein-Symposiums, Kirchberg am Wechsel, Österreich 1977.
WITTGENSTEIN AND HIS IMPACT ON CONTEMPORARY THOUGHT
Proceedings of the 2nd International Wittgenstein-Symposium, Kirchberg am Wechsel, Austria 1977.
Hrsg. E. und W. Leinfellner, H. Berghel, A. Hübner.
Wien 1978, 550 Seiten, kartoniert. ISBN 3-209-00204-5. öS 520,–/DM 74,50.

Band 3

WITTGENSTEIN, DER WIENER KREIS UND DER KRITISCHE RATIONALISMUS
Akten des 3. Internationalen Wittgenstein-Symposiums, Kirchberg am Wechsel, Österreich 1978.
WITTGENSTEIN, THE VIENNA CIRCLE AND CRITICAL RATIONALISM
Proceedings of the 3rd International Wittgenstein-Symposium, Kirchberg am Wechsel, Austria 1978.
Hrsg. H. Berghel, A. Hübner, E. Köhler.
Wien 1979, 544 Seiten, kartoniert. ISBN 3-209-00226-6. öS 590,–/DM 84,50.

Band 4

SPRACHE, LOGIK UND PHILOSOPHIE
Akten des 4. Internationalen Wittgenstein-Symposiums, Kirchberg am Wechsel, Österreich 1979.
LANGUAGE, LOGIC, AND PHILOSOHPHY
Proceedings of the 4th International Wittgenstein-Symposium, Kirchberg am Wechsel, Austria 1979.
Hrsg. Rudolf Haller und Wolfgang Grassl.
Wien 1980, 617 Seiten, kartoniert. ISBN 3-209-00249-5. öS 625,–/DM 89,50.

Band 5

SPRACHE UND ERKENNTNIS ALS SOZIALE TATSACHE
Beiträge des Wittgenstein-Symposiums von Rom 1979.
Hrsg. v. Rudolf Haller, Wien 1981, 147 Seiten, kart. ISBN 3-209-00278-9. öS 198,–/DM 28,50.

Band 6

WITTGENSTEIN – ÄSTHETIK UND TRANSZENDENTALE PHILOSOPHIE
Akten eines Symposiums in Bergen (Norwegen) 1980.
WITTGENSTEIN – AESTHETICS AND TRANSCENDENTAL PHILOSOPHY
Proceedings of a Symposium at Bergen (Norway) 1980.
Hrsg. Kjell S. Johannessen, Tore Nordenstam.
Wien 1981, 193 Seiten, kartoniert. ISBN 3-209-00279-7. öS 270,–/DM 39,–.

Verlag Hölder-Pichler-Tempsky

A-1096 Wien, Frankgasse 4, Postfach 127,
Telefon 0222/43 89 93 △

SCHRIFTENREIHE DER WITTGENSTEIN-GESELLSCHAFT

Herausgegeben von Elisabeth Leinfellner
Rudolf Haller, Adolf Hübner, Werner Leinfellner, Paul Weingartner

---

Band 7

ETHIK – GRUNDLAGEN, PROBLEME UND ANWENDUNGEN

Akten des 5. Internationalen Wittgenstein-Symposiums, Kirchberg am Wechsel, Österreich 1980.

ETHICS – FOUNDATIONS, PROBLEMS, AND APPLICATIONS

Proceedings of the 5th International Wittgenstein-Symposium, Kirchberg am Wechsel, Austria 1980.
Hrsg. Edgar Morscher, Rudolf Stranzinger.
Wien 1981, 525 Seiten, kartoniert. ISBN 3-209-00280-0. öS 738,–/DM 105,50.

Band 8

SPRACHE UND ONTOLOGIE

Akten des 6. Internationalen Wittgenstein-Symposiums, Kirchberg am Wechsel, Österreich 1981.

LANGUAGE AND ONTOLOGY

Proceedings of the 6th International Wittgenstein-Symposium, Kirchberg am Wechsel, Austria 1981.
Hrsg. Werner Leinfellner, Eric Kraemer, Jeffrey Schank.
Wien 1982, 544 Seiten, kartoniert. ISBN 3-209-00422-6. öS 738,–/DM 105,50.

Band 9

ERKENNTNIS- UND WISSENSCHAFTSTHEORIE

Akten des 7. Internationalen Wittgenstein-Symposiums, Kirchberg am Wechsel, Österreich 1982.

EPISTEMOLOGY AND PHILOSOPHY OF SCIENCE

Proceedings of the 7th International Wittgenstein-Symposium, Kirchberg am Wechsel, Austria 1982.
Hrsg. Paul Weingartner, Hans Czermak.
Wien 1983, 576 Seiten, kartoniert. ISBN 3-209-00499-4. öS 738,–/DM 105,50.

Band 10

ÄSTHETIK / AESTHETICS (Band 10/1)

RELIGIONSPHILOSOPHIE / PHILOSOPHY OF RELIGION (Band 10/2)

Akten des 8. Internationalen Wittgenstein-Symposiums, Kirchberg am Wechsel, Österreich 1983.
Proceedings of the 8th International Wittgenstein-Symposium, Kirchberg am Wechsel, Austria 1983.
Hrsg. Rudolf Haller und Wolfgang L. Gombocz.
Band 10/1: Wien 1984, 262 Seiten, kartoniert. ISBN 3-209-00547-8. öS 428,– / DM 62,–
Band 10/2: Wien 1984, 252 Seiten, kartoniert. ISBN 3-209-00548-6. öS 428,– / DM 62,–
Band 10/1 und Band 10/2 ZUSAMMEN (ISBN 3-209-00549-4): öS 778,– / DM 112,–

Band 11

PHILOSOPHIE DES GEISTES – PHILOSOPHIE DER PSYCHOLOGIE

Akten des 9. Internationalen Wittgenstein-Symposiums, Kirchberg am Wechsel, Österreich 1984.

PHILOSOPHY OF MIND – PHILOSOPHY OF PSYCHOLOGY

Proceedings of the 9th International Wittgenstein-Symposium, Kirchberg am Wechsel, Austria 1984.
Hrsg. R. H. Chisholm, J. C. Marek, J. T. Blackmore, A. Hübner.
Wien 1985, 662 Seiten, kartoniert. ISBN 3-209-00592-3. öS 840,– / DM 120,–

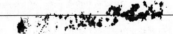

 Verlag Hölder-Pichler-Tempsky

A-1096 Wien, Frankgasse 4, Postfach 127,
Telefon 0222/43 89 93 △